Oxford
Concise
School
Dictionary

Compiled by   Joyce Hawkins
Andrew Delahunty
Fred McDonald

OXFORD
UNIVERSITY PRESS

OXFORD
UNIVERSITY PRESS

Great Clarendon Street, Oxford OX2 6DP

Oxford University Press is a department of the University of Oxford.
It furthers the University's objective of excellence in research,
scholarship, and education by publishing worldwide in

Oxford NewYork

Auckland Bangkok Buenos Aires Cape Town Chennai
Dar es Salaam Delhi Hong Kong Istanbul Karachi Kolkata
Kuala Lumpur Madrid Melbourne Mexico City Mumbai Nairobi
São Paulo Shanghai Taipei Tokyo Toronto
Oxford is a registered trade mark of Oxford University Press
in the UK and in certain other countries

© Oxford University Press 2004

This edition 2004 based on *The Oxford School Dictionary* 1997

Database right Oxford University Press (maker)

British Library cataloguing in Publication Data available

Part of a 6-part set. Not to be sold separately.

ISBN 0-19-911201-0 (complete set)

ISBN 0-19-911260-6 *Oxford Concise School Dictionary* (when part of
this set)

10 9 8 7 6 5 4 3 2 1

Printed in the UK by Cox and Wyman

Do you have a query about words, their origin, meaning, use, spelling,
pronunciation, or any other aspect of the English language? Visit our
website at www.askoxford.com where you will be able to find answers

Contents

Preface

This dictionary has been specially written for upper primary and lower secondary students aged 10–14 years, corresponding to key stages 2 and 3 of the English National Curriculum. It is written in a straightforward way avoiding difficult abbreviations and special conventions while seeking to familiarize users with the style in which most adult dictionaries are written.

Inflections of all verbs and plurals of nouns are spelt out in full, and comparatives and superlatives of adjectives and adverbs are also given when these present difficulties of form or spelling. Pronunciation of difficult words is given in a simple look-and-say system that avoids special symbols. Definitions are clearly expressed, with careful explanations of difficult concepts (e.g. *hindsight*, *hypothesis*, and *irony*), and there are many examples of words in use. Usage notes clarify grammatical points and words that are easily confused (e.g. *alternate* and *alternative*). Key prefixes and suffixes (such as *in-*, *re-*, and *-ation*) are given in the main text, and a fuller list is provided in Appendix 1. Word origins (etymologies) are given for a selection of words, chosen to illustrate the wide range of sources from which modern English words are derived (Old English; Old Norse; Latin and Greek, often via French; Sanskrit, Hindi, and other Indian languages; the languages of South America; and modern languages). The emphasis here is on historical interest, where there is a story to tell (as with *assassin*, *carnival*, *marathon*, and *scapegoat*). We hope this will stimulate users to look in larger dictionaries for further information about the origins of words.

The English language

English is the chief language of Britain, the USA, Australia, and a number of other countries. About 400 million people speak it as their first or their only language, and millions more in all parts of the world learn it as a foreign language for use in communicating with people of other nations. It is the official language used between airline pilots and their air traffic controllers in all countries, and in shipping, and the main language of international business, science, medicine, and computing.

All languages have a history: they are constantly changing and evolving. It is probable that nearly all the languages of Europe, and some of those in the Middle East and India, came from one ancient community, who lived in Eastern Europe about 5,000 years ago. Scholars call the language of this community Indo-European. As people moved away to the east and west they lost contact with each other and developed new and different lifestyles. Naturally their language needs changed too. They invented new words and forgot old ones, and the grammar of the language also changed. Many varied languages grew from the original parent tongue, until the time came when people with the same ancestors would no longer have understood each other.

Invasions and conquest complicated the process. The English language shows this very well, for invaders brought their own languages to Britain, and British travellers took theirs to lands overseas. The earliest known inhabitants of Britain spoke a form of Celtic, related to modern Welsh and Gaelic. Very little of this Celtic survived the waves of invasion that drove its speakers into western and highland parts of the country, but the names of some cities, rivers, and hills date back to Celtic times (e.g. *Carlisle, Avon, Pendle*).

Old English

Old English, which is also called Anglo-Saxon, does not look very much like modern English (for example *Fæder ure, Þu Þe eart on heofonum* = Our Father, who is in heaven) but many words, especially the most frequently used ones, can be traced back to it. *Eat, drink, sleep, speak, work, play*, and *sing* are all from Old

English; so are *house, door, meat, bread, milk, fish*; and *head, nose, eye, man, woman, husband, wife*. The prepositions and conjunctions that we use to join words together in sentences, such as *and*, *but*, *to*, and *from*, come from Old English, and so do many common adverbs, for example *up*, *down*, *here*, *there*, *over*, and *under*.

Old English did not originate in Britain. It was the language of the Angles, Saxons, and Jutes, Germanic tribes who came from the Continent in about AD450. By about AD700 the Anglo-Saxons had occupied most of the country and their language was the dominant one. Even the name of the country itself became 'England', which means 'land of the Angles', and from it came 'Englisc', the Old English spelling of 'English'.

The next great influence on Old English came from the Vikings, who arrived from Norway and Denmark in the 9th and 10th centuries and occupied much of northern and eastern England. They also settled in parts of Scotland, Wales, and Ireland. Their language was Old Norse, and from it we get many common words, such as *call, cast,* and *take*, and a number of words beginning with 'sc' or 'sk', including *scare, scrap, skirt,* and *sky*.

Middle English

In 1066 the Normans, led by William the Conqueror, invaded England. English life was greatly changed in the years that followed and the language changed too, so much so that, with a little practice, we can now read and understand the language of that time. These lines, for example, were written in about 1390: *This carpenter hadde wedded newe a wyf, Which that he lovede moore than his lyf.* We call this language 'Middle English' to distinguish it from Old English or Anglo-Saxon.

For much of this period the language used by the ruling classes was the French of the victorious Norman invaders, though most of the ordinary people still spoke English. Many words connected with government and law came into the language at this time through their French use, e.g. *advise, command, court, govern, people, reign, royalty, rule*.

Throughout all these centuries, although scholars in different countries spoke different languages, they all understood Latin, which had been the language of the ancient Roman Empire, and used it for writing about every subject that they studied. Some Latin words (e.g. *mint, pound, sack*, and *street*) had already been adopted by the Anglo-Saxons before they came to Britain, because they had lived on the fringe of the Roman Empire; others (e.g. *font, pope*, and *school*) arrived with the spread of Christianity. Then in the 14th–16th centuries (the *Renaissance*) people throughout Europe became especially interested in Greek and Roman literature, philosophy, art, and buildings, and many more words from Greek and Latin were introduced into English (e.g. *architecture, column, comedy, educate, history, physics, tributary*). The Christian Church in all western countries had always used Latin, and continued to use this (instead of English or other local languages) in all its services.

Modern English

From about 1500 onwards the English language continued to change, and developed enormously. It adopted words from other languages with which people came into contact through trade or travel, and it was exported to other lands when English-speaking people travelled abroad. In the early 17th century colonies began to be established, first in north America and in India, then in the West Indies, and later in Australia, New Zealand, Hong Kong, and Africa. To each country the settlers took the English language of their own time, and in each country it changed, little by little, until it differed in various ways not only from the English of the other settlements but from its parent form in Britain – where, of course, the language was changing too. Some words, such as names for birds and animals found only in one country, were adopted into the form of English used there and are not known elsewhere; others (e.g. *banana, potato*, and *tornado*) have made their way into international English and are known everywhere.

In the 20th century, people who came from the Caribbean and Asia to settle in England brought with them their own cultures and vocabulary, and many words from these have been adopted into standard English (e.g. *chapatti* and *reggae*).

Nowadays travel is not the only way in which people acquire words from other countries. Films made in one country are shown in many others, and television programmes from all over the world are received in people's homes. The result is that while American, Australian, and other vocabulary becomes familiar in Britain, British English continues to be exported.

Dialect

There are different forms of English not only in different parts of the world but within the British Isles. People from North Yorkshire, the Midlands, East Anglia, and Somerset have different words for different things, or use different grammatical forms. These forms of English are called **dialects**. Each is known, understood, and regarded as standard in its own area, but not outside of it.

The way the people of an area pronounce words is called an **accent**, and this too varies in different parts of the country.

Every language has a number of dialects and most languages have one dialect and style of pronunciation that is regarded as standard for the whole country. In Britain, 'Standard English' is based on the form of English used in southern England. It is the basis of the written language, known (unlike other dialects) in all parts of the country. It is taught in secondary schools, used for national news bulletins on radio and television, and learned by foreigners. People from outside southern England often speak Standard English with a local accent, and use it as well as their local dialect.

Formal and informal

We wear different clothes for different kinds of occasions, and often the words that we use when writing or speaking formally are different from those that we use informally to friends.

Very informal language (e.g. *nick* = to steal, *piffle* = nonsense) is called **slang**. It is used either for fun, or to express something in a more vivid or picturesque way than ordinary words would do, or to shock people or attract their attention. Often, special slang words are used by members of a group, and they recognize others who use them as belonging to it too.

Indo-European Languages

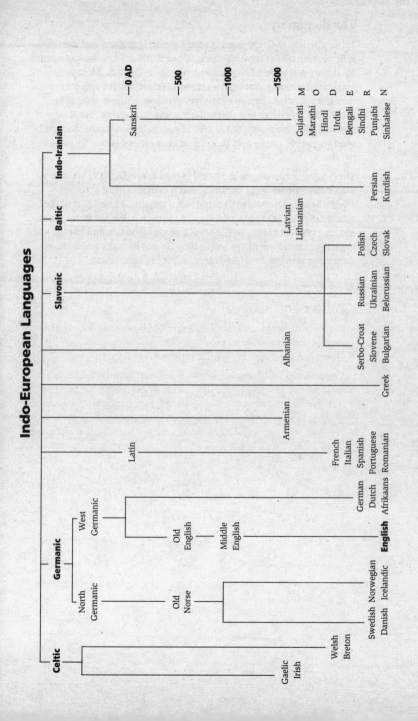

The dictionary

There are over 500,000 words in the English language, and the total is increasing all the time. Of these, about 3,000 are known and used by almost everyone whose native language is English. Most people know the meaning of at least another 5,000 words, though they may not use all of them in everyday speech or writing. In addition, those who specialize in a particular subject (e.g. music, chemistry, medicine, or computers) have a wide vocabulary of words that are used by people working in that subject but are not generally known to others.

The biggest dictionary in the world is the *Oxford English Dictionary*, which fills twenty large volumes, and it contains most of these words. Small dictionaries can find room for only a small part of the whole language; they include most of the words that are in common use, but (in order to make the book a convenient size and not too expensive) there are many words they cannot include, and a larger dictionary must be consulted for information about these.

Notes on the use of the dictionary

Dictionary entries

Words defined are arranged in alphabetical order. The words derived from each word (*derivatives*) are often included in the same entry without definitions if their meanings can easily be worked out from the meaning of the main word.

Words with the same spelling but with a different meaning or origin (*homographs*) are given separate entries with a space between them, and numbered with a raised figure, e.g.

peer[1] *verb* (**peers, peering, peered**)
  look at something closely or with difficulty.
peer[2] *noun* (*plural* **peers**)
  1 a noble. **2** someone who is equal to another in rank, merit, or age etc. ♦ *She had no peer.*
  peeress *noun* **peerage** *noun*

Pronunciation

Help is given with this when the word is difficult, or when two words with the same spelling are pronounced differently. The pronunciation is given in brackets with *say* or *rhymes with*, e.g.

toll[1] (rhymes with *hole*) *noun*
chaos (*say* kay-oss) *noun*

Words are broken up into small units (usually of one syllable), and the syllable that is spoken with most stress is shown in thick black letters. In the pronunciation guide, note the following distinctions:

I   shows the sound as in m**i**ne
oo "   "   "   " " s**oo**n
uu "   "   "   " " b**oo**k
th "   "   "   " " **th**in
th "   "   "   " " **th**is
zh "   "   "   " " vi**s**ion

Word classes (parts of speech)

These are printed in italic or sloping print (e.g. *noun, adjective, verb*) after the word and before its definition. Some words can be used as more than one word class (part of speech). When these are defined, no space is left between the entries, e.g.

barricade *noun* (*plural* **barricades**)
  a barrier, especially one put up hastily across a street or door.
barricade *verb* (**barricades, barricading, barricaded**)
  block a street or door with a barricade.

Inflections and plurals

Derived forms of verbs, plurals of nouns, and some comparative and superlative forms of adjectives and adverbs are given after the word class (part of speech).

The first verb form given (ending in *–s*) is used for the present tense. The second form given (ending in *–ing*) is the present participle. When three verb forms are given, e

admit *verb* (admits, admitting, admitted)
the third form is both the past tense (as in 'he *admitted* it') and the past participle ('it was *admitted*'). When four forms are given, e.g.

come *verb* (comes, coming, came, come)
freeze *verb* (freezes, freezing, froze, frozen)

the third is the past tense (as in 'he *came*'; it '*froze*'), and the fourth is the past participle ('he had *come*'; 'it was *frozen*').

Meanings

Many words have more than one meaning. Each meaning is numbered separately.

Labels

Words that are not standard English are labelled as *informal* or *slang* etc.

Examples

Examples of words in use are given in italic or sloping print *like this* to help make a definition clearer, e.g.

beware *verb*
be careful ♦ *Beware of pickpockets.*

Phrases

These are listed and defined under the word class (part of speech) to which they belong, e.g.

jump *verb* (jumps, jumping, jumped)
1 move up suddenly from the ground into the air. 2 go over something by jumping ♦ *The horse jumped the fence.* 3 pass over something; miss out part of a book etc. 4 move suddenly in surprise. 5 pass quickly to a different place or level.
jump at (*informal*) accept something eagerly.
jump on (*informal*) start criticizing someone.
jump the gun start before you should. **jump the queue** not wait your turn.

jump *noun* (*plural* jumps)
1 a jumping movement. 2 an obstacle to jump over. 3 a sudden rise or change.

Usage notes

The dictionary includes over 200 notes on correct usage, grammatical points, and words that are easily confused, e.g.

less *adjective & adverb*
smaller in amount; not so much ♦ *Make less noise.* ♦ *It is less important.*

ℹ USAGE Do not use *less* when you mean *fewer*. You should use *fewer* when you are talking about a number of individual things, and *less* when you are talking about a quantity or mass of something: ♦ *The less batter you make, the fewer pancakes you'll get.*

Origins of words

The derivation (or *etymology*) of a word is given in square brackets at the end of the entry, e.g.

alligator *noun* (*plural* **alligators**)
a large reptile of the crocodile family.
[from Spanish *el lagarto* = the lizard]

This etymology shows that the word *alligator* comes from a Spanish word. Other typical origins of English words are shown in the following examples:

across   [from French *a croix* = crosswise]
adder   [from Old English; originally called *a nadder*, which became *an adder*]
admiral   [from Arabic *amir* = commander]
barbecue   [via American Spanish from a Caribbean word. It originally meant a wooden frame for drying fish]
bard   [from a Celtic word used in Scottish, Irish, and Welsh]
chutney   [from Hindi *chatni*]
dope   [from Dutch *doop* = sauce]
husband   [from Old Norse *husbondi* = master of the house]
kibbutz   [from Hebrew *qibbus* = gathering]
mile   [from Latin *mille* = thousand (paces)]
narcotic   [from Greek *narke* = numbness]
pagoda   [via Portuguese from Persian]
soggy   [from a dialect word *sog* = swamp]
tattoo[1]   [from a Polynesian language]
tea   [via Dutch from Chinese]

Some words are shortenings of other words:

fax   [a shortening of *facsimile*]

Some words are made by putting other words together, sometimes in ways that are not immediately obvious:

honeymoon   [from *honey* + *moon* (because the first intensely passionate feelings gradually wane like the moon)]

Some words are made from the first letters of a phrase:

laser   [from the initials of 'light amplification by stimulated emission of radiation']

Others come from the names of people or places:

guillotine [named after Dr Guillotin, who suggested its use in France in 1789]
pasteurize [named after Louis Pasteur, a 19th-century French scientist who invented the process]
rugby   [named after Rugby School in Warwickshire, where it was first played]

Some origins have interesting stories attached to them:

scapegoat [from *escape* and *goat*, after the goat which the ancient Jews allowed to escape into the desert after the priest had symbolically laid the people's sins upon it]
talent   [from Greek *talanton* = sum of money. The meaning in English is based on the use of the word in a parable in the New Testament (Matthew 25:14–30), in which a man gives his servants 'talents' of money to put to good use]

A few words imitate a sound they represent or are associated with:

zap   [imitating the sound of a blow or shot]

Aa

a *adjective* (called the *indefinite article* and changing to **an** before most vowel sounds)
1 one (but not any special one) ♦ *Can you lend me a book?* **2** each; per ♦ *We see it once a day or once an hour.*

aback *adverb*
taken aback surprised.
[from Old English *on baec* = backwards]

abacus (*say* ab-a-kus) *noun* (*plural* **abacuses**)
a frame used for counting with beads sliding on wires.
[from a Greek word *abax* meaning 'slab'. An early form of abacus was a slab of wood with a coating of dust, for writing on and adding up figures]

abandon *verb* (**abandons, abandoning, abandoned**)
1 give up ♦ *We never abandoned hope.* **2** leave something without intending to return ♦ *Abandon ship!*
abandonment *noun*

abandon *noun*
a careless and uncontrolled manner ♦ *She was dancing with great abandon.*

abbey *noun* (*plural* **abbeys**)
1 a monastery or convent. **2** a church that was once part of a monastery ♦ *Westminster Abbey.*

abbot *noun* (*plural* **abbots**)
the head of an abbey.

abbreviate *verb* (**abbreviates, abbreviating, abbreviated**)
shorten something.

abbreviation *noun* (*plural* **abbreviations**)
1 a shortened form of a word or words, especially one using the initial letters, such as GCSE, St., USA. **2** abbreviating something.
[from Latin *brevis* = short]

abdicate *verb* (**abdicates, abdicating, abdicated**)
1 resign from a throne. **2** give up an important responsibility.
abdication *noun*

abdomen (*say* ab-dom-en) *noun* (*plural* **abdomens**)
1 the lower front part of a person's or animal's body, containing the stomach, intestines, and other digestive organs. **2** the rear section of an insect's body.
abdominal (*say* ab-**dom**-in-al) *adjective*

abduct *verb* (**abducts, abducting, abducted**)
take a person away illegally; kidnap.
abduction *noun* **abductor** *noun*

abhor *verb* (**abhors, abhorring, abhorred**)
(*formal*) hate something very much.
abhorrent *adjective* **abhorrence** *noun*

abide *verb* (**abides, abiding, abided**)
1 (*old use; past tense* **abode**) remain or dwell somewhere. **2** bear or tolerate ♦ *I can't abide wasps.*
abide by keep a promise etc.
[from Old English]

ability *noun* (*plural* **abilities**)
1 being able to do something. **2** cleverness or talent.

ablaze *adjective*
blazing; on fire.

able *adjective*
1 having the power or skill or opportunity to do something. **2** skilful or clever.
ably *adverb*

-able *suffix* (also **-ble**, **-ible**, and **-uble**)
forms adjectives (e.g. *readable*, *legible*). The nouns formed from these end in **-bility** (e.g. *readability*, *legibility*).

abnormal *adjective*
not normal; unusual.
abnormally *adverb* **abnormality** *noun*

aboard *adverb & preposition*
on or into a ship or aircraft or train.

abolish *verb* (**abolishes, abolishing, abolished**)
put an end to a law or custom etc.
abolition (*say* ab-ol-**ish**-on) *noun*

abominable *adjective*
very bad or unpleasant.
abominably *adverb* **abomination** *noun*

aborigine (*say* ab-er-ij-in-ee) *noun* (*plural* **aborigines**)
one of the original inhabitants of a country.
aboriginal *adjective & noun*
Aborigine one of the original inhabitants of Australia who lived there before the Europeans arrived.
[from Latin *ab origine* = from the beginning]

abort *verb* (**aborts, aborting, aborted**)
put an end to something before it has been completed ♦ *They aborted the space flight because of problems.*

abortion *noun* (*plural* **abortions**)
an operation to remove an unborn child from the womb before it has developed enough to survive.

abortive *adjective*
unsuccessful ♦ *an abortive attempt.*

abound *verb* (**abounds, abounding, abounded**)
1 be plentiful or abundant ♦ *Fish abound in the river.* **2** have something in great quantities ♦ *The river abounds in fish.*

about *preposition*
1 near in amount or size or time etc. ♦ *It costs about £5.* ♦ *Come about two o'clock.* 2 on the subject of; in connection with ♦ *Tell me about your holiday.* 3 all round; in various parts of ♦ *They ran about the playground.*

about *adverb*
1 in various directions ♦ *They were running about.* 2 not far away ♦ *He is somewhere about.*
be about to be going to do something.

above *preposition*
1 higher than. 2 more than.

above *adverb*
at or to a higher place.

abrasive *adjective*
1 that scrapes things away ♦ *an abrasive wheel.* 2 harsh ♦ *an abrasive manner.*

abreast *adverb*
1 side by side. 2 keeping up with something.

abridge *verb* (abridges, abridging, abridged)
shorten a book etc. by using fewer words ♦ *an abridged edition.*
abridgement *noun*

abroad *adverb*
in or to another country.

abrupt *adjective*
1 sudden or hasty ♦ *his abrupt departure.* 2 rather rude and unfriendly; curt ♦ *She has quite an abrupt manner.*
abruptly *adverb* **abruptness** *noun*

abscess (*say* ab-sis) *noun* (*plural* abscesses)
an inflamed place where pus has formed in the body.

abscond *verb* (absconds, absconding, absconded)
go away secretly ♦ *The cashier had absconded with the money.*

absent *adjective*
not here; not present ♦ *absent from school.*
absence *noun*

absent (*say* ab-sent) *verb* (absents, absenting, absented)
absent yourself stay away.

absentee *noun* (*plural* absentees)
a person who is absent.
absenteeism *noun*

absent-minded *adjective*
having your mind on other things; forgetful.

absolute *adjective*
complete; not restricted ♦ *absolute power.*
absolutely *adverb*

absolute zero *noun*
the lowest possible temperature, calculated as −273.15°C.

absolve *verb* (absolves, absolving, absolved)
1 clear a person of blame or guilt. 2 release a person from a promise or obligation.

absorb *verb* (absorbs, absorbing, absorbed)
1 soak up a liquid or gas. 2 receive something and reduce its effects ♦ *The buffers absorbed most of the shock.* 3 take up a person's attention or time.
absorption *noun*

absorbent *adjective*
able to soak up liquids easily ♦ *absorbent paper.*

abstain *verb* (abstains, abstaining, abstained)
1 keep yourself from doing something; refrain. 2 choose not to use your vote.
abstention *noun*

abstinence *noun*
abstaining, especially from alcohol.
abstinent *adjective*

abstract (*say* ab-strakt) *adjective*
1 concerned with ideas, not solid objects ♦ *Truth, hope, and danger are all abstract.* 2 (said about a painting or sculpture) showing the artist's ideas or feelings, not showing a recognizable person or thing.

absurd *adjective*
ridiculous or foolish.
absurdly *adverb* **absurdity** *noun*

abundance *noun*
a large amount, plenty.

abundant *adjective*
plentiful.
abundantly *adverb*

abuse (*say* ab-yooz) *verb* (abuses, abusing, abused)
1 use something badly or wrongly; misuse. 2 hurt someone or treat them cruelly. 3 say unpleasant things about a person or thing.

abuse (*say* ab-yooss) *noun* (*plural* abuses)
1 a misuse ♦ *the abuse of power.* 2 ill-treatment. 3 physical harm or cruelty done to someone.

abusive *adjective*
rude and insulting ♦ *abusive remarks.*

abysmal (*say* ab-iz-mal) *adjective*
extremely bad ♦ *abysmal ignorance.*

abyss (*say* ab-iss) *noun* (*plural* abysses)
an extremely deep pit.
[from Greek *abyssos* = bottomless]

AC *abbreviation*
alternating current.

academic *adjective*
1 to do with education or studying, especially at a school or college or university. 2 theoretical; having no practical use ♦ *an academic point.*

academic *noun* (*plural* academics)
a university or college teacher.

academy *noun* (*plural* **academies**)
1 a school or college, especially one for specialized training. **2** a society of scholars or artists ♦ *The Royal Academy.*
[from Greek *Akademeia*, the name of the garden where the Greek philosopher Plato taught his pupils. The garden was named after *Akademos*, one of the ancient heroes of Athens]

accelerate *verb* (**accelerates, accelerating, accelerated**)
make or become quicker; increase speed.

acceleration *noun* (*plural* **accelerations**)
1 the rate at which the speed of something increases. **2** the rate of change of velocity.

accelerator *noun* (*plural* **accelerators**)
1 the pedal that a driver presses to make a motor vehicle go faster. **2** a thing used to increase the speed of something.

accent (*say* ak-sent) *noun* (*plural* **accents**)
1 the way a person pronounces the words of a language ♦ *She has a French accent.* **2** the main emphasis or stress in a word ♦ *In 'strawberry', the accent is on 'straw-'.* **3** a mark placed over a letter to show how it is pronounced, e.g. on *fête.*

accept *verb* (**accepts, accepting, accepted**)
1 take a thing that is offered or presented. **2** say yes to an invitation, offer, etc.
acceptance *noun*

---

❶ USAGE Do not confuse with *except.*

---

acceptable *adjective*
good enough to accept; pleasing.
acceptably *adverb* **acceptability** *noun*

access (*say* ak-sess) *noun*
1 a way to enter or reach something. **2** the right to use or look at something.

access *verb* (**accesses, accessing, accessed**)
find information that has been stored in a computer.

accessible *adjective*
1 able to be reached. **2** able to be understood easily.
accessibly *adverb* **accessibility** *noun*

accessory (*say* ak-sess-er-ee) *noun* (*plural* **accessories**)
1 an extra thing that goes with something. **2** a person who helps another with a crime.

accident *noun* (*plural* **accidents**)
an unexpected happening, especially one causing injury or damage.
accidental *adjective* **accidentally** *adverb*
by accident by chance; without its being arranged in advance.

acclaim *verb* (**acclaims, acclaiming, acclaimed**)
welcome or applaud.
acclaim *noun* **acclamation** *noun*

accommodate *verb* (**accommodates, accommodating, accommodated**)
1 provide somebody with a place to live, work, or sleep overnight. **2** help by providing something ♦ *We can accommodate you with skis.*

accommodation *noun*
somewhere to live, work, or sleep overnight.

accompanist *noun* (*plural* **accompanists**)
a pianist etc. who accompanies a singer or another musician.

accompany *verb* (**accompanies, accompanying, accompanied**)
1 go somewhere with somebody. **2** be present with something ♦ *Thunder accompanied the storm.* **3** play music, especially on a piano, that supports a singer or another player etc.
accompaniment *noun*

accomplice (*say* a-kum-pliss) *noun* (*plural* **accomplices**)
a person who helps another in a crime etc.

accomplish *verb* (**accomplishes, accomplishing, accomplished**)
do something successfully.
accomplishment *noun*

accomplished *adjective*
skilled.

accord *noun*
agreement; consent.
of your own accord without being asked or compelled.

according *adverb*
according to 1 as stated by ♦ *According to him, we are stupid.* **2** in relation to ♦ *Price the apples according to their size.*

accordingly *adverb*
1 in the way that is required ♦ *I've given you your instructions and I expect you to act accordingly.* **2** therefore.

accordion *noun* (*plural* **accordions**)
a portable musical instrument like a large concertina with a set of piano-type keys at one end, played by squeezing it in and out and pressing the keys.

account *noun* (*plural* **accounts**)
1 a statement of money owed, spent, or received; a bill. **2** an arrangement to keep money in a bank etc. **3** a description or report.
on account of because of. **on no account** under no circumstances; certainly not. **take something into account** consider or include it when making a decision or calculation.

account *verb* (**accounts, accounting, accounted**)
account for make it clear why something happens.
[from early French *conter* = to count]

accountable *adjective*
responsible; having to explain why you have done something.
accountability *noun*

accountant *noun* (*plural* **accountants**)
a person whose job is keeping or inspecting financial accounts.
accountancy *noun*

accumulate *verb* (accumulates, accumulating, accumulated)
pile up or increase.
accumulation *noun*

accurate *adjective*
correct or exact.
accurately *adverb* accuracy *noun*

accuse *verb* (accuses, accusing, accused)
say that a person has committed a crime etc.; blame.
accusation *noun* accuser *noun*

ace *noun* (*plural* **aces**)
1 a playing card with one spot. 2 a very skilful person or thing. 3 (in tennis) a serve that is too good for the other player to reach.

ache *noun* (*plural* **aches**)
a dull continuous pain.

ache *verb* (aches, aching, ached)
have an ache.

achieve *verb* (achieves, achieving, achieved)
succeed in doing or producing something.
achievable *adjective* achievement *noun*

acid *noun* (*plural* **acids**)
a chemical substance that contains hydrogen and neutralizes alkalis. The hydrogen can be replaced by a metal to form a salt.
acidic *adjective* acidity *noun*

acid *adjective*
1 sharp-tasting; sour. 2 looking or sounding bitter ♦ *an acid reply*.
acidly *adverb*

acid rain *noun*
rain made acidic by mixing with waste gases from factories etc.

acknowledge *verb* (acknowledges, acknowledging, acknowledged)
1 admit that something is true. 2 state that you have received or noticed something ♦ *The college wrote back to acknowledge my letter*. 3 express thanks or appreciation for something.
acknowledgement *noun*

acne (*say* ak-nee) *noun*
inflamed red pimples on the face and neck.

acorn *noun* (*plural* **acorns**)
the seed of the oak tree.

acoustic (*say* a-koo-stik) *adjective*
1 to do with sound or hearing. 2 (said about a musical instrument) not electronic ♦ *an acoustic guitar*.
acoustically *adverb*
[from Greek *akouein* = hear]

acoustics (*say* a-**koo**-stiks) *plural noun*
1 the qualities of a hall etc. that make it good or bad for carrying sound. 2 the properties of sound.

acquaint *verb* (acquaints, acquainting, acquainted)
tell somebody about something ♦ *Acquaint him with the facts*.
be acquainted with know slightly.

acquaintance *noun* (*plural* **acquaintances**)
1 a person you know slightly. 2 familiarity with someone or something.

acquire *verb* (acquires, acquiring, acquired)
obtain.

acquisition *noun*
something you have obtained.

acquit *verb* (acquits, acquitting, acquitted)
decide that somebody is not guilty ♦ *The jury acquitted her*.
acquittal *noun*
acquit yourself well perform or do something well.

acre (*say* ay-ker) *noun* (*plural* **acres**)
an area of land measuring 4,840 square yards or 0.405 hectares.
acreage *noun*
[from Old English *aecer* = field]

acrobat *noun* (*plural* **acrobats**)
a person who performs spectacular gymnastic stunts for entertainment.
acrobatic *adjective* acrobatics *plural noun*

acronym (*say* ak-ron-im) *noun* (*plural* **acronyms**)
a word or name that is formed from the initial letters of other words and pronounced as a word in its own right ♦ *Nato is an acronym of North Atlantic Treaty Organization*.

across *preposition & adverb*
1 from one side to the other ♦ *Swim across the river.* ♦ *Are you across yet?* 2 on the opposite side ♦ *the house across the street*.

acrylic (*say* a-**kril**-ik) *noun*
a kind of fibre, plastic, or resin made from an organic acid.

act *noun* (*plural* **acts**)
1 something someone does. 2 a pretence ♦ *She is only putting on an act*. 3 one of the main divisions of a play or opera. 4 each short performance in a programme of entertainment ♦ *a juggling act*. 5 a law passed by a parliament.

act *verb* (acts, acting, acted)
1 do something; perform actions. **2** perform a part in a play or film etc. **3** function; have an effect.

action *noun* (*plural* **actions**)
1 doing something. **2** something done. **3** a battle; fighting ♦ *He was killed in action.* **4** a lawsuit.
out of action not working or functioning. **take action** do something.

activate *verb* (activates, activating, activated)
start something working.
activation *noun* **activator** *noun*

active *adjective*
1 taking part in many activities; energetic. **2** functioning or working; in operation ♦ *an active volcano.* **3** radioactive. **4** (said about a form of a verb) used when the subject of the verb is performing the action. In 'The shop *sells* videos' the verb is active; in 'Videos *are sold* by the shop' the verb is passive.
actively *adverb* **activeness** *noun*

activist *noun* (*plural* **activists**)
a person who is active and energetic, especially in politics.

activity *noun* (*plural* **activities**)
1 an action or occupation ♦ *outdoor activities.* **2** being active or lively.

actor *noun* (*plural* **actors**)
a person who acts a part in a play or film etc.

actress *noun* (*plural* **actresses**)
a woman who acts a part in a play or film etc.

actual *adjective*
real.
actually *adverb* **actuality** *noun*

acupuncture (*say* ak-yoo-punk-cher) *noun*
pricking parts of the body with needles to relieve pain or cure disease.
acupuncturist *noun*

acute *adjective*
1 sharp or strong ♦ *acute pain.* **2** having a sharp mind.
acutely *adverb* **acuteness** *noun*
[from Latin *acus* = needle]

acute accent *noun* (*plural* **acute accents**)
a mark over a vowel, as over *é* in *fiancé.*

acute angle *noun* (*plural* **acute angles**)
an angle of less than 90°.

AD *abbreviation*
Anno Domini (Latin = in the year of Our Lord), used in dates counted from the birth of Jesus Christ.

adamant (*say* ad-am-ant) *adjective*
firm and not giving way to requests.

adapt *verb* (adapts, adapting, adapted)
1 change something so that it is suitable for a new purpose. **2** to become used to a new situation.
adaptable *adjective* **adaptation** *noun*

adaptor *noun* (*plural* **adaptors**)
a device to connect pieces of electrical or other equipment.

add *verb* (adds, adding, added)
1 put one thing with another. **2** make another remark.
add up 1 make or find a total. **2** (*informal*) make sense; seem reasonable.

adder *noun* (*plural* **adders**)
a small poisonous snake.
[from Old English; originally called *a nadder*, which became *an adder*. The same change happened to other Old English words, e.g. *apron*]

addict *noun* (*plural* **addicts**)
a person who does or uses something that he or she cannot give up.
addicted *adjective* **addiction** *noun*

addictive *adjective*
causing a habit that people cannot give up ♦ *an addictive drug.*

addition *noun* (*plural* **additions**)
1 the process of adding. **2** something added.
additional *adjective* **additionally** *adverb*
in addition also; as an extra thing.

additive *noun* (*plural* **additives**)
a substance added to another in small amounts for a special purpose, e.g. as a flavouring.

address *noun* (*plural* **addresses**)
1 the details of the place where someone lives or of where letters etc. should be delivered to a person or firm. **2** (in computing) the part of an instruction that shows where a piece of information is stored in a computer's memory. **3** a speech to an audience.

address *verb* (addresses, addressing, addressed)
1 write an address on a letter etc. **2** make a speech or remark etc. to somebody.

adenoids *plural noun*
thick spongy flesh at the back of the nose and throat, which may hinder breathing.

adept (*say* a-dept) *adjective*
very skilful.

adequate *adjective*
enough or good enough.
adequately *adverb* **adequacy** *noun*

adhere *verb* (adheres, adhering, adhered)
stick to something.
adhesion *noun*

adhesive *adjective*
sticky; causing things to stick together.

adhesive *noun* (*plural* **adhesives**)
a substance used to stick things together; glue.

adjacent *adjective*
near or next to ♦ *I waited in an adjacent room.*

adjective noun (plural **adjectives**)
a word that describes a noun or adds to its
meaning, e.g. big, honest, strange, our.
adjectival adjective adjectivally adverb

adjourn (say a-jern) verb (**adjourns,
adjourning, adjourned**)
1 break off a meeting etc. until a later time.
2 break off and go somewhere else
♦ They adjourned to the library.
adjournment noun

adjudicate (say a-joo-dik-ayt) verb
(**adjudicates, adjudicating, adjudicated**)
act as judge in a competition etc.
adjudication noun adjudicator noun

adjust verb (**adjusts, adjusting, adjusted**)
1 put a thing into its proper position or order.
2 alter something so that it fits or is suitable.
adjustable adjective adjustment noun

ad lib verb (**ad libs, ad libbing, ad libbed**)
say or do something without any rehearsal or
preparation.

administer verb (**administers, administering,
administered**)
1 give or provide something ♦ He administered
medicine. 2 manage business affairs.

admirable adjective
worth admiring; excellent.
admirably adverb

admiral noun (plural **admirals**)
a naval officer of high rank.
[from Arabic amir = commander. The full title
was amir-al bahr = commander of the sea (bahr
= sea). Early Christian writers thought that
amir-al was one word meaning commander,
whereas it meant 'commander of the ...']

admire verb (**admires, admiring, admired**)
1 look at something and enjoy it. 2 think that
someone or something is very good.
admiration noun admirer noun

admission noun (plural **admissions**)
1 admitting. 2 the charge for being allowed to go
in. 3 a statement admitting something; a
confession.

admit verb (**admits, admitting, admitted**)
1 allow someone or something to come in.
2 state reluctantly that something is true;
confess ♦ We admit that the task is difficult.
♦ He admitted his crime.

admittance noun
being allowed to go in, especially to a private
place.

admonish verb (**admonishes, admonishing,
admonished**)
advise or warn someone firmly.
admonition noun

adolescent noun (plural **adolescents**)
a young person at the age between being a child
and being an adult.
adolescence noun adolescent adjective

adopt verb (**adopts, adopting, adopted**)
1 take someone into your family as your own
child. 2 accept something; take something and
use it ♦ They adopted new methods of working.
adoption noun

adore verb (**adores, adoring, adored**)
love a person or thing very much.
adorable adjective adoration noun

adorn verb (**adorns, adorning, adorned**)
decorate.
adornment noun

adrenalin (say a-dren-al-in) noun
a hormone that stimulates the nervous system,
making your heart beat faster and increasing
your energy and your ability to move quickly.

adrift adjective & adverb
drifting.

adulation noun
very great flattery.

adult (say ad-ult) noun (plural **adults**)
a fully grown or mature person.

adultery noun
being unfaithful to your wife or husband by
having sexual intercourse with someone else.
adulterer noun adulterous adjective

advance noun (plural **advances**)
1 a forward movement; progress. 2 an increase.
3 a loan; payment made before it is due.
in advance beforehand; ahead.

advance verb (**advances, advancing,
advanced**)
1 move forward; make progress. 2 lend or pay
money ahead of the proper time ♦ Can you
advance me a month's salary?
advancement noun

advantage noun (plural **advantages**)
1 something useful or helpful. 2 the next point
won after deuce in tennis.
advantageous adjective
take advantage of use a person or thing
profitably or unfairly. to advantage making a
good effect ♦ The painting can be seen to its best
advantage here. to your advantage profitable or
helpful to you.

Advent noun
the period just before Christmas, when
Christians celebrate the coming of Christ.

advent noun
the arrival of a new person or thing ♦ the advent
of computers.

adventure noun (plural **adventures**)
1 an exciting or dangerous experience.
2 willingness to take risks.
adventurer noun adventurous adjective

adverb *noun* (*plural* **adverbs**)
a word that adds to the meaning of a verb or
adjective or another adverb and tells how, when,
or where something happens, e.g. *gently*, *soon*,
and *upstairs*.
adverbial *adjective* **adverbially** *adverb*

adversary (*say* ad-ver-ser-ee) *noun* (*plural*
adversaries)
an opponent or enemy.

adverse *adjective*
unfavourable or harmful ♦ *adverse effects*.
adversely *adverb*

adversity *noun* (*plural* **adversities**)
trouble or misfortune.

advert *noun* (*plural* **adverts**) (*informal*)
an advertisement.

advertise *verb* (**advertises, advertising,
advertised**)
1 praise goods etc. in order to encourage people
to buy or use them. **2** make something publicly
known ♦ *advertise a meeting*. **3** ask or offer by a
public notice ♦ *advertise for a secretary*.
advertiser *noun*

advertisement *noun* (*plural* **advertisements**)
a public notice or announcement, especially one
advertising goods or services in newspapers, on
posters, or in broadcasts.

advice *noun*
1 telling a person what you think he or she
should do. **2** a piece of information ♦ *We
received advice that the goods had been
dispatched*.

❶ USAGE Do not confuse with the verb *advise*.

advisable *adjective*
to be recommended; sensible.
advisability *noun*

advise *verb* (**advises, advising, advised**)
1 give somebody advice; recommend. **2** inform.
adviser *noun* **advisory** *adjective*

aerial *adjective*
1 in or from the air. **2** to do with aircraft.

aerial *noun* (*plural* **aerials**)
a wire or rod etc. for receiving or transmitting
radio or television signals.

aerobics *plural noun*
exercises to stimulate breathing and strengthen
the heart and lungs.
aerobic *adjective*

aerodrome *noun* (*plural* **aerodromes**)
an airfield.

aerodynamic *adjective*
designed to move through the air quickly and
easily.

aeronautics *noun*
the study of aircraft and flying.
aeronautic *adjective* **aeronautical** *adjective*

aeroplane *noun* (*plural* **aeroplanes**)
a flying machine with wings.

aerosol *noun* (*plural* **aerosols**)
a container that holds a liquid under pressure
and can let it out in a fine spray.

aesthetic (*say* iss-thet-ik) *adjective*
to do with the appreciation of beautiful things.

afar *adverb*
far away ♦ *The din was heard from afar*.

affair *noun* (*plural* **affairs**)
1 an event or matter ♦ *The party was a grand
affair*. **2** a temporary sexual relationship
between two people who are not married to each
other.

affairs *plural noun*
the business and activities that are part of
private or public life ♦ *Keep out of my affairs*;
♦ *current affairs*.

affect *verb* (**affects, affecting, affected**)
1 have an effect on; influence. **2** pretend
♦ *She affected ignorance*.

❶ USAGE The word *affect* is a verb. Do not
confuse it with the noun *effect*.

affectation *noun* (*plural* **affectations**)
unnatural behaviour that is intended to impress
other people.

affected *adjective*
pretended and unnatural.

affection *noun* (*plural* **affections**)
a strong liking for a person.

affectionate *adjective*
showing affection; loving.
affectionately *adverb*

affirm *verb* (**affirms, affirming, affirmed**)
state something definitely or firmly.
affirmation *noun*

affirmative *adjective*
that says 'yes' ♦ *an affirmative reply*. (Compare
negative.)

afflict *verb* (**afflicts, afflicting, afflicted**)
cause somebody to suffer ♦ *He is afflicted with
arthritis*.
affliction *noun*

affluent (*say* af-loo-ent) *adjective*
rich.
affluence *noun*

afford *verb* (**affords, affording, afforded**)
1 have enough money to pay for something.
2 have enough time or resources etc. to do
something. **3** to be able to do something without
a risk ♦ *We can't afford to complain*.

affront *verb* (**affronts, affronting, affronted**)
insult or offend someone.

affront noun (plural **affronts**)
an insult.

afloat adjective & adverb
floating; on the sea.

afraid adjective
frightened or alarmed.
I'm afraid I regret ♦ I'm afraid I'm late.

afresh adverb
again; in a new way ♦ We must start afresh.

African adjective
to do with Africa or its people.
African noun (plural **Africans**)
an African person.

aft adverb
at or towards the back of a ship or aircraft.

after preposition
1 later than ♦ Come after tea. 2 behind in place
or order ♦ Which letter comes after H? 3 trying to
catch; pursuing ♦ Run after him. 4 in spite of
♦ We can come after all. 5 in imitation or honour
of ♦ She is named after her aunt. 6 about or
concerning ♦ He asked after you.
after adverb
1 behind ♦ Jill came tumbling after. 2 later
♦ It came a week after.

afternoon noun (plural **afternoons**)
the time from noon or lunchtime to evening.

aftershave noun
a pleasant-smelling lotion that men put on their
skin after shaving.

afterwards adverb
at a later time.

again adverb
1 another time; once more ♦ try again.
2 as before ♦ You will soon be well again.
3 besides; moreover.

against preposition
1 touching or hitting ♦ He leant against the wall.
2 in opposition to; not in favour of ♦ They voted
against the proposal. 3 in preparation for
♦ Protect them against the cold.

age noun (plural **ages**)
1 the length of time a person has lived or a thing
has existed. 2 a special period of history or
geology ♦ the ice age.
ages plural noun (informal) a very long time
♦ We've been waiting for ages. **come of age**
reach the age at which you have an adult's legal
rights and obligations (now at 18 years; formerly
21).
age verb (**ages, ageing, aged**)
make or become old.

aged adjective
1 (say ayjd) having the age of ♦ a girl aged 9.
2 (say **ay**-jid) very old ♦ an aged man.

agency noun (plural **agencies**)
1 the office or business of an agent ♦ a travel
agency. 2 the means by which something is done
♦ Flowers are pollinated by the agency of bees.

agenda (say a-**jen**-da) noun (plural **agendas**)
a list of things to be done or discussed
♦ The agenda is rather long.

agent noun (plural **agents**)
1 a person who organizes things for other
people. 2 a spy ♦ a secret agent.

aggravate verb (**aggravates, aggravating,
aggravated**)
1 make a thing worse or more serious.
2 (informal) annoy.
aggravation noun
[from Latin gravis = heavy]

aggregate noun (plural **aggregates**)
a total amount or score.

aggression noun
starting an attack or war etc.; aggressive
behaviour.

aggressive adjective
likely to attack people; forceful.
aggressively adverb **aggressiveness** noun
aggressor noun

aggrieved (say a-**greevd**) adjective
resentful because of being treated unfairly.

aghast adjective
horrified.

agile adjective
moving quickly or easily.
agilely adverb **agility** noun

agitate verb (**agitates, agitating, agitated**)
1 make someone feel upset or anxious.
2 stir up public interest or concern; campaign
♦ They agitated for a new bypass. 3 shake
something about.
agitation noun **agitator** noun

agnostic (say ag-**nost**-ik) noun (plural
agnostics)
a person who believes that it is impossible to
know whether God exists.
agnosticism noun
[from a- = not + Greek gnostikos = knowing.
The word was invented by the biologist Thomas
Huxley in the 19th century. He based it on the
word gnostic which meant 'relating to
knowledge']

ago adverb
in the past ♦ long ago.

agog adjective
eager and excited.

agony *noun* (*plural* **agonies**)
extremely great pain or suffering.
agonizing *adjective*

agree *verb* (**agrees, agreeing, agreed**)
1 think or say the same as another person etc.
2 consent ♦ *She agreed to come.* **3** suit a person's
health or digestion ♦ *Curry doesn't agree with
me.* **4** correspond in grammatical number,
gender, or person. In 'They were good teachers'
they agrees with *teachers* (both are plural forms)
and *were* agrees with *they*; *was* would be
incorrect because it is singular.

agreeable *adjective*
1 willing ♦ *We shall go if you are agreeable.*
2 pleasant ♦ *an agreeable place.*
agreeably *adverb*

agreement *noun* (*plural* **agreements**)
1 agreeing. **2** an arrangement that people have
agreed on.

agriculture *noun*
cultivating land on a large scale and rearing
livestock; farming.
agricultural *adjective*

aground *adverb* & *adjective*
stranded on the bottom in shallow water.

ahead *adverb*
1 further forward; in front. **2** forwards
♦ *Full steam ahead!*

aid *noun* (*plural* **aids**)
1 help. **2** something that helps ♦ *a hearing aid.*
3 money, food, etc. sent to another country to
help it ♦ *overseas aid.*
in aid of for the purpose of; to help something.

aid *verb* (**aids, aiding, aided**)
help.

Aids *noun*
a disease that greatly weakens a person's ability
to resist infections.
[from the initial letters of 'acquired immune
deficiency syndrome']

ailing *adjective*
1 ill; in poor health. **2** in difficulties; not
successful ♦ *the ailing ship industry.*

ailment *noun* (*plural* **ailments**)
a slight illness.

aim *verb* (**aims, aiming, aimed**)
1 point a gun etc. **2** throw or kick in a particular
direction. **3** try or intend to do something.

aim *noun* (*plural* **aims**)
1 aiming a gun etc. **2** a purpose or intention.

aimless *adjective*
without a purpose.
aimlessly *adverb*

air *noun* (*plural* **airs**)
1 the mixture of gases that surrounds the
earth and which everyone breathes. **2** the open
space above the earth. **3** a tune or melody.
4 an appearance or impression of something
♦ *an air of mystery.* **5** an impressive or haughty
manner ♦ *He puts on airs.*
by air in or by aircraft. **on the air** on radio or
television.

air *verb* (**airs, airing, aired**)
1 put clothes etc. in a warm place to finish
drying. **2** ventilate a room. **3** express ♦ *He aired
his opinions.*

air bag *noun* (*plural* **air bags**)
a safety device in a vehicle, which inflates in
front of the driver or passenger to reduce the
impact in a collision.

air-conditioning *noun*
a system for controlling the temperature, purity,
etc. of the air in a room or building.
air-conditioned *adjective*

aircraft *noun* (*plural* **aircraft**)
an aeroplane, glider, or helicopter etc.

aircraft carrier *noun* (*plural* **aircraft carriers**)
a large ship with a long deck where aircraft can
take off and land.

airfield *noun* (*plural* **airfields**)
an area equipped with runways etc. where
aircraft can take off and land.

air force *noun* (*plural* **air forces**)
the part of a country's armed forces that is
equipped with aircraft.

airline *noun* (*plural* **airlines**)
a company that provides a regular service of
transport by aircraft.

airliner *noun* (*plural* **airliners**)
a large aircraft for carrying passengers.

airlock *noun* (*plural* **airlocks**)
1 a compartment with an airtight door at each
end, through which people can go in and out of
a pressurized chamber. **2** a bubble of air that
stops liquid flowing through a pipe.

airmail *noun*
mail carried by air.

airman *noun* (*plural* **airmen**)
a man who is a member of an air force or of the
crew of an aircraft.

airport *noun* (*plural* **airports**)
a place where aircraft land and take off, with
passenger terminals and other buildings.

air raid *noun* (*plural* **air raids**)
an attack by aircraft.

airstrip *noun* (*plural* **airstrips**)
a strip of ground prepared for aircraft to land and
take off.

airtight *adjective*
not letting air in or out.

airy *adjective*
1 with plenty of fresh air. 2 light as air. 3 vague
and insincere ♦ *airy promises.*
airily *adverb*

aisle (*say* I'll) *noun* (*plural* **aisles**)
1 a passage between or beside rows of seats or
pews. 2 a side part of a church.

ajar *adverb* & *adjective*
slightly open ♦ *Leave the door ajar.*

akin *adjective*
related or similar to ♦ *a feeling akin to regret.*

alarm *noun* (*plural* **alarms**)
1 a warning sound or signal; a piece of
equipment for giving this. 2 a feeling of fear or
worry. 3 an alarm clock.
alarm *verb* (**alarms, alarming, alarmed**)
make someone frightened or anxious.
alarming *adjective*
[from Italian *all' arme!* = to arms!]

alarm clock *noun* (*plural* **alarm clocks**)
a clock that can be set to make a sound at a fixed
time to wake a sleeping person.

alas *interjection*
an exclamation of sorrow.

albatross *noun* (*plural* **albatrosses**)
a large seabird with very long wings.

albino (*say* al-**been**-oh) *noun* (*plural* **albinos**)
a person or animal with no colour in the skin and
hair (which are white).

album *noun* (*plural* **albums**)
1 a book with blank pages in which to keep a
collection of photographs, stamps, autographs,
etc. 2 a collection of songs on a CD, record, or
tape.

alcohol *noun*
1 a colourless liquid made by fermenting sugar
or starch. 2 drinks containing this liquid (e.g.
wine, beer, whisky), that can make people
drunk.
[The original meaning was a powdered cosmetic,
and it came from an Arabic word *al-kuhul*. The
meaning changed to any powder and then to a
refined liquid produced by purifying, as alcohol
is]

alcoholic *adjective*
containing alcohol.
alcoholic *noun* (*plural* **alcoholics**)
a person who is seriously addicted to alcohol.
alcoholism *noun*

ale *noun* (*plural* **ales**)
beer.

alert *adjective*
watching for something; ready to act.
alertly *adverb* **alertness** *noun*
alert *noun* (*plural* **alerts**)
a warning or alarm.
on the alert on the lookout; watchful.

alert *verb* (**alerts, alerting, alerted**)
warn someone of danger etc.; make someone
aware of something.
[from Italian *all' erta* = to the watchtower!]

A level *noun* (*plural* **A levels**)
advanced level in GCSE.

algae (*say* al-jee) *plural noun*
plants that grow in water, with no true stems or
leaves.

algebra (*say* al-jib-ra) *noun*
mathematics in which letters and symbols are
used to represent quantities.
algebraic (*say* al-jib-**ray**-ik) *adjective*
[from Arabic *al-jabr* = putting together broken
parts. It was part of the name of an Arabic
mathematical work written in the 9th century]

alias (*say* ay-lee-as) *noun* (*plural* **aliases**)
a false or different name.
alias *adverb*
also named ♦ *Clark Kent, alias Superman.*

alibi (*say* al-ib-I) *noun* (*plural* **alibis**)
evidence that a person accused of a crime was
somewhere else when it was committed.

alien (*say* ay-lee-en) *noun* (*plural* **aliens**)
1 a person who is not a citizen of the country
where he or she is living; a foreigner. 2 a being
from another world.
alien *adjective*
1 foreign. 2 unnatural ♦ *Cruelty is alien to her
nature.*

alienate (*say* ay-lee-en-ayt) *verb* (**alienates,
alienating, alienated**)
make a person become unfriendly or not willing
to help you.
alienation *noun*

alight *adjective*
1 on fire. 2 lit up.

alike *adjective* & *adverb*
like one another; in the same way ♦ *The twins
are very alike.* ♦ *Treat them alike.*

alimony *noun*
money paid by someone to their wife or husband
after they are separated or divorced;
maintenance.

alive *adjective*
1 living. 2 alert ♦ *Be alive to the possible
dangers.*

alkali (*say* alk-al-I) *noun* (*plural* **alkalis**)
a chemical substance that neutralizes an acid to
form a salt.
alkaline *adjective*
[from Arabic *al-kali* = the ashes (because alkalis
were first obtained from the ashes of seaweed)]

all *adjective*
the whole number or amount of ♦ *All my books
are here;* ♦ *all day.*

all *noun*
1 everything ♦ *That is all I know.* 2 everybody
♦ *All are agreed.*
all *adverb*
1 completely ♦ *She was dressed all in white.*
2 to each team or competitor ♦ *The score is
fifteen all.*
all in (*informal*) exhausted ♦ *I'm all in.*
all-in *adjective* including or allowing everything
♦ *an all-in price.* **all there** (*informal*) having an
alert mind. **all the same** in spite of this; making
no difference ♦ *I like him, all the same.*

Allah *noun*
the Muslim name of God.

allegation (*say* al-ig-ay-shon) *noun* (*plural
allegations*)
a statement made without proof.

allege (*say* a-lej) *verb* (**alleges, alleging,
alleged**)
say something without being able to prove it
♦ *He alleged that I had cheated.*
allegedly (*say* a-lej-id-lee) *adverb*

allegiance (*say* a-lee-jans) *noun* (*plural
allegiances*)
loyalty.

allegory (*say* al-ig-er-ee) *noun* (*plural
allegories*)
a story in which the characters and events
represent or symbolize a deeper meaning, e.g. to
teach a moral lesson.
allegorical (*say* al-ig-o-rik-al) *adjective*

alleluia *interjection*
praise to God.

allergy (*say* al-er-jee) *noun* (*plural* **allergies**)
something that a person is sensitive to and that
can make them ill ♦ *He has an allergy to cats.*
allergic (*say* al-er-jik) *adjective*

alley *noun* (*plural* **alleys**)
1 a narrow street or passage. 2 a place where you
can play bowls or skittles.

alliance (*say* a-leye-ans) *noun* (*plural
alliances*)
an association formed by countries or groups
who wish to support each other.

allied *adjective*
1 joined as allies; on the same side. 2 of the same
kind.

alligator *noun* (*plural* **alligators**)
a large reptile of the crocodile family.
[from Spanish *el lagarto* = the lizard]

alliteration *noun*
the repetition of the same letter or sound at the
beginning of several words to make a special
effect, e.g. in ♦ *Whisper words of wisdom.*

allotment *noun* (*plural* **allotments**)
1 a small rented piece of public land used for
growing vegetables, fruit, or flowers. 2 allotting;
the amount allotted.

allow *verb* (**allows, allowing, allowed**)
1 permit ♦ *Smoking is not allowed.* 2 permit
someone to have something; provide with
♦ *She was allowed £10 for books.* 3 agree
♦ *I allow that you have been patient.*
allowable *adjective*

allowance *noun* (*plural* **allowances**)
an amount of money that is given regularly for a
particular purpose.
make allowances be considerate; excuse
♦ *Make allowances for his age.*

alloy *noun* (*plural* **alloys**)
a metal formed by mixing two or more metals
etc.

all right *adjective* & *adverb*
1 satisfactory. 2 in good condition. 3 as desired.
4 yes, I consent.

all-round *adjective*
general; not specialist ♦ *an all-round athlete.*
all-rounder *noun*

allude *verb* (**alludes, alluding, alluded**)
refer to something without naming it.
allusion *noun*

---

❶ USAGE Do not confuse with *elude*.

---

allure *verb* (**allures, alluring, allured**)
attract or fascinate someone.
allure *noun* **alluring** *adjective*

ally (*say* al-eye) *noun* (*plural* **allies**)
1 a country in alliance with another. 2 a person
who cooperates with another.
ally *verb* (**allies, allying, allied**)
form an alliance.

almighty *adjective*
1 having complete power. 2 (*informal*) very
great ♦ *an almighty din.*

almond (*say* ah-mond) *noun* (*plural* **almonds**)
an oval edible nut.

almost *adverb*
near to being something but not quite ♦ *almost
ready.*

alone *adjective*
without any other people or things; without
help.

along *preposition*
following the length of something ♦ *Walk along
the path.*
along *adverb*
1 on or onwards ♦ *Push it along.*
2 accompanying somebody ♦ *I've brought my
brother along.*
along with as well as; together with

alongside *preposition* & *adverb*
next to something; beside.

aloof *adverb*
apart; not taking part ♦ *We stayed aloof from
their quarrels.*

aloof *adjective*
distant and not friendly in manner ♦ *She seemed aloof.*

aloud *adverb*
in a voice that can be heard.

alpha *noun*
the first letter of the Greek alphabet, = a.

alphabet *noun* (*plural* **alphabets**)
the letters used in a language, usually arranged in a set order.
alphabetical *adjective* **alphabetically** *adverb*
[from *alpha* and *beta*, the first two letters of the Greek alphabet. The Hebrew names *aleph* and *beth* are related to the Greek words]

already *adverb*
by now; before now.

Alsatian (*say* al-**say**-shan) *noun* (*plural* **Alsatians**)
a German shepherd dog.

also *adverb*
in addition; besides.

altar *noun* (*plural* **altars**)
a table or similar structure used in religious ceremonies.

---

❶ USAGE Do not confuse with the verb *alter*.

---

alter *verb* (**alters, altering, altered**)
make or become different; change.
alteration *noun*

---

❶ USAGE Do not confuse with the noun *altar*.

---

alternate (*say* ol-**tern**-at) *adjective*
1 happening or coming one after the other ♦ *alternate layers of sponge and cream.* 2 one in every two ♦ *We meet up on alternate Fridays.*
alternately *adverb*

---

❶ USAGE See the note at *alternative*.

---

alternate (*say* ol-**tern**-ayt) *verb* (**alternates, alternating, alternated**)
use or come alternately.
alternation *noun*

alternating current *noun* (*plural* **alternating currents**)
electric current that keeps reversing its direction at regular intervals.

alternative *adjective*
available instead of something else.
alternatively *adverb*

---

❶ USAGE Do not confuse *alternative* with *alternate*. If there are *alternative colours* it means that there is a choice of two or more colours, but *alternate colours* means that there is first one colour and then the other.

---

alternative *noun* (*plural* **alternatives**)
one of two or more possibilities.
no alternative no choice.

alternative energy *noun*
any form of energy that does not use up the earth's resources or harm the environment.

alternative medicine *noun*
types of medical treatment that are not based on ordinary medicine.

alternator *noun* (*plural* **alternators**)
a dynamo that generates an alternating current.

although *conjunction*
though.

altitude *noun* (*plural* **altitudes**)
the height of something, especially above sea level.

alto *noun* (*plural* **altos**)
1 an adult male singer with a very high voice.
2 a contralto.

altogether *adverb*
1 with all included; in total ♦ *The outfit costs £20 altogether.* 2 completely ♦ *The stream dries up altogether in summer.* 3 on the whole
♦ *Altogether, it was a good concert.*

---

❶ USAGE Do not confuse *altogether* and *all together*.

---

aluminium *noun*
a lightweight silver-coloured metal.

always *adverb*
1 at all times. 2 often ♦ *You are always crying.*
3 whatever happens ♦ *You can always sleep on the floor.*

Alzheimer's disease *noun*
a serious disease of the brain which affects some old people and makes them confused and forgetful.

a.m. *abbreviation*
before noon.

amalgamate *verb* (**amalgamates, amalgamating, amalgamated**)
mix or combine.
amalgamation *noun*

amateur (*say* am-at-er) *noun* (*plural* **amateurs**)
a person who does something as a hobby, not as a professional.

amateurish *adjective*
not done or made very well; not skilful.

amaze *verb* (**amazes, amazing, amazed**)
surprise somebody greatly; fill with wonder.
amazement *noun*

amazing *adjective*
very surprising or remarkable.

amazon noun (plural **amazons**)
a strong or athletic woman.
[The Amazons were a mythical race of women warriors. The Greeks thought that the name came from a- = without + mazos = breast, believing that the Amazons used to cut off their right breast in order to hold a bow better]

ambassador noun (plural **ambassadors**)
a person sent to a foreign country to represent his or her own government.

amber noun
1 a hard clear yellowish substance used for making ornaments. 2 a yellow traffic light shown as a signal for caution, placed between red (= stop) and green (= go).

ambidextrous adjective
able to use either your left hand or your right hand equally well.

ambiguous adjective
having more than one possible meaning; unclear.
ambiguously adverb ambiguity noun

ambition noun (plural **ambitions**)
1 a strong desire to achieve something.
2 the thing desired.

ambitious adjective
full of ambition.

ambivalent (say am-**biv**-al-ent) adjective
having mixed feelings about something (e.g. liking and disliking it).
ambivalence noun

amble verb (ambles, ambling, ambled)
walk at a slow easy pace.

ambulance noun (plural **ambulances**)
a vehicle equipped to carry sick or injured people.

ambush noun (plural **ambushes**)
a surprise attack from troops etc. who have concealed themselves.

ambush verb (ambushes, ambushing, ambushed)
attack someone after lying in wait for them.

amen interjection
a word used at the end of a prayer or hymn, meaning 'may it be so'.

amend verb (amends, amending, amended)
alter something in order to improve it.
amendment noun
make amends make up for having done something wrong; atone.

American adjective
1 to do with the continent of America. 2 to do with the United States of America.
American noun

amino acid (say a-**meen**-oh) noun (plural **amino acids**)
an acid found in proteins.

amiss adjective
wrong or faulty ♦ She knew something was amiss.

ammonia noun
a colourless gas or liquid with a strong smell.

ammunition noun
a supply of bullets, shells, grenades, etc. for use in fighting.

amnesia (say am-**nee**-zee-a) noun
loss of memory.

amnesty noun (plural **amnesties**)
a general pardon for people who have committed a crime.

amoeba (say a-**mee**-ba) noun (plural **amoebas**)
a microscopic creature consisting of a single cell which constantly changes shape and can split itself in two.

among or **amongst** preposition
1 surrounded by; in ♦ There were weeds among the flowers. 2 between ♦ Divide the sweets among the children.

amount noun (plural **amounts**)
1 a quantity. 2 a total.

amount verb (amounts, amounting, amounted)
amount to 1 add up to. 2 be equivalent to ♦ Their reply amounts to a refusal.

amp noun (plural **amps**)
1 an ampere. 2 (informal) an amplifier.

ampere (say am-pair) noun (plural **amperes**)
a unit for measuring electric current.

amphibian noun (plural **amphibians**)
1 an animal able to live both on land and in water, such as a frog, toad, or newt. 2 a vehicle that can move on both land and water.

amphibious adjective
able to live or move on both land and in water.

ample adjective
1 quite enough ♦ ample provisions. 2 large.
amply adverb

amplifier noun (plural **amplifiers**)
a piece of equipment for making a sound or electrical signal louder or stronger.

amplify verb (amplifies, amplifying, amplified)
1 make a sound or electrical signal louder or stronger. 2 give more details about something ♦ Could you amplify that point?

amplitude noun
1 (in science) the strength of a sound wave or electronic signal. 2 largeness or abundance.

amputate verb (amputates, amputating, amputated)
cut off an arm or leg by a surgical operation.
amputation noun

amuse *verb* (amuses, amusing, amused)
1 make a person laugh or smile. 2 make time pass pleasantly for someone.
amusing *adjective*

amusement *noun* (*plural* **amusements**)
1 being amused. 2 a way of passing time pleasantly.

an *adjective* SEE **a**.

anachronism (*say* an-ak-ron-izm) *noun* (*plural* **anachronisms**)
something wrongly placed in a particular historical period, or regarded as out of date ◆ *Bows and arrows would be an anachronism in modern warfare.*
[from Greek *chronos* = time]

anaemia (*say* a-nee-mee-a) *noun*
a poor condition of the blood that makes a person pale.
anaemic *adjective*

anaesthetic (*say* an-iss-**thet**-ik) *noun* (*plural* **anaesthetics**)
a substance or gas that makes you unable to feel pain.
anaesthesia *noun*

anaesthetist (*say* an-**ees**-thet-ist) *noun* (*plural* **anaesthetists**)
a person trained to give anaesthetics.
anaesthetize *verb*

anagram *noun* (*plural* **anagrams**)
a word or phrase made by rearranging the letters of another ◆ *'Trap' is an anagram of 'part'.*

anal (*say* **ay**-nal) *adjective*
to do with the anus.

analogy (*say* a-**nal**-oj-ee) *noun* (*plural* **analogies**)
a comparison between things that are alike in some ways ◆ *the analogy between the human heart and a pump.*
analogous *adjective*

analyse *verb* (analyses, analysing, analysed)
1 examine and interpret something ◆ *The book analyses the causes of the war.* 2 separate something into its parts.

analysis *noun* (*plural* **analyses**)
1 a separation of something into its parts. 2 a detailed examination of something.
analytic *adjective* **analytical** *adjective*

anarchist (*say* an-er-kist) *noun* (*plural* **anarchists**)
a person who believes that all forms of government are bad and should be abolished.

anarchy (*say* **an**-er-kee) *noun*
1 lack of government or control, resulting in lawlessness. 2 complete disorder.

anatomy (*say* an-**at**-om-ee) *noun*
the study of the structure of the bodies of humans or animals.
anatomical *adjective* **anatomist** *noun*

ancestor *noun* (*plural* **ancestors**)
anyone from whom a person is descended.
ancestral *adjective* **ancestry** *noun*

anchor *noun* (*plural* **anchors**)
a heavy object joined to a ship by a chain or rope and dropped to the bottom of the sea to stop the ship from moving.

anchor *verb* (anchors, anchoring, anchored)
1 fix or be fixed by an anchor. 2 fix something firmly.

ancient *adjective*
1 very old. 2 belonging to the distant past ◆ *ancient history.*

and *conjunction*
1 together with; in addition to ◆ *We had cakes and buns.* 2 so that; with this result ◆ *Work hard and you will pass.* 3 to ◆ *Go and buy a pen.*

android *noun* (*plural* **androids**)
(in science fiction) a robot that looks like a human being.

anecdote *noun* (*plural* **anecdotes**)
a short amusing or interesting story about a real person or thing.

angel *noun* (*plural* **angels**)
1 an attendant or messenger of God. 2 a very kind or beautiful person.
angelic (*say* an-**jel**-ik) *adjective*
[from Greek *angelos* = messenger]

anger *noun*
a strong feeling that you have towards someone who has done wrong or has done something you do not like.

anger *verb* (angers, angering, angered)
make a person angry.

angle *noun* (*plural* **angles**)
1 the space between two lines or surfaces that meet; the amount by which a line or surface must be turned to make it lie along another. 2 a point of view.

angle *verb* (angles, angling, angled)
1 put something in a slanting position. 2 present news etc. from one point of view.

angler *noun* (*plural* **anglers**)
a person who fishes with a fishing rod and line.
angling *noun*

Anglican *adjective*
to do with the Church of England.
Anglican *noun*

Anglo-Saxon *noun* (*plural* **Anglo-Saxons**)
1 an English person, especially of the time before the Norman conquest in 1066. 2 the form of English spoken from about 700 to 1150; Old English.

angry *adjective* (**angrier, angriest**)
feeling anger.
angrily *adverb*

angular *adjective*
1 having angles or sharp corners. **2** (said about a person) bony, not plump.

animal *noun* (*plural* **animals**)
1 a living thing that can feel and usually move about ♦ *Horses, birds, fish, bees, and people are all animals.* **2** a cruel or uncivilized person.

animate *verb* (**animates, animating, animated**)
make a thing lively.
animation *noun*

animated *adjective*
1 lively and excited. **2** (said about a film) made by photographing a series of still pictures and showing them rapidly one after another, so they appear to move.

ankle *noun* (*plural* **ankles**)
the part of the leg where it joins the foot.

annihilate (*say* an-I-il-ayt) *verb* (**annihilates, annihilating, annihilated**)
destroy something completely.
annihilation *noun*

anniversary *noun* (*plural* **anniversaries**)
a day when you remember something special that happened on the same day in a previous year.

announce *verb* (**announces, announcing, announced**)
make something known, especially by saying it publicly or to an audience.
announcement *noun* **announcer** *noun*

annoy *verb* (**annoys, annoying, annoyed**)
1 make a person slightly angry. **2** be troublesome to someone.
annoyance *noun*

annual *adjective*
1 happening once a year ♦ *her annual visit.* **2** calculated over one year ♦ *our annual income.* **3** living for one year or one season ♦ *an annual plant.*
annually *adverb*

annual *noun* (*plural* **annuals**)
1 a book that comes out once a year. **2** an annual plant.
[from Latin *annus* = year]

anode *noun* (*plural* **anodes**)
the electrode by which electric current enters a device. (Compare **cathode**.)

anoint *verb* (**anoints, anointing, anointed**)
put oil or ointment on something, especially in a religious ceremony.

anon *adverb* (*old use*)
soon ♦ *I will say more about this anon.*

anon. *abbreviation*
anonymous.

anonymous (*say* an-on-im-us) *adjective*
without the name of the person responsible being known or made public ♦ *an anonymous donor.*
anonymously *adverb* **anonymity** (*say* an-on-im-it-ee) *noun*

anorak *noun* (*plural* **anoraks**)
a thick warm jacket with a hood.
[from an Inuit word]

anorexia (*say* an-er-eks-ee-a) *noun*
an illness that makes a person so anxious to lose weight that he or she refuses to eat.
anorexic *adjective*

another *adjective* & *pronoun*
a different or extra person or thing ♦ *another day*; ♦ *choose another.*

answer *noun* (*plural* **answers**)
1 a reply. **2** the solution to a problem.

answer *verb* (**answers, answering, answered**)
1 give or find an answer to; reply. **2** respond to a signal ♦ *Answer the telephone.*
answer back reply cheekily. **answer for** be responsible for. **answer to** correspond to ♦ *This answers to the description of the stolen bag.*

ant *noun* (*plural* **ants**)
a very small insect that lives as one of an organized group.

antagonism (*say* an-tag-on-izm) *noun*
an unfriendly feeling; hostility.
antagonist *noun* **antagonistic** *adjective*

antagonize *verb* (**antagonizes, antagonizing, antagonized**)
make a person feel hostile or angry.

antelope *noun* (*plural* **antelope** or **antelopes**)
a fast-running animal like a deer, found in Africa and parts of Asia.

antenatal (*say* an-tee-nay-tal) *adjective*
before birth; during pregnancy.

antenna *noun*
1 (*plural* **antennae**) a feeler on the head of an insect or crustacean. **2** (*plural* **antennas**) an aerial.

anthem *noun* (*plural* **anthems**)
a religious or patriotic song, usually sung by a choir or group of people.

anthology *noun* (*plural* **anthologies**)
a collection of poems, stories, songs, etc. in one book.
[from Greek *anthos* = flower + *logia* = collection: early collections of poems were regarded as including the 'flowers', i.e. the most beautiful examples]

anthropoid *adjective*
like a human being ♦ *Gorillas are anthropoid apes.*

anthropology *noun*
the study of human beings and their customs.
anthropological *adjective* **anthropologist** *noun*

antibiotic *noun* (*plural* **antibiotics**)
a substance (e.g. penicillin) that destroys
bacteria or prevents them from growing.

antibody *noun* (*plural* **antibodies**)
a protein that forms in the blood as a defence
against certain substances which it then attacks
and destroys.

anticipate *verb* (**anticipates, anticipating,
anticipated**)
1 take action in advance about something you
are aware of ♦ *A good teacher learns to anticipate
what students will ask.* **2** act before someone else
does ♦ *Others may have anticipated Columbus in
discovering America.* **3** expect ♦ *We anticipate
that it will rain.*
anticipation *noun* **anticipatory** *adjective*

---

❶ USAGE Many people regard use 3 as incorrect;
it is better to avoid it and use 'expect'.

---

anticlimax *noun* (*plural* **anticlimaxes**)
a disappointing ending or result where
something exciting had been expected.

anticlockwise *adverb* & *adjective*
moving in the direction opposite to clockwise.

antics *plural noun*
funny or foolish actions.

anticyclone *noun* (*plural* **anticyclones**)
an area where air pressure is high, usually
producing fine settled weather.

antidote *noun* (*plural* **antidotes**)
something that acts against the effects of a poison
or disease.

antifreeze *noun*
a liquid added to water to make it less likely to
freeze.

antihistamine *noun* (*plural* **antihistamines**)
a drug that protects people against unpleasant
effects when they are allergic to something.

antimony *noun*
a brittle silvery metal.

antiquarian (*say* anti-**kwair**-ee-an) *adjective*
to do with the study of antiques.

antiquated *adjective*
old-fashioned.

antique (*say* an-**teek**) *adjective*
very old; belonging to the distant past.

antique *noun* (*plural* **antiques**)
something that is valuable because it is very old.

antiquity (*say* an-**tik**-wit-ee) *noun*
ancient times.

anti-Semitic (*say* anti-sim-**it**-ik) *adjective*
hostile or prejudiced towards Jews.
anti-Semitism (*say* anti-**sem**-it-izm) *noun*

antiseptic *adjective*
1 able to destroy bacteria, especially those that
cause things to become septic or to decay.
2 thoroughly clean and free from germs.

antiseptic *noun* (*plural* **antiseptics**)
a substance with an antiseptic effect.

antisocial *adjective*
unfriendly or inconsiderate towards other
people.

antler *noun* (*plural* **antlers**)
the branching horn of a deer.

anus (*say* **ay**-nus) *noun* (*plural* **anuses**)
the opening at the lower end of the alimentary
canal, through which solid waste matter is
passed out of the body.

anvil *noun* (*plural* **anvils**)
a large block of iron on which a blacksmith
hammers metal into shape.

anxious *adjective*
1 worried. **2** eager ♦ *She is anxious to please us.*
anxiously *adverb* **anxiety** *noun*

any *adjective* & *pronoun*
1 one or some ♦ *Have you any wool?* ♦ *There
isn't any.* **2** no matter which ♦ *Come any day you
like.* **3** every ♦ *Any fool knows that!*

any *adverb*
at all; in some degree ♦ *Is that any better?*

anybody *noun* & *pronoun*
any person.

anyhow *adverb*
1 anyway. **2** (*informal*) carelessly ♦ *He does his
work anyhow.*

anyone *noun* & *pronoun*
anybody.

anything *noun* & *pronoun*
any thing.

anyway *adverb*
whatever happens; whatever the situation
may be.

anywhere *adverb*
in or to any place.

anywhere *pronoun*
any place ♦ *Anywhere will do.*

aorta (*say* ay-**or**-ta) *noun* (*plural* **aortas**)
the main artery that carries blood away from the
left side of the heart.

apart *adverb*
1 away from each other; separately ♦ *Keep your
desks apart.* **2** into pieces ♦ *It fell apart.*
3 excluded ♦ *Joking apart, what do you think
of it?*
apart from excluding, other than.

apartheid (*say* a-**part**-hayt) *noun*
the political policy that used to be practised in
South Africa, of keeping people of different races
apart.
[Afrikaans, = being apart]

apartment *noun* (*plural* **apartments**)
1 a set of rooms. **2** (*American*) a flat.

apathy (*say* ap-ath-ee) *noun*
not being interested in something or caring much about it.
apathetic (*say* ap-a-**thet**-ik) *adjective*

ape *noun* (*plural* **apes**)
any of the four kinds of monkey (gorillas, chimpanzees, orang-utans, and gibbons) that do not have a tail.

ape *verb* (**apes, aping, aped**)
imitate or mimic.

aperture *noun* (*plural* **apertures**)
an opening.

apex (*say* **ay**-peks) *noun* (*plural* **apexes**)
the tip or highest point.

aplomb (*say* a-**plom**) *noun*
dignity and confidence ♦ *She handled the press conference with aplomb.*

apologetic *adjective*
making an apology.
apologetically *adverb*

apologize *verb* (**apologizes, apologizing, apologized**)
make an apology.

apology *noun* (*plural* **apologies**)
1 a statement saying that you are sorry for having done something wrong or badly.
2 something very poor ♦ *this feeble apology for a meal.*

apoplexy (*say* ap-op-lek-see) *noun*
1 sudden loss of the ability to feel and move, caused by the blocking or breaking of a blood vessel in the brain. **2** (*informal*) rage or anger.
apoplectic *adjective*

Apostle *noun* (*plural* **Apostles**)
any of the twelve men sent out by Christ to preach the Gospel.

apostrophe (*say* a-**poss**-trof-ee) *noun* (*plural* **apostrophes**)
the punctuation mark ' used to show that letters have been missed out (as in *I can't* = I cannot) or to show possession (as in *the boy's book*; *the boys' books*).

appalling *adjective*
shocking; very unpleasant.

apparatus *noun*
the equipment for a particular experiment or job etc.

apparent *adjective*
1 clear or obvious ♦ *His embarrassment was apparent to everyone.* **2** seeming; appearing to be true but not really so ♦ *I could not understand her apparent indifference.*
apparently *adverb*

apparition *noun* (*plural* **apparitions**)
1 a ghost. **2** something strange or surprising that appears.

appeal *verb* (**appeals, appealing, appealed**)
1 ask for something earnestly or formally ♦ *They appealed for funds.* **2** ask for a decision to be changed ♦ *He appealed against the prison sentence.* **3** seem attractive or interesting ♦ *Cricket doesn't appeal to me.*

appeal *noun* (*plural* **appeals**)
1 asking for something you badly need. **2** asking for a decision to be changed. **3** attraction or interest.

appear *verb* (**appears, appearing, appeared**)
1 come into sight. **2** seem. **3** take part in a play, film, or show etc.

appearance *noun* (*plural* **appearances**)
1 appearing. **2** what somebody looks like; what something appears to be.

appease *verb* (**appeases, appeasing, appeased**)
calm or pacify someone, especially by giving in to demands.
appeasement *noun*

appendage *noun* (*plural* **appendages**)
something added or attached; a thing that forms a natural part of something larger.

appendicitis *noun*
inflammation of the appendix.

appendix *noun*
1 (*plural* **appendixes**) a small tube leading off from the intestine. **2** (*plural* **appendices**) a section added at the end of a book.

appetite *noun* (*plural* **appetites**)
1 desire for food. **2** an enthusiasm for something ♦ *an appetite for violent films.*

appetizing *adjective*
(said about food) looking and smelling good to eat.

applaud *verb* (**applauds, applauding, applauded**)
show that you like something, especially by clapping your hands.

applause *noun*
clapping.

apple *noun* (*plural* **apples**)
a round fruit with a red, yellow, or green skin.

appliance *noun* (*plural* **appliances**)
a device or piece of equipment ♦ *electrical appliances.*

applicable (*say* ap-lik-a-bul) *adjective*
able to be applied; suitable or relevant.

applicant *noun* (*plural* **applicants**)
a person who applies for a job or position.

application *noun* (*plural* **applications**)
1 the action of applying. **2** a formal request.
3 the ability to apply yourself. **4** (in computing) a program or piece of software designed for a particular purpose.

applied *adjective*
put to practical use ♦ *applied maths.*

apply *verb* (applies, applying, applied)
1 put one thing on another. **2** start using something. **3** concern; be relevant ♦ *This rule does not apply to you.* **4** make a formal request ♦ *apply for a job.*
apply yourself give all your attention to a job; work diligently.

appoint *verb* (appoints, appointing, appointed)
1 choose a person for a job. **2** arrange something officially ♦ *They appointed a time for the meeting.*

appointment *noun* (*plural* **appointments**)
1 an arrangement to meet or visit somebody at a particular time. **2** choosing somebody for a job. **3** a job or position.

apposition *noun*
placing things together, especially nouns and phrases in a grammatical relationship. In *the reign of Elizabeth, our Queen,* 'our Queen' is in apposition to 'Elizabeth'.

appreciable *adjective*
enough to be noticed or felt; perceptible.
appreciably *adverb*

appreciate *verb* (appreciates, appreciating, appreciated)
1 enjoy or value something. **2** understand. **3** increase in value.
appreciation *noun* **appreciative** *adjective*

apprehend *verb* (apprehends, apprehending, apprehended)
1 seize or arrest someone. **2** understand.

apprehension *noun*
1 fear or worry. **2** understanding. **3** the arrest of a person.

apprehensive *adjective*
anxious or worried.

apprentice *noun* (*plural* **apprentices**)
a person who is learning a trade or craft by a legal agreement with an employer.
apprenticeship *noun*

apprentice *verb* (apprentices, apprenticing, apprenticed)
place a person as an apprentice.

approach *verb* (approaches, approaching, approached)
1 come near. **2** go to someone with a request or offer ♦ *They approached me for help.* **3** set about doing something or tackling a problem.

approach *noun* (*plural* **approaches**)
1 approaching. **2** a way or road.

appropriate (*say* a-**proh**-pree-at) *adjective*
suitable.
appropriately *adverb*

appropriate (*say* a-proh-pree-ayt) *verb* (appropriates, appropriating, appropriated)
take something and use it as your own.
appropriation *noun*

approval *noun*
approving somebody or something.
on approval received by a customer to examine before deciding to buy.

approve *verb* (approves, approving, approved)
1 say or think that a person or thing is good or suitable. **2** agree formally to something ♦ *The committee has approved the expenditure.*

approximate (*say* a-**proks**-im-at) *adjective*
almost exact or correct but not completely so.
approximately *adverb*

approximate (*say* a-**proks**-im-ayt) *verb* (approximates, approximating, approximated)
make or be almost the same as something.

apricot *noun* (*plural* **apricots**)
a juicy orange-coloured fruit with a stone in it.
[from Spanish or Portuguese]

April *noun*
the fourth month of the year.
[from Latin *Aprilis*]

apron *noun* (*plural* **aprons**)
1 a piece of clothing worn over the front of the body, especially to protect other clothes. **2** a hard-surfaced area on an airfield where aircraft are loaded and unloaded.

apt *adjective*
1 likely ♦ *He is apt to be careless.* **2** suitable ♦ *an apt quotation.*
aptly *adverb* **aptness** *noun*

aptitude *noun*
a talent or skill ♦ *an aptitude for languages.*

aquarium *noun* (*plural* **aquariums**)
a tank or building in which live fish and other water animals are displayed.

aquatic *adjective*
to do with water ♦ *aquatic sports.*

aqueduct *noun* (*plural* **aqueducts**)
a bridge carrying a water channel across low ground or a valley.

Arab *noun* (*plural* **Arabs**)
a member of a Semitic people living in parts of the Middle East and North Africa.
Arabian *adjective*

Arabic *adjective*
to do with the Arabs or their language.

Arabic *noun*
the language of the Arabs.

arabic numerals *plural noun*
the symbols 1, 2, 3, 4, etc. (Compare **Roman numerals**.)

arable *adjective*
suitable for ploughing or growing crops on
♦ *arable land.*

arbitrary (*say* ar-bit-rer-ee) *adjective*
chosen or done on an impulse, not according to
a rule or law ♦ *an arbitrary decision.*
arbitrarily *adverb*

arbitration *noun*
settling a dispute by calling in someone from
outside to make a decision.
arbitrate *verb* **arbitrator** *noun*

arbour (*say* ar-ber) *noun* (*plural* **arbours**)
a shady place among trees.

arc *noun* (*plural* **arcs**)
1 a curve; part of the circumference of a circle.
2 a luminous electric current passing between
two electrodes.

arcade *noun* (*plural* **arcades**)
a covered passage or area, especially for
shopping.

arch[1] *noun* (*plural* **arches**)
1 a curved structure that helps to support a
bridge or other building etc. 2 something shaped
like this.

arch *verb* (**arches, arching, arched**)
form something into an arch; curve ♦ *The cat
arched its back and hissed.*

arch[2] *adjective*
pretending to be playful; mischievous ♦ *an arch
smile.*
archly *adverb*

archaeology (*say* ar-kee-ol-oj-ee) *noun*
the study of ancient civilizations by digging for
the remains of their buildings, tools, coins, etc.
and examining them.
archaeological *adjective* **archaeologist** *noun*

archaic (*say* ar-kay-ik) *adjective*
belonging to former or ancient times.

archangel *noun* (*plural* **archangels**)
an angel of the highest rank.

archbishop *noun* (*plural* **archbishops**)
the chief bishop of a region.

arch-enemy *noun* (*plural* **arch-enemies**)
the chief enemy.

archer *noun* (*plural* **archers**)
a person who shoots with a bow and arrows.

archery *noun*
the sport of shooting at a target with a bow and
arrows.

archetype (*say* ark-i-typ) *noun* (*plural*
archetypes)
the original form or model from which others are
copied.

archipelago (*say* ark-i-**pel**-ag-oh) *noun* (*plural*
archipelagos)
a large group of islands, or the sea containing
these.

architect (*say* ark-i-tekt) *noun* (*plural*
architects)
a person who designs buildings.
[from Greek *arch-* = chief + Greek *tekton*
= builder]

architecture *noun*
1 the process of designing buildings.
2 a particular style of building ♦ *Elizabethan
architecture.*
architectural *adjective*

archives (*say* ark-I'vz) *plural noun*
the historical documents etc. of an organization
or community.

archway *noun* (*plural* **archways**)
an arched passage or entrance.

arc lamp or **arc light** *noun* (*plural* **arc lamps**
or **arc lights**)
a light using an electric arc.

arctic *adjective*
very cold ♦ *The weather was arctic.*

ardour (*say* ar-der) *noun*
enthusiasm or passion.

arduous *adjective*
needing much effort; laborious.
arduously *adverb*

area *noun* (*plural* **areas**)
1 the measurement of a surface, or the amount of
space a surface covers ♦ *The area of the room is
20 square metres.* 2 a particular region or piece of
land. 3 a subject or activity.

arena (*say* a-**reen**-a) *noun* (*plural* **arenas**)
the level area in the centre of an amphitheatre or
sports stadium.
[from Latin, = sand: the floors of Roman arenas
were covered with sand to soak up the blood that
was spilt in fighting between gladiators]

aren't (*mainly spoken*)
are not.
aren't I? (*informal*) am I not?

arguable *adjective*
possible but not certain.
arguably *adverb*

argue *verb* (**argues, arguing, argued**)
1 say that you disagree; exchange angry
comments. 2 state that something is true and
give reasons.

argument *noun* (*plural* **arguments**)
1 a disagreement or quarrel. 2 a reason or series
of reasons put forward.

argumentative *adjective*
fond of arguing.

aria (*say* ar-ee-a) *noun* (*plural* **arias**)
a solo in an opera or oratorio.

arid *adjective*
dry and barren.

arise *verb* (arises, arising, arose, arisen)
1 come into existence; come to people's notice
♦ *Problems arose.* 2 (*old use*) rise; stand up
♦ *Arise, Sir Francis.*

aristocracy (*say* a-ris-**tok**-ra-see) *noun*
people of the highest social rank; members of the nobility.

aristocrat (*say* a-ris-tok-rat) *noun* (*plural* aristocrats)
a member of the aristocracy.
aristocratic *adjective*

arithmetic *noun*
the science or study of numbers; calculating with numbers.
arithmetical *adjective*

ark *noun* (*plural* arks)
1 (in the Bible) the ship in which Noah and his family escaped the Flood. 2 a wooden box in which the writings of the Jewish Law were kept.

arm¹ *noun* (*plural* arms)
1 either of the two upper limbs of the body, between the shoulder and the hand. 2 a sleeve.
3 something shaped like an arm or jutting out from a main part. 4 the raised side part of a chair.
armful *noun*

arm² *verb* (arms, arming, armed)
1 supply someone with weapons. 2 prepare for war.

armada (*say* ar-**mah**-da) *noun* (*plural* armadas)
a fleet of warships.
the Armada or **Spanish Armada** the warships sent by Spain to invade England in 1588.

armadillo *noun* (*plural* armadillos)
a small burrowing South American animal whose body is covered with a shell of bony plates.

armature *noun* (*plural* armatures)
the current-carrying part of a dynamo or electric motor.

armchair *noun* (*plural* armchairs)
a chair with arms.

armed forces or **armed services** *plural noun*
a country's army, navy, and air force.

armistice *noun* (*plural* armistices)
an agreement to stop fighting in a war or battle.

armour *noun*
1 a protective covering for the body, formerly worn in fighting. 2 a metal covering on a warship, tank, or car to protect it from missiles.
armoured *adjective*

armpit *noun* (*plural* armpits)
the hollow underneath the top of the arm, below the shoulder.

arms *plural noun*
1 weapons. 2 a coat of arms.
up in arms protesting vigorously.

arms race *noun*
competition between nations in building up supplies of weapons, especially nuclear weapons.

army *noun* (*plural* armies)
1 a large number of people trained to fight on land. 2 a large group.

aroma (*say* a-**roh**-ma) *noun* (*plural* aromas)
a smell, especially a pleasant one.
aromatic (*say* a-ro-**mat**-ik) *adjective*

around *adverb* & *preposition*
all round; about.

arouse *verb* (arouses, arousing, aroused)
1 stir up a feeling in someone ♦ *You've aroused my curiosity.* 2 wake someone up.

arpeggio (*say* ar-**pej**-ee-oh) *noun* (*plural* arpeggios)
the notes of a musical chord played one after the other instead of together.

arrange *verb* (arranges, arranging, arranged)
1 put things into a certain order; adjust. 2 form plans for something ♦ *We arranged to be there.*
3 prepare music for a particular purpose.
arrangement *noun*

array *noun* (*plural* arrays)
1 a display. 2 an orderly arrangement.

arrears *plural noun*
1 money that is owing and ought to have been paid earlier. 2 a backlog of work etc.
in arrears behind with payments.

arrest *verb* (arrests, arresting, arrested)
1 seize a person by authority of the law. 2 stop a process or movement.

arrest *noun* (*plural* arrests)
1 arresting somebody ♦ *The police made several arrests.* 2 stopping something.

arrive *verb* (arrives, arriving, arrived)
1 reach the end of a journey or a point on it.
2 come ♦ *The great day arrived.*
arrival *noun*

arrogant *adjective*
behaving in an unpleasantly proud way because you think you are superior to other people.
arrogantly *adverb* **arrogance** *noun*

arrow *noun* (*plural* arrows)
1 a pointed stick to be shot from a bow. 2 a sign with an outward-pointing V at the end, used to show direction or position.
arrowhead *noun*
[from Old Norse]

arsenic *noun*
a very poisonous metallic substance.

arson *noun*
the crime of deliberately setting fire to a house or building.
arsonist *noun*

art *noun* (*plural* **arts**)
1 producing something beautiful, especially by painting or drawing; things produced in this way. 2 a skill ♦ *the art of sailing.*

artefact *noun* (*plural* **artefacts**)
an object made by humans, especially one from the past that is studied by archaeologists.

artery *noun* (*plural* **arteries**)
1 one of the tubes that carry blood away from the heart to all parts of the body. (Compare **vein**.) 2 an important road or route.
arterial (*say* ar-**teer**-ee-al) *adjective*

artesian well *noun* (*plural* **artesian wells**)
a well that is bored straight down into a place where water will rise easily to the surface.

artful *adjective*
crafty.
artfully *adverb*

arthritis (*say* arth-**ry**-tiss) *noun*
a disease that makes joints in the body stiff and painful.
arthritic (*say* arth-**rit**-ik) *adjective*

arthropod *noun* (*plural* **arthropods**)
an animal of the group that includes insects, spiders, crabs, and centipedes.

artichoke *noun* (*plural* **artichokes**)
a kind of plant with a flower head used as a vegetable.
[from Arabic]

article *noun* (*plural* **articles**)
1 a piece of writing published in a newspaper or magazine. 2 an object.
definite article the word 'the'. **indefinite article** the word 'a' or 'an'.

articulate (*say* ar-**tik**-yoo-lat) *adjective*
able to express things clearly and fluently.

articulate (*say* ar-**tik**-yoo-layt) *verb*
(**articulates, articulating, articulated**)
1 say or speak clearly. 2 connect by a joint.
articulation *noun*

articulated *adjective*
(said about a vehicle) in two sections that are connected by a flexible joint ♦ *an articulated lorry.*

artificial *adjective*
not natural; made by human beings in imitation of a natural thing.
artificially *adverb* **artificiality** *noun*

artificial intelligence *noun*
the use of computers to perform tasks normally requiring human intelligence, e.g. decision-making.

artificial respiration *noun*
helping somebody to start breathing again after their breathing has stopped.

artillery *noun*
1 large guns. 2 the part of the army that uses large guns.

artist *noun* (*plural* **artists**)
1 a person who produces works of art, especially a painter. 2 an entertainer.
artistry *noun*

artistic *adjective*
1 to do with art or artists. 2 having a talent for art.
artistically *adverb*

arts *plural noun*
subjects (e.g. languages, literature, or history) in which opinion and understanding are very important, as opposed to sciences where measurements and calculations are used.
the arts painting, music, and writing etc., considered together.

as *adverb*
equally or similarly ♦ *This is just as easy.*

as *preposition*
in the function or role of ♦ *Use it as a handle.*

as *conjunction*
1 when or while ♦ *She slipped as she got off the bus.* 2 because ♦ *As he was late, we missed the train.* 3 in a way that ♦ *Leave it as it is.*
as for with regard to ♦ *As for you, I despise you.*
as it were in a way ♦ *She became, as it were, her own enemy.* **as well** also.

A/S *abbreviation*
advanced subsidiary level in GCSE.

asbestos *noun*
a fireproof material made up of fine soft fibres.

ascend *verb* (**ascends, ascending, ascended**)
go up.
ascend the throne become king or queen.

ascent *noun* (*plural* **ascents**)
1 ascending. 2 a way up; an upward path or slope.

ascertain (*say* as-er-**tayn**) *verb* (**ascertains, ascertaining, ascertained**)
find something out by asking.
ascertainable *adjective*

ascetic (*say* a-**set**-ik) *adjective*
not allowing yourself pleasure and luxuries.
asceticism *noun*

ascribe *verb* (**ascribes, ascribing, ascribed**)
regard something as belonging to or caused by; attribute ♦ *She ascribes her success to good luck.*

asexual *adjective*
(in biology) not involving sexual activity ♦ *asexual reproduction.*

ash¹ *noun* (*plural* **ashes**)
the powder that is left after something has been burned.
ashy *adjective*

ash² *noun* (*plural* **ashes**)
a tree with silver-grey bark.

ashamed *adjective*
feeling shame.

Asian *adjective*
to do with Asia or its people.
Asian *noun* (*plural* **Asians**)
an Asian person.

Asiatic *adjective*
to do with Asia.

aside *adverb*
1 to or at one side ♦ *pull it aside.* 2 away; in reserve.
aside *noun* (*plural* **asides**)
words spoken so that only certain people will hear.

ask *verb* (**asks, asking, asked**)
1 speak so as to find out or get something.
2 invite ♦ *Ask her to the party.*

asleep *adverb* & *adjective*
sleeping.

asparagus *noun*
a plant whose young shoots are eaten as a vegetable.

aspect *noun* (*plural* **aspects**)
1 one part of a problem or situation ♦ *Violence was the worst aspect of the crime.* 2 a person's or thing's appearance ♦ *The forest had a sinister aspect.* 3 the direction a house etc. faces
♦ *This room has a southern aspect.*

asphalt (*say* ass-falt) *noun*
a sticky black substance like tar, often mixed with gravel to surface roads etc.

asphyxiate (*say* ass-fiks-ee-ayt) *verb*
(**asphyxiates, asphyxiating, asphyxiated**)
suffocate.
asphyxiation *noun*

aspidistra *noun* (*plural* **aspidistras**)
a house plant with broad leaves.

aspirate (*say* asp-er-at) *noun* (*plural* **aspirates**)
the sound of 'h'.

aspiration *noun* (*plural* **aspirations**)
ambition; strong desire.

aspire *verb* (**aspires, aspiring, aspired**)
have an ambition to achieve something
♦ *He aspired to be world champion.*

aspirin *noun* (*plural* **aspirins**)
a medicinal drug used to relieve pain or reduce fever.

ass *noun* (*plural* **asses**)
1 a donkey. 2 (*informal*) a stupid person.

assassin *noun* (*plural* **assassins**)
a person who assassinates somebody.
[from Arabic *hashishi* = hashish-takers: the word was used as a name for a group of Muslims at the time of the Crusades, who were believed to take hashish before going out to kill Christian leaders]

assassinate *verb* (**assassinates, assassinating, assassinated**)
kill an important person deliberately and violently, especially for political reasons.
assassination *noun*

assault *noun* (*plural* **assaults**)
a violent or illegal attack.
assault *verb* (**assaults, assaulting, assaulted**)
make an assault on someone.

assemble *verb* (**assembles, assembling, assembled**)
1 bring or come together. 2 fit or put together the parts of something.
assemblage *noun*

assembly *noun* (*plural* **assemblies**)
1 assembling. 2 a regular meeting, such as when everybody in a school meets together. 3 people who regularly meet for a special purpose; a parliament.

assent *verb* (**assents, assenting, assented**)
consent; say you agree.
assent *noun*
consent or approval.

assert *verb* (**asserts, asserting, asserted**)
state something firmly.
assertion *noun*
assert yourself use firmness or forcefulness.

assertive *adjective*
acting forcefully and with confidence.

assess *verb* (**assesses, assessing, assessed**)
decide or estimate the value or quality of a person or thing.
assessment *noun* **assessor** *noun*

asset *noun* (*plural* **assets**)
something useful.

assets *plural noun*
a person's or company's property that could be sold to pay debts or raise money.

assign *verb* (**assigns, assigning, assigned**)
1 give or allot. 2 appoint a person to perform a task.

assignment *noun* (*plural* **assignments**)
1 assigning. 2 something assigned; a task given to someone.

assimilate *verb* (**assimilates, assimilating, assimilated**)
take in and absorb something, e.g. nourishment into the body or knowledge into the mind.
assimilation *noun*

assist *verb* (assists, assisting, assisted)
help.
assistance *noun*

assistant *noun* (*plural* assistants)
1 a person who assists another; a helper.
2 a person who serves customers in a shop.

assistant *adjective*
helping a person and ranking next below him or
her ♦ *the assistant manager.*

associate *verb* (associates, associating,
associated)
1 connect things in your mind ♦ *I don't associate
Ryan with fitness and healthy living.* 2 spend
time or have dealings with a group of people.

associate *noun* (*plural* associates)
a colleague or companion; a partner.
associate *adjective*

association *noun* (*plural* associations)
1 an organization of people; a society.
2 associating. 3 a connection or link in your
mind.

Association football *noun*
a form of football using a round ball that may not
be handled during play except by the goalkeeper.

assonance (*say* ass-on-ans) *noun*
similarity of vowel sounds, e.g. in *vermin* and
furnish.

assorted *adjective*
of various sorts put together; mixed ♦ *assorted
sweets.*

assortment *noun* (*plural* assortments)
a mixed collection of things.

assume *verb* (assumes, assuming, assumed)
1 accept (without proof or question) that
something is true or sure to happen. 2 take on;
undertake ♦ *She assumed the extra
responsibility.* 3 put on ♦ *He assumed an
innocent expression.*
assumption *noun*
assumed name a false name.

assurance *noun* (*plural* assurances)
1 a promise or guarantee that something is true
or will happen. 2 a kind of life insurance.
3 confidence in yourself.

assure *verb* (assures, assuring, assured)
1 tell somebody confidently; promise. 2 make
certain.

asterisk *noun* (*plural* asterisks)
a star-shaped sign * used to draw attention to
something.

asteroid *noun* (*plural* asteroids)
one of the small planets found mainly between
the orbits of Mars and Jupiter.

asthma (*say* ass-ma) *noun*
a disease that makes breathing difficult.
asthmatic *adjective* & *noun*

astonish *verb* (astonishes, astonishing,
astonished)
surprise somebody greatly.
astonishment *noun*

astound *verb* (astounds, astounding,
astounded)
astonish; shock somebody greatly.

astray *adverb* & *adjective*
away from the right path or place or course of
action.
go astray be lost or mislaid. lead astray make
someone do something wrong.

astride *adverb* & *preposition*
with one leg on each side of something.

astringent *adjective*
1 causing skin or body tissue to contract. 2 harsh
or severe ♦ *astringent criticism.*

astrology *noun*
the study of how the stars and planets may
influence people's lives.
astrologer *noun* astrological *adjective*

astronaut *noun* (*plural* astronauts)
a person who travels in a spacecraft.
astronautics *noun*

astronomical *adjective*
1 to do with astronomy. 2 extremely large
♦ *The restaurant's prices are astronomical.*

astronomy *noun*
the study of the stars and planets and their
movements.
astronomer *noun*

astute *adjective*
clever and good at understanding situations
quickly; shrewd.
astutely *adverb* astuteness *noun*

asylum *noun* (*plural* asylums)
1 refuge and safety offered by one country to
political refugees from another. 2 (*old use*) a
hospital for mentally ill people.

asymmetrical (*say* ay-sim-et-rik-al) *adjective*
not symmetrical.
asymmetrically *adverb*

at *preposition*
This word is used to show 1 position (*at the top*),
2 time (*at midnight*), 3 condition (*Stand at
ease*), 4 direction towards something (*Aim at the
target*), 5 level or price etc. (*Sell them at £1
each*), 6 cause (*We were annoyed at his failure*).
at all in any way. at it doing or working at
something. at once 1 immediately. 2 at the
same time ♦ *It all came out at once.*

atheist (*say* ayth-ee-ist) *noun* (*plural* atheists)
a person who believes that there is no God.
atheism *noun*

athlete *noun* (*plural* athletes)
a person who is good at sport, especially
athletics.

athletic *adjective*
1 physically strong and active. 2 to do with athletes.
athletically *adverb*

athletics *plural noun*
physical exercises and sports, e.g. running, jumping, and throwing.

atlas *noun* (*plural* **atlases**)
a book of maps.
[named after Atlas, a giant in Greek mythology who was punished for taking part in a revolt against the gods by being made to support the sky on his shoulders. *Atlas* was used as the title of a 17th-century Flemish book of maps which had a picture of Atlas at the front]

atmosphere *noun* (*plural* **atmospheres**)
1 the air round the earth. 2 a feeling or mood given by surroundings ♦ *the happy atmosphere of the fairground.* 3 (in science) a unit of pressure, equal to the pressure of the atmosphere at sea level.
atmospheric *adjective*

atom *noun* (*plural* **atoms**)
the smallest particle of a substance.
[from Greek *atomos* = indivisible: people used to think that an atom could not be divided]

atom bomb or **atomic bomb** *noun* (*plural* **atom bombs** or **atomic bombs**)
a bomb that explodes from the energy produced by splitting atoms.

atomic *adjective*
1 to do with an atom or atoms. 2 to do with the energy produced by splitting atoms.

atomic number *noun* (*plural* **atomic numbers**)
(in science) the number of protons in the nucleus of the atom of a chemical element.

atrocity (*say* a-**tross**-it-ee) *noun* (*plural* **atrocities**)
something extremely bad or wicked; wickedness.

attach *verb* (**attaches, attaching, attached**)
1 fix or join to something else. 2 think that something is an important part of something else ♦ *We attach great importance to fitness.*
attachment *noun*
attached to fond of.

attack *noun* (*plural* **attacks**)
1 a violent attempt to hurt or overcome somebody. 2 a piece of strong criticism. 3 sudden illness or pain. 4 an attempt to score a goal in a game.
attack *verb* (**attacks, attacking, attacked**)
make an attack.
attacker *noun*

attain *verb* (**attains, attaining, attained**)
accomplish; succeed in doing or getting something.
attainable *adjective* **attainment** *noun*

attempt *verb* (**attempts, attempting, attempted**)
make an effort to do something; try.
attempt *noun* (*plural* **attempts**)
an effort to do something; a try.

attend *verb* (**attends, attending, attended**)
1 give care and thought to something; look and listen ♦ *Why don't you attend to your teacher?* 2 be present somewhere; go often to a place. 3 look after someone; be an attendant.
attendance *noun*

attendant *noun* (*plural* **attendants**)
a person who helps or accompanies someone.

attention *noun*
1 giving concentration and careful thought ♦ *Pay attention to what I'm saying.* 2 a position in which a soldier etc. stands with feet together and arms straight downwards.

attentive *adjective*
giving attention to something.
attentively *adverb* **attentiveness** *noun*

attic *noun* (*plural* **attics**)
a room in the roof of a house.

attitude *noun* (*plural* **attitudes**)
1 the way a person thinks or behaves. 2 the position of the body; posture.

attract *verb* (**attracts, attracting, attracted**)
1 get someone's attention or interest; seem pleasant to someone. 2 pull something by an invisible force ♦ *Magnets attract metal pins.*

attraction *noun*
1 something that attracts visitors ♦ *a tourist attraction.* 2 what is pleasant or appealing about something ♦ *City life has many attractions.*

attractive *adjective*
1 pleasant or good-looking. 2 interesting or appealing ♦ *an attractive plan.*
attractively *adverb* **attractiveness** *noun*

attribute (*say* a-**trib**-yoot) *verb* (**attributes, attributing, attributed**)
regard something as belonging to or created by ♦ *We attribute his success to hard work.*
attribution *noun*

attribute (*say* **at**-rib-yoot) *noun* (*plural* **attributes**)
a quality or characteristic ♦ *Kindness is one of his attributes.*

attributive (*say* a-**trib**-yoo-tiv) *adjective*
expressing an attribute and placed before the word it describes, e.g. *old* in *the old dog.* (Compare **predicative.**)
attributively *adverb*

auburn *adjective*
(said about hair) reddish-brown.

auction *noun* (*plural* **auctions**)
a public sale where things are sold to the person who offers the most money for them.

auction *verb* (auctions, auctioning, auctioned)
sell something by auction.
auctioneer *noun*

audacious (*say* aw-**day**-shus) *adjective*
bold or daring.
audaciously *adverb* audacity *noun*

audible *adjective*
loud enough to be heard.
audibly *adverb* audibility *noun*

audience *noun* (*plural* audiences)
1 people who have gathered to hear or watch
something. **2** a formal interview with an
important person.

audio *noun*
reproduced sounds.

audio-visual *adjective*
using both sound and pictures to give
information.

audit *noun* (*plural* audits)
an official examination of financial accounts to
see that they are correct.

audit *verb* (audits, auditing, audited)
make an audit of accounts.
auditor *noun*

audition *noun* (*plural* auditions)
a test to see if an actor or musician is suitable for
a job.
audition *verb*

auditorium *noun* (*plural* auditoriums)
the part of a theatre or hall where the audience
sits.

August *noun*
the eighth month of the year.
[named after Augustus Caesar, the first Roman
emperor]

aunt *noun* (*plural* aunts)
the sister of your father or mother; your uncle's
wife.

au pair (*say* oh **pair**) *noun* (*plural* au pairs)
a person from abroad, usually a young woman,
who works for a time in someone's home.

aura (*say* **or**-a) *noun* (*plural* auras)
a general feeling surrounding a person or thing
♦ *an aura of happiness.*

aural (*say* **or**-al) *adjective*
to do with the ear or hearing.
aurally *adverb*

❶ USAGE Do not confuse with *oral.*

aurora (*say* aw-**raw**-ra) *noun* (*plural* auroras)
bands of coloured light appearing in the sky at
night, the **aurora borealis** (*say* bor-ee-**ay**-liss)
in the northern hemisphere and the **aurora
australis** (*say* aw-**stray**-liss) in the southern
hemisphere.

auspices (*say* aw-**spiss**-eez) *plural noun*
protection or support ♦ *under the auspices of the
Red Cross.*

auspicious (*say* aw-**spish**-us) *adjective*
fortunate or favourable ♦ *an auspicious start.*

austere (*say* aw-**steer**) *adjective*
very simple and plain; without luxuries.
austerely *adverb* austerity *noun*

authentic *adjective*
genuine ♦ *an authentic signature.*
authentically *adverb* authenticity *noun*

author *noun* (*plural* authors)
the writer of a book, play, poem, etc.
authorship *noun*

authoritative *adjective*
having proper authority or expert knowledge;
official.

authority *noun* (*plural* authorities)
1 the right or power to give orders to other
people. **2** a person or organization with the right
to give orders. **3** an expert; a book etc. that gives
reliable information ♦ *an authority on spiders.*

authorize *verb* (authorizes, authorizing,
authorized)
give official permission for something.
authorization *noun*

autistic (*say* aw-**tist**-ik) *adjective*
having a disability that makes someone unable
to communicate with other people or respond to
surroundings.
autism *noun*

autobiography *noun* (*plural*
autobiographies)
the story of a person's life written by himself or
herself.
autobiographical *adjective*

autocrat *noun* (*plural* autocrats)
a ruler with unlimited power.
autocratic *adjective* autocratically *adverb*

autocue *noun* (*plural* autocues) (*trade mark*)
a device that displays the script for a television
presenter or newsreader to read.

autograph *noun* (*plural* autographs)
the signature of a famous person.

autograph *verb* (autographs, autographing,
autographed)
sign your name in a book etc.

automatic *adjective*
1 working on its own without continuous
attention or control by people. **2** done without
thinking.
automatically *adverb*

automation *noun*
making processes automatic; using machines
instead of people to do jobs.

automaton (*say* aw-**tom**-at-on) *noun* (*plural* **automatons**)
1 a robot. **2** a person who seems to act mechanically without thinking.

autonomy (*say* aw-**ton**-om-ee) *noun*
1 self-government. **2** the right to act independently without being told what to do.
autonomous *adjective*

autumn *noun* (*plural* **autumns**)
the season between summer and winter.
autumnal *adjective*

auxiliary *adjective*
giving help and support ♦ *auxiliary services*.
auxiliary *noun* (*plural* **auxiliaries**)
a helper.

auxiliary verb *noun* (*plural* **auxiliary verbs**)
a verb such as *do*, *have*, and *will*, which is used to form parts of other verbs, e.g. *have* in *I have finished*.

avail *noun*
to no avail without any success.

available *adjective*
ready or able to be used; obtainable.
availability *noun*

avalanche *noun* (*plural* **avalanches**)
a mass of snow or rock falling down the side of a mountain.

avenge *verb* (**avenges, avenging, avenged**)
take vengeance for something done to harm you.
avenger *noun*

avenue *noun* (*plural* **avenues**)
1 a wide street. **2** a road with trees along both sides.

average *noun* (*plural* **averages**)
1 the value obtained by adding several quantities together and dividing by the number of quantities. **2** the usual or ordinary standard.
average *adjective*
1 worked out as an average ♦ *Their average age is ten*. **2** of the usual or ordinary standard.
average *verb* (**averages, averaging, averaged**)
work out, produce, or amount to as an average.

aversion *noun*
a strong dislike.

avert *verb* (**averts, averting, averted**)
1 turn something away ♦ *People averted their eyes from the accident*. **2** prevent ♦ *We averted a disaster*.

aviary *noun* (*plural* **aviaries**)
a large cage or building for keeping birds.

aviation *noun*
the flying of aircraft.
aviator *noun*

avocado (*say* av-ok-**ah**-doh) *noun* (*plural* **avocados**)
a pear-shaped tropical fruit.
[via Spanish from Nahuatl (a Central American language)]

avoid *verb* (**avoids, avoiding, avoided**)
1 keep yourself away from someone or something. **2** keep yourself from doing something; refrain from ♦ *Avoid rash promises*.
avoidable *adjective* **avoidance** *noun*

avoirdupois (*say* av-wah-dew-**pwah**) *noun*
a system of weights using the unit of 16 ounces = 1 pound.

await *verb* (**awaits, awaiting, awaited**)
wait for.

awake *verb* (**awakes, awaking, awoke, awoken**)
wake up.
awake *adjective*
not asleep.

award *verb* (**awards, awarding, awarded**)
give something officially as a prize, payment, or penalty.
award *noun* (*plural* **awards**)
something awarded, such as a prize or a sum of money.

aware *adjective*
knowing or realizing something ♦ *Were you aware of the danger?*
awareness *noun*

away *adverb*
1 to or at a distance; not at the usual place.
2 out of existence ♦ *The water had boiled away*.
3 continuously or persistently ♦ *We worked away at it*.
away *adjective*
played on an opponent's ground ♦ *an away match*.

awe *noun*
fearful or deeply respectful wonder
♦ *The mountains always fill me with awe*.
awed *adjective* **awesome** *adjective* **awestricken** *adjective* **awestruck** *adjective*

awful *adjective*
1 very bad ♦ *an awful accident*. **2** (*informal*) very great ♦ *That's an awful lot of money*.
awfully *adverb*

awkward *adjective*
1 difficult to use or deal with; not convenient.
2 clumsy; not skilful.
awkwardly *adverb* **awkwardness** *noun*
[from Old Norse *afugr* = turned the wrong way]

awning *noun* (*plural* **awnings**)
a roof-like shelter made of canvas etc.

axe *noun* (*plural* **axes**)
1 a tool for chopping things. **2** (*informal*) being axed.
have an axe to grind have a personal interest in something and want to take care of it.
axe *verb* (**axes, axing, axed**)
1 cancel or abolish something. **2** reduce something greatly.

axis *noun* (*plural* axes)
1 a line through the centre of a spinning object.
2 a line dividing a thing in half. 3 the horizontal or vertical line on a graph.

axle *noun* (*plural* axles)
the rod through the centre of a wheel, on which the wheel turns.

ayatollah (*say* I-a-**tol**-a) *noun* (*plural* ayatollahs)
a Muslim religious leader in Iran.

aye (*say* I) *adverb*
yes.

azure *adjective*
sky-blue.

Bb

babble *verb* (babbles, babbling, babbled)
1 talk very quickly without making sense.
2 make a murmuring sound.
babble *noun* babbler *noun*

baboon *noun* (*plural* baboons)
a kind of large monkey from Africa and Asia. Baboons have long muzzles and short tails.

baby *noun* (*plural* babies)
a very young child or animal.
babyish *adjective*

babysitter *noun* (*plural* babysitters)
someone who looks after a child while the parents are out.

bachelor *noun* (*plural* bachelors)
a man who has not married.
Bachelor of Arts or **Science** a person who has taken a first degree in arts or science.

back *noun* (*plural* backs)
1 the part that is furthest from the front. 2 the back part of the body from the shoulders to the buttocks. 3 the part of a chair etc. that your back rests against. 4 a defending player near the goal in football, hockey, etc.

back *adjective*
1 placed at or near the back. 2 to do with the back ♦ *back pain*.

back *adverb*
1 to or towards the back. 2 to the place you have come from ♦ *Go back home*. 3 to an earlier time or position ♦ *Put the clocks back one hour*.

back *verb* (backs, backing, backed)
1 move backwards. 2 give someone support or help. 3 bet on something. 4 cover the back of something ♦ *Back the rug with canvas*.
backer *noun*
back out refuse to do what you agreed to do.
back up 1 give support or help to a person or thing. 2 (in computing) make a spare copy of a file or data. **back-up** *noun*

backbencher *noun* (*plural* backbenchers)
a Member of Parliament who does not hold an important position.

backbone *noun* (*plural* backbones)
the column of small bones down the centre of the back; the spine.

backfire *verb* (backfires, backfiring, backfired)
1 if a car backfires, it makes a loud noise, caused by an explosion in the exhaust pipe. 2 if a plan backfires, it goes wrong.

background *noun*
1 the back part of a picture, scene, or view etc. 2 the conditions influencing something.
3 a person's family, upbringing, and education.
in the background not noticeable or obvious.

backing *noun*
1 support. 2 material that is used to line the back of something. 3 musical accompaniment.

backlash *noun* (*plural* backlashes)
a violent reaction to an event.

backlog *noun* (*plural* backlogs)
an amount of work that should have been finished but is still waiting to be done.

backstroke *noun*
a way of swimming lying on your back.

backward *adjective*
1 going backwards. 2 slow at learning or developing.
backwardness *noun*

backward *adverb*
backwards.

❶ USAGE The adverb *backward* is mainly used in American English.

backwards *adverb*
1 to or towards the back. 2 with the back end going first. 3 in reverse order ♦ *Count backwards*.
backwards and forwards in each direction alternately; to and fro.

bacon *noun*
smoked or salted meat from the back or sides of a pig.

bacterium *noun* (*plural* bacteria)
a microscopic organism that can cause disease.
bacterial *adjective*

❶ USAGE Note that it is a mistake to use the plural form *bacteria* as if it were the singular. It is incorrect to say 'a bacteria' or 'this bacteria'; correct usage is *this bacterium* or *these bacteria*.

bad *adjective* (**worse, worst**)
1 not having the right qualities; not good.
2 wicked or evil. **3** serious or severe ♦ *a bad accident.* **4** ill or unhealthy. **5** harmful ♦ *Sweets are bad for your teeth.* **6** decayed or rotten ♦ *This meat has gone bad.*
badness *noun*
not bad quite good.

badge *noun* (*plural* **badges**)
a button or sign that you wear to show people who you are or what school or club etc. you belong to.

badger *noun* (*plural* **badgers**)
a grey burrowing animal with a black and white head.

badger *verb* (**badgers, badgering, badgered**)
keep asking someone to do something; pester.

badly *adverb* (**worse, worst**)
1 in a bad way; not well. **2** severely; causing much injury ♦ *He was badly wounded.* **3** very much ♦ *She badly wanted to win.*

baffle *verb* (**baffles, baffling, baffled**)
puzzle or confuse somebody.
bafflement *noun*

bag *noun* (*plural* **bags**)
a container made of a soft material, for holding or carrying things.
bags (*informal*) plenty ♦ *bags of room.*

bag *verb* (**bags, bagging, bagged**)
1 (*informal*) catch or claim something.
2 put something into bags.

baggage *noun*
luggage.

baggy *adjective*
(said about clothes) large and loose.

bagpipes *plural noun*
a musical instrument in which air is squeezed out of a bag into pipes. Bagpipes are played especially in Scotland.

bail¹ *noun*
money that is paid or promised as a guarantee that a person who is accused of a crime will return for trial if he or she is released in the meantime.

bail *verb* (**bails, bailing, bailed**)
provide bail for a person.

bail² *noun* (*plural* **bails**)
one of the two small pieces of wood placed on top of the stumps in cricket.

bail³ *verb* (**bails, bailing, bailed**)
scoop out water that has got into a boat.

bailiff *noun* (*plural* **bailiffs**)
1 a law officer who serves writs and performs arrests. **2** an official who takes people's property when they owe money.

bait *noun*
1 food that is put on a hook or in a trap to catch fish or animals. **2** something that is meant to tempt someone.

bait *verb* (**baits, baiting, baited**)
1 put bait on a hook or in a trap. **2** try to make someone angry by teasing them.

baize *noun*
the thick green cloth that is used for covering snooker tables.

bake *verb* (**bakes, baking, baked**)
1 cook in an oven. **2** make or become very hot.
3 make a thing hard by heating it.

baker *noun* (*plural* **bakers**)
a person who bakes and sells bread or cakes.
bakery *noun*

balance *noun* (*plural* **balances**)
1 a steady position, with the weight or amount evenly distributed. **2** a person's feeling of being steady. **3** a device for weighing things, with two containers hanging from a bar. **4** the difference between money paid into an account and money taken out. **5** the amount of money that someone still has to pay.

balance *verb* (**balances, balancing, balanced**)
make or be steady or equal.

balcony *noun* (*plural* **balconies**)
1 a platform that sticks out from an outside wall of a building. **2** the upstairs part of a theatre or cinema.

bald *adjective*
1 without hair on the top of the head. **2** with no details; blunt ♦ *a bald statement.*
baldly *adverb* **baldness** *noun*

ball¹ *noun* (*plural* **balls**)
1 a round object used in many games.
2 anything that has a round shape ♦ *a ball of string.*
ball of the foot the rounded part of the foot at the base of the big toe.

ball² *noun* (*plural* **balls**)
a formal party where people dance.

ballad *noun* (*plural* **ballads**)
a simple song or poem that tells a story.

ballast (*say* bal-ast) *noun*
heavy material that is carried in a ship to keep it steady.

ball bearings *plural noun*
small steel balls rolling in a groove on which machine parts can move easily.

ballerina (*say* bal-er-een-a) *noun* (*plural* **ballerinas**)
a female ballet dancer.

ballet (*say* bal-ay) *noun* (*plural* **ballets**)
a stage entertainment that tells a story with dancing, mime, and music.

ballistic missile noun (plural **ballistic missiles**)
a missile that is initially powered and guided and then falls under gravity on its target.

balloon noun (plural **balloons**)
1 a bag made of thin rubber that can be inflated and used as a toy or decoration. 2 a large round bag inflated with hot air or light gases to make it rise in the air, often carrying a basket for passengers to ride in. 3 an outline round spoken words in a strip cartoon.

ballot noun (plural **ballots**)
1 a secret method of voting, usually by making a mark on a piece of paper. 2 a piece of paper on which a vote is made.

ballot verb (**ballots, balloting, balloted**)
invite people to vote for something by a ballot.

ballpoint pen noun (plural **ballpoint pens**)
a pen with a tiny ball round which the ink flows.

balm noun
1 a sweet-scented ointment. 2 something that soothes you.

balmy adjective
1 sweet-scented like balm. 2 soft and warm
♦ a balmy breeze.

bamboo noun (plural **bamboos**)
1 a tall plant with hard hollow stems. 2 a stem of the bamboo plant.

ban verb (**bans, banning, banned**)
forbid something officially.

ban noun (plural **bans**)
an order that bans something.

banana noun (plural **bananas**)
a long curved fruit with a yellow or green skin.

band¹ noun (plural **bands**)
1 a strip or loop of something. 2 a range of values, wavelengths, etc.

band² noun (plural **bands**)
1 an organized group of people doing something together ♦ a band of robbers. 2 a group of people playing music together.

band verb (**bands, banding, banded**)
form an organized group.

bandage noun (plural **bandages**)
a strip of material for binding up a wound.
bandage verb

bandit noun (plural **bandits**)
a member of a gang of robbers who attack travellers.

bandwagon noun
jump or climb on the bandwagon join other people in something that is successful.

bandy verb (**bandies, bandying, bandied**)
if a word or story is bandied about, it is mentioned or told by a lot of different people.

bane noun
a cause of trouble or worry etc. ♦ Exams are the bane of our lives!

bang noun (plural **bangs**)
1 a sudden loud noise like that of an explosion. 2 a sharp blow or knock.

bang verb (**bangs, banging, banged**)
1 hit or shut something noisily. 2 make a sudden loud noise.

bang adverb
1 with a bang; suddenly. 2 (informal) exactly
♦ bang in the middle.

banish verb (**banishes, banishing, banished**)
1 punish a person by ordering them to leave a place. 2 drive away doubts or fears.
banishment noun

banisters plural noun
a handrail with upright supports beside a staircase.

banjo noun (plural **banjos**)
an instrument like a guitar with a round body.

bank¹ noun (plural **banks**)
1 a slope. 2 a long piled-up mass of sand, snow, cloud, etc. 3 a row of lights or switches etc.

bank verb (**banks, banking, banked**)
1 build or form a bank. 2 tilt sideways while changing direction ♦ The plane banked as it prepared to land.

bank² noun (plural **banks**)
1 a business that looks after people's money. 2 a reserve supply ♦ a blood bank.

bank verb (**banks, banking, banked**)
put money in a bank.
bank on rely on.

banker noun (plural **bankers**)
a person who runs a bank.

bank holiday noun (plural **bank holidays**)
a public holiday, when banks are officially closed.

bankrupt adjective
unable to pay your debts.
bankruptcy noun

banner noun (plural **banners**)
1 a flag. 2 a strip of cloth with a design or slogan on it, carried on a pole or two poles in a procession or demonstration.

banquet noun (plural **banquets**)
a formal public meal.
banqueting noun

banter noun
playful teasing or joking.
banter verb

baptism noun (plural **baptisms**)
the ceremony of baptizing someone.

Baptist noun (plural **Baptists**)
a member of a group of Christians who believe that a person should not be baptized until he or she is old enough to understand what baptism means.

baptize *verb* (**baptizes, baptizing, baptized**)
receive a person into the Christian Church in a ceremony in which he or she is sprinkled with or dipped in water, and usually given a name or names.

bar *noun* (*plural* **bars**)
1 a long piece of something hard ♦ *a gold bar.*
2 a counter or room where refreshments, especially alcoholic drinks, are served.
3 a barrier or obstruction. 4 one of the small equal sections into which music is divided ♦ *three beats to the bar.*
the Bar barristers.

bar *verb* (**bars, barring, barred**)
1 fasten something with a bar or bars. 2 block or obstruct ♦ *A man with a dog barred the way.*
3 forbid or ban.

barb *noun* (*plural* **barbs**)
the backward-pointing spike of a spear, arrow, or fish hook, which makes the point stay in.

barbarian *noun* (*plural* **barbarians**)
an uncivilized or brutal person.

barbaric *adjective*
savage and cruel.
barbarity *noun* **barbarism** *noun*

barbecue *noun* (*plural* **barbecues**)
1 a metal frame for grilling food over an open fire outdoors. 2 a party where food is cooked in this way.

barbecue *verb* (**barbecues, barbecuing, barbecued**)
cook food on a barbecue.
[via American Spanish from a Caribbean word. It originally meant a wooden frame for drying fish and meat]

barbed *adjective*
1 having a barb or barbs. 2 a barbed comment or remark is deliberately hurtful.

barbed wire *noun*
wire with small spikes in it, used to make fences.

barber *noun* (*plural* **barbers**)
a men's hairdresser.

bar chart *noun* (*plural* **bar charts**)
a diagram that shows amounts as bars of varying width or height.

bar code *noun* (*plural* **bar codes**)
a set of black lines that are printed on goods, library books, etc., and can be read by a computer to give information about the goods, books, etc.

bard *noun* (*plural* **bards**)
a poet or travelling singer.
[from a Celtic word used in Scottish, Irish, and Welsh]

bare *adjective*
1 without clothing or covering. 2 empty
♦ *The cupboard was bare.* 3 plain; without details ♦ *the bare facts.* 4 only just enough
♦ *the bare necessities of life.*
bareness *noun*

bare *verb* (**bares, baring, bared**)
uncover or reveal ♦ *The dog bared its teeth in a snarl.*

barely *adverb*
only just; with difficulty ♦ *We barely reached home in time.*

bargain *noun* (*plural* **bargains**)
1 an agreement about buying or selling or exchanging something. 2 something that you buy cheaply.

bargain *verb* (**bargains, bargaining, bargained**)
argue over the price to be paid or what you will do in return for something.
bargain for be prepared for or expect ♦ *He got more than he bargained for.*

barge *noun* (*plural* **barges**)
a long flat-bottomed boat used on canals.

barge *verb* (**barges, barging, barged**)
push or knock against roughly.
barge in rush into a room rudely.

baritone *noun* (*plural* **baritones**)
a male singer with a voice between a tenor and a bass.

barium (*say* bair-ee-um) *noun*
a soft silvery-white metal.

bark[1] *noun* (*plural* **barks**)
the short harsh sound made by a dog or fox.
bark *verb*
[from Old English *beorc*, imitating the sound]

bark[2] *noun*
the outer covering of a tree's branches or trunk.

barley *noun*
a cereal plant from which malt is made.

bar mitzvah *noun* (*plural* **bar mitzvahs**)
a religious ceremony for Jewish boys aged 13.

barn *noun* (*plural* **barns**)
a farm building for storing hay or grain etc.
barnyard *noun*

barnacle *noun* (*plural* **barnacles**)
a shellfish that attaches itself to rocks and the bottoms of ships.

barometer (*say* ba-rom-it-er) *noun* (*plural* **barometers**)
an instrument that measures air pressure, used in forecasting the weather.

baron *noun* (*plural* **barons**)
1 a member of the lowest rank of noblemen.
2 a powerful owner of an industry or business
♦ *a newspaper baron.*
barony *noun* **baronial** (*say* ba-roh-nee-al) *adjective*

baroness *noun* (*plural* **baronesses**)
a female baron or a baron's wife.

baronet *noun* (*plural* **baronets**)
a nobleman ranking below a baron but above a knight.
baronetcy *noun*

baroque (*say* ba-rok) *noun*
an elaborately decorated style of architecture used in the 17th and 18th centuries.

barracks *noun*
a large building or group of buildings for soldiers to live in.

barrage (*say* ba-rahzh) *noun* (*plural* **barrages**)
1 a dam built across a river. 2 heavy gunfire. 3 a large amount of something ♦ *a barrage of questions.*

barrel *noun* (*plural* **barrels**)
1 a large rounded container with flat ends. 2 the metal tube of a gun, through which the shot is fired.

barrel organ *noun* (*plural* **barrel organs**)
a musical instrument which you play by turning a handle.

barren *adjective*
1 (said about a woman) not able to have children. 2 (said about land) not fertile.

barricade *noun* (*plural* **barricades**)
a barrier, especially one put up hastily across a street or door.

barricade *verb* (**barricades, barricading, barricaded**)
block a street or door with a barricade.

barrier *noun* (*plural* **barriers**)
1 a fence or wall that prevents people from getting past. 2 something that stops you doing something.

barrister *noun* (*plural* **barristers**)
a lawyer who represents people in the higher lawcourts.

barrow *noun* (*plural* **barrows**)
1 a wheelbarrow. 2 a small cart that is pushed or pulled by hand.

barter *verb* (**barters, bartering, bartered**)
trade by exchanging goods for other goods, not for money.

---

❶ USAGE This word does not mean 'to bargain'.

---

barter *noun*
the system of bartering.

basalt (*say* bas-awlt) *noun*
a kind of dark volcanic rock.

base¹ *noun* (*plural* **bases**)
1 the lowest part of something; the part on which a thing stands. 2 a starting point or foundation; a basis. 3 a headquarters. 4 each of the four corners that must be reached by a runner in baseball. 5 a substance that can combine with an acid to form a salt. 6 the number in terms of which other numbers can be expressed in a number system. 10 is the base of the decimal system and 2 is the base of the binary system.

base *verb* (**bases, basing, based**)
use something as a starting point or foundation ♦ *The story is based on facts.*

base² *adjective*
1 dishonourable ♦ *base motives.* 2 not of great value ♦ *base metals.*
basely *adverb* **baseness** *noun*

baseball *noun* (*plural* **baseballs**)
1 an American game in which runs are scored by hitting a ball and running round a series of four bases. 2 the ball used in this game.

basement *noun* (*plural* **basements**)
a room or rooms below ground level.

bash *verb* (**bashes, bashing, bashed**)
hit hard.

bash *noun* (*plural* **bashes**)
1 a hard hit. 2 (*informal*) a try ♦ *Have a bash at it.*

bashful *adjective*
shy and self-conscious.
bashfully *adverb*

basic *adjective*
forming a basis or starting point ♦ *Bread is a basic food.*

basin *noun* (*plural* **basins**)
1 a deep bowl. 2 a washbasin. 3 a sheltered area of water for mooring boats. 4 the area from which water drains into a river ♦ *the Amazon basin.*

basis *noun* (*plural* **bases**)
something to start from or add to; the main principle or ingredient.

bask *verb* (**basks, basking, basked**)
sit or lie comfortably warming yourself in the sun.

basket *noun* (*plural* **baskets**)
a container for holding or carrying things, made of strips of flexible material or wire woven together.

basketball *noun* (*plural* **basketballs**)
1 a game in which goals are scored by putting a ball through high nets. 2 the ball used in this game.

bass (*say* bayss) *adjective*
deep-sounding; the bass part of a piece of music is the lowest part.

bass *noun* (*plural* **basses**)
1 a male singer with a very deep voice. 2 a bass instrument or part.

bassoon *noun* (*plural* **bassoons**)
a bass woodwind instrument.

bastard *noun* (*plural* **bastards**)
1 (*old use*) an illegitimate child. 2 (*slang*) an unpleasant or difficult person or thing.
bastardy *noun*

bat¹ *noun* (*plural* **bats**)
1 a shaped piece of wood used to hit the ball in cricket, baseball, etc. **2** a batsman ♦ *their opening bat.*
off your own bat without help from other people.
bat *verb* (**bats, batting, batted**)
use a bat in cricket etc.

bat² *noun* (*plural* **bats**)
a flying animal that looks like a mouse with wings.

batch *noun* (*plural* **batches**)
a set of things or people dealt with together.

bath *noun* (*plural* **baths**)
1 washing your whole body while sitting in water. **2** a large container for water in which to wash your whole body; this water ♦ *Your bath is getting cold.* **3** a liquid in which something is placed ♦ *an acid bath.*
bath *verb* (**baths, bathing, bathed**)
wash in a bath.

bathe *verb* (**bathes, bathing, bathed**)
1 go swimming. **2** wash something gently.
bathe *noun* **bather** *noun* **bathing suit** *noun*

bathroom *noun* (*plural* **bathrooms**)
a room containing a bath.

baths *plural noun*
1 a building with rooms where people can bath. **2** a public swimming pool.

batsman *noun* (*plural* **batsmen**)
a player who uses a bat in cricket etc.

battalion *noun* (*plural* **battalions**)
an army unit containing two or more companies.

batten *verb* (**battens, battening, battened**)
fasten something down firmly.

batter *verb* (**batters, battering, battered**)
hit hard and often.

batter *noun* (*plural* **batters**)
1 a beaten mixture of flour, eggs, and milk, used for making pancakes etc. **2** a player who is batting in baseball.

battery *noun* (*plural* **batteries**)
1 a device for storing and supplying electricity. **2** a set of similar pieces of equipment; a group of large guns. **3** a series of cages in which poultry or animals are kept close together ♦ *battery farming.*

battle *noun* (*plural* **battles**)
1 a fight between two armies. **2** a struggle.
battlefield *noun* **battleground** *noun*
battle *verb* (**battles, battling, battled**)
fight or struggle.

battlements *plural noun*
the top of a castle wall, often with gaps from which the defenders could fire at the enemy.

battleship *noun* (*plural* **battleships**)
a heavily armed warship.

bawl *verb* (**bawls, bawling, bawled**)
1 shout. **2** cry noisily.

bay¹ *noun* (*plural* **bays**)
a place where the shore curves inwards.

bay² *noun* (*plural* **bays**)
a compartment or small area set aside for something ♦ *a parking bay.*

bay³ *noun* (*plural* **bays**)
the long deep cry of a hunting hound or other large dog.
at bay cornered but defiantly facing attackers ♦ *a stag at bay.* **keep at bay** prevent something from coming near or causing harm ♦ *We need laws to keep poverty at bay.*

bayonet *noun* (*plural* **bayonets**)
a blade that can be fixed to the end of a rifle and used for stabbing.

bay window *noun* (*plural* **bay windows**)
a window that sticks out from the main wall of a house.

bazaar *noun* (*plural* **bazaars**)
1 a market place in an Eastern country. **2** a sale to raise money for a charity etc.

BBC *abbreviation*
British Broadcasting Corporation.

BC *abbreviation*
before Christ (used with dates counting back from the birth of Jesus Christ).

be *verb* (**am, are, is; was, were; being, been**)
1 exist; occupy a position ♦ *The shop is on the corner.* **2** happen; take place ♦ *The wedding is tomorrow.*
This verb is also used **1** to join subject and complement (*He is my teacher*). **2** to form parts of other verbs (*It is raining. He was killed*).
have been have gone to or come to as a visitor etc. ♦ *We have been to Rome.*

beach *noun* (*plural* **beaches**)
the part of the seashore nearest to the water.

beacon *noun* (*plural* **beacons**)
a light or fire used as a signal or warning.

bead *noun* (*plural* **beads**)
1 a small piece of a hard substance with a hole in it for threading with others on a string or wire, e.g. to make a necklace. **2** a drop of liquid ♦ *a bead of sweat.*
[from Old English *gebed*. The original meaning was 'prayer': people kept count of the prayers they said by moving the beads on a rosary, to which the meaning of *bead* was transferred]

beady *adjective*
(said about eyes) small and bright.

beak *noun* (*plural* **beaks**)
the hard horny part of a bird's mouth.
[via early French from Latin *beccus*]

beaker noun (plural **beakers**)
1 a tall drinking mug, often without a handle.
2 a glass container used for pouring liquids in a laboratory.

beam noun (plural **beams**)
1 a long thick bar of wood or metal. 2 a ray or stream of light or other radiation. 3 a happy smile.

beam verb (**beams, beaming, beamed**)
1 smile happily. 2 send out a beam of light or other radiation.

bean noun (plural **beans**)
1 a kind of plant with seeds growing in pods.
2 its seed or pod eaten as food. 3 the seed of coffee.

bear¹ noun (plural **bears**)
a large heavy animal with thick fur and large teeth and claws.

bear² verb (**bears, bearing, bore, borne**)
1 carry or support. 2 have or show a mark etc.
♦ She still bears the scar. 3 endure or stand
♦ I can't bear this pain. 4 produce or give birth to ♦ She bore him two sons.
bearer noun
bear in mind remember something and take it into account. **bear out** support or confirm.

bearable adjective
able to be endured; tolerable.

beard noun (plural **beards**)
hair on a man's chin.
bearded adjective
beard verb (**beards, bearding, bearded**)
come face to face with a person and challenge him or her boldly.

bearing noun (plural **bearings**)
1 the way a person stands, walks, behaves, etc.
2 relevance ♦ My friendship with Tom has no bearing on his selection for the team. 3 the direction or position of one thing in relation to another. 4 a device for preventing friction in a machine ♦ ball bearings.
get your bearings work out where you are in relation to things.

beast noun (plural **beasts**)
1 any large four-footed animal. 2 (informal) a cruel or vicious person.
beastly adjective

beat verb (**beats, beating, beat, beaten**)
1 hit often, especially with a stick. 2 shape or flatten something by beating it. 3 stir vigorously.
4 make repeated movements ♦ His heart beat faster. 5 do better than somebody; overcome.
beater noun
beat noun (plural **beats**)
1 a regular rhythm or stroke ♦ the beat of your heart. 2 emphasis in rhythm; the strong rhythm of pop music. 3 a policeman's regular route.

beautiful adjective
attractive to your senses or your mind.
beautifully adverb

beautify verb (**beautifies, beautifying, beautified**)
make someone beautiful.
beautification noun

beauty noun (plural **beauties**)
1 a quality that gives pleasure to your senses or your mind. 2 a person or thing that has beauty.
3 an excellent example of something.

beaver noun (plural **beavers**)
an animal with soft brown fur and strong teeth; it builds its home in a deep pool which it makes by damming a stream.

beaver verb (**beavers, beavering, beavered**)
work hard ♦ He's beavering away on the computer.

because conjunction
for the reason that.
because of for the reason of ♦ He limped because of his bad leg.

beck noun
at someone's beck and call always ready and waiting to do what he or she asks.

beckon verb (**beckons, beckoning, beckoned**)
make a sign to a person asking him or her to come.

become verb (**becomes, becoming, became, become**)
1 come or grow to be; begin to be ♦ It became dark. 2 be suitable for; make a person look attractive.
become of happen to ♦ What became of it?

bed noun (plural **beds**)
1 a piece of furniture that you sleep or rest on, especially one with a mattress and coverings.
2 a piece of a garden where plants are grown.
3 the bottom of the sea or of a river. 4 a flat base; a foundation. 5 a layer of rock or soil.

bedclothes plural noun
sheets, blankets, etc.

bedpan noun (plural **bedpans**)
a container for use as a lavatory by a bedridden person.

bedraggled (say bid-**rag**-eld) adjective
very untidy; wet and dirty.

bedridden adjective
too weak or ill to get out of bed.

bedrock noun
solid rock beneath soil.

bedroom noun (plural **bedrooms**)
a room for sleeping in.

bedtime noun (plural **bedtimes**)
the time for going to bed.

bee *noun* (*plural* bees)
a stinging insect with four wings that makes honey.

beech *noun* (*plural* beeches)
a tree with smooth bark and glossy leaves.

beef *noun*
meat from an ox, bull, or cow.
[via early French from Latin *bos bovis* = head of cattle]

beefy *adjective*
having a solid muscular body.
beefiness *noun*

beehive *noun* (*plural* beehives)
a box or other container for bees to live in.

beeline *noun*
make a beeline for go straight or quickly towards something.

beer *noun* (*plural* beers)
an alcoholic drink made from malt and hops.
beery *adjective*

beet *noun* (*plural* beet or beets)
a plant with a thick root used as a vegetable or for making sugar.

beetle *noun* (*plural* beetles)
an insect with hard shiny wing covers.

beetroot *noun* (*plural* beetroot)
the dark red root of beet used as a vegetable.

before *adverb*
at an earlier time ♦ *Have you been here before?*
before *preposition* & *conjunction*
1 earlier than ♦ *I was here before you!* 2 in front of ♦ *He came before the judge.*

beforehand *adverb*
earlier; in readiness.

befriend *verb* (befriends, befriending, befriended)
make friends with someone.

beg *verb* (begs, begging, begged)
1 ask to be given money, food, etc. 2 ask formally or desperately.
beg the question argue in an illogical way by relying on the result that you are trying to prove.
go begging be available. I beg your pardon I apologize; I did not hear what you said.

beggar *noun* (*plural* beggars)
1 a person who lives by begging. 2 (*informal*) a person ♦ *You lucky beggar!*
beggary *noun*

begin *verb* (begins, beginning, began, begun)
1 do the earliest or first part of something; start speaking. 2 come into existence ♦ *The problem began last year.* 3 have something as its first part ♦ *The word begins with B.*

beginner *noun* (*plural* beginners)
a person who is just beginning to learn a subject.

beginning *noun* (*plural* beginnings)
the start or first part of something.

begrudge *verb* (begrudges, begrudging, begrudged)
resent having to give or allow something; grudge.

beguile (*say* big-I'll) *verb* (beguiles, beguiling, beguiled)
1 amuse or fascinate. 2 deceive.

behalf *noun*
on behalf of for the benefit of someone else or as their representative ♦ *We are collecting money on behalf of cancer research.* on my behalf for me.

ⓘ USAGE Do not use♦ *on behalf of* (= for someone else) when you mean ♦ *on the part of* (= by someone). For example, do not say: ♦ *This was the worst performance on behalf of Arsenal that I can remember.*

behave *verb* (behaves, behaving, behaved)
1 act in a particular way ♦ *They behaved badly.* 2 show good manners ♦ *Behave yourself!*
behaviour *noun* **behavioural** *adjective*

behead *verb* (beheads, beheading, beheaded)
cut the head off a person or thing; execute a person in this way.

behind *adverb*
1 at or to the back; at a place people have left ♦ *Don't leave it behind.* 2 not making good progress; late ♦ *I'm behind with my rent.*
behind *preposition*
1 at or to the back of; on the further side of. 2 having made less progress than ♦ *He is behind the others in French.* 3 supporting; causing ♦ *What is behind all this trouble?*
behind a person's back kept secret from him or her deceitfully. behind the times out of date.

behind *noun* (*plural* behinds) (*informal*)
a person's bottom.

behindhand *adverb* & *adjective*
late or slow in doing something

beige (*say* bayzh) *noun* & *adjective*
a very light brown colour.

being *noun* (*plural* beings)
1 existence. 2 a creature.

belated *adjective*
coming very late or too late.
belatedly *adverb*

belch *verb* (belches, belching, belched)
1 send out wind from your stomach through your mouth noisily. 2 send out fire or smoke etc. from an opening.
belch *noun*

belief *noun* (*plural* beliefs)
1 believing. 2 something a person believes.

believe *verb* (believes, believing, believed)
think that something is true or that someone is telling the truth.
believable *adjective* **believer** *noun*
believe in think that something exists or is good or can be relied on.

belittle *verb* (belittles, belittling, belittled)
make something seem of little value ♦ *Do not belittle their success.*
belittlement *noun*

bell *noun* (*plural* bells)
1 a cup-shaped metal instrument that makes a ringing sound when struck by the clapper hanging inside it. **2** any device that makes a ringing or buzzing sound to attract attention. **3** a bell-shaped object.

belligerent (*say* bil-ij-er-ent) *adjective*
1 aggressive; eager to fight. **2** fighting; engaged in a war.
belligerently *adverb* **belligerence** *noun*

bellow *noun* (*plural* bellows)
1 the loud deep sound made by a bull or other large animal. **2** a deep shout.
bellow *verb* (bellows, bellowing, bellowed)
give a deep shout.

belly *noun* (*plural* bellies)
the abdomen; the stomach.

belong *verb* (belongs, belonging, belonged)
have a proper place ♦ *The pans belong in the kitchen.*
belong to be the property of; be a member of ♦ *We belong to the same club.*

belongings *plural noun*
a person's possessions.

beloved *adjective*
dearly loved.

below *adverb*
at or to a lower position; underneath ♦ *There's fire down below.*
below *preposition*
lower than; under ♦ *The temperature was ten degrees below zero.*

belt *noun* (*plural* belts)
1 a strip of cloth or leather etc. worn round the waist. **2** a band of flexible material used in machinery. **3** a long narrow area ♦ *a belt of rain.*
belt *verb* (belts, belting, belted)
1 put a belt round something. **2** (*slang*) hit or beat. **3** (*slang*) rush along.

bench *noun* (*plural* benches)
1 a long seat. **2** a long table for working at. **3** the seat where judges or magistrates sit; the judges or magistrates hearing a lawsuit.

bend *verb* (bends, bending, bent)
1 change from being straight. **2** turn downwards; stoop ♦ *She bent to pick it up.*
bend *noun* (*plural* bends)
a place where something bends; a curve or turn ♦ *a bend in the road.*

beneath *preposition*
1 under. **2** unworthy of ♦ *Cheating is beneath you.*
beneath *adverb*
underneath.

benefactor *noun* (*plural* benefactors)
a person who gives money or other help.

beneficial *adjective*
having a good or helpful effect; advantageous.

beneficiary (*say* ben-if-**ish**-er-ee) *noun* (*plural* beneficiaries)
a person who receives benefits, especially from a will.

benefit *noun* (*plural* benefits)
1 something that is helpful or profitable. **2** a payment to which a person is entitled from government funds or from an insurance policy.
benefit *verb* (benefits, benefiting, benefited)
1 do good to a person or thing. **2** receive a benefit.

benevolent *adjective*
1 kind and helpful. **2** formed for charitable purposes ♦ *a benevolent fund.*
benevolently *adverb* **benevolence** *noun*

benign (*say* bin-**l**'n) *adjective*
1 kindly. **2** favourable. **3** (said about a disease) mild, not malignant.
benignly *adverb*

benignant (*say* bin-**ig**-nant) *adjective*
kindly.

bent *adjective*
curved or crooked.
bent on intending to do something.
bent *noun*
a talent for something.

bequeath *verb* (bequeaths, bequeathing, bequeathed)
leave something to a person, especially in a will.

bequest *noun* (*plural* bequests)
something left to a person, especially in a will.

bereaved *adjective*
extremely sad because a relative or friend has died.
bereavement *noun*

berry *noun* (*plural* berries)
any small round juicy fruit without a stone.

berserk (*say* ber-**serk**) *adjective*
go berserk become uncontrollably violent.

berth *noun* (*plural* berths)
1 a sleeping place on a ship or train. **2** a place where a ship can moor.
give a wide berth to keep at a safe distance from a person or thing.
berth *verb* (berths, berthing, berthed)
moor in a berth.

beseech *verb* (beseeches, beseeching, beseeched or besought)
ask earnestly; implore.

beside *preposition*
1 by the side of; near. 2 compared with.
be beside himself or **herself** etc. be very excited or upset.

besides *preposition & adverb*
in addition to; also ♦ *Who came besides you?*
♦ *And besides, it's the wrong colour.*

besiege *verb* (**besieges, besieging, besieged**)
1 surround a place in order to capture it. 2 crowd round ♦ *Fans besieged the singer after the concert.*

besotted *adjective*
too fond of something; fond in a silly way.

besought *past tense* of **beseech.**

best *adjective*
of the most excellent kind; most able to do something.

best *adverb*
1 in the best way; most. 2 most usefully; most wisely ♦ *We had best go.*

best man *noun*
the bridegroom's chief attendant at a wedding.

bestow *verb* (**bestows, bestowing, bestowed**)
present to someone.
bestowal *noun*

best-seller *noun* (*plural* **best-sellers**)
a book that sells in large numbers.

bet *noun* (*plural* **bets**)
1 an agreement that you will receive money if you are correct in choosing the winner of a race, game, etc. or in saying something will happen, and will lose money if you are not correct.
2 the money you risk losing in a bet.

bet *verb* (**bets, betting, bet** or **betted**)
1 make a bet. 2 (*informal*) think most likely; predict ♦ *I bet he will forget.*

beta (*say* beet-a) *noun*
the second letter of the Greek alphabet, = b.

betray *verb* (**betrays, betraying, betrayed**)
1 be disloyal to a person or country etc. 2 reveal something without meaning to.
betrayal *noun* **betrayer** *noun*

betrothed *adjective* (*formal*)
engaged to be married.
betroth *verb* **betrothal** *noun*

better *adjective*
1 more excellent; more satisfactory. 2 recovered from illness.

better *adverb*
1 in a better way; more. 2 more usefully; more wisely ♦ *We had better go.*
get the better of defeat or outwit.

better *verb* (**betters, bettering, bettered**)
1 improve something. 2 do better than.
betterment *noun*

between *preposition & adverb*
1 within two or more given limits ♦ *between the walls.* 2 connecting two or more people, places, or things ♦ *The train runs between London and Glasgow.* 3 shared by ♦ *Divide this money between you.* 4 separating; comparing ♦ *Can you tell the difference between them?*

ℹ USAGE The preposition *between* should be followed by the object form of the pronoun (*me, her, him, them,* or *us*). The expression 'between you and I' is incorrect; say ♦ *between you and me.*

---

beverage *noun* (*plural* **beverages**)
any kind of drink.

bewail *verb* (**bewails, bewailing, bewailed**)
mourn for something.

beware *verb*
be careful ♦ *Beware of pickpockets.*

bewilder *verb* (**bewilders, bewildering, bewildered**)
puzzle someone hopelessly.
bewilderment *noun*

bewitch *verb* (**bewitches, bewitching, bewitched**)
1 put a magic spell on someone. 2 delight someone very much.

beyond *preposition & adverb*
1 further than; further on ♦ *Don't go beyond the fence.* 2 outside the range of; too difficult for
♦ *The problem is beyond me.*

bias *noun* (*plural* **biases**)
1 a feeling or influence for or against someone or something; a prejudice. 2 a tendency to swerve.
3 a slanting direction.

biased *adjective*
prejudiced.

bib *noun* (*plural* **bibs**)
1 a cloth or covering put under a baby's chin during meals. 2 the part of an apron above the waist.

Bible *noun* (*plural* **Bibles**)
the sacred book of the Jews (the Old Testament) and of the Christians (the Old and New Testament).
[from Greek *biblia* = books. The word originally meant rolls of papyrus from Byblos, a port now in Lebanon]

biblical *adjective*
to do with or in the Bible.

bibliography (*say* bib-lee-og-ra-fee) *noun* (*plural* **bibliographies**)
1 a list of books about a subject or by a particular author. 2 the study of books and their history.
bibliographical *adjective*

bicentenary (*say* by-sen-**teen**-er-ee) *noun*
(*plural* **bicentenaries**)
a 200th anniversary.
bicentennial (*say* by-sen-**ten**-ee-al) *adjective*

biceps (*say* by-seps) *noun* (*plural* **biceps**)
the large muscle at the front of the arm above the
elbow.

bicker *verb* (**bickers, bickering, bickered**)
quarrel over unimportant things; squabble.

bicycle *noun* (*plural* **bicycles**)
a two-wheeled vehicle driven by pedals.
bicyclist *noun*

bid¹ *noun* (*plural* **bids**)
1 the offer of an amount you are willing to pay
for something, especially at an auction. **2** an
attempt.
bid *verb* (**bids, bidding, bid**)
make a bid.
bidder *noun*

bid² *verb* (**bids, bidding, bid** (or *old use*) **bade**),
bid or **bidden**)
1 say as a greeting or farewell ♦ *I bid you all
good night.* **2** command ♦ *Do as you are bid* or
bidden.

bidding *noun*
if you do someone's bidding, you do what they
tell you to do.

bide *verb* (**bides, biding, bided**)
bide your time wait patiently for the right time
to do something.

biennial *noun* (*plural* **biennials**)
a plant that lives for two years, flowering and
dying in the second year.

bier (*say* beer) *noun* (*plural* **biers**)
a movable stand on which a coffin or a dead
body is placed before it is buried.

bifocal (*say* by-**foh**-kal) *adjective*
(said about lenses for glasses) made in two
sections, with the upper part for looking at
distant objects and the lower part for reading.

bifocals *plural noun*
bifocal glasses.

big *adjective* (**bigger, biggest**)
1 large. **2** important ♦ *the big match.* **3** more
grown-up; elder ♦ *my big sister.*

bigamy (*say* **big**-a-mee) *noun*
the crime of marrying a person when you are
already married to someone else.
bigamous *adjective* **bigamist** *noun*

bigot *noun* (*plural* **bigots**)
a bigoted person.

bigoted *adjective*
narrow-minded and intolerant.
bigotry *noun*

bike *noun* (*plural* **bikes**) (*informal*)
a bicycle or motorcycle.

bikini *noun* (*plural* **bikinis**)
a woman's two-piece swimsuit.
[named after the island of Bikini in the Pacific
Ocean, where an atomic bomb test was carried
out in 1946, at about the time the bikini was first
worn (both caused great excitement)]

bilateral *adjective*
1 of or on two sides. **2** between two people or
groups ♦ *a bilateral agreement.*

bile *noun*
a bitter liquid produced by the liver, helping to
digest fats.

bilingual (*say* by-**ling**-wal) *adjective*
1 able to speak two languages well. **2** written in
two languages.

bilious *adjective*
feeling sick; sickly.
biliousness *noun*

bill¹ *noun* (*plural* **bills**)
1 a written statement of charges for goods or
services that have been supplied. **2** a poster.
3 a list; a programme of entertainment.
4 the draft of a proposed law to be discussed
by Parliament. **5** (*American*) a banknote.
bill of fare a menu.

bill² *noun* (*plural* **bills**)
a bird's beak.

billabong *noun* (*plural* **billabongs**)
(in Australia) a backwater.

billboard *noun* (*plural* **billboards**)
a tall fence or hoarding for advertisements.

billiards *noun*
a game in which three balls are struck with cues
on a cloth-covered table (**billiard table**).

billion *noun* (*plural* **billions**)
1 a thousand million (1,000,000,000).
2 a million million (1,000,000,000,000).
billionth *adjective* & *noun*

---

❶ USAGE Although the word originally meant a
million million, nowadays it usually means a
thousand million.

---

billow *noun* (*plural* **billows**)
a huge wave.

bin *noun* (*plural* **bins**)
a large or deep container, especially one for
rubbish or litter.
[via Old English from a Celtic word]

binary (*say* **by**-ner-ee) *adjective*
involving sets of two; consisting of two parts.

binary digit *noun* (*plural* **binary digits**)
either of the two digits (0 and 1) used in the
binary system.

binary system or **binary notation** *noun*
(in computing) a system of expressing numbers
by using the digits 0 and 1 only.

bind *verb* (binds, binding, bound)
1 fasten material round something. 2 fasten the pages of a book into a cover. 3 tie up or tie together. 4 make somebody agree to do something.
binder *noun*
bind a person over make him or her agree not to break the law.

bind *noun* (*slang*)
a nuisance; a bore.

binding *noun* (*plural* **bindings**)
something that binds, especially the covers, glue, etc. of a book.

binding *adjective*
(said about an agreement or promise) that must be carried out or obeyed.

binge *noun* (*plural* **binges**) (*slang*)
a time spent eating a lot of food.

bingo *noun*
a game using cards on which numbered squares are crossed out as the numbers are called out at random.

binoculars *plural noun*
a device with lenses for both eyes, making distant objects seem nearer.

biochemistry *noun*
the study of the chemical composition and processes of living things.
biochemical *adjective* **biochemist** *noun*

biodegradable *adjective*
able to be broken down by bacteria in the environment ♦ *All our packaging is biodegradable.*

biography (*say* by-**og**-ra-fee) *noun* (*plural* **biographies**)
the story of a person's life.
biographical *adjective* **biographer** *noun*

biology *noun*
the study of the life and structure of living things.
biological *adjective* **biologist** *noun*

bionic (*say* by-**on**-ik) *adjective*
(said about a person or parts of the body) operated by electronic devices.

biopsy (*say* by-**op**-see) *noun* (*plural* **biopsies**)
examination of tissue from a living body.

biped (*say* by-ped) *noun* (*plural* **bipeds**)
a two-footed animal.

birch *noun* (*plural* **birches**)
1 a deciduous tree with slender branches.
2 a bundle of birch branches for flogging people.

bird *noun* (*plural* **birds**)
1 an animal with feathers, two wings, and two legs. 2 (*slang*) a young woman.
bird's-eye view a view from above.

bird of prey *noun* (*plural* **birds of prey**)
a bird that feeds on animal flesh, such as an eagle or hawk.

birth *noun* (*plural* **births**)
1 the process by which a baby or young animal comes out from its mother's body. 2 origin; parentage ♦ *He is of noble birth.*

birth control *noun*
ways of avoiding conceiving a baby.

birthday *noun* (*plural* **birthdays**)
the anniversary of the day a person was born.

birth rate *noun* (*plural* **birth rates**)
the number of children born in one year for every 1,000 people.

birthright *noun*
a right or privilege to which a person is entitled through being born into a particular family or country.

biscuit *noun* (*plural* **biscuits**)
a small flat kind of cake that has been baked until it is crisp.
[from Latin *bis* = twice + *coctus* = cooked: originally they were twice baked and then dried out in a cool oven to make them keep longer]

bisect (*say* by-**sekt**) *verb* (**bisects, bisecting, bisected**)
divide something into two equal parts.
bisection *noun* **bisector** *noun*

bishop *noun* (*plural* **bishops**)
1 an important member of the clergy in charge of all the churches in a city or district. 2 a chess piece shaped like a bishop's mitre.

bismuth *noun*
a greyish-white metal.

bison (*say* by-son) *noun* (*plural* **bison**)
a wild ox found in North America and Europe, with a large shaggy head.

bit¹ *noun* (*plural* **bits**)
1 a small piece or amount of something.
2 the metal part of a horse's bridle that is put into its mouth. 3 the part of a tool that cuts or grips things when twisted.
a bit 1 a short distance or time ♦ *Wait a bit.*
2 slightly ♦ *I'm a bit worried.* **bit by bit** gradually.

bit² *past tense* of **bite.**

bit³ *noun* (*plural* **bits**)
the smallest unit of information in a computer, expressed as a choice between two possibilities.

bitch *noun* (*plural* **bitches**)
1 a female dog, fox, or wolf. 2 (*informal*) a spiteful woman.
bitchy *adjective*

bite *verb* (**bites, biting, bit, bitten**)
1 cut or take something with your teeth.
2 penetrate; sting. 3 accept bait ♦ *The fish are biting.*
bite the dust die or be killed.

bite *noun* (*plural* **bites**)
1 an act of biting ♦ *She took a bite.* 2 a wound or
mark made by biting ♦ *an insect bite.*
3 a snack.

bitter *adjective*
1 tasting sharp, not sweet. 2 feeling or causing
mental pain or resentment ♦ *a bitter
disappointment.* 3 very cold.
bitterly *adverb* **bitterness** *noun*

bivalve *noun* (*plural* **bivalves**)
a shellfish (e.g. an oyster) that has a shell with
two hinged parts.

bizarre (*say* biz-**ar**) *adjective*
very odd in appearance or effect.

black *noun* (*plural* **blacks**)
1 the very darkest colour, like coal or soot.
2 a person with a very dark or black skin.

black *adjective*
1 of the colour black. 2 (said about a person)
having dark skin. 3 dismal; not hopeful
♦ *The outlook is black.* 4 hostile; disapproving
♦ *He gave me a black look.* 5 very dirty.
6 (said about coffee or tea) without milk.
blackly *adverb* **blackness** *noun*

black *verb* (**blacks, blacking, blacked**)
make a thing black.
black out 1 cover windows etc. so that no light
can penetrate. 2 faint, lose consciousness.
blackout *noun*

blackberry *noun* (*plural* **blackberries**)
a sweet black berry.

blackbird *noun* (*plural* **blackbirds**)
a European songbird, the male of which is black.

blackboard *noun* (*plural* **blackboards**)
a dark board for writing on with chalk.

black box *noun* (*plural* **black boxes**)
a flight recorder.

blacken *verb* (**blackens, blackening,
blackened**)
make or become black.

black eye *noun* (*plural* **black eyes**)
an eye with a bruise round it.

blackguard (*say* blag-**erd**) *noun* (*plural*
blackguards) (*old use*)
a wicked person.

black hole *noun* (*plural* **black holes**)
a region in outer space with such a strong
gravitational field that no matter or radiation can
escape from it.

black ice *noun*
thin transparent ice on roads.

blacklist *verb* (**blacklists, blacklisting,
blacklisted**)
put someone on a list of those who are
disapproved of.

blackmail *verb* (**blackmails, blackmailing,
blackmailed**)
demand money etc. from someone by threats.
blackmail *noun* **blackmailer** *noun*

black market *noun* (*plural* **black markets**)
illegal trading.

black sheep *noun*
a member of a family who behaves badly or has
a bad reputation.

blacksmith *noun* (*plural* **blacksmiths**)
a person who makes and repairs iron things,
especially one who makes and fits horseshoes.

black spot *noun* (*plural* **black spots**)
a dangerous place.

bladder *noun* (*plural* **bladders**)
1 the bag-like part of the body in which urine
collects. 2 the inflatable bag inside a football.

blade *noun* (*plural* **blades**)
1 the flat cutting edge of a knife, sword, axe, etc.
2 the flat wide part of an oar, spade, propeller,
etc. 3 a flat narrow leaf ♦ *blades of grass.*
4 a broad flat bone ♦ *shoulder blade.*

blame *verb* (**blames, blaming, blamed**)
1 say that somebody or something has caused
what is wrong ♦ *They blamed me.* 2 find fault
with someone ♦ *We can't blame them for
wanting a holiday.*
blame *noun*
responsibility for what is wrong.

blancmange (*say* bla-**monj**) *noun* (*plural*
blancmanges)
a jelly-like pudding made with milk.

bland *adjective*
1 having a mild flavour rather than a strong one.
2 lacking any interesting featues or qualities
♦ *a bland manner.*
blandly *adverb* **blandness** *noun*

blank *adjective*
1 not written or printed on; unmarked.
2 without interest or expression ♦ *a blank look.*
3 empty of thoughts ♦ *My mind's gone blank.*
blankly *adverb* **blankness** *noun*
blank *noun* (*plural* **blanks**)
1 an empty space. 2 a blank cartridge.

blanket *noun* (*plural* **blankets**)
1 a warm cloth covering used on a bed etc.
2 any thick soft covering ♦ *a blanket of snow.*
blanket *adjective*
covering all cases or instances ♦ *a blanket ban.*

blank verse *noun*
poetry without rhyme, usually in lines of ten
syllables.

blare *verb* (**blares, blaring, blared**)
make a loud harsh sound.
blare *noun*

blaspheme (*say* blas-**feem**) *verb* (**blasphemes,
blaspheming, blasphemed**)
talk or write irreverently about sacred things.

blasphemy (*say* blas-fim-ee) *noun* (*plural* blasphemies)
irreverent talk about sacred things.
blasphemous *adjective*

blast *noun* (*plural* blasts)
1 a strong rush of wind or air. 2 a loud noise ♦ *the blast of the trumpets.*

blast *verb* (blasts, blasting, blasted)
blow up with explosives.
blast off launch by the firing of rockets.
blast-off *noun*

blatant (*say* blay-tant) *adjective*
very obvious ♦ *a blatant lie.*
blatantly *adverb*

blaze *noun* (*plural* blazes)
a very bright flame, fire, or light.

blaze *verb* (blazes, blazing, blazed)
1 burn or shine brightly. 2 show great feeling ♦ *He was blazing with anger.*

blazer *noun* (*plural* blazers)
a kind of jacket, often with a badge or in the colours of a school or team etc.

bleach *verb* (bleaches, bleaching, bleached)
make or become white.

bleach *noun* (*plural* bleaches)
a substance used to bleach things.

bleak *adjective*
1 bare and cold ♦ *a bleak hillside.* 2 dreary or miserable ♦ *a bleak future.*
bleakly *adverb* bleakness *noun*

bleary *adjective*
watery and not seeing clearly ♦ *bleary eyes.*
blearily *adverb*

bleat *noun* (*plural* bleats)
the cry of a lamb, goat, or calf.

bleat *verb* (bleats, bleating, bleated)
make a bleat.

bleed *verb* (bleeds, bleeding, bled)
1 lose blood. 2 draw blood or fluid from.

blemish *noun* (*plural* blemishes)
a flaw; a mark that spoils a thing's appearance.
blemish *verb*

blench *verb* (blenches, blenching, blenched)
flinch.

blend *verb* (blends, blending, blended)
mix smoothly or easily.

blend *noun* (*plural* blends)
a mixture.

blender *noun* (*plural* blenders)
an electric machine used to mix food or turn it into liquid.

bless *verb* (blesses, blessing, blessed)
1 make sacred or holy. 2 bring God's favour on a person or thing.

blessing *noun* (*plural* blessings)
1 a prayer that blesses a person or thing; being blessed. 2 something that people are glad of.

blight *noun* (*plural* blights)
1 a disease that makes plants wither.
2 something that does a lot of harm ♦ *Vandalism is a blight on our community.*

blight *verb* (blights, blighting, blighted)
1 affect with blight. 2 spoil or damage something ♦ *Injuries have blighted his career.*

blind *adjective*
1 without the ability to see. 2 without any thought or understanding ♦ *blind obedience.*
3 (said about a tube, passage, or road) closed at one end.
blindly *adverb* blindness *noun*

blind *verb* (blinds, blinding, blinded)
make a person blind.

blind *noun* (*plural* blinds)
1 a screen for a window. 2 a deception; something used to hide the truth ♦ *His journey was a blind.*

blind date *noun* (*plural* blind dates)
a date between a man and woman who have not met before.

blindfold *noun* (*plural* blindfolds)
a strip of cloth tied round someone's eyes so that they cannot see.

blindfold *verb* (blindfolds, blindfolding, blindfolded)
cover someone's eyes with a blindfold.

blind spot *noun* (*plural* blind spots)
a subject that you do not understand or know much about.

blink *verb* (blinks, blinking, blinked)
shut and open your eyes rapidly.
blink *noun*

bliss *noun*
perfect happiness.
blissful *adjective* blissfully *adverb*

blister *noun* (*plural* blisters)
a swelling like a bubble, especially on skin.
blister *verb*

blizzard *noun* (*plural* blizzards)
a severe snowstorm.

bloated *adjective*
swollen by fat, gas, or liquid.

blob *noun* (*plural* blobs)
a small round mass of something ♦ *blobs of paint.*

block *noun* (*plural* blocks)
1 a solid piece of something. 2 an obstruction.
3 a large building divided into flats or offices.
4 a group of buildings.

block *verb* (blocks, blocking, blocked)
obstruct; prevent something from moving or being used.
blockage *noun*

blockade *noun* (*plural* blockades)
the blocking of a city or port etc. in order to prevent people and goods from going in or out.

blockade *verb* (blockades, blockading, blockaded)
set up a blockade of a place.

block letters *plural noun*
plain capital letters.

bloke *noun* (*plural* blokes) (*informal*)
a man.

blond or **blonde** *adjective*
fair-haired; fair.

blonde *noun* (*plural* blondes)
a fair-haired girl or woman.

blood *noun*
1 the red liquid that flows through veins and arteries. 2 family relationship; ancestry ♦ *He is of royal blood.*
in cold blood deliberately and cruelly.

blood bank *noun* (*plural* blood banks)
a supply of blood and plasma for transfusions.

bloodbath *noun* (*plural* bloodbaths)
a massacre.

blood donor *noun* (*plural* blood donors)
a person who gives blood for use in transfusions.

blood group *noun* (*plural* blood groups)
any of the classes or types of human blood.

bloodhound *noun* (*plural* bloodhounds)
a large dog that tracks people by their scent.

bloodshed *noun*
the killing or wounding of people.

bloodshot *adjective*
(said about eyes) streaked with red.

blood sport *noun* (*plural* blood sports)
a sport that involves wounding or killing animals.

bloodstream *noun*
the blood circulating in the body.

bloodthirsty *adjective*
eager for bloodshed.

blood vessel *noun* (*plural* blood vessels)
a tube carrying blood in the body; an artery, vein, or capillary.

bloody *adjective* (bloodier, bloodiest)
1 bloodstained. 2 with much bloodshed ♦ *a bloody battle.*
bloody-minded *adjective* deliberately awkward and not helpful.

bloom *noun* (*plural* blooms)
1 a flower. 2 the fine powder on fresh ripe grapes etc.

bloom *verb* (blooms, blooming, bloomed)
produce flowers.

blossom *noun* (*plural* blossoms)
a flower or mass of flowers, especially on a fruit tree.

blossom *verb* (blossoms, blossoming, blossomed)
1 produce flowers. 2 develop into something ♦ *She blossomed into a fine singer.*

blot *noun* (*plural* blots)
1 a spot of ink. 2 a flaw or fault; something ugly ♦ *a blot on the landscape.*

blot *verb* (blots, blotting, blotted)
1 make a blot or blots on something. 2 dry with blotting paper.
blot out 1 cross out thickly. 2 obscure ♦ *Fog blotted out the view.*

blotch *noun* (*plural* blotches)
an untidy patch of colour.
blotchy *adjective*

blotting paper *noun*
absorbent paper for soaking up ink from writing.

blouse *noun* (*plural* blouses)
a loose piece of clothing like a shirt, worn by women.

blow¹ *verb* (blows, blowing, blew, blown)
1 send out a current of air. 2 move in or with a current of air ♦ *His hat blew off.* 3 make or sound something by blowing ♦ *blow bubbles;* ♦ *blow the whistle.* 4 melt with too strong an electric current ♦ *A fuse has blown.* 5 (*slang*) damn ♦ *Blow you!*
blow up 1 inflate. 2 explode. 3 shatter by an explosion.

blow *noun* (*plural* blows)
the action of blowing.

blow² *noun* (*plural* blows)
1 a hard knock or hit. 2 a shock; a disaster.

blowlamp or **blowtorch** *noun* (*plural* blowlamps or blowtorches)
a device used for directing a very hot flame at a surface.

blubber *noun*
the fat of whales.

bludgeon (*say* bluj-on) *noun* (*plural* bludgeons)
a short stick with a thickened end, used as a weapon.

bludgeon *verb* (bludgeons, bludgeoning, bludgeoned)
hit someone several times with a heavy stick or other object.

blue *noun* (*plural* blues)
the colour of a cloudless sky.
out of the blue unexpectedly.

blue *adjective*
1 of the colour blue. 2 unhappy; depressed ♦ *feeling blue.* 3 indecent; obscene ♦ *blue films.*
blueness *noun*

bluebottle *noun* (*plural* bluebottles)
a large bluish fly.

blueprint *noun* (*plural* blueprints)
a detailed plan.

blues *noun*
a slow sad jazz song or tune.
the blues a very sad feeling; depression.

bluff¹ *verb* (bluffs, bluffing, bluffed)
deceive someone, especially by pretending to be someone else or to be able to do something.

bluff *noun* (*plural* **bluffs**)
the act of bluffing; a threat that you make but do not intend to carry out.

bluff² *adjective*
frank and hearty in manner.
bluffness *noun*

blunder *noun* (*plural* **blunders**)
a stupid mistake.

blunder *verb* (blunders, blundering, blundered)
1 make a blunder. **2** move clumsily and uncertainly.

blunt *adjective*
1 not sharp. **2** speaking in plain terms; straightforward ♦ *a blunt refusal.*
bluntly *adverb* **bluntness** *noun*

blunt *verb* (blunts, blunting, blunted)
make a thing blunt.

blur *verb* (blurs, blurring, blurred)
make or become indistinct or smeared.

blur *noun* (*plural* **blurs**)
an indistinct appearance ♦ *Without his glasses on, everything was a blur.*

blurt *verb* (blurts, blurting, blurted)
say something suddenly or tactlessly ♦ *He blurted it out.*

blush *verb* (blushes, blushing, blushed)
become red in the face because you are ashamed or embarrassed.

blush *noun* (*plural* **blushes**)
reddening in the face.

bluster *verb* (blusters, blustering, blustered)
1 blow in gusts; be windy. **2** talk loudly and aggressively.
blustery *adjective*

BMX *abbreviation*
a kind of bicycle for use in racing on a dirt track.

boar *noun* (*plural* **boars**)
1 a wild pig. **2** a male pig.

board *noun* (*plural* **boards**)
1 a flat piece of wood. **2** a flat piece of stiff material, e.g. a chessboard. **3** daily meals supplied in return for payment or work ♦ *board and lodging.* **4** a committee.
on board on or in a ship, aircraft, etc.

board *verb* (boards, boarding, boarded)
1 go on board a ship etc. **2** give or get meals and accommodation.
board up block with fixed boards.

boarder *noun* (*plural* **boarders**)
1 a pupil who lives at a boarding school during the term. **2** a lodger who receives meals.

boarding school *noun* (*plural* **boarding schools**)
a school where pupils live during the term.

boast *verb* (boasts, boasting, boasted)
1 speak with great pride and try to impress people. **2** have something to be proud of ♦ *The town boasts a fine park.*
boaster *noun* **boastful** *adjective* **boastfully** *adverb*

boast *noun* (*plural* **boasts**)
a boastful statement.

boat *noun* (*plural* **boats**)
a vehicle built to travel on water and carry people etc.
in the same boat in the same situation; suffering the same difficulties.

bob *verb* (bobs, bobbing, bobbed)
move quickly up and down.

bobsleigh or **bobsled** *noun* (*plural* **bobsleighs** or **bobsleds**)
a sledge with two sets of runners.

bodice *noun* (*plural* **bodices**)
the upper part of a dress.

bodily *adjective*
to do with your body ♦ *bodily functions.*

bodily *adverb*
by taking hold of someone ♦ *He was picked up bodily and bundled into a car.*

body *noun* (*plural* **bodies**)
1 the structure consisting of bones and flesh etc. of a person or animal; the main part of this apart from the head and limbs. **2** a corpse. **3** the main part of something. **4** a group or quantity regarded as a unit ♦ *the school's governing body.* **5** a distinct object or piece of matter ♦ *Stars and planets are heavenly bodies.*
bodily *adjective* & *adverb*

bodyguard *noun* (*plural* **bodyguards**)
a guard to protect a person's life.

bog *noun* (*plural* **bogs**)
an area of wet spongy ground.
boggy *adjective*
bogged down stuck and unable to make any progress.

bogus *adjective*
not real; sham.

boil¹ *verb* (boils, boiling, boiled)
1 make or become hot enough to bubble and give off steam. **2** cook or wash something in boiling water. **3** be very hot.

boil *noun*
boiling point ♦ *bring the milk to the boil.*
[via early French *boillir* from Latin *bullire* = to bubble]

boil² *noun* (*plural* **boils**)
an inflamed swelling under the skin.

boiler *noun* (*plural* **boilers**)
a container in which water is heated.

boisterous *adjective*
noisy and lively.

bold *adjective*
1 confident and courageous. 2 impudent. 3 (said about colours, designs, etc.) strong and bright.
boldly *adverb* **boldness** *noun*

bolster *noun* (*plural* **bolsters**)
a long pillow for placing across a bed under other pillows.

bolster *verb* (**bolsters, bolstering, bolstered**)
add extra support.

bolt *noun* (*plural* **bolts**)
1 a sliding bar for fastening a door. 2 a thick metal pin for fastening things together. 3 a sliding bar that opens and closes the breech of a rifle. 4 a shaft of lightning. 5 an arrow shot from a crossbow. 6 the action of bolting.
a bolt from the blue a surprise, usually an unpleasant one. **bolt upright** quite upright.

bolt *verb* (**bolts, bolting, bolted**)
1 fasten with a bolt or bolts. 2 run away or escape. 3 swallow food quickly.

bomb *noun* (*plural* **bombs**)
an explosive device.
the bomb an atomic or hydrogen bomb.

bomb *verb* (**bombs, bombing, bombed**)
attack a place with bombs.

bombard *verb* (**bombards, bombarding, bombarded**)
1 attack with gunfire or many missiles. 2 direct a large number of questions or comments etc. at somebody.
bombardment *noun*

bomber *noun* (*plural* **bombers**)
1 someone who plants or sets off a bomb. 2 an aeroplane from which bombs are dropped.

bombshell *noun* (*plural* **bombshells**)
a great shock.

bonanza (*say* bon-an-za) *noun* (*plural* **bonanzas**)
sudden great wealth or luck.

bond *noun* (*plural* **bonds**)
1 a close friendship or connection between two or more people. 2 **bonds** ropes or chains used to tie someone up. 3 a document stating an agreement.

bond *verb* (**bonds, bonding, bonded**)
become closely linked or connected.

bondage *noun*
slavery; captivity.

bone *noun* (*plural* **bones**)
one of the hard parts that make up the skeleton of a person's or animal's body.

bone *verb* (**bones, boning, boned**)
remove the bones from meat or fish.

bonfire *noun* (*plural* **bonfires**)
an outdoor fire to burn rubbish or celebrate something.
[originally *bone fire* = a fire to dispose of people's or animals' bones]

bonnet *noun* (*plural* **bonnets**)
1 a hat with strings that tie under the chin. 2 a Scottish beret. 3 the hinged cover over a car engine.

bonus (*say* boh-nus) *noun* (*plural* **bonuses**)
1 an extra payment in addition to a person's normal wages. 2 an extra benefit.

bony *adjective*
1 with large bones; having bones with little flesh on them. 2 full of bones. 3 like bones.

boo *verb* (**boos, booing, booed**)
shout 'boo' in disapproval.
boo *noun*

booby *noun* (*plural* **boobies**)
a babyish or stupid person.

booby prize *noun* (*plural* **booby prizes**)
a prize given as a joke to someone who comes last in a contest.

booby trap *noun* (*plural* **booby traps**)
something designed to hit or injure someone unexpectedly.

book *noun* (*plural* **books**)
a set of sheets of paper, usually with printing or writing on them, fastened together inside a cover.
bookseller *noun* **bookshop** *noun* **bookstall** *noun*

book *verb* (**books, booking, booked**)
1 reserve a place in a theatre, hotel, train, etc. 2 enter a person in a police record ♦ *The police booked him for speeding.*

bookcase *noun* (*plural* **bookcases**)
a piece of furniture with shelves for books.

bookkeeping *noun*
recording details of the money that is spent and received by a business.
bookkeeper *noun*

booklet *noun* (*plural* **booklets**)
a small thin book.

bookmaker *noun* (*plural* **bookmakers**)
a person whose business is taking bets.

bookmark *noun* (*plural* **bookmarks**)
something to mark a place in a book.

bookworm *noun* (*plural* **bookworms**)
a person who loves reading.

boom *verb* (**booms, booming, boomed**)
1 make a deep hollow sound. 2 be growing and prospering ♦ *Business is booming.*

boom *noun* (*plural* **booms**)
1 a deep hollow sound. 2 prosperity; growth.

boomerang *noun* (*plural* **boomerangs**)
a curved piece of wood that can be thrown so that it returns to the thrower, originally used by Australian Aborigines.
[from an Australian Aborginal word]

boor *noun* (*plural* **boors**)
an ill-mannered person.
boorish *adjective*

boost *verb* (**boosts, boosting, boosted**)
1 increase the strength, value, or reputation of a person or thing. 2 push something upwards.
booster *noun*

boost *noun* (*plural* **boosts**)
1 an increase. 2 an upward push.

boot *noun* (*plural* **boots**)
1 a shoe that covers the foot and ankle or leg. 2 the compartment for luggage in a car.
booted *adjective*

boot *verb* (**boots, booting, booted**)
1 kick hard. 2 switch on a computer.

booty *noun*
valuable goods taken away by soldiers after a battle.

booze *verb* (**boozes, boozing, boozed**) (*slang*)
drink alcohol.

booze *noun* (*slang*)
alcoholic drink.

border *noun* (*plural* **borders**)
1 the boundary of a country; the part near this. 2 an edge. 3 something placed round an edge to strengthen or decorate it. 4 a strip of ground round a garden or part of it.

border *verb* (**borders, bordering, bordered**)
put or be a border to something.

borderline *adjective*
only just belonging to a particular group or category ♦ *a borderline case.*

bore¹ *verb* (**bores, boring, bored**)
1 drill a hole. 2 get through by pushing.

bore² *verb* (**bores, boring, bored**)
make somebody feel uninterested by being dull.

bore *noun* (*plural* **bores**)
a boring person or thing.
boredom *noun*

bore³ *past tense* of **bear**².

bored *adjective*
weary and uninterested because something is so dull.

boring *adjective*
dull or tedious.

born *adjective*
1 having come into existence by birth. (See the note on *borne*.) 2 having a certain natural quality or ability ♦ *a born leader.*

borne *past participle* of **bear**².

---

❶ USAGE The word *borne* is used before *by* or after *have*, *has*, or *had*, e.g. *children borne by Eve*; *she had borne him a son.* The word *born* is used e.g. in *a son was born.*

---

bosom *noun* (*plural* **bosoms**)
a woman's breasts.

boss *noun* (*plural* **bosses**) (*informal*)
a manager; a person whose job is to give orders to workers etc.

boss *verb* (**bosses, bossing, bossed**) (*informal*)
order someone about.

bossy *adjective*
fond of ordering people about.
bossiness *noun*

botany *noun*
the study of plants.
botanical *adjective* **botanist** *noun*

both *adjective* & *pronoun*
the two; not only one ♦ *Are both films good?*
♦ *Both are old.*

both *adverb*
both … and not only … but also ♦ *The house is both small and ugly.*

bother *verb* (**bothers, bothering, bothered**)
1 cause somebody trouble or worry; pester. 2 take trouble; feel concern ♦ *Don't bother to reply.*

bother *noun*
trouble or worry.

bottle *noun* (*plural* **bottles**)
1 a narrow-necked container for liquids. 2 (*slang*) courage ♦ *She showed a lot of bottle.*

bottle *verb* (**bottles, bottling, bottled**)
put or store something in bottles.
bottle up if you bottle up your feelings, you keep them to yourself.
[via early French *botaille* from Latin *buttis* = cask]

bottle bank *noun* (*plural* **bottle banks**)
a large container in which used glass bottles are collected for recycling.

bottleneck *noun* (*plural* **bottlenecks**)
a narrow place where something, especially traffic, cannot flow freely.

bottom *noun* (*plural* **bottoms**)
1 the lowest part; the base. 2 the part furthest away ♦ *the bottom of the garden.* 3 a person's buttocks.

bottom *adjective*
lowest ♦ *the bottom shelf.*

bough *noun* (*plural* **boughs**)
a large branch coming from the trunk of a tree.

boulder *noun* (*plural* **boulders**)
a very large smooth stone.

bounce *verb* (**bounces, bouncing, bounced**)
1 spring back when thrown against something. 2 make a ball etc. bounce. 3 (said about a cheque) be sent back by the bank because there is not enough money in the account. 4 jump suddenly; move in a lively manner.

bounce *noun* (*plural* **bounces**)
1 the action or power of bouncing. 2 a lively confident manner ♦ *full of bounce.*
bouncy *adjective*

bound¹ *verb* (bounds, bounding, bounded)
jump or spring; run with jumping movements
♦ *The dogs were bounding along.*
bound *noun* (*plural* **bounds**)
a bounding movement.
bound² *past tense* of **bind**.
bound *adjective*
bound to certain to ♦ *He is bound to fail.* **bound
up with** closely connected with ♦ *Happiness is
bound up with success.*
bound³ *adjective*
going towards something ♦ *We are bound for
Spain.*
bound⁴ *verb* (bounds, bounding, bounded)
limit; be the boundary of ♦ *Their land is
bounded by the river.*
boundary *noun* (*plural* **boundaries**)
1 a line that marks a limit. **2** a hit to the
boundary of a cricket field.
bounds *plural noun*
limits ♦ *This was beyond the bounds of
possibility.*
out of bounds where you are not allowed to go.
bouquet (*say* boh-**kay**) *noun* (*plural*
bouquets)
a bunch of flowers.
bout *noun* (*plural* **bouts**)
1 a boxing or wrestling contest. **2** a period of
exercise or work or illness ♦ *a bout of flu.*
boutique (*say* boo-**teek**) *noun* (*plural*
boutiques)
a small shop selling fashionable clothes.
bow¹ (rhymes with *go*) *noun* (*plural* **bows**)
1 a strip of wood curved by a tight string joining
its ends, used for shooting arrows. **2** a wooden
rod with horsehair stretched between its ends,
used for playing a violin etc. **3** a knot made with
loops.
bow² (rhymes with *cow*) *verb* (**bows, bowing,
bowed**)
1 bend your body forwards to show respect or as
a greeting. **2** bend downwards ♦ *bowed by the
weight.*
bow *noun* (*plural* **bows**)
bowing your body.
bow³ (rhymes with *cow*) *noun* (*plural* **bows**)
the front part of a ship.
bowels *plural noun*
the intestines.
bowl¹ *noun* (*plural* **bowls**)
1 a rounded deep container for food or liquid.
2 the rounded part of a spoon or tobacco pipe etc.
bowl² *noun* (*plural* **bowls**)
a ball used in the game of **bowls** or in bowling,
when heavy balls are rolled towards skittles.

bowl *verb* (bowls, bowling, bowled)
1 send a ball to be played by a batsman. **2** get a
batsman out by bowling. **3** send a ball etc.
rolling.
bow-legged *adjective*
having legs that curve outwards at the knees;
bandy.
bowling *noun*
1 the game of bowls. **2** the game of knocking
down skittles with a heavy ball.
bow tie *noun* (*plural* **bow ties**)
a man's necktie tied into a bow.
bow window *noun* (*plural* **bow windows**)
a curved window.
box¹ *noun* (*plural* **boxes**)
1 a container made of wood, cardboard, etc.,
usually with a top or lid. **2** a rectangular space to
be filled in on a form, computer screen, etc.
3 a compartment in a theatre, lawcourt, etc.
♦ *the witness box.* **4** a hut or shelter ♦ *a sentry
box.* **5** a small evergreen shrub.
the box (*informal*) television.
box² *verb* (boxes, boxing, boxed)
fight with the fists as a sport.
boxer *noun* (*plural* **boxers**)
1 a person who boxes. **2** a dog that looks like a
bulldog.
Boxing Day *noun*
the first weekday after Christmas Day.
box office *noun* (*plural* **box offices**)
an office for booking seats at a theatre or cinema.
boy *noun* (*plural* **boys**)
1 a male child. **2** a young man.
boyhood *noun* **boyish** *adjective*
boycott *verb* (boycotts, boycotting,
boycotted)
refuse to use or have anything to do with ♦ *They
boycotted the buses when the fares went up.*
boycott *noun*
boyfriend *noun* (*plural* **boyfriends**)
a person's regular male companion in a romantic
or sexual relationship.
bra *noun* (*plural* **bras**)
a piece of underwear worn by women to support
their breasts.
brace *verb* (braces, bracing, braced)
support; make a thing firm against something.
bracelet *noun* (*plural* **bracelets**)
an ornament worn round the wrist.
braces *plural noun*
straps to hold trousers up, passing over the
shoulders.
bracing *adjective*
making you feel refreshed and healthy
♦ *the bracing sea breeze.*

bracken *noun*
a type of large fern that grows in open country;
a mass of these ferns.

bracket *noun* (*plural* **brackets**)
1 a mark used in pairs to enclose words or
figures ♦ *There are round brackets ( ) and square
brackets [ ].* 2 a support attached to a wall etc.
3 a group or range between certain limits
♦ *a high income bracket.*

bracket *verb* (**brackets, bracketing, bracketed**)
1 enclose in brackets. 2 put things together
because they are similar.

brahmin *noun* (*plural* **brahmins**)
a member of the highest Hindu class, originally
priests.

Braille (rhymes with *mail*) *noun*
a system of representing letters etc. by raised
dots which blind people can read by feeling
them.

brain *noun* (*plural* **brains**)
1 the organ inside the top of the head that
controls the body. 2 the mind; intelligence.

brainwash *verb* (**brainwashes, brainwashing,
brainwashed**)
force a person to give up one set of ideas or
beliefs and accept new ones; indoctrinate.

brainwave *noun* (*plural* **brainwaves**)
a sudden bright idea.

brainy *adjective*
clever; intelligent.

brake *noun* (*plural* **brakes**)
a device for slowing or stopping something.

brake *verb* (**brakes, braking, braked**)
use a brake.

bramble *noun* (*plural* **brambles**)
a blackberry bush or a prickly bush like it.

bran *noun*
ground-up husks of corn.

branch *noun* (*plural* **branches**)
1 a woody arm-like part of a tree or shrub.
2 a part of a railway, road, or river etc. that leads
off from the main part. 3 a shop or office etc. that
belongs to a large organization.

branch *verb* (**branches, branching, branched**)
form a branch.
branch out start something new.

brand *noun* (*plural* **brands**)
a particular make of goods.

brandish *verb* (**brandishes, brandishing,
brandished**)
wave something about.

brand new *adjective*
completely new.

brandy *noun* (*plural* **brandies**)
a strong alcoholic drink, usually made from
wine.

brash *adjective*
1 impudent. 2 reckless.

brass *noun* (*plural* **brasses**)
1 a metal that is an alloy of copper and zinc.
2 wind instruments made of brass, e.g. trumpets
and trombones.
brass *adjective*

brassy *adjective* (**brassier, brassiest**)
1 resembling brass in colour. 2 loud or showy.

bravado (*say* brav-ah-doh) *noun*
a display of boldness.

brave *adjective*
having or showing courage.
bravely *adverb* **bravery** *noun*

brave *verb* (**braves, braving, braved**)
face and endure something bravely.

brawl *noun* (*plural* **brawls**)
a noisy quarrel or fight.

brawl *verb* (**brawls, brawling, brawled**)
take part in a brawl.

brawny *adjective*
strong and muscular.

brazen *verb* (**brazens, brazening, brazened**)
brazen it out behave as if there is nothing to be
ashamed of when you have done wrong.

breach *noun* (*plural* **breaches**)
1 the breaking of an agreement or rule etc.
2 a broken place; a gap.

bread *noun* (*plural* **breads**)
a food made by baking flour and water, usually
with yeast.
breadcrumbs *plural noun*

breadth *noun*
width; broadness.

break *verb* (**breaks, breaking, broke, broken**)
1 divide or fall into pieces by hitting or pressing.
2 damage; stop working properly. 3 fail to
keep a promise or law etc. 4 stop for a time;
end ♦ *She broke her silence.* 5 change ♦ *the
weather broke.* 6 (said about waves) fall in foam.
7 go suddenly or with force ♦ *They broke
through.* 8 appear suddenly ♦ *Dawn had broken.*
breakage *noun*
break a record do better than anyone else has
done before. **break down** 1 stop working
properly. 2 collapse. **break out** 1 begin
suddenly. 2 escape. **break the news** make
something known. **break up** 1 break into small
parts. 2 leave for the holidays at the end of a
school term.

break *noun* (*plural* **breaks**)
1 a broken place; a gap. 2 an escape; a sudden
dash. 3 a short rest from work. 4 a number of
points scored continuously in snooker etc.
5 (*informal*) a piece of luck; a fair chance
♦ *Give me a break.*
break of day dawn.

breakdown noun (plural **breakdowns**)
1 breaking down; failure ♦ the breakdown of law and order. **2** a period of mental illness caused by anxiety or depression. **3** an analysis of accounts or statistics. **4** a sudden failure to work, esp. by a car ♦ We had a breakdown on the motorway.

breakfast noun (plural **breakfasts**)
the first meal of the day.

breakneck adjective
dangerously fast ♦ He had to drive at breakneck speed to get there on time.

breakthrough noun (plural **breakthroughs**)
an important advance or achievement.

breast noun (plural **breasts**)
1 one of the two fleshy parts on the upper front of a woman's body that produce milk to feed a baby. **2** a person's or animal's chest.

breastplate noun (plural **breastplates**)
a piece of armour covering the chest.

breath (say breth) noun (plural **breaths**)
1 air drawn into the lungs and sent out again. **2** a gentle blowing ♦ a breath of wind.
out of breath panting. **take your breath away** surprise or delight you greatly. **under your breath** in a whisper.

breathalyser noun (plural **breathalysers**)
a device for measuring the amount of alcohol in a person's breath.
breathalyse verb

breathe (say breeth) verb (**breathes, breathing, breathed**)
1 take air into the body and send it out again. **2** speak or utter ♦ Don't breathe a word of this.

breather (say bree-ther) noun (plural **breathers**)
a pause for rest ♦ Let's take a breather.

breathless adjective
out of breath.

breed verb (**breeds, breeding, bred**)
1 produce young creatures. **2** keep animals in order to produce young ones from them. **3** bring up or train. **4** create or produce ♦ Poverty breeds illness.
breeder noun

breed noun (plural **breeds**)
a variety of animals with qualities inherited from their parents.

breeze noun (plural **breezes**)
a wind.
breezy adjective

brevity noun
shortness; briefness.

brew verb (**brews, brewing, brewed**)
1 make beer or tea. **2** develop ♦ Trouble is brewing.

brew noun (plural **brews**)
a brewed drink.

brewery noun (plural **breweries**)
a place where beer is brewed.

bribe noun (plural **bribes**)
money or a gift offered to a person to influence him or her.

bribe verb (**bribes, bribing, bribed**)
give someone a bribe.
bribery noun

brick noun (plural **bricks**)
1 a small hard block of baked clay etc. used to build walls. **2** a rectangular block of something.

brick verb (**bricks, bricking, bricked**)
close something with bricks ♦ We bricked up the gap in the wall.

bricklayer noun (plural **bricklayers**)
a worker who builds with bricks.

bride noun (plural **brides**)
a woman on her wedding day.
bridal adjective

bridegroom noun (plural **bridegrooms**)
a man on his wedding day.

bridesmaid noun (plural **bridesmaids**)
a girl or unmarried woman who attends the bride at a wedding.

bridge[1] noun (plural **bridges**)
1 a structure built over and across a river, railway, or road etc. to allow people to cross it. **2** a high platform above a ship's deck, for the officer in charge. **3** the bony upper part of the nose. **4** something that connects things.

bridge verb (**bridges, bridging, bridged**)
make or form a bridge over something.

bridge[2] noun
a card game rather like whist.

bridle noun (plural **bridles**)
the part of a horse's harness that fits over its head.

bridleway or **bridle path** noun (plural **bridleways** or **bridle paths**)
a road suitable for horses but not for vehicles.

brief adjective
short.
briefly adverb **briefness** noun
in brief in a few words.

brief noun (plural **briefs**)
instructions and information given to someone, especially to a barrister.

brief verb (**briefs, briefing, briefed**)
1 give a brief to a barrister. **2** instruct or inform someone concisely in advance.

briefcase noun (plural **briefcases**)
a flat case for carrying documents etc.

briefing noun (plural **briefings**)
a meeting to give someone concise instructions or information.

briefs plural noun
very short knickers or underpants.

brigade noun (plural **brigades**)
1 a large unit of an army. 2 a group of people organized for a special purpose ♦ the fire brigade.

bright adjective
1 giving a strong light; shining. 2 clever. 3 cheerful.
brightly adverb **brightness** noun

brighten verb (**brightens**, **brightening**, **brightened**)
make or become brighter.

brilliant adjective
1 very bright; sparkling. 2 very clever.
brilliantly adverb **brilliance** noun

brim noun (plural **brims**)
1 the edge of a cup etc. 2 the bottom part of a hat that sticks out.

brim verb (**brims**, **brimming**, **brimmed**)
be full to the brim.
brim over overflow.

brimful adjective
full to the brim.

bring verb (**brings**, **bringing**, **brought**)
cause a person or thing to come; lead; carry.
bring about cause to happen. **bring off** achieve; do something successfully. **bring up 1** look after and train growing children. 2 mention a subject. 3 vomit. 4 cause to stop suddenly.

brisk adjective
quick and lively.
briskly adverb **briskness** noun

bristle noun (plural **bristles**)
1 a short stiff hair. 2 one of the stiff pieces of hair, wire, or plastic etc. in a brush.
bristly adjective

bristle verb (**bristles**, **bristling**, **bristled**)
1 (said about an animal) raise its bristles in anger or fear. 2 show indignation.
bristle with be full of ♦ The roof bristled with aerials.

brittle adjective
hard but easy to break or snap.
brittleness noun

broad adjective
1 large across; wide. 2 full and complete ♦ broad daylight. 3 in general terms; not detailed ♦ We are in broad agreement. 4 strong and unmistakable ♦ a broad hint; ♦ a broad accent.
broadly adverb **broadness** noun

broad bean noun (plural **broad beans**)
a bean with large flat seeds.

broadcast noun (plural **broadcasts**)
a programme sent out on the radio or on television.

broadcast verb (**broadcasts**, **broadcasting**, **broadcast**)
send out a programme on the radio or on television.
broadcaster noun

broaden verb (**broadens**, **broadening**, **broadened**)
make or become broader.

broad-minded adjective
tolerant; not easily shocked.

broccoli noun (plural **broccoli**)
a kind of cauliflower with greenish flower heads.

brochure (say broh-shoor) noun (plural **brochures**)
a booklet or pamphlet containing information.

broke adjective (informal)
having spent all your money.

broken-hearted adjective
extremely sad or upset about something.

broken home noun (plural **broken homes**)
a family lacking one parent through divorce or separation.

bronchitis (say bronk-I-tiss) noun
a disease with bronchial inflammation, which makes you cough a lot.

bronze noun (plural **bronzes**)
1 a metal that is an alloy of copper and tin. 2 something made of bronze. 3 a bronze medal, awarded as third prize. 4 yellowish-brown.
bronze adjective

Bronze Age noun
the time when tools and weapons were made of bronze.

brooch noun (plural **brooches**)
an ornament with a hinged pin for fastening it on to clothes.

brood noun (plural **broods**)
young birds that were hatched together.

brood verb (**broods**, **brooding**, **brooded**)
1 sit on eggs to hatch them. 2 keep thinking and worrying about something.

brook noun (plural **brooks**)
a small stream.

broom noun (plural **brooms**)
1 a brush with a long handle, for sweeping. 2 a shrub with yellow, white, or pink flowers.

broomstick noun (plural **broomsticks**)
the handle of a broom.

broth noun (plural **broths**)
a kind of thin soup.

brother noun (plural **brothers**)
1 a son of the same parents as another person. 2 a man who is a fellow member of a Church, trade union, etc.
brotherly adjective
[from Old English]

brother-in-law *noun* (*plural* **brothers-in-law**)
the brother of a married person's husband or
wife; the husband of a person's sister.

brow *noun* (*plural* **brows**)
1 an eyebrow. **2** the forehead. **3** the ridge at the
top of a hill; the edge of a cliff.

brown *noun* (*plural* **browns**)
the colour of earth.

brown *adjective*
1 of the colour brown. **2** having a brown skin;
suntanned.

Brownie *noun* (*plural* **Brownies**)
a member of a junior branch of the Guides.

browse *verb* (**browses, browsing, browsed**)
1 read or look at something casually. **2** feed on
grass or leaves. **3** (in computing) to look through
files or data, especially on the Internet.

browser *noun* (*plural* **browsers**)
(in computing) a program for searching the
Internet.

bruise *noun* (*plural* **bruises**)
a dark mark made on the skin by hitting it.

bruise *verb* (**bruises, bruising, bruised**)
give or get a bruise or bruises.

brunette *noun* (*plural* **brunettes**)
a woman with brown hair.

brunt *noun*
the chief impact or strain ♦ *They bore the brunt
of the attack.*

brush *noun* (*plural* **brushes**)
1 an implement used for cleaning or painting
things or for smoothing the hair, usually with
pieces of hair, wire, or plastic etc. set in a solid
base. **2** a fox's bushy tail. **3** brushing ♦ *Give it a
good brush.* **4** a short fight ♦ *They had a brush
with the enemy.*

brush *verb* (**brushes, brushing, brushed**)
1 use a brush on something. **2** touch gently in
passing.
brush up revise a subject.

brusque (*say* bruusk) *adjective*
curt and offhand in manner.
brusquely *adverb*

Brussels sprouts *plural noun*
the edible buds of a kind of cabbage.

brutal *adjective*
very cruel.
brutally *adverb* **brutality** *noun*

brute *noun* (*plural* **brutes**)
1 a brutal person. **2** an animal.
brutish *adjective*

BSE *abbreviation*
bovine spongiform encephalopathy; a fatal
disease of cattle that affects the nervous system
and makes the cow stagger about. BSE is
sometimes known as 'mad cow disease'.

bubble *noun* (*plural* **bubbles**)
1 a thin transparent ball of liquid filled with air
or gas. **2** a small ball of air in something.
bubbly *adjective*

bubble *verb* (**bubbles, bubbling, bubbled**)
1 send up bubbles; rise in bubbles. **2** show great
liveliness.

buccaneer *noun* (*plural* **buccaneers**)
a pirate.

buck *noun* (*plural* **bucks**)
a male deer, rabbit, or hare.

buck *verb* (**bucks, bucking, bucked**)
(said about a horse) jump with its back arched.
buck up (*informal*) **1** hurry. **2** cheer up.

bucket *noun* (*plural* **buckets**)
a container with a handle, for carrying liquids
etc.
bucketful *noun*

buckle *noun* (*plural* **buckles**)
a device through which a belt or strap is threaded
to fasten it.

buckle *verb* (**buckles, buckling, buckled**)
fasten something with a buckle.

bud *noun* (*plural* **buds**)
a flower or leaf before it opens.

Buddhism (*say* buud-izm) *noun*
a faith that started in Asia and follows the
teachings of the Indian philosopher Gautama
Buddha, who lived in the 5th century BC.
Buddhist *noun*

budge *verb* (**budges, budging, budged**)
if you cannot budge something, you cannot
move it at all.

budgerigar *noun* (*plural* **budgerigars**)
an Australian bird often kept as a pet in a cage.
[from Australian Aboriginal *budgeri* = good +
gar = cockatoo]

budget *noun* (*plural* **budgets**)
1 a plan for spending money wisely. **2** an
amount of money set aside for a purpose.
budgetary *adjective*
the Budget the Chancellor of the Exchequer's
statement of plans to raise money (e.g. by taxes).
[via early French *bougette* = little leather bag,
from Latin *bulga* = leather bag. In the 18th
century, the Chancellor presented his statement
by 'opening the budget']

buffalo *noun* (*plural* **buffalo** or **buffaloes**)
a large ox. Different kinds are found in Asia,
Africa, and North America (where they are also
called *bison*).

buffer *noun* (*plural* **buffers**)
1 something that softens a blow, especially a
device on a railway engine or wagon or at the
end of a track. **2** (in computing) a memory in
which text or data can be stored for a time.

buffet¹ (*say* buu-fay) *noun* (*plural* **buffets**)
1 a cafe at a station. 2 a meal where guests serve themselves to food.

buffet² (*say* buf-it) *noun* (*plural* **buffets**)
a hit, especially with the hand.

buffet *verb* (**buffets, buffeting, buffeted**)
hit or knock ♦ *Strong winds buffeted the aircraft.*

buffoon *noun* (*plural* **buffoons**)
a person who plays the fool.
buffoonery *noun*

bug *noun* (*plural* **bugs**)
1 an insect. 2 an error in a computer program that prevents it working properly. 3 (*informal*) a germ or virus. 4 (*informal*) a secret hidden microphone.

bug *verb* (**bugs, bugging, bugged**) (*informal*)
1 fit with a secret hidden microphone. 2 annoy.

bugbear *noun* (*plural* **bugbears**)
something that you fear or dislike.

buggy *noun* (*plural* **buggies**)
a pushchair for young children.

build *verb* (**builds, building, built**)
make something by putting parts together.
build in include. **built-in** *adjective*
build up 1 establish gradually. 2 accumulate.
3 cover an area with buildings. 4 make stronger or more famous ♦ *build up a reputation.*
built-up *adjective*

build *noun* (*plural* **builds**)
the shape of someone's body ♦ *of slender build.*

builder *noun* (*plural* **builders**)
someone who puts up buildings.

building *noun* (*plural* **buildings**)
1 the process of making houses and other structures. 2 a structure with walls and a roof that people can go into.

building society *noun* (*plural* **building societies**)
an organization that people can pay money into and that lends money to people who want to buy houses.

bulb *noun* (*plural* **bulbs**)
1 a thick rounded part of a plant from which a stem grows up and roots grow down.
2 a rounded part of something ♦ *the bulb of a thermometer.* 3 a glass globe that produces electric light.
bulbous *adjective*

bulge *noun* (*plural* **bulges**)
a rounded swelling; an outward curve.
bulgy *adjective*

bulge *verb* (**bulges, bulging, bulged**)
form or cause to form a bulge.

bulimia (*say* buu-lim-ia) *noun*
an illness that makes someone eat too much and then too little. People who suffer from bulimia often makes themselves vomit after eating.
bulimic *adjective*

bulk *noun* (*plural* **bulks**)
1 the size of something, especially when it is large. 2 the greater portion; the majority
♦ *The bulk of the population voted for it.*
in bulk in large amounts.

bulk *verb* (**bulks, bulking, bulked**)
increase the size or thickness of something
♦ *bulk it out.*

bulky *adjective* (**bulkier, bulkiest**)
taking up a lot of space.
bulkiness *noun*

bull *noun* (*plural* **bulls**)
1 a fully grown male of the cow family.
2 an adult male seal, whale, or elephant.

bulldog *noun* (*plural* **bulldogs**)
a dog of a powerful courageous breed with a short thick neck.

bulldozer *noun* (*plural* **bulldozers**)
a powerful tractor with a wide metal blade or scoop in front, used for shifting soil or clearing ground.

bullet *noun* (*plural* **bullets**)
a small piece of metal shot from a rifle or revolver.

bulletin *noun* (*plural* **bulletins**)
1 a brief news report on radio or television.
2 a regular letter or report giving information about an organization.

bullfight *noun* (*plural* **bullfights**)
a public entertainment in which bulls are tormented and killed in an arena.
bullfighter *noun*

bullock *noun* (*plural* **bullocks**)
a young castrated bull.

bullseye *noun* (*plural* **bullseyes**)
the centre of a target.

bully *verb* (**bullies, bullying, bullied**)
1 use strength or power to hurt or frighten a weaker person. 2 start play in hockey, when two opponents tap the ground and each other's stick
♦ *bully off.*

bully *noun* (*plural* **bullies**)
someone who bullies people.

bulwark *noun* (*plural* **bulwarks**)
a wall of earth built as a defence; a protection.

bumblebee *noun* (*plural* **bumblebees**)
a large bee with a loud hum.

bump *verb* (**bumps, bumping, bumped**)
1 knock against something. 2 move along with jolts.
bump into (*informal*) meet by chance. **bump off** (*slang*) kill.

bump *noun* (*plural* **bumps**)
1 the action or sound of bumping. 2 a swelling or lump.
bumpy *adjective*

bumper¹ *noun* (*plural* **bumpers**)
a bar along the front or back of a motor vehicle to protect it in collisions.

bumper² *adjective*
unusually large or plentiful ♦ *a bumper crop.*

bumpkin *noun* (*plural* **bumpkins**)
a country person with awkward manners.

bun *noun* (*plural* **buns**)
1 a small round sweet cake. 2 hair twisted into a round bunch at the back of the head.

bunch *noun* (*plural* **bunches**)
a number of things joined or fastened together.

bundle *noun* (*plural* **bundles**)
a number of things tied or wrapped together.

bundle *verb* (**bundles, bundling, bundled**)
1 make a number of things into a bundle. 2 push hurriedly or carelessly ♦ *They bundled him into a taxi.*

bungalow *noun* (*plural* **bungalows**)
a house without any upstairs rooms.
[from Hindi *bangla* = to do with Bengal, where there were houses of this kind]

bungle *verb* (**bungles, bungling, bungled**)
make a mess of doing something.
bungler *noun*

bunion *noun* (*plural* **bunions**)
a swelling at the side of the joint where the big toe joins the foot.

bunk *noun* (*plural* **bunks**)
a bed built like a shelf.

bunker *noun* (*plural* **bunkers**)
1 a container for storing fuel. 2 a sandy hollow built as an obstacle on a golf course. 3 an underground shelter.

bunny *noun* (*plural* **bunnies**) (*informal*)
a rabbit.

Bunsen burner *noun* (*plural* **Bunsen burners**)
a small gas burner used in scientific work.

bunting¹ *noun* (*plural* **buntings**)
a kind of small bird.

bunting² *noun*
strips of small flags hung up to decorate streets and buildings.

buoy (*say* boi) *noun* (*plural* **buoys**)
a floating object anchored to mark a channel or underwater rocks etc.

buoyant (*say* boi-ant) *adjective*
1 able to float. 2 light-hearted; cheerful.
buoyantly *adverb* **buoyancy** *noun*

bur *noun* (*plural* **burs**)
a different spelling of *burr* (seed case).

burden *noun* (*plural* **burdens**)
1 a heavy load that you have to carry.
2 something troublesome that you have to bear ♦ *Exams are a burden.*
burdensome *adjective*

burden *verb* (**burdens, burdening, burdened**)
cause someone work or trouble.

bureau (*say* bewr-oh) *noun* (*plural* **bureaux**)
1 a writing desk. 2 a business office ♦ *They will tell you at the Information Bureau.*

bureaucracy (*say* bewr-ok-ra-see) *noun*
the use of too many rules and forms by officials, especially in government departments.
bureaucratic (*say* bewr-ok-**rat**-ik) *adjective*

burger *noun* (*plural* **burgers**)
a hamburger.

burglar *noun* (*plural* **burglars**)
a person who breaks into a building in order to steal things.
burglary *noun*

burgle *verb* (**burgles, burgling, burgled**)
rob a place as a burglar.

burial *noun* (*plural* **burials**)
burying somebody.

burlesque (*say* ber-**lesk**) *noun* (*plural* **burlesques**)
a comical imitation.

burly *adjective* (**burlier, burliest**)
having a strong heavy body.

burn *verb* (**burns, burning, burned** or **burnt**)
1 blaze or glow with fire; produce heat or light by combustion. 2 damage or destroy something by fire, heat, or chemicals. 3 be damaged or destroyed by fire etc. 4 feel very hot.

---

❶ USAGE The word *burnt* (not *burned*) is always used when an adjective is required, e.g. in *burnt wood.* As parts of the verb, either *burned* or *burnt* may be used, e.g. *the wood had burned* or *had burnt completely.*

---

burn *noun* (*plural* **burns**)
1 a mark or injury made by burning. 2 the firing of a spacecraft's rockets.

burning *adjective*
1 intense ♦ *a burning ambition.* 2 very important; hotly discussed ♦ *a burning question.*

burr *noun* (*plural* **burrs**)
1 a plant's seed case or flower that clings to hair or clothes. 2 a whirring sound. 3 a soft country accent.

burrow *noun* (*plural* **burrows**)
a hole or tunnel dug by a rabbit or fox etc. as a dwelling.

burrow *verb* (**burrows, burrowing, burrowed**)
1 dig a burrow. 2 push your way through or into something; search deeply ♦ *She burrowed in her handbag.*

bursar noun (plural **bursars**)
a person who manages the finances and other business of a school or college.

burst verb (**bursts, bursting, burst**)
1 break or force apart. 2 come or start suddenly ♦ It burst into flame. ♦ They burst out laughing. 3 be very full ♦ bursting with energy.

burst noun (plural **bursts**)
1 a split caused by something bursting. 2 something short and forceful ♦ a burst of gunfire.

bury verb (**buries, burying, buried**)
1 place a dead body in the earth, a tomb, or the sea. 2 put underground; cover up.

bus noun (plural **buses**)
a large vehicle for passengers to travel in.

bush noun (plural **bushes**)
1 a shrub. 2 wild uncultivated land, especially in Africa and Australia.
bushy adjective

bushel noun (plural **bushels**)
a measure for grain and fruit (8 gallons or 4 pecks).

business (say **biz**-niss) noun (plural **businesses**)
1 a person's concern or responsibilities ♦ Mind your own business. 2 an affair or subject ♦ I'm tired of the whole business. 3 a shop or firm. 4 buying and selling things; trade.
businessman noun **businesswoman** noun

busking noun
playing music for money in the street.
busker noun

bust noun (plural **busts**)
1 a sculpture of a person's head, shoulders, and chest. 2 the upper front part of a woman's body.

bustle verb (**bustles, bustling, bustled**)
hurry in a busy or excited way.

bustle noun
hurried or excited activity.

busy adjective (**busier, busiest**)
1 having a lot to do; occupied. 2 full of activity. 3 (said about a telephone line) engaged.
busily adverb **busyness** noun

busy verb (**busies, busying, busied**)
busy yourself occupy yourself; keep busy.

busybody noun (plural **busybodies**)
a person who meddles or interferes.

but conjunction
however; nevertheless ♦ I wanted to go, but I couldn't.

but preposition
except ♦ There is no one here but me.

but adverb
only; no more than ♦ We can but try.

butcher noun (plural **butchers**)
1 a person who cuts up meat and sells it. 2 a person who kills cruelly or needlessly.
butchery noun

butcher verb (**butchers, butchering, butchered**)
kill cruelly or needlessly.

butler noun (plural **butlers**)
a male servant in charge of other servants in a large private house.
[from early French bouteillier = someone who carried the bottles]

butt¹ noun (plural **butts**)
1 the thicker end of a weapon or tool. 2 a stub ♦ cigarette butts.

butt² noun (plural **butts**)
a large cask or barrel.

butt³ noun (plural **butts**)
a person or thing that is a target for ridicule or teasing ♦ He was the butt of their jokes.

butt⁴ verb (**butts, butting, butted**)
1 push or hit with the head as a ram or goat does. 2 place the edges of things together.
butt in interrupt or meddle.

butter noun
a soft fatty food made by churning cream.
buttery adjective

buttercup noun (plural **buttercups**)
a wild plant with bright yellow cup-shaped flowers.

butterfly noun (plural **butterflies**)
1 an insect with large white or coloured wings. 2 a swimming stroke in which both arms are lifted at the same time.

buttock noun (plural **buttocks**)
either of the two fleshy rounded parts of your bottom.

button noun (plural **buttons**)
1 a knob or disc sewn on clothes as a fastening or ornament. 2 a small knob pressed to work an electric device.

button verb (**buttons, buttoning, buttoned**)
fasten something with a button or buttons.

buttonhole noun (plural **buttonholes**)
1 a slit through which a button passes to fasten clothes. 2 a flower worn on a lapel.

buttonhole verb (**buttonholes, buttonholing, buttonholed**)
stop somebody so that you can talk to him or her.

buttress noun (plural **buttresses**)
a support built against a wall.

buy verb (**buys, buying, bought**)
get something by paying for it.
buyer noun

buy noun (plural **buys**)
something that is bought.

buzz noun (plural **buzzes**)
a vibrating humming sound.

buzz verb (**buzzes, buzzing, buzzed**)
1 make a buzz. 2 threaten an aircraft by deliberately flying close to it.

by *preposition*
This word is used to show **1** closeness (*Sit by me*), **2** direction or route (*We got here by a short cut*), **3** time (*They came by night*), **4** manner or method (*cooking by gas*), **5** amount (*You missed it by inches*).
by the way incidentally. **by yourself** alone; without help.

by *adverb*
1 past ♦ *I can't get by.* **2** in reserve; for future use ♦ *Put it by.*
by and by soon; later on. **by and large** on the whole.

by-election *noun* (*plural* **by-elections**)
an election to replace a Member of Parliament who has died or resigned.

bygone *adjective*
belonging to the past.
let bygones be bygones forgive and forget.

bypass *noun* (*plural* **bypasses**)
1 a road taking traffic round a city or congested area. **2** a channel that allows something to flow when the main route is blocked.

bypass *verb* (**bypasses, bypassing, bypassed**)
avoid something by means of a bypass.

by-product *noun* (*plural* **by-products**)
something useful produced while something else is being made.

byroad *noun* (*plural* **byroads**)
a minor road.

bystander *noun* (*plural* **bystanders**)
a person standing near but taking no part when something happens.

byte *noun* (*plural* **bytes**)
a fixed number of bits (= binary digits) in a computer, often representing a single character.

byword *noun* (*plural* **bywords**)
a person or thing spoken of as a famous example ♦ *Their firm became a byword for quality.*

Cc

cab *noun* (*plural* **cabs**)
1 a taxi. **2** a compartment for the driver of a lorry, train, bus, or crane.

cabaret (*say* kab-er-ay) *noun* (*plural* **cabarets**)
an entertainment provided for the customers in a restaurant or nightclub.
[from early French *cabaret* = wooden inn or hut]

cabbage *noun* (*plural* **cabbages**)
a vegetable with green or purple leaves.
[from early French *caboche* = head]

cabin *noun* (*plural* **cabins**)
1 a hut or shelter. **2** a room for sleeping on a ship. **3** the part of an aircraft in which passengers sit. **4** a driver's cab.

Cabinet *noun*
the group of chief ministers, chosen by the Prime Minister, who meet to decide government policy.

cabinet *noun* (*plural* **cabinets**)
a cupboard or container with drawers or shelves.

cable *noun* (*plural* **cables**)
1 a thick rope of fibre or wire; a thick chain. **2** a covered group of wires laid underground for transmitting electrical signals. **3** a telegram sent overseas.

cable television *noun*
a system of television programmes transmitted by cables to people who have paid for them.

cackle *noun* (*plural* **cackles**)
1 a loud silly laugh. **2** noisy chatter. **3** the loud clucking noise a hen makes.
cackle *verb*

cactus *noun* (*plural* **cacti**)
a fleshy plant, usually with prickles, from a hot dry climate.

cad *noun* (*plural* **cads**)
a dishonourable man.

cadaverous (*say* kad-av-er-us) *adjective*
pale and gaunt.

caddie *noun* (*plural* **caddies**)
a person who carries a golfer's clubs during a game.

cadence (*say* kay-denss) *noun* (*plural* **cadences**)
1 rhythm; the rise and fall of the voice in speaking. **2** the final notes of a musical phrase.

cadenza (*say* ka-den-za) *noun* (*plural* **cadenzas**)
an elaborate passage for a solo instrument or singer, to show the performer's skill.

cadet *noun* (*plural* **cadets**)
a young person being trained for the armed forces or the police.

cadge *verb* (**cadges, cadging, cadged**)
get something by begging for it.
cadger *noun*

cadmium *noun*
a metal that looks like tin.

Caesarean or **Caesarean section** (*say* siz-air-ee-an) *noun* (*plural* **Caesareans** or **Caesarean sections**)
a surgical operation for taking a baby out of the mother's womb.

cafe (*say* kaf-ay) *noun* (*plural* **cafes**)
a small restaurant.

caffeine (*say* kaf-een) *noun*
a stimulant substance found in tea and coffee.

cage *noun* (*plural* **cages**)
1 a container with bars or wires, in which birds or animals are kept. 2 the enclosed platform of a lift.

cairn *noun* (*plural* **cairns**)
a pile of loose stones set up as a landmark or monument.

cajole *verb* (**cajoles, cajoling, cajoled**)
persuade someone to do something by flattering them; coax.

cake *noun* (*plural* **cakes**)
1 a baked food made from a mixture of flour, fat, eggs, sugar, etc. 2 a shaped or hardened mass
♦ *a cake of soap*; ♦ *fish cakes*.

caked *adjective*
covered with dried mud etc.

calamine *noun*
a pink powder used to make a soothing lotion for the skin.

calamity *noun* (*plural* **calamities**)
a disaster.
calamitous *adjective*

calcium *noun*
a chemical substance found in teeth, bones, and lime.

calculate *verb* (**calculates, calculating, calculated**)
1 work something out by using mathematics.
2 plan something deliberately; intend
♦ *Her remarks were calculated to hurt me*.
calculable *adjective* **calculation** *noun*

calculator *noun* (*plural* **calculators**)
a small electronic device for making calculations.

calculus *noun*
mathematics for working out problems about rates of change.

calendar *noun* (*plural* **calendars**)
a chart or set of pages showing the dates of the month or year.

calf¹ *noun* (*plural* **calves**)
a young cow, whale, seal, etc.

calf² *noun* (*plural* **calves**)
the fleshy back part of the leg below the knee.

calibre (*say* kal-ib-er) *noun* (*plural* **calibres**)
1 the diameter of a tube or gun barrel, or of a bullet etc. 2 ability; importance ♦ *someone of your calibre*.

call *noun* (*plural* **calls**)
1 a shout or cry. 2 a visit. 3 telephoning somebody. 4 a summons.

call *verb* (**calls, calling, called**)
1 shout or speak loudly, e.g. to attract someone's attention. 2 telephone somebody. 3 name a person or thing ♦ *They've decided to call the baby Alexander*. 4 tell somebody to come to you; summon. 5 make a short visit.
caller *noun*
call a person's bluff challenge a person to do what was threatened, and expose the fact that it was a bluff. **call for** 1 come and collect.
2 require ♦ *The scandal calls for investigation*.
call off cancel or postpone. **call up** summon to join the armed forces.

calligraphy (*say* kal-ig-raf-ee) *noun*
the art of beautiful handwriting.

calling *noun* (*plural* **callings**)
an occupation; a profession or trade.

callous (*say* kal-us) *adjective*
hard-hearted; unsympathetic.
callously *adverb* **callousness** *noun*

calm *adjective*
1 quiet and still; not windy. 2 not excited or agitated.
calmly *adverb* **calmness** *noun*
calm *verb* (**calms, calming, calmed**)
make or become calm.

calorie *noun* (*plural* **calories**)
a unit for measuring an amount of heat or the energy produced by food.
calorific *adjective*

calypso *noun* (*plural* **calypsos**)
a West Indian song about current happenings, made up as the singer goes along.

calyx (*say* kay-liks) *noun* (*plural* **calyces**)
a ring of leaves (*sepals*) forming the outer case of a bud.

camcorder *noun* (*plural* **camcorders**)
a combined video camera and sound recorder.

camel *noun* (*plural* **camels**)
a large animal with a long neck and either one or two humps on its back, used in desert countries for riding and for carrying goods.

cameo (*say* kam-ee-oh) *noun* (*plural* **cameos**)
1 a small hard piece of stone carved with a raised design in its upper layer. 2 a short part in a play or film, usually one played by a well-known actor.

camera *noun* (*plural* **cameras**)
a device for taking photographs, films, or television pictures.
cameraman *noun*
in camera in a judge's private room; in private.

camouflage (*say* kam-off-lah*zh*) *noun*
a way of hiding things by making them look like part of their surroundings.
camouflage *verb* (**camouflages, camouflaging, camouflaged**)
hide by camouflage.

camp noun (plural **camps**)
a place where people live in tents or huts etc.
camp verb (**camps, camping, camped**)
have a holiday in a tent.
camper noun

campaign noun (plural **campaigns**)
1 a series of battles in one area or with one
purpose. **2** a planned series of actions, usually to
arouse interest in something ♦ *an advertising
campaign.*
campaign verb (**campaigns, campaigning,
campaigned**)
take part in a campaign.
campaigner noun
[via French from Latin *campania* = a piece of
open ground (where armies camped and had
exercises)]

camphor noun
a strong-smelling white substance used in
medicine, mothballs, and making plastics.
camphorated adjective

campsite noun (plural **campsites**)
a place where people can have a camping
holiday.

campus noun (plural **campuses**)
the grounds of a university or college.

can¹ noun (plural **cans**)
1 a sealed tin in which food or drink is
preserved. **2** a metal or plastic container for
liquids.
can verb (**cans, canning, canned**)
preserve in a sealed can.
canner noun

can² auxiliary verb (past tense **could**)
1 be able to ♦ *He can play the violin.* **2** have
permission to ♦ *You can go.*

❶ USAGE Some people object to *can* being used
with the meaning 'have permission to' and insist
that you should only use *may* for this meaning.
Can is widely used in this meaning, however,
and in most situations there is little reason to
prefer *may*. *May* is appropriate, though, in
formal or official writing.

canal noun (plural **canals**)
1 an artificial river cut through land so that boats
can sail along it or so that it can drain or irrigate
an area. **2** a tube through which something
passes in the body ♦ *the alimentary canal.*

canary noun (plural **canaries**)
a small yellow bird that sings.

cancel verb (**cancels, cancelling, cancelled**)
1 say that something planned will not be done or
will not take place. **2** stop an order or instruction
for something. **3** mark a stamp or ticket etc. so
that it cannot be used again.
cancellation noun
cancel out stop each other's effect ♦ *The good
and harm cancel each other out.*

cancer noun (plural **cancers**)
1 a disease in which harmful growths form in the
body. **2** a tumour, especially a harmful one.
cancerous adjective

candid adjective
frank and honest.
candidly adverb **candour** noun

candidate noun (plural **candidates**)
1 a person who wants to be elected or chosen for
a particular job or position etc. **2** a person taking
an examination.
candidacy noun **candidature** noun

candle noun (plural **candles**)
a stick of wax with a wick through it, giving light
when burning.
candlelight noun

candyfloss noun (plural **candyflosses**)
a fluffy mass of very thin strands of spun sugar.

cane noun (plural **canes**)
1 the stem of a reed or tall grass etc. **2** a thin
stick.
cane verb (**canes, caning, caned**)
beat someone with a cane.

canine (say kayn-I'n) adjective
to do with dogs.
canine tooth a pointed tooth at the front of the
mouth.
canine noun (plural **canines**)
1 a dog. **2** a canine tooth.

canker noun
a disease that rots the wood of trees and plants or
causes ulcers and sores on animals.

cannabis noun
hemp, especially when smoked as a drug.

cannibal noun (plural **cannibals**)
1 a person who eats human flesh. **2** an animal
that eats animals of its own kind.
cannibalism noun

cannon noun
1 (plural **cannon**) a large heavy gun. **2** (plural
cannons) the hitting of two balls in billiards by
the third ball.
cannon verb (**cannons, cannoning, cannoned**)
bump into something heavily.

❶ USAGE Do not confuse with *canon*.

cannon ball noun (plural **cannon balls**)
a large solid ball fired from a cannon.

cannot
can not.

canoe noun (plural **canoes**)
a narrow lightweight boat, moved forwards with
paddles.
canoe verb (**canoes, canoeing, canoed**)
travel in a canoe.
canoeist noun

canon *noun* (*plural* **canons**)
1 a general principle or rule. **2** a clergyman of a cathedral.

---

❶ USAGE Do not confuse with *cannon*.

---

canopy *noun* (*plural* **canopies**)
1 a hanging cover forming a shelter above a throne, bed, or person etc. **2** the part of a parachute that spreads in the air.

cant *noun*
1 insincere talk. **2** jargon.

can't (*mainly spoken*)
cannot.

cantankerous *adjective*
bad-tempered.

canteen *noun* (*plural* **canteens**)
1 a restaurant for workers in a factory, office, etc. **2** a case or box containing a set of cutlery. **3** a soldier's or camper's water flask.

canter *noun*
a gentle gallop.

canter *verb* (**canters, cantering, cantered**)
go or ride at a canter.

cantilever *noun* (*plural* **cantilevers**)
a beam or girder fixed at one end only and used to support a bridge etc.

canvas *noun* (*plural* **canvases**)
1 a kind of strong coarse cloth. **2** a piece of canvas for painting on; a painting.

canvass *verb* (**canvasses, canvassing, canvassed**)
visit people to ask them for their support, especially in an election.
canvasser *noun*

canyon *noun* (*plural* **canyons**)
a deep valley, usually with a river running through it.

cap *noun* (*plural* **caps**)
1 a soft hat without a brim but often with a peak. **2** a special headdress, e.g. that worn by a nurse. **3** a cap showing membership of a sports team. **4** a cap-like cover or top. **5** something that makes a bang when fired in a toy pistol.

cap *verb* (**caps, capping, capped**)
1 put a cap or cover on something; cover. **2** award a sports cap to someone chosen to be in a team. **3** do better than something ♦ *Can you cap that joke?*

capable *adjective*
able to do something.
capably *adverb* **capability** *noun*

capacious (*say* ka-**pay**-shus) *adjective*
roomy; able to hold a large amount.

capacity *noun* (*plural* **capacities**)
1 the amount that something can hold. **2** ability; capability. **3** the position that someone occupies ♦ *In my capacity as your guardian I am responsible for you.*

cape[1] *noun* (*plural* **capes**)
a cloak.

cape[2] *noun* (*plural* **capes**)
a large piece of high land that sticks out into the sea.

caper *verb* (**capers, capering, capered**)
jump or run about playfully.

caper *noun* (*plural* **capers**)
1 jumping about playfully. **2** (*slang*) an activity or adventure.

capillary (*say* ka-**pil**-er-ee) *noun* (*plural* **capillaries**)
any of the very fine blood vessels that connect veins and arteries.

capital *adjective*
1 important. **2** (*informal*) excellent.

capital *noun* (*plural* **capitals**)
1 a capital city. **2** a capital letter. **3** the top part of a pillar. **4** money or property that can be used to produce more wealth.

capital city *noun* (*plural* **capital cities**)
the most important city in a country.

capitalism (*say* **kap**-it-al-izm) *noun*
an economic system in which trade and industry are controlled by private owners for profit, and not by the state. (Compare **Communism**.)

capitalist (*say* **kap**-it-al-ist) *noun* (*plural* **capitalists**)
1 a person who has a lot of wealth invested; a rich person. **2** a person who is in favour of capitalism.

capitalize (*say* **kap**-it-al-I'z) *verb* (**capitalizes, capitalizing, capitalized**)
1 write or print as a capital letter. **2** change something into capital; provide something with capital (= money).
capitalization *noun*
capitalize on profit by something; use it to your own advantage ♦ *You could capitalize on your skill at drawing.*

capital letter *noun* (*plural* **capital letters**)
a large letter of the kind used at the start of a name or sentence.

capital punishment *noun*
punishing criminals by putting them to death.

capitulate *verb* (**capitulates, capitulating, capitulated**)
admit that you are defeated and surrender.
capitulation *noun*

capricious (*say* ka-**prish**-us) *adjective*
deciding or changing your mind in an impulsive way.
capriciously *adverb* **capriciousness** *noun*

capsize *verb* (**capsizes, capsizing, capsized**)
overturn ♦ *the boat capsized.*

capsule noun (*plural* **capsules**)
1 a hollow pill containing medicine.
2 a plant's seed case that splits open when ripe.
3 a compartment of a spacecraft that can be separated from the main part.

captain noun (*plural* **captains**)
1 a person in command of a ship or aircraft.
2 the leader in a sports team. 3 an army officer ranking next below a major; a naval officer ranking next below a commodore.
captaincy noun

caption noun (*plural* **captions**)
1 the words printed with a picture to describe it.
2 a short title or heading in a newspaper or magazine.

captious (*say* kap-shus) *adjective*
pointing out small mistakes or faults.

captivate verb (**captivates, captivating, captivated**)
charm or delight someone.
captivation noun

captive noun (*plural* **captives**)
someone taken prisoner.
captive *adjective*
taken prisoner; unable to escape.
captivity noun

capture verb (**captures, capturing, captured**)
1 take someone prisoner. 2 take or obtain by force, trickery, skill, or attraction ♦ *He captured her heart.* 3 (in computing) put data in a form that can be stored in a computer.
capture noun
taking or obtaining by force; capturing.

car noun (*plural* **cars**)
1 a motor car. 2 a carriage of a train ♦ *the dining car.*

caramel noun (*plural* **caramels**)
1 a kind of toffee tasting like burnt sugar. 2 burnt sugar used for colouring and flavouring food.

carat noun (*plural* **carats**)
1 a measure of weight for precious stones.
2 a measure of the purity of gold ♦ *Pure gold is 24 carats.*

caravan noun (*plural* **caravans**)
1 a vehicle towed by a car and used for living in.
2 a group of people travelling together across desert country.
caravanning noun

carbohydrate noun (*plural* **carbohydrates**)
a compound of carbon, oxygen, and hydrogen (e.g. sugar or starch).

carbolic noun
a kind of disinfectant.

carbon noun (*plural* **carbons**)
1 a substance that is present in all living things and that occurs in its pure form as diamond and graphite. 2 carbon paper. 3 a carbon copy.

carbonate noun (*plural* **carbonates**)
a compound that gives off carbon dioxide when mixed with acid.

carbon dioxide noun
a gas formed when things burn, or breathed out by humans and animals.

carburettor noun (*plural* **carburettors**)
a device for mixing fuel and air in an engine.

carcass noun (*plural* **carcasses**)
1 the dead body of an animal. 2 the bony part of a bird's body after the meat has been eaten.

carcinogen noun (*plural* **carcinogens**)
any substance that produces cancer.

card noun (*plural* **cards**)
1 thick stiff paper or thin cardboard. 2 a small piece of stiff paper for writing or printing on, especially to send messages or greetings or to record information. 3 a small, oblong piece of plastic issued to a customer by a bank or building society, giving details of their account and allowing them to use cash machines etc.
4 a playing card.
cards plural noun a game using playing cards.
on the cards likely; possible.

cardboard noun
a kind of thin board made of layers of paper or wood fibre.

cardiac (*say* kard-ee-ak) *adjective*
to do with the heart.

cardigan noun (*plural* **cardigans**)
a knitted jersey fastened with buttons down the front.
[named after the Earl of Cardigan, a commander in the Crimean War in the 19th century, whose troops wore this kind of jersey]

cardinal noun (*plural* **cardinals**)
a senior priest in the Roman Catholic Church.
cardinal *adjective*
1 chief; most important ♦ *the cardinal features of our plan.* 2 deep scarlet (like a cardinal's cassock).

cardinal number noun (*plural* **cardinal numbers**)
a number for counting things, e.g. one, two, three, etc. (Compare **ordinal number**.)

cardinal points plural noun
the four main points of the compass (North, South, East, and West).

care noun (*plural* **cares**)
1 serious attention and thought ♦ *Plan your holiday with care.* 2 caution to avoid damage or loss ♦ *Glass—handle with care.* 3 protection or supervision ♦ *Leave the child in my care.*
4 worry or anxiety ♦ *freedom from care.*
take care be especially careful. **take care of** look after.

care *verb* (**cares, caring, cared**)
1 feel interested or concerned. 2 feel affection.
care for 1 have in your care. 2 be fond of.

career *noun* (*plural* **careers**)
a series of jobs that mark a person's progress
in the profession or work they choose to do
♦ *a career in journalism.*

career *verb* (**careers, careering, careered**)
rush along wildly.

carefree *adjective*
without worries or responsibilities.

careful *adjective*
1 giving serious thought and attention to
something. 2 avoiding damage or danger etc.;
cautious.
carefully *adverb* **carefulness** *noun*

careless *adjective*
not careful.
carelessly *adverb* **carelessness** *noun*

caress *noun* (*plural* **caresses**)
a gentle loving touch.

caress *verb* (**caresses, caressing, caressed**)
touch lovingly.

caretaker *noun* (*plural* **caretakers**)
a person employed to look after a school, block
of flats, etc.

cargo *noun* (*plural* **cargoes**)
goods carried in a ship or aircraft.

Caribbean *adjective*
to do with or from the Caribbean Sea, a part of
the Atlantic Ocean east of Central America.

caricature *noun* (*plural* **caricatures**)
an amusing or exaggerated picture of someone.

carnage *noun*
the killing of many people.

carnival *noun* (*plural* **carnivals**)
a festival, often with a procession in fancy dress.
[from Latin *carnis* = of flesh: originally this
meant the festivities before Lent, when meat was
given up until Easter]

carnivorous (*say* kar-niv-er-us) *adjective*
meat-eating. (Compare **herbivorous**.)
carnivore *noun*

carol *noun* (*plural* **carols**)
a Christmas hymn.
caroller *noun* **carolling** *noun*

carp¹ *noun* (*plural* **carp**)
an edible freshwater fish.

carp² *verb* (**carps, carping, carped**)
keep finding fault.

car park *noun* (*plural* **car parks**)
an area where cars may be parked.

carpenter *noun* (*plural* **carpenters**)
a person who makes things out of wood.
carpentry *noun*

carpet *noun* (*plural* **carpets**)
a thick soft covering for a floor.
carpeted *adjective* **carpeting** *noun*
[from early Italian *carpita*, from Latin *carpere*
= to pluck]

carriage *noun* (*plural* **carriages**)
1 one of the separate parts of a train, where
passengers sit. 2 a passenger vehicle pulled by
horses. 3 carrying goods from one place to
another; the cost of carrying goods ♦ *Carriage is
extra.* 4 a moving part carrying or holding
something in a machine.

carrier *noun* (*plural* **carriers**)
a person or thing that carries something.

carrot *noun* (*plural* **carrots**)
a plant with a thick orange-coloured root used as
a vegetable.

carry *verb* (**carries, carrying, carried**)
1 take something from one place to another.
2 support the weight of something. 3 take an
amount into the next column when adding
figures. 4 be heard a long way away ♦ *Sound
carries in the mountains.* 5 if a proposal at a
meeting is carried, it is approved by most people
at the meeting ♦ *The motion was carried by ten
votes to six.*
be carried away be very excited.
carry on 1 continue. 2 (*informal*) behave
excitedly. 3 (*informal*) complain. **carry out** put
into practice.

cart *noun* (*plural* **carts**)
an open vehicle for carrying loads.

cart *verb* (**carts, carting, carted**)
1 carry in a cart. 2 (*informal*) carry something
heavy or tiring ♦ *I've carted these books all round
the school.*

carthorse *noun* (*plural* **carthorses**)
a large strong horse used for pulling heavy loads.

cartilage *noun*
tough white flexible tissue attached to a bone.

carton *noun* (*plural* **cartons**)
a cardboard or plastic container.

cartoon *noun* (*plural* **cartoons**)
1 an amusing drawing. 2 a series of drawings
that tell a story; a comic strip. 3 an animated
film.
cartoonist *noun*

cartridge *noun* (*plural* **cartridges**)
1 a case containing the explosive for a bullet or
shell. 2 a container holding film for a camera,
ink for a pen, etc. 3 the device that holds the
stylus of a record player.

cartwheel *noun* (*plural* **cartwheels**)
1 the wheel of a cart. 2 a handstand balancing on
each hand in turn with arms and legs spread like
spokes of a wheel.

carve verb (**carves, carving, carved**)
1 make something by cutting wood or stone etc.
2 cut cooked meat into slices.
carver noun

case¹ noun (plural **cases**)
1 a container. 2 a suitcase.

case² noun (plural **cases**)
1 an example of something existing or occurring; a situation ♦ In every case we found that someone had cheated. 2 something investigated by police etc. or by a lawcourt ♦ a murder case. 3 a set of facts or arguments to support something ♦ She put forward a good case for equality.
4 the form of a word that shows how it is related to other words. Fred's is the possessive case of Fred; him is the objective case of he.
in any case anyway. **in case** because something may happen.

cash noun
1 money in coin or notes. 2 immediate payment for goods etc.

cash verb (**cashes, cashing, cashed**)
change a cheque etc. for cash.

cashew noun (plural **cashews**)
a small kidney-shaped nut.
[via Portuguese from Tupi (a South American language)]

cashier noun (plural **cashiers**)
a person who takes in and pays out money in a bank or takes payments in a shop.

cash machine or **cash dispenser** noun
(plural **cash machines** or **cash dispensers**)
a machine, usually outside a bank or building society, from which people can draw out cash by using a bank card.

cashpoint noun (plural **cashpoints**)
a cash machine.

cash register noun (plural **cash registers**)
a machine that records and stores the money received in a shop.

casing noun (plural **casings**)
a protective covering.

casino noun (plural **casinos**)
a public building or room for gambling.

cask noun (plural **casks**)
a barrel.

casket noun (plural **caskets**)
a small box for jewellery etc.

casserole noun (plural **casseroles**)
1 a covered dish in which food is cooked and served. 2 food cooked in a casserole.

cassette noun (plural **cassettes**)
a small sealed case containing recording tape, film, etc.

cast verb (**casts, casting, cast**)
1 throw. 2 shed or throw off. 3 make a vote.
4 make something of metal or plaster in a mould.
5 choose performers for a play or film etc.

cast noun (plural **casts**)
1 a shape made by pouring liquid metal or plaster into a mould. 2 all the performers in a play or film.

castaway noun (plural **castaways**)
a shipwrecked person.

caste noun (plural **castes**)
(in India) one of the social classes into which Hindus are born.

casting vote noun (plural **casting votes**)
the vote that decides which group wins when the votes on each side are equal.

castle noun (plural **castles**)
1 a large old fortified building. 2 a piece in chess, also called a **rook**.
castles in the air daydreams.

castor noun (plural **castors**)
a small wheel on the leg of a table, chair, etc.

castor sugar noun
finely ground white sugar.

castrate verb (**castrates, castrating, castrated**)
remove the testicles of a male animal. (Compare spay.)
castration noun

casual adjective
1 happening by chance; not planned.
2 not careful; not methodical. 3 informal; suitable for informal occasions ♦ casual clothes.
4 not permanent ♦ casual work.
casually adverb **casualness** noun

casualty noun (plural **casualties**)
1 a person who is killed or injured in war or in an accident. 2 a department of a hospital that deals with emergency patients.

cat noun (plural **cats**)
1 a small furry domestic animal. 2 a wild animal of the same family as a domestic cat, e.g. a lion, tiger, or leopard. 3 (informal) a spiteful girl or woman.
let the cat out of the bag reveal a secret.

cataclysm (say kat-a-klizm) noun (plural **cataclysms**)
a violent upheaval or disaster.

catalogue noun (plural **catalogues**)
1 a list of things (e.g. of books in a library), usually arranged in order. 2 a book containing a list of things that can be bought ♦ a Christmas catalogue.

catalogue verb (**catalogues, cataloguing, catalogued**)
enter something in a catalogue.

catalyst (say kat-a-list) noun (plural **catalysts**)
1 (in science) something that starts or speeds up a chemical reaction. 2 something that causes a change.

catalytic converter noun (plural **catalytic converters**)
a device fitted to a car's exhaust system, with a catalyst for converting pollutant gases into less harmful ones.

catapult noun (plural **catapults**)
1 a device with elastic for shooting small stones.
2 an ancient military weapon for hurling stones etc.

catapult verb (**catapults, catapulting, catapulted**)
hurl or rush violently.

cataract noun (plural **cataracts**)
1 a large waterfall or rush of water. 2 a cloudy area that forms in the eye and prevents a person from seeing clearly.

catastrophe (say ka-**tass**-trof-ee) noun (plural **catastrophes**)
a sudden great disaster.
catastrophic (say kat-a-**strof**-ik) adjective
catastrophically adverb

catch verb (**catches, catching, caught**)
1 take and hold something. 2 arrest or capture. 3 overtake. 4 be in time to get on a bus or train etc. 5 be infected with an illness.
6 hear ♦ I didn't catch what he said. 7 discover someone doing something wrong♦ They were caught smoking in the playground. 8 make or become fixed or unable to move; entangle
♦ I caught my dress on a nail. 9 hit; strike
♦ The blow caught him on the nose.
catch fire start burning. **catch it** (informal) be scolded or punished. **catch on** (informal)
1 become popular. 2 understand. **catch out** discover someone in a mistake.

catch noun (plural **catches**)
1 catching something. 2 something caught or worth catching. 3 a hidden difficulty. 4 a device for fastening something.

catching adjective
infectious.

catchment area noun (plural **catchment areas**)
1 the area from which a school takes pupils or a hospital takes patients. 2 the whole area from which water drains into a river or reservoir.

catchphrase noun (plural **catchphrases**)
a popular phrase.

catchy adjective
easy to remember; soon becoming popular
♦ a catchy tune.

category noun (plural **categories**)
a set of people or things classified as being similar to each other.

cater verb (**caters, catering, catered**)
1 provide food, especially for a lot of people.
2 provide what is needed.
caterer noun

caterpillar noun (plural **caterpillars**)
the creeping worm-like creature that will turn into a butterfly or moth.

cathedral noun (plural **cathedrals**)
the most important church of a district, usually containing the bishop's throne.

Catherine wheel noun (plural **Catherine wheels**)
a firework that spins round.

cathode noun (plural **cathodes**)
the electrode by which electric current leaves a device. (Compare **anode**.)

Catholic adjective
1 belonging to the Roman Catholic Church.
2 of all Christians ♦ the Holy Catholic Church.
Catholicism noun
Catholic noun (plural **Catholics**)
a Roman Catholic.

catholic adjective
including most things ♦ Her taste in literature is catholic.

cattle plural noun
animals with horns and hoofs, kept by farmers for their milk and beef.

catty adjective (**cattier, cattiest**)
speaking or spoken spitefully.

catwalk noun (plural **catwalks**)
a long platform that models walk along at a fashion show.

cauldron noun (plural **cauldrons**)
a large deep pot for boiling things in.

cauliflower noun (plural **cauliflowers**)
a cabbage with a large head of white flowers.

cause noun (plural **causes**)
1 a person or thing that makes something happen or produces an effect. 2 a reason ♦ There is no cause for worry. 3 a purpose for which people work; an organization or charity.
cause verb (**causes, causing, caused**)
be the cause of; make something happen.

causeway noun (plural **causeways**)
a raised road across low or marshy ground.

caustic adjective
1 able to burn or wear things away by chemical action. 2 sarcastic.
caustically adverb

caution noun (plural **cautions**)
1 care taken in order to avoid danger etc.
2 a warning.
caution verb (**cautions, cautioning, cautioned**)
warn someone.

cautionary adjective
giving a warning.

cautious adjective
showing caution.
cautiously adverb **cautiousness** noun

Cavalier *noun* (*plural* **Cavaliers**)
a supporter of King Charles I in the English Civil War (1642–9).

cavalry *noun*
soldiers who fight on horseback or in armoured vehicles. (Compare **infantry**.)

cave *noun* (*plural* **caves**)
a large hollow place in the side of a hill or cliff, or underground.

cave *verb* (**caves, caving, caved**)
cave in **1** fall inwards. **2** give way in an argument.

cavern *noun* (*plural* **caverns**)
a large cave.
cavernous *adjective*

cavity *noun* (*plural* **cavities**)
a hollow or hole.

cavort (*say* ka-**vort**) *verb* (**cavorts, cavorting, cavorted**)
jump or run about excitedly.

caw *noun* (*plural* **caws**)
the harsh cry of a crow etc.

cc *abbreviation*
cubic centimetre(s).

CCTV *abbreviation*
closed circuit television, a security device.

CD *abbreviation*
compact disc.

CD-ROM *abbreviation*
compact disc read-only memory; a compact disc on which large amounts of data can be stored and then displayed on a computer screen.

cease *verb* (**ceases, ceasing, ceased**)
stop or end.

cease *noun*
without cease not ceasing.

ceasefire *noun* (*plural* **ceasefires**)
a signal to stop firing.

ceaseless *adjective*
not ceasing.

cedar *noun* (*plural* **cedars**)
an evergreen tree with hard fragrant wood.
cedarwood *noun*

cedilla (*say* sid-il-a) *noun* (*plural* **cedillas**)
a mark under *c* in certain languages to show that it is pronounced as *s*, e.g. in *façade*.

ceiling *noun* (*plural* **ceilings**)
1 the flat surface under the top of a room.
2 the highest limit that something can reach.

celebrate *verb* (**celebrates, celebrating, celebrated**)
1 do something special or enjoyable to show that a day or event is important. **2** perform a religious ceremony.
celebrant *noun* **celebration** *noun*

celebrated *adjective*
famous.

celebrity *noun* (*plural* **celebrities**)
1 a famous person. **2** fame; being famous.

celery *noun*
a vegetable with crisp white or green stems.

celestial (*say* sil-est-ee-al) *adjective*
1 to do with the sky. **2** to do with heaven; divine.
celestial bodies *plural noun* stars etc.

cell *noun* (*plural* **cells**)
1 a small room where a prisoner is locked up.
2 a small room in a monastery. **3** a microscopic unit of living matter. **4** a compartment of a honeycomb. **5** a device for producing electric current chemically. **6** a small group or unit in an organization etc.

cellar *noun* (*plural* **cellars**)
an underground room.

cello (*say* chel-oh) *noun* (*plural* **cellos**)
a musical instrument like a large violin, placed between the knees of a player.
cellist *noun*

cellular *adjective*
1 consisting of living cells. **2** (said about a mobile telephone system) using a number of short-range radio stations to cover the area it serves.

cellulose *noun*
1 tissue that forms the main part of all plants and trees. **2** paint made from cellulose.

Celsius (*say* sel-see-us) *adjective*
measuring temperature on a scale using 100 degrees, where water freezes at 0° and boils at 100°.
[named after A. Celsius, a Swedish astronomer, who invented it]

Celtic *adjective*
to do with the Celts, a group of peoples living in parts of Europe and Asia before Roman times, or to the languages spoken by them, including Irish, Scottish Gaelic, and Welsh.

cement *noun*
1 a mixture of lime and clay used in building, to join bricks together, etc. **2** a strong glue.

cement *verb* (**cements, cementing, cemented**)
1 put cement on something. **2** join firmly; strengthen.

cemetery (*say* sem-et-ree) *noun* (*plural* **cemeteries**)
a place where people are buried.

censor *noun* (*plural* **censors**)
a person who examines films, books, letters, etc. and removes or bans anything that seems harmful.
censor *verb* **censorship** *noun*

❶ USAGE Do not confuse with *censure*.

censure (*say* sen-sher) *noun*
strong criticism or disapproval of something.
censure *verb*

ℹ️ USAGE Do not confuse with *censor*.

census *noun* (*plural* **censuses**)
an official count or survey of the population of a
country or area.

cent *noun* (*plural* **cents**)
a coin worth one-hundredth of a dollar.

centenary (*say* sen-**teen**-er-ee) *noun* (*plural*
centenaries)
a 100th anniversary.
centennial (*say* sen-**ten**-ee-al) *adjective*

centigrade *adjective*
measuring temperature on a scale using 100
degrees, where water freezes at 0° and boils at
100°; Celsius.

centimetre *noun* (*plural* **centimetres**)
one-hundredth of a metre, about four-tenths of
an inch.

centipede *noun* (*plural* **centipedes**)
a small crawling creature with a long body and
many legs.

central *adjective*
1 to do with or at the centre. **2** most important.
centrally *adverb*

central heating *noun*
a system of heating a building from one source
by circulating hot water or hot air or steam in
pipes or by linked radiators.

centre *noun* (*plural* **centres**)
1 the middle point or part. **2** an important place
♦ *a centre of the film industry*. **3** a building or
place for a special purpose ♦ *a sports centre*.
centre *verb* (**centres, centring, centred**)
place something at the centre.
centre on or **centre around 1** be concentrated
in. **2** have as its main subject or concern.

centre of gravity *noun* (*plural* **centres of
gravity**)
the point in an object around which its mass is
perfectly balanced.

century *noun* (*plural* **centuries**)
1 a period of one hundred years. **2** a hundred
runs scored by a batsman in an innings at
cricket.

ceramic *adjective*
to do with or made of pottery.

cereal *noun* (*plural* **cereals**)
1 a grass producing seeds which are used as
food, e.g. wheat, barley, or rice. **2** a breakfast
food made from these seeds.

ℹ️ USAGE Do not confuse with *serial*.

cerebral (*say* se-rib-ral) *adjective*
to do with the brain.

cerebral palsy *noun*
a condition caused by brain damage before birth
that makes a person suffer from spasms of the
muscles and jerky movements.

ceremonial *adjective*
to do with or used in a ceremony; formal.
ceremonially *adverb*

ceremonious *adjective*
full of ceremony; elaborately performed.

ceremony *noun* (*plural* **ceremonies**)
the formal actions carried out on an important
occasion, e.g. at a wedding or a funeral.

certain *adjective*
sure; without doubt.
a certain person or **thing** a person or thing that
is known but not named.

certainty *noun* (*plural* **certainties**)
1 something that is sure to happen. **2** being sure.

certificate *noun* (*plural* **certificates**)
an official written or printed statement giving
information about a person etc. ♦ *a birth
certificate*.

certitude *noun*
a feeling of certainty.

cervix *noun* (*plural* **cervices** (*say* ser-vis-ees))
the entrance to the womb.
cervical *adjective*

cesspit or **cesspool** *noun* (*plural* **cesspits** or
cesspools)
a covered pit where liquid waste or sewage is
stored temporarily.

CFC *abbreviation*
chlorofluorocarbon; a gas containing chlorine
and fluorine that is thought to be harmful to the
ozone layer in the Earth's atmosphere.

chaff[1] *noun*
husks of corn, separated from the seed.

chaff[2] *verb*
tease someone.

chain *noun* (*plural* **chains**)
1 a row of metal rings fastened together.
2 a connected series of things ♦ *a chain of
mountains*; ♦ *a chain of events*. **3** a number of
shops, hotels, or other businesses owned by the
same company.
chain *verb* (**chains, chaining, chained**)
fasten something with a chain or chains.

chain letter *noun* (*plural* **chain letters**)
a letter that you are asked to copy and send to
several other people, who are supposed to do the
same.

chain reaction *noun* (*plural* **chain reactions**)
a series of happenings in which each causes the
next.

chain store *noun* (*plural* **chain stores**)
one of a number of similar shops owned by the
same firm.

chair noun (plural **chairs**)
1 a movable seat, with a back, for one person.
2 the person in charge at a meeting.
chair verb (**chairs, chairing, chaired**)
be in control of a meeting ♦ Who will chair this meeting?

chairman noun (plural **chairmen**)
the person who is in control of a meeting.
chairmanship noun

---

❶ USAGE The word chairman may be used of a man or of a woman; they are addressed formally as ♦ Mr Chairman and ♦ Madam Chairman.

---

chairperson noun (plural **chairpersons**)
a chairman.

chalk noun (plural **chalks**)
1 a soft white or coloured stick used for writing on blackboards or for drawing. 2 soft white limestone.
chalky adjective

challenge noun (plural **challenges**)
1 a call to someone to take part in a contest.
2 a task or activity that is new and exciting but also difficult.
challenge verb (**challenges, challenging, challenged**)
1 make a challenge to someone. 2 be a challenge to someone. 3 question whether something is true or correct.
challenger noun

chamber noun (plural **chambers**)
1 (old use) a room. 2 a hall used for meetings of a parliament etc.; the members of the group using it. 3 a compartment in machinery etc.

chambermaid noun (plural **chambermaids**)
a woman employed to clean bedrooms at a hotel etc.

chamber music noun
classical music for a small group of players.

chamber pot noun (plural **chamber pots**)
a receptacle for urine etc., used in a bedroom.

chameleon (say kam-ee-lee-on) noun (plural **chameleons**)
a small lizard that can change its colour to that of its surroundings.

champagne (say sham-**payn**) noun
a bubbly white wine, especially from the Champagne region in France.

champion noun (plural **champions**)
1 a person or thing that has defeated all the others in a sport or competition etc. 2 someone who supports a cause by fighting, speaking, etc.
championship noun
champion verb (**champions, championing, championed**)
support a cause by fighting or speaking for it.

chance noun (plural **chances**)
1 an opportunity or possibility ♦ Now is your chance to escape. 2 the way things happen without being planned ♦ I met her by chance.
take a chance take a risk.

chancellor noun (plural **chancellors**)
1 an important government or legal official.
2 the chief minister of the government in some European countries.
Chancellor of the Exchequer the government minister in charge of a country's finances.
[from Latin cancellarius = secretary]

change verb (**changes, changing, changed**)
1 make or become different. 2 exchange.
3 put on different clothes. 4 go from one train or bus etc. to another. 5 give smaller units of money, or money in another currency, for an amount of money ♦ Can you change £20?
change noun (plural **changes**)
1 changing; a difference in doing something.
2 coins or notes of small values. 3 money given back to the payer when the price is less than the amount handed over. 4 a fresh set of clothes.
5 a variation in routine ♦ Let's walk home for a change.

changeable adjective
likely to change; changing frequently
♦ changeable weather.

channel noun (plural **channels**)
1 a stretch of water connecting two seas.
2 a broadcasting wavelength. 3 a way for water to flow along. 4 the part of a river or sea etc. that is deep enough for ships.
channel verb (**channels, channelling, channelled**)
1 make a channel in something. 2 direct something through a channel or other route.

chant noun (plural **chants**)
1 a tune to which words with no regular rhythm are fitted, especially one used in church music.
2 a rhythmic call or shout.
chant verb (**chants, chanting, chanted**)
1 sing. 2 call out words in a rhythm.

chaos (say **kay**-oss) noun
great disorder.
chaotic adjective **chaotically** adverb
[from Greek, = vast chasm or pit]

chap noun (plural **chaps**) (informal)
a man.

chapatti noun (plural **chapattis**)
a flat cake of unleavened bread, used in Indian cookery.

chapel noun (plural **chapels**)
1 a small building or room used for Christian worship. 2 a section of a large church, with its own altar.
[via early French chapele from Latin capella = little cloak: the first chapel had as a relic the cloak of St Martin]

chaplain *noun* (*plural* **chaplains**)
a member of the clergy who regularly works in a college, hospital, prison, regiment, etc.

chapped *adjective*
with skin split or cracked from cold etc.

chapter *noun* (*plural* **chapters**)
1 a division of a book. 2 the clergy of a cathedral or members of a monastery. The room where they meet is called a **chapter house**.

character *noun* (*plural* **characters**)
1 a person in a story, film, or play. 2 all the qualities that make a person or thing what he, she, or it is. 3 a letter of the alphabet or other written symbol.

characteristic *noun* (*plural* **characteristics**)
a quality that forms part of a person's or thing's character.

characteristic *adjective*
typical of a person or thing.
characteristically *adverb*

charade (*say* sha-**rahd**) *noun* (*plural* **charades**)
1 a scene in the game of **charades**, in which people try to guess a word from other people's acting. 2 a pretence.

charcoal *noun*
a black substance made by burning wood slowly. Charcoal can be used for drawing with.

charge *noun* (*plural* **charges**)
1 the price asked for something. 2 a rushing attack. 3 the amount of explosive needed to fire a gun etc. 4 electricity in something. 5 an accusation that someone has committed a crime. 6 a person or thing in someone's care.
in charge in control; deciding what shall happen to a person or thing.

charge *verb* (**charges, charging, charged**)
1 ask a particular price. 2 rush forward in an attack. 3 give an electric charge to something. 4 accuse someone of committing a crime. 5 entrust someone with a responsibility or task.

chariot *noun* (*plural* **chariots**)
a horse-drawn vehicle with two wheels, used in ancient times for fighting, racing, etc.
charioteer *noun*

charity *noun* (*plural* **charities**)
1 an organization set up to help people who are poor, ill, or disabled or have suffered a disaster. 2 giving money or help etc. to the needy. 3 kindness and sympathy towards others; being unwilling to think badly of people.
charitable *adjective* **charitably** *adverb*

charm *noun* (*plural* **charms**)
1 the power to please or delight people; attractiveness. 2 a magic spell. 3 a small object believed to bring good luck. 4 an ornament worn on a bracelet etc.

charm *verb* (**charms, charming, charmed**)
1 give pleasure or delight to people. 2 put a spell on someone; bewitch.
charmer *noun*

chart *noun* (*plural* **charts**)
1 a map for people sailing ships or flying aircraft. 2 an outline map showing special information
♦ *a weather chart.* 3 a diagram, list, or table giving information in an orderly way.
the charts a list of the records that are most popular.

chart *verb* (**charts, charting, charted**)
make a chart of something; map.

charter *noun* (*plural* **charters**)
1 an official document giving somebody certain rights etc. 2 chartering an aircraft, ship, or vehicle.

charter *verb* (**charters, chartering, chartered**)
1 hire an aircraft, ship, or vehicle. 2 give a charter to someone.

charwoman *noun* (*plural* **charwomen**)
a woman employed as a cleaner.

chase *verb* (**chases, chasing, chased**)
go quickly after a person or thing in order to capture or catch them up or drive them away.
chase *noun*

chasm (*say* kazm) *noun* (*plural* **chasms**)
a deep opening in the ground.

chassis (*say* shas-ee) *noun* (*plural* **chassis**)
the framework under a car etc., on which other parts are mounted.

chaste *adjective*
not having sexual intercourse at all, or only with the person you are married to.
chastity *noun*

chat *noun* (*plural* **chats**)
a friendly conversation.

chat *verb* (**chats, chatting, chatted**)
have a friendly conversation.

chatter *verb* (**chatters, chattering, chattered**)
1 talk quickly about unimportant things; keep on talking. 2 (said about the teeth) make a rattling sound because you are cold or frightened.
chatterer *noun*

chatter *noun*
chattering talk or sound.

chauvinism (*say* shoh-vin-izm) *noun*
1 prejudiced belief that your own country is superior to others. 2 the belief of some men that men are superior to women.
chauvinist *noun* **chauvinistic** *adjective*

cheap *adjective*
1 low in price; not expensive. 2 of poor quality; of low value.
cheaply *adverb* **cheapness** *noun*

cheapen *verb* (**cheapens, cheapening, cheapened**)
make cheap.

cheat *verb* (**cheats, cheating, cheated**)
1 try to do well in an examination or game by breaking the rules. 2 trick or deceive somebody so they lose something.

cheat *noun* (*plural* **cheats**)
a person who cheats.

check¹ *verb* (**checks, checking, checked**)
1 make sure that something is correct or in good condition. 2 make something stop or go slower. 3 in chess, to put an opponent's king in check.

check *noun* (*plural* **checks**)
1 checking something. 2 stopping or slowing; a pause. 3 a receipt; a bill in a restaurant. 4 in chess, the situation in which a king is threatened with capture.
[via early French from a Persian word meaning 'king': the chess meaning is the oldest]

check² *noun* (*plural* **checks**)
a pattern of squares.
checked *adjective*

checkmate *noun*
the winning situation in chess.
checkmate *verb*

checkout *noun* (*plural* **checkouts**)
a place where goods are paid for in a self-service shop.

check-up *noun* (*plural* **check-ups**)
a routine medical or dental examination.

cheek *noun* (*plural* **cheeks**)
1 the side of the face below the eye. 2 rude or disrespectful behaviour; impudence.

cheeky *adjective*
rude or disrespectful; impudent.
cheekily *adverb* **cheekiness** *noun*

cheer *noun* (*plural* **cheers**)
1 a shout of praise or pleasure or encouragement. 2 cheerfulness ♦ *full of good cheer.*

cheer *verb* (**cheers, cheering, cheered**)
1 give a cheer. 2 gladden or encourage somebody.
cheer up make or become cheerful.

cheerful *adjective*
1 looking or sounding happy. 2 pleasantly bright or colourful.
cheerfully *adverb* **cheerfulness** *noun*

cheerless *adjective*
gloomy or dreary.

cheery *adjective*
bright and cheerful.

cheese *noun* (*plural* **cheeses**)
a solid food made from milk.

cheetah *noun* (*plural* **cheetahs**)
a large spotted animal of the cat family that can run extremely fast.

chemical *adjective*
to do with or produced by chemistry.

chemical *noun* (*plural* **chemicals**)
a substance obtained by or used in chemistry.

chemist *noun* (*plural* **chemists**)
1 a person who makes or sells medicines. 2 a shop selling medicines, cosmetics, etc. 3 an expert in chemistry.

chemistry *noun*
1 the way that substances combine and react with one another. 2 the study of substances and their reactions etc.

chemotherapy *noun*
the treatment of disease, especially cancer, by the use of chemical substances.

cheque *noun* (*plural* **cheques**)
a printed form on which you write instructions to a bank to pay out money from your account.

cherish *verb* (**cherishes, cherishing, cherished**)
1 look after a person or thing lovingly. 2 be fond of.

cherry *noun* (*plural* **cherries**)
a small soft round fruit with a stone.

chess *noun*
a game for two players with sixteen pieces each (called **chessmen**) on a board of 64 squares (a **chessboard**).

chest *noun* (*plural* **chests**)
1 the front part of the body between the neck and the waist. 2 a large strong box for storing things in.

chestnut *noun* (*plural* **chestnuts**)
1 a tree that produces hard brown nuts. 2 the nut of this tree. 3 an old joke or story.

chest of drawers *noun* (*plural* **chests of drawers**)
a piece of furniture with drawers for storing clothes etc.

chew *verb* (**chews, chewing, chewed**)
grind food between the teeth.
chewy *adjective*

chewing gum *noun*
a sticky flavoured type of sweet for chewing.

chick *noun* (*plural* **chicks**)
a very young bird.

chicken *noun* (*plural* **chickens**)
1 a young hen. 2 a hen's flesh used as food.

chicken *adjective* (*slang*)
afraid to do something; cowardly.

chicken *verb* (**chickens, chickening, chickened**)
chicken out (*slang*) not take part in something because you are afraid.

chickenpox *noun*
a disease that produces red spots on the skin.

chief *noun* (*plural* **chiefs**)
1 a leader or ruler of a people, especially of a Native American tribe. **2** a person with the highest rank or authority.
chief *adjective*
most important; main.
chiefly *adverb*

chieftain *noun* (*plural* **chieftains**)
the chief of a tribe or clan.

child *noun* (*plural* **children**)
1 a young person; a boy or girl. **2** someone's son or daughter.

childhood *noun* (*plural* **childhoods**)
the time when a person is a child.

childish *adjective*
1 like a child; unsuitable for a grown person. **2** silly and immature.
childishly *adverb*

childminder *noun* (*plural* **childminders**)
a person who is paid to look after children while their parents are out at work.

chill *noun* (*plural* **chills**)
1 unpleasant coldness. **2** an illness that makes you shiver.
chill *verb* (**chills, chilling, chilled**)
make a person or thing cold.

chilli *noun* (*plural* **chillies**)
the hot-tasting pod of a red pepper.
[via Spanish from Nahuatl (a Central American language)]

chilly *adjective*
1 rather cold. **2** unfriendly ♦ *We got a chilly reception.*
chilliness *noun*

chime *noun* (*plural* **chimes**)
a series of notes sounded by a set of bells each making a different musical sound.

chimney *noun* (*plural* **chimneys**)
a tall pipe or structure that carries smoke away from a fire.

chimney pot *noun* (*plural* **chimney pots**)
a pipe fitted to the top of a chimney.

chimpanzee *noun* (*plural* **chimpanzees**)
an African ape, smaller than a gorilla.

chin *noun* (*plural* **chins**)
the lower part of the face below the mouth.

china *noun*
thin delicate pottery.

chink *noun* (*plural* **chinks**)
1 a narrow opening ♦ *a chink in the curtains.* **2** a chinking sound.
chink *verb* (**chinks, chinking, chinked**)
make a sound like glasses or coins being struck together.

chip *noun* (*plural* **chips**)
1 a thin piece cut or broken off something hard. **2** a fried oblong strip of potato. **3** a place where a small piece has been knocked off something. **4** a small counter used in games. **5** a microchip.
a chip off the old block a child who is very like their father or mother. **have a chip on your shoulder** feel resentful or defensive about something.
chip *verb* (**chips, chipping, chipped**)
1 knock small pieces off something. **2** cut a potato into chips.

chipolata *noun* (*plural* **chipolatas**)
a small spicy sausage.

chiropody (*say* ki-**rop**-od-ee) *noun*
medical treatment of the feet, e.g. corns.
chiropodist *noun*

chirp *verb* (**chirps, chirping, chirped**)
make short sharp sounds like a small bird.
chirp *noun*

chisel *noun* (*plural* **chisels**)
a tool with a sharp end for shaping wood, stone, etc.
chisel *verb* (**chisels, chiselling, chiselled**)
shape or cut something with a chisel.

chivalrous (*say* shiv-al-rus) *adjective*
being considerate and helpful towards people less strong than yourself.
chivalry *noun*

chlorine (*say* **klor**-een) *noun*
a greenish-yellow gas used to disinfect water etc.

chloroform (*say* **klo**-ro-form) *noun*
a liquid that gives off a vapour that makes people unconscious.

chlorophyll (*say* **klo**-ro-fil) *noun*
the substance that makes plants green.

chock-full *adjective*
crammed full.

chocolate *noun* (*plural* **chocolates**)
1 a solid brown food or powder made from roasted cacao seeds. **2** a drink made with this powder. **3** a sweet made of or covered with chocolate.
[via French or Spanish from Nahuatl (a Central American language)]

choice *noun* (*plural* **choices**)
1 choosing between things. **2** the range of things from which someone can choose ♦ *There is a wide choice of holidays.* **3** a person or thing chosen.
choice *adjective*
of the best quality ♦ *choice bananas.*

choir *noun* (*plural* **choirs**)
a group of people trained to sing together, especially in a church.
choirboy *noun* **choirgirl** *noun*

choke *verb* (**chokes, choking, choked**)
1 cause somebody to stop breathing properly.
2 be unable to breathe properly. 3 clog.
choke *noun* (*plural* **chokes**)
a device controlling the flow of air into the engine of a motor vehicle.

cholera (*say* kol-er-a) *noun*
an infectious disease that is often fatal.

cholesterol (*say* kol-**est**-er-ol) *noun*
a fatty substance that can clog the arteries.

choose *verb* (**chooses, choosing, chose, chosen**)
decide which you are going to take from among a number of people or things.
choosy *adjective*

chop *verb* (**chops, chopping, chopped**)
cut or hit something with a heavy blow.
chop *noun* (*plural* **chops**)
1 a chopping blow. 2 a small thick slice of meat, usually on a rib.

choppy *adjective* (**choppier, choppiest**)
(said about the sea) not smooth; full of small waves.
choppiness *noun*

chopsticks *plural noun*
a pair of thin sticks used for lifting Chinese and Japanese food to your mouth.

choral *adjective*
to do with or sung by a choir or chorus.

chord¹ (*say* kord) *noun* (*plural* **chords**)
a number of musical notes sounded together.

chord² (*say* kord) *noun* (*plural* **chords**)
a straight line joining two points on a curve.

ⓘ USAGE Do not confuse with *cord*.

---

chore (*say* chor) *noun* (*plural* **chores**)
a regular or dull task.

choreography (*say* ko-ree-**og**-ra-fee) *noun*
the art of writing the steps for ballets or stage dances.
choreographer *noun*

chorus *noun* (*plural* **choruses**)
1 the words repeated after each verse of a song or poem. 2 music sung by a group of people.
3 a group singing together.
chorus *verb* (**choruses, chorusing, chorused**)
sing or speak in chorus.

christen *verb* (**christens, christening, christened**)
1 baptize. 2 give a name or nickname to a person or thing.
christening *noun*

Christian *noun* (*plural* **Christians**)
a person who believes in Jesus Christ and his teachings.
Christian *adjective*
to do with Christians or their beliefs.
Christianity *noun*

Christian name *noun* (*plural* **Christian names**)
a name given to a person at his or her christening; a person's first name.

Christmas *noun* (*plural* **Christmases**)
the day (25 December) when Christians commemorate the birth of Jesus Christ; the days round it.

Christmas pudding *noun* (*plural* **Christmas puddings**)
a dark pudding containing dried fruit etc., eaten at Christmas.

Christmas tree *noun* (*plural* **Christmas trees**)
an evergreen or artificial tree decorated at Christmas.

chromatic (*say* krom-**at**-ik) *adjective*
to do with colours.
chromatic scale *noun* a musical scale going up or down in semitones.

chromium (*say* **kroh**-mee-um) *noun*
a shiny silvery metal.

chromosome (*say* kroh-mos-ohm) *noun* (*plural* **chromosomes**)
a tiny thread-like part of an animal cell or plant cell, carrying genes.

chronic *adjective*
lasting for a long time ♦ *a chronic illness.*
chronically *adverb*

chronicle *noun* (*plural* **chronicles**)
a record of events in the order that they happened.

chronology (*say* kron-**ol**-oj-ee) *noun*
the order of events in the sequence in which they happened, e.g. in history.
chronological *adjective*

chrysalis *noun* (*plural* **chrysalises**)
the hard cover a caterpillar makes round itself before it changes into a butterfly or moth.

chrysanthemum *noun* (*plural* **chrysanthemums**)
a garden flower that blooms in autumn.

chubby *adjective* (**chubbier, chubbiest**)
plump.
chubbiness *noun*

chuckle *noun* (*plural* **chuckles**)
a quiet laugh.
chuckle *verb* (**chuckles, chuckling, chuckled**)
laugh quietly.

chum *noun* (*plural* **chums**) (*informal*)
a friend.
chummy *adjective*

chunk *noun* (*plural* **chunks**)
a thick piece of something.
chunky *adjective*

church *noun* (*plural* **churches**)
1 a public building for Christian worship.
2 a religious service in a church ♦ *I will see you after church.* 3 a particular Christian religion, e.g. the Church of England.

churlish *adjective*
ill-mannered and unfriendly; surly.

churn *noun* (*plural* **churns**)
1 a large can in which milk is carried from a farm. 2 a machine in which milk is beaten to make butter.

churn *verb* (**churns, churning, churned**)
1 make butter in a churn. 2 stir or swirl vigorously.
churn out produce something in large quantities.

chute (*say* shoot) *noun* (*plural* **chutes**)
a steep channel for people or things to slide down.

chutney *noun* (*plural* **chutneys**)
a strong-tasting mixture of fruit, peppers, etc., eaten with meat.
[from Hindi *chatni*]

cider *noun* (*plural* **ciders**)
an alcoholic drink made from apples.

cigar *noun* (*plural* **cigars**)
a roll of compressed tobacco leaves for smoking.

cigarette *noun* (*plural* **cigarettes**)
a small roll of shredded tobacco in thin paper for smoking.

cinder *noun* (*plural* **cinders**)
a small piece of partly burnt coal or wood.

cine-camera (*say* sin-ee) *noun* (*plural* **cine-cameras**)
a camera used for taking moving pictures.

cinema *noun* (*plural* **cinemas**)
1 a place where films are shown. 2 the business or art of making films.

cipher (*say* sy-fer) *noun* (*plural* **ciphers**)
1 a kind of code. 2 the symbol 0, representing nought or zero.

circle *noun* (*plural* **circles**)
1 a perfectly round flat shape or thing.
2 a number of people with similar interests.
3 the balcony of a cinema or theatre.

circle *verb* (**circles, circling, circled**)
move in a circle; go round something.

circuit (*say* ser-kit) *noun* (*plural* **circuits**)
1 a circular line or journey. 2 a track for motor racing. 3 the path of an electric current.

circular *adjective*
1 shaped like a circle; round. 2 moving round a circle.
circularity *noun*

circular *noun* (*plural* **circulars**)
a letter or advertisement etc. sent to a number of people.

circulate *verb* (**circulates, circulating, circulated**)
1 go round something continuously ♦ *Blood circulates in the body.* 2 pass from place to place.
3 send something round to a number of people.

circulation *noun* (*plural* **circulations**)
1 the movement of blood around the body.
2 the number of copies of each issue of a newspaper or magazine that are sold or distributed.

circumcise *verb* (**circumcises, circumcising, circumcised**)
cut off the fold of skin at the tip of the penis.
circumcision *noun*

circumference *noun* (*plural* **circumferences**)
the line or distance round something, especially round a circle.

circumflex accent *noun* (*plural* **circumflex accents**)
a mark over a vowel, as over *e* in *fête*.

circumnavigate *verb* (**circumnavigates, circumnavigating, circumnavigated**)
sail completely round something.
circumnavigation *noun*

circumscribe *verb* (**circumscribes, circumscribing, circumscribed**)
1 draw a line round something. 2 limit or restrict something ♦ *Her powers are circumscribed by many regulations.*

circumspect *adjective*
cautious and watchful.
circumspection *noun*

circumstance *noun* (*plural* **circumstances**)
a fact or condition connected with an event or person or action.

circumstantial (*say* ser-kum-**stan**-shal) *adjective*
consisting of facts that strongly suggest something but do not actually prove it
♦ *circumstantial evidence.*

circus *noun* (*plural* **circuses**)
a travelling show usually performed in a tent, with clowns, acrobats, and sometimes trained animals.
[from Latin, = ring; related to *circle*]

cistern *noun* (*plural* **cisterns**)
a tank for storing water.

citizen *noun* (*plural* **citizens**)
a person belonging to a particular city or country.
citizenship *noun*

citrus fruit *noun* (*plural* **citrus fruits**)
a lemon, orange, grapefruit, or other sharp-tasting fruit.

city *noun* (*plural* **cities**)
a large important town, usually with special rights given by a charter.

civic *adjective*
1 to do with a city or town. 2 to do with citizens.

civil *adjective*
1 polite and courteous. 2 to do with citizens.
3 to do with civilians; not military ♦ *civil aviation.*
civilly *adverb*

civilian *noun* (*plural* **civilians**)
a person who is not serving in the armed forces.

civility *noun* (*plural* **civilities**)
politeness.

civilization *noun* (*plural* **civilizations**)
1 a society or culture at a particular time in history ♦ *ancient civilizations.* 2 a developed or organized way of life ♦ *We were far from civilization.*

civilize *verb* (**civilizes, civilizing, civilized**)
bring culture and education to a primitive community.

Civil Service *noun*
people employed by the government in various departments other than the armed forces.

civil war *noun* (*plural* **civil wars**)
war between groups of people of the same country.

claim *verb* (**claims, claiming, claimed**)
1 ask for something to which you believe you have a right. 2 declare; state something without being able to prove it.
claimant *noun*

claim *noun* (*plural* **claims**)
1 claiming. 2 something claimed. 3 a piece of ground claimed or assigned to someone for mining etc.

clairvoyant *noun* (*plural* **clairvoyants**)
a person who is said to be able to predict future events or communicate mentally with people who are dead or far away.
clairvoyance *noun*

clamber *verb* (**clambers, clambering, clambered**)
climb with difficulty.

clammy *adjective*
damp and slimy.

clamour *noun* (*plural* **clamours**)
1 a loud confused noise. 2 an outcry; a loud protest or demand.
clamorous *adjective*

clamour *verb* (**clamours, clamouring, clamoured**)
make a loud protest or demand.

clamp *noun* (*plural* **clamps**)
a device for holding things tightly.

clamp *verb* (**clamps, clamping, clamped**)
1 fix something with a clamp. 2 fix something firmly.
clamp down on become stricter about something or put a stop to it.

clan *noun* (*plural* **clans**)
a group sharing the same ancestor, especially in Scotland.

clang *noun* (*plural* **clangs**)
a loud ringing sound.
clang *verb*

clank *noun* (*plural* **clanks**)
a sound like heavy pieces of metal banging together.
clank *verb*

clap *verb* (**claps, clapping, clapped**)
1 strike the palms of the hands together loudly, especially as applause. 2 slap in a friendly way ♦ *She clapped him on the shoulder.* 3 put quickly ♦ *They clapped him in gaol.*

clap *noun* (*plural* **claps**)
1 a sudden sharp noise ♦ *a clap of thunder.*
2 a round of clapping ♦ *Give the winners a clap.*
3 a friendly slap.

claret *noun* (*plural* **clarets**)
a kind of red wine.

clarify *verb* (**clarifies, clarifying, clarified**)
make something clear or easier to understand.
clarification *noun*

clarinet *noun* (*plural* **clarinets**)
a woodwind instrument.
clarinettist *noun*

clarity *noun*
clearness.

clash *verb* (**clashes, clashing, clashed**)
1 make a loud sound like that of cymbals banging together. 2 conflict. 3 (said about two or more events) happen inconveniently at the same time. 4 (said about colours) look unpleasant together.
clash *noun*

clasp *noun* (*plural* **clasps**)
1 a device for fastening things, with parts that lock together. 2 a tight grasp.

clasp *verb* (**clasps, clasping, clasped**)
1 grasp or hold tightly. 2 fasten with a clasp.

class *noun* (*plural* **classes**)
1 a group of children, students, etc. who are taught together. 2 a group of similar people, animals, or things. 3 people of the same social or economic level. 4 level of quality ♦ *first class.*

class *verb* (**classes, classing, classed**)
arrange things in classes or groups; classify.

classic *adjective*
generally agreed to be excellent or important.

classic *noun* (*plural* **classics**)
a classic book, film, writer, etc.

classical *adjective*
1 to do with ancient Greek or Roman literature, art, or history. 2 serious or conventional in style ♦ *classical music.*

classified *adjective*
1 put into classes or groups. 2 (said about information) declared officially to be secret and available only to certain people.

classify *verb* (classifies, classifying, classified)
arrange things in classes or groups.
classification *noun*

classroom *noun* (*plural* classrooms)
a room where a class of children or students is taught.

clatter *verb* (clatters, clattering, clattered)
make a sound like hard objects rattling together.
clatter *noun*

clause *noun* (*plural* clauses)
1 a single part of a treaty, law, or contract.
2 part of a complex sentence, with its own verb
♦ *There are two clauses in 'We choose what we want'.*

claustrophobia *noun*
fear of being inside an enclosed space.

claw *noun* (*plural* claws)
1 a sharp nail on a bird's or animal's foot.
2 a claw-like part or device used for grasping.

clay *noun*
a kind of stiff sticky earth that becomes hard when baked, used for making bricks and pottery.
clayey *adjective*

clean *adjective*
1 without any dirt or marks or stains. 2 fresh; not yet used. 3 honourable; not unfair ♦ *a clean fight.* 4 not indecent. 5 a clean catch is one made skilfully with no fumbling.
cleanness *noun*

clean *verb* (cleans, cleaning, cleaned)
make a thing clean.

clean *adverb*
completely ♦ *I clean forgot.*

clear *adjective*
1 transparent; not muddy or cloudy. 2 easy to see or hear or understand; distinct. 3 free from obstacles or unwanted things. 4 free from guilt ♦ *a clear conscience.* 5 complete ♦ *Give three clear days' notice.*
clearly *adverb* **clearness** *noun*

clear *adverb*
1 distinctly; clearly ♦ *We heard you loud and clear.* 2 completely ♦ *He got clear away.* 3 apart; not in contact ♦ *Stand clear of the doors.*

clear *verb* (clears, clearing, cleared)
1 make or become clear. 2 show that someone is innocent or reliable. 3 jump over something without touching it. 4 get approval or authorization for something ♦ *Clear this with the headmaster.*
clear away remove used plates etc. after a meal.
clear off or **out** (*informal*) go away. **clear up**
1 make things tidy. 2 become better or brighter.
3 solve ♦ *clear up the mystery.*

clearing *noun* (*plural* clearings)
an open space in a forest.

clef *noun* (*plural* clefs)
a symbol on a stave in music, showing the pitch of the notes ♦ *treble clef*; ♦ *bass clef.*

cleft *noun* (*plural* clefts)
a split in something.

clemency *noun*
gentleness or mildness; mercy.

clench *verb* (clenches, clenching, clenched)
close your teeth or fingers tightly.

clergy *noun*
the people who have been ordained as priests or ministers of the Christian Church.
clergyman *noun* **clergywoman** *noun*

clerical *adjective*
1 to do with the routine work in an office, such as filing and writing letters. 2 to do with the clergy.

clerk (*say* klark) *noun* (*plural* clerks)
a person employed to keep records or accounts, deal with papers in an office, etc.

clever *adjective*
1 quick at learning and understanding things.
2 skilful.
cleverly *adverb* **cleverness** *noun*

cliché (*say* klee-shay) *noun* (*plural* clichés)
a phrase or idea that is used so often that it has little meaning.

click *noun* (*plural* clicks)
a short sharp sound.
click *verb*

client *noun* (*plural* clients)
a person who gets help or advice from a professional person such as a lawyer, accountant, architect, etc.; a customer.

cliff *noun* (*plural* cliffs)
a steep rock face, especially on a coast.

climate *noun* (*plural* climates)
the regular weather conditions of an area.
climatic (*say* kly-mat-ik) *adjective*

climax *noun* (*plural* climaxes)
the most interesting or important point of a story, series of events, etc.

climb *verb* (climbs, climbing, climbed)
1 go up or over or down something.
2 grow upwards. 3 go higher.
climb *noun* **climber** *noun*
climb down admit that you have been wrong.

clinch *verb* (clinches, clinching, clinched)
1 settle something definitely ♦ *We hope to clinch the deal today.* 2 (said about boxers) be clasping each other.
clinch *noun*

cling *verb* (clings, clinging, clung)
hold on tightly.

clinic noun (plural **clinics**)
a place where people see doctors etc. for treatment or advice.

clinical adjective
1 to do with the medical treatment of patients.
2 coldly efficient or aloof.

clink noun (plural **clinks**)
a thin sharp sound like glasses being struck together.
clink verb

clip¹ noun (plural **clips**)
a fastener for keeping things together, usually worked by a spring.
clip verb (**clips, clipping, clipped**)
fasten with a clip.

clip² verb (**clips, clipping, clipped**)
1 cut with shears or scissors etc. 2 (informal) hit.
clip noun (plural **clips**)
1 a short piece of film shown on its own.
2 (informal) a hit on the head.

clippers plural noun
an instrument for cutting hair.

clique (say kleek) noun (plural **cliques**)
a small group of people who stick together and keep others out.

cloak noun (plural **cloaks**)
a sleeveless piece of outdoor clothing that hangs loosely from the shoulders.
cloak verb (**cloaks, cloaking, cloaked**)
cover or conceal.

cloakroom noun (plural **cloakrooms**)
1 a place where people can leave outdoor clothes, luggage, etc. 2 a lavatory.

clock noun (plural **clocks**)
1 a device that shows what the time is.
2 a measuring device with a dial or digital display.
clock verb (**clocks, clocking, clocked**)
clock in or **out** register the time you arrive at work or leave work. **clock up** reach a certain speed.

clockwise adverb & adjective
moving round a circle in the same direction as a clock's hands.

clockwork noun
a mechanism with a spring that has to be wound up.
like clockwork very regularly.

clod noun (plural **clods**)
a lump of earth or clay.

clog noun (plural **clogs**)
a shoe with a wooden sole.
clog verb (**clogs, clogging, clogged**)
block up.

cloister noun (plural **cloisters**)
a covered path along the side of a church or monastery etc., round a courtyard.

clone noun (plural **clones**)
an animal or plant made from the cells of another animal or plant and therefore exactly like it.
clone verb (**clones, cloning, cloned**)
produce a clone of an animal or plant.

close¹ (say klohss) adjective
1 near. 2 detailed or concentrated ♦ with close attention. 3 tight; with little empty space ♦ a close fit. 4 in which competitors are nearly equal ♦ a close contest. 5 stuffy.
closely adverb **closeness** noun

close adverb
closely ♦ close behind.

close noun (plural **closes**)
1 a street that is closed at one end. 2 an enclosed area, especially round a cathedral.

close² (say klohz) verb (**closes, closing, closed**)
1 shut. 2 end.
close in 1 get nearer. 2 if the days are closing in, they are getting shorter.

close noun
end ♦ at the close of play.

close-up noun (plural **close-ups**)
a photograph or piece of film taken at close range.

closure noun (plural **closures**)
closing.

clot noun (plural **clots**)
1 a small mass of blood, cream, etc. that has become solid. 2 (slang) a stupid person.
clot verb (**clots, clotting, clotted**)
form clots.

cloth noun (plural **cloths**)
1 woven material or felt. 2 a piece of this material. 3 a tablecloth.

clothes plural noun
things worn to cover the body.

clothing noun
clothes.

cloud noun (plural **clouds**)
1 a mass of condensed water vapour floating in the sky. 2 a mass of smoke, dust, etc., in the air.

cloudy adjective (**cloudier, cloudiest**)
1 full of clouds. 2 not transparent ♦ The liquid became cloudy.
cloudiness noun

clover noun
a small plant usually with three leaves on each stalk.
in clover in ease and luxury.

clown noun (plural **clowns**)
1 a performer who does amusing tricks and actions, especially in a circus. 2 a person who does silly things.

cloying adjective
sickeningly sweet.

club *noun* (*plural* **clubs**)
1 a heavy stick used as a weapon. **2** a stick with a shaped head used to hit the ball in golf. **3** a group of people who meet because they are interested in the same thing; the building where they meet. **4** a playing card with black clover leaves on it. **5** a nightclub.

club *verb* (**clubs, clubbing, clubbed**)
hit with a heavy stick.
club together join with other people in order to pay for something ♦ *club together to buy a boat.*

cluck *verb* (**clucks, clucking, clucked**)
make a hen's throaty cry.
cluck *noun*

clue *noun* (*plural* **clues**)
something that helps a person to solve a puzzle or a mystery.
not have a clue (*informal*) be stupid or helpless.

clump *noun* (*plural* **clumps**)
1 a cluster or mass of things. **2** a clumping sound.

clump *verb* (**clumps, clumping, clumped**)
1 form a cluster or mass. **2** walk with a heavy tread.

clumsy *adjective* (**clumsier, clumsiest**)
1 heavy and ungraceful; likely to knock things over or drop things. **2** not skilful; not tactful ♦ *a clumsy apology.*
clumsily *adverb* **clumsiness** *noun*

cluster *noun* (*plural* **clusters**)
a small close group.

cluster *verb* (**clusters, clustering, clustered**)
form a cluster.

clutch *verb* (**clutches, clutching, clutched**)
grasp tightly.

clutch *noun* (*plural* **clutches**)
1 a tight grasp. **2** a device for connecting and disconnecting the engine of a motor vehicle from its gears.

clutter *noun*
things lying about untidily.

clutter *verb* (**clutters, cluttering, cluttered**)
fill with clutter ♦ *Piles of papers cluttered her desk.*

Co. *abbreviation*
Company.

c/o *abbreviation*
care of.

co- *prefix*
1 together, jointly (as in *coexistence, cooperate*). **2** joint (as in *co-pilot*).

coach *noun* (*plural* **coaches**)
1 a bus used for long journeys. **2** a carriage of a railway train. **3** a large horse-drawn carriage with four wheels. **4** an instructor in sports. **5** a teacher giving private specialized tuition.

coach *verb* (**coaches, coaching, coached**)
instruct or train somebody, especially in sports.

coagulate *verb* (**coagulates, coagulating, coagulated**)
change from liquid to semi-solid; clot.
coagulation *noun*

coal *noun* (*plural* **coals**)
a hard black mineral substance used for burning to supply heat; a piece of this.

coalesce (*say* koh-a-**less**) *verb* (**coalesces, coalescing, coalesced**)
combine and form one whole thing.
coalescence *noun*

coalition *noun* (*plural* **coalitions**)
a temporary alliance, especially of two or more political parties in order to form a government.

coarse *adjective*
1 not smooth or delicate; rough. **2** composed of large particles. **3** not refined; vulgar.
coarsely *adverb* **coarseness** *noun*

coarsen *verb* (**coarsens, coarsening, coarsened**)
make or become coarse.

coast *noun* (*plural* **coasts**)
the seashore or the land close to it.
coastal *adjective* **coastline** *noun*
the coast is clear there is no chance of being seen or hindered.

coastguard *noun* (*plural* **coastguards**)
a person whose job is to keep watch on the coast, detect or prevent smuggling, etc.

coat *noun* (*plural* **coats**)
1 a piece of clothing with sleeves, worn over other clothes. **2** the hair or fur on an animal's body. **3** a covering layer ♦ *a coat of paint.*

coat *verb* (**coats, coating, coated**)
cover something with a coating.

coating *noun* (*plural* **coatings**)
a thin covering or layer.

coat of arms *noun* (*plural* **coats of arms**)
a design on a shield, used as an emblem by a family or institution.

coax *verb* (**coaxes, coaxing, coaxed**)
persuade someone gently or patiently.

cobalt *noun*
a hard silvery-white metal.

cobble *noun* (*plural* **cobbles**)
a rounded stone used for paving streets etc.
cobbled *adjective* **cobblestone** *noun*

cobra (*say* **koh**-bra) *noun* (*plural* **cobras**)
a poisonous snake that can rear up.

cobweb *noun* (*plural* **cobwebs**)
the thin sticky net made by a spider to trap insects.

cocaine *noun*
a drug made from the leaves of a tropical plant called *coca.*

cock *noun* (*plural* **cocks**)
1 a male chicken. **2** a male bird. **3** a stopcock.
4 a lever in a gun.
cock *verb* (**cocks, cocking, cocked**)
1 make a gun ready to fire by raising the cock.
2 turn something upwards or in a particular
direction ♦ *The dog cocked its ears.*

cockatoo *noun* (*plural* **cockatoos**)
a crested parrot.

cockerel *noun* (*plural* **cockerels**)
a young male chicken.

cocker spaniel *noun* (*plural* **cocker spaniels**)
a kind of small spaniel.

cockpit *noun* (*plural* **cockpits**)
the compartment where the pilot of an aircraft
sits.

cockroach *noun* (*plural* **cockroaches**)
a dark brown beetle-like insect, often found in
dirty houses.

cocksure *adjective*
very sure; too confident.

cocoa *noun* (*plural* **cocoas**)
1 a hot drink made from a powder of crushed
cacao seeds. **2** this powder.

coconut *noun* (*plural* **coconuts**)
1 a large round nut that grows on a kind of palm
tree. **2** its white lining, used in sweets and
cookery.

cocoon *noun* (*plural* **cocoons**)
1 the covering round a chrysalis. **2** a protective
wrapping.

cod *noun* (*plural* **cod**)
a large edible sea fish.

code *noun* (*plural* **codes**)
1 a word or phrase used to represent a message
in order to keep its meaning secret. **2** a set of
signs used in sending messages by machine etc.
♦ *the Morse code.* **3** a set of numbers that
represents an area in telephoning ♦ *Do you know
the code for Norwich?* **4** a set of laws or rules
♦ *the Highway Code.*
code *verb* (**codes, coding, coded**)
put a message into code.

coeducation *noun*
educating boys and girls together.
coeducational *adjective*

coefficient *noun* (*plural* **coefficients**)
a number by which another number is
multiplied; a factor.

coexist *verb* (**coexists, coexisting, coexisted**)
exist together or at the same time.
coexistence *noun* **coexistent** *adjective*

coffee *noun* (*plural* **coffees**)
1 a hot drink made from the roasted ground
seeds (**coffee beans**) of a tropical plant.
2 these seeds.

coffin *noun* (*plural* **coffins**)
a long box in which a body is buried or
cremated.

cog *noun* (*plural* **cogs**)
one of a number of tooth-like parts round the
edge of a wheel, fitting into and pushing those on
another wheel.

cogent (*say* koh-jent) *adjective*
convincing ♦ *a cogent argument.*

cogitate *verb* (**cogitates, cogitating,
cogitated**)
think deeply about something.
cogitation *noun*

coherent (*say* koh-**heer**-ent) *adjective*
clear, reasonable, and making sense.
coherently *adverb*

coil *noun* (*plural* **coils**)
something wound into a spiral.
coil *verb* (**coils, coiling, coiled**)
wind something into a coil.

coin *noun* (*plural* **coins**)
a piece of metal, usually round, used as money.
coin *verb* (**coins, coining, coined**)
1 manufacture coins. **2** invent a word or phrase.

coincide *verb* (**coincides, coinciding,
coincided**)
1 happen at the same time as something
else. **2** be in the same place. **3** be the same
♦ *My opinion coincided with hers.*

coincidence *noun* (*plural* **coincidences**)
the happening of similar events at the same time
by chance.

colander *noun* (*plural* **colanders**)
a bowl-shaped container with holes in it, used
for straining water from vegetables etc. after
cooking.

cold *adjective*
1 having a low temperature; not warm.
2 not friendly or loving; not enthusiastic.
coldly *adverb* **coldness** *noun*
get cold feet have doubts about doing
something bold or ambitious. **give someone the
cold shoulder** be deliberately unfriendly.

cold *noun* (*plural* **colds**)
1 lack of warmth; low temperature; cold
weather. **2** an infectious illness that makes your
nose run, your throat sore, etc.

cold-blooded *adjective*
1 having a body temperature that changes
according to the surroundings. **2** callous;
deliberately cruel.

collaborate *verb* (**collaborates, collaborating,
collaborated**)
work together on a job.
collaboration *noun* **collaborator** *noun*

collapse *verb* (**collapses, collapsing, collapsed**)
1 break or fall to pieces; fall in. **2** become very
weak or ill. **3** fold up.

collapse *noun* (*plural* **collapses**)
1 collapsing. 2 a breakdown.

collapsible *adjective*
able to be folded up ♦ *a collapsible bed.*

collar *noun* (*plural* **collars**)
1 the part of a piece of clothing that goes round your neck. 2 a band that goes round the neck of a dog, cat, horse, etc.

colleague *noun* (*plural* **colleagues**)
a person you work with.

collect (*say* kol-ekt) *verb* (**collects, collecting, collected**)
1 bring people or things together from various places. 2 obtain examples of things as a hobby ♦ *She collects stamps.* 3 come together. 4 ask for money or contributions etc. from people. 5 fetch ♦ *Collect your coat from the cleaners.*
collector *noun*

collection *noun* (*plural* **collections**)
1 collecting. 2 things collected. 3 money collected for a charity etc.

collective noun *noun* (*plural* **collective nouns**)
a noun that is singular in form but refers to many individuals taken as a unit, e.g. *army, herd.*

college *noun* (*plural* **colleges**)
a place where people can continue learning something after they have left school.

collide *verb* (**collides, colliding, collided**)
crash into something.
collision *noun*

colloquial (*say* col-oh-kwee-al) *adjective*
suitable for conversation but not for formal speech or writing.
colloquially *adverb* **colloquialism** *noun*

colon¹ *noun* (*plural* **colons**)
a punctuation mark (:), often used to introduce lists.

colon² *noun* (*plural* **colons**)
the largest part of the intestine.

colonel (*say* ker-nel) *noun* (*plural* **colonels**)
an army officer in charge of a regiment.

colonial *adjective*
to do with a colony.

colonize *verb* (**colonizes, colonizing, colonized**)
establish a colony in a country.
colonist *noun* **colonization** *noun*

colony *noun* (*plural* **colonies**)
1 an area of land that the people of another country settle in and control. 2 the people of a colony. 3 a group of people or animals of the same kind living close together.

colossal *adjective*
immense; enormous.
[from *colossus* = huge statue, from the bronze statue of Apollo at Rhodes, called the *Colossus of Rhodes*]

colour *noun* (*plural* **colours**)
1 the effect produced by waves of light of a particular wavelength. 2 the use of various colours, not only black and white. 3 the colour of someone's skin. 4 a substance used to colour things. 5 the special flag of a ship or regiment.

colour *verb* (**colours, colouring, coloured**)
1 put colour on; paint or stain. 2 blush. 3 influence what someone says or believes.
colouring *noun*

colour-blind *adjective*
unable to see the difference between certain colours.

coloured *adjective*
1 having colour. 2 having a dark skin.

ℹ USAGE The word *coloured*, used to describe people, is often considered to be insulting. It is better to use *black*.

colourful *adjective*
1 full of colour. 2 lively; with vivid details.

column *noun* (*plural* **columns**)
1 a pillar. 2 something long or tall and narrow ♦ *a column of smoke.* 3 a vertical section of a page ♦ *There are two columns on this page.* 4 a regular article in a newspaper.
columnist *noun*

coma (*say* koh-ma) *noun* (*plural* **comas**)
a state of deep unconsciousness, especially in someone who is ill or injured.
[from Greek *koma* = deep sleep]

comb *noun* (*plural* **combs**)
1 a strip of wood or plastic etc. with teeth, used to tidy hair or hold it in place. 2 something used like this, e.g. to separate strands of wool. 3 the red crest on a fowl's head. 4 a honeycomb.

comb *verb* (**combs, combing, combed**)
1 tidy hair with a comb. 2 search thoroughly.

combat *noun* & *verb* (**combats, combating, combated**)
fight.
combatant (*say* kom-ba-tant) *noun*

combination *noun* (*plural* **combinations**)
1 combining. 2 a number of people or things that are combined.
combination lock a lock that is opened by using a special sequence of numbers or letters.

combine (*say* komb-I'n) *verb* (**combines, combining, combined**)
join or mix together.

combustion *noun*
the process of burning, a chemical process (accompanied by heat) in which substances combine with oxygen in air.

come verb (comes, coming, came, come)
1 move towards somewhere ♦ *Come here!*
2 arrive at or reach a place or condition or result
♦ *They came to a city.* ♦ *We came to a decision.*
3 happen ♦ *How did you come to lose it?* 4 occur
or be present ♦ *It comes on the next page.* 5 result
♦ *That's what comes of being careless.*
come by obtain. **come in for** receive a share of.
come to 1 amount to. 2 become conscious
again. **come to pass** (*old use*) happen.

comedian noun (*plural* comedians)
someone who entertains people by making them
laugh.

comedy noun (*plural* comedies)
1 a play or film etc. that makes people laugh.
2 humour.
[from Greek *komos* = noisy fun + *oide* = song]

comet noun (*plural* comets)
an object moving across the sky with a bright tail
of light.

comfort noun (*plural* comforts)
1 a comfortable feeling or condition. 2 soothing
somebody who is unhappy or in pain. 3 a person
or thing that gives comfort.

comfort verb (comforts, comforting,
comforted)
make a person less unhappy; soothe.

comfortable adjective
1 (said about a person) physically relaxed and
feeling good. 2 making someone physically
relaxed ♦ *a comfortable chair.*
comfortably adverb

comic adjective
making people laugh.
comical adjective **comically** adverb
comic strip noun a series of drawings telling a
story, especially a funny one.

comic noun (*plural* comics)
1 a paper full of comic strips. 2 a comedian.

comma noun (*plural* commas)
a punctuation mark (,) used to mark a pause in
a sentence or to separate items in a list.

command noun (*plural* commands)
1 a statement telling somebody to do something;
an order. 2 authority; control. 3 ability to use
something; mastery ♦ *She has a good command
of Spanish.*

command verb (commands, commanding,
commanded)
1 give a command to somebody; order.
2 have authority over. 3 deserve and get ♦ *They
command our respect.*
commander noun

commandeer verb (commandeers,
commandeering, commandeered)
take or seize something for military purposes or
for your own use.

commandment noun (*plural*
commandments)
a sacred command, especially one of the Ten
Commandments given to Moses.

commando noun (*plural* commandos)
a soldier trained for making dangerous raids.

commemorate verb (commemorates,
commemorating, commemorated)
be a celebration or reminder of some past event
or person etc.
commemoration noun **commemorative**
adjective

commence verb (commences, commencing,
commenced)
begin.
commencement noun

commend verb (commends, commending,
commended)
1 praise ♦ *He was commended for bravery.*
2 entrust ♦ *We commend him to your care.*
commendation noun

comment noun (*plural* comments)
an opinion given about an event etc. or to
explain something.

comment verb (comments, commenting,
commented)
make a comment.

commentary verb (*plural* commentaries)
a description of an event by someone who is
watching it, especially for radio or television.
commentate verb **commentator** noun

commercial adjective
1 to do with commerce. 2 paid for by firms etc.
whose advertisements are included
♦ *commercial radio.* 3 profitable.
commercially adverb

commercial noun (*plural* commercials)
a broadcast advertisement.

commiserate verb (commiserates,
commiserating, commiserated)
sympathize.
commiseration noun

commission noun (*plural* commissions)
1 a task formally given to someone
♦ *a commission to paint a portrait.*
2 an appointment to be an officer in the armed
forces. 3 a group of people given authority to do
or investigate something. 4 payment to someone
for selling your goods etc.

commission verb (commissions,
commissioning, commissioned)
give a commission to a person or for a task etc.

commit verb (commits, committing,
committed)
1 do or perform ♦ *commit a crime.* 2 place in
someone's care or custody ♦ *He was committed
to prison.* 3 promise that you will make your
time etc. available for a particular purpose
♦ *Don't commit all your spare time to helping
him.*

commitment *noun* (*plural* **commitments**)
something you have agreed to do or to be
involved in; an obligation.

committee *noun* (*plural* **committees**)
a group of people appointed to deal with
something.

commodity *noun* (*plural* **commodities**)
a useful thing; a product.

commodore *noun* (*plural* **commodores**)
1 a naval officer ranking next below a rear
admiral. **2** the commander of part of a fleet.

common *adjective*
1 ordinary; usual; found or occurring frequently
♦ *a common weed.* **2** of all or most people ♦ *They
worked for the common good.* **3** shared ♦ *Music is
their common interest.* **4** vulgar.
commonly *adverb* **commonness** *noun*
in common shared by two or more people or
things.

Common Market *noun*
a group of European countries that trade freely
together.

commonplace *adjective*
ordinary; usual.

common sense *noun*
normal good sense in thinking or behaviour.

commonwealth *noun*
1 a group of countries cooperating together.
2 a country made up of an association of states
♦ *the Commonwealth of Australia.*
the Commonwealth 1 an association of Britain
and various other countries that used to be part
of the British Empire, including Canada,
Australia, and New Zealand. **2** the republic set
up in Britain by Oliver Cromwell, lasting from
1649 to 1660.

commotion *noun*
an uproar; a fuss.

commune (*say* kom-yoon) *noun* (*plural*
communes)
1 a group of people living together and sharing
everything. **2** a district of local government in
France and some other countries.

communicate *verb* (**communicates,
communicating, communicated**)
1 pass news, information, etc. to other people.
2 (said about rooms etc.) have a connecting
door.

communication *noun* (*plural*
communications)
1 communicating. **2** something communicated;
a message.
communications *plural noun* links between
places (e.g. roads, railways, telephones, or
radio).

communicative *adjective*
willing to talk.

communion *noun*
the act of sharing thoughts or feelings.
Communion or **Holy Communion** the Christian
ceremony in which consecrated bread and wine
are given to worshippers.

communism *noun*
a political system where the state controls
property, production, trade, etc. (Compare
capitalism.)
communist *noun*

community *noun* (*plural* **communities**)
1 the people living in one area. **2** a group with
similar interests or origins.

commute *verb* (**commutes, commuting,
commuted**)
1 travel a fairly long way by train, bus, or car to
and from your daily work. **2** alter a punishment
to something less severe.

commuter *noun* (*plural* **commuters**)
a person who commutes to and from work.

compact *adjective*
1 closely or neatly packed together. **2** concise.
compactly *adverb* **compactness** *noun*

compact *noun* (*plural* **compacts**)
a small flat container for face powder.

compact disc *noun* (*plural* **compact discs**)
a small plastic disc on which music, information,
etc. is stored as digital signals and is read by a
laser beam.

companion *noun* (*plural* **companions**)
1 a person you spend time with or travel with.
2 one of a matching pair of things. **3** (in book
titles) a guidebook or reference book ♦ *The
Oxford Companion to Music.*
companionship *noun*

company *noun* (*plural* **companies**)
1 a number of people together. **2** a business firm.
3 having people with you; companionship.
4 visitors ♦ *We've got company.* **5** a section of a
battalion.

comparative *adjective*
comparing a thing with something else ♦ *They
live in comparative comfort.*
comparatively *adverb*

comparative *noun* (*plural* **comparatives**)
the form of an adjective or adverb that expresses
'more' ♦ *The comparative of 'big' is 'bigger'.*

compare *verb* (**compares, comparing,
compared**)
put things together so as to tell in what ways
they are similar or different.
compare notes share information. **compare
with 1** be similar to. **2** be as good as ♦ *Our art
gallery cannot compare with Tate Modern.*

ℹ USAGE When *compare* is used with an object, it
can be followed by either *to* or *with.*
Traditionally *to* is used when you are showing
the similarity between two things: ♦ *She
compared me to a pig. With* is used when you are
looking at the similarities and differences
between things: ♦ *Just compare this year's
profits with last year's.*

comparison *noun* (*plural* **comparisons**)
the act of comparing things.

compartment *noun* (*plural* **compartments**)
1 one of the spaces into which something is divided; a separate room or enclosed space.
2 a division of a railway carriage.

compass *noun* (*plural* **compasses**)
a device that shows direction, with a magnetized needle pointing to the north.
compasses or **pair of compasses** a device for drawing circles, usually with two rods hinged together at one end.

compassion *noun*
pity or mercy.
compassionate *adjective* **compassionately** *adverb*

compel *verb* (**compels, compelling, compelled**)
force somebody to do something.

compensate *verb* (**compensates, compensating, compensated**)
1 give a person money etc. to make up for a loss or injury. 2 have a balancing effect ♦ *This victory compensates for our earlier defeats.*
compensation *noun* **compensatory** *adjective*

compete *verb* (**competes, competing, competed**)
take part in a competition.

competent *adjective*
able to do a particular thing.
competently *adverb* **competence** *noun*

competition *noun* (*plural* **competitions**)
1 a game or race or other contest in which people try to win. 2 competing. 3 the people competing with yourself.
competitive *adjective*

competitor *noun* (*plural* **competitors**)
someone who competes; a rival.

compile *verb* (**compiles, compiling, compiled**)
put things together into a list or collection, e.g. to form a book.
compiler *noun* **compilation** *noun*

complacent *adjective*
smugly satisfied with the way things are, and feeling that no change or action is necessary.
complacently *adverb* **complacency** *noun*

complain *verb* (**complains, complaining, complained**)
say that you are annoyed or unhappy about something.

complaint *noun* (*plural* **complaints**)
1 a statement complaining about something.
2 an illness.

complement *noun* (*plural* **complements**)
1 the quantity needed to fill or complete something ♦ *The ship had its full complement of sailors.* 2 the word or words used after verbs such as *be* and *become* to complete the sense. In *She was brave* and *He became king of England*, the complements are *brave* and *king of England*.

❶ USAGE Do not confuse with *compliment*.

complementary *adjective*
completing; forming a complement.

complementary angle *noun* (*plural* **complementary angles**)
either of two angles that add up to 90°.

complete *adjective*
1 having all its parts. 2 finished. 3 thorough; in every way ♦ *a complete stranger.*
completely *adverb* **completeness** *noun*

complete *verb* (**completes, completing, completed**)
make a thing complete; add what is needed.
completion *noun*

complex *adjective*
1 made up of parts. 2 complicated.
complexity *noun*

complex *noun* (*plural* **complexes**)
1 a set of buildings made up of related parts ♦ *a sports complex.* 2 a group of feelings or ideas that influence a person's behaviour etc.
♦ *a persecution complex.*

complexion *noun* (*plural* **complexions**)
1 the natural colour and appearance of the skin of the face. 2 the way things seem ♦ *That puts a different complexion on the matter.*

complicated *adjective*
1 made up of many parts. 2 difficult to understand or do.

complication *noun* (*plural* **complications**)
1 something that complicates things or adds difficulties. 2 a complicated condition.

compliment *noun* (*plural* **compliments**)
something said or done to show that you approve of a person or thing ♦ *He paid me a compliment.*
compliments *plural noun* formal greetings given in a message.

compliment *verb* (**compliments, complimenting, complimented**)
pay someone a compliment; congratulate.

❶ USAGE Do not confuse with *complement*.

complimentary *adjective*
1 expressing a compliment. 2 given free of charge ♦ *complimentary tickets.*

component *noun* (*plural* **components**)
each of the parts of which a thing is made up.

compose *verb* (**composes, composing, composed**)
1 form or make up ♦ *The class is composed of 20 students.* 2 write music or poetry etc. 3 arrange in good order. 4 make calm ♦ *compose yourself.*

composer *noun* (*plural* **composers**)
a person who composes music etc.

composite (*say* kom-poz-it) *adjective*
made up of a number of parts or different styles.

composition *noun* (*plural* **compositions**)
1 composing. **2** something composed, especially a piece of music. **3** an essay or story written as a school exercise. **4** the parts that make something ♦ *the composition of the soil.*

compost *noun*
1 decayed leaves and grass etc. used as a fertilizer. **2** a soil-like mixture for growing seedlings, cuttings, etc.

composure *noun*
calmness of manner.

compound *adjective*
made of two or more parts or ingredients.
compound *noun* (*plural* **compounds**)
a compound substance.
compound *verb* (**compounds, compounding, compounded**)
put together; combine.

comprehensible *adjective*
understandable.

comprehensive *adjective*
including all or many kinds of people or things.
comprehensive *noun* (*plural* **comprehensives**)
a comprehensive school.

comprehensive school *noun* (*plural* **comprehensive schools**)
a secondary school for all or most of the children of an area.

compress (*say* kom-press) *verb* (**compresses, compressing, compressed**)
press together or into a smaller space.
compression *noun* **compressor** *noun*

compromise (*say* kom-prom-I'z) *noun* (*plural* **compromises**)
an agreement reached by each side accepting less than it asked for.
compromise *verb* (**compromises, compromising, compromised**)
1 settle a dispute by a compromise.
2 expose someone to danger or suspicion etc.
♦ *His confession compromises his sister.*

compulsion *noun* (*plural* **compulsions**)
a strong and uncontrollable desire to do something.

compulsory *adjective*
required by law or rule; not optional ♦ *Wearing seat belts is compulsory.*

compunction *noun*
a guilty feeling ♦ *She felt no compunction about hitting the burglar.*

compute *verb* (**computes, computing, computed**)
calculate.
computation *noun*

computer *noun* (*plural* **computers**)
an electronic machine for making calculations, storing and analysing information put into it, or controlling machinery automatically.

comrade *noun* (*plural* **comrades**)
a companion who shares in your activities.
comradeship *noun*

concave *adjective*
curved like the inside of a ball or circle. (The opposite is *convex*.)
concavity *noun*

conceal *verb* (**conceals, concealing, concealed**)
hide; keep something secret.
concealment *noun*

concede *verb* (**concedes, conceding, conceded**)
1 admit that something is true. **2** grant or allow something ♦ *They conceded us the right to cross their land.* **3** admit that you have been defeated.

conceit *noun*
being too proud of yourself; vanity.
conceited *adjective*

conceive *verb* (**conceives, conceiving, conceived**)
1 become pregnant; form a baby in the womb.
2 form an idea or plan; imagine ♦ *I can't conceive why you want to come.*

concentrate *verb* (**concentrates, concentrating, concentrated**)
1 give your full attention or effort to something.
2 bring or come together in one place. **3** make a liquid etc. less dilute.

concentration *noun* (*plural* **concentrations**)
1 concentrating. **2** the amount dissolved in each part of a liquid.

concentric *adjective*
having the same centre ♦ *concentric circles.*

concept *noun* (*plural* **concepts**)
an idea.

conception *noun* (*plural* **conceptions**)
1 the conceiving of a baby. **2** an idea.

concern *verb* (**concerns, concerning, concerned**)
1 be important to or affect somebody.
2 worry somebody. **3** be about; have as its subject ♦ *The story concerns a group of rabbits.*
concern *noun* (*plural* **concerns**)
1 something that concerns you; a responsibility.
2 worry. **3** a business.

concert *noun* (*plural* **concerts**)
a musical entertainment.

concerto (*say* kon-chert-oh) *noun* (*plural* **concertos**)
a piece of music for a solo instrument and an orchestra.

concession noun (plural concessions)
1 conceding. 2 something conceded.
3 a reduction in price for a certain category of person.
concessionary adjective

conciliate verb (conciliates, conciliating, conciliated)
1 win over an angry or hostile person by friendliness. 2 help people who disagree to come to an agreement.
conciliation noun

concise adjective
brief; giving much information in a few words.
concisely adverb conciseness noun

conclude verb (concludes, concluding, concluded)
1 bring or come to an end. 2 decide; form an opinion by reasoning ♦ The jury concluded that he was guilty.

conclusion noun (plural conclusions)
1 an ending. 2 an opinion formed by reasoning.

conclusive adjective
putting an end to all doubt.
conclusively adverb

concoct verb (concocts, concocting, concocted)
1 make something by putting ingredients together. 2 invent ♦ We'll have to concoct an excuse.
concoction noun

concord noun
friendly agreement or harmony.

concrete noun
cement mixed with sand and gravel, used in building.

concrete adjective
1 able to be touched and felt; not abstract.
2 definite ♦ We need concrete evidence, not theories.

concurrent adjective
happening or existing at the same time.

concussion noun
a temporary injury to the brain caused by a hard knock.
concussed adjective

condemn verb (condemns, condemning, condemned)
1 say that you strongly disapprove of something.
2 convict or sentence a criminal ♦ He was condemned to death. 3 make someone suffer something unpleasant ♦ They were condemned to a life of poverty. 4 declare that houses etc. are not fit to be used.
condemnation noun

condense verb (condenses, condensing, condensed)
1 make a liquid denser or more compact.
2 put something into fewer words. 3 change from gas or vapour to liquid ♦ Steam condenses on windows.
condensation noun condenser noun

condescend verb (condescends, condescending, condescended)
1 behave in a way which shows that you feel superior to others. 2 allow yourself to do something that seems unsuitable for a person of your high rank.
condescension noun

condition noun (plural conditions)
1 the state or fitness of a person or thing
♦ This bicycle is in good condition. 2 the situation or surroundings etc. that affect something
♦ working conditions. 3 something required as part of an agreement.
on condition that only if; on the understanding that something will be done.

condition verb (conditions, conditioning, conditioned)
1 put something into a good or proper condition.
2 train someone to behave in a particular way or become used to a particular situation.

conditional adjective
depending on a condition or requirement being met ♦ a conditional offer.
conditionally adverb

condom noun (plural condoms)
a rubber sheath worn on the penis during sexual intercourse as a contraceptive and as a protection against disease.

condone verb (condones, condoning, condoned)
forgive or ignore wrongdoing ♦ We do not condone violence.

conduct (say kon-dukt) verb (conducts, conducting, conducted)
1 lead or guide. 2 be the conductor of an orchestra or choir. 3 manage or direct something
♦ conduct an experiment. 4 allow heat, light, sound, or electricity to pass along or through.
5 behave ♦ They conducted themselves with dignity.

conduction noun
the conducting of heat or electricity etc.

conductor noun (plural conductors)
1 a person who directs the performance of an orchestra or choir by movements of the arms.
2 a person who collects the fares on a bus etc.
3 something that conducts heat or electricity etc.
conductress noun

cone noun (plural **cones**)
1 an object that is circular at one end and narrows to a point at the other end. **2** an ice cream cornet. **3** the dry cone-shaped fruit of a pine, fir, or cedar tree.

confectionery noun
sweets, cakes, and sweet biscuits.

confederate adjective
allied; joined by an agreement or treaty.

confederate noun (plural **confederates**)
1 a member of a confederacy. **2** an ally; an accomplice.

confederation noun (plural **confederations**)
1 the process of joining in an alliance. **2** a group of people, organizations, or states joined together by an agreement or treaty.

conference noun (plural **conferences**)
a meeting for holding a discussion.

confess verb (**confesses, confessing, confessed**)
say openly that you have done something wrong or have a weakness; admit.

confession noun (plural **confessions**)
saying that you have done something wrong.

confetti noun
tiny pieces of coloured paper thrown by wedding guests at the bride and bridegroom.

confide verb (**confides, confiding, confided**)
1 tell someone a secret ♦ I decided to confide in my sister. **2** entrust something to someone.

confidence noun (plural **confidences**)
1 firm trust. **2** a feeling of certainty or boldness; being sure that you can do something. **3** something told confidentially.
in confidence as a secret. **in a person's confidence** trusted with his or her secrets.

confidence trick noun (plural **confidence tricks**)
swindling a person after persuading him or her to trust you.

confident adjective
showing or feeling confidence; bold.
confidently adverb

confidential adjective
meant to be kept secret.
confidentially adverb **confidentiality** noun

confine verb (**confines, confining, confined**)
1 keep something within limits; restrict
♦ Please confine your remarks to the subject being discussed. **2** keep somebody in a place.

confirm verb (**confirms, confirming, confirmed**)
1 prove that something is true or correct.
2 make a thing definite ♦ Please write to confirm your booking. **3** make a person a full member of the Christian Church.
confirmation noun **confirmatory** adjective

confiscate verb (**confiscates, confiscating, confiscated**)
take something away as a punishment.
confiscation noun

conflagration noun (plural **conflagrations**)
a great and destructive fire.

conflict (say **kon**-flikt) noun (plural **conflicts**)
a fight, struggle, or disagreement.

conflict (say kon-**flikt**) verb (**conflicts, conflicting, conflicted**)
have a conflict; differ or disagree.

conform verb (**conforms, conforming, conformed**)
keep to accepted rules, customs, or ideas.
conformist noun **conformity** noun

confound verb (**confounds, confounding, confounded**)
1 astonish or puzzle someone. **2** confuse.

confront verb (**confronts, confronting, confronted**)
1 come or bring face to face, especially in a hostile way. **2** be present and have to be dealt with ♦ Problems confront us.
confrontation noun

confuse verb (**confuses, confusing, confused**)
1 make a person puzzled or muddled. **2** mistake one thing for another.
confusion noun

confute verb (**confutes, confuting, confuted**)
prove a person or statement to be wrong.
confutation noun

congeal (say kon-jeel) verb (**congeals, congealing, congealed**)
become jelly-like instead of liquid, especially in cooling ♦ congealed blood.

congenital (say kon-jen-it-al) adjective
existing in a person from birth.
congenitally adverb

congested adjective
crowded or blocked up ♦ congested streets
♦ congested lungs.
congestion noun

conglomeration noun (plural **conglomerations**)
a mass of different things put together.

congratulate verb (**congratulates, congratulating, congratulated**)
tell a person that you are pleased about his or her success or good fortune.
congratulation noun **congratulatory** adjective

congregate verb (**congregates, congregating, congregated**)
assemble; flock together.

congregation noun (plural **congregations**)
a group of people who have come together to take part in religious worship.

Congress noun
the parliament of the USA.

congruent *adjective*
congruent triangles have exactly the same shape and size.
congruence *noun*

conic *adjective*
to do with a cone.

conical *adjective*
cone-shaped.
conically *adverb*

conifer (*say* kon-if-er) *noun* (*plural* conifers)
an evergreen tree with cones.
coniferous *adjective*

conjecture *noun* (*plural* conjectures)
guesswork or a guess.
conjecture *verb* **conjectural** *adjective*

conjugate *verb* (conjugates, conjugating, conjugated)
give all the different forms of a verb.
conjugation *noun*

conjunction *noun* (*plural* conjunctions)
1 a word that joins words or phrases or sentences, e.g. *and*, *but*. 2 combination or union ♦ *The four armies acted in conjunction.*

conjure *verb* (conjures, conjuring, conjured)
perform tricks that look like magic.
conjuror *noun*
conjure up produce in your mind ♦ *Mention of the Arctic conjures up visions of snow.*

connect *verb* (connects, connecting, connected)
1 join together; link. 2 think of things or people as being associated with each other.

connection *noun* (*plural* connections)
1 a point where two things are connected; a link ♦ *We all know there is a connection between smoking and cancer.* 2 a train, bus, etc. that leaves a station soon after another arrives, so that passengers can change from one to the other.

connoisseur (*say* kon-a-ser) *noun* (*plural* connoisseurs)
a person with great experience and appreciation of something ♦ *a connoisseur of wine.*

conquer *verb* (conquers, conquering, conquered)
defeat or overcome.
conqueror *noun*

conquest *noun* (*plural* conquests)
1 a victory over someone. 2 conquered territory.

conscience (*say* kon-shens) *noun* (*plural* consciences)
knowing what is right and wrong, especially in your own actions.

conscientious (*say* kon-shee-en-shus) *adjective*
careful and honest about doing your work properly.
conscientiously *adverb*

conscientious objector *noun* (*plural* conscientious objectors)
a person who refuses to serve in the armed forces because he or she believes it is morally wrong.

conscious (*say* kon-shus) *adjective*
1 awake and knowing what is happening.
2 aware of something ♦ *I was not conscious of the time.* 3 done deliberately ♦ *a conscious decision.*
consciously *adverb* **consciousness** *noun*

conscript (*say* kon-skript) *verb* (conscripts, conscripting, conscripted)
make a person join the armed forces.
conscription *noun*

conscript (*say* kon-skript) *noun* (*plural* conscripts)
a conscripted person.

consecrate *verb* (consecrates, consecrating, consecrated)
officially say that a thing, especially a building, is holy.
consecration *noun*

consecutive *adjective*
following one after another.
consecutively *adverb*

consensus *noun* (*plural* consensuses)
general agreement; the opinion of most people.

consent *noun*
agreement to what someone wishes; permission.

consent *verb* (consents, consenting, consented)
say that you are willing to do or allow what someone wishes.

consequence *noun* (*plural* consequences)
1 something that happens as the result of an event or action. 2 importance ♦ *It is of no consequence.*

consequent *adjective*
happening as a result.
consequently *adverb*

conservation *noun*
conserving; preservation, especially of the natural environment.
conservationist *noun*

Conservative *noun* (*plural* Conservatives)
a person who supports the Conservative Party, a political party that favours private enterprise and freedom from state control.
Conservative *adjective*

conservative *adjective*
1 liking traditional ways and disliking changes. 2 moderate or cautious; not extreme ♦ *a conservative estimate.*
conservatively *adverb* **conservatism** *noun*

conserve *verb* (conserves, conserving, conserved)
prevent something valuable from being changed, spoilt, or wasted.

consider *verb* (considers, considering, considered)
1 think carefully about or give attention to something, especially in order to make a decision. **2** have an opinion; think to be ♦ *Consider yourself lucky.*

considerable *adjective*
fairly great ♦ *a considerable amount.*
considerably *adverb*

considerate *adjective*
taking care not to inconvenience or hurt others.
considerately *adverb*

consideration *noun* (*plural* **considerations**)
1 being considerate. **2** careful thought or attention. **3** a fact that must be kept in mind. **4** payment given as a reward.
take into consideration allow for.

considering *preposition*
taking something into consideration ♦ *The car runs well, considering its age.*

consist *verb* (consists, consisting, consisted)
be made up or composed of ♦ *The flat consists of three rooms.*

consistency *noun* (*plural* **consistencies**)
1 being consistent. **2** thickness or stiffness, especially of a liquid.

consistent *adjective*
1 keeping to a regular pattern or style; not changing. **2** not contradictory.
consistently *adverb*

consolation *noun* (*plural* **consolations**)
1 consoling. **2** something that consoles someone.

console¹ (*say* kon-**sohl**) *verb* (consoles, consoling, consoled)
comfort someone who is unhappy or disappointed.

console² (*say* kon-**sohl**) *noun* (*plural* **consoles**)
a panel or unit containing the controls for equipment.

consolidate *verb* (consolidates, consolidating, consolidated)
1 make or become secure and strong. **2** combine two or more organizations, funds, etc. into one.
consolidation *noun*

consonant *noun* (*plural* **consonants**)
a letter that is not a vowel ♦ *b, c, d, f, etc. are consonants.*

conspicuous *adjective*
easily seen; noticeable.
conspicuously *adverb* **conspicuousness** *noun*

conspiracy *noun* (*plural* **conspiracies**)
planning with others to do something illegal; a plot.
conspirator *noun*

constable *noun* (*plural* **constables**)
a police officer of the lowest rank.

constant *adjective*
1 not changing; happening all the time. **2** faithful or loyal.
constantly *adverb* **constancy** *noun*

constant *noun* (*plural* **constants**)
1 a thing that does not vary. **2** (in science and mathematics) a number or value that does not change.

constellation *noun* (*plural* **constellations**)
a group of stars.

constipated *adjective*
unable to empty the bowels easily or regularly.
constipation *noun*

constituency *noun* (*plural* **constituencies**)
a district represented by a Member of Parliament elected by the people who live there.

constituent *noun* (*plural* **constituents**)
1 one of the parts that form a whole thing. **2** someone who lives in a particular constituency.
constituent *adjective*

constitute *verb* (constitutes, constituting, constituted)
make up or form something ♦ *Twelve months constitute a year.*

constitution *noun* (*plural* **constitutions**)
1 the group of laws or principles that state how a country is to be organized and governed. **2** the nature of the body in regard to healthiness ♦ *She has a strong constitution.* **3** constituting. **4** the composition of something.
constitutional *adjective*

constrict *verb* (constricts, constricting, constricted)
squeeze or tighten something by making it narrower.
constriction *noun*

construct *verb* (constructs, constructing, constructed)
make something by placing parts together; build.
constructor *noun*

construction *noun* (*plural* **constructions**)
1 constructing. **2** something constructed; a building. **3** two or more words put together to form a phrase or clause or sentence. **4** an explanation or interpretation ♦ *They put a bad construction on our refusal.*

constructive *adjective*
helpful and positive ♦ *constructive suggestions.*

consult *verb* (consults, consulting, consulted)
go to a person or book etc. for information or advice.
consultation *noun*

consultant *noun* (*plural* **consultants**)
a person who is qualified to give expert advice.

consume *verb* (**consumes, consuming, consumed**)
1 eat or drink something. **2** use up ♦ *Much time was consumed in waiting.* **3** destroy ♦ *Fire consumed the building.*

consumer *noun* (*plural* **consumers**)
a person who buys or uses goods or services.

consummate (*say* kon-**sum**-at) *adjective*
perfect; highly skilled ♦ *a consummate artist.*

consumption *noun*
1 consuming. **2** (*old use*) tuberculosis of the lungs.

contact *noun* (*plural* **contacts**)
1 touching. **2** being in touch; communication. **3** a person to communicate with when you need information or help.

contact *verb* (**contacts, contacting, contacted**)
get in touch with a person.

contact lens *noun* (*plural* **contact lenses**)
a tiny lens worn against the eyeball, instead of glasses.

contagious *adjective*
spreading by contact with an infected person ♦ *a contagious disease.*

contain *verb* (**contains, containing, contained**)
1 have inside ♦ *The box contains chocolates.* **2** consist of ♦ *A gallon contains 8 pints.* **3** restrain; hold back ♦ *Try to contain your laughter.*

container *noun* (*plural* **containers**)
1 a box or bottle etc. designed to contain something. **2** a large box-like object of standard design in which goods are transported.

contaminate *verb* (**contaminates, contaminating, contaminated**)
make a thing dirty or impure or diseased etc.; pollute.
contamination *noun*

contemplate *verb* (**contemplates, contemplating, contemplated**)
1 look at something thoughtfully. **2** consider or think about doing something ♦ *We are contemplating a visit to London.*
contemplation *noun* **contemplative** *adjective*

contemporary *adjective*
1 belonging to the same period ♦ *Dickens was contemporary with Thackeray.* **2** modern; up-to-date ♦ *contemporary furniture.*

contemporary *noun* (*plural* **contemporaries**)
a person who is contemporary with another or who is about the same age ♦ *She was my contemporary at college.*

contempt *noun*
a feeling of despising a person or thing.

contemptible *adjective*
deserving contempt ♦ *Hurting her feelings like that was a contemptible thing to do.*

contemptuous *adjective*
feeling or showing contempt ♦ *She gave me a contemptuous look.*
contemptuously *adverb*

content¹ (*say* kon-**tent**) *adjective*
contented.
contentment *noun*

content² (*say* **kon**-tent) *noun* or **contents** *plural noun*
what something contains.

contented *adjective*
happy with what you have; satisfied.
contentedly *adverb*

contest (*say* **kon**-test) *noun* (*plural* **contests**)
a competition; a struggle in which rivals try to obtain something or to do best.

contestant *noun* (*plural* **contestants**)
a person taking part in a contest; a competitor.

context *noun* (*plural* **contexts**)
1 the words that come before and after a particular word or phrase and help to fix its meaning. **2** the background to an event that helps to explain it.

continent *noun* (*plural* **continents**)
one of the main masses of land in the world ♦ *The continents are Europe, Asia, Africa, North America, South America, Australia, and Antarctica.*
continental *adjective*
the Continent the mainland of Europe, not including the British Isles.

continual *adjective*
happening all the time, usually with breaks in between ♦ *Stop this continual quarrelling!*
continually *adverb*

❶ USAGE Do not confuse with *continuous. Continual* is used to describe something that happens very frequently (*there were continual interruptions*) while *continuous* is used to describe something that happens without a pause (*there was continuous rain all day*).

continue *verb* (**continues, continuing, continued**)
1 do something without stopping. **2** begin again after stopping ♦ *The game will continue after lunch.*
continuation *noun*

continuous *adjective*
going on and on; without a break.
continuously *adverb* **continuity** *noun*

❶ USAGE See note at *continual.*

contort *verb* (contorts, contorting, contorted)
twist or force out of the usual shape or meaning.
contortion *noun*

contortionist *noun* (*plural* contortionists)
a person who can twist his or her body into
unusual positions.

contour *noun* (*plural* contours)
1 a line on a map joining the points that are the
same height above sea level. 2 an outline.

contraband *noun*
smuggled goods.

contraception *noun*
a way of preventing pregnancy; birth control.

contraceptive *noun* (*plural* contraceptives)
a substance or device that prevents pregnancy.

contract (*say* kon-trakt) *noun* (*plural*
contracts)
1 a formal agreement to do something.
2 a document stating the terms of an agreement.

contract (*say* kon-**trakt**) *verb* (contracts,
contracting, contracted)
1 make or become smaller. 2 make a contract.
3 get an illness ♦ *She contracted measles.*

contraction *noun* (*plural* contractions)
1 contracting. 2 a shortened form of a word or
words. *Can't* is a contraction of *cannot.*

contractor *noun* (*plural* contractors)
a person who makes a contract, especially for
building.

contradict *verb* (contradicts, contradicting,
contradicted)
1 say that something said is not true or that
someone is wrong. 2 say the opposite of
♦ *These rumours contradict previous ones.*
contradiction *noun* contradictory *adjective*

contraflow *noun* (*plural* contraflows)
a flow of road traffic travelling in the opposite
direction to the usual flow and close beside it.

contralto *noun* (*plural* contraltos)
a female singer with a low voice.

contraption *noun* (*plural* contraptions)
a strange-looking device or machine.

contrary *adjective*
1 (*say* **kon**-tra-ree) of the opposite kind or
direction etc.; opposed; unfavourable.
2 (*say* kon-**trair**-ee) awkward and obstinate.
contrary (*say* kon-tra-ree) *noun*
the opposite.
on the contrary the opposite is true.

contrast *noun* (*plural* contrasts)
1 a difference clearly seen when things are
compared. 2 something showing a clear
difference.

contrast *verb* (contrasts, contrasting,
contrasted)
1 compare or oppose two things in order to show
that they are clearly different. 2 be clearly
different when compared.

contravene *verb* (contravenes, contravening,
contravened)
act against a rule or law.
contravention *noun*

contribute *verb* (contributes, contributing,
contributed)
1 give money or help along with other people.
2 write something for a newspaper or magazine
etc. 3 help to cause something ♦ *Tiredness
contributed to the accident.*
contribution *noun* contributor *noun*
contributory *adjective*

contrite *adjective*
very sorry for having done wrong.

contrive *verb* (contrives, contriving,
contrived)
plan cleverly; find a way of doing or making
something.

control *verb* (controls, controlling, controlled)
1 have the power to make someone or something
do what you want. 2 hold something, especially
anger, in check; restrain.
controller *noun*

control *noun*
controlling a person or thing; authority.
in control having control of something.
out of control no longer able to be controlled.

controls *plural noun*
the switches etc. used to control a machine.

controversial *adjective*
causing controversy.

controversy (*say* **kon**-tro-ver-see or
kon-**trov**-er-see) *noun* (*plural* controversies)
a long argument or disagreement.

conundrum *noun* (*plural* conundrums)
a riddle; a hard question.

convalesce *verb* (convalesces, convalescing,
convalesced)
be recovering from an illness.
convalescence *noun* convalescent *adjective* &
noun

convection *noun*
the passing on of heat within liquid, air, or gas
by circulation of the warmed parts.

convenience *noun* (*plural* conveniences)
1 being convenient. 2 something that is
convenient. 3 a public lavatory.
at your convenience whenever you find
convenient; as it suits you.

convenient *adjective*
easy to use or deal with or reach.
conveniently *adverb*

conventional *adjective*
1 done or doing things in the accepted way;
traditional. 2 (said about weapons) not nuclear.
conventionally *adverb* conventionality *noun*

conversation *noun* (*plural* **conversations**)
talk between people.
conversational *adjective*

convert (*say* kon-**vert**) *verb* (**converts,
converting, converted**)
1 change. **2** cause a person to change his or her
beliefs. **3** kick a goal after scoring a try at rugby
football.
converter *noun* **conversion** *noun*

convex *adjective*
curved like the outside of a ball or circle. (The
opposite is **concave**.)
convexity *noun*

convey *verb* (**conveys, conveying, conveyed**)
1 transport. **2** communicate a message or idea
etc.
conveyor *noun*

conveyor belt *noun* (*plural* **conveyor belts**)
a continuous moving belt for moving objects
from one place to another.

convict (*say* kon-**vikt**) *verb* (**convicts,
convicting, convicted**)
prove or declare that a certain person is guilty of
a crime.

convict (*say* kon-vikt) *noun* (*plural* **convicts**)
a convicted person who is in prison.

conviction *noun* (*plural* **convictions**)
1 convicting or being convicted of a crime.
2 being convinced. **3** a firm opinion or belief.
carry conviction be convincing.

convince *verb* (**convinces, convincing,
convinced**)
make a person feel certain that something is true.

convoy *noun* (*plural* **convoys**)
a group of ships or lorries travelling together.

convulsion *noun* (*plural* **convulsions**)
1 a violent movement of the body. **2** a violent
upheaval.

coo *verb* (**coos, cooing, cooed**)
make a dove's soft murmuring sound.
coo *noun*

cook *verb* (**cooks, cooking, cooked**)
make food ready to eat by heating it.
cook up (*informal*) if you cook up a story or
plan, you invent it.

cook *noun* (*plural* **cooks**)
a person who cooks.

cookery *noun*
the skill of cooking food.

cool *adjective*
1 fairly cold; not hot or warm. **2** calm; not
enthusiastic.
coolly *adverb* **coolness** *noun*

cool *verb* (**cools, cooling, cooled**)
make or become cool.
cooler *noun*

cooped up *adjective*
having to stay in a place which is small and
uncomfortable.

cooperate *verb* (**cooperates, cooperating,
cooperated**)
work helpfully with other people.
cooperation *noun* **cooperative** *adjective*

coordinate *verb* (**coordinates, coordinating,
coordinated**)
organize people or things to work properly
together.
coordination *noun* **coordinator** *noun*

coordinate *noun* (*plural* **coordinates**)
either of the pair of numbers or letters used to fix
the position of a point on a graph or map.

cope *verb* (**copes, coping, coped**)
manage or deal with something successfully.

copious *adjective*
plentiful; in large amounts.
copiously *adverb*

copper *noun* (*plural* **coppers**)
1 a reddish-brown metal used to make wire,
coins, etc. **2** a reddish-brown colour. **3** a coin
made of copper or metal of this colour.
copper *adjective*

copse *noun* (*plural* **copses**)
a small group of trees.

copulate *verb* (**copulates, copulating,
copulated**)
have sexual intercourse with someone.
copulation *noun*

copy *noun* (*plural* **copies**)
1 a thing made to look like another. **2** something
written or typed out again from its original form.
3 one of a number of specimens of the same book
or newspaper etc.

copy *verb* (**copies, copying, copied**)
1 make a copy of something. **2** do the same as
someone else; imitate.

copyright *noun*
the legal right to print a book, reproduce a
picture, record a piece of music, etc.

coral *noun*
1 a hard red, pink, or white substance formed by
the skeletons of tiny sea creatures massed
together. **2** a pink colour.

cord *noun* (*plural* **cords**)
1 a long thin flexible strip of twisted threads or
strands. **2** a piece of flex. **3** a cord-like structure
in the body ◆ *the spinal cord*. **4** corduroy.

---

❶ USAGE Do not confuse with *chord*.

---

cordial *adjective*
warm and friendly.
cordially *adverb* **cordiality** *noun*

corduroy *noun*
cotton cloth with velvety ridges.

core *noun* (*plural* **cores**)
1 the part in the middle of something. **2** the hard
central part of an apple or pear etc., containing
the seeds.

corgi *noun* (*plural* **corgis**)
a small dog with short legs and upright ears.

cork *noun* (*plural* **corks**)
1 the lightweight bark of a kind of oak tree.
2 a stopper for a bottle, made of cork or other material.

cork *verb* (**corks, corking, corked**)
close something with a cork.

corkscrew *noun* (*plural* **corkscrews**)
1 a device for removing corks from bottles.
2 a spiral.

corn¹ *noun*
1 the seed of wheat and similar plants. 2 a plant, such as wheat, grown for its grain.

corn² *noun* (*plural* **corns**)
a small hard painful lump on the foot.

cornea *noun* (*plural* **corneas**)
the transparent covering over the pupil of the eye.
corneal *adjective*

corner *noun* (*plural* **corners**)
1 the angle or area where two lines or sides or walls meet or where two streets join. 2 a free hit or kick from the corner of a hockey or football field. 3 a region ♦ *a quiet corner of the world*.

corner *verb* (**corners, cornering, cornered**)
1 drive someone into a corner or other position from which it is difficult to escape. 2 travel round a corner. 3 obtain possession of all or most of something ♦ *corner the market*.

cornet *noun* (*plural* **cornets**)
1 a cone-shaped wafer etc. holding ice cream.
2 a musical instrument rather like a trumpet.

cornflakes *plural noun*
toasted maize flakes eaten as a breakfast cereal.

cornucopia *noun*
1 a horn-shaped container overflowing with fruit and flowers. 2 a plentiful supply of good things.

corny *adjective* (**cornier, corniest**) (*informal*)
1 repeated so often that people are tired of it
♦ *a corny joke*. 2 sentimental.

corollary (*say* ker-ol-er-ee) *noun* (*plural* **corollaries**)
a fact etc. that logically results from another
♦ *The work is difficult and, as a corollary, tiring.*

coronary *noun* (*plural* **coronaries**)
short for **coronary thrombosis**, blockage of an artery carrying blood to the heart.
[from Latin *corona* = crown: the coronary arteries encircle the heart like a crown]

coronation *noun* (*plural* **coronations**)
the crowning of a king or queen.

corporal *noun* (*plural* **corporals**)
a soldier ranking next below a sergeant.

corporal punishment *noun*
punishment on the body, such as spanking or caning.

corps (*say* kor) *noun* (*plural* **corps** (*say* korz))
1 a special army unit ♦ *the Medical Corps*.
2 a large group of soldiers. 3 a set of people doing the same job ♦ *the diplomatic corps*.
[from French, from Latin *corpus* = body]

corpse *noun* (*plural* **corpses**)
a dead body.

corpuscle *noun* (*plural* **corpuscles**)
one of the red or white cells in blood.

correct *adjective*
1 true; accurate; without any mistakes. 2 proper; done or said in an approved way.
correctly *adverb* **correctness** *noun*

correct *verb* (**corrects, correcting, corrected**)
1 make a thing correct by altering or adjusting it.
2 mark the mistakes in something. 3 point out or punish a person's faults.
correction *noun* **corrective** *adjective*

correspond *verb* (**corresponds, corresponding, corresponded**)
1 write letters to each other. 2 agree; match
♦ *Your story corresponds with his.* 3 be similar or equivalent ♦ *Their assembly corresponds to our parliament.*

correspondence *noun*
1 letters; writing letters. 2 similarity; agreement.

corridor *noun* (*plural* **corridors**)
a passage in a building.

corroborate *verb* (**corroborates, corroborating, corroborated**)
help to confirm a statement etc.
corroboration *noun*

corrode *verb* (**corrodes, corroding, corroded**)
destroy metal gradually by chemical action.
corrosion *noun* **corrosive** *adjective*

corrugated *adjective*
shaped into alternate ridges and grooves
♦ *corrugated iron*.

corrupt *adjective*
1 dishonest; accepting bribes. 2 wicked.
3 decaying.

corrupt *verb* (**corrupts, corrupting, corrupted**)
1 cause someone to become dishonest or wicked.
2 spoil; cause something to decay.
corruption *noun* **corruptible** *adjective*

cosine *noun* (*plural* **cosines**)
(in a right-angled triangle) the ratio of the length of a side adjacent to one of the acute angles to the length of the hypotenuse. (Compare **sine**.)

cosmetic *noun* (*plural* **cosmetics**)
a substance (e.g. face powder or lipstick) put on the skin to make it look more attractive.

cosmetic surgery *noun*
surgery carried out to make people look more attractive.

cosmic *adjective*
1 to do with the universe. 2 to do with outer space ♦ *cosmic rays*.

cosmopolitan *adjective*
from many countries; containing people from
many countries.

cosmos (*say* koz-moss) *noun*
the universe.

cost *noun* (*plural* costs)
1 the amount of money needed to buy, do, or
make something. **2** the effort or loss needed to
achieve something.
at all costs or **at any cost** no matter what the
cost or difficulty may be.

cost *verb* (costs, costing, cost)
1 have a certain amount as its price or charge.
2 cause the loss of ♦ *This war has cost many
lives*. **3** (*past tense* is **costed**) estimate the cost of
something.

costly *adjective* (costlier, costliest)
expensive.
costliness *noun*

costume *noun* (*plural* costumes)
clothes, especially for a particular purpose or of
a particular place or period.

cosy *adjective* (cosier, cosiest)
warm and comfortable.
cosily *adverb* **cosiness** *noun*

cot *noun* (*plural* cots)
a baby's bed with high sides.
[from Hindi *khat* = framework of a bed]

cottage *noun* (*plural* cottages)
a small simple house, especially in the country.

cotton *noun*
1 a soft white substance covering the seeds of a
tropical plant; the plant itself. **2** thread made
from this substance. **3** cloth made from cotton
thread.

cotton wool *noun*
soft fluffy material originally made from cotton.

couch *noun* (*plural* couches)
1 a long soft seat like a sofa but with only one
end raised. **2** a sofa or settee.

couch *verb* (couches, couching, couched)
express in words of a certain kind ♦ *The request
was couched in polite terms*.

cough (*say* kof) *verb* (coughs, coughing,
coughed)
send out air from the lungs with a sudden sharp
sound.

cough *noun* (*plural* coughs)
1 the act or sound of coughing. **2** an illness that
makes you cough.

could *past tense* of **can²**.

couldn't (*mainly spoken*)
could not.

council *noun* (*plural* councils)
a group of people chosen or elected to organize
or discuss something, especially those elected to
organize the affairs of a town or county.

❶ USAGE Do not confuse with *counsel*.

councillor *noun* (*plural* councillors)
a member of a town or county council.

council tax *noun* (*plural* council taxes)
a tax paid to a local authority to pay for local
services, based on the estimated value of
someone's house or flat.

counsel *noun* (*plural* counsels)
1 advice ♦ *give counsel*. **2** a barrister or group of
barristers representing someone in a lawsuit.
take counsel with consult.

❶ USAGE Do not confuse with *council*.

counsel *verb* (counsels, counselling,
counselled)
give advice to someone; recommend.

count¹ *verb* (counts, counting, counted)
1 say numbers in their proper order. **2** find the
total of something by using numbers. **3** include
in a total ♦ *There are six of us, counting the dog*.
4 be important ♦ *It's what you do that counts*.
5 regard; consider ♦ *I should count it an honour
to be invited*.
count on rely on.

count *noun* (*plural* counts)
1 counting. **2** a number reached by counting;
a total. **3** any of the points being considered,
e.g. in accusing someone of crimes ♦ *guilty on
all counts*.

count² *noun* (*plural* counts)
a foreign nobleman.

countdown *noun* (*plural* countdowns)
counting numbers backwards to zero before an
event, especially the launching of a space rocket.

counter¹ *noun* (*plural* counters)
1 a flat surface over which customers are served
in a shop, bank, etc. **2** a small round playing
piece used in board games. **3** a device for
counting things.

counter² *verb* (counters, countering,
countered)
1 counteract. **2** counter-attack; return an
opponent's blow by hitting back.

counteract *verb* (counteracts, counteracting,
counteracted)
act against something and reduce or prevent its
effects.
counteraction *noun*

counterbalance *noun* (*plural*
counterbalances)
a weight or influence that balances another.
counterbalance *verb*

counterfeit (*say* kownt-er-feet) *adjective*
fake; not genuine.

counterfeit *verb* (counterfeits,
counterfeiting, counterfeited)
forge or make an imitation of something.

counterfoil *noun* (*plural* counterfoils)
a section of a cheque or receipt etc. that is torn
off and kept as a record.

counterpart noun (plural **counterparts**)
a person or thing that corresponds to another
♦ *Their President is the counterpart of our Prime Minister.*
countless adjective
too many to count.
country noun (plural **countries**)
1 the land occupied by a nation. 2 all the people of a country. 3 the countryside.
countryside noun
an area with fields, woods, villages, etc. away from towns.
county noun (plural **counties**)
each of the main areas that a country is divided into for local government.
coup (say koo) noun (plural **coups**)
a sudden action taken to win power; a clever victory.
couple noun (plural **couples**)
two people or things considered together; a pair.
couple verb (**couples, coupling, coupled**)
fasten or link two things together.
couplet noun (plural **couplets**)
a pair of lines in rhyming verse.
coupon noun (plural **coupons**)
a piece of paper that gives you the right to receive or do something.
courage noun
the ability to face danger or difficulty or pain even when you are afraid; bravery.
courageous adjective
courier (say koor-ee-er) noun (plural **couriers**)
1 a messenger. 2 a person employed to guide and help a group of tourists.
course noun (plural **courses**)
1 the direction in which something goes; a route ♦ *the ship's course.* 2 a series of events or actions etc. ♦ *Your best course is to start again.* 3 a series of lessons, exercises, etc. 4 part of a meal ♦ *the meat course.* 5 a racecourse. 6 a golf course.
of course without a doubt; as we expected.
court noun (plural **courts**)
1 the royal household. 2 a lawcourt; the judges etc. in a lawcourt. 3 an enclosed area for games such as tennis and netball. 4 a courtyard.
court verb (**courts, courting, courted**)
try to win somebody's love or support.
[from early French, from Latin *cohors* = a crowd of people]
courteous (say ker-tee-us) adjective
polite.
courteously adverb **courtesy** noun
courtier noun (plural **courtiers**) (old use)
one of a king's or queen's companions at court.
courtly adjective
dignified and polite.
courtship noun
1 courting someone, especially a boyfriend or girlfriend. 2 the mating ritual of some birds and animals.

courtyard noun (plural **courtyards**)
a space surrounded by walls or buildings.
cousin noun (plural **cousins**)
a child of your uncle or aunt.
cover verb (**covers, covering, covered**)
1 place one thing over or round another; conceal. 2 travel a certain distance ♦ *We covered ten miles a day.* 3 aim a gun at somebody ♦ *I've got you covered.* 4 protect by insurance or a guarantee ♦ *These goods are covered against fire or theft.* 5 be enough money to pay for something ♦ *£10 should cover my fare.* 6 deal with or include ♦ *The book covers all kinds of farming.*
coverage noun
cover up conceal something, especially an awkward fact or piece of information.
cover noun (plural **covers**)
1 a thing used for covering something else; a lid, wrapper, envelope, etc. 2 the binding of a book. 3 something that hides or shelters or protects you.
cow noun (plural **cows**)
the fully grown female of cattle or of certain other large animals (e.g. elephant, whale, or seal).
coward noun (plural **cowards**)
a person who has no courage and shows fear in a shameful way.
cowardice noun **cowardly** adjective
cowboy noun (plural **cowboys**)
a man in charge of grazing cattle on a ranch in the USA.
cower verb (**cowers, cowering, cowered**)
crouch or shrink back in fear.
coy adjective
pretending to be shy or modest; bashful.
coyly adverb **coyness** noun
crab noun (plural **crabs**)
a shellfish with ten legs, the first pair being a set of pincers.
crab apple noun (plural **crab apples**)
a small sour apple.
crack noun (plural **cracks**)
1 a line on the surface of something where it has broken but not come completely apart. 2 a narrow gap. 3 a sudden sharp noise. 4 a knock ♦ *a crack on the head.* 5 (informal) a joke; a wisecrack. 6 a drug made from cocaine.
crack adjective (informal)
first-class ♦ *He is a crack shot.*
crack verb (**cracks, cracking, cracked**)
1 make or get a crack; split. 2 make a sudden sharp noise. 3 break down ♦ *He cracked under the strain.*
crack a joke tell a joke. **crack down on** (informal) stop something that is illegal or against rules. **get cracking** (informal) get busy.
cracker noun (plural **crackers**)
1 a paper tube that bangs when pulled apart. 2 a thin biscuit.

crackle verb (crackles, crackling, crackled)
make small cracking sounds ♦ *The fire crackled in the grate.*
crackle noun

cradle noun (plural **cradles**)
1 a small cot for a baby. 2 a supporting framework.
cradle verb (cradles, cradling, cradled)
hold gently.

craft noun (plural **crafts**)
1 a job that needs skill, especially with the hands. 2 skill. 3 cunning; trickery. 4 (plural **craft**) a ship or boat; an aircraft or spacecraft.

craftsman noun (plural **craftsmen**)
a person who is good at a craft.
craftsmanship noun

crafty adjective (craftier, craftiest)
cunning.
craftily adverb **craftiness** noun

crag noun (plural **crags**)
a steep piece of rough rock.
craggy adjective **cragginess** noun
[from a Celtic word]

cram verb (crams, cramming, crammed)
1 push many things into something so that it is very full. 2 learn as many facts as you can in a short time just before an examination.

cramp noun (plural **cramps**)
pain caused by a muscle tightening suddenly.
cramp verb (cramps, cramping, cramped)
hinder someone's freedom or growth etc.

cramped adjective
in a space that is too small or tight.

crane noun (plural **cranes**)
1 a machine for lifting and moving heavy objects. 2 a large wading bird with long legs and neck.
crane verb (cranes, craning, craned)
stretch your neck to try and see something.

crank noun (plural **cranks**)
1 an L-shaped part used for changing the direction of movement in machinery. 2 a person with strange or fanatical ideas.
cranky adjective

cranny noun (plural **crannies**)
a crevice.

crash noun (plural **crashes**)
1 the loud noise of something breaking or colliding. 2 a violent collision or fall. 3 a sudden drop or failure.
crash verb (crashes, crashing, crashed)
1 make or have a crash; cause to crash. 2 move with a crash. 3 (said about a computer) stop working suddenly.
crash adjective
intensive ♦ *a crash course.*

crash helmet noun (plural **crash helmets**)
a padded helmet worn by cyclists and motorcyclists to protect the head.

crass adjective
1 very obvious or shocking; gross ♦ *crass ignorance.* 2 very stupid.

crate noun (plural **crates**)
1 a packing case made of strips of wood. 2 an open container with compartments for carrying bottles.

crater noun (plural **craters**)
1 the mouth of a volcano. 2 a bowl-shaped cavity or hollow caused by an explosion or impact.

craving noun (plural **cravings**)
a strong desire; a longing.

crawl verb (crawls, crawling, crawled)
1 move with the body close to the ground or other surface, or on hands and knees. 2 move slowly. 3 be covered with crawling things.
crawler noun
crawl noun
1 a crawling movement. 2 a very slow pace. 3 an overarm swimming stroke.

crayon noun (plural **crayons**)
a stick or pencil of coloured wax etc. for drawing.

craze noun (plural **crazes**)
a temporary enthusiasm.

crazy adjective (crazier, craziest)
1 insane. 2 very foolish ♦ *this crazy idea.*
crazily adverb **craziness** noun

crazy paving noun
paving made of oddly shaped pieces of stone etc.

creak noun (plural **creaks**)
a harsh squeak like that of a stiff door hinge.
creaky adjective
creak verb (creaks, creaking, creaked)
make a creak.

cream noun (plural **creams**)
1 the fatty part of milk. 2 a yellowish-white colour. 3 a food containing or looking like cream ♦ *chocolate cream.* 4 a soft substance ♦ *face cream.* 5 the best part.
creamy adjective
cream verb (creams, creaming, creamed)
make creamy; beat butter etc. until it is soft like cream.
cream off remove the best part of something.

crease noun (plural **creases**)
1 a line made in something by folding, pressing, or crushing it. 2 a line on a cricket pitch marking a batsman's or bowler's position.
crease verb (creases, creasing, creased)
make a crease or creases in something.

create verb (creates, creating, created)
1 bring into existence; make or produce, especially something that no one has made before. 2 (slang) make a fuss; grumble.
creation noun **creator** noun

creative *adjective*
showing imagination and thought ♦ *a creative use of language.*
creativity *noun*

creature *noun* (*plural* **creatures**)
a living being, especially an animal.

crèche (*say* kresh) *noun* (*plural* **crèches**)
a place where babies and young children are looked after while their parents are at work.

credentials *plural noun*
documents showing a person's identity, qualifications, etc.

credible *adjective*
able to be believed; convincing.
credibly *adverb* **credibility** *noun*

---

❶ USAGE Do not confuse with *creditable* or *credulous.*

---

credit *noun* (*plural* **credits**)
1 a source of pride or honour ♦ *a credit to the school.* **2** praise or acknowledgement given for some achievement or good quality ♦ *I must give you credit for persistence.* **3** an arrangement trusting a person to pay for something later on. **4** an amount of money in an account at a bank etc., or entered in a financial account as paid in. (Compare **debit**.) **5** belief or trust ♦ *I put no credit in this rumour.*
credits a list of people who have helped to produce a film or television programme.
credit *verb* (**credits, crediting, credited**)
1 believe. **2** attribute; say that a person has done or achieved something ♦ *Columbus is credited with the discovery of America.* **3** enter something as a credit in a financial account. (Compare **debit**.)

creditable *adjective*
deserving praise.

---

❶ USAGE Do not confuse with *credible* or *credulous.*

---

credit card *noun* (*plural* **credit cards**)
a card authorizing a person to buy on credit.

creditor *noun* (*plural* **creditors**)
a person to whom money is owed.

credulous *adjective*
too ready to believe things; gullible.

---

❶ USAGE Do not confuse with *credible* or *creditable.*

---

creed *noun* (*plural* **creeds**)
a set or formal statement of beliefs.

creep *verb* (**creeps, creeping, crept**)
1 move along close to the ground. **2** move quietly. **3** come gradually. **4** prickle with fear ♦ *It makes my flesh creep.*

creep *noun* (*plural* **creeps**)
1 a creeping movement. **2** (*informal*) an unpleasant person, especially one who seeks to win favour.
the creeps (*informal*) a nervous feeling caused by fear or dislike.

creeper *noun* (*plural* **creepers**)
a plant that grows along the ground or up a wall etc.

creepy *adjective* (**creepier, creepiest**)
frightening and sinister.

cremate *verb* (**cremates, cremating, cremated**)
burn a dead body to ashes.
cremation *noun*

crematorium *noun* (*plural* **crematoria**)
a place where corpses are cremated.

crescendo (*say* krish-end-oh) *noun* (*plural* **crescendos**)
a gradual increase in loudness.

crescent *noun* (*plural* **crescents**)
1 a narrow curved shape coming to a point at each end. **2** a curved street.

cress *noun*
a plant with hot-tasting leaves, used in salads and sandwiches.

crest *noun* (*plural* **crests**)
1 a tuft of hair, skin, or feathers on an animal's or bird's head. **2** the top of a hill or wave etc. **3** a design used on notepaper etc.
crested *adjective*

crestfallen *adjective*
disappointed or dejected.

crevasse (*say* kri-vass) *noun* (*plural* **crevasses**)
a deep open crack, especially in a glacier.

crevice *noun* (*plural* **crevices**)
a narrow opening, especially in a rock or wall.

crew¹ *noun* (*plural* **crews**)
1 the people working in a ship or aircraft. **2** a group working together ♦ *the camera crew.*

crew² *past tense* of **crow**².

crib *noun* (*plural* **cribs**)
1 a baby's cot. **2** a framework holding fodder for animals. **3** a model representing the Nativity of Jesus Christ. **4** something cribbed. **5** a translation for use by students.
crib *verb* (**cribs, cribbing, cribbed**)
copy someone else's work.

crick *noun* (*plural* **cricks**)
painful stiffness in the neck or back.

cricket¹ *noun*
a game played outdoors between teams with a ball, bats, and two wickets.
cricketer *noun*

cricket² *noun* (*plural* **crickets**)
a brown insect like a grasshopper.

crime *noun* (*plural* **crimes**)
1 an action that breaks the law. **2** law-breaking.

criminal *noun* (*plural* **criminals**)
a person who has committed a crime or crimes.
criminal *adjective* **criminally** *adverb*

crimson *adjective*
deep-red.
crimson *noun*

cringe *verb* (**cringes, cringing, cringed**)
shrink back in fear; cower.

cripple *noun* (*plural* **cripples**)
a person who is permanently lame.
cripple *verb* (**cripples, crippling, crippled**)
1 make a person lame. 2 weaken or damage
something seriously.

crisis *noun* (*plural* **crises**)
an important and dangerous or difficult
situation.

crisp *adjective*
1 very dry so that it breaks with a snap.
2 fresh and stiff ♦ *a crisp £5 note.* 3 cold and dry
♦ *a crisp morning.* 4 brisk and sharp ♦ *a crisp
manner.*
crisply *adverb* **crispness** *noun*

crisp *noun* (*plural* **crisps**)
a very thin fried slice of potato, usually sold in
packets.

criss-cross *adjective* & *adverb*
with crossing lines.

criterion (*say* kry-**teer**-ee-on) *noun* (*plural*
criteria)
a standard by which something is judged or
decided.

critic *noun* (*plural* **critics**)
1 a person who gives opinions on books, plays,
films, music, etc. 2 a person who criticizes.

critical *adjective*
1 criticizing. 2 to do with critics or criticism.
3 to do with or at a crisis; very serious.
critically *adverb*

criticism *noun* (*plural* **criticisms**)
1 criticizing; pointing out faults. 2 the work of a
critic.

criticize *verb* (**criticizes, criticizing, criticized**)
say that a person or thing has faults.

croak *noun* (*plural* **croaks**)
a deep hoarse sound like that of a frog.
croak *verb*

crockery *noun*
household china.

crocodile *noun* (*plural* **crocodiles**)
1 a large tropical reptile with a thick skin, long
tail, and huge jaws. 2 a long line of
schoolchildren walking in pairs.
crocodile tears sorrow that is not sincere (so
called because the crocodile was said to weep
while it ate its victim).

crocus *noun* (*plural* **crocuses**)
a small plant with yellow, purple, or white
flowers.

crony *noun* (*plural* **cronies**)
a close friend or companion.

crook *noun* (*plural* **crooks**)
1 a shepherd's stick with a curved end.
2 something bent or curved. 3 (*informal*) a
person who makes a living dishonestly.

crooked *adjective*
1 bent or twisted; not straight. 2 dishonest.

croon *verb* (**croons, crooning, crooned**)
sing softly and gently.

crop *noun* (*plural* **crops**)
1 something grown for food ♦ *a good crop of
wheat.* 2 a whip with a loop instead of a lash.
3 part of a bird's throat. 4 a very short haircut.
crop *verb* (**crops, cropping, cropped**)
1 cut or bite off ♦ *sheep were cropping the grass.*
2 produce a crop.
crop up happen unexpectedly.

croquet (*say* kroh-**kay**) *noun*
a game played with wooden balls and mallets.

cross *noun* (*plural* **crosses**)
1 a mark or shape made like + or ×.
2 an upright post with another piece of wood
across it, used in ancient times for crucifixion;
the Cross the cross on which Christ was
crucified, used as a symbol of Christianity.
3 a mixture of two different things.

cross *verb* (**crosses, crossing, crossed**)
1 go across something. 2 draw a line or lines
across something. 3 make the sign or shape of a
cross ♦ *Cross your fingers for luck.* 4 produce
something from two different kinds.
cross out draw a line across something because
it is unwanted, wrong, etc.

cross *adjective*
1 annoyed or bad-tempered. 2 going from one
side to another ♦ *There were cross winds on the
bridge.*
crossly *adverb* **crossness** *noun*

crossbar *noun* (*plural* **crossbars**)
a horizontal bar, especially between two
uprights.

cross-breed *verb* (**cross-breeds,
cross-breeding, cross-bred**)
breed by mating an animal with one of a
different kind.
cross-breed *noun* (Compare **hybrid**.)

cross-examine *verb* (**cross-examines,
cross-examining, cross-examined**)
cross-question someone, especially in a
lawcourt.
cross-examination *noun*

cross-eyed *adjective*
with eyes that look or seem to look towards the
nose.

crossing *noun* (*plural* **crossings**)
a place where people can cross a road or railway.

cross-legged *adjective & adverb*
with ankles crossed and knees spread apart.

cross-question *verb* (cross-questions, cross-questioning, cross-questioned)
question someone carefully in order to test answers given to previous questions.

cross-reference *noun* (*plural* cross-references)
a note telling people to look at another part of a book etc. for more information.

crossroads *noun* (*plural* crossroads)
a place where two or more roads cross one another.

cross-section *noun* (*plural* cross-sections)
1 a drawing of something as if it has been cut through. 2 a typical sample.

crossword *noun* (*plural* crosswords)
a puzzle in which words have to be guessed from clues and then written into the blank squares in a diagram.

crotchet *noun* (*plural* crotchets)
a note in music, which usually represents one beat (written ♩).

crouch *verb* (crouches, crouching, crouched)
lower your body, with your arms and legs bent.

crow¹ *noun* (*plural* crows)
a large black bird.
as the crow flies in a straight line.

crow² *verb* (crows, crowing, crowed or crew)
1 make a shrill cry as a cock does. 2 boast; be triumphant.
crow *noun*

crowbar *noun* (*plural* crowbars)
an iron bar used as a lever.

crowd *noun* (*plural* crowds)
a large number of people in one place.

crowd *verb* (crowds, crowding, crowded)
1 come together in a crowd. 2 cram; fill uncomfortably full.

crown *noun* (*plural* crowns)
1 an ornamental headdress worn by a king or queen. 2 (often **Crown**) the sovereign ♦ *This land belongs to the Crown.* 3 the highest part ♦ *the crown of the road.* 4 a former coin worth 5 shillings (25p).
Crown Prince or **Crown Princess** the heir to the throne.

crown *verb* (crowns, crowning, crowned)
1 place a crown on someone as a symbol of royal power or victory. 2 form or cover or decorate the top of something. 3 reward; make a successful end to something ♦ *Our efforts were crowned with victory.* 4 (*slang*) hit someone on the head.

crucial (*say* kroo-shal) *adjective*
most important.
crucially *adverb*

crucifix *noun* (*plural* crucifixes)
a model of the Cross or of Jesus Christ on the Cross.

crucify *verb* (crucifies, crucifying, crucified)
put a person to death by nailing or binding the hands and feet to a cross.
crucifixion *noun*

crude *adjective*
1 in a natural state; not yet refined ♦ *crude oil.* 2 not well finished; rough ♦ *a crude carving.* 3 vulgar.
crudely *adverb* **crudity** *noun*

cruel *adjective* (crueller, cruellest)
causing pain or suffering.
cruelly *adverb* **cruelty** *noun*

cruise *noun* (*plural* cruises)
a pleasure trip in a ship.

cruise *verb* (cruises, cruising, cruised)
1 sail or travel at a moderate speed. 2 have a cruise.

cruiser *noun* (*plural* cruisers)
1 a fast warship. 2 a large motor boat.

crumb *noun* (*plural* crumbs)
a tiny piece of bread etc.

crumble *verb* (crumbles, crumbling, crumbled)
break or fall into small fragments.
crumbly *adjective*

crumpet *noun* (*plural* crumpets)
a soft flat cake made with yeast, eaten toasted with butter.

crumple *verb* (crumples, crumpling, crumpled)
1 crush or become crushed into creases. 2 collapse loosely.

crunch *verb* (crunches, crunching, crunched)
crush something noisily, for example between your teeth.

crunch *noun* (*plural* crunches)
a crunching sound.
crunchy *adjective*
the crunch (*informal*) a crucial event or turning point.

Crusade *noun* (*plural* Crusades)
a military expedition made by Christians in the Middle Ages to recover Palestine from the Muslims who had conquered it.
Crusader *noun*

crusade *noun* (*plural* crusades)
a campaign against something bad.

crush *verb* (crushes, crushing, crushed)
1 press something so that it gets broken or harmed. 2 squeeze tightly. 3 defeat.

crush *noun* (*plural* crushes)
1 a crowd of people pressed together. 2 a drink made with crushed fruit.

crust *noun* (*plural* crusts)
1 the hard outer layer of something, especially bread. 2 the rocky outer layer of the earth.

crustacean (*say* krust-ay-shon) *noun* (*plural* crustaceans)
an animal with a shell, e.g. a crab, lobster, or shrimp.

crutch *noun* (*plural* crutches)
a support like a long walking stick for helping a lame person to walk.

cry *noun* (*plural* cries)
1 a loud wordless sound expressing pain, grief, joy, etc. **2** a shout. **3** crying ♦ *Have a good cry.*

cry *verb* (cries, crying, cried)
1 shed tears; weep. **2** call out loudly.

cryptic *adjective*
hiding its meaning in a puzzling way.
cryptically *adverb*

crystal *noun* (*plural* crystals)
1 a transparent colourless mineral rather like glass. **2** very clear high-quality glass. **3** a small solid piece of a substance with a symmetrical shape ♦ *ice crystals.*
crystalline *adjective*

crystallize *verb* (crystallizes, crystallizing, crystallized)
1 form into crystals. **2** become definite in form.
crystallization *noun*

cub *noun* (*plural* cubs)
a young lion, tiger, fox, bear, etc.

Cub or **Cub Scout** *noun* (*plural* Cubs or Cub Scouts)
a member of the junior branch of the Scout Association.

cubby hole *noun* (*plural* cubby holes)
a small compartment.

cube *noun* (*plural* cubes)
1 an object that has six equal square sides, e.g. a box or dice. **2** the number produced by multiplying something by itself twice ♦ *The cube of 3 is 3 ×3 ×3 = 27.*

cube *verb* (cubes, cubing, cubed)
1 multiply a number by itself twice ♦ *4 cubed is 4 ×4 ×4 = 64.* **2** cut something into small cubes.

cube root *noun* (*plural* cube roots)
the number that gives a particular number if it is multiplied by itself twice ♦ *The cube root of 27 is 3.*

cubic *adjective*
three-dimensional.
cubic metre, **cubic foot**, etc., the volume of a cube with sides one metre, foot, etc. long, used as a unit of measurement for volume.

cubicle *noun* (*plural* cubicles)
a compartment of a room.

cuckoo *noun* (*plural* cuckoos)
a bird that makes a sound like 'cuck-oo'.

cucumber *noun* (*plural* cucumbers)
a long green-skinned vegetable eaten raw or pickled.

cuddle *verb* (cuddles, cuddling, cuddled)
put your arms closely round a person or animal that you love.
cuddle *noun*

cuddly *adjective*
pleasantly soft and plump; nice to cuddle.

cue[1] *noun* (*plural* cues)
something said or done that acts as a signal for an actor etc. to say or do something.

cue[2] *noun* (*plural* cues)
a long stick for striking the ball in billiards or snooker.

cuff *noun* (*plural* cuffs)
1 the end of a sleeve that fits round the wrist. **2** hitting somebody with your hand; a slap.
off the cuff without rehearsal or preparation.

cuff *verb* (cuffs, cuffing, cuffed)
hit somebody with your hand.

cul-de-sac *noun* (*plural* culs-de-sac)
a street with an opening at one end only; a dead end.

cull *verb* (culls, culling, culled)
1 pick out and kill surplus animals from a flock. **2** select and use ♦ *I've culled lines from several poems.*
cull *noun*

culpable *adjective*
deserving blame.

culprit *noun* (*plural* culprits)
the person who has done something wrong.

cult *noun* (*plural* cults)
1 a religious sect. **2** a film, TV programme, rock group, etc. that is very popular with a particular group of people.

cultivate *verb* (cultivates, cultivating, cultivated)
1 use land to grow crops. **2** grow or develop things by looking after them.
cultivation *noun* **cultivator** *noun*

culture *noun* (*plural* cultures)
1 appreciation and understanding of literature, art, music, etc. **2** the customs and traditions of a people ♦ *West Indian culture.* **3** (in science) a quantity of bacteria or cells grown for study. **4** improvement by care and training ♦ *physical culture.* **5** cultivating things.
cultural *adjective*

cumbersome *adjective*
clumsy to carry or manage.

cumulative *adjective*
accumulating; increasing by continuous additions.

cunning *adjective*
1 clever at deceiving people. **2** cleverly designed or planned.

cunning *noun*
1 skill in deceiving people; craftiness. **2** skill or ingenuity.
[originally = clever, skilful: perhaps from an Old Norse word meaning 'knowledge']

cup *noun* (*plural* **cups**)
1 a small bowl-shaped container for drinking from. 2 anything shaped like a cup.
3 a goblet-shaped ornament given as a prize.
cupful *noun*

cup *verb* (**cups, cupping, cupped**)
form into the shape of a cup ♦ *cup your hands.*

cupboard *noun* (*plural* **cupboards**)
a piece of furniture with a door, for storing things.

cur *noun* (*plural* **curs**)
a scruffy or bad-tempered dog.

curate *noun* (*plural* **curates**)
a member of the clergy who helps a vicar.

curator (*say* kewr-ay-ter) *noun* (*plural* **curators**)
a person in charge of a museum or other collection.

curb *verb* (**curbs, curbing, curbed**)
restrain ♦ *You need to curb your impatience.*

curb *noun* (*plural* **curbs**)
a restraint ♦ *Put a curb on spending.*

❶ USAGE Do not confuse with *kerb*.

curd *noun* or **curds** *plural noun*
a thick substance formed when milk turns sour.

curdle *verb* (**curdles, curdling, curdled**)
form into curds.
make someone's blood curdle horrify or terrify them.

cure *verb* (**cures, curing, cured**)
1 get rid of someone's illness. 2 stop something bad. 3 treat food in order to preserve it.

cure *noun* (*plural* **cures**)
1 something that cures a person or thing;
a remedy. 2 curing; being cured ♦ *We cannot promise a cure.*

curfew *noun* (*plural* **curfews**)
a time or signal after which people must remain indoors until the next day.

curious *adjective*
1 wanting to find out about things; inquisitive.
2 strange; unusual.
curiously *adverb*

curiosity *noun* (*plural* **curiosities**)
1 being curious. 2 something unusual and interesting.

curl *noun* (*plural* **curls**)
a curve or coil, e.g. of hair.

curl *verb* (**curls, curling, curled**)
form into curls.
curl up sit or lie with your knees drawn up.

curly *adjective*
having curls.

currant *noun* (*plural* **currants**)
1 a small black dried grape used in cookery.
2 a small round red, black, or white berry.

❶ USAGE Do not confuse with *current*.

currency *noun* (*plural* **currencies**)
1 the money in use in a country. 2 the general use of something ♦ *Some words have no currency now.*

current *adjective*
happening now; used now.
currently *adverb*

current *noun* (*plural* **currents**)
1 water or air etc. moving in one direction.
2 the flow of electricity along a wire etc. or through something.

❶ USAGE Do not confuse with *currant*.

curriculum *noun* (*plural* **curricula**)
a course of study in a school or university.

curry[1] *noun* (*plural* **curries**)
food cooked with spices that taste hot.
curried *adjective*

curry[2] *verb* (**curries, currying, curried**)
curry favour seek to win favour by flattering someone.

curse *noun* (*plural* **curses**)
1 a call or prayer for a person or thing to be harmed; the evil produced by this. 2 something very unpleasant. 3 an angry word or words.

curse *verb* (**curses, cursing, cursed**)
1 make a curse. 2 use a curse against a person or thing.
be cursed with something suffer from it.

cursor *noun* (*plural* **cursors**)
a movable indicator, usually a flashing light, on a computer screen, showing where new data will go.

curt *adjective*
brief and hasty or rude ♦ *a curt reply.*
curtly *adverb* **curtness** *noun*

curtain *noun* (*plural* **curtains**)
1 a piece of material hung at a window or door.
2 the large cloth screen hung at the front of a stage.

curtsy *noun* (*plural* **curtsies**)
a movement of respect made by women and girls, putting one foot behind the other and bending the knees.

curtsy *verb* (**curtsies, curtsying, curtsied**)
make a curtsy.

curvature *noun* (*plural* **curvatures**)
curving; a curved shape.

curve *verb* (**curves, curving, curved**)
bend smoothly.

curve *noun* (*plural* **curves**)
a curved line or shape.
curvy *adjective*

cushion *noun* (*plural* **cushions**)
1 a bag, usually of cloth, filled with soft material so that it is comfortable to sit on or lean against.
2 anything soft or springy that protects or supports something ♦ *The hovercraft travels on a cushion of air.*

cushion *verb* (**cushions, cushioning, cushioned**)
protect from the effects of a knock or shock etc.
♦ *A pile of boxes cushioned his fall.*

custard *noun* (*plural* **custards**)
1 a sweet yellow sauce made with milk.
2 a pudding made with beaten eggs and milk.

custody *noun*
1 care and supervision; guardianship.
2 imprisonment.
take into custody arrest.
[from Latin *custos* = guardian]

custom *noun* (*plural* **customs**)
1 the usual way of behaving or doing something.
2 regular business from customers.

customary *adjective*
according to custom; usual.
customarily *adverb*

customer *noun* (*plural* **customers**)
a person who uses a shop, bank, or other business.

customs *plural noun*
1 taxes charged on goods brought into a country.
2 the place at a port or airport where officials examine your luggage.

cut *verb* (**cuts, cutting, cut**)
1 divide or wound or separate something by using a knife, axe, scissors, etc. 2 make a thing shorter or smaller; remove part of something
♦ *They are cutting all their prices.* 3 divide a pack of playing cards. 4 hit a ball with a chopping movement. 5 go through or across something.
6 switch off electrical power or an engine etc.
2 (in a film) move to another shot or scene.
3 make a sound recording.
cut a corner pass round it very closely.
cut and dried already decided. **cut in** interrupt.

cut *noun* (*plural* **cuts**)
1 cutting; the result of cutting. 2 a small wound.
3 (*slang*) a share.
be a cut above something be superior.

cute *adjective* (*informal*)
1 attractive. 2 clever.
cutely *adverb* **cuteness** *noun*

cutlass *noun* (*plural* **cutlasses**)
a short sword with a broad curved blade.

cutlery *noun*
knives, forks, and spoons.

cutlet *noun* (*plural* **cutlets**)
a thick slice of meat for cooking.

cutting *noun* (*plural* **cuttings**)
1 a steep-sided passage cut through high ground for a road or railway. 2 something cut out of a newspaper or magazine. 3 a piece cut from a plant to form a new plant.

cycle *noun* (*plural* **cycles**)
1 a bicycle or motorcycle. 2 a series of events that are regularly repeated in the same order.
cyclic *adjective* **cyclical** *adjective*

cycle *verb* (**cycles, cycling, cycled**)
ride a bicycle or tricycle.
cyclist *noun*

cyclone *noun* (*plural* **cyclones**)
a wind that rotates round a calm central area.
cyclonic *adjective*

cygnet (*say* sig-nit) *noun* (*plural* **cygnets**)
a young swan.

cylinder *noun* (*plural* **cylinders**)
an object with straight sides and circular ends.
cylindrical *adjective*

cymbal *noun* (*plural* **cymbals**)
a percussion instrument consisting of a metal plate that is hit to make a ringing sound.

---

❶ USAGE Do not confuse with *symbol*.

---

cynic (*say* sin-ik) *noun* (*plural* **cynics**)
a person who believes that people's reasons for doing things are selfish or bad, and shows this by sneering at them.
cynical *adjective* **cynically** *adverb* **cynicism** *noun*
[from Greek *kynikos* = surly: probably from the name *Kynosarges*, the gymnasium where the Greek philosopher Aristotle taught, but popularly associated with the Greek word *kuon* = dog]

cypress *noun* (*plural* **cypresses**)
an evergreen tree with dark leaves.

Dd

dab *noun* (*plural* **dabs**)
1 a quick gentle touch, usually with something wet. 2 a small lump ♦ *a dab of butter.*

dab *verb* (**dabs, dabbing, dabbed**)
touch something quickly and gently.

dabble *verb* (**dabbles, dabbling, dabbled**)
1 splash something about in water. 2 do something as a hobby ♦ *dabble in chemistry.*

dachshund (*say* daks-huund) *noun* (*plural* **dachshunds**)
a small dog with a long body and very short legs.

daffodil *noun* (*plural* **daffodils**)
a yellow flower that grows from a bulb.

daft *adjective* (*informal*)
silly or stupid.

dagger *noun* (*plural* **daggers**)
a pointed knife with two sharp edges, used as a weapon.

daily *adverb & adjective*
every day.

dainty *adjective* (**daintier, daintiest**)
small, delicate, and pretty.
daintily *adverb* **daintiness** *noun*

dairy *noun* (*plural* **dairies**)
a place where milk, butter, etc. are produced or sold.

daisy *noun* (*plural* **daisies**)
a small flower with white petals and a yellow centre.

dam¹ *noun* (*plural* **dams**)
a wall built to hold water back.
dam *verb* (**dams, damming, dammed**)
hold water back with a dam.

dam² *noun* (*plural* **dams**)
the mother of a horse or dog etc. (Compare **sire.**)

damage *noun*
harm or injury done to something.
damage *verb* (**damages, damaging, damaged**)
harm or spoil something.

damages *plural noun*
money paid as compensation for an injury or loss.

Dame *noun* (*plural* **Dames**)
the title of a woman who has been given the equivalent of a knighthood.

dame *noun* (*plural* **dames**)
a comic middle-aged woman in a pantomime, usually played by a man.

damn *verb* (**damns, damning, damned**)
curse or condemn.

damnation *noun*
being condemned to hell.

damned *adjective*
hateful or annoying.

damp *adjective*
slightly wet; not quite dry.
damply *adverb* **dampness** *noun*
damp *noun*
moisture in the air or on a surface or all through something.

damp course *noun* (*plural* **damp courses**)
a layer of material built into a wall to prevent dampness in the ground from rising.

dampen *verb* (**dampens, dampening, dampened**)
1 make something damp. 2 reduce the strength of something.

damsel *noun* (*plural* **damsels**) (*old use*)
a young woman.

dance *verb* (**dances, dancing, danced**)
move about in time to music.

dance *noun* (*plural* **dances**)
1 a set of movements used in dancing. 2 a piece of music for dancing to. 3 a party or gathering where people dance.
dancer *noun*

dandelion *noun* (*plural* **dandelions**)
a yellow wild flower with jagged leaves.

dandruff *noun*
tiny white flakes of dead skin in a person's hair.

D and T *abbreviation*
design and technology.

danger *noun* (*plural* **dangers**)
1 something that is not safe or could harm you.
2 the possibility of suffering harm or death.

dangerous *adjective*
likely to kill or harm you.
dangerously *adverb*

dangle *verb* (**dangles, dangling, dangled**)
hang or swing loosely.

dappled *adjective*
marked with patches of a different colour.

dare *verb* (**dares, daring, dared**)
1 be brave or bold enough to do something.
2 challenge a person to do something risky.
dare *noun* (*plural* **dares**)
a challenge to do something risky.

dark *adjective*
1 with little or no light. 2 not light in colour
♦ *a dark suit.* 3 having dark hair. 4 sinister or evil.
darkly *adverb* **darkness** *noun*
dark *noun*
1 absence of light ♦ *Cats can see in the dark.*
2 the time when darkness has come ♦ *She went out after dark.*

darken *verb* (**darkens, darkening, darkened**)
make or become dark.

darling *noun* (*plural* **darlings**)
someone who is loved very much.

darn *verb* (**darns, darning, darned**)
mend a hole by weaving threads across it.
darn *noun* (*plural* **darns**)
a place that has been darned.

dart *noun* (*plural* **darts**)
1 an object with a sharp point, thrown at a target. 2 a darting movement. 3 a tapering tuck stitched in something to make it fit.
dart *verb* (**darts, darting, darted**)
run suddenly and quickly.

darts *noun*
a game in which darts are thrown at a circular board (**dartboard**).

dash *verb* (**dashes, dashing, dashed**)
1 run quickly; rush. 2 throw a thing violently against something ♦ *The storm dashed the ship against the rocks.*

dash *noun* (*plural* **dashes**)
1 a short quick run; a rush. **2** energy or liveliness. **3** a small amount ♦ *Add a dash of brandy.* **4** a short line (—) used in writing or printing.

dashboard *noun* (*plural* **dashboards**)
a panel fitted in a vehicle in front of the driver, with dials and controls.

dashing *adjective*
lively and showy.

data (*say* **day**-ta) *noun*
pieces of information.

---

❶ USAGE Strictly speaking, this word is a plural noun (the singular is *datum*), so it should be used with a plural verb: *Here are the data.* However, the word is widely used nowadays as if it were a singular noun and most people do not regard this as wrong: *Here is the data.*

---

database *noun* (*plural* **databases**)
a store of information held in a computer.

date¹ *noun* (*plural* **dates**)
1 the time when something happens or happened or was written, stated as the day, month, and year (or any of these). **2** an appointment to meet someone, especially someone of the opposite sex.

date *verb* (**dates, dating, dated**)
1 give a date to something. **2** have existed from a particular time ♦ *The church dates from 1684.* **3** seem old-fashioned.

date² *noun* (*plural* **dates**)
a small sweet brown fruit that grows on a kind of palm tree.

daub *verb* (**daubs, daubing, daubed**)
paint or smear something clumsily.
daub *noun*

daughter *noun* (*plural* **daughters**)
a girl or woman who is someone's child.

daughter-in-law *noun* (*plural* **daughters-in-law**)
a son's wife.

daunt *verb* (**daunts, daunting, daunted**)
make somebody afraid or discouraged.
daunting *adjective*

dawdle *verb* (**dawdles, dawdling, dawdled**)
go slowly and lazily.
dawdler *noun*

dawn *noun* (*plural* **dawns**)
the time when the sun rises.

dawn *verb* (**dawns, dawning, dawned**)
1 begin to grow light in the morning. **2** begin to be realized ♦ *The truth dawned on them.*

day *noun* (*plural* **days**)
1 the 24 hours between midnight and the next midnight. **2** the light part of this time. **3** a particular day ♦ *sports day.* **4** a period of time ♦ *in Queen Victoria's day.*

daybreak *noun*
dawn.

daydream *noun* (*plural* **daydreams**)
pleasant thoughts of something you would like to happen.

daydream *verb* (**daydreams, daydreaming, daydreamed**)
have daydreams.

day-to-day *adjective*
ordinary; happening every day.

dazed *adjective*
unable to think or see clearly.
daze *noun*
[from Old Norse *dasathr* = weary]

dazzle *verb* (**dazzles, dazzling, dazzled**)
1 make a person unable to see clearly because of too much bright light. **2** amaze or impress a person by a splendid display.

DC *abbreviation*
direct current.

de- *prefix*
1 removing (as in *defrost*). **2** down, away (as in *descend*). **3** completely (as in *denude*).

dead *adjective*
1 no longer alive. **2** not lively. **3** not functioning; no longer in use. **4** exact or complete ♦ *a dead loss.*

deaden *verb* (**deadens, deadening, deadened**)
make pain or noise etc. weaker.

dead end *noun* (*plural* **dead ends**)
1 a road or passage with one end closed.
2 a situation where there is no chance of making progress.

dead heat *noun* (*plural* **dead heats**)
a race in which two or more winners finish exactly together.

deadline *noun* (*plural* **deadlines**)
a time limit.
[originally this meant a line round an American military prison. If prisoners went beyond it they could be shot]

deadlock *noun* (*plural* **deadlocks**)
a situation in which no progress can be made.

deadly *adjective* (**deadlier, deadliest**)
likely to kill.

deaf *adjective*
1 unable to hear. **2** unwilling to hear.
deafness *noun*

deafen *verb* (**deafens, deafening, deafened**)
make somebody become deaf, especially by a very loud noise.
deafening *adjective*

deal *verb* (**deals, dealing, dealt**)
1 hand something out; give. **2** give out cards for a card game. **3** do business; buy and sell ♦ *He deals in scrap metal.*
dealer *noun*
deal with 1 be concerned with ♦ *This book deals with words and meanings.* **2** do what is needed ♦ *I'll deal with the washing-up.*
deal *noun* (*plural* **deals**)
1 an agreement or bargain. **2** someone's turn to deal at cards.
a good deal or **a great deal** a large amount.

dear *adjective*
1 loved very much. **2** a polite greeting in letters ♦ *Dear Sir.* **3** expensive.
dearly *adverb*

death *noun* (*plural* **deaths**)
dying; the end of life.

debatable *adjective*
questionable; that can be argued against.

debate *noun* (*plural* **debates**)
a formal discussion.

debate *verb* (**debates, debating, debated**)
hold a debate.
debater *noun*

debilitating *adjective*
causing weakness.

debit *noun* (*plural* **debits**)
an entry in an account showing how much money is owed.

debit *verb* (**debits, debiting, debited**)
enter something as a debit in a financial account.
[from Latin *debitum* = something owed]

debris (*say* deb-ree) *noun*
scattered fragments or wreckage.

debt (*say* det) *noun* (*plural* **debts**)
something that you owe someone.
in debt owing money etc.
[from Latin *debitum* = something owed]

debtor (*say* **det**-or) *noun* (*plural* **debtors**)
a person who owes money to someone.

decade (*say* **dek**-ayd) *noun* (*plural* **decades**)
a period of ten years.

decadent (*say* **dek**-a-dent) *adjective*
falling to lower moral standards, especially in order to enjoy pleasure.
decadence *noun*

decaffeinated *adjective*
(said about coffee or tea) with the caffeine removed.

decapitate *verb* (**decapitates, decapitating, decapitated**)
cut someone's head off; behead.
decapitation *noun*

decathlon (*say* **decathlons**)
an athletic contest in which each competitor takes part in ten events.

decay *verb* (**decays, decaying, decayed**)
1 go bad; rot. **2** become less good or less strong.
decay *noun*

deceased *adjective*
dead.

deceit (*say* dis-**eet**) *noun* (*plural* **deceits**)
making a person believe something that is not true.
deceitful *adjective* **deceitfully** *adverb*

deceive *verb* (**deceives, deceiving, deceived**)
make a person believe something that is not true.
deceiver *noun*

December *noun*
the twelfth month of the year.
[from Latin *decem* = ten, because it was the tenth month of the ancient Roman calendar]

decent *adjective*
1 respectable and honest. **2** reasonable or adequate. **3** (*informal*) kind.
decently *adverb* **decency** *noun*

deception *noun* (*plural* **deceptions**)
deceiving someone.
deceptive *adjective* **deceptively** *adverb*

decibel (*say* **dess**-ib-el) *noun* (*plural* **decibels**)
a unit for measuring the loudness of sound.

decide *verb* (**decides, deciding, decided**)
1 make up your mind; make a choice. **2** settle a contest or argument.
decider *noun*

decided *adjective*
1 having clear and definite opinions. **2** noticeable ♦ *a decided difference.*
decidedly *adverb*

deciduous (*say* dis-**id**-yoo-us) *adjective*
a deciduous tree is one that loses its leaves in autumn.

decimal *adjective*
using tens or tenths.

decimal *noun* (*plural* **decimals**)
a decimal fraction.

decimal currency *noun* (*plural* **decimal currencies**)
a currency in which each unit is ten or one hundred times the value of the one next below it.

decimal fraction *noun* (*plural* **decimal fractions**)
a fraction with tenths shown as numbers after a dot ($\frac{3}{10}$ is 0.3; $1\frac{1}{2}$ is 1.5).

decimal point *noun* (*plural* **decimal points**)
the dot in a decimal fraction.

decipher (*say* dis-**I**-fer) *verb* (**deciphers, deciphering, deciphered**)
1 work out the meaning of a coded message. **2** work out the meaning of something written badly.
decipherment *noun*

decision *noun* (*plural* **decisions**)
1 deciding; what you have decided.
2 determination.

decisive (*say* dis-I-siv) *adjective*
1 that settles or ends something ♦ *a decisive battle*. 2 able to make decisions quickly and firmly.
decisively *adverb* **decisiveness** *noun*

deck *noun* (*plural* **decks**)
1 a floor on a ship or bus. 2 a pack of playing cards. 3 a turntable on a record player.

deckchair *noun* (*plural* **deckchairs**)
a folding chair with a canvas or plastic seat.

declaim *verb* (**declaims, declaiming, declaimed**)
make a speech etc. loudly and dramatically.
declamation *noun*

declare *verb* (**declares, declaring, declared**)
1 say something clearly or firmly. 2 tell customs officials that you have goods on which you ought to pay duty. 3 end a cricket innings before all the batsmen are out.
declaration *noun*
declare war announce that you are starting a war against someone.

decline *verb* (**declines, declining, declined**)
1 refuse. 2 become weaker or smaller.
3 slope downwards. 4 state the forms of a noun, pronoun, or adjective that correspond to particular cases, numbers, and genders.

decline *noun* (*plural* **declines**)
a gradual decrease or loss of strength.

decode *verb* (**decodes, decoding, decoded**)
work out the meaning of something written in code.
decoder *noun*

decompose *verb* (**decomposes, decomposing, decomposed**)
decay or rot.
decomposition *noun*

decorate *verb* (**decorates, decorating, decorated**)
1 make something look more beautiful or colourful. 2 put fresh paint or paper on walls.
3 give somebody a medal.
decoration *noun* **decorator** *noun* **decorative** *adjective*

decorous (*say* dek-er-us) *adjective*
polite and dignified.
decorously *adverb*

decoy (*say* dee-koi) *noun* (*plural* **decoys**)
something used to tempt a person or animal into a trap or into danger.

decoy (*say* dik-oi) *verb* (**decoys, decoying, decoyed**)
tempt a person or animal into a trap etc.

decrease *verb* (**decreases, decreasing, decreased**)
make or become smaller or fewer.

decrease *noun* (*plural* **decreases**)
decreasing; the amount by which something decreases.

decree *noun* (*plural* **decrees**)
an official order or decision.

decree *verb* (**decrees, decreeing, decreed**)
make a decree.

decrepit (*say* dik-rep-it) *adjective*
old and weak.
decrepitude *noun*

dedicate *verb* (**dedicates, dedicating, dedicated**)
1 devote all your time or energy to something ♦ *She dedicated her life to nursing*. 2 name a person as a mark of respect, e.g. at the beginning of a book.
dedication *noun*

deduce *verb* (**deduces, deducing, deduced**)
work something out by reasoning from facts that you know are true.
deducible *adjective*

deduct *verb* (**deducts, deducting, deducted**)
subtract part of something.

deduction *noun* (*plural* **deductions**)
1 deducting; something deducted. 2 deducing; something deduced.

deed *noun* (*plural* **deeds**)
1 something that someone has done; an act.
2 a legal document.

deep *adjective*
1 going a long way down or back or in ♦ *a deep well*; ♦ *deep cupboards*. 2 measured from top to bottom or front to back ♦ *a hole six feet deep*.
3 intense or strong ♦ *deep colours*; ♦ *deep feelings*. 4 low-pitched, not shrill ♦ *a deep voice*.
deeply *adverb* **deepness** *noun*

deepen *verb* (**deepens, deepening, deepened**)
make or become deeper.

deer *noun* (*plural* **deer**)
a fast-running graceful animal, the male of which usually has antlers.

deface *verb* (**defaces, defacing, defaced**)
spoil the surface of something, e.g. by scribbling on it.
defacement *noun*

default *verb* (**defaults, defaulting, defaulted**)
fail to do what you have agreed to do, especially to pay back a loan.
defaulter *noun*

default *noun* (*plural* **defaults**)
1 failure to do something. 2 (in computing) what a computer does unless you give it another command.
by default because something has failed to happen.

defeat *verb* (**defeats, defeating, defeated**)
1 win a victory over someone. 2 baffle; be too difficult for someone.

defeat *noun* (*plural* **defeats**)
1 defeating someone. 2 being defeated; a lost game or battle.

defect (*say* dif-**ekt** or **dee**-fekt) *noun* (*plural* **defects**)
a flaw.

defect (*say* dif-**ekt**) *verb* (**defects, defecting, defected**)
desert your own country etc. and join the enemy.
defection *noun* **defector** *noun*

defective *adjective*
having defects; incomplete.
defectiveness *noun*

defence *noun* (*plural* **defences**)
1 defending something. 2 something that defends or protects. 3 a reply put forward by a defendant.

defend *verb* (**defends, defending, defended**)
1 protect, especially against an attack. 2 try to prove that a statement is true or that an accused person is not guilty.
defender *noun*

defendant *noun* (*plural* **defendants**)
a person accused of something in a lawcourt.

defensive *adjective*
used or done for defence; protective.
defensively *adverb*
on the defensive ready to defend yourself.

defer¹ *verb* (**defers, deferring, deferred**)
postpone.
deferment *noun* **deferral** *noun*

defer² *verb* (**defers, deferring, deferred**)
give way to a person's wishes or authority; yield.

deference (*say* **def**-er-ens) *noun*
polite respect.
deferential (*say* def-er-**en**-shal) *adjective*
deferentially *adverb*

defiant *adjective*
defying; openly disobedient.
defiantly *adverb* **defiance** *noun*

deficiency *noun* (*plural* **deficiencies**)
1 a lack or shortage. 2 a defect.
deficient *adjective*

defile *verb* (**defiles, defiling, defiled**)
make a thing dirty or impure.
defilement *noun*

define *verb* (**defines, defining, defined**)
1 explain what a word or phrase means.
2 show clearly what something is; specify.
3 show a thing's outline.
definable *adjective*

definite *adjective*
1 clearly stated; exact ♦ *Fix a definite time.*
2 certain or settled ♦ *Is it definite that we are to move?*

definite article *noun* (*plural* **definite articles**)
(in grammar) the word 'the'.

definitely *adverb*
certainly; without doubt.

definition *noun* (*plural* **definitions**)
1 a statement of what a word or phrase means or of what a thing is. 2 being distinct; clearness of outline (e.g. in a photograph).

deflate *verb* (**deflates, deflating, deflated**)
1 let out air from a tyre or balloon etc.
2 make someone feel less proud or confident. 3 reduce or reverse inflation.
deflation *noun* **deflationary** *adjective*

deflect *verb* (**deflects, deflecting, deflected**)
make something turn aside.
deflection *noun* **deflector** *noun*

deforest *verb* (**deforests, deforesting, deforested**)
clear away the trees from an area.
deforestation *noun*

deform *verb* (**deforms, deforming, deformed**)
spoil a thing's shape or appearance.
deformation *noun*

deft *adjective*
skilful and quick.
deftly *adverb* **deftness** *noun*

defuse *verb* (**defuses, defusing, defused**)
1 remove the fuse from a bomb so that it cannot explode. 2 make a situation less dangerous or tense.

defy *verb* (**defies, defying, defied**)
1 resist something openly; refuse to obey
♦ *They defied the law.* 2 challenge a person to do something you believe cannot be done
♦ *I defy you to prove this.* 3 prevent something being done ♦ *The door defied all efforts to open it.*

degenerate (*say* di-**jen**-e-rayt) *verb* (**degenerates, degenerating, degenerated**)
become worse or lower in standard.
degeneration *noun*

degenerate (*say* di-**jen**-e-ret) *adjective*
having become immoral or bad.
degeneracy *noun*

degrade *verb* (**degrades, degrading, degraded**)
1 humiliate or dishonour someone. 2 reduce to a simpler molecular form.
degradation (*say* deg-ra-**day**-shon) *noun*

degree *noun* (*plural* **degrees**)
1 a unit for measuring temperature. 2 a unit for measuring angles. 3 extent ♦ *to some degree.*
4 an award to someone at a university or college who has successfully finished a course.

dehydrated *adjective*
dried up, with all moisture removed.
dehydration *noun*

deity (*say* **dee**-it-ee or **day**-it-ee) *noun* (*plural* **deities**)
a god or goddess.

dejected *adjective*
sad or depressed.
dejectedly *adverb* **dejection** *noun*

delay *verb* (delays, delaying, delayed)
1 make someone or something late. **2** postpone.

delay *noun* (*plural* **delays**)
delaying; the time for which something is
delayed ♦ *a two-hour delay.*

delegate (*say* del-ig-at) *noun* (*plural*
delegates)
a person who represents others and acts on their
instructions.

delegate (*say* del-ig-ayt) *verb* (delegates,
delegating, delegated)
1 give someone a task or duty to do on your
behalf ♦ *I'm going to delegate this job to my
assistant.* **2** appoint someone as a delegate
♦ *We delegated Jones to represent us.*

delegation (*say* del-ig-**ay**-shon) *noun* (*plural*
delegations)
1 delegating. **2** a group of delegates.

delete (*say* dil-**eet**) *verb* (deletes, deleting,
deleted)
cross out or remove something written or printed
or stored on a computer.
deletion *noun*

deliberate (*say* dil-ib-er-at) *adjective*
1 done on purpose; intentional. **2** slow and
careful.
deliberately *adverb*

deliberate (*say* dil-ib-er-ayt) *verb* (deliberates,
deliberating, deliberated)
discuss or think carefully.
deliberation *noun*

delicacy *noun* (*plural* **delicacies**)
1 being delicate. **2** a delicious food.

delicate *adjective*
1 fine and graceful ♦ *delicate embroidery.*
2 fragile and easily damaged. **3** pleasant and
not strong or intense. **4** becoming ill easily.
5 using or needing great care ♦ *a delicate
situation.*
delicately *adverb* **delicateness** *noun*

delicious *adjective*
tasting or smelling very pleasant.
deliciously *adverb*

delight *verb* (delights, delighting, delighted)
1 please someone greatly. **2** take great pleasure
in something.

delight *noun* (*plural* **delights**)
great pleasure.
delightful *adjective* **delightfully** *adverb*

delinquent (*say* dil-**ing**-kwent) *noun* (*plural*
delinquents)
a young person who breaks the law.
delinquent *adjective* **delinquency** *noun*

delirious (*say* di-li-ri-us) *adjective*
1 affected with delirium. **2** extremely excited or
enthusiastic.
deliriously *adverb*

delirium (*say* dil-irri-um) *noun*
1 a state of mental confusion and agitation
during a feverish illness. **2** wild excitement.

deliver *verb* (delivers, delivering, delivered)
1 take letters or goods etc. to someone's house or
place of work. **2** give a speech or lecture etc.
3 help with the birth of a baby. **4** aim or strike a
blow or an attack. **5** rescue; set free.
deliverer *noun* **deliverance** *noun* **delivery** *noun*

delta *noun* (*plural* **deltas**)
a triangular area at the mouth of a river where it
spreads into branches.

delude *verb* (deludes, deluding, deluded)
deceive or mislead someone.

deluge *noun* (*plural* **deluges**)
1 a large flood. **2** a heavy fall of rain.
3 something coming in great numbers ♦ *a deluge
of questions.*

deluge *verb* (deluges, deluging, deluged)
overwhelm by a deluge.

delusion *noun* (*plural* **delusions**)
a false belief.

demagogue (*say* dem-a-gog) *noun* (*plural*
demagogues)
a leader who wins support by making emotional
speeches rather than by careful reasoning.

demand *verb* (demands, demanding,
demanded)
1 ask for something firmly or forcefully.
2 need ♦ *This work demands great skill.*

demand *noun* (*plural* **demands**)
1 a firm or forceful request. **2** a desire to have or
buy something ♦ *There is a great demand for
computers.*
in demand wanted or needed.

demanding *adjective*
needing a lot of effort or attention
♦ *a demanding job*; ♦ *a demanding child.*

demarcation (*say* dee-mar-**kay**-shon) *noun*
marking the boundary or limits of something.

demented *adjective*
driven mad; crazy.

demigod *noun* (*plural* **demigods**)
a partly divine being.

democracy *noun* (*plural* **democracies**)
1 government of a country by representatives
elected by the whole people. **2** a country
governed in this way.
democrat *noun* **democratic** *adjective*
democratically *adverb*

Democrat *noun* (*plural* **Democrats**)
a member of the Democratic Party in the USA.

demolish *verb* (demolishes, demolishing,
demolished)
1 knock a building down and break it up.
2 destroy something completely.
demolition *noun*

demon *noun* (*plural* **demons**)
1 a devil; an evil spirit. 2 a fierce or forceful person.
demonic (*say* dim-on-ik) *adjective*

demonstrate *verb* (**demonstrates, demonstrating, demonstrated**)
1 show or prove something. 2 take part in a demonstration.
demonstrator *noun*

demonstration *noun* (*plural* **demonstrations**)
1 demonstrating; showing how to do or work something. 2 a march or meeting held to show everyone what you think about something.

demonstrative (*say* dim-on-strat-iv) *adjective*
1 showing or proving something. 2 showing feelings or affections openly. 3 (in grammar) pointing out the person or thing referred to. *This, that, these,* and *those* are demonstrative adjectives and pronouns.
demonstratively *adverb* **demonstrativeness** *noun*

demoralize *verb* (**demoralizes, demoralizing, demoralized**)
dishearten someone; weaken someone's confidence or morale.
demoralization *noun*

demote *verb* (**demotes, demoting, demoted**)
reduce a person to a lower position or rank.
demotion *noun*

demure *adjective*
shy and modest.
demurely *adverb* **demureness** *noun*

den *noun* (*plural* **dens**)
1 a lair. 2 a person's private room. 3 a place where something illegal happens ♦ *a gambling den.*

denial *noun* (*plural* **denials**)
denying or refusing something.

denim *noun*
a kind of strong, usually blue, cotton cloth used to make jeans etc.

denomination *noun* (*plural* **denominations**)
1 a name or title. 2 a religious group with a special name ♦ *Baptists, Methodists, and other denominations.* 3 a unit of weight or of money ♦ *coins of small denomination.*

denominator *noun* (plural **denominators**)
the number below the line in a fraction, showing how many parts the whole is divided into, e.g. 4 in $\frac{1}{4}$. (Compare **numerator**.)

denounce *verb* (**denounces, denouncing, denounced**)
speak strongly against something; accuse ♦ *They denounced him as a spy.*
denunciation *noun*

dense *adjective*
1 thick; packed close together ♦ *dense fog;* ♦ *dense crowds.* 2 (*informal*) stupid.
densely *adverb*

density *noun* (*plural* **densities**)
1 thickness. 2 (in science) the proportion of mass to volume.

dent *noun* (*plural* **dents**)
a hollow left in a surface where something has pressed or hit it.

dent *verb* (**dents, denting, dented**)
make a dent in something.

dental *adjective*
to do with the teeth or with dentistry.

dentist *noun* (*plural* **dentists**)
a person who is trained to treat teeth, fill or extract them, fit false ones, etc.
dentistry *noun*

denture *noun* (*plural* **dentures**)
a set of false teeth.

denude *verb* (**denudes, denuding, denuded**)
make bare or naked; strip something away.
denudation *noun*

denunciation *noun* (*plural* **denunciations**)
denouncing.

deny *verb* (**denies, denying, denied**)
1 say that something is not true. 2 refuse to give or allow something ♦ *deny a request.*

deodorant (*say* dee-oh-der-ant) *noun* (*plural* **deodorants**)
a substance that removes smells.

depart *verb* (**departs, departing, departed**)
go away; leave.
departure *noun*
[from early French *départir* = separate]

department *noun* (*plural* **departments**)
one section of a large organization or shop.
departmental *adjective*

depend *verb* (**depends, depending, depended**)
depend on 1 rely on ♦ *We depend on your help.* 2 be controlled by something else ♦ *It all depends on the weather.*

dependant *noun* (*plural* **dependants**)
a person who depends on another, especially financially ♦ *She has two dependants.*

ⓘ USAGE Note that the spelling ends in -*ant* for this noun but -*ent* for the adjective *dependent.*

---

dependent *adjective*
depending ♦ *She has two dependent children;* ♦ *they are dependent on her.*
dependence *noun*

deplore *verb* (**deplores, deploring, deplored**)
be very upset or annoyed by something.
deplorable *adjective* **deplorably** *adverb*

deport *verb* (**deports, deporting, deported**)
send an unwanted foreign person out of a
country.
deportation *noun*

depose *verb* (**deposes, deposing, deposed**)
remove a person from power.

deposit *noun* (*plural* **deposits**)
1 an amount of money paid into a bank etc.
2 money paid as a first instalment. **3** a layer of
solid matter in or on the earth.

deposit *verb* (**deposits, depositing, deposited**)
1 put something down. **2** pay money as a
deposit.
depositor *noun*

depot (*say* dep-oh) *noun* (*plural* **depots**)
1 a place where things are stored. **2** a place
where buses or trains are kept and repaired. -
3 a headquarters.

depraved *adjective*
behaving wickedly; of bad character.
depravity *noun*

depress *verb* (**depresses, depressing,
depressed**)
1 make somebody sad. **2** lower the value of
something ♦ *Threat of war depressed prices.*
3 press down ♦ *Depress the lever.*
depressive *adjective*

depression *noun* (*plural* **depressions**)
1 a feeling or great sadness or hopelessness.
2 a long period when trade is very slack because
many people cannot afford to buy things, with
widespread unemployment. **3** a shallow hollow
in the ground or on a surface. **4** an area of low air
pressure which may bring rain. **5** pressing
something down.

deprive *verb* (**deprives, depriving, deprived**)
take or keep something away from somebody.
deprival *noun* **deprivation** *noun*

depth *noun* (*plural* **depths**)
1 being deep; how deep something is.
2 the deepest or lowest part.
in depth thoroughly. **out of your depth** **1** in
water that is too deep to stand in. **2** trying to do
something that is too difficult for you.

deputation *noun* (*plural* **deputations**)
a group of people sent as representatives of
others.

deputy *noun* (*plural* **deputies**)
a person appointed to act as a substitute for
another.

deranged *adjective*
insane.
derangement *noun*

derby (*say* dar-bi) *noun* (*plural* **derbies**)
a sports match between two teams from the same
city or area.
[from the name of the Earl of Derby, who in 1780
founded the famous horse race called the Derby
which is run at Epsom in Surrey]

derelict (*say* derri-likt) *adjective*
abandoned and left to fall into ruin.
dereliction *noun*

deride *verb* (**derides, deriding, derided**)
laugh at with contempt or scorn; ridicule.
derision *noun*

derive *verb* (**derives, deriving, derived**)
1 obtain something from a source ♦ *She derived
great enjoyment from music.* **2** form or originate
from something ♦ *Some English words are
derived from Latin words.*
derivation *noun* **derivative** *adjective*

descend *verb* (**descends, descending,
descended**)
go down.
descent *noun*
be descended from have as an ancestor; come
by birth from a certain person or family.

descendant *noun* (*plural* **descendants**)
a person who is descended from someone.

describe *verb* (**describes, describing,
described**)
1 say what someone or something is like.
2 draw in outline; move in a pattern ♦ *The orbit
of the Earth around the Sun describes an ellipse.*
description *noun* **descriptive** *adjective*

desert (*say* dez-ert) *noun* (*plural* **deserts**)
a large area of dry often sandy land.

desert (*say* diz-ert) *verb* (**deserts, deserting,
deserted**)
leave a person or place without intending to
return.
deserter *noun* **desertion** *noun*

desert island *noun* (*plural* **desert islands**)
an uninhabited island.

deserve *verb* (**deserves, deserving, deserved**)
have a right to something; be worthy of
something.
deservedly *adverb*

design *noun* (*plural* **designs**)
1 a drawing that shows how something is to be
made. **2** the way something is made or arranged.
3 lines and shapes that form a decoration;
a pattern. **4** a mental plan or scheme.
have designs on plan to get hold of.

design *verb* (**designs, designing, designed**)
1 draw a design for something. **2** plan or intend
something for a special purpose.
designer *noun*

desirable *adjective*
1 causing people to desire it; worth having.
2 worth doing; advisable.
desirability *noun*

desire *noun* (*plural* **desires**)
a feeling of wanting something very much.
desirous *adjective*

desire *verb* (**desires, desiring, desired**)
have a desire for something.

desk *noun* (*plural* **desks**)
1 a piece of furniture with a flat top and often
drawers, used when writing or doing work.
2 a counter at which a cashier or receptionist
sits.

desktop *adjective*
suitable to be used on a desk ♦ *a desktop
computer.*

desolate *adjective*
1 lonely and sad. **2** uninhabited.
desolation *noun*

despair *noun*
a feeling of hopelessness.

despair *verb* (**despairs, despairing, despaired**)
feel despair.

desperate *adjective*
1 extremely serious or hopeless ♦ *a desperate
situation.* **2** having a great need or desire for
something ♦ *She is desperate to get a ticket.*
3 reckless and ready to do anything.
desperately *adverb* **desperation** *noun*

despise *verb* (**despises, despising, despised**)
think someone or something is inferior or
worthless.

despite *preposition*
in spite of.

despondent *adjective*
sad or gloomy.
despondently *adverb* **despondency** *noun*

dessert (*say* diz-ert) *noun* (*plural* **desserts**)
fruit or a sweet food served as the last course of
a meal.

destination *noun* (*plural* **destinations**)
the place to which a person or thing is travelling.

destined *adjective*
having as a destiny; intended.

destiny *noun* (*plural* **destinies**)
what will happen or has happened to somebody
or something; fate.

destitute *adjective*
left without anything; living in extreme poverty.
destitution *noun*

destroy *verb* (**destroys, destroying,
destroyed**)
ruin or put an end to something.
destruction *noun* **destructive** *adjective*

destroyer *noun* (*plural* **destroyers**)
a fast warship.

detach *verb* (**detaches, detaching, detached**)
unfasten or separate.
detachable *adjective* **detachment** *noun*

detached *adjective*
1 separated. **2** (said about a house) not joined to
another. **3** impartial; not involved in something.

detail *noun* (*plural* **details**)
1 a very small part of a design or plan or
decoration etc. **2** a small piece of information.
detailed *adjective*
in detail describing or dealing with everything
fully.

detain *verb* (**detains, detaining, detained**)
1 keep someone waiting. **2** keep someone at a
place.

detect *verb* (**detects, detecting, detected**)
discover.
detection *noun* **detector** *noun*

detective *noun* (*plural* **detectives**)
a person who investigates crimes.

detention *noun* (*plural* **detentions**)
1 detaining; being detained. **2** being made to stay
late in school as a punishment.

deter *verb* (**deters, deterring, deterred**)
discourage or prevent a person from doing
something.

detergent *noun* (*plural* **detergents**)
a substance used for cleaning or washing things.

deteriorate (*say* dit-eer-ee-er-ayt) *verb*
(**deteriorates, deteriorating, deteriorated**)
become worse.
deterioration *noun*

determination *noun*
1 the firm intention to achieve what you have
decided to achieve. **2** determining or deciding
something.

determine *verb* (**determines, determining,
determined**)
1 decide ♦ *determine what is to be done.*
2 find out; calculate ♦ *determine the height of the
mountain.*

determined *adjective*
full of determination; with your mind firmly
made up.

determiner *noun* (*plural* **determiners**)
(in grammar) a word (such as *a, the, many*) that
modifies a noun.

deterrent *noun* (*plural* **deterrents**)
something that deters people, such as a powerful
weapon or a threat of punishment.

detest *verb* (**detests, detesting, detested**)
dislike something very much; loathe.
detestable *adjective* **detestation** *noun*

detonate (*say* det-on-ayt) *verb* (**detonates,
detonating, detonated**)
explode or cause something to explode.
detonation *noun* **detonator** *noun*

detour (*say* dee-toor) *noun* (*plural* **detours**)
a roundabout route instead of the normal one.

detriment (*say* det-rim-ent) *noun*
harm or disadvantage ♦ *She worked long hours, to the detriment of her health.*

detrimental (*say* det-rim-**en**-tal) *adjective*
harmful or disadvantageous.
detrimentally *adverb*

deuce *noun* (*plural* **deuces**)
a score in tennis where both sides have 40 points and must gain two consecutive points to win.

devalue *verb* (**devalues, devaluing, devalued**)
1 reduce a thing's value. **2** reduce the value of a country's currency in relation to other currencies or to gold.
devaluation *noun*

devastate *verb* (**devastates, devastating, devastated**)
1 ruin or cause great destruction to something. **2** cause great shock or grief to someone.
devastating *adjective* **devastation** *noun*

develop *verb* (**develops, developing, developed**)
1 make or become bigger or better. **2** come gradually into existence ♦ *Storms developed.* **3** begin to have or use ♦ *They developed bad habits.* **4** use an area of land for building houses, shops, factories, etc. **5** treat photographic film with chemicals so that pictures appear.
developer *noun* **development** *noun*

deviate (*say* dee-vee-ayt) *verb* (**deviates, deviating, deviated**)
turn aside from a course or from what is usual or true.
deviation *noun*

device *noun* (*plural* **devices**)
1 something made for a particular purpose ♦ *a device for opening tins.* **2** a design used as a decoration or emblem.
leave someone to their own devices leave them to do as they wish.

devil *noun* (*plural* **devils**)
1 an evil spirit. **2** a wicked, cruel, or annoying person.
devilish *adjective* **devilry** *noun*

devilment *noun*
mischief.

devious (*say* dee-vee-us) *adjective*
1 roundabout; not direct ♦ *a devious route.* **2** not straightforward; underhand.
deviously *adverb* **deviousness** *noun*

devise *verb* (**devises, devising, devised**)
invent or plan.

devoid *adjective*
lacking or without something ♦ *His work is devoid of merit.*

devolution *noun*
handing over power from central government to local or regional government.

devolve *verb* (**devolves, devolving, devolved**)
pass or be passed to a deputy or successor.

devote *verb* (**devotes, devoting, devoted**)
give completely ♦ *He devoted his time to sport.*

devoted *adjective*
very loving or loyal.

devotee (*say* dev-o-**tee**) *noun* (*plural* **devotees**)
a person who is devoted to something; an enthusiast.

devotion *noun*
great love or loyalty.

devotions *plural noun*
prayers.

devour *verb* (**devours, devouring, devoured**)
eat or swallow something hungrily or greedily.

devout *adjective*
earnestly religious or sincere.
devoutly *adverb* **devoutness** *noun*

dew *noun*
tiny drops of water that form during the night on surfaces of things in the open air.
dewdrop *noun* **dewy** *adjective*

dexterity (*say* deks-**terri**-tee) *noun*
skill in handling things.

dhoti *noun* (*plural* **dhotis**)
the loincloth worn by male Hindus.

diabetes (*say* dy-a-**bee**-teez) *noun*
a disease in which there is too much sugar in a person's blood.
diabetic (*say* dy-a-**bet**-ik) *adjective* & *noun*

diabolical *adjective*
1 like a devil; very wicked. **2** very clever or annoying.

diadem (*say* **dy**-a-dem) *noun* (*plural* **diadems**)
a crown or headband worn by a royal person.

diagnose *verb* (**diagnoses, diagnosing, diagnosed**)
find out what disease a person has or what is wrong.
diagnosis *noun* **diagnostic** *adjective*

diagonal (*say* dy-**ag**-on-al) *noun* (*plural* **diagonals**)
a straight line joining opposite corners.
diagonal *adjective* **diagonally** *adverb*

diagram *noun* (*plural* **diagrams**)
a kind of drawing or picture that shows the parts of something or how it works.

dial *noun* (*plural* **dials**)
a circular object with numbers or letters round it.
dial *verb* (**dials, dialling, dialled**)
telephone a number by turning a telephone dial or pressing numbered buttons.

dialect *noun* (*plural* **dialects**)
the words and pronunciations used by people in one district but not in the rest of a country.

dialogue noun (plural **dialogues**)
1 the words spoken by characters in a play, film, or story. 2 a conversation.

dialysis (say dy-al-iss-iss) noun
a way of removing harmful substances from the blood by letting it flow through a machine.

diameter (say dy-am-it-er) noun (plural **diameters**)
1 a line drawn straight across a circle or sphere and passing through its centre. 2 the length of this line.

diametrically adverb
completely ♦ diametrically opposite.

diamond noun (plural **diamonds**)
1 a very hard precious stone, a form of carbon, that looks like clear glass. 2 a shape with four equal sides and four angles that are not right angles. 3 a playing card with red diamond shapes on it.

diaper noun (plural **diapers**) (American)
a baby's nappy.

diaphanous (say dy-af-an-us) adjective
(said about fabric) almost transparent.

diaphragm (say dy-a-fram) noun (plural **diaphragms**)
1 the muscular layer inside the body that separates the chest from the abdomen and is used in breathing. 2 a dome-shaped contraceptive device that fits over the cervix.

diarist noun (plural **diarists**)
a person who keeps a diary.

diarrhoea (say dy-a-ree-a) noun
too frequent and too watery emptying of the bowels.

diary noun (plural **diaries**)
a book in which someone writes down what happens each day.

diatribe noun (plural **diatribes**)
a strong verbal attack.

dice noun
(strictly this is the plural of **die²**, but it is often used as a singular, plural **dice**) a small cube marked with dots (1 to 6) on its sides, used in games.

dice verb (**dices, dicing, diced**)
1 cut meat, vegetables, etc. into small cubes.
2 gamble or take risks with ♦ dice with death.

dictate verb (**dictates, dictating, dictated**)
1 speak or read something aloud for someone else to write down. 2 give orders in a bossy way.
dictation noun

dictates (say dik-tayts) plural noun
orders or commands.

dictator noun (plural **dictators**)
a ruler who has unlimited power.
dictatorial (say dik-ta-tor-ee-al) adjective
dictatorship noun

diction noun
1 a person's way of speaking words ♦ clear diction. 2 a writer's choice of words.

dictionary noun (plural **dictionaries**)
a book that contains words in alphabetical order so that you can find out how to spell them and what they mean.

didactic (say dy-dak-tik) adjective
having the manner of someone who is lecturing people.
didactically adverb

diddle verb (**diddles, diddling, diddled**) (slang)
cheat or swindle.

didn't (mainly spoken)
did not.

die¹ verb (**dies, dying, died**)
1 stop living or existing. 2 stop burning or functioning ♦ The fire had died down.
be dying for or **to** (informal) want to have or do something very much ♦ We are all dying to see you again.

die² noun singular of **dice**.

die³ noun (plural **dies**)
a device that stamps a design on coins etc. or that cuts or moulds metal.

diehard noun (plural **diehards**)
a person who obstinately refuses to give up old ideas or policies.

diesel (say dee-zel) noun (plural **diesels**)
1 an engine that works by burning oil in compressed air. 2 fuel for this kind of engine.

diet¹ noun (plural **diets**)
1 special meals that someone eats in order to be healthy or to lose weight. 2 the sort of foods usually eaten by a person or animal.
diet verb (**diets, dieting, dieted**)
keep to a diet.

diet² noun (plural **diets**)
the parliament of certain countries (e.g. Japan).

dietitian (say dy-it-ish-an) noun (plural **dietitians**)
an expert in diet and nutrition.

differ verb (**differs, differing, differed**)
1 be different. 2 disagree.

difference noun (plural **differences**)
1 being different; the way in which things differ.
2 the remainder left after one number is subtracted from another ♦ The difference between 8 and 3 is 5. 3 a disagreement.

different adjective
unlike; not the same.
differently adverb

---

❶ USAGE It is regarded as more acceptable to say different from rather than different to, which is common in less formal use. The phrase different than is used in American English but not in standard British English.

---

differential *noun* (*plural* **differentials**)
1 a difference in wages between one group of workers and another. 2 a differential gear.

differential gear *noun* (*plural* **differential gears**)
a system of gears that makes a vehicle's driving wheels revolve at different speeds when going round corners.

differentiate *verb* (**differentiates, differentiating, differentiated**)
1 be a difference between things; make one thing different from another ♦ *What are the features that differentiate one breed from another?*
2 distinguish; recognize differences ♦ *We do not differentiate between them.*
differentiation *noun*

difficult *adjective*
needing a lot of effort or skill; not easy.

difficulty *noun* (*plural* **difficulties**)
1 being difficult. 2 something that causes a problem.

diffident (*say* dif-id-ent) *adjective*
shy and not self-confident; hesitating to put yourself or your ideas forward.
diffidently *adverb* **diffidence** *noun*

diffract *verb* (**diffracts, diffracting, diffracted**)
break up a beam of light etc.
diffraction *noun*

diffuse (*say* dif-yooz) *verb* (**diffuses, diffusing, diffused**)
1 spread something widely or thinly ♦ *diffused lighting.* 2 mix slowly ♦ *diffusing gases.*
diffusion *noun*

diffuse (*say* dif-yooss) *adjective*
1 spread widely; not concentrated. 2 using many words; not concise.
diffusely *adverb* **diffuseness** *noun*

dig *verb* (**digs, digging, dug**)
1 break up soil and move it; make a hole or tunnel by moving soil. 2 poke something in ♦ *Dig a knife into it.* 3 seek or discover by investigating ♦ *We dug up some facts.*
digger *noun*

dig *noun* (*plural* **digs**)
1 a piece of digging, especially an archaeological excavation. 2 a poke. 3 a critical remark.

digest (*say* dy-jest) *verb* (**digests, digesting, digested**)
1 soften and change food in the stomach etc. so that the body can absorb it. 2 take information into your mind and think it over.
digestible *adjective* **digestion** *noun*

digest (*say* dy-jest) *noun* (*plural* **digests**)
a summary of news, information, etc.

digestive *adjective*
to do with digestion ♦ *the digestive system.*

digestive biscuit *noun* (*plural* **digestive biscuits**)
a wholemeal biscuit (because it is supposed to be easy to digest).

digit (*say* dij-it) *noun* (*plural* **digits**)
1 any of the numbers from 0 to 9. 2 a finger or toe.

digital *adjective*
1 to do with or using digits. 2 (said about a watch or clock) showing the time with a row of figures. 3 (said about a computer, recording, etc.) storing the data or sound as a series of binary digits.

dignified *adjective*
having dignity.

dignitary *noun* (*plural* **dignitaries**)
an important official.

dignity *noun*
a calm and serious manner.
beneath your dignity not considered worthy enough for you to do.

dilapidated *adjective*
falling to pieces.
dilapidation *noun*

dilemma (*say* dil-em-a) *noun* (*plural* **dilemmas**)
a situation where someone has to choose between two or more possible actions, each of which will bring difficulties.

❶ USAGE Do not use *dilemma* to mean simply a problem or difficult situation. There should be some idea of choosing between two (or perhaps more) things.

diligent (*say* dil-ij-ent) *adjective*
hard-working.
diligently *adverb* **diligence** *noun*

dilute *verb* (**dilutes, diluting, diluted**)
make a liquid weaker by adding water or other liquid.
dilution *noun*

dilute *adjective*
diluted ♦ *a dilute acid.*

dim *adjective* (**dimmer, dimmest**)
1 not bright or clear; only faintly lit. 2 (*informal*) stupid.
dimly *adverb* **dimness** *noun*

dim *verb* (**dims, dimming, dimmed**)
make or become dim.
dimmer *noun*

dimension *noun* (*plural* **dimensions**)
1 a measurement such as length, width, area, or volume. 2 size or extent.
dimensional *adjective*

diminish *verb* (**diminishes, diminishing, diminished**)
make or become smaller.
diminution *noun*

diminutive (*say* dim-in-yoo-tiv) *adjective*
very small.

dimple *noun* (*plural* **dimples**)
a small hollow or dent, especially in the skin.
dimpled *adjective*

din *noun*
a loud annoying noise.

dine *verb* (**dines, dining, dined**) (*formal*)
have dinner.
diner *noun*

dinghy (*say* ding-ee) *noun* (*plural* **dinghies**)
a kind of small boat.
[from Hindi *dingi* = a small river boat]

dingy (*say* din-jee) *adjective*
dirty-looking.
dingily *adverb* **dinginess** *noun*

dinner *noun* (*plural* **dinners**)
1 the main meal of the day, either at midday or
in the evening. **2** a formal evening meal in
honour of something.

dinosaur (*say* dy-noss-or) *noun* (*plural*
dinosaurs)
a prehistoric reptile, often of enormous size.

diocese (*say* dy-oss-iss) *noun* (*plural* **dioceses**)
a district under the care of a bishop.

dioxide *noun*
an oxide with two atoms of oxygen to one of
another element ♦ *carbon dioxide*.

dip *verb* (**dips, dipping, dipped**)
put down or go down, especially into a liquid.

dip *noun* (*plural* **dips**)
1 dipping. **2** a downward slope. **3** a quick swim.
4 a substance into which things are dipped.

diploma *noun* (*plural* **diplomas**)
a certificate awarded by a college etc. for skill in
a particular subject.

diplomacy *noun*
1 the work of making agreements with other
countries. **2** skill in dealing with people and
gently persuading them to agree to things; tact.

diplomat *noun* (*plural* **diplomats**)
1 a person employed in diplomacy on behalf of
his or her country. **2** a tactful person.
diplomatic *adjective*

direct *adjective*
1 as straight as possible. **2** going straight to the
point; frank. **3** exact ♦ *the direct opposite*.

direct *verb* (**directs, directing, directed**)
1 tell someone the way. **2** guide or aim in a
certain direction. **3** control or manage.
4 order ♦ *He directed his troops to advance*.

direct current *noun*
electric current flowing only in one direction.

direction *noun* (*plural* **directions**)
1 directing. **2** the line along which something
moves or faces.
directional *adjective*

directly *adverb*
immediately; by a direct route.

direct object *noun* (*plural* **direct objects**)
the word that receives the action of the verb. In
'she hit him', 'him' is the direct object.

director *noun* (*plural* **directors**)
1 a person who is in charge of something.
2 a person who decides how a film, programme,
or play should be made or performed.

directory *noun* (*plural* **directories**)
a book containing a list of people with their
telephone numbers, addresses, etc.

direct speech *noun*
someone's words written down exactly in the
way they were said.

dirge *noun* (*plural* **dirges**)
a slow sad song.

dirt *noun*
earth, soil; anything that is not clean.
[from an Old Norse word meaning 'excrement']

dirty *adjective* (**dirtier, dirtiest**)
1 not clean; soiled. **2** unfair; dishonourable
♦ *a dirty trick*. **3** indecent; obscene.
dirtily *adverb* **dirtiness** *noun*

dis- *prefix* (changing to **dif-** before words
beginning with *f*, and to **di-** before some
consonants)
1 not; the reverse of (as in *dishonest*).
2 apart; separated (as in *disarm, disperse*).

disabled *adjective*
unable to use part of your body properly because
of illness or injury.
disability *noun* **disablement** *noun*

disadvantage *noun* (*plural* **disadvantages**)
something that hinders or is unhelpful.

disagree *verb* (**disagrees, disagreeing,
disagreed**)
1 have or express a different opinion from
someone. **2** have a bad effect ♦ *Rich food
disagrees with me*.
disagreement *noun*

disagreeable *adjective*
unpleasant.

disappear *verb* (**disappears, disappearing,
disappeared**)
stop being visible; vanish.
disappearance *noun*

disappoint *verb* (**disappoints, disappointing,
disappointed**)
fail to do what someone hopes for.
disappointment *noun*

disapprove *verb* (**disapproves, disapproving,
disapproved**)
have an unfavourable opinion of something; not
approve.
disapproval *noun*

disarm *verb* (disarms, disarming, disarmed)
1 reduce the size of armed forces. **2** take away someone's weapons. **3** overcome a person's anger or doubt ♦ *Her friendliness disarmed their suspicions.*
disarming *adjective*

disarmament *noun*
reduction of a country's armed forces or weapons.

disaster *noun* (*plural* disasters)
1 a very bad accident or misfortune. **2** a complete failure.
disastrous *adjective* **disastrously** *adverb*

disbelief *noun*
refusal or unwillingness to believe something.
disbelieve *verb*

disc *noun* (*plural* discs)
1 any round flat object. **2** a layer of cartilage between vertebrae in the spine. **3** a CD or record.

discerning *adjective*
perceptive; showing good judgement.

discharge *verb* (discharges, discharging, discharged)
1 release a person. **2** send something out ♦ *discharge smoke.* **3** pay or do what was agreed ♦ *discharge the debt.*

disciple *noun* (*plural* disciples)
1 a person who accepts the teachings of another whom he or she regards as a leader. **2** any of the original followers of Jesus Christ.

discipline *noun* (*plural* disciplines)
1 orderly and obedient behaviour. **2** a subject for study.
disciplinary (*say* dis-ip-lin-er-ee) *adjective*

disc jockey *noun* (*plural* disc jockeys)
a person who plays recorded music on the radio or at a disco or nightclub.

disco *noun* (*plural* discos)
a place where CDs or records are played for dancing.

discolour *verb* (discolours, discolouring, discoloured)
spoil a thing's colour; stain.
discoloration *noun*

disconcert (*say* dis-kon-**sert**) *verb* (disconcerts, disconcerting, disconcerted)
make a person feel uneasy.

disconnect *verb* (disconnects, disconnecting, disconnected)
break a connection; detach ♦ *The phone has been disconnected.*
disconnection *noun*

disconsolate (*say* dis-**kon**-sol-at) *adjective*
disappointed.

discontent *noun*
lack of contentment; dissatisfaction.
discontented *adjective* **discontentment** *noun*

discontinue *verb* (discontinues, discontinuing, discontinued)
put an end to something.

discord *noun* (*plural* discords)
1 disagreement; quarrelling. **2** musical notes sounded together and producing a harsh or unpleasant sound.
discordant *adjective*

discount *noun* (*plural* discounts)
an amount by which a price is reduced.

discount *verb* (discounts, discounting, discounted)
ignore or disregard something ♦ *We cannot discount the possibility.*

discourage *verb* (discourages, discouraging, discouraged)
1 take away someone's enthusiasm or confidence. **2** try to persuade someone not to do something.
discouragement *noun*

discover *verb* (discovers, discovering, discovered)
1 find or find out. **2** be the first person to find something.
discoverer *noun* **discovery** *noun*

discredit *verb* (discredits, discrediting, discredited)
1 cause something to be doubted. **2** damage someone's reputation.

discredit *noun*
damage to someone's reputation.
discreditable *adjective*

discreet *adjective*
1 not giving away secrets. **2** not showy.
discreetly *adverb*

ℹ USAGE Do not confuse with *discrete*.

---

discrepancy (*say* dis-**krep**-an-see) *noun* (*plural* discrepancies)
lack of agreement between things which should be the same ♦ *There are several discrepancies in the two accounts.*

discrete *adjective*
separate; distinct from each other.

ℹ USAGE Do not confuse with *discreet*.

---

discretion (*say* dis-**kresh**-on) *noun*
1 being discreet; keeping secrets ♦ *I hope I can count on your discretion.* **2** freedom to decide things and take action according to your own judgement ♦ *You can use your discretion.*

discriminate *verb* (discriminates, discriminating, discriminated)
1 notice the differences between things; distinguish; prefer one thing to another.
2 treat people differently or unfairly, e.g. because of their race, sex, or religion.
discrimination *noun*

discus noun (plural **discuses**)
a thick heavy disc thrown in athletic contests.

discuss verb (**discusses, discussing, discussed**)
talk with other people about a subject.
discussion noun

disease noun (plural **diseases**)
an unhealthy condition; an illness.
diseased adjective

disembark verb (**disembarks, disembarking, disembarked**)
get off a ship or aircraft.
disembarkation noun

disentangle verb (**disentangles, disentangling, disentangled**)
free from tangles or confusion.

disfigure verb (**disfigures, disfiguring, disfigured**)
spoil the appearance of a person or thing.
disfigurement noun

disgrace noun
1 shame; loss of approval or respect.
2 something that causes shame.
disgraceful adjective **disgracefully** adverb

disgrace verb (**disgraces, disgracing, disgraced**)
bring disgrace on someone.

disguise verb (**disguises, disguising, disguised**)
1 make a person or thing look different in order to deceive people. 2 conceal your feelings.

disguise noun (plural **disguises**)
something used for disguising.

disgust noun
a feeling that something is very unpleasant or disgraceful.

disgust verb (**disgusts, disgusting, disgusted**)
give someone a feeling of disgust.
disgusted adjective **disgusting** adjective

dish noun (plural **dishes**)
1 a plate or bowl for food. 2 food prepared for eating. 3 a satellite dish.

dish verb (**dishes, dishing, dished**) (informal)
dish out give out portions of something to people.

dishevelled (say dish-ev-eld) adjective
ruffled and untidy.
dishevelment noun

dishonest adjective
not honest.
dishonestly adverb **dishonesty** noun

dishonour verb (**dishonours, dishonouring, dishonoured**)
disgrace someone.
dishonour noun **dishonourable** adjective

disillusion verb (**disillusions, disillusioning, disillusioned**)
get rid of someone's wrong beliefs.
disillusionment noun

disinclined adjective
unwilling to do something.

disinfect verb (**disinfects, disinfecting, disinfected**)
destroy the germs in something.
disinfection noun

disinfectant noun (plural **disinfectants**)
a substance used for disinfecting things.

disintegrate verb (**disintegrates, disintegrating, disintegrated**)
break up into small parts or pieces.
disintegration noun

disinterested adjective
impartial; not influenced by the hope of gaining something yourself ♦ She gave us some disinterested advice.

> ❶ USAGE It is not accepted as part of standard English to use this word as if it meant 'not interested' or 'bored'. If this is what you mean, use uninterested.

disjointed adjective
(said about talk or writing) not having parts that fit together well and so difficult to understand.

disk noun (plural **disks**)
a computer storage device consisting of magnetically coated plates.

dislike verb (**dislikes, disliking, disliked**)
not like somebody or something.

dislocate verb (**dislocates, dislocating, dislocated**)
1 move or force a bone from its proper position in one of the joints. 2 disrupt ♦ Fog dislocated the traffic.
dislocation noun

dislodge verb (**dislodges, dislodging, dislodged**)
move or force something from its place.

disloyal adjective
not loyal.
disloyally adverb **disloyalty** noun

dismal adjective
1 gloomy. 2 of poor quality.
dismally adverb

dismantle verb (**dismantles, dismantling, dismantled**)
take something to pieces.

dismay noun
a feeling of surprise and discouragement.
dismayed adjective

dismiss verb (**dismisses, dismissing, dismissed**)
1 send someone away. 2 tell a person that you will no longer employ him or her. 3 put something out of your thoughts because it is not worth thinking about. 4 get a batsman or cricket side out.
dismissal noun **dismissive** adjective

dismount *verb* (dismounts, dismounting, dismounted)
get off a horse or bicycle.

disobey *verb* (disobeys, disobeying, disobeyed)
not obey; disregard orders.
disobedient *adjective* **disobedience** *noun*

disorder *noun* (*plural* disorders)
1 untidiness. 2 a disturbance. 3 an illness.
disorderly *adjective*

disorganized *adjective*
muddled and badly organized.
disorganization *noun*

dispatch *verb* (dispatches, dispatching, dispatched)
1 send off to a destination. 2 kill.
dispatch *noun* (*plural* dispatches)
1 dispatching. 2 a report or message sent.
3 promptness; speed.

dispel *verb* (dispels, dispelling, dispelled)
drive away; scatter ♦ *Wind dispels fog.*

dispensary *noun* (*plural* dispensaries)
a place where medicines are dispensed.

dispense *verb* (dispenses, dispensing, dispensed)
1 distribute; deal out. 2 prepare medicine
according to prescriptions.
dispensation *noun*
dispense with do without something.

dispenser *noun* (*plural* dispensers)
a device that supplies a quantity of something
♦ *a cash dispenser.*

disperse *verb* (disperses, dispersing, dispersed)
scatter.
dispersal *noun* **dispersion** *noun*

displace *verb* (displaces, displacing, displaced)
1 shift from its place. 2 take a person's or thing's
place.
displacement *noun*

display *verb* (displays, displaying, displayed)
show; arrange something so that it can be clearly
seen.
display *noun* (*plural* displays)
1 the displaying of something; an exhibition.
2 something displayed. 3 (in computing) an
electronic device for visually presenting data.

disposable *adjective*
made to be thrown away after it has been used
♦ *disposable nappies.*

dispose *verb* (disposes, disposing, disposed)
1 make a person ready or willing to do
something ♦ *I feel disposed to help him.* 2 place
in position; arrange ♦ *Dispose your troops in two
lines.*
be well disposed be friendly. **dispose of** get rid
of.

disposition *noun* (*plural* dispositions)
1 a person's nature or qualities. 2 arrangement.

disproportionate *adjective*
out of proportion; too large or too small.

disprove *verb* (disproves, disproving, disproved)
show that something is not true.

dispute *verb* (disputes, disputing, disputed)
1 argue; debate. 2 quarrel. 3 raise an objection to
♦ *We dispute their claim.*
dispute *noun* (*plural* disputes)
1 an argument or debate. 2 a quarrel.
in dispute being argued about.

disqualify *verb* (disqualifies, disqualifying, disqualified)
bar someone from a competition etc. because he
or she has broken the rules or is not properly
qualified to take part.
disqualification *noun*

disregard *verb* (disregards, disregarding, disregarded)
ignore.
disregard *noun*
the act of ignoring something.

disrepair *noun*
bad condition caused by not doing repairs
♦ *The old mill is in a state of disrepair.*

disreputable *adjective*
not respectable.

disrespect *noun*
lack of respect; rudeness.
disrespectful *adjective* **disrespectfully** *adverb*

disrupt *verb* (disrupts, disrupting, disrupted)
put into disorder; interrupt a continuous flow
♦ *Fog disrupted traffic.*
disruption *noun* **disruptive** *adjective*

dissatisfied *adjective*
not satisfied.
dissatisfaction *noun*

dissect (*say* dis-sekt) *verb* (dissects, dissecting, dissected)
cut something up in order to examine it.
dissection *noun*

dissent *noun*
disagreement over an idea, proposal, etc.
dissent *verb* (dissents, dissenting, dissented)
disagree.

dissident *noun* (*plural* dissidents)
a person who disagrees, especially someone who
opposes their government.
dissident *adjective* **dissidence** *noun*

dissolute *adjective*
having an immoral way of life.

dissolution *noun* (*plural* dissolutions)
1 putting an end to a marriage or partnership etc.
2 the formal ending of a parliament or assembly.

dissolve *verb* (dissolves, dissolving, dissolved)
1 mix something with a liquid so that it becomes part of the liquid. 2 make or become liquid; melt. 3 put an end to a marriage or partnership etc. 4 formally end a parliament, assembly, or other gathering ♦ *Parliament was dissolved and a general election was held*.

dissuade *verb* (dissuades, dissuading, dissuaded)
persuade somebody not to do something.
dissuasion *noun*

distance *noun* (*plural* distances)
the amount of space between two places.
in the distance far away but visible.

distant *adjective*
1 far away. 2 not friendly; not sociable. 3 not closely related ♦ *distant cousins*.
distantly *adverb*

distaste *noun*
dislike.

distasteful *adjective*
unpleasant.

distemper *noun*
1 a disease of dogs and certain other animals. 2 a kind of paint.

distil *verb* (distils, distilling, distilled)
purify a liquid by boiling it and condensing the vapour.
distillation *noun* **distiller** *noun*

distinct *adjective*
1 easily heard or seen; noticeable. 2 clearly separate or different.
distinctly *adverb* **distinctness** *noun*

---

❶ USAGE See note at *distinctive*.

---

distinction *noun* (*plural* distinctions)
1 a difference. 2 excellence or honour. 3 an award for excellence; a high mark in an examination.

distinctive *adjective*
that distinguishes one thing from another or others ♦ *The school has a distinctive uniform*.
distinctively *adverb*

---

❶ USAGE Do not confuse this word with *distinct*. A *distinct* mark is a clear mark; a *distinctive* mark is one that is not found anywhere else.

---

distinguish *verb* (distinguishes, distinguishing, distinguished)
1 make or notice differences between things. 2 see or hear something clearly. 3 bring honour to ♦ *He distinguished himself by his bravery*.
distinguishable *adjective*

distinguished *adjective*
1 important and famous. 2 dignified in appearance.

distort *verb* (distorts, distorting, distorted)
1 pull or twist out of its normal shape. 2 misrepresent; give a false account of something ♦ *distort the truth*.
distortion *noun*

distract *verb* (distracts, distracting, distracted)
take a person's attention away from something.

distraction *noun* (*plural* distractions)
1 something that distracts attention. 2 an amusement. 3 great worry or distress.

distress *noun* (*plural* distresses)
great sorrow, pain, or trouble.

distribute *verb* (distributes, distributing, distributed)
1 deal or share out. 2 spread or scatter.
distribution *noun* **distributor** *noun*

district *noun* (*plural* districts)
part of a town or country.

distrust *noun*
lack of trust; suspicion.
distrustful *adjective*

distrust *verb* (distrusts, distrusting, distrusted)
have little trust in.

disturb *verb* (disturbs, disturbing, disturbed)
1 spoil someone's peace or rest. 2 cause someone to worry. 3 move a thing from its position.
disturbance *noun*

disuse *noun*
the state of being no longer used.
disused *adjective*

ditch *noun* (*plural* ditches)
a trench dug to hold water or carry it away, or to serve as a boundary.
[from Old English]

ditto *noun*
(used in lists) the same again.

dive *verb* (dives, diving, dived)
1 go under water, especially head first. 2 move down quickly.
dive *noun*

diverse (*say* dy-**verss**) *adjective*
varied; of several different kinds.
diversity *noun*

diversify *verb* (diversifies, diversifying, diversified)
make or become varied; involve yourself in different kinds of things.
diversification *noun*

diversion *noun* (*plural* diversions)
1 diverting something from its course. 2 an alternative route for traffic when a road is closed. 3 a recreation or entertainment.

divert *verb* (diverts, diverting, diverted)
1 turn something aside from its course. 2 entertain or amuse.
diverting *adjective*

divide *verb* (**divides, dividing, divided**)
1 separate from something or into smaller parts;
split up. 2 find how many times one number is
contained in another ♦ *Divide six by three*
$(6 \div 3 = 2)$.
divider *noun*

divine *adjective*
1 belonging to or coming from God. 2 like a god.
3 (*informal*) excellent; extremely beautiful.
divinely *adverb* **divinity** *noun*

division *noun* (*plural* **divisions**)
1 dividing. 2 a dividing line; a partition.
3 one of the parts into which something is
divided. 4 (in Parliament) separation of
members into two sections for counting votes.
divisional *adjective*

divisive (*say* div-I-siv) *adjective*
causing disagreement within a group.

divorce *noun* (*plural* **divorces**)
the legal ending of a marriage.

divorce *verb* (**divorces, divorcing, divorced**)
1 end a marriage by divorce. 2 separate; think of
things separately.

Diwali (*say* di-**wah**-lee) *noun*
a Hindu religious festival at which lamps are lit,
held in October or November.

DIY *abbreviation*
do-it-yourself.

dizzy *adjective* (**dizzier, dizziest**)
having or causing the feeling that everything is
spinning round; giddy.
dizzily *adverb* **dizziness** *noun*

DJ *abbreviation*
disc jockey.

DNA *abbreviation*
deoxyribonucleic acid; a substance in
chromosomes that stores genetic information.

do *verb* (**does, doing, did, done**)
This word has many different uses, most of
which mean performing or dealing with
something (*Do your best. I can't do this. She is
doing well at school*) or being suitable or enough
(*This will do*).
The verb is also used with other verbs
1 in questions (*Do you want this?*),
2 in statements with 'not' (*He does not want it*),
3 for emphasis (*I do like nuts*), 4 to avoid
repeating a verb that has just been used (*We
work as hard as they do*).
do away with get rid of. **do up 1** fasten
♦ *Do your coat up.* 2 repair or redecorate ♦ *Do up
the spare room.*

dock¹ *noun* (*plural* **docks**)
a part of a harbour where ships are loaded,
unloaded, or repaired.

dock *verb* (**docks, docking, docked**)
1 bring or come into a dock. 2 when two
spacecraft dock, they join together in space.

dock² *noun*
an enclosure for the prisoner on trial in a
lawcourt.

dock³ *noun*
a weed with broad leaves.

dock⁴ *verb* (**docks, docking, docked**)
1 cut short an animal's tail. 2 reduce or take
away part of someone's wages or supplies etc.

docker *noun* (*plural* **dockers**)
a labourer who loads and unloads ships.

doctor *noun* (*plural* **doctors**)
1 a person who is trained to treat sick or injured
people. 2 a person who holds an advanced
degree (a **doctorate**) at a university ♦ *Doctor of
Music.*

doctrine *noun* (*plural* **doctrines**)
a belief held by a religious, political, or other
group.
doctrinal *adjective*

document *noun* (*plural* **documents**)
a written or printed paper giving information or
evidence about something.
documentation *noun*

documentary *adjective*
1 consisting of documents ♦ *documentary
evidence.* 2 showing real events or situations.

documentary *noun* (*plural* **documentaries**)
a film giving information about real events.

dodge *verb* (**dodges, dodging, dodged**)
move quickly to avoid someone or something.

dodge *noun* (*plural* **dodges**)
1 a dodging movement. 2 (*informal*) a trick;
a clever way of doing something.

dodgy *adjective* (*informal*)
1 awkward or tricky. 2 not working properly.
3 dishonest.

dodo *noun* (*plural* **dodos**)
a large heavy bird that used to live on an island
in the Indian Ocean but has been extinct for over
200 years.

doe *noun* (*plural* **does**)
a female deer, rabbit, or hare.

doesn't (*mainly spoken*)
does not.

dog *noun* (*plural* **dogs**)
a four-legged animal that barks, often kept as a
pet.

dog *verb* (**dogs, dogging, dogged**)
follow closely or persistently ♦ *Reporters dogged
his footsteps.*
[from Old English]

dog-eared *adjective*
(said about a book) having the corners of the
pages bent from constant use.

dogged (*say* **dog**-id) *adjective*
persistent or obstinate.
doggedly *adverb*

dogma noun (plural **dogmas**)
a belief or principle that a Church or other authority declares is true and must be accepted.

dogmatic adjective
expressing ideas in a very firm authoritative way.
dogmatically adverb

do-it-yourself adjective
suitable for an amateur to do or make at home.

dole verb (**doles, doling, doled**)
dole out distribute.

dole noun (informal)
money paid by the state to unemployed people.

doll noun (plural **dolls**)
a toy model of a person.

dollar noun (plural **dollars**)
a unit of money in the USA and some other countries.

dolphin noun (plural **dolphins**)
a sea animal like a small whale with a beak-like snout.
[via early French from Greek delphis]

domain (say dom-**ayn**) noun (plural **domains**)
1 a kingdom. **2** an area of knowledge, interest, etc.

dome noun (plural **domes**)
a roof shaped like the top half of a ball.
domed adjective

domestic adjective
1 to do with the home or household.
2 (said about animals) kept by people, not wild.
domestically adverb **domesticated** adjective

dominate verb (**dominates, dominating, dominated**)
1 control by being stronger or more powerful.
2 be conspicuous or prominent ♦ The mountain dominated the whole landscape.
dominant adjective **dominance** noun
domination noun

domineer verb (**domineers, domineering, domineered**)
behave in a dominating way.
domineering adjective

dominion noun (plural **dominions**)
1 authority to rule others; control. **2** an area over which someone rules; a domain.

domino noun (plural **dominoes**)
a small flat oblong piece of wood or plastic with dots (1 to 6) or a blank space at each end, used in the game of dominoes.

donkey noun (plural **donkeys**)
an animal that looks like a small horse with long ears.

donor noun (plural **donors**)
someone who gives something ♦ a blood donor.

don't (mainly spoken)
do not.

doom noun
a grim fate that you cannot avoid, especially death or destruction ♦ a sense of impending doom.

doomed adjective
destined to fail or be destroyed.

door noun (plural **doors**)
a movable barrier on hinges (or one that slides or revolves), used to open or close an entrance.
doorknob noun **doormat** noun

doorstep noun (plural **doorsteps**)
the step or piece of ground just outside a door.

doorway noun (plural **doorways**)
the opening into which a door fits.

dope noun (plural **dopes**)
1 (informal) a drug, especially one taken or given illegally. **2** (informal) a stupid person.
dopey adjective

dope verb (**dopes, doping, doped**) (informal)
give a drug to a person or animal.
[from Dutch doop = sauce]

dormant adjective
1 sleeping. **2** living or existing but not active; not extinct ♦ a dormant volcano.

dormitory noun (plural **dormitories**)
a room for several people to sleep in, especially in a school or institution.
dormitory town or **suburb** a place from which people travel to work elsewhere.

dormouse noun (plural **dormice**)
an animal like a large mouse that hibernates in winter.

dose noun (plural **doses**)
an amount of medicine etc. taken at one time.

dot noun (plural **dots**)
a tiny spot.

dot verb (**dots, dotting, dotted**)
mark something with dots.

double adjective
1 twice as much; twice as many. **2** having two things or parts that form a pair ♦ a double-barrelled gun. **3** suitable for two people ♦ a double bed.
doubly adverb

double noun (plural **doubles**)
1 a double quantity or thing. **2** a person or thing that looks exactly like another.

double verb (**doubles, doubling, doubled**)
1 make or become twice as much or as many.
2 bend or fold in two. **3** turn back sharply ♦ The fox doubled back on its tracks.
[via early French from Latin duplus]

double bass noun (plural **double basses**)
a musical instrument with strings, like a large cello.

double-cross verb (**double-crosses, double-crossing, double-crossed**)
deceive or cheat someone who thinks you are working with them.

double-decker *noun* (*plural* **double-deckers**)
a bus with two floors, one above the other.

doubt *noun* (*plural* **doubts**)
a feeling of not being sure about something.

doubt *verb* (**doubts, doubting, doubted**)
feel doubt.
doubter *noun*

doubtful *adjective*
1 feeling doubt. 2 making you feel doubt.
doubtfully *adverb*

dough *noun*
1 a thick mixture of flour and water used for making bread, pastry, etc. 2 (*slang*) money.
doughy *adjective*

doughnut *noun* (*plural* **doughnuts**)
a round bun that has been fried and covered in sugar.

dour (*say* doo-er) *adjective*
stern and gloomy-looking.
dourly *adverb*

dove *noun* (*plural* **doves**)
a kind of pigeon.

dovetail *noun* (*plural* **dovetails**)
a wedge-shaped joint used to join two pieces of wood.

dovetail *verb* (**dovetails, dovetailing, dovetailed**)
1 join pieces of wood with a dovetail. 2 fit neatly together ♦ *My plans dovetailed with hers.*

dowager *noun* (*plural* **dowagers**)
a woman who holds a title or property after her husband has died ♦ *the dowager duchess.*

dowdy *adjective* (**dowdier, dowdiest**)
shabby; unfashionable.
dowdily *adverb*

down¹ *adverb*
1 to or in a lower place or position or level ♦ *She fell down.* 2 to a source or place etc. ♦ *Track them down.* 3 in writing ♦ *Take down these instructions.* 4 as a payment ♦ *We will pay £5 down and the rest later.* 5 unhappy or depressed.
be down on disapprove of ♦ *She is down on smoking.*

down *preposition*
downwards through or along or into ♦ *Pour it down the drain.*

down² *noun*
very fine soft feathers or hair.
downy *adjective*

down³ *noun* (*plural* **downs**)
a grass-covered hill ♦ *the South Downs.*
downland *noun*

downhill *adverb* & *adjective*
down a slope.

download *verb* (**downloads, downloading, downloaded**)
transfer data from a large computer system to a smaller one.

downpour *noun* (*plural* **downpours**)
a heavy fall of rain.

downright *adverb* & *adjective*
complete or completely ♦ *a downright lie.*

Down's syndrome *noun*
a medical condition caused by a chromosome defect that causes intellectual impairment and physical abnormalities such as short stature and a broad flattened skull.

down-to-earth *adjective*
sensible and practical.

downward *adjective* & *adverb*
going towards what is lower.
downwards *adverb*

dowry *noun* (*plural* **dowries**)
property or money brought by a bride to her husband when she marries him.

doze *verb* (**dozes, dozing, dozed**)
sleep lightly.

doze *noun*
a light sleep.
dozy *adjective*

dozen *noun* (*plural* **dozens**)
a set of twelve.

ℹ USAGE Correct use is *ten dozen* (not *ten dozens*).

---

drab *adjective* (**drabber, drabbest**)
1 not colourful. 2 dull or uninteresting ♦ *a drab life.*
drably *adverb* **drabness** *noun*

draft *noun* (*plural* **drafts**)
1 a rough sketch or plan. 2 a written order for a bank to pay out money.

draft *verb* (**drafts, drafting, drafted**)
1 prepare a draft. 2 select for a special duty ♦ *She was drafted to our office in Paris.*

ℹ USAGE This is also the American spelling of *draught.*

---

drag *verb* (**drags, dragging, dragged**)
1 pull something heavy along. 2 search a river or lake etc. with nets and hooks. 3 continue slowly and tediously.

drag *noun*
1 something that is tedious or a nuisance. 2 (*slang*) women's clothes worn by men.

dragon *noun* (*plural* **dragons**)
1 a mythological monster, usually with wings and able to breathe out fire. 2 a fierce person, especially a woman.

dragonfly *noun* (*plural* **dragonflies**)
an insect with a long thin body and two pairs of transparent wings.

drain *noun* (*plural* **drains**)
  1 a pipe or ditch etc. for taking away water or other liquid. **2** something that takes away strength or resources.
  drainpipe *noun*

drain *verb* (**drains, draining, drained**)
  1 take away water etc. through a drain. **2** flow or trickle away. **3** empty liquid out of a container. **4** take away strength etc.; exhaust.
  drainage *noun*

drake *noun* (*plural* **drakes**)
  a male duck.

drama *noun* (*plural* **dramas**)
  1 a play. **2** writing or performing plays. **3** a series of exciting events.
  dramatic *adjective* **dramatist** *noun* **dramatize** *verb*
  [from Greek *drama*, from *dran* = to do, to act]

drape *verb* (**drapes, draping, draped**)
  hang cloth etc. loosely over something.

draper *noun* (*plural* **drapers**) (*old use*)
  a shopkeeper who sells cloth or clothes.
  drapery *noun*

drastic *adjective*
  having a strong or violent effect.
  drastically *adverb*

draught (*say* drahft) *noun* (*plural* **draughts**)
  1 a current of usually cold air indoors.
  2 the depth of water needed to float a ship.
  3 a swallow of liquid.
  draughty *adjective*

draught (*say* drahft) *adjective*
  (said about beer) served from a cask or barrel rather than a bottle or can.

draughts *noun*
  a game played with 24 round pieces on a chessboard.

draw *verb* (**draws, drawing, drew, drawn**)
  1 produce a picture or outline by making marks on a surface. **2** pull. **3** take out ♦ *draw water.*
  4 attract ♦ *The fair drew large crowds.* **5** end a game or contest with the same score on both sides. **6** move or come ♦ *The ship drew nearer.*
  7 write out a cheque to be cashed.
  draw a conclusion form an opinion about something by thinking about the evidence.

draw *noun* (*plural* **draws**)
  1 the drawing of lots (SEE **lot**). **2** the drawing out of a gun etc. ♦ *He was quick on the draw.*
  3 an attraction. **4** a drawn game.

---

❶ USAGE Do not confuse this word with *drawer*.

---

drawback *noun* (*plural* **drawbacks**)
  a disadvantage.

drawbridge *noun* (*plural* **drawbridges**)
  a bridge over a moat, hinged at one end so that it can be raised or lowered.

drawer *noun* (*plural* **drawers**)
  1 a sliding box-like compartment in a piece of furniture. **2** a person who draws something.
  3 someone who draws (= writes out) a cheque.

drawing *noun* (*plural* **drawings**)
  a picture or outline drawn.

drawing pin *noun* (*plural* **drawing pins**)
  a short pin with a flat top to be pressed with your thumb, used for fastening paper etc. to a surface.

drawing room *noun* (*plural* **drawing rooms**)
  a sitting room.

drawl *verb* (**drawls, drawling, drawled**)
  speak very slowly or lazily.

drawl *noun* (*plural* **drawls**)
  a drawling way of speaking.

dread *noun*
  great fear.

dread *verb* (**dreads, dreading, dreaded**)
  fear something very much.

dreadful *adjective* (*informal*)
  very bad ♦ *dreadful weather.*
  dreadfully *adverb*

dreadlocks *plural noun*
  hair worn in many ringlets or plaits, especially by Rastafarians.

dream *noun* (*plural* **dreams**)
  1 a series of pictures or events in a sleeping person's mind. **2** something imagined; an ambition or ideal.
  dreamy *adjective* **dreamily** *adverb*

dream *verb* (**dreams, dreaming, dreamt or dreamed**)
  1 have a dream or dreams. **2** have an ambition.
  3 think something might happen ♦ *I never dreamt she would leave.*
  dreamer *noun*
  dream up invent or imagine a plan, idea, etc.

dreary *adjective* (**drearier, dreariest**)
  1 dull or boring. **2** gloomy.
  drearily *adverb* **dreariness** *noun*

dredge *verb* (**dredges, dredging, dredged**)
  drag something up, especially by scooping at the bottom of a river or the sea.
  dredger *noun*

dregs *plural noun*
  the last drops of a liquid at the bottom of a glass, barrel, etc., together with any sediment.

drench *verb* (**drenches, drenching, drenched**)
  make wet all through; soak.

dress *noun* (*plural* **dresses**)
  1 a woman's or girl's piece of clothing with a bodice and skirt. **2** clothes; costume ♦ *fancy dress.*

dress *verb* (**dresses, dressing, dressed**)
  1 put clothes on. **2** arrange a display in a window etc.; decorate ♦ *dress the shop windows.*
  3 prepare food for cooking or eating. **4** put a dressing on a wound.
  dresser *noun*

dresser *noun* (*plural* **dressers**)
a sideboard with shelves at the top for dishes etc.

dressing *noun* (*plural* **dressings**)
1 a bandage, plaster, or ointment etc. for a wound. **2** a sauce of oil, vinegar, etc. for a salad. **3** manure or other fertilizer for spreading on the soil.

dressing gown *noun* (*plural* **dressing gowns**)
a loose garment for wearing when you are not fully dressed.

dress rehearsal *noun* (*plural* **dress rehearsals**)
a rehearsal at which the cast wear their costumes.

dribble *verb* (**dribbles, dribbling, dribbled**)
1 let saliva trickle out of your mouth. **2** (said about a liquid) flow in drops. **3** move the ball forward in football or hockey with slight touches of your feet or stick.

drift *verb* (**drifts, drifting, drifted**)
1 be carried gently along by water or air. **2** move along slowly and casually. **3** live casually with no definite objective.
drifter *noun*

drift *noun* (*plural* **drifts**)
1 a drifting movement. **2** a mass of snow or sand piled up by the wind. **3** the general meaning of what someone says.

driftwood *noun*
wood floating on the sea or washed ashore by it.

drill *noun* (*plural* **drills**)
1 a tool for making holes; a machine for boring holes or wells. **2** repeated exercises, e.g. in military training.

drill *verb* (**drills, drilling, drilled**)
1 make a hole etc. with a drill. **2** teach someone to do something by making them do repeated exercises.

drink *verb* (**drinks, drinking, drank, drunk**)
1 swallow liquid. **2** drink a lot of alcoholic drinks.
drinker *noun*

drink *noun* (*plural* **drinks**)
1 a liquid for drinking; an amount of liquid swallowed. **2** an alcoholic drink.

drip *verb* (**drips, dripping, dripped**)
fall or let something fall in drops.

drip *noun* (*plural* **drips**)
1 liquid falling in drops; the sound it makes. **2** apparatus for dripping liquid into the veins of a sick person.

drip-dry *adjective*
made of material that dries easily and does not need ironing.

dripping *noun*
fat melted from roasted meat and allowed to set.

drive *verb* (**drives, driving, drove, driven**)
1 make something or someone move. **2** operate a motor vehicle or a train etc. **3** force or compel someone to do something ♦ *Hunger drove them to steal.* **4** force someone into a state ♦ *She is driving me crazy.* **5** rush; move rapidly ♦ *Rain drove against the window.*
driver *noun*

drive *noun* (*plural* **drives**)
1 a journey in a vehicle. **2** a hard stroke in cricket or golf etc. **3** the transmitting of power to machinery ♦ *four-wheel drive.* **4** energy or enthusiasm. **5** an organized effort ♦ *a sales drive.* **6** a track for vehicles through the grounds of a house.

drive-in *adjective*
that you can use without getting out of your car.

drivel *noun*
silly talk; nonsense.

drizzle *noun*
very fine rain.

drone *verb* (**drones, droning, droned**)
1 make a deep humming sound. **2** talk in a boring voice.

drone *noun* (*plural* **drones**)
1 a droning sound. **2** a male bee.

drool *verb* (**drools, drooling, drooled**)
dribble.
drool over be very emotional about liking something.

droop *verb* (**droops, drooping, drooped**)
hang down weakly.

drop *noun* (*plural* **drops**)
1 a tiny amount of liquid. **2** a fall or decrease. **3** a descent. **4** a small round sweet. **5** a hanging ornament.

drop *verb* (**drops, dropping, dropped**)
1 fall. **2** let something fall. **3** become lower or less. **4** put down a passenger etc. ♦ *Drop me at the station.*
drop in visit someone casually.

dropout *noun* (*plural* **dropouts**)
a person who has dropped out of society or a course of study.

droppings *plural noun*
the dung of animals or birds.

drought (*say* drout) *noun* (*plural* **droughts**)
a long period of dry weather.

drown *verb* (**drowns, drowning, drowned**)
1 die or kill by suffocation under water. **2** flood or drench. **3** make so much noise that another sound cannot be heard. **drowsy** *adjective*
sleepy.
drowsily *adverb* **drowsiness** *noun*

drudge *noun* (*plural* **drudges**)
a person who does hard or tedious work.
drudgery *noun*

drug *noun* (*plural* **drugs**)
1 a substance used in medicine. 2 a substance that affects your senses or your mind, especially one causing addiction.

drug *verb* (**drugs, drugging, drugged**)
give a drug to someone, especially to make them unconscious.

drum *noun* (*plural* **drums**)
1 a musical instrument made of a cylinder with a skin or parchment stretched over one or both ends. 2 a cylindrical object or container
♦ *an oil drum.*

drum *verb* (**drums, drumming, drummed**)
1 play a drum or drums. 2 tap repeatedly on something.
drummer *noun*

drum into drive a lesson, facts etc. into a person's mind by constant repetition.

drumstick *noun* (*plural* **drumsticks**)
1 a stick for beating a drum. 2 the lower part of a cooked bird's leg.

drunk *adjective*
not able to control your behaviour through drinking too much alcohol.

drunk *noun* (*plural* **drunks**)
a person who is drunk.

drunkard *noun* (*plural* **drunkards**)
a person who is often drunk.

drunken *adjective*
1 drunk ♦ *a drunken man.* 2 caused by drinking alcohol ♦ *a drunken brawl.*

dry *adjective* (**drier, driest**)
1 without water or moisture. 2 thirsty. 3 boring or dull. 4 (said about remarks or humour) said in a matter-of-fact or ironical way ♦ *dry wit.*
drily *adverb* **dryness** *noun*

dry *verb* (**dries, drying, dried**)
make or become dry.

dry-cleaning *noun*
a method of cleaning clothes etc. using a liquid that evaporates quickly.

dual carriageway *noun* (*plural* **dual carriageways**)
a road with a dividing strip between lanes of traffic in opposite directions.

dub² *verb* (**dubs, dubbing, dubbed**)
change or add new sound to the soundtrack of a film or to a recording.

dubious (*say* **dew-bee-us**) *adjective*
doubtful.
dubiously *adverb*

duchess *noun* (*plural* **duchesses**)
a duke's wife or widow.

duchy *noun* (*plural* **duchies**)
the territory of a duke ♦ *the duchy of Cornwall.*

duck *noun* (*plural* **ducks**)
1 a swimming bird with a flat beak; the female of this. 2 a batsman's score of nought at cricket. 3 a ducking movement.

duck *verb* (**ducks, ducking, ducked**)
1 bend down quickly to avoid something. 2 go or push quickly under water. 3 dodge; avoid doing something.

duckling *noun* (*plural* **ducklings**)
a young duck.

duct *noun* (*plural* **ducts**)
a tube or channel through which liquid, gas, air, or cables can pass.

ductile *adjective*
(said about metal) able to be drawn out into fine strands.

due *adjective*
1 expected; scheduled to do something or to arrive ♦ *The train is due in ten minutes.* 2 owing; needing to be paid. 3 that ought to be given; rightful ♦ *Treat her with due respect.*
due to as a result of.

---

❶ USAGE Traditionally, correct use is as in *His lateness was due to an accident.* Some people object to the use of 'due to' without a preceding noun (e.g. 'lateness') to which it refers. However, such uses as *He was late, due to an accident* are nowadays widely regarded as acceptable. But if you prefer, you can use *because of* or *owing to* instead.

---

due *adverb*
exactly ♦ *We sailed due east.*

due *noun* (*plural* **dues**)
1 something you deserve or have a right to; proper respect ♦ *Give him his due.* 2 a fee ♦ *harbour dues.*

duel *noun* (*plural* **duels**)
a fight between two people, especially with pistols or swords.
duelling *noun* **duellist** *noun*

duet *noun* (*plural* **duets**)
a piece of music for two players or singers.

duffel coat *noun* (*plural* **duffel coats**)
a thick overcoat with a hood, fastened with toggles.

duffer *noun* (*plural* **duffers**)
a person who is stupid or not good at doing something.

duke *noun* (*plural* **dukes**)
a member of the highest rank of noblemen.
dukedom *noun*
[via early French from Latin *dux* = leader]

dull *adjective*
1 not bright or clear ♦ *dull weather.* 2 stupid. 3 boring ♦ *a dull concert.* 4 not sharp ♦ *a dull pain;* ♦ *a dull thud.*
dully *adverb* **dullness** *noun*

dumb *adjective*
1 without the ability to speak. 2 silent.
3 (*informal*) stupid.
dumbly *adverb* **dumbness** *noun*

dumbfound *verb* (**dumbfounds,
dumbfounding, dumbfounded**)
astonish; strike a person dumb with surprise.

dummy *noun* (*plural* **dummies**)
1 something made to look like a person or thing.
2 an imitation teat given to a baby to suck.

dump *noun* (*plural* **dumps**)
1 a place where something (especially rubbish)
is left or stored. 2 (*informal*) a dull or
unattractive place.

dump *verb* (**dumps, dumping, dumped**)
1 get rid of something that is not wanted.
2 put something down carelessly.

dumpling *noun* (*plural* **dumplings**)
a lump of dough cooked in a stew etc. or baked
with fruit inside.

dumpy *adjective*
short and fat.

dunce *noun* (*plural* **dunces**)
a person who is slow at learning.
[from John Duns Scotus, a Scottish philosopher
in the Middle Ages. His opponents said that his
followers could not understand new ideas]

dune *noun* (*plural* **dunes**)
a mound of loose sand shaped by the wind.

dung *noun*
solid waste matter excreted by an animal.

dungarees *plural noun*
overalls made of thick strong cloth.
[from Hindi *dungri* = the cloth they were
made of]

dungeon (*say* **dun**-jon) *noun* (*plural*
dungeons)
an underground cell for prisoners.

duo (*say* **dew**-oh) *noun* (*plural* **duos**)
a pair of people, especially playing music.

duodenum (*say* dew-o-**deen**-um) *noun* (*plural*
duodenums)
the part of the small intestine that is just below
the stomach.
duodenal *adjective*

dupe *verb* (**dupes, duping, duped**)
deceive.

duplicate (*say* **dyoop**-lik-at) *noun* (*plural*
duplicates)
1 something that is exactly the same as
something else. 2 an exact copy.

duplicate (*say* **dyoop**-lik-ayt) *verb* (**duplicates,
duplicating, duplicated**)
make or be a duplicate.
duplication *noun* **duplicator** *noun*

duplicity (*say* dew-**plis**-it-ee) *noun*
deceitfulness.

durable *adjective*
strong and likely to last.
durably *adverb* **durability** *noun*

during *preposition*
while something else is going on.

dusk *noun* (*plural* **dusks**)
twilight in the evening.

dust *noun*
tiny particles of earth or other solid material.

dust *verb* (**dusts, dusting, dusted**)
1 wipe away dust. 2 sprinkle with dust or
something powdery.

dustbin *noun* (*plural* **dustbins**)
a bin for household rubbish.

dustman *noun* (*plural* **dustmen**)
a person employed to empty dustbins and take
away rubbish.

dustpan *noun* (*plural* **dustpans**)
a pan into which dust is brushed from a floor.

dusty *adjective* (**dustier, dustiest**)
1 covered with dust. 2 like dust.

dutiful *adjective*
doing your duty; obedient.
dutifully *adverb*

duty *noun* (*plural* **duties**)
1 what you ought to do or must do. 2 a task that
must be done. 3 a tax charged on imports and on
certain other things.
on or **off duty** actually doing (or not doing)
what is your regular work.

duvet (*say* doo-vay) *noun* (*plural* **duvets**)
a kind of quilt used instead of other bedclothes.

DVD *abbreviation*
digital versatile disc (formerly digital videodisc);
a disc used for storing large amounts of audio or
video information, especially films.

dwarf *noun* (*plural* **dwarfs** or **dwarves**)
a very small person or thing.

dwarf *verb* (**dwarfs, dwarfing, dwarfed**)
make something seem small by contrast
♦ *The ocean liner dwarfed the tugs that were
towing it.*

dwelling *noun* (*plural* **dwellings**)
a house etc. to live in.

dwindle *verb* (**dwindles, dwindling,
dwindled**)
get smaller gradually.

dye *verb* (**dyes, dyeing, dyed**)
colour something by putting it into a liquid.
dyer *noun*

dye *noun* (*plural* **dyes**)
a substance used to dye things.

dynamic *adjective*
1 energetic or forceful. 2 (said about a force)
producing motion.
dynamically *adverb*

dynamics *noun*
the scientific study of force and motion.

dynamite *noun*
1 a powerful explosive. 2 something likely to make people very excited or angry.

dynamo *noun* (*plural* **dynamos**)
a machine that makes electricity.

dynasty (*say* **din**-a-stee) *noun* (*plural* **dynasties**)
a line of rulers or powerful people all from the same family.
dynastic *adjective*

dyslexia (*say* dis-**leks**-ee-a) *noun*
special difficulty in being able to read and spell, caused by a brain condition.
dyslexic *adjective*

dystrophy (*say* **dis**-trof-ee) *noun*
a disease that weakens the muscles.

Ee

E. *abbreviation*
east; eastern.

each *adjective & pronoun*
every; every one ♦ *each child*; ♦ *each of you*.

> ❶ USAGE In standard English, the pronoun *each* should be used with a singular verb and singular pronouns: ♦ *Each has chosen her own outfit.*

eager *adjective*
strongly wanting to do something; enthusiastic.
eagerly *adverb* **eagerness** *noun*

eagle *noun* (*plural* **eagles**)
a large bird of prey with very strong sight.

ear¹ *noun* (*plural* **ears**)
1 the organ of the body that is used for hearing.
2 hearing ability ♦ *She has a good ear for music.*

ear² *noun* (*plural* **ears**)
the spike of seeds at the top of a stalk of corn.

eardrum *noun* (*plural* **eardrums**)
a membrane in the ear that vibrates when sounds reach it.

earl *noun* (*plural* **earls**)
a British nobleman.
earldom *noun*

early *adjective & adverb* (**earlier**, **earliest**)
1 before the usual or expected time. 2 near the beginning ♦ *early in the book.*
earliness *noun*

earmark *verb* (**earmarks**, **earmarking**, **earmarked**)
put something aside for a particular purpose.

earn *verb* (**earns**, **earning**, **earned**)
get something by working or in return for what you have done.

earnest *adjective*
showing serious feelings or intentions.
earnestly *adverb* **earnestness** *noun*
in earnest 1 more seriously or with more determination ♦ *We began to shovel the snow in earnest.* 2 meaning what you say

earshot *noun*
the distance within which a sound can be heard.

earth *noun* (*plural* **earths**)
1 the planet (**Earth**) that we live on. 2 the ground; soil. 3 the hole where a fox or badger lives. 4 connection to the ground to complete an electrical circuit.

earth *verb* (**earths**, **earthing**, **earthed**)
connect an electrical circuit to the ground.

earthenware *noun*
pottery made of coarse baked clay.

earthly *adjective*
concerned with life on earth rather than with life after death.

earthquake *noun* (*plural* **earthquakes**)
a violent movement of part of the earth's surface.

earthy *adjective*
1 like earth or soil. 2 direct and unembarrassed about bodily functions or sexual subjects.

earwig *noun* (*plural* **earwigs**)
a crawling insect with pincers at the end of its body.
[called this because it was thought to crawl into people's ears]

ease *noun*
freedom from trouble or effort or pain
♦ *She climbed the tree with ease.*
at ease relaxed.

ease *verb* (**eases**, **easing**, **eased**)
1 make less painful or less tight or troublesome.
2 move gently into position. 3 become less severe ♦ *The pressure eased.*

easel *noun* (*plural* **easels**)
a stand for supporting a blackboard or a painting.

easily *adverb*
1 without difficulty; with ease. 2 by far ♦ *easily the best.* 3 very likely ♦ *He could easily be lying.*

east *noun*
1 the direction where the sun rises. 2 the eastern part of a country, city, etc.

east *adjective & adverb*
towards or in the east; coming from the east.
easterly *adjective* **eastern** *adjective* **easterner** *noun* **easternmost** *adjective*

Easter *noun*
the Sunday (in March or April) when Christians commemorate the resurrection of Christ; the days around it.

eastward *adjective & adverb*
towards the east.
eastwards *adverb*

easy *adjective* (**easier, easiest**)
able to be done or used or understood without
trouble.
easiness *noun*

easy *adverb*
with ease; comfortably ♦ *Take it easy!*

eat *verb* (**eats, eating, ate, eaten**)
1 chew and swallow as food. **2** have a meal
♦ *When do we eat?* **3** use up; destroy gradually
♦ *Extra expenses ate up our savings.*
[from Old English]

eaves *plural noun*
the overhanging edges of a roof.

eavesdrop *verb* (**eavesdrops, eavesdropping,
eavesdropped**)
listen secretly to a private conversation.
eavesdropper *noun*

ebb *noun* (*plural* **ebbs**)
1 the movement of the tide when it is going out,
away from the land. **2** a low point ♦ *Our courage
was at a low ebb.*

eccentric (*say* ik-**sen**-trik) *adjective*
behaving strangely.
eccentrically *adverb* **eccentricity** (*say*
ek-sen-**triss**-it-ee) *noun*

ecclesiastical (*say* ik-lee-zee-**ast**-ik-al)
adjective
to do with the Church or the clergy.

echo *noun* (*plural* **echoes**)
a sound that is heard again as it is reflected off
something.

echo *verb* (**echoes, echoing, echoed**)
1 make an echo. **2** repeat a sound or saying.

eclair (*say* ay-**klair**) *noun* (*plural* **eclairs**)
a finger-shaped cake of pastry with a creamy
filling.

eclipse *noun* (*plural* **eclipses**)
the blocking of the sun's or moon's light when
the moon or the earth is in the way.

ecology (*say* ee-kol-o-jee) *noun*
the study of living things in relation to each other
and to where they live.
ecological *adjective* **ecologically** *adverb*
ecologist *noun*

economic (*say* ee-kon-om-ik) *adjective*
1 to do with economy or economics. **2** profitable.

economical *adjective*
using as little of something as possible.
economically *adverb*

economics *noun*
the study of how money is used and how goods
and services are provided and used.
economist *noun*

economize *verb* (**economizes, economizing,
economized**)
be economical; use or spend less ♦ *We need to
economize on fuel.*

economy *noun* (*plural* **economies**)
1 a country's or household's income (e.g. from
what it sells or earns) and the way this is spent
(e.g. on goods and services). **2** being
economical. **3** a saving ♦ *You need to make
economies.*

ecstasy (*say* ek-sta-see) *noun*
1 a feeling of great delight. **2** an illegal drug that
makes people feel very energetic and can cause
hallucinations.

ecstatic (*say* ik-**stat**-ik) *adjective* **ecstatically**
adverb

eddy *noun* (*plural* **eddies**)
a swirling patch of water or air or smoke etc.

edge *noun* (*plural* **edges**)
1 the part along the side or end of something.
2 the sharp part of a knife or axe or other cutting
instrument.
be on edge be tense and irritable.

edgy *adjective*
tense and irritable.
edginess *noun*

edible *adjective*
suitable for eating, not poisonous ♦ *edible fruits.*

edit *verb* (**edits, editing, edited**)
1 be the editor of a newspaper or other
publication. **2** make written material ready for
publishing. **3** choose and put the parts of a film
or tape recording etc. into order.

edition *noun* (*plural* **editions**)
1 the form in which something is published
♦ *a paperback edition.* **2** all the copies of a book
etc. issued at the same time ♦ *the first edition.*
3 an individual television or radio programme in
a series.

editor *noun* (*plural* **editors**)
1 the person in charge of a newspaper or a
section of it. **2** a person who edits something.

editorial *adjective*
to do with editing or editors.

editorial *noun* (*plural* **editorials**)
a newspaper article giving the editor's comments
on something.

educate *verb* (**educates, educating, educated**)
provide people with education.
educative *adjective* **educator** *noun*

educated *adjective*
showing a high standard of knowledge and culture, as a result of a good education.

education *noun*
the process of training people's minds and abilities so that they acquire knowledge and develop skills.
educational *adjective* **educationally** *adverb*
educationist *noun*

EEC *abbreviation*
European Economic Community (= the Common Market).

eel *noun* (*plural* **eels**)
a long fish that looks like a snake.

eerie *adjective* (**eerier, eeriest**)
strange in a frightening or mysterious way.
eerily *adverb* **eeriness** *noun*

effect *noun* (*plural* **effects**)
1 a change that is produced by an action or cause; a result. 2 an impression that is produced by something ♦ *a cheerful effect.*

---

❶ USAGE Do not confuse with *affect.*

---

effective *adjective*
1 producing the effect that is wanted.
2 impressive and striking.
effectively *adverb* **effectiveness** *noun*

effeminate *adjective*
(said about a man) having qualities that are thought to be feminine.
effeminacy *noun*

efficient *adjective*
doing work well; effective.
efficiently *adverb* **efficiency** *noun*

effort *noun* (*plural* **efforts**)
1 the use of energy; the energy used.
2 something difficult or tiring. 3 an attempt
♦ *This painting is a good effort.*

e.g. *abbreviation*
for example.

---

❶ USAGE Do not confuse with *i.e.*

---

egg¹ *noun* (*plural* **eggs**)
1 a more or less round object produced by the female of birds, fish, reptiles, and insects, which may develop into a new individual if fertilized. 2 a hen's or duck's egg used as food. 3 an ovum.

egg² *verb* (**eggs, egging, egged**)
encourage someone with taunts or dares etc.
♦ *We egged him on.*

ego (*say* eeg-oh) *noun* (*plural* **egos**)
a person's self or self-respect.

Eid (*say* eed) *noun*
a Muslim festival marking the end of the fast of Ramadan.

eiderdown *noun* (*plural* **eiderdowns**)
a quilt stuffed with soft material.

eight *adjective* & *noun*(*plural* **eights**)
the number 8.
eighth *adjective* & *noun*

eighteen *adjective* & *noun*
the number 18.
eighteenth *adjective* & *noun*

eighty *adjective* & *noun*(*plural* **eighties**)
the number 80.
eightieth *adjective* & *noun*

either *adjective* & *pronoun*
1 one or the other of two ♦ *Either team can win*; ♦ *either of them.* 2 both of two ♦ *There are fields on either side of the river.*

either *adverb*
also; similarly ♦ *If you won't go, I won't either.*

either *conjunction* (used with *or*)
the first of two possibilities ♦ *He is either ill or drunk.* ♦ *Either come right in or go away.*

ejaculate *verb* (**ejaculates, ejaculating, ejaculated**)
1 (said about a man) produce semen from the penis. 2 (*formal*) suddenly say something.
ejaculation *noun*

eject *verb* (**ejects, ejecting, ejected**)
1 send something out forcefully. 2 force someone to leave. 3 (said about a pilot) be thrown out of an aircraft in a special seat in an emergency.
ejection *noun* **ejector** *noun*

elaborate (*say* il-ab-er-at) *adjective*
having many parts or details; complicated.
elaborately *adverb* **elaborateness** *noun*
elaborate (*say* il-ab-er-ayt) *verb* (**elaborates, elaborating, elaborated**)
explain or work something out in detail.
elaboration *noun*

elastic *noun*
cord or material woven with strands of rubber etc. so that it can stretch.

elastic *adjective*
able to be stretched or squeezed and then go back to its original length or shape.
elasticity *noun*

elbow *noun* (*plural* **elbows**)
the joint in the middle of the arm.

elbow *verb* (**elbows, elbowing, elbowed**)
push with the elbow.

elder¹ *adjective*
older ♦ *my elder brother.*

elder *noun* (*plural* **elders**)
1 an older person ♦ *Respect your elders!*
2 an official in certain Churches.

elder² *noun* (*plural* **elders**)
a tree with white flowers and black berries.
elderberry *noun*

elderly *adjective*
rather old.

eldest *adjective*
oldest.

elect *verb* (**elects, electing, elected**)
1 choose by voting. **2** choose to do something; decide.

election *noun* (*plural* **elections**)
electing; the process of electing Members of Parliament.

electorate *noun* (*plural* **electorates**)
all the electors.

electric *adjective*
1 to do with or worked by electricity. **2** causing sudden excitement ♦ *The news had an electric effect.*
electrical *adjective* **electrically** *adverb*

electric chair *noun*
an electrified chair used for capital punishment in the USA.

electrician *noun* (*plural* **electricians**)
a person whose job is to deal with electrical equipment.

electricity *noun*
a form of energy carried by certain particles of matter (electrons and protons), used for lighting and heating and for making machines work.

electrify *verb* (**electrifies, electrifying, electrified**)
1 give an electric charge to something. **2** supply something with electric power; cause something to work with electricity. **3** thrill with sudden excitement.
electrification *noun*

electrocute *verb* (**electrocutes, electrocuting, electrocuted**)
kill by electricity.
electrocution *noun*

electrode *noun* (*plural* **electrodes**)
a solid conductor through which electricity enters or leaves a vacuum tube.

electromagnet *noun* (*plural* **electromagnets**)
a magnet worked by electricity.
electromagnetic *adjective*

electron *noun* (*plural* **electrons**)
a particle of matter with a negative electric charge.

electronic *adjective*
produced or worked by a flow of electrons.
electronically *adverb*

electronic mail *noun*
a system of sending messages and data from one computer to another by means of a network.

electronics *noun*
the use or study of electronic devices.

elegant *adjective*
graceful and dignified.
elegantly *adverb* **elegance** *noun*

element *noun* (*plural* **elements**)
1 each of the parts that make up a whole thing. **2** each of about 100 substances composed of atoms that have the same number of protons. **3** a basic or elementary principle ♦ *the elements of algebra.* **4** a wire or coil that gives out heat in an electric fire or cooker etc. **5** the environment or circumstances that suit you best ♦ *Karen is really in her element at parties.*
the elements the forces of weather, such as rain, wind, and cold.

elementary *adjective*
dealing with the simplest stages of something; easy.

elephant *noun* (*plural* **elephants**)
a very large animal with a trunk and tusks.

elevate *verb* (**elevates, elevating, elevated**)
lift or raise something to a higher position.
elevation *noun*

eleven *adjective* & *noun*(*plural* **elevens**)
the number 11.
eleventh *adjective* & *noun*

elicit (*say* ill-**iss**-it) *verb* (**elicits, eliciting, elicited**)
draw out information by reasoning or questioning.

eligible (*say* el-**ij**-ib-ul) *adjective*
qualified or suitable for something.
eligibility *noun*

eliminate *verb* (**eliminates, eliminating, eliminated**)
get rid of something.
elimination *noun*

elision (*say* il-**lizh**-on) *noun*
omitting part of a word in pronouncing it, e.g. in saying *I'm* for *I am.*

elite (*say* ay-**leet**) *noun*
a group of people given privileges which are not given to others.

ellipse (*say* il-**ips**) *noun* (*plural* **ellipses**)
an oval shape.

elliptical (*say* il-**ip**-tik-al) *adjective*
1 shaped like an ellipse. **2** with some words omitted ♦ *an elliptical phrase.*
elliptically *adverb*

elm *noun* (*plural* **elms**)
a tall tree with rough leaves.

elocution (*say* el-o-**kew**-shon) *noun*
the art of speaking clearly and correctly.

elongated *adjective*
made longer; lengthened.
elongation *noun*

elope *verb* (**elopes, eloping, eloped**)
run away secretly to get married.
elopement *noun*

eloquent *adjective*
speaking fluently and expressing ideas vividly.
eloquently *adverb* **eloquence** *noun*

else *adverb*
1 besides; other ♦ *Nobody else knows.*
2 otherwise; if not ♦ *Run or else you'll be late.*

elsewhere *adverb*
somewhere else.

elude (*say* il-ood) *verb* (**eludes, eluding, eluded**)
avoid being caught by someone ♦ *The fox eluded the hounds.*
elusive *adjective*

---

❶ USAGE Do not confuse with *allude*.

---

email *noun*
electronic mail.

emancipate (*say* im-an-sip-ayt) *verb* (**emancipates, emancipating, emancipated**)
set free from slavery or other restraints.
emancipation *noun*

embalm *verb* (**embalms, embalming, embalmed**)
preserve a corpse from decay by using spices or chemicals.

embankment *noun* (*plural* **embankments**)
a long bank of earth or stone to hold back water or support a road or railway.

embargo *noun* (*plural* **embargoes**)
an official ban, especially on trade with a country.

embark *verb* (**embarks, embarking, embarked**)
put or go on board a ship or aircraft.
embarkation *noun*
embark on begin ♦ *They embarked on a dangerous exercise.*

embarrass *verb* (**embarrasses, embarrassing, embarrassed**)
make someone feel awkward or ashamed.
embarrassment *noun*

embassy *noun* (*plural* **embassies**)
1 an ambassador and his or her staff.
2 the building where they work.

embellish *verb* (**embellishes, embellishing, embellished**)
ornament something; add details to it.
embellishment *noun*

embers *plural noun*
small pieces of glowing coal or wood in a dying fire.

embezzle *verb* (**embezzles, embezzling, embezzled**)
take dishonestly money that was left in your care.
embezzlement *noun*

emblem *noun* (*plural* **emblems**)
a symbol that represents something ♦ *The crown is a royal emblem.*
emblematic *adjective*

embody *verb* (**embodies, embodying, embodied**)
1 express principles or ideas in a visible form ♦ *The house embodies our idea of a modern home.* **2** include or contain ♦ *Parts of the old treaty are embodied in the new one.*
embodiment *noun*

embrace *verb* (**embraces, embracing, embraced**)
1 hold someone closely in your arms. **2** include a number of things. **3** accept or adopt a cause or belief.

embrace *noun* (*plural* **embraces**)
a hug.

embroider *verb* (**embroiders, embroidering, embroidered**)
1 decorate cloth with needlework. **2** add made-up details to a story to make it more interesting.
embroidery *noun*

embryo (*say* em-bree-oh) *noun* (*plural* **embryos**)
1 a baby or young animal as it starts to grow in the womb; a young bird growing in an egg.
2 anything in its earliest stages of development.
embryonic (*say* em-bree-on-ik) *adjective*

emend *verb* (**emends, emending, emended**)
remove errors from a piece of writing.

emerald *noun* (*plural* **emeralds**)
1 a bright-green precious stone. **2** its colour.

emerge *verb* (**emerges, emerging, emerged**)
1 come out or appear. **2** become known.
emergence *noun* **emergent** *adjective*

emergency *noun* (*plural* **emergencies**)
a sudden serious happening needing prompt action.

emigrate *verb* (**emigrates, emigrating, emigrated**)
leave your own country and go and live in another.
emigration *noun* **emigrant** *noun*

---

❶ USAGE People are *emigrants* from the country they leave and *immigrants* in the country where they settle.

---

eminent *adjective*
1 famous and respected. **2** outstanding and conspicuous.
eminently *adverb* **eminence** *noun*

emit *verb* (**emits, emitting, emitted**)
send out light, heat, fumes, etc.
emission *noun*

emotion *noun* (*plural* **emotions**)
a strong feeling in the mind, such as love or hate.
emotional *adjective* **emotionally** *adverb*

emperor *noun* (*plural* **emperors**)
a man who rules an empire.

emphasis (*say* em-fa-sis) *noun* (*plural*
emphases)
1 special importance given to something.
2 stress put on a word or part of a word.
emphasize *verb*

emphatic (*say* im-**fat**-ik) *adjective*
using emphasis.
emphatically *adverb*

empire *noun* (*plural* **empires**)
1 a group of countries controlled by one person
or government. **2** a large business organization
controlled by one person or group.

employ *verb* (**employs, employing, employed**)
1 pay a person to work for you. **2** make use of
♦ *Our doctor employs the most modern methods.*
employment *noun*

employee *noun* (*plural* **employees**)
a person employed by someone.

employer *noun* (*plural* **employers**)
a person or organization that employs people.

empress *noun* (*plural* **empresses**)
1 a woman who rules an empire. **2** an emperor's
wife.

empty *adjective*
1 with nothing in it. **2** with nobody in it.
3 with no meaning or no effect ♦ *empty
promises.*
emptily *adverb* **emptiness** *noun*

empty *verb* (**empties, emptying, emptied**)
make or become empty.

emulsion *noun* (*plural* **emulsions**)
1 a creamy or slightly oily liquid. **2** a kind of
water-based paint. **3** the coating on photographic
film which is sensitive to light.

enable *verb* (**enables, enabling, enabled**)
give the means or ability to do something.

enamel *noun* (*plural* **enamels**)
1 a shiny substance for coating metal. **2** paint
that dries hard and shiny. **3** the hard shiny
surface of teeth.

encamp *verb* (**encamps, encamping,
encamped**)
settle in a camp.

encampment *noun* (*plural* **encampments**)
a camp.

enchant *verb* (**enchants, enchanting,
enchanted**)
1 put someone under a magic spell. **2** fill
someone with intense delight.
enchanter *noun* **enchantment** *noun*
enchantress *noun*

encircle *verb* (**encircles, encircling, encircled**)
surround.
encirclement *noun*

enclose *verb* (**encloses, enclosing, enclosed**)
1 put a wall or fence round; shut in on all sides.
2 put something into a box or envelope etc.

enclosure *noun* (*plural* **enclosures**)
1 enclosing. **2** an enclosed area. **3** something
enclosed with a letter or parcel.

encore (*say* on-kor) *noun* (*plural* **encores**)
an extra item performed at a concert etc. after
previous items have been applauded.

encounter *verb* (**encounters, encountering,
encountered**)
1 meet someone unexpectedly. **2** experience
♦ *We encountered some difficulties.*

encounter *noun* (*plural* **encounters**)
1 an unexpected meeting. **2** a battle.

encourage *verb* (**encourages, encouraging,
encouraged**)
1 give confidence or hope; hearten. **2** try to
persuade; urge. **3** stimulate; help to develop
♦ *We need to encourage healthy eating.*
encouragement *noun*

encroach *verb* (**encroaches, encroaching,
encroached**)
intrude upon someone's rights; go further than
the proper limits ♦ *The extra work would
encroach on their free time.*
encroachment *noun*

encrust *verb* (**encrusts, encrusting, encrusted**)
cover with a crust or layer.
encrustation *noun*

encumber *verb* (**encumbers, encumbering,
encumbered**)
be a burden to; hamper.
encumbrance *noun*

encyclopedia *noun* (*plural* **encyclopedias**)
a book or set of books containing all kinds of
information.
encyclopedic *adjective*

end *noun* (*plural* **ends**)
1 the last part or extreme point of something.
2 the half of a sports pitch or court defended or
occupied by one team or player. **3** destruction or
death. **4** purpose ♦ *She did it to gain her own
ends.*

end *verb* (**ends, ending, ended**)
bring or come to an end.

endanger *verb* (**endangers, endangering,
endangered**)
cause danger to.

endless *adjective*
1 never stopping. **2** with the ends joined to make
a continuous strip for use in machinery etc.
♦ *an endless belt.*
endlessly *adverb*

endow *verb* (**endows, endowing, endowed**)
1 provide a source of income to establish
something ♦ *She endowed a scholarship.*
2 provide with an ability or quality ♦ *He was
endowed with great talent.*
endowment *noun*

endure *verb* (**endures, enduring, endured**)
1 suffer or put up with pain or hardship etc.
2 continue to exist; last.
endurable *adjective* **endurance** *noun*

enemy *noun* (*plural* **enemies**)
1 one who hates and opposes or seeks to harm
another. **2** a nation or army etc. at war with
another.

energetic *adjective*
full of energy.
energetically *adverb*

energy *noun* (*plural* **energies**)
1 strength to do things, liveliness. **2** the ability of
matter or radiation to do work. Energy is
measured in joules. **3** power obtained from fuel
and other resources and used for light and heat,
the operation of machinery, etc.

enforce *verb* (**enforces, enforcing, enforced**)
compel people to obey a law or rule.
enforcement *noun* **enforceable** *adjective*

engage *verb* (**engages, engaging, engaged**)
1 arrange to employ or use ♦ *Engage a typist.*
2 occupy the attention of ♦ *They engaged her in
conversation.* **3** begin a battle with ♦ *We engaged
the enemy.*

engaged *adjective*
1 having promised to marry somebody.
2 in use; occupied.

engagement *noun* (*plural* **engagements**)
1 engaging something. **2** a promise to marry
somebody. **3** an arrangement to meet somebody
or do something. **4** a battle.

engaging *adjective*
attractive or charming.

engine *noun* (*plural* **engines**)
1 a machine that provides power. **2** a vehicle that
pulls a railway train; a locomotive.
[from old French: it originally meant 'cleverness'
and is related to *ingenious*]

engineer *noun* (*plural* **engineers**)
an expert in engineering.
engineer *verb* (**engineers, engineering,
engineered**)
plan and construct or cause to happen
♦ *He engineered a meeting between them.*

engineering *noun*
the design and building or control of machinery
or of structures such as roads and bridges.

engrave *verb* (**engraves, engraving,
engraved**)
carve words or lines etc. on a surface.
engraver *noun* **engraving** *noun*

enigma (*say* in-**ig**-ma) *noun* (*plural* **enigmas**)
something very difficult to understand; a puzzle.

enigmatic (*say* en-ig-**mat**-ik) *adjective*
mysterious and puzzling.
enigmatically *adverb*

enjoy *verb* (**enjoys, enjoying, enjoyed**)
get pleasure from something.
enjoyable *adjective* **enjoyment** *noun*

enlarge *verb* (**enlarges, enlarging, enlarged**)
make bigger.
enlargement *noun*

enlighten *verb* (**enlightens, enlightening,
enlightened**)
give more knowledge or information to a person.
enlightenment *noun*

enlist *verb* (**enlists, enlisting, enlisted**)
1 join the armed forces. **2** obtain someone's
support or services etc. ♦ *enlist their help.*
enlistment *noun*

enmity *noun*
being somebody's enemy; hostility.

enormous *adjective*
very large; huge.
enormously *adverb* **enormousness** *noun*

enough *adjective* & *noun* & *adverb*
as much or as many as necessary ♦ *enough food;*
♦ *I have had enough;* ♦ *Are you warm enough?*

enquire *verb* (**enquires, enquiring, enquired**)
1 ask for information ♦ *He enquired if I was well.*
2 investigate something carefully.

❶ USAGE See the note at *inquire.*

enquiry *noun* (*plural* **enquiries**)
1 a question. **2** an investigation.

enrage *verb* (**enrages, enraging, enraged**)
make someone very angry.

enrich *verb* (**enriches, enriching, enriched**)
make richer.
enrichment *noun*

enrol *verb* (**enrols, enrolling, enrolled**)
1 become a member of a society etc.
2 make someone into a member.
enrolment *noun*

ensemble (*say* on-**somb**l) *noun* (*plural*
ensembles)
1 a group of things that go together. **2** a group of
musicians. **3** a matching outfit of clothes.

enslave *verb* (**enslaves, enslaving, enslaved**)
make a slave of someone; force someone into
slavery.
enslavement *noun*

ensure *verb* (**ensures, ensuring, ensured**)
make certain of; guarantee ♦ *Good food will
ensure good health.*

❶ USAGE Do not confuse with *insure.*

entail *verb* (entails, entailing, entailed)
make a thing necessary; involve ♦ *This plan entails danger.*
entailment *noun*

entangle *verb* (entangles, entangling, entangled)
tangle.
entanglement *noun*

enter *verb* (enters, entering, entered)
1 come in or go in. 2 put something into a list or book. 3 type something into a computer. 4 register as a competitor.

enterprise *noun* (*plural* **enterprises**)
1 being enterprising; adventurous spirit. 2 an undertaking or project. 3 business activity ♦ *private enterprise.*

enterprising *adjective*
willing to undertake new or adventurous projects.

entertain *verb* (entertains, entertaining, entertained)
1 amuse. 2 have people as guests and give them food and drink. 3 consider ♦ *He refused to entertain the idea.*
entertainer *noun*

entertainment *noun* (*plural* **entertainments**)
1 entertaining; being entertained. 2 something performed before an audience to amuse or interest them.

enthusiasm *noun* (*plural* **enthusiasms**)
a strong liking, interest, or excitement.
enthusiast *noun* **enthusiastic** *adjective*

entire *adjective*
whole or complete.
entirely *adverb*

entirety (*say* int-I-rit-ee) *noun*
the whole of something.
in its entirety in its complete form.

entitle *verb* (entitles, entitling, entitled)
give the right to have something ♦ *This coupon entitles you to a ticket.*
entitlement *noun*

entitled *adjective*
having as a title ♦ *a short poem entitled 'Spring'.*

entomology (*say* en-tom-**ol**-o-jee) *noun*
the study of insects.
entomologist *noun*

entrance¹ (*say* en-trans) *noun* (*plural* entrances)
1 the way into a place. 2 entering ♦ *Her entrance is the signal for applause.*

entrance² (*say* in-**trahns**) *verb* (entrances, entrancing, entranced)
fill with intense delight; enchant.

entrant *noun* (*plural* **entrants**)
someone who enters for an examination or contest etc.

entrench *verb* (entrenches, entrenching, entrenched)
1 fix or establish firmly ♦ *These ideas are entrenched in his mind.* 2 settle in a well-defended position.
entrenchment *noun*

entrust *verb* (entrusts, entrusting, entrusted)
place a person or thing in someone's care.

entry *noun* (*plural* **entries**)
1 an entrance. 2 something entered in a list, diary, or reference book. 3 something entered in a competition ♦ *Send your entries to this address.*

entwine *verb* (entwines, entwining, entwined)
twine round.

enumerate *verb* (enumerates, enumerating, enumerated)
count; list one by one.

envelop (*say* en-vel-op) *verb* (envelops, enveloping, enveloped)
cover or wrap round something completely.

envelope (*say* en-vel-ohp) *noun* (*plural* envelopes)
a wrapper or covering, especially a folded cover for a letter.

envious *adjective*
feeling envy.
enviously *adverb*

environment *noun* (*plural* **environments**)
1 surroundings, especially as they affect people's lives. 2 the natural world of the land, sea, and air.
environmental *adjective* **environmentally** *adverb*

environmentalist *noun* (*plural* environmentalists)
a person who wants to protect or improve the environment.

environmentally friendly *adjective*
not harmful to the environment.

envy *noun*
1 a feeling of discontent you have when someone possesses things that you would like to have for yourself. 2 something causing this ♦ *Their car is the envy of all their friends.*

envy *verb* (envies, envying, envied)
feel envy towards someone.

enzyme *noun* (*plural* **enzymes**)
a kind of substance that assists chemical processes.

epic *noun* (*plural* **epics**)
1 a long poem or story about heroic deeds or history. 2 a spectacular film.

epicentre *noun* (*plural* **epicentres**)
the point where an earthquake reaches the earth's surface.

epidemic noun (plural **epidemics**)
an outbreak of a disease that spreads quickly among the people of an area.

epigram noun (plural **epigrams**)
a short witty saying.

epilepsy noun
a disease of the nervous system, causing convulsions.
epileptic adjective & noun

epilogue (say ep-il-og) noun (plural **epilogues**)
a short section at the end of a book or play etc.

episode noun (plural **episodes**)
1 one event in a series of happenings.
2 one programme in a radio or television serial.

epitaph noun (plural **epitaphs**)
words written on a tomb or describing a person who has died.

epithet noun (plural **epithets**)
an adjective; words expressing something special about a person or thing, e.g. 'the Great' in Alfred the Great.

equal adjective
1 the same in amount, size, or value etc.
2 having the necessary strength, courage, or ability etc. ♦ She was equal to the task.
equally adverb

equal noun (plural **equals**)
a person or thing that is equal to another ♦ She has no equal.

equal verb (**equals, equalling, equalled**)
1 be the same in amount, size, or value etc.
2 match or be as good as ♦ No one has yet equalled this score.

equality noun
being equal.

equalize verb (**equalizes, equalizing, equalized**)
make things equal.
equalization noun

equation noun (plural **equations**)
(in mathematics) a statement that two amounts etc. are equal, e.g. $3 + 4 = 2 + 5$.

equator noun (plural **equators**)
an imaginary line round the Earth at an equal distance from the North and South Poles.

equatorial (say ek-wa-tor-ee-al) adjective
to do with or near the equator.

equilateral (say ee-kwi-lat-er-al) adjective
(said about a triangle) having all sides equal.

equilibrium (say ee-kwi-lib-ree-um) noun
1 a balance between different forces, influences, etc. 2 a balanced state of mind.

equinox (say ek-win-oks) noun (plural **equinoxes**)
the time of year when day and night are equal in length (about 20 March in spring, about 22 September in autumn).
equinoctial adjective

equip verb (**equips, equipping, equipped**)
supply with what is needed.

equipment noun
the things needed for a particular purpose.

equivalent adjective
equal in importance, meaning, value, etc.
equivalence noun

-er¹ and **-ier** suffix
can form the comparative of adjectives and adverbs (e.g. high/higher, lazy/lazier).

-er² suffix
can form nouns meaning 'a person or thing that does something' (e.g. farmer, computer).

era (say eer-a) noun (plural **eras**)
a period of history.

eradicate verb (**eradicates, eradicating, eradicated**)
get rid of something; remove all traces of it.
eradication noun

erase verb (**erases, erasing, erased**)
1 rub something out. 2 wipe out a recording on magnetic tape.
eraser noun

erect adjective
standing straight up.

erect verb (**erects, erecting, erected**)
set up or build something.
erection noun **erector** noun

erosion noun
the wearing away of the earth's surface by the action of water, wind, etc.

erotic adjective
arousing sexual feelings.
erotically adverb

errand noun (plural **errands**)
a short journey to take a message or fetch goods etc.

erratic (say ir-at-ik) adjective
1 not regular. 2 not reliable.
erratically adverb

error noun (plural **errors**)
a mistake.

erupt verb (**erupts, erupting, erupted**)
1 burst out. 2 when a volcano erupts, it shoots out lava.
eruption noun

escalate verb (**escalates, escalating, escalated**)
make or become greater, more serious, or more intense ♦ The riots escalated into a war.
escalation noun

escalator noun (plural **escalators**)
a staircase with an endless line of steps moving up or down.

escapade (say es-ka-**payd**) noun (plural **escapades**)
a reckless adventure.

escape verb (**escapes, escaping, escaped**)
1 get yourself free; get out or away. 2 avoid something ♦ He escaped punishment.
3 be forgotten by someone ♦ Her name escapes me for the moment.

escape noun (plural **escapes**)
1 escaping. 2 a way to escape.

escapism noun
escaping from the difficulties of life by thinking about or doing more pleasant things.
escapist adjective

escort (say ess-kort) noun (plural **escorts**)
a person or group accompanying a person or thing, especially to give protection.

escort (say iss-**kort**) verb (**escorts, escorting, escorted**)
act as an escort to somebody or something.

especially adverb
1 in particular. 2 to a great extent.

espionage (say ess-pee-on-ah*zh*) noun
spying.

espresso noun (plural **espressos**)
coffee made by forcing steam through ground coffee beans.

Esq. abbreviation
(short for **Esquire**) a title written after a man's surname where no title is used before his name.

-ess suffix
forms feminine nouns (e.g. lioness, princess).

essay (say ess-ay) noun (plural **essays**)
1 a short piece of writing in prose. 2 an attempt.

essence noun (plural **essences**)
1 the most important quality or element of something. 2 a concentrated liquid.

essential adjective
not able to be done without.
essentially adverb

essential noun (plural **essentials**)
an essential thing.

-est or **-iest** suffix
can form the superlative of adjectives and adverbs (e.g. high/highest, lazy/laziest).

establish verb (**establishes, establishing, established**)
1 set up a business, government, or relationship etc. on a firm basis. 2 show something to be true; prove ♦ He established his innocence.
the established Church a country's national Church, officially recognized as such by law.

establishment noun (plural **establishments**)
1 establishing something. 2 a business firm or other institution.
the Establishment people who are established in positions of power and influence.

estate noun (plural **estates**)
1 an area of land with a set of houses or factories on it. 2 a large area of land owned by one person. 3 all that a person owns when he or she dies.
4 (old use) a condition or status ♦ the holy estate of matrimony.

estate agent noun (plural **estate agents**)
a person whose business is selling or letting houses and land.

esteem verb (**esteems, esteeming, esteemed**)
think that a person or thing is excellent.

esteem noun
respect and admiration.

estimable adjective
worthy of esteem.

estimate (say ess-tim-at) noun (plural **estimates**)
a rough calculation or guess about an amount or value.

estimate (say ess-tim-ayt) verb (**estimates, estimating, estimated**)
make an estimate.
estimation noun

estuary (say ess-tew-er-ee) noun (plural **estuaries**)
the mouth of a river where it reaches the sea and the tide flows in and out.

etc. abbreviation
(short for **et cetera**) and other similar things; and so on.

etch verb (**etches, etching, etched**)
1 engrave a picture with acid on a metal plate, especially for printing. 2 if something is etched on your mind or memory, it has made a deep impression and you will never forget it.
etcher noun

eternal adjective
lasting for ever; not ending or changing.
eternally adverb **eternity** noun

ether (say ee-ther) noun
1 a colourless liquid that evaporates easily into fumes that are used as an anaesthetic.
2 the upper air.

ethereal (say ith-**eer**-ee-al) adjective
light and delicate.
ethereally adverb

ethical (say eth-ik-al) adjective
1 to do with ethics. 2 morally right; honourable.
ethically adverb

ethics (say eth-iks) plural noun
standards of right behaviour; moral principles.

ethnic *adjective*
belonging to a particular racial group within a larger set of people.

ethnic cleansing *noun*
the mass expulsion or killing of one ethnic group by another in an area.

etiquette (*say* et-ik-et) *noun*
the rules of correct behaviour.

etymology (*say* et-im-ol-o-jee) *noun* (*plural* etymologies)
1 an account of the origin of a word and its meaning. 2 the study of the origins of words.
etymological *adjective*

EU *abbreviation*
European Union.

eucalyptus (*say* yoo-kal-**ip**-tus) *noun* (*plural* eucalyptuses)
1 a kind of evergreen tree. 2 a strong-smelling oil obtained from its leaves.

Eucharist (*say* yoo-ker-ist) *noun*
the Christian sacrament in which bread and wine are consecrated and swallowed, commemorating the Last Supper of Christ and his disciples.

eulogy (*say* yoo-loj-ee) *noun* (*plural* eulogies)
a piece of praise for a person or thing.

euphemism (*say* yoo-fim-izm) *noun* (*plural* euphemisms)
a mild word or phrase used instead of an offensive or frank one; *'to pass away'* is a euphemism for *'to die'*.
euphemistic *adjective* **euphemistically** *adverb*

euro *noun* (*plural* euros or euro)
the currency which replaced the national currencies of several EU states in 2002.

European *adjective*
to do with Europe or its people.
European *noun*

euthanasia (*say* yooth-an-**ay**-zee-a) *noun*
causing somebody to die gently and without pain, especially when they are suffering from a painful incurable disease.

evacuate *verb* (evacuates, evacuating, evacuated)
1 move people away from a dangerous place.
2 make a thing empty of air or other contents.
evacuation *noun*

evacuee *noun* (*plural* evacuees)
a person who has been evacuated.

evade *verb* (evades, evading, evaded)
avoid a person or thing by cleverness or trickery.

evaluate *verb* (evaluates, evaluating, evaluated)
estimate the value of something; assess.
evaluation *noun*

evaporate *verb* (evaporates, evaporating, evaporated)
1 change from liquid into steam or vapour.
2 cease to exist ♦ *Their enthusiasm had evaporated.*
evaporation *noun*

evasion *noun* (*plural* evasions)
1 evading. 2 an evasive answer or excuse.

evasive *adjective*
trying to avoid answering something; not frank or straightforward.
evasively *adverb* **evasiveness** *noun*

even *adjective*
1 level and smooth. 2 not varying. 3 calm; not easily upset ♦ *an even temper.* 4 equal ♦ *Our scores were even.* 5 able to be divided exactly by two ♦ *Six and fourteen are even numbers.* (Compare **odd**.)
evenly *adverb* **evenness** *noun*
get even take revenge.

even *verb* (evens, evening, evened)
make or become even.

even *adverb*
(used to emphasize a word or statement)
♦ *She ran even faster.*
even so although that is correct.

even-handed *adjective*
fair and impartial.

evening *noun* (*plural* evenings)
the time at the end of the day before most people go to bed.

event *noun* (*plural* events)
1 something that happens, especially something important. 2 a race or competition that forms part of a sports contest.

eventful *adjective*
full of happenings.

eventual *adjective*
happening at last ♦ *his eventual success.*
eventually *adverb*

ever *adverb*
1 at any time ♦ *the best thing I ever did.* 2 always ♦ *ever hopeful.* 3 (*informal,* used for emphasis) ♦ *Why ever didn't you tell me?*

evergreen *adjective*
having green leaves all the year.
evergreen *noun*

every *adjective*
each without any exceptions ♦ *We enjoyed every minute.*
every one each one. **every other day** or **week** etc., each alternate one; every second one.

---

❶ USAGE Follow with a singular verb, e.g. *Every one of them is growing* (not 'are growing').

---

everybody *pronoun*
every person.

everyday *adjective*
ordinary; usual ♦ *everyday clothes.*

everyone *pronoun*
everybody.

everything *pronoun*
1 all things; all. 2 the only or most important thing ♦ *Beauty is not everything.*

everywhere *adverb*
in every place.

evict *verb* (evicts, evicting, evicted)
make people move out from where they are living.
eviction *noun*

evidence *noun*
1 anything that gives people reason to believe something. 2 statements made or objects produced in a lawcourt to prove something.

evident *adjective*
obvious; clearly seen.
evidently *adverb*

evil *adjective*
morally bad; wicked.
evilly *adverb*

evil *noun* (*plural* evils)
1 wickedness. 2 something unpleasant or harmful.

evolution (*say* ee-vol-oo-shon) *noun*
1 gradual change into something different.
2 the development of animals and plants from earlier or simpler forms.
evolutionary *adjective*

evolve *verb* (evolves, evolving, evolved)
develop gradually or naturally.

ewe (*say* yoo) *noun* (*plural* ewes)
a female sheep.

ex- *prefix* (changing to **ef-** before words beginning with *f*; shortened to **e-** before many consonants)
1 out; away (as in *extract*). 2 up, upwards; thoroughly (as in *extol*). 3 formerly (as in *ex-president*).

exact *adjective*
1 correct. 2 clearly stated; giving all details ♦ *exact instructions.*
exactly *adverb* **exactness** *noun*

exact *verb* (exacts, exacting, exacted)
insist on something and obtain it ♦ *He exacted obedience from the recruits.*
exaction *noun*

exaggerate *verb* (exaggerates, exaggerating, exaggerated)
make something seem bigger, better, or worse etc. than it really is.
exaggeration *noun*

examination *noun* (*plural* examinations)
1 a test of a person's knowledge or skill.
2 examining something; an inspection ♦ *a medical examination.*

examine *verb* (examines, examining, examined)
1 test a person's knowledge or skill. 2 look at something closely or in detail.
examiner *noun*

example *noun* (*plural* examples)
1 anything that shows what others of the same kind are like or how they work. 2 a person or thing good enough to be worth imitating.

exasperate *verb* (exasperates, exasperating, exasperated)
annoy someone.
exasperation *noun*

excavate *verb* (excavates, excavating, excavated)
dig out; uncover by digging.
excavation *noun* **excavator** *noun*

exceed *verb* (exceeds, exceeding, exceeded)
1 be greater than; surpass. 2 do more than you need or ought to do; go beyond a thing's limits ♦ *He has exceeded his authority.*

excel *verb* (excels, excelling, excelled)
be better than others at doing something.

Excellency *noun* (*plural* Excellencies)
the title of high officials such as ambassadors and governors.

excellent *adjective*
extremely good.
excellently *adverb* **excellence** *noun*

except *preposition*
excluding; not including ♦ *They all left except me.*

except *verb* (excepts, excepting, excepted)
exclude; leave out ♦ *I blame you all, no one is excepted.*

> ❶ USAGE Do not confuse with *accept.*

exception *noun* (*plural* exceptions)
a person or thing that is left out or does not follow the general rule.
take exception raise objections to something.
with the exception of except.

exceptional *adjective*
1 very unusual. 2 outstandingly good.
exceptionally *adverb*

excess *noun* (*plural* excesses)
too much of something.
in excess of more than.

excessive *adjective*
too much or too great ♦ *Do not use excessive force.*
excessively *adverb*

exchange *verb* (exchanges, exchanging, exchanged)
give something and receive something else for it.
exchangeable *adjective*

exchange noun (plural **exchanges**)
1 exchanging. 2 a place where things (especially stocks and shares) are bought and sold ♦ a stock exchange. 3 a place where telephone lines are connected to each other when a call is made.

exchequer noun (plural **exchequers**)
a national treasury into which public funds (such as taxes) are paid.

excitable adjective
easily excited.

excite verb (**excites, exciting, excited**)
1 make someone eager and enthusiastic about something ♦ The thought of finding gold excited them. 2 cause a feeling or reaction ♦ The invention excited great interest.
excited adjective **excitedly** adverb

excitement noun (plural **excitements**)
a strong feeling of eagerness or pleasure.

exclaim verb (**exclaims, exclaiming, exclaimed**)
shout or cry out in eagerness or surprise.

exclamation noun (plural **exclamations**)
1 exclaiming. 2 a word or words cried out expressing joy or pain or surprise etc.

exclamation mark noun (plural **exclamation marks**)
the punctuation mark (!) placed after an exclamation.

exclude verb (**excludes, excluding, excluded**)
1 keep somebody or something out. 2 leave something out ♦ Do not exclude the possibility of rain.
exclusion noun

exclusive adjective
1 allowing only certain people to be members etc. ♦ an exclusive club. 2 not shared with others ♦ This newspaper has an exclusive report.
exclusively adverb **exclusiveness** noun
exclusive of excluding, not including ♦ This is the price exclusive of meals.

excrement (say eks-kri-ment) noun
waste matter from the body.

excrete verb (**excretes, excreting, excreted**)
get rid of waste matter from the body.
excretion noun **excretory** adjective
[from ex- = out + Latin cretum = separated]

excruciating (say iks-**kroo**-shee-ayt-ing) adjective
extremely painful; agonizing.
excruciatingly adverb
[from ex- = out + Latin cruciatum = tortured]

excursion noun (plural **excursions**)
a short journey made for pleasure.
[from ex- = out + Latin cursus = course]

excuse (say iks-**kewz**) verb (**excuses, excusing, excused**)
1 forgive. 2 allow someone not to do something or to leave a room etc. ♦ Please may I be excused swimming?

excuse (say iks-**kewss**) noun (plural **excuses**)
a reason given to explain why something wrong has been done.

execute verb (**executes, executing, executed**)
1 put someone to death as a punishment.
2 perform or produce something ♦ She executed the somersault perfectly.
execution noun
[from Latin executare = to carry out, to punish]

executive (say ig-**zek**-yoo-tiv) noun (plural **executives**)
a senior person with authority in a business or government organization.

exempt adjective
not having to do something that others have to do ♦ Charities are exempt from paying tax.
exemption noun

exercise noun (plural **exercises**)
1 using your body to make it strong and healthy.
2 a piece of work done for practice.

exercise verb (**exercises, exercising, exercised**)
1 do exercises. 2 give exercise to an animal etc.
3 use ♦ You must exercise more patience.

exert verb (**exerts, exerting, exerted**)
use power or influence etc. ♦ He exerted all his strength.
exertion noun
exert yourself make an effort.

exhale verb (**exhales, exhaling, exhaled**)
breathe out.
exhalation noun

exhaust verb (**exhausts, exhausting, exhausted**)
1 make somebody very tired. 2 use up something completely.
exhaustion noun

exhaust noun (plural **exhausts**)
1 the waste gases or steam from an engine.
2 the pipe etc. through which they are sent out.

exhaustive adjective
thorough; trying everything possible ♦ We made an exhaustive search.
exhaustively adverb

exhibit verb (**exhibits, exhibiting, exhibited**)
show or display something in public.
exhibitor noun

exhibit noun (plural **exhibits**)
something on display in a gallery or museum.

exhibition noun (plural **exhibitions**)
a collection of things put on display for people to look at.

exhilarate (*say* ig-zil-er-ayt) *verb* (**exhilarates, exhilarating, exhilarated**)
make someone very happy and excited.
exhilaration *noun*

exhort (*say* ig-zort) *verb* (**exhorts, exhorting, exhorted**)
try hard to persuade someone to do something.
exhortation *noun*

exile *verb* (**exiles, exiling, exiled**)
banish.

exile *noun* (*plural* **exiles**)
1 having to live away from your own country
♦ *He was in exile for ten years.* **2** a banished person.

exist *verb* (**exists, existing, existed**)
1 be present as part of what is real ♦ *Do ghosts exist?* **2** stay alive ♦ *We cannot exist without food.*
existence *noun* **existent** *adjective*

exit *noun* (*plural* **exits**)
1 the way out of a building. **2** going off the stage
♦ *The actress made her exit.*

exit *verb*
(in stage directions) he or she leaves the stage.
[from Latin *exit*, = he or she goes out]

exorcize *verb* (**exorcizes, exorcizing, exorcized**)
drive out an evil spirit.
exorcism *noun* **exorcist** *noun*

exotic *adjective*
1 very unusual ♦ *exotic clothes.* **2** from another part of the world ♦ *exotic plants.*
exotically *adverb*

expand *verb* (**expands, expanding, expanded**)
make or become larger or fuller.
expansion *noun* **expansive** *adjective*

expect *verb* (**expects, expecting, expected**)
1 think or believe that something will happen or that someone will come. **2** think that something ought to happen ♦ *She expects obedience.*

expectant *adjective*
1 expecting something to happen; hopeful.
2 an expectant mother is a woman who is pregnant.
expectantly *adverb* **expectancy** *noun*

expectation *noun* (*plural* **expectations**)
1 expecting something; being hopeful.
2 something you expect to happen or get.

expedient (*say* iks-pee-dee-ent) *adjective*
1 suitable or convenient. **2** useful and practical though perhaps unfair.
expediently *adverb* **expediency** *noun*

expedient *noun* (*plural* **expedients**)
a means of doing something, especially when in difficulty.

expedition *noun* (*plural* **expeditions**)
1 a journey made in order to do something
♦ *a climbing expedition.* **2** speed or promptness.
expeditionary *adjective*

expel *verb* (**expels, expelling, expelled**)
1 send or force something out ♦ *This fan expels stale air.* **2** make a person leave a school or country etc.

expendable *adjective*
able to be sacrificed or got rid of in order to gain something.

expenditure *noun* (*plural* **expenditures**)
the spending or using up of money or effort etc.

expense *noun* (*plural* **expenses**)
the cost of doing something.

expensive *adjective*
costing a lot.
expensively *adverb* **expensiveness** *noun*

experience *noun* (*plural* **experiences**)
1 what you learn from doing or seeing things.
2 something that has happened to you.

experience *verb* (**experiences, experiencing, experienced**)
have something happen to you.

experienced *adjective*
having great skill or knowledge from much experience.

experiment *noun* (*plural* **experiments**)
a test made in order to find out what happens or to prove something.
experimental *adjective* **experimentally** *adverb*

experiment *verb* (**experiments, experimenting, experimented**)
carry out an experiment.
experimentation *noun*

expert *noun* (*plural* **experts**)
a person with great knowledge or skill in something.

expert *adjective*
having great knowledge or skill.
expertly *adverb* **expertness** *noun*

expire *verb* (**expires, expiring, expired**)
1 come to an end; stop being usable
♦ *Your season ticket has expired.* **2** die.
3 breathe out air.
expiration *noun* **expiry** *noun*

explain *verb* (**explains, explaining, explained**)
1 make something clear to somebody else; show its meaning. **2** account for something
♦ *That explains his absence.*
explanation *noun*

explicit (*say* iks-pliss-it) *adjective*
stated or stating something openly and exactly.
(Compare **implicit**.)
explicitly *adverb*

explode *verb* (**explodes, exploding, exploded**)
1 burst or suddenly release energy with a loud noise. **2** cause a bomb to go off. **3** increase suddenly or quickly.

exploit (*say* iks-**ploit**) *verb* (**exploits, exploiting, exploited**)
1 use or develop resources. **2** use a person or thing selfishly.
exploitation *noun*

explore *verb* (**explores, exploring, explored**)
1 travel through a country etc. in order to learn about it. **2** examine a subject or idea carefully ♦ *We explored the possibilities.*
exploration *noun* **explorer** *noun* **exploratory** *adjective*

explosion *noun* (*plural* **explosions**)
1 the exploding of a bomb etc.; the noise made by exploding. **2** a sudden great increase.

explosive *adjective*
able to explode.

explosive *noun* (*plural* **explosives**)
an explosive substance.

exponent *noun* (*plural* **exponents**)
1 a person who puts forward an idea etc.
2 someone who is good at an activity.
3 (in mathematics) the raised number etc. written to the right of another (e.g. 3 in 2^3) showing how many times the first one is to be multiplied by itself; the index.

export *verb* (**exports, exporting, exported**)
send goods abroad to be sold.
exportation *noun* **exporter** *noun*

export *noun* (*plural* **exports**)
1 exporting things. **2** something exported.

expose *verb* (**exposes, exposing, exposed**)
1 reveal or uncover. **2** allow light to reach a photographic film so as to take a picture.
exposure *noun*

express *adjective*
1 going or sent quickly. **2** clearly stated ♦ *This was done against my express orders.*

express *noun* (*plural* **expresses**)
a fast train stopping at only a few stations.

express *verb* (**expresses, expressing, expressed**)
1 put ideas etc. into words; make your feelings known. **2** press or squeeze out ♦ *Express the juice.*

expression *noun* (*plural* **expressions**)
1 the look on a person's face that shows his or her feelings. **2** a word or phrase etc. **3** a way of speaking or of playing music etc. so as to show your feelings. **4** expressing ♦ *this expression of opinion.*

expressive *adjective*
full of expression.

expulsion *noun* (*plural* **expulsions**)
expelling or being expelled.

exquisite (*say* eks-**kwiz**-it) *adjective*
very beautiful.
exquisitely *adverb*

extend *verb* (**extends, extending, extended**)
1 stretch out. **2** make something become longer or larger. **3** offer or give ♦ *Extend a warm welcome to our friends.*
extendible *adjective*

extension *noun* (*plural* **extensions**)
1 extending or being extended. **2** something added on; an addition to a building. **3** one of a set of telephones in an office or house etc.

extensive *adjective*
covering a large area or range ♦ *extensive gardens.*
extensively *adverb* **extensiveness** *noun*

extent *noun* (*plural* **extents**)
1 the area or length over which something extends. **2** the amount, level, or scope of something ♦ *the full extent of his power.*

exterior *adjective*
outer.

exterior *noun* (*plural* **exteriors**)
the outside of something.

exterminate *verb* (**exterminates, exterminating, exterminated**)
destroy or kill all the members or examples.
extermination *noun* **exterminator** *noun*

external *adjective*
outside.
externally *adverb*

extinct *adjective*
1 not existing any more ♦ *The dodo is an extinct bird.* **2** not burning; not active ♦ *an extinct volcano.*

extinction *noun*
1 making or becoming extinct. **2** extinguishing; being extinguished.

extinguish *verb* (**extinguishes, extinguishing, extinguished**)
1 put out a fire or light. **2** put an end to; destroy ♦ *Our hopes of victory were extinguished.*

extort *verb* (**extorts, extorting, extorted**)
obtain something by force or threats.
extortion *noun*

extortionate *adjective*
charging or demanding far too much.

extra *adjective*
additional; more than is usual ♦ *extra strength.*

extra *adverb*
more than usually ♦ *extra strong.*

extra *noun* (*plural* **extras**)
1 an extra person or thing. **2** a person acting as part of a crowd in a film or play.

extract (*say* iks-**trakt**) *verb* (**extracts, extracting, extracted**)
take out; remove.
extractor *noun*

extract (*say* **eks**-trakt) *noun* (*plural* **extracts**)
1 a passage taken from a book, speech, film, etc.
2 a substance separated or obtained from another.

extraction *noun*
1 extracting. 2 someone's descent ♦ *He is of Chinese extraction.*

extraordinary *adjective*
very unusual or strange.
extraordinarily *adverb*

extrasensory *adjective*
outside the range of the known human senses.

extraterrestrial *adjective*
from beyond the earth's atmosphere; from outer space.

extraterrestrial *noun* (*plural* **extraterrestrials**)
a being from outer space.

extravagant *adjective*
spending or using too much.
extravagantly *adverb* **extravagance** *noun*

extreme *adjective*
1 very great or intense ♦ *extreme cold.* 2 furthest away ♦ *the extreme north.* 3 going to great lengths in actions or opinions; not moderate.
extremely *adverb*

extreme *noun* (*plural* **extremes**)
1 something extreme. 2 either end of something.

extricate (*say* **eks**-trik-ayt) *verb* (**extricates, extricating, extricated**)
free someone or something from a difficult position or situation.
extrication *noun*

extrovert *noun* (*plural* **extroverts**)
a person who is generally friendly and likes company. (The opposite is *introvert.*)

exuberant (*say* ig-**zew**-ber-ant) *adjective*
very lively and cheerful.
exuberantly *adverb* **exuberance** *noun*

exude *verb* (**exudes, exuding, exuded**)
1 give off moisture, a smell, etc. 2 display a feeling or quality openly ♦ *She exuded confidence.*

exult *verb* (**exults, exulting, exulted**)
rejoice greatly.
exultant *adjective* **exultation** *noun*

eye *noun* (*plural* **eyes**)
1 the organ of the body that is used for seeing.
2 the power of seeing ♦ *She has sharp eyes.*
3 the small hole in a needle. 4 the centre of a storm.

eye *verb* (**eyes, eyeing, eyed**)
look at something with interest.
[from Old English]

eyeball *noun* (*plural* **eyeballs**)
the ball-shaped part of the eye inside the eyelids.

eyebrow *noun* (*plural* **eyebrows**)
the fringe of hair growing on the face above the eye.

eyelash *noun* (*plural* **eyelashes**)
one of the short hairs that grow on an eyelid.

eyelid *noun* (*plural* **eyelids**)
either of the two folds of skin that can close over the eyeball.

eyepiece *noun* (*plural* **eyepieces**)
the lens of a telescope or microscope etc. that you put to your eye.

eyesight *noun*
the ability to see.

eyewitness *noun* (*plural* **eyewitnesses**)
a person who actually saw an accident or crime etc.

fable *noun* (*plural* **fables**)
a short story that teaches about behaviour, often with animals as characters.
[from Latin *fabula* = story]

fabric *noun* (*plural* **fabrics**)
1 cloth. 2 the basic framework of something, especially the walls, floors, and roof of a building.

fabricate *verb* (**fabricates, fabricating, fabricated**)
1 construct or manufacture something.
2 invent ♦ *fabricate an excuse.*
fabrication *noun*

fabulous *adjective*
1 wonderful. 2 incredibly great ♦ *fabulous wealth.* 3 told of in fables and myths.
fabulously *adverb*

façade (*say* fas-**ahd**) *noun* (*plural* **façades**)
1 the front of a building. 2 an outward appearance, especially a deceptive one.

face *noun* (*plural* **faces**)
1 the front part of the head. 2 the expression on a person's face. 3 the front or upper side of something. 4 a surface ♦ *A cube has six faces.*

face *verb* (**faces, facing, faced**)
1 look or have the front towards something ♦ *Our room faced the sea.* 2 meet and have to deal with something; encounter ♦ *Explorers face many dangers.* 3 cover a surface with a layer of different material.

facetious (*say* fas-**ee**-shus) *adjective*
trying to be funny at an unsuitable time
♦ *facetious remarks*.
facetiously *adverb*

facilitate (*say* fas-**il**-it-ayt) *verb* (**facilitates, facilitating, facilitated**)
make something easier to do.
facilitation *noun*

facility (*say* fas-**il**-it-ee) *noun* (*plural* **facilities**)
1 something that provides you with the means to do things ♦ *There are sports facilities*. 2 ease or skill in doing something ♦ *She reads music with great facility*.

facsimile (*say* fak-**sim**-il-ee) *noun* (*plural* **facsimiles**)
1 an exact reproduction of a document etc.
2 a fax.

fact *noun* (*plural* **facts**)
something that is certainly true.
the facts of life information about how babies are conceived.

faction *noun* (*plural* **factions**)
a small united group within a larger one, especially in politics.

factor *noun* (*plural* **factors**)
1 something that helps to bring about a result
♦ *Hard work was a factor in her success.*
2 a number by which a larger number can be divided exactly ♦ *2 and 3 are factors of 6.*

factory *noun* (*plural* **factories**)
a large building where machines are used to make things.

faculty *noun* (*plural* **faculties**)
1 any of the powers of the body or mind (e.g. sight, speech, or understanding). 2 a department teaching a particular subject in a university or college ♦ *the faculty of music.*

fad *noun* (*plural* **fads**)
1 a person's particular like or dislike.
2 a temporary fashion or craze.
faddy *adjective*

fade *verb* (**fades, fading, faded**)
1 lose colour or freshness or strength.
2 disappear gradually. 3 make a sound etc. become gradually weaker (*fade it out*) or stronger (*fade it in* or *up*).

faeces (*say* **fee**-seez) *plural noun*
solid waste matter passed out of the body.

Fahrenheit *adjective*
measuring temperature on a scale where water freezes at 32° and boils at 212°.
[named after G. D. Fahrenheit, a German scientist, who invented the mercury thermometer]

fail *verb* (**fails, failing, failed**)
1 try to do something but be unable to do it.
2 become weak or useless; break down
♦ *The brakes failed.* 3 not do something
♦ *He failed to warn me.* 4 not get enough marks to pass an examination. 5 judge that someone has not passed an examination.

fail *noun*
without fail for certain; whatever happens.

failing *noun* (*plural* **failings**)
a weakness or a fault.

failure *noun* (*plural* **failures**)
1 not being able to do something. 2 a person or thing that has failed.

faint *adjective*
1 pale or dim; not distinct. 2 weak or giddy; nearly unconscious. 3 slight ♦ *a faint hope.*
faintly *adverb* **faintness** *noun*

faint *verb* (**faints, fainting, fainted**)
become unconscious for a short time.

❶ USAGE Do not confuse with *feint*.

fair[1] *adjective*
1 right or just; according to the rules ♦ *a fair fight.* 2 (said about hair or skin) light in colour; (said about a person) having fair hair. 3 (*old use*) beautiful. 4 fine or favourable ♦ *fair weather.*
5 moderate; quite good ♦ *a fair number of people.*
fairness *noun*

fair *adverb*
fairly ♦ *Play fair!*

fair[2] *noun* (*plural* **fairs**)
1 a group of outdoor entertainments such as roundabouts, sideshows, and stalls.
2 an exhibition or market.
fairground *noun*

fairly *adverb*
1 justly; according to the rules. 2 moderately
♦ *It is fairly hard.*

fairy *noun* (*plural* **fairies**)
an imaginary very small creature with magic powers.
fairyland *noun* **fairy tale** *noun*

faith *noun* (*plural* **faiths**)
strong belief or trust.
in good faith with honest intentions.

faithful *adjective*
1 loyal and trustworthy. 2 true to the facts
♦ *a faithful account.* 3 sexually loyal to one partner.
faithfully *adverb* **faithfulness** *noun*
Yours faithfully see *yours*.

fake *noun* (*plural* **fakes**)
something that looks genuine but is not; a forgery.

fake *verb* (**fakes, faking, faked**)
1 make something that looks genuine, in order to deceive people. **2** pretend to have or be something ♦ *He used to fake illness to miss games.*
faker *noun*

falcon *noun* (*plural* **falcons**)
a kind of hawk often used in the sport of hunting other birds or game.
falconry *noun*

fall *verb* (**falls, falling, fell, fallen**)
1 come or go down without being pushed or thrown etc. **2** decrease; become lower ♦ *Prices fell.* **3** be captured or overthrown ♦ *The city fell.* **4** die in battle. **5** happen ♦ *Silence fell.* **6** become ♦ *She fell asleep.*
fall back retreat. **fall back on** use for support or in an emergency. **fall for 1** be attracted by a person. **2** be taken in by a deception. **fall out** quarrel. **fall through** fail ♦ *plans fell through.*

fall *noun* (*plural* **falls**)
1 the action of falling. **2** (*American*) autumn, when leaves fall.

fallacy (*say* fal-a-see) *noun* (*plural* **fallacies**)
a false or mistaken idea or belief.
fallacious (*say* fal-ay-shus) *adjective*

Fallopian tube *noun* (*plural* **Fallopian tubes**)
one of the two tubes in a woman's body along which the eggs travel from the ovaries to the uterus.

fallout *noun*
particles of radioactive material carried in the air after a nuclear explosion.

false *adjective*
1 untrue or incorrect. **2** not genuine; artificial ♦ *false teeth.* **3** treacherous or deceitful.
falsely *adverb* **falseness** *noun* **falsity** *noun*

falter *verb* (**falters, faltering, faltered**)
1 hesitate when you move or speak. **2** become weaker; begin to give way ♦ *His courage began to falter.*

fame *noun*
being famous.
famed *adjective*

familiar *adjective*
1 well-known; often seen or experienced. **2** knowing something well ♦ *Are you familiar with this book?* **3** very friendly.
familiarly *adverb* **familiarity** *noun*

family *noun* (*plural* **families**)
1 parents and their children, sometimes including grandchildren and other relations. **2** a group of things that are alike in some way. **3** a group of related plants or animals ♦ *Lions belong to the cat family.*

family planning *noun*
birth control.

family tree *noun* (*plural* **family trees**)
a diagram showing how people in a family are related.

famine *noun* (*plural* **famines**)
a very bad shortage of food in an area.

famished *adjective*
very hungry.

famous *adjective*
known to very many people.

famously *adverb* (*informal*)
very well ♦ *They get on famously.*

fan[1] *noun* (*plural* **fans**)
an object or machine for making air move about so as to cool people or things.
fan *verb* (**fans, fanning, fanned**)
send a current of air on something.
fan out spread out in the shape of a fan.

fan[2] *noun* (*plural* **fans**)
an enthusiastic admirer or supporter.

fanatic *noun* (*plural* **fanatics**)
a person who is very enthusiastic or too enthusiastic about something.
fanatical *adjective* **fanatically** *adverb* **fanaticism** *noun*

fanciful *adjective*
1 imagining things. **2** imaginary.

fancy *noun* (*plural* **fancies**)
1 a liking or desire for something. **2** imagination.
fancy *adjective*
decorated or elaborate; not plain.
fancy *verb* (**fancies, fancying, fancied**)
1 have a liking or desire for something. **2** imagine. **3** believe ♦ *I fancy it's raining.*

fancy dress *noun*
unusual costume worn for a party, often to make you look like a famous person.

fantastic *adjective*
1 (*informal*) excellent. **2** strange or unusual. **3** designed in a very fanciful way.
fantastically *adverb*

fantasy *noun* (*plural* **fantasies**)
something imaginary or fantastic.

far *adverb*
1 at or to a great distance ♦ *We didn't go far.* **2** much; by a great amount ♦ *This is far better.*
far *adjective*
distant or remote ♦ *On the far side of the river.*

farce *noun* (*plural* **farces**)
1 an exaggerated comedy. **2** a situation or series of events that is ridiculous or a pretence ♦ *The trial was a complete farce.*
farcical *adjective*

fare *noun* (*plural* **fares**)
1 the price charged for a passenger to travel. **2** food and drink ♦ *There was only very plain fare.*

farewell *interjection* & *noun* (*plural* **farewells**)
goodbye.

farm *noun* (*plural* **farms**)
1 an area of land where someone grows crops or keeps animals for food or other use. 2 the farmer's house.
farmhouse *noun* **farmyard** *noun*
farm *verb* (**farms, farming, farmed**)
1 grow crops or keep animals for food etc. 2 use land for growing crops; cultivate.
farmer *noun* (*plural* **farmers**)
a person who owns or manages a farm.
farther *adverb* & *adjective*
at or to a greater distance; more distant.

> ❶ USAGE *Farther* and *farthest* are used only in connection with distance (e.g. *She lives farther from the school than I do*), but even in such cases many people prefer to use *further*. Only *further* can be used to mean 'additional', e.g. in *We must make further inquiries*. If you are not sure which is right, use *further*.

farthest *adverb* & *adjective*
at or to the greatest distance; most distant.

> ❶ USAGE See the note at *farther*.

farthing *noun* (*plural* **farthings**)
a former British coin worth one-quarter of a penny.
fascinate *verb* (**fascinates, fascinating, fascinated**)
be very attractive or interesting to somebody.
fascination *noun* **fascinator** *noun*
fascist *noun* (*plural* **fascists**)
someone who believes in or practises very oppressive and nationalistic forms of government.
fascism *noun* [from *fasces*, the rods of office in ancient Rome, used as an emblem by the Italian Fascist party in the 1920s]
fashion *noun* (*plural* **fashions**)
1 the style of clothes or other things that most people like at a particular time. 2 a way of doing something ♦ *Continue in the same fashion*.
fashionable *adjective*
following the fashion of the time; popular.
fashionably *adverb*
fast¹ *adjective*
1 moving or done quickly; rapid. 2 allowing fast movement ♦ *a fast road*. 3 showing a time later than the correct time ♦ *Your watch is fast*. 4 firmly fixed or attached. 5 not likely to fade ♦ *fast colours*.
fastness *noun*
fast *adverb*
1 quickly ♦ *Run fast!* 2 firmly ♦ *His leg was stuck fast in the mud*.
fast asleep in a deep sleep.

fast² *verb* (**fasts, fasting, fasted**)
go without food.
fast *noun*
fasten *verb* (**fastens, fastening, fastened**)
fix one thing firmly to another.
fastener *noun* **fastening** *noun*
fat *noun* (*plural* **fats**)
1 the white greasy part of meat. 2 oil or grease used in cooking.
the fat of the land the best food.
fat *adjective* (**fatter, fattest**)
1 having a very thick round body. 2 thick ♦ *a fat book*. 3 full of fat.
fatness *noun*
fatal *adjective*
causing death or disaster ♦ *a fatal accident*.
fatally *adverb*
fate *noun* (*plural* **fates**)
1 a power that is thought to make things happen. 2 what will happen or has happened to somebody or something; destiny.
[from Latin *fatum* = what has been spoken]
father *noun* (*plural* **fathers**)
1 a male parent. 2 the title of certain priests.
fatherly *adjective*
[from Old English]
father-in-law *noun* (*plural* **fathers-in-law**)
the father of a married person's husband or wife.
fatigue *noun*
1 tiredness. 2 weakness in metals, caused by stress.
fatigued *adjective*
fatten *verb* (**fattens, fattening, fattened**)
make or become fat.
fatty *adjective*
like fat; containing fat.
fatuous *adjective*
silly or foolish.
fatuously *adverb* **fatuousness** *noun* **fatuity** *noun*
fault *noun* (*plural* **faults**)
1 anything that makes a person or thing imperfect; a flaw or mistake. 2 the responsibility for something wrong ♦ *It wasn't your fault*. 3 a break in a layer of rock, caused by movement of the earth's crust.
faulty *adjective*
at fault responsible for a mistake or failure.
fault *verb* (**faults, faulting, faulted**)
find faults in something.
fauna *noun*
the animals of a certain area or period of time. (Compare **flora**.)
favour *noun* (*plural* **favours**)
1 a kind or helpful act. 2 friendly support or approval ♦ *The visitors soon won the favour of the local people*.
be in favour of like or support.

favour *verb* (**favours, favouring, favoured**)
be in favour of something; show favour to a person.

favourable *adjective*
1 helpful or advantageous. 2 showing approval.
favourably *adverb*

favourite *adjective*
liked more than others.

favourite *noun*
1 a person or thing that someone likes most.
2 a competitor that is generally expected to win.

fax *noun* (*plural* **faxes**)
1 a machine that sends an exact copy of a document electronically. 2 a copy produced by this.

fax *verb* (**faxes, faxing, faxed**)
send a copy of a document using a fax machine.
[a shortening of *facsimile*]

fear *noun* (*plural* **fears**)
a feeling that something unpleasant may happen.

fear *verb* (**fears, fearing, feared**)
feel fear; be afraid of somebody or something.

fearful *adjective*
1 feeling fear; afraid. 2 causing fear or horror
♦ *a fearful monster.* 3 (*informal*) very great or bad.
fearfully *adverb*

fearsome *adjective*
frightening.

feasible *adjective*
1 able to be done; possible. 2 likely or probable
♦ *a feasible explanation.*
feasibly *adverb* **feasibility** *noun*

---

❶ USAGE The use of *feasible* to mean 'likely or probable' has not become generally accepted in standard English, so it is better to avoid it in writing or formal situations.

---

feast *noun* (*plural* **feasts**)
1 a large splendid meal. 2 a religious festival.
feast *verb*
[from old French; related to *fête*]

feather *noun* (*plural* **feathers**)
one of the very light coverings that grow from a bird's skin.
feathery *adjective*

feather *verb* (**feathers, feathering, feathered**)
cover or line something with feathers.

feature *noun* (*plural* **features**)
1 any part of the face (e.g. the mouth, nose, or eyes). 2 an important or noticeable part; a characteristic. 3 a special newspaper article or programme that deals with a particular subject.
4 the main film in a cinema programme.

February *noun*
the second month of the year.
[named after *februa*, the ancient Roman feast of purification held in this month]

fed *past tense* of **feed**.
fed up (*informal*) discontented.

federal *adjective*
to do with a system in which several states are ruled by a central government but are responsible for their own internal affairs.

federation *noun* (*plural* **federations**)
a group of federal states.

fee *noun* (*plural* **fees**)
a charge for something.

feeble *adjective*
weak; without strength.
feebly *adverb* **feebleness** *noun*

feed *verb* (**feeds, feeding, fed**)
1 give food to a person or animal. 2 take food.
3 supply something to a machine etc.
feeder *noun*

feed *noun*
food for animals or babies.

feedback *noun*
1 the response you get from people to something you have done. 2 the harsh noise produced when some of the sound from an amplifier goes back into it.

feel *verb* (**feels, feeling, felt**)
1 touch something to find out what it is like.
2 be aware of something; have an opinion.
3 experience an emotion. 4 give a certain sensation ♦ *the sand feels warm.*
feel like want.

feeler *noun* (*plural* **feelers**)
1 a long thin projection on an insect's or crustacean's body, used for feeling; an antenna.
2 a cautious question or suggestion etc. to test people's reactions.

feeling *noun* (*plural* **feelings**)
1 the ability to feel things; the sense of touch.
2 what a person feels in the mind; emotion
♦ *I didn't mean to hurt your feelings.* 3 what you think about something ♦ *I have a feeling that we are going to win.*

feint (*say* faynt) *noun* (*plural* **feints**)
a pretended attack or punch meant to deceive an opponent.

feint *verb* (**feints, feinting, feinted**)
make a feint.

---

❶ USAGE Do not confuse with *faint*.

---

fell¹ *past tense* of **fall**.

fell² *verb* (**fells, felling, felled**)
make something fall; cut or knock down
♦ *They were felling the trees.*

fellow *noun* (*plural* **fellows**)
1 a friend or companion; one who belongs to the same group. 2 a man or boy. 3 a member of a learned society.

fellow *adjective*
of the same group or kind ♦ *Her fellow teachers supported her.*

fellowship *noun* (*plural* **fellowships**)
1 friendship. 2 a group of friends; a society.

felt¹ *past tense* of **feel.**

felt² *noun*
a thick fabric made of fibres of wool or fur etc. pressed together.

female *adjective*
of the sex that can bear offspring or produce eggs or fruit.

female *noun* (*plural* **females**)
a female person, animal, or plant.

feminine *adjective*
1 to do with or like women; suitable for women. 2 (in some languages) belonging to the class of words which includes the words referring to women.
femininity *noun*

feminist *noun* (*plural* **feminists**)
a person who believes that women should have the same rights and status as men.
feminism *noun*

fence *noun* (*plural* **fences**)
1 a barrier made of wood or wire etc. round an area. 2 a structure for a horse to jump over. 3 a person who buys stolen goods and sells them again.

fence *verb* (**fences, fencing, fenced**)
1 put a fence round or along something. 2 fight with long narrow swords (called **foils**) as a sport.
fencer *noun*

fend *verb* (**fends, fending, fended**)
fend for yourself take care of yourself. **fend off** keep a person or thing away from you.

ferment (*say* fer-ment) *verb* (**ferments, fermenting, fermented**)
bubble and change chemically by the action of a substance such as yeast.
fermentation *noun*

ferment (*say* fer-ment) *noun*
1 fermenting. 2 an excited or agitated condition.

fern *noun* (*plural* **ferns**)
a plant with feathery leaves and no flowers.

ferocious *adjective*
fierce or savage.
ferociously *adverb* **ferocity** *noun*

ferry *verb* (**ferries, ferrying, ferried**)
transport people or things, especially across water.

ferry *noun* (*plural* **ferries**)
a boat or ship used for transporting people or things across a short stretch of water.

fertile *adjective*
1 producing good crops ♦ *fertile soil.* 2 able to produce offspring. 3 able to produce ideas ♦ *a fertile imagination.*
fertility *noun*

fertilize *verb* (**fertilizes, fertilizing, fertilized**)
1 add substances to the soil to make it more fertile. 2 put pollen into a plant or sperm into an egg or female animal so that it develops seed or young.
fertilization *noun*

fertilizer *noun* (*plural* **fertilizers**)
chemicals or manure added to the soil to make it more fertile.

fervent *adjective*
strongly passionate.

festival *noun* (*plural* **festivals**)
1 a time of celebration, especially for religious reasons. 2 an organized series of concerts, films, performances, etc., especially one held every year.

festivity *noun* (*plural* **festivities**)
a festive occasion or celebration.

festoon *noun* (*plural* **festoons**)
a chain of flowers or ribbons etc. hung as a decoration.

festoon *verb* (**festoons, festooning, festooned**)
decorate something with ornaments.

fetch *verb* (**fetches, fetching, fetched**)
1 go for and bring back ♦ *fetch some milk;* ♦ *fetch a doctor.* 2 be sold for a particular price ♦ *The chairs fetched £20.*

fête (*say* fayt) *noun* (*plural* **fêtes**)
an outdoor entertainment with stalls and sideshows.

fetter *noun* (*plural* **fetters**)
a chain or shackle put round a prisoner's ankle.

fetus or **foetus** (*say* fee-tus) *noun* (*plural* **fetuses** or **foetuses**)
a developing embryo, especially an unborn human baby.
fetal *adjective*
[from Latin, = offspring]

feud (*say* fewd) *noun* (*plural* **feuds**)
a long-lasting quarrel, especially between two families.

feudal (*say* few-dal) *adjective*
to do with the system used in the Middle Ages in which people could farm land in exchange for work done for the owner.
feudalism *noun*

fever *noun* (*plural* **fevers**)
1 an abnormally high body temperature, usually with an illness. 2 excitement or agitation.
fevered *adjective* **feverish** *adjective* **feverishly** *adverb*

few *adjective*
not many.

few *noun*
a small number of people or things.
quite a few or **a good few** a fairly large number

ℹ USAGE See the note at *less*.

fiancé (*say* fee-**ahn**-say) *noun* (*plural* **fiancés**)
a man who is engaged to be married.

fiancée (*say* fee-**ahn**-say) *noun* (*plural* **fiancées**)
a woman who is engaged to be married.

fiasco (*say* fee-**as**-koh) *noun* (*plural* **fiascos**)
a complete failure.

fibre *noun* (*plural* **fibres**)
1 a very thin thread. **2** a substance made of thin threads. **3** indigestible material in certain foods that stimulates the action of the intestines.
fibrous *adjective*

fibreglass *noun*
1 fabric made from glass fibres. **2** plastic containing glass fibres.

fickle *adjective*
constantly changing; not loyal to one person or group etc.
fickleness *noun*

fiction *noun* (*plural* **fictions**)
1 writings about events that have not really happened; stories and novels. **2** something imagined or untrue.
fictional *adjective*

fiddle *noun* (*plural* **fiddles**)
1 a violin. **2** (*informal*) a swindle.
fiddle *verb* (**fiddles, fiddling, fiddled**)
1 play the violin. **2** fidget or tinker with something, using your fingers. **3** (*informal*) alter accounts or records dishonestly.
fiddler *noun*

fidget *verb* (**fidgets, fidgeting, fidgeted**)
make small restless movements.
fidgety *adjective*

field *noun* (*plural* **fields**)
1 a piece of land with grass or crops growing on it. **2** an area of interest or study ♦ *recent advances in the field of genetics.* **3** those who are taking part in a race or outdoor game etc.
field *verb* (**fields, fielding, fielded**)
1 stop or catch the ball in cricket etc. **2** be on the side not batting in cricket etc. **3** put a team into a match, contest, etc. ♦ *They fielded their best players for the final.*
fielder *noun* **fieldsman** *noun*

fieldwork *noun*
practical work or research done in various places, not in a library or museum or laboratory etc.

fiend (*say* feend) *noun* (*plural* **fiends**)
1 an evil spirit; a devil. **2** a very wicked or cruel person. **3** an enthusiast ♦ *a fresh-air fiend.*

fiendish *adjective*
1 very wicked or cruel. **2** extremely difficult or complicated.
fiendishly *adverb*

fierce *adjective*
1 angry and violent or cruel. **2** intense ♦ *fierce heat.*
fiercely *adverb* **fierceness** *noun*

fifteen *adjective & noun*
1 the number 15. **2** a team in rugby union football.
fifteenth *adjective & noun*

fifth *adjective & noun* (*plural* **fifths**)
next after the fourth.
fifthly *adverb*

fifty *adjective & noun* (*plural* **fifties**)
the number 50.
fiftieth *adjective & noun*

fifty-fifty *adjective & adverb*
1 shared equally between two people or groups ♦ *We'll split the money fifty-fifty.* **2** evenly balanced ♦ *a fifty-fifty chance.*

fig *noun* (*plural* **figs**)
a soft fruit full of small seeds.

fight *noun* (*plural* **fights**)
1 a struggle against somebody using hands, weapons, etc. **2** an attempt to achieve or overcome something ♦ *the fight against poverty.*
fight *verb* (**fights, fighting, fought**)
1 have a fight. **2** attempt to achieve or overcome something.
fighter *noun*

figure *noun* (*plural* **figures**)
1 the symbol of a number. **2** an amount or value. **3** a diagram or illustration. **4** a shape. **5** the shape of a person's, especially a woman's, body. **6** a person. **7** a representation of a person or animal in painting, sculpture, etc.
figure *verb* (**figures, figuring, figured**)
appear or take part in something ♦ *She figures in some of the stories about King Arthur.*
figure out work something out.

figurehead *noun* (*plural* **figureheads**)
1 a carved figure decorating the prow of a sailing ship. **2** a person who is head of a country or organization but has no real power.

figure of speech *noun* (*plural* **figures of speech**)
a word or phrase used for special effect and not intended literally, e.g. *'a flood of letters'.*

filament *noun* (*plural* **filaments**)
a thread or thin wire, especially one in a light bulb.

file¹ *noun* (*plural* **files**)
a metal tool with a rough surface that is rubbed on things to shape them or make them smooth.
file *verb* (**files, filing, filed**)
shape or smooth something with a file.

file² *noun* (*plural* **files**)
1 a folder or box etc. for keeping papers in order.
2 a collection of data stored under one name in a computer. 3 a line of people one behind the other.

file *verb* (**files, filing, filed**)
1 put something into a file. 2 walk in a file
♦ *They filed out.*

filings *plural noun*
tiny pieces of metal rubbed off by a file
♦ *iron filings.*

fill *verb* (**fills, filling, filled**)
1 make or become full. 2 block up a hole or cavity. 3 hold a position, or appoint a person to a vacant post.
filler *noun*

fill *noun*
enough to fill a person or thing ♦ *We ate our fill.*

filling station *noun* (*plural* **filling stations**)
a place where petrol is sold from pumps.

film *noun* (*plural* **films**)
1 a motion picture, such as those shown in cinemas or on television. 2 a rolled strip or sheet of thin plastic coated with material that is sensitive to light, used for taking photographs or making a motion picture. 3 a very thin layer
♦ *a film of grease.*

film *verb* (**films, filming, filmed**)
record something on film; make a film of a story etc.

filter *noun* (*plural* **filters**)
1 a device for holding back dirt or other unwanted material from a liquid or gas etc. that passes through it. 2 a system for filtering traffic.

filter *verb* (**filters, filtering, filtered**)
1 pass through a filter. 2 move gradually
♦ *They filtered into the hall.* ♦ *News began to filter out.* 3 (said about traffic) move in a particular direction while other traffic is held up.

filth *noun*
disgusting dirt.

filthy *adjective* (**filthier, filthiest**)
1 disgustingly dirty. 2 obscene or offensive.
filthiness *noun*

fin *noun* (*plural* **fins**)
1 a thin flat part sticking out from a fish's body, that helps it to swim. 2 a small part that sticks out on an aircraft or rocket etc., for helping its balance.

final *adjective*
1 coming at the end; last. 2 that puts an end to an argument etc. ♦ *You must go, and that's final!*
finally *adverb* **finality** *noun*

final *noun* (*plural* **finals**)
the last in a series of contests.

finalist *noun* (*plural* **finalists**)
a competitor in a final.

finance *noun*
1 the use or management of money. 2 the money used to pay for something.
financial *adjective*
finances *plural noun* money resources; funds.

finance *verb* (**finances, financing, financed**)
provide the money for something.
financier *noun*

find *verb* (**finds, finding, found**)
1 get or see something by looking for it or by chance. 2 learn something by experience
♦ *He found that digging was hard work.*
3 decide and give a verdict ♦ *The jury found him guilty.*
find out get or discover some information.

find *noun* (*plural* **finds**)
something found.

findings *plural noun*
the conclusions reached from an investigation.

fine¹ *adjective*
1 of high quality; excellent. 2 dry and clear; sunny ♦ *fine weather.* 3 very thin; consisting of small particles. 4 in good health; well
♦ *I'm fine.*
finely *adverb* **fineness** *noun*

fine *adverb*
1 finely ♦ *chop it fine.* 2 (*informal*) very well
♦ *That will suit me fine.*

fine² *noun* (*plural* **fines**)
money which has to be paid as a punishment.

fine *verb* (**fines, fining, fined**)
make somebody pay a fine.

finger *noun* (*plural* **fingers**)
1 one of the separate parts of the hand.
2 a narrow piece of something ♦ *fish fingers.*

finger *verb* (**fingers, fingering, fingered**)
touch or feel something with your fingers.

fingernail *noun* (*plural* **fingernails**)
the hard covering at the end of a finger.

fingerprint *noun* (*plural* **fingerprints**)
a mark made by the tiny ridges on the fingertip, used as a way of identifying someone.

finish *verb* (**finishes, finishing, finished**)
bring or come to an end.

finish *noun* (*plural* **finishes**)
1 the last stage of something; the end.
2 the surface or coating on woodwork etc.

finite (*say* **fy**-nyt) *adjective*
limited; not infinite ♦ *We have only a finite supply of coal.*

finicky *adjective*
very fussy.

fir *noun* (*plural* **firs**)
an evergreen tree with needle-like leaves, that produces cones.

fire *noun* (*plural* **fires**)
1 the process of burning that produces light and heat. 2 coal and wood etc. burning in a grate or furnace to give heat. 3 a device using electricity or gas to heat a room. 4 the shooting of guns ♦ *Hold your fire!*
on fire burning. **set fire to** start something burning.

fire *verb* (**fires, firing, fired**)
1 set fire to. 2 bake pottery or bricks etc. in a kiln. 3 shoot a gun; send out a bullet or missile. 4 dismiss someone from a job. 5 excite ♦ *fire them with enthusiasm.*
firer *noun*

firearm *noun* (*plural* **firearms**)
a small gun; a rifle, pistol, or revolver.

fire brigade *noun* (*plural* **fire brigades**)
a team of people organized to fight fires.

fire engine *noun* (*plural* **fire engines**)
a large vehicle that carries firefighters and equipment to put out large fires.

fire escape *noun* (*plural* **fire escapes**)
a special staircase by which people may escape from a burning building etc.

fire extinguisher *noun* (*plural* **fire extinguishers**)
a metal cylinder from which water or foam can be sprayed to put out a fire.

firefighter *noun* (*plural* **firefighters**)
a member of a fire brigade.

fireplace *noun* (*plural* **fireplaces**)
an open structure for holding a fire in a room.

firewood *noun*
wood for use as fuel.

firework *noun* (*plural* **fireworks**)
a device containing chemicals that burn or explode attractively and noisily.

firing squad *noun* (*plural* **firing squads**)
a group of soldiers given the duty of shooting a condemned person.

firm *noun* (*plural* **firms**)
a business organization.

firm *adjective*
1 not giving way when pressed; hard or solid. 2 steady; not shaking or moving. 3 definite and not likely to change ♦ *a firm belief.*
firmly *adverb* **firmness** *noun*

firm *verb* (**firms, firming, firmed**)
make something become firm.

first *adjective*
coming before all others in time or order or importance.
firstly *adverb*

first *adverb*
before everything else ♦ *Finish this work first.*

first aid *noun*
treatment given to an injured person before a doctor comes.

first-class *adjective*
1 using the best class of a service ♦ *first-class post.* 2 excellent.

fish *noun* (*plural* **fish** or **fishes**)
an animal with gills and fins that always lives and breathes in water.

fish *verb* (**fishes, fishing, fished**)
1 try to catch fish. 2 search for something; try to get something ♦ *He is only fishing for compliments.*
[from Old English]

fisherman *noun* (*plural* **fishermen**)
a person who tries to catch fish.

fishmonger *noun* (*plural* **fishmongers**)
a shopkeeper who sells fish.

fishy *adjective* (**fishier, fishiest**)
1 smelling or tasting of fish. 2 (*informal*) causing doubt or suspicion ♦ *a fishy excuse.*
fishily *adverb* **fishiness** *noun*

fission *noun*
1 splitting something. 2 splitting the nucleus of an atom so as to release energy.

fist *noun* (*plural* **fists**)
a tightly closed hand with the fingers bent into the palm.

fit¹ *adjective* (**fitter, fittest**)
1 suitable or good enough ♦ *a meal fit for a king.* 2 healthy, in good physical condition ♦ *Keep fit!* 3 ready or likely ♦ *They worked till they were fit to collapse.*
fitness *noun*

fit *verb* (**fits, fitting, fitted**)
1 be the right size and shape for something; be suitable. 2 put something into place ♦ *Fit a lock on the door.* 3 alter something to make it the right size and shape. 4 make suitable for something ♦ *His training fits him for the job.*
fitter *noun*

fit *noun*
the way something fits ♦ *a good fit.*

fit² *noun* (*plural* **fits**)
1 a sudden illness, especially one that makes you move violently or become unconscious. 2 an outburst ♦ *a fit of rage.*

fitful *adjective*
happening in short periods, not steadily.
fitfully *adverb*

fitting *adjective*
proper or appropriate ♦ *This statue is a fitting memorial to an extraordinary woman.*

five *adjective* & *noun*(*plural* **fives**)
the number 5.

fix *verb* (**fixes, fixing, fixed**)
1 fasten or place firmly. **2** make permanent and unable to change. **3** decide or arrange ♦ *We fixed a date for the party.* **4** repair; put into working condition ♦ *He is fixing my bike.*
fixer *noun*
fix up arrange or organize something.
fix *noun* (*plural* **fixes**)
1 (*informal*) an awkward situation ♦ *I'm in a fix.* **2** finding the position of something, by using a compass, radar, etc. **3** (*informal*) an addict's dose of a drug.

fixedly *adverb*
with a fixed expression.

fixture *noun* (*plural* **fixtures**)
1 something fixed in its place. **2** a sports event planned for a particular day.

fizz *verb* (**fizzes, fizzing, fizzed**)
make a hissing or spluttering sound; produce a lot of small bubbles.

fizzy *adjective*
(said about a drink) having a lot of small bubbles.
fizziness *noun*

flabby *adjective*
fat and soft, not firm.
flabbily *adverb* **flabbiness** *noun*

flag¹ *noun* (*plural* **flags**)
1 a piece of cloth with a coloured pattern or shape on it, used as a sign or signal. **2** a small piece of paper or plastic that looks like a flag.
flagpole *noun* **flagstaff** *noun*
flag *verb* (**flags, flagging, flagged**)
1 become weak; droop. **2** signal with a flag or by waving.
flag² *noun* (*plural* **flags**)
a flat slab of stone used for paving.

flagrant (*say* flay-grant) *adjective*
very bad and noticeable ♦ *flagrant disobedience.*
flagrantly *adverb* **flagrancy** *noun*

flagship *noun* (*plural* **flagships**)
1 a ship that carries an admiral and flies his flag. **2** a company's best or most important product, store, etc.

flair *noun*
a natural ability or talent ♦ *Ian has a flair for languages.*

❶ USAGE Do not confuse with *flare.*

flake *noun* (*plural* **flakes**)
1 a very light thin piece of something. **2** a small flat piece of falling snow.
flaky *adjective*

flamboyant *adjective*
very showy in appearance or manner.

flame *noun* (*plural* **flames**)
a tongue-shaped portion of fire or burning gas.

flame *verb* (**flames, flaming, flamed**)
1 produce flames. **2** become bright red.

flamingo *noun* (*plural* **flamingoes**)
a wading bird with long legs, a long neck, and pinkish feathers.

flammable *adjective*
able to be set on fire.
flammability *noun*

❶ USAGE See note at *inflammable.*

flank *noun* (*plural* **flanks**)
the side of something, especially an animal's body or an army.

flannel *noun* (*plural* **flannels**)
1 a soft cloth for washing yourself. **2** a soft woollen material.

flap *verb* (**flaps, flapping, flapped**)
1 wave about. **2** (*informal*) panic or fuss about something.
flap *noun* (*plural* **flaps**)
1 a part that is fixed at one edge onto something else, often to cover an opening. **2** the action or sound of flapping. **3** (*informal*) a panic or fuss ♦ *Don't get in a flap.*

flare *verb* (**flares, flaring, flared**)
1 blaze with a sudden bright flame. **2** become angry suddenly. **3** become gradually wider ♦ *flaring nostrils.*
flare *noun* (*plural* **flares**)
1 a sudden bright flame or light, especially one used as a signal. **2** a gradual widening, especially in skirts or trousers.

❶ USAGE Do not confuse with *flair.*

flash *noun* (*plural* **flashes**)
1 a sudden bright flame or light. **2** a device for making a sudden bright light for taking photographs. **3** a sudden display of anger, wit, etc. **4** a short item of news.
flash *verb* (**flashes, flashing, flashed**)
1 make a flash. **2** appear suddenly; move quickly ♦ *The train flashed past us.*

flashback *noun* (*plural* **flashbacks**)
going back in a film or story to something that happened earlier.

flashy *adjective*
gaudy or showy.

flask *noun* (*plural* **flasks**)
1 a bottle with a narrow neck. **2** a vacuum flask.

flat *adjective* (**flatter, flattest**)
1 with no curves or bumps; smooth and level. **2** spread out; lying at full length ♦ *Lie flat on the ground.* **3** (said about a tyre) with no air inside. **4** (said about feet) without the normal arch underneath. **5** absolute ♦ *a flat refusal.* **6** dull; not changing. **7** (said about a drink) no longer fizzy. **8** (said about a battery) unable to produce any more electric current. **9** (in music) one semitone lower than the natural note ♦ *E flat.*
flatly *adverb* **flatness** *noun*

flat *noun* (*plural* **flats**)
1 a set of rooms for living in, usually on one floor of a building. 2 (in music) a note one semitone lower than the natural note; the sign (♭) that indicates this. 3 a punctured tyre.

flatten *verb* (**flattens, flattening, flattened**)
make or become flat.

flatter *verb* (**flatters, flattering, flattered**)
1 praise somebody more than he or she deserves. 2 make a person or thing seem better or more attractive than they really are.
flatterer *noun* **flattery** *noun*

flaunt *verb* (**flaunts, flaunting, flaunted**)
display something proudly in a way that annoys people; show it off ♦ *He liked to flaunt his expensive clothes and cars.*

---

❶ USAGE Do not confuse this word with *flout*, which has a different meaning.

---

flavour *noun* (*plural* **flavours**)
the taste of something.

flavour *verb* (**flavours, flavouring, flavoured**)
give something a flavour; season it.
flavouring *noun*

flaw *noun* (*plural* **flaws**)
something that makes a person or thing imperfect.
flawed *adjective*

flea *noun* (*plural* **fleas**)
a small jumping insect that sucks blood.

fleck *noun* (*plural* **flecks**)
1 a very small patch of colour. 2 a particle; a speck ♦ *flecks of dirt.*
flecked *adjective*

fledged *adjective*
(said about young birds) having grown feathers and able to fly.
fully-fledged *adjective* fully trained
♦ *a fully-fledged engineer.*

fledgeling *noun* (*plural* **fledgelings**)
a young bird that is just fledged.

fleece *noun* (*plural* **fleeces**)
1 the woolly hair of a sheep or similar animal. 2 a warm piece of clothing made from a soft fabric.
fleecy *adjective*

fleece *verb* (**fleeces, fleecing, fleeced**)
1 shear the fleece from a sheep. 2 swindle a person out of some money.

fleet *noun* (*plural* **fleets**)
a number of ships, aircraft, or vehicles owned by one country or company.

fleeting *adjective*
passing quickly; brief.

flesh *noun*
1 the soft substance of the bodies of people and animals, consisting of muscle and fat. 2 the body as opposed to the mind or soul. 3 the pulpy part of fruits and vegetables.
fleshy *adjective*

flex *verb* (**flexes, flexing, flexed**)
bend or stretch something that is flexible
♦ *Try flexing your muscles.*

flex *noun* (*plural* **flexes**)
flexible insulated wire for carrying electric current.

flexible *adjective*
1 easy to bend or stretch. 2 able to be changed or adapted ♦ *Our plans are flexible.*
flexibility *noun*

flick *noun* (*plural* **flicks**)
a quick light hit or movement.

flick *verb* (**flicks, flicking, flicked**)
hit or move with a flick.

flicker *verb* (**flickers, flickering, flickered**)
1 burn or shine unsteadily. 2 move quickly to and fro.

flicker *noun* (*plural* **flickers**)
a flickering light or movement.

flight¹ *noun* (*plural* **flights**)
1 flying. 2 a journey in an aircraft. 3 a series of stairs. 4 a group of flying birds or aircraft. 5 the feathers or fins on a dart or arrow.

flight² *noun* (*plural* **flights**)
fleeing; an escape.

flight recorder *noun* (*plural* **flight recorders**)
an electronic device in an aircraft that records technical information about its flight. It is used after an accident to help find the cause.

flimsy *adjective* (**flimsier, flimsiest**)
made of something thin or weak.
flimsily *adverb* **flimsiness** *noun*

flinch *verb* (**flinches, flinching, flinched**)
move or shrink back because you are afraid; wince.
flinch *noun*

fling *verb* (**flings, flinging, flung**)
throw something violently or carelessly.

fling *noun* (*plural* **flings**)
1 a short time of enjoyment ♦ *a final fling before the exams.* 2 a brief romantic affair. 3 a vigorous dance ♦ *the Highland fling.*

flint *noun* (*plural* **flints**)
1 a very hard kind of stone. 2 a piece of flint or hard metal used to produce sparks.
flinty *adjective*

flip *verb* (**flips, flipping, flipped**)
1 flick. 2 (*slang*) become crazy or very angry.

flip *noun* (*plural* **flips**)
a flipping movement.

flippant *adjective*
not showing proper seriousness.
flippantly *adverb* **flippancy** *noun*

flirt *verb* (flirts, flirting, flirted)
behave as though you are sexually attracted to
someone to amuse yourself.
flirtation *noun*

flirt *noun* (*plural* **flirts**)
a person who flirts.
flirtatious *adjective* **flirtatiously** *adverb*

float *verb* (floats, floating, floated)
1 stay or move on the surface of a liquid or in air.
2 make something float. **3** launch a business by
getting financial support from the sale of shares.
floater *noun*

float *noun* (*plural* **floats**)
1 a device designed to float. **2** a vehicle with a
platform used for delivering milk or for carrying
a display in a parade etc. **3** a small amount of
money kept for paying small bills or giving
change etc.

flock *noun* (*plural* **flocks**)
a group of sheep, goats, or birds.

flock *verb* (flocks, flocking, flocked)
gather or move in a crowd.

flog *verb* (flogs, flogging, flogged)
1 beat a person or animal hard with a whip or
stick as a punishment. **2** (*slang*) sell.
flogging *noun*

flood *noun* (*plural* **floods**)
1 a large amount of water spreading over a place
that is usually dry. **2** a great amount ♦ *a flood of
requests*. **3** the movement of the tide when it is
coming in towards the land.

flood *verb* (floods, flooding, flooded)
1 cover with a flood. **2** come in great amounts
♦ *Letters flooded in*.

floodlight *noun* (*plural* **floodlights**)
a lamp that makes a broad bright beam to light
up a stage, stadium, important building, etc.
floodlit *adjective*

floor *noun* (*plural* **floors**)
1 the part of a room that people walk on.
2 a storey of a building; all the rooms at the same
level.

---

❶ USAGE In Britain, the *ground floor* of a
building is the one at street level, and the one
above it is the *first floor*. In the USA, the *first
floor* is the one at street level, and the one above
it is the *second floor*.

---

floor *verb* (floors, flooring, floored)
1 put a floor into a building. **2** knock a person
down. **3** baffle somebody.
[from Old English]

flop *verb* (flops, flopping, flopped)
1 fall or sit down clumsily. **2** hang or sway
heavily and loosely. **3** (*slang*) be a failure.
floppy *adjective*

floppy disk *noun* (*plural* **floppy disks**)
a flexible disc holding data for use in a computer.

flora *noun*
the plants of a particular area or period.
(Compare **fauna**.)

florist *noun* (*plural* **florists**)
a shopkeeper who sells flowers.

floss *noun*
1 silky thread or fibres. **2** a soft medicated thread
pulled between the teeth to clean them.
flossy *adjective*

flotsam *noun*
wreckage or cargo found floating after a
shipwreck.
flotsam and jetsam odds and ends.

flounce *verb* (flounces, flouncing, flounced)
go in an impatient or annoyed manner
♦ *She flounced out of the room.*
flounce *noun*

flounder *verb* (flounders, floundering,
floundered)
1 move clumsily and with difficulty. **2** make
mistakes or become confused when trying to do
something.

flour *noun*
a fine powder of wheat or other grain, used in
cooking.
floury *adjective*

flourish *verb* (flourishes, flourishing,
flourished)
1 grow or develop strongly. **2** be successful;
prosper. **3** wave something about dramatically.

flourish *noun* (*plural* **flourishes**)
a showy or dramatic sweeping movement, curve,
or passage of music.

flout *verb* (flouts, flouting, flouted)
disobey a rule or instruction openly and
scornfully ♦ *She shaved her head one day, just
because she loved to flout convention.*

---

❶ USAGE Do not confuse this word with *flaunt*,
which has a different meaning.

---

flow *verb* (flows, flowing, flowed)
1 move along smoothly or continuously. **2** gush
out ♦ *Water flowed from the tap.* **3** hang loosely
♦ *flowing hair.* **4** (said about the tide) come in
towards the land.

flow *noun* (*plural* **flows**)
1 a flowing movement or mass. **2** a steady
continuous stream of something ♦ *a flow of
ideas*. **3** the movement of the tide when it is
coming in towards the land ♦ *the ebb and flow of
the tide.*

flower *noun* (*plural* **flowers**)
1 the part of a plant from which seed and fruit
develops. **2** a blossom and its stem used for
decoration, usually in groups.

flower *verb* (flowers, flowering, flowered)
produce flowers.

flowery *adjective*
1 full of flowers. 2 (said about language) elaborate, full of ornamental phrases.

flu *noun*
influenza.

fluctuate *verb* (**fluctuates, fluctuating, fluctuated**)
rise and fall; vary ♦ *Prices fluctuated.*
fluctuation *noun*

fluent (*say* **floo**-ent) *adjective*
1 skilful at speaking clearly and without hesitating. 2 able to speak a foreign language easily and well.
fluently *adverb* **fluency** *noun*

fluff *noun*
a fluffy substance.

fluffy *adjective*
having a mass of soft fur or fibres.
fluffiness *noun*

fluid *noun* (*plural* **fluids**)
a substance that is able to flow freely as liquids and gases do.

fluid *adjective*
1 able to flow freely. 2 not fixed ♦ *My plans for Christmas are fluid.*
fluidity *noun*

fluke *noun* (*plural* **flukes**)
a success that you achieve by unexpected good luck.

fluorescent (*say* floo-er-**ess**-ent) *adjective*
creating light from radiation ♦ *a fluorescent lamp.*
fluorescence *noun*

fluoridation *noun*
adding fluoride to drinking water in order to help prevent tooth decay.

fluoride *noun*
a chemical substance that is thought to prevent tooth decay.

flurry *noun* (*plural* **flurries**)
1 a sudden whirling gust of wind, rain, or snow. 2 a short period of activity or excitement.

flush¹ *verb* (**flushes, flushing, flushed**)
1 blush. 2 clean or remove something with a fast flow of water.

flush *noun* (*plural* **flushes**)
1 a blush. 2 a fast flow of water. 3 (in card games) a hand of cards of the same suit.

flush² *adjective*
1 level with the surrounding surface ♦ *The doors are flush with the walls.* 2 (*informal*) having plenty of money.

fluster *verb* (**flusters, flustering, flustered**)
make somebody nervous and confused.
fluster *noun*

flute *noun* (*plural* **flutes**)
a musical instrument consisting of a long pipe with holes that are stopped by fingers or keys.

flutter *verb* (**flutters, fluttering, fluttered**)
1 flap wings quickly. 2 move or flap quickly and irregularly.

flutter *noun* (*plural* **flutters**)
1 a fluttering movement. 2 a nervously excited condition. 3 (*informal*) a small bet ♦ *Have a flutter!*

fly¹ *noun* (*plural* **flies**)
1 a small flying insect with two wings. 2 a real or artificial fly used as bait in fishing.

fly² *verb* (**flies, flying, flew, flown**)
1 move through the air by means of wings or in an aircraft. 2 travel through the air or through space. 3 wave in the air ♦ *Flags were flying.*
4 make something fly ♦ *They flew model aircraft.* 5 move or pass quickly ♦ *Time flies.*
6 flee from ♦ *You must fly the country!*
flyer *noun*

fly *noun* (*plural* **flies**)
the front opening of a pair of trousers.

flying saucer *noun* (*plural* **flying saucers**)
a mysterious saucer-shaped object reported to have been seen in the sky and believed by some people to be an alien spacecraft.

flyleaf *noun* (*plural* **flyleaves**)
a blank page at the beginning or end of a book.

flyover *noun* (*plural* **flyovers**)
a bridge that carries one road or railway over another.

flywheel *noun* (*plural* **flywheels**)
a heavy wheel used to regulate machinery.

foal *noun* (*plural* **foals**)
a young horse.

foam *noun*
1 a white mass of tiny bubbles on a liquid; froth. 2 a spongy kind of rubber or plastic.
foamy *adjective*

foam *verb* (**foams, foaming, foamed**)
form bubbles or froth.

fob *verb* (**fobs, fobbing, fobbed**)
fob off get rid of someone by an excuse or a trick.

focal *adjective*
to do with or at a focus.

focus *noun* (*plural* **focuses** or **foci**)
1 the distance from an eye or lens at which an object appears clearest. 2 the point at which rays etc. seem to meet. 3 something that is a centre of interest or attention etc.
in focus appearing clearly. **out of focus** not appearing clearly.

focus *verb* (**focuses, focusing, focused**)
1 adjust the focus of your eye or a lens so that objects appear clearly. 2 concentrate
♦ *She focused her attention on the screen.*

fodder *noun*
food for horses and farm animals.

foetus (*say* fee-tus) *noun* (*plural* **foetuses**)
another spelling of **fetus**.

fog *noun*
thick mist.
foggy *adjective*

foghorn *noun* (*plural* **foghorns**)
a loud horn for warning ships in fog.

foil[1] *noun* (*plural* **foils**)
1 a very thin sheet of metal ♦ *cooking foil.*
2 a person or thing that makes another look
better in contrast.

foil[2] *noun* (*plural* **foils**)
a long narrow sword used in the sport of fencing.

foil[3] *verb* (**foils, foiling, foiled**)
prevent something from being successful
♦ *We foiled his evil plan.*

foist *verb* (**foists, foisting, foisted**)
make a person accept something inferior or
unwelcome ♦ *They foisted the job on me.*

fold *verb* (**folds, folding, folded**)
bend or move so that one part lies on another
part.

fold *noun* (*plural* **folds**)
a line where something is folded.

folder *noun* (*plural* **folders**)
a folding cover for loose papers.

folk *noun*
people.

folk dance *nouns* (*plural* **folk dances**)
a dance in the traditional style of a country.

folklore *noun*
old beliefs and legends.

folk song *noun* (*plural* **folk songs**)
a song in the traditional style of a country.

follow *verb* (**follows, following, followed**)
1 go or come after. 2 do a thing after something
else. 3 take a person or thing as a guide or
example. 4 take an interest in the progress of
events or a sport or team etc. 5 understand
♦ *Did you follow what he said?* 6 result from
something.
follower *noun*

following *preposition*
after, as a result of ♦ *Following the burglary, we
had new locks fitted.*

folly *noun* (*plural* **follies**)
foolishness; a foolish action etc.

fond *adjective*
1 loving or liking a person or thing. 2 foolishly
hopeful ♦ *fond hopes.*
fondly *adverb* **fondness** *noun*

fondle *verb* (**fondles, fondling, fondled**)
touch or stroke lovingly.

food *noun* (*plural* **foods**)
any substance that a person or animal can eat in
order to grow and be healthy.

food chain *noun* (*plural* **food chains**)
a series of plants and animals each of which
serves as food for the one above it in the series.

fool *noun* (*plural* **fools**)
1 a stupid person; someone who acts unwisely.
2 a jester or clown ♦ *Stop playing the fool.*
3 a creamy pudding with crushed fruit in it
♦ *gooseberry fool.*
fool's errand a useless errand. **fool's paradise**
happiness that comes only from being mistaken
about something.

fool *verb* (**fools, fooling, fooled**)
1 behave in a joking way; play about. 2 trick or
deceive someone.

foolish *adjective*
without good sense or judgement; unwise.
foolishly *adverb* **foolishness** *noun*

foolproof *adjective*
easy to use or do correctly.

foot *noun* (*plural* **feet**)
1 the lower part of the leg below the ankle.
2 any similar part, e.g. one used by certain
animals to move or attach themselves to
things. 3 the lowest part ♦ *the foot of the hill.*
4 a measure of length, 12 inches or about 30
centimetres ♦ *a ten-foot pole*; ♦ *it is ten feet long.*
5 a unit of rhythm in a line of poetry, e.g. each of
the four divisions in *Jack / and Jill / went up / the
hill.*
on foot walking.

foot-and-mouth disease *noun*
a serious contagious disease that affects cattle,
sheep, and other animals.

football *noun* (*plural* **footballs**)
1 a game played by two teams which try to kick
an inflated leather ball into their opponents'
goal. 2 the ball used in this game.
footballer *noun*

foothill *noun* (*plural* **foothills**)
a low hill near the bottom of a mountain or range
of mountains.

foothold *noun* (*plural* **footholds**)
1 a place to put your foot when climbing.
2 a small but firm position from which further
progress can be made.

footing *noun*
1 having your feet placed on something; a
foothold ♦ *He lost his footing and slipped.*
2 the status or nature of a relationship ♦ *We are
on a friendly footing with that
country.*

footlights *plural noun*
a row of lights along the front of the floor of a
stage.

footnote *noun* (*plural* **footnotes**)
a note printed at the bottom of the page.

footpath *noun* (*plural* **footpaths**)
a path for pedestrians.

footprint noun (plural **footprints**)
a mark made by a foot or shoe.

footstep noun (plural **footsteps**)
1 a step taken in walking or running.
2 the sound of this.

for preposition
This word is used to show 1 purpose or direction (*This letter is for you; We set out for home*),
2 distance or time (*Walk for six miles or two hours*), 3 price or exchange (*We bought it for £2; New lamps for old*), 4 cause (*She was fined for speeding*), 5 defence or support (*He fought for his country; Are you for us or against us?*),
6 reference (*For all her wealth, she is bored*),
7 similarity or correspondence (*We took him for a fool*).
for ever for all time; always.

for conjunction
because ♦ *They hesitated, for they were afraid.*

forbear verb (**forbears, forbearing, forbore, forborne**)
1 refrain from something ♦ *We forbore to mention it.* 2 be patient or tolerant.
forbearance noun

forbid verb (**forbids, forbidding, forbade, forbidden**)
1 order someone not to do something. 2 refuse to allow ♦ *We shall forbid the marriage.*

forbidding adjective
looking stern or unfriendly.

force noun (plural **forces**)
1 strength or power. 2 (in science) an influence, which can be measured, that causes something to move. 3 an organized group of police, soldiers, etc.
in or **into force** in or into effectiveness
♦ *The new law comes into force next week.*
the forces a country's armed forces.

force verb (**forces, forcing, forced**)
1 use force in order to get or do something, or to make somebody obey. 2 break something open by force. 3 cause plants to grow or bloom earlier than is normal ♦ *You can force them in a greenhouse.*

forceful adjective
strong and vigorous.
forcefully adverb

forcible adjective
done by force; forceful.
forcibly adverb

ford noun (plural **fords**)
a shallow place where you can walk across a river.

ford verb (**fords, fording, forded**)
cross a river at a ford.

fore adjective & adverb
at or towards the front ♦ *fore and aft.*

fore noun
the front part.
to the fore to or at the front; in or to a prominent position.

forearm[1] noun (plural **forearms**)
the arm from the elbow to the wrist or fingertips.

forearm[2] verb (**forearms, forearming, forearmed**)
prepare in advance against possible danger.

forecast noun (plural **forecasts**)
a statement that tells in advance what is likely to happen.

forecast verb (**forecasts, forecasting, forecast**)
make a forecast.
forecaster noun

forefinger noun (plural **forefingers**)
the finger next to the thumb.

foregone conclusion noun (plural **foregone conclusions**)
a result that can be foreseen easily or is bound to happen.

foreground noun
the part of a scene, picture, or view that is nearest to you.

forehand noun (plural **forehands**)
a stroke made in tennis etc. with the palm of the hand turned forwards.

forehead (say **forrid** or **for**-hed) noun (plural **foreheads**)
the part of the face above the eyes.

foreign adjective
1 belonging to or in another country. 2 not belonging naturally to a place or to someone's nature ♦ *Lying is foreign to her nature.*

foreigner noun (plural **foreigners**)
a person from another country.

foreman noun (plural **foremen**)
1 a worker in charge of a group of other workers. 2 a member of a jury who is in charge of the jury's discussions and who speaks on its behalf.

foremost adjective & adverb
first in position or rank; most important.

forensic (say fer-en-sik) adjective
to do with or used in lawcourts.

forensic medicine noun
medical knowledge used in legal matters or in solving crimes.

forerunner noun (plural **forerunners**)
a person or thing that comes before another; a sign of what is to come.

foresee verb (**foresees, foreseeing, foresaw, foreseen**)
realize what is going to happen.

foreshadow verb (**foreshadows, foreshadowing, foreshadowed**)
be a sign of something that is to come.

foreshorten *verb* (foreshortens, foreshortening, foreshortened)
show an object in a drawing etc. with some lines shortened to give an effect of distance or depth.

foresight *noun*
the ability to foresee and prepare for future needs.

forest *noun* (*plural* forests)
trees and undergrowth covering a large area.
forested *adjective*

forestry *noun*
planting forests and looking after them.
forester *noun*

foretaste *noun* (*plural* foretastes)
an experience of something that is to come in the future.

foretell *verb* (foretells, foretelling, foretold)
tell in advance; prophesy.

forethought *noun*
careful thought and planning for the future.

foreword *noun* (*plural* forewords)
a preface.

forfeit (*say* for-fit) *verb* (forfeits, forfeiting, forfeited)
pay or give up something as a penalty.
forfeiture *noun*

forfeit *noun* (*plural* forfeits)
something forfeited.

forge¹ *noun* (*plural* forges)
a place where metal is heated and shaped; a blacksmith's workshop.

forge *verb* (forges, forging, forged)
1 shape metal by heating and hammering.
2 copy something in order to deceive people.
forger *noun* **forgery** *noun*

forge² *verb* (forges, forging, forged)
forge ahead move forward by a strong effort.

forget *verb* (forgets, forgetting, forgot, forgotten)
1 fail to remember. 2 stop thinking about ♦ *Forget your troubles*.
forget yourself behave rudely or thoughtlessly.

forgetful *adjective*
tending to forget.
forgetfully *adverb* **forgetfulness** *noun*

forgive *verb* (forgives, forgiving, forgave, forgiven)
stop feeling angry with somebody about something.
forgiveness *noun*

fork *noun* (*plural* forks)
1 a small device with prongs for lifting food to your mouth. 2 a large device with prongs used for digging or lifting things. 3 a place where something separates into two or more parts ♦ *a fork in the road*.

fork *verb* (forks, forking, forked)
1 lift or dig with a fork. 2 form a fork by separating into two branches. 3 follow one of these branches ♦ *Fork left*.
fork out (*slang*) pay out money.

fork-lift truck *noun* (*plural* fork-lift trucks)
a truck with two metal bars at the front for lifting and moving heavy loads.

forlorn *adjective*
left alone and unhappy.
forlorn hope the only faint hope left.

form *noun* (*plural* forms)
1 the shape, appearance, or condition of something. 2 the way something exists ♦ *Ice is a form of water*. 3 a class in school. 4 a bench.
5 a piece of paper with spaces to be filled in.

form *verb* (forms, forming, formed)
1 shape or construct something; create.
2 come into existence; develop ♦ *Icicles formed*.

formal *adjective*
1 strictly following the accepted rules or customs; ceremonious ♦ *a formal occasion*;
♦ *formal dress*. 2 rather serious and stiff in your manner.
formally *adverb*

format *noun* (*plural* formats)
1 the shape and size of something.
2 the way something is arranged or organized.
3 (in computing) the way data is organized for processing or storage by a computer.

formation *noun* (*plural* formations)
1 the act of forming something. 2 a thing formed.
3 a special arrangement or pattern ♦ *flying in formation*.

former *adjective*
of an earlier time.
formerly *adverb*
the former the first of two people or things just mentioned.

formidable (*say* for-mid-a-bul) *adjective*
1 difficult to deal with or do ♦ *a formidable task*.
2 fearsome or frightening.
formidably *adverb*

formula *noun* (*plural* formulae)
1 a set of chemical symbols showing what a substance consists of. 2 a rule or statement expressed in symbols or numbers. 3 a list of substances needed for making something.
4 a fixed wording for a ceremony etc. 5 one of the groups into which racing cars are placed according to the size of their engines ♦ *Formula One*.

formulate *verb* (formulates, formulating, formulated)
express an idea or plan clearly and exactly.
formulation *noun*

fort *noun* (*plural* forts)
a fortified building.

forth adverb
1 out; into view. 2 onwards or forwards
♦ from this day forth.
and so forth and so on.

forthcoming adjective
1 happening soon ♦ forthcoming events. 2 made
available when needed ♦ Money for the trip was
not forthcoming. 3 willing to give information.

forthright adjective
frank and outspoken.

fortification noun (plural **fortifications**)
1 fortifying something. 2 a wall or building
constructed to make a place strong against
attack.

fortify verb (**fortifies, fortifying, fortified**)
1 make a place strong against attack, especially
by building fortifications. 2 strengthen.

fortnight noun (plural **fortnights**)
a period of two weeks.
fortnightly adverb & adjective

fortress noun (plural **fortresses**)
a fortified building or town.

fortunate adjective
lucky.
fortunately adverb

fortune noun (plural **fortunes**)
1 luck, especially good luck. 2 a great amount of
money.
tell someone's fortune predict what will
happen to them in the future.

forty adjective & noun(plural **forties**)
the number 40.
fortieth adjective & noun
forty winks a short sleep; a nap.

forward adjective
1 going forwards. 2 placed in the front. 3 having
made more than the normal progress. 4 too eager
or bold.
forwardness noun
forward adverb
forwards.
forward noun (plural **forwards**)
a player in the front line of a team in football,
hockey, etc.

forwards adverb
1 to or towards the front. 2 in the direction you
are facing.

fossil noun (plural **fossils**)
the remains or traces of a prehistoric animal or
plant that has been buried in the ground for a
very long time and become hardened in rock.
fossilized adjective

fossil fuel (plural **fossil fuels**)
a natural fuel such as coal or gas formed in the
geological past.

foster verb (**fosters, fostering, fostered**)
1 bring up someone else's child as if he or she
was your own. 2 help to grow or develop.
foster child noun **foster parent** noun

foul adjective
1 disgusting; tasting or smelling unpleasant.
2 (said about weather) rough; stormy. 3 unfair;
breaking the rules of a game. 4 very disagreeable
or unpleasant ♦ a foul mood.
foully adverb **foulness** noun

foul noun (plural **fouls**)
an action that breaks the rules of a game.

foul verb (**fouls, fouling, fouled**)
1 make or become foul ♦ Smoke had fouled the
air. 2 commit a foul against a player in a game.

found¹ past tense of **find**.

found² verb (**founds, founding, founded**)
1 establish; provide money for starting
♦ They founded a hospital. 2 base ♦ This novel is
founded on fact.

foundation noun (plural **foundations**)
1 the solid base on which a building is built up.
2 the basis for something. 3 the founding of
something. 4 a fund of money set aside for a
charitable purpose.
foundation stone noun

founder¹ noun (plural **founders**)
a person who founds something ♦ the founder of
the hospital.

founder² verb (**founders, foundering,
foundered**)
1 fill with water and sink ♦ The ship foundered.
2 stumble or fall. 3 fail completely ♦ Their plans
foundered.

fountain noun (plural **fountains**)
an ornamental structure in which a jet of water
shoots up into the air.

four adjective & noun(plural **fours**)
the number 4.
on all fours on hands and knees.

fourteen adjective & noun
the number 14.
fourteenth adjective & noun

fourth adjective
next after the third.
fourthly adverb

fourth noun (plural **fourths**)
1 the fourth person or thing. 2 one of four equal
parts; a quarter.

fowl noun (plural **fowls**)
a bird, especially one kept on a farm etc. for its
eggs or meat.

fox noun (plural **foxes**)
a wild animal that looks like a dog with a long
furry tail.
foxy adjective

fraction noun (plural **fractions**)
1 a number that is not a whole number, e.g. $\frac{1}{2}$,
0.5. **2** a tiny part.
fractional adjective **fractionally** adverb

fracture noun (plural **fractures**)
the breaking of something, especially of a bone.
fracture verb (**fractures, fracturing, fractured**)
break.

fragile adjective
easy to break or damage.
fragility noun

fragment noun (plural **fragments**)
1 a small piece broken off. **2** a small part.
fragmentary adjective **fragmentation** noun
fragmented adjective

fragrant adjective
having a pleasant smell.
fragrance noun

frail adjective
1 (said about people) not strong or healthy
♦ a frail old man. **2** (said about things) fragile.
frailty noun

frame noun (plural **frames**)
1 a holder that fits round the outside of a picture.
2 a rigid structure that supports something.
3 a human or animal body ♦ He has a small
frame. **4** a single exposure on a cinema film.
frame of mind the way you think or feel for a
while.
frame verb (**frames, framing, framed**)
1 put a frame on or round. **2** construct or form
♦ They framed the question badly. **3** make an
innocent person seem guilty by arranging false
evidence.

framework noun (plural **frameworks**)
1 a frame supporting something. **2** a basic plan
or system.

franc noun (plural **francs**)
a unit of money used in many countries and
replaced in some by the euro in 2002.

frank adjective
making your thoughts and feelings clear to
people; candid.
frankly adverb **frankness** noun

frantic adjective
wildly agitated or excited.
frantically adverb

fraud noun (plural **frauds**)
1 the crime of swindling people. **2** a dishonest
trick. **3** an impostor; a person or thing that is not
what it pretends to be.
fraudulent adjective **fraudulently** adverb
fraudulence noun

fray[1] noun (plural **frays**)
a fight or conflict ♦ ready for the fray.

fray[2] verb (**frays, fraying, frayed**)
1 make or become ragged so that loose threads
show. **2** (said about tempers or nerves) become
strained or upset.

freak noun (plural **freaks**)
a very strange or abnormal person, animal, or
thing.
freakish adjective

freckle noun (plural **freckles**)
a small brown spot on the skin.
freckled adjective
[from Old Norse]

free adjective (**freer, freest**)
1 able to do what you want to do or go where
you want to go. **2** not costing anything.
3 not fixed ♦ Leave one end free. **4** not having or
being affected by something ♦ The harbour is
free of ice. **5** available; not being used or
occupied. **6** generous ♦ She is very free with her
money.
freely adverb
free verb (**frees, freeing, freed**)
set free.

freedom noun (plural **freedoms**)
being free; independence.

freehand adjective
(said about a drawing) done without a ruler or
compasses, or without tracing it ♦ Draw a circle
freehand.

free-range adjective
1 free-range hens are not kept in small cages but
are allowed to move about freely. **2** free-range
eggs are ones laid by these hens.

freewheel verb (**freewheels, freewheeling,
freewheeled**)
ride a bicycle without pedalling.

freeze verb (**freezes, freezing, froze, frozen**)
1 turn into ice; become covered with ice. **2** make
or be very cold. **3** keep wages or prices etc. at a
fixed level. **4** suddenly stand completely still.

freezer noun (plural **freezers**)
a refrigerator in which food can be frozen
quickly and stored.

freezing point noun (plural **freezing points**)
the temperature at which a liquid freezes.

French window noun (plural **French
windows**)
a long window that serves as a door on an
outside wall.

frenzy noun
wild excitement or agitation.
frenzied adjective **frenziedly** adverb

frequency noun (plural **frequencies**)
1 being frequent. **2** how often something
happens. **3** the number of vibrations made each
second by a wave of sound, radio, or light.

frequent (*say* **freek**-went) *adjective*
happening often.
frequently *adverb*

frequent (*say* frik-**went**) *verb* (**frequents, frequenting, frequented**)
be in or go to a place often ♦ *They frequented the club.*

fresh *adjective*
1 newly made or produced or arrived; not stale ♦ *fresh bread.* 2 not tinned or preserved ♦ *fresh fruit.* 3 cool and clean ♦ *fresh air.* 4 (said about water) not salty.
freshly *adverb* **freshness** *noun*

freshen *verb* (**freshens, freshening, freshened**)
make or become fresh.

fret¹ *verb* (**frets, fretting, fretted**)
worry about something.
fretful *adjective* **fretfully** *adverb*

fret² *noun* (*plural* **frets**)
a bar or ridge on the fingerboard of a guitar etc.

friar *noun* (*plural* **friars**)
a man who is a member of a Roman Catholic religious order and has vowed to live a life of poverty.
friary *noun*

friction *noun*
1 rubbing of one thing against another. 2 bad feeling between people; quarrelling.
frictional *adjective*

Friday *noun*
the day of the week following Thursday.
[from Old English *Frigedaeg* = day of Frigga, a Norse goddess]

fridge *noun* (*plural* **fridges**)
a refrigerator.

friend *noun* (*plural* **friends**)
1 a person you like who likes you. 2 a helpful or kind person.

friendly *adjective* (**friendlier, friendliest**)
behaving like a friend.
friendliness *noun*

friendship *noun* (*plural* **friendships**)
being friends.

frieze (*say* freez) *noun* (*plural* **friezes**)
a strip of designs or pictures round the top of a wall.

fright *noun* (*plural* **frights**)
1 sudden great fear. 2 a person or thing that looks ridiculous.

frighten *verb* (**frightens, frightening, frightened**)
make someone afraid.
be frightened of be afraid of.

frightful *adjective*
awful; very great or bad.
frightfully *adverb*

frill *noun* (*plural* **frills**)
1 a decorative gathered or pleated trimming on a dress, curtain, etc. 2 something extra that is pleasant but unnecessary ♦ *a simple life with no frills.*
frilled *adjective* **frilly** *adjective*

fringe *noun* (*plural* **fringes**)
1 a decorative edging with many threads hanging down loosely. 2 a straight line of hair hanging down over the forehead. 3 the edge of something.
fringed *adjective*

frisk *verb* (**frisks, frisking, frisked**)
1 jump or run about playfully. 2 search somebody by running your hands over his or her clothes.

frisky *adjective*
playful or lively.
friskily *adverb* **friskiness** *noun*

fritter¹ *noun* (*plural* **fritters**)
a slice of meat or fruit or potato etc. coated in batter and fried.

fritter² *verb* (**fritters, frittering, frittered**)
waste something gradually; spend money or time on trivial things.

frivolous *adjective*
seeking pleasure in a light-hearted way; not serious.
frivolously *adverb* **frivolity** *noun*

frizzy *adjective*
(said about hair) in tight curls.
frizziness *noun*

fro *adverb*
to and fro backwards and forwards.

frock *noun* (*plural* **frocks**)
a girl's or woman's dress.

frog *noun* (*plural* **frogs**)
a small jumping animal that can live both in water and on land.
a frog in your throat hoarseness.

frolic *noun* (*plural* **frolics**)
a lively cheerful game or entertainment.
frolicsome *adjective*

frolic *verb* (**frolics, frolicking, frolicked**)
play about in a lively cheerful way.

from *preposition*
This word is used to show 1 starting point in space or time or order (*We flew from London to Paris. We work from 9 to 5 o'clock. Count from one to ten*), 2 source or origin (*Get water from the tap*), 3 separation or release (*Take the gun from him. She was freed from prison*), 4 difference (*Can you tell margarine from butter?*), 5 cause (*I suffer from headaches*).

frond *noun* (*plural* **fronds**)
a leaf-like part of a fern, palm tree, etc.

front *noun* (*plural* **fronts**)
1 the part or side that comes first or is the most important or furthest forward. **2** a road or promenade along the seashore. **3** the place where fighting is happening in a war.
4 (in weather systems) the forward edge of an approaching mass of air.
frontal *adjective*

front *adjective*
of the front; in front.

frontier *noun* (*plural* **frontiers**)
the boundary between two countries or regions.

frontispiece *noun* (*plural* **frontispieces**)
an illustration opposite the title page of a book.

frost *noun* (*plural* **frosts**)
1 powdery ice that forms on things in freezing weather. **2** weather with a temperature below freezing point.

frosted *adjective*
covered with frost.

frostbite *noun*
harm done to the body by very cold weather.
frostbitten *adjective*

frosty *adjective* (**frostier, frostiest**)
1 cold with frost. **2** unfriendly and unwelcoming ♦ *a frosty look.*
frostily *adverb*

froth *noun*
a white mass of tiny bubbles on a liquid.
frothy *adjective*

frown *verb* (**frowns, frowning, frowned**)
wrinkle your forehead because you are angry or worried.

frown *noun* (*plural* **frowns**)
a frowning movement or look.

fruit *noun* (*plural* **fruits** or **fruit**)
1 the seed container that grows on a tree or plant and is often used as food. **2** the result of doing something ♦ *the fruits of his efforts.*
fruity *adjective*

fruit *verb* (**fruits, fruiting, fruited**)
produce fruit.

fruitful *adjective*
producing good results ♦ *fruitful discussions.*
fruitfully *adverb*

fruitless *adjective*
producing no results.
fruitlessly *adverb*

frustrate *verb* (**frustrates, frustrating, frustrated**)
prevent somebody from doing something; prevent something from being successful ♦ *A lack of money has frustrated our plans.*
frustration *noun*

fry *verb* (**fries, frying, fried**)
cook something in very hot fat.
fryer *noun*

fudge *noun*
a soft sugary sweet.

fuel *noun* (*plural* **fuels**)
something that is burnt to produce heat or power.

fuel *verb* (**fuels, fuelling, fuelled**)
supply something with fuel.

fugitive (*say* few-jit-iv) *noun* (*plural* **fugitives**)
a person who is running away from something.

fulcrum *noun* (*plural* **fulcrums** or **fulcra**)
the point on which a lever rests.

fulfil *verb* (**fulfils, fulfilling, fulfilled**)
1 do what is required; satisfy; carry out
♦ *You must fulfil your promises.* **2** make something come true ♦ *It fulfilled an ancient prophecy.* **3** give you satisfaction.
fulfilment *noun*

full *adjective*
1 containing as much or as many as possible.
2 having many people or things ♦ *full of ideas.*
3 complete ♦ *the full story.* **4** the greatest possible ♦ *at full speed.* **5** fitting loosely; with many folds ♦ *a full skirt.*
fully *adverb* **fullness** *noun*
in full with nothing left out ♦ *We have paid in full.*

full *adverb*
completely and directly ♦ *It hit him full in the face.*
[from Old English]

full-blown *adjective*
fully developed.

full moon *noun* (*plural* **full moons**)
the moon when you can see the whole of it as a bright disc.

full stop *noun* (*plural* **full stops**)
the dot used as a punctuation mark at the end of a sentence or an abbreviation.

fully *adverb*
completely.

fumble *verb* (**fumbles, fumbling, fumbled**)
hold or handle something clumsily.

fume *noun* or **fumes** *plural noun*
strong-smelling smoke or gas.

fume *verb* (**fumes, fuming, fumed**)
1 give off fumes. **2** be very angry.

fumigate (*say* few-mig-ayt) *verb* (**fumigates, fumigating, fumigated**)
disinfect something by fumes.
fumigation *noun*

fun *noun*
amusement or enjoyment.
make fun of make people laugh at a person or thing.

function *noun* (*plural* **functions**)
1 what somebody or something is there to
do ♦ *The function of a knife is to cut things.*
2 an important event or party. 3 a basic
operation in a computer or calculator.
4 a variable quantity whose value depends on
the value of other variable quantities ♦ *X is a
function of Y and Z.*

function *verb* (**functions, functioning,
functioned**)
perform a function; work properly.

fund *noun* (*plural* **funds**)
1 money collected or kept for a special purpose.
2 a stock or supply.

fund *verb* (**funds, funding, funded**)
supply with money.

fundamental *adjective*
basic.
fundamentally *adverb*

funeral *noun* (*plural* **funerals**)
the ceremony when a dead person is buried or
cremated.

funfair *noun* (*plural* **funfairs**)
a fair consisting of amusements and sideshows.

fungus *noun* (*plural* **fungi** (*say* fung-I))
a plant without leaves or flowers that grows on
other plants or on decayed material, such as
mushrooms and toadstools.
[from Latin]

funnel *noun* (*plural* **funnels**)
1 a metal chimney on a ship or steam engine.
2 a tube that is wide at the top and narrow at the
bottom to help you pour things into a narrow
opening.
[from Latin *fundere* = pour]

funny *adjective* (**funnier, funniest**)
1 making you laugh or smile. 2 strange or odd
♦ *a funny smell.*
funnily *adverb*

fur *noun* (*plural* **furs**)
1 the soft hair that covers some animals.
2 animal skin with the fur on it, used for
clothing; fabric that looks like animal fur.

furious *adjective*
1 very angry. 2 violent or intense ♦ *furious heat.*
furiously *adverb*

furnace *noun* (*plural* **furnaces**)
a device in which great heat can be produced,
e.g. for melting metals or making glass.

furnish *verb* (**furnishes, furnishing, furnished**)
1 provide a place with furniture. 2 provide or
supply with something.

furniture *noun*
tables, chairs, and other movable things that you
need in a house or school or office etc.

furrow *noun* (plural **furrows**)
1 a long cut in the ground made by a plough or
other implement. 2 a groove. 3 a deep wrinkle in
the skin.

furry *adjective*
like fur; covered with fur.

further *adverb* & *adjective*
1 at or to a greater distance; more distant.
2 more; additional ♦ *We made further enquiries.*

❶ USAGE See the note at *farther.*

further *verb* (**furthers, furthering, furthered**)
help something to progress ♦ *This success will
further your career.*
furtherance *noun*

further education *noun*
education for people above school age.

furthest *adverb* & *adjective*
at or to the greatest distance; most distant.

fury *noun* (*plural* **furies**)
wild anger; rage.

fuse¹ *noun* (*plural* **fuses**)
a safety device containing a short piece of wire
that melts if too much electricity is passed
through it.

fuse *verb* (**fuses, fusing, fused**)
1 stop working because a fuse has melted.
2 blend together, especially through melting.

fuse² *noun* (*plural* **fuses**)
a length of material that burns easily, used for
setting off an explosive.

fusion *noun*
1 the action of blending or uniting things.
2 the uniting of atomic nuclei, usually releasing
energy.

fuss *noun* (*plural* **fusses**)
1 unnecessary excitement or bustle.
2 an agitated protest.
make a fuss of treat someone with great
kindness and attention.

fuss *verb* (**fusses, fussing, fussed**)
make a fuss about something.

fussy *adjective* (**fussier, fussiest**)
1 fussing; inclined to make a fuss. 2 choosing
very carefully; hard to please. 3 full of
unnecessary details or decorations.
fussily *adverb* **fussiness** *noun*

future *noun*
1 time that will come; what is going to
happen then. 2 (in grammar) the tense of a verb
that indicates something happening in the
future, expressed by using 'shall', 'will', or 'be
going to'.

future *adjective*
belonging or referring to the future.

fuzz *noun*
something fluffy or frizzy.

fuzzy *adjective*
1 like fuzz; covered with fuzz. 2 blurred; not
clear.
fuzzily *adverb* **fuzziness** *noun*

Gg

gabble *verb* (gabbles, gabbling, gabbled)
talk so quickly that it is difficult to know what is
being said.

gadget *noun* (*plural* gadgets)
any small useful tool.
gadgetry *noun*
[probably from French *gâchette*, = lock
mechanism]

Gaelic (*say* gay-lik) *noun*
the Celtic languages of Scotland and Ireland.

gag *noun* (*plural* gags)
1 something put into a person's mouth or tied
over it to prevent them from speaking. **2** a joke.
gag *verb* (gags, gagging, gagged)
1 put a gag on a person. **2** prevent someone from
making comments ♦ *We cannot gag the press.*
3 retch.

gaggle *noun* (*plural* gaggles)
a flock of geese.

gaiety *noun*
1 cheerfulness. **2** brightly coloured appearance.

gaily *adverb*
in a cheerful way.

gain *verb* (gains, gaining, gained)
1 get something that you did not have before;
obtain. **2** a clock or watch gains when it becomes
ahead of the correct time. **3** reach; arrive at
♦ *At last we gained the shore.*
gain on come closer to a person or thing when
chasing them or in a race.
gain *noun* (*plural* gains)
something gained; a profit or improvement.
gainful *adjective*

galaxy *noun* (*plural* galaxies)
a very large group of stars.
galactic (*say* ga-lak-tik) *adjective*

gale *noun* (*plural* gales)
a very strong wind.

gallant (*say* gal-lant) *adjective*
1 brave or heroic ♦ *a gallant effort.* **2** (*say*
gal-lant or ga-**lant**) courteous towards women.
gallantly *adverb* **gallantry** *noun*

gallery *noun* (*plural* galleries)
1 a room or building for showing works of art.
2 a platform jutting out from the wall in a church
or hall. **3** the highest balcony in a cinema or
theatre. **4** a long room or passage.

gallon *noun* (*plural* gallons)
a unit used to measure liquids, 8 pints or 4.546
litres.

gallop *noun* (*plural* gallops)
1 the fastest pace that a horse can go. **2** a fast ride
on a horse.

gallop *verb* (gallops, galloping, galloped)
go or ride at a gallop.

gallows *noun* (*plural* gallows)
a framework with a noose for hanging criminals.

galoshes *plural noun*
a pair of waterproof shoes worn over ordinary
shoes.

galvanize *verb* (galvanizes, galvanizing,
galvanized)
1 stimulate someone into sudden activity.
2 coat iron with zinc to protect it from rust.
galvanization *noun*

gambit *noun* (*plural* gambits)
1 a kind of opening move in chess. **2** an action or
remark intended to gain an advantage.

gamble *verb* (gambles, gambling, gambled)
1 bet on the result of a game, race, or other
event. **2** take great risks in the hope of gaining
something.
gambler *noun*
gamble *noun* (*plural* gambles)
1 a bet or chance ♦ *a gamble on the lottery.*
2 a risky attempt.

gambol *verb* (gambols, gambolling,
gambolled)
jump or skip about in play.

game *noun* (*plural* games)
1 a form of play or sport, especially one with
rules ♦ *a game of football;* ♦ *a computer game.*
2 a section of a long game such as tennis or
whist. **3** a scheme or plan; a trick ♦ *Whatever his
game is, he won't succeed.* **4** wild animals or
birds hunted for sport or food.
give the game away reveal a secret.
game *adjective*
1 able and willing to do something ♦ *'Shall we
swim to the island?' 'I'm game!'* **2** brave.
gamely *adverb*

gamekeeper *noun* (*plural* gamekeepers)
a person employed to protect game birds and
animals, especially from poachers.

gamma *noun*
the third letter of the Greek alphabet, = g.

gamma rays *plural noun*
very short X-rays emitted by radioactive
substances.

gander *noun* (*plural* ganders)
a male goose.

gang *noun* (*plural* gangs)
1 a group of people who do things together.
2 a group of criminals.
gang *verb* (gangs, ganging, ganged)
join in a gang ♦ *gang together.*
gang up on form a group to fight or oppose
someone.

gangling *adjective*
tall, thin, and awkward-looking.

gangplank *noun* (*plural* **gangplanks**)
a plank placed so that people can walk into or out of a boat.

gangrene (*say* gang-green) *noun*
decay of body tissue in a living person.

gangster *noun* (*plural* **gangsters**)
a member of a gang of violent criminals.

gangway *noun* (*plural* **gangways**)
1 a gap left for people to pass between rows of seats or through a crowd. **2** a movable bridge placed so that people can walk onto or off a ship.

gaol (*say* jayl) *noun* (*plural* **gaols**)
a different spelling of **jail**.
gaol *verb* **gaoler** *noun*

gap *noun* (*plural* **gaps**)
1 a break or opening in something continuous such as a hedge or fence. **2** an interval. **3** a wide difference in ideas.

gape *verb* (**gapes, gaping, gaped**)
1 have your mouth open. **2** stare with your mouth open. **3** be open wide.

garage (*say* ga-rah*z*h or ga-rij) *noun* (*plural* **garages**)
1 a building in which a motor vehicle or vehicles may be kept. **2** a place where motor vehicles are repaired or serviced and where petrol is sold.

garbage *noun*
rubbish, especially household rubbish.

garble *verb* (**garbles, garbling, garbled**)
give a confused account of a story or message so that it is misunderstood.

garden *noun* (*plural* **gardens**)
a piece of ground where flowers, fruit, or vegetables are grown.
gardener *noun* **gardening** *noun*

gargle *verb* (**gargles, gargling, gargled**)
hold a liquid at the back of the mouth and breathe air through it to wash the inside of the throat.
gargle *noun*

gargoyle *noun* (*plural* **gargoyles**)
an ugly or comical face or figure carved on a building, especially on a water spout.

garland *noun* (*plural* **garlands**)
a wreath of flowers worn or hung as a decoration.
garland *verb*

garlic *noun*
a plant with a bulb divided into smaller bulbs (**cloves**), which have a strong smell and taste and are used for flavouring food.

garment *noun* (*plural* **garments**)
a piece of clothing.

garnish *verb* (**garnishes, garnishing, garnished**)
decorate something, especially food.

garnish *noun*
something used to decorate food or give it extra flavour.

garret *noun* (*plural* **garrets**)
an attic.

garrison *noun* (*plural* **garrisons**)
1 troops who stay in a town or fort to defend it. **2** the building they occupy.
garrison *verb*

garter *noun* (*plural* **garters**)
a band of elastic to hold up a sock or stocking.

gas¹ *noun* (*plural* **gases**)
1 a substance that (like air) can move freely and is not liquid or solid at ordinary temperatures. **2** a gas that can be burned, used for lighting, heating, or cooking.
gas *verb* (**gasses, gassing, gassed**)
1 kill or injure someone with gas. **2** (*informal*) talk idly for a long time.

gas² *noun* (*American*)
gasoline.

gaseous (*say* gas-ee-us) *adjective*
in the form of a gas.

gash *noun* (*plural* **gashes**)
a long deep cut or wound.
gash *verb* (**gashes, gashing, gashed**)
make a gash in something.

gasoline *noun* (*American*)
petrol.

gasp *verb* (**gasps, gasping, gasped**)
1 breathe in suddenly when you are shocked or surprised. **2** struggle to breathe with your mouth open when you are tired or ill. **3** speak in a breathless way.
gasp *noun*

gassy *adjective*
fizzy.

gastric *adjective*
to do with the stomach.

gastronomy (*say* gas-tron-om-ee) *noun*
the art or science of good eating.
gastronomic *adjective*

gastropod *noun* (*plural* **gastropods**)
an animal (e.g. a snail) that moves by means of a fleshy 'foot' on its stomach.

gate *noun* (*plural* **gates**)
1 a movable barrier, usually on hinges, used as a door in a wall or fence. **2** a barrier for controlling the flow of water in a dam or lock. **3** a place where you wait before you board an aircraft. **4** the number of people attending a football match etc.

gatecrash *verb* (**gatecrashes, gatecrashing, gatecrashed**)
go to a private party without being invited.
gatecrasher *noun*

gateway *noun* (*plural* **gateways**)
1 an opening containing a gate. **2** a way to reach something ♦ *The gateway to success.*

gather *verb* (**gathers, gathering, gathered**)
1 come or bring together. **2** collect; obtain gradually ♦ *We've been gathering information.* **3** collect as harvest; pluck ♦ *Gather the corn when it is ripe;* ♦ *gather flowers.* **4** understand or learn ♦ *I gather you've been on holiday.* **5** pull cloth into folds by running a thread through it. **6** a sore gathers when it swells up and forms pus.
gather speed move gradually faster.

gathering *noun* (*plural* **gatherings**)
an assembly or meeting of people; a party.

gaudy *adjective*
too showy and bright.
gaudily *adverb* **gaudiness** *noun*

gauge (*say* gayj) *noun* (*plural* **gauges**)
1 a standard measurement. **2** the distance between a pair of rails on a railway. **3** a measuring instrument.

gauge *verb* (**gauges, gauging, gauged**)
1 measure. **2** estimate; form a judgement.

gaunt *adjective*
(said about a person) lean and haggard.
gauntness *noun*

gauntlet[1] *noun* (*plural* **gauntlets**)
a glove with a wide cuff covering the wrist.
throw down the gauntlet offer a challenge.

gauntlet[2] *noun*
run the gauntlet have to suffer continuous severe criticism or risk.

gauze *noun*
1 thin transparent woven material. **2** fine wire mesh.
gauzy *adjective*

gay *adjective*
1 homosexual. **2** cheerful. **3** brightly coloured.
gayness *noun*

ⓘ USAGE Nowadays the most common meaning of *gay* is 'homosexual'. The older meanings 'cheerful' and 'brightly coloured' can still be used but are becoming less and less common in everyday use. ♦ *Gayness* is the noun from meaning 1 of *gay*. The noun that relates to the other two meanings is *gaiety*.

gaze *verb* (**gazes, gazing, gazed**)
look at something steadily for a long time.
gaze *noun* (*plural* **gazes**)
a long steady look.

gazetteer (*say* gaz-it-**eer**) *noun* (*plural* **gazetteers**)
a list of place names.

GCSE *abbreviation*
General Certificate of Secondary Education.

gear *noun* (*plural* **gears**)
1 a cogwheel, especially one of a set in a motor vehicle that turn power from the engine into movement of the wheels. **2** equipment or apparatus ♦ *camping gear.*

gear *verb* (**gears, gearing, geared**)
gear to make something match or be suitable for something else ♦ *Health care should be geared to people's needs, not to whether they can pay.* **gear up** get ready for ♦ *We were all geared up to play cricket, but then it rained.*

Geiger counter (*say* gy-ger) *noun* (*plural* **Geiger counters**)
an instrument that detects and measures radioactivity.

gel *noun* (*plural* **gels**)
a jelly-like substance, especially one used to give a style to hair.

gelatine *noun*
a clear jelly-like substance made by boiling animal tissue and used to make jellies and other foods and in photographic film.
gelatinous (*say* jil-**at**-in-us) *adjective*

gem *noun* (*plural* **gems**)
1 a precious stone. **2** an excellent person or thing.

gender *noun* (*plural* **genders**)
1 the group in which a noun is classed in the grammar of some languages, e.g. masculine, feminine, or neuter. **2** a person's sex ♦ *Jobs should be open to all, regardless of race or gender.*

gene (*say* jeen) *noun* (*plural* **genes**)
the part of a living cell that controls which characteristics (such as the colour of hair or eyes) are inherited from parents.

genealogy (*say* jeen-ee-**al**-o-jee) *noun* (*plural* **genealogies**)
1 a list or diagram showing how people are descended from an ancestor. **2** the study of family history and ancestors.
genealogical (*say* jeen-ee-a-**loj**-ik-al) *adjective*

genera (*say* **jen**-e-ra) *plural noun*
plural of **genus**.

general *adjective*
1 to do with or involving most people or things ♦ *This drug is now in general use.* **2** not detailed; broad ♦ *I've got the general idea.* **3** chief or head ♦ *the general manager.*
in general as a general rule; usually.

general *noun* (*plural* **generals**)
a senior army officer.

general election *noun* (*plural* **general elections**)
an election of Members of Parliament for the whole country.

generally *adverb*
1 usually. **2** in a general sense; without regard to details ♦ *I was speaking generally.*

general practitioner noun (plural **general practitioners**)
a doctor who treats all kinds of diseases. He or she is the first doctor that people see when they are ill.

generate verb (**generates, generating, generated**)
produce or create.

generation noun (plural **generations**)
1 generating. 2 a single stage in a family ♦ Three generations were included: children, parents, and grandparents. 3 all the people born at about the same time ♦ our parents' generation.

generator noun (plural **generators**)
1 an apparatus for producing gases or steam. 2 a machine for converting mechanical energy into electricity.

generous adjective
1 willing to give things or share them. 2 given freely; plentiful ♦ a generous helping.
generously adverb **generosity** noun

genetic (say jin-**et**-ik) adjective
1 to do with genes. 2 to do with characteristics inherited from parents or ancestors.
genetically adverb
genetically modified (said about an animal or plant) containing genes that have been artificially altered.

genetics noun
the study of genes and genetic behaviour.

genial (say **jee**-nee-al) adjective
kindly and cheerful.
genially adverb **geniality** (say jee-nee-**al**-it-ee) noun

genital (say **jen**-it-al) adjective
to do with animal reproduction or reproductive organs.

genitals (say **jen**-it-alz) plural noun
external sexual organs.

genius noun (plural **geniuses**)
1 an unusually clever or creative person. 2 a very great natural ability ♦ He has a real genius for music.

genocide (say **jen**-o-syd) noun
deliberate extermination of a race of people.

gentle adjective
1 mild or kind; not rough. 2 not harsh or severe ♦ a gentle breeze.
gently adverb **gentleness** noun

gentleman noun (plural **gentlemen**)
1 a well-mannered or honourable man. 2 a man of good social position. 3 (in polite use) a man.

genuine adjective
real; not faked or pretending.
genuinely adverb **genuineness** noun

genus (say **jee**-nus) noun (plural **genera** (say **jen**-er-a))
a group of similar animals or plants ♦ Lions and tigers belong to the same genus.

geography (say jee-**og**-ra-fee) noun
the study of the earth's surface and of its climate, peoples, and products.
geographer noun **geographical** adjective
geographically adverb
[from geo- = earth + -graphy = description]

geology (say jee-**ol**-o-jee) noun
the study of the structure of the earth's crust and its layers.
geological adjective **geologically** adverb
geologist noun

geometry (say jee-**om**-it-ree) noun
the study of lines, angles, surfaces, and solids in mathematics.
geometric adjective **geometrical** adjective
geometrically adverb

gerbil (say **jer**-bil) noun (plural **gerbils**)
a small brown rodent with long hind legs, often kept as a pet.

geriatric (say je-ree-**at**-rik) adjective
to do with the care of old people and their health.
[from Greek geras = old age + iatros = doctor]

germ noun (plural **germs**)
1 a micro-organism, especially one that can cause disease. 2 a tiny living structure from which a plant or animal may develop. 3 part of the seed of a cereal plant.
[from Latin germen = seed or sprout]

German measles noun
rubella.

German shepherd dog noun (plural **German shepherd dogs**)
a large strong dog, often used by the police.

germinate verb (**germinates, germinating, germinated**)
when a seed germinates, it begins to develop, and roots and shoots grow from it.
germination noun

gesticulate (say jes-**tik**-yoo-layt) verb (**gesticulates, gesticulating, gesticulated**)
make expressive movements with your hands and arms.
gesticulation noun

gesture (say **jes**-cher) noun (plural **gestures**)
1 a movement that expresses what a person feels. 2 an action that shows goodwill ♦ It would be a nice gesture to send her some flowers.
gesture verb (**gestures, gesturing, gestured**)
tell a person something by making a gesture ♦ She gestured me to be quiet.

get *verb* (**gets, getting, got**)
This word has many different uses, including
1 obtain or receive ♦ *She got first prize.*
2 become ♦ *Don't get angry!* **3** reach a place
♦ *We got there by midnight.* **4** put or move
♦ *I can't get my shoe on.* **5** prepare ♦ *Will you get
the tea?* **6** persuade or order ♦ *Get him to wash
up.* **7** catch or suffer from an illness. **8** (*informal*)
understand ♦ *Do you get what I mean?*
get away with 1 escape with something.
2 avoid being punished for what you have done.
get by (*informal*) manage. **get on 1** make
progress. **2** be friendly with somebody. **get over**
recover from an illness etc. **get up 1** stand up.
2 get out of your bed in the morning. **3** prepare
or organize ♦ *We got up a concert.* **get your own
back** (*informal*) have your revenge. **have got to**
must.

geyser (*say* **gee**-zer *or* **gy**-zer) *noun* (*plural*
geysers)
1 a natural spring that shoots up columns of hot
water. **2** a kind of water heater.
[from *Geysir* = gusher, the name of a geyser in
Iceland]

ghastly *adjective*
1 very unpleasant or bad. **2** looking pale and ill.
ghastliness *noun*
[from Old English *gaestan* = terrify]

ghost *noun* (*plural* **ghosts**)
the spirit of a dead person that appears to the
living.
ghostly *adjective*

ghoulish (*say* **gool**-ish) *adjective*
enjoying things that are grisly or unpleasant.
ghoulishly *adverb* **ghoulishness** *noun*
[from Arabic *gul* = a demon that eats dead
bodies]

giant *noun* (*plural* **giants**)
1 (in myths or fairy tales) a creature like a huge
man. **2** a man, animal, or plant that is much
larger than the usual size.
[via early French from Greek *gigas*]

gibberish (*say* **jib**-er-ish) *noun*
meaningless speech; nonsense.

gibbet (*say* **jib**-it) *noun* (*plural* **gibbets**)
1 a gallows. **2** an upright post with an arm from
which a criminal's body was hung after
execution, as a warning to others.

gibbon *noun* (*plural* **gibbons**)
a small ape from south-east Asia. Gibbons have
very long arms to help them swing through the
trees where they live.

giddy *adjective*
1 feeling that everything is spinning round
and that you might fall. **2** causing this feeling
♦ *We looked down from the giddy height of the
cliff.*
giddily *adverb* **giddiness** *noun*

gift *noun* (*plural* **gifts**)
1 a present. **2** a natural talent ♦ *She has a gift for
music.*

gifted *adjective*
having a special talent.

gig *noun* (*plural* **gigs**) (*informal*)
a live performance by a musician, comedian, etc.

gigabyte (*say* **gi**-ga-byt *or* **ji**-ga-byt) *noun*
(*plural* **gigabytes**)
(in computing) a unit of information equal to
one thousand million bytes, or (more precisely)
2^{30} bytes.

gigantic (*say* jy-**gan**-tik) *adjective*
extremely large; huge.

giggle *verb* (**giggles, giggling, giggled**)
laugh in a silly way.

giggle *noun* (*plural* **giggles**)
1 a silly laugh. **2** (*informal*) something amusing;
a bit of fun.

gild *verb* (**gilds, gilding, gilded**)
cover something with a thin layer of gold or gold
paint.

gills *plural noun*
the part of the body through which fish and
certain other water animals breathe.

gilt *noun*
a thin covering of gold or gold paint.

gimmick *noun* (*plural* **gimmicks**)
something unusual or silly done or used just to
attract people's attention.

gin *noun*
a colourless alcoholic drink flavoured with
juniper berries.

ginger *noun*
1 the hot-tasting root of a tropical plant, or a
flavouring made from this root, used especially
in drinks and Eastern cooking. **2** liveliness or
energy. **3** a reddish-yellow colour.
ginger *adjective*

ginger *verb* (**gingers, gingering, gingered**)
make something more lively ♦ *This will ginger
things up!*
[via Old English, Latin, and Greek from
Dravidian (a group of languages spoken in
southern India)]

gingerly *adverb*
cautiously.

giraffe *noun* (*plural* **giraffe** *or* **giraffes**)
an African animal with long legs and a very long
neck, the world's tallest mammal.
[from Arabic]

girder *noun* (*plural* **girders**)
a metal beam supporting part of a building or a
bridge.

girdle *noun* (*plural* **girdles**)
1 a belt or cord worn round the waist.
2 a woman's elastic corset covering from
the waist to the thigh.

girl noun (plural **girls**)
1 a female child. **2** a young woman.
girlhood noun **girlish** adjective

girlfriend noun (plural **girlfriends**)
a person's regular female companion in a
romantic or sexual relationship.

giro (say jy-roh) noun
a system of sending money directly from one
bank account or post office account to another.

gist (say jist) noun
the essential points or general sense of what
someone says.

give verb (**gives, giving, gave, given**)
1 let someone have something. **2** make or do
something ♦ He gave a laugh. **3** be flexible or
springy; bend or collapse when pressed.
giver noun
give in acknowledge that you are defeated; yield.
give up 1 stop trying. **2** end a habit.

given adjective
named or stated in advance ♦ All the people in a
given area.

glacial (say glay-shal) adjective
icy; made of or produced by ice.
glacially adverb

glacier (say glas-ee-er) noun (plural **glaciers**)
a mass of ice that moves very slowly down a
mountain valley.

glad adjective
1 pleased; expressing joy. **2** giving pleasure
♦ We brought the glad news.
gladly adverb **gladness** noun
glad of grateful for or pleased with something.

gladden verb (**gladdens, gladdening,
gladdened**)
make a person glad.

glade noun (plural **glades**)
an open space in a forest.

gladiator (say glad-ee-ay-ter) noun (plural
gladiators)
a man trained to fight for public entertainment in
ancient Rome.
gladiatorial (say glad-ee-at-or-ee-al) adjective
[from Latin gladius = sword]

glamorous adjective
excitingly attractive.

glamour noun
an attractive and exciting quality.

glance verb (**glances, glancing, glanced**)
1 look at something briefly. **2** strike something at
an angle and slide off it ♦ The ball glanced off his
bat.
glance noun

gland noun (plural **glands**)
an organ of the body that separates substances
from the blood so that they can be used or
secreted (passed out of the body).
glandular adjective

glare verb (**glares, glaring, glared**)
1 shine with a bright or dazzling light.
2 stare angrily or fiercely.
glare noun

glasnost noun
the open reporting of news or giving of
information, especially in the former Soviet
Union.
[from Russian, = openness]

glass noun (plural **glasses**)
1 a hard brittle substance that is usually
transparent. **2** a container made of glass for
drinking from. **3** a mirror. **4** a lens.
glassy adjective

glasses plural noun
1 a pair of lenses in a frame, worn over the eyes
to help improve eyesight. **2** binoculars.

glaze verb (**glazes, glazing, glazed**)
1 fit a window or building with glass. **2** give a
shiny surface to something. **3** (said of a person's
eyes) lose brightness and animation.

gleam noun (plural **gleams**)
1 a beam of soft light, especially one that comes
and goes. **2** a small amount of hope, humour,
etc.

gleam verb (**gleams, gleaming, gleamed**)
shine brightly, especially after cleaning or
polishing.

glee noun
great delight.
gleeful adjective **gleefully** adverb

glen noun (plural **glens**)
a narrow valley, especially in Scotland.
[from Scottish Gaelic or Irish]

glib adjective
speaking or writing readily but not sincerely or
thoughtfully.
glibly adverb **glibness** noun

glide verb (**glides, gliding, glided**)
1 move along smoothly. **2** fly without using an
engine. **3** birds glide when they fly without
beating their wings.
glide noun

glider noun (plural **gliders**)
an aircraft without an engine that flies by
floating on warm air currents called thermals.

glimmer noun (plural **glimmers**)
1 a faint light. **2** a small sign or trace of
something ♦ a glimmer of hope.

glimmer verb (**glimmers, glimmering,
glimmered**)
shine with a faint, flickering light.

glimpse noun (plural **glimpses**)
a brief view.

glimpse verb (**glimpses, glimpsing, glimpsed**)
see something briefly.

glint *noun* (*plural* **glints**)
a very brief flash of light.
glint *verb* (**glints, glinting, glinted**)
shine with a flash of light.
glisten (*say* glis-en) *verb* (**glistens, glistening, glistened**)
shine like something wet or oily.
glitter *verb* (**glitters, glittering, glittered**)
shine with tiny flashes of light; sparkle.
glitter *noun*
tiny sparkling pieces used for decoration.
gloat *verb* (**gloats, gloating, gloated**)
be pleased in an unkind way that you have succeeded or that someone else has been hurt or upset.
global *adjective*
1 to do with the whole world; worldwide.
2 to do with the whole of a system.
globally *adverb*
global warming *noun*
the increase in the temperature of the earth's atmosphere, caused by the greenhouse effect.
globe *noun* (*plural* **globes**)
1 something shaped like a ball, especially one with a map of the whole world on it. 2 the world ♦ *She has travelled all over the globe.* 3 a hollow round glass object.
gloom *noun*
1 darkness. 2 sadness or despair.
gloomy *adjective* (**gloomier, gloomiest**)
1 almost dark. 2 depressed or depressing.
gloomily *adverb* **gloominess** *noun*
glorify *verb* (**glorifies, glorifying, glorified**)
1 give great praise or great honour to. 2 make a thing seem more splendid or attractive than it really is ♦ *It is a film that glorifies war.*
glorification *noun*
glorious *adjective*
splendid or magnificent.
gloriously *adverb*
glory *noun* (*plural* **glories**)
1 fame and honour. 2 praise. 3 beauty or magnificence.
glory *verb* (**glories, glorying, gloried**)
rejoice; pride yourself ♦ *They gloried in victory.*
gloss¹ *noun* (*plural* **glosses**)
the shine on a smooth surface.
gloss *verb* (**glosses, glossing, glossed**)
make a thing glossy.
gloss² *verb* (**glosses, glossing, glossed**)
gloss over mention a fault or mistake etc. only briefly to make it seem less serious than it really is.
glossary *noun* (*plural* **glossaries**)
a list of difficult words with their meanings explained.

glossy *adjective* (**glossier, glossiest**)
smooth and shiny.
glossily *adverb* **glossiness** *noun*
glove *noun* (*plural* **gloves**)
a covering for the hand, usually with separate divisions for each finger and thumb.
gloved *adjective*
glow *noun*
1 brightness and warmth without flames.
2 a warm or cheerful feeling ♦ *We felt a glow of pride.*
glow *verb* (**glows, glowing, glowed**)
shine with a soft, warm light.
glue *noun* (*plural* **glues**)
a sticky substance used for joining things together.
gluey *adjective*
glue *verb* (**glues, gluing, glued**)
1 stick with glue. 2 attach or hold closely
♦ *His ear was glued to the keyhole.*
glum *adjective*
miserable or depressed.
glumly *adverb* **glumness** *noun*
glut *noun* (*plural* **gluts**)
an excessive supply.
glutinous (*say* gloo-tin-us) *adjective*
glue-like or sticky.
glutton *noun* (*plural* **gluttons**)
a person who eats too much.
gluttonous *adjective* **gluttony** *noun*
glutton for punishment a person who seems to enjoy doing something difficult or unpleasant.
gm *abbreviation*
gram.
GMT *abbreviation*
Greenwich Mean Time.
gnarled (*say* narld) *adjective*
twisted and knobbly, like an old tree.
gnash (*say* nash) *verb* (**gnashes, gnashing, gnashed**)
grind your teeth together.
gnat (*say* nat) *noun* (*plural* **gnats**)
a tiny fly that bites.
gnaw (*say* naw) *verb* (**gnaws, gnawing, gnawed**)
keep on biting something hard so that it wears away.
gnome (*say* nohm) *noun* (*plural* **gnomes**)
a kind of dwarf in fairy tales, usually living underground.
GNVQ *abbreviation*
General National Vocational Qualification.

go *verb* (**goes, going, went, gone**)
This word has many uses, including **1** move from one place to another ♦ *Where are you going?* **2** leave ♦ *I must go.* **3** lead from one place to another ♦ *The road goes to Bristol.* **4** become ♦ *The milk has gone sour.* **5** make a sound ♦ *The gun went bang.* **6** belong in some place or position ♦ *Plates go on that shelf.* **7** be sold ♦ *The house went very cheaply.*
go off 1 explode. **2** become stale or decayed. **3** stop liking something. **go on** continue. **go out** stop burning or shining. **go through** experience something unpleasant or difficult.

go *noun* (*plural* **goes**)
1 a turn or try ♦ *May I have a go?* **2** (*informal*) energy or liveliness ♦ *She is full of go.*
make a go of make a success of something.
on the go active; always working or moving.

goad *noun* (*plural* **goads**)
a stick with a pointed end for prodding cattle to move onwards.

goad *verb* (**goads, goading, goaded**)
stir into action by being annoying ♦ *He goaded me into fighting.*

goal *noun* (*plural* **goals**)
1 the place where a ball must go to score a point in football, hockey, etc. **2** a point scored in this way. **3** something that you are trying to reach or achieve.

goalkeeper *noun* (*plural* **goalkeepers**)
the player who stands in the goal to try and keep the ball from entering.

goat *noun* (*plural* **goats**)
a mammal with horns and a beard, closely related to the sheep. Domestic goats are kept for their milk.
[from Old English]

gobble *verb* (**gobbles, gobbling, gobbled**)
eat quickly and greedily.
[from early French *gober* = to swallow]

go-between *noun* (*plural* **go-betweens**)
a person who acts as a messenger or negotiator between others.

God *noun*
the creator of the universe in Christian, Jewish, and Muslim belief.

god *noun* (*plural* **gods**)
a male being that is worshipped ♦ *Mars was a Roman god.*

godchild *noun* (*plural* **godchildren**)
a child that has a godparent.
god-daughter *noun* **godson** *noun*

goddess *noun* (*plural* **goddesses**)
a female being that is worshipped.

godparent *noun* (*plural* **godparents**)
a person at a child's christening who promises to see that the child has a religious education.
godfather *noun* **godmother** *noun*

godsend *noun* (*plural* **godsends**)
a piece of unexpected good luck.

goggle *verb* (**goggles, goggling, goggled**)
stare with wide open eyes.

going *present participle* of **go.**
be going to do something be ready or likely to do it.

gold *noun* (*plural* **golds**)
1 a precious yellow metal. **2** a deep yellow colour. **3** a gold medal, awarded as first prize.
gold *adjective*

golden *adjective*
1 made of gold. **2** coloured like gold. **3** precious or excellent ♦ *a golden opportunity.*

golden wedding *noun* (*plural* **golden weddings**)
a couple's fiftieth wedding anniversary.

goldfish *noun* (*plural* **goldfish**)
a small red or orange fish, often kept as a pet.

golf *noun*
an outdoor game played by hitting a small white ball with a club into a series of holes on a specially prepared ground (a **golf course** or **golf links**) and taking as few strokes as possible.
golfer *noun* **golfing** *noun*

gong *noun* (*plural* **gongs**)
a large metal disc that makes an echoing sound when it is hit.

good *adjective* (**better, best**)
1 having the right qualities; of the kind that people like ♦ *a good book.* **2** kind ♦ *It was good of you to help us.* **3** well-behaved ♦ *Be a good boy.* **4** skilled or talented ♦ *a good pianist.* **5** healthy; giving benefit ♦ *Exercise is good for you.* **6** thorough ♦ *Give it a good clean.* **7** large; considerable ♦ *It's a good distance from the shops.*

good *noun*
1 something good ♦ *Do good to others.* **2** benefit ♦ *It's for your own good.*
for good for ever. **no good** useless.

ⓘ USAGE In standard English, *good* cannot be used as an adverb. You can say *She's a good player* but not *She played good.* The adverb that goes with *good* is *well.*

---

goodbye *interjection*
a word used when you leave somebody or at the end of a phone call.

goods *plural noun*
1 things that are bought and sold. **2** things that are carried on trains or lorries.

goose *noun* (*plural* **geese**)
a long-necked water bird with webbed feet, larger than a duck.

gooseberry *noun* (*plural* **gooseberries**)
1 a small green fruit that grows on a prickly bush. **2** (*informal*) an unwanted extra person.

goose pimples or **goosebumps** *plural noun*
skin that has turned rough with small bumps on
it because a person is cold or afraid.

gorge *noun* (*plural* **gorges**)
a narrow valley with steep sides.

gorge *verb* (**gorges, gorging, gorged**)
eat greedily; stuff with food.

gorgeous *adjective*
magnificent or beautiful.
gorgeously *adverb*

gorilla *noun* (*plural* **gorillas**)
a large powerful African ape, the largest of all
the apes.

---

❶ USAGE Do not confuse with *guerrilla*, which
can be pronounced in the same way.

---

gospel *noun*
the Gospels the first four books of the New
Testament, telling of the life and teachings of
Jesus Christ.

gospel music *noun*
a fervent style of black American religious
singing.

gossip *verb* (**gossips, gossiping, gossiped**)
talk a lot about other people.

gossip *noun* (*plural* **gossips**)
1 talk, especially rumours, about other people.
2 a person who enjoys gossiping.
gossipy *adjective*

got *past tense of* **get**.
have got possess ♦ *Have you got a car?*

Gothic *noun*
the style of building common in Europe in the
12th–16th centuries, with pointed arches and
much decorative carving.

gouge (*say* gowj) *verb* (**gouges, gouging,
gouged**)
scoop or force out by pressing.

gourmet (*say* goor-may) *noun* (*plural*
gourmets)
a person who understands and appreciates good
food and drink.

govern *verb* (**governs, governing, governed**)
be in charge of the public affairs of a country or
region.

governess *noun* (*plural* **governesses**)
a woman employed to teach children in a private
household.

government *noun* (*plural* **governments**)
1 the group of people who are in charge of the
public affairs of a country. **2** the process of
governing.
governmental *adjective*

governor *noun* (*plural* **governors**)
1 a person who governs a state or a colony etc.
2 a member of the governing body of a school or
other institution. **3** the person in charge of a
prison.

gown *noun* (*plural* **gowns**)
1 a woman's long dress. **2** a loose robe worn by
lawyers, members of a university, etc.

GP *abbreviation*
general practitioner.

grab *verb* (**grabs, grabbing, grabbed**)
take hold of something firmly or suddenly.

grace *noun*
1 beauty, especially of movement. **2** goodwill or
favour. **3** dignity or good manners ♦ *At least he
had the grace to apologize.* **4** a short prayer of
thanks before or after a meal. **5** the title of a
duke, duchess, or archbishop ♦ *His Grace the
Duke of Kent.*

grace *verb* (**graces, gracing, graced**)
bring honour or dignity to something ♦ *The
mayor himself graced us with his presence.*

graceful *adjective*
beautiful and elegant in movement or shape.
gracefully *adverb* **gracefulness** *noun*

gracious *adjective*
behaving kindly and honourably.
graciously *adverb* **graciousness** *noun*

grade *noun* (*plural* **grades**)
1 a step in a scale of quality or value or rank.
2 a mark showing the quality of a student's
work.

grade *verb* (**grades, grading, graded**)
sort or divide into grades.

gradient (*say* gray-dee-ent) *noun* (*plural*
gradients)
a slope or the steepness of a slope.

gradual *adjective*
happening slowly but steadily.
gradually *adverb*

graduate (*say* grad-yoo-at) *noun* (*plural*
graduates)
a person who has a university or college degree.

graduate (*say* grad-yoo-ayt) *verb* (**graduates,
graduating, graduated**)
be awarded a university or college degree.

graffiti *noun*
words or drawings scribbled or sprayed on a
wall.

---

❶ USAGE Strictly speaking, this word is a plural
noun (the singular is *graffito*), so it should be
used with a plural verb: *There are graffiti all over
the wall.* However, the word is widely used
nowadays as if it were a singular noun and most
people do not regard this as wrong: *There is
graffiti all over the wall.*

---

graft *noun* (*plural* **grafts**)
1 a shoot from one plant or tree fixed into
another to form a new growth. **2** a piece of living
tissue transplanted by a surgeon to replace what
is diseased or damaged ♦ *a skin graft.*

graft *verb* (**grafts, grafting, grafted**)
insert or transplant as a graft.

grain *noun* (*plural* **grains**)
1 a small hard seed or similar particle. **2** cereal plants when they are growing or after being harvested. **3** a very small amount ♦ *a grain of truth.* **4** the pattern of lines made by the fibres in a piece of wood or paper.
grainy *adjective*

gram *noun* (*plural* **grams**)
a unit of mass or weight in the metric system.

grammar *noun* (*plural* **grammars**)
1 the rules for using words correctly. **2** a book about these rules.
grammatical *adjective*

grammar school *noun* (*plural* **grammar schools**)
a secondary school for children with academic ability.

grand *adjective*
1 splendid and impressive. **2** most important or highest-ranking. **3** including everything; complete.
grandly *adverb* **grandness** *noun*

grandchild *noun* (*plural* **grandchildren**)
the child of a person's son or daughter.
granddaughter *noun* **grandson** *noun*

grandeur (*say* grand-yer) *noun*
impressive beauty; splendour.

grandfather *noun* (*plural* **grandfathers**)
the father of a person's father or mother.

grandiose (*say* grand-ee-ohss) *adjective*
large and impressive; trying to seem impressive.

grandmother *noun* (*plural* **grandmothers**)
the mother of a person's father or mother.

grandparent *noun* (*plural* **grandparents**)
a grandfather or grandmother.

grand piano *noun* (*plural* **grand pianos**)
a large piano with the strings fixed horizontally.

grandstand *noun* (*plural* **grandstands**)
a building with a roof and rows of seats for spectators at a racecourse or sports ground.

grand total *noun*
the sum of other totals.

granite *noun*
a very hard kind of rock used for building.

grant *verb* (**grants, granting, granted**)
1 give or allow someone what they have asked for ♦ *We have decided to grant your request.* **2** admit; agree that something is true.
take for granted assume that something is true or will happen

grant *noun* (*plural* **grants**)
something granted, especially a sum of money.

Granth (*say* grunt) *noun*
the sacred scriptures of the Sikhs.

grape *noun* (*plural* **grapes**)
a small green or purple berry that grows in bunches on a vine. Grapes are used to make wine.

grapefruit *noun* (*plural* **grapefruit**)
a large round yellow citrus fruit.

grapevine *noun* (*plural* **grapevines**)
1 a vine on which grapes grow. **2** a way by which news spreads unofficially, with people passing it on from one to another.

graph *noun* (*plural* **graphs**)
a diagram showing how two quantities or variables are related.

graphic *adjective*
1 to do with drawing or painting ♦ *a graphic artist.* **2** giving a lively description.
graphically *adverb*

grapple *verb* (**grapples, grappling, grappled**)
1 struggle or wrestle. **2** seize or hold firmly. **3** try to deal with a problem etc. ♦ *I've been grappling with this essay all day.*

grasp *verb* (**grasps, grasping, grasped**)
1 seize and hold firmly. **2** understand.

grasp *noun*
1 a person's understanding of something ♦ *a good grasp of electronics.* **2** a firm hold.

grasping *adjective*
greedy for money or possessions.

grass *noun* (*plural* **grasses**)
1 a plant with green blades and stalks. **2** ground covered with grass; lawn.
grassy *adjective*

grasshopper *noun* (*plural* **grasshoppers**)
a jumping insect that makes a shrill noise.

grass roots *plural noun*
the ordinary people in a political party or other group.

grate¹ *noun* (*plural* **grates**)
1 a metal framework that keeps fuel in a fireplace. **2** a fireplace.

grate² *verb* (**grates, grating, grated**)
1 shred something into small pieces by rubbing it on a rough surface. **2** make an unpleasant noise by rubbing. **3** sound harshly.
grate on have an irritating effect.

grateful *adjective*
feeling or showing that you are thankful for something that has been done for you.
gratefully *adverb*

gratify *verb* (**gratifies, gratifying, gratified**)
1 give pleasure. **2** satisfy a feeling or desire ♦ *May we gratify our curiosity and have a look?*
gratification *noun*

grating *noun* (*plural* **gratings**)
a framework of metal bars placed across an opening.

gratitude *noun*
being grateful.

grave¹ *noun* (*plural* **graves**)
the place where a dead body is buried.

grave² *adjective*
serious or solemn.
gravely *adverb*

grave accent (rhymes with *starve*) *noun*
(*plural* **grave accents**)
a backward-sloping mark over a vowel, as in
vis-à-vis.

gravel *noun*
small stones mixed with coarse sand, used to
make paths.
gravelled *adjective* **gravelly** *adjective*

graveyard *noun* (*plural* **graveyards**)
a burial ground.

gravity *noun*
1 the force that pulls all objects in the universe
towards each other. **2** the force that pulls
everything towards the earth. **3** seriousness.

gravy *noun*
a hot brown sauce made from meat juices.

graze *verb* (**grazes, grazing, grazed**)
1 feed on growing grass. **2** scrape your skin
slightly ♦ *I grazed my elbow on the wall.* **3** touch
something lightly in passing.

graze *noun* (*plural* **grazes**)
a raw place where skin has been scraped.

grease *noun*
1 any thick oily substance. **2** melted fat.
greasy *adjective*

grease *verb* (**greases, greasing, greased**)
put grease on something.

great *adjective*
1 very large; much above average. **2** very
important or talented ♦ *a great composer.*
3 (*informal*) very good or enjoyable ♦ *It's great
to see you again.* **4** older or younger by one
generation ♦ *great-grandfather.*
greatly *adverb* **greatness** *noun*

greed *noun*
being greedy.

greedy *adjective* (**greedier, greediest**)
wanting more food, money, or other things than
you need.
greedily *adverb* **greediness** *noun*

green *noun* (*plural* **greens**)
1 the colour of grass, leaves, etc. **2** an area of
grassy land ♦ *the village green;* ♦ *a putting
green.*

green *adjective*
1 of the colour green. **2** concerned with
protecting the natural environment.
3 inexperienced and likely to make mistakes.
greenness *noun*

green belt *noun* (*plural* **green belts**)
an area kept as open land round a city.

greenery *noun*
green leaves or plants.

greengrocer *noun* (*plural* **greengrocers**)
a person who keeps a shop that sells fruit and
vegetables.
greengrocery *noun*

greenhouse *noun* (*plural* **greenhouses**)
a glass building where plants are protected from
cold.

greenhouse effect *noun*
the warming of the earth's surface when heat
from the sun is trapped in the earth's atmosphere
by gases such as carbon dioxide and methane.

greens *plural noun*
green vegetables, such as cabbage and spinach.

Greenwich Mean Time (*say* gren-ich) *noun*
the time on the line of longitude which passes
through Greenwich in London, used as a basis
for calculating time throughout the world.

greet *verb* (**greets, greeting, greeted**)
1 speak to a person who arrives. **2** receive
♦ *They greeted the song with applause.* **3** present
itself to ♦ *A strange sight greeted our eyes.*

greeting *noun* (*plural* **greetings**)
words or actions used to greet somebody.

grey *noun* (*plural* **greys**)
the colour between black and white, like ashes
or dark clouds.
grey *adjective* **greyness** *noun*

greyhound *noun* (*plural* **greyhounds**)
a slender dog with smooth hair, used in racing.

grid *noun* (*plural* **grids**)
1 a framework or pattern of bars or lines crossing
each other. **2** a network of cables or wires for
carrying electricity over a large area.

grid reference *noun* (*plural* **grid references**)
a set of numbers that allows you to describe the
exact position of something on a map.

grief *noun*
deep sorrow, especially at a person's death.
come to grief suffer a disaster.

grievance *noun* (*plural* **grievances**)
something that people are discontented about.

grieve *verb* (**grieves, grieving, grieved**)
1 feel deep sorrow, especially at a person's
death. **2** make a person feel very sad.

grill *noun* (*plural* **grills**)
1 a heated element on a cooker, for sending heat
downwards. **2** food cooked under this. **3** a grille.

grill *verb* (**grills, grilling, grilled**)
1 cook under a grill. **2** question closely and
severely ♦ *The police grilled him for an hour.*

grim *adjective* (**grimmer, grimmest**)
1 stern or severe. **2** unpleasant or unattractive
♦ *a grim prospect.*
grimly *adverb* **grimness** *noun*

grimace (*say* grim-**ayss** or grim-**as**) *noun* (*plural* **grimaces**)
a twisted expression on the face made in pain or disgust.
grimace *verb* (**grimaces, grimacing, grimaced**)
make a grimace.

grime *noun*
dirt in a layer on a surface or on the skin.
grimy *adjective*

grin *noun* (*plural* **grins**)
a broad smile showing your teeth.
grin *verb* (**grins, grinning, grinned**)
smile broadly showing your teeth.

grind *verb* (**grinds, grinding, ground**)
1 crush something into tiny pieces or powder.
2 sharpen or smooth something by rubbing it on a rough surface. 3 rub harshly together ♦ *He ground his teeth in fury.*
grinder *noun*
grind to a halt stop suddenly with a loud noise.

grip *verb* (**grips, gripping, gripped**)
1 hold something firmly. 2 hold a person's attention ♦ *The opening chapter really gripped me.*
grip *noun* (*plural* **grips**)
1 a firm hold. 2 a handle, especially on a sports racket, bat, etc. 3 a travelling bag. 4 control or power ♦ *The country is in the grip of lottery fever.*
get to grips with begin to deal with successfully.

gristle *noun*
tough rubbery tissue in meat.
gristly *adjective*

grit *noun*
1 tiny pieces of stone or sand. 2 courage and endurance.
gritty *adjective* **grittiness** *noun*
grit *verb* (**grits, gritting, gritted**)
1 spread a road or path with grit. 2 clench your teeth when in pain or trouble.

grizzled *adjective*
streaked with grey hairs.

grizzly bear *noun* (*plural* **grizzly bears**)
a large fierce bear of North America.

groan *verb* (**groans, groaning, groaned**)
1 make a long deep sound in pain, distress, or disapproval. 2 creak loudly under a heavy load.
groan *noun* **groaner** *noun*

grocer *noun* (*plural* **grocers**)
a person who keeps a shop that sells food and household goods.

groceries *plural noun*
goods sold by a grocer.

groom *noun* (*plural* **grooms**)
1 a person whose job is to look after horses.
2 a bridegroom.

groom *verb* (**grooms, grooming, groomed**)
1 clean and brush a horse or other animal.
2 make something neat and trim. 3 train a person for a certain job or position ♦ *Evans is being groomed for the captaincy.*

groove *noun* (*plural* **grooves**)
a long narrow furrow or channel cut in the surface of something.
grooved *adjective*

grope *verb* (**gropes, groping, groped**)
feel about for something you cannot see.

gross (*say* grohss) *adjective*
1 fat and ugly. 2 very obvious or shocking ♦ *gross stupidity.* 3 having bad manners; vulgar.
4 (*informal*) disgusting. 5 total; without anything being deducted ♦ *our gross income.* (Compare net².)
grossly *adverb* **grossness** *noun*
gross *noun* (*plural* **gross**)
twelve dozen (144) of something ♦ *ten gross* = *1440.*

grotesque (*say* groh-**tesk**) *adjective*
fantastically ugly or very strangely shaped.
grotesquely *adverb* **grotesqueness** *noun*
[from Italian *pittura grottesca* = painting like one found in a grotto]

grotto *noun* (*plural* **grottoes**)
a small pretty cave, especially an artificial one.
[from Italian]

ground¹ *past tense* of **grind**.

ground² *noun* (*plural* **grounds**)
1 the solid surface of the earth. 2 a sports field. 3 land of a certain kind ♦ *marshy ground.*
4 the amount of a subject that is dealt with ♦ *The course covers a lot of ground.*
ground *verb* (**grounds, grounding, grounded**)
1 prevent a plane from flying ♦ *All aircraft are grounded because of the fog.* 2 stop a child from going out, as a punishment. 3 give a good basic training to someone ♦ *Ground them in the rules of spelling.* 4 base ♦ *This theory is grounded on reliable evidence.*

grounds *plural noun*
1 the gardens of a large house. 2 solid particles that sink to the bottom ♦ *coffee grounds.*
3 reasons ♦ *There are grounds for suspicion.*

group *noun* (*plural* **groups**)
1 a number of people, animals, or things that come together or belong together in some way.
2 a band of musicians.
group *verb* (**groups, grouping, grouped**)
put together or come together in a group or groups.

grouse¹ *noun* (*plural* **grouse**)
a bird with feathered feet, hunted as game.

grouse² *verb* (**grouses, grousing, groused**) (*informal*)
grumble or complain.
grouse *noun* **grouser** *noun*

grove *noun* (*plural* **groves**)
a group of trees; a small wood.

grovel *verb* (**grovels, grovelling, grovelled**)
1 crawl on the ground, especially in a show of fear or humility. 2 act in an excessively humble way, for example by apologizing a lot.
groveller *noun*

grow *verb* (**grows, growing, grew, grown**)
1 become bigger or greater. 2 develop.
3 cultivate; plant and look after ♦ *She grows roses.* 4 become ♦ *He grew rich.*
grower *noun*
grow up become an adult.

growl *verb* (**growls, growling, growled**)
make a deep angry sound in the throat.
growl *noun*

grown-up *noun* (*plural* **grown-ups**)
an adult person.
grown-up *adjective*

growth *noun* (*plural* **growths**)
1 growing or developing. 2 something that has grown. 3 a lump that has grown on or inside a person's body; a tumour.

grub *noun* (*plural* **grubs**)
1 a tiny worm-like creature that will become an insect; a larva. 2 (*slang*) food.

grub *verb* (**grubs, grubbing, grubbed**)
1 dig up by the roots. 2 turn things over or move them about while looking for something; rummage.

grubby *adjective* (**grubbier, grubbiest**)
rather dirty.
grubbiness *noun*

grudge *noun* (*plural* **grudges**)
a feeling of resentment or ill will ♦ *She isn't the sort of person who bears a grudge.*

grudge *verb* (**grudges, grudging, grudged**)
resent having to give or allow something.

gruff *adjective*
having a rough or unfriendly voice or manner.
gruffly *adverb* **gruffness** *noun*

grumble *verb* (**grumbles, grumbling, grumbled**)
complain in a bad-tempered way.
grumble *noun* **grumbler** *noun*

grunt *verb* (**grunts, grunting, grunted**)
1 make a pig's gruff snort. 2 speak or say gruffly.
grunt *noun*

guarantee *noun* (*plural* **guarantees**)
a formal promise to do something or to repair something you have sold if it breaks or goes wrong.

guarantee *verb* (**guarantees, guaranteeing, guaranteed**)
1 give a guarantee; promise. 2 make it certain that something will happen ♦ *Money does not guarantee happiness.*
guarantor *noun*

guard *verb* (**guards, guarding, guarded**)
1 protect; keep safe. 2 watch over and prevent from escaping.
guard against try to prevent something happening.

guard *noun* (*plural* **guards**)
1 guarding; protection ♦ *Keep the prisoners under close guard.* 2 someone who guards a person or place. 3 a group of soldiers or police officers etc. acting as a guard. 4 a railway official in charge of a train. 5 a protecting device ♦ *a fireguard.*
on guard alert for possible danger or difficulty.

guardian *noun* (*plural* **guardians**)
1 someone who guards. 2 a person who is legally in charge of a child whose parents cannot look after him or her.
guardianship *noun*

guerrilla (*say* ger-il-a) *noun* (*plural* **guerrillas**)
a member of a small unofficial army who fights by making surprise attacks.

❶ USAGE Do not confuse with *gorilla.*

guess *noun* (*plural* **guesses**)
an opinion or answer that you give without making careful calculations or without certain knowledge.

guess *verb* (**guesses, guessing, guessed**)
make a guess.
guesser *noun*

guesswork *noun*
something you think of or work out by guessing.

guest *noun* (*plural* **guests**)
1 a person who is invited to visit or stay at another's house. 2 a person staying at a hotel.
3 a person who takes part in another's show as a visiting performer.

guidance *noun*
1 guiding. 2 advising or advice on problems.

Guide *noun* (*plural* **Guides**)
a member of the Girl Guides Association, an organization for girls.

guide *noun* (*plural* **guides**)
1 a person who shows others the way or points out interesting sights. 2 a book giving information about a place or subject.

guide *verb* (**guides, guiding, guided**)
show someone the way or how to do something.

guidebook *noun* (*plural* **guidebooks**)
a book of information about places that tourists visit.

guide dog *noun* (*plural* **guide dogs**)
a dog trained to lead a blind person.

guile (rhymes with *mile*) *noun*
craftiness.

guillotine (*say* gil-ot-een) *noun* (*plural*
guillotines)
a machine with a heavy blade for beheading
criminals, formerly used in France.
[named after Dr Guillotin, who suggested its use
in France in 1789]

guilt *noun*
1 the fact that you have committed an offence.
2 a feeling that you are to blame for something
that has happened.

guilty *adjective*
1 having done wrong ♦ *He was found guilty of
murder.* **2** feeling or showing guilt ♦ *a guilty
conscience.*
guiltily *adverb*

guinea pig *noun* (*plural* **guinea pigs**)
1 a small furry animal without a tail. **2** a person
who is used as the subject of an experiment.

guitar *noun* (*plural* **guitars**)
a musical instrument played by plucking its
strings.
guitarist *noun*

gulf *noun* (*plural* **gulfs**)
1 a large area of the sea that is partly surrounded
by land. **2** a wide gap; a great difference.

gull *noun* (*plural* **gulls**)
a seagull.
[a Celtic word]

gullible *adjective*
easily deceived.

gulp *verb* (**gulps, gulping, gulped**)
1 swallow hastily or greedily. **2** make a loud
swallowing noise, especially because of fear.
gulp *noun* (*plural* **gulps**)
1 the act of gulping. **2** a large mouthful of liquid.

gum[1] *noun* (*plural* **gums**)
the firm flesh in which your teeth are rooted.

gum[2] *noun* (*plural* **gums**)
1 a sticky substance produced by some trees
and shrubs, used as glue. **2** a sweet made with
gum or gelatine ♦ *a fruit gum.* **3** chewing gum.
4 a gum tree.
gummy *adjective*
gum *verb* (**gums, gumming, gummed**)
cover or stick something with gum.

gum tree *noun* (*plural* **gum trees**)
a eucalyptus.

gun *noun* (*plural* **guns**)
1 a weapon that fires shells or bullets from a
metal tube. **2** a starting pistol. **3** a device that
forces a substance out of a tube ♦ *a grease gun.*
gunfire *noun* **gunshot** *noun*
gun *verb* (**guns, gunning, gunned**)
gun down shoot someone with a gun.

gunpowder *noun*
an explosive made from a powdered mixture of
potassium nitrate, charcoal, and sulphur.

gurgle *verb* (**gurgles, gurgling, gurgled**)
make a low bubbling sound.
gurgle *noun*

guru *noun* (*plural* **gurus**)
1 a Hindu religious leader. **2** an influential
teacher; a mentor.

gush *verb* (**gushes, gushing, gushed**)
1 flow suddenly or quickly. **2** talk too
enthusiastically or emotionally.
gush *noun*

gust *noun* (*plural* **gusts**)
a sudden rush of wind, rain, or smoke.
gusty *adjective* **gustily** *adverb*
gust *verb* (**gusts, gusting, gusted**)
blow in gusts.

gut *noun* (*plural* **guts**)
the lower part of the digestive system; the
intestine.
gut *verb* (**guts, gutting, gutted**)
1 remove the guts from a dead fish or other
animal. **2** remove or destroy the inside of
something ♦ *The fire gutted the factory.*

guts *plural noun*
1 the digestive system; the insides of a person or
thing. **2** (*informal*) courage.

gutted *adjective* (*informal*)
extremely disappointed or upset.

gutter *noun* (*plural* **gutters**)
a long narrow channel at the side of a street, or
along the edge of a roof, for carrying away
rainwater.
gutter *verb* (**gutters, guttering, guttered**)
a candle gutters when it burns unsteadily so that
melted wax runs down.

guttural (*say* gut-er-al) *adjective*
throaty and harsh-sounding ♦ *a guttural voice.*

guy[1] *noun* (*plural* **guys**)
1 a figure representing Guy Fawkes, burnt on 5
November in memory of the Gunpowder Plot
which planned to blow up Parliament on that
day in 1605. **2** (*informal*) a man.

guy[2] or **guy-rope** *noun* (*plural* **guys** or
guy-ropes)
a rope used to hold something in place,
especially a tent.

gym (*say* jim) *noun* (*plural* **gyms**) (*informal*)
1 a gymnasium. **2** gymnastics.

gymkhana (*say* jim-kah-na) *noun* (*plural*
gymkhanas)
a series of horse-riding contests and other sports
events.
[from Urdu]

gymnasium *noun* (*plural* **gymnasia** or
gymnasiums)
a place equipped for gymnastics.
[from Greek *gymnasion*, from *gymnos* = naked
(because Greek men exercised naked)]

gymnastics *plural noun*
exercises performed to develop the muscles or to show the performer's agility.
gymnastic *adjective*

gypsy *noun* (*plural* **gypsies**)
a member of a community of people, also called travellers, who live in caravans or similar vehicles and travel from place to place.
[from *Egyptian*, because gypsies were originally thought to have come from Egypt]

gyrate (*say* jy-**rayt**) *verb* (**gyrates, gyrating, gyrated**)
revolve; move in circles or spirals.
gyration *noun*

gyroscope (*say* jy-ro-skohp) *noun* (*plural* **gyroscopes**)
a device used in navigation, which keeps steady because of a heavy wheel spinning inside it.
[from Greek *gyros* = a ring or circle + *skopein* = to look at (because gyroscopes were once used to study the earth's rotation)]

Hh

haberdashery *noun*
small articles used in sewing, e.g. ribbons, buttons, and thread.
haberdasher *noun*

habit *noun* (*plural* **habits**)
1 something that you do without thinking because you have done it so often; a settled way of behaving. **2** something that is hard to give up ♦ *a smoking habit*. **3** the long dress worn by a monk or nun.
habitual *adjective* **habitually** *adverb*

habitat *noun* (*plural* **habitats**)
where an animal or plant lives naturally.

habitation *noun* (*plural* **habitations**)
1 a place to live in. **2** inhabiting a place.

hack *verb* (**hacks, hacking, hacked**)
1 chop or cut roughly. **2** (*informal*) break into a computer system.
hacker *noun*

hackles *plural noun*
make someone's hackles rise make someone angry or indignant.

haddock *noun* (*plural* **haddock**)
a sea fish like cod but smaller, used as food.

hadn't (*mainly spoken*)
had not.

haemoglobin (*say* heem-a-**gloh**-bin) *noun*
the red substance that carries oxygen in the blood.

haemophilia (*say* heem-o-**fil**-ee-a) *noun*
a disease that causes people to bleed dangerously from even a slight cut.
haemophiliac *noun*

haemorrhage (*say* hem-**er**-ij) *noun*
bleeding, especially inside a person's body.

hag *noun* (*plural* **hags**)
an ugly old woman.

haggard *adjective*
looking ill or very tired.

haggis *noun* (*plural* **haggises**)
a Scottish food made from sheep's offal.

hail¹ *noun*
frozen drops of rain.
hail *verb* **hailstone** *noun* **hailstorm** *noun*

hail² *interjection* (*old use*)
an exclamation of greeting.
hail *verb* (**hails, hailing, hailed**)
call out to somebody.
hail from come from ♦ *He hails from Ireland.*

hair *noun* (*plural* **hairs**)
1 a soft covering that grows on the heads and bodies of people and animals. **2** one of the strands that make up this covering.
hairbrush *noun* **haircut** *noun* **hairstyle** *noun*
keep your hair on (*informal*) do not lose your temper. **split hairs** make petty or unimportant distinctions of meaning. **hair-splitting** *noun*

hairdresser *noun* (*plural* **hairdressers**)
a person whose job is to cut and arrange people's hair.

hairpin *noun* (*plural* **hairpins**)
a U-shaped pin for keeping hair in place.

hairpin bend *noun* (*plural* **hairpin bends**)
a sharp bend in a road.

hair-raising *adjective*
terrifying.

hairy *adjective*
1 with a lot of hair. **2** (*informal*) dangerous or risky.

hajj *noun*
the pilgrimage to Mecca which all Muslims are expected to make at least once.

halal *noun*
meat prepared according to Muslim law.

halcyon (*say* hal-see-on) *adjective*
happy and peaceful ♦ *halcyon days.*

half *noun* (*plural* **halves**)
one of the two equal parts or amounts into which something is or can be divided.

half *adverb*
partly; not completely ♦ *This meat is only half cooked*.
not half (*slang*) extremely ♦ *Was she cross? Not half!*

half-brother *noun* (*plural* **half-brothers**)
a brother to whom you are related by one parent but not by both parents.

half-hearted *adjective*
not very enthusiastic.
half-heartedly *adverb*

half-life *noun* (*plural* **half-lives**)
the time taken for the radioactivity of a substance to fall to half its original value.

half mast *noun*
a point about halfway up a flagpole, to which a flag is lowered as a mark of respect for a person who has died.

halfpenny (*say* **hayp**-nee) *noun* (*plural* **halfpennies** for separate coins, **halfpence** for a sum of money)
a former coin worth half a penny.

half-sister *noun* (*plural* **half-sisters**)
a sister to whom you are related by one parent but not by both parents.

half-term *noun* (*plural* **half-terms**)
a short holiday in the middle of a term.

halfway *adjective* & *adverb*
between two others and equally distant from each.

hall *noun* (*plural* **halls**)
1 a space or passage just inside the front entrance of a house. 2 a very large room or building used for meetings, concerts, etc. 3 a large country house.

Hallowe'en *noun*
31 October, traditionally a time when ghosts and witches are believed to appear.

hallucination *noun* (*plural* **hallucinations**)
something you think you can see or hear that is not really there.
hallucinate *verb*

halo *noun* (*plural* **haloes**)
a circle of light round something, especially round the head of a saint etc. in paintings.

halt *verb* (**halts, halting, halted**)
stop.

halt *noun* (*plural* **halts**)
1 a stop or standstill ♦ *Work came to a halt*. 2 a small stopping place on a railway.

halve *verb* (**halves, halving, halved**)
1 divide something into halves. 2 reduce something to half its size.

ham *noun* (*plural* **hams**)
1 meat from a pig's leg. 2 (*informal*) an actor who overacts. 3 (*informal*) someone who operates a radio to send and receive messages as a hobby.

hamburger *noun* (*plural* **hamburgers**)
a flat round cake of minced beef served fried, often in a bread roll.

hammer *noun* (*plural* **hammers**)
a tool with a heavy metal head used for driving nails in, breaking things, etc.

hammer *verb* (**hammers, hammering, hammered**)
1 hit something with a hammer. 2 knock loudly ♦ *Someone was hammering on the door*. 3 (*informal*) defeat.

hammock *noun* (*plural* **hammocks**)
a bed made of a strong net or piece of cloth hung by cords.
[via Spanish from Taino (a South American language)]

hamper[1] *noun* (*plural* **hampers**)
a large box-shaped basket with a lid.

hamper[2] *verb* (**hampers, hampering, hampered**)
hinder; prevent from moving or working freely.

hamster *noun* (*plural* **hamsters**)
a small furry animal with cheek pouches for carrying grain.

hamstring *noun* (*plural* **hamstrings**)
any of the five tendons at the back of a person's knee.

hand *noun* (*plural* **hands**)
1 the end part of the arm below the wrist. 2 a pointer on a clock or dial. 3 a worker; a member of a ship's crew ♦ *All hands on deck!* 4 the cards held by one player in a card game. 5 side or direction ♦ *the right-hand side*; ♦ *on the other hand*. 6 help or aid ♦ *Give me a hand with these boxes*.
at hand near. **by hand** using your hand or hands. **give** or **receive a big hand** applaud or be applauded. **hands down** winning easily. **in good hands** in the care or control of someone who can be trusted. **in hand** in your possession; being dealt with. **on hand** available. **out of hand** out of control.

hand *verb* (**hands, handing, handed**)
give or pass something to somebody ♦ *Hand it over*.
hand down pass something from one generation to another.

handbag *noun* (*plural* **handbags**)
a small bag for holding a purse and personal articles.

handbook *noun* (*plural* **handbooks**)
a small book that gives useful facts about something.

handcuff *noun* (*plural* **handcuffs**)
one of a pair of metal rings linked by a chain, for fastening a prisoner's wrists together.

handcuff *verb* (handcuffs, handcuffing, handcuffed)
fasten with handcuffs.

handful *noun* (*plural* **handfuls**)
1 as much as can be carried in one hand. **2** a few people or things. **3** (*informal*) a troublesome person or task.

handicap *noun* (*plural* **handicaps**)
1 a disadvantage. **2** a physical or mental disability.
handicapped *adjective*

handkerchief *noun* (*plural* **handkerchiefs**)
a small square of cloth for wiping the nose or face.

handle *noun* (*plural* **handles**)
the part of a thing by which it is held, carried, or controlled.

handle *verb* (handles, handling, handled)
1 touch or feel something with your hands. **2** deal with; manage ♦ *Will you handle the catering.*
handler *noun*

handlebar *noun* or **handlebars** *plural noun*
the bar, with a handle at each end, that steers a bicycle or motorcycle etc.

handsome *adjective*
1 good-looking. **2** generous ♦ *a handsome offer.*
handsomely *adverb*

handstand *noun* (*plural* **handstands**)
balancing on your hands with your feet in the air.

handwriting *noun*
writing done by hand; a person's style of writing.
handwritten *adjective*

handy *adjective* (handier, handiest)
1 convenient or useful. **2** good at using the hands.
handily *adverb* **handiness** *noun*

hang *verb* (hangs, hanging, hung)
1 fix the top or side of something to a hook or nail etc.; be supported in this way. **2** stick wallpaper to a wall. **3** decorate with drapery or hanging ornaments etc. ♦ *The tree was hung with lights.* **4** droop or lean ♦ *People hung over the gate.* **5** remain in the air or as something unpleasant ♦ *Smoke hung over the city.* ♦ *The threat is still hanging over him.*
6 (with *past tense & past participle* **hanged**) execute someone by hanging them from a rope that tightens round the neck ♦ *He was hanged in 1950.*
hang about 1 loiter. **2** not go away. **hang back** hesitate to go forward or to do something. **hang on 1** hold tightly. **2** (*informal*) wait. **hang up** end a telephone conversation by putting back the receiver.

hang *noun*
get the hang of (*informal*) learn how to do or use something.

hang-glider *noun* (*plural* **hang-gliders**)
a framework in which a person can glide through the air.
hang-gliding *noun*

hangover *noun* (*plural* **hangovers**)
an unpleasant feeling after drinking too much alcohol.

hank *noun* (*plural* **hanks**)
a coil or piece of wool, thread, etc.

hanker *verb* (hankers, hankering, hankered)
feel a longing for something.

haphazard *adjective*
done or chosen at random, not by planning.

happen *verb* (happens, happening, happened)
1 take place; occur. **2** do something by chance ♦ *I happened to see him.*

happy *adjective* (happier, happiest)
1 pleased or contented. **2** fortunate ♦ *a happy coincidence.* **3** willing ♦ *I'd be happy to help.*
happily *adverb* **happiness** *noun*

harangue (*say* ha-rang) *verb* (harangues, haranguing, harangued)
make a long aggressive speech to somebody.
harangue *noun*

harass (*say* ha-ras) *verb* (harasses, harassing, harassed)
trouble or annoy somebody often.
harassment (*say* ha-ras-ment) *noun*

harbour *noun* (*plural* **harbours**)
a place where ships can shelter or unload.

harbour *verb* (harbours, harbouring, harboured)
1 give shelter to somebody, especially a criminal.
2 keep a strong or hostile thought in your mind ♦ *I think she still harbours a grudge against them.*

hard *adjective*
1 firm or solid; not soft. **2** difficult ♦ *hard sums.*
3 severe or stern. **4** causing suffering ♦ *hard luck.* **5** using great effort ♦ *a hard worker.*
6 hard drugs are strong and addictive ones.
hardness *noun*
hard of hearing slightly deaf. **hard up** (*informal*) short of money.

hard *adverb*
1 so as to be hard ♦ *The ground froze hard.*
2 with great effort; intensively ♦ *We worked hard.* ♦ *It is raining hard.* **3** with difficulty ♦ *hard-earned.*

hard disk *noun* (*plural* **hard disks**)
a disk fixed inside a computer, able to store large amounts of data.

harden *verb* (hardens, hardening, hardened)
make or become hard.
hardener *noun*

hardly *adverb*
only just; only with difficulty ♦ *She can hardly walk.*

🛈 USAGE It is not acceptable in standard English to use 'not' with *hardly*, as in 'she can't hardly walk'.

hardship *noun* (*plural* **hardships**)
difficult conditions that cause discomfort or suffering ♦ *a life of hardship.*

hardware *noun*
1 metal implements and tools etc.; machinery. 2 the machinery of a computer as opposed to the software. (Compare **software**.)

hard water *noun*
water containing minerals that prevent soap from making much lather.

hardy *adjective* (**hardier, hardiest**)
able to endure cold or difficult conditions. **hardiness** *noun*

hare *noun* (*plural* **hares**)
an animal like a rabbit but larger.

harm *verb* (**harms, harming, harmed**)
damage or injure.

harm *noun*
damage or injury.
harmful *adjective* **harmless** *adjective*

harmonica *noun* (*plural* **harmonicas**)
a mouth organ.

harmonious *adjective*
1 combining together in a pleasant, attractive, or effective way. 2 sounding pleasant. 3 peaceful and friendly.

harmony *noun* (*plural* **harmonies**)
1 a pleasant combination, especially of musical notes. 2 being friendly to each other.

harness *noun* (*plural* **harnesses**)
the straps put round a horse's head and neck for controlling it.

harness *verb* (**harnesses, harnessing, harnessed**)
1 put a harness on a horse. 2 control and use something ♦ *Could we harness the power of the wind?*

harp *noun* (*plural* **harps**)
a musical instrument with strings stretched across a frame and plucked by the fingers. **harpist** *noun*

harpoon *noun* (*plural* **harpoons**)
a spear attached to a rope, used for catching whales etc.
harpoon *verb*

harrowing *adjective*
very upsetting or distressing.

harsh *adjective*
1 rough and unpleasant. 2 severe or cruel.
harshly *adverb* **harshness** *noun*

harvest *noun* (*plural* **harvests**)
1 the time when farmers gather in the corn, fruit, or vegetables that they have grown. 2 the crop that is gathered in.

hash *noun*
a mixture of small pieces of meat and vegetables, usually fried.
make a hash of (*informal*) make a mess of something; bungle.

hasn't (*mainly spoken*)
has not.

haste *noun*
a hurry.
make haste act quickly.

hasten *verb* (**hastens, hastening, hastened**)
hurry.

hasty *adjective*
hurried; done too quickly.
hastily *adverb* **hastiness** *noun*

hat *noun* (*plural* **hats**)
a covering for the head, worn out of doors.
keep something under your hat keep it a secret.

hatch[1] *noun* (*plural* **hatches**)
an opening in a floor, wall, or door, usually with a covering.

hatch[2] *verb* (**hatches, hatching, hatched**)
1 break out of an egg. 2 keep an egg warm until a baby bird comes out. 3 plan ♦ *They hatched a plot.*

hatchet *noun* (*plural* **hatchets**)
a small axe.

hate *verb* (**hates, hating, hated**)
dislike very strongly.

hate *noun*
extreme dislike.

hatred *noun*
extreme dislike.

hat-trick *noun* (*plural* **hat-tricks**)
achieving three goals, wickets, or victories one after the other.

haughty *adjective* (**haughtier, haughtiest**)
proud of yourself and looking down on other people.
haughtily *adverb* **haughtiness** *noun*

haul *verb* (**hauls, hauling, hauled**)
pull or drag with great effort.
haulage *noun*

haul *noun* (*plural* **hauls**)
1 hauling. 2 the amount obtained by an effort; booty ♦ *The thieves' haul came to £2 million.* 3 a distance to be covered ♦ *a long haul.*

haunt *verb* (**haunts, haunting, haunted**)
1 (said about ghosts) appear often in a place or to a person. 2 visit a place often. 3 stay in your mind ♦ *The memory haunts me still.*
haunted *adjective*

haunt *noun* (*plural* **haunts**)
a place that you often visit ♦ *my favourite haunt.*

have *verb* (**has, having, had**)
This word has many uses, including **1** possess or own ♦ *We have two dogs.* **2** contain ♦ *This tin has sweets in it.* **3** experience ♦ *He had a shock.* **4** be obliged to do something ♦ *We have to go now.* **5** allow ♦ *I won't have him bullied.* **6** receive or accept ♦ *Will you have a sweet?* **7** get something done ♦ *I'm having my watch mended.* **8** (*slang*) cheat or deceive ♦ *We've been had!*
have somebody on (*informal*) fool him or her.

have *auxiliary verb*
used to form the past tense of verbs, e.g. *He has gone.*

haven *noun* (*plural* **havens**)
a safe place or refuge.

haven't (*mainly spoken*)
have not.

havoc *noun*
great destruction or disorder.
play havoc with disrupt something completely.

hawk *noun* (*plural* **hawks**)
a bird of prey with very strong eyesight.

hawthorn *noun* (*plural* **hawthorns**)
a thorny tree with small red berries (called **haws**).

hay *noun*
dried grass for feeding to animals.

hay fever *noun*
irritation of the nose, throat, and eyes, caused by pollen or dust.

hazard *noun* (*plural* **hazards**)
1 a danger or risk. **2** an obstacle.
hazardous *adjective*

hazy *adjective*
1 misty. **2** vague or uncertain.
hazily *adverb* **haziness** *noun*

he *pronoun*
1 the male person or animal being talked about. **2** a person (male or female) ♦ *He who hesitates is lost.*

head *noun* (*plural* **heads**)
1 the part of the body containing the brains, eyes, and mouth. **2** your brains or mind; intelligence ♦ *Use your head!* **3** a talent or ability ♦ *She has a good head for figures.* **4** the side of a coin on which someone's head is shown ♦ *Heads or tails?* **5** a person ♦ *It costs £2 per head.* **6** the top or front of something ♦ *a pinhead;* ♦ *at the head of the procession.* **7** the chief; the person in charge. **8** a headteacher.
come to a head reach a crisis point. **keep your head** stay calm. **off the top of your head** without preparation or thinking carefully.

head *verb* (**heads, heading, headed**)
1 be at the top or front of something. **2** hit a ball with your head. **3** move in a particular direction ♦ *We headed for the coast.* **4** force someone to turn aside by getting in front of them ♦ *Let's see if we can head him off.*
[from Old English]

headache *noun* (*plural* **headaches**)
1 a pain in the head. **2** (*informal*) a worrying problem.

heading *noun* (*plural* **headings**)
a word or words put at the top of a piece of printing or writing.

headland *noun* (*plural* **headlands**)
a large piece of high land that sticks out into the sea.

headlight *noun* (*plural* **headlights**)
a powerful light at the front of a car, engine, etc.

headline *noun* (*plural* **headlines**)
a heading in a newspaper.
the headlines the main items of news.

headlong *adverb* & *adjective*
1 falling head first. **2** in a hasty or thoughtless way.

headmaster *noun* (*plural* **headmasters**)
a male headteacher.

headmistress *noun* (*plural* **headmistresses**)
a female headteacher.

head-on *adverb* & *adjective*
with the front parts colliding ♦ *a head-on collision.*

headquarters *noun*
the place from which an organization is controlled.

headstrong *adjective*
determined to do as you want.

headteacher *noun* (*plural* **headteachers**)
the person in charge of a school.

headway *noun*
make headway make progress.

heal *verb* (**heals, healing, healed**)
1 make or become healthy flesh again ♦ *The wound healed slowly.* **2** (*old use*) cure ♦ *healing the sick.*

health *noun*
1 the condition of a person's body or mind ♦ *His health is bad.* **2** being healthy ♦ *in sickness and in health.*

healthy *adjective* (**healthier, healthiest**)
1 being well; free from illness. **2** producing good health ♦ *Fresh air is healthy.*
healthily *adverb* **healthiness** *noun*

heap *noun* (*plural* **heaps**)
a pile, especially an untidy one.
heaps *plural noun* (*informal*) a great amount; plenty ♦ *There's heaps of time.*

heap *verb* (heaps, heaping, heaped)
1 make things into a heap. 2 to load heavily with ♦ *She heaped the plate with food.*

hear *verb* (hears, hearing, heard)
1 take in sounds through the ears. 2 receive news or information etc. 3 listen to and try a case in a lawcourt.
hearer *noun*
hear! hear! (in a debate) I agree. **not hear of** refuse to allow something ♦ *He wouldn't hear of my paying for it.*

hearing *noun* (*plural* hearings)
1 the ability to hear. 2 a chance to be heard; a trial in a lawcourt.

hearing aid *noun* (*plural* hearing aids)
a device to help a deaf person to hear.

heart *noun* (*plural* hearts)
1 the organ of the body that makes the blood circulate. 2 a person's feelings or emotions; sympathy. 3 enthusiasm; courage ♦ *Take heart.* 4 the middle or most important part. 5 a curved shape representing a heart. 6 a playing card with red heart shapes on it.
break someone's heart make someone very unhappy. **heartbroken** *adjective* **by heart** memorized.

heart attack *noun* (*plural* heart attacks)
a sudden failure of the heart to work properly, which results in great pain or sometimes death.

hearten *verb* (heartens, heartening, heartened)
make a person feel encouraged.

heartfelt *adjective*
felt deeply.

hearth *noun* (*plural* hearths)
the floor of a fireplace, or the area in front of it.

heartless *adjective*
without pity or sympathy.

hearty *adjective*
1 strong and vigorous. 2 enthusiastic and sincere ♦ *hearty congratulations.* 3 (said about a meal) large.
heartily *adverb* **heartiness** *noun*

heat *noun* (*plural* heats)
1 hotness or (in scientific use) the form of energy causing this. 2 hot weather. 3 strong feeling, especially anger. 4 a race or contest to decide who will take part in the final.
on heat (said about a female mammal) ready for mating.

heat *verb* (heats, heating, heated)
make or become hot.

heathen *noun* (*plural* heathens)
a person who does not believe in any of the world's chief religions.

heather *noun*
an evergreen plant with small purple, pink, or white flowers.

heatwave *noun* (*plural* heatwaves)
a long period of hot weather.

heave *verb* (heaves, heaving, heaved)
1 lift or move something heavy. 2 (*informal*) throw. 3 rise and fall. 4 (said about the stomach) feel uncomfortable, making you want to vomit.
heave *noun*
heave a sigh utter a deep sigh.

heaven *noun* (*plural* heavens)
1 the place where God and angels are thought to live. 2 a very pleasant place or condition.
the heavens the sky.

heavy *adjective* (heavier, heaviest)
1 weighing a lot; difficult to lift or carry. 2 great in amount or force etc. ♦ *heavy rain;* ♦ *a heavy penalty.* 3 needing much effort ♦ *heavy work.* 4 full of sadness or worry ♦ *with a heavy heart.*
heavily *adverb* **heaviness** *noun*

heavyweight *noun* (*plural* heavyweights)
1 a heavy person. 2 a boxer of the heaviest weight.
heavyweight *adjective*

Hebrew *noun*
the language of the Jews in ancient Palestine and modern Israel.

hectare (*say* hek-tar) *noun* (*plural* hectares)
a unit of area equal to 10,000 square metres or nearly $2\frac{1}{2}$ acres.

hedge *noun* (*plural* hedges)
a row of bushes forming a barrier or boundary.

hedgehog *noun* (*plural* hedgehogs)
a small animal covered with long prickles.

heed *noun*
take or **pay heed** give attention to something.
heedful *adjective* **heedless** *adjective*

heel *noun* (*plural* heels)
1 the back part of the foot. 2 the part round or under the heel of a sock or shoe etc.
take to your heels run away.

hefty *adjective* (heftier, heftiest)
large and strong.
heftily *adverb*

height *noun* (*plural* heights)
1 how high something is; the distance from the base to the top or from head to foot. 2 a high place. 3 the highest or most intense part ♦ *at the height of the holiday season.*

heighten *verb* (heightens, heightening, heightened)
make or become higher or more intense.

heir (air) *noun* (*plural* heirs)
a person who inherits something.

heiress (*say* air-ess) *noun* (*plural* heiresses)
a female heir, especially to great wealth.

heirloom (*say* air-loom) *noun* (*plural* heirlooms)
a valued possession that has been handed down in a family for several generations.

helicopter *noun* (*plural* helicopters)
a kind of aircraft with a large horizontal propeller or rotor.
[from Greek *helix* = coil + Greek *pteron* = wing]

helium (*say* hee-lee-um) *noun*
a light colourless gas that does not burn.

helix (*say* hee-liks) *noun* (*plural* helices (*say* hee-liss-eez))
a spiral.
[from Greek, = coil]

hell *noun*
1 a place where, in some religions, wicked people are thought to be punished after they die. 2 a very unpleasant place or experience.
hell for leather (*informal*) at high speed.
[from Old English]

hello *interjection*
a word used to greet somebody or to attract their attention.

helmet *noun* (*plural* helmets)
a strong covering worn to protect the head.

help *verb* (helps, helping, helped)
1 do part of another person's work for him or her. 2 benefit; make something better or easier ♦ *This will help you to sleep.* 3 if you cannot help doing something, you cannot avoid doing it ♦ *I can't help coughing.* 4 serve food etc. to somebody ♦ *just help yourself.*
helper *noun* **helpful** *adjective* **helpfully** *adverb*

help *noun*
1 helping somebody. 2 a person or thing that helps.
[from Old English]

helping *noun* (*plural* helpings)
a portion of food.

helpless *adjective*
not able to do things.
helplessly *adverb* **helplessness** *noun*

helpline *noun* (*plural* helplines)
a telephone service giving advice on problems.

hem *noun* (*plural* hems)
the edge of a piece of cloth that is folded over and sewn down.

hem *verb* (hems, hemming, hemmed)
put a hem on something.
hem in surround and restrict.

hemisphere *noun* (*plural* hemispheres)
1 half a sphere. 2 half the earth ♦ *Australia is in the southern hemisphere.*
hemispherical *adjective*

hen *noun* (*plural* hens)
1 a female bird. 2 a female fowl.

hence *adverb*
1 henceforth. 2 therefore. 3 (*old use*) from here.

henchman *noun* (*plural* henchmen)
a trusty supporter.

her *pronoun*
the form of **she** used as the object of a verb or after a preposition.

her *adjective*
belonging to her ♦ *her book.*

herald *noun* (*plural* heralds)
an official in former times who made announcements and carried messages for a king or queen.

heraldry *noun*
the study of coats of arms.
heraldic (*say* hir-al-dik) *adjective*

herb *noun* (*plural* herbs)
a plant used for flavouring or for making medicine.
herbal *adjective*

herbivorous (*say* her-biv-er-us) *adjective*
plant-eating. (Compare **carnivorous**.)
herbivore *noun*

herd *noun* (*plural* herds)
1 a group of cattle or other animals that feed together. 2 a mass of people; a mob.
herdsman *noun*

herd *verb* (herds, herding, herded)
1 gather or move or send in a herd ♦ *We all herded into the dining room.* 2 look after a herd of animals.

here *adverb*
in or to this place etc.
here and there in various places or directions.

hereby *adverb*
by this act or decree etc.

hereditary *adjective*
1 inherited ♦ *a hereditary disease.* 2 inheriting a position ♦ *Our Queen is a hereditary monarch.*

heredity (*say* hir-ed-it-ee) *noun*
the process of inheriting physical or mental characteristics from parents or ancestors.

heresy (*say* herri-see) *noun* (*plural* heresies)
an opinion that disagrees with the beliefs generally accepted by the Christian Church or other authority.

heretic (*say* herri-tik) *noun* (*plural* heretics)
a person who supports a heresy.
heretical (*say* hi-ret-ik-al) *adjective*

heritage *noun*
the things that someone has inherited.

hermetically *adverb*
so as to be airtight ♦ *The tin is hermetically sealed.*

hermit *noun* (*plural* hermits)
a person who lives alone and keeps away from people.

hero noun (plural **heroes**)
1 a man or boy who is admired for doing something very brave or great. **2** the chief male character in a story etc.
heroic adjective **heroically** adverb **heroism** noun

heroin noun
a very strong drug, made from morphine.

heroine noun (plural **heroines**)
1 a woman or girl who is admired for doing something very brave or great. **2** the chief female character in a story etc.

heron noun (plural **herons**)
a wading bird with long legs and a long neck.

herring noun (plural **herring** or **herrings**)
a sea fish used as food.

hers possessive pronoun
belonging to her ♦ Those books are hers.

❶ USAGE It is incorrect to write her's.

herself pronoun
she or her and nobody else. The word is used to refer back to the subject of a sentence (e.g. She cut herself) or for emphasis (e.g. She herself has said it).
by herself alone; on her own.

hertz noun (plural **hertz**)
a unit of frequency of electromagnetic waves, = one cycle per second.

hesitate verb (**hesitates, hesitating, hesitated**)
be slow or uncertain in speaking, moving, etc.
hesitant adjective **hesitation** noun

heterogeneous (say het-er-o-**jeen**-ee-us) adjective
composed of people or things of different kinds.

heterosexual adjective
attracted to people of the opposite sex; not homosexual.
heterosexual noun

hexagon noun (plural **hexagons**)
a flat shape with six sides and six angles.
hexagonal adjective

hibernate verb (**hibernates, hibernating, hibernated**)
spend the winter in a state like deep sleep.
hibernation noun
[from Latin hiberna = winter quarters]

hiccup noun (plural **hiccups**)
1 a high gulping sound made when your breath is briefly interrupted. **2** a brief hitch or setback.
hiccup verb

hide¹ verb (**hides, hiding, hid, hidden**)
1 get into a place where you cannot be seen.
2 keep a person or thing from being seen.
3 keep a thing secret.

hide² noun (plural **hides**)
an animal's skin.

hide-and-seek noun
a game in which one person looks for others who are hiding.

hideous adjective
very ugly or unpleasant.
hideously adverb

hiding¹ noun
being hidden ♦ She went into hiding.
hiding place noun

hiding² noun (plural **hidings**)
a thrashing or beating.

hierarchy (say **hyr**-ark-ee) noun (plural **hierarchies**)
an organization that ranks people one above another according to the power or authority that they hold.

hieroglyphics (say hyr-o-**glif**-iks) plural noun
pictures or symbols used in ancient Egypt to represent words.

hi-fi noun (plural **hi-fis**) (informal)
1 high fidelity. **2** equipment for reproducing recorded sound with very little distortion.

higgledy-piggledy adverb & adjective
completely mixed up; in great disorder.

high adjective
1 reaching a long way upwards ♦ high hills.
2 far above the ground or above sea level ♦ high clouds. **3** measuring from top to bottom ♦ two metres high. **4** above average level in importance, quality, amount, etc. ♦ high rank; ♦ high prices. **5** (said about meat) beginning to go bad. **6** (informal) affected by a drug.
it is high time it is already the time for something to happen ♦ It's high time we left.

high adverb
at or to a high level or position etc. ♦ They flew high above us.

highbrow adjective
intellectual.

higher education noun
education at a university or college.

high fidelity noun
reproducing recorded sound with very little distortion.

high jump noun
an athletic contest in which competitors try to jump over a high bar.

highlight noun (plural **highlights**)
1 the most interesting part of something ♦ The highlight of the holiday was the trip to Pompeii. **2** a light area in a painting etc.
3 a light-coloured streak in a person's hair.

highly adverb
1 extremely ♦ highly amusing. **2** very favourably ♦ We think highly of her.

Highness noun (plural **Highnesses**)
the title of a prince or princess.

high road noun (plural **high roads**)
the main road.

high school noun (plural **high schools**)
a secondary school.

high street noun (plural **high streets**)
a town's main street.

high tea noun
a meal eaten in the late afternoon or early
evening.

highway noun (plural **highways**)
a main road or route.

highwayman noun (plural **highwaymen**)
a man who robbed travellers on highways in
former times.

hijack verb (**hijacks, hijacking, hijacked**)
seize control of an aircraft or vehicle during a
journey.
hijack noun **hijacker** noun

hike noun (plural **hikes**)
a long walk.
hike verb **hiker** noun

hilarious adjective
very funny.
hilariously adverb **hilarity** noun

hill noun (plural **hills**)
a piece of land that is higher than the ground
around it.
hillside noun **hilly** adjective

hilt noun (plural **hilts**)
the handle of a sword, dagger, or knife.
to the hilt completely.

him pronoun
the form of **he** used as the object of a verb or after
a preposition.

himself pronoun
he or him and nobody else. (Compare **herself**.)

hind adjective
at the back ♦ the hind legs.

hinder verb (**hinders, hindering, hindered**)
get in someone's way or make things difficult for
them.
hindrance noun

hindquarters plural noun
an animal's hind legs and rear parts.

hindsight noun
looking back on an event with knowledge or
understanding that you did not have at the time.

Hindu noun (plural **Hindus**)
a person who believes in Hinduism, which is one
of the religions of India.

hinge noun (plural **hinges**)
a joining device on which a lid or door etc. turns
when it opens.
hinge verb (**hinges, hinging, hinged**)
1 fix something with a hinge. **2** depend
♦ Everything hinges on this meeting.

hint noun (plural **hints**)
1 a slight indication or suggestion ♦ Give me a
hint of what you want. **2** a useful idea or piece of
advice ♦ household hints.
hint verb (**hints, hinting, hinted**)
make a hint.

hip¹ noun (plural **hips**)
the bony part at the side of the body between the
waist and the thigh.

hip² noun (plural **hips**)
the fruit of the wild rose.

hippopotamus noun (plural
hippopotamuses)
a very large African animal that lives near water.

hire verb (**hires, hiring, hired**)
1 pay to borrow something. **2** lend something for
payment ♦ He hires out bicycles.
hirer noun
hire noun
hiring something ♦ bikes for hire.

hire purchase noun
a system of buying something by paying for it in
instalments.

his adjective & possessive pronoun
belonging to him ♦ That is his book. ♦ That book
is his.

hiss verb (**hisses, hissing, hissed**)
make a sound like an s ♦ The snakes were
hissing.
hiss noun

histogram noun (plural **histograms**)
a chart showing amounts as rectangles of
varying sizes.

historian noun (plural **historians**)
a person who writes or studies history.

historic adjective
famous or important in history; likely to be
remembered ♦ a historic town; ♦ a historic
meeting.

ⓘ USAGE Do not confuse with *historical*.

---

historical adjective
1 to do with history. **2** that actually existed or
took place in the past ♦ The novel is based on
historical events.

ⓘ USAGE Do not confuse with *historic*.

---

history noun (plural **histories**)
1 what happened in the past. **2** study of past
events. **3** a description of important events.
[from Greek *historia* = learning or finding out]

hit verb (**hits, hitting, hit**)
1 come forcefully against a person or thing;
knock or strike. **2** have a bad effect on ♦ Famine
has hit the poor countries. **3** reach ♦ I can't hit
that high note.
hit on discover something by chance.

hit *noun* (*plural* **hits**)
1 hitting; a knock or stroke. 2 a shot that hits the target. 3 a success. 4 a successful song, show, etc.

hitch *verb* (**hitches, hitching, hitched**)
1 raise or pull with a slight jerk. 2 fasten with a loop or hook etc. 3 hitch-hike.

hitch *noun* (*plural* **hitches**)
1 a slight difficulty causing delay. 2 a hitching movement. 3 a knot.

hitch-hike *verb* (**hitch-hikes, hitch-hiking, hitch-hiked**)
travel by getting lifts from passing vehicles.
hitch-hiker *noun*

hi-tech *adjective*
using the most advanced technology, especially electronic devices and computers.

hither *adverb*
to or towards this place.

hitherto *adverb*
until this time.

HIV *abbreviation*
human immunodeficiency virus; a virus that causes Aids.

hive *noun* (*plural* **hives**)
1 a beehive. 2 the bees living in a beehive.
hive of industry a place full of people working busily.

hoard *noun* (*plural* **hoards**)
a carefully saved store of money, treasure, food, etc.

hoard *verb* (**hoards, hoarding, hoarded**)
store something away.
hoarder *noun*

---

❶ USAGE Do not confuse with *horde*.

---

hoarding *noun* (*plural* **hoardings**)
a tall fence covered with advertisements.

hoar frost *noun*
a white frost.

hoarse *adjective*
having a rough or croaking voice.
hoarsely *adverb* **hoarseness** *noun*

hoax *verb* (**hoaxes, hoaxing, hoaxed**)
deceive somebody as a joke.
hoax *noun* **hoaxer** *noun*

hobble *verb* (**hobbles, hobbling, hobbled**)
limp or walk with difficulty.

hobby *noun* (*plural* **hobbies**)
something you do for pleasure in your spare time.

hobby horse *noun* (*plural* **hobby horses**)
1 a stick with a horse's head, used as a toy.
2 a subject that a person likes to talk about whenever he or she gets the chance.

hobgoblin *noun* (*plural* **hobgoblins**)
a mischievous or evil spirit.

hockey *noun*
a game played by two teams with curved sticks and a hard ball.

hoe *noun* (*plural* **hoes**)
a tool for scraping up weeds.

hoe *verb* (**hoes, hoeing, hoed**)
scrape or dig with a hoe.

hog *noun* (*plural* **hogs**)
1 a male pig. 2 (*informal*) a greedy person.
go the whole hog (*informal*) do something completely or thoroughly.

Hogmanay *noun*
New Year's Eve in Scotland.
[perhaps from early French *aguillanneuf* = a gift at new year]

hoist *verb* (**hoists, hoisting, hoisted**)
lift something up, especially by using ropes or pulleys.

hold *verb* (**holds, holding, held**)
1 have and keep, especially in your hands.
2 have room for ♦ *The jug holds two pints.*
3 support ♦ *This plank won't hold my weight.*
4 stay the same; continue ♦ *Will the fine weather hold?* 5 believe or consider ♦ *We shall hold you responsible.* 6 cause something to take place ♦ *hold a meeting.* 7 restrain someone or stop them getting away ♦ *The police are holding three men for the robbery.*
hold forth make a long speech. **hold out** refuse to give in. **hold up** 1 hinder. 2 stop and rob somebody by threats or force. **hold with** approve of ♦ *We don't hold with bullying.* **hold your tongue** (*informal*) stop talking.

hold *noun* (*plural* **holds**)
1 holding something; a grasp. 2 something to hold on to for support. 3 the part of a ship where cargo is stored, below the deck.
get hold of 1 grasp. 2 obtain. 3 make contact with a person.

hold-up *noun* (*plural* **hold-ups**)
1 a delay. 2 a robbery with threats or force.

hole *noun* (*plural* **holes**)
1 a hollow place; a gap or opening. 2 a burrow.
3 one of the small holes into which you have to hit the ball in golf. 4 (*informal*) an unpleasant place.
holey *adjective*
in a hole in an awkward situation.

hole *verb* (**holes, holing, holed**)
1 make a hole or holes in something. 2 hit a golf ball into one of the holes.

holiday *noun* (*plural* **holidays**)
1 a day or week etc. when people do not go to work or to school. 2 a time when you go away to enjoy yourself.

holiness *noun*
being holy or sacred.
His Holiness the title of the Pope.

hollow *adjective*
with an empty space inside; not solid.
hollowly *adverb*

hollow *noun* (*plural* **hollows**)
a hollow or sunken place.

hollow *verb* (**hollows, hollowing, hollowed**)
make a thing hollow.

holly *noun* (*plural* **hollies**)
an evergreen bush with shiny prickly leaves and
red berries.

holocaust *noun* (*plural* **holocausts**)
an immense destruction, especially by fire
♦ *the nuclear holocaust.*
the Holocaust the mass murder of the Jews by
the Nazis from 1939 to 1945.

hologram *noun* (*plural* **holograms**)
a type of photograph made by laser beams that
produces a three-dimensional image.

holy *adjective* (**holier, holiest**)
1 belonging or devoted to God. **2** consecrated
♦ *holy water.*
holiness *noun*

homage *noun* (*plural* **homages**)
an act or expression of respect or honour
♦ *We paid homage to his achievements.*

home *noun* (*plural* **homes**)
1 the place where you live. **2** the place where
you were born or where you feel you belong.
3 a place where those who need help are looked
after ♦ *an old people's home.* **4** the place to be
reached in a race or in certain games.

home *adjective*
1 to do with your own home or country
♦ *home industries.* **2** played on a team's own
ground ♦ *a home match.*

home *adverb*
1 to or at home ♦ *Is she home yet?* **2** to the point
aimed at ♦ *Push the bolt home.*
bring something home to somebody make
him or her realize it.

home *verb* (**homes, homing, homed**)
make for a target ♦ *The missile homed in.*

home economics *noun*
the study of cookery and how to run a home.

homeless *adjective*
having no home.

homely *adjective*
simple and ordinary ♦ *a homely meal.*
homeliness *noun*

home-made *adjective*
made at home, not bought from a shop.

homeopathy *noun*
the treatment of disease by tiny doses of drugs
that in a healthy person would produce
symptoms of the disease.
homeopathic *adjective*

home page *noun* (*plural* **home pages**)
the first page of an Internet website, with a
summary of all the information it gives.

homesick *adjective*
sad because you are away from home.
homesickness *noun*

homeward *adjective* & *adverb*
going towards home.
homewards *adverb*

homework *noun*
school work that has to be done at home.

homicide *noun* (*plural* **homicides**)
the killing of one person by another.
homicidal *adjective*

homogeneous (*say* hom-o-**jeen**-ee-us)
adjective
formed of people or things of the same kind.

homograph *noun* (*plural* **homographs**)
a word that is spelt like another but has a
different meaning or origin, e.g. *bat* (a flying
animal) and *bat* (for hitting a ball).

homonym (*say* hom-o-nim) *noun* (*plural*
homonyms)
a homograph or homophone.

homophone *noun* (*plural* **homophones**)
a word with the same sound as another, e.g. *son,
sun.*

Homo sapiens *noun*
human beings regarded as a species of animal.
[Latin, = wise man or person]

homosexual *adjective*
attracted to people of the same sex.
homosexual *noun* **homosexuality** *noun*

honest *adjective*
not stealing or cheating or telling lies; truthful.
honestly *adverb* **honesty** *noun*

honey *noun*
a sweet sticky food made by bees.

honeycomb *noun* (*plural* **honeycombs**)
a wax structure of small six-sided sections made
by bees to hold their honey and eggs.

honeycombed *adjective*
with many holes or tunnels.

honeymoon *noun* (*plural* **honeymoons**)
a holiday spent together by a newly married
couple.
[from *honey* + *moon* (because the first intensely
passionate feelings gradually wane like the
moon)]

honeysuckle *noun*
a climbing plant with fragrant yellow or pink
flowers.

honk *noun* (*plural* **honks**)
a loud sound like that made by a goose or an
old-fashioned car horn.
honk *verb*

honorary *adjective*
1 given or received as an honour ♦ *an honorary degree.* 2 unpaid ♦ *the honorary treasurer of the club.*

❶ USAGE Do not confuse with *honourable.*

honour *noun* (*plural* **honours**)
1 great respect or reputation. 2 a person or thing that brings honour. 3 something a person is proud to do ♦ *It is an honour to meet you.* 4 honesty and loyalty ♦ *a man of honour.* 5 an award for distinction.
in honour of as an expression of respect for.
honour *verb* (**honours, honouring, honoured**)
1 feel or show honour for a person. 2 keep to the terms of an agreement or promise.

honourable *adjective*
deserving honour; honest and loyal.
honourably *adverb*

❶ USAGE Do not confuse with *honorary.*

hood *noun* (*plural* **hoods**)
1 a covering of soft material for the head and neck. 2 a folding roof or cover.
hooded *adjective*
hoodwink *verb* (**hoodwinks, hoodwinking, hoodwinked**)
deceive.

hoof *noun* (*plural* **hoofs** or **hooves**)
the horny part of the foot of a horse etc.

hook *noun* (*plural* **hooks**)
a bent or curved piece of metal etc. for hanging things on or for catching hold of something.
hook *verb* (**hooks, hooking, hooked**)
1 fasten something with or on a hook. 2 catch a fish etc. with a hook. 3 hit a ball in a curving path.
be hooked on something (*slang*) be addicted to it.

hooked *adjective*
hook-shaped.

hooligan *noun* (*plural* **hooligans**)
a rough and violent young person.
hooliganism *noun*

hoop *noun* (*plural* **hoops**)
a ring made of metal or wood.

hoot *noun* (*plural* **hoots**)
1 the sound made by an owl or a vehicle's horn or a steam whistle. 2 a cry of scorn or disapproval. 3 an outburst of laughter. 4 (*informal*) something funny.
hoot *verb* **hooter** *noun*

hop' *verb* (**hops, hopping, hopped**)
1 jump on one foot. 2 (said about an animal) spring from all feet at once. 3 (*informal*) move quickly ♦ *Here's the car—hop in!*
hop it (*informal*) go away.

hop *noun* (*plural* **hops**)
a hopping movement.

hop² *noun* (*plural* **hops**)
a climbing plant used to give beer its flavour.

hope *noun* (*plural* **hopes**)
1 the feeling of wanting something to happen, and thinking that it will happen. 2 a person or thing that gives hope ♦ *You are our only hope.*
hope *verb* (**hopes, hoping, hoped**)
feel hope; want and expect something.

hopeful *adjective*
1 feeling hope. 2 likely to be good or successful.

hopefully *adverb*
1 it is to be hoped; I hope that. 2 in a hopeful way.

❶ USAGE Some people say it is incorrect to use *hopefully* to mean 'I hope that' or 'let's hope', and say that it should only be used to mean 'in a hopeful way'. This first use is very common in informal language but you should avoid it when you are writing or speaking formally.

hopeless *adjective*
1 without hope. 2 very bad at something.
hopelessly *adverb* **hopelessness** *noun*

hopscotch *noun*
a game of hopping into squares drawn on the ground.

horde *noun* (*plural* **hordes**)
a large group or crowd.

❶ USAGE Do not confuse with *hoard.*

horizon *noun* (*plural* **horizons**)
the line where the earth and the sky seem to meet.

horizontal *adjective*
level, so as to be parallel to the horizon; going across from left to right. (The opposite is *vertical.*)
horizontally *adverb*

hormone *noun* (*plural* **hormones**)
a substance produced by glands in the body and carried by the blood to stimulate other organs in the body.
hormonal *adjective*

horn *noun* (*plural* **horns**)
1 a hard substance that grows into a point on the head of a bull, cow, ram, etc. 2 a pointed part. 3 a brass instrument played by blowing. 4 a device for making a warning sound.
horned *adjective* **horny** *adjective*

horoscope *noun* (*plural* **horoscopes**)
an astrologer's forecast of future events.

horrendous *adjective*
extremely unpleasant.

horrible *adjective*
1 horrifying. 2 very unpleasant or nasty.
horribly *adverb*

horrid *adjective*
horrible.
horridly *adverb*

horrify *verb* (**horrifies, horrifying, horrified**)
1 make somebody feel very afraid or disgusted.
2 shock.

horror *noun* (*plural* **horrors**)
1 great fear or disgust. 2 a person or thing
causing horror.

horse *noun* (*plural* **horses**)
1 a large four-legged animal used for riding on
and for pulling carts etc. 2 a framework for
hanging clothes on to dry.
on horseback mounted on a horse.

horse chestnut *noun* (*plural* **horse
chestnuts**)
a large tree that produces dark-brown nuts
(conkers).

horsepower *noun*
a unit for measuring the power of an engine,
equal to 746 watts.

horseshoe *noun* (*plural* **horseshoes**)
a U-shaped piece of metal nailed to a horse's
hoof.

horticulture *noun*
the art of cultivating gardens.
horticultural *adjective*

hose *noun* (*plural* **hoses**)
1 (also **hosepipe**) a flexible tube for taking
water to something. 2 (*old use*) breeches
♦ *doublet and hose.*

hospitable *adjective*
welcoming; liking to give hospitality.
hospitably *adverb*

hospital *noun* (*plural* **hospitals**)
a place providing medical and surgical treatment
for people who are ill or injured.

hospitality *noun*
welcoming guests or strangers and giving them
food and entertainment.

host¹ *noun* (*plural* **hosts**)
1 a person who has guests and looks after them.
2 the presenter of a television or radio
programme.
[from Latin *hospes*]

host² *noun* (*plural* **hosts**)
a large number of people or things.
[from Latin *hostis* = enemy or army]

host³ *noun* (*plural* **hosts**)
the bread consecrated at Holy Communion.
[from Latin *hostia* = sacrifice]

hostage *noun* (*plural* **hostages**)
a person who is held prisoner until the holder's
demands are met.

hostel *noun* (*plural* **hostels**)
a building where travellers, students, or other
groups can stay or live.

hostess *noun* (*plural* **hostesses**)
a woman who has guests and looks after them.

hostile *adjective*
1 unfriendly ♦ *a hostile glance.* 2 opposed to
something. 3 to do with an enemy ♦ *hostile
aircraft.*
hostility *noun*

hot *adjective* (**hotter, hottest**)
1 having great heat or a high temperature.
2 giving a burning sensation when tasted.
3 passionate or excitable ♦ *a hot temper.*
hotly *adverb* **hotness** *noun*
in hot water (*informal*) in trouble or disgrace.

hotel *noun* (*plural* **hotels**)
a building where people pay to have meals and
stay for the night.

hound *noun* (*plural* **hounds**)
a dog used in hunting or racing.
[from Old English]

hour *noun* (*plural* **hours**)
1 one twenty-fourth part of a day and night;
sixty minutes. 2 a time ♦ *Why are you up at
this hour?*
hours *plural noun* a fixed period for work
♦ *Office hours are 9 a.m. to 5 p.m.*

hourly *adverb* & *adjective*
every hour.

house (*say* howss) *noun* (*plural* **houses**)
1 a building made for people to live in, usually
designed for one family. 2 a building or
establishment for a special purpose ♦ *the opera
house.* 3 a building for a government assembly;
the assembly itself ♦ *the House of Commons;*
♦ *the House of Lords.* 4 one of the divisions of a
school for sports competitions etc. 5 a family or
dynasty ♦ *the royal house of Tudor.*

house (*say* howz) *verb* (**houses, housing,
housed**)
provide accommodation or room for someone or
something.
[from Old English]

household *noun* (*plural* **households**)
all the people who live together in the same
house.
[from *house* + an old sense of *hold* =
possession]

householder *noun* (*plural* **householders**)
a person who owns or rents a house.

housekeeper *noun* (*plural* **housekeepers**)
a person employed to look after a household.

housekeeping *noun*
1 looking after a household. 2 (*informal*) the
money for a household's food and other
necessities.

housemaid *noun* (*plural* **housemaids**)
a woman servant in a house, especially one who cleans rooms.

house-proud *adjective*
very careful to keep a house clean and tidy.

house-trained *adjective*
(said about an animal) trained to be clean in the house.

housewife *noun* (*plural* **housewives**)
a woman who does the housekeeping for her family.

housework *noun*
the cleaning and cooking etc. done in housekeeping.

housing *noun* (*plural* **housings**)
1 accommodation; houses. 2 a stiff cover or guard for a piece of machinery.

housing estate *noun* (*plural* **housing estates**)
a set of houses planned and built together in one area.

hovel *noun* (*plural* **hovels**)
a small shabby house.

hover *verb* (**hovers, hovering, hovered**)
1 stay in one place in the air. 2 wait about near someone or something.

hovercraft *noun* (*plural* **hovercraft**)
a vehicle that travels just above the surface of land or water, supported by a strong current of air sent downwards from its engines.

how *adverb*
1 in what way; by what means ♦ *How did you do it?* 2 to what extent or amount etc. ♦ *How high can you jump?* 3 in what condition ♦ *How are you?*
how about would you like ♦ *How about a game of football?* **how do you do?** a formal greeting.

however *adverb*
1 in whatever way; to whatever extent ♦ *You will never catch him, however hard you try.* 2 all the same; nevertheless ♦ *Later, however, he decided to go.*

howl *noun* (*plural* **howls**)
a long loud sad-sounding cry or sound, such as that made by a dog or wolf.

howl *verb* (**howls, howling, howled**)
1 make a howl. 2 weep loudly.

howler *noun* (*plural* **howlers**) (*informal*)
a foolish mistake.

HQ *abbreviation*
headquarters.

hub *noun* (*plural* **hubs**)
1 the central part of a wheel. 2 the central point of interest or activity.

hubbub *noun*
a loud confused noise of voices.

huddle *verb* (**huddles, huddling, huddled**)
1 crowd together with other people, often for warmth. 2 curl your body closely.
huddle *noun*

huff *noun*
in a huff offended or sulking about something ♦ *She went away in a huff.*
huffy *adjective*

hug *verb* (**hugs, hugging, hugged**)
1 clasp someone tightly in your arms. 2 keep close to something ♦ *The ship hugged the shore.*
hug *noun* (*plural* **hugs**)
a tight embrace.

huge *adjective*
extremely large; enormous.
hugely *adverb* **hugeness** *noun*

hulk *noun* (*plural* **hulks**)
1 the body or wreck of an old ship. 2 a large clumsy person or thing.
hulking *adjective*

hull *noun* (*plural* **hulls**)
the framework of a ship.

hullabaloo *noun* (*plural* **hullabaloos**)
an uproar.

hum *verb* (**hums, humming, hummed**)
1 sing a tune with your lips closed. 2 make a low continuous sound like that of a bee.

human *adjective*
to do with human beings.

human being *noun* (*plural* **human beings**)
a man, woman, or child.

humane (*say* hew-**mayn**) *adjective*
kind-hearted and merciful.
humanely *adverb*

humanitarian *adjective*
concerned with people's welfare and the reduction of suffering.
humanitarian *noun*

humanity *noun*
1 human beings; people. 2 being human. 3 being humane.
humanities *plural noun* arts subjects such as history, literature, and music, not sciences.

humble *adjective*
1 modest; not proud or showy. 2 of low rank or importance.
humbly *adverb* **humbleness** *noun*

humbug *noun* (*plural* **humbugs**)
1 insincere or dishonest talk or behaviour. 2 a hard peppermint sweet.

humdrum *adjective*
dull and not exciting; commonplace.

humid (*say* hew-**mid**) *adjective*
(said about air) moist and damp.
humidity *noun*

humiliate *verb* (humiliates, humiliating,
humiliated)
make a person feel disgraced or ashamed.
humiliation *noun*

humility *noun*
being humble.

hummingbird *noun* (*plural* hummingbirds)
a small tropical bird that makes a humming
sound by beating its wings rapidly.

humorous *adjective*
full of humour; amusing.

humour *noun*
1 being amusing; what makes people laugh.
2 the ability to enjoy comical things ♦ *a sense of
humour*. 3 a mood ♦ *in a good humour*.

humour *verb* (humours, humouring,
humoured)
keep a person contented by doing what he or she
wants.

hump *noun* (*plural* humps)
1 a rounded lump or mound. 2 an abnormal
outward curve at the top of a person's back.

humpback bridge *noun* (*plural* humpback
bridges)
a small bridge that curves steeply upwards in the
middle.

humus (*say* hew-mus) *noun*
rich earth made by decayed plants.

hunch[1] *noun* (*plural* hunches)
a feeling that you can guess what is going to
happen.

hunch[2] *verb* (hunches, hunching, hunched)
bend your shoulders upward so that your back is
rounded.

hunchback *noun* (*plural* hunchbacks)
someone with a hump on their back.
hunchbacked *adjective*

hundred *noun* & *adjective*(*plural* hundreds)
the number 100.
hundredth *adjective* & *noun*

hundredweight *noun* (*plural*
hundredweight)
a unit of weight equal to 112 pounds (about 50.8
kilograms).

hunger *noun*
the feeling that you have when you have not
eaten for some time; need for food.

hunger strike *noun* (*plural* hunger strikes)
refusing to eat, as a way of making a protest.

hungry *adjective* (hungrier, hungriest)
feeling hunger.
hungrily *adverb*

hunk *noun* (*plural* hunks)
1 a large piece of something. 2 (*informal*) a
muscular, good-looking man.

hunt *verb* (hunts, hunting, hunted)
1 chase and kill animals for food or as a sport.
2 search for something.
hunter *noun* huntsman *noun*

hurdle *noun* (*plural* hurdles)
1 an upright frame to be jumped over in
hurdling. 2 an obstacle or difficulty.

hurdling *noun*
racing in which the runners jump over hurdles.
hurdler *noun*

hurl *verb* (hurls, hurling, hurled)
throw something with great force.

hurray or **hurrah** *interjection*
a shout of joy or approval; a cheer.

hurricane *noun* (*plural* hurricanes)
a storm with violent wind.

hurry *verb* (hurries, hurrying, hurried)
1 move quickly; do something quickly. 2 try to
make somebody or something be quick.
hurried *adjective* hurriedly *adverb*

hurry *noun*
hurrying; a need to hurry.

hurt *verb* (hurts, hurting, hurt)
1 cause pain or injury to someone. 2 suffer pain
♦ *My leg hurts*. 3 upset or offend ♦ *I'm sorry if I
hurt your feelings*.

hurt *noun*
physical or mental pain or injury.
hurtful *adjective*

hurtle *verb* (hurtles, hurtling, hurtled)
move rapidly ♦ *The train hurtled along*.

husband *noun* (*plural* husbands)
the man to whom a woman is married.
[from Old Norse *husbondi* = master of the
house]

hush *verb* (hushes, hushing, hushed)
make or become silent or quiet.
hush up prevent something from becoming
generally known.

husk *noun* (*plural* husks)
the dry outer covering of some seeds and fruits.

husky *adjective* (huskier, huskiest)
1 hoarse. 2 big and strong; burly.
huskily *adverb* huskiness *noun*

hustle *verb* (hustles, hustling, hustled)
1 hurry. 2 push or shove rudely.
hustle *noun* hustler *noun*

hut *noun* (*plural* huts)
a small roughly made house or shelter.

hutch *noun* (*plural* hutches)
a box-like cage for a pet rabbit etc.

hybrid *noun* (*plural* hybrids)
1 a plant or animal produced by combining two
different species or varieties. 2 something that
combines parts or characteristics of two different
things.

hydrant noun (plural **hydrants**)
a special water tap to which a large hose can be
attached for fire-fighting or street-cleaning etc.

hydraulic adjective
worked by the force of water or other fluid
♦ hydraulic brakes.

hydrochloric acid noun
a colourless acid containing hydrogen and
chlorine.

hydroelectric adjective
using water power to produce electricity.
hydroelectricity noun

hydrogen noun
a lightweight gas that combines with oxygen to
form water.

hydrogen bomb noun (plural **hydrogen
bombs**)
a very powerful bomb using energy created by
the fusion of hydrogen nuclei.

hyena noun (plural **hyenas**)
a wild animal that looks like a wolf and makes a
shrieking howl.

hygiene (say hy-jeen) noun
keeping things clean in order to remain healthy
and prevent disease.
hygienic adjective **hygienically** adverb

hymn noun (plural **hymns**)
a religious song, usually one praising God.
hymn book noun

hype noun (informal)
extravagant publicity or advertising.

hyperactive adjective
unable to relax and always moving about or
doing things.

hyperbola (say hy-**per**-bol-a) noun (plural
hyperbolas)
a kind of curve.

hyphen noun (plural **hyphens**)
a short dash used to join words or parts of words
together (e.g. in hitch-hiker).

hypnosis (say hip-**noh**-sis) noun
a condition like a deep sleep in which a person's
actions may be controlled by someone else.

hypnotize verb (**hypnotizes, hypnotizing,
hypnotized**)
produce hypnosis in somebody.
hypnotism noun **hypnotic** adjective **hypnotist**
noun

hypochondriac (say hy-po-**kon**-dree-ak) noun
(plural **hypochondriacs**)
a person who constantly imagines that he or she
is ill.
hypochondria noun

hypocrite (say **hip**-o-krit) noun (plural
hypocrites)
a person who pretends to be more virtuous than
he or she really is.
hypocrisy (say hip-**ok**-riss-ee) noun **hypocritical**
adjective

hypodermic adjective
injecting something under the skin
♦ a hypodermic syringe.

hypotenuse (say hy-**pot**-i-newz) noun (plural
hypotenuses)
the side opposite the right angle in a right-angled
triangle.

hypothermia noun
the condition of having a body temperature well
below normal.

hypothesis (say hy-**poth**-i-sis) noun (plural
hypotheses)
a suggestion or guess that tries to explain
something.

hypothetical (say hy-po-**thet**-ikal) adjective
based on a theory or possibility, not on proven
facts.

hysteria noun
wild uncontrollable excitement, panic, or
emotion.
hysterics noun

hysterical adjective
1 in a state of hysteria. **2** (informal) extremely
funny.
hysterically adverb

Ii

I pronoun
a word used by a person to refer to himself or
herself.

-ible SEE **-able**.

ice noun (plural **ices**)
1 frozen water, a brittle transparent solid
substance. **2** an ice cream.

ice age noun (plural **ice ages**)
a period in the past when most of the earth's
surface was covered with ice.

iceberg noun (plural **icebergs**)
a large mass of ice floating in the sea with most
of it under water.
[from Dutch ijs = ice + berg = hill]

ice cream noun (plural **ice creams**)
a sweet creamy frozen food.

ice hockey noun
a form of hockey played on ice.

ice rink noun (plural **ice rinks**)
a place made for skating.

icicle noun (plural **icicles**)
a pointed hanging piece of ice formed when
dripping water freezes.

icing *noun*
a sugary substance for decorating cakes.

icon (*say* I-kon) *noun* (*plural* **icons**)
1 a sacred painting of a holy person. **2** a small symbol or picture on a computer screen.

icy *adjective* (**icier, iciest**)
1 covered with ice. **2** very cold.
icily *adverb* **iciness** *noun*

idea *noun* (*plural* **ideas**)
1 a plan or thought formed in the mind.
2 an opinion or belief. **3** a feeling that something is likely.
[from Greek, = form, pattern]

ideal *adjective*
perfect; completely suitable.
ideally *adverb*

ideal *noun* (*plural* **ideals**)
a person or thing regarded as perfect or a standard worth trying to achieve.

identical *adjective*
exactly the same.
identically *adverb*

identify *verb* (**identifies, identifying, identified**)
1 recognize as being a certain person or thing.
2 treat something as being identical to something else ♦ *Don't identify wealth with happiness.*
3 think of yourself as sharing someone's feelings etc. ♦ *We can identify with the hero of this play.*
identification *noun*

identity *noun* (*plural* **identities**)
1 who or what a person or thing is. **2** being identical; sameness. **3** distinctive character.

idiom *noun* (*plural* **idioms**)
a phrase that means something different from the meanings of the words in it, e.g. *in hot water* (= in disgrace), *hell for leather* (= at high speed).
idiomatic *adjective* **idiomatically** *adverb*
[from Greek *idios* = your own]

idiosyncrasy (*say* id-ee-o-**sink**-ra-see) *noun*
(*plural* **idiosyncrasies**)
one person's own way of behaving or doing something.
[from Greek *idios* = your own + *syn-*
= together + *krasis* = mixture]

idiot *noun* (*plural* **idiots**)
a stupid or foolish person.
idiocy *noun* **idiotic** *adjective* **idiotically** *adverb*
[from Greek *idiotes* = private citizen, uneducated person]

idle *adjective*
1 doing no work; lazy. **2** not in use
♦ *The machines were idle.* **3** useless; with no special purpose ♦ *idle gossip.*
idly *adverb* **idleness** *noun*

idol *noun* (*plural* **idols**)
1 a statue or image that is worshipped as a god.
2 a famous person who is widely admired.
[from Greek *eidolon* = image]

idolize *verb* (**idolizes, idolizing, idolized**)
admire someone greatly.

i.e. *abbreviation*
that is ♦ *The world's highest mountain (i.e. Mount Everest) is in the Himalayas.*

❶ USAGE Do not confuse with *e.g.*

-ier SEE **-er.**

if *conjunction*
1 on condition that; supposing that ♦ *He will do it if you pay him.* **2** even though ♦ *I'll finish this job if it kills me.* **3** whether ♦ *Do you know if dinner is ready?*
if only I wish ♦ *If only I were rich!*

ignite *verb* (**ignites, igniting, ignited**)
catch fire, or set on fire.

ignition *noun* (*plural* **ignitions**)
1 igniting. **2** the part of a motor engine that starts the fuel burning.

ignominious *adjective*
humiliating; bringing disgrace.
ignominy *noun*

ignorant *adjective*
1 not knowing about something. **2** knowing very little.
ignorantly *adverb* **ignorance** *noun*

ignore *verb* (**ignores, ignoring, ignored**)
take no notice of a person or thing.

ilk *noun*
of that ilk (*informal*) of that kind.

ill *adjective*
1 unwell; in bad health. **2** bad or harmful
♦ *There were no ill effects.*

ill *adverb*
badly ♦ *She was ill-treated.*
ill at ease uncomfortable or embarrassed.

illegal *adjective*
not legal; against the law.
illegally *adverb* **illegality** *noun*

illegible *adjective*
impossible to read.
illegibly *adverb* **illegibility** *noun*

illegitimate *adjective*
born of parents who are not married to each other.
illegitimately *adverb* **illegitimacy** *noun*

illiterate *adjective*
unable to read or write.
illiterately *adverb* **illiteracy** *noun*

illness *noun* (*plural* **illnesses**)
1 being ill. **2** a particular form of bad health; a disease.

illogical *adjective*
not logical; not reasoning correctly.
illogically *adverb* **illogicality** *noun*

illuminate *verb* (illuminates, illuminating, illuminated)
1 light something up. 2 decorate streets etc. with lights. 3 decorate a manuscript with coloured designs. 4 clarify or help to explain something.
illumination *noun*

illusion *noun* (*plural* illusions)
1 something that seems to be real or actually happening but is not, especially something that deceives the eye. 2 a false idea or belief. (Compare **delusion**.)
illusive *adjective* **illusory** *adjective*

illustrate *verb* (illustrates, illustrating, illustrated)
1 show something by pictures, examples, etc. 2 put illustrations in a book.
illustrator *noun*

illustration *noun* (*plural* illustrations)
1 a picture in a book etc. 2 illustrating something. 3 an example that helps to explain something.

illustrious *adjective*
famous and distinguished.

image *noun* (*plural* images)
1 a picture or statue of a person or thing. 2 the appearance of something as seen in a mirror or through a lens etc. 3 a person or thing that is very much like another ♦ *He is the image of his father.* 4 a word or phrase that describes something in an imaginative way. 5 a person's public reputation.

imaginary *adjective*
existing only in the imagination; not real.

imagination *noun* (*plural* imaginations)
the ability to imagine things, especially in a creative or inventive way.
imaginative *adjective*

imagine *verb* (imagines, imagining, imagined)
1 form pictures or ideas in your mind. 2 suppose or think ♦ *I don't imagine there'll be any tickets left.*

imitate *verb* (imitates, imitating, imitated)
copy or mimic something.
imitation *noun* **imitator** *noun* **imitative** *adjective*

immaculate *adjective*
1 perfectly clean; spotless. 2 without any fault or blemish.
immaculately *adverb*

immature *adjective*
not mature.
immaturity *noun*

immediate *adjective*
1 happening or done without any delay. 2 nearest; with nothing or no one between ♦ *our immediate neighbours.*
immediately *adverb* **immediacy** *noun*

immense *adjective*
exceedingly great; huge.
immensely *adverb* **immensity** *noun*

immersion heater *noun* (*plural* immersion heaters)
a device that heats up water by means of an electric element in the water in a tank etc.

immigrate *verb* (immigrates, immigrating, immigrated)
come into a country to live there.
immigration *noun* **immigrant** *noun*

ℹ️ USAGE See the note at *emigrate.*

imminent *adjective*
likely to happen at any moment ♦ *an imminent storm.*
imminence *noun*

immobilize *verb* (immobilizes, immobilizing, immobilized)
stop a thing from moving or working.
immobilization *noun*

immoral *adjective*
morally wrong; wicked.
immorally *adverb* **immorality** *noun*

immortal *adjective*
1 living for ever; not mortal. 2 famous for all time.
immortal *noun* **immortality** *noun* **immortalize** *verb*

immune *adjective*
safe from danger or attack, especially from disease ♦ *immune from* (or *against* or *to*) *infection* etc.
immunity *noun*

immunize *verb* (immunizes, immunizing, immunized)
make a person immune from a disease etc., e.g. by vaccination.
immunization *noun*

impact *noun* (*plural* impacts)
1 a collision; the force of a collision. 2 an influence or effect ♦ *the impact of computers on our lives.*

impale *verb* (impales, impaling, impaled)
pierce or fix something on a sharp pointed object.

impartial *adjective*
not favouring one side more than the other; not biased.
impartially *adverb* **impartiality** *noun*

impatient *adjective*
not patient; in a hurry
impatiently *adverb* **impatience** *noun*

impel verb (impels, impelling, impelled)
1 urge or drive someone to do something
♦ *Curiosity impelled her to investigate.*
2 drive forward; propel.

impending adjective
soon to happen; imminent.

impenetrable adjective
1 impossible to get through.
2 incomprehensible.

imperative adjective
1 expressing a command. 2 essential ♦ *Speed is imperative.*

imperative noun (plural **imperatives**)
a command; the form of a verb used in making commands (e.g. 'come' in *Come here!*).

imperceptible adjective
too small or gradual to be noticed.

imperfect adjective
1 not perfect. 2 (said about a tense of a verb) showing a continuous action, e.g. ♦ *She was singing.*
imperfectly adverb **imperfection** noun

imperial adjective
1 to do with an empire or its rulers. 2 (said about weights and measures) formerly fixed by British law; non-metric.
imperially adverb

imperious adjective
haughty and bossy.

impermeable adjective
not allowing liquid to pass through it.

impersonal adjective
1 not affected by personal feelings; showing no emotion. 2 not referring to a particular person.
impersonally adverb

impersonal verb noun (plural **impersonal verbs**)
a verb used only with 'it', e.g. in ♦ *It is raining.*

impertinent adjective
insolent; not showing proper respect.
impertinently adverb **impertinence** noun

imperturbable adjective
not excitable; calm.
imperturbably adverb

impervious adjective
1 not allowing water, heat, etc. to pass through ♦ *impervious to water.* 2 not able to be affected by something ♦ *impervious to criticism.*

impetuous adjective
acting hastily without thinking.

impetus noun
1 the force that makes an object start moving and that keeps it moving. 2 the influence that causes something to develop more quickly ♦ *The ceasefire gave an impetus to peace talks.*

implacable adjective
not able to be placated; relentless.
implacably adverb

implant verb (implants, implanting, implanted)
insert; fix something in.
implantation noun

implant noun (plural **implants**)
an organ or piece of tissue inserted in the body.

implement noun (plural **implements**)
a tool.

implicate verb (implicates, implicating, implicated)
involve a person in a crime etc.; show that a person is involved ♦ *His evidence implicates his sister.*

implication noun (plural **implications**)
1 implicating. 2 implying; something that is implied.

implicit (say im-**pliss**-it) adjective
1 implied but not stated openly. (Compare **explicit**.) 2 absolute; unquestioning ♦ *She expects implicit obedience.*
implicitly adverb

implore verb (implores, imploring, implored)
beg somebody to do something.

imply verb (implies, implying, implied)
suggest something without actually saying it.
implication noun

impolite adjective
not polite.

import verb (imports, importing, imported)
bring in goods etc. from another country.

import noun (plural **imports**)
1 importing; something imported. 2 (formal) meaning or importance ♦ *The message was of great import.*

important adjective
1 having or able to have a great effect. 2 having great authority or influence.
importantly adverb **importance** noun

impose verb (imposes, imposing, imposed)
put or inflict ♦ *It imposes a strain upon us.*
impose on somebody put an unfair burden on him or her.

imposing adjective
impressive.

imposition noun (plural **impositions**)
1 something imposed; an unfair burden or inconvenience. 2 imposing something.

impossible adjective
1 not possible. 2 (informal) very annoying; unbearable ♦ *He really is impossible!*
impossibly adverb **impossibility** noun

impostor noun (plural **impostors**)
a person who dishonestly pretends to be someone else.

impotent *adjective*
1 powerless; unable to take action. 2 (said about a man) unable to have sexual intercourse.
impotently *adverb* **impotence** *noun*

impoverish *verb* (impoverishes, impoverishing, impoverished)
1 make a person poor. 2 make a thing poor in quality ♦ *impoverished soil.*
impoverishment *noun*

impracticable *adjective*
not able to be done in practice.

impractical *adjective*
not practical.

imprecise *adjective*
not precise.

impregnable *adjective*
strong enough to be safe against attack.

impregnate *verb* (impregnates, impregnating, impregnated)
1 fertilize; make pregnant. 2 saturate; fill throughout ♦ *The air was impregnated with the scent.*
impregnation *noun*

impress *verb* (impresses, impressing, impressed)
1 make a person admire something or think it is very good. 2 fix something firmly in the mind ♦ *He impressed on them the need for secrecy.*
3 press a mark into something.

impression *noun* (*plural* **impressions**)
1 an effect produced on the mind ♦ *The book made a big impression on me.* 2 a vague idea. 3 an imitation of a person or a sound etc. 4 a reprint of a book.

impressionable *adjective*
easily influenced or affected.

impressive *adjective*
making a strong impression; seeming to be very good.

imprison *verb* (imprisons, imprisoning, imprisoned)
put someone in prison; shut someone up in a place.
imprisonment *noun*

improbable *adjective*
unlikely.
improbably *adverb* **improbability** *noun*

impromptu *adjective* & *adverb*
done without any rehearsal or preparation.

improper *adjective*
1 unsuitable or wrong. 2 indecent.
improperly *adverb* **impropriety** (*say* im-pro-**pry**-it-ee) *noun*

improper fraction *noun* (*plural* **improper fractions**)
a fraction that is greater than 1, with the numerator greater than the denominator, e.g. $\frac{5}{3}$.

improve *verb* (improves, improving, improved)
make or become better.
improvement *noun*

improvise *verb* (improvises, improvising, improvised)
1 compose or perform something without any rehearsal or preparation. 2 make something quickly with whatever is available.
improvisation *noun*

imprudent *adjective*
unwise or rash.

impudent *adjective*
cheeky or disrespectful.
impudently *adverb* **impudence** *noun*

impulse *noun* (*plural* **impulses**)
1 a sudden desire to do something ♦ *I did it on impulse.* 2 a push or impetus. 3 (in science) a force acting for a very short time ♦ *electrical impulses.*

impulsive *adjective*
done or acting on impulse, not after careful thought.
impulsively *adverb* **impulsiveness** *noun*

impure *adjective*
not pure.
impurity *noun*

in *preposition*
This word is used to show position or condition, e.g. 1 at or inside; within the limits of something (*in a box; in two hours*), 2 into (*He fell in a puddle*), 3 arranged as; consisting of (*a serial in four parts*), 4 occupied with; a member of (*He is in the army*), 5 by means of (*We paid in cash*).
in all in total number; altogether.

in *adverb*
1 so as to be in something or inside (*Get in*). 2 inwards (*The top caved in*). 3 at home; indoors (*Is anybody in?*). 4 in action; (in cricket) batting. 5 having arrived (*The train is in*).
in for likely to get ♦ *You're in for a shock.*
in on (*informal*) aware of or sharing in ♦ *I want to be in on this project.*

in- *prefix* (changing to **il-** before *l*, **im-** before *b, m, p,* **ir-** before *r*)
1 in; into; on; towards (as in *include, invade*). 2 not (as in *incorrect, indirect*).

inability *noun*
being unable.

inaccessible *adjective*
not able to be reached.

inaccurate *adjective*
not accurate.

inadequate *adjective*
1 not enough. 2 not able to cope or deal with something.
inadequately *adverb* **inadequacy** *noun*

inadvisable *adjective*
not advisable.

inanimate *adjective*
1 not living. 2 showing no sign of life.

inappropriate *adjective*
not appropriate.

inarticulate *adjective*
1 not able to speak or express yourself clearly
♦ *inarticulate with rage.* 2 not expressed in
words ♦ *an inarticulate cry.*

inaudible *adjective*
not able to be heard.
inaudibly *adverb* **inaudibility** *noun*

inaugurate *verb* (**inaugurates, inaugurating,**
inaugurated)
1 start or introduce something new and
important. 2 formally establish a person in office
♦ *inaugurate a new President.*
inaugural *adjective* **inauguration** *noun*
inaugurator *noun*

inborn *adjective*
present in a person or animal from birth
♦ *an inborn ability.*

inbred *adjective*
1 inborn. 2 produced by inbreeding.

inbreeding *noun*
breeding from closely related individuals.

incalculable *adjective*
not able to be calculated or predicted.

incandescent *adjective*
giving out light when heated; shining.
incandescence *noun*

incantation *noun* (*plural* **incantations**)
a spoken spell or charm; the chanting of this.

incapable *adjective*
not able to do something ♦ *They seem incapable
of understanding.*

incapacitate *verb* (**incapacitates,**
incapacitating, incapacitated)
make a person or thing unable to do something;
disable.

incarnate *adjective*
having a body or human form ♦ *a devil
incarnate.*
incarnation *noun*
the Incarnation the embodiment of God in
human form as Jesus Christ.

incautious *adjective*
rash.

incendiary *adjective*
starting or designed to start a fire
♦ *an incendiary bomb.*

incentive *noun* (*plural* **incentives**)
something that encourages a person to do
something or to work harder.

incest *noun*
sexual intercourse between two people who are
so closely related that they cannot marry each
other.
incestuous *adjective*

inch *noun* (*plural* **inches**)
a measure of length, one-twelfth of a foot (about
$2\frac{1}{2}$ centimetres).

inch *verb* (**inches, inching, inched**)
move slowly and gradually ♦ *I inched along the
ledge.*
[from Old English]

incident *noun* (*plural* **incidents**)
an event.

incidental *adjective*
happening as a minor part of something else
♦ *incidental expenses.*

incidentally *adverb*
by the way.

incinerate *verb* (**incinerates, incinerating,**
incinerated)
destroy something by burning.
incineration *noun*

incinerator *noun* (*plural* **incinerators**)
a device for burning rubbish.

incision *noun* (*plural* **incisions**)
a cut, especially one made in a surgical
operation.

incisive *adjective*
clear and sharp ♦ *incisive comments.*

incisor (*say* in-sy-zer) *noun* (*plural* **incisors**)
each of the sharp-edged front teeth in the upper
and lower jaws.

incite *verb* (**incites, inciting, incited**)
urge a person to do something; stir up
♦ *They incited a riot.*
incitement *noun*

inclination *noun* (*plural* **inclinations**)
1 a tendency. 2 a liking or preference.
3 a slope or slant.

incline *verb* (**inclines, inclining, inclined**)
1 lean or slope. 2 bend the head or body
forward, as in a nod or bow. 3 cause or influence
♦ *Her frank manner inclines me to believe her.*
be inclined have a tendency or willingness
♦ *The door is inclined to bang.* ♦ *I'm inclined to
agree with you.*

include *verb* (**includes, including, included**)
make or consider something as part of a group of
things.
inclusion *noun*

inclusive *adjective*
including everything; including all the things
mentioned ♦ *Read pages 20 to 28 inclusive.*

incoherent *adjective*
not speaking or reasoning in an orderly way.

income *noun* (*plural* **incomes**)
money received regularly from doing work or
from investments.

income tax *noun*
tax charged on income.

incomparable *adjective*
without an equal; not surpassed ♦ *incomparable
beauty.*

incompatible *adjective*
not able to exist or be used together.

incompetent *adjective*
not able or skilled enough to do something
properly.

incomplete *adjective*
not complete.

incomprehensible *adjective*
not able to be understood.
incomprehension *noun*

incongruous *adjective*
out of place or unsuitable.
incongruously *adverb* **incongruity** *noun*

inconsiderate *adjective*
not considerate towards other people.

inconsistent *adjective*
not consistent.
inconsistently *adverb* **inconsistency** *noun*

inconspicuous *adjective*
not conspicuous.
inconspicuously *adverb*

incontinent *adjective*
not able to control the bladder or bowels.
incontinence *noun*

incontrovertible *adjective*
unable to be denied; indisputable.

inconvenience *noun* (*plural* **inconveniences**)
being inconvenient.

inconvenience *verb* (**inconveniences,
inconveniencing, inconvenienced**)
cause inconvenience or slight difficulty to
someone.

inconvenient *adjective*
not convenient.

incorporate *verb* (**incorporates,
incorporating, incorporated**)
include something as a part of something larger.
incorporation *noun*

incorporated *adjective*
(said about a business firm) formed into a legal
corporation.

incorrect *adjective*
not correct.
incorrectly *adverb*

incorruptible *adjective*
1 not able to decay. 2 not able to be bribed.

increase *verb* (**increases, increasing,
increased**)
make or become larger or more.

increase *noun* (*plural* **increases**)
increasing; the amount by which a thing
increases.

incredible *adjective*
unbelievable.
incredibly *adverb* **incredibility** *noun*

ℹ USAGE Do not confuse with *incredulous.*

---

incredulous *adjective*
not believing somebody; showing disbelief.
incredulously *adverb* **incredulity** *noun*

ℹ USAGE Do not confuse with *incredible.*

---

incriminate *verb* (**incriminates, incriminating,
incriminated**)
show a person to have been involved in a crime
etc.
incrimination *noun*

incubate *verb* (**incubates, incubating,
incubated**)
1 hatch eggs by keeping them warm.
2 cause bacteria or a disease etc. to develop.
incubation *noun*

incubator *noun* (*plural* **incubators**)
1 a device in which a baby born prematurely
can be kept warm and supplied with oxygen.
2 a device for incubating eggs etc.

incur *verb* (**incurs, incurring, incurred**)
bring something on yourself ♦ *I hope you don't
incur too much expense.*

indebted *adjective*
owing money or gratitude to someone.

indecent *adjective*
not decent; improper.
indecently *adverb* **indecency** *noun*

indecisive *adjective*
not decisive.

indeed *adverb*
1 really; truly ♦ *I am indeed surprised*; (used to
strengthen a meaning) ♦ *very nice indeed.*
2 admittedly ♦ *It is, indeed, his first attempt.*

indefensible *adjective*
unable to be defended or justified
♦ *an indefensible decision.*

indefinite *adjective*
not definite; vague.

indefinite article *noun* (*plural* **indefinite
articles**)
(in grammar) the word 'a' or 'an'.

indefinitely *adverb*
for an indefinite or unlimited time.

indelible *adjective*
impossible to rub out or remove.
indelibly *adverb*

indelicate *adjective*
1 slightly indecent. 2 tactless.
indelicacy *noun*

independent *adjective*
1 not dependent on any other person or thing for help, money, or support. **2** (said about a country) governing itself. **3** (said about broadcasting) not financed by money from licences.
independently *adverb* **independence** *noun*

indestructible *adjective*
unable to be destroyed.
indestructibility *noun*

indeterminate *adjective*
not fixed or decided exactly; left vague.

index *noun*
1 (*plural* **indexes**) an alphabetical list of things, especially at the end of a book. **2** a number showing how prices or wages have changed from a previous level. **3** (*plural* **indices**) (in mathematics) the raised number etc. written to the right of another (e.g. 3 in 2^3) showing how many times the first one is to be multiplied by itself.

Indian *adjective*
1 to do with India or its people. **2** to do with Native Americans.
Indian *noun*

---

❶ USAGE The preferred term for the descendants of the original inhabitants of North and South America is *Native American*. *American Indian* is usually acceptable but the term *Red Indian* is now regarded as offensive and should not be used.

---

india rubber *noun* (*plural* **india rubbers**)
a rubber.

indicate *verb* (**indicates, indicating, indicated**)
1 point something out or make it known.
2 be a sign of. **3** when drivers indicate, they signal which direction they are turning by using their indicators.
indication *noun*

indicative *adjective*
giving an indication.

indicative *noun*
the form of a verb used in making a statement (e.g. 'he said' or 'he is coming'), not in a command or question, or wish.

indicator *noun* (*plural* **indicators**)
1 a thing that indicates or points to something.
2 a flashing light used to signal that a motor vehicle is turning. **3** (in science) a chemical compound, such as litmus, that changes colour in the presence of a particular substance or condition.

indifferent *adjective*
1 not caring about something; not interested.
2 not very good ♦ *an indifferent cricketer.*
indifferently *adverb* **indifference** *noun*

indigenous (*say* in-dij-in-us) *adjective*
growing or originating in a particular country; native ♦ *The koala bear is indigenous to Australia.*

indigestible *adjective*
difficult or impossible to digest.

indigestion *noun*
pain or discomfort caused by difficulty in digesting food.

indignant *adjective*
angry at something that seems unfair or wicked.
indignantly *adverb* **indignation** *noun*

indignity *noun* (*plural* **indignities**)
treatment that makes a person feel undignified or humiliated; an insult.

indirect *adjective*
not direct.
indirectly *adverb*

indirect speech *noun*
someone's words given in a changed form reported by someone else, as in ♦ *He said that he would come* (reporting the words 'I will come').

indiscreet *adjective*
1 not discreet; revealing secrets. **2** not cautious; rash.
indiscreetly *adverb* **indiscretion** *noun*

indiscriminate *adjective*
showing no discrimination; not making a careful choice.
indiscriminately *adverb*

indispensable *adjective*
not able to be dispensed with; essential.
indispensability *noun*

indisputable *adjective*
undeniable.

indistinct *adjective*
not distinct.
indistinctly *adverb* **indistinctness** *noun*

indistinguishable *adjective*
not able to be told apart; not distinguishable.

individual *adjective*
1 of or for one person. **2** single or separate
♦ *Count each individual word.*
individually *adverb*

individual *noun* (*plural* **individuals**)
one person, animal, or plant.

individuality *noun*
the things that make one person or thing different from another; distinctive identity.

indivisible *adjective*
not able to be divided or separated.
indivisibly *adverb*

indoctrinate *verb* (indoctrinates, indoctrinating, indoctrinated)
fill a person's mind with particular ideas or beliefs, so that they come to accept them without thinking.
indoctrination *noun*

indomitable *adjective*
not able to be overcome or conquered.

indoor *adjective*
used or placed or done etc. inside a building ♦ *indoor games*.

indoors *adverb*
inside a building.

induce *verb* (induces, inducing, induced)
1 persuade. **2** produce or cause ♦ *Some substances induce sleep.* **3** if a pregnant woman is induced, labour is brought on artificially with drugs.
induction *noun*

indulge *verb* (indulges, indulging, indulged)
allow a person to have or do what they want.
indulgence *noun* indulgent *adjective*
indulge in allow yourself to have or do something that you like.

industrial *adjective*
to do with industry; working or used in industry.
industrially *adverb*

industrial action *noun*
ways for workers to protest, such as striking or working to rule.

industrialized *adjective*
(said about a country or district) having many industries.
industrialization *noun*

Industrial Revolution *noun*
the rapid expansion of British industry by the use of machines during the late 18th and early 19th centuries.

industrious *adjective*
working hard.
industriously *adverb*

industry *noun* (*plural* industries)
1 making or producing goods etc., especially in factories. **2** a particular branch of this, or any business activity ♦ *the motor industry*; ♦ *the tourist industry*. **3** being industrious.

ineffective *adjective*
not effective; inefficient.
ineffectively *adverb*

ineffectual *adjective*
not achieving anything.

inefficient *adjective*
not efficient.
inefficiently *adverb* inefficiency *noun*

inept *adjective*
lacking any skill; clumsy.
ineptly *adverb* ineptitude *noun*

inert *adjective*
not moving or reacting.
inertly *adverb*

inert gas *noun* (*plural* inert gases)
a gas that almost never combines with other substances.

inertia (*say* in-er-sha) *noun*
1 inactivity; being inert or slow to take action. **2** the tendency for a moving thing to keep moving in a straight line.

inevitable *adjective*
unavoidable; sure to happen.
inevitably *adverb* inevitability *noun*

inexhaustible *adjective*
so great that it cannot be used up completely ♦ *Ben has an inexhaustible supply of jokes.*

inexorable (*say* in-eks-er-a-bul) *adjective*
1 relentless. **2** not able to be persuaded by requests or entreaties.
inexorably *adverb*

inexperience *noun*
lack of experience.
inexperienced *adjective*

infallible *adjective*
1 never wrong. **2** never failing ♦ *an infallible remedy*.
infallibly *adverb* infallibility *noun*

infancy *noun*
1 early childhood; babyhood. **2** an early stage of development.

infant *noun* (*plural* infants)
a baby or young child.

infantile *adjective*
1 to do with infants. **2** very childish.

infantry *noun*
soldiers who fight on foot. (Compare **cavalry**.)

infatuated *adjective*
filled with foolish or unreasoning love.
infatuation *noun*

infect *verb* (infects, infecting, infected)
pass on a disease or bacteria to a person, animal, or plant.

infection *noun* (*plural* infections)
1 infecting. **2** an infectious disease or condition.

infectious *adjective*
1 (said about a disease) able to be spread by air or water etc. (Compare **contagious**.) **2** quickly spreading to others ♦ *His fear was infectious.*

inferior *adjective*
less good or less important; low or lower in position, quality, etc.
inferiority *noun*

inferior *noun* (*plural* inferiors)
a person who is lower in position or rank than someone else.

infernal *adjective*
1 to do with or like hell ♦ *the infernal regions.*
2 (*informal*) detestable or tiresome ♦ *that infernal noise.*
infernally *adverb*

inferno *noun* (*plural* **infernos**)
a raging fire.

infertile *adjective*
not fertile.
infertility *noun*

infest *verb* (**infests, infesting, infested**)
(said about pests) be numerous and troublesome in a place.
infestation *noun*

infidelity *noun*
unfaithfulness.

infiltrate *verb* (**infiltrates, infiltrating, infiltrated**)
get into a place or organization gradually and without being noticed.
infiltration *noun* **infiltrator** *noun*

infinite *adjective*
1 endless; without a limit. 2 too great to be measured.
infinitely *adverb*

infinitesimal *adjective*
extremely small.
infinitesimally *adverb*

infinitive *noun* (*plural* **infinitives**)
(in grammar) the form of a verb that does not change to indicate a particular tense or number or person, in English used with or without *to*, e.g. *go* in 'Let him go' or 'Allow him to go'.

infinity *noun*
an infinite number or distance or time.

inflame *verb* (**inflames, inflaming, inflamed**)
1 produce strong feelings or anger in people.
2 cause redness, heat, and swelling in a body part.

inflammable *adjective*
able to be set on fire.

---

❶ USAGE This word means the same as *flammable*. If you want to say that something is not able to be set on fire, use *non-flammable*.

---

inflammation *noun*
painful redness or swelling in a part of the body.

inflate *verb* (**inflates, inflating, inflated**)
1 fill something with air or gas so that it expands.
2 increase something too much. 3 raise prices or wages etc. more than is justifiable.

inflation *noun*
1 inflating. 2 a general rise in prices and fall in the purchasing power of money.
inflationary *adjective*

inflect *verb* (**inflects, inflecting, inflected**)
1 change the ending or form of a word to show its tense or its grammatical relation to other words, e.g. *sing* changes to *sang* or *sung*; *child* changes to *children*. 2 alter the voice in speaking.

inflection *noun* (*plural* **inflections**)
an ending or form of a word used to inflect, e.g. *-ed*.

inflexible *adjective*
not able to be bent or changed or persuaded.
inflexibly *adverb* **inflexibility** *noun*

influence *noun* (*plural* **influences**)
1 the power to produce an effect. 2 a person or thing with this power.

influence *verb* (**influences, influencing, influenced**)
have influence on a person or thing.

influential *adjective*
having great influence.

influenza *noun*
an infectious disease that causes fever, catarrh, and pain.

inform *verb* (**informs, informing, informed**)
give information to somebody.
informant *noun*

informal *adjective*
not formal.
informally *adverb* **informality** *noun*

---

❶ USAGE In this dictionary, words marked *informal* are used in talking but not when you are writing or speaking formally.

---

information *noun*
facts told or heard or discovered, or put into a computer etc.

informative *adjective*
giving a lot of useful information.

informed *adjective*
knowing about something.

infra-red *adjective*
below or beyond red in the colour spectrum.

infuriate *verb* (**infuriates, infuriating, infuriated**)
make a person very angry.
infuriation *noun*

ingenious *adjective*
1 clever at inventing things. 2 cleverly made or thought out.
ingeniously *adverb* **ingenuity** *noun*

ingrained *adjective*
1 (said about dirt) marking a surface deeply.
2 (said about feelings or habits etc.) firmly fixed.

ingratiate verb (ingratiates, ingratiating, ingratiated)
ingratiate yourself get yourself into favour with someone, especially by flattering them or always agreeing with their ideas or opinions.
ingratiation noun

ingratitude noun
lack of gratitude.

ingredient noun (plural ingredients)
one of the parts of a mixture; one of the things used in a recipe.

inhabit verb (inhabits, inhabiting, inhabited)
live in a place.
inhabitant noun

inhale verb (inhales, inhaling, inhaled)
breathe in.
inhalation noun

inhaler noun (plural inhalers)
a device used for relieving asthma etc. by inhaling.

inherent (say in-heer-ent) adjective
existing in something as one of its natural or permanent qualities.
inherently adverb inherence noun

inherit verb (inherits, inheriting, inherited)
1 receive money, property, or a title etc. when its previous owner dies. 2 get certain qualities etc. from parents or predecessors.
inheritance noun inheritor noun

inhibition noun (plural inhibitions)
a feeling of embarrassment or worry that prevents you from doing something or expressing your emotions.
inhibited adjective

inhospitable adjective
1 unfriendly to visitors. 2 (said about a place) not giving any shelter or good weather.

inhuman adjective
cruel; without pity or kindness.
inhumanity noun

inimitable adjective
impossible to imitate.

initial noun (plural initials)
the first letter of a word or name.

initial adjective
at the beginning ♦ the initial stages.
initially adverb

initiative (say in-ish-a-tiv) noun
1 the power or right to get something started.
2 the ability to make decisions and take action on your own without being told what to do.
take the initiative take action to start something happening.

inject verb (injects, injecting, injected)
1 put a medicine or drug into the body by means of a syringe. 2 add a new quality ♦ Inject some humour into the story.
injection noun

injure verb (injures, injuring, injured)
harm or hurt someone.
injury noun injurious (say in-joor-ee-us) adjective

injustice noun (plural injustices)
1 lack of justice. 2 an unjust action or treatment.

ink noun (plural inks)
a black or coloured liquid used in writing and printing.

inkling noun (plural inklings)
a slight idea or suspicion ♦ I had no inkling of your artistic talents.

inky adjective
1 stained with ink. 2 black like ink
♦ inky darkness.

inland adjective & adverb
in or towards the interior of a country; away from the coast.

Inland Revenue noun
the government department responsible for collecting taxes and similar charges inland (not at a port).

in-laws plural noun (informal)
relatives by marriage.

inlet noun (plural inlets)
a strip of water reaching into the land from a sea or lake.

inmost adjective
most inward.

inn noun (plural inns)
a hotel or public house, especially in the country.
innkeeper noun

innards plural noun
the internal organs of a person or animal; the inner parts of a machine.

inner adjective
inside; nearer to the centre.
innermost adjective

innings noun (plural innings)
the time when a cricket team or player is batting.

innocent adjective
1 not guilty. 2 not wicked; lacking experience of evil. 3 harmless.
innocently adverb innocence noun

innocuous adjective
harmless.

innovation noun (plural innovations)
1 introducing new things or new methods.
2 a newly introduced process or way of doing things.
innovative adjective innovator noun

innumerable adjective
countless.

inoculate *verb* (inoculates, inoculating, inoculated)
inject or treat someone with a vaccine or serum as a protection against a disease.
inoculation *noun*

ℹ️ USAGE Note the spelling of this word. It has one 'n' and one 'c'.

inoffensive *adjective*
harmless.

inorganic *adjective*
not of living organisms; of mineral origin.

input *noun*
what is put into something, especially data put into a computer.
input *verb*

inquest *noun* (*plural* inquests)
an official inquiry to find out how a person died.

inquire *verb* (inquires, inquiring, inquired)
1 investigate something carefully. **2** ask for information.

ℹ️ USAGE You can spell this word *inquire* or *enquire* in either of its meanings. It is probably more common for *inquire* to be used for 'investigate' and *enquire* to be used for 'ask for information', but there is no real need to follow this distinction.

inquiry *noun* (*plural* inquiries)
1 an official investigation. **2** a question.

inquisitive *adjective*
always asking questions or trying to find out things.
inquisitively *adverb*

inroads *plural noun*
make inroads on or **into** use up large quantities of supplies or resources.

insane *adjective*
not sane; mad.
insanely *adverb* **insanity** *noun*

insanitary *adjective*
unclean and likely to be harmful to health.

insatiable (*say* in-say-sha-bul) *adjective*
impossible to satisfy ♦ *an insatiable appetite*.

inscribe *verb* (inscribes, inscribing, inscribed)
write or carve words etc. on something.

inscription *noun* (*plural* inscriptions)
words written or carved on a monument, coin, stone, etc. or written in the front of a book.

insect *noun* (*plural* insects)
a small animal with six legs, no backbone, and a body divided into three parts (head, thorax, abdomen).

insecticide *noun* (*plural* insecticides)
a substance for killing insects.

insectivorous *adjective*
feeding on insects and other small invertebrate creatures.
insectivore *noun*

insecure *adjective*
1 not secure or safe. **2** lacking confidence about yourself.
insecurely *adverb* **insecurity** *noun*

inseminate *verb* (inseminates, inseminating, inseminated)
insert semen into the womb.
insemination *noun*

insensitive *adjective*
not sensitive or thinking about other people's feelings.
insensitively *adverb* **insensitivity** *noun*

inseparable *adjective*
1 not able to be separated. **2** liking to be constantly together ♦ *inseparable friends*.
inseparably *adverb*

insert *verb* (inserts, inserting, inserted)
put a thing into something else.
insertion *noun*

inside *noun* (*plural* insides)
the inner side, surface, or part.
inside out with the inside turned to face outwards. **insides** (*informal*) the organs in the abdomen; the stomach and bowels.

inside *adverb* & *preposition*
on or to the inside of something; in ♦ *Come inside*. ♦ *It's inside that box*.

insider *noun* (*plural* insiders)
a member of a certain group, especially someone with access to private information.

insight *noun* (*plural* insights)
being able to perceive the truth about things; understanding.

insignificant *adjective*
not important or influential.
insignificance *noun*

insincere *adjective*
not sincere.
insincerely *adverb* **insincerity** *noun*

insinuate *verb* (insinuates, insinuating, insinuated)
1 hint something unpleasant. **2** introduce a thing or yourself gradually or craftily into a place.
insinuation *noun*

insist *verb* (insists, insisting, insisted)
be very firm in saying or asking for something ♦ *I insist on seeing the manager*.
insistent *adjective* **insistence** *noun*

insolent *adjective*
very rude and insulting.
insolently *adverb* **insolence** *noun*

insoluble *adjective*
1 impossible to solve ♦ *an insoluble problem.*
2 impossible to dissolve.
insolubility *noun*

insomnia *noun*
being unable to sleep.
insomniac *noun*

inspect *verb* (**inspects, inspecting, inspected**)
examine something carefully and critically.
inspection *noun*

inspector *noun* (*plural* **inspectors**)
1 a person whose job is to inspect or supervise
things. 2 a police officer ranking next above a
sergeant.

inspiration *noun* (*plural* **inspirations**)
1 a sudden brilliant idea. 2 inspiring; an
inspiring influence.

inspire *verb* (**inspires, inspiring, inspired**)
fill a person with enthusiasm or creative feelings
or ideas ♦ *The applause inspired us with
confidence.*

install *verb* (**installs, installing, installed**)
1 put something in position and ready to use
♦ *They installed central heating.* 2 put a person
into an important position with a ceremony
♦ *He was installed as Pope.*
installation *noun*

instalment *noun* (*plural* **instalments**)
each of the parts in which something is given or
paid for over a period of time ♦ *an instalment of
a serial;* ♦ *You can pay by instalments.*

instance *noun* (*plural* **instances**)
an example ♦ *for instance.*
for instance for example.

instant *adjective*
1 happening immediately ♦ *instant success.*
2 (said about food) designed to be prepared
quickly and easily ♦ *instant coffee.*
instantly *adverb*
instant *noun* (*plural* **instants**)
a moment ♦ *not an instant too soon.*

instantaneous *adjective*
happening immediately.
instantaneously *adverb*

instead *adverb*
in place of something else.

instinct *noun* (*plural* **instincts**)
a natural tendency or ability ♦ *Birds fly by
instinct.*
instinctive *adjective* **instinctively** *adverb*

institute *noun* (*plural* **institutes**)
a society or organization; the building used by
this.

institution *noun* (*plural* **institutions**)
1 an institute; a public organization, e.g. a
hospital or university. 2 a habit or custom.
3 instituting something.
institutional *adjective*

instruct *verb* (**instructs, instructing,
instructed**)
1 teach a person a subject or skill. 2 inform.
2 tell a person what he or she must do.
instructive *adjective* **instructor** *noun*

instruction *noun* (*plural* **instructions**)
1 teaching a subject or skill. 2 an order or piece
of information ♦ *Follow the instructions
carefully.*

instrument *noun* (*plural* **instruments**)
1 a device for producing musical sounds.
2 a tool used for delicate or scientific work.
3 a measuring device.

instrumental *adjective*
1 performed on musical instruments, without
singing. 2 being the means of doing something
♦ *She was instrumental in getting me a job.*

insubordinate *adjective*
disobedient or rebellious.
insubordination *noun*

insufferable *adjective*
unbearable.

insular *adjective*
1 to do with or like an island. 2 narrow-minded.

insulate *verb* (**insulates, insulating, insulated**)
cover or protect something to prevent heat, cold,
or electricity etc. from passing in or out.
insulation *noun* **insulator** *noun*

insulin *noun*
a substance that controls the amount of sugar in
the blood. The lack of insulin causes diabetes.

insult (*say* in-sult) *verb* (**insults, insulting,
insulted**)
hurt a person's feelings or pride.

insult (*say* in-sult) *noun* (*plural* **insults**)
an insulting remark or action.

insuperable *adjective*
unable to be overcome ♦ *an insuperable
difficulty.*

insurance *noun*
an agreement to compensate someone for a loss,
damage, or injury etc., in return for a payment
(called a **premium**) made in advance.

insure *verb* (**insures, insuring, insured**)
protect with insurance ♦ *Is your jewellery
insured?*

❶ USAGE Do not confuse with *ensure.*

intact *adjective*
not damaged; complete.
[from Latin *intactum* = not touched]

intake *noun* (*plural* **intakes**)
1 taking something in. 2 the number of people or
things taken in ♦ *We have a high intake of
students this year.*

integer *noun* (*plural* **integers**)
a whole number (e.g. 0, 3, 19), not a fraction.

integral (*say* in-tig-ral) *adjective*
1 being an essential part of a whole thing
♦ *An engine is an integral part of a car.*
2 whole or complete.

integrate *verb* (integrates, integrating, integrated)
1 make parts into a whole; combine. **2** bring people together harmoniously into a single community.
integration *noun*

integrity (*say* in-teg-rit-ee) *noun*
honesty.

intellect *noun* (*plural* intellects)
the ability to think and work things out with the mind.

intellectual *adjective*
1 to do with or using the intellect. **2** having a good intellect and a liking for knowledge.
intellectually *adverb*

intellectual *noun* (*plural* intellectuals)
an intellectual person.

intelligence *noun*
1 being intelligent. **2** information, especially of military value; the people who collect and study this information.

intelligent *adjective*
able to learn and understand things; having great mental ability.
intelligently *adverb*

intend *verb* (intends, intending, intended)
1 have something in mind as what you want to do. **2** plan that something should be used or understood in a particular way.

intense *adjective*
1 very strong or great. **2** feeling things very strongly and seriously ♦ *He's a very intense young man.*
intensely *adverb* **intensity** *noun*

intent *noun* (*plural* intents)
intention.

intent *adjective*
with concentrated attention; very interested.
intently *adverb*
intent on eager or determined to do something.

intention *noun* (*plural* intentions)
what a person intends; a purpose or plan.

intentional *adjective*
deliberate, not accidental.
intentionally *adverb*

interact *verb* (interacts, interacting, interacted)
have an effect upon one another.
interaction *noun*

interactive *adjective*
(in computing) allowing information to be sent immediately in either direction between a computer system and its user.

interbreed *verb* (interbreeds, interbreeding, interbred)
breed with each other; cross-breed.

intercept *verb* (intercepts, intercepting, intercepted)
stop or catch a person or thing that is going from one place to another.
interception *noun*

interchange *verb* (interchanges, interchanging, interchanged)
1 put each of two things into the other's place. **2** exchange things. **3** alternate.
interchangeable *adjective*

interchange *noun* (*plural* interchanges)
1 interchanging. **2** a road junction where vehicles can move from one motorway etc. to another.

intercourse *noun*
1 communication or dealings between people. **2** sexual intercourse.

interdependent *adjective*
dependent upon each other.

interest *noun* (*plural* interests)
1 a feeling of wanting to know about or help with something. **2** a thing that interests somebody ♦ *Science fiction is one of my interests.* **3** an advantage or benefit ♦ *She looks after her own interests.* **4** money paid regularly in return for money lent or deposited.

interest *verb* (interests, interesting, interested)
attract a person's interest.
interested *adjective* **interesting** *adjective*

interface *noun* (*plural* interfaces)
(in computing) a connection between two parts of a computer system.

interfere *verb* (interferes, interfering, interfered)
1 take part in something that has nothing to do with you. **2** get in the way; obstruct.
interference *noun*

interior *adjective*
inner.

interior *noun* (*plural* interiors)
the inside of something; the central or inland part of a country.

interjection *noun* (*plural* interjections)
a word or words exclaimed expressing joy or pain or surprise, such as *oh!* or *wow!* or *good heavens!*

interlude *noun* (*plural* interludes)
1 an interval. **2** something happening in an interval or between other events.

intermediate *adjective*
coming between two things in time, place, or order.

interminable *adjective*
seeming to be endless; long and boring.
interminably *adverb*

intermission *noun* (*plural* **intermissions**)
an interval, especially between parts of a film.

intermittent *adjective*
happening at intervals; not continuous.
intermittently *adverb*

internal *adjective*
inside.
internally *adverb*

internal-combustion engine *noun* (*plural* **internal-combustion engines**)
an engine that produces power by burning fuel inside the engine itself.

international *adjective*
to do with or belonging to more than one country; agreed between nations.
internationally *adverb*

international *noun* (*plural* **internationals**)
1 a sports contest between teams representing different countries. 2 a sports player who plays for his or her country.

Internet *noun*
a computer network that allows users all over the world to communicate and exchange information.
[from *inter* = among, between + *net*]

interplanetary *adjective*
between planets.

interpolate *verb* (**interpolates, interpolating, interpolated**)
1 interject a remark in a conversation. 2 insert words; put terms into a mathematical series.
interpolation *noun*

interpose *verb* (**interposes, interposing, interposed**)
place something between two things.

interpret *verb* (**interprets, interpreting, interpreted**)
1 explain what something means. 2 translate what someone says into another language orally. 3 perform music etc. in a way that shows your feelings about its meaning.
interpretation *noun* **interpreter** *noun*

interrogate *verb* (**interrogates, interrogating, interrogated**)
question someone closely or formally.
interrogation *noun* **interrogator** *noun*

interrogative *adjective*
questioning; expressing a question.
interrogatory *adjective*

interrupt *verb* (**interrupts, interrupting, interrupted**)
1 break in on what someone is saying by inserting a remark. 2 prevent something from continuing.
interruption *noun*

intersect *verb* (**intersects, intersecting, intersected**)
1 divide a thing by passing or lying across it. 2 (said about lines or roads etc.) cross each other.
intersection *noun*

interval *noun* (*plural* **intervals**)
1 a time between two events or parts of a play etc. 2 a space between two things.
at intervals with some time or distance between each one.
[from Latin *intervallum* = space between the ramparts of a fortification, from *vallum* = rampart]

intervene *verb* (**intervenes, intervening, intervened**)
1 come between two events ♦ *in the intervening years*. 2 interrupt a discussion or fight etc. to try and stop it or change its result.
intervention *noun*

interview *noun* (*plural* **interviews**)
a formal meeting with someone to ask him or her questions or to obtain information.

interview *verb* (**interviews, interviewing, interviewed**)
hold an interview with someone.
interviewer *noun*

intestine *noun* (*plural* **intestines**)
the long tube along which food passes while being absorbed by the body, between the stomach and the anus.
intestinal *adjective*

intimate (*say* in-tim-at) *adjective*
1 very friendly with someone. 2 private and personal ♦ *intimate thoughts*. 3 detailed ♦ *an intimate knowledge of the country*.
intimately *adverb* **intimacy** *noun*

intimidate *verb* (**intimidates, intimidating, intimidated**)
frighten a person by threats into doing something.
intimidation *noun*

into *preposition*
used to express 1 movement to the inside (*Go into the house*), 2 change of condition or occupation etc. (*It broke into pieces; She went into politics*), 3 (in division) *4 into 20* = 20 divided by 4.

intolerable *adjective*
unbearable.
intolerably *adverb*

intoxicate *verb* (**intoxicates, intoxicating, intoxicated**)
make a person drunk or very excited.
intoxication *noun*

intransitive *adjective*
(said about a verb) used without a direct object after it, e.g. *hear* in *we can hear* (but not in *we can hear you*). (Compare **transitive**.)
intransitively *adverb*

intravenous (*say* in-tra-**veen**-us) *adjective*
directly into a vein.

intricate *adjective*
very complicated.
intricately *adverb* **intricacy** *noun*

intrigue (*say* in-**treeg**) *verb* (**intrigues, intriguing, intrigued**)
1 interest someone very much ♦ *The subject intrigues me.* **2** plot with someone in an underhand way.

introduce *verb* (**introduces, introducing, introduced**)
1 bring an idea or practice into use. **2** make a person known to other people. **3** announce a broadcast, speaker, etc.

introduction *noun* (*plural* **introductions**)
1 introducing somebody or something.
2 an explanation put at the beginning of a book or speech etc.
introductory *adjective*

introvert *noun* (*plural* **introverts**)
a shy person who does not like to talk about his or her own thoughts and feelings with other people. (The opposite is *extrovert*.)

intrude *verb* (**intrudes, intruding, intruded**)
come in or join in without being wanted.
intrusion *noun* **intrusive** *adjective*

intruder *noun* (*plural* **intruders**)
1 someone who intrudes. **2** a burglar.

intuition *noun*
the power to know or understand things without having to think hard or without being taught.
intuitive *adjective* **intuitively** *adverb*

Inuit (*say* in-**yoo**-it) *noun* (*plural* **Inuit**)
1 a member of a people living in northern Canada and Greenland. **2** the language of the Inuit.

ℹ USAGE This name is now preferred to *Eskimo*.

---

inundate *verb* (**inundates, inundating, inundated**)
flood or overwhelm a place ♦ *We've been inundated with letters about the programme.*
inundation *noun*

invade *verb* (**invades, invading, invaded**)
1 attack and enter a country etc. **2** crowd into a place ♦ *Tourists invade Oxford in summer.*
invader *noun*

invalid (*say* in-va-**lid**) *noun* (*plural* **invalids**)
a person who is ill or who is weakened by illness.

invalid (*say* in-**val**-id) *adjective*
not valid ♦ *This passport is invalid.*
invalidity *noun*
[from *in-* = not + Latin *validus* = strong or powerful]

invaluable *adjective*
having a value that is too great to be measured; extremely valuable.

invariable *adjective*
not variable; never changing.
invariably *adverb*

invasion *noun* (*plural* **invasions**)
attacking and entering a country etc.

invent *verb* (**invents, inventing, invented**)
1 be the first person to make or think of a particular thing. **2** make up a false story ♦ *She had to invent an excuse.*
invention *noun* **inventor** *noun* **inventive** *adjective*

invertebrate *noun* (*plural* **invertebrates**)
an animal without a backbone.
invertebrate *adjective*

inverted commas *plural noun*
punctuation marks " " or ' ' put round quotations and spoken words.

invest *verb* (**invests, investing, invested**)
1 use money to make a profit, e.g. by lending it in return for interest to be paid, or by buying stocks and shares or property. **2** give somebody an honour, medal, or special title in a formal ceremony.
investment *noun* **investor** *noun*

investigate *verb* (**investigates, investigating, investigated**)
find out as much as you can about something; make a systematic inquiry.
investigation *noun* **investigator** *noun* **investigative** *adjective*

invigilate *verb* (**invigilates, invigilating, invigilated**)
supervise candidates at an examination.
invigilation *noun* **invigilator** *noun*

invigorate *verb* (**invigorates, invigorating, invigorated**)
give a person strength or courage. (Compare **vigour**.)

invincible *adjective*
not able to be defeated.
invincibly *adverb* **invincibility** *noun*

invisible *adjective*
not visible; not able to be seen.
invisibly *adverb* **invisibility** *noun*

invite *verb* (**invites, inviting, invited**)
1 ask a person to come or do something.
2 be likely to cause something to happen ♦ *You are inviting disaster.*
invitation *noun*

invoice noun (plural **invoices**)
a list of goods sent or work done, with the prices charged.

involuntary adjective
not deliberate; unintentional.
involuntarily adverb

involve verb (**involves, involving, involved**)
1 have as a part; make a thing necessary ♦ The job involves hard work. **2** make someone share or take part in something ♦ They involved us in their charity work.
involvement noun

inward adjective
1 on the inside. **2** going or facing inwards.
inward adverb
inwards.

inwards adverb
towards the inside.

iodine noun
a chemical substance used as an antiseptic.

ion noun (plural **ions**)
an electrically charged particle.

ionosphere (say I-on-os-feer) noun
a region of the upper atmosphere, containing ions.

IQ abbreviation
intelligence quotient; a number showing how a person's intelligence compares with that of an average person.

IRA abbreviation
Irish Republican Army.

iridescent adjective
showing rainbow-like colours.
iridescence noun

iron noun (plural **irons**)
1 a hard grey metal. **2** a device with a flat base that is heated for smoothing clothes or cloth. **3** a tool made of iron ♦ a branding iron.
iron adjective

iron verb (**irons, ironing, ironed**)
smooth clothes or cloth with an iron.
iron out sort out a difficulty or problem.

Iron Age noun
the time when tools and weapons were made of iron.

ironic (say I-ron-ik) adjective
using irony; full of irony.
ironical adjective **ironically** adverb

ironmonger noun (plural **ironmongers**)
a shopkeeper who sells tools and other metal objects.
ironmongery noun

irony (say I-ron-ee) noun (plural **ironies**)
1 saying the opposite of what you mean in order to emphasize it, e.g. saying 'What a lovely day' when it is pouring with rain. **2** an oddly contradictory situation ♦ The irony of it is that I tripped while telling someone else to be careful.

irrational adjective
not rational; illogical.
irrationally adverb

irregular adjective
1 not regular; uneven. **2** against the rules or usual custom. **3** (said about troops) not in the regular armed forces.
irregularly adverb **irregularity** noun

irrepressible adjective
unable to be repressed; always lively and cheerful.
irrepressibly adverb

irreproachable adjective
blameless or faultless.
irreproachably adverb

irresistible adjective
too strong or attractive to be resisted.
irresistibly adverb

irrespective adjective
not taking something into account ♦ Prizes are awarded to winners, irrespective of age.

irresponsible adjective
not showing a proper sense of responsibility.
irresponsibly adverb **irresponsibility** noun

irrigate verb (**irrigates, irrigating, irrigated**)
supply land with water so that crops etc. can grow.
irrigation noun

irritable adjective
easily annoyed; bad-tempered.
irritably adverb **irritability** noun

irritate verb (**irritates, irritating, irritated**)
1 annoy. **2** cause itching.
irritation noun **irritant** adjective & noun

Islam noun
the religion of Muslims.
Islamic adjective

island noun (plural **islands**)
1 a piece of land surrounded by water. **2** something that resembles an island because it is isolated or detached ♦ a traffic island.

isn't (mainly spoken)
is not.

isobar (say I-so-bar) noun (plural **isobars**)
a line on a map connecting places that have the same atmospheric pressure.

isolate verb (**isolates, isolating, isolated**)
place a person or thing apart or alone; separate.
isolation noun

isosceles (say I-soss-il-eez) adjective
an isosceles triangle has two sides of equal length.

isotope noun (plural **isotopes**)
(in science) a form of an element that differs from other forms in the structure of its nucleus but has the same chemical properties as the other forms.

ISP *abbreviation*
Internet service provider, a company providing individual users with a connection to the Internet.

issue *verb* (**issues, issuing, issued**)
1 come or go out; flow out. 2 supply; give out ♦ *We issued one blanket to each refugee.* 3 send out ♦ *They issued a gale warning.* 4 put out for sale; publish. 5 come or go out; flow out.

issue *noun* (*plural* **issues**)
1 a subject for discussion or concern ♦ *What are the real issues?* 2 a particular edition of a newspaper or magazine ♦ *The Christmas issue of Radio Times.* 3 issuing something ♦ *The issue of passports is held up.* 4 (*formal*) heirs ♦ *He died without issue.*
take issue with disagree with.

isthmus (*say* iss-mus) *noun* (*plural* **isthmuses**)
a narrow strip of land connecting two larger pieces of land.

IT *abbreviation*
information technology.

it *pronoun*
1 the thing being talked about. 2 the player who has to catch others in a game. 3 used in statements about the weather or about circumstances etc. ♦ *It is raining;* ♦ *It is six miles to York.* 4 used as an indefinite object ♦ *Run for it!* 5 used to refer to a phrase ♦ *It is unlikely that she will fail.*

italic (*say* it-al-ik) *adjective*
printed with sloping letters (called **italics**) *like this*.

itch *verb* (**itches, itching, itched**)
1 have or feel a tickling sensation in the skin that makes you want to scratch it. 2 long to do something.

item *noun* (*plural* **items**)
1 one thing in a list or group of things. 2 one piece of news, article, etc. in a newspaper or bulletin.

its *possessive pronoun*
belonging to it ♦ *The cat hurt its paw.*

❶ USAGE Do not put an apostrophe into *its* unless you mean 'it is' or 'it has' (see the next entry).

it's (*mainly spoken*)
1 it is ♦ *It's very hot.* 2 it has ♦ *It's broken all records.*

❶ USAGE Do not confuse with *its*.

itself *pronoun*
it and nothing else.
by itself on its own; alone.

ITV *abbreviation*
Independent Television.

ivory *noun*
1 the hard creamy-white substance that forms elephants' tusks. 2 a creamy-white colour.

ivy *noun* (*plural* **ivies**)
a climbing evergreen plant with shiny leaves.

-ize or **-ise** *suffix*
forms verbs meaning 'bring or come into a certain condition' (e.g. *civilize*), or 'treat in a certain way' (e.g. *pasteurize*), or 'have a certain feeling' (e.g. *sympathize*).

Jj

jab *verb* (**jabs, jabbing, jabbed**)
poke roughly; push a thing into something.

jack *noun* (*plural* **jacks**)
1 a device for lifting something heavy off the ground. 2 a playing card with a picture of a young man. 3 a small white ball aimed at in bowls.
jack of all trades someone who can do many different kinds of work.

jackdaw *noun* (*plural* **jackdaws**)
a kind of small crow.

jacket *noun* (*plural* **jackets**)
1 a short coat, usually reaching to the hips. 2 a cover to keep the heat in a water tank etc. 3 a paper wrapper for a book. 4 the skin of a potato that is baked without being peeled.

jackpot *noun* (*plural* **jackpots**)
an amount of prize money that increases until someone wins it.
hit the jackpot 1 win a large prize.
2 have remarkable luck or success.

Jacuzzi (*say* ja-**koo**-zi) *noun* (*plural* **Jacuzzis**)
(*trademark*) a large bath in which underwater jets of water massage the body.

jagged (*say* **jag**-id) *adjective*
having an uneven edge with sharp points.

jaguar *noun* (*plural* **jaguars**)
a large fierce South American animal rather like a leopard.
[via Portuguese from Tupi (a South American language)]

jail *noun* (*plural* **jails**)
a prison.

Jain (*say* jayn) *noun* (*plural* **Jains**)
a believer in an Indian religion rather like Buddhism.

jam *noun* (*plural* **jams**)
1 a sweet food made of fruit boiled with sugar until it is thick. 2 a lot of people, cars, or logs etc. crowded together so that movement is difficult.
in a jam in a difficult situation.

jam *verb* (**jams, jamming, jammed**)
1 make or become fixed and difficult to move ♦ *The window has jammed.* **2** crowd or squeeze into a space. **3** push something forcibly ♦ *jam the brakes on.* **4** block a broadcast by causing interference with the transmission.

jamboree *noun* (*plural* **jamborees**)
a large party or celebration

jangle *verb* (**jangles, jangling, jangled**)
make a loud harsh ringing sound.
jangle *noun*

janitor *noun* (*plural* **janitors**)
a caretaker.

January *noun*
the first month of the year.
[named after *Janus*, a Roman god of gates and beginnings, usually shown with two faces that look in opposite directions]

jar¹ *noun* (*plural* **jars**)
a container made of glass or pottery.

jar² *verb* (**jars, jarring, jarred**)
1 cause an unpleasant jolt or shock. **2** sound harshly ♦ *Her voice really jars on me.*
jar *noun* (*plural* **jars**)
a jarring effect.

jargon *noun*
words or expressions used by a profession or group that are difficult for other people to understand ♦ *computer jargon.*

jaunt *noun* (*plural* **jaunts**)
a short trip.
jaunting *noun*

jaunty *adjective* (**jauntier, jauntiest**)
lively and cheerful.
jauntily *adverb* **jauntiness** *noun*

javelin *noun* (*plural* **javelins**)
a lightweight spear.

jaw *noun* (*plural* **jaws**)
1 either of the two bones that form the framework of the mouth. **2** the lower part of the face. **3** something shaped like the jaws or used for gripping things. **4** (*slang*) talking.

jazz *noun*
a kind of music with strong rhythm, often improvised.
jazzy *adjective*

jealous *adjective*
1 unhappy or resentful because you feel that someone is your rival or is better or luckier than yourself. **2** careful in keeping something ♦ *He is very jealous of his own rights.*
jealously *adverb* **jealousy** *noun*

jeans *plural noun*
trousers made of strong cotton fabric.

Jeep *noun* (*plural* **Jeeps**)
(*trademark*) a small sturdy motor vehicle with four-wheel drive, especially one used in the army.

jeer *verb* (**jeers, jeering, jeered**)
laugh or shout at somebody rudely or scornfully.
jeer *noun*

jelly *noun* (*plural* **jellies**)
1 a soft transparent food. **2** any soft slippery substance.
jellied *adjective*

jellyfish *noun* (*plural* **jellyfish**)
a sea animal with a body like jelly.

jerk *verb* (**jerks, jerking, jerked**)
1 make a sudden sharp movement.
2 pull something suddenly.
jerk *noun* (*plural* **jerks**)
1 a sudden sharp movement. **2** (*slang*) a stupid person.
jerky *adjective* **jerkily** *adverb*

jerkin *noun* (*plural* **jerkins**)
a sleeveless jacket.

jersey *noun* (*plural* **jerseys**)
1 a pullover with sleeves. **2** a plain machine-knitted material used for making clothes.

jest *noun* (*plural* **jests**)
a joke.
[from Middle English *gest* = a story]

jester *noun* (*plural* **jesters**)
a professional entertainer at a royal court in the Middle Ages.

jet *noun* (*plural* **jets**)
1 a stream of water, gas, flame, etc. shot out from a narrow opening. **2** a spout or nozzle from which a jet comes. **3** an aircraft driven by engines that send out a high-speed jet of hot gases at the back.

jet lag *noun*
extreme tiredness that a person feels after a long flight between different time zones.

jettison *verb* (**jettisons, jettisoning, jettisoned**)
1 throw something overboard. **2** get rid of something that is no longer wanted. **3** release or drop something from an aircraft or spacecraft in flight.

jetty *noun* (*plural* **jetties**)
a small landing stage.

Jew *noun* (*plural* **Jews**)
a member of a people descended from the ancient tribes of Israel, or who practises the religion of this people.
Jewish *adjective*

jewel *noun* (*plural* **jewels**)
1 a precious stone. **2** an ornament containing precious stones.
jewelled *adjective*
[from early French]

jewellery *noun*
jewels and similar ornaments for wearing.

jigsaw *noun* (*plural* **jigsaws**)
1 a picture cut into irregular pieces which are then shuffled and fitted together again for amusement. **2** a saw that can cut curved shapes.

jilt *verb* (**jilts, jilting, jilted**)
abandon a boyfriend or girlfriend, especially after promising to marry him or her.

jingle *verb* (**jingles, jingling, jingled**)
make or cause to make a tinkling sound.

jingle *noun* (*plural* **jingles**)
1 a jingling sound. **2** a very simple verse or tune, especially one used in advertising.

jitters *plural noun* (*informal*)
a feeling of extreme nervousness.
jittery *adjective*

job *noun* (*plural* **jobs**)
1 work that someone does regularly to earn a living. **2** a piece of work to be done. **3** (*informal*) a difficult task ♦ *You'll have a job to lift that box.* **4** (*informal*) a thing; a state of affairs ♦ *It's a good job you're here.*
just the job (*informal*) exactly what you want or need.

jockey *noun* (*plural* **jockeys**)
a person who rides horses in races.

jodhpurs (*say* jod-perz) *plural noun*
trousers for horse riding, fitting closely from the knee to the ankle.
[named after *Jodhpur*, a city in India, where similar trousers are worn]

jog *verb* (**jogs, jogging, jogged**)
1 run or trot slowly, especially for exercise. **2** give something a slight push.
jogger *noun*
jog someone's memory help someone to remember something.

jogtrot *noun*
a slow steady trot.

join *verb* (**joins, joining, joined**)
1 put or come together; fasten or connect. **2** take part with others in doing something ♦ *We all joined in the chorus.* **3** become a member of a group or organization etc. ♦ *Join the Navy.*
join up enlist in the armed forces.

joint *noun* (*plural* **joints**)
1 a place where two things are joined. **2** the place where two bones fit together. **3** a large piece of meat cut ready for cooking. **4** (*informal*) a cannabis cigarette.

joint *adjective*
shared or done by two or more people, nations, etc. ♦ *a joint project.*
jointly *adverb*

joke *noun* (*plural* **jokes**)
something said or done to make people laugh.

joke *verb* (**jokes, joking, joked**)
1 make jokes. **2** tease someone or not be serious ♦ *I'm only joking.*

joker *noun* (*plural* **jokers**)
1 someone who jokes. **2** an extra playing card with a jester on it.

jolly *adjective* (**jollier, jolliest**)
cheerful and good-humoured.
jollity *noun*

jolly *adverb* (*informal*)
very ♦ *jolly good.*

jolt *verb* (**jolts, jolting, jolted**)
1 shake or dislodge something with a sudden sharp movement. **2** move along jerkily, e.g. on a rough road. **3** give someone a shock.

jolt *noun* (*plural* **jolts**)
1 a jolting movement. **2** a shock.

jostle *verb* (**jostles, jostling, jostled**)
push roughly, especially in a crowd.

jot *verb* (**jots, jotting, jotted**)
write something quickly ♦ *Let me jot down that phone number.*

jotter *noun* (*plural* **jotters**)
a notepad or notebook.

joule (*say* jool) *noun* (*plural* **joules**)
a unit of work or energy.

journal *noun* (*plural* **journals**)
1 a newspaper or magazine. **2** a diary.

journalist *noun* (*plural* **journalists**)
a person who writes for a newspaper or magazine.
journalism *noun* **journalistic** *adjective*

journey *noun* (*plural* **journeys**)
1 going from one place to another. **2** the distance or time taken to travel somewhere ♦ *two days' journey.*

journey *verb* (**journeys, journeying, journeyed**)
make a journey.

jovial *adjective*
cheerful and good-humoured.
jovially *adverb* **joviality** *noun*

joy *noun* (*plural* **joys**)
1 a feeling of great pleasure or happiness. **2** a thing that causes joy.
joyful *adjective* **joyfully** *adverb* **joyfulness** *noun* **joyous** *adjective* **joyously** *adverb*

joyride *noun* (*plural* **joyrides**)
a drive in a stolen car for amusement.
joyrider *noun* **joyriding** *noun*

joystick *noun* (*plural* **joysticks**)
1 the control lever of an aircraft. **2** a device for moving a cursor or image on a VDU screen, especially in computer games.

JP *abbreviation*
Justice of the Peace.

jubilant *adjective*
rejoicing or triumphant.
jubilantly *adverb* **jubilation** *noun*

jubilee (*say* joo-bil-ee) *noun* (*plural* **jubilees**)
a special anniversary: *silver* (25th), *golden* (50th), and *diamond* (60th) *jubilee*.

Judaism (*say* joo-day-izm) *noun*
the religion of the Jewish people.

judge *noun* (*plural* **judges**)
1 a person appointed to hear cases in a lawcourt and decide what should be done. **2** a person deciding who has won a contest or competition. **3** someone who is good at forming opinions or making decisions ♦ *She's a good judge of character.*

judge *verb* (**judges, judging, judged**)
1 act as a judge. **2** form and give an opinion. **3** estimate ♦ *He judged the distance carefully.*

judgement *noun* (*plural* **judgements**)
1 judging. **2** the decision made by a lawcourt. **3** someone's opinion. **4** the ability to judge wisely. **5** something considered as a punishment from God ♦ *It's a judgement on you!*

judicial *adjective*
to do with lawcourts, judges, or judgements ♦ *the British judicial system.*
judicially *adverb*

❶ USAGE Do not confuse with *judicious*.

judicious (*say* joo-**dish**-us) *adjective*
having or showing good sense or good judgement.
judiciously *adverb*

❶ USAGE Do not confuse with *judicial*.

judo *noun*
a Japanese method of self-defence without using weapons.
[from Japanese *ju* = gentle + *do* = way]

jug *noun* (*plural* **jugs**)
a container for holding and pouring liquids, with a handle and a lip.

juggernaut *noun* (*plural* **juggernauts**)
a huge lorry.
[named after a Hindu god whose image was dragged in procession on a huge wheeled vehicle]

juggle *verb* (**juggles, juggling, juggled**)
1 toss and catch a number of objects skilfully for entertainment, keeping one or more in the air at any time. **2** rearrange or alter things skilfully or in order to deceive people.
juggler *noun*

jugular *adjective*
to do with the throat or neck ♦ *the jugular veins.*

juice *noun* (*plural* **juices**)
1 the liquid from fruit, vegetables, or other food. **2** a liquid produced by the body ♦ *the digestive juices.*
juicy *adjective*

jukebox *noun* (*plural* **jukeboxes**)
a machine that automatically plays a record you have selected when you put a coin in.

July *noun*
the seventh month of the year.
[named after Julius Caesar, who was born in this month]

jumble *verb* (**jumbles, jumbling, jumbled**)
mix things up into a confused mass.

jumble *noun*
a confused mixture of things; a muddle.

jumble sale *noun* (*plural* **jumble sales**)
a sale of second-hand goods.

jumbo *noun* (*plural* **jumbos**)
1 something very large; a jumbo jet. **2** an elephant.

jumbo jet *noun* (*plural* **jumbo jets**)
a very large jet aircraft.

jump *verb* (**jumps, jumping, jumped**)
1 move up suddenly from the ground into the air. **2** go over something by jumping ♦ *The horse jumped the fence.* **3** pass over something; miss out part of a book etc. **4** move suddenly in surprise. **5** pass quickly to a different place or level.
jump at (*informal*) accept something eagerly.
jump on (*informal*) start criticizing someone.
jump the gun start before you should.
jump the queue not wait your turn.

jump *noun* (*plural* **jumps**)
1 a jumping movement. **2** an obstacle to jump over. **3** a sudden rise or change.

jumper *noun* (*plural* **jumpers**)
a jersey.
[from French *jupe* = tunic]

jumpy *adjective*
nervous and edgy.

junction *noun* (*plural* **junctions**)
1 a join. **2** a place where roads or railway lines meet.

June *noun*
the sixth month of the year.
[named after the Roman goddess Juno]

jungle *noun* (*plural* **jungles**)
a thick tangled forest, especially in the tropics.
jungly *adjective*
[from Hindi]

junior *adjective*
1 younger. **2** for young children ♦ *a junior school.* **3** lower in rank or importance ♦ *junior officers.*
[from Latin, = younger]

junk *noun*
rubbish; things of no value.

junk food *noun*
food that is not nourishing.

junk mail *noun*
unwanted advertising material sent by post.

jury *noun* (*plural* **juries**)
a group of people (usually twelve) appointed to give a verdict about a case in a lawcourt.
juryman *noun* **jurywoman** *noun*
[from Latin *jurare* = take an oath]

just *adjective*
1 giving proper consideration to everyone's claims. **2** deserved; right in amount etc.
♦ *a just reward.*
justly *adverb* **justness** *noun*

just *adverb*
1 exactly ♦ *It's just what I wanted.* **2** only; simply ♦ *I just wanted to see him.* **3** barely; by only a small amount ♦ *just below the knee.*
4 at this moment or only a little while ago ♦ *She has just gone.*

justice *noun* (*plural* **justices**)
1 being just; fair treatment. **2** legal proceedings ♦ *a court of justice.* **3** a judge or magistrate.
[via early French from Latin *jus* = law]

justify *verb* (**justifies, justifying, justified**)
show that something is fair, just, or reasonable.
justifiable *adjective* **justification** *noun*

jut *verb* (**juts, jutting, jutted**)
stick out.

jute *noun*
fibre from tropical plants, used for making sacks etc.

juvenile *adjective*
to do with or for young people.

juvenile *noun* (*plural* **juveniles**)
a young person, not old enough to be legally considered an adult.

juvenile delinquent *noun* (*plural* **juvenile delinquents**)
a young person who has broken the law.

Kk

kaleidoscope (*say* kal-I-dos-kohp) *noun*
(*plural* **kaleidoscopes**)
a tube that you look through to see brightly coloured patterns which change as you turn the end of the tube.
kaleidoscopic *adjective*

kangaroo *noun* (*plural* **kangaroos**)
an Australian animal that jumps along on its strong hind legs. (See **marsupial**.)
[an Australian Aboriginal word]

karaoke *noun* (*say* ka-ra-oh-ki)
a form of entertainment in which people sing well-known songs against a pre-recorded backing.
[from Japanese, = empty orchestra]

karate (*say* ka-rah-tee) *noun*
a Japanese method of self-defence in which the hands and feet are used as weapons.
[from Japanese *kara* = empty + *te* = hand]

KB or **Kb** *abbreviation*
kilobyte(s).

keel *noun* (*plural* **keels**)
the long piece of wood or metal along the bottom of a boat.
on an even keel steady.

keel *verb* (**keels, keeling, keeled**)
keel over fall down or overturn ♦ *The ship keeled over.*

keen *adjective*
1 enthusiastic; very interested in or eager to do something ♦ *a keen swimmer.* **2** sharp ♦ *a keen edge.* **3** piercingly cold ♦ *a keen wind.*
keenly *adverb* **keenness** *noun*

keep *verb* (**keeps, keeping, kept**)
1 have something and look after it or not get rid of it. **2** stay or cause to stay in the same condition etc. ♦ *keep still;* ♦ *keep it hot.* **3** do something continually ♦ *She keeps laughing.* **4** last without going bad ♦ *How long will this milk keep?*
5 respect and not break ♦ *keep a promise.*
6 make entries in ♦ *keep a diary.*
keep to observe or respect. **keep up 1** make the same progress as others. **2** continue something.

keep *noun* (*plural* **keeps**)
1 maintenance; the food etc. that you need to live ♦ *She earns her keep.* **2** a strong tower in a castle.
for keeps (*informal*) permanently; to keep ♦ *Is this football mine for keeps?*

keeper *noun* (*plural* **keepers**)
1 a person who looks after an animal, building, etc. ♦ *the park keeper.* **2** a goalkeeper or wicketkeeper.

keeping *noun*
care; looking after something ♦ *in safe keeping.*

keg *noun* (*plural* **kegs**)
a small barrel.

kelvin *noun* (*plural* **kelvins**)
the SI unit of thermodynamic temperature.

kennel *noun* (*plural* **kennels**)
a shelter for a dog.

kerb *noun* (*plural* **kerbs**)
the edge of a pavement.

kernel *noun* (*plural* **kernels**)
the part inside the shell of a nut etc.

ketchup *noun*
a thick sauce made from tomatoes and vinegar etc.
[probably from Chinese *k'e chap* = tomato juice]

kettle noun (plural **kettles**)
a container with a spout and handle, for boiling water in.

kettledrum noun (plural **kettledrums**)
a large drum shaped like a bowl.

key noun (plural **keys**)
1 a piece of metal shaped so that it will open a lock. 2 a device for winding up a clock or clockwork toy etc. 3 a small lever to be pressed by a finger, e.g. on a piano, typewriter, or computer. 4 a system of notes in music ♦ *the key of C major.* 5 a fact or clue that explains or solves something ♦ *the key to the mystery.*
6 a list of symbols used in a map or table, showing what they mean.

key verb (**keys, keying, keyed**)
key in type information into a computer using a keyboard.

keyboard noun (plural **keyboards**)
the set of keys on a piano, typewriter, computer, etc.

keyhole noun (plural **keyholes**)
the hole through which a key is put into a lock.

keyhole surgery noun
surgery carried out through a very small cut in the patient's body, using special instruments.

keypad noun (plural **keypads**)
a small keyboard or set of buttons used to operate a telephone, television, etc.

kg abbreviation
kilogram(s).

khaki noun
a dull yellowish-brown colour, used for military uniforms.
[from Urdu *khaki* = dust-coloured]

kibbutz noun (plural **kibbutzim**)
a commune in Israel, especially for farming.
[from Hebrew *qibbus* = gathering]

kick verb (**kicks, kicking, kicked**)
1 hit or move a person or thing with your foot.
2 move your legs about vigorously. 3 (said about a gun) recoil when fired.
kick off 1 start a football match. 2 (*informal*) start doing something. **kick out** get rid of; dismiss. **kick up** (*informal*) make a noise or fuss.

kick noun (plural **kicks**)
1 a kicking movement. 2 the recoiling movement of a gun. 3 (*informal*) a thrill.
4 (*informal*) an interest or activity ♦ *He's on a health kick.*

kick-off noun (plural **kick-offs**)
the start of a football match.

kid noun (plural **kids**)
1 (*informal*) a child. 2 a young goat.
3 fine leather made from goatskin.

kidnap verb (**kidnaps, kidnapping, kidnapped**)
take someone away by force, especially in order to obtain a ransom.
kidnapper noun

kidney noun (plural **kidneys**)
either of the two organs in the body that remove waste products from the blood and excrete urine into the bladder.

kill verb (**kills, killing, killed**)
1 make a person or thing die. 2 destroy or put an end to something.
killer noun
kill time occupy time idly while waiting.

killing noun (plural **killings**)
an act causing death.

kilo noun (plural **kilos**)
a kilogram.

kilogram noun (plural **kilograms**)
a unit of mass or weight equal to 1,000 grams (about 2.2 pounds).

kilometre (*say* kil-o-meet-er *or* kil-**om**-it-er) noun (plural **kilometres**)
a unit of length equal to 1,000 metres (about ⅗ of a mile).

kilowatt noun (plural **kilowatts**)
a unit of electrical power equal to 1,000 watts.

kilt noun (plural **kilts**)
a kind of pleated skirt worn especially by Scotsmen.
kilted adjective

kin plural noun
a person's family and relatives.

kind¹ noun (plural **kinds**)
a class of similar things or animals; a sort or type.
in kind (said about payment) made in goods or services and not in money. **kind of** (*informal*) in a way, to some extent ♦ *I felt kind of sorry for him.*

---

❶ USAGE Correct use is ♦ *this kind of thing* or ♦ *these kinds of things* (not 'these kind of things').

---

kind² adjective
friendly and helpful; considerate.
kind-hearted adjective **kindness** noun

kindergarten noun (plural **kindergartens**)
a school or class for very young children.

kindle verb (**kindles, kindling, kindled**)
1 start a flame; set light to something.
2 begin burning.

kinetic adjective
to do with or produced by movement ♦ *kinetic energy.*

king *noun* (*plural* **kings**)
1 a man who is the ruler of a country through inheriting the position. 2 a person or thing regarded as supreme ♦ *the lion is the king of beasts.* 3 the most important piece in chess. 4 a playing card with a picture of a king.
kingly *adjective* **kingship** *noun*
[from Old English]

kingdom *noun* (*plural* **kingdoms**)
1 a country ruled by a king or queen. 2 a major division of the natural world ♦ *the animal kingdom.*

kingfisher *noun* (*plural* **kingfishers**)
a small bird with blue feathers that dives to catch fish.

kink *noun* (*plural* **kinks**)
1 a short twist in a rope, wire, piece of hair, etc. 2 a peculiarity.

kinky *adjective*
involving peculiar sexual behaviour.

kiosk *noun* (*plural* **kiosks**)
1 a telephone box. 2 a small hut or stall where newspapers, sweets, etc. are sold.

kiss *noun* (*plural* **kisses**)
touching somebody with your lips as a sign of affection.

kiss *verb* (**kisses, kissing, kissed**)
give somebody a kiss.

kiss of life *noun*
blowing air from your mouth into another person's to help the other person to start breathing again, especially after an accident.

kit *noun* (*plural* **kits**)
1 equipment or clothes for a particular occupation. 2 a set of parts sold ready to be fitted together.

kitchen *noun* (*plural* **kitchens**)
a room in which meals are prepared and cooked.

kite *noun* (*plural* **kites**)
1 a light framework covered with cloth, paper, etc. and flown in the wind on the end of a long piece of string. 2 a large hawk.

kitten *noun* (*plural* **kittens**)
a very young cat.

kiwi *noun* (*plural* **kiwis**)
a New Zealand bird that cannot fly.
[from a Maori word]

kleptomania *noun*
an uncontrollable urge to steal things.
kleptomaniac *noun*

km *abbreviation*
kilometre(s).

knack *noun*
a special skill ♦ *There's a knack to putting up a deckchair.*

knapsack *noun* (*plural* **knapsacks**)
a bag carried on the back by soldiers, hikers, etc.

knave *noun* (*plural* **knaves**)
1 (*old use*) a dishonest man; a rogue. 2 a jack in playing cards.

knead *verb* (**kneads, kneading, kneaded**)
press and stretch something soft (especially dough) with your hands.

knee *noun* (*plural* **knees**)
the joint in the middle of the leg.

kneecap *noun* (*plural* **kneecaps**)
the small bone covering the front of the knee joint.

kneel *verb* (**kneels, kneeling, knelt**)
be or get yourself in a position on your knees.

knickers *plural noun*
underpants worn by women and girls.

knife *noun* (*plural* **knives**)
a cutting instrument consisting of a sharp blade set in a handle.

knight *noun* (*plural* **knights**)
1 a man who has been given the rank that allows him to put 'Sir' before his name. 2 (in the Middle Ages) a warrior of high social rank, usually mounted and in armour. 3 a piece in chess, with a horse's head.
knighthood *noun*

knit *verb* (**knits, knitting, knitted** or **knit**)
make something by looping together wool or other yarn, using long needles or a machine.
knitter *noun* **knitting needle** *noun*
knit your brow frown.

knob *noun* (*plural* **knobs**)
1 the round handle of a door, drawer, etc. 2 a round lump on something. 3 a round button or switch on a dial or machine. 4 a small round piece of something ♦ *a knob of butter.*
knobbly *adjective* **knobby** *adjective*

knock *verb* (**knocks, knocking, knocked**)
1 hit a thing hard or so as to make a noise. 2 produce by hitting ♦ *We need to knock a hole in the wall.* 3 (*informal*) criticize unfavourably ♦ *People are always knocking this country.*
knock off 1 (*informal*) stop working. 2 deduct something from a price. 3 (*informal*) steal.
knock out make a person unconscious, especially by a blow to the head.

knockout *noun* (*plural* **knockouts**)
1 knocking someone out. 2 a contest in which the loser in each round has to drop out. 3 (*informal*) an amazing person or thing.

knot *noun* (*plural* **knots**)
1 a place where a piece of string, rope, or ribbon etc. is twisted round itself or another piece. 2 a tangle or lump. 3 a round spot on a piece of wood where a branch joined it. 4 a cluster of people or things. 5 a unit for measuring the speed of ships and aircraft, equal to 2,025 yards (= 1,852 metres or 1 nautical mile) per hour.

knot *verb* (**knots, knotting, knotted**)
1 tie or fasten with a knot. 2 entangle.

know *verb* (**knows, knowing, knew, known**)
1 have something in your mind that you
have learned or discovered. 2 recognize or be
familiar with a person or place ♦ *I've known him
for years.* 3 understand ♦ *She knows how to
please us.*

knowing *adjective*
showing that you know something ♦ *a knowing
look.*

knowingly *adverb*
1 in a knowing way. 2 deliberately.

knowledge *noun*
1 knowing. 2 all that a person knows. 3 all that
is known.
to my knowledge as far as I know.

knowledgeable *adjective*
well-informed.
knowledgeably *adverb*

knuckle *noun* (*plural* **knuckles**)
a joint in the finger.

knuckle *verb* (**knuckles, knuckling, knuckled**)
knuckle down begin to work hard. **knuckle
under** yield or submit.

koala (*say* koh-**ah**-la) *noun* (*plural* **koalas**)
an Australian animal that looks like a small
bear.
[an Australian Aboriginal word]

Koran (*say* kor-**ahn**) *noun*
the sacred book of Islam, written in Arabic,
believed by Muslims to contain the words of
Allah revealed to the prophet Muhammad.

kosher *adjective*
keeping to Jewish laws about the preparation of
food ♦ *kosher meat.*

kw *abbreviation*
kilowatt(s).

label *noun* (*plural* **labels**)
a small piece of paper, cloth, or metal etc. fixed
on or beside something to show what it is or
what it costs, or its owner or destination, etc.
label *verb* (**labels, labelling, labelled**)
put a label on something.

laboratory *noun* (*plural* **laboratories**)
a room or building equipped for scientific
experiments.

laborious *adjective*
1 needing or using a lot of hard work.
2 explaining something at great length and with
obvious effort.
laboriously *adverb*

Labour *noun*
the Labour Party, a British political party formed
to represent the interests of working people.

labour *noun* (*plural* **labours**)
1 hard work. 2 a task. 3 working people.
4 the contractions of the womb when a baby is
being born.

labour *verb* (**labours, labouring, laboured**)
1 work hard. 2 explain or discuss something at
great length and with obvious effort ♦ *I will not
labour the point.*

labourer *noun* (*plural* **labourers**)
a person who does hard manual work, especially
outdoors.

laburnum *noun* (*plural* **laburnums**)
a tree with hanging yellow flowers.

labyrinth *noun* (*plural* **labyrinths**)
a complicated arrangement of passages or paths;
a maze.

lace *noun* (*plural* **laces**)
1 net-like material with decorative patterns of
holes in it. 2 a piece of thin cord or leather for
fastening a shoe etc.

lack *noun*
being without something.

lack *verb* (**lacks, lacking, lacked**)
be without something ♦ *He lacks courage.*

lacquer *noun*
a hard glossy varnish.
lacquered *adjective*

lacrosse *noun*
a game in which players use a stick with a net on
it (a **crosse**) to catch and throw a ball.

lacy *adjective*
made of lace or like lace.

lad *noun* (*plural* **lads**)
a boy or youth.

ladder *noun* (*plural* **ladders**)
1 two upright pieces of wood or metal etc. and
crosspieces (**rungs**), used for climbing up or
down. 2 a vertical ladder-like flaw in a stocking
etc. where a stitch has become undone.

ladle *noun* (*plural* **ladles**)
a large deep spoon with a long handle, used for
lifting and pouring liquids.

lady *noun* (*plural* **ladies**)
1 a well-mannered woman. 2 a woman of good
social position. 3 (in polite use) a woman.
ladylike *adjective* **ladyship** *noun*
Lady *noun* the title of a noblewoman.
[from Old English *hlaefdige* = person who
makes the bread (compare **lord**)]

ladybird noun (plural **ladybirds**)
a small flying beetle, usually red with black spots.

lag¹ verb (**lags, lagging, lagged**)
go too slowly and fail to keep up with others.

lag² verb (**lags, lagging, lagged**)
wrap pipes or boilers etc. in insulating material (**lagging**) to prevent loss of heat.

lager (say lah-ger) noun (plural **lagers**)
a light beer.

lagoon noun (plural **lagoons**)
a salt-water lake separated from the sea by sandbanks or reefs.

laid past tense of lay.

laid-back adjective
(informal) relaxed and calm.

lain past participle of lie².

lair noun (plural **lairs**)
a sheltered place where a wild animal lives.

lake noun (plural **lakes**)
a large area of water entirely surrounded by land.
[from Latin lacus = pool, lake]

lamb noun (plural **lambs**)
1 a young sheep. 2 meat from a lamb.
lambswool noun

lame adjective
1 unable to walk normally. 2 weak; not convincing ♦ a lame excuse.
lamely adverb **lameness** noun

lament noun (plural **laments**)
a statement, song, or poem expressing grief or regret.

lament verb (**laments, lamenting, lamented**)
express grief or regret about something.
lamentation noun

lamentable (say lam-in-ta-bul) adjective
regrettable or deplorable.

lamp noun (plural **lamps**)
a device for producing light from electricity, gas, or oil.
lamplight noun **lampshade** noun

lamp post noun (plural **lamp posts**)
a tall post in a street etc., with a lamp at the top.

lance noun (plural **lances**)
a long spear.

lance corporal noun (plural **lance corporals**)
a soldier ranking between a private and a corporal.

land noun (plural **lands**)
1 the part of the earth's surface not covered by sea. 2 the ground or soil; an area of country ♦ forest land. 3 the area occupied by a nation; a country.

land verb (**lands, landing, landed**)
1 arrive or put on land from a ship or aircraft etc. 2 reach the ground after jumping or falling. 3 bring a fish out of the water. 4 obtain ♦ She landed an excellent job. 5 arrive or cause to arrive at a certain place or position etc. ♦ They landed up in gaol. 6 present with a problem ♦ He landed me with this task.
[from Old English]

landing noun (plural **landings**)
1 the level area at the top of a flight of stairs. 2 bringing or coming to land ♦ The pilot made a smooth landing. 3 a place where people can get on and off a boat.

landing stage noun (plural **landing stages**)
a platform on which people and goods are taken on and off a boat.

landlady noun (plural **landladies**)
1 a woman who lets rooms to lodgers. 2 a woman who runs a pub.

landlord noun (plural **landlords**)
1 a person who lets a house, room, or land to a tenant. 2 a person who runs a pub.

landmark noun (plural **landmarks**)
1 an object that is easily seen in a landscape. 2 an important event in the history or development of something.

landmine noun (plural **landmines**)
an explosive mine laid on or just under the surface of the ground.

landowner noun (plural **landowners**)
a person who owns a large amount of land.

landscape noun (plural **landscapes**)
1 a view of a particular area of countryside or town. 2 a picture of the countryside.

landslide noun (plural **landslides**)
1 a huge mass of soil and rocks sliding down a slope. 2 an overwhelming victory in an election ♦ She won the general election by a landslide.

lane noun (plural **lanes**)
1 a narrow road, especially in the country. 2 a strip of road for a single line of traffic. 3 a strip of track or water for one runner, swimmer, etc. in a race.

language noun (plural **languages**)
1 words and their use. 2 the words used in a particular country or by a particular group of people. 3 a system of signs or symbols giving information, especially in computing.

languid adjective
slow because of tiredness, weakness, or laziness.
languidly adverb **languor** noun

languish verb (**languishes, languishing, languished**)
1 live in miserable conditions; be neglected ♦ He has been languishing in prison for three years. 2 become weak or listless.

lank *adjective*
(said about hair) long and limp.

lanky *adjective* (**lankier, lankiest**)
awkwardly thin and tall.
lankiness *noun*

lantern *noun* (*plural* **lanterns**)
a transparent case for holding a light and
shielding it from the wind.

lap¹ *noun* (*plural* **laps**)
1 the level place formed by the front of the legs
above the knees when a person is sitting down.
2 going once round a racecourse. **3** one section
of a journey ♦ *the last lap.*
lap *verb* (**laps, lapping, lapped**)
overtake another competitor in a race to become
one or more laps ahead.

lap² *verb* (**laps, lapping, lapped**)
1 take up liquid by moving the tongue, as a cat
does. **2** make a gentle splash against something
♦ *Waves lapped the shore.*

lapel (*say* la-**pel**) *noun* (*plural* **lapels**)
a flap folded back at the front edge of a coat or
jacket.

lapse *noun* (*plural* **lapses**)
1 a slight mistake or failure ♦ *a lapse of memory.*
2 an amount of time elapsed ♦ *after a lapse of six
months.*
lapse *verb* (**lapses, lapsing, lapsed**)
1 pass or slip gradually ♦ *He lapsed into
unconsciousness.* **2** be no longer valid, through
not being renewed ♦ *My insurance policy has
lapsed.*

laptop *noun* (*plural* **laptops**)
a portable computer for use while travelling.

larch *noun* (*plural* **larches**)
a tall deciduous tree that bears small cones.

lard *noun*
a white greasy substance prepared from pig fat
and used in cooking.

larder *noun* (*plural* **larders**)
a cupboard or small room for storing food.

large *adjective*
of more than the ordinary or average size; big.
largeness *noun*
at large **1** free to roam about, not captured
♦ *The escaped prisoners are still at large.*
2 in general, as a whole ♦ *She is respected by the
country at large.*
[from Latin *largus* = abundant or generous]

largely *adverb*
to a great extent ♦ *You are largely responsible for
the accident.*

lark¹ *noun* (*plural* **larks**)
a small sandy-brown bird; the skylark.

lark² *noun* (*plural* **larks**) (*informal*)
something amusing; a bit of fun ♦ *We did it for
a lark.*

larva *noun* (*plural* **larvae**)
an insect in the first stage of its life, after it comes
out of the egg.
larval *adjective*
[from Latin, = ghost or mask]

laser *noun* (*plural* **lasers**)
a device that makes a very strong narrow beam
of light or other electromagnetic radiation.
[from the initials of 'light amplification by
stimulated emission of radiation']

lash *noun* (*plural* **lashes**)
1 a stroke with a whip or stick. **2** the cord or
cord-like part of a whip. **3** an eyelash.
lash *verb* (**lashes, lashing, lashed**)
1 strike with a whip; beat violently. **2** tie with
cord etc. ♦ *Lash the sticks together.*
lash down (said about rain) pour or beat down
forcefully. **lash out** **1** speak or hit out angrily.
2 spend money extravagantly.

lass *noun* (*plural* **lasses**)
a girl or young woman.
lassie *noun*

lasso *noun* (*plural* **lassoes** or **lassos**)
a rope with a sliding noose at the end, used for
catching cattle etc.
[via Spanish *lazo* from Latin *laqueus* = noose]

last¹ *adjective* & *adverb*
1 coming after all others; final. **2** latest; most
recent ♦ *last night.* **3** least likely ♦ *She is the last
person I'd have chosen.*
the last straw a final thing that makes problems
unbearable.
last *noun*
1 a person or thing that is last. **2** the end
♦ *He was brave to the last.*
at last or **at long last** finally; after much delay.

last² *verb* (**lasts, lasting, lasted**)
1 continue; go on existing or living or being
usable. **2** be enough for ♦ *The food will last us
for three days.*

lasting *adjective*
able to last for a long time ♦ *a lasting peace.*

lastly *adverb*
in the last place; finally.

latch *noun* (*plural* **latches**)
a small bar fastening a door or gate, lifted by a
lever or spring.
latchkey *noun*
latch *verb* (**latches, latching, latched**)
fasten with a latch.
latch onto **1** meet someone and follow them
around all the time. **2** understand something.

late *adjective* & *adverb*
1 after the usual or expected time. **2** near the end
♦ *late in the afternoon.* **3** recent ♦ *the latest
news.* **4** who has died recently ♦ *the late king.*
of late recently.

lately *adverb*
recently.

latent heat *noun*
the heat needed to change a solid into a liquid or vapour, or a liquid into a vapour, without a change in temperature.

lathe (*say* layth) *noun* (*plural* **lathes**)
a machine for holding and turning pieces of wood while they are being shaped.

lather *noun*
a mass of froth.

lather *verb* (**lathers, lathering, lathered**)
1 cover with lather. **2** form a lather.

Latin *noun*
the language of the ancient Romans.

Latin America *noun*
the parts of Central and South America where the main language is Spanish or Portuguese.

latitude *noun* (*plural* **latitudes**)
1 the distance of a place from the equator, measured in degrees. **2** freedom from restrictions on what people can do or believe.

latrine (*say* la-**treen**) *noun* (*plural* **latrines**)
a lavatory in a camp or barracks etc.

latter *adjective*
later ♦ *the latter part of the year.*
the latter the second of two people or things just mentioned. (Compare **former**.)

lattice *noun* (*plural* **lattices**)
a framework of crossed laths or bars with spaces between.

laudable *adjective*
deserving praise.
laudably *adverb*

laugh *verb* (**laughs, laughing, laughed**)
make the sounds that show you are happy or think something is funny.

laugh *noun* (*plural* **laughs**)
the sound of laughing.

laughable *adjective*
deserving to be laughed at.

laughing stock *noun* (*plural* **laughing stocks**)
a person or thing that is the object of ridicule and scorn.

laughter *noun*
the act, sound, or manner of laughing.

launch[1] *verb* (**launches, launching, launched**)
1 send a ship from the land into the water.
2 send a rocket etc. into space. **3** set a thing moving by throwing or pushing it. **4** make a new product available for the first time ♦ *Our new model will be launched in April.* **5** start into action ♦ *launch an attack.*

launch[2] *noun* (*plural* **launches**)
a large motor boat.

launderette *noun* (*plural* **launderettes**)
a place fitted with washing machines that people pay to use.

laundry *noun* (*plural* **laundries**)
1 a place where clothes etc. are washed and ironed for customers. **2** clothes etc. needing to be washed or after being washed.

laureate (*say* **lorri**-at) *adjective*
Poet Laureate a person appointed to write poems for national occasions.

laurel *noun* (*plural* **laurels**)
an evergreen shrub with smooth shiny leaves.

lava *noun*
molten rock that flows from a volcano; the solid rock formed when it cools.

lavatory *noun* (*plural* **lavatories**)
1 a toilet. **2** a room containing a toilet.

lavender *noun*
1 a shrub with sweet-smelling purple flowers.
2 a light-purple colour.

lavish *adjective*
1 generous. **2** plentiful.
lavishly *adverb* **lavishness** *noun*

law *noun* (*plural* **laws**)
1 a rule or set of rules that everyone must obey.
2 the profession of lawyers. **3** (*informal*) the police. **4** a scientific statement of something that always happens ♦ *the law of gravity.*

law-abiding *adjective*
obeying the law.

lawcourt *noun* (*plural* **lawcourts**)
a room or building in which a judge or magistrate hears evidence and decides whether someone has broken the law.

lawful *adjective*
allowed or accepted by the law.
lawfully *adverb*

lawless *adjective*
1 not obeying the law. **2** without proper laws ♦ *a lawless country.*
lawlessly *adverb* **lawlessness** *noun*

lawn *noun* (*plural* **lawns**)
an area of closely cut grass in a garden or park.

lawnmower *noun* (*plural* **lawnmowers**)
a machine for cutting the grass of lawns.

lawn tennis *noun*
tennis played on an outdoor grass or hard court.

lawsuit *noun* (*plural* **lawsuits**)
a dispute or claim that is brought to a lawcourt to be settled.

lawyer *noun* (*plural* **lawyers**)
a person who is qualified to give advice in matters of law.

laxative *noun* (*plural* **laxatives**)
a medicine that stimulates the bowels to empty.

lay¹ *verb* (**lays, laying, laid**)
1 put something down in a particular place or way. **2** arrange things, especially for a meal ♦ *Can you lay the table?* **3** place ♦ *He laid the blame on his sister.* **4** form or prepare ♦ *We laid our plans.* **5** produce an egg.
lay off 1 stop employing somebody for a while. **2** (*informal*) stop doing something. **lay on** supply or provide. **lay out 1** arrange or prepare. **2** (*informal*) knock a person unconscious. **3** prepare a corpse for burial.

---

❶ USAGE Do not confuse *lay/laid/laying* = 'put down', with *lie/lay/lain/lying* = 'be in a flat position'. Correct uses are as follows: ♦ *Go and lie down;* ♦ *she went and lay down;* ♦ *please lay it on the floor.* 'Go and lay down' is incorrect.

---

lay² *past tense* of **lie².**

lay³ *adjective*
1 not belonging to the clergy ♦ *a lay preacher.* **2** not professionally qualified ♦ *a lay magistrate.*

lay-by *noun* (*plural* **lay-bys**)
a place where vehicles can stop beside a main road.

layer *noun* (*plural* **layers**)
a single thickness or coating.

layman *noun* (*plural* **laymen**)
1 a person who does not have specialized knowledge or training (e.g. as a doctor or lawyer). **2** a person who is not ordained as a member of the clergy.

layout *noun* (*plural* **layouts**)
an arrangement of parts of something according to a plan.

lazy *adjective* (**lazier, laziest**)
not wanting to work; doing little work.
lazily *adverb* **laziness** *noun*

lead¹ (*say* leed) *verb* (**leads, leading, led**)
1 take or guide someone, especially by going in front. **2** be winning in a race or contest etc.; be ahead. **3** be in charge of a group of people. **4** be a way or route ♦ *This path leads to the beach.* **5** play the first card in a card game. **6** live or experience ♦ *He leads a dull life.*
lead to result in; cause.

lead (*say* leed) *noun* (*plural* **leads**)
1 a leading place or part or position ♦ *She took the lead on the final bend.* **2** guidance or example ♦ *We should be taking a lead on this issue.* **3** a clue to be followed. **4** a strap or cord for leading a dog or other animal. **5** an electrical wire attached to something.

lead² (*say* led) *noun* (*plural* **leads**)
1 a soft heavy grey metal. **2** the writing substance (graphite) in a pencil.
lead *adjective*

leader *noun* (*plural* **leaders**)
1 the person in charge of a group of people; a chief. **2** the person who is winning. **3** a newspaper article giving the editor's opinion.
leadership *noun*

leaf *noun* (*plural* **leaves**)
1 a flat, usually green, part of a plant, growing out from its stem, branch, or root. **2** the paper forming one page of a book. **3** a very thin sheet of metal *gold leaf.* **4** a flap that makes a table larger.
leafy *adjective* **leafless** *adjective*
turn over a new leaf make a fresh start and improve your behaviour.

leaflet *noun* (*plural* **leaflets**)
a piece of paper printed with information.

league¹ *noun* (*plural* **leagues**)
1 a group of teams who compete against each other for a championship. **2** a group of people or nations who agree to work together.
in league with working or plotting together.

league² *noun* (*plural* **leagues**)
an old measure of distance, about 3 miles.

leak *noun* (*plural* **leaks**)
1 a hole or crack etc. through which liquid or gas accidentally escapes. **2** the revealing of secret information.
leaky *adjective*

leak *verb* (**leaks, leaking, leaked**)
1 get out or let out through a leak. **2** reveal secret information.
leakage *noun*

lean¹ *adjective*
1 with little or no fat ♦ *lean meat.* **2** thin ♦ *a lean body.*

lean² *verb* (**leans, leaning, leaned** or **leant**)
1 bend your body towards or over something. **2** put or be in a sloping position. **3** rest against something. **4** rely or depend on someone for help.

leaning *noun* (*plural* **leanings**)
a tendency or preference.

leap *verb* (**leaps, leaping, leaped** or **leapt**)
jump vigorously.
leap *noun*

leapfrog *noun*
a game in which each player jumps with legs apart over another who is bending down.

leap year *noun* (*plural* **leap years**)
a year with an extra day in it (29 February).

learn *verb* (**learns, learning, learned** or **learnt**)
1 get knowledge or skill through study or training. **2** find out about something.

---

❶ USAGE It is not acceptable in standard English to use *learn* to mean 'to teach'.

---

learned (*say* ler-nid) *adjective*
having much knowledge obtained by study.

learner noun (plural **learners**)
a person who is learning something, especially to drive a car.

learning noun
knowledge obtained by study.

lease noun (plural **leases**)
an agreement to allow someone to use a building or land etc. for a fixed period in return for payment.
leaseholder noun
a new lease of life a chance to be healthy, active, or usable again.

lease verb (leases, leasing, leased)
allow or obtain the use of something by lease.

leash noun (plural **leashes**)
a dog's lead.

least adjective & adverb
very small in amount etc. ♦ the least bit;
♦ the least expensive bike.
at least 1 not less than what is mentioned
♦ It will cost at least £40. 2 anyway ♦ He's at home, or at least I think he is.

leather noun
material made from animal skins.
leathery adjective

leave verb (leaves, leaving, left)
1 go away from a person or place.
2 stop belonging to a group or stop working somewhere. 3 cause or allow something to stay where it is or as it is ♦ You left the door open.
4 go away without taking something ♦ I left my book at home. 5 let someone deal with something ♦ Leave the washing-up to me.
6 put something to be collected or passed on
♦ Would you like to leave a message?
leave off cease. leave out omit; not include.

leave noun
1 permission. 2 official permission to be away from work; the time for which this permission lasts ♦ three days' leave.
[from Old English]

lecture noun (plural **lectures**)
1 a talk about a subject to an audience or a class.
2 a long serious warning or reprimand given to someone.

lecture verb (lectures, lecturing, lectured)
give a lecture.
lecturer noun
[from Latin lectura = reading, or something to be read]

led past tense of **lead**¹.

ledge noun (plural **ledges**)
a narrow shelf ♦ a window ledge; ♦ a mountain ledge.

ledger noun (plural **ledgers**)
an account book.
[probably from Dutch]

leech noun (plural **leeches**)
a small blood-sucking worm that lives in water.

leek noun (plural **leeks**)
a long green and white vegetable of the onion family.

leer verb (leers, leering, leered)
look at someone in a sly or unpleasant way.
leer noun

leeway noun
1 extra space or time available. 2 a drift to leeward or off course.
make up leeway make up lost time; regain a lost position.

left¹ adjective & adverb
1 on or towards the west if you think of yourself as facing north. 2 (said about political groups) in favour of socialist or radical views.
left-hand adjective

left noun
the left-hand side or part etc.
[from Old English lyft = weak]

left² past tense of **leave**.

left-handed adjective
using the left hand in preference to the right hand.

leg noun (plural **legs**)
1 one of the limbs on a person's or animal's body, on which it stands or moves. 2 the part of a piece of clothing covering a leg. 3 each of the supports of a chair or other piece of furniture.
4 one part of a journey. 5 one of a pair of matches between the same teams.
[from Old Norse]

legacy noun (plural **legacies**)
1 something left to a person in a will.
2 something that results from what people have done in the past ♦ a legacy of distrust.

legal adjective
1 lawful. 2 to do with the law or lawyers.
legally adverb **legality** noun

legend noun (plural **legends**)
1 an old story handed down from the past, which may or may not be true. (Compare **myth**.)
2 a very famous person.
legendary adjective
[from Latin legenda = things to be read]

legible adjective
clear enough to read.
legibly adverb **legibility** noun
[from Latin legere = to read]

legion noun (plural **legions**)
1 a division of the ancient Roman army.
2 a group of soldiers or former soldiers.

legislate verb (legislates, legislating, legislated)
make laws.
legislation noun **legislator** noun

legitimate *adjective*
1 lawful. 2 born when parents are married to each other.
legitimately *adverb* **legitimacy** *noun*

leisure *noun*
time that is free from work, when you can do what you like.
leisured *adjective* **leisurely** *adjective*
at leisure having leisure; not hurried. **at your leisure** when you have time.

lemming *noun* (*plural* **lemmings**)
a small mouse-like animal of Arctic regions that migrates in large numbers and is said to run headlong into the sea and drown.

lemon *noun* (*plural* **lemons**)
1 an oval yellow citrus fruit with a sour taste.
2 a pale yellow colour.

lemonade *noun*
a lemon-flavoured drink.

lemur (*say* lee-mer) *noun* (*plural* **lemurs**)
a monkey-like animal.

lend *verb* (**lends, lending, lent**)
1 allow a person to use something of yours for a short time. 2 provide someone with money that they must repay, usually in return for payments (called **interest**). 3 give or add a quality ♦ *She lent dignity to the occasion.*
lender *noun*
lend a hand help somebody.

---

❶ USAGE Do not use *lend* to mean *borrow*.

---

length *noun* (*plural* **lengths**)
1 how long something is. 2 a piece of cloth, rope, wire, etc. cut from a larger piece. 3 the distance of a swimming pool from one end to the other.
4 the amount of thoroughness in an action ♦ *They went to great lengths to make us comfortable.*
at length 1 after a long time. 2 taking a long time; in detail.

lengthen *verb* (**lengthens, lengthening, lengthened**)
make or become longer.

lengthy *adjective*
going on for a long time.
lengthily *adverb*

lenient (*say* lee-nee-ent) *adjective*
merciful; not severe.
leniently *adverb* **lenience** *noun*

lens *noun* (*plural* **lenses**)
1 a curved piece of glass or plastic used to focus things. 2 the transparent part of the eye, immediately behind the pupil.
[Latin, = lentil (because of its shape)]

Lent *noun*
a time of fasting and penitence observed by Christians for about six weeks before Easter.
Lenten *adjective*
[from Old English *lencten* = the spring]

lent *past tense* of **lend**.

lentil *noun* (*plural* **lentils**)
a kind of small bean.

leopard (*say* lep-erd) *noun* (*plural* **leopards**)
a large spotted mammal of the cat family, also called a panther.
leopardess *noun*

leper *noun* (*plural* **lepers**)
a person who has leprosy.

leprosy *noun*
an infectious disease that makes parts of the body waste away.
leprous *adjective*

lesbian *noun* (*plural* **lesbians**)
a homosexual woman.
[named after the Greek island of Lesbos (because Sappho, a poetess who lived there about 600BC, wrote poetry about love between women)]

less *adjective* & *adverb*
smaller in amount; not so much ♦ *Make less noise.* ♦ *It is less important.*

---

❶ USAGE Do not use *less* when you mean *fewer*. You should use *fewer* when you are talking about a number of individual things, and *less* when you are talking about a quantity or mass of something: ♦ *The less batter you make, the fewer pancakes you'll get.*

---

less *noun*
a smaller amount.

less *preposition*
minus; deducting ♦ *She earned £100, less tax.*

-less *suffix*
forms adjectives meaning 'without' (e.g. *colourless*) or 'unable to be ...' (e.g. *countless*).

lesser *adjective*
not so great as the other ♦ *the lesser evil.*

lesson *noun* (*plural* **lessons**)
1 an amount of teaching given at one time. 2 something to be learnt by a pupil.
3 an example or experience from which you should learn ♦ *Let this be a lesson to you!*
4 a passage from the Bible read aloud as part of a church service.

lest *conjunction* (*old use*)
so that something should not happen ♦ *Remind us, lest we forget.*

let *verb* (**lets, letting, let**)
1 allow somebody or something to do something; not prevent or forbid ♦ *Let me see it.* 2 cause to ♦ *Let us know what happens.* 3 allow or cause to come or go or pass ♦ *Let me out!* 4 allow someone to use a house or building etc. in return for payment (**rent**). 5 leave ♦ *Let it alone.*
let down 1 deflate. 2 disappoint somebody. **let off** 1 cause to explode. 2 excuse somebody from a duty or punishment etc. **let on** (*informal*) reveal a secret. **let up** (*informal*) relax.
let-up *noun*

lethal (*say* **lee**-thal) *adjective*
deadly; causing death.
lethally *adverb*

lethargy (*say* **leth**-er-jee) *noun*
extreme lack of energy or vitality.
lethargic (*say* lith-**ar**-jik) *adjective*

letter *noun* (*plural* **letters**)
1 a symbol representing a sound used in speech. 2 a written message, usually sent by post.
to the letter paying strict attention to every detail.

letter box *noun* (*plural* **letter boxes**)
1 a slot in a door, through which letters are delivered. 2 a postbox.

lettering *noun*
letters drawn or painted.

lettuce *noun* (*plural* **lettuces**)
a garden plant with broad crisp leaves used in salads.

leukaemia (*say* lew-**kee**-mee-a) *noun*
a disease in which there are too many white corpuscles in the blood.
[from Greek *leukos* = white + *haima* = blood]

level *adjective*
1 flat or horizontal. 2 at the same height or position as something else.

level *noun* (*plural* **levels**)
1 height, depth, position, or value etc. ♦ *Fix the shelves at eye level.* 2 a level surface. 3 a device that shows whether something is level.
on the level (*informal*) honest.

level *verb* (**levels, levelling, levelled**)
1 make or become level. 2 aim a gun or missile. 3 direct an accusation at a person.

level crossing *noun* (*plural* **level crossings**)
a place where a road crosses a railway at the same level.

lever *noun* (*plural* **levers**)
1 a bar that turns on a fixed point (the **fulcrum**) in order to lift something or force something open. 2 a bar used as a handle to operate machinery etc. ♦ *a gear lever.*

lever *verb* (**levers, levering, levered**)
lift or move something by means of a lever.

leverage *noun*
1 the force you need when you use a lever. 2 influence.

levity *noun*
being humorous, especially at an unsuitable time.

levy *verb* (**levies, levying, levied**)
impose or collect a tax or other payment by the use of authority or force.

levy *noun* (*plural* **levies**)
an amount of money paid in tax.

liability *noun* (*plural* **liabilities**)
1 being legally responsible for something. 2 a debt or obligation. 3 a disadvantage or handicap.

liable *adjective*
1 likely to do or suffer something ♦ *She is liable to colds.* ♦ *The cliff is liable to crumble.* 2 legally responsible for something.

liaison (*say* lee-**ay**-zon) *noun* (*plural* **liaisons**)
1 communication and cooperation between people or groups. 2 a person who is a link or go-between. 3 a sexual affair.

liar *noun* (*plural* **liars**)
a person who tells lies.

libel (*say* **ly**-bel) *noun* (*plural* **libels**)
an untrue written, printed, or broadcast statement that damages a person's reputation. (Compare **slander**.)
libellous *adjective*

libel *verb* (**libels, libelling, libelled**)
make a libel against someone.

liberal *adjective*
1 giving generously. 2 given in large amounts. 3 not strict; tolerant.
liberally *adverb* **liberality** *noun*

Liberal Democrat *noun* (*plural* **Liberal Democrats**)
a member of the Liberal Democrat political party.

liberate *verb* (**liberates, liberating, liberated**)
set free.
liberation *noun* **liberator** *noun*

liberty *noun* (*plural* **liberties**)
freedom.
take liberties behave too casually or in too familiar a way.

librarian *noun* (*plural* **librarians**)
a person in charge of or working in a library.
librarianship *noun*

library (*say* **ly**-bra-ree) *noun* (*plural* **libraries**)
1 a place where books are kept for people to use or borrow. 2 a collection of books, records, films, etc.

lice *plural* of **louse**.

licence *noun* (*plural* **licences**)
1 an official permit to do or use or own something ♦ *a driving licence.* 2 special freedom to avoid the usual rules or customs.

license *verb* (**licenses, licensing, licensed**)
give a licence to a person; authorize ♦ *We are licensed to sell tobacco.*

lichen (*say* **ly**-ken or **lich**-en) *noun* (*plural* **lichens**)
a dry-looking plant that grows on rocks, walls, trees, etc.

lick *verb* (**licks, licking, licked**)
1 move your tongue over something. **2** (said about a wave or flame) move like a tongue; touch lightly. **3** (*slang*) defeat.
a lick of paint a light covering of paint. **at a lick** (*informal*) at a fast pace.

lid *noun* (*plural* **lids**)
1 a cover for a box or pot etc. **2** an eyelid.

lie¹ *noun* (*plural* **lies**)
a statement that the person who makes it knows to be untrue.

lie *verb* (**lies, lying, lied**)
tell a lie or lies; be deceptive.

lie² *verb* (**lies, lying, lay, lain**)
1 be or get in a flat or resting position ♦ *He lay on the grass.* ♦ *The cat has lain here all night.* **2** be or remain ♦ *The island lies near the coast.* ♦ *The machinery lay idle.*
lie low keep yourself hidden.

---

❶ USAGE See the note at **lay¹**.

---

lieutenant (*say* lef-**ten**-ant) *noun* (*plural* **lieutenants**)
1 an officer in the army or navy. **2** a deputy or chief assistant.

life *noun* (*plural* **lives**)
1 the period between birth and death.
2 being alive and able to function and grow.
3 living things ♦ *Is there life on Mars?*
4 liveliness ♦ *full of life.* **5** a biography.
6 the length of time that something exists or functions ♦ *The battery has a life of two years.*

lifebelt *noun* (*plural* **lifebelts**)
a ring of material that will float, used to support someone's body in water.

lifeboat *noun* (*plural* **lifeboats**)
a boat for rescuing people at sea.

life cycle *noun* (*plural* **life cycles**)
the series of changes in the life of a living thing.

lifeguard *noun* (*plural* **lifeguards**)
someone whose job is to rescue swimmers who are in difficulty.

life insurance *noun*
insurance that pays out a sum of money when the insured person dies.

life jacket *noun* (*plural* **life jackets**)
a jacket of material that will float, used to support someone's body in water.

lifeless *adjective*
1 without life. **2** unconscious.
lifelessly *adverb*

lifelike *adjective*
looking exactly like a real person or thing.

lifestyle *noun* (*plural* **lifestyles**)
the way of life of a person or a group of people.

lifetime *noun* (*plural* **lifetimes**)
the time for which someone is alive.

lift *verb* (**lifts, lifting, lifted**)
1 raise or pick up something. **2** rise or go upwards. **3** remove or abolish something ♦ *The ban has been lifted.* **4** (*informal*) steal.

lift *noun* (*plural* **lifts**)
1 lifting. **2** a device for taking people or goods from one floor or level to another in a building. **3** a free ride in somebody else's vehicle ♦ *Can you give me a lift to the station?*
[from Old Norse]

ligament *noun* (*plural* **ligaments**)
a piece of the tough flexible tissue that holds your bones together.
[from Latin *ligare* = bind]

light¹ *noun* (*plural* **lights**)
1 radiation that stimulates the sense of sight and makes things visible. **2** something that provides light, especially an electric lamp. **3** a flame.
bring or **come to light** make or become known.

light *adjective*
1 full of light; not dark. **2** pale ♦ *light blue.*

light *verb* (**lights, lighting, lit** or **lighted**)
1 start a thing burning; begin to burn. **2** provide light for something.
light up 1 put lights on, especially at dusk.
2 make or become light or bright.

---

❶ USAGE Say ♦ *He lit the lamps*; ♦ *the lamps were lit* (not 'lighted'), but ♦ *She carried a lighted torch* (not 'a lit torch').

---

light² *adjective*
1 having little weight; not heavy. **2** small in amount or force etc. ♦ *light rain*; ♦ *a light punishment.* **3** needing little effort ♦ *light work.* **4** cheerful, not sad ♦ *with a light heart.* **5** not serious or profound ♦ *light music.*
lightly *adverb* **lightness** *noun*

light *adverb*
lightly; with only a small load ♦ *We were travelling light.*
[from Old English *liht*]

lighten¹ *verb* (**lightens, lightening, lightened**)
make or become lighter or brighter.

lighten² *verb* (**lightens, lightening, lightened**)
make or become lighter or less heavy.

light-hearted *adjective*
1 cheerful and free from worry. **2** not serious.

lighthouse *noun* (*plural* **lighthouses**)
a tower with a bright light at the top to guide or warn ships.

lightning *noun*
a flash of bright light produced by natural electricity during a thunderstorm.
like lightning with very great speed.

lightning conductor *noun* (*plural* **lightning conductors**)
a metal rod or wire fixed on a building to divert lightning into the earth.

light year *noun* (*plural* **light years**)
the distance that light travels in one year (about 9.5 million million km).

like¹ *verb* (**likes, liking, liked**)
1 think a person or thing is pleasant or satisfactory. 2 wish ♦ *I'd like to come.*

like² *adjective*
similar; having some or all of the qualities of another person or thing ♦ *They are as like as two peas.*

like *noun*
a similar person or thing ♦ *We shall not see his like again.*

like *preposition*
1 similar to; in the manner of ♦ *He swims like a fish.* 2 in a suitable state for ♦ *It looks like rain.*
♦ *I feel like a cup of tea.*

likelihood *noun*
being likely; probability.

likely *adjective* (**likelier, likeliest**)
1 probable; expected to happen or be true etc.
♦ *Rain is likely.* 2 expected to be suitable or successful ♦ *a likely spot.*

liken *verb* (**likens, likening, likened**)
compare ♦ *He likened the human heart to a pump.*

likeness *noun* (*plural* **likenesses**)
1 a similarity in appearance; a resemblance.
2 a portrait.

liking *noun*
a feeling that you like something ♦ *She has a liking for ice cream.*

lilac *noun*
1 a bush with fragrant purple or white flowers.
2 pale purple.

lilt *noun* (*plural* **lilts**)
a light pleasant rhythm in a voice or tune.
lilting *adjective*

lily *noun* (*plural* **lilies**)
a garden plant with trumpet-shaped flowers, growing from a bulb.

limb *noun* (*plural* **limbs**)
1 a leg, arm, or wing. 2 a large branch of a tree.
out on a limb isolated; without any support.

limber *verb* (**limbers, limbering, limbered**)
limber up do exercises in preparation for an athletic activity.

lime¹ *noun*
a white chalky substance (calcium oxide) used in making cement and as a fertilizer.

lime² *noun* (*plural* **limes**)
1 a green fruit like a small round lemon.
2 a drink made from the juice of this fruit.

lime³ *noun* (*plural* **limes**)
a tree with yellow flowers.

limelight *noun*
in the limelight receiving a lot of publicity and attention.

limerick *noun* (*plural* **limericks**)
a type of amusing poem with five lines.
[named after Limerick, a town in Ireland, possibly because people sang `will you come up to Limerick' as a refrain]

limestone *noun*
a kind of rock from which lime (calcium oxide) is obtained.

limit *noun* (*plural* **limits**)
1 a line, point, or level where something ends.
2 the greatest amount allowed ♦ *the speed limit.*

limit *verb* (**limits, limiting, limited**)
1 keep something within certain limits.
2 be a limit to something.
limitation *noun*

limited company *noun* (*plural* **limited companies**)
a business company whose shareholders would have to pay only some of its debts if it went bankrupt.

limp¹ *verb* (**limps, limping, limped**)
walk lamely.

limp *noun* (*plural* **limps**)
a limping walk.

limp² *adjective*
1 not stiff or firm. 2 without strength or energy.
limply *adverb* **limpness** *noun*

limpet *noun* (*plural* **limpets**)
a small shellfish that attaches itself firmly to rocks.

line¹ *noun* (*plural* **lines**)
1 a long thin mark. 2 a row or series of people or things; a row of words. 3 a length of rope, string, wire, etc. used for a special purpose
♦ *a fishing line.* 4 a railway; a line of railway track. 5 a company operating a transport service of ships, aircraft, or buses. 6 a way of doing things or behaving; a type of business.
7 a telephone connection.
in line 1 forming a straight line. 2 conforming.

line *verb* (**lines, lining, lined**)
1 mark something with lines ♦ *Use lined paper.*
2 form something into a line or lines ♦ *Line them up.*

line² *verb* (**lines, lining, lined**)
cover the inside of something.

lineage (*say* lin-ee-ij) *noun* (*plural* **lineages**)
ancestry; a line of descendants from an ancestor.

linear (*say* lin-ee-er) *adjective*
1 arranged in a line. 2 to do with a line or length.

linen *noun*
1 cloth made from flax. **2** shirts, sheets, and tablecloths etc. (which were formerly made of linen).

liner *noun* (*plural* **liners**)
a large passenger ship.

linger *verb* (**lingers, lingering, lingered**)
stay for a long time, as if unwilling to leave; be slow to leave.

lingerie (*say* **lan**-zher-ee) *noun*
women's underwear.

linguistics *noun*
the study of languages.
linguistic *adjective*

lining *noun* (*plural* **linings**)
a layer that covers the inside of something.

link *noun* (*plural* **links**)
1 one of the rings or loops of a chain. **2** a connection or relationship.
link *verb* (**links, linking, linked**)
join things together; connect.
linkage *noun*

links *plural noun*
a golf course, especially one near the sea.

linoleum *noun*
a stiff shiny floor covering.

linseed *noun*
the seed of flax, from which oil is obtained.

lint *noun*
a soft material for covering wounds.

lion *noun* (*plural* **lions**)
a large strong flesh-eating animal of the cat family found in Africa and India.
lioness *noun*

lip *noun* (*plural* **lips**)
1 either of the two fleshy edges of the mouth. **2** the edge of something hollow, such as a cup or crater. **3** the pointed part at the top of a jug etc., from which you pour things.

lip-read *verb* (**lip-reads, lip-reading, lip-read**)
understand what a person says by watching the movements of their lips, not by hearing.

lipstick *noun* (*plural* **lipsticks**)
a stick of a waxy substance for colouring the lips.

liqueur (*say* lik-**yoor**) *noun* (*plural* **liqueurs**)
a strong sweet alcoholic drink.

liquid *noun* (*plural* **liquids**)
a substance like water or oil that flows freely but (unlike a gas) has a constant volume.
liquid *adjective*
1 in the form of a liquid; flowing freely. **2** easily converted into cash ♦ *the firm's liquid assets.*
liquidity *noun*

liquor *noun*
1 alcoholic drink. **2** juice produced in cooking; liquid in which food has been cooked.

liquorice (*say* **lick**-er-ish) *noun*
1 a black substance used in medicine and as a sweet. **2** the plant from whose root this substance is obtained.

lisp *noun* (*plural* **lisps**)
a fault in speech in which *s* and *z* are pronounced like *th*.
lisp *verb*

list *noun* (*plural* **lists**)
a number of names, items, or figures etc. written or printed one after another.
list *verb* (**lists, listing, listed**)
make a list of people or things.

listen *verb* (**listens, listening, listened**)
pay attention in order to hear something.
listener *noun*

listless *adjective*
too tired to be active or enthusiastic.
listlessly *adverb* **listlessness** *noun*

lit *past tense* of **light**[1].

literacy *noun*
the ability to read and write.

literal *adjective*
1 meaning exactly what is said, not metaphorical or exaggerated. **2** word for word ♦ *a literal translation.*

literally *adverb*
really; exactly as stated ♦ *The noise made me literally jump out of my seat.*

literature *noun*
books and other writings, especially those considered to have been written well.

litigation *noun* (*plural* **litigations**)
a lawsuit; the process of carrying on a lawsuit.

litmus *noun*
a blue substance that is turned red by acids and can be turned back to blue by alkalis.

litmus paper *noun*
paper stained with litmus.

litre *noun* (*plural* **litres**)
a measure of liquid, about $1\frac{3}{4}$ pints.

litter *noun* (*plural* **litters**)
1 rubbish or untidy things left lying about. **2** the young animals born to one mother at one time. **3** absorbent material put down on a tray for a cat to urinate and defecate in indoors. **4** a kind of stretcher.
litter *verb* (**litters, littering, littered**)
make a place untidy with litter.

little *adjective* (**less, least**)
small in amount or size or intensity etc.; not great or big or much.
a little 1 a small amount ♦ *Have a little sugar.* **2** slightly ♦ *I'm a little tired.* **little by little** gradually; by a small amount at a time.
little *adverb*
not much ♦ *He was little known in this country.*

live¹ (rhymes with *give*) *verb* (**lives, living, lived**)
1 have life; be alive. 2 have your home ♦ *She lives in Glasgow.* 3 pass your life in a certain way ♦ *He lived as a hermit.*
live down if you cannot live down a mistake or embarrassment, you cannot make people forget it. **live on** use something as food; depend on for your living.

live² (rhymes with *hive*) *adjective*
1 alive. 2 connected to a source of electric current. 3 broadcast while it is actually happening, not from a recording. 4 burning ♦ *live coals.*

livelihood *noun* (*plural* **livelihoods**)
a way of earning money or providing enough food to support yourself.

lively *adjective* (**livelier, liveliest**)
full of life or action; vigorous and cheerful.
liveliness *noun*

liver *noun* (*plural* **livers**)
1 a large organ of the body, found in the abdomen, that processes digested food and purifies the blood. 2 an animal's liver used as food.

livestock *noun*
farm animals.

livid *adjective*
1 bluish-grey ♦ *a livid bruise.* 2 furiously angry.

living *noun*
1 being alive. 2 the way that a person lives ♦ *a good standard of living.* 3 a way of earning money or providing enough food to support yourself.

living room *noun* (*plural* **living rooms**)
a room for general use during the day.

lizard *noun* (*plural* **lizards**)
a reptile with a rough or scaly skin, four legs, and a long tail.

llama *noun* (*plural* **llamas**)
a South American animal with woolly fur. [via Spanish from Quechua (a South American language)]

load *noun* (*plural* **loads**)
1 something carried; a burden. 2 the quantity that can be carried. 3 the total amount of electric current supplied. 4 (*informal*) a large amount ♦ *It's a load of nonsense.* ♦ *You could earn loads of money.*
loads (*informal*) plenty ♦ *We've got loads of time.*

load *verb* (**loads, loading, loaded**)
1 put a load in or on something. 2 fill heavily. 3 weight with something heavy ♦ *loaded dice.* 4 put a bullet or shell into a gun; put a film into a camera. 5 enter programs or data into a computer.

loaf¹ *noun* (*plural* **loaves**)
a shaped mass of bread baked in one piece.
use your loaf (*informal*) think; use common sense.
[from Old English]

loaf² *verb* (**loafs, loafing, loafed**)
spend time idly; loiter or stand about.
loafer *noun*

loam *noun*
rich soil containing clay, sand, and decayed leaves etc.
loamy *adjective*

loan *noun* (*plural* **loans**)
1 something lent, especially money. 2 lending; being lent ♦ *These books are on loan from the library.*

loathe (rhymes with *clothe*) *verb* (**loathes, loathing, loathed**)
feel great hatred and disgust for something.
loathing *noun*

loathsome *adjective*
making you feel great hatred and disgust; repulsive.

lob *verb* (**lobs, lobbing, lobbed**)
throw, hit, or kick a ball etc. high into the air, especially in a high arc.

lobby *noun* (*plural* **lobbies**)
1 an entrance hall. 2 a group who lobby MPs etc. ♦ *the anti-hunting lobby.*

lobby *verb* (**lobbies, lobbying, lobbied**)
try to persuade an MP or other person to support your cause, by speaking to them in person or writing letters.

lobster *noun* (*plural* **lobsters**)
a large shellfish with eight legs and two long claws.

local *adjective*
belonging to a particular place or a small area.
locally *adverb*

local *noun* (*plural* **locals**) (*informal*)
1 someone who lives in a particular district. 2 a pub near a person's home.
[from Latin *locus* = a place]

local anaesthetic *noun* (*plural* **local anaesthetics**)
an anaesthetic affecting only the part of the body where it is applied.

localized *adjective*
restricted to a particular place ♦ *localized showers.*

locate *verb* (**locates, locating, located**)
discover where something is ♦ *I have located the fault.*
be located be situated in a particular place ♦ *The cinema is located in the High Street.*

location noun (plural **locations**)
1 the place where something is situated.
2 discovering where something is; locating.
on location filmed in natural surroundings, not in a studio.

lock¹ noun (plural **locks**)
1 a fastening that is opened with a key or other device. 2 a section of a canal or river fitted with sluice gates so that boats can be raised or lowered to the level beyond each gate. 3 the distance that a vehicle's front wheels can turn. 4 a wrestling hold that keeps an opponent's arm or leg from moving.
lock, stock, and barrel completely.

lock verb (**locks, locking, locked**)
1 fasten or secure something by means of a lock. 3 store something away securely. 3 become fixed in one place; jam.

lock² noun (plural **locks**)
a clump of hair.

locker noun (plural **lockers**)
a small cupboard or compartment where things can be stowed safely.

locket noun (plural **lockets**)
a small ornamental case for holding a portrait or lock of hair etc., worn on a chain round the neck.

locks plural noun
a person's hair.

locomotive noun (plural **locomotives**)
a railway engine.

locomotive adjective
to do with movement or the ability to move
♦ locomotive power.
locomotion noun

locus (say loh-kus) noun (plural **loci** (say loh-ky))
1 (in mathematics) the path traced by a moving point, or made by points placed in a certain way.
2 the exact place of something.

locust noun (plural **locusts**)
a kind of grasshopper that travels in large swarms which eat all the plants in an area.

lodge noun (plural **lodges**)
1 a small house, especially at the gates of a park.
2 a porter's room at the entrance to a college, factory, etc. 3 a beaver's or otter's lair.

lodge verb (**lodges, lodging, lodged**)
1 stay somewhere as a lodger. 2 provide a person with somewhere to live temporarily. 3 become stuck or caught somewhere ♦ The ball lodged in the tree.
lodge a complaint complain formally.

lodger noun (plural **lodgers**)
a person who pays to live in another person's house.

lodgings plural noun
a room or rooms, not in a hotel, rented for living in.

loft noun ('plural **lofts**)
a room or storage space under the roof of a house or barn etc.

lofty adjective
1 tall. 2 noble. 3 haughty.
loftily adverb **loftiness** noun

log¹ noun (plural **logs**)
1 a large piece of a tree that has fallen or been cut down; a piece cut off this. 2 a detailed record kept of a voyage or flight, kept in a **logbook**.

log verb (**logs, logging, logged**)
enter facts in a log.
log in (or **on**) start using a computer. **log out** (or **off**) finish using a computer.

log² noun (plural **logs**)
a logarithm ♦ log tables.

logarithm noun (plural **logarithms**)
one of a series of numbers set out in tables which make it possible to do sums by adding and subtracting instead of multiplying and dividing.

loggerheads plural noun
at loggerheads disagreeing or quarrelling.

logic noun
1 reasoning; a system or method of reasoning.
2 the principles used in designing a computer; the circuits involved in this.

logical adjective
using logic; reasoning or reasoned correctly.
logically adverb **logicality** noun

logo (say loh-goh or log-oh) noun (plural **logos**)
a printed symbol used by a business company etc. as its emblem.

loiter verb (**loiters, loitering, loitered**)
linger or stand about idly.
loiterer noun

lollipop noun (plural **lollipops**)
a large round hard sweet on a stick.

lonely adjective (**lonelier, loneliest**)
1 sad because you are on your own. 2 solitary.
3 far from inhabited places; not often visited or used ♦ a lonely road.
loneliness noun

long¹ adjective
1 measuring a lot from one end to the other.
2 taking a lot of time ♦ a long holiday. 3 having a certain length ♦ The river is 10 miles long.

long adverb
1 for a long time ♦ Have you been waiting long? 2 at a long time before or after ♦ They left long ago. 3 throughout a time ♦ all night long.
as long as or **so long as** provided that; on condition that. **before long** soon. **no longer** not any more.

long² verb (**longs, longing, longed**)
feel a strong desire.

long division *noun*
dividing one number by another and writing down all the calculations.

longing *noun* (*plural* **longings**)
a strong desire.

longitude *noun* (*plural* **longitudes**)
the distance east or west, measured in degrees, from the Greenwich meridian.

long jump *noun*
an athletic contest in which competitors jump as far as possible along the ground in one leap.

long-sighted *adjective*
able to see distant things clearly but not things close to you.

long wave *noun*
a radio wave of a wavelength above one kilometre and a frequency less than 300 kilohertz.

long-winded *adjective*
talking or writing at great length.

look *verb* (**looks, looking, looked**)
1 use your eyes; turn your eyes in a particular direction. 2 face in a particular direction. 3 have a certain appearance; seem ♦ *You look sad.* **look after** 1 protect or take care of someone. 2 be in charge of something. **look down on** despise. **look forward to** be waiting eagerly for something you expect. **look into** investigate. **look out** be careful. **look up** 1 search for information about something. 2 improve in prospects ♦ *Things are looking up.* **look up to** admire or respect.

look *noun* (*plural* **looks**)
1 the act of looking; a gaze or glance.
2 appearance ♦ *I don't like the look of this place.*

looking glass *noun* (*plural* **looking glasses**)
a glass mirror.

lookout *noun* (*plural* **lookouts**)
1 looking out or watching for something.
2 a place from which you can keep watch.
3 a person whose job is to keep watch.
4 a future prospect ♦ *It's a poor lookout for us.* 5 (*informal*) a person's own fault or concern ♦ *If he wastes his money, that's his lookout.*

loom¹ *noun* (*plural* **looms**)
a machine for weaving cloth.

loom² *verb* (**looms, looming, loomed**)
appear suddenly; seem large or close and threatening ♦ *An iceberg loomed up through the fog.*

loop *noun* (*plural* **loops**)
the shape made by a curve crossing itself; a piece of string, ribbon, wire, etc. made into this shape.

loophole *noun* (*plural* **loopholes**)
a way of avoiding a law or rule or promise etc. without actually breaking it.

loose *adjective*
1 not tight; not firmly fixed ♦ *a loose tooth.*
2 not tied up or shut in ♦ *There's a lion loose!*
3 not packed in a box or packet etc. 4 not exact
♦ *a loose translation.*
loosely *adverb* **looseness** *noun*
at a loose end with nothing to do. **on the loose** escaped or free.

loosen *verb* (**loosens, loosening, loosened**)
make or become loose or looser.

loot *noun*
stolen things; goods taken from an enemy.

loot *verb* (**loots, looting, looted**)
1 rob a place or an enemy, especially in a time of war or disorder. 2 take something as loot.
looter *noun*
[from a Hindi word, = to rob]

lop *verb* (**lops, lopping, lopped**)
cut away branches or twigs; cut off.

lopsided *adjective*
with one side lower or smaller than the other.

lord *noun* (*plural* **lords**)
1 a nobleman, especially one who is allowed to use the title 'Lord' in front of his name.
2 a master or ruler.
lordly *adjective* **lordship** *noun*
[from Old English *hlaford* = person who keeps the bread (compare **lady**)]

lorry *noun* (*plural* **lorries**)
a large strong motor vehicle for carrying heavy goods or troops.

lose *verb* (**loses, losing, lost**)
1 be without something that you once had, especially because you cannot find it. 2 fail to keep or obtain something ♦ *We lost control.*
3 be defeated in a contest or argument etc.
4 cause the loss of ♦ *That one mistake lost us the game.* 5 (said about a clock or watch) become behind the correct time.
loser *noun*
be lost or **lose your way** not know where you are or which is the right path. **lose your life** be killed. **lost cause** an idea or policy etc. that is failing.

loss *noun* (*plural* **losses**)
1 losing something. 2 something lost.
be at a loss not know what to do or say.

lot *noun* (*plural* **lots**)
1 a large number or amount ♦ *You have a lot of friends.* ♦ *There's lots of time.* 2 one of a set of objects used in choosing or deciding something by chance ♦ *We drew lots to see who should go first.* 3 a person's share or fate. 4 something for sale at an auction. 5 a piece of land.
a lot very much ♦ *I feel a lot better.* **the lot** or **the whole lot** everything; all.

lotion *noun* (*plural* **lotions**)
a liquid for putting on the skin.

lottery *noun* (*plural* **lotteries**)
a way of raising money by selling numbered tickets and giving prizes to people who hold winning numbers, which are chosen by a method depending on chance (compare **lot** 2).

loud *adjective*
1 easily heard; producing much noise.
2 unpleasantly bright; gaudy ♦ *loud colours.*
loudly *adverb* **loudness** *noun*

loudspeaker *noun* (*plural* **loudspeakers**)
a device that changes electrical signals into sound, for reproducing music or voices.

lounge *noun* (*plural* **lounges**)
a sitting room.

lounge *verb* (**lounges, lounging, lounged**)
sit or stand in a lazy and relaxed way.

louse *noun* (*plural* **lice**)
a small insect that lives as a parasite on animals or plants.

lousy *adjective* (**lousier, lousiest**)
1 full of lice. **2** (*slang*) very bad or unpleasant.

lout *noun* (*plural* **louts**)
a bad-mannered man.

lovable *adjective*
easy to love.

love *noun* (*plural* **loves**)
1 great liking or affection. **2** sexual affection or passion. **3** a loved person; a sweetheart.
4 (in tennis) no score; nil.
in love feeling strong love. **make love** have sexual intercourse.

love *verb* (**loves, loving, loved**)
feel love for a person or thing.
lover *noun* **lovingly** *adverb*
[from Old English]

love affair *noun* (*plural* **love affairs**)
a romantic or sexual relationship between two people in love.

lovely *adjective* (**lovelier, loveliest**)
1 beautiful. **2** very pleasant or enjoyable.
loveliness *noun*

lover *noun* (*plural* **lovers**)
1 a person who someone is having a sexual relationship with but is not married to.
2 someone who loves something ♦ *an art lover.*

lovesick *adjective*
longing for someone you love, especially someone who does not love you.

low *adjective*
1 only reaching a short way up; not high.
2 below average in importance, quality, amount, etc. ♦ *low prices*; ♦ *of low rank.*
3 unhappy ♦ *I'm feeling low.* **4** not high-pitched; not loud ♦ *low notes*; ♦ *a low voice.*
lowness *noun*

low *adverb*
at or to a low level or position etc. ♦ *The plane was flying low.*

lower *adjective* & *adverb*
less high.

lower *verb* (**lowers, lowering, lowered**)
make or become lower.

loyal *adjective*
always firmly supporting your friends or group or country etc.
loyally *adverb* **loyalty** *noun*

lozenge *noun* (*plural* **lozenges**)
1 a small flavoured tablet, especially one containing medicine. **2** a diamond shape.

Ltd. *abbreviation*
limited.

lubricant *noun* (*plural* **lubricants**)
a lubricating substance.

lubricate *verb* (**lubricates, lubricating, lubricated**)
oil or grease something so that it moves smoothly.
lubrication *noun*

lucid *adjective*
1 clear and easy to understand. **2** thinking clearly; not confused in your mind.
lucidly *adverb* **lucidity** *noun*

luck *noun*
1 the way things happen without being planned; chance. **2** good fortune ♦ *It will bring you luck.*

lucky *adjective* (**luckier, luckiest**)
having or bringing or resulting from good luck.
luckily *adverb*

ludicrous *adjective*
ridiculous or laughable.
ludicrously *adverb*

luggage *noun*
suitcases and bags etc. holding things for taking on a journey.

lukewarm *adjective*
1 only slightly warm; tepid. **2** not very enthusiastic ♦ *lukewarm applause.*

lull *verb* (**lulls, lulling, lulled**)
soothe or calm; send someone to sleep.

lull *noun* (*plural* **lulls**)
a short period of quiet or inactivity.

lullaby *noun* (*plural* **lullabies**)
a song that is sung to send a baby to sleep.

lumbago *noun*
pain in the muscles of the lower back.

lumber *noun*
1 unwanted furniture etc.; junk. **2** (*American*) timber.

lumber *verb* (**lumbers, lumbering, lumbered**)
1 leave someone with an unwanted or unpleasant task. **2** move in a heavy clumsy way.

luminous *adjective*
glowing in the dark.
luminosity *noun*

lump¹ *noun* (*plural* **lumps**)
1 a solid piece of something. **2** a swelling.
lumpy *adjective*

lump *verb* (**lumps, lumping, lumped**)
put or treat things together in a group because
you regard them as alike in some way.

lump² *verb* (**lumps, lumping, lumped**)
lump it (*informal*) put up with something you
dislike.

lump sum *noun* (*plural* **lump sums**)
a single payment, especially one covering a
number of items.

lunacy *noun* (*plural* **lunacies**)
insanity or great foolishness.

lunatic *noun* (*plural* **lunatics**)
an insane person.
lunatic *adjective*

lunch *noun* (*plural* **lunches**)
a meal eaten in the middle of the day.
lunch *verb*

lung *noun* (*plural* **lungs**)
either of the two parts of the body, in the chest,
used in breathing.

lunge *verb* (**lunges, lunging, lunged**)
thrust the body forward suddenly.
lunge *noun*

lupin *noun* (*plural* **lupins**)
a garden plant with tall spikes of flowers.

lurch¹ *verb* (**lurches, lurching, lurched**)
stagger; lean suddenly to one side.
lurch *noun*

lurch² *noun*
leave somebody in the lurch leave somebody in
difficulties.

lure *verb* (**lures, luring, lured**)
tempt a person or animal into a trap; entice.
lure *noun*

lurid (*say* **lewr**-id) *adjective*
1 in very bright colours; gaudy. **2** sensational
and shocking ♦ *the lurid details of the murder*.
luridly *adverb* **luridness** *noun*

lurk *verb* (**lurks, lurking, lurked**)
wait where you cannot be seen.

luscious (*say* **lush**-us) *adjective*
delicious.
lusciously *adverb* **lusciousness** *noun*

lush *adjective*
1 growing thickly and strongly ♦ *lush grass*.
2 luxurious.
lushly *adverb* **lushness** *noun*

lust *noun* (*plural* **lusts**)
powerful desire, especially sexual desire.
lustful *adjective*

lust *verb* (**lusts, lusting, lusted**)
have a powerful desire for a person or thing
♦ *people who lust after power*.

lusty *adjective* (**lustier, lustiest**)
strong and vigorous.
lustily *adverb* **lustiness** *noun*

lute *noun* (*plural* **lutes**)
a stringed musical instrument with a
pear-shaped body, popular in the 14th–17th
centuries.

luxuriant *adjective*
growing abundantly.

ℹ USAGE Do not confuse with *luxurious*.

luxurious *adjective*
expensive and comfortable.
luxuriously *adverb*

ℹ USAGE Do not confuse with *luxuriant*.

luxury *noun* (*plural* **luxuries**)
1 something expensive that you enjoy but do not
really need. **2** expensive and comfortable
surroundings ♦ *a life of luxury*.
[from Latin *luxus* = plenty]

-ly *suffix*
forms **1** adjectives (e.g. *friendly, heavenly,
sickly*), **2** adverbs from adjectives (e.g. *boldly,
sweetly, thoroughly*).

Lycra *noun* (*trademark*)
a thin stretchy material used especially for sports
clothing.

lying *present participle* of **lie¹** and **lie²**.

lynch *verb* (**lynches, lynching, lynched**)
join together to execute or punish someone
violently without a proper trial, especially by
hanging them.

lyric (*say* **li**-rik) *noun* (*plural* **lyrics**)
1 a short poem that expresses thoughts and
feelings. **2** the words of a song.
lyrical *adjective* **lyrically** *adverb*

Mm

MA *abbreviation*
Master of Arts.

mac *noun* (*plural* **macs**) (*informal*)
a mackintosh.

macaroni *noun*
pasta in the form of short tubes.
[via Italian from Greek *makaria* = food made
from barley]

macaroon *noun* (*plural* **macaroons**)
a small sweet cake or biscuit made with ground
almonds.

machine noun (plural **machines**)
something with parts that work together to do a job.

machine gun noun (plural **machine guns**)
a gun that can keep firing bullets quickly one after another.

machinery noun
1 machines. 2 the moving parts of a machine. 3 an organized system for doing something ♦ the machinery of local government.

mackerel noun (plural **mackerel**)
a sea fish used as food.

mackintosh noun (plural **mackintoshes**)
a raincoat.

mad adjective (**madder, maddest**)
1 having something wrong with the mind; insane. 2 extremely foolish. 3 very keen ♦ He is mad about football. 4 (informal) very excited or annoyed.
madly adverb **madness** noun **madman** noun
like mad (informal) with great speed, energy, or enthusiasm.

madam noun
a word used when speaking politely to a woman ♦ Can I help you, madam?

mad cow disease noun
BSE.

madden verb (**maddens, maddening, maddened**)
make a person mad or angry.
maddening adjective

mafia noun
1 a large organization of criminals in Italy, Sicily, and the United States of America. 2 any group of people believed to act together in a sinister way.

magazine noun (plural **magazines**)
1 a paper-covered publication that comes out regularly, with articles, stories, or features by several writers. 2 the part of a gun that holds the cartridges. 3 a store for weapons and ammunition or for explosives. 4 a device that holds film for a camera or slides for a projector. [from Arabic makhazin = storehouses]

magenta (say ma-jen-ta) noun
a colour between bright red and purple. [named after Magenta, a town in north Italy, where Napoleon III won a battle in the year when the dye was discovered (1859)]

maggot noun (plural **maggots**)
the larva of some kinds of fly.
maggoty adjective

magic noun
1 the art of making things happen by supernatural powers. 2 mysterious tricks performed for entertainment. 3 a mysterious and enchanting quality ♦ the magic of the East.
magic adjective **magical** adjective **magically** adverb

magician noun (plural **magicians**)
1 a person who does magic tricks. 2 a wizard.

magistrate noun (plural **magistrates**)
an official who hears and judges minor cases in a local court.
magistracy noun
[from Latin magister = master]

magnanimous (say mag-nan-im-us) adjective
generous and forgiving, not petty-minded.
magnanimously adverb **magnanimity** noun

magnate noun (plural **magnates**)
a wealthy influential person, especially in business.

magnesium noun
a silvery-white metal that burns with a very bright flame.

magnet noun (plural **magnets**)
a piece of iron or steel that can attract iron and that points north and south when it is hung up.
magnetism noun

magnetic adjective
1 having the powers of a magnet. 2 having the power to attract people ♦ a magnetic personality.
magnetically adverb

magnetize verb (**magnetizes, magnetizing, magnetized**)
1 make into a magnet. 2 attract like a magnet.
magnetization noun

magneto (say mag-neet-oh) noun (plural **magnetos**)
a small electric generator using magnets.

magnificent adjective
1 grand or splendid in appearance etc. 2 excellent.
magnificently adverb **magnificence** noun
[from Latin magnificus = splendid]

magnify verb (**magnifies, magnifying, magnified**)
make something look or seem bigger than it really is.
magnification noun **magnifier** noun

magnifying glass noun (plural **magnifying glasses**)
a lens that magnifies things.

magnitude noun (plural **magnitudes**)
1 size or extent. 2 importance.

magpie noun (plural **magpies**)
a noisy bird with black and white feathers, related to the crow.
[from Mag (short for Margaret) + an old word pie = magpie]

mahogany noun
a hard brown wood.

maid noun (plural **maids**)
1 a female servant. 2 (old use) a girl.
maidservant noun

maiden *noun* (*plural* **maidens**) (*old use*)
a girl.
maidenhood *noun*

maiden *adjective*
1 not married ♦ *a maiden aunt.* 2 first
♦ *a maiden voyage.*

maiden name *noun* (*plural* **maiden names**)
a woman's family name before she married.

maiden over *noun* (*plural* **maiden overs**)
a cricket over in which no runs are scored.

mail¹ *noun*
letters and parcels sent by post.

mail² *noun*
armour made of metal rings joined together
♦ *a suit of chain mail.*

mailing list *noun* (*plural* **mailing lists**)
a list of names and addresses of people to whom
an organization sends information from time to
time.

mail order *noun*
a system for buying and selling goods by post.

maim *verb* (**maims, maiming, maimed**)
injure a person so that part of their body is made
useless.

main *adjective*
largest or most important.

main *noun*
1 the main pipe or cable in a public system
carrying water, gas, or (usually called **mains**)
electricity to a building. 2 (*old use*) the seas
♦ *Drake sailed the Spanish main.*
in the main for the most part; on the whole.

main clause *noun* (*plural* **main clauses**)
a clause that can be used as a complete sentence.
(Compare **subordinate clause**.)

mainland *noun*
the main part of a country or continent, not the
islands round it.

mainly *adverb*
1 chiefly. 2 almost completely. 3 usually.

mainstream *noun*
the most widely accepted ideas or opinions about
something ♦ *Fascism is not in the mainstream of
British politics.*

maintain *verb* (**maintains, maintaining,
maintained**)
1 cause something to continue; keep in
existence. 2 keep a thing in good condition.
3 provide money for a person to live on.
4 state that something is true.

maintenance *noun*
1 maintaining or keeping something in good
condition. 2 money for food and clothing.
3 money to be paid by a husband or wife to the
other partner after a divorce.

maize *noun*
a tall kind of corn with large seeds on cobs.

majestic *adjective*
1 stately and dignified. 2 imposing.
majestically *adverb*

majesty *noun* (*plural* **majesties**)
1 the title of a king or queen ♦ *Her Majesty the
Queen.* 2 being majestic.

major *adjective*
1 greater; very important ♦ *major roads.*
2 of the musical scale that has a semitone after
the 3rd and 7th notes. (Compare **minor**.)

major *noun* (*plural* **majors**)
an army officer ranking next above a captain.
[from Latin, = larger, greater]

majority *noun* (*plural* **majorities**)
1 the greatest part of a group of people or things.
(Compare **minority**.) 2 the amount by which the
winner in an election beats the loser ♦ *She had a
majority of 25 over her opponent.* 3 the age at
which a person becomes an adult according to
the law (now usually 18) ♦ *He has attained his
majority.*

make *verb* (**makes, making, made**)
1 bring something into existence, especially
by putting things together. 2 cause or
compel ♦ *Make him repeat it.* 3 gain or earn
♦ *She makes £25,000 a year.* 4 achieve or reach
♦ *He made 25 runs.* ♦ *The swimmer just made
the shore.* 5 reckon ♦ *What do you make the
time?* 6 result in or add up to ♦ *4 and 6 make 10.*
7 perform an action etc. ♦ *make an effort.*
8 arrange for use ♦ *make the beds.* 9 cause to be
successful or happy ♦ *Her visit made my day.*
make do manage with something that is not
what you really want. **make for** go towards.
make love 1 have sexual intercourse. 2 (*old
use*) try to win someone's love. **make off** go
away quickly. **make out** 1 manage to see, hear,
or understand something. 2 claim or pretend that
something is true. **make up** 1 build or put
together. 2 invent a story etc. 3 be friendly again
after a disagreement. 4 compensate for
something. 5 put on make-up. **make up your
mind** decide.

make *noun* (*plural* **makes**)
1 making; how something is made. 2 a brand of
goods; something made by a particular firm.

makeshift *adjective*
improvised or used because you have nothing
better ♦ *We used a box as a makeshift table.*

make-up *noun*
1 cosmetics. 2 the way something is made up.
3 a person's character.

maladjusted *adjective*
unable to fit in or cope with other people or your
own circumstances.

malapropism *noun* (*plural* **malapropisms**)
a comical confusion of words, e.g. using
hooligan instead of *hurricane.*

malaria *noun*
a feverish disease spread by mosquitoes.
malarial *adjective*

male *adjective*
1 belonging to the sex that reproduces by
fertilizing egg cells produced by the female.
2 of men ♦ *a male voice choir.*
male *noun* (*plural* **males**)
a male person, animal, or plant.

male chauvinist *noun* (*plural* **male
chauvinists**)
a man who thinks that women are not as good as
men.

malevolent (*say* ma-lev-ol-ent) *adjective*
wishing to harm people.
malevolently *adverb* **malevolence** *noun*

malfunction *noun* (*plural* **malfunctions**)
faulty functioning ♦ *a malfunction in the
computer.*
malfunction *verb* (**malfunctions,
malfunctioning, malfunctioned**)
fail to work properly.

malice *noun*
the desire to harm other people.
malicious *adjective* **maliciously** *adverb*

malign (*say* mal-I'n) *adjective*
1 harmful ♦ *a malign influence.* **2** showing
malice.
malignity (*say* mal-**ig**-nit-ee) *noun*

malignant *adjective*
1 (said about a tumour) growing uncontrollably.
2 full of malice.
malignantly *adverb* **malignancy** *noun*

malleable *adjective*
1 able to be pressed or hammered into shape.
2 easy to influence; adaptable.
malleability *noun*

mallet *noun* (*plural* **mallets**)
1 a large hammer, usually made of wood.
2 an implement with a long handle, used in
croquet or polo for striking the ball.

malnutrition *noun*
bad health because you do not have enough food
or the right kind of food.
malnourished *adjective*

malt *noun*
dried barley used in brewing, making vinegar,
etc.
malted *adjective*

maltreat *verb* (**maltreats, maltreating,
maltreated**)
ill-treat.
maltreatment *noun*

mammal *noun* (*plural* **mammals**)
any animal of which the female gives birth to
live babies which are fed with milk from her own
body.
mammalian (*say* mam-**ay**-lee-an) *adjective*

mammoth *noun* (*plural* **mammoths**)
an extinct elephant with a hairy skin and curved
tusks.
mammoth *adjective*
huge.

man *noun* (*plural* **men**)
1 a grown-up male human being. **2** an individual
person. **3** mankind. **4** a piece used in chess or
other board games.
man *verb* (**mans, manning, manned**)
supply with people to work something
♦ *Man the pumps!*
[from Old English]

manacle *noun* (*plural* **manacles**)
a fetter or handcuff.
manacle *verb* (**manacles, manacling,
manacled**)
fasten with manacles.

manage *verb* (**manages, managing, managed**)
1 be able to cope with something difficult.
2 be in charge of a business or part of it, or a
group of people.
manageable *adjective*

management *noun*
1 managing. **2** managers; the people in charge.

manager *noun* (*plural* **managers**)
a person who manages something.
manageress *noun* **managerial** (*say*
man-a-**jeer**-ee-al) *adjective*

mandarin *noun* (*plural* **mandarins**)
1 an important official. **2** a kind of small orange.

mane *noun* (*plural* **manes**)
the long hair on a horse's or lion's neck.

manganese *noun*
a hard brittle metal.

manger *noun* (*plural* **mangers**)
a trough in a stable for horses or cattle to feed
from.

mangle *verb* (**mangles, mangling, mangled**)
damage something by crushing or cutting it
roughly.

mango *noun* (*plural* **mangoes**)
a tropical fruit with yellow pulp.

manhandle *verb* (**manhandles, manhandling,
manhandled**)
treat or push roughly.

manhole *noun* (*plural* **manholes**)
a space or opening, usually with a cover, by
which a person can get into a sewer or boiler etc.
to inspect or repair it.

manhood *noun*
1 the condition of being a man. **2** manly
qualities.

mania *noun* (*plural* **manias**)
1 violent madness. **2** great enthusiasm
♦ *a mania for sport.*
maniac *noun* **manic** *adjective*

manicure noun (plural **manicures**)
care and treatment of the hands and nails.
manicure verb manicurist noun

manifest adjective
clear and obvious.
manifestly adverb

manifesto noun (plural **manifestos**)
a public statement of a group's or person's policy
or principles.

manifold adjective
of many kinds; very varied.

manipulate verb (**manipulates, manipulating,
manipulated**)
1 handle or arrange something skilfully.
2 get someone to do what you want by treating
them cleverly.
manipulation noun manipulator noun

mankind noun
human beings in general.

manly adjective
1 suitable for a man. 2 brave and strong.
manliness noun

manner noun
1 the way something happens or is done.
2 a person's way of behaving. 3 a sort or type
♦ all manner of things.

mannerism noun (plural **mannerisms**)
a person's own particular gesture or way of
speaking.

manners plural noun
how a person behaves with other people;
politeness.

manoeuvre (say man-oo-ver) noun (plural
manoeuvres)
a difficult or skilful or cunning action.

manoeuvre verb (**manoeuvres, manoeuvring,
manoeuvred**)
move carefully and skilfully.
manoeuvrable adjective

manor noun (plural **manors**)
1 a manor house. 2 the land belonging to a
manor house.
manorial adjective
[from early French, related to mansion]

manor house noun (plural **manor houses**)
a large important house in the country.

manpower noun
the number of people who are working or
needed or available for work on something.

mansion noun (plural **mansions**)
a large stately house.
[from Latin mansio = a place to stay, a dwelling]

manslaughter noun
killing a person unlawfully but without meaning
to.

mantelpiece noun (plural **mantelpieces**)
a shelf above a fireplace.

mantle noun (plural **mantles**)
1 a cloak. 2 a covering ♦ a mantle of snow.

manual adjective
worked by or done with the hands ♦ a manual
typewriter; ♦ manual work.
manually adverb

manual noun (plural **manuals**)
a handbook containing instructions etc.

manufacture verb (**manufactures,
manufacturing, manufactured**)
make things, especially on a large scale.
manufacture noun manufacturer noun

manure noun
fertilizer, especially dung.

manuscript noun (plural **manuscripts**)
something written or typed but not printed.

Manx adjective
to do with the Isle of Man.

many adjective (**more, most**)
great in number; numerous ♦ many people.

many noun
many people or things ♦ Many were found.

Maori (rhymes with flowery) noun (plural
Maoris)
1 a member of the aboriginal people of New
Zealand. 2 their language.

map noun (plural **maps**)
a diagram of part or all of the earth's surface or
of the sky.

map verb (**maps, mapping, mapped**)
make a map of an area.
map out plan the details of something.

marathon noun (plural **marathons**)
a long-distance running race, especially one
covering 26 miles 385 yards (42.195 km).
[named after Marathon in Greece, from which a
messenger is said to have run to Athens (about
40 kilometres) to announce that the Greeks had
defeated the Persian army]

March noun
the third month of the year.
[named after Mars, the Roman god of war]

marauding adjective
going about in search of plunder or prey.
marauder noun

marble noun (plural **marbles**)
1 a small glass ball used in games. 2 a kind of
limestone polished and used in sculpture or
building.

march verb (**marches, marching, marched**)
1 walk with regular steps. 2 make somebody
walk somewhere ♦ He marched them up the hill.
marcher noun

march noun (plural **marches**)
1 marching. 2 music suitable for marching to.

mare noun (plural **mares**)
a female horse or donkey.

margarine (*say* mar-ja-**reen** or mar-ga-**reen**) *noun*
a substance used like butter, made from animal or vegetable fats.

margin *noun* (*plural* **margins**)
1 an edge or border. 2 the blank space between the edge of a page and the writing or pictures etc. on it. 3 the difference between two scores or prices etc. ♦ *She won by a narrow margin.*

marginal *adjective*
1 in a margin ♦ *marginal notes.* 2 very slight ♦ *a marginal difference.*
marginally *adverb*

marginal seat *noun* (*plural* **marginal seats**)
a constituency where an MP was elected with only a small majority and may be defeated in the next election.

marine (*say* ma-**reen**) *adjective*
to do with the sea; living in the sea.

marine *noun* (*plural* **marines**)
a member of the troops who are trained to serve at sea as well as on land.

marionette *noun* (*plural* **marionettes**)
a puppet worked by strings or wires.

marital *adjective*
to do with marriage.

maritime *adjective*
1 to do with the sea or ships. 2 found near the sea.

mark¹ *noun* (*plural* **marks**)
1 a spot, dot, line, or stain etc. on something. 2 a number or letter etc. put on a piece of work to show how good it is. 3 a distinguishing feature. 4 a sign or symbol ♦ *They all stood as a mark of respect.* 5 a target.
on your marks! a command to runners to get ready to begin a race. **up to the mark** of the normal or expected standard.

mark *verb* (**marks, marking, marked**)
1 put a mark on something. 2 give a mark to a piece of work. 3 pay attention to something ♦ *Mark my words!* 4 keep close to an opposing player in football etc.
marker *noun*
mark time 1 march on the spot without moving forward. 2 occupy your time without making any progress.

mark² *noun* (*plural* **marks**)
a German unit of money replaced by the euro in 2002.

marked *adjective*
noticeable ♦ *a marked improvement.*
markedly *adverb*

market *noun* (*plural* **markets**)
1 a place where things are bought and sold, usually from stalls in the open air. 2 demand for things ♦ *Is there a market for typewriters now?*
marketplace *noun*
on the market offered for sale.

market research *noun*
the study of what people need or want to buy.

marksman *noun* (*plural* **marksmen**)
an expert in shooting at a target.
marksmanship *noun*

marmalade *noun*
jam made from oranges, lemons, or other citrus fruit.

maroon *verb* (**maroons, marooning, marooned**)
abandon or isolate somebody in a deserted place; strand.

marquee (*say* mar-**kee**) *noun* (*plural* **marquees**)
a large tent used for a party or exhibition etc.

marquis *noun* (*plural* **marquises**)
a nobleman ranking next above an earl.

marriage *noun* (*plural* **marriages**)
1 the state of being married. 2 a wedding.

marrow *noun* (*plural* **marrows**)
1 a large gourd eaten as a vegetable. 2 the soft substance inside bones.

marry *verb* (**marries, marrying, married**)
1 become a person's husband or wife. 2 join two people as husband and wife; be in charge of a marriage ceremony.

marsh *noun* (*plural* **marshes**)
a low-lying area of very wet ground.
marshy *adjective*

marshal *noun* (*plural* **marshals**)
1 an official who supervises a contest or ceremony etc. 2 an officer of very high rank ♦ *a Field Marshal.*

marshmallow *noun* (*plural* **marshmallows**)
a soft spongy sweet, usually pink or white.

marsupial (*say* mar-**soo**-pee-al) *noun* (*plural* **marsupials**)
an animal such as a kangaroo or wallaby. The female has a pouch on the front of its body in which its babies are carried.

martial *adjective*
to do with war; warlike.

martial arts *plural noun*
fighting sports, such as judo and karate.

martial law *noun*
government of a country by the armed forces during a crisis.

martyr *noun* (*plural* **martyrs**)
a person who is killed or made to suffer because of his or her beliefs.
martyrdom *noun*

marvel *noun* (*plural* **marvels**)
a wonderful thing.
marvellous *adjective*

marzipan *noun*
a soft sweet food made of ground almonds, eggs, and sugar.

mascot *noun* (*plural* **mascots**)
a person, animal, or thing that is believed to
bring good luck.

masculine *adjective*
1 to do with men. **2** typical of or suitable for
men. **3** (in some languages) belonging to the
class of words which includes the words
referring to men, such as *garçon* and *livre* in
French.
masculinity *noun*

mash *verb* (**mashes, mashing, mashed**)
crush into a soft mass.

mask *noun* (*plural* **masks**)
a covering worn over the face to disguise or
protect it.

masochist (*say* mas-ok-ist) *noun* (*plural*
masochists)
a person who enjoys things that seem painful or
tiresome.
masochism *noun*

mason *noun* (*plural* **masons**)
a person who builds or works with stone.

masonry *noun*
1 the stone parts of a building; stonework.
2 a mason's work.

masquerade *noun* (*plural* **masquerades**)
a pretence.

masquerade *verb* (**masquerades,
masquerading, masqueraded**)
pretend to be something ♦ *He masqueraded as a
policeman.*

Mass *noun* (*plural* **Masses**)
the Communion service in a Roman Catholic
church.

mass *noun* (*plural* **masses**)
1 a large amount. **2** a heap or other collection of
matter. **3** (in science) the quantity of physical
matter that a thing contains.

mass *adjective*
involving a large number of people ♦ *mass
murder.*

massacre *noun* (*plural* **massacres**)
the killing of a large number of people.
massacre *verb*

massage (*say* mas-ahzh) *verb* (**massages,
massaging, massaged**)
rub and press the body to make it less stiff or less
painful.
massage *noun* **masseur** *noun* **masseuse** *noun*

massive *adjective*
large and heavy; huge.

mass media *noun*
the main media of news information, especially
newspapers and broadcasting.

mass production *noun*
manufacturing goods in large quantities.
mass-produced *adjective*

mast *noun* (*plural* **masts**)
a tall pole that holds up a ship's sails or a flag or
an aerial.

master *noun* (*plural* **masters**)
1 a man who is in charge of something. **2** a male
teacher. **3** a great artist, composer, sportsman,
etc. **4** something from which copies are made.
5 (*old use*) a title put before a boy's name.

masterful *adjective*
1 domineering. **2** very skilful.
masterfully *adverb*

master key *noun* (*plural* **master keys**)
a key that will open several different locks.

masterly *adjective*
very skilful. .

Master of Arts *noun* (*plural* **Masters of Arts**)
a person who has taken the next degree after
Bachelor of Arts.

master of ceremonies *noun* (*plural* **masters
of ceremonies**)
a person who introduces the speakers at a formal
event, or the entertainers at a variety show.

Master of Science *noun* (*plural* **Masters of
Science**)
a person who has taken the next degree after
Bachelor of Science.

masterpiece *noun* (*plural* **masterpieces**)
1 an excellent piece of work. **2** a person's best
piece of work.

mastery *noun*
complete control or thorough knowledge or skill
in something.

mastiff *noun* (*plural* **mastiffs**)
a large kind of dog.

masturbate *verb* (**masturbates,
masturbating, masturbated**)
get sexual pleasure by rubbing your genitals.
masturbation *noun*

mat *noun* (*plural* **mats**)
1 a small carpet. **2** a doormat. **3** a small piece of
material put on a table to protect the surface.

matador *noun* (*plural* **matadors**)
a bullfighter who fights on foot.

match¹ *noun* (*plural* **matches**)
a small thin stick with a head made of a
substance that gives a flame when rubbed on
something rough.
matchbox *noun* **matchstick** *noun*

match² *noun* (*plural* **matches**)
1 a game or contest between two teams or
players. **2** one person or thing that matches
another. **3** a marriage.

match *verb* (**matches, matching, matched**)
1 be equal or similar to another person or thing. ·
2 put teams or players to compete against each
other. **3** find something that is similar or
corresponding.

mate¹ *noun* (*plural* **mates**)
1 a companion or friend. **2** each of a mated pair
of birds or animals. **3** an officer on a merchant
ship.

mate *verb* (**mates, mating, mated**)
1 come together or bring two together in order to breed. **2** put things together as a pair or because they correspond.

mate² *noun & verb* (*in chess*)
checkmate.

material *noun* (*plural* **materials**)
1 anything used for making something else. **2** cloth or fabric.

materialize *verb* (**materializes, materializing, materialized**)
1 become visible; appear ♦ *The ghost didn't materialize.* **2** become a fact; happen ♦ *The trip did not materialize.*
materialization *noun*

maternal *adjective*
1 to do with a mother. **2** motherly.
maternally *adverb*

maternity *noun*
motherhood.

maternity *adjective*
to do with having a baby ♦ *a maternity ward.*

mathematics *noun*
the study of numbers, measurements, and shapes.
mathematical *adjective* **mathematically** *adverb*
mathematician *noun*
[from Greek *mathema* = science, from *manthanein* = to learn]

matriarch (*say* **may**-tree-ark) *noun* (*plural* **matriarchs**)
a woman who is head of a family or tribe. (Compare **patriarch**.)
matriarchal *adjective* **matriarchy** *noun*

matrix (*say* **may**-triks) *noun* (*plural* **matrices** (*say* **may**-tri-seez))
1 (in mathematics) a set of quantities arranged in rows and columns. **2** a mould or framework in which something is made or allowed to develop.

matron *noun* (*plural* **matrons**)
1 a mature married woman. **2** a woman in charge of nursing in a school etc. or (formerly) of the nursing staff in a hospital.
matronly *adjective*

matted *adjective*
tangled into a mass.

matter *noun* (*plural* **matters**)
1 something you can touch or see, not spirit or mind or qualities etc. **2** a substance ♦ *Peat consists mainly of vegetable matter.* **3** things of a certain kind ♦ *printed matter.* **4** something to be thought about or done ♦ *It's a serious matter.* **5** a quantity ♦ *in a matter of minutes.*
a matter of course the natural or expected thing ♦ *I always lock my bike, as a matter of course.*
as a matter of fact in fact. **no matter** it does not matter. **what is the matter?** what is wrong?

matter *verb* (**matters, mattering, mattered**)
be important.

matter-of-fact *adjective*
keeping to facts; not imaginative or emotional ♦ *She talked about death in a very matter-of-fact way.*

mattress *noun* (*plural* **mattresses**)
soft or springy material in a fabric covering, used on or as a bed.

mature *adjective*
1 fully grown or developed. **2** grown-up.
maturely *adverb* **maturity** *noun*

mature *verb* (**matures, maturing, matured**)
make or become mature.

maul *verb* (**mauls, mauling, mauled**)
injure by handling or clawing ♦ *He was mauled by a lion.*

mauve (*say* mohv) *noun*
pale purple.

maxim *noun* (*plural* **maxims**)
a short saying giving a general truth or rule of behaviour, e.g. 'Waste not, want not'.

maximize *verb* (**maximizes, maximizing, maximized**)
increase something to a maximum.

maximum *noun* (*plural* **maxima** or **maximums**)
the greatest possible number or amount. (The opposite is **minimum**.)

May *noun*
the fifth month of the year.
[named after Maia, a Roman goddess]

may¹ *auxiliary verb* (**may, might**)
used to express **1** permission (*You may go now*), **2** possibility (*It may be true*), **3** wish (*Long may she reign*), uncertainty (*whoever it may be*).

ⓘ USAGE See note at *can.*

may² *noun*
hawthorn blossom.

maybe *adverb*
perhaps; possibly.

mayfly *noun* (*plural* **mayflies**)
an insect that lives for only a short time, in spring.

mayhem *noun*
violent confusion or damage ♦ *The mob caused mayhem.*

mayonnaise *noun*
a creamy sauce made from eggs, oil, vinegar, etc., usually eaten with salad or in sandwiches.

mayor *noun* (*plural* **mayors**)
the person in charge of the council in a town or city.
mayoral *adjective* **mayoress** *noun*
[from early French, related to *major*]

maze *noun* (*plural* **mazes**)
a network of paths, especially one designed as a puzzle in which to try and find your way.

Mb *abbreviation*
megabyte(s).

MD *abbreviation*
Doctor of Medicine.

me *pronoun*
the form of *I* used as the object of a verb or after a preposition.

meadow (*say* med-oh) *noun* (*plural* **meadows**)
a field of grass.

meagre *adjective*
scanty in amount; barely enough ♦ *a meagre diet.*

meal¹ *noun* (*plural* **meals**)
food served and eaten at one sitting.
[from Old English *mael*]

meal² *noun*
coarsely ground grain.
mealy *adjective*
[from Old English *melu*]

mean¹ *verb* (**means, meaning, meant** (*say* ment))
1 have as an equivalent or explanation
♦ *'Maybe' means 'perhaps'.* 2 have as a purpose; intend ♦ *I mean to win.* 3 indicate ♦ *Dark clouds mean rain.* 4 have as a result ♦ *It means I'll have to get the early train.*

mean² *adjective* (**meaner, meanest**)
1 not generous; miserly. 2 unkind or spiteful
♦ *a mean trick.* 3 poor in quality or appearance
♦ *a mean little house.*
meanly *adverb* **meanness** *noun*

mean³ *noun* (*plural* **means**)
a point or number midway between two extremes; the average of a set of numbers.
mean *adjective*
midway between two points; average.

meander (*say* mee-an-der) *verb* (**meanders, meandering, meandered**)
take a winding course; wander.
meander *noun*
[named after the Maeander, a river in south-west Turkey (now Mendere or Menderes)]

meaning *noun* (*plural* **meanings**)
what something means.
meaningful *adjective* **meaningless** *adjective*

means *noun*
a way of achieving something or producing a result ♦ *a means of transport.*
by all means certainly. **by means of** by this method; using this. **by no means** not at all.
means *plural noun*
money or other wealth.
live beyond your means spend more than you can afford.

meantime *noun*
in the meantime in the time between two events or while something else is happening.

meanwhile *adverb*
in the time between two events or while something else is happening.

measles *noun*
an infectious disease that causes small red spots on the skin.

measure *verb* (**measures, measuring, measured**)
1 find the size, amount, or extent of something by comparing it with a fixed unit or with an object of known size. 2 be a certain size
♦ *The room measures 3 × 4 metres.*
measurable *adjective* **measurement** *noun*

measure *noun* (*plural* **measures**)
1 a unit used for measuring ♦ *A kilometre is a measure of length.* 2 a device used in measuring. 3 the size or quantity of something. 4 something done for a particular purpose ♦ *We took measures to stop vandalism.*

meat *noun* (*plural* **meats**)
animal flesh used as food.
meaty *adjective*

mechanic *noun* (*plural* **mechanics**)
a person who maintains or repairs machinery.

mechanical *adjective*
1 to do with machines. 2 produced or worked by machines. 3 done or doing things without thought.
mechanically *adverb*

mechanics *noun*
1 the study of movement and force. 2 the study or use of machines.

mechanism *noun* (*plural* **mechanisms**)
1 the moving parts of a machine. 2 the way a machine works. 3 the process by which something is done.

medal *noun* (*plural* **medals**)
a piece of metal shaped like a coin, star, or cross, given to a person for bravery or for achieving something.

meddle *verb* (**meddles, meddling, meddled**)
1 interfere. 2 tinker ♦ *Don't meddle with it.*
meddler *noun* **meddlesome** *adjective*

media *plural* of **medium** *noun*
the media newspapers, radio, and television, which convey information and ideas to the public. (See **medium**.)

ℹ USAGE This word is a plural. Although it is commonly used with a singular verb, this is not generally approved of. Say *The media are* (not 'is') *very influential*. It is incorrect to speak of one of them (e.g. television) as 'this media'.

mediate *verb* (**mediates, mediating, mediated**)
negotiate between the opposing sides in a dispute.
mediation *noun* **mediator** *noun*

medical *adjective*
to do with the treatment of disease.
medically *adverb*

medicine *noun* (*plural* **medicines**)
1 a substance, usually swallowed, used to try to cure a disease. **2** the study and treatment of diseases.
medicinal (*say* med-**iss**-in-al) *adjective*
medicinally *adverb*

medieval (*say* med-ee-**ee**-val) *adjective*
belonging to or to do with the Middle Ages.

mediocre (*say* mee-dee-**oh**-ker) *adjective*
not very good; of only medium quality.
mediocrity *noun*

meditate *verb* (**meditates, meditating, meditated**)
think deeply and quietly.
meditation *noun* **meditative** *adjective*

Mediterranean *adjective*
to do with the Mediterranean Sea (which lies between Europe and Africa) or the countries round it.

medium *adjective*
neither large nor small; moderate.

medium *noun* (*plural* **media**)
1 a thing in which something exists, moves, or is expressed ♦ *Air is the medium in which sound travels.* ♦ *Television is used as a medium for advertising.* (See **media**.) **2** (*plural* **mediums**) a person who claims to be able to communicate with the dead.

medium wave *noun*
a radio wave of a frequency between 300 kilohertz and 3 megahertz.

meek *adjective* (**meeker, meekest**)
quiet and obedient.
meekly *adverb* **meekness** *noun*

meet *verb* (**meets, meeting, met**)
1 come together from different places ♦ *We all met in London.* **2** get to know someone ♦ *We met at a party.* **3** come into contact; touch.
4 go to receive an arrival ♦ *We will meet your train.* **5** pay a bill or the cost of something.
6 satisfy or fulfil ♦ *I hope this meets your needs.*

meet *noun* (*plural* **meets**)
a gathering of riders and hounds for a hunt.

meeting *noun* (*plural* **meetings**)
1 coming together. **2** a number of people who have come together for a discussion, contest, etc.

megabyte *noun* (*plural* **megabytes**)
(in computing) a unit of information roughly equal to one million bytes.

megalomania *noun*
an exaggerated idea of your own importance.
megalomaniac *noun*

megaphone *noun* (*plural* **megaphones**)
a funnel-shaped device for amplifying a person's voice.

melancholy *adjective*
sad; gloomy.

melancholy *noun*
sadness or depression.
[from Greek *melas* = black + *chole* = bile. Black bile in the body was once thought to cause this feeling]

mellow *adjective* (**mellower, mellowest**)
1 not harsh; soft and rich in flavour, colour, or sound. **2** having become more kindly and sympathetic with age.
mellowness *noun*

mellow *verb* (**mellows, mellowing, mellowed**)
make or become mellow.

melodious *adjective*
like a melody; pleasant to listen to.

melodrama *noun* (*plural* **melodramas**)
a play full of dramatic excitement and emotion.
melodramatic *adjective*

melody *noun* (*plural* **melodies**)
a tune, especially a pleasing tune.

melt *verb* (**melts, melting, melted**)
1 make or become liquid by heating. **2** disappear slowly ♦ *The crowd just melted away.* **3** soften ♦ *a pudding that melts in the mouth.*

melting pot *noun* (*plural* **melting pots**)
a place where people of many different races and cultures live and influence each other.

member *noun* (*plural* **members**)
1 a person or thing that belongs to a particular society or group. **2** a part of something.
membership *noun*

membrane *noun* (*plural* **membranes**)
a thin skin or similar covering.
membranous *adjective*

memoir (*say* mem-**wahr**) *noun* (*plural* **memoirs**)
a biography, especially one written by someone who knew the person.

memorable *adjective*
1 worth remembering. **2** easy to remember.
memorably *adverb*

memorandum *noun* (*plural* **memoranda** or **memorandums**)
1 a note to remind yourself of something.
2 a note from one person to another in the same firm.

memorial *noun* (*plural* **memorials**)
something to remind people of a person or event ♦ *a war memorial.*
memorial *adjective*

memorize *verb* (**memorizes, memorizing, memorized**)
get something into your memory.

memory noun (plural **memories**)
1 the ability to remember things. **2** something that you remember. **3** the part of a computer where information is stored.
in memory of in honour of a person or event remembered.

menace noun (plural **menaces**)
1 a threat or danger. **2** a troublesome person or thing.

menace verb (**menaces, menacing, menaced**)
threaten with harm or danger.

mend verb (**mends, mending, mended**)
1 repair. **2** make or become better; improve.
mender noun

mend noun (plural **mends**)
a repair.
on the mend getting better after an illness.

menopause noun
the time of life when a woman gradually ceases to menstruate.

menstruate verb (**menstruates, menstruating, menstruated**)
bleed from the womb about once a month, as girls and women normally do from their teens until middle age.
menstruation noun **menstrual** adjective

-ment suffix
used to make nouns, as in amusement and oddments.

mental adjective
1 to do with or in the mind. **2** (informal) mad.
mentally adverb

mentality noun (plural **mentalities**)
a person's mental ability or attitude.

mention verb (**mentions, mentioning, mentioned**)
speak or write about a person or thing briefly; refer to.

mention noun (plural **mentions**)
an example of mentioning something
♦ Our school got a mention in the local paper.

menu (say men-yoo) noun (plural **menus**)
1 a list of the food available in a restaurant or served at a meal. **2** (in computing) a list of possible actions, shown on a screen, from which you decide what you want a computer to do.

MEP abbreviation
Member of the European Parliament.

mercenary adjective
working only for money or some other reward.

mercenary noun (plural **mercenaries**)
a soldier hired to serve in a foreign army.

merchandise noun
goods for sale.

merchant noun (plural **merchants**)
a person involved in trade.

merchant navy noun
the ships and sailors that carry goods for trade.

merciful adjective
showing mercy.
mercifully adverb

mercury noun
a heavy silvery metal that is usually liquid, used in thermometers.
mercuric adjective

mercy noun (plural **mercies**)
1 kindness or pity shown in not punishing a wrongdoer severely or not harming a defeated enemy etc. **2** something to be thankful for.
at the mercy of completely in the power of.

mere adjective
not more than ♦ He's a mere child.

merely adverb
only; simply.

merge verb (**merges, merging, merged**)
combine or blend.

merger noun (plural **mergers**)
the combining of two business companies etc. into one.

meridian noun (plural **meridians**)
a line on a map or globe from the North Pole to the South Pole. The meridian that passes through Greenwich is shown on maps as 0° longitude.

meringue (say mer-ang) noun (plural **meringues**)
a crisp cake made from egg white and sugar.

merit noun (plural **merits**)
1 a quality that deserves praise. **2** excellence.
meritorious adjective

mermaid noun (plural **mermaids**)
a mythical sea creature with a woman's body but with a fish's tail instead of legs.
merman noun

merry adjective (**merrier, merriest**)
cheerful and lively.
merrily adverb **merriment** noun

merry-go-round noun (plural **merry-go-rounds**)
a roundabout at a fair.

mesh noun (plural **meshes**)
1 the open spaces in a net, sieve, or other criss-cross structure. **2** material made like a net.

mesmerize verb (**mesmerizes, mesmerizing, mesmerized**)
1 (old use) hypnotize. **2** fascinate or hold a person's attention completely.
mesmerism noun **mesmeric** adjective

mess noun (plural **messes**)
1 a dirty or untidy condition or thing.
2 a difficult or confused situation; trouble.
3 (in the armed forces) a dining room.
make a mess of bungle.

mess *verb* (**messes, messing, messed**)
mess about behave stupidly or idly. **mess up**
1 make a thing dirty or untidy. 2 bungle or spoil
♦ *They've messed up our plans.* **mess with**
interfere or tinker with.
[from early French *mes* = a portion of food]

message *noun* (*plural* **messages**)
1 a piece of information etc. sent from one
person to another. 2 the main theme or moral of
a book, film, etc.

messenger *noun* (*plural* **messengers**)
a person who carries a message.

Messiah (*say* mis-I-a) *noun* (*plural* **Messiahs**)
1 the saviour of the world expected by the
Jewish people. 2 Jesus Christ, who Christians
believe to be this saviour.
Messianic *adjective*
[from Hebrew *mashiah* = anointed]

messy *adjective* (**messier, messiest**)
dirty and untidy.
messily *adverb* **messiness** *noun*

metabolism (*say* mit-ab-ol-izm) *noun*
the process by which food is built up into living
material in a plant or animal, or used to supply it
with energy.
metabolic *adjective* **metabolize** *verb*

metal *noun* (*plural* **metals**)
a chemical substance, usually hard, that
conducts heat and electricity and melts when it
is heated, e.g. gold, silver, copper, iron, and
uranium.
metallic *adjective*

metamorphosis (*say* met-a-**mor**-fo-sis) *noun*
(*plural* **metamorphoses** (*say*
met-a-**mor**-fo-seez))
a change of form or character, especially one
made by a living thing.
metamorphose *verb*

metaphor *noun* (*plural* **metaphors**)
using a word or phrase in a way that is not
literal, e.g. 'The pictures of starving people
touched our hearts'.
metaphorical *adjective* **metaphorically** *adverb*

meteor (*say* **meet**-ee-er) *noun* (*plural*
meteors)
a piece of rock or metal that moves through
space and burns up when it enters the earth's
atmosphere.

meteorite *noun* (*plural* **meteorites**)
the remains of a meteor that has landed on the
earth.

meter *noun* (*plural* **meters**)
a device for measuring something, e.g. the
amount supplied ♦ *a gas meter.*
meter *verb*

ⓘ USAGE Do not confuse with *metre.*

---

methane (*say* mee-thayn) *noun*
an inflammable gas produced by decaying
matter.

method *noun* (*plural* **methods**)
1 a procedure or way of doing something.
2 methodical behaviour; orderliness.

methodical *adjective*
doing things in an orderly or systematic way.
methodically *adverb*

methylated spirit or **spirits** *noun*
a liquid fuel made from alcohol.

metre *noun* (*plural* **metres**)
1 a unit of length in the metric system, about $39\frac{1}{2}$
inches. 2 rhythm in poetry.

ⓘ USAGE Do not confuse with *meter.*

---

metric *adjective*
1 to do with the metric system. 2 to do with
metre in poetry.
metrically *adverb*

metric system *noun*
a measuring system based on decimal units (the
metre, litre, and gram).

metric ton *noun* (*plural* **metric tons**)
1,000 kilograms.

metronome *noun* (*plural* **metronomes**)
a device that makes a regular clicking noise to
help a person keep in time when practising
music.

mew *verb* (**mews, mewing, mewed**)
make a cat's cry.
mew *noun*

mice *plural* of **mouse.**

microbe *noun* (*plural* **microbes**)
a micro-organism.

microchip *noun* (*plural* **microchips**)
a very small piece of silicon etc. made to work
like a complex wired electric circuit.

microcosm *noun* (*plural* **microcosms**)
a world in miniature; something regarded as
resembling something else on a very small scale.

microfilm *noun*
a length of film on which written or printed
material is photographed in greatly reduced size.

micron *noun* (*plural* **microns**)
a unit of measurement, one millionth of a metre.

microphone *noun* (*plural* **microphones**)
an electrical device that picks up sound waves
for recording, amplifying, or broadcasting.
[from Greek *mikros* = small + *phone* = sound]

microprocessor *noun* (*plural*
microprocessors)
the central processing unit of a computer,
consisting of one or more microchips.

microscope noun (plural **microscopes**)
an instrument with lenses that magnify tiny objects or details.
[from Greek mikros = small + skopein = to look at]

microscopic adjective
1 extremely small; too small to be seen without the aid of a microscope. 2 to do with a microscope.

microwave noun (plural **microwaves**)
1 a very short electromagnetic wave.
2 a microwave oven.

microwave oven noun (plural **microwave ovens**)
an oven that uses microwaves to heat or cook food very quickly.

mid adjective
1 in the middle of ♦ mid-July; ♦ He's in his mid thirties.

midday noun
the middle of the day; noon.

middle noun (plural **middles**)
1 the place or part of something that is at the same distance from all its sides or edges or from both its ends. 2 someone's waist.
in the middle of during or halfway through a process or activity ♦ I'm just in the middle of cooking.

middle adjective
1 placed or happening in the middle. 2 moderate in size or rank etc.

middle-aged adjective
aged between about 40 and 60.

Middle Ages noun
the period in history from about AD 1000 to 1400.

middle class or **classes** noun
the class of people between the upper class and the working class, including business and professional people such as teachers, doctors, and lawyers.
middle-class adjective

Middle East noun
the countries from Egypt to Iran inclusive.

Middle English noun
the English language from about 1150 to 1500.

middle school noun (plural **middle schools**)
a school for children aged from about 9 to 13.

middling adjective
of medium size or quality.

middling adverb
fairly or moderately.

midge noun (plural **midges**)
a small insect like a gnat.

midget noun (plural **midgets**)
an extremely small person or thing.
midget adjective

midland adjective
1 to do with the middle part of a country.
2 to do with the Midlands.

Midlands plural noun
the central part of England.

midnight noun
twelve o'clock at night.

midst noun
in the midst of in the middle of or surrounded by. **in our midst** among us.

midsummer noun
the middle of summer, about 21 June in the northern hemisphere.

midway adverb
halfway.

midwife noun (plural **midwives**)
a person trained to look after a woman who is giving birth to a baby.
midwifery (say mid-wif-ri) noun

might¹ noun
great strength or power.
with all your might using all your strength and determination.

might² auxiliary verb
used 1 as the past tense of **may¹** (We told her she might go), 2 to express possibility (It might be true).

mighty adjective
very strong or powerful.
mightily adverb **mightiness** noun

migraine (say mee-grayn or my-grayn) noun (plural **migraines**)
a severe kind of headache.

migrate verb (**migrates, migrating, migrated**)
1 leave one place or country and settle in another. 2 (said about birds or animals) move periodically from one area to another.
migration noun **migratory** adjective

mild adjective (**milder, mildest**)
1 gentle; not harsh or severe. 2 (said about weather) quite warm and pleasant. 3 (said about food) not strongly flavoured.
mildly adverb **mildness** noun

mildew noun
a tiny fungus that forms a white coating on things kept in damp conditions.
mildewed adjective

mile noun (plural **miles**)
a measure of distance equal to 1,760 yards (about 1.6 kilometres).
[from Latin mille = thousand. A Roman mile was reckoned as 1,000 paces]

milestone noun (plural **milestones**)
1 a stone of a kind that used to be fixed beside a road to mark the distance between towns.
2 an important event in life or history.

militant *adjective*
1 eager to fight. 2 forceful or aggressive
♦ *a militant protest.*
militant *noun* **militancy** *noun*

military *adjective*
to do with soldiers or the armed forces.
the military a country's armed forces.

milk *noun*
1 a white liquid that female mammals produce in
their bodies to feed their babies. 2 the milk of
cows, sheep, or goats used as food by human
beings. 3 a milky liquid, e.g. that in a coconut.
milk *verb* (**milks, milking, milked**)
get the milk from a cow or other animal.
[from Old English]

milkman *noun* (*plural* **milkmen**)
a man who delivers milk to customers' houses.

milkshake *noun* (*plural* **milkshakes**)
a cold frothy drink made from milk whisked
with sweet fruit flavouring.

milky *adjective* (**milkier, milkiest**)
1 like milk. 2 white.

Milky Way *noun*
the broad band of stars formed by our galaxy.

mill *noun* (*plural* **mills**)
1 machinery for grinding corn to make flour; a
building containing this machinery. 2 a grinding
machine ♦ *a pepper mill.* 3 a factory for
processing certain materials ♦ *a paper mill.*

millennium *noun* (*plural* **millenniums**)
a period of 1,000 years.

millennium bug *noun*
a fault in older computer systems that made it
impossible for programs to deal with dates later
than 1999.

million *noun* (*plural* **millions**)
one thousand thousand (1,000,000).
millionth *adjective* & *noun*

millionaire *noun* (*plural* **millionaires**)
a person who has at least a million pounds or
dollars; an extremely rich person.

millipede *noun* (*plural* **millipedes**)
a small crawling creature with many legs.

millstone *noun* (*plural* **millstones**)
either of a pair of large circular stones between
which corn is ground.
a millstone around someone's neck a heavy
responsibility or burden.

mimic *verb* (**mimics, mimicking, mimicked**)
imitate someone, especially to amuse people.
mimicry *noun*
mimic *noun* (*plural* **mimics**)
a person who mimics others.

mince *verb* (**minces, mincing, minced**)
1 cut into very small pieces in a machine.
2 walk in an affected way with short quick steps.
mincer *noun*
not to mince matters speak bluntly.

mince *noun*
minced meat.

mincemeat *noun*
a sweet mixture of currants, raisins, apple, etc.
used in pies.

mince pie *noun* (*plural* **mince pies**)
a pie containing mincemeat, traditionally eaten
at Christmas.

mind *noun* (*plural* **minds**)
1 the ability to think, feel, understand, and
remember, originating in the brain. 2 a person's
thoughts, opinion, or intention ♦ *Have you made
your mind up?* ♦ *I changed my mind.*
in two minds not able to decide. **out of your
mind** insane.
mind *verb* (**minds, minding, minded**)
1 look after ♦ *He was minding the baby.*
2 be careful about ♦ *Mind the step.* 3 be sad or
upset about something; object to ♦ *We don't
mind waiting.*
minder *noun*

mindless *adjective*
done without thinking; stupid or pointless.

mine¹ *possessive pronoun*
belonging to me.

mine² *noun* (*plural* **mines**)
1 a place where coal, metal, precious stones, etc.
are dug out of the ground. 2 an explosive placed
in or on the ground or in the sea etc. to destroy
people or things that come close to it.
mine *verb* (**mines, mining, mined**)
1 dig from a mine. 2 lay explosive mines in a
place.

minefield *noun* (*plural* **minefields**)
1 an area where explosive mines have been laid.
2 something with hidden dangers or problems.

miner *noun* (*plural* **miners**)
a person who works in a mine.

mineral *noun* (*plural* **minerals**)
1 a hard inorganic substance found in the
ground. 2 a cold fizzy non-alcoholic drink.

mingle *verb* (**mingles, mingling, mingled**)
mix or blend.

mingy *adjective* (**mingier, mingiest**) (*informal*)
not generous; mean.

miniature *adjective*
1 very small. 2 copying something on a very
small scale ♦ *a miniature railway.*
miniature *noun* (*plural* **miniatures**)
1 a very small portrait. 2 a small-scale model.

minim *noun* (*plural* **minims**)
a note in music, lasting twice as long as a
crotchet (written ♩).

minimize *verb* (**minimizes, minimizing,
minimized**)
make something as small as possible.

minimum *noun* (*plural* **minima** or **minimums**)
the lowest possible number or amount. (The
opposite is **maximum**.)
minimal *adjective*

minister *noun* (*plural* **ministers**)
1 a person in charge of a government
department. **2** a member of the clergy.
ministerial *adjective*

ministry *noun* (*plural* **ministries**)
1 a government department ♦ *the Ministry of
Defence*. **2** the work of the clergy.

minnow *noun* (*plural* **minnows**)
a tiny freshwater fish.

minor *adjective*
1 not very important, especially when compared
to something else. **2** to do with the musical scale
that has a semitone after the second note.
(Compare **major**.)

minor *noun* (*plural* **minors**)
a person under the age of legal responsibility.

minority *noun* (*plural* **minorities**)
1 the smallest part of a group of people or things.
2 a small group that is different from others.
(Compare **majority**.)

minstrel *noun* (*plural* **minstrels**)
a travelling singer and musician in the Middle
Ages.

mint¹ *noun* (*plural* **mints**)
1 a plant with fragrant leaves that are used for
flavouring things. **2** peppermint or a sweet
flavoured with this.
[from Latin *mentha* = mint]

mint² *noun* (*plural* **mints**)
the place where a country's coins are made.
in mint condition in perfect condition, as though
it had never been used.

mint *verb* (**mints, minting, minted**)
make coins.
[from Latin *moneta* = money]

minus *preposition*
with the next number or thing subtracted
♦ *Ten minus four equals six (10 − 4 = 6).*

minus *adjective*
less than zero ♦ *temperatures of minus ten
degrees (−10°).*
[from Latin, = less]

minute¹ (*say* min-it) *noun* (*plural* **minutes**)
1 one-sixtieth of an hour. **2** a very short time;
a moment. **3** a particular time ♦ *Come here this
minute!* **4** one-sixtieth of a degree (used in
measuring angles).

minute² (*say* my-**newt**) *adjective*
1 very small ♦ *a minute insect.* **2** very detailed
♦ *a minute examination.*
minutely *adverb*

minutes *plural noun*
a written summary of what was said at a
meeting.

miracle *noun* (*plural* **miracles**)
something wonderful and good that happens,
especially something believed to have a
supernatural or divine cause.
miraculous *adjective* **miraculously** *adverb*

mirage (*say* mi-rahzh) *noun* (*plural* **mirages**)
an illusion; something that seems to be there but
is not, especially when a lake seems to appear in
a desert.

mirror *noun* (*plural* **mirrors**)
a device or surface of reflecting material, usually
glass.

mirror *verb* (**mirrors, mirroring, mirrored**)
reflect in or like a mirror.

mis- *prefix*
badly or wrongly. (Compare **amiss**.)

misbehave *verb* (**misbehaves, misbehaving,
misbehaved**)
behave badly.
misbehaviour *noun*

miscalculate *verb* (**miscalculates,
miscalculating, miscalculated**)
calculate incorrectly.
miscalculation *noun*

miscarriage *noun* (*plural* **miscarriages**)
1 the birth of a baby before it has developed
enough to live. **2** failure to achieve the right
result ♦ *a miscarriage of justice.*

miscellaneous (*say* mis-el-**ay**-nee-us) *adjective*
of various kinds; mixed.
miscellany (*say* mis-el-an-ee) *noun*

mischief *noun*
1 naughty or troublesome behaviour. **2** trouble
caused by this.
mischievous *adjective* **mischievously** *adverb*

misconception *noun* (*plural* **misconceptions**)
a mistaken idea.

misconduct *noun*
bad behaviour by someone in a responsible
position ♦ *professional misconduct.*

miser *noun* (*plural* **misers**)
a person who hoards money and spends as little
as possible.
miserly *adjective* **miserliness** *noun*

miserable *adjective*
1 full of misery; very unhappy, poor, or
uncomfortable. **2** disagreeable or unpleasant
♦ *miserable weather.*
miserably *adverb*

misery *noun* (*plural* **miseries**)
1 great unhappiness or discomfort or suffering,
especially lasting for a long time. **2** (*informal*) a
person who is always unhappy or complaining.

misfire *verb* (**misfires, misfiring, misfired**)
1 fail to fire. **2** fail to function correctly or to have
the required effect ♦ *The joke misfired.*

misfit *noun* (*plural* **misfits**)
a person who does not fit in well with other people or who is not well suited to his or her work.

misfortune *noun* (*plural* **misfortunes**)
1 bad luck. **2** an unlucky event or accident.

misgiving *noun* (*plural* **misgivings**)
a feeling of doubt or slight fear or mistrust.

misguided *adjective*
guided by mistaken ideas or beliefs.

mishap (*say* mis-hap) *noun* (*plural* **mishaps**)
an unlucky accident.

misinterpret *verb* (**misinterprets, misinterpreting, misinterpreted**)
interpret incorrectly.
misinterpretation *noun*

mislay *verb* (**mislays, mislaying, mislaid**)
lose something for a short time because you cannot remember where you put it.

mislead *verb* (**misleads, misleading, misled**)
give somebody a wrong idea or impression deliberately.

misnomer *noun* (*plural* **misnomers**)
an unsuitable name for something.

misogynist (*say* mis-oj-in-ist) *noun* (*plural* **misogynists**)
a man who hates women.
misogyny *noun*

misplaced *adjective*
1 placed wrongly. **2** inappropriate ♦ *misplaced loyalty.*
misplacement *noun*

misprint *noun* (*plural* **misprints**)
a mistake in printing.

misrepresent *verb* (**misrepresents, misrepresenting, misrepresented**)
represent in a false or misleading way.
misrepresentation *noun*

Miss *noun* (*plural* **Misses**)
a title put before a girl's or unmarried woman's name.
[short for *mistress*]

miss *verb* (**misses, missing, missed**)
1 fail to hit, reach, catch, see, hear, or find something. **2** be sad because someone or something is not with you. **3** notice that something has gone.
miss out 1 leave out. **2** not get the benefit.

miss *noun* (*plural* **misses**)
missing something ♦ *Was that shot a hit or a miss?*

misshapen *adjective*
badly shaped.

missile *noun* (*plural* **missiles**)
a weapon or other object for firing or throwing at a target.

missing *adjective*
1 lost; not in the proper place. **2** absent.

mission *noun* (*plural* **missions**)
1 an important job that somebody is sent to do or feels they must do. **2** a place or building where missionaries work. **3** a military or scientific expedition.

missionary *noun* (*plural* **missionaries**)
a person who is sent to another country to spread a religious faith.

misspell *verb* (**misspells, misspelling, misspelt** or **misspelled**)
spell a word wrongly.

mist *noun* (*plural* **mists**)
1 damp cloudy air near the ground. **2** condensed water vapour on a window, mirror, etc.
mist *verb*

mistake *noun* (*plural* **mistakes**)
1 something done wrongly. **2** an incorrect opinion.

mistake *verb* (**mistakes, mistaking, mistook, mistaken**)
1 misunderstand ♦ *Don't mistake my meaning.* **2** choose or identify wrongly ♦ *We mistook her for her sister.*

mistaken *adjective*
1 incorrect. **2** having an incorrect opinion.

mister *noun* (*informal*)
a form of address to a man.

mistletoe *noun*
a plant with white berries that grows as a parasite on trees.

mistress *noun* (*plural* **mistresses**)
1 a woman who is in charge of something. **2** a woman who is a man's lover but not his wife. **3** a woman teacher. **4** the woman owner of a dog or other animal.

mistrust *verb* (**mistrusts, mistrusting, mistrusted**)
feel no trust in somebody or something.
mistrust *noun*

misty *adjective* (**mistier, mistiest**)
1 full of mist. **2** not clear or distinct.
mistily *adverb* **mistiness** *noun*

misunderstand *verb* (**misunderstands, misunderstanding, misunderstood**)
get a wrong idea or impression of something.
misunderstanding *noun*

misuse (*say* mis-yooz) *verb* (**misuses, misusing, misused**)
1 use incorrectly. **2** treat badly.
misuse (*say* mis-yooss) *noun*

mitten *noun* (*plural* **mittens**)
a kind of glove without separate parts for the fingers.

mix *verb* (**mixes, mixing, mixed**)
1 put different things together so that they are no longer distinct; blend or combine. **2** (said about a person) get together with others.
mixer *noun*
mix up 1 mix thoroughly. **2** confuse.

mix *noun* (*plural* **mixes**)
a mixture.

mixed *adjective*
containing two or more kinds of things or people.

mixture *noun* (*plural* **mixtures**)
1 something made of different things mixed together. **2** the process of mixing.

mnemonic (*say* nim-on-ik) *noun* (*plural* **mnemonics**)
a verse or saying that helps you to remember something.
[from Greek *mneme* = memory]

moan *verb* (**moans, moaning, moaned**)
1 make a long low sound of pain or suffering. **2** grumble.
moan *noun*

moat *noun* (*plural* **moats**)
a deep wide ditch round a castle, usually filled with water.
moated *adjective*

mob *noun* (*plural* **mobs**)
1 a large disorderly crowd. **2** a gang.

mobile *adjective*
moving easily.
mobility *noun*

mobile *noun* (*plural* **mobiles**)
1 a decoration for hanging up so that its parts move in currents of air. **2** a mobile phone.

mobile home *noun* (*plural* **mobile homes**)
a large caravan permanently parked and used for living in.

mobile phone *noun* (*plural* **mobile phones**)
a phone you can carry about that uses a cellular radio system.

mobilize *verb* (**mobilizes, mobilizing, mobilized**)
assemble people or things for a particular purpose, especially for war.
mobilization *noun*

mock *verb* (**mocks, mocking, mocked**)
1 make fun of a person or thing. **2** imitate someone or something to make people laugh.
mockery *noun*
mock *adjective*
imitation, not real ♦ *mock exams*.

mock-up *noun* (*plural* **mock-ups**)
a model of something, made in order to test or study it.

mode *noun* (*plural* **modes**)
1 the way a thing is done. **2** what is fashionable.

model *noun* (*plural* **models**)
1 a copy of an object, usually on a smaller scale. **2** a particular design. **3** a person who poses for an artist or displays clothes by wearing them. **4** a person or thing that is worth copying.

model *verb* (**models, modelling, modelled**)
1 make a model of something. **2** design or plan something using another thing as an example. **3** work as an artist's model or a fashion model.

modem (*say* moh-dem) *noun* (*plural* **modems**)
a device that links a computer to a telephone line for transmitting data.

moderate *adjective*
1 medium; not extremely small or great or hot etc. ♦ *a moderate climate*. **2** not extreme or unreasonable ♦ *moderate opinions*.
moderately *adverb*

moderate (*say* mod-er-ayt) *verb* (**moderates, moderating, moderated**)
make or become moderate.
moderation *noun*
in moderation in moderate amounts.

modern *adjective*
1 belonging to the present or recent times. **2** in fashion now.
modernity *noun*

modernize *verb* (**modernizes, modernizing, modernized**)
make a thing more modern.
modernization *noun*

modest *adjective*
1 not vain or boastful. **2** moderate in size or amount ♦ *a modest income*. **3** not showy or splendid. **4** behaving or dressing decently or decorously.
modestly *adverb* **modesty** *noun*

modify *verb* (**modifies, modifying, modified**)
1 change something slightly. **2** describe a word or limit its meaning ♦ *Adjectives modify nouns*.
modification *noun*

modulate *verb* (**modulates, modulating, modulated**)
1 adjust or regulate. **2** vary in pitch or tone etc. **3** alter an electronic wave to allow signals to be sent.
modulation *noun* **modulator** *noun*

module *noun* (*plural* **modules**)
1 an independent part of a spacecraft, building, etc. **2** a unit; a section of a course of study.
modular *adjective*

moist *adjective*
slightly wet.
moistly *adverb* **moistness** *noun*

moisten *verb* (**moistens, moistening, moistened**)
make or become moist.

moisture *noun*
water in the air or making a thing moist.

moisturizer *noun*
a cream used to make the skin less dry.

mole¹ *noun* (*plural* **moles**)
1 a small furry animal that burrows under the ground. 2 a spy working within an organization and passing information to another organization or country.

mole² *noun* (*plural* **moles**)
a small dark spot on skin.

molecule *noun* (*plural* **molecules**)
the smallest part into which a substance can be divided without changing its chemical nature; a group of atoms.
molecular (*say* mo-lek-yoo-ler) *adjective*

molehill *noun* (*plural* **molehills**)
a small pile of earth thrown up by a burrowing mole.

molest *verb* (**molests, molesting, molested**)
1 annoy or pester. 2 attack or abuse someone sexually.

mollusc *noun* (*plural* **molluscs**)
any of a group of animals including snails, slugs, and mussels, with soft bodies, no backbones, and sometimes external shells.

molten *adjective*
melted; made liquid by great heat.

moment *noun* (*plural* **moments**)
1 a very short time. 2 a particular time
♦ *Call me the moment she arrives.*

momentary *adjective*
lasting for only a moment.
momentarily *adverb*

momentous (*say* mo-ment-us) *adjective*
very important.

momentum *noun*
1 the ability something has to keep moving or developing. 2 (in science) the quantity of motion of a moving object, measured as its mass multiplied by its velocity.

monarch *noun* (*plural* **monarchs**)
a king, queen, emperor, or empress ruling a country.
monarchic *adjective*

monarchy *noun* (*plural* **monarchies**)
a country ruled by a monarch.
monarchist *noun*

monastery *noun* (*plural* **monasteries**)
a building where monks live and work.
monastic *adjective*

Monday *noun*
the day of the week following Sunday.
[from Old English *monandaeg* = day of the moon]

monetary *adjective*
to do with money.

money *noun*
1 coins and banknotes. 2 wealth.

mongrel (*say* mung-rel) *noun* (*plural* **mongrels**)
a dog of mixed breeds.

monitor *noun* (*plural* **monitors**)
1 a device for watching or testing how something is working. 2 a screen that displays data and images produced by a computer. 3 a pupil who is given a special responsibility in a school.

monitor *verb* (**monitors, monitoring, monitored**)
watch or test how something is working.

monk *noun* (*plural* **monks**)
a member of a community of men who live according to the rules of a religious organization. (Compare **nun**.)

monkey *noun* (*plural* **monkeys**)
1 an animal with long arms, hands with thumbs, and often a tail. 2 a mischievous person, especially a child.

monocle *noun* (*plural* **monocles**)
a lens worn over one eye, like half of a pair of glasses.

monogram *noun* (*plural* **monograms**)
a design made up of a letter or letters, especially a person's initials.
monogrammed *adjective*

monolith *noun* (*plural* **monoliths**)
a large single upright block of stone.

monolithic *adjective*
1 to do with or like a monolith. 2 huge and difficult to move or change.

monologue *noun* (*plural* **monologues**)
a long speech by one person.

monopolize *verb* (**monopolizes, monopolizing, monopolized**)
take the whole of something for yourself
♦ *One girl monopolized my attention.*
monopolization *noun*

monopoly *noun* (*plural* **monopolies**)
the exclusive right to own something or to provide a service.

monosyllable *noun* (*plural* **monosyllables**)
a word with only one syllable.
monosyllabic *adjective*

monotone *noun*
a level unchanging tone of voice in speaking or singing.

monotonous *adjective*
boring because it does not change ♦ *monotonous work.*
monotonously *adverb* **monotony** *noun*

monsoon *noun* (*plural* **monsoons**)
1 a strong wind in and near the Indian Ocean, bringing heavy rain in summer. 2 the rainy season brought by this wind.

monster *noun* (*plural* **monsters**)
1 a large frightening creature. 2 a huge thing. 3 a wicked or cruel person.

monster *adjective*
huge.

monstrosity *noun* (*plural* **monstrosities**)
a monstrous thing.

monstrous *adjective*
1 like a monster; huge. 2 very shocking or outrageous.

month *noun* (*plural* **months**)
each of the twelve parts into which a year is divided.

monthly *adjective* & *adverb*
happening or done once a month.

monument *noun* (*plural* **monuments**)
a statue, building, or column etc. put up as a memorial of some person or event.

monumental *adjective*
1 built as a monument. 2 very large or important.

moo *verb* (**moos, mooing, mooed**)
make the low deep sound of a cow.
-moo *noun*

mood *noun* (*plural* **moods**)
the way someone feels ♦ *She is in a cheerful mood.*

moody *adjective* (**moodier, moodiest**)
1 gloomy or sullen. 2 having sudden changes of mood for no apparent reason.
moodily *adverb* **moodiness** *noun*

moon *noun* (*plural* **moons**)
1 the natural satellite of the earth that can be seen in the sky at night. 2 a satellite of any planet.
moonbeam *noun* **moonlight** *noun* **moonlit** *adjective*

moor¹ *noun* (*plural* **moors**)
an area of rough land covered with heather, bracken, and bushes.
moorland *noun*

moor² *verb* (**moors, mooring, moored**)
fasten a boat etc. to a fixed object by means of a cable.

mooring *noun* (*plural* **moorings**)
a place where a boat can be moored.

mop *noun* (*plural* **mops**)
1 a bunch or pad of soft material fastened on the end of a stick, used for cleaning floors etc. 2 a thick mass of hair.

mop *verb* (**mops, mopping, mopped**)
clean or wipe with a mop etc.
mop up 1 wipe or soak up liquid. 2 deal with the last parts of something ♦ *The army is mopping up the last of the rebels.*

mope *verb* (**mopes, moping, moped**)
be sad.

moped (*say* moh-ped) *noun* (*plural* **mopeds**)
a kind of small motorcycle.

moral *adjective*
1 connected with what is right and wrong in behaviour. 2 good or virtuous.
morally *adverb* **morality** *noun*
moral support help in the form of encouragement.

moral *noun* (*plural* **morals**)
a lesson in right behaviour taught by a story or event.

❶ USAGE Do not confuse with *morale*.

morale (*say* mor-ahl) *noun*
the level of confidence and good spirits in a person or group of people ♦ *Morale was high after the victory.*

❶ USAGE Do not confuse with *moral*.

morals *plural noun*
standards of behaviour.

morbid *adjective*
1 thinking about gloomy or unpleasant things. 2 (in medicine) unhealthy ♦ *a morbid growth.*
morbidly *adverb* **morbidity** *noun*

more *adjective* (comparative of **much** and **many**)
greater in amount etc.

more *noun*
a greater amount.

more *adverb*
1 to a greater extent ♦ *more beautiful.* 2 again ♦ *once more.*
more or less 1 approximately. 2 nearly or practically.

moreover *adverb*
besides; in addition to what has been said.

Mormon *noun* (*plural* **Mormons**)
a member of a religious group founded in the USA.

morning *noun* (*plural* **mornings**)
the early part of the day, before noon or before lunchtime.

moron *noun* (*plural* **morons**) (*informal*)
a very stupid person.
moronic *adjective*

morose (*say* mo-rohss) *adjective*
bad-tempered and miserable.
morosely *adverb* **moroseness** *noun*

Morse code *noun*
a signalling code using short and long sounds or flashes of light (dots and dashes) to represent letters.

morsel *noun* (*plural* **morsels**)
a small piece of food.

mortal *adjective*
1 not living for ever ♦ *All of us are mortal.*
2 causing death; fatal ♦ *a mortal wound.*
3 deadly ♦ *mortal enemies.*
mortally *adverb* **mortality** *noun*

mortal *noun* (*plural* **mortals**)
a human being, as compared to a god or immortal spirit.

mortar *noun* (*plural* **mortars**)
1 a mixture of sand, cement, and water used in building to stick bricks together. **2** a hard bowl in which substances are pounded with a pestle. **3** a short cannon for firing shells at a high angle.

mortgage (*say* mor-gij) *noun* (*plural* **mortgages**)
an arrangement to borrow money to buy a house, with the house as security for the loan.

mortgage *verb* (**mortgages, mortgaging, mortgaged**)
offer a house etc. as security in return for a loan.

mortify *verb* (**mortifies, mortifying, mortified**)
humiliate someone or make them feel very ashamed.
mortification *noun*

mortuary *noun* (*plural* **mortuaries**)
a place where dead bodies are kept before being buried or cremated.

mosaic (*say* mo-zay-ik) *noun* (*plural* **mosaics**)
a picture or design made from small coloured pieces of stone or glass.

mosque (*say* mosk) *noun* (*plural* **mosques**)
a building where Muslims worship.

mosquito *noun* (*plural* **mosquitoes**)
a kind of gnat that sucks blood.

moss *noun* (*plural* **mosses**)
a plant that grows in damp places and has no flowers.
mossy *adjective*

most *adjective* (superlative of **much** and **many**)
greatest in amount or degree ♦ *Most people came by bus.*

most *noun*
the greatest amount ♦ *Most of the food was eaten.*

most *adverb*
1 to the greatest extent; more than any other ♦ *most beautiful.* **2** very or extremely ♦ *most impressive.*

mostly *adverb*
mainly.

motel *noun* (*plural* **motels**)
a hotel providing accommodation for motorists and their cars.

moth *noun* (*plural* **moths**)
an insect rather like a butterfly, that usually flies at night.

mother *noun* (*plural* **mothers**)
a female parent.
motherhood *noun*

mother *verb* (**mothers, mothering, mothered**)
look after someone in a motherly way.
[from Old English]

mother-in-law *noun* (*plural* **mothers-in-law**)
the mother of a married person's husband or wife.

motherly *adjective*
kind and gentle like a mother.
motherliness *noun*

motion *noun* (*plural* **motions**)
1 a way of moving; movement. **2** a formal statement to be discussed and voted on at a meeting.

motion *verb* (**motions, motioning, motioned**)
signal by a gesture ♦ *She motioned him to sit beside her.*

motivation *noun*
what gives a person a reason for doing something.
motivate *verb*

motive *noun* (*plural* **motives**)
what makes a person do something ♦ *a motive for murder.*

motor *noun* (*plural* **motors**)
a machine providing power to drive machinery etc.; an engine.

motor *verb* (**motors, motoring, motored**)
go or take someone in a car.

motorcycle or **motorbike** *noun* (*plural* **motorcycles** or **motorbikes**)
a two-wheeled road vehicle with an engine.
motorcyclist *noun*

motorist *noun* (*plural* **motorists**)
a person who drives a car.

motorway *noun* (*plural* **motorways**)
a wide road for fast long-distance traffic.

motto *noun* (*plural* **mottoes**)
1 a short saying used as a guide for behaviour ♦ *Their motto is 'Who dares, wins'.* **2** a short verse or riddle etc. found inside a cracker.

mould¹ *noun* (*plural* **moulds**)
a hollow container of a particular shape, in which a liquid or soft substance is put to set into this shape.

mould *verb* (**moulds, moulding, moulded**)
make something have a particular shape or character.

mould² *noun*
a furry growth of very small fungi.
mouldy *adjective*

moulder *verb* (**moulders, mouldering, mouldered**)
rot away or decay into dust.

moult *verb* (**moults, moulting, moulted**)
shed feathers, hair, or skin etc. while a new growth forms.

mound *noun* (*plural* **mounds**)
1 a pile of earth or stones etc. **2** a small hill.

mount verb (mounts, mounting, mounted)
1 climb or go up; ascend. 2 get on a horse or bicycle etc. 3 increase in amount ♦ Our costs mounted. 4 place or fix in position for use or display ♦ Mount your photos in an album.

mount noun (plural mounts)
1 a mountain ♦ Mount Everest. 2 something on which an object is mounted. 3 a horse etc. for riding.
[from Latin mons = mountain]

mountain noun (plural mountains)
1 a very high hill. 2 a large heap or pile or quantity.
mountainous adjective

mountaineer noun (plural mountaineers)
a person who climbs mountains.
mountaineering noun

mounted adjective
serving on horseback ♦ mounted police.

mourn verb (mourns, mourning, mourned)
be sad, especially because someone has died.
mourner noun

mournful adjective
sad and sorrowful.
mournfully adverb

mouse noun (plural mice)
1 a small animal with a long thin tail and a pointed nose. 2 (plural mouses or mice) a small device which you move around on a mat to control the movements of a cursor on a VDU screen.
mousetrap noun **mousy** adjective

mousse (say mooss) noun (plural mousses)
1 a creamy pudding flavoured with fruit or chocolate. 2 a frothy creamy substance put on the hair so that it can be styled more easily.

moustache (say mus-tahsh) noun (plural moustaches)
hair allowed to grow on a man's upper lip.

mouth noun (plural mouths)
1 the opening through which food is taken into the body. 2 the place where a river enters the sea. 3 an opening or outlet.
mouthful noun

mouth organ noun (plural mouth organs)
a small musical instrument that you play by blowing and sucking while passing it along your lips.

mouthpiece noun (plural mouthpieces)
the part of a musical instrument or other device that you put to your mouth.

move verb (moves, moving, moved)
1 take or go from one place to another; change a person's or thing's position. 2 affect a person's feelings ♦ Their sad story moved us deeply. 3 put forward a formal statement (a **motion**) to be discussed and voted on at a meeting.
mover noun

move noun (plural moves)
1 a movement or action. 2 a player's turn to move a piece in chess or other games.
get a move on (informal) hurry up.
on the move moving or making progress.

movement noun (plural movements)
1 moving or being moved. 2 a group of people working together to achieve something. 3 one of the main divisions of a symphony or other long musical work.

mow verb (mows, mowing, mowed, mown)
cut down grass etc.
mower noun
mow down knock down and kill.

MP abbreviation
Member of Parliament.

Mr (say mist-er) noun (plural Messrs)
a title put before a man's name.

Mrs (say mis-iz) noun (plural Mrs)
a title put before a married woman's name.

Ms (say miz) noun
a title put before a woman's name.

ⓘ USAGE You put Ms before the name of a woman if she does not wish to be called 'Miss' or 'Mrs', or if you do not know whether she is married.

M.Sc. abbreviation
Master of Science.

Mt abbreviation
mount or mountain.

much adjective (more, most)
existing in a large amount ♦ much noise.

much noun
a large amount of something.

much adverb
1 greatly or considerably ♦ much to my surprise. 2 approximately ♦ It is much the same.

muck noun
1 farmyard manure. 2 (informal) dirt or filth. 3 (informal) a mess.
mucky adjective

muck verb
muck about (informal) mess about. **muck out** clean out the place where an animal is kept.
muck up (informal) 1 make dirty. 2 make a mess of; spoil.
[probably from a Scandinavian language]

mud noun
wet soft earth.
muddy adjective **muddiness** noun

muddle verb (muddles, muddling, muddled)
1 jumble or mix things up. 2 confuse.
muddler noun

muddle noun (plural muddles)
a muddled condition or thing; confusion or disorder.

mudguard noun (plural **mudguards**)
a curved cover over the top part of the wheel of a bicycle etc. to protect the rider from the mud and water thrown up by the wheel.

muff noun (plural **muffs**)
a short tube-shaped piece of warm material into which the hands are pushed from opposite ends.

muffin noun (plural **muffins**)
1 a flat bun eaten toasted and buttered. **2** a small sponge cake, usually containing fruit, chocolate chips, etc.

muffle verb (**muffles, muffling, muffled**)
1 cover or wrap something to protect it or keep it warm. **2** deaden the sound of something ♦ a muffled scream.

muffler noun (plural **mufflers**)
a warm scarf.

mug noun (plural **mugs**)
1 a kind of large cup with straight sides. **2** (slang) a fool; a person who is easily deceived. **3** (slang) a person's face.

mug verb (**mugs, mugging, mugged**)
attack and rob somebody in the street.
mugger noun

mule noun (plural **mules**)
an animal that is the offspring of a donkey and a mare, known for being stubborn.
mulish adjective

mull¹ verb (**mulls, mulling, mulled**)
heat wine or beer with sugar and spices, as a drink ♦ mulled ale.

mull² verb (**mulls, mulling, mulled**)
mull something over think about something carefully; ponder.

multicultural adjective
made up of people of many different races, religions, and cultures.

multilateral adjective
(said about an agreement or treaty) made between three or more people or countries etc.

multimedia adjective
using more than one medium ♦ a multimedia show with pictures, lights, and music.

multimedia noun
a computer program with sound and still and moving pictures linked to the text.

multimillionaire noun (plural **multimillionaires**)
a person with a fortune of several million pounds or dollars.

multinational noun (plural **multinationals**)
a large business company which works in several countries.

multiple adjective
having many parts or elements.

multiple noun (plural **multiples**)
a number that contains another number (a **factor**) an exact amount of times with no remainder ♦ 8 and 12 are multiples of 4.

multiple sclerosis noun
a disease of the nervous system which makes a person unable to control their movements, and may affect their sight.

multiply verb (**multiplies, multiplying, multiplied**)
1 take a number a given quantity of times ♦ Five multiplied by four equals twenty (5 × 4 = 20). **2** make or become many; increase.
multiplication noun **multiplier** noun

multiracial adjective
consisting of people of many different races.

multitude noun (plural **multitudes**)
a great number of people or things.
multitudinous adjective

mumble verb (**mumbles, mumbling, mumbled**)
speak indistinctly so that you are not easy to hear.
mumble noun **mumbler** noun

mumbo-jumbo noun
talk that sounds mysterious but has no real meaning.

mummy noun (plural **mummies**)
a corpse wrapped in cloth and treated with oils etc. before being buried so that it does not decay, as was the custom in ancient Egypt.
mummify verb

mumps noun
an infectious disease that makes the neck swell painfully.

munitions plural noun
military weapons, ammunition, and equipment.

mural adjective
on or to do with a wall.

mural noun (plural **murals**)
a picture painted on a wall.

murder verb (**murders, murdering, murdered**)
kill a person unlawfully and deliberately.
murderer noun **murderess** noun

murder noun (plural **murders**)
the murdering of somebody.
murderous adjective

murky adjective (**murkier, murkiest**)
dark and gloomy.
murk noun **murkiness** noun

murmur verb (**murmurs, murmuring, murmured**)
1 make a low continuous sound. **2** speak in a soft voice.
murmur noun

muscle *noun* (*plural* **muscles**)
1 a band or bundle of fibrous tissue that can contract and relax and so produce movement in parts of the body. **2** the power of muscles; strength.
muscular *adjective* **muscularity** *noun*

museum *noun* (*plural* **museums**)
a place where interesting, old, or valuable objects are displayed for people to see.
[from Greek *mouseion* = place of the Muses, the goddesses of the arts and sciences]

mush *noun*
soft pulp.
mushy *adjective*

mushroom *noun* (*plural* **mushrooms**)
an edible fungus with a stem and a dome-shaped top.

music *noun*
1 a pattern of pleasant or interesting sounds made by instruments or by the voice. **2** printed or written symbols which stand for musical sounds.
[from Greek *mousike tekhne* = art of the Muses (see **museum**)]

musical *adjective*
1 to do with music. **2** producing music. **3** good at music or interested in it.
musically *adverb*

musical *noun* (*plural* **musicals**)
a play or film containing a lot of songs.

musician *noun* (*plural* **musicians**)
someone who plays a musical instrument.

Muslim *noun* (*plural* **Muslims**)
a person who follows the religious teachings of Muhammad (who lived in about 570–632), set out in the Koran.

must *auxiliary verb*
used to express **1** necessity or obligation (*You must go*), **2** certainty (*You must be joking!*).

mustard *noun*
a yellow paste or powder used to give food a hot taste.
mustard and cress small green plants eaten in salads.

muster *noun* (*plural* **musters**)
an assembly of people or things.
pass muster be up to the required standard.

mustn't (*mainly spoken*)
must not.

musty *adjective* (**mustier, mustiest**)
smelling or tasting mouldy or stale.
mustiness *noun*

mutation *noun* (*plural* **mutations**)
a change in the form of a living creature because of changes in its genes.
mutate *verb* **mutant** *noun*

mute *adjective*
1 silent; not speaking or able to speak.
2 not pronounced ♦ *The g in 'gnat' is mute.*
mutely *adverb* **muteness** *noun*

mutilate *verb* (**mutilates, mutilating, mutilated**)
damage something by breaking or cutting off part of it.
mutilation *noun*

mutineer *noun* (*plural* **mutineers**)
a person who mutinies.

mutiny *noun* (*plural* **mutinies**)
rebellion against authority, especially refusal by members of the armed forces to obey orders.
mutinous *adjective* **mutinously** *adverb*

mutiny *verb* (**mutinies, mutinying, mutinied**)
take part in a mutiny.

mutter *verb* (**mutters, muttering, muttered**)
1 speak in a low voice. **2** grumble.
mutter *noun*

mutton *noun*
meat from a sheep.
[from early French, probably from Celtic]

mutual (*say* **mew**-tew-al) *adjective*
1 given or done to each other ♦ *mutual destruction.* **2** shared by two or more people ♦ *a mutual friend.*
mutually *adverb*

muzzle *noun* (*plural* **muzzles**)
1 an animal's nose and mouth. **2** a cover put over an animal's nose and mouth so that it cannot bite. **3** the open end of a gun.

muzzle *verb* (**muzzles, muzzling, muzzled**)
1 put a muzzle on an animal. **2** silence; prevent a person from expressing opinions.

my *adjective*
belonging to me.

myself *pronoun*
I or me and nobody else.

mysterious *adjective*
full of mystery; puzzling.
mysteriously *adverb*

mystery *noun* (*plural* **mysteries**)
something that cannot be explained or understood; something puzzling.
[from Greek *mysterion* = a secret thing or ceremony]

mystic *adjective*
1 having a spiritual meaning. **2** mysterious and filling people with wonder.
mystical *adjective* **mystically** *adverb* **mysticism** *noun*

mystic *noun* (*plural* **mystics**)
a person who seeks to obtain spiritual contact with God by deep religious meditation.
[from Greek *mystikos* = secret]

mystify *verb* (**mystifies, mystifying, mystified**)
puzzle or bewilder.
mystification *noun*

myth (*say* mith) *noun* (*plural* **myths**)
1 an old story containing ideas about ancient times or about supernatural beings. (Compare **legend**.) 2 an untrue story or belief.

mythical *adjective*
imaginary; found only in myths ♦ *a mythical animal.*

mythology *noun*
myths or the study of myths.
mythological *adjective*

Nn

N. *abbreviation*
1 north. 2 northern.

nag *verb* (**nags, nagging, nagged**)
1 pester a person by keeping on criticizing, complaining, or asking for things. 2 keep on hurting or bothering you ♦ *a nagging pain.*

nail *noun* (*plural* **nails**)
1 the hard covering over the end of a finger or toe. 2 a small sharp piece of metal hammered in to fasten pieces of wood etc. together.

nail *verb* (**nails, nailing, nailed**)
1 fasten with a nail or nails. 2 (*informal*) catch; arrest.

naked *adjective*
1 without any clothes or coverings on. 2 obvious; not hidden ♦ *the naked truth.*
nakedly *adverb* **nakedness** *noun*

naked eye *noun*
the eye when it is not helped by a telescope or microscope etc.

name *noun* (*plural* **names**)
1 the word or words by which a person, animal, place, or thing is known. 2 a person's reputation.

name *verb* (**names, naming, named**)
1 give a name to. 2 state the name or names of. 3 say what you want something to be ♦ *Name your price.*
name the day decide when something, especially a wedding, is to take place or happen ♦ *Have you two named the day yet?*

namely *adverb*
that is to say ♦ *My two favourite subjects are sciences, namely chemistry and biology.*

nanny *noun* (*plural* **nannies**)
a woman employed to look after young children.

nap *noun* (*plural* **naps**)
a short sleep.
catch a person napping catch a person unprepared for something or not alert.

napkin *noun* (*plural* **napkins**)
1 a piece of cloth or paper used at meals to protect your clothes or for wiping your lips or fingers. 2 (*old use*) a nappy.

nappy *noun* (*plural* **nappies**)
a piece of cloth or other fabric put round a baby's bottom.

narcotic *noun* (*plural* **narcotics**)
a drug that makes a person sleepy or unconscious.
narcotic *adjective* **narcosis** *noun*
[from Greek *narke* = numbness]

narrative *noun* (*plural* **narratives**)
a spoken or written account of something.

narrow *adjective*
1 not wide or broad. 2 uncomfortably close; with only a small margin of safety ♦ *a narrow escape.*
narrowly *adverb*

narrow-minded *adjective*
not tolerant of other people's beliefs and ways.

nasal *adjective*
to do with the nose.
[from Latin *nasus* = nose]

nasty *adjective* (**nastier, nastiest**)
1 unpleasant. 2 unkind.
nastily *adverb* **nastiness** *noun*

nation *noun* (*plural* **nations**)
a large community of people most of whom have the same ancestors, language, history, and customs, and who usually live in the same part of the world under one government.
national *adjective* & *noun* **nationally** *adverb*

national anthem *noun* (*plural* **national anthems**)
a nation's official song, which is played or sung on important occasions.

national curriculum *noun*
an official list of the subjects that must be taught by state schools.

nationalist *noun* (*plural* **nationalists**)
1 a person who is very patriotic. 2 a person who wants his or her country to be independent rather than being part of another country ♦ *Scottish Nationalists.*
nationalism *noun* **nationalistic** *adjective*

nationality *noun* (*plural* **nationalities**)
the condition of belonging to a particular nation ♦ *What is his nationality?*

nationalize *verb* (**nationalizes, nationalizing, nationalized**)
put an industry or business under state ownership or control.
nationalization *noun*

national park *noun* (*plural* **national parks**)
an area of natural beauty which is protected by the government and which the public may visit.

nationwide *adjective* & *adverb*
over the whole of a country.

native *noun* (*plural* **natives**)
a person born in a particular place ♦ *He is a native of Sweden.*

native *adjective*
1 belonging to a person because of the place of his or her birth ♦ *my native country.* **2** grown or originating in a particular place ♦ *a plant native to China.* **3** natural; belonging to a person by nature ♦ *native ability.*

Native American *noun* (*plural* **Native Americans**)
one of the original inhabitants of North and South America.

---

❶ USAGE See note at **Indian**.

---

natural *adjective*
1 produced or done by nature, not by people or machines. **2** normal; not surprising. **3** having a quality or ability that you were born with ♦ *a natural leader.* **4** (said about a note in music) neither sharp nor flat.
naturally *adverb* **naturalness** *noun*

natural *noun* (*plural* **naturals**)
1 a person who is naturally good at something. **2** a natural note in music; a sign (♮) that shows this.

natural history *noun*
the study of plants and animals.

naturalist *noun* (*plural* **naturalists**)
an expert in natural history.

natural science *noun*
the study of physics, chemistry, and biology.

natural selection *noun*
Darwin's theory that only the plants and animals suited to their surroundings will survive and breed.

nature *noun* (*plural* **natures**)
1 everything in the world that was not made by people. **2** the characteristics of a person or thing ♦ *She has a loving nature.* **3** a kind or sort of thing ♦ *He likes things of that nature.*

naughty *adjective* (**naughtier, naughtiest**)
1 badly behaved or disobedient. **2** slightly rude or indecent ♦ *naughty pictures.*
naughtily *adverb* **naughtiness** *noun*

nausea (*say* naw-zee-a) *noun*
a feeling of sickness or disgust.
nauseous *adjective* **nauseating** *adjective*

nautical *adjective*
to do with ships or sailors.

nautical mile *noun* (*plural* **nautical miles**)
a measure of distance used at sea, equal to 2,025 yards (1.852 kilometres).

naval *adjective*
to do with a navy.
[from Latin *navis* = ship]

navel *noun* (*plural* **navels**)
the small hollow in the centre of the abdomen, where the umbilical cord was attached.
[from Old English]

navigate *verb* (**navigates, navigating, navigated**)
1 sail in or through a river or sea etc. ♦ *The ship navigated the Suez Canal.* **2** make sure that a ship, aircraft, or vehicle is going in the right direction.
navigation *noun* **navigator** *noun*

navy *noun* (*plural* **navies**)
1 a country's warships and the people trained to use them. **2** (also **navy blue**) a very dark blue, the colour of naval uniform.

Nazi (*say* nah-tsee) *noun* (*plural* **Nazis**)
a member of the National Socialist Party in Germany in Hitler's time, with fascist beliefs.
Nazism *noun*

NB *abbreviation*
take note that (Latin *nota bene* = note well).

NE *abbreviation*
1 north-east. **2** north-eastern.

near *adverb* & *adjective*
not far away.
near by not far away ♦ *They live near by.*

near *preposition*
not far away from ♦ *near the shops.*

nearby *adjective*
near ♦ *a nearby house.*

nearly *adverb*
almost ♦ *We have nearly finished.*

neat *adjective* (**neater, neatest**)
1 simple and clean and tidy. **2** skilful. **3** undiluted ♦ *neat whisky.*
neatly *adverb* **neatness** *noun*

neaten *verb* (**neatens, neatening, neatened**)
make or become neat.

nebula *noun* (*plural* **nebulae**)
a bright or dark patch in the sky, caused by a distant galaxy or a cloud of dust or gas.

nebulous *adjective*
indistinct or vague ♦ *nebulous ideas.*

necessary *adjective*
not able to be done without; essential.
necessarily *adverb*

necessity *noun* (*plural* **necessities**)
1 need ♦ *the necessity of buying food and clothing.* **2** something necessary.

neck *noun* (*plural* **necks**)
1 the part of the body that joins the head to the shoulders. **2** the part of a garment round the neck. **3** a narrow part of something, especially of a bottle.
neck and neck almost exactly together in a race or contest.

necklace *noun* (*plural* **necklaces**)
an ornament worn round the neck.

necktie *noun* (*plural* **neckties**)
a strip of material worn passing under the collar
of a shirt and knotted in front.

need *verb* (**needs, needing, needed**)
1 be without something you should have;
require ♦ *We need two more chairs.* **2** (as an
auxiliary verb) have to do something ♦ *You need
not answer.*

need *noun* (*plural* **needs**)
1 something needed; a necessary thing.
2 a situation where something is necessary
♦ *There is no need to cry.* **3** great poverty or
hardship.
needful *adjective* **needless** *adjective*

needle *noun* (*plural* **needles**)
1 a very thin pointed piece of steel used in
sewing. **2** something long and thin and sharp
♦ *a knitting needle*; ♦ *pine needles.* **3** the pointer
of a meter or compass.

needlework *noun*
sewing or embroidery.

needy *adjective* (**needier, neediest**)
very poor; lacking things necessary for life.
neediness *noun*

negative *adjective*
1 that says 'no' ♦ *a negative answer.* **2** looking
only at the bad aspects of a situation ♦ *Don't be
so negative.* **3** showing no sign of what is being
tested for ♦ *Her pregnancy test was negative.*
4 less than nought; minus. **5** (in science) to do
with the kind of electric charge carried by
electrons.
negatively *adverb*

❶ USAGE The opposite of sense 1 is **affirmative**,
and of senses 2, 3, 4 **positive**.

negative *noun* (*plural* **negatives**)
1 a negative statement. **2** a photograph on film
with the dark parts light and the light parts dark,
from which a positive print (with the dark and
light or colours correct) can be made.

neglect *verb* (**neglects, neglecting, neglected**)
1 not look after or pay attention to a person or
thing. **2** not do something; forget ♦ *He neglected
to shut the door.*

neglect *noun*
neglecting or being neglected.
neglectful *adjective*

negligence *noun*
lack of proper care or attention; carelessness.
negligent *adjective* **negligently** *adverb*

negligible *adjective*
not big enough or important enough to be worth
bothering about.

negotiable *adjective*
able to be changed after being discussed
♦ *The salary is negotiable.*

negotiate *verb* (**negotiates, negotiating,
negotiated**)
1 bargain or discuss with others in order to
reach an agreement. **2** arrange after discussion
♦ *They negotiated a treaty.* **3** get over an obstacle
or difficulty.
negotiation *noun* **negotiator** *noun*

neigh *verb* (**neighs, neighing, neighed**)
make the high-pitched cry of a horse.
neigh *noun*

neighbour *noun* (*plural* **neighbours**)
a person who lives next door or near to another.
neighbouring *adjective* **neighbourly** *adjective*
[from Old English *neahgebur* = near dweller]

neighbourhood *noun* (*plural*
neighbourhoods)
1 the surrounding district or area. **2** a part of a
town where people live ♦ *a quiet neighbourhood.*

neither (*say* **ny**-ther or **nee**-ther) *adjective* &
pronoun
not either.

❶ USAGE Correct use is ♦ *Neither of them likes it.*
♦ *Neither he nor his children like it.* Use a
singular verb (e.g. *likes*) unless one of its
subjects is plural (e.g. *children*).

neither *adverb* & *conjunction*
neither ... nor not one thing and not the other
♦ *She neither knew nor cared.*

❶ USAGE Say ♦ *I don't know that either* (not
'neither').

neolithic (*say* nee-o-**lith**-ik) *adjective*
belonging to the later part of the Stone Age.

neon *noun*
a gas that glows when electricity passes through
it, used in glass tubes to make illuminated signs.

nephew *noun* (*plural* **nephews**)
the son of a person's brother or sister.

nerve *noun* (*plural* **nerves**)
1 any of the fibres in the body that carry
messages to and from the brain, so that parts of
the body can feel and move. **2** courage; calmness
in a dangerous situation ♦ *Don't lose your nerve.*
3 impudence ♦ *You've got a nerve!*
get on someone's nerves irritate someone.
nerves *plural noun* nervousness.

nerve *verb* (**nerves, nerving, nerved**)
give strength or courage to someone.

nervous *adjective*
1 easily upset or agitated; excitable.
2 slightly afraid; timid. **3** to do with the nerves
♦ *a nervous illness.*
nervously *adverb* **nervousness** *noun*

nervous breakdown *noun* (*plural* **nervous
breakdowns**)
a state of severe depression and anxiety, so that
the person cannot cope with life.

nervous system *noun* (*plural* **nervous systems**)
the system, consisting of the brain, spinal cord, and nerves, which sends electrical messages from one part of the body to another.

-ness *suffix*
forming nouns from adjectives (e.g. *kindness*, *sadness*).

nest *noun* (*plural* **nests**)
1 a structure or place in which a bird lays its eggs and feeds its young. **2** a place where some small creatures (e.g. mice or wasps) live. **3** a set of similar things that fit inside each other ♦ *a nest of tables*.

nest *verb* (**nests, nesting, nested**)
1 have or make a nest. **2** fit inside something.

nest egg *noun* (*plural* **nest eggs**)
a sum of money saved up for future use.

nestle *verb* (**nestles, nestling, nestled**)
curl up comfortably.

net[1] *noun* (*plural* **nets**)
1 material made of pieces of thread, cord, or wire etc. joined together in a criss-cross pattern with holes between. **2** something made of this.
the Net the Internet.

net *verb* (**nets, netting, netted**)
cover or catch with a net.

net[2] *adjective*
remaining when nothing more is to be deducted ♦ *The net weight, without the box, is 100 grams.* (Compare **gross**.)

net *verb* (**nets, netting, netted**)
obtain or produce as net profit.

netball *noun*
a game in which two teams try to throw a ball into a high net hanging from a ring.

netting *noun*
a piece of net.

nettle *noun* (*plural* **nettles**)
a wild plant with leaves that sting when they are touched.

nettle *verb* (**nettles, nettling, nettled**)
annoy or provoke someone.

network *noun* (*plural* **networks**)
1 a net-like arrangement or pattern of intersecting lines or parts ♦ *the railway network.* **2** an organization with many connecting parts that work together ♦ *a spy network.* **3** a group of radio or television stations which broadcast the same programmes. **4** a set of computers which are linked to each other.

neuron or **neurone** *noun* (*plural* **neurons** or **neurones**)
a cell that is part of the nervous system and sends impulses to and from the brain.

neurotic (*say* newr-ot-ik) *adjective*
always very worried about something.

neuter *adjective*
1 neither masculine nor feminine. **2** (in some languages) belonging to the class of words which are neither masculine nor feminine, such as *Fenster* in German.

neuter *verb* (**neuters, neutering, neutered**)
remove an animal's sex organs so that it cannot breed.

neutral *adjective*
1 not supporting either side in a war or quarrel. **2** not very distinctive ♦ *a neutral colour such as grey.* **3** neither acid nor alkaline.
neutrally *adverb* **neutrality** *noun*

neutral gear *noun*
a gear that is not connected to the driving parts of an engine.

neutron *noun* (*plural* **neutrons**)
(in science) a particle of matter with no electric charge.

never *adverb*
1 at no time; not ever. **2** not at all.

nevertheless *adverb* & *conjunction*
in spite of this; although this is a fact.

new *adjective*
not existing before; just made, invented, discovered, or received etc.
newly *adverb* **newness** *noun*

new *adverb*
newly *newborn*; *new-laid.*

newcomer *noun* (*plural* **newcomers**)
a person who has arrived recently.

newfangled *adjective*
disliked because it is new in method or style.

newly *adverb*
1 recently. **2** in a new way.

new moon *noun* (*plural* **new moons**)
the moon at the beginning of its cycle, when only a thin crescent can be seen.

news *noun*
1 information about recent events or a broadcast report of this. **2** a piece of new information ♦ *That's news to me.*

newsagent *noun* (*plural* **newsagents**)
a shopkeeper who sells newspapers.

newspaper *noun* (*plural* **newspapers**)
1 a daily or weekly publication on large sheets of paper, containing news reports, articles, etc. **2** the sheets of paper forming a newspaper ♦ *Wrap it in newspaper.*

newt *noun* (*plural* **newts**)
a small animal rather like a lizard, that lives near or in water.
[from Old English: originally *an ewt*]

newton *noun* (*plural* **newtons**)
a unit for measuring force.

New Year's Day *noun*
1 January.

next *adjective*
nearest; coming immediately after ♦ *on the next day.*

next *adverb*
1 in the next place. **2** on the next occasion ♦ *What happens next?*

next door *adverb & adjective*
in the next house or room.

nib *noun* (*plural* **nibs**)
the pointed metal part of a pen.

nibble *verb* (**nibbles, nibbling, nibbled**)
take small, quick, or gentle bites.

nice *adjective* (**nicer, nicest**)
1 pleasant or kind. **2** precise or careful ♦ *Dictionaries make nice distinctions between meanings of words.*
nicely *adverb* **niceness** *noun*

nick *noun* (*plural* **nicks**)
1 a small cut or notch. **2** (*informal*) a police station or prison.
in good nick (*informal*) in good condition.
in the nick of time only just in time.

nickel *noun* (*plural* **nickels**)
1 a silvery-white metal. **2** (*American*) a 5-cent coin.

nickname *noun* (*plural* **nicknames**)
a name given to a person instead of his or her real name.

nicotine *noun*
a poisonous substance found in tobacco.
[from the name of J. Nicot, who introduced tobacco into France in 1560]

niece *noun* (*plural* **nieces**)
the daughter of a person's brother or sister.

niggardly *adjective*
mean or stingy.
niggardliness *noun*

night *noun* (*plural* **nights**)
1 the dark hours between sunset and sunrise. **2** a particular night or evening ♦ *the first night of the play.*

nightclub *noun* (*plural* **nightclubs**)
a place that is open at night where people go to drink and dance.

nightdress *noun* (*plural* **nightdresses**)
a loose dress that girls or women wear in bed.

nightingale *noun* (*plural* **nightingales**)
a small brown bird that sings sweetly.

nightmare *noun* (*plural* **nightmares**)
1 a frightening dream. **2** an unpleasant experience ♦ *the journey was a nightmare.*
nightmarish *adjective*
[from *night* + Middle English *mare* = an evil spirit thought to lie on people asleep and suffocate them]

nil *noun*
nothing or nought.

nimble *adjective*
able to move quickly; agile.
nimbly *adverb*

nine *adjective & noun* (*plural* **nines**)
the number 9.
ninth *adjective & noun*

nineteen *noun & adjective*
the number 19.
nineteenth *adjective & noun*

ninety *adjective & noun* (*plural* **nineties**)
the number 90.
ninetieth *adjective & noun*

nip *verb* (**nips, nipping, nipped**)
1 pinch or bite quickly. **2** (*informal*) go quickly.

nip *noun* (*plural* **nips**)
1 a quick pinch or bite. **2** sharp coldness ♦ *There's a nip in the air.* **3** a small drink of a spirit ♦ *a nip of brandy.*

nippers *plural noun*
pincers.

nipple *noun* (*plural* **nipples**)
the small part that sticks out at the front of a person's breast, from which babies suck milk.

nirvana *noun*
(in Buddhism and Hinduism) the highest state of knowledge and understanding, achieved by meditation.
[from Sanskrit]

nit *noun* (*plural* **nits**)
a parasitic insect or its egg, found in people's hair.

nit-picking *noun*
pointing out very small faults.

nitrate *noun* (*plural* **nitrates**)
1 a chemical compound containing nitrogen. **2** potassium or sodium nitrate, used as a fertilizer.

nitrogen (*say* ny-tro-jen) *noun*
a gas that makes up about four-fifths of the air.

no *adjective*
not any ♦ *We have no money.*

no *adverb*
1 used to deny or refuse something ♦ *Will you come? No.* **2** not at all ♦ *She is no better.*

No. or **no.** *abbreviation* (*plural* **Nos.** or **nos.**)
number.

noble *adjective* (**nobler, noblest**)
1 of high social rank; aristocratic. **2** having a very good character or qualities ♦ *a noble king.* **3** stately or impressive ♦ *a noble building.*
nobly *adverb* **nobility** *noun*

noble *noun* (*plural* **nobles**)
a person of high social rank.
nobleman *noun* **noblewoman** *noun*

nobody *pronoun*
no person; no one.

nobody *noun* (*plural* **nobodies**) (*informal*)
an unimportant or unimpressive person; a nonentity.

nocturnal *adjective*
1 happening at night. **2** active at night ♦ *Badgers are nocturnal animals.*

nod *verb* (**nods, nodding, nodded**)
1 move the head up and down, especially as a way of agreeing with somebody or as a greeting. **2** be drowsy.
nod *noun*

noise *noun* (*plural* **noises**)
a sound, especially one that is loud or unpleasant.
noisy *adjective* **noisily** *adverb* **noiseless** *adjective*

nomad *noun* (*plural* **nomads**)
a member of a tribe that moves from place to place looking for pasture for their animals.
nomadic *adjective*

no man's land *noun*
an area that does not belong to anybody, especially the land between opposing armies.

nominate *verb* (**nominates, nominating, nominated**)
propose someone as a candidate in an election or to be appointed to a post.
nomination *noun* **nominator** *noun*

non- *prefix*
not.

non-commissioned officer *noun* (*plural* **non-commissioned officers**)
a member of the armed forces, such as a corporal or sergeant, who has not been commissioned as an officer but has been promoted from the ranks of ordinary soldiers.

non-committal *adjective*
not committing yourself; not showing what you think.

nondescript *adjective*
having no special or distinctive qualities and therefore difficult to describe.

none *pronoun*
1 not any. **2** no one ♦ *None can tell.*

❶ USAGE It is better to use a singular verb (e.g. ♦ *None of them is here*), but the plural is not incorrect (e.g. ♦ *None of them are here*).

nonentity (*say* non-en-tit-ee) *noun* (*plural* **nonentities**)
an unimportant person.

non-existent *adjective*
not existing or unreal.

non-fiction *noun*
writings that are not fiction; books about real people and things and true events.

non-flammable *adjective*
not able to be set on fire.

❶ USAGE See note at *inflammable.*

nonplussed *adjective*
puzzled or confused.

nonsense *noun*
1 words put together in a way that does not mean anything. **2** stupid ideas or behaviour.
nonsensical (*say* non-sens-ik-al) *adjective*

non-stop *adjective* & *adverb*
1 not stopping ♦ *They talked non-stop for hours.* **2** not stopping between two main stations ♦ *a non-stop train.*

noodles *plural noun*
pasta made in narrow strips, used in soups etc. [from German *Nudel*]

nook *noun* (*plural* **nooks**)
a sheltered corner; a recess.

noon *noun*
twelve o'clock midday.

no one *noun*
no person; nobody.

noose *noun* (*plural* **nooses**)
a loop in a rope that gets smaller when the rope is pulled.

nor *conjunction*
and not ♦ *She cannot do it; nor can I.*

normal *adjective*
1 usual or ordinary. **2** natural and healthy; without a physical or mental illness.
normally *adverb* **normality** *noun*

Norman *noun* (*plural* **Normans**)
a member of the people of Normandy in northern France, who conquered England in 1066.
Norman *adjective*

north *noun*
1 the direction to the left of a person who faces east. **2** the northern part of a country, city, etc.
north *adjective* & *adverb*
towards or in the north.
northerly *adjective* **northern** *adjective*
northerner *noun* **northernmost** *adjective*

north-east *noun, adjective,* & *adverb*
midway between north and east.
north-easterly *adjective* **north-eastern** *adjective*

northward *adjective* & *adverb*
towards the north.
northwards *adverb*

north-west *noun, adjective,* & *adverb*
midway between north and west.
north-westerly *adjective* **north-western** *adjective*

Nos. or **nos.** *plural* of **No.** or **no.**

nose *noun* (*plural* **noses**)
1 the part of the face that is used for breathing and for smelling things. **2** the front end or part.

nosedive *noun* (*plural* **nosedives**)
a steep downward dive, especially of an aircraft.
nosedive *verb*

nostalgia (*say* nos-tal-ja) *noun*
sentimental remembering or longing for the past.
nostalgic *adjective* **nostalgically** *adverb*

nostril *noun* (*plural* **nostrils**)
either of the two openings in the nose.

nosy *adjective* (**nosier, nosiest**)
inquisitive.
nosily *adverb* **nosiness** *noun*

not *adverb*
used to change the meaning of something to its
opposite or absence.

notation *noun* (*plural* **notations**)
a system of symbols representing numbers,
quantities, musical notes, etc.

notch *noun* (*plural* **notches**)
a small V-shape cut into a surface.

note *noun* (*plural* **notes**)
1 something written down as a reminder or
as a comment or explanation. **2** a short letter.
3 a banknote ♦ *a £5 note.* **4** a single sound in
music. **5** any of the black or white keys on a
piano etc. (see **key** 3). **6** a sound or quality that
indicates something ♦ *a note of warning.*
7 notice or attention ♦ *Take note.*

note *verb* (**notes, noting, noted**)
1 make a note about something; write down.
2 notice or pay attention to ♦ *Note what we say.*

notebook *noun* (*plural* **notebooks**)
a book with blank pages on which to write notes.

notepaper *noun*
paper for writing letters.

nothing *noun*
1 no thing; not anything. **2** no amount; nought.
for nothing 1 without payment, free. **2** without
a result.

notice *noun* (*plural* **notices**)
1 something written or printed and displayed for
people to see. **2** attention ♦ *It escaped my notice.*
3 warning that something is going to happen
4 formal information that you are about to end
an agreement or a person's employment etc.
♦ *We gave him a month's notice.*

notice *verb* (**notices, noticing, noticed**)
see or become aware of something.

noticeable *adjective*
easily seen or noticed.
noticeably *adverb*

notion *noun* (*plural* **notions**)
an idea, especially one that is vague or incorrect.

notorious *adjective*
well-known for something bad.
notoriously *adverb* **notoriety** (*say*
noh-ter-I-it-ee) *noun*

notwithstanding *preposition*
in spite of.

nought (*say* nawt) *noun*
1 the figure 0. **2** nothing.

noun *noun* (*plural* **nouns**)
a word that stands for a person, place, or thing.
Common nouns are words such as *boy, dog, river,
sport, table,* which are used of a whole kind of
people or things; *proper nouns* are words such as
Charles, Thames, and *London* which name a
particular person or thing.

nourish *verb* (**nourishes, nourishing,
nourished**)
keep a person, animal, or plant alive and well by
means of food.
nourishing *adjective* **nourishment** *noun*

novel *noun* (*plural* **novels**)
a story that fills a whole book.

novel *adjective*
of a new and unusual kind ♦ *a novel experience.*
[from Latin *novus* = new]

novelist *noun* (*plural* **novelists**)
a person who writes novels.

novelty *noun* (*plural* **novelties**)
1 newness and originality. **2** something new and
unusual. **3** a cheap toy or ornament.

November *noun*
the eleventh month of the year.
[from Latin *novem* = nine, because it was the
ninth month of the ancient Roman calendar]

novice *noun* (*plural* **novices**)
1 a beginner. **2** a person preparing to be a monk
or nun.

now *adverb*
1 at this time. **2** by this time. **3** immediately
♦ *You must go now.* **4** I wonder, or I am telling
you ♦ *Now why didn't I think of that?*
now and again or **now and then** sometimes;
occasionally.

now *conjunction*
as a result of or at the same time as something
♦ *Now that you have come, we'll start.*

now *noun*
this moment ♦ *They will be at home by now.*

nowadays *adverb*
at the present time, as contrasted with years ago.

nowhere *adverb*
not anywhere.

nowhere *noun*
no place ♦ *Nowhere is as beautiful as Scotland.*

nozzle *noun* (*plural* **nozzles**)
the spout of a hose, pipe, or tube.

nuclear *adjective*
1 to do with a nucleus, especially of an atom.
2 using the energy that is created by reactions in
the nuclei of atoms ♦ *nuclear power;* ♦ *nuclear
weapons.*

nucleus *noun* (*plural* **nuclei**)
1 the part in the centre of something, round which other things are grouped. **2** the central part of an atom or of a seed or a biological cell.

nude *adjective*
not wearing any clothes; naked.
nudity *noun*

nudge *verb* (**nudges, nudging, nudged**)
1 poke a person gently with your elbow.
2 push slightly or gradually.
nudge *noun*

nugget *noun* (*plural* **nuggets**)
1 a rough lump of gold or platinum found in the earth. **2** a small but useful fact.

nuisance *noun* (*plural* **nuisances**)
an annoying person or thing.

numb *adjective*
unable to feel or move.
numbly *adverb* **numbness** *noun*

number *noun* (*plural* **numbers**)
1 a symbol or word indicating how many; a numeral or figure. **2** a numeral given to a thing to identify it ♦ *a telephone number.* **3** a quantity of people or things ♦ *the number of people present.* **4** one issue of a magazine or newspaper. **5** a song or piece of music.

---

❶ USAGE Note that *a number of*, meaning 'several', should be followed by a plural verb:
♦ *A number of problems remain.*

---

number *verb* (**numbers, numbering, numbered**)
1 mark with numbers. **2** count. **3** amount to
♦ *The crowd numbered 10,000.*

numeral *noun* (*plural* **numerals**)
a symbol that represents a certain number; a figure.

numerate (*say* new-mer-at) *adjective*
having a good basic knowledge of mathematics.
numeracy *noun*

numerator *noun* (plural numerators)
the number above the line in a fraction, showing how many parts are to be taken, e.g. 2 in $\frac{2}{3}$. (Compare **denominator**.)

numerical (*say* new-merri-kal) *adjective*
to do with or consisting of numbers
♦ *in numerical order.*
numerically *adverb*

numerous *adjective*
many.

nun *noun* (*plural* **nuns**)
a member of a community of women who live according to the rules of a religious organization. (Compare **monk**.)

nunnery *noun* (*plural* **nunneries**)
a convent.

nurse *noun* (*plural* **nurses**)
1 a person trained to look after people who are ill or injured. **2** (*old use*) a woman employed to look after young children.

nurse *verb* (**nurses, nursing, nursed**)
1 look after someone who is ill or injured. **2** feed a baby at the breast. **3** have a feeling for a long time ♦ *She's been nursing a grudge against him for years.* **4** hold carefully.

nursemaid *noun* (*plural* **nursemaids**)
(*old use*) a young woman employed to look after young children.

nursery *noun* (*plural* **nurseries**)
1 a place where young children are looked after or play. **2** a place where young plants are grown and are usually for sale.

nursery rhyme *noun* (*plural* **nursery rhymes**)
a simple rhyme or song of the kind that young children like.

nursery school *noun* (*plural* **nursery schools**)
a school for children below primary school age.

nursing home *noun* (*plural* **nursing homes**)
a small hospital or home for invalids.

nut *noun* (*plural* **nuts**)
1 a fruit with a hard shell. **2** a kernel. **3** a small piece of metal with a hole in the middle, for screwing onto a bolt. **4** (*slang*) the head. **5** (*slang*) a mad or eccentric person.
nutty *adjective*

nutcrackers *plural noun*
pincers for cracking nuts.

nutrition (*say* new-**trish**-on) *noun*
1 nourishment. **2** the study of what nourishes people.
nutritional *adjective* **nutritionally** *adverb*

nutritious (*say* new-**trish**-us) *adjective*
nourishing; giving good nourishment.
nutritiousness *noun*

nutshell *noun* (*plural* **nutshells**)
the shell of a nut.
in a nutshell stated very briefly.

nuzzle *verb* (**nuzzles, nuzzling, nuzzled**)
rub gently with the nose.

NVQ *abbreviation*
National Vocational Qualification.

NW *abbreviation*
1 north-west. **2** north-western.

nylon *noun*
a synthetic, strong, lightweight cloth or fibre.

NZ *abbreviation*
New Zealand.

Oo

O *interjection*
oh.

oaf *noun* (*plural* **oafs**)
a stupid lout.

oak *noun* (*plural* **oaks**)
a large deciduous tree with seeds called acorns.
oaken *adjective*

oar *noun* (*plural* **oars**)
a pole with a flat blade at one end, used for
rowing a boat.
oarsman *noun* **oarsmanship** *noun*

oasis (*say* oh-ay-sis) *noun* (*plural* **oases**)
a fertile place in a desert, with a spring or well of
water.

oath *noun* (*plural* **oaths**)
1 a solemn promise to do something or that
something is true, sometimes appealing to God
as witness. **2** a swear word.
on or **under oath** having sworn to tell the truth
in a lawcourt.

oats *plural noun*
a cereal used to make food (*oats* for horses,
oatmeal for people).

obedient *adjective*
doing what you are told; willing to obey.
obediently *adverb* **obedience** *noun*

obey *verb* (**obeys, obeying, obeyed**)
do what you are told to do by a person, law, etc.

obituary *noun* (*plural* **obituaries**)
an announcement in a newspaper of a person's
death, often with a short account of his or her
life.

object (*say* ob-jikt) *noun* (*plural* **objects**)
1 something that can be seen or touched.
2 a purpose or intention. **3** a person or thing to
which some action or feeling is directed ♦ *She
has become an object of pity.* **4** (in grammar) the
word or words naming who or what is acted
upon by a verb or by a preposition, e.g. *him* in
the dog bit him and *against him.*

object (*say* ob-jekt) *verb* (**objects, objecting,
objected**)
say that you are not in favour of something or do
not agree; protest.
objector *noun*

objection *noun* (*plural* **objections**)
1 objecting to something. **2** a reason for
objecting.

objectionable *adjective*
unpleasant or nasty.
objectionably *adverb*

objective *noun* (*plural* **objectives**)
what you are trying to reach or do; an aim.
objective *adjective*
1 real or actual ♦ *Is there any objective evidence
to prove his claims?* **2** not influenced by personal
feelings or opinions ♦ *an objective account of the
quarrel.* (Compare **subjective**.)
objectively *adverb* **objectivity** *noun*

obligation *noun* (*plural* **obligations**)
1 being obliged to do something. **2** what you are
obliged to do; a duty.
under an obligation owing gratitude to
someone who has helped you.

obligatory (*say* ob-lig-a-ter-ee) *adjective*
compulsory, not optional.

oblige *verb* (**obliges, obliging, obliged**)
1 force or compel. **2** help and please someone
♦ *Can you oblige me with a loan?*
be obliged to someone feel gratitude to a
person who has helped you.

obliging *adjective*
polite and helpful.

oblique (*say* ob-leek) *adjective*
1 slanting. **2** not saying something
straightforwardly ♦ *an oblique reply.*
obliquely *adverb*

obliterate *verb* (**obliterates, obliterating,
obliterated**)
blot out; destroy and remove all traces of
something.
obliteration *noun*

oblong *adjective*
rectangular in shape and longer than it is wide.
oblong *noun*

obnoxious *adjective*
very unpleasant; objectionable.

oboe *noun* (*plural* **oboes**)
a high-pitched woodwind instrument.
oboist *noun*

obscene (*say* ob-seen) *adjective*
indecent in a very offensive way.
obscenely *adverb* **obscenity** *noun*

obscure *adjective*
1 difficult to see or to understand; not clear.
2 not well-known.
obscurely *adverb* **obscurity** *noun*
obscure *verb* (**obscures, obscuring, obscured**)
make a thing obscure; darken or conceal
♦ *Clouds obscured the sun.*

observant *adjective*
quick at observing or noticing things.
observantly *adverb*

observation *noun* (*plural* **observations**)
1 observing or watching. **2** a comment or
remark.

observatory *noun* (*plural* **observatories**)
a building with telescopes etc. for observing the
stars or weather.

observe *verb* (**observes, observing, observed**)
1 see and notice; watch carefully. **2** obey a law.
3 keep or celebrate a custom or religious festival
etc. **4** make a remark.
observer *noun*

obsolescent *adjective*
becoming obsolete; going out of use or fashion.
obsolescence *noun*

obsolete *adjective*
not used any more; out of date.

obstacle *noun* (*plural* **obstacles**)
something that stands in the way or obstructs
progress.

obstinate *adjective*
1 keeping firmly to your own ideas or ways,
even though they may be wrong. **2** difficult to
overcome or remove ♦ *an obstinate problem.*
obstinately *adverb* **obstinacy** *noun*

obstreperous (*say* ob-**strep**-er-us) *adjective*
noisy and unruly.

obstruct *verb* (**obstructs, obstructing,
obstructed**)
stop a person or thing from getting past; hinder.
obstruction *noun* **obstructive** *adjective*

obtain *verb* (**obtains, obtaining, obtained**)
get or be given something.
obtainable *adjective*

obtrusive *adjective*
unpleasantly noticeable.
obtrusiveness *noun*

obtuse angle *noun* (*plural* **obtuse angles**)
an angle of more than 90° but less than 180°.
(Compare **acute angle**.)

obvious *adjective*
easy to see or understand.
obviously *adverb*

occasion *noun* (*plural* **occasions**)
1 the time when something happens. **2** a special
event. **3** a suitable time; an opportunity.
on occasion from time to time.

occasional *adjective*
1 happening from time to time but not regularly
or frequently. **2** for special occasions
♦ *occasional music.*
occasionally *adverb*

occult *adjective*
to do with the supernatural or magic ♦ *occult
powers.*

occupation *noun* (*plural* **occupations**)
1 a person's job or profession. **2** something you
do to pass your time. **3** capturing a country etc.
by military force.

occupational *adjective*
caused by an occupation ♦ *an occupational
disease.*

occupational therapy *noun*
creative work designed to help people to recover
from certain illnesses.

occupy *verb* (**occupies, occupying, occupied**)
1 live in a place; inhabit. **2** fill a space or
position. **3** capture a country etc. and place
troops there. **4** keep somebody busy.
occupier *noun*

occur *verb* (**occurs, occurring, occurred**)
1 happen or exist. **2** be found; appear ♦ *These
plants occur in ponds.* **3** come into a person's
mind ♦ *An idea occurred to me.*

ocean *noun* (*plural* **oceans**)
the seas that surround the continents of the
earth, especially one of the large named areas of
this ♦ *the Pacific Ocean.*
oceanic *adjective*

o'clock *adverb*
by the clock ♦ *Lunch is at one o'clock.*

octagon *noun* (*plural* **octagons**)
a flat shape with eight sides and eight angles.
octagonal *adjective*

octave *noun* (*plural* **octaves**)
the interval of eight steps between one musical
note and the next note of the same name above
or below it.

October *noun*
the tenth month of the year.
[from Latin *octo* = eight, because it was the
eighth month of the ancient Roman calendar]

octopus *noun* (*plural* **octopuses**)
a sea creature with eight long tentacles.
[from Greek *okto* = eight + *pous* = foot]

oculist *noun* (*plural* **oculists**)
a doctor who treats diseases of the eye.

odd *adjective*
1 strange or unusual. **2** (said about a number)
not able to be divided exactly by 2; not even.
3 left over from a pair or set ♦ *I've got one odd
sock.* **4** of various kinds; not regular ♦ *odd jobs.*
oddly *adverb* **oddness** *noun*

oddity *noun* (*plural* **oddities**)
a strange person or thing.

oddments *plural noun*
scraps or pieces left over from a larger piece or
set.

odds *plural noun*
1 the chances that a certain thing will happen.
2 the proportion of money that you will win if a
bet is successful ♦ *When the odds are 10 to 1, you
will win £10 if you bet £1.*
odds and ends oddments.

odious (*say* oh-dee-us) *adjective*
extremely unpleasant; hateful.
odiously *adverb* **odiousness** *noun*

odour *noun* (*plural* **odours**)
a smell, especially an unpleasant one.
odorous *adjective* **odourless** *adjective*

odyssey (*say* od-iss-ee) *noun* (*plural* **odysseys**)
a long adventurous journey.

o'er *preposition* & *adverb* (*poetic*)
over.

oesophagus (*say* ee-sof-a-gus) *noun* (*plural* **oesophagi** (*say* ee-sof-a-gl))
the tube leading from the throat to the stomach; the gullet.

oestrogen (*say* ees-tro-jen) *noun*
a hormone which develops and maintains female sexual and physical characteristics.

of *preposition*
(used to indicate relationships) **1** belonging to ♦ *the mother of the child*. **2** concerning; about ♦ *news of the disaster*. **3** made from ♦ *built of stone*. **4** from ♦ *north of the town*.

off *preposition*
1 not on; away or down from ♦ *He fell off the ladder*. **2** not taking or wanting ♦ *She is off her food*. **3** deducted from ♦ *£5 off the price*.

off *adverb*
1 away or down from something ♦ *His hat blew off*. **2** not working or happening ♦ *The heating is off*. ♦ *The match is off because of snow*. **3** to the end; completely ♦ *Finish it off*. **4** as regards money or supplies ♦ *How are you off for cash?* **5** behind or at the side of a stage ♦ *There were noises off*. **6** (said about food) beginning to go bad.

offal *noun*
the organs of an animal (e.g. liver or kidneys) sold as food.

off-colour *adjective*
slightly unwell.

offence *noun* (*plural* **offences**)
1 an illegal action. **2** a feeling of annoyance or resentment.
give offence hurt someone's feelings. **take offence** be upset by something said or done.

offend *verb* (**offends, offending, offended**)
1 cause offence to someone; hurt a person's feelings. **2** do wrong or commit a crime.
offender *noun*

offensive *adjective*
1 causing offence; insulting. **2** disgusting ♦ *an offensive smell*. **3** used in attacking ♦ *offensive weapons*.
offensively *adverb* **offensiveness** *noun*

offensive *noun* (*plural* **offensives**)
an attack.
take the offensive be the first to attack.

offer *verb* (**offers, offering, offered**)
1 present something so that people can accept it if they want to. **2** say that you are willing to do or give something or to pay a certain amount.

offer *noun* (*plural* **offers**)
1 offering something. **2** an amount of money offered. **3** a specially reduced price.

offhand *adjective*
1 said or done without preparation. **2** (said about a remark etc.) rather casual and rude; curt.
offhanded *adjective*

office *noun* (*plural* **offices**)
1 a room or building used for business; the people who work there. **2** a government department ♦ *the Foreign and Commonwealth Office*. **3** an important job or position.
be in office hold an official position.

officer *noun* (*plural* **officers**)
1 a person who is in charge of others, especially in the armed forces. **2** an official. **3** a member of the police.

official *adjective*
1 done or said by someone with authority. **2** done as part of your job or position ♦ *official duties*.
officially *adverb*

official *noun* (*plural* **officials**)
a person who holds a position of authority.

offing *noun*
in the offing likely to happen soon.

off-licence *noun* (*plural* **off-licences**)
a shop with a licence to sell alcoholic drinks to be drunk away from the shop.

off-putting *adjective*
making you less keen on something; disconcerting.

offshoot *noun* (*plural* **offshoots**)
1 a side shoot on a plant. **2** a by-product.

offside *adjective* & *adverb*
(said about a player in football etc.) in a position where the rules do not allow him or her to play the ball.

often *adverb*
many times; in many cases.

ogre *noun* (*plural* **ogres**)
1 a cruel giant in fairy tales. **2** a terrifying person.

oh *interjection*
an exclamation of pain, surprise, delight, etc., or used for emphasis ♦ *Oh yes I will!*

ohm *noun* (*plural* **ohms**)
a unit of electrical resistance.

oil *noun* (*plural* **oils**)
1 a thick slippery liquid that will not dissolve in water. **2** a kind of petroleum used as fuel. **3** oil paint.

oil *verb* (**oils, oiling, oiled**)
put oil on something, especially to make it work smoothly.

oilfield *noun*
an area where oil is found.

oil rig *noun* (*plural* **oil rigs**)
a structure with equipment for drilling for oil.

oil well *noun* (*plural* **oil wells**)
a hole drilled in the ground or under the sea to get oil.

oily *adjective*
1 containing or like oil; covered or soaked with oil. **2** behaving in an insincerely polite way.
oiliness *noun*

ointment *noun* (*plural* **ointments**)
a cream or slippery paste for putting on sore skin and cuts.

OK or **okay** *adverb* & *adjective* (*informal*)
all right.

old *adjective*
1 not new; born or made or existing from a long time ago. **2** of a particular age ♦ *I'm ten years old.* **3** former or original ♦ *in its old place.*
4 (*informal*), used casually or for emphasis) ♦ *good old mum!*
oldness *noun*
[from Old English]

old age *noun*
the time when a person is old.

Old English *noun*
the English language from about 700 to 1150, also called **Anglo-Saxon**.

old-fashioned *adjective*
of the kind that was usual a long time ago; no longer fashionable.

Old Norse *noun*
the language spoken by the Vikings, the ancestor of modern Scandinavian languages.

olive *noun* (*plural* **olives**)
1 an evergreen tree with a small bitter fruit.
2 this fruit, from which an oil (**olive oil**) is made.
3 a shade of green like an unripe olive.

olive branch *noun* (*plural* **olive branches**)
something you do or offer that shows you want to make peace.
[from a story in the Bible, in which a dove brings Noah an olive branch as a sign that God is no longer angry with the human race]

Olympic Games or **Olympics** *plural noun*
a series of international sports contests held every four years in a different part of the world.

omega (*say* oh-**meg**-a) *noun*
the last letter of the Greek alphabet, a long *o.*

omelette *noun* (*plural* **omelettes**)
eggs beaten together and cooked in a pan, often with a filling.

omen *noun* (*plural* **omens**)
an event regarded as a sign of what is going to happen.

ominous *adjective*
suggesting that trouble is coming.
ominously *adverb*

omit *verb* (**omits, omitting, omitted**)
1 miss something out. **2** fail to do something.
omission *noun*

omnibus *noun* (*plural* **omnibuses**)
1 a single book, television programme, etc., containing several instalments that were previously published or broadcast separately.
2 (*old use*) a bus.

omniscient (*say* om-**niss**-ee-ent) *adjective*
knowing everything.
omniscience *noun*

omnivorous (*say* om-**niv**-er-us) *adjective*
feeding on all kinds of food. (Compare **carnivorous, herbivorous**.)

on *preposition*
1 supported by; covering; added or attached to ♦ *the sign on the door.* **2** close to; towards ♦ *The army advanced on Paris.* **3** during; at the time of ♦ *on my birthday.* **4** by reason of ♦ *Arrest him on suspicion of murder.* **5** concerning ♦ *a book on butterflies.* **6** in a state of; using or showing ♦ *The house was on fire.*

on *adverb*
1 so as to be on something ♦ *Put it on.*
2 further forward ♦ *Move on.* **3** working; in action ♦ *Is the heater on?*
on and off not continually.

once *adverb*
1 for one time or on one occasion only ♦ *They came only once.* **2** formerly ♦ *They once lived here.*

once *noun*
one time ♦ *Once is enough.*

once *conjunction*
as soon as ♦ *You can go once I have taken your names.*

oncoming *adjective*
approaching; coming towards you ♦ *oncoming traffic.*

one *adjective*
1 single. **2** individual or united.

one *noun*
1 the smallest whole number, 1. **2** a person or thing alone.
one another each other.

one *pronoun*
any person or thing ♦ *I need a pen but I can't find one.* ♦ *One likes to help.*
oneself *pronoun*

one-sided *adjective*
1 with one side or person in a contest, conversation etc. being much stronger or doing a lot more than the other ♦ *a one-sided match.*
2 showing only one point of view in an unfair way ♦ *This is a very one-sided account of the conflict.*

onion *noun* (*plural* **onions**)
a round vegetable with a strong flavour.
oniony *adjective*

onlooker *noun* (*plural* **onlookers**)
a spectator.

only *adjective*
being the one person or thing of a kind; sole ♦ *my only wish.*
only child a child who has no brothers or sisters.

only *adverb*
no more than; and that is all ♦ *There are only three cakes left.*

only *conjunction*
but then; however ♦ *He makes promises, only he never keeps them.*

onomatopoeia (*say* on-om-at-o-**pee**-a) *noun*
the formation of words that imitate what they stand for, e.g. *cuckoo, plop.*
onomatopoeic *adjective*

onshore *adjective*
from the sea towards the land ♦ *an onshore breeze.*

onslaught *noun* (*plural* **onslaughts**)
a fierce attack.

onto *preposition*
to a position on.

onward *adverb & adjective*
going forward; further on.
onwards *adverb*

ooze *verb* (**oozes, oozing, oozed**)
1 flow out slowly; trickle. **2** allow something to flow out slowly ♦ *The wound oozed blood.*
ooze *noun*
mud at the bottom of a river or sea.

opal *noun* (*plural* **opals**)
a kind of stone in which small points of shifting colour can be seen.
opalescent *adjective*

opaque (*say* o-**payk**) *adjective*
not able to be seen through; not transparent or translucent.

open *adjective*
1 allowing people or things to go in and out; not closed or fastened. **2** not covered or blocked up. **3** spread out; unfolded. **4** not limited or restricted ♦ *an open championship.* **5** letting in visitors or customers. **6** with wide empty spaces ♦ *open country.* **7** honest and frank; not secret or secretive ♦ *Be open about the danger.* **8** willing to listen to other ideas ♦ *an open mind.*
♦ *I'm open to suggestions.*
openness *noun*
in the open air not inside a house or building.
open-air *adjective*
open *verb* (**opens, opening, opened**)
1 make or become open or more open. **2** begin.
opener *noun*

opencast *adjective*
(said about a mine) worked by removing layers of earth from the surface, not underground.

opening *noun* (*plural* **openings**)
1 a space or gap; a place where something opens.
2 the beginning of something. **3** an opportunity.

openly *adverb*
without secrecy.

opera *noun* (*plural* **operas**)
a drama set to music, with singers acting the story.
operatic *adjective*

operate *verb* (**operates, operating, operated**)
1 make a machine work. **2** be in action; work.
3 perform a surgical operation on somebody.
operable *adjective*

operating system *noun* (*plural* **operating systems**)
(in computing) the software that controls a computer's basic functions.

operation *noun* (*plural* **operations**)
1 a piece of work or method of working.
2 something done to a patient's body to take away or repair a damaged part. **3** a planned military activity.
operational *adjective*
in operation working or in use ♦ *When does the new system come into operation?*

operator *noun* (*plural* **operators**)
a person who works something, especially a telephone switchboard or exchange.

opinion *noun* (*plural* **opinions**)
what you think of something; a belief or judgement.

opinion poll *noun* (*plural* **opinion polls**)
an estimate of what people think, made by questioning a sample of them.

opium *noun*
a drug made from the juice of certain poppies, used in medicine.

opponent *noun* (*plural* **opponents**)
a person or group opposing another in a contest or war.

opportunist *noun* (*plural* **opportunists**)
a person who is quick to seize opportunities.
opportunism *noun*

opportunity *noun* (*plural* **opportunities**)
a good chance to do a particular thing.

oppose *verb* (**opposes, opposing, opposed**)
1 argue or fight against; resist. **2** contrast
♦ *'Soft' is opposed to 'hard'.*
as opposed to in contrast with. **be opposed to** be strongly against ♦ *We are opposed to parking in the town centre.*

opposite *adjective*
1 placed on the other or further side; facing
♦ *on the opposite side of the road.* **2** moving away from or towards each other ♦ *The trains were travelling in opposite directions.*
3 completely different ♦ *opposite characters.*
opposite *noun* (*plural* **opposites**)
an opposite person or thing.
opposite *preposition*
opposite to ♦ *They live opposite the school.*

opposition *noun*
1 opposing something; resistance. **2** the people who oppose something.
the Opposition the chief political party opposing the one that is in power.

oppress *verb* (oppresses, oppressing, oppressed)
1 govern or treat somebody cruelly or unjustly.
2 weigh somebody down with worry or sadness.
oppression *noun* **oppressive** *adjective*
oppressor *noun*

opt *verb* (opts, opting, opted)
choose.
opt out decide not to take part in something.

optical *adjective*
to do with sight; aiding sight ♦ *optical instruments.*
optically *adverb*

optical illusion *noun* (*plural* optical illusions)
a deceptive appearance that makes you think you see something that is not really there.

optician *noun* (*plural* opticians)
a person who tests people's eyesight and makes or sells glasses and contact lenses.

optimist *noun* (*plural* optimists)
a person who expects that things will turn out well. (Compare **pessimist**.)
optimism *noun* **optimistic** *adjective*
optimistically *adverb*

optimum *adjective*
best; most favourable.
optimum *noun* **optimal** *adjective*

option *noun* (*plural* options)
1 the right or power to choose something.
2 something chosen or that may be chosen.

optional *adjective*
that you can choose, not compulsory.
optionally *adverb*

or *conjunction*
used to show that there is a choice or an alternative ♦ *Do you want a bun or a biscuit?*

-or *suffix*
forms nouns meaning 'a person or thing that does something' (e.g. *tailor*, *refrigerator*).

oracle *noun* (*plural* oracles)
1 a shrine where the ancient Greeks consulted one of their gods for advice or a prophecy.
2 a wise or knowledgeable adviser.
oracular (*say* or-ak-yoo-ler) *adjective*

oral *adjective*
1 spoken, not written. 2 to do with or using the mouth.
orally *adverb*

---

❶ USAGE Do not confuse with *aural.*

---

orange *noun* (*plural* oranges)
1 a round juicy citrus fruit with reddish-yellow peel. 2 a reddish-yellow colour.

orangeade *noun*
an orange-flavoured drink.

orang-utan *noun* (*plural* orang-utans)
a large ape of Borneo and Sumatra.

orator *noun* (*plural* orators)
a person who is good at making speeches in public.
oratorical *adjective* **oratory** *noun*

orbit *noun* (*plural* orbits)
1 the curved path taken by something moving round a planet, moon, or star. 2 the range of someone's influence or control.
orbital *adjective*

orbit *verb* (orbits, orbiting, orbited)
move in an orbit round something ♦ *The satellite has been orbiting the earth since 1986.*

orchard *noun* (*plural* orchards)
a piece of ground planted with fruit trees.

orchestra *noun* (*plural* orchestras)
a large group of people playing various musical instruments together.
orchestral *adjective*
[from Greek, = the space where the chorus danced during a play]

orchid *noun* (*plural* orchids)
a kind of plant with brightly coloured, often unevenly shaped, flowers.

ordain *verb* (ordains, ordaining, ordained)
1 make a person a member of the clergy in the Christian Church ♦ *He was ordained in 1981.*
2 declare or order something by law.

ordeal *noun* (*plural* ordeals)
a difficult or horrific experience.

order *noun* (*plural* orders)
1 a command. 2 a request for something to be supplied. 3 the way things are arranged ♦ *in alphabetical order.* 4 a neat arrangement; a proper arrangement or condition ♦ *in working order.* 5 obedience to rules or laws ♦ *law and order.* 6 a kind or sort ♦ *She showed courage of the highest order.* 7 a group of monks or nuns who live by certain religious rules.
in order that or **in order to** for the purpose of.

order *verb* (orders, ordering, ordered)
1 command. 2 ask for something to be supplied.
3 put something into order; arrange neatly.

orderly *adjective*
1 arranged neatly or well; methodical.
2 well-behaved and obedient.
orderliness *noun*

ordinal number *noun* (*plural* ordinal numbers)
a number that shows a thing's position in a series, e.g. first, fifth, twentieth, etc. (Compare **cardinal number**.)

ordinary *adjective*
normal or usual; not special.
ordinarily *adverb*
out of the ordinary unusual.

ordination *noun* (*plural* ordinations)
ordaining or being ordained as a member of the clergy.

Ordnance Survey *noun*
an official survey organization that makes
detailed maps of the British Isles.

ore *noun* (*plural* **ores**)
rock with metal or other useful substances in it
♦ *iron ore.*

organ *noun* (*plural* **organs**)
1 a musical instrument from which sounds are
produced by air forced through pipes, played by
keys and pedals. 2 a part of the body with a
particular function ♦ *the digestive organs.*

organic *adjective*
1 to do with the organs of the body ♦ *organic
diseases.* 2 to do with or formed from living
things ♦ *organic matter.* 3 organic food is grown
or produced without the use of chemical
fertilizers, pesticides, etc. ♦ *organic farming.*
organically *adverb*

organism *noun* (*plural* **organisms**)
a living thing; an individual animal or plant.

organist *noun* (*plural* **organists**)
a person who plays the organ.

organization *noun* (*plural* **organizations**)
1 an organized group of people, such as a
business, charity, government department, etc.
2 the organizing of something.
organizational *adjective*

organize *verb* (**organizes, organizing,
organized**)
1 plan and prepare something ♦ *We organized a
picnic.* 2 form people into a group to work
together. 3 put things in order.
organizer *noun*

orgasm *noun* (*plural* **orgasms**)
the climax of sexual excitement.

orgy *noun* (*plural* **orgies**)
1 a wild party that involves a lot of drinking and
sex. 2 an extravagant activity ♦ *an orgy of
spending.*

oriental *adjective*
to do with the countries east of the
Mediterranean Sea, especially China and Japan.

orientate *verb* (**orientates, orientating,
orientated**)
1 place something or face in a certain direction.
2 get your bearings ♦ *I'm just trying to orientate
myself.*
orientation *noun*

origami (*say* o-rig-ah-mee) *noun*
folding paper into decorative shapes.
[from Japanese *ori* = fold + *kami* = paper]

origin *noun* (*plural* **origins**)
1 the start of something; the point or cause
from which something began. 2 a person's
family background ♦ *a man of humble origins.*
3 the point where two or more axes on a graph
meet.
[from Latin *oriri* = to rise]

original *adjective*
1 existing from the start; earliest ♦ *the original
inhabitants.* 2 new in its design etc.; not a copy.
3 producing new ideas; inventive.
originally *adverb* **originality** *noun*

originate *verb* (**originates, originating,
originated**)
1 cause something to begin; create. 2 have its
origin ♦ *The quarrel originated in rivalry.*
origination *noun* **originator** *noun*

ornament *noun* (*plural* **ornaments**)
an object displayed or worn as a decoration.
ornamental *adjective*

ornament *verb* (**ornaments, ornamenting,
ornamented**)
decorate something with beautiful things.
ornamentation *noun*

ornithology *noun*
the study of birds.
ornithologist *noun* **ornithological** *adjective*

orphan *noun* (*plural* **orphans**)
a child whose parents are dead.

orthodox *adjective*
1 holding beliefs that are correct or generally
accepted. 2 conventional or normal.
orthodoxy *noun*

Orthodox Church *noun*
the Christian Churches of eastern Europe.

orthopaedics (*say* orth-o-**pee**-diks) *noun*
the treatment of deformities and injuries to bones
and muscles.
orthopaedic *adjective*
[from Greek *orthos* = straight + *paideia* =
rearing of children (because the treatment was
originally of children)]

oscillate *verb* (**oscillates, oscillating,
oscillated**)
1 move to and fro like a pendulum; vibrate.
2 waver or vary.
oscillation *noun* **oscillator** *noun*

osmosis *noun*
the passing of fluid through a porous partition
into another more concentrated fluid.

ostentatious *adjective*
making a showy display of something to impress
people.
ostentatiously *adverb* **ostentation** *noun*

osteopath *noun* (*plural* **osteopaths**)
a person who treats certain medical conditions,
diseases, etc. by manipulating a patient's bones
and muscles.
osteopathy *noun* **osteopathic** *adjective*

ostrich *noun* (*plural* **ostriches**)
a large long-legged African bird that can run very
fast but cannot fly. It was said to bury its head in
the sand when pursued, in the belief that it
cannot then be seen.

other *adjective*
1 different ♦ *some other tune.* **2** remaining ♦ *Try the other shoe.* **3** additional ♦ *my other friends.* **4** just recent or past ♦ *I saw him the other day.*

other *pronoun & noun(plural* **others)**
the other person or thing ♦ *Where are the others?*

otherwise *adverb*
1 if things happen differently; if you do not ♦ *Write it down, otherwise you'll forget.* **2** in other ways ♦ *It rained, but otherwise the holiday was good.* **3** differently ♦ *We could not do otherwise.*

otter *noun (plural* **otters)**
a fish-eating animal with webbed feet, a flat tail, and thick brown fur, living near water. [from Old English]

ought *auxiliary verb*
expressing duty (*We ought to feed them*), rightness or advisability (*You ought to take more exercise*), or probability (*At this speed, we ought to be there by noon*).

oughtn't (*mainly spoken*)
ought not.

ounce *noun (plural* **ounces)**
a unit of weight equal to $\frac{1}{16}$ of a pound (about 28 grams).

our *adjective*
belonging to us.

ours *possessive pronoun*
belonging to us ♦ *These seats are ours.*

---

❶ USAGE It is incorrect to write ♦ *our's.*

---

ourselves *pronoun*
we or us and nobody else.

oust *verb* (**ousts, ousting, ousted**)
drive a person out from a position or office.

out *adverb*
1 away from or not in a particular place or position or state etc.; not at home. **2** into the open; into existence or sight etc. ♦ *The sun came out.* **3** no longer burning or shining. **4** in error ♦ *Your estimate was 10% out.* **5** to or at an end; completely ♦ *sold out;* ♦ *tired out.* **6** without restraint; boldly or loudly ♦ *Speak out!* **7** (in cricket) no longer batting.
be out for or **out to** be seeking or wanting ♦ *They are out to make trouble.* **be out of** have no more of something left. **out of date** **1** old-fashioned. **2** not valid any more. **out of doors** in the open air. **out of the way** remote.

---

❶ USAGE Use hyphens when *out of date* is used as an adjective before a noun, e.g. *out-of-date information* (but *The information is out of date*).

---

out and out *adjective*
thorough or complete ♦ *an out and out villain.*

outboard motor *noun (plural* **outboard motors)**
a motor fitted to the outside of a boat's stern.

outbreak *noun (plural* **outbreaks)**
the start of a disease or war or anger etc.

outburst *noun (plural* **outbursts)**
a sudden bursting out of anger or laughter etc.

outcast *noun (plural* **outcasts)**
a person who has been rejected by family, friends, or society.

outcrop *noun (plural* **outcrops)**
a piece of rock from a lower level that sticks out on the surface of the ground.

outcry *noun (plural* **outcries)**
a strong protest.

outdo *verb* (**outdoes, outdoing, outdid, outdone)**
do better than another person.

outdoors *adverb*
in the open air.

outer *adjective*
outside or external; nearer to the outside.
outermost *adjective*

outer space *noun*
the universe beyond the earth's atmosphere.

outfit *noun (plural* **outfits)**
1 a set of clothes worn together. **2** a set of equipment. **3** (*informal*) a team or organization.

outgrow *verb* (**outgrows, outgrowing, outgrew, outgrown)**
1 grow out of clothes or habits etc. **2** grow faster or larger than another person or thing.

outhouse *noun (plural* **outhouses)**
a small building (e.g. a shed or barn) that belongs to a house but is separate from it.

outing *noun (plural* **outings)**
a journey for pleasure.

outlandish *adjective*
looking or sounding strange or foreign.

outlast *verb* (**outlasts, outlasting, outlasted)**
last longer than something else.

outlaw *noun (plural* **outlaws)**
a person who is punished by being excluded from legal rights and the protection of the law, especially a robber or bandit.

outlay *noun (plural* **outlays)**
what is spent on something.

outlet *noun (plural* **outlets)**
1 a way for something to get out. **2** a way of expressing strong feelings. **3** a place from which goods are sold or distributed.

outline *noun (plural* **outlines)**
1 a line round the outside of something, showing its boundary or shape. **2** a summary.

outlook *noun* (*plural* **outlooks**)
1 a view on which people look out. 2 a person's mental attitude to something. 3 future prospects ♦ *The outlook is bleak.*

outlying *adjective*
far from the centre; remote ♦ *the outlying districts.*

outmoded *adjective*
out of date.

outnumber *verb* (**outnumbers, outnumbering, outnumbered**)
be more numerous than another group.

outpatient *noun* (*plural* **outpatients**)
a person who visits a hospital for treatment but does not stay there.

outpost *noun* (*plural* **outposts**)
a distant settlement.

output *noun* (*plural* **outputs**)
1 the amount produced. 2 the information or results produced by a computer.

outrage *noun* (*plural* **outrages**)
1 something that shocks people by being very wicked or cruel. 2 great anger.
outrageous *adjective* **outrageously** *adverb*
outrage *verb* (**outrages, outraging, outraged**)
shock and anger people greatly.

outright *adverb*
1 completely; not gradually ♦ *This drug should be banned outright.* 2 frankly ♦ *We told him this outright.*

outright *adjective*
thorough or complete ♦ *an outright fraud.*

outrun *verb* (**outruns, outrunning, outran, outrun**)
run faster or further than another.

outset *noun*
the beginning of something ♦ *from the outset of his career.*

outside *noun* (*plural* **outsides**)
the outer side, surface, or part.
at the outside at the most ♦ *a mile at the outside.*

outside *adjective*
1 on or coming from the outside ♦ *the outside edge.* 2 greatest possible ♦ *the outside price.* 3 remote or slight ♦ *an outside chance.*

outside *adverb*
on or to the outside; outdoors ♦ *Leave it outside.* ♦ *It's cold outside.*

outside *preposition*
on or to the outside of ♦ *Leave it outside the door.*

outside broadcast *noun* (*plural* **outside broadcasts**)
a broadcast made on location and not in a studio.

outsider *noun* (*plural* **outsiders**)
1 a person who does not belong to a certain group. 2 a horse or person thought to have no chance of winning a race or competition.

outsize *adjective*
much larger than average.

outskirts *plural noun*
the outer parts or districts, especially of a town.

outspoken *adjective*
speaking or spoken very frankly.

outstanding *adjective*
1 extremely good or distinguished. 2 not yet paid or dealt with.

outstrip *verb* (**outstrips, outstripping, outstripped**)
1 run faster or further than another; outrun. 2 surpass in achievement or success.

outward *adjective*
1 going outwards. 2 on the outside.
outwardly *adverb* **outwards** *adverb*

outwit *verb* (**outwits, outwitting, outwitted**)
deceive somebody by being crafty.

ova *plural* of **ovum.**

oval *adjective*
shaped like a 0, rounded and longer than it is broad.
oval *noun*

ovary *noun* (*plural* **ovaries**)
1 either of the two organs in which ova or egg cells are produced in a woman's or female animal's body. 2 part of the pistil in a plant, from which fruit is formed.

oven *noun* (*plural* **ovens**)
a closed space in which things are cooked or heated.

over *preposition*
1 above. 2 more than ♦ *It's over a mile away.* 3 concerning ♦ *They quarrelled over money.* 4 across the top of; on or to the other side of ♦ *They rowed the boat over the lake.* 5 during ♦ *We can talk over dinner.* 6 in superiority or preference to ♦ *their victory over United.*

over *adverb*
1 out and down from the top or edge; from an upright position ♦ *He fell over.* 2 so that a different side shows ♦ *Turn it over.* 3 at or to a place; across ♦ *Walk over to our house.* 4 remaining ♦ *There is nothing left over.* 5 all through; thoroughly ♦ *Think it over.* 6 at an end ♦ *The lesson is over.*
over and over many times; repeatedly.

over *noun* (*plural* **overs**)
a series of six balls bowled in cricket.
[from Old English]

overact *verb* (**overacts, overacting, overacted**)
(said about an actor) act in an exaggerated manner.

overall *adjective*
including everything; total ♦ *the overall cost.*

overalls *plural noun*
a piece of clothing like a shirt and trousers combined, worn over other clothes to protect them.

overarm *adjective & adverb*
with the arm lifted above shoulder level and coming down in front of the body ♦ *bowling overarm.*

overawe *verb* (overawes, overawing, overawed)
overcome a person with awe.

overbalance *verb* (overbalances, overbalancing, overbalanced)
lose balance and fall over.

overbearing *adjective*
domineering.

overblown *adjective*
1 exaggerated or pretentious. 2 (said about a flower) too fully open; past its best.

overboard *adverb*
from in or on a ship into the water ♦ *She jumped overboard.*

overcast *adjective*
covered with cloud.

overcoat *noun* (*plural* overcoats)
a warm outdoor coat.

overcome *verb* (overcomes, overcoming, overcame, overcome)
1 win a victory over somebody; defeat. 2 have a strong physical or emotional effect on someone and make them helpless ♦ *He was overcome by the fumes.* 3 find a way of dealing with a problem etc.

overdo *verb* (overdoes, overdoing, overdid, overdone)
1 do something too much. 2 cook food for too long.

overdose *noun* (*plural* overdoses)
too large a dose of a drug.

overdraft *noun* (*plural* overdrafts)
the amount by which a bank account is overdrawn.

overdraw *verb* (overdraws, overdrawing, overdrew, overdrawn)
draw more money from a bank account than the amount you have in it.

overdue *adjective*
late; not paid or arrived etc. by the proper time.

overhaul *verb* (overhauls, overhauling, overhauled)
1 examine something thoroughly and repair it if necessary. 2 overtake.
overhaul *noun*

overhead *adjective & adverb*
1 above the level of your head. 2 in the sky.

overheads *plural noun*
the expenses of running a business.

overhear *verb* (overhears, overhearing, overheard)
hear something accidentally or without the speaker intending you to hear it.

overjoyed *adjective*
filled with great joy.

overlap *verb* (overlaps, overlapping, overlapped)
1 lie across part of something. 2 happen partly at the same time.
overlap *noun*

overlay *verb* (overlays, overlaying, overlaid)
cover with a layer; lie on top of something.

overload *verb* (overloads, overloading, overloaded)
put too great a load on someone or something.

overlook *verb* (overlooks, overlooking, overlooked)
1 not notice or consider something. 2 deliberately ignore something wrong; not punish an offence. 3 have a view over something.

overpower *verb* (overpowers, overpowering, overpowered)
defeat someone by greater strength or numbers.

overpowering *adjective*
very strong.

overrate *verb* (overrates, overrating, overrated)
have too high an opinion of something.

override *verb* (overrides, overriding, overrode, overridden)
1 overrule. 2 be more important than ♦ *Safety overrides all other considerations.*
overriding *adjective*

overrule *verb* (overrules, overruling, overruled)
reject a suggestion etc. by using your authority ♦ *We voted for having a disco but the headteacher overruled the idea.*

overrun *verb* (overruns, overrunning, overran, overrun)
1 spread over and occupy or harm something ♦ *Mice overran the place.* 2 go on for longer than it should ♦ *The broadcast overran by ten minutes.*

oversee *verb* (oversees, overseeing, oversaw, overseen)
watch over or supervise people working.
overseer *noun*

oversight *noun* (*plural* oversights)
a mistake made by not noticing something.

overtake *verb* (overtakes, overtaking, overtook, overtaken)
1 pass a moving vehicle or person etc. 2 catch up with someone.

overthrow *verb* (overthrows, overthrowing, overthrew, overthrown)
remove someone from power by force
♦ *They overthrew the king.*

overtime *noun*
time spent working outside the normal hours; payment for this.

overture *noun* (*plural* **overtures**)
1 a piece of music written as an introduction to an opera, ballet, etc. 2 a friendly attempt to start a discussion ♦ *They made overtures of peace.*

overturn *verb* (overturns, overturning, overturned)
1 turn over or upside down. 2 reverse a legal decision.

overwhelm *verb* (overwhelms, overwhelming, overwhelmed)
1 bury or drown beneath a huge mass. 2 overcome completely.
overwhelming *adjective*

ovum (*say* oh-vum) *noun* (*plural* **ova**)
a female cell that can develop into a new individual when it is fertilized.
[from Latin, = egg]

owe *verb* (owes, owing, owed)
1 have a duty to pay or give something to someone, especially money. 2 have something because of the action of another person or thing ♦ *They owed their lives to the pilot's skill.*
owing to because of; caused by.

❶ USAGE The use of *owing to* as a preposition meaning 'because of' is entirely acceptable, unlike this use of *due to*, which some people object to. See note at *due*.

owl *noun* (*plural* **owls**)
a bird of prey with large eyes, usually flying at night.

own *adjective*
belonging to yourself or itself.
get your own back get revenge. **on your own** alone.

own *verb* (owns, owning, owned)
1 possess; have something as your property. 2 acknowledge or admit something ♦ *I own that I made a mistake.*
own up confess; admit guilt.

owner *noun* (*plural* **owners**)
the person who owns something.
ownership *noun*

own goal *noun* (*plural* **own goals**)
a goal scored by a member of a team against their own side.

ox *noun* (*plural* **oxen**)
a large animal kept for its meat and for pulling carts.

oxide *noun* (*plural* **oxides**)
a compound of oxygen and one other element.

oxygen *noun*
a colourless odourless tasteless gas that exists in the air and is essential for living things.

oyster *noun* (*plural* **oysters**)
a kind of shellfish whose shell sometimes contains a pearl.

ozone *noun*
a form of oxygen with a sharp smell.

ozone layer *noun*
a layer of ozone high in the atmosphere, protecting the earth from harmful amounts of the sun's radiation.

Pp

p *abbreviation*
penny or pence.

p. *abbreviation* (*plural* **pp.**)
page.

pace *noun* (*plural* **paces**)
1 one step in walking, marching, or running. 2 speed ♦ *He set a fast pace.*

pacemaker *noun* (*plural* **pacemakers**)
1 a person who sets the pace for another in a race. 2 an electrical device to keep the heart beating.

pacifist (*say* pas-if-ist) *noun* (*plural* **pacifists**)
a person who believes that war is always wrong.
pacifism *noun*

pacify *verb* (pacifies, pacifying, pacified)
1 calm a person down. 2 bring peace to a country or to people who are fighting.
pacification *noun*

pack *noun* (*plural* **packs**)
1 a bundle or collection of things wrapped or tied together. 2 a set of playing cards (usually 52). 3 a bag carried on your back. 4 a large amount ♦ *a pack of lies.* 5 a group of hounds or wolves etc. 6 a group of people; a group of Brownies or Cub Scouts.

pack *verb* (packs, packing, packed)
1 put things into a suitcase, bag, or box etc. in order to move or store them. 2 crowd together; fill tightly.
pack off (*informal*) send a person away. **send a person packing** (*informal*) dismiss him or her.

package *noun* (*plural* **packages**)
1 a parcel or packet. 2 a number of things offered or accepted together.
packaging *noun*

package holiday *noun* (*plural* **package holidays**)
a holiday with all the travel and accommodation arranged and included in the price.

packet *noun* (*plural* **packets**)
a small parcel.

pack ice *noun*
a mass of pieces of ice floating in the sea.

pad *noun* (*plural* **pads**)
1 a soft thick mass of material, used e.g. to protect or stuff something. **2** a piece of soft material worn to protect your leg in cricket and other games. **3** a set of sheets of paper fastened together at one edge. **4** the soft fleshy part under an animal's foot or the end of a finger or toe. **5** a flat surface from which rockets are launched or where helicopters take off and land.

pad *verb* (**pads, padding, padded**)
put a pad on or in something.
pad out make a book, speech, etc. longer than it needs to be.

padding *noun*
material used to pad things.

paddle¹ *verb* (**paddles, paddling, paddled**)
walk about in shallow water.
paddle *noun*

paddle² *noun* (*plural* **paddles**)
a short oar with a broad blade; something shaped like this.

paddle *verb* (**paddles, paddling, paddled**)
move a boat along with a paddle or paddles; row gently.

paddock *noun* (*plural* **paddocks**)
a small field where horses are kept.

padlock *noun* (*plural* **padlocks**)
a detachable lock with a metal loop that passes through a ring or chain etc.
padlock *verb*

paediatrics (*say* peed-ee-at-riks) *noun*
the study of children's diseases.
paediatric *adjective* **paediatrician** *noun*
[from Greek *paidos* = of a child + *iatros* = doctor]

pagan (*say* pay-gan) *noun* (*plural* **pagans**)
a person who does not believe in one of the chief religions; a heathen.
pagan *adjective*
[from Latin *paganus* = country dweller, civilian. In Christian Latin the word was used of anyone who was a 'civilian' in the sense of not being in the 'army' of Christ]

page¹ *noun* (*plural* **pages**)
a piece of paper that is part of a book or newspaper etc.; one side of this.

page² *noun* (*plural* **pages**)
1 a boy or man employed to go on errands or be an attendant. **2** a young boy attending a bride at a wedding.

pageant *noun* (*plural* **pageants**)
1 a play or entertainment about historical events and people. **2** a procession of people in costume as an entertainment.
pageantry *noun*

pagoda (*say* pag-oh-da) *noun* (*plural* **pagodas**)
a Buddhist tower, or a Hindu temple shaped like a pyramid, in India and the Far East.
[via Portuguese from Persian]

paid *past tense* of **pay**.
put paid to (*informal*) put an end to someone's activity or hope etc.

pail *noun* (*plural* **pails**)
a bucket.

pain *noun* (*plural* **pains**)
1 an unpleasant feeling caused by injury or disease. **2** suffering in the mind.
painful *adjective* **painfully** *adverb* **painless** *adjective*
take pains make a careful effort with work etc.

painkiller *noun* (*plural* **painkillers**)
a medicine or drug that relieves pain.

painstaking *adjective*
very careful and thorough.

paint *noun* (*plural* **paints**)
a liquid substance put on something to colour it.
paintbox *noun* **paintbrush** *noun*

paint *verb* (**paints, painting, painted**)
1 put paint on something. **2** make a picture with paints.

painting *noun* (*plural* **paintings**)
1 a painted picture. **2** using paints to make a picture.

pair *noun* (*plural* **pairs**)
1 a set of two things or people; a couple. **2** something made of two joined parts ♦ *a pair of scissors.*

pair *verb* (**pairs, pairing, paired**)
put two things together as a pair.
pair off or **up** form a couple.

palace *noun* (*plural* **palaces**)
a mansion where a king, queen, or other important person lives.

palatable *adjective*
tasting pleasant.

palate *noun* (*plural* **palates**)
1 the roof of your mouth. **2** a person's sense of taste.

pale¹ *adjective*
1 almost white ♦ *a pale face.* **2** not bright in colour or light ♦ *pale green;* ♦ *the pale moonlight.*
palely *adverb* **paleness** *noun*

pale² *noun* (*plural* **pales**)
a boundary.
beyond the pale beyond the limits of good taste or behaviour etc.

palindrome *noun* (*plural* **palindromes**)
a word or phrase that reads the same backwards
as forwards, e.g. *radar* or *Madam, I'm Adam*.
[from Greek *palindromos* = running back again]

paling *noun* (*plural* **palings**)
a fence made of wooden posts or railings; one of
its posts.

pall[1] (*say* pawl) *noun* (*plural* **palls**)
1 a cloth spread over a coffin. **2** a dark covering
♦ *A pall of smoke lay over the town*.

pall[2] (*say* pawl) *verb* (**palls, palling, palled**)
become uninteresting or boring to someone
♦ *The novelty of the new computer game soon
began to pall*.

palliative *noun* (*plural* **palliatives**)
something that lessens pain or suffering.
palliative *adjective*

palm *noun* (*plural* **palms**)
1 the inner part of the hand, between the fingers
and the wrist. **2** a palm tree.
palm off deceive a person into accepting
something.

palm tree *noun* (*plural* **palm trees**)
a tropical tree with large leaves and no branches.

palpitate *verb* (**palpitates, palpitating,
palpitated**)
1 (said about the heart) beat hard and quickly.
2 (said about a person) quiver with fear or
excitement.
palpitation *noun*

pampas *noun*
wide grassy plains in South America.

pamper *verb* (**pampers, pampering,
pampered**)
treat or look after someone very kindly and
indulgently.

pamphlet *noun* (*plural* **pamphlets**)
a leaflet or booklet giving information on a
subject.
[from *Pamphilet*, the name of a long
12th-century poem in Latin]

pan *noun* (*plural* **pans**)
1 a wide container with a flat base, used for
cooking etc. **2** something shaped like this.
3 the bowl of a lavatory.

pancake *noun* (*plural* **pancakes**)
a thin round cake of batter fried on both sides.

panda *noun* (*plural* **pandas**)
a large bear-like black-and-white animal found
in China.

pandemonium *noun*
uproar and complete confusion.
[from *Pandemonium*, John Milton's name for the
capital of hell in his poem 'Paradise Lost', from
pan- = all + *demon*]

pane *noun* (*plural* **panes**)
a sheet of glass in a window.

panel *noun* (*plural* **panels**)
1 a long flat piece of wood, metal, etc. that is
part of a door, wall, piece of furniture, etc.
2 a flat board with controls or instruments on it.
3 a group of people chosen to discuss or decide
something.
panelled *adjective* **panelling** *noun*

pang *noun* (*plural* **pangs**)
a sudden sharp pain.

panic *noun*
sudden uncontrollable fear.
panic-stricken *adjective* **panicky** *adjective*
panic *verb* (**panics, panicking, panicked**)
fill or be filled with panic.

panorama *noun* (*plural* **panoramas**)
a view or picture of a wide area.
panoramic *adjective*

pant *verb* (**pants, panting, panted**)
take short quick breaths, usually after running or
working hard.

panther *noun* (*plural* **panthers**)
a leopard, especially a black one.

pantomime *noun* (*plural* **pantomimes**)
1 a Christmas entertainment, usually based on a
fairy tale. **2** mime.

pantry *noun* (*plural* **pantries**)
a small room for storing food; a larder.

pants *plural noun* (*informal*)
1 underpants or knickers. **2** (*American*) trousers.

paper *noun* (*plural* **papers**)
1 a substance made in thin sheets from wood,
rags, etc. and used for writing or printing
or drawing on or for wrapping things.
2 a newspaper. **3** wallpaper. **4** a document.
5 a set of examination questions ♦ *a history
paper*.
paper *verb* (**papers, papering, papered**)
cover a wall or room with wallpaper.

paperback *noun* (*plural* **paperbacks**)
a book with a thin flexible cover.

papier mâché (*say* pap-yay mash-ay) *noun*
paper made into pulp and moulded to make
models, ornaments, etc.

parable *noun* (*plural* **parables**)
a story told to teach people something, especially
one of those told by Jesus Christ.

parabola (*say* pa-rab-ol-a) *noun* (*plural*
parabolas)
a curve like the path of an object thrown into the
air and falling down again.
parabolic *adjective*

parachute *noun* (*plural* **parachutes**)
an umbrella-like device on which people or
things can float slowly to the ground from an
aircraft.
parachute *verb* **parachutist** *noun*

parade *noun* (*plural* **parades**)
1 a procession that displays people or things.
2 an assembly of troops for inspection, drill, etc.;
a ground for this. **3** a public square, promenade,
or row of shops.
parade *verb* (**parades, parading, paraded**)
1 move in a parade. **2** assemble for a parade.

paradise *noun*
1 heaven; a heavenly place. **2** the Garden of
Eden.

paradox *noun* (*plural* **paradoxes**)
a statement that seems to contradict itself but is
in fact true.
paradoxical *adjective* **paradoxically** *adverb*

paraffin *noun*
a kind of oil used as fuel.

paragraph *noun* (*plural* **paragraphs**)
one or more sentences on a single subject,
forming a section of a piece of writing and
beginning on a new line, usually slightly in from
the margin of the page.

parallel *adjective*
1 (said about lines etc.) side by side and the
same distance apart from each other for their
whole length, like railway lines. **2** similar or
corresponding ♦ *When petrol prices rise there is
a parallel rise in bus fares.*
parallelism *noun*
parallel *noun* (*plural* **parallels**)
1 something similar or corresponding.
2 a comparison ♦ *You can draw a parallel
between the two situations.* **3** a line that is
parallel to another. **4** a line of latitude.

❶ USAGE Take care with the spelling of this word:
one 'r', two 'l's, then one 'l'.

parallelogram *noun* (*plural* **parallelograms**)
a quadrilateral with its opposite sides equal and
parallel.

paralyse *verb* (**paralyses, paralysing,
paralysed**)
1 cause paralysis in a person etc. **2** make
something be unable to move ♦ *She was
paralysed with fear.*

paralysis *noun*
being unable to move, especially because of a
disease or an injury to the nerves.
paralytic (*say* pa-ra-**lit**-ik) *adjective*

paramedic *noun* (*plural* **paramedics**)
a person who is trained to do medical work,
especially emergency first aid, but is not a fully
qualified doctor.

parameter (*say* pa-**ram**-it-er) *noun* (*plural*
parameters)
a quantity, quality, or factor that is variable and
affects other things by its changes.

❶ USAGE Do not confuse with *perimeter*.

paramount *adjective*
more important than anything else ♦ *Secrecy is
paramount.*

parapet *noun* (*plural* **parapets**)
a low wall along the edge of a balcony, bridge,
roof, etc.

paraphernalia *noun*
numerous pieces of equipment, belongings, etc.

paraphrase *verb* (**paraphrases, paraphrasing,
paraphrased**)
give the meaning of something by using different
words.
paraphrase *noun*

parasite *noun* (*plural* **parasites**)
an animal or plant that lives in or on another,
from which it gets its food.
parasitic *adjective*
[from Greek *parasitos* = guest at a meal]

paratroops *plural noun*
troops trained to be dropped from aircraft by
parachute.
paratrooper *noun*

parcel *noun* (*plural* **parcels**)
something wrapped up to be sent by post or
carried.
parcel *verb* (**parcels, parcelling, parcelled**)
1 wrap something up as a parcel. **2** divide
something into portions ♦ *parcel out the work.*
[from old French, related to *particle*]

parched *adjective*
very dry or thirsty.

parchment *noun* (*plural* **parchments**)
a kind of heavy paper, originally made from
animal skins.
[from the city of Pergamum, now in Turkey,
where parchment was made in ancient times]

pardon *noun*
1 forgiveness. **2** the cancelling of a punishment
♦ *a free pardon.*
pardon *verb* (**pardons, pardoning, pardoned**)
1 forgive or excuse somebody. **2** cancel a
person's punishment.
pardonable *adjective* **pardonably** *adverb*
pardon *interjection*
used to mean 'I didn't hear or understand what
you said'.

parent *noun* (*plural* **parents**)
1 a father or mother; a living thing that has
produced others of its kind. **2** a source from
which others are derived ♦ *the parent company.*
parenthood *noun* **parenting** *noun* **parental**
(*say* pa-**rent**-al) *adjective*

parenthesis (*say* pa-ren-thi-sis) *noun* (*plural*
parentheses)
1 something extra that is inserted in a sentence,
usually between brackets or dashes. **2** either of
the pair of brackets (like these) used to mark off
words from the rest of a sentence.
parenthetical *adjective*

parish noun (plural **parishes**)
a district with its own church.
parishioner noun
[from Greek *paroikia* = neighbourhood]

park noun (plural **parks**)
1 a large garden or recreation ground for public
use. 2 an area of grassland or woodland
belonging to a country house.
park verb (**parks, parking, parked**)
leave a vehicle somewhere for a time.

parliament noun (plural **parliaments**)
the assembly that makes a country's laws.
parliamentary adjective
[from early French *parlement* = speaking]

parlour noun (plural **parlours**) (*old use*)
a sitting room.

parody noun (plural **parodies**)
an amusing imitation of the style of a writer,
composer, literary work, etc.
parody verb (**parodies, parodying, parodied**)
make or be a parody of a person or thing.

parole noun
the release of a prisoner before the end of his or
her sentence on condition of good behaviour
♦ *He was on parole.*
parole verb

paroxysm (*say* pa-roks-izm) noun (*plural*
paroxysms)
a sudden outburst of rage, jealousy, laughter,
etc.

parrot noun (plural **parrots**)
a brightly coloured tropical bird that can learn to
repeat words etc.

parsley noun
a plant with crinkled green leaves used to flavour
and decorate food.

parsnip noun (plural **parsnips**)
a plant with a pointed pale yellow root used as a
vegetable.

parson noun (plural **parsons**)
a member of the clergy, especially a rector or
vicar.

part noun (plural **parts**)
1 some but not all of a thing or number of
things; anything that belongs to something
bigger. 2 the character played by an actor or
actress. 3 the words spoken by a character in a
play. 4 how much a person or thing is involved
in something ♦ *She played a huge part in her
daughter's success.* 5 one side in an agreement or
in a dispute or quarrel.
take in good part not be offended at something.
take part join in an activity.
part verb (**parts, parting, parted**)
separate or divide.
part with give away or get rid of something.

part exchange noun
giving something that you own as part of the
price of what you are buying.

partial adjective
1 not complete or total ♦ *a partial eclipse.*
2 favouring one side more than the other; biased
or unfair.
partially adverb **partiality** noun
be partial to be fond of something.

participate verb (**participates, participating,
participated**)
take part or have a share in something.
participant noun **participation** noun
participator noun

participle noun (plural **participles**)
a word formed from a verb (e.g. *gone, going;
guided, guiding*) and used with an auxiliary verb
to form certain tenses (e.g. *It has gone. It is
going*) or the passive (e.g. *We were guided to our
seats*), or as an adjective (e.g. *a guided missile; a
guiding light*). The **past participle** (e.g. *gone,
guided*) describes a completed action or past
condition. The **present participle** (which ends
in *-ing*) describes a continuing action or
condition.

particle noun (plural **particles**)
a very small piece or amount.

particular adjective
1 of this one and no other; individual ♦ *This
particular stamp is very rare.* 2 special ♦ *Take
particular care of it.* 3 giving something close
attention; choosing carefully ♦ *He is very
particular about his clothes.*
particularly adverb **particularity** noun
particular noun (plural **particulars**)
a detail or single fact ♦ *Can you give me some
particulars of the job?*
in particular 1 especially ♦ *We liked this one in
particular.* 2 special ♦ *We did nothing in
particular.*

parting noun (plural **partings**)
1 leaving or separation. 2 a line where hair is
combed away in different directions.

partisan noun (plural **partisans**)
1 a strong supporter of a party or group etc.
2 a member of an organization resisting the
authorities in a conquered country.

partition noun (plural **partitions**)
1 a thin wall that divides a room or space.
2 dividing something, especially a country, into
separate parts.
partition verb (**partitions, partitioning,
partitioned**)
1 divide something into separate parts. 2 divide
a room or space by means of a partition.

partly adverb
to some extent but not completely.

partner *noun* (*plural* **partners**)
1 one of a pair of people who do something together, such as dancing or playing a game. **2** a person who jointly owns a business with one or more other people. **3** the person that someone is married to or is having a sexual relationship with.
partnership *noun*

part of speech *noun* (*plural* **parts of speech**)
any of the groups (also called **word classes**) into which words are divided in grammar (noun, pronoun, adjective, verb, adverb, preposition, conjunction, and interjection).

partridge *noun* (*plural* **partridges**)
a game bird with brown feathers.

part-time *adjective* & *adverb*
working for only some of the normal hours.
part-timer *noun*

party *noun* (*plural* **parties**)
1 a gathering of people to enjoy themselves ♦ *a birthday party*. **2** a group working or travelling together. **3** an organized group of people with similar political beliefs ♦ *the Labour Party*. **4** a person who is involved in an action or lawsuit etc. ♦ *the guilty party*.

pass *verb* (**passes, passing, passed**)
1 go past something; go or move in a certain direction. **2** move something in a certain direction ♦ *Pass the cord through the ring*. **3** give or transfer something to another person ♦ *Could you pass the butter?* **4** (in ball games) kick or throw the ball to another player of your own side. **5** be successful in a test or examination. **6** approve or accept ♦ *They passed a law*. **7** occupy time ♦ *They passed several hours chatting together*. **8** happen ♦ *We heard what passed when they met*. **9** come to an end. **10** utter ♦ *Pass a remark*. **11** (in a game, quiz, etc.) let your turn go by or choose not to answer.
pass out 1 complete your military training. **2** faint.

pass *noun* (*plural* **passes**)
1 passing something. **2** a success in an examination. **3** (in ball games) kicking or throwing the ball to another player of your own side. **4** a permit to go in or out of a place. **5** a route through a gap in a range of mountains. **6** a critical state of affairs ♦ *Things have come to a pretty pass!*

passage *noun* (*plural* **passages**)
1 a way through something; a corridor. **2** a journey by sea or air. **3** a section of a piece of writing or music. **4** passing ♦ *the passage of time*.
passageway *noun*

passenger *noun* (*plural* **passengers**)
a person who is driven or carried in a car, train, ship, or aircraft etc.

passer-by *noun* (*plural* **passers-by**)
a person who happens to be going past something.

passion *noun* (*plural* **passions**)
1 strong emotion. **2** great enthusiasm.
the Passion the sufferings of Jesus Christ at the Crucifixion.
[from Latin *passio* = suffering]

passionate *adjective*
full of passion.
passionately *adverb*

passive *adjective*
1 not resisting or fighting against something. **2** acted upon and not active. **3** (in grammar, said about a form of a verb) used when the subject of the sentence receives the action, e.g. *was hit* in 'She was hit on the head'. (Compare **active**.) **4** (said about an activity) that you get the effect of because other people are doing it ♦ *passive smoking*.
passively *adverb* **passiveness** *noun* **passivity** *noun*

Passover *noun*
a Jewish religious festival commemorating the freeing of the Jews from slavery in Egypt.
[from *pass over*, because according to the Bible God spared the Jews from the fate which affected the Egyptians]

passport *noun* (*plural* **passports**)
an official document that entitles the person holding it to travel abroad.

password *noun* (*plural* **passwords**)
1 a secret word or phrase used to distinguish friends from enemies. **2** a word you need to key in to gain access to certain computer files.

past *adjective*
of the time gone by ♦ *during the past week*.

past *noun*
the time gone by.

past *preposition*
1 beyond ♦ *Walk past the school*. **2** after ♦ *It is past midnight*.
past it (*slang*) too old to be able to do something.

paste *noun* (*plural* **pastes**)
1 a soft, moist, and sticky substance. **2** a glue, especially for paper. **3** a soft edible mixture ♦ *tomato paste*. **4** a hard glassy substance used to make imitation jewellery.

paste *verb* (**pastes, pasting, pasted**)
1 stick something onto a surface by using paste. **2** coat something with paste. **3** (*slang*) beat or thrash someone.

pastel *noun* (*plural* **pastels**)
1 a crayon that is like chalk. **2** a light delicate colour.

pasteurize *verb* (pasteurizes, pasteurizing, pasteurized)
purify milk by heating and then cooling it.
[named after Louis Pasteur, a 19th-century French scientist who invented the process]

pastille *noun* (*plural* pastilles)
a small flavoured sweet for sucking.

pastime *noun* (*plural* pastimes)
something you do to make time pass pleasantly; a hobby or game.

pastoral *adjective*
to do with country life ♦ *a pastoral scene.*

pastry *noun* (*plural* pastries)
1 dough made with flour, fat, and water, rolled flat and baked. 2 something made of pastry.

pasture *noun* (*plural* pastures)
land covered with grass etc. that cattle, sheep, or horses can eat.

pasture *verb* (pastures, pasturing, pastured)
put animals to graze in a pasture.

pasty¹ (*say* pas-tee) *noun* (*plural* pasties)
pastry with a filling of meat and vegetables, baked without a dish to shape it.

pasty² (*say* pay-stee) *adjective*
looking pale and unhealthy.

pat *verb* (pats, patting, patted)
tap gently with the hand open or with something flat.

pat *noun* (*plural* pats)
1 a patting movement or sound. 2 a small piece of butter or other soft substance.
a pat on the back praise.

patch *noun* (*plural* patches)
1 a piece of material or metal etc. put over a hole or damaged place. 2 an area that is different from its surroundings. 3 a piece of ground ♦ *the cabbage patch.* 4 a small area or piece of something ♦ *There are patches of fog.*
not a patch on (*informal*) not nearly as good as.

patch *verb* (patches, patching, patched)
put a patch on something.
patch up 1 repair something roughly.
2 settle a quarrel.

patchwork *noun*
needlework in which small pieces of different cloth are sewn edge to edge.

patchy *adjective*
occurring in patches; uneven.
patchily *adverb* **patchiness** *noun*

pâté (*say* pat-ay) *noun* (*plural* pâtés)
paste made of meat or fish.

pâté de foie gras (*say* pat-ay der fwah grah) *noun*
a rich paste made from goose liver.

patent (*say* pat-ent or pay-tent) *noun* (*plural* patents)
the official right given to an inventor to make or sell his or her invention and to prevent other people from copying it.

patent *verb* (patents, patenting, patented)
get a patent for something.

patent *adjective*
obvious.
patently *adverb*

paternal *adjective*
1 to do with a father. 2 fatherly.
paternally *adverb*

paternalistic *adjective*
treating people in a paternal way; providing for people's needs but giving them no responsibility.
paternalism *noun*

paternity *noun*
1 fatherhood. 2 being the father of a particular baby.

path *noun* (*plural* paths)
1 a narrow way along which people or animals can walk. 2 a line along which a person or thing moves. 3 a course of action.

pathetic *adjective*
1 making you feel pity or sympathy. 2 miserably inadequate or useless ♦ *a pathetic attempt.*
pathetically *adverb*

pathos (*say* pay-thoss) *noun*
a quality of making people feel pity or sympathy.

patience *noun*
1 being patient. 2 a card game for one person.

patient *adjective*
able to wait or put up with trouble or inconvenience without becoming anxious or angry.
patiently *adverb*

patient *noun* (*plural* patients)
a person who has treatment from a doctor or dentist etc.

patio *noun* (*plural* patios)
a paved area beside a house.
[from Spanish, = courtyard]

patriarch (*say* pay-tree-ark) *noun* (*plural* patriarchs)
1 the male who is head of a family or tribe. 2 a bishop of high rank in the Orthodox Christian churches.
patriarchal *adjective*

patriot (*say* pay-tree-ot or pat-ree-ot) *noun* (*plural* patriots)
a person who loves his or her country and supports it loyally.
patriotic *adjective* **patriotically** *adverb*
patriotism *noun*

patrol *verb* (patrols, patrolling, patrolled)
walk or travel regularly over an area in order to guard it and see that all is well.

patrol *noun* (*plural* **patrols**)
1 a patrolling group of people, ships, aircraft, etc.
2 a group of Scouts or Guides.
on patrol patrolling.

patron (*say* pay-tron) *noun* (*plural* **patrons**)
1 someone who supports a person or cause with money or encouragement. 2 a regular customer.
patronage (*say* pat-ron-ij) *noun*

patronize (*say* pat-ron-I'z) *verb* (**patronizes, patronizing, patronized**)
1 be a regular customer of a particular shop, restaurant, etc. 2 talk to someone in a way that shows you think they are stupid or inferior to you.

patter¹ *noun*
a series of light tapping sounds.

patter *verb* (**patters, pattering, pattered**)
make light tapping sounds ♦ *Rain pattered on the window panes.*

patter² *noun*
the quick talk of a comedian, conjuror, salesperson, etc.
[originally = recite a prayer: from Latin *pater noster* = Our Father, the first words of a Christian prayer]

pattern *noun* (*plural* **patterns**)
1 a repeated arrangement of lines, shapes, or colours etc. 2 a thing to be copied in order to make something ♦ *a dress pattern.* 3 the regular way in which something happens ♦ *Our French classes follow a set pattern.* 4 an excellent example or model.
patterned *adjective*

paunch *noun* (*plural* **paunches**)
a large belly.

pauper *noun* (*plural* **paupers**)
a person who is very poor.

pause *noun* (*plural* **pauses**)
a temporary stop in speaking or doing something.

pause *verb* (**pauses, pausing, paused**)
1 stop speaking or doing something for a short time. 2 temporarily interrupt the playing of a CD, videotape, etc.

pave *verb* (**paves, paving, paved**)
lay a hard surface on a road or path etc.
paving stone *noun*
pave the way prepare for something.

pavement *noun* (*plural* **pavements**)
a paved path along the side of a street.

pavilion *noun* (*plural* **pavilions**)
1 a building for use by players and spectators etc., especially at a cricket ground. 2 an ornamental building or shelter used for dances, concerts, exhibitions, etc.

paw *noun* (*plural* **paws**)
the foot of an animal that has claws.

paw *verb* (**paws, pawing, pawed**)
touch or scrape something with a hand or foot.

pawn¹ *noun* (*plural* **pawns**)
1 the least valuable piece in chess. 2 a person whose actions are controlled by somebody else.

pawn² *verb* (**pawns, pawning, pawned**)
leave something with a pawnbroker as security for a loan.

pawnbroker *noun* (*plural* **pawnbrokers**)
a shopkeeper who lends money to people in return for objects that they leave as security.
pawnshop *noun*

pay *verb* (**pays, paying, paid**)
1 give money in return for goods or services.
2 give what is owed ♦ *pay your debts;* ♦ *pay the rent.* 3 be profitable or worthwhile ♦ *It pays to advertise.* 4 give or express ♦ *Try to pay attention.* ♦ *It's time we paid them a visit.*
♦ *He doesn't often pay people compliments.*
5 suffer a penalty. 6 let out a rope by loosening it gradually.
payer *noun*
pay off 1 pay in full what you owe.
2 be worthwhile or have good results ♦ *All the preparation she did really paid off.* **pay up** pay the full amount you owe.

pay *noun*
salary or wages.

payable *adjective*
that must be paid.

payment *noun* (*plural* **payments**)
1 paying. 2 money paid.

payphone *noun* (*plural* **payphones**)
a public telephone operated by coins or a card.

PC *abbreviation*
1 personal computer. 2 police constable.

PE *abbreviation*
physical education.

pea *noun* (*plural* **peas**)
the small round green seed of a climbing plant, growing inside a pod and used as a vegetable; the plant bearing these pods.

peace *noun*
1 a time when there is no war, violence, or disorder. 2 quietness and calm.

peaceable *adjective*
fond of peace; not quarrelsome or warlike.
peaceably *adverb*

peaceful *adjective*
quiet and calm.
peacefully *adverb* **peacefulness** *noun*

peach *noun* (*plural* **peaches**)
1 a round soft juicy fruit with a pinkish or yellowish skin and a large stone. 2 (*informal*) an extremely good thing ♦ *a peach of a shot.*

peacock noun (plural **peacocks**)
a large male bird with a long brightly coloured
tail that it can spread out like a fan.
peahen noun

peak noun (plural **peaks**)
1 a pointed top, especially of a mountain.
2 the highest or most intense part of something
♦ Traffic reaches its peak at 5 p.m. 3 the part of
a cap that sticks out in front.
peaked adjective

peak verb (peaks, peaking, peaked)
reach its highest point or value.

peal noun (plural **peals**)
1 the loud ringing of a bell or set of bells.
2 a loud burst of thunder or laughter.

peal verb (peals, pealing, pealed)
(said about bells) ring loudly.

peanut noun (plural **peanuts**)
a small round nut that grows in a pod in the
ground.

pear noun (plural **pears**)
a juicy fruit that gets narrower near the stalk.

pearl noun (plural **pearls**)
a small shiny white ball found in the shells of
some oysters and used as a jewel.
pearly adjective

peasant noun (plural **peasants**)
a person who belongs to a farming community,
especially in poor areas of the world.
peasantry noun
[from Latin paganus = country dweller]

peat noun
rotted plant material that can be dug out of the
ground and used as fuel or in gardening.
peaty adjective
[from Latin peta, probably from a Celtic word]

pebble noun (plural **pebbles**)
a small round stone.
pebbly adjective

peck verb (pecks, pecking, pecked)
1 bite at something quickly with the beak.
2 kiss someone lightly on the cheek.

peck noun (plural **pecks**)
1 a quick bite by a bird. 2 a light kiss on the
cheek.

peckish adjective (informal)
hungry.

peculiar adjective
1 strange or unusual. 2 belonging to a particular
person, place, or thing; restricted ♦ This custom
is peculiar to this tribe.
peculiarly adverb **peculiarity** noun

pedal noun (plural **pedals**)
a lever pressed by the foot to operate a bicycle,
car, machine, etc. or in certain musical
instruments.

pedal verb (pedals, pedalling, pedalled)
use a pedal; move or work something, especially
a bicycle, by means of pedals.

pedantic adjective
too concerned with minor details or with
sticking strictly to formal rules.
pedantically adverb

peddle verb (peddles, peddling, peddled)
1 go from house to house selling goods. 2 sell
illegal drugs. 3 try to get people to accept an idea,
way of life, etc. **pedestal** noun (plural
pedestals)
the raised base on which a statue or pillar etc.
stands.
put someone on a pedestal admire him or her
greatly.

pedestrian noun (plural **pedestrians**)
a person who is walking.

pedestrian adjective
ordinary and dull.

pedestrian crossing noun (plural **pedestrian
crossings**)
a place where pedestrians can cross the road
safely.

pedigree noun (plural **pedigrees**)
a list of a person's or animal's ancestors,
especially to show how well an animal has been
bred.
[from early French pé de grue = crane's foot
(from the shape made by the lines on a family
tree)]

pedlar noun (plural **pedlars**)
a person who goes from house to house selling
small things.
[from Middle English ped = a hamper or basket
(in which a pedlar carried his goods)]

peel noun (plural **peels**)
the skin of certain fruits and vegetables.

peel verb (peels, peeling, peeled)
1 remove the peel or covering from something.
2 come off in strips or layers. 3 lose a covering or
skin.

peelings plural noun
strips of skin peeled from potatoes etc.

peep verb (peeps, peeping, peeped)
1 look quickly or secretly. 2 look through a
narrow opening. 3 come slowly or briefly into
view ♦ The moon peeped out from behind the
clouds.
peep noun **peephole** noun

peer¹ verb (peers, peering, peered)
look at something closely or with difficulty.

peer² noun (plural **peers**)
1 a noble. 2 someone who is equal to another in
rank, merit, or age etc. ♦ She had no peer.
peeress noun **peerage** noun

peer group noun (plural **peer groups**)
a group of people of roughly the same age or
status.

peerless adjective
without an equal; better than the others.

peevish *adjective*
irritable.

peg *noun* (*plural* **pegs**)
a piece of wood or metal or plastic for fastening things together or for hanging things on.

peg *verb* (**pegs, pegging, pegged**)
1 fix something with pegs. 2 keep wages or prices at a fixed level.
peg away work diligently; persevere. **peg out** (*slang*) die.

Pekinese or **Pekingese** *noun* (*plural*
Pekinese or **Pekingese**)
a small kind of dog with short legs, a flat face, and long silky hair.
[from *Peking*, the old name of Beijing, the capital of China (where the breed came from)]

pelican *noun* (*plural* **pelicans**)
a large bird with a pouch in its long beak for storing fish.

pelican crossing *noun* (*plural* **pelican crossings**)
a place where pedestrians can cross a street safely by operating lights that signal traffic to stop.

pellet *noun* (*plural* **pellets**)
a tiny ball of metal, food, paper, etc.

pelt¹ *verb* (**pelts, pelting, pelted**)
1 throw a lot of things at someone. 2 run fast. 3 rain very hard.
at full pelt as fast as possible.

pelt² *noun* (*plural* **pelts**)
an animal skin, especially with the fur still on it.

pen¹ *noun* (*plural* **pens**)
an instrument with a point for writing with ink.

pen² *noun* (*plural* **pens**)
an enclosure for cattle, sheep, hens, or other animals.

pen *verb* (**pens, penning, penned**)
shut animals etc. into a pen or other enclosed space.

penalize *verb* (**penalizes, penalizing, penalized**)
punish; give someone a penalty.
penalization *noun*

penalty *noun* (*plural* **penalties**)
1 a punishment. 2 a point or advantage given to one side in a game when a member of the other side has broken a rule, e.g. a free kick at goal in football.

pence *plural noun* SEE **penny**.

pencil *noun* (*plural* **pencils**)
an instrument for drawing or writing, made of a thin stick of graphite or coloured chalk etc. enclosed in a cylinder of wood or metal.

pendant *noun* (*plural* **pendants**)
an ornament worn hanging on a cord or chain round the neck.

pending *preposition*
1 until ♦ *Please take charge, pending his return.*
2 during ♦ *pending these discussions.*

pending *adjective*
1 waiting to be decided or settled. 2 about to happen.

pendulum *noun* (*plural* **pendulums**)
a weight hung so that it can swing to and fro, especially in the works of a clock.

penetrate *verb* (**penetrates, penetrating, penetrated**)
make or find a way through or into something; pierce.
penetration *noun* **penetrative** *adjective*

penfriend *noun* (*plural* **penfriends**)
a friend you write to regularly without meeting.

penguin *noun* (*plural* **penguins**)
an Antarctic seabird that cannot fly but uses its wings as flippers for swimming.

penicillin *noun*
an antibiotic obtained from mould.

peninsula *noun* (*plural* **peninsulas**)
a piece of land that is almost surrounded by water.
peninsular *adjective*
[from Latin *paene* = almost + *insula* = island]

penis (*say* **peen**-iss) *noun* (*plural* **penises**)
the part of the body with which a male urinates and has sexual intercourse.

penitence *noun*
regret for having done wrong.
penitent *adjective* **penitently** *adverb*

penknife *noun* (*plural* **penknives**)
a small folding knife.

pen-name *noun* (*plural* **pen-names**)
a name used by an author instead of his or her real name.

penniless *adjective*
having no money; very poor.

penny *noun* (*plural* **pennies** for separate coins, **pence** for a sum of money)
1 a British coin worth $\frac{1}{100}$ of a pound. 2 a former coin worth $\frac{1}{12}$ of a shilling.

pension *noun* (*plural* **pensions**)
an income consisting of regular payments made to someone who is retired, widowed, or disabled.

pensioner *noun* (*plural* **pensioners**)
a person who receives a pension.

pentagon *noun* (*plural* **pentagons**)
a flat shape with five sides and five angles.
pentagonal (*say* pent-**ag**-on-al) *adjective*
the Pentagon a five-sided building in Washington, headquarters of the leaders of the American armed forces.
[from Greek *pente* = five + *gonia* = angle]

pentameter *noun* (*plural* **pentameters**)
a line of verse with five rhythmic beats.
[from Greek *pente* = five + *metron* = measure]

pentathlon *noun* (*plural* **pentathlons**)
an athletic contest consisting of five events.
[from Greek *pente* = five + *athlon* = contest]

Pentecost *noun*
1 the Jewish harvest festival, fifty days after
Passover. **2** Whit Sunday.
[from Greek *pentekoste* = fiftieth (day)]

pent-up *adjective*
shut in ♦ *pent-up feelings.*

penultimate *adjective*
last but one.

peony *noun* (*plural* **peonies**)
a plant with large round red, pink, or white
flowers.

people *plural noun*
human beings; persons, especially those
belonging to a particular country, area, or
group etc.

people *noun* (*plural* **peoples**)
a community or nation ♦ *a warlike people*;
♦ *the English-speaking peoples.*

pepper *noun* (*plural* **peppers**)
1 a hot-tasting powder used to flavour food.
2 a bright green, red, or yellow vegetable.
peppery *adjective*

pepper *verb* (**peppers, peppering, peppered**)
1 sprinkle with pepper. **2** pelt with many small
objects.

peppermint *noun* (*plural* **peppermints**)
1 a kind of mint used for flavouring. **2** a sweet
flavoured with this mint.

per *preposition*
for each ♦ *The charge is £2 per person.*

perceive *verb* (**perceives, perceiving,
perceived**)
see, notice, or understand something.

per cent *adverb*
for or in every hundred ♦ *three per cent* (3%).

percentage *noun* (*plural* **percentages**)
an amount or rate expressed as a proportion of
100.

perceptible *adjective*
able to be seen or noticed.
perceptibly *adverb* **perceptibility** *noun*

perception *noun* (*plural* **perceptions**)
the ability to see, notice, or understand
something.

perceptive *adjective*
quick to notice or understand things.

perch¹ *noun* (*plural* **perches**)
1 a place where a bird sits or rests. **2** a seat high
up.

perch *verb* (**perches, perching, perched**)
rest or place on a perch.

perch² *noun* (*plural* **perch**)
an edible freshwater fish.

percolate *verb* (**percolates, percolating,
percolated**)
flow through small holes or spaces.
percolation *noun*

percolator *noun* (*plural* **percolators**)
a pot for making coffee, in which boiling water
percolates through coffee grounds.

percussion *noun*
1 musical instruments (e.g. drums or cymbals)
played by being struck or shaken. **2** the striking
of one thing against another.
percussive *adjective*

perdition *noun*
eternal damnation.

peregrine *noun* (*plural* **peregrines**)
a kind of falcon.

perennial *adjective*
lasting for many years; keeping on recurring.
perennially *adverb*

perennial *noun* (*plural* **perennials**)
a plant that lives for many years.

perfect (*say* per-fikt) *adjective*
1 so good that it cannot be made any better.
2 complete ♦ *a perfect stranger.* **3** (in grammar,
said about a tense of a verb) showing a
completed action, e.g. ♦ *He has arrived.*
perfectly *adverb*

perfect (*say* per-fekt) *verb* (**perfects,
perfecting, perfected**)
make a thing perfect.
perfection *noun*
to perfection perfectly.

perfectionist *noun* (*plural* **perfectionists**)
a person who is only satisfied if something is
done perfectly.

perforate *verb* (**perforates, perforating,
perforated**)
1 make tiny holes in something, especially so
that it can be torn off easily. **2** pierce.
perforated *adjective* **perforation** *noun*

perform *verb* (**performs, performing,
performed**)
1 do something in front of an audience
♦ *The school will perform a play.* **2** do or carry
out something ♦ *Surgeons had to perform an
emergency operation.*
performance *noun* **performer** *noun*

perfume *noun* (*plural* **perfumes**)
1 a pleasant smell. **2** a liquid for giving
something a pleasant smell; scent.
perfume *verb* **perfumery** *noun*
[originally used of pleasant-smelling smoke from
something burning: via French from old Italian
parfumare = to smoke through]

perfunctory

perfunctory *adjective*
done without much care or interest
♦ *a perfunctory glance.*
perfunctorily *adverb*

perhaps *adverb*
it may be; possibly.

peril *noun* (*plural* **perils**)
danger.
perilous *adjective* **perilously** *adverb*
at your peril at your own risk.

perimeter *noun* (*plural* **perimeters**)
1 the outer edge or boundary of something.
2 the distance round the edge.

---

❶ USAGE Do not confuse with *parameter.*

---

period *noun* (*plural* **periods**)
1 a length of time. 2 the time allowed for a lesson
in school. 3 the time when a woman
menstruates. 4 (in punctuation) a full stop.

periodic *adjective*
occurring at regular intervals.
periodically *adverb*

periodical *noun* (*plural* **periodicals**)
a magazine published at regular intervals (e.g.
monthly).

periodic table *noun*
a table in which the chemical elements are
arranged in order of increasing atomic number.

periscope *noun* (*plural* **periscopes**)
a device with a tube and mirrors with which a
person in a trench or submarine etc. can see
things that are otherwise out of sight.

perish *verb* (**perishes, perishing, perished**)
1 die; be destroyed. 2 rot ♦ *The rubber ring has
perished.*
perishable *adjective*

perjure *verb* (**perjures, perjuring, perjured**)
perjure yourself commit perjury.

perjury *noun*
telling a lie while you are on oath to speak the
truth.

perk¹ *verb* (**perks, perking, perked**)
perk up make or become more cheerful.

perk² *noun* (*plural* **perks**) (*informal*)
something extra given to a worker ♦ *Free bus
travel is one of the perks of the job.*

perky *adjective*
lively and cheerful.
perkily *adverb*

perm or **permanent wave** *noun* (*plural*
permanent waves)
treatment of the hair to give it long-lasting
waves.

permafrost *noun*
a permanently frozen layer of soil in polar
regions.

permanent *adjective*
lasting for always or for a very long time.
permanently *adverb* **permanence** *noun*

permeate *verb* (**permeates, permeating,
permeated**)
spread into every part of something; pervade
♦ *Smoke had permeated the hall.*
permeation *noun*

permissible *adjective*
permitted or allowed.

permission *noun*
the right to do something, given by someone in
authority; authorization.

permissive *adjective*
letting people do what they wish; tolerant or
liberal.

permit (*say* per-mit) *verb* (**permits, permitting,
permitted**)
give permission or consent or a chance to do
something; allow.

permit (*say* per-mit) *noun* (*plural* **permits**)
written or printed permission to do something or
go somewhere.

permutation *noun* (*plural* **permutations**)
1 changing the order of a set of things.
2 a changed order ♦ *3, 1, 2 is a permutation of 1,
2, 3.*

peroxide *noun*
a chemical used for bleaching hair.

perpendicular *adjective*
upright; at a right angle (90°) to a line or surface.

perpetrate *verb* (**perpetrates, perpetrating,
perpetrated**)
commit or be guilty of ♦ *perpetrate a crime.*
perpetration *noun* **perpetrator** *noun*

perpetual *adjective*
lasting for a long time; continual.
perpetually *adverb*

perplex *verb* (**perplexes, perplexing,
perplexed**)
bewilder or puzzle somebody.
perplexity *noun*

persecute *verb* (**persecutes, persecuting,
persecuted**)
be continually cruel to somebody, especially
because you disagree with his or her beliefs.
persecution *noun* **persecutor** *noun*

persevere *verb* (**perseveres, persevering,
persevered**)
go on doing something even though it is difficult.
perseverance *noun*

Persian *adjective*
to do with Persia, a country in the Middle East
now called Iran.

Persian *noun*
the language of Persia.

persist verb (persists, persisting, persisted)
1 continue firmly or obstinately ♦ She persists in breaking the rules. 2 continue to exist ♦ The custom persists in some countries.
persistent adjective **persistently** adverb **persistence** noun **persistency** noun

person noun (plural **people** or **persons**)
1 a human being; a man, woman, or child. 2 (in grammar) any of the three groups of personal pronouns and forms taken by verbs. The **first person** (= I, me, we, us) refers to the person(s) speaking; the **second person** (= you) refers to the person(s) spoken to; the **third person** (= he, him, she, her, it, they, them) refers to the person(s) spoken about.
in person being actually present oneself ♦ She hopes to be there in person.
[from Latin persona = mask used by an actor]

personal adjective
1 belonging to, done by, or concerning a particular person ♦ personal belongings. 2 private ♦ We have personal business to discuss. 3 criticizing a person's appearance, character, or private affairs ♦ making personal remarks.
personally adverb

❶ USAGE Do not confuse with personnel.

personal computer noun (plural **personal computers**)
a small computer designed to be used by one person at a time.

personality noun (plural **personalities**)
1 a person's character ♦ She has a cheerful personality. 2 a well-known person ♦ a TV personality.

personify verb (personifies, personifying, personified)
represent a quality or idea etc. as a person.
personification noun

personnel noun
the people employed by a firm or other large organization.

❶ USAGE Do not confuse with personal.

perspective noun (plural **perspectives**)
1 the impression of depth and space in a picture or scene. 2 a person's point of view.
in perspective giving a well-balanced view of things.

perspire verb (perspires, perspiring, perspired)
sweat.
perspiration noun

persuade verb (persuades, persuading, persuaded)
make someone believe or agree to do something.
persuasion noun **persuasive** adjective

pert adjective
cheeky.
pertly adverb **pertness** noun

perturb verb (perturbs, perturbing, perturbed)
worry someone.
perturbation noun

pervade verb (pervades, pervading, pervaded)
spread all through something.
pervasion noun **pervasive** adjective

perverse adjective
obstinately doing something different from what is reasonable or required.
perversely adverb **perversity** noun

pervert (say per-vert) verb (perverts, perverting, perverted)
1 turn something from the right course of action ♦ By giving false evidence they perverted the course of justice. 2 make a person behave wickedly or abnormally.
perversion noun

pervert (say per-vert) noun (plural **perverts**)
a person whose sexual behaviour is thought to be unnatural or disgusting.

pessimist noun (plural **pessimists**)
a person who expects that things will turn out badly. (Compare **optimist**.)
pessimism noun **pessimistic** adjective **pessimistically** adverb

pest noun (plural **pests**)
1 a destructive insect or animal, such as a locust or a mouse. 2 a nuisance.

pester verb (pesters, pestering, pestered)
keep annoying someone by frequent questions or requests.

pesticide noun (plural **pesticides**)
a substance for killing harmful insects and other pests.

pestilence noun (plural **pestilences**)
a deadly epidemic.

pestle (say pes-el) noun
a heavy tool with a rounded end, used for crushing substances in a mortar.
[from Latin pinsere = to pound]

pet noun (plural **pets**)
1 a tame animal kept for companionship and pleasure. 2 a person treated as a favourite ♦ a teacher's pet.

pet adjective
favourite ♦ my pet subject.

pet verb (pets, petting, petted)
treat or fondle someone affectionately.

petal noun (plural **petals**)
one of the separate coloured outer parts of a flower.

peter *verb* (peters, petering, petered)
peter out become gradually less and cease to exist.

petition *noun* (*plural* **petitions**)
a formal request for something, especially a written one signed by many people.

petrify *verb* (petrifies, petrifying, petrified)
1 make someone so terrified that he or she cannot move. **2** turn to stone.
petrifaction *noun*

petrol *noun*
a liquid made from petroleum, used as fuel for engines.

petroleum *noun*
an oil found underground that is refined to make fuel (e.g. petrol or paraffin) or for use in dry-cleaning etc.

petticoat *noun* (*plural* **petticoats**)
a woman's or girl's dress-length piece of underwear worn under a skirt or dress.

petting *noun*
affectionate touching or fondling.

petty *adjective* (pettier, pettiest)
1 unimportant or trivial ♦ *petty regulations*.
2 mean and small-minded.
pettily *adverb* **pettiness** *noun*

petty cash *noun*
cash kept by an office for small payments.

pew *noun* (*plural* **pews**)
a long wooden seat, usually fixed in rows, in a church.

pewter *noun*
a grey alloy of tin and lead.

pH *noun*
a measure of the acidity or alkalinity of a solution. Pure water has a pH of 7, acids have a pH between 0 and 7, and alkalis have a pH between 7 and 14.

phantom *noun* (*plural* **phantoms**)
1 a ghost. **2** something that does not really exist.

Pharaoh (*say* **fair**-oh) *noun* (*plural* **Pharaohs**)
the title of the king of ancient Egypt.

pharmacy *noun* (*plural* **pharmacies**)
1 a shop selling medicines; a dispensary.
2 the job of preparing medicines.

phase *noun* (*plural* **phases**)
a stage in the progress or development of something.

phase *verb* (phases, phasing, phased)
do something in stages, not all at once
♦ *a phased withdrawal*.

Ph.D. *abbreviation*
Doctor of Philosophy; a university degree awarded to someone who has done advanced research in their subject.

pheasant (*say* **fez**-ant) *noun* (*plural* **pheasants**)
a game bird with a long tail.

phenomenal *adjective*
amazing or remarkable.
phenomenally *adverb*

phenomenon *noun* (*plural* **phenomena**)
an event or fact, especially one that is remarkable.

ℹ USAGE Note that *phenomena* is a plural. It is incorrect to say 'this phenomena' or 'these phenomenas'.

---

phial *noun* (*plural* **phials**)
a small glass bottle.

philanthropy *noun*
concern for fellow human beings, especially as shown by kind and generous acts that benefit large numbers of people.
philanthropist *noun* **philanthropic** *adjective*

philistine (*say* **fil**-ist-I'n) *noun* (*plural* **philistines**)
a person who dislikes art, poetry, etc.

philosopher *noun* (*plural* **philosophers**)
an expert in philosophy.

philosophical *adjective*
1 to do with philosophy. **2** calm and not upset after a misfortune or disappointment
♦ *Be philosophical about losing.*
philosophically *adverb*

philosophy *noun* (*plural* **philosophies**)
1 the study of truths about life, morals, etc.
2 a set of ideas or principles or beliefs.

phobia (*say* **foh**-bee-a) *noun* (*plural* **phobias**)
great or abnormal fear of something.

phone *noun* (*plural* **phones**)
a telephone.

phone *verb* (phones, phoning, phoned)
telephone.

phone-in *noun* (*plural* **phone-ins**)
a radio or television programme in which people telephone the studio and take part in a discussion.

phonetic (*say* fon-**et**-ik) *adjective*
1 to do with speech sounds. **2** representing speech sounds.
phonetically *adverb*

phosphorus *noun*
a chemical substance that glows in the dark.

photo *noun* (*plural* **photos**)
a photograph.

photograph *noun* (*plural* **photographs**)
a picture made by the effect of light or other radiation on film or special paper, using a camera.

photograph *verb* (photographs,
photographing, photographed)
take a photograph of a person or thing.
photographer *noun*

photography *noun*
taking photographs.
photographic *adjective*

photosynthesis *noun*
the process by which green plants use sunlight to
turn carbon dioxide and water into complex
substances, giving off oxygen.

phrase *noun* (*plural* phrases)
1 a group of words that form a unit in a sentence
or clause, e.g. *in the garden* in 'The Queen was
in the garden'. 2 a short section of a tune.

physical *adjective*
1 to do with the body rather than the mind or
feelings. 2 to do with things that you can touch
or see. 3 to do with physics.
physically *adverb*

physical education or **physical training**
noun
exercises and sports done to keep the body
healthy.

physician *noun* (*plural* physicians)
a doctor, especially one who is not a surgeon.

physicist (*say* fiz-i-sist) *noun* (*plural*
physicists)
an expert in physics.

physics (*say* fiz-iks) *noun*
the study of the properties of matter and energy
(e.g. heat, light, sound, movement).
[from Greek *physikos* = natural]

physiotherapy (*say* fiz-ee-o-therra-pee) *noun*
the treatment of a disease or weakness by
massage, exercises, etc.
physiotherapist *noun*

physique (*say* fiz-eek) *noun* (*plural*
physiques)
a person's build.

pi *noun*
the symbol (π) for the ratio of the circumference
of a circle to its diameter. The value of pi is
approximately 3.14159.

pianist *noun* (*plural* pianists)
a person who plays the piano.

piano *noun* (*plural* pianos)
a large musical instrument with a keyboard.

piccolo *noun* (*plural* piccolos)
a small high-pitched flute.

pick¹ *verb* (picks, picking, picked)
1 separate a flower or fruit from its plant
♦ *We picked apples.* 2 choose; select carefully.
3 pull bits off or out of something. 4 open a lock
by using something pointed, not with a key.
pick a quarrel deliberately provoke a quarrel
with somebody. **pick holes in** find fault with.
pick on single someone out for criticism or
unkind treatment. **pick someone's pocket** steal
from it. **pick up 1** lift or take up. **2** collect.
3 take someone into a vehicle. 4 manage to hear
something. 5 get better or recover.

pick *noun*
1 choice ♦ *take your pick.* 2 the best of a group.

pick² *noun* (*plural* picks)
1 a pickaxe. 2 a plectrum.

pickaxe *noun* (*plural* pickaxes)
a heavy pointed tool with a long handle, used for
breaking up hard ground etc.

picket *noun* (*plural* pickets)
1 a striker or group of strikers who try to
persuade other people not to go into a place of
work during a strike. 2 a pointed post as part of
a fence.

picket *verb* (pickets, picketing, picketed)
stand outside a place of work to try to persuade
other people not to go in during a strike.

pickle *noun* (*plural* pickles)
1 a strong-tasting food made of pickled
vegetables. 2 (*informal*) a mess.

pickle *verb* (pickles, pickling, pickled)
preserve food in vinegar or salt water.

pickpocket *noun* (*plural* pickpockets)
a thief who steals from people's pockets or bags.

pick-up *noun* (*plural* pick-ups)
1 an open truck for carrying small loads.
2 the part of a record player that holds the stylus.

picnic *noun* (*plural* picnics)
a meal eaten in the open air away from home.

picnic *verb* (picnics, picnicking, picnicked)
have a picnic.
picnicker *noun*

picture *noun* (*plural* pictures)
1 a representation of a person or thing made by
painting, drawing, or photography. 2 a film at
the cinema. 3 how something seems; an
impression.
in the picture fully informed about something.

picture *verb* (pictures, picturing, pictured)
1 show in a picture. 2 imagine.

picturesque *adjective*
1 forming an attractive scene ♦ *a picturesque
village.* 2 vividly described; expressive
♦ *picturesque language.*
picturesquely *adverb*

pie *noun* (*plural* pies)
a baked dish of meat, fish, or fruit covered with
pastry.

piece *noun* (*plural* **pieces**)
1 a part or portion of something; a fragment.
2 a separate thing or example ♦ *a fine piece of work.* **3** something written, composed, or painted etc. ♦ *a piece of music.* **4** one of the objects used to play a game on a board ♦ *a chess piece.* **5** a coin ♦ *a 50p piece.*

piece *verb* (**pieces, piecing, pieced**)
put pieces together to make something.

piecemeal *adjective* & *adverb*
done or made one piece at a time.

pie chart *noun* (*plural* **pie charts**)
a circle divided into sectors to represent the way in which a quantity is divided up.

pier *noun* (*plural* **piers**)
1 a long structure built out into the sea for people to walk on. **2** a pillar supporting a bridge or arch.

pierce *verb* (**pierces, piercing, pierced**)
make a hole through something; penetrate.

piety *noun*
being very religious and devout; piousness.

pig *noun* (*plural* **pigs**)
1 a fat animal with short legs and a blunt snout, kept for its meat. **2** (*informal*) someone greedy, dirty, or unpleasant.
piggy *adjective* & *noun*

pigeon *noun* (*plural* **pigeons**)
a bird with a fat body and a small head.

pigeonhole *noun* (*plural* **pigeonholes**)
a small compartment above a desk etc., used for holding letters or papers.

piggyback *adverb*
carried on somebody else's back or shoulders.
piggyback *noun*

pig-headed *adjective*
obstinate.

piglet *noun* (*plural* **piglets**)
a young pig.

pigment *noun* (*plural* **pigments**)
a substance that colours something.
pigmented *adjective* **pigmentation** *noun*

pigsty *noun* (*plural* **pigsties**)
1 a partly covered pen for pigs. **2** a filthy room or house.

pigtail *noun* (*plural* **pigtails**)
a plait of hair worn hanging at the back of the head.

pike *noun* (*plural* **pikes**)
1 a heavy spear. **2** (*plural* **pike**) a large freshwater fish.

pile¹ *noun* (*plural* **piles**)
1 a number of things on top of one another. **2** (*informal*) a large quantity; a lot of money. **3** (*informal*) a large impressive building.

pile *verb* (**piles, piling, piled**)
put things into a pile; make a pile.

pile² *noun* (*plural* **piles**)
a heavy beam made of metal, concrete, or timber driven into the ground to support something.

pile³ *noun*
a raised surface on fabric, made of upright threads ♦ *a carpet with a thick pile.*

pile-up *noun* (*plural* **pile-ups**)
a road accident that involves a number of vehicles.

pilfer *verb* (**pilfers, pilfering, pilfered**)
steal small things.
pilferer *noun* **pilferage** *noun*

pilgrim *noun* (*plural* **pilgrims**)
a person who travels to a holy place for religious reasons.
pilgrimage *noun*

pill *noun* (*plural* **pills**)
a small solid piece of medicine for swallowing.
the pill a contraceptive pill.

pillage *verb* (**pillages, pillaging, pillaged**)
carry off goods using force, especially in a war; plunder.
pillage *noun*

pillar *noun* (*plural* **pillars**)
a tall stone or wooden post.

pillar box *noun* (*plural* **pillar boxes**)
a postbox standing in a street.

pillion *noun* (*plural* **pillions**)
a seat behind the driver on a motorcycle.

pillow *noun* (*plural* **pillows**)
a cushion for a person's head to rest on, especially in bed.
[from Latin *pulvinus* = cushion]

pillowcase or **pillowslip** *noun* (*plural* **pillowcases** or **pillowslips**)
a cloth cover for a pillow.

pilot *noun* (*plural* **pilots**)
1 a person who works the controls for flying an aircraft. **2** a person qualified to steer a ship in and out of a port or through a difficult stretch of water. **3** a guide.

pilot *verb* (**pilots, piloting, piloted**)
1 be pilot of an aircraft or ship. **2** guide or steer.

pilot *adjective*
testing on a small scale how something will work ♦ *a pilot scheme.*
[from Greek *pedon* = oar or rudder]

pilot light *noun* (*plural* **pilot lights**)
1 a small flame that lights a larger burner on a gas cooker etc. **2** an electric indicator light.

pimp *noun* (*plural* **pimps**)
a man who gets clients for prostitutes and lives off their earnings.

pimple *noun* (*plural* **pimples**)
a small round raised spot on the skin.
pimply *adjective*

PIN *abbreviation*
personal identification number; a number used as a person's password so that he or she can use a cash dispenser, computer, etc.

pin *noun* (*plural* **pins**)
1 a short thin piece of metal with a sharp point and a rounded head, used to fasten pieces of cloth or paper etc. together. **2** a pointed device for fixing or marking something.
pins and needles a tingling feeling in the skin.

pin *verb* (**pins, pinning, pinned**)
1 fasten something with a pin or pins. **2** make a person or thing unable to move ♦ *He was pinned under the wreckage.* **3** fix blame or responsibility on someone ♦ *They pinned the blame on her sister.*

pincer *noun* (*plural* **pincers**)
the claw of a shellfish such as a lobster.

pincers *plural noun*
a tool with two parts that are pressed together for gripping and holding things.

pinch *verb* (**pinches, pinching, pinched**)
1 squeeze something tightly or painfully between two things, especially between the finger and thumb. **2** (*informal*) steal.

pinch *noun* (*plural* **pinches**)
1 a pinching movement. **2** the amount that can be held between the tips of the thumb and forefinger ♦ *a pinch of salt.*
at a pinch in time of difficulty; if necessary.
feel the pinch suffer from lack of money.

pincushion *noun* (*plural* **pincushions**)
a small pad into which pins are stuck to keep them ready for use.

pine¹ *noun* (*plural* **pines**)
an evergreen tree with needle-shaped leaves.

pine² *verb* (**pines, pining, pined**)
1 feel an intense longing for somebody or something. **2** become weak through longing for somebody or something.

pineapple *noun* (*plural* **pineapples**)
a large tropical fruit with a tough prickly skin and yellow flesh.

ping-pong *noun*
table tennis.

pinion *noun* (*plural* **pinions**)
a bird's wing, especially the outer end.

pinion *verb* (**pinions, pinioning, pinioned**)
1 clip a bird's wings to prevent it from flying. **2** hold or fasten someone's arms or legs in order to prevent them from moving.

pink *adjective*
pale red.
pinkness *noun*

pink *noun* (*plural* **pinks**)
1 a pink colour. **2** a garden plant with fragrant flowers, often pink or white.

pinnacle *noun* (*plural* **pinnacles**)
1 a pointed ornament on a roof. **2** a high pointed piece of rock. **3** the highest point of something ♦ *It was the pinnacle of her career.*

pinpoint *adjective*
exact or precise ♦ *with pinpoint accuracy.*

pinpoint *verb* (**pinpoints, pinpointing, pinpointed**)
find or identify something precisely.

pinstripe *noun* (*plural* **pinstripes**)
one of the very narrow stripes that form a pattern in cloth.
pinstriped *adjective*

pint *noun* (*plural* **pints**)
a measure for liquids, equal to one-eighth of a gallon.

pin-up *noun* (*plural* **pin-ups**) (*informal*)
a picture of an attractive or famous person for pinning on a wall.

pioneer *noun* (*plural* **pioneers**)
one of the first people to go to a place or do or investigate something.
pioneer *verb*

pious *adjective*
very religious; devout.
piously *adverb* **piousness** *noun*

pip *noun* (*plural* **pips**)
1 a small hard seed of an apple, pear, orange, etc. **2** one of the stars on the shoulder of an army officer's uniform. **3** a short high-pitched sound ♦ *She heard the six pips of the time signal on the radio.*

pip *verb* (**pips, pipping, pipped**) (*informal*)
defeat someone by a small amount.

pipe *noun* (*plural* **pipes**)
1 a tube through which water or gas etc. can flow from one place to another. **2** a short narrow tube with a bowl at one end in which tobacco can burn for smoking. **3** a tube forming a musical instrument or part of one.
the pipes bagpipes.

pipe *verb* (**pipes, piping, piped**)
1 send something along pipes. **2** transmit music or other sound by wire or cable. **3** play music on a pipe or the bagpipes. **4** decorate a cake with thin lines of icing, cream, etc.
pipe down (*informal*) be quiet. **pipe up** begin to say something.

pipe dream *noun* (*plural* **pipe dreams**)
an impossible wish.

pipeline *noun* (*plural* **pipelines**)
a pipe for carrying oil or water etc. a long distance.
in the pipeline in the process of being made or organized.

piping *noun*
1 pipes; a length of pipe. 2 a decorative line of icing, cream, etc. on a cake or other dish. 3 a long narrow pipe-like fold decorating clothing, upholstery, etc.

piping *adjective*
shrill ♦ *a piping voice.*
piping hot very hot.

pirate *noun* (*plural* **pirates**)
1 a person on a ship who attacks and robs other ships at sea. 2 someone who produces or publishes or broadcasts illegally ♦ *a pirate radio station*; ♦ *pirate videos.*
piratical *adjective* **piracy** *noun*

pirouette (*say* pir-oo-et) *noun* (*plural* **pirouettes**)
a spinning movement of the body made while balanced on the point of the toe or on one foot.
pirouette *verb*
[from French, = spinning top]

pistil *noun*
the female organs of a flower.

pistol *noun* (*plural* **pistols**)
a small handgun.

piston *noun* (*plural* **pistons**)
a disc or cylinder that fits inside a tube in which it moves up and down as part of an engine or pump etc.

pit *noun* (*plural* **pits**)
1 a deep hole. 2 a hollow. 3 a coal mine. 4 the part of a race circuit where racing cars are refuelled and repaired during a race.

pit *verb* (**pits, pitting, pitted**)
1 make holes or hollows in something ♦ *The ground was pitted with craters.* 2 put somebody in competition with somebody else ♦ *He was pitted against the champion in the final.*
pitted *adjective* **pitch**¹ *noun* (*plural* **pitches**)
1 a piece of ground marked out for cricket, football, or another game. 2 the highness or lowness of a voice or a musical note. 3 intensity or strength ♦ *Excitement was at fever pitch.* 4 the steepness of a slope ♦ *the pitch of the roof.*

pitch *verb* (**pitches, pitching, pitched**)
1 throw or fling. 2 set up a tent or camp. 3 fall heavily ♦ *He pitched forward as the bus braked suddenly.* 4 move up and down on a rough sea. 5 set something at a particular level ♦ *They pitched their hopes high.* 6 (said about a bowled ball in cricket) strike the ground.
pitch in (*informal*) start working or doing something vigorously.

pitch² *noun*
a black sticky substance rather like tar.
pitch-black or **pitch-dark** *adjectives* very black or very dark.

pitched battle *noun* (*plural* **pitched battles**)
a battle between troops in prepared positions.

pitcher *noun* (*plural* **pitchers**)
a large jug.

pitchfork *noun* (*plural* **pitchforks**)
a large fork with two prongs, used for lifting hay.

pitchfork *verb* (**pitchforks, pitchforking, pitchforked**)
1 lift something with a pitchfork. 2 put a person somewhere suddenly.

pitfall *noun* (*plural* **pitfalls**)
an unsuspected danger or difficulty.

pitiable *adjective*
making you feel pity.

pitiful *adjective*
1 making you feel pity. 2 very bad or inadequate.
pitifully *adverb*

pity *noun*
1 the feeling of being sorry because someone is in pain or trouble. 2 a cause for regret ♦ *It's a pity that you can't come.*
take pity on feel sorry for someone and help them.

pity *verb* (**pities, pitying, pitied**)
feel pity for someone.

pivot *noun* (*plural* **pivots**)
a point or part on which something turns or balances.
pivotal *adjective*

pivot *verb* (**pivots, pivoting, pivoted**)
turn or place something to turn on a pivot.

pixel (*say* piks-el) *noun* (*plural* **pixels**)
one of the tiny dots on a computer display screen from which the image is formed.
[short for *picture element*]

pixie *noun* (*plural* **pixies**)
a small fairy; an elf.

pizza (*say* peets-a) *noun* (*plural* **pizzas**)
an Italian food that consists of a layer of dough baked with a savoury topping.
[from Italian, = pie]

pizzicato (*say* pits-i-kah-toh) *adjective* & *adverb*
plucking the strings of a musical instrument.

placard *noun* (*plural* **placards**)
a poster or notice, especially one carried at a demonstration.
[from early French *plaquier* = to lay flat]

placate *verb* (**placates, placating, placated**)
make someone feel calmer and less angry.

place *noun* (*plural* **places**)
1 a particular part of space, especially where something belongs; an area or position. 2 a seat ♦ *Save me a place.* 3 a job; employment. 4 a building; a home ♦ *Come round to our place.* 5 a duty or function ♦ *It's not my place to interfere.* 6 a point in a series of things ♦ *In the first place, the date is wrong.*
in place 1 in the right position. 2 suitable.
in place of instead of. **out of place** 1 in the wrong position. 2 unsuitable.

place *verb* (places, placing, placed)
put something in a particular place.
placement *noun*

placid *adjective*
calm and peaceful; not easily made anxious or
upset.
placidly *adverb* **placidity** *noun*

plagiarize (*say* play-jee-er-I'z) *verb*
(plagiarizes, plagiarizing, plagiarized)
take someone else's writings or ideas and use
them as if they were your own.
plagiarism *noun* **plagiarist** *noun*

plague *noun* (*plural* plagues)
1 a dangerous illness that spreads very quickly.
2 a large number of pests ♦ *a plague of locusts.*

plague *verb* (plagues, plaguing, plagued)
pester or annoy ♦ *We've been plagued by wasps
all afternoon.*

plain *adjective*
1 simple; not decorated or elaborate. **2** not
beautiful. **3** easy to see or hear or understand.
4 frank and straightforward.
plainly *adverb* **plainness** *noun*

plain *noun* (*plural* plains)
a large area of flat country.

---

❶ USAGE Do not confuse with *plane.*

---

plain clothes *noun*
civilian clothes worn instead of a uniform, e.g.
by police.

plaintiff *noun* (*plural* plaintiffs)
the person who brings a complaint against
somebody else to a lawcourt. (Compare
defendant.)

plaintive *adjective*
sounding sad ♦ *a plaintive cry.*

plait (*say* plat) *verb* (plaits, plaiting, plaited)
weave three or more strands of hair or rope to
form one length.

plait *noun* (*plural* plaits)
a length of hair or rope that has been plaited.

plan *noun* (*plural* plans)
1 a way of doing something thought out in
advance. **2** a drawing showing the arrangement
of parts of something. **3** a map of a town or
district.

plan *verb* (plans, planning, planned)
make a plan for something.
planner *noun*

plane¹ *noun* (*plural* planes)
1 an aeroplane. **2** a tool for making wood smooth
by scraping its surface. **3** a flat or level surface.

plane *verb* (planes, planing, planed)
smooth wood with a plane.

plane *adjective*
flat or level ♦ *a plane surface.*

---

❶ USAGE Do not confuse with *plain.*

---

plane² *noun* (*plural* planes)
a tall tree with broad leaves.

planet *noun* (*plural* planets)
one of the bodies that move in an orbit round the
sun. The main planets are Mercury, Venus,
Earth, Mars, Jupiter, Saturn, Uranus, Neptune,
and Pluto.
planetary *adjective*

plank *noun* (*plural* planks)
a long flat piece of wood.

plankton *noun*
microscopic plants and animals that float in the
sea, lakes, etc.

plant *noun* (*plural* plants)
1 a living thing that cannot move, makes its food
from chemical substances, and usually has a
stem, leaves, and roots. **2** a small plant, not a
tree or shrub. **3** a factory or its equipment.
4 (*informal*) something deliberately placed for
other people to find, usually to mislead people or
cause trouble.

plant *verb* (plants, planting, planted)
1 put something in soil for growing. **2** fix
something firmly in place. **3** place something
where it will be found, usually to mislead people
or cause trouble.
planter *noun*

plantation *noun* (*plural* plantations)
1 a large area of land where cotton, tobacco, or
tea etc. is planted. **2** a group of planted trees.

plaque (*say* plak) *noun* (*plural* plaques)
1 a flat piece of metal or porcelain fixed on a wall
as an ornament or memorial. **2** a filmy substance
that forms on teeth and gums, where bacteria
can live.

plaster *noun* (*plural* plasters)
1 a small covering put over the skin around a cut
or wound to protect it. **2** a mixture of lime, sand,
and water etc. for covering walls and ceilings.
3 plaster of Paris, or a cast made of this to hold
broken bones in place.

plaster *verb* (plasters, plastering, plastered)
1 cover a wall etc. with plaster. **2** cover
something thickly; daub.

plaster of Paris *noun*
a white paste used for making moulds or for
casts round a broken leg or arm.

plastic *noun* (*plural* plastics)
a strong light synthetic substance that can be
moulded into a permanent shape.

plastic *adjective*
1 made of plastic. **2** soft and easy to mould
♦ *Clay is a plastic substance.*
plasticity *noun*
[from Greek *plastos* = moulded or formed]

plastic surgery *noun*
surgery to repair deformed or injured parts of the
body.
plastic surgeon *noun*

plate 284 **plimsoll**

plate *noun* (*plural* **plates**)
1 an almost flat usually circular object from which food is eaten or served. 2 a thin flat sheet of metal, glass, or other hard material. 3 an illustration on special paper in a book.
plateful *noun*

plate *verb* (**plates, plating, plated**)
1 coat metal with a thin layer of gold, silver, tin, etc. 2 cover something with sheets of metal.

plateau (*say* plat-oh) *noun* (*plural* **plateaux** (*say* plat-ohz))
a flat area of high land.

platform *noun* (*plural* **platforms**)
1 a flat raised area along the side of a line at a railway station. 2 a flat surface above the level of the floor, especially one from which someone speaks to an audience. 3 the policies that a political party puts forward.

platinum *noun*
a valuable silver-coloured metal that does not tarnish.

platitude *noun* (*plural* **platitudes**)
a trite or over-used remark.
platitudinous *adjective*

plausible *adjective*
seeming to be honest or worth believing but perhaps deceptive ♦ *a plausible excuse.*
plausibly *adverb* **plausibility** *noun*

play *verb* (**plays, playing, played**)
1 take part in a game, sport, or other amusement. 2 make music or sound with a musical instrument, record player, etc. 3 perform a part in a play or film.
player *noun*
play about or **play around** have fun or be mischievous. **play down** give people the impression that something is not important. **play up** (*informal*) tease or annoy someone.

play *noun* (*plural* **plays**)
1 a story acted on a stage or on radio or television. 2 playing or having fun.
[from Old English]

playful *adjective*
1 wanting to play; full of fun. 2 done in fun; not serious.
playfully *adverb* **playfulness** *noun*

playground *noun* (*plural* **playgrounds**)
a piece of ground for children to play on.

playgroup *noun* (*plural* **playgroups**)
a group of very young children who play together regularly, supervised by adults.

playing card *noun* (*plural* **playing cards**)
each of a set of cards (usually 52) used for playing games.

playing field *noun* (*plural* **playing fields**)
a field used for outdoor games.

playmate *noun* (*plural* **playmates**)
a person you play games with.

play-off *noun* (*plural* **play-offs**)
an extra match that is played to decide a draw or tie.

plaything *noun* (*plural* **playthings**)
a toy.

playwright *noun* (*plural* **playwrights**)
a person who writes plays.

PLC or **p.l.c.** *abbreviation*
public limited company.

plea *noun* (*plural* **pleas**)
1 a request or appeal ♦ *a plea for mercy.* 2 an excuse ♦ *He stayed at home on the plea of a headache.* 3 a formal statement of 'guilty' or 'not guilty' made in a lawcourt by someone accused of a crime.

plead *verb* (**pleads, pleading, pleaded**)
1 beg someone to do something. 2 state formally in a lawcourt that you are guilty or not guilty of a crime. 3 give something as an excuse ♦ *She didn't come on holiday with us, pleading poverty.*

pleasant *adjective*
pleasing; giving pleasure.
pleasantly *adverb* **pleasantness** *noun*

please *verb* (**pleases, pleasing, pleased**)
1 make a person feel satisfied or glad. 2 (used to make a request or an order polite) ♦ *Please ring the bell.* 3 like; think suitable ♦ *Do as you please.*

pleasure *noun* (*plural* **pleasures**)
1 a feeling of satisfaction or gladness; enjoyment. 2 something that pleases you.

plectrum *noun* (*plural* **plectra**)
a small piece of metal or bone etc. for plucking the strings of a musical instrument.

pledge *noun* (*plural* **pledges**)
1 a solemn promise. 2 a thing handed over as security for a loan or contract.

pledge *verb* (**pledges, pledging, pledged**)
1 promise solemnly to do or give something. 2 hand something over as security.

plenty *noun*
quite enough; as much as is needed or wanted.

plenty *adverb* (*informal*)
quite or fully ♦ *It's plenty big enough.*

pliable *adjective*
1 easy to bend; flexible. 2 easy to influence or control.
pliability *noun*

pliers *plural noun*
pincers that have jaws with flat surfaces for gripping things.

plight *noun* (*plural* **plights**)
a difficult or dangerous situation.

plimsoll *noun* (*plural* **plimsolls**)
a canvas sports shoe with a rubber sole.
[same origin as **Plimsoll line** (because the thin sole reminded people of a Plimsoll line)]

Plimsoll line noun (plural **Plimsoll lines**)
a mark on a ship's side showing how deeply it
may legally go down in the water when loaded.
[named after an English politician, S. Plimsoll,
who in the 1870s protested about ships being
overloaded]

PLO abbreviation
Palestine Liberation Organization.

plod verb (**plods, plodding, plodded**)
1 walk slowly and heavily. **2** work slowly but
steadily.
plodder noun

plop noun (plural **plops**)
the sound of something dropping into water.
plop verb

plot noun (plural **plots**)
1 a secret plan. **2** the story in a play, novel, or
film. **3** a small piece of land.

plot verb (**plots, plotting, plotted**)
1 make a secret plan. **2** make a chart or graph of
something ♦ We plotted the ship's route on our
map.

plough noun (plural **ploughs**)
a farming implement for turning the soil over, in
preparation for planting seeds.

plough verb (**ploughs, ploughing, ploughed**)
1 turn over soil with a plough. **2** go through
something with great effort or difficulty
♦ He ploughed through the book.
ploughman noun
plough back reinvest profits in the business that
produced them.

pluck verb (**plucks, plucking, plucked**)
1 pick a flower or fruit. **2** pull the feathers off a
bird. **3** pull something up or out. **4** pull a string
(e.g. on a guitar) and let it go again.
pluck up courage summon up courage and
overcome fear.

pluck noun
courage or spirit.

plucky adjective (**pluckier, pluckiest**)
brave or spirited.
pluckily adverb

plug noun (plural **plugs**)
1 something used to stop up a hole ♦ a bath
plug. **2** a device that fits into a socket to connect
wires to a supply of electricity. **3** (informal) a
piece of publicity for something.

plug verb (**plugs, plugging, plugged**)
1 stop up a hole. **2** (informal) publicize
something.
plug in put a plug into an electrical socket.

plum noun (plural **plums**)
1 a soft juicy fruit with a pointed stone in the
middle. **2** a reddish-purple colour. **3** (informal)
something very good ♦ a plum job.

plumb verb (**plumbs, plumbing, plumbed**)
1 measure how deep something is. **2** get to the
bottom of a matter ♦ We could not plumb the
mystery. **3** fit a room or building with a
plumbing system.

plumb adjective
exactly upright; vertical ♦ The wall was plumb.

plumb adverb (informal)
exactly ♦ It fell plumb in the middle.

plumber noun (plural **plumbers**)
a person who fits and mends plumbing.

plumbing noun
1 the water pipes, water tanks, and drainage
pipes in a building. **2** the work of a plumber.

plumb line noun
a line with a heavy object tied to it, used for
finding a vertical line on an upright surface or for
testing the depth of water.

plume noun (plural **plumes**)
1 a large feather. **2** something shaped like a
feather ♦ a plume of smoke.

plummet noun (plural **plummets**)
a plumb line or the weight on its end.

plummet verb (**plummets, plummeting,
plummeted**)
1 drop downwards quickly. **2** decrease rapidly in
value ♦ Prices have plummeted.

plump¹ adjective
slightly fat; rounded.
plumpness noun

plump verb (**plumps, plumping, plumped**)
make something rounded ♦ plump up a cushion.

plump² verb (**plumps, plumping, plumped**)
plump for (informal) choose.

plunder verb (**plunders, plundering,
plundered**)
rob a person or place using force, especially
during a war or riot.
plunderer noun

plunder noun
1 plundering. **2** goods etc. that have been
plundered.

plunge verb (**plunges, plunging, plunged**)
1 go or push forcefully into something; dive.
2 fall or go downwards suddenly. **3** go or force
into action etc. ♦ They plunged the world into
war.

plunge noun (plural **plunges**)
a sudden fall or dive.
take the plunge start a bold course of action.

plural noun (plural **plurals**)
the form of a noun or verb used when it stands
for more than one person or thing ♦ The plural
of 'child' is 'children'. (Compare **singular**.)
plural adjective **plurality** noun

plus preposition
with the next number or thing added ♦ 2 plus 2
equals four (2 + 2 = 4).
[from Latin, = more]

plush *noun*
a thick velvety cloth used in furnishings.
plushy *adjective*

plutonium *noun*
a radioactive substance used in nuclear weapons and reactors.
[named after the planet Pluto]

ply¹ *noun* (*plural* **plies**)
1 a thickness or layer of wood or cloth etc.
2 a strand in yarn ♦ *4-ply wool.*

ply² *verb* (**plies, plying, plied**)
1 use or wield a tool or weapon. 2 work at ♦ *Tailors plied their trade.* 3 keep offering ♦ *They plied her with food* or *with questions.*
4 go regularly ♦ *The boat plies between the two harbours.* 5 drive or wait about looking for custom ♦ *Taxis are allowed to ply for hire.*

plywood *noun*
strong thin board made of layers of wood glued together.

PM *abbreviation*
Prime Minister.

p.m. *abbreviation*
after noon.

pneumatic (*say* new-mat-ik) *adjective*
filled with or worked by compressed air ♦ *a pneumatic drill.*
pneumatically *adverb*
[from Greek *pneuma* = wind]

pneumonia (*say* new-moh-nee-a) *noun*
a serious illness caused by inflammation of one or both lungs.
[from Greek *pneumon* = lung]

PO *abbreviation*
1 Post Office. 2 postal order.

poach *verb* (**poaches, poaching, poached**)
1 cook an egg (removed from its shell) in or over boiling water. 2 cook fish or fruit etc. in a small amount of liquid. 3 steal game or fish from someone else's land or water. 4 take something unfairly ♦ *One club was poaching members from another.*
poacher *noun*

pocket *noun* (*plural* **pockets**)
1 a small bag-shaped part, especially in a piece of clothing. 2 a person's supply of money ♦ *The expense is beyond my pocket.* 3 an isolated part or area ♦ *small pockets of rain.*
pocketful *noun*
be out of pocket have spent more money than you have gained.

pocket *adjective*
small enough to carry in a pocket ♦ *a pocket calculator.*

pocket *verb* (**pockets, pocketing, pocketed**)
put something into a pocket.
[from old French *pochet* = little pouch]

pocket money *noun*
money given to a child to spend as he or she likes.

pod *noun* (*plural* **pods**)
a long seed container of the kind found on a pea or bean plant.

poem *noun* (*plural* **poems**)
a piece of poetry.

poet *noun* (*plural* **poets**)
a person who writes poetry.
poetess *noun*

poetry *noun*
writing arranged in short lines, usually with a particular rhythm and sometimes with rhymes.
poetic *adjective* **poetical** *adjective* **poetically** *adverb*

poignant (*say* poin-yant) *adjective*
very distressing; affecting the feelings ♦ *poignant memories.*
poignancy *noun*

point *noun* (*plural* **points**)
1 the narrow or sharp end of something. 2 a dot ♦ *the decimal point.* 3 a particular place or time ♦ *At this point she was winning.* 4 a detail or characteristic ♦ *He has his good points.*
5 the important or essential idea ♦ *Keep to the point!* 6 purpose or value ♦ *There is no point in hurrying.* 7 an electrical socket. 8 a device for changing a train from one track to another.

point *verb* (**points, pointing, pointed**)
1 show where something is, especially by holding out a finger etc. towards it. 2 aim or direct ♦ *She pointed a gun at me.* 3 fill in the parts between bricks with mortar or cement.
point out draw attention to something.

point-blank *adjective*
1 aimed or fired from close to the target. 2 direct and straightforward ♦ *a point-blank refusal.*

point-blank *adverb*
in a point-blank manner ♦ *He refused point-blank.*

pointed *adjective*
1 with a point at the end. 2 clearly directed at a person ♦ *a pointed remark.*
pointedly *adverb*

pointer *noun* (*plural* **pointers**)
1 a stick, rod, or mark etc. used to point at something. 2 a dog that points with its muzzle towards birds that it scents. 3 an indication or hint.

pointless *adjective*
without a point; with no purpose.
pointlessly *adverb*

poise *verb* (**poises, poising, poised**)
balance.

poise *noun*
1 a dignified self-confident manner. 2 balance.

poison *noun* (*plural* **poisons**)
a substance that can harm or kill a living thing if swallowed or absorbed into the body.
poisonous *adjective*

poison *verb* (**poisons, poisoning, poisoned**)
1 give poison to; kill somebody with poison.
2 put poison in something. **3** corrupt or spoil something ♦ *He poisoned their minds.*
poisoner *noun*
[via early French from Latin *potio* = potion]

poke *verb* (**pokes, poking, poked**)
1 prod or jab. **2** push out or forward; stick out.
3 search ♦ *I was poking about in the attic.*
poke fun at ridicule.

poke *noun* (*plural* **pokes**)
a poking movement; a prod.

poker[1] *noun* (*plural* **pokers**)
a stiff metal rod for poking a fire.

poker[2] *noun*
a card game in which players bet on who has the best cards.

polar *adjective*
1 to do with or near the North Pole or South Pole.
2 to do with either pole of a magnet.
polarity *noun*

polar bear *noun* (*plural* **polar bears**)
a white bear living in Arctic regions.

polarize *verb* (**polarizes, polarizing, polarized**)
1 keep vibrations of light waves etc. to a single direction. **2** divide into two groups of completely opposite extremes of feeling or opinion
♦ *Opinions had polarized.*
polarization *noun*

Polaroid camera *noun* (*plural* **Polaroid cameras**) (*trade mark*)
a camera that takes a picture and produces the finished photograph a few seconds later.

pole[1] *noun* (*plural* **poles**)
a long slender rounded piece of wood or metal.

pole[2] *noun* (*plural* **poles**)
1 a point on the earth's surface that is as far north (**North Pole**) or as far south (**South Pole**) as possible. **2** either of the ends of a magnet.
3 either terminal of an electric cell or battery.

pole star *noun*
the star above the North Pole.

pole vault *noun*
an athletic contest in which competitors jump over a high bar with the help of a long flexible pole.

police *noun*
the people whose job is to catch criminals and make sure that the law is kept.
policeman *noun* **police officer** *noun*
policewoman *noun*

police *verb* (**polices, policing, policed**)
keep order in a place by means of police.

policy[1] *noun* (*plural* **policies**)
the aims or plan of action of a person or group.

policy[2] *noun* (*plural* **policies**)
a document stating the terms of a contract of insurance.

polish *verb* (**polishes, polishing, polished**)
1 make a thing smooth and shiny by rubbing.
2 make a thing better by making corrections and alterations.
polisher *noun*
polish off finish off.

polish *noun* (*plural* **polishes**)
1 a substance used in polishing. **2** a shine.
3 elegance of manner.

polite *adjective*
having good manners.
politely *adverb* **politeness** *noun*

political *adjective*
connected with the governing of a country or region.
politically *adverb*

politician *noun* (*plural* **politicians**)
a person who is involved in politics.

politics *noun*
political matters; the business of governing a country or region.

poll (rhymes with *pole*) *noun* (*plural* **polls**)
1 voting or votes at an election. **2** an opinion poll. **3** (*old use*) the head.

poll *verb* (**polls, polling, polled**)
1 vote at an election. **2** receive a stated number of votes in an election.
polling booth *noun* **polling station** *noun*

pollen *noun*
powder produced by flowers, containing male cells for fertilizing other flowers.

pollen count *noun* (*plural* **pollen counts**)
a measurement of the amount of pollen in the air, given as a warning for people who are allergic to pollen.

pollinate *verb* (**pollinates, pollinating, pollinated**)
fertilize a plant with pollen.
pollination *noun*

poll tax *noun* (*plural* **poll taxes**)
a tax that every adult has to pay regardless of income.

pollute *verb* (**pollutes, polluting, polluted**)
make the air, water, etc. dirty or impure.
pollutant *noun* **pollution** *noun*

polygamy (*say* pol-ig-a-mee) *noun*
having more than one wife at a time.
polygamous *adjective* **polygamist** *noun*

polygon *noun* (*plural* **polygons**)
a shape with many sides. Hexagons and octagons are polygons.
polygonal *adjective*

polyhedron *noun* (*plural* **polyhedrons**)
a solid shape with many sides.

polytechnic *noun* (*plural* **polytechnics**)
a college giving instruction in many subjects at degree level or below. In 1992 the British polytechnics were able to change their names and call themselves universities.

polythene *noun*
a lightweight plastic used to make bags, wrappings, etc.

pomegranate *noun* (*plural* **pomegranates**)
a tropical fruit with many seeds.
[from Latin *pomum* = apple + *granatum* = having many seeds]

pomp *noun*
the ceremonial splendour that is traditional on important public occasions.

pompous *adjective*
full of excessive dignity and self-importance.
pompously *adverb* **pomposity** *noun*

pond *noun* (*plural* **ponds**)
a small lake.

ponder *verb* (**ponders, pondering, pondered**)
think deeply and seriously.

ponderous *adjective*
1 heavy and awkward. 2 laborious and dull
♦ *He writes in a ponderous style.*
ponderously *adverb*

pontificate *verb* (**pontificates, pontificating, pontificated**)
give your opinions in a pompous way.
pontification *noun*

pony *noun* (*plural* **ponies**)
a small horse.

ponytail *noun* (*plural* **ponytails**)
a bunch of long hair tied at the back of the head.

poodle *noun* (*plural* **poodles**)
a dog with thick curly hair.

pool¹ *noun* (*plural* **pools**)
1 a pond. 2 a puddle. 3 a swimming pool.

pool² *noun* (*plural* **pools**)
1 the fund of money staked in a gambling game. 2 a group of things shared by several people. 3 a game resembling billiards.
the pools gambling based on the results of football matches.

pool *verb* (**pools, pooling, pooled**)
put money or things together for sharing.

poor *adjective*
1 with very little money or other resources.
2 not good; inadequate ♦ *a poor piece of work.*
3 unfortunate; deserving pity ♦ *Poor fellow!*
poorness *noun*

poorly *adverb*
in a poor way ♦ *We've played poorly this season.*

poorly *adjective*
rather ill ♦ *You look poorly.*

pop¹ *noun* (*plural* **pops**)
1 a small explosive sound. 2 a fizzy drink.

pop *verb* (**pops, popping, popped**)
1 make a pop. 2 (*informal*) go or put quickly
♦ *Pop down to the shop.* ♦ *I'll just pop this pie into the microwave.*

pop² *noun*
modern popular music.

Pope *noun* (*plural* **Popes**)
the leader of the Roman Catholic Church.

pop-eyed *adjective*
with bulging eyes.

poplar *noun* (*plural* **poplars**)
a tall slender tree.

poppadom *noun* (*plural* **poppadoms**)
a thin crisp biscuit made of lentil flour, eaten with Indian food.

poppy *noun* (*plural* **poppies**)
a plant with large red flowers.

popular *adjective*
1 liked or enjoyed by many people. 2 believed by many people ♦ *popular opinion.* 3 intended for the general public.
popularly *adverb* **popularity** *noun*

populate *verb* (**populates, populating, populated**)
supply with a population; inhabit.

population *noun* (*plural* **populations**)
the people who live in a district or country; the total number of these people.

porcelain *noun*
the finest kind of china.

porch *noun* (*plural* **porches**)
a shelter outside the entrance to a building.

porcupine *noun* (*plural* **porcupines**)
a small animal covered with long prickles.

pore¹ *noun* (*plural* **pores**)
a tiny opening on the skin through which moisture can pass in or out.

pore² *verb* (**pores, poring, pored**)
pore over study with close attention ♦ *He was poring over his books.*

❶ USAGE Do not confuse with *pour.*

pork *noun*
meat from a pig.
[from Latin *porcus* = pig]

pornography (*say* porn-**og**-ra-fee) *noun*
obscene pictures or writings.
pornographic *adjective*

porpoise (*say* **por**-pus) *noun* (*plural* **porpoises**)
a sea animal rather like a small whale.

porridge *noun*
a food made by boiling oatmeal to a thick paste.
[from an old word *pottage* = soup]

port[1] *noun* (*plural* **ports**)
1 a harbour. 2 a city or town with a harbour.
3 the left-hand side of a ship or aircraft when you
are facing forward. (Compare **starboard**.)
[from Latin *portus* = harbour]

port[2] *noun*
a strong red Portuguese wine.
[from the city of Oporto in Portugal]

portable *adjective*
able to be carried.
[from Latin *portare* = carry]

portcullis *noun* (*plural* **portcullises**)
a strong heavy vertical grating that can be
lowered in grooves to block the gateway to a
castle.
[from early French *porte coleice* = sliding door]

porter[1] *noun* (*plural* **porters**)
a person whose job is to carry luggage or other
goods.
[from Latin *portare* = carry]

porter[2] *noun* (*plural* **porters**)
a person whose job is to look after the entrance
to a large building.
[from Latin *porta* = gate]

porthole *noun* (*plural* **portholes**)
a small window in the side of a ship or aircraft.

portion *noun* (*plural* **portions**)
a part or share given to somebody.

portion *verb* (**portions, portioning, portioned**)
divide something into portions ♦ *Portion it out.*

portly *adjective* (**portlier, portliest**)
rather fat.
portliness *noun*

portrait *noun* (*plural* **portraits**)
1 a picture of a person or animal. 2 a description
in words.

pose *noun* (*plural* **poses**)
1 a position or posture of the body, e.g. for a
portrait or photograph. 2 a way of behaving that
someone adopts to give a particular impression.

pose *verb* (**poses, posing, posed**)
1 take up a pose. 2 put someone into a pose.
3 pretend. 4 put forward or present ♦ *It poses
several problems for us.*

posh *adjective* (*informal*)
1 very smart; high-class ♦ *a posh restaurant.*
2 upper-class ♦ *a posh accent.*

position *noun* (*plural* **positions**)
1 the place where something is or should be.
2 the way a person or thing is placed or arranged
♦ *in a sitting position.* 3 a situation or condition
♦ *I am in no position to help you.* 4 paid
employment; a job.
positional *adjective*

positive *adjective*
1 definite or certain ♦ *Are you positive you saw
him?* ♦ *We have positive proof that he is guilty.*
2 agreeing; saying 'yes' ♦ *We received a positive
reply.* 3 confident and hopeful. 4 showing signs
of what is being tested for ♦ *Her pregnancy test
was positive.* 5 greater than nought. 6 to do with
the kind of electric charge that lacks electrons.
7 (in grammar, said about an adjective or
adverb) in the simple form, not comparative or
superlative ♦ *The positive form is 'big', the
comparative is 'bigger', the superlative is
'biggest'.*
positively *adverb*

❶ USAGE The opposite of senses 1–4 is **negative**.

possess *verb* (**possesses, possessing,
possessed**)
1 have or own something. 2 control someone's
thoughts or behaviour ♦ *I don't know what
possessed you to do such a thing!*
possessor *noun*

possessed *adjective*
seeming to be controlled by strong emotion or an
evil spirit ♦ *He fought like a man possessed.*

possession *noun* (*plural* **possessions**)
1 something you possess or own. 2 owning
something.

possessive *adjective*
1 wanting to possess and keep things for
yourself. 2 (in grammar) showing that
somebody owns something ♦ *a possessive
pronoun* (see **pronoun**).

possibility *noun* (*plural* **possibilities**)
1 being possible. 2 something that may exist or
happen etc.

possible *adjective*
able to exist, happen, be done, or be used.

possibly *adverb*
1 in any way ♦ *I can't possibly do it.* 2 perhaps.

post[1] *noun* (*plural* **posts**)
1 an upright piece of wood, concrete, or metal
etc. set in the ground. 2 the starting point or
finishing point of a race ♦ *He was left at the post.*

post *verb* (**posts, posting, posted**)
put up a notice or poster etc. to announce
something.

post[2] *noun*
1 the collecting and delivering of letters, parcels,
etc. 2 these letters and parcels etc.

post *verb* (**posts, posting, posted**)
put a letter or parcel etc. into a postbox for
collection.
keep me posted keep me informed.

post[3] *noun* (*plural* **posts**)
1 a position of paid employment; a job. 2 the
place where someone is on duty ♦ *a sentry post.*
3 a place occupied by soldiers, traders, etc.

post *verb* (posts, posting, posted)
place someone on duty ♦ *We posted sentries.*

postage *noun*
the charge for sending something by post.

postage stamp *noun* (*plural* **postage stamps**)
a stamp for sticking on things to be posted, showing the amount paid.

postal *adjective*
to do with or by the post.

postal order *noun* (*plural* **postal orders**)
a document bought from a post office for sending money by post.

postbox *noun* (*plural* **postboxes**)
a box into which letters are put for collection.

postcard *noun* (*plural* **postcards**)
a card for sending messages by post without an envelope.

postcode *noun* (*plural* **postcodes**)
a group of letters and numbers included in an address to help in sorting the post.

poster *noun* (*plural* **posters**)
a large sheet of paper announcing or advertising something, for display in a public place.

posterity *noun*
future generations of people ♦ *These letters and diaries should be preserved for posterity.*

postman *noun* (*plural* **postmen**)
a person who delivers or collects letters etc.

postmark *noun* (*plural* **postmarks**)
an official mark put on something sent by post to show where and when it was posted.

post-mortem *noun* (*plural* **post-mortems**)
an examination of a dead body to discover the cause of death.

posthumous (*say* poss-tew-mus) *adjective*
coming after a person's death ♦ *a posthumous award for bravery.*
posthumously *adverb*

post office *noun* (*plural* **post offices**)
1 a building or room where postal business is carried on. 2 the national organization responsible for postal services.

postpone *verb* (postpones, postponing, postponed)
fix a later time for something ♦ *They postponed the meeting for a fortnight.*
postponement *noun*

postscript *noun* (*plural* **postscripts**)
something extra added at the end of a letter (after the writer's signature) or at the end of a book.

posture *noun* (*plural* **postures**)
a particular position of the body, or the way in which a person stands, sits, or walks.

post-war *adjective*
happening during the time after a war.

pot¹ *noun* (*plural* **pots**)
1 a deep, usually round, container. 2 (*informal*) a lot of something ♦ *He has got pots of money.*
go to pot (*informal*) lose quality; be ruined.
take pot luck (*informal*) take whatever is available.

pot *verb* (pots, potting, potted)
put into a pot.

pot² *noun* (*informal*)
cannabis.

potassium *noun*
a soft silvery-white metal substance that is essential for living things.

potato *noun* (*plural* **potatoes**)
a starchy white tuber growing underground, used as a vegetable.
[via Spanish from a Caribbean word]

potentate (*say* poh-ten-tayt) *noun* (*plural* **potentates**)
a powerful monarch or ruler.

potential (*say* po-**ten**-shal) *adjective*
capable of happening or being used or developed ♦ *a potential winner.*
potentially *adverb* **potentiality** *noun*

potential *noun*
1 the ability of a person or thing to develop in the future. 2 (in science) the voltage between two points.

pothole *noun* (*plural* **potholes**)
1 a deep natural hole in the ground. 2 a hole in a road.

potion *noun* (*plural* **potions**)
a liquid for drinking as a medicine etc.

potted *adjective*
1 shortened or abridged ♦ *a potted account of the story.* 2 preserved in a pot ♦ *potted shrimps.*

potter¹ *noun* (*plural* **potters**)
a person who makes pottery.

potter² *verb* (potters, pottering, pottered)
work or move about in a leisurely way ♦ *I spent the afternoon pottering around in the garden.*

pottery *noun* (*plural* **potteries**)
1 cups, plates, ornaments, etc. made of baked clay. 2 the craft of making these things. 3 a place where a potter works.

pouch *noun* (*plural* **pouches**)
1 a small bag. 2 a fold of skin in which a kangaroo etc. keeps its young. 3 something shaped like a bag.

poultry *noun*
birds (e.g. chickens, geese, and turkeys) kept for their eggs and meat.

pounce *verb* (pounces, pouncing, pounced)
jump or swoop down quickly on something.
pounce *noun*

pound¹ *noun* (*plural* **pounds**)
1 a unit of money (in Britain = 100 pence).
2 a unit of weight equal to 16 ounces or about 454 grams.
[from Old English *pund*]

pound² *noun* (*plural* **pounds**)
1 a place where stray animals are taken.
2 a public enclosure for vehicles officially removed.
[origin unknown]

pound³ *verb* (**pounds, pounding, pounded**)
1 hit something often, especially in order to crush it. **2** run or go heavily ♦ *He pounded down the stairs.* **3** thump ♦ *My heart was pounding.*
[from Old English *punian*]

pour *verb* (**pours, pouring, poured**)
1 flow or make something flow. **2** rain heavily
♦ *It poured all day.* **3** come or go in large amounts ♦ *Letters poured in.*
pourer *noun*

> ❶ USAGE Do not confuse with *pore.*

pout *verb* (**pouts, pouting, pouted**)
push out your lips when you are annoyed or sulking.
pout *noun*

poverty *noun*
1 being poor. **2** a lack or scarcity ♦ *a poverty of ideas.*

powder *noun* (*plural* **powders**)
1 a mass of fine dry particles of something.
2 a medicine or cosmetic etc. made as a powder.
3 gunpowder.
powdery *adjective*

powder *verb* (**powders, powdering, powdered**)
1 put powder on something. **2** make something into powder.

power *noun* (*plural* **powers**)
1 strength or energy. **2** the ability to do something ♦ *the power of speech.* **3** political authority or control. **4** a powerful country, person, or organization. **5** mechanical or electrical energy; the electricity supply
♦ *There was a power failure after the storm.*
6 (in science) the rate of doing work, measured in watts or horsepower. **7** (in mathematics) the product of a number multiplied by itself a given number of times ♦ *The third power of 2 = 2 ×2 ×2 = 8.*
powered *adjective* **powerless** *adjective*

powerful *adjective*
having great power, strength, or influence.
powerfully *adverb*

power station *noun* (*plural* **power stations**)
a building where electricity is produced.

pp. *abbreviation*
pages.

practicable *adjective*
able to be done.

> ❶ USAGE Do not confuse with *practical.*

practical *adjective*
1 able to do or make useful things ♦ *a practical person.* **2** likely to be useful ♦ *a very practical invention.* **3** actually doing something, rather than just learning or thinking about it ♦ *She has had practical experience.*
practicality *noun*

> ❶ USAGE Do not confuse with *practicable.*

practical *noun* (*plural* **practicals**)
a lesson or examination in which you actually do or make something rather than reading or writing about it ♦ *a chemistry practical.*

practical joke *noun* (*plural* **practical jokes**)
a trick played on somebody.

practically *adverb*
1 in a practical way. **2** almost ♦ *I've practically finished.*

practice *noun* (*plural* **practices**)
1 doing something repeatedly in order to become better at it ♦ *Have you done your piano practice?*
2 actually doing something; action, not theory
♦ *It works well in practice.* **3** the professional business of a doctor, dentist, lawyer, etc.
4 a habit or custom ♦ *It is his practice to work until midnight.*
out of practice no longer skilful because you have not practised recently.

> ❶ USAGE See the note on *practise.*

practise *verb* (**practises, practising, practised**)
1 do something repeatedly in order to become better at it. **2** do something actively or habitually
♦ *Practise what you preach.* **3** work as a doctor, dentist, or lawyer.

> ❶ USAGE Note the spelling: *practice* is a noun, *practise* is a verb.

practised *adjective*
experienced or expert.

prairie *noun* (*plural* **prairies**)
a large area of flat grass-covered land in North America.

praise *verb* (**praises, praising, praised**)
1 say that somebody or something is very good.
2 honour God in words.
praise *noun*
words that praise somebody or something.
praiseworthy *adjective*

pram noun (plural **prams**)
a four-wheeled carriage for a baby, pushed by a person walking.

prance verb (**prances, prancing, pranced**)
move about in a lively or happy way.

prank noun (plural **pranks**)
a trick played for mischief; a practical joke.
prankster noun

prattle verb (**prattles, prattling, prattled**)
chatter like a young child.
prattle noun

prawn noun (plural **prawns**)
an edible shellfish like a large shrimp.

pray verb (**prays, praying, prayed**)
1 talk to God. **2** ask earnestly for something.
3 (formal) please ♦ Pray be seated.

prayer noun (plural **prayers**)
praying; words used in praying.

pre- prefix
before (as in prehistoric).

preach verb (**preaches, preaching, preached**)
give a religious or moral talk.
preacher noun

precarious (say pri-**kair**-ee-us) adjective
not very safe or secure.
precariously adverb

precaution noun (plural **precautions**)
something done to prevent future trouble or danger.
precautionary adjective

precede verb (**precedes, preceding, preceded**)
come or go before someone or something else.

---

❶ USAGE Do not confuse with proceed.

---

precedence (say **press**-i-dens) noun
the right of someone or something to be first.
take precedence have priority.

precedent (say **press**-i-dent) noun (plural **precedents**)
a previous case that is taken as an example to be followed.

precinct (say **pree**-sinkt) noun (plural **precincts**)
1 the area round a place, especially round a cathedral. **2** a part of a town where traffic is not allowed ♦ a shopping precinct.

precious adjective
1 very valuable. **2** greatly loved.
preciousness noun
precious adverb (informal)
very ♦ We have precious little time.

precipice noun (plural **precipices**)
a very steep place, such as the face of a cliff.

précis (say **pray**-see) noun (plural **précis** (say **pray**-seez))
a summary.

precise adjective
exact; clearly stated.
precisely adverb **precision** noun

precocious (say prik-**oh**-shus) adjective
(said about a child) very advanced or developed for his or her age.
precociously adverb **precocity** noun

predator (say **pred**-a-ter) noun (plural **predators**)
an animal that hunts or preys upon others.
predatory adjective

predecessor (say **pree**-dis-ess-er) noun (plural **predecessors**)
an earlier person or thing, e.g. an ancestor or the former holder of a job.

predicate noun (plural **predicates**)
the part of a sentence that says something about the subject, e.g. 'is short' in ♦ life is short.

predicative (say prid-**ik**-a-tiv) adjective
forming part of the predicate, e.g. old in
♦ The dog is old. (Compare **attributive**.)
predicatively adverb

predict verb (**predicts, predicting, predicted**)
say what will happen in the future; foretell or prophesy.
predictable adjective **prediction** noun **predictor** noun

predispose verb (**predisposes, predisposing, predisposed**)
make you likely to be in favour of something
♦ We are predisposed to help them.
predisposition noun

predominate verb (**predominates, predominating, predominated**)
be the largest or most important or most powerful.
predominant adjective **predominance** noun

pre-eminent adjective
excelling others; outstanding.
pre-eminently adverb **pre-eminence** noun

preen verb (**preens, preening, preened**)
(said about a bird) smooth its feathers with its beak.
preen yourself smarten your appearance.

preface (say **pref**-as) noun (plural **prefaces**)
an introduction at the beginning of a book or speech.
preface verb

prefect noun (plural **prefects**)
1 a senior pupil in a school, given authority to help to keep order. **2** a regional official in France, Japan, and other countries.

prefer verb (**prefers, preferring, preferred**)
1 like one person or thing more than another.
2 (formal) put forward ♦ They preferred charges of forgery against him.
preference noun

preferable (*say* pref-er-a-bul) *adjective*
liked better; more desirable.
preferably *adverb*

prefix *noun* (*plural* **prefixes**)
a word or syllable joined to the front of a word to
change or add to its meaning, as in *dis*order,
*out*stretched, *un*happy.

pregnant *adjective*
having a baby developing in the womb.
pregnancy *noun*

prehensile *adjective*
(said about an animal's foot or tail etc.) able to
grasp things.

prehistoric *adjective*
belonging to very ancient times, before written
records of events were made.
prehistory *noun*

prejudice *noun* (*plural* **prejudices**)
an unfavourable opinion or dislike formed
without examining the facts fairly.
prejudiced *adjective*

preliminary *adjective*
coming before an important action or event and
preparing for it.

prelude *noun* (*plural* **preludes**)
1 a thing that introduces or leads up to
something else. 2 a short piece of music,
especially one that introduces a longer piece.

premature *adjective*
too early; coming before the usual or proper
time.
prematurely *adverb*

premeditated *adjective*
planned beforehand ♦ *a premeditated crime.*

premier *noun* (*plural* **premiers**)
a prime minister or other head of government.

première (*say* prem-**yair**) *noun* (*plural*
premières)
the first public performance of a play or film.

premises *plural noun*
a building and its grounds.

premium *noun* (*plural* **premiums**)
1 an amount or instalment paid to an insurance
company. 2 an extra charge or payment.
at a premium in demand but scarce.

Premium Bond *noun* (*plural* **Premium Bonds**)
a savings certificate that gives the person who
holds it a chance to win a prize of money.

premonition *noun* (*plural* **premonitions**)
a feeling that something is about to happen,
especially something bad.

preoccupied *adjective*
having your thoughts completely busy with
something.
preoccupation *noun*

prep *noun* (*informal*)
homework.

preparation *noun* (*plural* **preparations**)
1 getting something ready. 2 something done in
order to get ready for an event or activity
♦ *last-minute preparations.*

preparatory school *noun* (*plural*
preparatory schools)
a school that prepares pupils for a higher school.

prepare *verb* (**prepares, preparing, prepared**)
get ready; make something ready.
be prepared to be willing to do something.

preposition *noun* (*plural* **prepositions**)
a word used with a noun or pronoun to show
place, position, time, or means, e.g. *at* home, *in*
the hall, *on* Sunday, *by* train.

preposterous *adjective*
completely absurd or ridiculous.

prep school *noun* (*plural* **prep schools**)
a preparatory school.

Presbyterian (*say* prez-bit-**eer**-ee-an) *noun*
(*plural* **Presbyterians**)
a member of a Christian Church governed by
elders who are all of equal rank, especially the
national Church of Scotland.

prescribe *verb* (**prescribes, prescribing,
prescribed**)
1 advise a person to use a particular medicine or
treatment etc. 2 say what should be done.

prescription *noun* (*plural* **prescriptions**)
1 a doctor's written order for a medicine.
2 the medicine prescribed. 3 prescribing.

presence *noun*
1 being present in a place ♦ *Your presence is
required.* 2 a person's impressive appearance or
manner.

presence of mind *noun*
the ability to act quickly and sensibly in an
emergency.

present¹ *adjective*
1 in a particular place ♦ *No one else was present.*
2 belonging or referring to what is happening
now; existing now ♦ *the present Queen.*

present *noun*
present times or events.
at present now, for the time being.

present² *noun* (*plural* **presents**)
something given or received without payment;
a gift.

present (*say* priz-**ent**) *verb* (**presents,
presenting, presented**)
1 give something, especially with a ceremony
♦ *Who is to present the prizes?* 2 introduce
someone to another person. 3 introduce a radio
or television programme to an audience. 4 put on
a play or other entertainment. 5 show. 6 cause or
provide a problem or difficulty.
presentation *noun* **presenter** *noun*

presently *adverb*
1 soon ♦ *I shall be with you presently.*
2 now ♦ *the person who is presently in charge.*

preservative *noun* (*plural* **preservatives**)
a substance added to food to preserve it.

preserve *verb* (**preserves, preserving, preserved**)
keep something safe or in good condition.
preserver *noun* **preservation** *noun*

preserve *noun* (*plural* **preserves**)
1 jam made with preserved fruit. 2 an activity
that belongs to a particular person or group.

preside *verb* (**presides, presiding, presided**)
be in charge of a meeting etc.

president *noun* (*plural* **presidents**)
1 the person in charge of a club, society, or
council etc. 2 the head of a republic.
presidency *noun* **presidential** *adjective*

press *verb* (**presses, pressing, pressed**)
1 put weight or force steadily on something;
squeeze. 2 make something by pressing. 3 make
clothes smooth by ironing them. 4 urge; make
demands ♦ *They pressed for an increase in
wages.*

press *noun* (*plural* **presses**)
1 a device for pressing things ♦ *a trouser press.*
2 a machine for printing things. 3 a firm that
prints or publishes books etc. ♦ *Oxford
University Press.* 4 newspapers; journalists.

pressing *adjective*
needing immediate action; urgent ♦ *a pressing
need.*

press-up *noun* (*plural* **press-ups**)
an exercise in which you lie face downwards and
press down with your hands to lift your body.

pressure *noun* (*plural* **pressures**)
1 continuous pressing. 2 the force with which
something presses. 3 the force of the atmosphere
on the earth's surface ♦ *a band of high pressure.*
4 an influence that persuades or compels you to
do something.

prestige (*say* pres-**teej**) *noun*
good reputation.
prestigious *adjective*
[from Latin *praestigium* = an illusion, glamour]

presumably *adverb*
according to what you may presume.

presume *verb* (**presumes, presuming, presumed**)
1 suppose; assume something to be true
♦ *I presumed that they were dead.* 2 (*formal*)
take the liberty of doing something; venture
♦ *May we presume to advise you?*
presumption *noun*

presumptuous *adjective*
too bold or confident.
presumptuously *adverb*

presuppose *verb* (**presupposes, presupposing, presupposed**)
suppose or assume something beforehand.
presupposition *noun*

pretence *noun* (*plural* **pretences**)
an attempt to pretend that something is true.
false pretences pretending to be something that
you are not in order to deceive people ♦ *You've
invited me here under false pretences.*

pretend *verb* (**pretends, pretending, pretended**)
behave as if something is true or real when you
know that it is not, either in play or so as to
deceive people.

pretender *noun* (*plural* **pretenders**)
a person who claims a throne or title.

pretentious *adjective*
1 trying to impress by claiming greater
importance or merit than is actually the case.
2 showy or ostentatious.
pretentiously *adverb* **pretentiousness** *noun*

pretext *noun* (*plural* **pretexts**)
a reason put forward to conceal the true reason.

pretty *adjective* (**prettier, prettiest**)
attractive in a delicate way.
prettily *adverb* **prettiness** *noun*
pretty *adverb* (*informal*)
quite ♦ *It's pretty cold.*
[from Old English]

prevent *verb* (**prevents, preventing, prevented**)
1 stop something from happening. 2 stop a
person from doing something.
preventable *adjective* **prevention** *noun*
preventive *or* **preventative** *adjective*

preview *noun* (*plural* **previews**)
a showing of a film or play etc. before it is shown
to the general public.

previous *adjective*
coming before this; preceding.
previously *adverb*

prey (rhymes with *pray*) *noun*
an animal that is hunted or killed by another for
food.

prey *verb* (**preys, preying, preyed**)
prey on 1 hunt or take as prey. 2 cause to worry
♦ *The problem preyed on his mind.*

price *noun* (*plural* **prices**)
1 the amount of money for which something is
bought or sold. 2 what must be given or done in
order to achieve something.

priceless *adjective*
1 very valuable. 2 (*informal*) very amusing.

prick *verb* (**pricks, pricking, pricked**)
1 make a tiny hole in something. 2 hurt
somebody with a pin or needle etc.
prick *noun*
prick up your ears start listening suddenly.

prickle *noun* (*plural* **prickles**)
1 a small thorn. **2** a sharp spine on a hedgehog or cactus etc. **3** a feeling that something is pricking you.
prickly *adjective*

prickle *verb* (**prickles, prickling, prickled**)
feel or cause a pricking feeling.

pride *noun* (*plural* **prides**)
1 a feeling of deep pleasure or satisfaction when you have done something well. **2** something that makes you feel proud. **3** dignity or self-respect. **4** too high an opinion of yourself. **5** a group of lions.
pride of place the most important or most honoured position.

pride *verb* (**prides, priding, prided**)
pride yourself on be proud of.

priest *noun* (*plural* **priests**)
1 a member of the clergy in certain Christian Churches. **2** a person who conducts religious ceremonies in a non-Christian religion.
priestess *noun* **priesthood** *noun* **priestly** *adjective*

prig *noun* (*plural* **prigs**)
a self-righteous person.
priggish *adjective*

prim *adjective* (**primmer, primmest**)
formal and correct in manner; disliking anything rough or rude.
primly *adverb* **primness** *noun*

primary *adjective*
first; most important. (Compare **secondary**.)
primarily (*say* pry-mer-il-ee) *adverb*

primary colour *noun* (*plural* **primary colours**)
one of the colours from which all others can be made by mixing (red, yellow, and blue for paint; red, green, and violet for light).

primary school *noun* (*plural* **primary schools**)
a school for the first stage of a child's education.

primate (*say* pry-mayt) *noun* (*plural* **primates**)
1 an animal of the group that includes human beings, apes, and monkeys. **2** an archbishop.

prime *adjective*
1 chief; most important ♦ *the prime cause.* **2** excellent; first-rate ♦ *prime beef.*

prime *noun*
the best time or stage of something ♦ *in the prime of life.*

prime *verb* (**primes, priming, primed**)
1 prepare something for use or action. **2** put a coat of liquid on something to prepare it for painting. **3** equip a person with information.

prime minister *noun* (*plural* **prime ministers**)
the leader of a government.

prime number *noun* (*plural* **prime numbers**)
a number (e.g. 2, 3, 5, 7, 11) that can be divided exactly only by itself and one.

primeval (*say* pry-mee-val) *adjective*
belonging to the earliest times of the world.

primitive *adjective*
1 at an early stage of civilization. **2** at an early stage of development; not complicated or advanced ♦ *primitive technology.*

primrose *noun* (*plural* **primroses**)
a pale yellow flower that blooms in spring.
[from Latin *prima rosa* = first rose]

prince *noun* (*plural* **princes**)
1 the son of a king or queen. **2** a man or boy in a royal family.
princely *adjective*

princess *noun* (*plural* **princesses**)
1 the daughter of a king or queen. **2** a woman or girl in a royal family. **3** the wife of a prince.

principal *adjective*
chief; most important.
principally *adverb*

principal *noun* (*plural* **principals**)
the head of a college or school.
[from Latin *principalis* = first or chief]

ⓘ USAGE Do not confuse with *principle.*

principle *noun* (*plural* **principles**)
1 a general truth, belief, or rule ♦ *She taught me the principles of geometry.* **2** a rule of conduct ♦ *Cheating is against his principles.*
in principle as a general idea, without going into details. **on principle** because of your principles of behaviour.
[from Latin *principium* = source]

ⓘ USAGE Do not confuse with *principal.*

print *verb* (**prints, printing, printed**)
1 put words or pictures on paper by using a machine. **2** write with letters that are not joined together. **3** press a mark or design etc. on a surface. **4** make a picture from the negative of a photograph.

print *noun* (*plural* **prints**)
1 printed lettering or words. **2** a mark made by something pressing on a surface. **3** a printed picture, photograph, or design.
in print available from a publisher. **out of print** no longer available from a publisher.

printed circuit *noun* (*plural* **printed circuits**)
an electric circuit made by pressing thin metal strips on to a board.

printer *noun* (*plural* **printers**)
1 a machine that prints on paper from data in a computer. **2** someone who prints books or newspapers.

printout *noun* (*plural* **printouts**)
information etc. produced in printed form by a computer.

priority *noun* (*plural* **priorities**)
1 being earlier or more important than something else; precedence. 2 something considered more important than other things ♦ *Safety is a priority.*

prise *verb* (**prises, prising, prised**)
lever something out or open ♦ *Prise the lid off the crate.*

prism (*say* prizm) *noun* (*plural* **prisms**)
1 a solid shape with ends that are triangles or polygons which are equal and parallel. 2 a glass prism that breaks up light into the colours of the rainbow.
prismatic *adjective*

prison *noun* (*plural* **prisons**)
a place where criminals are kept as a punishment.
[from early French]

prisoner *noun* (*plural* **prisoners**)
1 a person kept in prison. 2 a captive.

private *adjective*
1 belonging to a particular person or group ♦ *private property.* 2 confidential ♦ *private talks.* 3 quiet and secluded. 4 not holding public office ♦ *a private citizen.* 5 independent or commercial; not run by the government ♦ *private education;* ♦ *a private hospital.*
privately *adverb* **privacy** (*say* priv-a-see) *noun*
in private where only particular people can see or hear; not in public.

private *noun* (*plural* **privates**)
a soldier of the lowest rank.

privatize *verb* (**privatizes, privatizing, privatized**)
transfer the running of a business or industry from the state to private owners.
privatization *noun*

privilege *noun* (*plural* **privileges**)
a special right or advantage given to one person or group.
privileged *adjective*

Privy Council *noun*
a group of distinguished people who advise the sovereign.

prize *noun* (*plural* **prizes**)
1 an award given to the winner of a game or competition etc. 2 something taken from an enemy.

prize *verb* (**prizes, prizing, prized**)
value something greatly.

pro *noun* (*plural* **pros**) (*informal*)
a professional.

probable *adjective*
likely to happen or be true.
probably *adverb* **probability** *noun*

probation *noun*
the testing of a person's character and abilities, e.g. to see whether they are suitable for a job they have recently started.
probationary *adjective*
on probation being supervised by a probation officer instead of being sent to prison.

probation officer *noun* (*plural* **probation officers**)
an official who supervises the behaviour of a convicted criminal who is not in prison.

probe *noun* (*plural* **probes**)
1 a long thin instrument used to look closely at something such as a wound. 2 an unmanned spacecraft used for exploring. 3 an investigation.

probe *verb* (**probes, probing, probed**)
1 explore something with a probe. 2 investigate.

problem *noun* (*plural* **problems**)
1 something difficult to deal with or understand. 2 something that has to be done or answered.
problematic *or* **problematical** *adjective*

procedure *noun* (*plural* **procedures**)
an orderly way of doing something.

proceed *verb* (**proceeds, proceeding, proceeded**)
1 go forward or onward. 2 continue; go on to do something ♦ *She proceeded to explain the plan.*

❶ USAGE Do not confuse with *precede*.

proceedings *plural noun*
1 things that happen; activities. 2 a lawsuit.

proceeds *plural noun*
the money made from a sale or event.

process (*say* proh-sess) *noun* (*plural* **processes**)
a series of actions for making or doing something.
in the process of in the course of doing something.

process *verb* (**processes, processing, processed**)
put something through a manufacturing or other process ♦ *processed cheese.*

procession *noun* (*plural* **processions**)
a number of people or vehicles etc. moving steadily forward following each other.

processor *noun* (*plural* **processors**)
1 a machine that processes things. 2 the part of a computer that controls all its operations.

proclaim *verb* (**proclaims, proclaiming, proclaimed**)
announce something officially or publicly.
proclamation *noun*

prod *verb* (**prods, prodding, prodded**)
1 poke. 2 stimulate someone into action.
prod *noun*

prodigal *adjective*
wasteful or extravagant.
prodigally *adverb* **prodigality** *noun*

prodigious *adjective*
wonderful or enormous.
prodigiously *adverb*

prodigy *noun* (*plural* **prodigies**)
1 a person with wonderful abilities.
2 a wonderful thing.

produce *verb* (**produces, producing, produced**)
1 make or create something; bring something into existence. 2 bring something out so that it can be seen. 3 organize the performance of a play, making of a film, etc. 4 supervise the making of a musical recording.
producer *noun*

produce (*say* prod-yooss) *noun*
things produced, especially by farmers.

product *noun* (*plural* **products**)
1 something produced. 2 the result of multiplying two numbers. (Compare **quotient**.)

production *noun* (*plural* **productions**)
1 the process of making or creating something.
2 the amount produced ♦ *Oil production increased last year.*

productive *adjective*
producing a lot of useful things or results.
productivity *noun*

profanity(*plural* **profanities**)
words or language that show disrespect for religion.

profession *noun* (*plural* **professions**)
1 an occupation that needs special education or training, such as medicine or law. 2 a declaration♦ *they made professions of loyalty.*
[from Latin *professio* = public declaration]

professional *adjective*
1 to do with a profession. 2 doing a certain kind of work as a full-time job for payment, not as an amateur ♦ *a professional footballer.* 2 done with a high standard of skill.
professional *noun* **professionally** *adverb*

professor *noun* (*plural* **professors**)
a university lecturer of the highest rank.
professorship *noun*

profile *noun* (*plural* **profiles**)
1 a side view of a person's face. 2 a short description of a person's character or career.
keep a low profile try not to attract attention.
[from early Italian *profilare* = draw in outline]

profit *noun* (*plural* **profits**)
1 the extra money obtained by selling something for more than it cost to buy or make.
2 an advantage gained by doing something.
profitable *adjective* **profitably** *adverb*

profit *verb* (**profits, profiting, profited**)
gain an advantage or benefit from something.

profiteer *noun* (*plural* **profiteers**)
a person who makes a great profit unfairly.
profiteering *noun*

profound *adjective*
1 very deep or intense ♦ *We take a profound interest in it.* 2 showing considerable knowledge or thought ♦ *a profound remark.*
profoundly *adverb* **profundity** *noun*

prognosis (*say* prog-**noh**-sis) *noun* (*plural* **prognoses**)
a forecast or prediction, especially about a disease.
prognostication *noun*

program *noun* (*plural* **programs**)
(in computing) a series of coded instructions for a computer to carry out.

program *verb* (**programs, programming, programmed**)
put instructions into a computer by means of a program.
programmer *noun*

programme *noun* (*plural* **programmes**)
1 a list of planned events. 2 a leaflet giving details of a play, concert, match, etc. 3 a show, play, or talk etc. on radio or television.

progress (*say* **proh**-gress) *noun*
1 forward movement; an advance.
2 a development or improvement.
in progress taking place.

progress (*say* pro-**gress**) *verb* (**progresses, progressing, progressed**)
1 move forward. 2 improve.
progression *noun* **progressive** *adjective*

prohibit *verb* (**prohibits, prohibiting, prohibited**)
forbid or ban ♦ *Smoking is prohibited.*
prohibition *noun*

prohibitive *adjective*
1 prohibiting. 2 (said about prices) so high that people will not buy things.

project (*say* **proj**-ekt) *noun* (*plural* **projects**)
1 a plan or scheme. 2 the task of finding out as much as you can about something and writing about it.

project (*say* pro-**jekt**) *verb* (**projects, projecting, projected**)
1 stick out. 2 show a picture on a screen.
3 give people a particular impression ♦ *He likes to project an image of absent-minded brilliance.*
projection *noun*

projectile *noun* (*plural* **projectiles**)
a missile.

projector *noun* (*plural* **projectors**)
a machine for showing films or photographs on a screen.

prolific *adjective*
producing a lot ♦ *a prolific author.*
prolifically *adverb*

prologue (*say* proh-log) *noun* (*plural*
prologues)
an introduction to a poem or play etc.

prolong *verb* (**prolongs, prolonging,
prolonged**)
make a thing longer or make it last for a long
time.
prolongation *noun*

prom *noun* (*plural* **proms**) (*informal*)
1 a promenade. 2 a promenade concert.

promenade (*say* prom-in-ahd) *noun* (*plural*
promenades)
1 a place suitable for walking, especially beside
the seashore. 2 a leisurely walk.
promenade *verb*

promenade concert (*plural* **promenade
concerts**)
a concert where part of the audience may stand
or walk about.

prominent *adjective*
1 easily seen; conspicuous ♦ *The house stood in
a prominent position.* 2 sticking out.
3 important.
prominently *adverb* **prominence** *noun*

promiscuous *adjective*
1 having many casual sexual relationships.
2 indiscriminate.
promiscuously *adverb* **promiscuity** *noun*

promise *noun* (*plural* **promises**)
1 a statement that you will definitely do or not do
something. 2 an indication of future success or
good results ♦ *His work shows promise.*
promise *verb* (**promises, promising, promised**)
make a promise.

promote *verb* (**promotes, promoting,
promoted**)
1 move a person to a higher rank or position.
2 help the progress of something ♦ *He has done
much to promote the cause of peace.*
promoter *noun* **promotion** *noun*

prompt *adjective*
1 without delay ♦ *a prompt reply.* 2 punctual.
promptly *adverb* **promptness** *noun*
promptitude *noun*

prompt *verb* (**prompts, prompting, prompted**)
1 cause or encourage a person to do something.
2 remind an actor or speaker of words when he
or she has forgotten them.
prompter *noun*

prone *adjective*
be prone to be likely to do or suffer from
something ♦ *He is prone to jealousy.*

prong *noun* (*plural* **prongs**)
one of the spikes on a fork.
pronged *adjective*

pronoun *noun* (*plural* **pronouns**)
a word used instead of a noun. **demonstrative
pronouns** are *this that these those*;
interrogative pronouns are *who?, what?,
which?,* etc.; **personal pronouns** are *I, me, we,
us, thou, thee, you, ye, he, him, she, her, it, they,
them*; **possessive pronouns** are *mine, yours,
theirs,* etc.; **reflexive pronouns** are *myself,
yourself,* etc.; **relative pronouns** are *who, what,
which, that.*

pronounce *verb* (**pronounces, pronouncing,
pronounced**)
1 say a sound or word in a particular way
♦ *'Two' and 'too' are pronounced the same.*
2 declare something formally ♦ *I now pronounce
you man and wife.*

pronounced *adjective*
noticeable ♦ *This street has a pronounced slope.*

pronunciation *noun* (*plural* **pronunciations**)
the way a word is pronounced.

ℹ USAGE Note the spelling; this word should not
be written or spoken as 'pronounciation'.

---

proof *noun* (*plural* **proofs**)
1 a fact or thing that shows something is true.
2 a printed copy of a book or photograph etc.
made for checking before other copies are
printed.

proof *adjective*
able to resist something or not be penetrated
♦ *a bulletproof jacket.*

prop[1] *noun* (*plural* **props**)
a support, especially one made of a long piece of
wood or metal.

prop *verb* (**props, propping, propped**)
support something by leaning it against
something else.

prop[2] *noun* (*plural* **props**)
an object or piece of furniture used on a theatre
stage or in a film.

propaganda *noun*
biased or misleading publicity intended to make
people believe something.

propel *verb* (**propels, propelling, propelled**)
push something forward.

propeller *noun* (*plural* **propellers**)
a device with blades that spin round to drive an
aircraft or ship.

proper *adjective*
1 suitable or right ♦ *the proper way to hold a bat.*
2 respectable ♦ *prim and proper.* 3 (*informal*)
complete or thorough ♦ *You're a proper
nuisance!*
properly *adverb*

proper fraction *noun* (*plural* **proper
fractions**)
a fraction that is less than 1, with the numerator
less than the denominator, e.g. $\frac{3}{5}$.

proper noun *noun* (*plural* **proper nouns**)
the name of an individual person or thing, e.g.
Mary, London, Spain, usually written with a
capital first letter.

property *noun* (*plural* **properties**)
1 a thing or things that belong to somebody.
2 a building or someone's land. 3 a quality or
characteristic ♦ *It has the property of becoming
soft when heated.*

prophecy *noun* (*plural* **prophecies**)
1 a statement that prophesies something.
2 the action of prophesying.

prophesy *verb* (**prophesies, prophesying,
prophesied**)
say what will happen in the future; foretell.

prophet *noun* (*plural* **prophets**)
1 a person who makes prophecies. 2 a religious
teacher who is believed to be inspired by God.
prophetess *noun* **prophetic** *adjective*
the Prophet Muhammad, who founded the
Muslim faith.

proportion *noun* (*plural* **proportions**)
1 a part or share of a whole thing. 2 a ratio.
3 the correct relationship in size, amount, or
importance between two things ♦ *You've drawn
his head out of proportion.*
proportional *adjective* **proportionally** *adverb*
proportionate *adjective*
proportions *plural noun* size ♦ *a ship of large
proportions.*

proportional representation *noun*
a system in which each political party has a
number of Members of Parliament in proportion
to the number of votes for all its candidates.

proposal *noun* (*plural* **proposals**)
1 something that is proposed; a formal
suggestion. 2 an offer of marriage.

propose *verb* (**proposes, proposing,
proposed**)
1 suggest an idea or plan etc. 2 plan or intend to
do something. 3 ask a person to marry you.

proposition *noun* (*plural* **propositions**)
1 a suggestion or offer. 2 a statement.
3 (*informal*) an undertaking or problem
♦ *a difficult proposition.*

proprietor *noun* (*plural* **proprietors**)
the owner of a shop or business.
proprietress *noun*

prosaic *adjective*
plain or dull and ordinary.
prosaically *adverb*

prose *noun*
writing or speech that is not in verse.

prosecute *verb* (**prosecutes, prosecuting,
prosecuted**)
1 make someone go to a lawcourt to be tried for
a crime. 2 continue with something; pursue
♦ *prosecuting their trade.*
prosecution *noun* **prosecutor** *noun*

prospect *noun* (*plural* **prospects**)
1 a possibility or expectation of something
♦ *There is no prospect of success.* 2 a wide view.

prospect (*say* pro-**spekt**) *verb* (**prospects,
prospecting, prospected**)
explore in search of gold or some other mineral.
prospector *noun*

prospective *adjective*
expected to be or to happen; possible
♦ *prospective customers.*

prospectus *noun* (*plural* **prospectuses**)
a booklet describing and advertising a school,
business company, etc.

prosperous *adjective*
successful or rich.
prosperity *noun*

prostitute *noun* (*plural* **prostitutes**)
a person who takes part in sexual acts for
payment.
prostitution *noun*

protect *verb* (**protects, protecting, protected**)
keep safe from harm or injury.
protection *noun* **protective** *adjective* **protector**
noun

protein *noun* (*plural* **proteins**)
a substance that is found in all living things and
is an essential part of the food of animals.

protest (*say* proh-test) *noun* (*plural* **protests**)
a statement or action showing that you
disapprove of something.

protest (*say* pro-test) *verb* (**protests,
protesting, protested**)
1 make a protest. 2 declare firmly ♦ *They
protested their innocence.*
protestation *noun*

Protestant *noun* (*plural* **Protestants**)
a member of any of the western Christian
Churches that are separate from the Roman
Catholic Church.

proton *noun* (*plural* **protons**)
a particle of matter with a positive electric
charge.

prototype *noun* (*plural* **prototypes**)
the first model of something, from which others
are copied or developed.

protractor *noun* (*plural* **protractors**)
a device for measuring angles, usually a
semicircle marked off in degrees.

protrude *verb* (**protrudes, protruding,
protruded**)
stick out from a surface.

proud *adjective*
1 very pleased with yourself or with someone
else who has done well ♦ *We are all so proud of
you.* 2 causing pride ♦ *This is a proud moment
for us.* 3 full of self-respect and independence
♦ *They were too proud to ask for help.* 4 having
too high an opinion of yourself.
proudly *adverb*
[via Old English from old French *prud* = brave]

prove *verb* (proves, proving, proved)
1 show that something is true. 2 turn out
♦ *The forecast proved to be correct.*
provable *adjective*

proverb *noun* (*plural* proverbs)
a short well-known saying that states a truth,
e.g. 'Many hands make light work'.

proverbial *adjective*
1 referred to in a proverb. 2 well-known.

provide *verb* (provides, providing, provided)
1 make something available; supply. 2 prepare
for something ♦ *Try to provide for emergencies.*
provider *noun*

provided *conjunction*
on condition ♦ *You can stay provided that you
help.*

providing *conjunction*
provided.

province *noun* (*plural* provinces)
1 a section of a country. 2 the area of a person's
special knowledge or responsibility ♦ *I'm afraid
carpentry is not my province.*
provincial *adjective*
the provinces the parts of a country outside its
capital city.

provision *noun* (*plural* provisions)
1 providing something. 2 a statement in a
document ♦ *the provisions of the treaty.*

provisional *adjective*
arranged or agreed upon temporarily but
possibly to be altered later.
provisionally *adverb*

provisions *plural noun*
supplies of food and drink.

provoke *verb* (provokes, provoking,
provoked)
1 make a person angry. 2 cause or give rise to
something ♦ *The joke provoked laughter.*
provocation *noun* **provocative** *adjective*

prow *noun* (*plural* prows)
the front end of a ship.

prowl *verb* (prowls, prowling, prowled)
move about quietly or cautiously, like a hunter.
prowl *noun* **prowler** *noun*

proxy *noun* (*plural* proxies)
a person authorized to represent or act for
another person ♦ *I will be abroad, so I have
arranged to vote by proxy.*

prude *noun* (*plural* prudes)
a person who is easily shocked.
prudish *adjective* **prudery** *noun*

prudent *adjective*
careful, not rash or reckless.
prudently *adverb* **prudence** *noun* **prudential**
adjective

prune¹ *noun* (*plural* prunes)
a dried plum.

prune² *verb* (prunes, pruning, pruned)
cut off unwanted parts of a tree or bush etc.

pry *verb* (pries, prying, pried)
look into or ask about someone else's private
business.

PS *abbreviation*
postscript.

psalm (*say* sahm) *noun* (*plural* psalms)
a religious song, especially one from the Book of
Psalms in the Bible.
psalmist *noun*

pseudonym *noun* (*plural* pseudonyms)
a false name used by an author.

psychiatrist (*say* sy-ky-a-trist) *noun* (*plural*
psychiatrists)
a doctor who treats mental illnesses.
psychiatry *noun* **psychiatric** *adjective*

psychic (*say* sy-kik) *adjective*
1 supernatural. 2 having supernatural powers,
especially being able to predict the future. 3 to do
with the mind or soul.
psychical *adjective*

psychoanalysis *noun*
investigation of a person's mental processes,
especially in the treatment of mental illness.
psychoanalyst *noun*

psychology *noun*
the study of the mind and how it works.
psychological *adjective* **psychologist** *noun*

PT *abbreviation*
physical training.

pterodactyl (*say* te-ro-dak-til) *noun* (*plural*
pterodactyls)
an extinct flying reptile.

PTO *abbreviation*
please turn over.

pub *noun* (*plural* pubs)
a building licensed to serve alcoholic drinks to
the public.

puberty (*say* pew-ber-tee) *noun*
the time when a young person is developing
physically into an adult.

public *adjective*
belonging to or known by everyone, not private.
publicly *adverb*

public *noun*
people in general.
in public openly, not in private.

publication *noun* (*plural* publications)
1 publishing. 2 a published book or newspaper
etc.

public house *noun* (*plural* public houses)
(*formal*) a pub.

publicity *noun*
public attention; doing things (e.g. advertising)
to draw people's attention to something.

public school noun (plural **public schools**)
1 a secondary school that charges fees. **2** (in Scotland and the USA) a school run by a local authority or by the state.

publish verb (**publishes, publishing, published**)
1 have something printed and sold to the public. **2** announce something in public.
publisher noun

pucker verb (**puckers, puckering, puckered**)
wrinkle.

pudding noun (plural **puddings**)
1 a cooked sweet food eaten at the end of a meal. **2** the sweet course of a meal. **3** a savoury food made with suet and flour.

puddle noun (plural **puddles**)
a shallow patch of liquid, especially of rainwater on a road.

puff noun (plural **puffs**)
1 a short blowing of breath, wind, or smoke etc. **2** a soft pad for putting powder on the skin. **3** a cake of very light pastry filled with cream.

puff verb (**puffs, puffing, puffed**)
1 blow out puffs of smoke etc. **2** breathe with difficulty; pant. **3** inflate or swell something
♦ *He puffed out his chest.*

puffy adjective
puffed out; swollen.
puffiness noun

pugnacious adjective
wanting to fight; aggressive.
pugnaciously adverb **pugnacity** noun

puke verb (**pukes, puking, puked**) (informal)
vomit.

pull verb (**pulls, pulling, pulled**)
1 make a thing come towards or after you by using force on it. **2** move by a driving force
♦ *The car pulled out into the road.*
pull noun
pull a face make a strange face. **pull in 1** (said about a vehicle) move to the side of the road and stop. **2** (said about a train) come to a station and stop. **pull somebody's leg** tease him or her. **pull off** achieve something. **pull through** recover from an illness. **pull up** (said about a vehicle) stop abruptly. **pull yourself together** become calm or sensible.

pulley noun (plural **pulleys**)
a wheel with a rope, chain, or belt over it, used for lifting or moving heavy things.

pullover noun (plural **pullovers**)
a knitted piece of clothing for the top half of the body.

pulp noun
1 the soft moist part of fruit. **2** any soft moist mass.
pulpy adjective

pulpit noun (plural **pulpits**)
a small enclosed platform for the preacher in a church or chapel.

pulsate verb (**pulsates, pulsating, pulsated**)
expand and contract rhythmically; vibrate.
pulsation noun

pulse[1] noun (plural **pulses**)
1 the rhythmical movement of the arteries as blood is pumped through them by the beating of the heart ♦ *The pulse can be felt in a person's wrists.* **2** a throb.
pulse verb (**pulses, pulsing, pulsed**)
throb or pulsate.

pulse[2] noun (plural **pulses**)
the edible seed of peas, beans, lentils, etc.

pulverize verb (**pulverizes, pulverizing, pulverized**)
crush something into powder.
pulverization noun

puma noun (plural **pumas**)
a large brown animal of western America; a mountain lion.
[via Spanish from Quechua (a South American language)]

pump[1] noun (plural **pumps**)
a device that pushes air or liquid into or out of something, or along pipes.
pump verb (**pumps, pumping, pumped**)
1 move air or liquid with a pump. **2** (informal) question a person to obtain information.
pump up inflate.

pump[2] noun (plural **pumps**)
a canvas sports shoe with a rubber sole.

pumpkin noun (plural **pumpkins**)
a very large round fruit with a hard orange skin.
[from Greek *pepon*, a kind of large melon]

pun noun (plural **puns**)
a joking use of a word sounding the same as another, e.g. 'Deciding where to bury him was a grave decision'.

punch[1] verb (**punches, punching, punched**)
1 hit someone with your fist. **2** make a hole in something.
punch noun (plural **punches**)
1 a hit with a fist. **2** a device for making holes in paper, metal, leather, etc. **3** vigour.

punch[2] noun
a drink made by mixing wine or spirits and fruit juice in a bowl.

punchline noun (plural **punchlines**)
words that give the climax of a joke or story.

punctual adjective
doing things exactly at the time arranged; not late.
punctually adverb **punctuality** noun

punctuate verb (**punctuates, punctuating, punctuated**)
1 put punctuation marks into something. **2** put something in at intervals ♦ *His speech was punctuated with cheers.*

punctuation *noun*
marks such as commas, full stops, and brackets put into a piece of writing to make it easier to read.

puncture *noun* (*plural* **punctures**)
a small hole made by something sharp, especially in a tyre.

puncture *verb* (**punctures, puncturing, punctured**)
make a puncture in something.

pungent (*say* pun-jent) *adjective*
1 having a strong taste or smell. 2 (said about remarks) sharp.
pungently *adverb* **pungency** *noun*

punish *verb* (**punishes, punishing, punished**)
make a person suffer because he or she has done something wrong.
punishable *adjective* **punishment** *noun*

punk *noun* (*plural* **punks**)
1 (also **punk rock**) a loud aggressive style of rock music. 2 a person who likes this music.

punt[1] *noun* (*plural* **punts**)
a flat-bottomed boat, usually moved by pushing a pole against the bottom of a river while standing in the punt.

punt *verb* (**punts, punting, punted**)
move a punt with a pole.

punt[2] *verb* (**punts, punting, punted**)
kick a football after dropping it from your hands and before it touches the ground.

pupa (*say* pew-pa) *noun* (*plural* **pupae**)
a chrysalis.

pupil *noun* (*plural* **pupils**)
1 someone who is being taught by a teacher, especially at school. 2 the opening in the centre of the eye.

puppet *noun* (*plural* **puppets**)
1 a kind of doll that can be made to move by fitting it over your hand or working it by strings or wires. 2 a person whose actions are controlled by someone else.
puppetry *noun*

puppy *noun* (*plural* **puppies**)
a young dog.

purchase *verb* (**purchases, purchasing, purchased**)
buy.
purchaser *noun*

purchase *noun* (*plural* **purchases**)
1 something bought. 2 buying. 3 a firm hold or grip.

pure *adjective*
1 not mixed with anything else ♦ *pure olive oil*. 2 clean or clear ♦ *pure spring water*. 3 free from evil or sin. 4 mere; nothing but ♦ *pure nonsense*.
purely *adverb* **pureness** *noun* **purity** *noun*

purée (*say* pewr-ay) *noun* (*plural* **purées**)
fruit or vegetables made into pulp.

purge *verb* (**purges, purging, purged**)
get rid of unwanted people or things.
purge *noun*

purify *verb* (**purifies, purifying, purified**)
make a thing pure.
purification *noun* **purifier** *noun*

Puritan *noun* (*plural* **Puritans**)
a Protestant in the 16th and 17th centuries who wanted simpler religious ceremonies and strictly moral behaviour.

purple *noun*
a deep reddish-blue colour.

purpose *noun* (*plural* **purposes**)
1 what you intend to do; a plan or aim. 2 determination ♦ *walk with purpose*.
purposeful *adjective* **purposefully** *adverb*
on purpose by intention, not by accident.

purr *verb* (**purrs, purring, purred**)
make the low murmuring sound that a cat does when it is pleased.
purr *noun*

purse *noun* (*plural* **purses**)
a small pouch for carrying money.

purse *verb* (**purses, pursing, pursed**)
purse your lips draw them tightly together because you are annoyed or frustrated.

pursue *verb* (**pursues, pursuing, pursued**)
1 chase someone in order to catch them. 2 continue with something; work at ♦ *We are pursuing our enquiries*.
pursuer *noun*

pursuit *noun* (*plural* **pursuits**)
1 pursuing. 2 a regular activity.

pus *noun*
a thick yellowish substance produced in inflamed or infected tissue, e.g. in an abscess or boil.

push *verb* (**pushes, pushing, pushed**)
1 make a thing go away from you by using force on it. 2 move yourself by using force ♦ *He pushed in front of me.* 3 try to force someone to do or use something; urge.
push off (*informal*) go away.

push *noun* (*plural* **pushes**)
a pushing movement or effort.
at a push if necessary but only with difficulty.
get the push (*informal*) be dismissed from a job.

pushchair *noun* (*plural* **pushchairs**)
a folding chair on wheels, for pushing a young child along.

pusher *noun* (*plural* **pushers**)
a person who sells illegal drugs.

pushy *adjective*
unpleasantly self-confident and eager to do things.

puss *noun* (*informal*)
a cat.

put *verb* (**puts, putting, put**)
1 move a person or thing to a place or position
♦ *Put the lamp on the table.* **2** make a person
or thing do or experience something or be
in a certain condition ♦ *Put the light on.*
♦ *The news put me in a good mood.* **3** express
in words ♦ *She put it tactfully.*
be hard put have difficulty in doing something.
put off 1 postpone. **2** dissuade. **3** stop someone
wanting something ♦ *The smell puts me off.*
put out 1 stop a fire from burning or a light
from shining. **2** annoy or inconvenience ♦ *Our
lateness has put her out.* **put up 1** construct or
build. **2** raise. **3** give someone a place to sleep
♦ *Can you put me up for the night?* **put up with**
endure or tolerate.

putt *verb* (**putts, putting, putted**)
hit a golf ball gently towards the hole.
putt *noun* **putter** *noun* **putting green** *noun*

putty *noun*
a soft paste that sets hard, used for fitting the
glass into a window frame.

puzzle *noun* (*plural* **puzzles**)
1 a difficult question or problem. **2** a game or toy
that sets a problem to solve or a difficult task to
complete. **3** a jigsaw puzzle.

puzzle *verb* (**puzzles, puzzling, puzzled**)
1 give someone a problem so that they have to
think hard. **2** think patiently about how to solve
something.
puzzlement *noun*

pygmy (*say* pig-mee) *noun* (*plural* **pygmies**)
1 a very small person or thing. **2** a member of
certain unusually short peoples in parts of
Africa.

pyjamas *plural noun*
a loose jacket and trousers worn in bed.
[from Persian or Urdu *pay* = leg + *jamah*
= clothing]

pylon *noun* (*plural* **pylons**)
a tall framework made of strips of steel,
supporting electric cables.
[from Greek, = monumental gateway, which a
modern pylon resembles in shape]

pyramid *noun* (*plural* **pyramids**)
1 a structure with a square base and with sloping
sides that meet in a point at the top. **2** an ancient
Egyptian tomb shaped like this.
pyramidal (*say* pir-am-id-al) *adjective*

python *noun* (*plural* **pythons**)
a large snake that kills its prey by coiling round
and crushing it.
[from the name of a large serpent or monster in
Greek legend, killed by Apollo]

Qq

QC *abbreviation*
Queen's Counsel.

QED *abbreviation*
quod erat demonstrandum (Latin, = which was
the thing that had to be proved).

quack[1] *verb* (**quacks, quacking, quacked**)
make the harsh cry of a duck.
quack *noun*
[imitating the sound]

quack[2] *noun* (*plural* **quacks**)
a person who falsely claims to have medical skill
or have remedies to cure diseases.
[from Dutch *quacken* = to boast]

quadratic equation *noun* (*plural* **quadratic
equations**)
an equation that involves quantities or variables
raised to the power of two, but no higher than
two.

quadrilateral *noun* (*plural* **quadrilaterals**)
a flat geometric shape with four sides.

quadruped *noun* (*plural* **quadrupeds**)
an animal with four feet.

quagmire (*say* kwog-mire) *noun* (*plural*
quagmires)
a bog or marsh.

quail[1] *noun* (*plural* **quail** or **quails**)
a bird related to the partridge.

quail[2] *verb* (**quails, quailing, quailed**)
feel or show fear.

quaint *adjective*
attractively odd or old-fashioned.
quaintly *adverb* **quaintness** *noun*

quake *verb* (**quakes, quaking, quaked**)
tremble; shake with fear.

Quaker *noun* (*plural* **Quakers**)
a member of a religious group called the Society
of Friends, founded by George Fox in the 17th
century.
[originally an insult, probably from George Fox's
saying that people should 'tremble at the name of
the Lord']

qualification *noun* (*plural* **qualifications**)
1 a skill or ability that makes someone suitable
for a job. **2** an exam that you have passed or a
course of study that you have completed.
3 something that qualifies a remark or
statement.

qualify *verb* (**qualifies, qualifying, qualified**)
1 make or become able to do something through
having certain qualities or training, or by passing
an exam. **2** make a remark or statement less
extreme; limit its meaning. **3** (in grammar, said
about an adjective) add meaning to a noun.

quality *noun* (*plural* **qualities**)
1 how good or bad something is.
2 a characteristic; something that is special in a person or thing.

qualm (*say* kwahm) *noun* (*plural* **qualms**)
a misgiving or scruple.

quandary *noun* (*plural* **quandaries**)
a difficult situation where you are uncertain what to do.

quantity *noun* (*plural* **quantities**)
1 how much there is of something; how many things there are of one sort. **2** a large amount.

quantum leap or **quantum jump** *noun*
(*plural* **quantum leaps** or **quantum jumps**)
a sudden large increase or advance.

quarantine *noun*
keeping a person or animal isolated in case they have a disease which could spread to others.
[from Italian *quaranta* = forty (because the original period of isolation was 40 days)]

quarrel *noun* (*plural* **quarrels**)
an angry disagreement.

quarrel *verb* (**quarrels, quarrelling, quarrelled**)
have a quarrel.
quarrelsome *adjective*

quarry¹ *noun* (*plural* **quarries**)
an open place where stone or slate is dug or cut out of the ground.

quarry *verb* (**quarries, quarrying, quarried**)
dig or cut from a quarry.

quarry² *noun* (*plural* **quarries**)
an animal etc. being hunted or pursued.

quart *noun* (*plural* **quarts**)
two pints, a quarter of a gallon.

quarter *noun* (*plural* **quarters**)
1 each of four equal parts into which a thing is or can be divided. **2** three months, one-fourth of a year. **3** a district or region ♦ *People came from every quarter.*
at close quarters very close together. **give no quarter** show no mercy.

quarter *verb* (**quarters, quartering, quartered**)
1 divide something into quarters. **2** put soldiers etc. into lodgings.

quarter-final *noun* (*plural* **quarter-finals**)
each of the matches or rounds before a semi-final, in which there are eight contestants or teams.

quarters *plural noun*
lodgings.

quartet *noun* (*plural* **quartets**)
1 a group of four musicians. **2** a piece of music for four musicians. **3** a set of four people or things.

quartz *noun*
a hard mineral, often in crystal form.
[via German from a Polish dialect word *kwardy* = hard]

quaver *verb* (**quavers, quavering, quavered**)
tremble or quiver.

quaver *noun* (*plural* **quavers**)
1 a quavering sound. **2** a note in music (♪) lasting half as long as a crotchet.

quay (*say* kee) *noun* (*plural* **quays**)
a landing place where ships can be tied up for loading and unloading; a wharf.
quayside *noun*

queasy *adjective*
feeling slightly sick.
queasily *adverb* **queasiness** *noun*

queen *noun* (*plural* **queens**)
1 a woman who is the ruler of a country through inheriting the position. **2** the wife of a king.
3 a female bee or ant that produces eggs.
4 an important piece in chess. **5** a playing card with a picture of a queen on it.
queenly *adjective*
[from Old English]

Queen's Counsel *noun* (*plural* **Queen's Counsels**)
a senior barrister.

queer *adjective*
1 strange or eccentric. **2** slightly ill or faint.
queerly *adverb* **queerness** *noun*

queer *verb* (**queers, queering, queered**)
queer a person's pitch spoil his or her chances beforehand.
[perhaps from German *quer* = perverse]

quell *verb* (**quells, quelling, quelled**)
1 crush a rebellion. **2** stop yourself from feeling fear, anger etc.; suppress.

quench *verb* (**quenches, quenching, quenched**)
1 satisfy your thirst by drinking. **2** put out a fire or flame.

query (*say* kweer-ee) *noun* (*plural* **queries**)
1 a question. **2** a question mark.

query *verb* (**queries, querying, queried**)
question whether something is true or correct.
[from Latin *quaere* = ask!]

quest *noun* (*plural* **quests**)
a long search for something ♦ *the quest for gold.*

question *noun* (*plural* **questions**)
1 a sentence asking something. **2** a problem to be discussed or solved ♦ *Parliament debated the question of education.* **3** doubt ♦ *Whether we shall win is open to question.*
in question being discussed or disputed
♦ *His honesty is not in question.* **out of the question** impossible.

question *verb* (**questions, questioning, questioned**)
1 ask someone questions. **2** say that you are doubtful about something.
questioner *noun*

questionable *adjective*
causing doubt; not certainly true or honest or
advisable.

question mark *noun* (*plural* **question marks**)
the punctuation mark ? placed after a question.

questionnaire *noun* (*plural* **questionnaires**)
a written set of questions asked to provide
information for a survey.

queue (*say* kew) *noun* (*plural* **queues**)
a line of people or vehicles waiting for
something.

queue *verb* (**queues, queueing, queued**)
wait in a queue.
[via French from Latin *cauda* = tail. *Queue*
originally meant an animal's tail as a term in
heraldry]

quibble *noun* (*plural* **quibbles**)
a trivial complaint or objection.

quibble *verb* (**quibbles, quibbling, quibbled**)
make trivial complaints or objections.

quick *adjective*
1 taking only a short time to do something.
2 done in a short time. 3 able to notice or learn
or think quickly. 4 (*old use*) alive ♦ *the quick
and the dead.*
quickly *adverb* **quickness** *noun*

quicksand *noun* (*plural* **quicksands**)
an area of loose wet deep sand that sucks in
anything resting or falling on top of it.
[from *quick* in the old sense 'alive' (because the
sand moves as if it were alive and 'eats' things)]

quid *noun* (*plural* **quid**) (*informal*)
£1.

quiet *adjective*
1 silent ♦ *Be quiet!* 2 with little sound; not loud
or noisy. 3 calm and peaceful; without
disturbance ♦ *a quiet life.* 4 (said about colours)
not bright.
quietly *adverb* **quietness** *noun*

quiet *noun*
quietness.

quieten *verb* (**quietens, quietening,
quietened**)
make or become quiet.

quill *noun* (*plural* **quills**)
1 a large feather. 2 a pen made from a large
feather. 3 one of the spines on a hedgehog.

quilt *noun* (*plural* **quilts**)
a padded bedcover.
[from Latin *culcita* = mattress or cushion]

quintet *noun* (*plural* **quintets**)
1 a group of five musicians. 2 a piece of music
for five musicians.

quirk *noun* (*plural* **quirks**)
1 a peculiarity of a person's behaviour.
2 a trick of fate.
quirky *adjective*

quit *verb* (**quits, quitting, quitted** or **quit**)
1 leave or abandon. 2 (*informal*) stop doing
something.
quitter *noun*

quite *adverb*
1 completely or entirely ♦ *I am quite all right.*
2 somewhat; to some extent ♦ *She is quite a good
swimmer.* 3 really ♦ *It's quite a change.*

quits *adjective*
even or equal after retaliating or paying someone
back ♦ *I think you and I are quits now.*

quiver¹ *noun* (*plural* **quivers**)
a container for arrows.

quiver² *verb* (**quivers, quivering, quivered**)
tremble.
quiver *noun*

quiz *noun* (*plural* **quizzes**)
a series of questions, especially as an
entertainment or competition.

quiz *verb* (**quizzes, quizzing, quizzed**)
question someone closely.

quoit (*say* koit) *noun* (*plural* **quoits**)
a ring thrown at a peg in the game of **quoits**.

quota *noun* (*plural* **quotas**)
1 a fixed share that must be given or received or
done. 2 a limited amount.

quotation *noun* (*plural* **quotations**)
1 quoting. 2 something quoted. 3 a statement of
the price of goods or services that can be
supplied.

quotation marks *plural noun*
inverted commas, used to mark a quotation.

quote *verb* (**quotes, quoting, quoted**)
1 repeat words that were first written or spoken
by someone else. 2 mention something as proof.
3 state the price of goods or services that you can
supply.

quote *noun* (*plural* **quotes**)
a quotation.

quotient (*say* kwoh-shent) *noun* (*plural*
quotients)
the result of dividing one number by another.
(Compare **product**.)
[from Latin *quotiens* = how many times?]

Rr

rabbi (*say* rab-I) *noun* (*plural* **rabbis**)
a Jewish religious leader.

rabbit *noun* (*plural* **rabbits**)
a furry animal with long ears that digs burrows.

rabble *noun* (*plural* **rabbles**)
a disorderly crowd or mob.

rabid (*say* **rab**-id) *adjective*
1 fanatical ♦ *a rabid tennis fan.* **2** suffering from rabies.

rabies (*say* **ray**-beez) *noun*
a fatal disease that affects dogs, cats, etc. and can be passed to humans by the bite of an infected animal.

race¹ *noun* (*plural* **races**)
1 a competition to be the first to reach a particular place or to do something. **2** a strong fast current of water ♦ *the tidal race.*
race *verb* (**races, racing, raced**)
1 compete in a race. **2** move very fast.
racer *noun*
[from Old Norse]

race² *noun* (*plural* **races**)
a very large group of people thought to have the same ancestors and with physical characteristics (e.g. colour of skin and hair, shape of eyes and nose) that differ from those of other groups.
racial *adjective*
[via French from Italian *razza*]

racehorse *noun* (*plural* **racehorses**)
a horse bred or kept for racing.

racetrack *noun* (*plural* **racetracks**)
a track for horse or vehicle races.

racism (*say* **ray**-sizm) *noun*
1 belief that a particular race of people is better than others. **2** discrimination against or hostility towards people of other races.
racist *noun*

rack¹ *noun* (*plural* **racks**)
1 a framework used as a shelf or container.
2 a bar or rail with cogs into which the cogs of a gear or wheel etc. fit. **3** an ancient device for torturing people by stretching them.
rack *verb* (**racks, racking, racked**)
torment ♦ *He was racked with guilt.*
rack your brains think hard in trying to solve a problem.

rack² *noun*
go to rack and ruin gradually become worse in condition from neglect.
[a different spelling of *wreck*]

racket¹ *noun* (*plural* **rackets**)
a bat with strings stretched across a frame, used in tennis, badminton, and squash.
[from Arabic *rahat* = palm of the hand]

racket² *noun* (*plural* **rackets**)
1 a loud noise; a din. **2** a dishonest or illegal business ♦ *a drugs racket.*
[perhaps imitating the sound of clattering]

racy *adjective* (**racier, raciest**)
lively and slightly shocking in style ♦ *She gave a racy account of her travels.*

radar *noun*
a system or apparatus that uses radio waves to show on a screen etc. the position of objects that cannot be seen because of darkness, fog, distance, etc.

radiant *adjective*
1 radiating light or heat etc. **2** radiated ♦ *radiant heat.* **3** looking very bright and happy.
radiantly *adverb* **radiance** *noun*

radiate *verb* (**radiates, radiating, radiated**)
1 send out light, heat, or other energy in rays. **2** give out a strong feeling or quality ♦ *She radiated confidence.* **3** spread out from a central point like the spokes of a wheel.

radiation *noun*
1 light, heat, or other energy radiated.
2 the energy or particles sent out by a radioactive substance. **3** the process of radiating.

radiator *noun* (*plural* **radiators**)
1 a device that gives out heat, especially a metal case that is heated electrically or through which steam or hot water flows. **2** a device that cools the engine of a motor vehicle.

radical *adjective*
1 basic and thorough ♦ *radical changes.*
2 wanting to make great reforms ♦ *a radical politician.*
radically *adverb*
radical *noun* (*plural* **radicals**)
a person who wants to make great reforms.

radio *noun* (*plural* **radios**)
1 the process of sending and receiving sound or pictures by means of electromagnetic waves.
2 an apparatus for receiving sound (a **receiver**) or sending it out (a **transmitter**) in this way.
3 sound broadcasting.
[from Latin *radius* = a spoke or ray]

radioactive *adjective*
having atoms that break up spontaneously and send out radiation which produces electrical and chemical effects and penetrates things.
radioactivity *noun*

radiocarbon dating *noun*
the use of a kind of radioactive carbon that decays at a steady rate, to find out how old something is.

radio telescope *noun* (*plural* **radio telescopes**)
an instrument that can detect radio waves from space.

radiotherapy *noun*
the use of radioactive substances in treating diseases such as cancer.

radish *noun* (*plural* **radishes**)
a small hard round red vegetable, eaten raw in salads.

radium *noun*
a radioactive metal, often used in radiotherapy.
[from Latin *radius* = a spoke or ray]

radius *noun* (*plural* **radii** or **radiuses**)
1 a straight line from the centre of a circle or
sphere to the circumference; the length of this
line. 2 a range or distance from a central point
♦ *The school takes pupils living within a radius
of ten kilometres.*

radon *noun*
a radioactive gas used in radiotherapy.

raffle *noun* (*plural* **raffles**)
a kind of lottery, usually to raise money for a
charity.

raffle *verb* (**raffles, raffling, raffled**)
offer something as a prize in a raffle.

raft *noun* (*plural* **rafts**)
a flat floating structure made of wood etc., used
as a boat.

rafter *noun* (*plural* **rafters**)
any of the long sloping pieces of wood that hold
up a roof.

rag¹ *noun* (*plural* **rags**)
1 an old or torn piece of cloth. 2 a piece of
ragtime music.

rag² *noun* (*plural* **rags**)
a series of entertainments and activities held by
students to collect money for charity.

rag *verb* (**rags, ragging, ragged**) (*slang*)
tease.

rage *noun* (*plural* **rages**)
great or violent anger.
all the rage very popular or fashionable for a
time.

rage *verb* (**rages, raging, raged**)
1 be very angry. 2 continue violently or with
great force ♦ *A storm was raging.*

ragged *adjective*
1 torn or frayed. 2 wearing torn clothes.
3 irregular or uneven ♦ *a ragged performance.*
[from Old Norse *roggvathr* = tufted]

raid *noun* (*plural* **raids**)
1 a sudden attack. 2 a surprise visit by police etc.
to arrest people or seize illegal goods.

raid *verb* (**raids, raiding, raided**)
make a raid on a place.
raider *noun*

rail¹ *noun* (*plural* **rails**)
1 a level or sloping bar for hanging things on or
forming part of a fence, banisters, etc. 2 a long
metal bar forming part of a railway track.
by rail on a train.
[from old French; related to *rule*]

rail² *verb* (**rails, railing, railed**)
protest angrily or bitterly.
[via French from Latin *rugire* = to bellow]

railings *plural noun*
a fence made of metal bars.

railway *noun*
1 the parallel metal bars that trains travel on.
2 (*plural* **railways**) a system of transport using
rails.

rain *noun*
drops of water that fall from the sky.
rainy *adjective*

rain *verb* (**rains, raining, rained**)
1 fall as rain or like rain. 2 send down like rain
♦ *They rained blows on him.*

rainbow *noun* (*plural* **rainbows**)
an arch of all the colours of the spectrum formed
in the sky when the sun shines through rain.

rainfall *noun*
the amount of rain that falls in a particular place
or time.

rainforest *noun* (*plural* **rainforests**)
a dense tropical forest in an area of very heavy
rainfall.

raise *verb* (**raises, raising, raised**)
1 move something to a higher place or an upright
position. 2 increase the amount or level of
something ♦ *We are trying to raise standards.*
3 collect; manage to obtain ♦ *They raised £100
for charity.* 4 bring up young children or animals
♦ *She had to raise her family alone.* 5 rouse or
cause ♦ *He raised a laugh with his joke.* 6 put
forward ♦ *We raised objections.* 7 end a siege.
[from Old Norse]

raisin *noun* (*plural* **raisins**)
a dried grape.
[from French, = grape]

rake *noun* (*plural* **rakes**)
a gardening tool with a row of short spikes fixed
to a long handle.

rake *verb* (**rakes, raking, raked**)
1 gather or smooth with a rake. 2 search.
rake up 1 collect. 2 remind people of an
old scandal etc. that would be best forgotten
♦ *Don't rake that up.*

rally *noun* (*plural* **rallies**)
1 a large meeting to support something or share
an interest. 2 a competition to test skill in driving
♦ *the Monte Carlo Rally.* 3 a series of strokes in
tennis before a point is scored. 4 a recovery.

rally *verb* (**rallies, rallying, rallied**)
1 bring or come together for a united effort
♦ *They rallied support.* ♦ *People rallied round.*
2 revive; recover strength.

RAM *abbreviation*
(in computing) random-access memory, with
contents that can be retrieved or stored directly
without having to read through items already
stored.

ram *noun* (*plural* **rams**)
1 a male sheep. 2 a device for ramming things.

ram *verb* (**rams, ramming, rammed**)
push one thing hard against another.

Ramadan *noun*
the ninth month of the Muslim year, when Muslims do not eat or drink between sunrise and sunset.
[Arabic, from *ramida* = to be parched]

ramble *noun* (*plural* **rambles**)
a long walk in the country.

ramble *verb* (**rambles, rambling, rambled**)
1 go for a ramble; wander. **2** talk or write a lot without keeping to the subject.
rambler *noun*

ramifications *plural noun*
1 the branches of a structure. **2** the many effects of a plan or action.

ramp *noun* (*plural* **ramps**)
a slope joining two different levels.
[from French *ramper* = to climb]

rampage *verb* (**rampages, rampaging, rampaged**)
rush about wildly or destructively.
on the rampage rampaging.

rampant *adjective*
1 growing or spreading uncontrollably ♦ *Disease was rampant in the poorer districts.* **2** (said about an animal on coats of arms) standing upright on a hind leg ♦ *a lion rampant.*

rampart *noun* (*plural* **ramparts**)
a wide bank of earth built as a fortification or a wall on top of this.

ramshackle *adjective*
badly made and rickety ♦ *a ramshackle hut.*

ranch *noun* (*plural* **ranches**)
a large cattle farm in America.

rancid *adjective*
smelling or tasting unpleasant like stale fat.

random *noun*
at random using no particular order or method ♦ *numbers chosen at random.*

random *adjective*
done or taken at random ♦ *a random sample.*

range *noun* (*plural* **ranges**)
1 a set of different things of the same type ♦ *a wide range of backgrounds*; ♦ *a lovely range of colours.* **2** the limits between which things exist or are available; an extent ♦ *the age range 15 to 18.* **3** the distance that a gun can shoot, an aircraft can travel, a sound can be heard, etc. **4** a place with targets for shooting practice. **5** a line or series of mountains or hills. **6** a large open area of grazing land or hunting ground. **7** a kitchen fireplace with ovens.

range *verb* (**ranges, ranging, ranged**)
1 exist between two limits; extend ♦ *Prices ranged from £1 to £50.* **2** arrange. **3** move over a wide area; wander.

ranger *noun* (*plural* **rangers**)
someone who looks after or patrols a park, forest, etc.

rank¹ *noun* (*plural* **ranks**)
1 a line of people or things. **2** a place where taxis stand to await customers. **3** a position in a series of different levels ♦ *He holds the rank of sergeant.*

rank *verb* (**ranks, ranking, ranked**)
1 put things in order according to their rank. **2** have a certain rank or place ♦ *She ranks among the greatest novelists.*

rank² *adjective* (**ranker, rankest**)
1 growing too thickly and coarsely. **2** smelling very unpleasant. **3** unmistakably bad ♦ *rank injustice.*
rankly *adverb* **rankness** *noun*

rank and file *noun*
the ordinary people or soldiers, not the leaders.

ransack *verb* (**ransacks, ransacking, ransacked**)
1 search thoroughly or roughly. **2** rob or pillage a place.

ransom *noun* (*plural* **ransoms**)
money that has to be paid for a prisoner to be set free.
hold to ransom hold someone captive or in your power and demand ransom.

ransom *verb* (**ransoms, ransoming, ransomed**)
1 free someone by paying a ransom. **2** get a ransom for someone.

rant *verb* (**rants, ranting, ranted**)
speak loudly and violently.
[from Dutch *ranten* = talk nonsense]

rap *verb* (**raps, rapping, rapped**)
1 knock loudly. **2** (*informal*) reprimand. **3** (*informal*) chat. **4** perform rap music.

rap *noun* (*plural* **raps**)
1 a rapping movement or sound. **2** (*informal*) blame or punishment ♦ *take the rap.* **3** (*informal*) a chat. **4** a type of popular music in which words are spoken rhythmically to an instrumental backing.

rapacious (*say* ra-pay-shus) *adjective*
1 greedy. **2** using threats or force to get everything you can.
rapaciously *adverb* **rapacity** *noun*

rape¹ *noun* (*plural* **rapes**)
the act of having sexual intercourse with a person without their consent.

rape *verb* (**rapes, raping, raped**)
force someone to have sexual intercourse against their will.
rapist *noun*
[from Latin *rapere* = take by force]

rape² *noun*
a plant with bright yellow flowers, grown as food for sheep and for its seed from which oil is obtained.
[from Latin *rapum* = turnip (to which it is related)]

rapid *adjective*
moving very quickly; swift.
rapidly *adverb* **rapidity** *noun*

rapids *plural noun*
part of a river where the water flows very
quickly.

rapt *adjective*
very intent and absorbed.
raptly *adverb*

rapture *noun*
very great delight.
rapturous *adjective* **rapturously** *adverb*

rare[1] *adjective* (**rarer, rarest**)
1 unusual; not often found or happening.
2 (said about air) thin; below normal pressure.
rarely *adverb* **rareness** *noun* **rarity** *noun*

rare[2] *adjective*
(said about meat) only lightly cooked;
undercooked.

rarefied *adjective*
1 (said about air) rare. **2** remote from everyday
life ♦ *the rarefied atmosphere of the university.*

rascal *noun* (*plural* **rascals**)
a dishonest or mischievous person; a rogue.
rascally *adjective*

rash[1] *adjective*
doing something or done without thinking of the
possible risks or effects.
rashly *adverb* **rashness** *noun*

rash[2] *noun* (*plural* **rashes**)
1 an outbreak of spots or patches on the skin.
2 a number of (usually unwelcome) events
happening in a short time ♦ *a rash of accidents.*

rasher *noun* (*plural* **rashers**)
a slice of bacon.

rasp *noun* (*plural* **rasps**)
1 a file with sharp points on its surface.
2 a rough grating sound.

rasp *verb* (**rasps, rasping, rasped**)
1 scrape roughly. **2** make a rough grating sound
or effect.

raspberry *noun* (*plural* **raspberries**)
a small soft red fruit.

Rastafarian *noun* (*plural* **Rastafarians**)
a member of a religious group that started in
Jamaica.

rat *noun* (*plural* **rats**)
1 an animal like a large mouse. **2** (*informal*) an
unpleasant or treacherous person.

rate *noun* (*plural* **rates**)
1 speed ♦ *The train travelled at a great rate.*
2 a measure of cost, value, etc. ♦ *Postage rates
went up.* **3** quality or standard ♦ *first-rate.*
at any rate anyway.

rate *verb* (**rates, rating, rated**)
1 put a value on something. **2** regard as
♦ *He rated me among his friends.*

rates *plural noun*
a local tax paid by owners of commercial land
and buildings.

rather *adverb*
1 slightly or somewhat ♦ *It's rather dark.*
2 preferably or more willingly ♦ *I would rather
not go.* **3** more exactly; instead of ♦ *He is lazy
rather than stupid.* **4** (*informal*) definitely, yes
♦ *'Will you come?' 'Rather!'*

rating *noun* (*plural* **ratings**)
1 the way something is rated. **2** a sailor who is
not an officer.

ratio (*say* ray-shee-oh) *noun* (*plural* **ratios**)
1 the relationship between two numbers, given
by the quotient ♦ *The ratio of 2 to 10 = 2:10 =*
$\frac{2}{10} = \frac{1}{5}$. **2** proportion ♦ *Mix flour and butter in the
ratio of two to one* (= two measures of flour to
one measure of butter).

ration *noun* (*plural* **rations**)
an amount allowed to one person.

ration *verb* (**rations, rationing, rationed**)
share something out in fixed amounts.

rational *adjective*
1 reasonable or sane. **2** able to reason.
rationally *adverb* **rationality** *noun*

rationalize *verb* (**rationalizes, rationalizing,
rationalized**)
1 make a thing logical and consistent ♦ *Attempts
to rationalize English spelling have failed.*
2 justify something by inventing a reasonable
explanation for it ♦ *They rationalized their
meanness by calling it economy.* **3** make an
industry etc. more efficient by reorganizing it.
rationalization *noun*

rations *plural noun*
a fixed daily amount of food issued to a soldier
etc.

rattle *verb* (**rattles, rattling, rattled**)
1 make a series of short sharp hard sounds.
2 make a person nervous or flustered.
rattle off say or recite rapidly.

rattle *noun* (*plural* **rattles**)
1 a rattling sound. **2** a device or baby's toy that
rattles.

rattlesnake *noun* (*plural* **rattlesnakes**)
a poisonous American snake with a tail that
rattles.

raucous (*say* raw-kus) *adjective*
loud and harsh ♦ *a raucous voice.*

ravages *plural noun*
damaging effects ♦ *the ravages of war.*

rave *verb* (**raves, raving, raved**)
1 talk wildly or angrily or madly. **2** talk
enthusiastically about something.

rave *noun* (*plural* **raves**)
a large party or event with dancing to loud fast
electronic music.

ravenous *adjective*
very hungry.
ravenously *adverb*

ravine (*say* ra-**veen**) *noun* (*plural* **ravines**)
a deep narrow gorge or valley.

ravishing *adjective*
very beautiful.

raw *adjective*
1 not cooked. 2 in the natural state; not yet processed ♦ *raw materials.* 3 without experience ♦ *raw recruits.* 4 with the skin removed ♦ *a raw wound.* 5 cold and damp ♦ *a raw morning.*
rawness *noun*
a raw deal (*informal*) unfair treatment.

raw material *noun* (*plural* **raw materials**)
natural substances used in industry ♦ *rich in iron ore, coal, and other raw materials.*

ray *noun* (*plural* **rays**)
1 a thin line of light, heat, or other radiation.
2 each of a set of lines or parts extending from a centre. 3 a slight trace of something ♦ *a ray of hope.*

raze *verb* (**razes, razing, razed**)
destroy a building or town completely ♦ *The fort was razed to the ground.*

razor *noun* (*plural* **razors**)
a device with a very sharp blade, especially one used for shaving.

re- *prefix*
1 again (as in *rebuild*). 2 back again, to an earlier condition (as in *reopen*). 3 in return; to each other (as in *react*). 4 against (as in *rebel*).
5 away or down (as in *recede*).

reach *verb* (**reaches, reaching, reached**)
1 go as far as; arrive at a place or thing. 2 stretch out your hand to get or touch something.
3 succeed in achieving something ♦ *The cheetah can reach a speed of 70 m.p.h.* ♦ *Have you reached a decision?*
reachable *adjective*

reach *noun* (*plural* **reaches**)
1 the distance a person or thing can reach.
2 a distance you can easily travel ♦ *We live within reach of the sea.* 3 a straight stretch of a river or canal.
[from Old English]

react *verb* (**reacts, reacting, reacted**)
1 respond to something; have a reaction.
2 (in science) undergo a chemical change.

reaction *noun* (*plural* **reactions**)
1 an effect or feeling etc. produced in one person or thing by another. 2 (in science) a chemical change caused when substances act upon each other.

reactionary *adjective*
opposed to progress or reform.

reactor *noun* (*plural* **reactors**)
an apparatus for producing nuclear power in a controlled way.

read *verb* (**reads, reading, read** (*say* red))
1 look at something written or printed and understand it or say it aloud. 2 (in computing) copy, search, or extract data. 3 indicate or register ♦ *The thermometer reads 20° Celsius.*
readable *adjective*

reader *noun* (*plural* **readers**)
1 a person who reads. 2 a book that helps you learn to read.

readily (*say* **red**-il-ee) *adverb*
1 willingly. 2 easily; without any difficulty.

reading *noun* (*plural* **readings**)
1 reading books. 2 the figure shown on a meter, gauge, or other instrument. 3 a gathering of people at which something is read aloud ♦ *a poetry reading.*

ready *adjective* (**readier, readiest**)
able or willing to do something or be used immediately; prepared.
readiness *noun*
at the ready ready for use or action.

ready *adverb*
beforehand ♦ *This meat is ready cooked.*
ready-made *adjective*

real *adjective*
1 existing or true; not imaginary. 2 genuine; not an imitation ♦ *real pearls.* 3 (said about food or drink) regarded as superior because it is produced by traditional methods ♦ *real ale.*

realism *noun*
seeing or showing things as they really are.
realist *noun*

realistic *adjective*
1 true to life; showing things as they really are.
2 sensible and practical about what is possible.
realistically *adverb*

reality *noun* (*plural* **realities**)
1 what is real ♦ *You must face reality.*
2 something real ♦ *Her worst fears had become a reality.*

realize *verb* (**realizes, realizing, realized**)
1 be fully aware of something; accept something as true. 2 make a hope or plan etc. happen ♦ *She realized her ambition to become a racing driver.*
3 obtain money in exchange for something by selling it.
realization *noun*

really *adverb*
1 truly or in fact. 2 very ♦ *She's really clever.*

realm (*say* relm) *noun* (*plural* **realms**)
1 a kingdom. 2 an area of knowledge, interest, etc. ♦ *in the realms of science.*

reams *plural noun*
a large quantity of writing.

reap *verb* (reaps, reaping, reaped)
1 cut down and gather corn when it is ripe.
2 obtain as the result of something done
♦ *They reaped great benefit from their training.*
reaper *noun*

rear¹ *noun*
the back part.
rear *adjective*
placed at the rear.

rear² *verb* (rears, rearing, reared)
1 bring up young children or animals. 2 rise up;
raise itself on hind legs ♦ *The horse reared in
fright.* 3 (said of a building) to appear very large
or high.

rearguard *noun* (*plural* **rearguards**)
troops protecting the rear of an army.
fight a rearguard action go on defending or
resisting something even though you are losing.

rearrange *verb* (rearranges, rearranging,
rearranged)
arrange in a different way or order.
rearrangement *noun*

reason *noun* (*plural* **reasons**)
1 a cause or explanation of something.
2 reasoning; common sense ♦ *You must listen to
reason.*

---

❶ USAGE Do not use the phrase *the reason is* with
the word *because* (which means the same thing).
Correct usage is ♦ *We cannot come. The reason is
that we both have flu* (not 'The reason is because
…').

---

reason *verb* (reasons, reasoning, reasoned)
1 use your ability to think and draw conclusions.
2 try to persuade someone by giving reasons
♦ *We reasoned with the rebels.*

reasonable *adjective*
1 ready to use or listen to reason; sensible or
logical. 2 fair or moderate; not expensive
♦ *reasonable prices.* 3 acceptable or fairly good
♦ *a reasonable standard of living.*
reasonably *adverb*

reassure *verb* (reassures, reassuring,
reassured)
restore someone's confidence by removing
doubts and fears.
reassurance *noun*

rebel (*say* rib-el) *verb* (rebels, rebelling,
rebelled)
refuse to obey someone in authority, especially
the government; fight against the rulers of your
own country.

rebel (*say* reb-el) *noun* (*plural* **rebels**)
someone who rebels against the government, or
against accepted standards of behaviour.
[from *re-* = again + Latin *bellum* = war
(originally referring to a defeated enemy who
began to fight again)]

rebellion *noun* (*plural* **rebellions**)
organized armed resistance to the government; a
revolt.
rebellious *adjective*

reboot *verb* (reboots, rebooting, rebooted)
switch a computer off and then on again.

rebound *verb* (rebounds, rebounding,
rebounded)
bounce back after hitting something.
rebound *noun*

rebuff *noun* (*plural* **rebuffs**)
an unkind refusal; a snub.
rebuff *verb*
[from *re-* = again + Italian *buffo* = a gust]

rebuke *verb* (rebukes, rebuking, rebuked)
speak severely to a person who has done wrong.
rebuke *noun*

recalcitrant *adjective*
disobedient or uncooperative.
recalcitrance *noun*
[from Latin *recalcitrare* = to kick back]

recall *verb* (recalls, recalling, recalled)
1 bring back into the mind; remember. 2 ask a
person to come back. 3 ask for something to be
returned.
recall *noun*

recapitulate *verb* (recapitulates,
recapitulating, recapitulated)
state again the main points of what has been
said.
recapitulation *noun*

recapture *verb* (recaptures, recapturing,
recaptured)
1 capture again. 2 bring or get back a mood or
feeling.
recapture *noun*

recede *verb* (recedes, receding, receded)
go back from a certain point ♦ *The floods have
receded.*

receipt (*say* ris-eet) *noun* (*plural* **receipts**)
1 a written statement that money has been paid
or something has been received. 2 receiving
something.
[via early French from Latin *recipire* = to
receive]

receive *verb* (receives, receiving, received)
1 take or get something that is given or sent to
you. 2 experience something ♦ *He received
injuries to his face and hands* 3 greet someone
who comes.

receiver *noun* (*plural* **receivers**)
1 a person or thing that receives something.
2 a person who buys and sells stolen goods.
3 an official who takes charge of a bankrupt
person's property. 4 a radio or television set that
receives broadcasts. 5 the part of a telephone that
receives the sound and is held to a person's ear.

recent *adjective*
happening or made or done a short time ago.
recently *adverb*

reception *noun* (*plural* **receptions**)
1 the way a person or thing is received.
2 a formal party to receive guests ♦ *a wedding reception.* **3** a place in a hotel or office etc. where visitors are received and registered. **4** the first class in an infant school. **5** the quality of television or radio signals.

receptionist *noun* (*plural* **receptionists**)
a person whose job is to greet and deal with visitors, clients, patients, etc.

receptive *adjective*
quick or willing to receive ideas etc.

recess *noun* (*plural* **recesses**)
1 a small space set back in a wall. **2** a time when work or business is stopped for a while.

recession *noun* (*plural* **recessions**)
1 a reduction in a country's trade or prosperity.
2 receding from a point.

recharge *verb* (**recharges, recharging, recharged**)
refill or reload something, especially put an electric charge into a used battery.

recipe (*say* **ress**-ip-ee) *noun* (*plural* **recipes**)
instructions for preparing or cooking food.

reciprocal (*say* ris-**ip**-rok-al) *adjective*
given and received; mutual ♦ *reciprocal help.*
reciprocally *adverb* **reciprocity** *noun*

reciprocal *noun* (*plural* **reciprocals**)
a reversed fraction, ♦ $\frac{3}{2}$ is the reciprocal of $\frac{2}{3}$.

recital *noun* (*plural* **recitals**)
1 reciting something. **2** a musical entertainment given by one performer or group.

recite *verb* (**recites, reciting, recited**)
say a poem etc. aloud from memory.
recitation *noun*

reckless *adjective*
rash; ignoring risk or danger.
recklessly *adverb* **recklessness** *noun*

reckon *verb* (**reckons, reckoning, reckoned**)
1 calculate or count up. **2** have as an opinion; feel confident ♦ *I reckon we shall win.*
reckon with think about or deal with
♦ *We didn't reckon with the train strike when we planned our journey.*

reclaim *verb* (**reclaims, reclaiming, reclaimed**)
1 claim or get something back. **2** make a thing usable again ♦ *reclaimed land.*
reclamation *noun*

recognize *verb* (**recognizes, recognizing, recognized**)
1 know who someone is or what something is because you have seen that person or thing before. **2** realize ♦ *She recognized the truth of what he was saying.* **3** accept something as genuine, welcome, or lawful etc. ♦ *Nine countries recognized the island's new government.*
recognition *noun* **recognizable** *adjective*

recoil *verb* (**recoils, recoiling, recoiled**)
1 move back suddenly in shock or disgust.
2 (said about a gun) jerk backwards when it is fired.

recollect *verb* (**recollects, recollecting, recollected**)
remember.
recollection *noun*

recommend *verb* (**recommends, recommending, recommended**)
say that a person or thing would be good or suitable for a particular job or purpose.
recommendation *noun*

reconcile *verb* (**reconciles, reconciling, reconciled**)
1 make people who have quarrelled become friendly again. **2** persuade a person to put up with something ♦ *New frames reconciled him to wearing glasses.* **3** make things agree ♦ *I cannot reconcile what you say with what you do.*
reconciliation *noun*

recondition *verb* (**reconditions, reconditioning, reconditioned**)
overhaul and repair.

reconnaissance (*say* rik-**on**-i-suns) *noun*
an exploration of an area, especially in order to gather information about it for military purposes.

reconstruct *verb* (**reconstructs, reconstructing, reconstructed**)
1 construct or build something again. **2** create or act past events again ♦ *Police reconstructed the robbery.*
reconstruction *noun*

record (*say* **rek**-ord) *noun* (*plural* **records**)
1 information kept in a permanent form, e.g. written or printed. **2** a disc on which sound has been recorded. **3** the best performance in a sport etc., or the most remarkable event of its kind ♦ *He holds the record for the high jump.*
4 facts known about a person's past life or career etc. ♦ *She has a good school record.*

record (*say* rik-**ord**) *verb* (**records, recording, recorded**)
1 put something down in writing or other permanent form. **2** store sounds or scenes (e.g. television pictures) on a disc or magnetic tape etc. so that you can play or show them later.

recorder *noun* (*plural* **recorders**)
1 a kind of flute held downwards from the player's mouth. **2** a person or thing that records something.

recover *verb* (**recovers, recovering, recovered**)
1 get something back again after losing it; regain.
2 get well again after being ill or weak.
recovery *noun*

recreation *noun* (*plural* **recreations**)
1 refreshing or entertaining yourself with an enjoyable activity. **2** a game or hobby etc. that is an enjoyable pastime.
recreational *adjective*

recruit *noun* (*plural* **recruits**)
1 a person who has just joined the armed forces. **2** a new member of a society, company, or other group.

recruit *verb* (**recruits, recruiting, recruited**)
enlist recruits.
recruitment *noun*

rectangle *noun* (*plural* **rectangles**)
a shape with four sides and four right angles.
rectangular *adjective*

rector *noun* (*plural* **rectors**)
a member of the Church of England clergy in charge of a parish.

rectum *noun* (*plural* **rectums**)
the last part of the large intestine, ending at the anus.

recuperate *verb* (**recuperates, recuperating, recuperated**)
get better after an illness.
recuperation *noun*

recur *verb* (**recurs, recurring, recurred**)
happen again; keep on happening.
recurrent *adjective* **recurrence** *noun*

recurring decimal *noun* (*plural* **recurring decimals**)
(in mathematics) a decimal fraction in which a digit or group of digits is repeated indefinitely, e.g. 0.666 ...

recycle *verb* (**recycles, recycling, recycled**)
convert waste material into a form in which it can be reused.

red *adjective* (**redder, reddest**)
1 of the colour of blood or a colour rather like this. **2** to do with communists; favouring communism.
redness *noun*

red *noun*
1 red colour. **2** a communist.
in the red in debt (because debts were entered in red in account books). **see red** become suddenly angry.

redden *verb* (**reddens, reddening, reddened**)
make or become red.

redeem *verb* (**redeems, redeeming, redeemed**)
1 buy something back or pay off a debt. **2** save a person from damnation ♦ *Christians believe that Christ redeemed us all.* **3** make up for faults ♦ *His one redeeming feature is his kindness.*
redeemer *noun* **redemption** *noun*

red-handed *adjective*
catch red-handed catch while actually committing a crime.

red herring *noun* (*plural* **red herrings**)
something that draws attention away from the main subject; a misleading clue.

red-hot *adjective*
very hot; so hot that it has turned red.

Red Indian *noun* (*plural* **Red Indians**) (*old use*)
a Native American from North America.

---

❶ USAGE See note at *Indian.*

---

red tape *noun*
use of too many rules and forms in official business.

reduce *verb* (**reduces, reducing, reduced**)
1 make or become smaller or less. **2** force someone into a condition or situation ♦ *She was reduced to tears.*
reduction *noun*

redundant *adjective*
no longer needed, especially for a particular job.
redundancy *noun*

re-echo *verb* (**re-echoes, re-echoing, re-echoed**)
echo; go on echoing.

reed *noun* (*plural* **reeds**)
1 a tall plant that grows in water or marshy ground. **2** a thin strip that vibrates to make the sound in a clarinet, saxophone, oboe, etc.

reef *noun* (*plural* **reefs**)
a ridge of rock, coral, or sand, especially one near the surface of the sea.

reek *verb* (**reeks, reeking, reeked**)
smell strongly or unpleasantly.
reek *noun*

reel *noun* (*plural* **reels**)
1 a round device on which cotton, thread, film, etc. is wound. **2** a lively Scottish dance.

reel *verb* (**reels, reeling, reeled**)
1 wind something onto or off a reel. **2** stagger. **3** feel giddy or confused ♦ *I am still reeling from the shock.*
reel off say something quickly.

refer *verb* (**refers, referring, referred**)
pass a problem etc. to someone else ♦ *My doctor referred me to a specialist.*
referral *noun*
refer to 1 mention or speak about ♦ *I wasn't referring to you.* **2** look in a book etc. for information ♦ *We referred to our dictionary.*

referee *noun* (*plural* **referees**)
someone appointed to see that people keep to the rules of a game.

reference *noun* (*plural* **references**)
1 referring to something ♦ *There was no reference to recent events.* **2** a direction to a book or page or file etc. where information can be found. **3** a letter from a previous employer describing someone's abilities and qualities.
in or **with reference to** concerning or about.

reference book noun (plural **reference books**)
a book (such as a dictionary or encyclopedia) that gives information systematically.

referendum noun (plural **referendums** or **referenda**)
a vote on a particular question by all the people of a country.
[from Latin, = something to be referred]

refill verb (**refills, refilling, refilled**)
fill again.

refill noun (plural **refills**)
a container holding a substance which is used to refill something ♦ This pen needs a refill.

refine verb (**refines, refining, refined**)
1 purify. 2 improve something, especially by making small changes.
[from re- = again + Middle English fine = make pure]

refined adjective
1 purified. 2 having good taste or good manners.

refinement noun (plural **refinements**)
1 the action of refining. 2 being refined. 3 something added to improve a thing.

refinery noun (plural **refineries**)
a factory for refining something ♦ an oil refinery.

reflect verb (**reflects, reflecting, reflected**)
1 send back light, heat, or sound etc. from a surface. 2 form an image of something as a mirror does. 3 think something over; consider. 4 be a sign of something; be influenced by something ♦ Prices reflect the cost of producing things.
reflection noun **reflective** adjective **reflector** noun

reflex noun (plural **reflexes**)
a movement or action done without any conscious thought.

reflexive pronoun noun (plural **reflexive pronouns**)
any of the pronouns myself, herself, himself, etc. (as in 'She cut herself'), which refer back to the subject of the verb.

reflexive verb noun (plural **reflexive verbs**)
a verb in which the subject and the object are the same person or thing, as in 'They hurt themselves', 'The cat washed itself'.

reform verb (**reforms, reforming, reformed**)
1 make changes in something in order to improve it. 2 give up a criminal or immoral lifestyle, or make someone do this.
reformer noun **reformative** adjective **reformatory** adjective

reform noun (plural **reforms**)
1 reforming. 2 a change made in order to improve something.

reformation noun
reforming.
the Reformation a religious movement in Europe in the 16th century intended to reform certain teachings and practices of the Roman Catholic Church, which resulted in the establishment of the Reformed or Protestant Churches.

refract verb (**refracts, refracting, refracted**)
bend a ray of light at the point where it enters water or glass etc. at an angle.
refraction noun **refractor** noun **refractive** adjective

refrain[1] verb (**refrains, refraining, refrained**)
stop yourself from doing something ♦ Please refrain from talking.

refrain[2] noun (plural **refrains**)
the chorus of a song.

refresh verb (**refreshes, refreshing, refreshed**)
make a tired person etc. feel fresh and strong again.
refresh someone's memory remind someone of something by going over previous information.

refreshing adjective
1 producing new strength ♦ a refreshing sleep. 2 pleasantly different or unusual ♦ refreshing honesty.

refreshments plural noun
drinks and snacks provided at an event.

refrigerator noun (plural **refrigerators**)
a cabinet or room in which food is stored at a very low temperature.

refuge noun (plural **refuges**)
a place where a person is safe from pursuit or danger.
take refuge go somewhere or do something so that you are protected.

refugee noun (plural **refugees**)
someone who has had to leave their home or country and seek refuge elsewhere, e.g. because of war or persecution or famine.

refund verb (**refunds, refunding, refunded**)
pay money back.

refund noun (plural **refunds**)
money paid back.

refuse (say ri-fewz) verb (**refuses, refusing, refused**)
say that you are unwilling to do or give or accept something.
refusal noun

refuse (*say* ref-yooss) *noun*
waste material ♦ *Lorries collected the refuse.*

regain *verb* (**regains, regaining, regained**)
1 get something back after losing it. 2 reach a place again.

regalia (*say* rig-ayl-i-a) *plural noun*
the emblems of royalty or rank ♦ *The royal regalia include the crown, sceptre, and orb.*

regard *verb* (**regards, regarding, regarded**)
1 think of in a certain way; consider to be ♦ *We regard the matter as serious.* 2 look or gaze at.

regard *noun*
1 a gaze. 2 consideration or heed ♦ *You acted without regard to people's safety.* 3 respect ♦ *We have a great regard for her.* 4 a gaze.
with regard to concerning.

regarding *preposition*
concerning ♦ *There are laws regarding drugs.*

regardless *adverb*
without considering something ♦ *Do it, regardless of the cost.*

regards *plural noun*
kind wishes sent in a message ♦ *Give him my regards.*

regatta *noun* (*plural* **regattas**)
a meeting for boat or yacht races.

regenerate *verb* (**regenerates, regenerating, regenerated**)
give new life or strength to something.
regeneration *noun*

regent *noun* (*plural* **regents**)
a person appointed to rule a country while the monarch is too young or unable to rule.

reggae (*say* reg-ay) *noun*
a West Indian style of music with a strong beat.

regime (*say* ray-zheem) *noun* (*plural* **regimes**)
a system of government or organization ♦ *a Fascist regime.*

regiment *noun* (*plural* **regiments**)
an army unit, usually divided into battalions or companies.
regimental *adjective*

region *noun* (*plural* **regions**)
an area; a part of a country or of the world ♦ *in tropical regions.*
regional *adjective* **regionally** *adverb*
in the region of near ♦ *The cost will be in the region of £100.*

register *noun* (*plural* **registers**)
1 an official list of things or names etc. 2 a book in which information about school attendances is recorded. 3 the range of a voice or musical instrument.

register *verb* (**registers, registering, registered**)
1 list something in a register. 2 indicate; show ♦ *The thermometer registered 100°.* 3 make an impression on someone's mind. 4 pay extra for a letter or parcel to be sent with special care.
registration *noun*

register office *noun* (*plural* **register offices**)
an office where marriages are performed and records of births, marriages, and deaths are kept.

---

❶ USAGE The name *registry office* is also used, and is the official name in Scotland

---

regret *noun* (*plural* **regrets**)
a feeling of sorrow or disappointment about something that has happened or been done.
regretful *adjective* **regretfully** *adverb*

regret *verb* (**regrets, regretting, regretted**)
feel regret about something.
regrettable *adjective* **regrettably** *adverb*

regular *adjective*
1 always happening or doing something at certain times ♦ *Try to eat regular meals.*
2 even or symmetrical ♦ *regular teeth.* 3 normal, standard, or correct ♦ *the regular procedure.*
4 belonging to a country's permanent armed forces ♦ *a regular soldier.*
regularly *adverb* **regularity** *noun*

regulate *verb* (**regulates, regulating, regulated**)
1 control, especially by rules. 2 make a machine work at a certain speed.
regulator *noun*

regulation *noun*
1 regulating. 2 a rule or law.

rehabilitation *noun*
restoring a person to a normal life or a building etc. to a good condition.
rehabilitate *verb*

rehearse *verb* (**rehearses, rehearsing, rehearsed**)
practise something before performing to an audience.
rehearsal *noun*

reign *verb* (**reigns, reigning, reigned**)
1 rule a country as king or queen. 2 be supreme; be the strongest influence ♦ *Silence reigned.*

reign *noun*
the time when someone reigns.

reimburse *verb* (**reimburses, reimbursing, reimbursed**)
repay money that has been spent ♦ *Your travelling expenses will be reimbursed.*
reimbursement *noun*

rein *noun* (*plural* **reins**)
a strap used to guide a horse.

reincarnation *noun*
being born again into a new body.

reindeer *noun* (*plural* **reindeer**)
a kind of deer that lives in Arctic regions.

reinforce *verb* (**reinforces, reinforcing, reinforced**)
strengthen by adding extra people or supports etc.

reinforcements *plural noun*
extra troops or ships etc. sent to strengthen a force.

reiterate *verb* (**reiterates, reiterating, reiterated**)
say something again or repeatedly.
reiteration *noun*

reject (*say* ri-jekt) *verb* (**rejects, rejecting, rejected**)
1 refuse to accept a person or thing. 2 throw away or discard.
rejection *noun*

reject (*say* ree-jekt) *noun* (*plural* **rejects**)
a person or thing that is rejected, especially because of being faulty or poorly made.

rejoice *verb* (**rejoices, rejoicing, rejoiced**)
feel or show great joy.

rejuvenate *verb* (**rejuvenates, rejuvenating, rejuvenated**)
make a person seem young again.
rejuvenation *noun*

relapse *verb* (**relapses, relapsing, relapsed**)
return to a previous condition; become worse after improving.
relapse *noun*

relate *verb* (**relates, relating, related**)
1 narrate. 2 connect or compare one thing with another. 3 understand and get on well with
♦ *Some people cannot relate to animals.*

related *adjective*
belonging to the same family.

relation *noun* (*plural* **relations**)
1 a relative. 2 the way one thing is related to another.

relationship *noun* (*plural* **relationships**)
1 how people or things are related. 2 how people get on with each other. 3 an emotional or sexual association between two people.

relative *noun* (*plural* **relatives**)
a person who is related to another.

relative *adjective*
connected or compared with something; compared with the average ♦ *They live in relative comfort.*
relatively *adverb*
relative pronoun see **pronoun.**

relax *verb* (**relaxes, relaxing, relaxed**)
1 stop working; rest. 2 become less anxious or worried. 3 make a rule etc. less strict or severe. 4 make a limb or muscle less stiff or tense.
relaxation *noun*

relay (*say* ri-lay) *verb* (**relays, relaying, relayed**)
pass on a message or broadcast.

relay (*say* re-lay) *noun* (*plural* **relays**)
1 a fresh group taking the place of another
♦ *The firemen worked in relays.* 2 a relay race.
3 a device for relaying a broadcast.

relay race *noun* (*plural* **relay races**)
a race between teams in which each person covers part of the distance.

release *verb* (**releases, releasing, released**)
1 set free or unfasten. 2 let a thing fall or fly or go out. 3 make a film or record etc. available to the public.

release *noun* (*plural* **releases**)
1 being released. 2 something released, such as a new film or record. 3 a device that unfastens something.

relegate *verb* (**relegates, relegating, relegated**)
1 put into a less important place. 2 put a sports team into a lower division of a league.
relegation *noun*

relent *verb* (**relents, relenting, relented**)
become less severe or more merciful.

relentless *adjective*
not stopping or relenting; pitiless.
relentlessly *adverb*

relevant *adjective*
connected with what is being discussed or dealt with. (The opposite is **irrelevant.**)
relevance *noun*

reliable *adjective*
able to be relied on; trustworthy.
reliably *adverb* **reliability** *noun*

relic *noun* (*plural* **relics**)
something that has survived from an earlier period of history.

relief *noun* (*plural* **reliefs**)
1 the ending or lessening of pain, trouble, boredom, etc. 2 something that gives relief or help. 3 help given to people in need ♦ *a relief fund for the earthquake victims.* 4 a person who takes over a turn of duty when another finishes.
5 a method of making a design etc. that stands out from a surface.

relief map *noun* (*plural* **relief maps**)
a map that shows hills and valleys by shading or moulding.

relieve *verb* (**relieves, relieving, relieved**)
give relief to a person or thing.
relieve of take something from a person
♦ *The thief relieved him of his wallet.*

religion *noun* (*plural* **religions**)
1 what people believe about God or gods, and how they worship. 2 a particular system of beliefs and worship.

religious *adjective*
1 to do with religion. 2 believing firmly in a religion and taking part in its customs.
religiously *adverb*

relish *noun* (*plural* **relishes**)
1 great enjoyment. 2 a tasty sauce or pickle that adds flavour to plainer food.

relish *verb* (**relishes, relishing, relished**)
enjoy greatly.

relive *verb* (**relives, reliving, relived**)
remember something that happened very vividly, as though it was happening again.

reluctant *adjective*
unwilling or not keen.
reluctantly *adverb* **reluctance** *noun*

rely *verb* (**relies, relying, relied**)
rely on 1 trust a person or thing to help or support you. 2 be dependent on something ♦ *Many people rely on this local bus service.*

remain *verb* (**remains, remaining, remained**)
1 be there after other parts have gone or been dealt with; be left over. 2 continue to be in the same place or condition; stay.

remainder *noun*
1 the remaining part or people or things.
2 the number left after subtraction or division.

remains *plural noun*
1 all that is left over after other parts have been removed or destroyed. 2 ancient ruins or objects; relics. 3 a dead body.

remand *verb* (**remands, remanding, remanded**)
send a prisoner back into custody while further evidence is being gathered.
remand *noun*
on remand in prison while waiting for a trial.

remark *noun* (*plural* **remarks**)
something said; a comment.

remark *verb* (**remarks, remarking, remarked**)
1 make a remark; say. 2 notice.

remarkable *adjective*
unusual or extraordinary.
remarkably *adverb*

remedial *adjective*
1 helping children who learn slowly. 2 helping to cure an illness or deficiency.

remedy *noun* (*plural* **remedies**)
something that cures or relieves a disease etc. or that puts a matter right.

remember *verb* (**remembers, remembering, remembered**)
1 keep something in your mind. 2 bring something back into your mind.
remembrance *noun*

remind *verb* (**reminds, reminding, reminded**)
1 help or make a person remember something ♦ *Remind me to buy some stamps.* 2 make a person think of something because of being similar ♦ *She reminds me of my history teacher.*
reminder *noun*

reminisce (*say* rem-in-**iss**) *verb* (**reminisces, reminiscing, reminisced**)
think or talk about things that you remember.
reminiscence *noun* **reminiscent** *adjective*

remiss *adjective*
negligent; careless about doing what you ought to do.

remnant *noun* (*plural* **remnants**)
a part or piece left over from something.

remonstrate *verb* (**remonstrates, remonstrating, remonstrated**)
make a protest ♦ *We remonstrated with him about his behaviour.*

remorse *noun*
deep regret for having done wrong.
remorseful *adjective* **remorsefully** *adverb*

remote *adjective*
1 far away or isolated. 2 some but very little; unlikely ♦ *a remote chance.*
remotely *adverb* **remoteness** *noun*

remote control *noun*
controlling something from a distance, usually by electricity or radio.

removal *noun*
removing or moving something.

remove *verb* (**removes, removing, removed**)
take something away or off.

remove *noun* (*plural* **removes**)
a distance or degree away from something ♦ *That is several removes from the truth.*

Renaissance (*say* ren-**ay**-sans) *noun*
the revival of classical styles of art and literature in Europe in the 14th–16th centuries.
[from French, = new birth]

rename *verb* (**renames, renaming, renamed**)
give a new name to a person or thing.

render *verb* (**renders, rendering, rendered**)
1 cause to become ♦ *This news rendered us speechless.* 2 give or perform something ♦ *The local community was quick to render help to the victims.*

rendezvous (*say* rond-ay-voo) *noun* (*plural* **rendezvous** (*say* **rond**-ay-vooz))
1 a meeting with somebody. 2 a place arranged for this.
[from French, = present yourselves]

renew *verb* (**renews, renewing, renewed**)
1 restore something to its original condition or replace it with something new. 2 begin or make or give again ♦ *We renewed our request.*
renewal *noun*

renewable resource noun (plural
renewable resources)
a resource (such as power from the sun, wind, or
waves) that can never be used up, or which can
be renewed.

renounce verb (renounces, renouncing,
renounced)
give up or reject.
renunciation noun

renovate verb (renovates, renovating,
renovated)
repair a thing and make it look new.
renovation noun

renowned adjective
well-known or famous.

rent[1] noun (plural rents)
a regular payment for the use of something,
especially a house that belongs to another
person.
rent verb (rents, renting, rented)
have or allow the use of something in return for
rent.

rent[2] noun (plural rents)
a torn place; a split.

reorganize verb (reorganizes, reorganizing,
reorganized)
change the way in which something is
organized.
reorganization noun

repair verb (repairs, repairing, repaired)
put something into good condition after it has
been damaged or broken etc.
repairable adjective
repair noun (plural repairs)
1 repairing ♦ closed for repair. 2 a mended place
♦ the repair is hardly visible.
in good repair in good condition; well
maintained.

repartee noun
witty replies and remarks.

repatriate verb (repatriates, repatriating,
repatriated)
send a person back to his or her own country.
repatriation noun

repeal verb (repeals, repealing, repealed)
cancel a law officially.
repeal noun

repeat verb (repeats, repeating, repeated)
1 say or do the same thing again. 2 tell another
person about something told to you.
repeatedly adverb
repeat noun (plural repeats)
1 the action of repeating. 2 something that is
repeated, especially a television programme.

repel verb (repels, repelling, repelled)
1 drive back or away ♦ They fought bravely
and repelled the attackers. 2 push something
away from itself by means of a physical force
♦ One north magnetic pole repels another.
3 disgust somebody.
repellent adjective & noun

repent verb (repents, repenting, repented)
be sorry for what you have done.
repentance noun **repentant** adjective

repercussion noun (plural repercussions)
a result or reaction produced indirectly by
something.

repertoire (say rep-er-twahr) noun
a stock of songs or plays etc. that a person or
company knows and can perform.

repetition noun (plural repetitions)
1 repeating. 2 something repeated.
repetitious adjective

repetitive adjective
full of repetitions.
repetitively adverb

replace verb (replaces, replacing, replaced)
1 put a thing back in its place. 2 take the place of
another person or thing. 3 put a new or different
thing in place of something.
replacement noun

replay noun (plural replays)
1 a sports match played again after a draw.
2 the playing or showing again of a recording.
replay verb

replica noun (plural replicas)
an exact copy.
[from Italian]

reply noun (plural replies)
something said or written to deal with a
question, letter, etc.; an answer.
reply verb (replies, replying, replied)
give a reply to; answer.

report verb (reports, reporting, reported)
1 describe something that has happened or that
you have done or studied. 2 make a complaint or
accusation against somebody. 3 go and tell
somebody that you have arrived or are ready for
work.
report noun (plural reports)
1 a description or account of something.
2 a regular statement of how someone has
worked or behaved, e.g. at school. 3 an explosive
sound.

reported speech noun
indirect speech.

reporter noun (plural reporters)
a person whose job is to collect and report news
for a newspaper, radio or television programme,
etc.

repose noun
calm, rest, or sleep.
repose verb (reposes, reposing, reposed)
rest or lie somewhere.

repossess verb (repossesses, repossessing,
repossessed)
take something back because it has not been paid
for.

reprehensible *adjective*
extremely bad and deserving blame or rebuke.

represent *verb* (represents, representing, represented)
1 help someone by speaking or doing something on their behalf. **2** symbolize or stand for ♦ *In Roman numerals, V represents 5.* **3** be an example or equivalent of something. **4** show a person or thing in a picture or play etc. **5** describe a person or thing in a particular way.
representation *noun*

representative *noun* (*plural* **representatives**)
a person or thing that represents another or others.

representative *adjective*
1 representing others. **2** typical of a group.

repress *verb* (represses, repressing, repressed)
1 keep down; control by force. **2** restrain or suppress.
repression *noun* **repressive** *adjective*

reprieve *noun* (*plural* **reprieves**)
postponement or cancellation of a punishment etc., especially the death penalty.

reprimand *noun* (*plural* **reprimands**)
a rebuke, especially a formal or official one.

reprimand *verb* (reprimands, reprimanding, reprimanded)
give someone a reprimand.

reprisal *noun* (*plural* **reprisals**)
an act of revenge.

reproach *verb* (reproaches, reproaching, reproached)
tell someone you are upset and disappointed by something he or she has done.
reproach *noun* **reproachful** *adjective* **reproachfully** *adverb*

reproduce *verb* (reproduces, reproducing, reproduced)
1 cause to be seen or heard or happen again. **2** make a copy of something. **3** produce offspring.
reproduction *noun* **reproductive** *adjective*

reprove *verb* (reproves, reproving, reproved)
rebuke or reproach.
reproof *noun*

reptile *noun* (*plural* **reptiles**)
a cold-blooded animal that has a backbone and very short legs or no legs at all, e.g. a snake, lizard, crocodile, or tortoise.
[from Latin *reptilis* = crawling]

republic *noun* (*plural* **republics**)
a country that has a president, especially one who is elected. (Compare **monarchy**.)
republican *adjective*
[from Latin *res publica* = public affairs]

repudiate *verb* (repudiates, repudiating, repudiated)
reject or deny.
repudiation *noun*

repulsive *adjective*
1 disgusting. **2** repelling things. (The opposite is **attractive**.)
repulsively *adverb* **repulsiveness** *noun*

reputable (*say* rep-yoo-ta-bul) *adjective*
having a good reputation; respected.
reputably *adverb*

reputation *noun* (*plural* **reputations**)
what people say about a person or thing.

reputed *adjective*
said or thought to be something ♦ *This is reputed to be the best hotel.*
reputedly *adverb*

request *verb* (requests, requesting, requested)
1 ask for a thing. **2** ask a person to do something.

request *noun* (*plural* **requests**)
1 asking for something. **2** a thing asked for.

require *verb* (requires, requiring, required)
1 need. **2** make somebody do something; oblige ♦ *Drivers are required to pass a test.*

requirement *noun* (*plural* **requirements**)
what is required; a need.

rescue *verb* (rescues, rescuing, rescued)
save from danger, harm, etc.; free from captivity.
rescuer *noun*

rescue *noun* (*plural* **rescues**)
the action of rescuing.

research *noun*
careful study or investigation to discover facts or information.

research (*say* ri-serch) *verb* (researches, researching, researched)
do research into something.
[from early French *recerche* = careful search]

resemblance *noun* (*plural* **resemblances**)
likeness or similarity.

resemble *verb* (resembles, resembling, resembled)
be like another person or thing.

resent *verb* (resents, resenting, resented)
feel indignant about or insulted by something.
resentful *adjective* **resentfully** *adverb* **resentment** *noun*

reservation *noun* (*plural* **reservations**)
1 reserving. **2** something reserved ♦ *a hotel reservation.* **3** an area of land kept for a special purpose. **4** a limit on how far you agree with something ♦ *I believe most of his story, but I have some reservations.*

reserve *verb* (reserves, reserving, reserved)
1 keep or order something for a particular person or a special use. **2** postpone ♦ *reserve judgement.*

reserve noun (plural **reserves**)
1 a person or thing kept ready to be used if necessary. **2** an extra player chosen in case a substitute is needed in a team. **3** an area of land kept for a special purpose ♦ a nature reserve. **4** shyness; being slow to reveal opinions or emotions.

reservoir (say **rez-er-vwar**) noun (plural **reservoirs**)
a place where water is stored, especially an artificial lake.

residence noun (plural **residences**)
a place where a person lives.

resident noun (plural **residents**)
a person living in a particular place.
resident adjective

residential adjective
1 containing people's homes ♦ a residential area. **2** providing accommodation ♦ a residential course.

residue noun (plural **residues**)
what is left over.
residual adjective

resign verb (**resigns, resigning, resigned**)
give up your job or position.
resignation noun
be resigned or **resign yourself to something** accept that you must put up with it.

resist verb (**resists, resisting, resisted**)
oppose; fight or act against something.

resistance noun
1 resisting ♦ The troops came up against armed resistance. **2** the ability of a substance to hinder the flow of electricity.
resistant adjective

resolute adjective
showing great determination.
resolutely adverb

resolution noun (plural **resolutions**)
1 being resolute. **2** something you have resolved to do ♦ New Year resolutions. **3** a formal decision made by a committee etc. **4** the solving of a problem etc.

resolve verb (**resolves, resolving, resolved**)
1 decide firmly or formally. **2** solve a problem etc. **3** overcome doubts or disagreements.
resolve noun
1 something you have decided to do; a resolution. **2** great determination.

resort verb (**resorts, resorting, resorted**)
turn to or make use of something ♦ They resorted to violence.
resort noun (plural **resorts**)
1 a place where people go for relaxation or holidays. **2** resorting ♦ without resort to cheating.
the last resort something to be tried when everything else has failed.

resounding adjective
1 loud and echoing. **2** very great; outstanding ♦ a resounding victory.

resource noun (plural **resources**)
1 something that can be used; an asset ♦ The country's natural resources include coal and oil. **2** an ability; ingenuity.

resourceful adjective
clever at finding ways of doing things.
resourcefully adverb **resourcefulness** noun

respect noun (plural **respects**)
1 admiration for a person's or thing's good qualities. **2** politeness or consideration ♦ Have respect for people's feelings. **3** a detail or aspect ♦ In this respect he is like his sister. **4** reference ♦ The rules with respect to bullying are quite clear.

respect verb (**respects, respecting, respected**)
have respect for a person or thing.

respectable adjective
1 having good manners and character etc. **2** fairly good ♦ a respectable score.
respectably adverb **respectability** noun

respectful adjective
showing respect.
respectfully adverb

respective adjective
belonging separately to each one of several ♦ We went to our respective rooms.

respectively adverb
in the same order as the people or things already mentioned ♦ Ruth and Emma finished first and second respectively.

respiration noun
breathing.
respiratory adjective

respirator noun (plural **respirators**)
1 a device that fits over a person's nose and mouth to purify air before it is breathed. **2** an apparatus for giving artificial respiration.

resplendent adjective
brilliant with colour or decorations.

respond verb (**responds, responding, responded**)
1 reply. **2** act in answer to, or because of, something; react.

response noun (plural **responses**)
1 a reply. **2** a reaction.

responsibility noun (plural **responsibilities**)
1 being responsible. **2** something for which a person is responsible.

responsible adjective
1 looking after a person or thing and having to take the blame if something goes wrong. **2** reliable and trustworthy. **3** with important duties ♦ a responsible job. **4** causing something ♦ His carelessness was responsible for their deaths.
responsibly adverb

rest¹ *noun* (*plural* **rests**)
1 a time of sleep or freedom from work as a way of regaining strength. **2** a support ♦ *a chin rest.* **3** an interval of silence between notes in music.

rest *verb* (**rests, resting, rested**)
1 have a rest; be still. **2** allow to rest ♦ *Sit down and rest your feet.* **3** lean or place something so it is supported; be supported ♦ *Rest the ladder against the wall.* **4** be left without further investigation etc. ♦ *And there the matter rests.*

rest² *noun*
the rest the remaining part; the others.

rest *verb* (**rests, resting, rested**)
remain ♦ *Rest assured, it will be a success.*
rest with be left to someone to deal with
♦ *It rests with you to suggest a date.*

restaurant *noun* (*plural* **restaurants**)
a place where you can buy a meal and eat it.

restful *adjective*
giving rest or a feeling of rest.

restive *adjective*
restless or impatient because of delay, boredom, etc.

restless *adjective*
unable to rest or keep still.
restlessly *adverb*

restore *verb* (**restores, restoring, restored**)
1 put something back to its original place or condition. **2** clean and repair a work of art or building etc. so that it looks as good as it did originally.
restoration *noun*

restrain *verb* (**restrains, restraining, restrained**)
hold a person or thing back; keep under control.
restraint *noun*

restrict *verb* (**restricts, restricting, restricted**)
keep within certain limits.
restriction *noun* **restrictive** *adjective*

result *noun* (*plural* **results**)
1 something produced by an action or condition etc.; an effect or consequence. **2** the score or situation at the end of a game, competition, or race etc. **3** the answer to a sum or calculation.

result *verb* (**results, resulting, resulted**)
1 happen as a result. **2** have a particular result
♦ *The match resulted in a draw.*
resultant *adjective*

resurrect *verb* (**resurrects, resurrecting, resurrected**)
bring back into use or existence ♦ *It is time to resurrect this old custom.*

resurrection *noun*
1 coming back to life after being dead.
2 the revival of something.
the Resurrection in the Christian religion, the resurrection of Jesus Christ three days after his death.

resuscitate *verb* (**resuscitates, resuscitating, resuscitated**)
revive a person from unconsciousness or apparent death.
resuscitation *noun*

retail *noun*
selling to the general public. (Compare **wholesale.**)
retailer *noun*

retain *verb* (**retains, retaining, retained**)
1 continue to have something; keep in your possession or memory etc. **2** hold something in place.

retaliate *verb* (**retaliates, retaliating, retaliated**)
repay an injury or insult etc. with a similar one; attack someone in return for a similar attack.
retaliation *noun*

reticent (*say* ret-i-sent) *adjective*
not telling people what you feel or think; discreet.
reticence *noun*

retina *noun* (*plural* **retinas**)
a layer of membrane at the back of the eyeball, sensitive to light.

retinue *noun* (*plural* **retinues**)
a group of people accompanying an important person.

retire *verb* (**retires, retiring, retired**)
1 give up your regular work when you reach a certain age. **2** retreat or withdraw. **3** go to bed or to your private room.
retirement *noun*

retiring *adjective*
shy; avoiding company.

retort *noun* (*plural* **retorts**)
1 a quick or witty or angry reply. **2** a glass bottle with a long downward bent neck, used in distilling liquids. **3** a receptacle used in making steel etc.

retort *verb* (**retorts, retorting, retorted**)
make a quick, witty, or angry reply.

retract *verb* (**retracts, retracting, retracted**)
1 pull back or in ♦ *The snail retracts its horns.*
2 withdraw an offer or statement.
retraction *noun* **retractable** *adjective*

retreat *verb* (**retreats, retreating, retreated**)
go back after being defeated or to avoid danger or difficulty etc.; withdraw.

retreat *noun* (*plural* **retreats**)
1 retreating. **2** a quiet place to which someone can withdraw.

retribution *noun* (*plural* **retributions**)
a deserved punishment.

retrieve *verb* (**retrieves, retrieving, retrieved**)
1 bring or get something back. **2** rescue.
retrievable *adjective* **retrieval** *noun*

retriever noun (plural **retrievers**)
a kind of dog that is often trained to retrieve game.

retrograde adjective
1 going backwards. 2 becoming less good.

retrospect noun
in retrospect when you look back at what has happened.

retrospective adjective
1 looking back on the past. 2 applying to the past as well as the future ♦ The law could not be made retrospective.
retrospection noun

return verb (**returns, returning, returned**)
1 come back or go back. 2 bring, give, put, or send back. 3 elect to parliament.
return noun (plural **returns**)
1 returning. 2 something returned. 3 profit ♦ He gets a good return on his savings. 4 a return ticket.

return match noun (plural **return matches**)
a second match played between the same teams.

return ticket noun (plural **return tickets**)
a ticket for a journey to a place and back again.

reunion noun (plural **reunions**)
1 reuniting. 2 a meeting of people who have not met for some time.

reunite verb (**reunites, reuniting, reunited**)
unite again after being separated.

reuse verb (**reuses, reusing, reused**)
use something again.
reusable adjective
reuse noun
using something again.

reveal verb (**reveals, revealing, revealed**)
let something be seen or known.

revel verb (**revels, revelling, revelled**)
1 take great delight in something. 2 hold revels.
reveller noun

revelation noun (plural **revelations**)
1 revealing. 2 something revealed, especially something surprising.

revels plural noun
lively and noisy festivities.

revenge noun
harming somebody in return for harm that they have done to you.
revenge verb (**revenges, revenging, revenged**)
revenge yourself take vengeance.

revenue noun (plural **revenues**)
1 a country's income from taxes etc., used for paying public expenses. 2 a company's income.

reverberate verb (**reverberates, reverberating, reverberated**)
resound or re-echo.
reverberation noun

reverence noun
a feeling of awe and deep or religious respect.

Reverend noun
the title of a member of the clergy ♦ the Reverend John Smith.

❶ USAGE Do not confuse with reverent.

reverent adjective
feeling or showing reverence.
reverently adverb

❶ USAGE Do not confuse with Reverend.

reverie (say rev-er-ee) noun (plural **reveries**)
a daydream.

reversal noun (plural **reversals**)
1 reversing or being reversed. 2 a piece of bad luck; a reverse.

reverse adjective
opposite in direction, order, or manner etc.
reverse noun (plural **reverses**)
1 the reverse side, order, manner, etc. 2 a piece of misfortune ♦ They suffered several reverses.
in reverse the opposite way round.
reverse verb (**reverses, reversing, reversed**)
1 turn in the opposite direction or order etc.; turn something inside out or upside down. 2 move backwards. 3 cancel a decision or decree.
reversible adjective

reverse gear noun
a gear that allows a vehicle to be driven backwards.

review noun (plural **reviews**)
1 an inspection or survey. 2 a published description and opinion of a book, film, play, etc.
review verb (**reviews, reviewing, reviewed**)
1 write a review of a book, film, play, etc.
2 reconsider. 3 inspect or survey.
reviewer noun

❶ USAGE Do not confuse with revue.

revise verb (**revises, revising, revised**)
1 go over work that you have already done, especially in preparing for an examination.
2 alter or correct something.
revision noun

revive verb (**revives, reviving, revived**)
come or bring back to life, strength, activity, or use etc.
revival noun

revolt verb (**revolts, revolting, revolted**)
1 rebel. 2 disgust somebody.
revolt noun (plural **revolts**)
a rebellion.

revolting adjective
disgusting.

revolution noun (plural **revolutions**)
1 a rebellion that overthrows the government.
2 a complete change. 3 revolving or rotation;
one complete turn of a wheel, engine, etc.
revolutionary adjective

revolve verb (**revolves, revolving, revolved**)
1 turn in a circle round a central point.
2 have something as the most important
element ♦ Her life revolves around her work.

revolver noun (plural **revolvers**)
a pistol with a revolving mechanism that makes
it possible to fire it a number of times without
reloading.

revue noun (plural **revues**)
an entertainment consisting of songs, sketches,
etc., often about current events.

ℹ USAGE Do not confuse with review.

---

revulsion noun
a feeling of disgust.

reward noun (plural **rewards**)
1 something given in return for something good
you have done. 2 a sum of money offered for
help in catching a criminal or finding lost
property.

reward verb (**rewards, rewarding, rewarded**)
give a reward to someone.

rewarding adjective
giving satisfaction and a feeling of achievement
♦ a rewarding job.

rewind verb (**rewinds, rewinding, rewound**)
wind a cassette or videotape back to or towards
the beginning.

rhetorical question noun (plural **rhetorical
questions**)
a question asked for dramatic effect and not
intended to get an answer, e.g. 'Who cares?'
(= nobody cares).

rheumatism noun
a disease that causes pain and stiffness in joints
and muscles.
rheumatic adjective **rheumatoid** adjective
[from Greek rheuma, a substance in the body
which was once believed to cause rheumatism]

rhino noun (plural **rhino** or **rhinos**) (informal)
a rhinoceros.

rhinoceros noun (plural **rhinoceros** or
rhinoceroses)
a large heavy animal with a horn or two horns
on its nose.
[from Greek rhinos = of the nose + keras =
horn]

rhizome noun (plural **rhizomes**)
a thick underground stem which produces roots
and new plants.

rhododendron noun (plural **rhododendrons**)
an evergreen shrub with large trumpet-shaped
flowers.
[from Greek rhodon = rose + dendron = tree]

rhombus noun (plural **rhombuses**)
a shape with four equal sides but no right angles,
like the diamond on playing cards.

rhubarb noun
a plant with thick reddish stalks that are cooked
and eaten as fruit.

rhyme noun (plural **rhymes**)
1 a similar sound in the endings of words,
e.g. bat/fat/mat or batter/fatter/matter.
2 a poem with rhymes. 3 a word that rhymes
with another.

rhyme verb (**rhymes, rhyming, rhymed**)
1 form a rhyme. 2 have rhymes.

rhythm noun (plural **rhythms**)
a regular pattern of beats, sounds, or
movements.
rhythmic adjective **rhythmical** adjective
rhythmically adverb

rib noun (plural **ribs**)
1 each of the curved bones round the chest.
2 a curved part that looks like a rib or supports
something ♦ the ribs of an umbrella.
ribbed adjective

ribbon noun (plural **ribbons**)
1 a narrow strip of silk or nylon etc. used for
decoration or for tying something. 2 a long
narrow strip of inked material used in a
typewriter etc.

rice noun
a cereal plant grown in flooded fields in hot
countries, or its seeds.

rich adjective
1 having a lot of money or property; wealthy.
2 having a large supply of something ♦ The
country is rich in natural resources. 3 (said about
colour, sound, or smell) pleasantly deep or
strong. 4 (said about food) containing a lot of fat,
butter, eggs, etc. 5 expensive or luxurious.
richness noun

richly adverb
1 in a rich or luxurious way. 2 fully or
thoroughly ♦ This award is richly deserved.

rickety adjective
shaky; likely to break or fall down.

rickshaw noun (plural **rickshaws**)
a two-wheeled carriage pulled by one or more
people, used in the Far East.
[from Japanese jin-riki-sha =
person-power-vehicle]

ricochet (say rik-osh-ay) verb (**ricochets,
ricocheting, ricocheted**)
bounce off something; rebound ♦ The bullets
ricocheted off the wall.
ricochet noun
[from French, = the skipping of a flat stone on
water]

ricotta *noun*
a kind of soft Italian cheese made from sheep's milk.
[from Italian]

rid *verb* (**rids, ridding, rid**)
make a person or place free from something unwanted ♦ *He rid the town of rats.*
get rid of remove something or throw it away.

riddle¹ *noun* (*plural* **riddles**)
a puzzling question, especially as a joke.

riddle² *verb* (**riddles, riddling, riddled**)
pierce with many holes ♦ *The car was riddled with bullets.*

ride (**rides, riding, rode, ridden**)
1 sit on a horse, bicycle, etc. and be carried along on it. **2** travel in a car, bus, train, etc. **3** float or be supported on something ♦ *The ship rode the waves.*

ride *noun* (*plural* **rides**)
1 a journey on a horse, bicycle, etc. or in a vehicle. **2** a roundabout etc. that you ride on at a fair or amusement park.

ridge *noun* (*plural* **ridges**)
1 a long narrow part higher than the rest of something. **2** a long narrow range of hills or mountains.
ridged *adjective*

ridicule *verb* (**ridicules, ridiculing, ridiculed**)
make fun of a person or thing.
ridicule *noun*

ridiculous *adjective*
so silly that it makes people laugh or despise it.
ridiculously *adverb*

rifle *noun* (*plural* **rifles**)
a long gun with spiral grooves (called **rifling**) inside the barrel that make the bullet spin and so travel more accurately.

rifle *verb* (**rifles, rifling, rifled**)
search and rob ♦ *They rifled his desk.*

rift valley *noun* (*plural* **rift valleys**)
a steep-sided valley formed where the land has sunk.

rig¹ *verb* (**rigs, rigging, rigged**)
1 provide a ship with ropes, spars, sails, etc.
2 set something up quickly or out of makeshift materials♦ *We managed to rig up a shelter for the night.*
rig out provide with clothes or equipment.

rig *noun* (*plural* **rigs**)
1 a framework supporting the machinery for drilling an oil well. **2** the way a ship's masts and sails etc. are arranged. **3** (*informal*) an outfit of clothes.
[probably from a Scandinavian language]

rig² *verb* (**rigs, rigging, rigged**)
arrange the result of an election or contest dishonestly.
[origin unknown]

rigging *noun*
the ropes etc. that support a ship's mast and sails.

right *adjective*
1 on or towards the east if you think of yourself as facing north. **2** correct; true ♦ *the right answer.* **3** morally good; fair or just ♦ *Is it right to cheat?* **4** (said about political groups) conservative; not in favour of socialist reforms.
right-hand *adjective* **rightly** *adverb* **rightness** *noun*

right *adverb*
1 on or towards the right-hand side ♦ *Turn right here.* **2** straight ♦ *Go right on.* **3** completely
♦ *Turn right round.* **4** exactly ♦ *right in the middle.* **5** correctly or appropriately ♦ *Did I do that right?*
right away immediately.

right *noun* (*plural* **rights**)
1 the right-hand side or part etc. **2** what is morally good or fair or just. **3** something that people are allowed to do or have ♦ *People over 18 have the right to vote in elections.*

right *verb* (**rights, righting, righted**)
1 make a thing right or upright ♦ *They righted the boat.* **2** put right ♦ *The fault might right itself.*

right angle *noun*
an angle of 90°.

rightful *adjective*
deserved or proper ♦ *in her rightful place.*
rightfully *adverb*

right hand *noun* (*plural* **right hands**)
the hand that most people use more than the left, on the right side of the body.

right-handed *adjective*
using the right hand in preference to the left hand.

right of way *noun* (*plural* **rights of way**)
1 a public path across private land. **2** the right of one vehicle to pass or cross a junction etc. before another.

rigid *adjective*
1 stiff or firm; not bending ♦ *a rigid support.*
2 strict ♦ *rigid rules.*
rigidly *adverb* **rigidity** *noun*

rigmarole *noun* (*plural* **rigmaroles**)
1 a long rambling statement. **2** a complicated procedure.

rigorous *adjective*
1 strict or severe. **2** careful and thorough.
rigorously *adverb*

rim *noun* (*plural* **rims**)
the outer edge of a cup, wheel, or other round object.

rind *noun*
the tough skin on bacon, cheese, or fruit.

ring¹ *noun* (*plural* **rings**)
1 a circle. 2 a thin circular piece of metal worn on a finger. 3 the space where a circus performs. 4 a square area in which a boxing match or wrestling match takes place.

ring *verb* (**rings, ringing, ringed**)
put a ring round something; encircle.

ring² *verb* (**rings, ringing, rang, rung**)
1 cause a bell to sound. 2 make a loud clear sound like that of a bell. 3 be filled with sound ♦ *The hall rang with cheers.* 4 telephone ♦ *Please ring me tomorrow.*
ringer *noun*

ring *noun* (*plural* **rings**)
the act or sound of ringing.
give someone a ring (*informal*) telephone someone.

ringleader *noun* (*plural* **ringleaders**)
a person who leads others in rebellion, mischief, crime, etc.

ringmaster *noun* (*plural* **ringmasters**)
the person in charge of a performance in a circus ring.

ring road *noun* (*plural* **ring roads**)
a road that runs around the edge of a town so that traffic does not have to go through the centre.

rink *noun* (*plural* **rinks**)
a place made for skating.

rinse *verb* (**rinses, rinsing, rinsed**)
1 wash something lightly. 2 wash in clean water to remove soap.

rinse *noun* (*plural* **rinses**)
1 rinsing. 2 a liquid for colouring the hair.

riot *noun* (*plural* **riots**)
wild or violent behaviour by a crowd of people.
run riot behave or spread in an unruly or uncontrolled way.

riot *verb* (**riots, rioting, rioted**)
take part in a riot.

riotous *adjective*
1 disorderly or unruly. 2 boisterous ♦ *riotous laughter.*

RIP *abbreviation*
may he or she (or they) rest in peace.

rip *verb* (**rips, ripping, ripped**)
1 tear roughly. 2 rush.
rip off (*informal*) swindle or charge too much.
rip *noun*
a torn place.

ripe *adjective* (**riper, ripest**)
1 ready to be harvested or eaten. 2 ready and suitable ♦ *The time is ripe for revolution.*
ripeness *noun*
a ripe old age a great age.

ripen *verb* (**ripens, ripening, ripened**)
make or become ripe.

rip-off *noun* (*plural* **rip-offs**)
(*informal*) a swindle or excessive charge.

ripple *noun* (*plural* **ripples**)
a small wave or series of waves.

ripple *verb* (**ripples, rippling, rippled**)
form ripples.

rise *verb* (**rises, rising, rose, risen**)
1 go upwards. 2 increase ♦ *Prices are expected to rise.* 3 get up from lying, sitting, or kneeling. 4 get out of bed. 5 rebel ♦ *They rose in revolt against the tyrant.* 6 (said about bread or cake etc.) swell up by the action of yeast. 7 (said about a river) begin its course. 8 (said about the wind) begin to blow more strongly.

rise *noun* (*plural* **rises**)
1 the action of rising; an upward movement. 2 an increase in amount etc. or in wages. 3 an upward slope.
give rise to cause.

rising *noun* (*plural* **risings**)
a revolt.

risk *noun* (*plural* **risks**)
a chance of danger or loss.

risk *verb* (**risks, risking, risked**)
1 take the chance of damaging or losing something. ♦ *They were risking their lives.* 2 accept the risk of something unpleasant happening ♦ *He risks injury.*

risky *adjective* (**riskier, riskiest**)
full of risk.

rissole *noun* (*plural* **rissoles**)
a fried cake of minced meat or fish.

ritual *noun* (*plural* **rituals**)
the series of actions used in a religious or other ceremony.
ritual *adjective* **ritually** *adverb*

rival *noun* (*plural* **rivals**)
a person or thing that competes with another or tries to do the same thing.
rivalry *noun*
[from Latin *rivalis* = someone using the same stream (from *rivus* = stream)]

river *noun* (*plural* **rivers**)
a large stream of water flowing in a natural channel.

rivet *noun* (*plural* **rivets**)
a strong nail or bolt for holding pieces of metal together. The end opposite the head is flattened to form another head when it is in place.

rivet *verb* (**rivets, riveting, riveted**)
1 fasten with rivets. 2 hold firmly ♦ *He stood riveted to the spot.* 3 fascinate ♦ *The concert was riveting.*
riveter *noun*

road *noun* (*plural* **roads**)
1 a level way with a hard surface made for traffic to travel on. 2 a way or course ♦ *the road to success.*
[from Old English]

roadblock noun (plural **roadblocks**)
a barrier across a road, set up by the police or army to stop and check vehicles.

road rage noun
violent or aggressive behaviour by a driver towards other drivers.

roadworthy adjective
safe to be used on roads.

roam verb (**roams, roaming, roamed**)
wander.
roam noun

roar noun (plural **roars**)
a loud deep sound like that made by a lion.
roar verb (**roars, roaring, roared**)
1 make a roar. 2 laugh loudly.
do a roaring trade do very good business.

roast verb (**roasts, roasting, roasted**)
1 cook meat etc. in an oven or by exposing it to heat. 2 make or be very hot.
roast adjective
roasted ♦ roast beef.
roast noun (plural **roasts**)
1 meat for roasting. 2 roast meat.
[from early French]

rob verb (**robs, robbing, robbed**)
take or steal from somebody ♦ He robbed me of my watch.
robber noun **robbery** noun

robe noun (plural **robes**)
a long loose garment.

robin noun (plural **robins**)
a small brown bird with a red breast.
[from early French, = Robert]

robot noun (plural **robots**)
1 a machine that looks or acts like a person.
2 a machine operated by remote control.
robotic adjective
[from Czech robota = forced labour]

robust adjective
strong and vigorous.
robustly adverb **robustness** noun

rock¹ noun (plural **rocks**)
1 a large stone or boulder. 2 the hard part of the earth's crust, under the soil. 3 a hard sweet usually shaped like a stick and sold at the seaside.

rock² verb (**rocks, rocking, rocked**)
1 move gently backwards and forwards while supported on something. 2 shake violently
♦ The earthquake rocked the city.
rock noun
1 a rocking movement. 2 rock music.

rock and roll or **rock 'n' roll** noun
a kind of popular dance music with a strong beat, originating in the 1950s.

rock-bottom adjective
at the lowest level ♦ rock-bottom prices.

rockery noun (plural **rockeries**)
a mound or bank in a garden, where plants are made to grow between large rocks.

rocket noun (plural **rockets**)
1 a firework that shoots high into the air.
2 a structure that flies by expelling burning gases, used to send up a missile or a spacecraft.
rocket verb (**rockets, rocketing, rocketed**)
move quickly upwards or away.

rocking horse noun (plural **rocking horses**)
a model of a horse that can be rocked by a child sitting on it.

rock music noun
popular music with a heavy beat.

rocky¹ adjective (**rockier, rockiest**)
1 like rock. 2 full of rocks.

rocky² adjective (**rockier, rockiest**)
unsteady.
rockiness noun

rod noun (plural **rods**)
1 a long thin stick or bar. 2 a stick with a line attached for fishing.

rodent noun (plural **rodents**)
an animal that has large front teeth for gnawing things. Rats, mice, and squirrels are rodents.

rodeo (say roh-di-oh) noun (plural **rodeos**)
a display of cowboys' skill in riding, controlling horses, etc.

roe¹ noun
a mass of eggs or reproductive cells in a fish's body.

roe² noun (plural **roes** or **roe**)
a kind of small deer of Europe and Asia. The male is called a **roebuck**.

rogue noun (plural **rogues**)
1 a dishonest person. 2 a mischievous person.
roguery noun

role noun (plural **roles**)
1 a performer's part in a play or film etc.
2 someone's or something's purpose or function
♦ the role of computers in education.

role model noun (plural **role models**)
a person admired by others as an example of how to behave.

roll verb (**rolls, rolling, rolled**)
1 move along by turning over and over, like a ball or wheel. 2 form something into the shape of a cylinder or ball. 3 flatten something by rolling a rounded object over it. 4 rock from side to side.
5 pass steadily ♦ The years rolled on. 6 make a long vibrating sound ♦ The thunder rolled.

roll noun (plural **rolls**)
1 a cylinder made by rolling something up.
2 a small individual portion of bread baked in a rounded shape. 3 an official list of names.
4 a long vibrating sound ♦ a drum roll.

roll-call *noun* (*plural* **roll-calls**)
the calling of a list of names to check that
everyone is present.

roller *noun* (*plural* **rollers**)
1 a cylinder for rolling over things, or on which
something is wound. **2** a long swelling sea wave.

Rollerblade *noun* (*plural* **Rollerblades**) (*trade mark*)
a boot like an ice-skating boot, with a line of
wheels in place of the skate, for rolling smoothly
on hard ground.
rollerblading *noun*

roller coaster *noun* (*plural* **roller coasters**)
a type of railway used for amusement at
fairgrounds etc. with a series of alternate steep
descents and ascents.

roller skate *noun* (*plural* **roller skates**)
a framework with wheels, fitted under a shoe so
that the wearer can roll smoothly over the
ground.
roller-skating *noun*

rolling pin *noun*
a heavy cylinder for rolling over pastry to
flatten it.

ROM *abbreviation*
(in computing) read-only memory, a type of
memory with contents that can be searched or
copied but not changed.

Roman *adjective*
to do with ancient or modern Rome or its people.
Roman *noun*

Roman alphabet *noun*
the alphabet used by the ancient Romans, in
which most European languages are written.

Roman Catholic *adjective*
belonging to or to do with the Christian Church
that has the Pope as its leader.

Roman Catholic *noun* (*plural* **Roman Catholics**)
a member of this Church.

romance (*say* ro-**manss**) *noun* (*plural* **romances**)
1 tender feelings, experiences, and qualities
connected with love. **2** a love story. **3** a love
affair. **4** an imaginative story about the
adventures of heroes ♦ *a romance of King
Arthur's court.*

Roman numerals *plural noun*
letters that represent numbers (I = 1, V = 5,
X = 10, etc.), used by the ancient Romans.
(Compare **arabic numerals.**)

romantic *adjective*
1 to do with love or romance. **2** sentimental or
idealistic; not realistic or practical.
romantically *adverb*

romp *verb* (**romps, romping, romped**)
play in a lively way.
romp *noun*

roof *noun* (*plural* **roofs**)
1 the part that covers the top of a building,
shelter, or vehicle. **2** the top inside surface of
something ♦ *the roof of the mouth.*

rook[1] *noun* (*plural* **rooks**)
a black crow that nests in large groups.

rook *verb* (**rooks, rooking, rooked**) (*informal*)
swindle; charge people an unnecessarily high
price.

rook[2] *noun* (*plural* **rooks**)
a chess piece shaped like a castle.

room *noun* (*plural* **rooms**)
1 a part of a building with its own walls and
ceiling. **2** enough space ♦ *Is there room for me?*
roomful *noun*

roost *verb* (**roosts, roosting, roosted**)
(said about birds) perch or settle for sleep.

roost *noun* (*plural* **roosts**)
a place where birds roost.

root[1] *noun* (*plural* **roots**)
1 that part of a plant that grows under the
ground and absorbs water and nourishment
from the soil. **2** a source or basis ♦ *The love of
money is the root of all evil.* **3** a number in
relation to the number it produces when
multiplied by itself ♦ *9 is the square root of 81 (9
×9 = 81).*
take root 1 grow roots. **2** become established.

root *verb* (**roots, rooting, rooted**)
1 take root; cause something to take root.
2 fix firmly ♦ *Fear rooted us to the spot.*
root out get rid of something.

root[2] *verb* (**roots, rooting, rooted**)
1 (said about an animal) turn up ground in
search of food. **2** rummage; find something by
doing this ♦ *I've managed to root out some facts
and figures.*

rope *noun* (*plural* **ropes**)
a strong thick cord made of twisted strands of
fibre.
show someone the ropes show him or her how
to do something.

rope *verb* (**ropes, roping, roped**)
fasten with a rope.
rope in persuade a person to take part in
something.

rose[1] *noun* (*plural* **roses**)
1 a shrub that has showy flowers, often with
thorny stems. **2** a deep pink colour. **3** a nozzle
with many holes, e.g. on a watering can or
hosepipe.

rose[2] *past tense* of **rise.**

Rosh Hashanah or **Rosh Hashana** *noun*
the Jewish New Year.

roster *noun* (*plural* **rosters**)
a list showing people's turns to be on duty etc.

rosy *adjective* (**rosier, rosiest**)
1 deep pink. 2 hopeful or cheerful ♦ *a rosy future.*
rosiness *noun*

rot *verb* (**rots, rotting, rotted**)
go soft or bad and become useless; decay.

rot *noun*
1 rotting or decay. 2 (*informal*) nonsense.

rota (*say* roh-ta) *noun* (*plural* **rotas**)
a list of people to do things or of things to be done in turn.

rotate *verb* (**rotates, rotating, rotated**)
1 go round like a wheel; revolve. 2 arrange or happen in a series; take turns at doing something.
rotation *noun* **rotary** *adjective* **rotatory** *adjective*

rote *noun*
by rote from memory or by routine, without full understanding of the meaning ♦ *We used to learn French songs by rote.*

rotor *noun* (*plural* **rotors**)
a rotating part of a machine or helicopter.

rotten *adjective*
1 rotted ♦ *rotten apples.* 2 (*informal*) very bad or unpleasant ♦ *rotten weather.*
rottenness *noun*

rouble (*say* roo-bul) *noun* (*plural* **roubles**)
the unit of money in Russia.

rouge (*say* roozh) *noun*
a reddish cosmetic for colouring the cheeks.
rouge *verb*

rough *adjective* (**rougher, roughest**)
1 not smooth; uneven. 2 not gentle or careful; violent ♦ *a rough push.* 3 not exact ♦ *a rough guess.* 4 (said about weather or the sea) wild and stormy.
roughly *adverb* **roughness** *noun*

rough *verb* (**roughs, roughing, roughed**)
rough it do without ordinary comforts. **rough out** draw or plan something roughly. **rough up** (*slang*) treat a person violently.

roughen *verb* (**roughens, roughening, roughened**)
make or become rough.

round *adjective*
1 shaped like a circle or ball or cylinder; curved. 2 full or complete ♦ *a round dozen.* 3 returning to the start ♦ *a round trip.*
roundness *noun*
in round figures approximately, without giving exact units.

round *adverb*
1 in a circle or curve; round something ♦ *Go round to the back of the house.* 2 in every direction or to every person ♦ *Hand the cakes round.* 3 in a new direction ♦ *Turn your chair round.* 4 to someone's house or office etc. ♦ *Go round after dinner.*
come round become conscious again.
round about 1 near by. 2 approximately.

round *preposition*
1 on all sides of ♦ *Put a fence round the field.* 2 in a curve or circle at an even distance from ♦ *The earth moves round the sun.* 3 to all parts of ♦ *Show them round the house.* 4 on the further side of ♦ *The shop is round the corner.*

round *noun* (*plural* **rounds**)
1 a series of visits made by a doctor, postman, etc. 2 one section or stage in a competition ♦ *Winners go on to the next round.* 3 a shot or volley of shots from a gun; ammunition for this. 4 a whole slice of bread; a sandwich made with two slices of bread. 5 a song in which people sing the same words but start at different times. 6 a set of drinks bought for all the members of a group.

round *verb* (**rounds, rounding, rounded**)
1 make or become round. 2 travel round ♦ *The car rounded the corner.*
round off finish something. **round up** gather people or animals together.

roundabout *noun* (*plural* **roundabouts**)
1 a road junction where traffic has to pass round a circular structure in the road. 2 a circular revolving ride at a fair.

roundabout *adjective*
indirect; not using the shortest way of going or of saying or doing something ♦ *I heard the news in a roundabout way.*

rounders *noun*
a game in which players try to hit a ball and run round a circuit.

round-the-clock *adjective*
lasting or happening all day and all night.

round trip *noun* (*plural* **round trips**)
a trip to one or more places and back to where you started.

round-up *noun* (*plural* **round-ups**)
1 a gathering-up of cattle or people ♦ *a police round-up of suspects.* 2 a summary ♦ *a round-up of the news.*

rouse *verb* (**rouses, rousing, roused**)
1 make or become awake. 2 cause to become active or excited.

rousing *adjective*
loud or exciting ♦ *three rousing cheers.*

rout *verb* (**routs, routing, routed**)
defeat and chase away an enemy.
rout *noun*

route (*say* root) *noun* (*plural* **routes**)
the way taken to get to a place.

routine (*say* roo-teen) *noun* (*plural* **routines**)
a regular way of doing things.
routinely *adverb*

rove *verb* (**roves, roving, roved**)
roam or wander.
rover *noun*

row¹ (rhymes with *go*) *noun* (*plural* **rows**)
a line of people or things.

row² (rhymes with *go*) *verb* (**rows, rowing, rowed**)
make a boat move by using oars.
rower *noun* **rowing boat** *noun*

row³ (rhymes with *cow*) *noun* (*plural* **rows**)
1 a loud noise. 2 a quarrel.

rowdy *adjective* (**rowdier, rowdiest**)
noisy and disorderly.
rowdiness *noun*

royal *adjective*
to do with a king or queen.
royally *adverb*
[via early French from Latin *regalis*]

royalty *noun*
1 being royal. 2 a royal person or people ♦ *in the presence of royalty.* 3 (*plural* **royalties**) a payment made to an author or composer etc. for each copy of a work sold or for each performance.

RSVP *abbreviation*
répondez s'il vous plaît.
[French, = please reply]

rub *verb* (**rubs, rubbing, rubbed**)
move something backwards and forwards while pressing it on something else.
rub *noun*
rub out remove something by rubbing.

rubber *noun* (*plural* **rubbers**)
1 a strong elastic substance used for making tyres, balls, hoses, etc. 2 a piece of rubber for rubbing out pencil or ink marks.
rubbery *adjective*

rubbish *noun*
1 things that are worthless or not wanted. 2 nonsense.

rubble *noun*
broken pieces of brick or stone.

rubella (*say* roo-bel-la) *noun*
an infectious disease which causes a red rash, and which can damage a baby if the mother catches it early in pregnancy.
[from Latin *rubellus* = reddish]

ruby *noun* (*plural* **rubies**)
a red jewel.
[from Latin *rubeus* = red]

rucksack *noun* (*plural* **rucksacks**)
a bag on straps for carrying on the back.
[from German *Rücken* = back + *Sack* = bag, sack]

rudder *noun* (*plural* **rudders**)
a hinged upright piece at the back of a ship or aircraft, used for steering.

ruddy *adjective* (**ruddier, ruddiest**)
red and healthy-looking ♦ *a ruddy complexion.*

rude *adjective* (**ruder, rudest**)
1 impolite. 2 indecent or improper. 3 roughly made; crude ♦ *a rude shelter.* 4 vigorous and hearty ♦ *in rude health.*
rudely *adverb* **rudeness** *noun*

rudimentary *adjective*
1 to do with rudiments; elementary. 2 not fully developed ♦ *Penguins have rudimentary wings.*

rudiments (*say* rood-i-ments) *plural noun*
the basic principles of a subject ♦ *She taught me the rudiments of chemistry.*

ruff *noun* (*plural* **ruffs**)
1 a starched pleated frill worn round the neck in the 16th century. 2 a collar-like ring of feathers or fur round a bird's or animal's neck.

ruffian *noun* (*plural* **ruffians**)
a violent lawless person.
ruffianly *adjective*

ruffle *verb* (**ruffles, ruffling, ruffled**)
1 disturb the smoothness of a thing. 2 upset or annoy someone.

ruffle *noun* (*plural* **ruffles**)
a gathered ornamental frill.

rug *noun* (*plural* **rugs**)
1 a thick mat for the floor. 2 a piece of thick fabric used as a blanket.

rugby or **rugby football** *noun*
a kind of football game using an oval ball that players may carry or kick.
[named after Rugby School in Warwickshire, where it was first played]

rugged *adjective*
1 having an uneven surface or outline; craggy. 2 sturdy.

rugger *noun*
rugby football.

ruin *noun* (*plural* **ruins**)
1 severe damage or destruction to something. 2 a building that has fallen down.
ruin *verb* (**ruins, ruining, ruined**)
damage or destroy a thing so severely that it is useless.
ruination *noun*

ruinous *adjective*
1 causing ruin. 2 in ruins; ruined.

rule *noun* (*plural* **rules**)
1 something that people have to obey. 2 ruling; governing ♦ *under French rule.* 3 a carpenter's ruler.
as a rule usually; more often than not.
rule *verb* (**rules, ruling, ruled**)
1 govern or reign. 2 make a decision ♦ *The referee ruled that it was a foul.* 3 draw a straight line with a ruler or other straight edge.
[from early French]

ruler *noun* (*plural* **rulers**)
1 a person who governs. 2 a strip of wood, metal, or plastic with straight edges, used for measuring and drawing straight lines.

ruling *noun* (*plural* **rulings**)
a judgement.

rum *noun*
a strong alcoholic drink made from sugar or
molasses.

rumble *verb* (**rumbles, rumbling, rumbled**)
make a deep heavy continuous sound like
thunder.
rumble *noun*

ruminant *adjective*
ruminating.

ruminant *noun* (*plural* **ruminants**)
an animal that chews the cud (see **cud**).

ruminate *verb* (**ruminates, ruminating,
ruminated**)
1 chew the cud. **2** meditate or ponder.
rumination *noun* **ruminative** *adjective*

rummage *verb* (**rummages, rummaging,
rummaged**)
turn things over or move them about while
looking for something.
rummage *noun*

rumour *noun* (*plural* **rumours**)
information that spreads to a lot of people but
may not be true.
rumour *verb*
be rumoured be spread as a rumour.
[from Latin *rumor* = noise]

rump *noun* (*plural* **rumps**)
the hind part of an animal.

rumple *verb* (**rumples, rumpling, rumpled**)
crumple; make a thing untidy.

rump steak *noun* (*plural* **rump steaks**)
a piece of meat from the rump of a cow.

rumpus *noun* (*plural* **rumpuses**) (*informal*)
an uproar; an angry protest.

run *verb* (**runs, running, ran, run**)
1 move with quick steps so that both or all
feet leave the ground at each stride. **2** go or
travel; flow ♦ *Tears ran down his cheeks.*
3 produce a flow of liquid ♦ *Run some water into
it.* **4** work or function ♦ *The engine was running
smoothly.* **5** manage or organize ♦ *She runs a
corner shop.* **6** compete in a contest ♦ *He ran for
President.* **7** extend ♦ *A fence runs round the
estate.* **8** go or take in a vehicle ♦ *I'll run you to
the station.*
run a risk take a chance. run away leave a
place secretly or quickly. run down 1 run over.
2 stop gradually; decline. 3 (*informal*) say
unkind or unfair things about someone. run into
1 collide with. 2 happen to meet. run out 1 have
used up your stock of something. 2 knock over
the wicket of a running batsman. run over
knock down or crush with a moving vehicle.
run through examine or rehearse.

run *noun* (*plural* **runs**)
1 the action of running; a time spent running
♦ *I went for a run.* **2** a point scored in cricket or
baseball. **3** a continuous series of events, etc.
♦ *She had a run of good luck.* **4** an enclosure for
animals ♦ *a chicken run.* **5** a series of damaged
stitches in a pair of tights or stockings. **6** a track
♦ *a ski run.*
on the run running away, especially from the
police.
[from Old English]

runaway *noun* (*plural* **runaways**)
someone who has run away.

runaway *adjective*
1 having run away or out of control.
2 won easily ♦ *a runaway victory.*

run-down *adjective*
1 tired and in bad health. **2** in bad condition;
dilapidated.

rung[1] *noun* (*plural* **rungs**)
one of the crossbars on a ladder.

rung[2] *past participle* of **ring**[2].

runner *noun* (*plural* **runners**)
1 a person or animal that runs, especially in a
race. **2** a stem that grows away from a plant and
roots itself. **3** a groove, rod, or roller for a thing
to move on; each of the long strips under a
sledge. **4** a long narrow strip of carpet or
covering.

runner bean *noun* (*plural* **runner beans**)
a kind of climbing bean with long green pods
which are eaten.

runner-up *noun* (*plural* **runners-up**)
someone who comes second in a competition.

running *present participle* of **run**.
in the running competing and with a chance of
winning.

running *adjective*
continuous or consecutive; without an interval
♦ *It rained for four days running.*

runny *adjective* (**runnier, runniest**)
1 flowing like liquid ♦ *runny honey.* **2** producing
a flow of liquid ♦ *a runny nose.*

runway *noun* (*plural* **runways**)
a long hard surface on which aircraft take off and
land.

rural *adjective*
to do with or belonging to the countryside.

ruse *noun* (*plural* **ruses**)
a deception or trick.

rush[1] *verb* (**rushes, rushing, rushed**)
1 move or do something quickly. **2** make
someone hurry. **3** attack or capture by dashing
forward suddenly.

rush *noun* (*plural* **rushes**)
1 a hurry. **2** a sudden movement towards
something. **3** a sudden great demand for
something.

rush² *noun* (*plural* **rushes**)
a plant with a thin stem that grows in marshy places.

rush hour *noun* (*plural* **rush hours**)
the time when traffic is busiest.

rusk *noun* (*plural* **rusks**)
a kind of hard, dry biscuit, especially for feeding babies.

rust *noun*
1 a red or brown substance that forms on iron or steel exposed to damp and corrodes it.
2 a reddish-brown colour.

rust *verb* (**rusts, rusting, rusted**)
make or become rusty.

rustic *adjective*
1 rural. 2 made of rough timber or branches
♦ *a rustic bridge.*

rustle *verb* (**rustles, rustling, rustled**)
1 make a sound like paper being crumpled.
2 (*American*) steal horses or cattle ♦ *cattle rustling.*
rustle *noun* **rustler** *noun*
rustle up (*informal*) produce ♦ *rustle up a meal.*

rusty *adjective* (**rustier, rustiest**)
1 coated with rust. 2 weakened by lack of use or practice ♦ *My French is a bit rusty.*
rustiness *noun*

rut *noun* (*plural* **ruts**)
1 a deep track made by wheels in soft ground.
2 a settled and usually dull way of life ♦ *We are getting into a rut.*
rutted *adjective*

ruthless *adjective*
pitiless, merciless, or cruel.
ruthlessly *adverb* **ruthlessness** *noun*
[from Middle English *ruth* = pity]

rye *noun*
a cereal used to make bread, biscuits, etc.

Ss

S. *abbreviation*
1 south. 2 southern.

sabbath *noun* (*plural* **sabbaths**)
a weekly day for rest and prayer, Saturday for Jews, Sunday for Christians.
[from Hebrew *shabat* = rest]

sabotage *noun*
deliberate damage or disruption to hinder an enemy, employer, etc.
sabotage *verb* **saboteur** *noun*
[from French *saboter* = make a noise with *sabots* (= wooden clogs)]

saccharin (*say* sak-er-in) *noun*
a very sweet substance used as a substitute for sugar.

sack¹ *noun* (*plural* **sacks**)
a large bag made of strong material.
sacking *noun*
the sack (*informal*) dismissal from a job
♦ *He got the sack.*
sack *verb* (**sacks, sacking, sacked**) (*informal*)
dismiss someone from a job.
[via Old English and Latin from Greek *sakkos*]

sack² *verb* (**sacks, sacking, sacked**) (*old use*)
plunder a captured town in a violent destructive way.
sack *noun*
[from French *mettre à sac* = put (booty) in a sack]

sacrament *noun* (*plural* **sacraments**)
an important Christian religious ceremony such as baptism or Holy Communion.

sacred *adjective*
holy; to do with God or a god.

sacrifice *noun* (*plural* **sacrifices**)
1 an offering to a god of a killed animal or other special thing. 2 giving up a thing you value, so that something good may happen. 3 a thing sacrificed.
sacrificial *adjective*
sacrifice *verb* (**sacrifices, sacrificing, sacrificed**)
offer something or give it up as a sacrifice.

sacrilege (*say* sak-ril-ij) *noun*
disrespect or damage to something people regard as sacred.
sacrilegious *adjective*

sad *adjective* (**sadder, saddest**)
unhappy; showing or causing sorrow.
sadly *adverb* **sadness** *noun*
[from Old English]

sadden *verb* (**saddens, saddening, saddened**)
make a person sad.

saddle *noun* (*plural* **saddles**)
1 a seat for putting on the back of a horse or other animal. 2 the seat of a bicycle. 3 a ridge of high land between two peaks.
saddle *verb* (**saddles, saddling, saddled**)
put a saddle on a horse etc.
saddle someone with burden someone with a task or problem.

sadist (*say* say-dist) *noun* (*plural* **sadists**)
a person who enjoys hurting or humiliating other people.
sadism *noun* **sadistic** *adjective*
[named after an 18th-century French novelist, the Marquis de Sade, noted for the cruelties in his stories]

safari *noun* (*plural* **safaris**)
an expedition to see or hunt wild animals.
[from Arabic *safar* = a journey]

safari park noun (plural **safari parks**)
a park where wild animals are kept in large enclosures to be seen by visitors.

safe adjective
1 not in danger. **2** not dangerous ♦ a safe speed.
safely adverb **safeness** noun **safety** noun

safe noun (plural **safes**)
a strong cupboard or box in which valuables can be locked safely.

safeguard noun (plural **safeguards**)
a protection.

safe sex noun
sexual activity using a condom or other precautions to prevent the spread of infection.

safety pin noun (plural **safety pins**)
a U-shaped pin with a clip fastening over the point.

sag verb (**sags, sagging, sagged**)
hang or go down in the middle from its own weight or because something heavy is pressing on it.
sag noun

saga (say **sah-ga**) noun (plural **sagas**)
a long story with many episodes or adventures.

sage¹ noun
a kind of herb used in cooking and formerly used in medicine.

sage² adjective
wise.
sagely adverb

sage noun (plural **sages**)
a wise and respected person.

sago noun
a starchy white food used to make puddings.

said past tense of say.

sail noun (plural **sails**)
1 a large piece of strong cloth attached to a mast etc. to catch the wind and make a ship or boat move. **2** a short voyage. **3** an arm of a windmill.
set sail start on a voyage in a ship.

sail verb (**sails, sailing, sailed**)
1 travel in a ship or boat. **2** start a voyage ♦ We sail at noon. **3** control a ship or boat.
4 move quickly and smoothly.
sailing ship noun

sailboard noun (plural **sailboards**)
a flat board with a mast and sail, used in windsurfing.

sailor noun (plural **sailors**)
a person who sails; a member of a ship's crew or of a navy.

saint noun (plural **saints**)
a holy or very good person.
saintly adjective **saintliness** noun

sake noun
for the sake of so as to help or please a person, get a thing, etc. **for someone's sake** so as to help or please them ♦ Don't go to any trouble for my sake.

salad noun (plural **salads**)
a mixture of vegetables eaten raw or cold.

salary noun (plural **salaries**)
a regular wage, usually for a year's work, paid in monthly instalments.
salaried adjective

sale noun (plural **sales**)
1 selling. **2** a time when things are sold at reduced prices.
for sale or **on sale** available to be bought.

salient (say **say-lee-ent**) adjective
most important or noticeable ♦ the salient features of the plan.

saliva noun
the natural liquid in a person's or animal's mouth.
salivary adjective

sallow adjective
(said about the skin) slightly yellow.
sallowness noun

salmon (say **sam-on**) noun (plural **salmon**)
a large edible fish with pink flesh.

salon noun (plural **salons**)
1 a large elegant room. **2** a room or shop where a hairdresser etc. receives customers.

saloon noun (plural **saloons**)
1 a car with a hard roof and a separate boot.
2 a comfortable room in a pub or bar.

salt noun (plural **salts**)
1 sodium chloride, the white substance that gives sea water its taste and is used for flavouring food. **2** a chemical compound of a metal and an acid.
salty adjective

salt verb (**salts, salting, salted**)
flavour or preserve food with salt.

salt cellar noun (plural **salt cellars**)
a small dish or perforated pot holding salt for use at meals.

salute verb (**salutes, saluting, saluted**)
1 raise your right hand to your forehead as a sign of respect. **2** greet. **3** say that you respect or admire something ♦ We salute this achievement.
salute noun (plural **salutes**)
1 the act of saluting. **2** the firing of guns as a sign of greeting or respect.

salvage verb (**salvages, salvaging, salvaged**)
save or rescue something such as a damaged ship's cargo so that it can be used again.
salvage noun

salvation noun
1 saving from loss or damage etc. **2** (in Christian teaching) saving the soul from sin and its consequences.

same adjective
1 of one kind, exactly alike or equal.
2 not changing; not different.
sameness noun

samosa *noun* (*plural* **samosas**)
a triangular, thin pastry case filled with spicy
meat or vegetables, fried and eaten as a snack.

sample *noun* (*plural* **samples**)
a small amount that shows what something is
like; a specimen.

sample *verb* (**samples, sampling, sampled**)
1 take a sample of something. **2** try part of
something.

sanatorium *noun* (*plural* **sanatoriums** or
sanatoria)
a hospital for treating long-term diseases or
people recovering from diseases.

sanctimonious *adjective*
making a show of being virtuous or pious.

sanction *noun* (*plural* **sanctions**)
1 action taken against a nation that is considered
to have broken an international law etc.
♦ *Sanctions against that country include refusing
to trade with it.* **2** a penalty for disobeying a law.
3 permission or authorization.

sanction *verb* (**sanctions, sanctioning,
sanctioned**)
permit or authorize.

sanctity *noun*
being sacred; holiness.

sanctuary *noun* (*plural* **sanctuaries**)
1 a safe place; a refuge. **2** an area where wildlife
is protected♦ *a bird sanctuary.* **3** a sacred place;
the part of a church where the altar stands.

sand *noun*
the tiny particles that cover the ground in
deserts, seashores, etc.

sand *verb* (**sands, sanding, sanded**)
smooth or polish with sandpaper or some other
rough material.
sander *noun*

sandal *noun* (*plural* **sandals**)
a lightweight shoe with straps over the foot.
sandalled *adjective*

sandpaper *noun*
strong paper coated with sand or a similar
substance, rubbed on rough surfaces to make
them smooth.

sandwich *noun* (*plural* **sandwiches**)
two or more slices of bread with jam, meat, or
cheese etc. between them.

sandwich *verb* (**sandwiches, sandwiching,
sandwiched**)
put a thing between two other things.
[named after the Earl of Sandwich (1718–92),
who invented them so that he could eat while
gambling]

sandy *adjective*
1 like sand. **2** covered with sand. **3** yellowish-red
♦ *sandy hair.*
sandiness *noun*

sane *adjective*
1 having a healthy mind; not mad. **2** sensible.
sanely *adverb* **sanity** *noun*

sanitary *adjective*
1 free from germs and dirt; hygienic. **2** to do with
sanitation.

sanitary towel *noun* (*plural* **sanitary towels**)
an absorbent pad worn by women during
menstruation.

sanitation *noun*
arrangements for drainage and the disposal of
sewage.

sanity *noun*
being sane.

Sanskrit *noun*
an ancient language of India.

sap *noun*
the liquid inside a plant, carrying food to all its
parts.

sap *verb* (**saps, sapping, sapped**)
take away a person's strength gradually.

sapling *noun* (*plural* **saplings**)
a young tree.

sapphire *noun* (*plural* **sapphires**)
a bright blue jewel.

sarcastic *adjective*
saying amusing or contemptuous things that
hurt someone's feelings.
sarcastically *adverb* **sarcasm** *noun*

sardine *noun* (*plural* **sardines**)
a small sea fish, usually sold in tins, packed
tightly in oil.

sari *noun* (*plural* **saris**)
a length of cloth worn wrapped round the body
as a dress, especially by Indian women and girls.
[from Hindi]

sash *noun* (*plural* **sashes**)
a strip of cloth worn round the waist or over one
shoulder.
[from Arabic *shash* = turban]

satchel *noun* (*plural* **satchels**)
a bag worn on the shoulder or the back,
especially for carrying books to and from school.
[from Latin *saccellus* = little sack]

satellite *noun* (*plural* **satellites**)
1 a spacecraft put in orbit round a planet to
collect information or transmit communications
signals. **2** a moon moving in an orbit round a
planet. **3** a country that is under the influence of
a more powerful country.

satellite dish *noun* (*plural* **satellite dishes**)
a bowl-shaped aerial for receiving broadcasting
signals transmitted by satellite.

satin *noun*
a silky material that is shiny on one side.
satiny *adjective*
[from an Arabic word = 'from Tsinkiang',
a town in China]

satire noun (plural **satires**)
1 using humour or exaggeration to criticize people in authority. **2** a play or sketch that does this.
satirical adjective **satirically** adverb **satirist** noun **satirize** verb

satisfaction noun
1 satisfying a need or want. **2** a feeling of pleasure arising from having what you need or want. **3** something that satisfies a desire etc.

satisfactory adjective
good enough; sufficient.
satisfactorily adverb

satisfy verb (**satisfies, satisfying, satisfied**)
1 give someone what they need or want. **2** make someone feel certain; convince ♦ *The police are satisfied that the death was accidental.* **3** fulfil ♦ *You have satisfied all our requirements.*

saturate verb (**saturates, saturating, saturated**)
1 make a thing very wet. **2** make something take in as much as possible of a substance or goods etc.
saturation noun

Saturday noun
the day of the week following Friday.
[from Old English *Saeternesdaeg* = day of Saturn, a Roman god]

sauce noun (plural **sauces**)
1 a thick liquid served with food to add flavour. **2** (*informal*) being cheeky; impudence.
[from Latin *salsus* = salted]

saucepan noun (plural **saucepans**)
a metal cooking pan with a handle at the side.

saucer noun (plural **saucers**)
a small shallow object on which a cup etc. is placed.
[from early French *saussier* = container for sauce]

saucy adjective (**saucier, sauciest**)
cheeky or impudent.
saucily adverb **sauciness** noun

sauna noun (plural **saunas**)
a room or compartment filled with steam, used as a kind of bath.
[from Finnish]

saunter verb (**saunters, sauntering, sauntered**)
walk slowly and casually.
saunter noun

sausage noun (plural **sausages**)
a tube of skin or plastic stuffed with minced meat and other filling.
[from early French; related to *sauce*]

savage adjective
wild and fierce; cruel.
savagely adverb **savageness** noun **savagery** noun

savage noun (plural **savages**)
1 a savage person. **2** (*old use*) a member of a people thought of as primitive or uncivilized.

savage verb (**savages, savaging, savaged**)
attack by biting or wounding ♦ *The sheep had been savaged by a dog.*

save verb (**saves, saving, saved**)
1 keep safe; free a person or thing from danger or harm. **2** keep something, especially money, so that it can be used later. **3** avoid wasting something ♦ *This will save time.*
4 (in computing) keep data by storing it in the computer's memory or on a disk. **5** (in sports) prevent an opponent from scoring.
save noun **saver** noun

savings plural noun
money saved.

saviour noun (plural **saviours**)
a person who saves someone.
the or **our Saviour** (in Christianity) Jesus Christ.

savoury adjective
1 tasty but not sweet. **2** having an appetizing taste or smell.

saw[1] noun (plural **saws**)
a tool with a zigzag edge for cutting wood or metal etc.

saw verb (**saws, sawing, sawed, sawn**)
1 cut something with a saw. **2** move to and fro as a saw does.
[from Old English]

saw[2] past tense of **see**.

sawdust noun
powder that comes from wood cut by a saw.

saxophone noun (plural **saxophones**)
a brass wind instrument with a reed in the mouthpiece.
saxophonist noun
[named after a 19th-century Belgian instrument maker, Adolphe Sax, who invented it]

say verb (**says, saying, said**)
1 speak or express something in words. **2** give an opinion.

say noun
the power to decide something ♦ *I have no say in the matter.*

saying noun (plural **sayings**)
a well-known phrase or proverb or other statement.

scab noun (plural **scabs**)
a hard crust that forms over a cut or graze while it is healing.
scabby adjective
[from Old Norse]

scaffold noun (plural **scaffolds**)
a platform on which criminals are executed.

scaffolding *noun*
a structure of poles or tubes and planks making platforms for workers to stand on while building or repairing a house etc.

scald *verb* (**scalds, scalding, scalded**)
1 burn yourself with very hot liquid or steam. **2** heat milk until it is nearly boiling. **3** clean pans etc. with boiling water.
scald *noun*

scale¹ *noun* (*plural* **scales**)
1 a series of units, degrees, or qualities etc. for measuring something. **2** a series of musical notes going up or down in a fixed pattern. **3** proportion or ratio ♦ *The scale of this map is one centimetre to the kilometre.* **4** the relative size or importance of something ♦ *They organize parties on a large scale.*
to scale with the parts in the same proportions as those of an original ♦ *The architect's plans were drawn to scale.*

scale *verb* (**scales, scaling, scaled**)
climb ♦ *She scaled the ladder.*
scale down or **up** reduce or increase at a fixed rate, or in proportion to something else.
[from Latin *scala* = ladder]

scale² *noun* (*plural* **scales**)
1 each of the thin overlapping parts on the outside of fish, snakes, etc.; a thin flake or part like this. **2** a hard substance formed in a kettle or boiler by hard water, or on teeth.
scaly *adjective*

scale *verb* (**scales, scaling, scaled**)
remove scales or scale from something.
[from old French; related to *scales*]

scale model *noun* (*plural* **scale models**)
a model of something, made to scale.

scales *plural noun*
a device for weighing things.
[from Old Norse *skal* = bowl]

scalp *noun* (*plural* **scalps**)
the skin on the top of the head.

scamp *noun* (*plural* **scamps**)
a rascal.

scamper *verb* (**scampers, scampering, scampered**)
run quickly, lightly, or playfully.
scamper *noun*

scan *verb* (**scans, scanning, scanned**)
1 look at every part of something. **2** glance at something. **3** count the beats of a line of poetry; be correct in rhythm ♦ *This line doesn't scan.* **4** sweep a radar or electronic beam over an area to examine it or in search of something. **5** (in computing) use a scanner to convert printed text or pictures into digital form for storing in a computer.

scan *noun* (*plural* **scans**)
1 scanning. **2** an examination using a scanner ♦ *a brain scan.*

scandal *noun* (*plural* **scandals**)
1 something shameful or disgraceful. **2** gossip about people's faults and wrongdoings.
scandalous *adjective*
[from Greek *skandalon* = stumbling block]

scandalize *verb* (**scandalizes, scandalizing, scandalized**)
shock a person by something considered shameful or disgraceful.

scanner *noun* (*plural* **scanners**)
1 a machine that examines things by means of light or other rays. **2** a machine that converts printed text, pictures, etc. into a form that can be stored in a computer.

scant *adjective*
barely enough or adequate ♦ *We paid scant attention.*

scanty *adjective* (**scantier, scantiest**)
small in amount or extent; meagre ♦ *a scanty harvest.*
scantily *adverb* **scantiness** *noun*

scapegoat *noun* (*plural* **scapegoats**)
a person who is made to bear the blame or punishment for what others have done.
[from *escape* and *goat*, after the goat which the ancient Jews allowed to escape into the desert after the priest had symbolically laid the people's sins upon it]

scar *noun* (*plural* **scars**)
1 the mark left by a cut or burn etc. after it has healed. **2** a lasting bad effect left by an unpleasant experience.

scar *verb* (**scars, scarring, scarred**)
make a scar or scars on skin etc.

scarce *adjective* (**scarcer, scarcest**)
1 not enough to supply people. **2** rare.
scarcity *noun*
make yourself scarce (*informal*) go away; keep out of the way.

scarcely *adverb*
only just; only with difficulty ♦ *She could scarcely walk.*

scare *verb* (**scares, scaring, scared**)
frighten.

scare *noun* (*plural* **scares**)
1 a fright. **2** a sudden widespread sense of alarm about something♦ *a bomb scare.*
[from Old Norse]

scarecrow *noun* (*plural* **scarecrows**)
a figure of a person dressed in old clothes, set up to frighten birds away from crops.

scarf *noun* (*plural* **scarves**)
a strip of material worn round the neck or head.

scarlet *adjective* & *noun*
bright red.

scary *adjective* (*informal*)
frightening.

scathing (*say* skay*th*-ing) *adjective*
severely criticizing a person or thing.

scatter *verb* (**scatters, scattering, scattered**)
1 throw or send or move in various directions.
2 run or leave quickly in all directions.

scavenge *verb* (**scavenges, scavenging, scavenged**)
1 search for useful things amongst rubbish.
2 (said about a bird or animal) search for decaying flesh as food.
scavenger *noun*

scene *noun* (*plural* **scenes**)
1 the place where something has happened
♦ *the scene of the crime.* **2** a part of a play or film.
3 a view as seen by a spectator. **4** an angry or noisy outburst ♦ *He made a scene about the money.* **5** stage scenery. **6** an area of activity
♦ *the local music scene.*

scenery *noun*
1 the natural features of a landscape. **2** things put on a stage to make it look like a place.

scent *noun* (*plural* **scents**)
1 a pleasant smell. **2** a liquid perfume.
3 an animal's smell that other animals can detect.
scented *adjective*

sceptical (*say* skep-tik-al) *adjective*
inclined to question things; not believing easily.
sceptically *adverb* **scepticism** *noun*

sceptre (*say* sep-ter) *noun* (*plural* **sceptres**)
a rod carried by a king or queen as a symbol of power.

schedule (*say* shed-yool) *noun* (*plural* **schedules**)
a programme or timetable of planned events or work.

schematic (*say* skee-mat-ik) *adjective*
in the form of a diagram or chart.

scheme *noun* (*plural* **schemes**)
a plan of action.

scheme *verb* (**schemes, scheming, schemed**)
make plans; plot.
schemer *noun*

scholar *noun* (*plural* **scholars**)
1 a person who has studied a subject thoroughly.
2 a person who has been awarded a scholarship.
scholarly *adjective*

scholarship *noun* (*plural* **scholarships**)
1 a grant of money given to someone to help to pay for his or her education. **2** scholars' knowledge or methods; advanced study.

school¹ *noun* (*plural* **schools**)
1 a place where teaching is done, especially of pupils aged 5–18. **2** the pupils in a school.
3 the time when teaching takes place in a school
♦ *School begins at 9 a.m.* **4** a group of people who have the same beliefs or style of work etc.

school *verb* (**schools, schooling, schooled**)
teach or train ♦ *She was schooling her horse for the competition.*
[from Greek *skhole*]

school² *noun* (*plural* **schools**)
a shoal of fish or whales etc.
[from early German or Dutch *schole* = a troop]

schoolchild *noun* (*plural* **schoolchildren**)
a child who goes to school.
schoolboy *noun* **schoolgirl** *noun*

schooling *noun*
1 training. **2** education, especially in a school.

schoolteacher *noun* (*plural* **schoolteachers**)
a person who teaches in a school.
schoolmaster *noun* **schoolmistress** *noun*

science *noun*
the study of the physical world by means of observation and experiment.
[from Latin *scientia* = knowledge]

science fiction *noun*
stories about imaginary scientific discoveries or space travel and life on other planets.

science park *noun* (*plural* **science parks**)
an area set up for industries using science or for organizations doing scientific research.

scientific *adjective*
1 to do with science or scientists. **2** studying things systematically and testing ideas carefully.
scientifically *adverb*

scientist *noun* (*plural* **scientists**)
1 an expert in science. **2** someone who uses scientific methods.

scintillating *adjective*
1 shining brightly; sparkling. **2** very lively and witty.

scissors *plural noun*
a cutting instrument used with one hand, with two blades pivoted so that they can close against each other.

scoff *verb* (**scoffs, scoffing, scoffed**)
1 jeer; speak contemptuously. **2** (*informal*) eat greedily
scoffer *noun*

scold *verb* (**scolds, scolding, scolded**)
speak angrily; tell someone off.
scolding *noun*

scone (*say* skon or skohn) *noun* (*plural* **scones**)
a soft flat cake, usually eaten with butter.

scoop *noun* (*plural* **scoops**)
1 a kind of deep spoon for serving ice cream etc. **2** a deep shovel for lifting grain, sugar, etc.
3 a scooping movement. **4** an important piece of news published by only one newspaper.

scoop *verb* (**scoops, scooping, scooped**)
lift or hollow something out with a scoop.

scoot *verb* (**scoots, scooting, scooted**)
1 propel a bicycle or scooter by sitting or standing on it and pushing it along with one foot.
2 (*informal*) run or go away quickly.

scooter *noun* (*plural* **scooters**)
1 a kind of motorcycle with small wheels.
2 a board with wheels and a long handle, which you ride on by scooting.

scope *noun*
1 opportunity or possibility for something,
♦ *There is scope for improvement.* 2 the range or extent of a subject.

scorch *verb* (**scorches, scorching, scorched**)
make something go brown by burning it slightly.

scorched-earth policy *noun*
the burning of crops and destruction of anything that might be useful to an opposing army.

score *noun* (*plural* **scores** or, in sense 2, **score**)
1 the number of points or goals made in a game; a result. 2 (*old use*) twenty ♦ *'Three score years and ten' means* $3 \times 20 + 10 = 70$ *years.*
3 written or printed music.
on that score for that reason, because of that
♦ *You needn't worry on that score.*

score *verb* (**scores, scoring, scored**)
1 get a point or goal in a game. 2 keep a count of the score. 3 mark with lines or cuts. 4 write out a musical score.
scorer *noun*
[from Old Norse]

scores *plural noun*
many; a large number.

scorn *noun*
contempt.
scornful *adjective* **scornfully** *adverb*

scorn *verb* (**scorns, scorning, scorned**)
1 treat someone with contempt. 2 refuse something scornfully.

scorpion *noun* (*plural* **scorpions**)
an animal that looks like a tiny lobster, with a poisonous sting.

Scot *noun* (*plural* **Scots**)
a person who comes from Scotland.

scotch¹ *noun*
whisky made in Scotland.

scotch² *verb* (**scotches, scotching, scotched**)
put an end to an idea or rumour etc.

scot-free *adjective*
without harm or punishment.

Scots *adjective*
from or belonging to Scotland.

  ❶ USAGE See note at *Scottish.*

Scottish *adjective*
to do with or belonging to Scotland.

  ❶ USAGE *Scottish* is the most widely used word for describing things to do with Scotland: *Scottish education*, *Scottish mountains.* *Scots* is less common and is mainly used to describe people: *a Scots girl. Scotch* is only used in fixed expressions like *Scotch terrier*, a breed of terrier with rough hair.

scoundrel *noun* (*plural* **scoundrels**)
a wicked or dishonest person.

scour¹ *verb* (**scours, scouring, scoured**)
1 rub something until it is clean and bright.
2 clear a channel or pipe by the force of water flowing through it.
scourer *noun*

scour² *verb* (**scours, scouring, scoured**)
search thoroughly.

scourge (*say* skerj) *noun* (*plural* **scourges**)
1 a whip for flogging people. 2 something that inflicts suffering or punishment.

Scout *noun* (*plural* **Scouts**)
a member of the Scout Association, an organization for boys.

scout *noun* (*plural* **scouts**)
someone sent out to collect information.

scout *verb* (**scouts, scouting, scouted**)
1 act as a scout. 2 search an area thoroughly.

scowl *noun* (*plural* **scowls**)
a bad-tempered frown.

scowl *verb* (**scowls, scowling, scowled**)
make a scowl.

scrabble *verb* (**scrabbles, scrabbling, scrabbled**)
1 scratch or claw at something with the hands or feet. 2 grope or struggle to get something.

scraggy *adjective*
thin and bony.

scramble *verb* (**scrambles, scrambling, scrambled**)
1 move quickly and awkwardly. 2 struggle to do or get something. 3 (said about aircraft or their crew) hurry and take off quickly. 4 cook eggs by mixing them up and heating them in a pan.
5 mix things together. 6 alter a radio or telephone signal so that it cannot be used without a decoding device.
scrambler *noun*

scramble *noun* (*plural* **scrambles**)
1 a climb or walk over rough ground.
2 a struggle to do or get something.
3 a motorcycle race over rough ground.

scrap¹ *noun* (*plural* **scraps**)
1 a small piece. 2 rubbish; waste material, especially metal that is suitable for reprocessing.

scrap *verb* (**scraps, scrapping, scrapped**)
get rid of something that is useless or unwanted.

scrap² *noun* (*plural* **scraps**) (*informal*)
a fight.

scrap *verb* (**scraps, scrapping, scrapped**)
(*informal*)
fight.

scrape *verb* (**scrapes, scraping, scraped**)
1 clean or smooth or damage something by
passing something hard over it. **2** make a harsh
sound by rubbing against a rough or hard
surface. **3** remove by scraping ♦ *Scrape the mud
off your shoes.* **4** get something by great effort or
care ♦ *They scraped together enough money for a
holiday.*
scraper *noun*
scrape through only just succeed, pass an exam,
etc.

scrape *noun* (*plural* **scrapes**)
1 a scraping movement or sound. **2** a mark etc.
made by scraping. **3** (*informal*) an awkward
situation caused by mischief or foolishness.

scrappy *adjective*
1 made of scraps or bits or disconnected things.
2 carelessly done.
scrappiness *noun*

scratch *verb* (**scratches, scratching, scratched**)
1 mark or cut the surface of a thing with
something sharp. **2** rub the skin with fingernails
or claws because it itches. **3** withdraw from a
race or competition.

scratch *noun* (*plural* **scratches**)
1 a mark made by scratching. **2** the action of
scratching.
scratchy *adjective*
start from scratch start from the beginning or
with nothing prepared. **up to scratch** up to the
proper standard.

scratch card *noun* (*plural* **scratch cards**)
a lottery card on which you scratch off part of the
surface to see if you have won a prize.

scrawl *noun* (*plural* **scrawls**)
untidy handwriting.

scrawl *verb* (**scrawls, scrawling, scrawled**)
write in a scrawl.

scrawny *adjective*
scraggy.

scream *noun* (*plural* **screams**)
1 a loud cry of pain, fear, anger, or excitement.
2 a loud piercing sound. **3** (*informal*) a very
amusing person or thing.

scream *verb* (**screams, screaming, screamed**)
make a scream.

screech *noun* (*plural* **screeches**)
a harsh high-pitched scream or sound.
screech *verb*

screen *noun* (*plural* **screens**)
1 a special surface for displaying films, television
pictures, or computer data. **2** a movable panel
used to hide, protect, or divide something.
3 a vehicle's windscreen.

screen *verb* (**screens, screening, screened**)
1 protect, hide, or divide with a screen. **2** show a
film or television pictures on a screen. **3** carry
out tests on someone to find out if they have a
disease. **4** check whether a person is suitable for
a job.

screenplay *noun* (*plural* **screenplays**)
the script of a film, with instructions to the actors
etc.

screw *noun* (*plural* **screws**)
1 a metal pin with a spiral ridge (the **thread**)
round it, holding things together by being
twisted in. **2** a twisting movement. **3** something
twisted. **4** a propeller, especially for a ship or
motor boat.

screw *verb* (**screws, screwing, screwed**)
1 fasten with a screw or screws. **2** fit or turn
something by twisting.

screwdriver *noun* (*plural* **screwdrivers**)
a tool for turning screws.

scribble *verb* (**scribbles, scribbling, scribbled**)
1 write quickly or untidily or carelessly.
2 make meaningless marks.
scribble *noun*

script *noun* (*plural* **scripts**)
1 handwriting. **2** the text of a play, film,
broadcast talk, etc.

scripture *noun* (*plural* **scriptures**)
1 sacred writings. **2** (in Christianity) the Bible.

scroll *noun* (*plural* **scrolls**)
1 a roll of paper or parchment used for writing
on. **2** a spiral design.

scroll *verb* (**scrolls, scrolling, scrolled**)
move the display on a computer screen up or
down to see what comes before or after it.

scrounge *verb* (**scrounges, scrounging,
scrounged**)
get something without paying for it.
scrounger *noun*

scrub¹ *verb* (**scrubs, scrubbing, scrubbed**)
1 rub with a hard brush, especially to clean
something. **2** (*informal*) cancel.
scrub *noun*

scrub² *noun*
1 low trees and bushes. **2** land covered with
these.

scruff *noun*
the back of the neck.

scruffy *adjective*
shabby and untidy.
scruffily *adverb* **scruffiness** *noun*

scrum *noun* (*plural* **scrums**)
1 (also **scrummage**) a group of players from
each side in rugby football who push against
each other and try to kick back the ball when it
is thrown between them. **2** a crowd pushing
against each other.

scruple *noun* (*plural* **scruples**)
a feeling of doubt or hesitation when your conscience tells you that an action would be wrong.

scruple *verb* (**scruples, scrupling, scrupled**)
have scruples ♦ *He would not scruple to betray us.*
[from Latin *scrupum*, literally = rough pebble]

scrupulous *adjective*
1 very careful and conscientious. **2** strictly honest or honourable.
scrupulously *adverb*

scrutinize *verb* (**scrutinizes, scrutinizing, scrutinized**)
look at something carefully.
scrutiny *noun*

scuba diving *noun*
swimming underwater using a tank of air strapped to your back.
[from the initials of *self-contained underwater breathing apparatus*]

scuff *verb* (**scuffs, scuffing, scuffed**)
1 drag your feet while walking. **2** scrape with your foot; mark or damage something by doing this.

scuffle *noun* (*plural* **scuffles**)
a confused fight or struggle.

scuffle *verb* (**scuffles, scuffling, scuffled**)
take part in a scuffle.
[probably from a Scandinavian language]

scullery *noun* (*plural* **sculleries**)
a room where dishes etc. are washed up.

sculptor *noun* (*plural* **sculptors**)
a person who makes sculptures.
sculpt *verb*

sculpture *noun* (*plural* **sculptures**)
1 making shapes by carving wood or stone or casting metal. **2** a shape made in this way.
sculpture *verb*

scum *noun*
1 froth or dirt on top of a liquid. **2** worthless people.

scuttle[1] *noun* (*plural* **scuttles**)
a bucket or container for coal in a house.

scuttle[2] *verb* (**scuttles, scuttling, scuttled**)
scurry; hurry away.

scuttle[3] *verb* (**scuttles, scuttling, scuttled**)
sink a ship deliberately by letting water into it.

scythe *noun* (*plural* **scythes**)
a tool with a long curved blade for cutting grass or corn.

scythe *verb* (**scythes, scything, scythed**)
cut with a scythe.

SE *abbreviation*
1 south-east. **2** south-eastern.

sea *noun* (*plural* **seas**)
1 the salt water that covers most of the earth's surface; a part of this. **2** a large lake ♦ *the Sea of Galilee.* **3** a large area of something ♦ *a sea of faces.*
at sea **1** on the sea. **2** not knowing what to do.

sea anemone *noun* (*plural* **sea anemones**)
a sea creature with short tentacles round its mouth.

seaboard *noun* (*plural* **seaboards**)
a coastline or coastal region.

seafaring *adjective* & *noun*
working or travelling on the sea.
seafarer *noun*

seafood *noun*
fish or shellfish from the sea eaten as food.

seagull *noun* (*plural* **seagulls**)
a seabird with long wings.

seal[1] *noun* (*plural* **seals**)
a sea mammal with thick fur or bristles, that breeds on land.
[from Old English]

seal[2] *noun* (*plural* **seals**)
1 a piece of metal with an engraved design for pressing on a soft substance to leave an impression. **2** an impression made on a piece of wax. **3** something designed to close an opening and prevent air or liquid etc. from getting in or out. **4** a confirmation or guarantee ♦ *a seal of approval.*

seal *verb* (**seals, sealing, sealed**)
1 close something by sticking two parts together. **2** close securely; stop up. **3** press a seal on something. **4** settle or decide ♦ *His fate was sealed.*
seal off prevent people getting to an area.
[from early French; related to *sign*]

sea level *noun*
the level of the sea halfway between high and low tide.

sealing wax *noun*
a substance that is soft when heated but hardens when cooled, used for sealing documents or for marking with a seal.

sea lion *noun* (*plural* **sea lions**)
a kind of large seal that lives in the Pacific Ocean.

seam *noun* (*plural* **seams**)
1 the line where two edges of cloth or wood etc. join. **2** a layer of coal in the ground.

seamanship *noun*
skill in seafaring.

seamy *adjective*
seamy side the less attractive side or part ♦ *Police see a lot of the seamy side of life.*
[originally, the 'wrong' side of a piece of sewing, where the rough edges of the seams show]

sear *verb* (**sears, searing, seared**)
scorch or burn the surface of something.

search *verb* (**searches, searching, searched**)
look very hard or carefully in order to find something.
search *noun* **searcher** *noun*

search engine noun (plural **search engines**)
(in computing) a program that searches for data, especially on the Internet.

searchlight noun (plural **searchlights**)
a light with a strong beam that can be turned in any direction.

search party noun (plural **search parties**)
a group of people organized to search for a missing person or thing.

search warrant noun (plural **search warrants**)
an official document giving the police permission to search private property.

seasick adjective
sick because of the movement of a ship.
seasickness noun

seaside noun
a place by the sea where people go for holidays.

season noun (plural **seasons**)
1 each of the four main parts of the year (spring, summer, autumn, and winter). 2 the time of year when something happens ♦ the football season.
in season available and ready for eating
♦ Strawberries are in season in the summer.

season verb (**seasons, seasoning, seasoned**)
1 give extra flavour to food by adding salt, pepper, or other strong-tasting substances.
2 dry and treat timber etc. to make it ready for use.

seasonable adjective
suitable for the season ♦ Hot weather is seasonable in summer.
seasonably adverb

ℹ USAGE Do not confuse with seasonal.

---

seasonal adjective
1 for or to do with a season. 2 happening in a particular season ♦ Fruit-picking is seasonal work.
seasonally adverb

ℹ USAGE Do not confuse with seasonable.

---

seasoning noun (plural **seasonings**)
a substance used to season food.

season ticket noun (plural **season tickets**)
a ticket that can be used as often as you like throughout a period of time.

seat noun (plural **seats**)
1 a thing made or used for sitting on. 2 the right to be a member of a council, committee, parliament, etc. ♦ She won the seat ten years ago.
3 the buttocks; the part of a skirt or trousers covering these. 4 the place where something is based or located ♦ London is the seat of our government.

seat verb (**seats, seating, seated**)
1 place in or on a seat. 2 have seats for
♦ The theatre seats 3,000 people.

seat belt noun (plural **seat belts**)
a strap to hold a person securely in a seat.

seating noun
1 the seats in a place ♦ seating for 400.
2 the arrangement of seats ♦ a seating plan.

sea urchin noun (plural **sea urchins**)
a sea animal with a round shell covered in sharp spikes.

seaweed noun
a plant or plants that grow in the sea.

seaworthy adjective
(said about a ship) fit for a sea voyage.
seaworthiness noun

secateurs plural noun
clippers held in the hand for pruning plants.

secluded adjective
quiet or sheltered from view ♦ a secluded beach.
seclusion noun

second¹ adjective
1 next after the first. 2 another ♦ a second chance. 3 less good ♦ second quality.
secondly adverb
have second thoughts wonder whether a decision you have made was the right one.

second noun (plural **seconds**)
1 a person or thing that is second. 2 an attendant of a fighter in a boxing match, duel, etc. 3 a thing that is not of the best quality, often sold cheaply.
4 one-sixtieth of a minute of time or of a degree used in measuring angles.

second verb (**seconds, seconding, seconded**)
1 assist someone. 2 support a proposal, motion, etc.
seconder noun

second² (say sik-**ond**) verb (**seconds, seconding, seconded**)
transfer a person temporarily to another job or department etc.
secondment noun

secondary adjective
1 coming after or from something. 2 less important. 3 (said about education etc.) for children of more than about 11 years old
♦ a secondary school. (Compare **primary**.)

second-hand adjective
1 bought or used after someone else has owned it. 2 selling used goods ♦ a second-hand shop.

second nature noun
behaviour that has become automatic or a habit
♦ Lying is second nature to him.

second-rate adjective
inferior; not very good.

secret adjective
1 that must not be told or shown to other people.
2 not known by everybody. 3 working secretly.
secretly adverb **secrecy** noun

secret noun (plural **secrets**)
something secret.

secretary (*say* sek-rit-ree) *noun* (*plural* secretaries)
1 a person whose job is to help with letters, answer the telephone, and make business arrangements for a person or organization.
2 the chief assistant of a government minister or ambassador.
secretarial *adjective*
[from Latin *secretarius* = an officer or servant allowed to know his employer's secrets]

secrete (*say* sik-reet) *verb* (**secretes, secreting, secreted**)
1 hide something. 2 produce a substance in the body ♦ *Saliva is secreted in the mouth.*
secretion *noun*

secretive (*say* seek-rit-iv) *adjective*
liking or trying to keep things secret.
secretively *adverb* **secretiveness** *noun*

secret service *noun*
a government department responsible for espionage.

sect *noun* (*plural* sects)
a group of people whose beliefs differ from others in the same religion.

section *noun* (*plural* sections)
1 a part of something. 2 a cross-section.

sector *noun* (*plural* sectors)
1 one part of an area. 2 a part of something ♦ *the private sector of industry.*
3 (in mathematics) a section of a circle between two lines drawn from its centre to its circumference. **secular** *adjective*
to do with worldly affairs, not spiritual or religious matters.

secure *adjective*
1 safe, especially against attack. 2 certain not to slip or fail. 3 reliable.
securely *adverb*

secure *verb* (**secures, securing, secured**)
1 make a thing secure. 2 fasten something firmly. 3 obtain ♦ *We secured two tickets for the show.*

security *noun* (*plural* securities)
1 being secure; safety. 2 precautions against theft or spying etc. 3 something given as a guarantee that a promise will be kept or a debt repaid. 4 investments such as stocks and shares.

sedate *adjective*
calm and dignified.
sedately *adverb* **sedateness** *noun*

sedate *verb* (**sedates, sedating, sedated**)
give a sedative to.
sedation *noun*

sedative (*say* sed-a-tiv) *noun* (*plural* sedatives)
a medicine that makes a person calm.

sedentary (*say* sed-en-ter-ee) *adjective*
done sitting down ♦ *sedentary work.*

Seder (*say* say-der) *noun* (*plural* Seders)
(in Judaism) a ritual and a ceremonial meal to mark the beginning of Passover.

sedge *noun*
a grass-like plant growing in marshes or near water.

sediment *noun*
fine particles of solid matter that float in liquid or sink to the bottom of it.

sedimentary *adjective*
formed from particles that have settled on a surface ♦ *sedimentary rocks.*

sedition *noun*
speeches or actions intended to make people rebel against the authority of the State.
seditious *adjective*

seduce *verb* (**seduces, seducing, seduced**)
1 persuade a person to have sexual intercourse.
2 attract or lead astray by offering temptations.
seducer *noun* **seduction** *noun* **seductive** *adjective*

see *verb* (**sees, seeing, saw, seen**)
1 perceive with the eyes. 2 meet or visit somebody ♦ *See a doctor about your cough.*
3 understand ♦ *She saw what I meant.* 4 imagine ♦ *Can you see yourself as a teacher?* 5 consider ♦ *I will see what can be done.* 6 make sure ♦ *See that the windows are shut.* 7 discover ♦ *See who is at the door.* 8 escort ♦ *See her to the door.*
see through not be deceived by something.
see to attend to.

seed *noun* (*plural* seeds or seed)
1 a fertilized part of a plant, capable of growing into a new plant. 2 (*old use*) descendants.
3 a seeded player.

seed *verb* (**seeds, seeding, seeded**)
1 plant or sprinkle seeds in something. 2 name the best players and arrange for them not to play against each other in the early rounds of a tournament.

seedling *noun* (*plural* seedlings)
a very young plant growing from a seed.

seedy *adjective* (**seedier, seediest**)
1 full of seeds. 2 shabby and disreputable.
seediness *noun*

seeing *conjunction*
considering ♦ *Seeing that we have all finished, let's go.*

seek *verb* (**seeks, seeking, sought**)
1 search for. 2 try to do or obtain something ♦ *to seek fame.*

seem *verb* (**seems, seeming, seemed**)
give the impression of being something ♦ *She seems worried about her work.*
seemingly *adverb*

seemly *adjective* (*old use*)
(said about behaviour etc.) proper or suitable.
seemliness *noun*
[from an old sense of *seem* = be suitable]

seep *verb* (**seeps, seeping, seeped**)
ooze slowly out or through something.
seepage *noun*

see-saw *noun* (*plural* **see-saws**)
a plank balanced in the middle so that two
people can sit, one on each end, and make it go
up and down.

seethe *verb* (**seethes, seething, seethed**)
1 bubble and surge like water boiling. 2 be very
angry or excited.

segment *noun* (*plural* **segments**)
a part that is cut off or separates naturally from
other parts ♦ *the segments of an orange*.
segmented *adjective*

segregate *verb* (**segregates, segregating,
segregated**)
1 separate people of different religions, races,
etc. 2 isolate a person or thing.
segregation *noun*

seismic (*say* sy-zmik) *adjective*
to do with earthquakes or other vibrations of the
earth.

seize *verb* (**seizes, seizing, seized**)
1 take hold of a person or thing suddenly or
forcibly. 2 take possession of something by force
or by legal authority ♦ *Customs officers seized a
lot of smuggled goods*. 3 take eagerly ♦ *Seize your
chance!* 4 have a sudden effect on ♦ *Panic seized
us*.
seize up become jammed, especially because of
friction or overheating.

seizure *noun* (*plural* **seizures**)
1 seizing. 2 a sudden fit, as in epilepsy or a heart
attack.

seldom *adverb*
rarely; not often.

select *verb* (**selects, selecting, selected**)
choose a person or thing.
selector *noun*

select *adjective*
1 carefully chosen. ♦ *a select group* 2 (said about
a club etc.) choosing its members carefully;
exclusive.

selection *noun* (*plural* **selections**)
1 selecting; being selected. 2 a person or thing
selected. 3 a group selected from a larger group.
4 a range of goods from which to choose.

self *noun* (*plural* **selves**)
1 a person as an individual. 2 a person's
particular nature ♦ *She has recovered and is
her old self again*. 3 a person's own advantage
♦ *He always puts self first*.

self-assured *adjective*
confident.

self-catering *noun*
catering for yourself (instead of having meals
provided).

self-centred *adjective*
selfish.

self-confident *adjective*
confident of your own abilities.

self-conscious *adjective*
embarrassed or unnatural because you know
that people are watching you.

self-contained *adjective*
(said about accommodation) complete in itself;
containing all the necessary facilities.

self-control *noun*
the ability to control your own behaviour.
self-controlled *adjective*

self-denial *noun*
deliberately going without things you would like
to have.

self-determination *noun*
a country's right to rule itself and to choose its
own method of government.

self-employed *adjective*
working independently, not for an employer.

self-esteem *noun*
your own opinion of yourself and your own
worth.

self-evident *adjective*
obvious and not needing proof or explanation.

self-important *adjective*
pompous.

selfish *adjective*
doing what you want and not thinking of other
people; keeping things for yourself.
selfishly *adverb* **selfishness** *noun*

selfless *adjective*
unselfish.

self-made *adjective*
rich or successful because of your own efforts.

self-pity *noun*
too much sorrow and pity for yourself and your
own problems.

self-possessed *adjective*
calm and dignified.

self-raising *adjective*
(said about flour) making cakes rise without
needing to have baking powder etc. added.

self-respect *noun*
your own proper respect for yourself.

self-righteous *adjective*
smugly sure that you are behaving virtuously.

self-service *adjective*
where customers help themselves to things and
pay a cashier for what they have taken.

self-sufficient *adjective*
able to produce or provide what you need
without help from others.

self-supporting *adjective*
earning enough to keep yourself without
needing money from others.

sell *verb* (**sells, selling, sold**)
1 exchange something for money. 2 be on sale at
a certain price ◆ *It sells for £5.99.*
seller *noun*
sell out 1 sell all your stock of something.
2 (*informal*) betray someone. 3 abandon your
principles for reasons of convenience because it
suits you.

sell *noun*
hard sell putting pressure on someone to buy
something. **sell-by date** a mark on the
packaging of food showing the date by which it
must be sold. **soft sell** selling by gentle
persuasion.

sell-out *noun* (*plural* **sell-outs**)
an entertainment, sporting event, etc. for which
all the tickets have been sold.

selves *plural* of **self**.

semaphore *noun*
a system of signalling by holding flags out with
your arms in positions that indicate letters of the
alphabet.

semen (*say* **seem**-en) *noun*
a white liquid produced by males and containing
sperm.

semibreve *noun* (*plural* **semibreves**)
the longest musical note normally used ($\mathbf{o}$),
lasting four times as long as a crotchet.

semicircle *noun* (*plural* **semicircles**)
half a circle.
semicircular *adjective*

semicolon *noun* (*plural* **semicolons**)
a punctuation mark (;) used to mark a break that
is more than that marked by a comma.

semiconductor *noun* (*plural*
semiconductors)
a substance that can conduct electricity but not
as well as most metals do.

semi-detached *adjective*
(said about a house) joined to another house on
one side.

semifinal *noun* (*plural* **semifinals**)
a match or round whose winner will take part in
the final.

seminar *noun* (*plural* **seminars**)
a meeting for advanced discussion and research
on a subject.

semiquaver *noun* (*plural* **semiquavers**)
a note in music (♪), equal in length to one
quarter of a crotchet.

Semitic (*say* sim-it-ik) *adjective*
to do with the Semites, the group of people that
includes the Jews and Arabs.
Semite (*say* **see**-my't) *noun*

semitone *noun* (*plural* **semitones**)
half a tone in music.

semolina *noun*
hard round grains of wheat used to make milk
puddings and pasta.

senate *noun* (*plural* **senates**)
1 the governing council in ancient Rome.
2 the upper house of the parliament of the United
States, France, and certain other countries.
senator *noun*

send *verb* (**sends, sending, sent**)
1 make a person or thing go or be taken
somewhere. 2 cause to become ◆ *The noise is
sending me crazy.*
sender *noun*
send for order a person or thing to come or be
brought to you. **send up** (*informal*) make fun of
something by imitating it.

senile (*say* **seen**-I'll) *adjective*
weak or confused and forgetful because of old
age.
senility *noun*

senior *adjective*
1 older than someone else. 2 higher in rank.
3 for older children ◆ *a senior school.*
seniority *noun*

senior *noun* (*plural* **seniors**)
1 a person who is older or higher in rank than
you are ◆ *He is my senior.* 2 a member of a senior
school.

senior citizen *noun* (*plural* **senior citizens**)
an elderly person, especially a pensioner.

sensation *noun* (*plural* **sensations**)
1 a feeling ◆ *a sensation of warmth.* 2 a very
excited condition; something causing this
◆ *The news caused a great sensation.*

sensational *adjective*
1 causing great excitement, interest, or shock.
2 (*informal*) very good; wonderful.
sensationally *adverb*

sense *noun* (*plural* **senses**)
1 the ability to see, hear, smell, touch, or taste
things. 2 the ability to feel or appreciate
something ◆ *a sense of guilt;* ◆ *a sense of
humour.* 3 the power to think or make wise
decisions ◆ *Hasn't he got the sense to come in out
of the rain?* 4 meaning ◆ *The word 'run' has
many senses.*
make sense 1 have a meaning. 2 be a sensible
idea.

sense *verb* (**senses, sensing, sensed**)
1 feel; get an impression ◆ *I sensed that she did
not like me.* 2 detect something ◆ *This device
senses radioactivity.*

senseless *adjective*
1 stupid; not showing good sense.
2 unconscious.

senses *plural noun*
sanity ♦ *He is out of his senses.*

sensible *adjective*
wise; having or showing good sense.
sensibly *adverb*

sensitive *adjective*
1 affected by something ♦ *Photographic paper is sensitive to light.* 2 receiving impressions quickly and easily ♦ *sensitive fingers.* 3 easily hurt or offended ♦ *She is very sensitive about her age.*
4 considerate about other people's feelings.
5 needing to be dealt with tactfully ♦ *a sensitive subject.*
sensitively *adverb* **sensitivity** *noun*

sensor *noun* (*plural* **sensors**)
a device or instrument for detecting a physical property such as light, heat, or sound.

sentence *noun* (*plural* **sentences**)
1 a group of words that express a complete thought and form a statement, question, exclamation, or command. 2 the punishment announced to a convicted person in a lawcourt.
sentence *verb* (**sentences, sentencing, sentenced**)
give someone a sentence in a lawcourt
♦ *The judge sentenced him to a year in prison.*
[from Latin *sententia* = opinion]

sententious *adjective*
giving moral advice in a pompous way.

sentiment *noun* (*plural* **sentiments**)
1 an opinion. 2 sentimentality.

sentimental *adjective*
showing or arousing tenderness or romantic feeling or foolish emotion.
sentimentally *adverb* **sentimentality** *noun*

sentinel *noun* (*plural* **sentinels**)
a guard or sentry.

sentry *noun* (*plural* **sentries**)
a soldier guarding something.

separate *adjective*
1 not joined to anything. 2 not shared.
separately *adverb*
separate *verb* (**separates, separating, separated**)
1 make or keep separate; divide. 2 become separate. 3 stop living together as a married couple.
separation *noun* **separator** *noun*

September *noun*
the ninth month of the year.
[from Latin *septem* = seven, because it was the seventh month of the ancient Roman calendar]

septic *adjective*
infected with harmful bacteria that cause pus to form.

sepulchre (*say* sep-ul-ker) *noun* (*plural* **sepulchres**)
a tomb.

sequel *noun* (*plural* **sequels**)
1 a book or film etc. that continues the story of an earlier one. 2 something that follows or results from an earlier event.

sequence *noun* (*plural* **sequences**)
1 the following of one thing after another; the order in which things happen. 2 a series of things.

seraph *noun* (*plural* **seraphim** or **seraphs**)
a kind of angel.

serenade *noun* (*plural* **serenades**)
a song or tune of a kind played by a man under his lover's window.
serenade *verb* (**serenades, serenading, serenaded**)
sing or play a serenade to someone.

serene *adjective*
calm and cheerful.
serenely *adverb* **serenity** *noun*

serf *noun* (*plural* **serfs**)
a farm labourer who worked for a landowner in the Middle Ages, and who was not allowed to leave.
serfdom *noun*

sergeant (*say* sar-jent) *noun* (*plural* **sergeants**)
a soldier or policeman who is in charge of others.

sergeant major *noun* (*plural* **sergeant majors**)
a soldier who is one rank higher than a sergeant.

serial *noun* (*plural* **serials**)
a story or film etc. that is presented in separate parts.

---

❶ USAGE Do not confuse with *cereal.*

---

serial killer *noun* (*plural* **serial killers**)
a person who commits a series of murders.

serial number *noun* (*plural* **serial numbers**)
a number put onto an object, usually by the manufacturers, to distinguish it from other identical objects.

series *noun* (*plural* **series**)
1 a number of things following or connected with each other. 2 a number of games or matches between the same competitors. 3 a number of separate radio or television programmes with the same characters or on the same subject.

serious *adjective*
1 solemn and thoughtful; not smiling. 2 sincere; not casual or light-hearted ♦ *a serious talk*;
♦ *a serious attempt.* 3 causing anxiety, not trivial
♦ *a serious accident.*
seriously *adverb* **seriousness** *noun*

sermon *noun* (*plural* **sermons**)
a talk given by a preacher, especially as part of a religious service.

serpent *noun* (*plural* **serpents**)
a snake.

serried *adjective*
arranged in rows close together ♦ *serried ranks of troops*.

servant *noun* (*plural* **servants**)
a person whose job is to work or serve in someone else's house.

serve *verb* (**serves, serving, served**)
1 work for a person or organization or country etc. **2** sell things to people in a shop. **3** give out food to people at a meal. **4** spend time in something; undergo ♦ *He has served a prison sentence.* **5** be suitable for something ♦ *This will serve our purpose.* **6** start play in tennis etc. by hitting the ball.
server *noun*
it serves you right you deserve it.

serve *noun* (*plural* **serves**)
a service in tennis etc.

service *noun* (*plural* **services**)
1 working for a person or organization or country etc. **2** something that helps people or supplies what they want ♦ *a bus service.* **3** the army, navy, or air force ♦ *the armed services.* **4** a religious ceremony. **5** providing people with goods, food, etc. ♦ *The service at the restaurant was slow.* **6** a set of dishes and plates etc. for a meal ♦ *a dinner service.* **7** the servicing of a vehicle or machine etc. **8** the action of serving in tennis etc.

service *verb* (**services, servicing, serviced**)
1 repair or keep a vehicle or machine etc. in working order. **2** supply with services.

serviceable *adjective*
usable; suitable for ordinary use or wear.

service station *noun* (*plural* **service stations**)
a place beside a major road where motorists can stop for fuel, light meals, etc.

serviette *noun* (*plural* **serviettes**)
a piece of cloth or paper used to keep your clothes or hands clean at a meal.

serving *noun* (*plural* **servings**)
a helping of food.

session *noun* (*plural* **sessions**)
1 a meeting or series of meetings ♦ *The Queen will open the next session of Parliament.* **2** a time spent doing one thing ♦ *a recording session.*

set *verb* (**sets, setting, set**)
1 put or fix ♦ *Set the vase on the table.* ♦ *They've set a date for the wedding.* **2** make ready to work ♦ *I'd better set the alarm.* **3** make or become firm or hard ♦ *Leave the jelly to set.* **4** give someone a task ♦ *This sets us a problem.* **5** put into a condition ♦ *Set them free.* **6** go down below the horizon ♦ *The sun was setting.*

set about 1 start doing something. **2** (*informal*) attack somebody. **set off 1** begin a journey. **2** start something happening. **3** cause something to explode. **set out 1** begin a journey. **2** display or make known. **set sail** begin a voyage. **set to 1** begin doing something vigorously. **2** begin fighting or arguing. **set up 1** place in position. **2** arrange or establish ♦ *set up house.* **3** cause or start ♦ *set up a din.*

set *noun* (*plural* **sets**)
1 a group of people or things that belong together. **2** a radio or television receiver. **3** (in mathematics) a collection of things that have a common property. **4** the way something is placed ♦ *the set of his jaw.* **5** the scenery or stage for a play or film. **6** a group of games in a tennis match. **7** a badger's burrow.

set *adjective*
1 fixed or arranged in advance ♦ *a set time.* **2** ready or prepared to do something.
set on determined about doing something.

setback *noun* (*plural* **setbacks**)
something that stops progress or slows it down.

set book *noun* (*plural* **set books**)
a book that must be studied for a literature examination.

set square *noun* (*plural* **set squares**)
a device shaped like a right-angled triangle, used in drawing lines parallel to each other etc.

settee *noun* (*plural* **settees**)
a long soft seat with a back and arms.

setter *noun* (*plural* **setters**)
a dog of a long-haired breed that can be trained to stand rigid when it scents game.

setting *noun* (*plural* **settings**)
1 the way or place in which something is set. **2** music for the words of a song etc. **3** a set of cutlery or crockery for one person at a meal.

settle *verb* (**settles, settling, settled**)
1 arrange; decide or solve something ♦ *That settles the problem.* **2** make or become calm or comfortable or orderly; stop being restless ♦ *Stop chattering and settle down!* **3** go and live somewhere ♦ *They settled in Canada.* **4** sink; come to rest on something ♦ *Dust had settled on his books.* **5** pay a bill or debt.

settlement *noun* (*plural* **settlements**)
1 settling something. **2** the way something is settled. **3** a small number of people or houses established in a new area.

settler *noun* (*plural* **settlers**)
one of the first people to settle in a new country.

set-up *noun* (*informal*)
the way something is organized or arranged.

seven *noun* & *adjective* (*plural* **sevens**)
the number 7.
seventh *adjective* & *noun*

seventeen *noun* & *adjective*
the number 17.
seventeenth *adjective* & *noun*

seventy *noun* & *adjective*(*plural* **seventies**)
the number 70.
seventieth *adjective* & *noun*

several *adjective* & *noun*
more than two but not many.

severe *adjective*
1 strict; not gentle or kind. **2** intense or forceful
♦ *severe gales.* **3** very plain ♦ *a severe style of
dress.*
severely *adverb* **severity** *noun*

sew *verb* (**sews, sewing, sewed, sewn** or
sewed)
1 join things together by using a needle and
thread. **2** work with a needle and thread or with
a sewing machine.

---

❶ USAGE Do not confuse with *sow.*

---

sewage (*say* soo-ij) *noun*
liquid waste matter carried away in drains.

sewer (*say* soo-er) *noun* (*plural* **sewers**)
a large underground drain for carrying away
sewage.

sewing machine *noun* (*plural* **sewing
machines**)
a machine for sewing things.

sex *noun* (*plural* **sexes**)
1 each of the two groups (*male* and *female*)
into which living things are placed according to
their functions in the process of reproduction.
2 the instinct that causes members of the two
sexes to be attracted to one another. **3** sexual
intercourse.

sexism *noun*
discrimination against people of a particular sex,
especially women.
sexist *adjective* & *noun*

sexual *adjective*
1 to do with sex or the sexes. **2** (said about
reproduction) happening by the fusion of male
and female cells.
sexually *adverb* **sexuality** *noun*

sexual intercourse *noun*
an intimate act between two people, in which the
man puts his penis into the woman's vagina, to
express love, for pleasure, or to conceive a child.

sexy *adjective* (**sexier, sexiest**) (*informal*)
1 sexually attractive. **2** concerned with sex.

SF *abbreviation*
science fiction.

shabby *adjective* (**shabbier, shabbiest**)
1 in a poor or worn-out condition; dilapidated.
2 poorly dressed. **3** unfair or dishonourable
♦ *a shabby trick.*
shabbily *adverb* **shabbiness** *noun*

shack *noun* (*plural* **shacks**)
a roughly built hut.

shackle *noun* (*plural* **shackles**)
an iron ring for fastening a prisoner's wrist or
ankle to something.

shackle *verb* (**shackles, shackling, shackled**)
put shackles on a prisoner.

shade *noun* (*plural* **shades**)
1 slight darkness produced where something
blocks the sun's light. **2** a device that reduces or
shuts out bright light. **3** a colour; how light or
dark a colour is. **4** a slight difference ♦ *The word
had several shades of meaning.* **5** (*poetical*) a
ghost.

shade *verb* (**shades, shading, shaded**)
1 shelter something from bright light. **2** make
part of a drawing darker than the rest. **3** move
gradually from one state or quality to another
♦ *evening shading into night.*

shadow *noun* (*plural* **shadows**)
1 the dark shape that falls on a surface when
something is between the surface and a light.
2 an area of shade. **3** a slight trace ♦ *a shadow of
doubt.*
shadowy *adjective*

shadow *verb* (**shadows, shadowing,
shadowed**)
1 cast a shadow on something. **2** follow a person
secretly.

Shadow Cabinet *noun*
members of the Opposition in Parliament who
each have responsibility for a particular area of
policy.

shady *adjective* (**shadier, shadiest**)
1 giving shade ♦ *a shady tree.* **2** in the shade
♦ *a shady place.* **3** (*informal*) not completely
honest; disreputable ♦ *a shady deal.*

shaft *noun* (*plural* **shafts**)
1 a long slender rod or straight part ♦ *the shaft
of an arrow.* **2** a ray of light. **3** a deep narrow
hole ♦ *a mine shaft.*

shaggy *adjective* (**shaggier, shaggiest**)
1 having long rough hair or fibre. **2** rough, thick,
and untidy ♦ *shaggy hair.*

shake *verb* (**shakes, shaking, shook, shaken**)
1 move quickly up and down or from side to
side. **2** shock or upset ♦ *The news shook us.*
3 tremble; be unsteady ♦ *His voice was shaking.*
shaker *noun*
shake hands clasp a person's right hand with
yours in greeting or parting or as a sign of
agreement.

shake *noun* (*plural* **shakes**)
shaking; a shaking movement.
shaky *adjective* **shakily** *adverb*
in two shakes very soon.

shall *auxiliary verb*
1 used with *I* and *we* to refer to the future
♦ *I shall arrive tomorrow.* 2 used with *I* and *we*
in questions when making a suggestion or offer
or asking for advice ♦ *Shall I shut the door?*
3 (*old-fashioned use*) used with words other than
I and *we* in promises or to express determination
♦ *Trust me, you shall have a party.*

shallow *adjective* (**shallower, shallowest**)
1 not deep ♦ *shallow water.* 2 not capable of
deep feelings ♦ *a shallow character.*
shallowness *noun*

sham *noun* (*plural* **shams**)
something that is not genuine; a pretence.
sham *adjective*

sham *verb* (**shams, shamming, shammed**)
pretend.

shamble *verb* (**shambles, shambling,
shambled**)
walk or run in a lazy or awkward way.

shame *noun*
1 a feeling of great sorrow or guilt because you
have done wrong. 2 dishonour or disgrace.
3 something you regret; a pity ♦ *It's a shame
that it rained.*
shameful *adjective* **shamefully** *adverb*

shame *verb* (**shames, shaming, shamed**)
make a person feel ashamed.

shameless *adjective*
not feeling or looking ashamed.
shamelessly *adverb*

shampoo *noun* (*plural* **shampoos**)
1 a liquid substance for washing the hair.
2 a substance for cleaning a carpet etc. or
washing a car. 3 a wash with shampoo
♦ *a shampoo and set.*

shampoo *verb* (**shampoos, shampooing,
shampooed**)
wash or clean with a shampoo.
[originally = to massage: from Hindi *champo*
= press]

shan't (*mainly spoken*)
shall not.

shanty¹ *noun* (*plural* **shanties**)
a shack.
[from Canadian French]

shanty² *noun* (*plural* **shanties**)
a sailors' song with a chorus.
[probably from French *chanter* = sing]

shanty town *noun* (*plural* **shanty towns**)
a settlement consisting of shacks.

shape *noun* (*plural* **shapes**)
1 a thing's outline; the appearance an outline
produces. 2 proper form or condition ♦ *Get it
into shape.* 3 the general form or condition of
something ♦ *the shape of British industry.*

shape *verb* (**shapes, shaping, shaped**)
1 make into a particular shape. 2 develop
♦ *The plan is shaping up nicely.*
[from Old English]

shapeless *adjective*
having no definite shape.

shapely *adjective* (**shapelier, shapeliest**)
having an attractive shape.

share *noun* (*plural* **shares**)
1 a part given to one person or thing out of
something that is being divided. 2 each of the
equal parts forming a business company's
capital, giving the person who holds it the right
to receive a portion (a **dividend**) of the
company's profits.

share *verb* (**shares, sharing, shared**)
1 give portions of something to two or more
people. 2 have or use or experience something
jointly with others ♦ *She shared a house with
me.*

shark *noun* (*plural* **sharks**)
a large sea fish with sharp teeth.

sharp *adjective*
1 with an edge or point that can cut or make
holes. 2 quick at noticing or learning things
♦ *sharp eyes.* 3 steep or pointed; not gradual
♦ *a sharp bend.* 4 forceful or severe ♦ *a sharp
frost.* 5 distinct; loud and shrill ♦ *a sharp cry.*
6 slightly sour. 7 (in music) one semitone higher
than the natural note ♦ *C sharp.*
sharply *adverb* **sharpness** *noun*

sharp *adverb*
1 sharply ♦ *Turn sharp right here.* 2 punctually
♦ *I'll see you at six o'clock sharp.* 3 (in music)
above the correct pitch ♦ *You were singing
sharp.*

sharp *noun* (*plural* **sharps**)
(in music) a note one semitone higher than the
natural note; the sign (#) that indicates this.

sharpen *verb* (**sharpens, sharpening,
sharpened**)
make or become sharp.
sharpener *noun*

sharp practice *noun*
dishonest or barely honest dealings in business.

shatter *verb* (**shatters, shattering, shattered**)
1 break violently into small pieces. 2 destroy
♦ *It shattered our hopes.* 3 upset greatly
♦ *We were shattered by the news.*

shave *verb* (**shaves, shaving, shaved**)
1 scrape growing hair off the skin with a razor.
2 cut or scrape a thin slice off something.
shaven *adjective* **shaver** *noun*

shave *noun* (*plural* **shaves**)
the act of shaving the face.
close shave (*informal*) a narrow escape.

shavings *plural noun*
thin strips shaved off a piece of wood or metal.

shawl noun (plural **shawls**)
a large piece of material worn round the shoulders or head or wrapped round a baby. [from Persian or Urdu]

she pronoun
the female person or animal being talked about.

sheaf noun (plural **sheaves**)
1 a bundle of cornstalks tied together. 2 a bundle of arrows, papers, etc. held together.

shear verb (**shears, shearing, sheared, sheared** or, in sense 1, **shorn**)
1 cut or trim; cut the wool off a sheep. 2 break because of a sideways or twisting force ♦ One of the bolts sheared off.
shearer noun

---

❶ USAGE Do not confuse with sheer.

---

shears plural noun
a cutting tool shaped like a very large pair of scissors and worked with both hands.

sheath noun (plural **sheaths**)
1 a cover for the blade of a knife or sword etc. 2 a close-fitting cover. 3 a condom.

shed¹ noun (plural **sheds**)
a simply made building used for storing things or sheltering animals, or as a workshop.

shed² verb (**sheds, shedding, shed**)
1 let something fall or flow ♦ The tree shed its leaves. ♦ We shed tears. 2 give off ♦ the candle shed soft light on the table. 3 get rid of ♦ The company has shed 200 workers.

sheen noun
a shine or gloss.

sheep noun (plural **sheep**)
an animal that eats grass and has a thick fleecy coat, kept in flocks for its wool and its meat. [from Old English]

sheepdog noun (plural **sheepdogs**)
a dog trained to guard and herd sheep.

sheepish adjective
1 bashful. 2 embarrassed or shamefaced.
sheepishly adverb **sheepishness** noun

sheer¹ adjective
1 complete or thorough ♦ sheer stupidity. 2 vertical, with almost no slope ♦ a sheer drop. 3 (said about material) very thin; transparent.

sheer² verb (**sheers, sheering, sheered**)
swerve; move sharply away.

---

❶ USAGE Do not confuse with shear.

---

sheet noun (plural **sheets**)
1 a large piece of lightweight material used on a bed to sleep under. 2 a whole flat piece of paper, glass, or metal. 3 a wide area of water, ice, flame, etc.

sheikh (say shayk or sheek) noun (plural **sheikhs**)
the leader of an Arab tribe or village.

shelf noun (plural **shelves**)
1 a flat piece of wood, metal, or glass etc. fixed to a wall or in a piece of furniture so that things can be placed on it. 2 a flat level surface that sticks out; a ledge.

shell noun (plural **shells**)
1 the hard outer covering of an egg, nut, etc., or of an animal such as a snail, crab, or tortoise. 2 the walls or framework of a building, ship, etc. 3 a metal case filled with explosive, fired from a large gun.

shell verb (**shells, shelling, shelled**)
1 take something out of its shell. 2 fire explosive shells at something.
shell out (informal) pay out money.

shellfish noun (plural **shellfish**)
a sea animal that has a shell.

shelter noun (plural **shelters**)
1 something that protects people from rain, wind, danger, etc. ♦ The bus stop has a shelter beside it. 2 protection ♦ The villagers sought shelter from the storm.

shelter verb (**shelters, sheltering, sheltered**)
1 provide with shelter. 2 protect. 3 find a shelter ♦ They sheltered under the trees.

shelve verb (**shelves, shelving, shelved**)
1 put things on a shelf or shelves. 2 fit a wall or cupboard etc. with shelves. 3 postpone or reject a plan etc. 4 slope ♦ The bed of the river shelves steeply.

shepherd noun (plural **shepherds**)
a person whose job is to look after sheep.

shepherd verb (**shepherds, shepherding, shepherded**)
guide or direct people.

sheriff noun (plural **sheriffs**)
the chief law officer of a county, whose duties vary in different countries.

sherry noun (plural **sherries**)
a kind of strong wine.

Shetland pony noun (plural **Shetland ponies**)
a kind of small, strong, shaggy pony, originally from the Shetland Isles.

shield noun (plural **shields**)
1 a large piece of metal, wood, etc. carried to protect the body. 2 a model of a triangular shield used as a trophy. 3 a protection.

shield verb (**shields, shielding, shielded**)
protect from harm or from being discovered.

shift verb (**shifts, shifting, shifted**)
1 move or cause to move. 2 (said about an opinion or situation) change slightly.
shift for yourself manage without help; rely on your own efforts.

shift *noun* (*plural* **shifts**)
1 a change of position or condition etc. 2 a group
of workers who start work as another group
finishes; the time when they work ♦ *the night
shift*. 3 a straight dress with no waist.

shifty *adjective*
evasive, not straightforward; untrustworthy.
shiftily *adverb* **shiftiness** *noun*

shilling *noun* (*plural* **shillings**)
a former British coin, equal to 5p.

shilly-shally *verb* (**shilly-shallies,
shilly-shallying, shilly-shallied**)
be unable to make up your mind.

shimmer *verb* (**shimmers, shimmering,
shimmered**)
shine with a quivering light ♦ *The sea
shimmered in the moonlight.*
shimmer *noun*

shin *noun* (*plural* **shins**)
the front of the leg between the knee and the
ankle.

shin *verb* (**shins, shinning, shinned**)
climb by using the arms and legs, not on a
ladder.

shine *verb* (**shines, shining, shone** or, in sense
4, **shined**)
1 give out or reflect light; be bright.
2 be excellent ♦ *He doesn't shine in maths.*
3 aim a light ♦ *Shine your torch on it.* 4 polish
♦ *Have you shined your shoes?*

shingle *noun*
pebbles on a beach.

shingles *noun*
a disease caused by the chicken pox virus,
producing a painful rash.

shiny *adjective* (**shinier, shiniest**)
shining or glossy.

ship *noun* (*plural* **ships**)
a large boat, especially one that goes to sea.

ship *verb* (**ships, shipping, shipped**)
transport goods etc., especially by ship.

-ship *suffix*
forms nouns meaning 'condition' (e.g.
friendship, hardship), position (e.g.
chairmanship), or skill (e.g. *seamanship*).

shipping *noun*
1 ships ♦ *Britain's shipping.* 2 transporting
goods by ship.

shipshape *adjective*
in good order; tidy.

shipwreck *noun* (*plural* **shipwrecks**)
1 the wrecking of a ship by storm or accident.
2 a wrecked ship.
shipwrecked *adjective*

shipyard *noun* (*plural* **shipyards**)
a place where ships are built or repaired.

shire *noun* (*plural* **shires**)
a county.
the Shires the country areas of (especially
central) England, away from the cities.

shirk *verb* (**shirks, shirking, shirked**)
avoid a duty or work etc. selfishly or unfairly.
shirker *noun*
[probably from German *Schurke* = scoundrel]

shirt *noun* (*plural* **shirts**)
a piece of clothing for the top half of the body,
made of light material and with a collar and
sleeves.
in your shirtsleeves not wearing a jacket over
your shirt.

shiver *verb* (**shivers, shivering, shivered**)
tremble with cold or fear.
shiver *noun* **shivery** *adjective*

shoal¹ *noun* (*plural* **shoals**)
a large number of fish swimming together.

shoal² *noun* (*plural* **shoals**)
1 a shallow place. 2 an underwater sandbank.

shock¹ *noun* (*plural* **shocks**)
1 a sudden unpleasant surprise. 2 great
weakness caused by pain or injury etc.
3 the effect of a violent shake or knock.
4 an effect caused by electric current passing
through the body.

shock *verb* (**shocks, shocking, shocked**)
1 give someone a shock; surprise or upset a
person greatly. 2 seem very improper or
scandalous to a person.

shock² *noun* (*plural* **shocks**)
a bushy mass of hair.

shocking *adjective*
1 causing indignation or disgust. 2 (*informal*)
very bad ♦ *shocking weather.*

shock wave *noun* (*plural* **shock waves**)
a sharp change in pressure in the air around an
explosion or an object moving very quickly.

shod *past tense* of **shoe.**

shoddy *adjective* (**shoddier, shoddiest**)
of poor quality; badly made or done ♦ *shoddy
work.*
shoddily *adverb* **shoddiness** *noun*

shoe *noun* (*plural* **shoes**)
1 a strong covering for the foot. 2 a horseshoe.
3 something shaped or used like a shoe.
be in somebody's shoes be in his or her
situation.

shoe *verb* (**shoes, shoeing, shod**)
fit with a shoe or shoes.

shoelace *noun* (*plural* **shoelaces**)
a cord for lacing up and fastening a shoe.

shoot *verb* (**shoots, shooting, shot**)
1 fire a gun or missile etc. **2** hurt or kill by shooting. **3** move or send very quickly ♦ *The car shot past us.* **4** kick or hit a ball at a goal. **5** (said about a plant) put out buds or shoots. **6** slide the bolt of a door into or out of its fastening. **7** film or photograph something ♦ *The film was shot in Africa.*

shoot *noun* (*plural* **shoots**)
1 a young branch or new growth of a plant. **2** an expedition for shooting animals.

shooting star *noun* (*plural* **shooting stars**)
a meteor.

shop *noun* (*plural* **shops**)
1 a building or room where goods or services are on sale to the public. **2** a workshop. **3** talk that is about your own work or job ♦ *She is always talking shop.*

shop *verb* (**shops, shopping, shopped**)
go and buy things at shops.
shopper *noun*
shop around compare goods and prices in several shops before buying.

shop floor *noun*
1 the workers in a factory, not the managers. **2** the place where they work.

shopkeeper *noun* (*plural* **shopkeepers**)
a person who owns or manages a shop.

shoplifter *noun* (*plural* **shoplifters**)
a person who steals goods from a shop after entering as a customer.
shoplifting *noun*

shopping *noun*
1 buying goods in shops. **2** the goods bought.

shore¹ *noun* (*plural* **shores**)
the land along the edge of a sea or of a lake.
[from early German or Dutch *schore*]

shore² *verb* (**shores, shoring, shored**)
prop something up with a piece of wood etc.
[from early German or Dutch *schoren*]

shorn *past participle* of **shear**.

short *adjective*
1 not long; occupying a small distance or time ♦ *a short walk.* **2** not tall ♦ *a short person.* **3** not enough; not having enough of something ♦ *Water is short in hot weather.* ♦ *We are short of water.* **4** bad-tempered or curt. **5** (said about pastry) rich and crumbly because it contains a lot of fat.
shortness *noun*
for short as an abbreviation ♦ *Raymond is called Ray for short.* **short for** an abbreviation ♦ *'Ray' is short for Raymond.* **short of** without going to the length of ♦ *I'll do anything to help, short of breaking the law.*

short *adverb*
suddenly ♦ *She stopped short.*

shortage *noun* (*plural* **shortages**)
lack or scarcity of something; insufficiency.

shortbread *noun*
a rich sweet biscuit, made with butter.

short circuit *noun* (*plural* **short circuits**)
a fault in an electrical circuit in which current flows along a shorter route than the normal one.
short-circuit *verb*

shortcoming *noun* (*plural* **shortcomings**)
a fault or failure to reach a good standard.

short cut *noun* (*plural* **short cuts**)
a route or method that is quicker than the usual one.

shorten *verb* (**shortens, shortening, shortened**)
make or become shorter.

shorthand *noun*
a set of special signs for writing words down as quickly as people say them.

short-handed *adjective*
not having enough workers or helpers.

shortly *adverb*
1 in a short time; soon ♦ *They will arrive shortly.* **2** in a few words. **3** curtly.

shorts *plural noun*
trousers with legs that do not reach to the knee.

short-sighted *adjective*
1 unable to see things clearly when they are further away. **2** lacking imagination or foresight.

short-tempered *adjective*
easily becoming angry.

short wave *noun*
a radio wave of a wavelength between 10 and 100 metres and a frequency of about 3 to 30 megahertz.

shot¹ *past tense* of **shoot**.

shot² *noun* (*plural* **shots**)
1 the firing of a gun or missile etc.; the sound of this. **2** something fired from a gun; lead pellets for firing from small guns. **3** a person judged by skill in shooting ♦ *He's a good shot.* **4** a heavy metal ball thrown as a sport. **5** a stroke in tennis, cricket, billiards, etc. **6** a photograph; a filmed scene. **7** (*informal*) an attempt ♦ *Have a shot at the crossword.* **8** an injection of a drug or vaccine.

shot *adjective*
(said about fabric) woven so that different colours show at different angles ♦ *shot silk.*

should *auxiliary verb*
1 used for saying what someone ought to do ♦ *You should have told me.* **2** used for saying what someone expects ♦ *They should be here by ten o'clock.* **3** used for saying what might happen ♦ *If you should happen to see him, tell him to come.* **4** used with *I* and *we* to make a polite statement (*I should like to come*) or in a conditional clause (*If they had supported us we should have won*).

ℹ **USAGE** In sense 4, although *should* is strictly correct, many people nowadays use *would* and this is not regarded as wrong.

shoulder *noun* (*plural* **shoulders**)
1 the part of the body between the neck and the arm, foreleg, or wing. **2** a side that juts out ♦ *the shoulder of the bottle.*

shoulder *verb* (**shoulders, shouldering, shouldered**)
1 take something on your shoulder or shoulders. **2** push with your shoulder. **3** accept responsibility or blame.

shoulder blade *noun* (*plural* **shoulder blades**)
either of the two large flat bones at the top of your back.

shouldn't (*mainly spoken*)
should not.

shout *noun* (*plural* **shouts**)
a loud cry or call.

shout *verb* (**shouts, shouting, shouted**)
give a shout; speak or call loudly.

shove *verb* (**shoves, shoving, shoved**)
push roughly.
shove *noun*
shove off (*informal*) go away.

shovel *noun* (*plural* **shovels**)
a tool like a spade with the sides turned up, used for lifting coal, earth, snow, etc.

shovel *verb* (**shovels, shovelling, shovelled**)
1 move or clear with a shovel. **2** scoop or push roughly ♦ *He was shovelling food into his mouth.*

show *verb* (**shows, showing, showed, shown**)
1 allow or cause something to be seen ♦ *Show me your new bike.* **2** make a person understand; demonstrate ♦ *Show me how to use it.* **3** guide ♦ *Show him in.* **4** treat in a certain way ♦ *She showed us much kindness.* **5** be visible ♦ *That scratch won't show.* **6** prove your ability to someone ♦ *We'll show them!*
show off 1 show something proudly. **2** try to impress people. **show up 1** make or be clearly visible; reveal a fault etc. **2** (*informal*) arrive.

show *noun* (*plural* **shows**)
1 a display or exhibition ♦ *a flower show.* **2** an entertainment. **3** (*informal*) something that happens or is done ♦ *He runs the whole show.*

showdown *noun* (*plural* **showdowns**)
a final test or confrontation.

shower *noun* (*plural* **showers**)
1 a brief fall of rain or snow. **2** a lot of small things coming or falling like rain ♦ *a shower of stones.* **3** a device or cabinet for spraying water to wash a person's body; a wash in this.

shower *verb* (**showers, showering, showered**)
1 fall or send things in a shower. **2** wash under a shower.

showman *noun* (*plural* **showmen**)
1 a person who presents entertainments. **2** someone who is good at attracting attention.
showmanship *noun*

show-off *noun* (*plural* **show-offs**) (*informal*)
a person who tries to impress people boastfully.

showpiece *noun* (*plural* **showpieces**)
a fine example of something for people to see and admire.

showy *adjective* (**showier, showiest**)
likely to attract attention; brightly or highly decorated.
showily *adverb* **showiness** *noun*

shrapnel *noun*
pieces of metal scattered from an exploding shell.

shred *noun* (*plural* **shreds**)
1 a tiny piece torn or cut off something. **2** a small amount ♦ *There is not a shred of evidence.*

shred *verb* (**shreds, shredding, shredded**)
cut into shreds.
shredder *noun*

shrew *noun* (*plural* **shrews**)
1 a small mouse-like animal. **2** (*old use*) a bad-tempered woman who is constantly scolding people.
shrewish *adjective*

shrewd *adjective*
having common sense and good judgement; clever.
shrewdly *adverb* **shrewdness** *noun*

shriek *noun* (*plural* **shrieks**)
a shrill cry or scream.

shriek *verb* (**shrieks, shrieking, shrieked**)
give a shriek.

shrill *adjective*
sounding very high and piercing.
shrilly *adverb* **shrillness** *noun*

shrimp *noun* (*plural* **shrimps**)
a small shellfish, pink when boiled.

shrine *noun* (*plural* **shrines**)
an altar, chapel, or other sacred place.

shrink *verb* (**shrinks, shrinking, shrank, shrunk**)
1 make or become smaller. **2** move back to avoid something. **3** avoid doing something because of fear, conscience, embarrassment, etc.
shrinkage *noun* **shrunken** *adjective*

shrivel *verb* (**shrivels, shrivelling, shrivelled**)
make or become dry and wrinkled.

shroud *noun* (*plural* **shrouds**)
1 a cloth in which a dead body is wrapped. **2** each of a set of ropes supporting a ship's mast.

Shrove Tuesday *noun*
the day before Lent, when pancakes are eaten, originally to use up fat before the fast.

shrub *noun* (*plural* **shrubs**)
a woody plant smaller than a tree; a bush.
shrubby *adjective*

shrubbery noun (plural **shrubberies**)
an area planted with shrubs.

shrug verb (**shrugs, shrugging, shrugged**)
raise your shoulders as a sign that you do not
care, do not know, etc.
shrug noun
shrug something off treat it as unimportant.

shudder verb (**shudders, shuddering,
shuddered**)
1 shiver violently with horror, fear, or cold.
2 make a strong shaking movement.
shudder noun

shuffle verb (**shuffles, shuffling, shuffled**)
1 walk without lifting the feet from the ground.
2 slide playing cards over each other to get them
into random order. 3 shift or rearrange.
shuffle noun

shun verb (**shuns, shunning, shunned**)
avoid; deliberately keep away from something.

shunt verb (**shunts, shunting, shunted**)
1 move a train or wagons on to another track.
2 divert to a less important place or position.
shunt noun **shunter** noun

shut verb (**shuts, shutting, shut**)
1 move a door, lid, or cover etc. so that it blocks
an opening; make or become closed. 2 bring or
fold parts together ♦ Shut the book.
shut down 1 stop something working.
2 stop business. **shut up** 1 shut securely.
2 (informal) stop talking or making a noise.

shutter noun (plural **shutters**)
1 a panel or screen that can be closed over a
window. 2 the device in a camera that opens and
closes to let light fall on the film.
shuttered adjective

shuttle noun (plural **shuttles**)
1 a holder carrying the weft thread across a loom
in weaving. 2 a train, bus, or aircraft that makes
frequent short journeys between two points.
shuttle verb (**shuttles, shuttling, shuttled**)
move, travel, or send backwards and forwards.

shy adjective (**shyer, shyest**)
afraid to meet or talk to other people; timid.
shyly adverb **shyness** noun

shy verb (**shies, shying, shied**)
jump or move suddenly in alarm.

SI noun
an internationally recognized system of metric
units of measurement, including the metre and
kilogram.

Siamese cat noun (plural **Siamese cats**)
a cat with short pale fur with darker face, ears,
tail, and feet.

Siamese twins plural noun
twins who are born with their bodies joined
together.

sick adjective
1 ill; physically or mentally unwell. 2 vomiting
or likely to vomit ♦ I feel sick. 3 distressed or
disgusted. 4 making fun of death, disability, or
misfortune in an unpleasant way.
sick of tired of.

sicken verb (**sickens, sickening, sickened**)
1 begin to be ill. 2 make or become distressed or
disgusted ♦ Vandalism sickens us all.
sickening adjective

sickle noun (plural **sickles**)
a tool with a narrow curved blade, used for
cutting corn etc.

sickly adjective
1 often ill; unhealthy. 2 making people feel sick
♦ a sickly smell. 3 weak ♦ a sickly smile.

sickness noun (plural **sicknesses**)
1 illness. 2 a disease. 3 vomiting.

side noun (plural **sides**)
1 a surface, especially one joining the top and
bottom of something. 2 a line that forms part of
the boundary of a triangle, square, etc. 3 either
of the two halves into which something can be
divided by a line down its centre. 4 the part near
the edge and away from the centre. 5 the place or
region next to a person or thing ♦ He stood at my
side. 6 one aspect or view of something ♦ Study
all sides of the problem. 7 one of two groups or
teams etc. who oppose each other.
on the side as a sideline. **side by side** next to
each other. **take sides** support one person or
group in a dispute or disagreement and not the
other.

side verb (**sides, siding, sided**)
side with take a person's side in an argument.

side effect noun (plural **side effects**)
an effect, especially an unpleasant one, that a
medicine has on you as well as the effect
intended.

sidelight noun (plural **sidelights**)
1 a light at the side of a vehicle or ship.
2 light from one side.

sideline noun (plural **sidelines**)
1 something done in addition to your main work
or activity. 2 each of the lines on the two long
sides of a sports pitch.

sidelong adjective
towards one side; sideways ♦ a sidelong glance.

sidetrack verb (**sidetracks, sidetracking,
sidetracked**)
take someone's attention away from the main
subject or problem.

sideways adverb & adjective
1 to or from one side ♦ Move it sideways.
2 with one side facing forwards ♦ We sat
sideways in the bus.

siding noun (plural **sidings**)
a short railway line by the side of a main line.

siege *noun* (*plural* **sieges**)
the surrounding of a place in order to capture it
or force someone to surrender.
lay siege to begin a siege of a place.

sieve (*say* siv) *noun* (*plural* **sieves**)
a device made of mesh or perforated metal or
plastic, used to separate the smaller or soft parts
of something from the larger or hard parts.
sieve *verb* (**sieves, sieving, sieved**)
put something through a sieve.

sift *verb* (**sifts, sifting, sifted**)
1 sieve. 2 examine and analyse facts or evidence
etc. carefully.
sifter *noun*

sigh *noun* (*plural* **sighs**)
a sound made by breathing out heavily when
you are sad, tired, relieved, etc.
sigh *verb* (**sighs, sighing, sighed**)
make a sigh.

sight *noun* (*plural* **sights**)
1 the ability to see. 2 a thing that can be seen or
is worth seeing ♦ *Our garden is a lovely sight in
May.* 3 something ugly or ridiculous to look at
♦ *You do look a sight in those clothes!* 4 a device
looked through to help aim a gun or telescope
etc.
at sight or **on sight** as soon as a person or thing
has been seen. **catch sight of** to see or glimpse
for a moment. **in sight** 1 visible. 2 clearly near
♦ *Victory was in sight.*

❶ USAGE Do not confuse with *site*.

sight *verb* (**sights, sighting, sighted**)
1 see or observe something. 2 aim a gun or
telescope etc.
[from Old English]

sighted *adjective*
able to see; not blind.

sight-reading *noun*
playing or singing music at sight, without
preparation.

sightseeing *noun*
visiting interesting places in a town etc.
sightseer *noun*

sign *noun* (*plural* **signs**)
1 something that shows that a thing exists
♦ *There are signs of decay.* 2 a mark, device, or
notice etc. that gives a special meaning ♦ *a road
sign.* 3 an action or movement giving
information or a command etc. 4 any of the
twelve divisions of the zodiac, represented by a
symbol.
sign *verb* (**signs, signing, signed**)
1 make a sign or signal. 2 write your signature
on something; accept a contract etc. by doing
this. 3 use signing.
sign on 1 accept a job etc. by signing a contract.
2 sign a form to say that you are unemployed
and want to claim benefit.

signal *noun* (*plural* **signals**)
1 a device, gesture, or sound etc. that gives
information or a command. 2 a message made
up of such things. 3 a sequence of electrical
impulses or radio waves.
signal *verb* (**signals, signalling, signalled**)
make a signal to somebody.
signaller *noun*

❶ USAGE Do not use this word in mistake for
single in the phrase *to single out.*

signal box *noun* (*plural* **signal boxes**)
a building from which railway signals, points,
etc. are controlled.

signature *noun* (*plural* **signatures**)
1 a person's name written by himself or herself.
2 (in music) a set of sharps and flats after the clef
in a score, showing the key the music is written
in (the **key signature**), or the sign, often a
fraction such as $\frac{3}{4}$ (the **time signature**), showing
the number of beats in the bar and their rhythm.

signature tune *noun* (*plural* **signature tunes**)
a special tune always used to announce a
particular programme, performer, etc.

significant *adjective*
1 having a meaning; full of meaning.
2 important ♦ *a significant event.*
significantly *adverb* **significance** *noun*

signing or **sign language** *noun*
a way of communicating by using movements of
the arms and hands, used mainly by and for deaf
people.

signpost *noun* (*plural* **signposts**)
a sign at a road junction etc. showing the names
and distances of places down each road.

Sikh (*say* seek) *noun* (*plural* **Sikhs**)
a member of a religion founded in northern
India, believing in one God and accepting some
Hindu and some Islamic beliefs.
Sikhism *noun*

silence *noun* (*plural* **silences**)
absence of sound or speaking.
in silence without speaking or making a sound.
silence *verb* (**silences, silencing, silenced**)
make a person or thing silent.

silencer *noun* (*plural* **silencers**)
a device for reducing the sound made by a gun
or a vehicle's exhaust system etc.

silent *adjective*
1 without any sound. 2 not speaking.
silently *adverb*

silhouette (*say* sil-oo-**et**) *noun* (*plural*
silhouettes)
a dark shadow seen against a light background.
silhouette *verb*

silicon *noun*
a substance found in many rocks, used in
making transistors, chips for microprocessors,
etc.

silk *noun* (*plural* **silks**)
1 a fine soft thread or cloth made from the fibre produced by silkworm caterpillars for making their cocoons. **2** a length of silk thread used for embroidery.
silken *adjective* **silky** *adjective*

silly *adjective* (**sillier, silliest**)
foolish or unwise.
silliness *noun*

silt *noun*
sediment laid down by a river or sea etc.

silt *verb* (**silts, silting, silted**)
silt up block or clog or become blocked with silt.

silver *noun*
1 a shiny white precious metal. **2** the colour of silver. **3** coins or objects made of silver or silver-coloured metal. **4** a silver medal, usually given as second prize.
silver *adjective* **silvery** *adjective*

silver *verb* (**silvers, silvering, silvered**)
make or become silvery.

silver wedding *noun* (*plural* **silver weddings**)
a couple's 25th wedding anniversary.

similar *adjective*
1 nearly the same as another person or thing; of the same kind. **2** (in mathematics) having the same shape but not the same size ♦ *similar triangles*.
similarly *adverb* **similarity** *noun*

simile (*say* sim-il-ee) *noun* (*plural* **similes**)
a comparison of one thing with another (e.g. *He is as strong as a horse* or *We ran like the wind*).

simmer *verb* (**simmers, simmering, simmered**)
boil very gently.
simmer down calm down.

simper *verb* (**simpers, simpering, simpered**)
smile in a silly affected way.
simper *noun*

simple *adjective* (**simpler, simplest**)
1 easy ♦ *a simple question*. **2** not complicated or elaborate. **3** plain, not showy ♦ *a simple cottage*. **4** without much sense or intelligence. **5** not of high rank; ordinary ♦ *a simple countryman*.
simplicity *noun*

simple-minded *adjective*
not having much intelligence.

simplify *verb* (**simplifies, simplifying, simplified**)
make a thing simple or easy to understand.
simplification *noun*

simply *adverb*
1 in a simple way ♦ *Explain it simply*. **2** without doubt; completely ♦ *It's simply marvellous*. **3** only or merely ♦ *It's simply a question of time*.

simulator *noun* (*plural* **simulators**)
a machine or device for simulating actual conditions or events, often used for training ♦ *a flight simulator*.

simultaneous (*say* sim-ul-**tay**-nee-us) *adjective*
happening at the same time.
simultaneously *adverb*

sin *noun* (*plural* **sins**)
1 the breaking of a religious or moral law. **2** a very bad action.

sin *verb* (**sins, sinning, sinned**)
commit a sin.
sinner *noun*

since *conjunction*
1 from the time when ♦ *Where have you been since I last saw you?* **2** because ♦ *Since we have missed the bus we must walk home*.

since *preposition*
from a certain time ♦ *She has been here since Christmas*.

since *adverb*
between then and now ♦ *He ran away and hasn't been seen since*.

sincere *adjective*
without pretence; truly felt or meant ♦ *my sincere thanks*.
sincerely *adverb* **sincerity** *noun*
Yours sincerely see **yours.**

sine *noun* (*plural* **sines**)
(in a right-angled triangle) the ratio of the length of a side opposite one of the acute angles to the length of the hypotenuse. (Compare **cosine.**)

sinew *noun* (*plural* **sinews**)
strong tissue that connects a muscle to a bone.
sinewy *adjective*

sinful *adjective*
1 guilty of sin. **2** wicked.
sinfully *adverb* **sinfulness** *noun*

sing *verb* (**sings, singing, sang, sung**)
1 make musical sounds with the voice.
2 perform a song.
singer *noun*

singe (*say* sinj) *verb* (**singes, singeing, singed**)
burn something slightly.

single *adjective*
1 one only; not double or multiple. **2** suitable for one person ♦ *single beds*. **3** separate ♦ *We sold every single thing*. **4** not married. **5** for the journey to a place but not back again ♦ *a single ticket*.
singly *adverb*

single *noun* (*plural* **singles**)
1 a single person or thing. **2** a single ticket.
3 a record with one short piece of music on each side.

single *verb* (**singles, singling, singled**)
single out pick out or distinguish from other people or things.

single file *noun*
in single file in a line, one behind the other.

single-handed *adjective*
without help.

single-minded *adjective*
with your mind set on one purpose only.

singsong *adjective*
having a monotonous tone or rhythm
♦ *a singsong voice.*

singular *noun* (*plural* **singulars**)
the form of a noun or verb used when it stands
for only one person or thing ♦ *The singular is
'man', the plural is 'men'.*

singular *adjective*
1 to do with the singular. **2** uncommon or
extraordinary ♦ *a woman of singular courage.*
singularly *adverb* **singularity** *noun*

sinister *adjective*
1 looking evil or harmful. **2** wicked ♦ *a sinister
motive.*
[from Latin, = on the left (which was thought to
be unlucky)]

sink *verb* (**sinks, sinking, sank, sunk**)
1 go or cause to go under the surface or to the
bottom of the sea etc. ♦ *The ship sank.* ♦ *They
sank the ship.* **2** go or fall slowly downwards
♦ *He sank to his knees.* **3** push something sharp
deeply into something soft ♦ *The dog sank its
teeth into my leg.* **4** dig or drill ♦ *They sank a
well.* **5** invest money in something.
sink in become understood. **sink** *noun* (*plural*
sinks)
a fixed basin with a drainpipe and usually a tap
or taps to supply water.

sip *verb* (**sips, sipping, sipped**)
drink in small mouthfuls.
sip *noun*

siphon *noun* (*plural* **siphons**)
1 a pipe or tube in the form of an upside-down U,
arranged so that liquid is forced up it and down
to a lower level. **2** a bottle containing soda water
which is released through a tube.
siphon *verb* (**siphons, siphoning, siphoned**)
flow or draw out through a siphon.

sir *noun*
1 a word used when speaking politely to a man
♦ *Please sir, may I go?* **2 Sir** the title given to a
knight or baronet ♦ *Sir John Moore.*

siren *noun* (*plural* **sirens**)
1 a device that makes a long loud sound as a
signal. **2** a dangerously attractive woman.
[named after the Sirens in Greek legend, women
who by their sweet singing lured seafarers to
shipwreck on the rocks]

sissy *noun* (*plural* **sissies**) (*informal*)
a timid or cowardly person.
[from *sis*, a shortening of *sister*]

sister *noun* (*plural* **sisters**)
1 a daughter of the same parents as another
person. **2** a woman who is a fellow member of an
association etc. **3** a nun. **4** a senior hospital
nurse, especially one in charge of a ward.
sisterly *adjective*
[from Old English]

sister-in-law *noun* (*plural* **sisters-in-law**)
1 the sister of a married person's husband or
wife. **2** the wife of a person's brother.

sit *verb* (**sits, sitting, sat**)
1 rest with your body supported on the buttocks;
occupy a seat ♦ *We were sitting in the front row.*
2 seat; cause someone to sit. **3** (said about birds)
perch; stay on the nest to hatch eggs. **4** be a
candidate for an examination. **5** be situated; stay.
6 (said about Parliament or a lawcourt etc.) be
assembled for business.

sitcom *noun* (*plural* **sitcoms**) (*informal*)
a radio or television comedy based on characters
reacting to unusual or comic situations.
[short for *situation comedy*]

site *noun* (*plural* **sites**)
the place where something happens or happened
or is built etc. ♦ *a camping site.*
[from Latin *situs* = position]

---

❶ USAGE Do not confuse with *sight*.

---

sit-in *noun* (*plural* **sit-ins**)
a protest in which people sit down or occupy a
public place and refuse to move.

sitter *noun* (*plural* **sitters**)
a person who looks after children, pets, or a
house while the owners are away.

sitting *noun* (*plural* **sittings**)
the time when people are served a meal or when
an official body of people does business.

sitting room *noun* (*plural* **sitting rooms**)
a room with comfortable chairs for sitting in.

situation *noun* (*plural* **situations**)
1 a position, with its surroundings. **2** a state of
affairs at a certain time ♦ *The police faced a
difficult situation.* **3** a job.

six *noun* & *adjective*(*plural* **sixes**)
the number 6.
sixth *adjective* & *noun*
at sixes and sevens in disorder or disagreement.

sixteen *noun* & *adjective*
the number 16.
sixteenth *adjective* & *noun*

sixth form *noun* (*plural* **sixth forms**)
a form for students aged 16–18 in a secondary
school.

sixth sense *noun*
the ability to know something by instinct rather
than by using any of the five senses; intuition.

sixty *noun* & *adjective*(*plural* **sixties**)
the number 60.
sixtieth *adjective* & *noun*

size *noun* (*plural* **sizes**)
1 the measurements or extent of something.
2 any of the series of standard measurements in which certain things are made ♦ *a size eight shoe.*
size *verb* (**sizes, sizing, sized**)
arrange things according to their size.
size up 1 estimate the size of something. **2** form an opinion or judgement about a person or thing.

sizeable *adjective*
large or fairly large.

sizzle *verb* (**sizzles, sizzling, sizzled**)
make a crackling or hissing sound.

skate *noun* (*plural* **skates**)
1 a boot with a steel blade attached to the sole, used for sliding smoothly over ice.
2 a roller-skate.
skate *verb* (**skates, skating, skated**)
move on skates.
skater *noun*

skateboard *noun* (*plural* **skateboards**)
a small board with wheels, used for standing and riding on as a sport.
skateboarder, skateboarding *nouns*

skein *noun* (*plural* **skeins**)
a coil of yarn or thread.

skeleton *noun* (*plural* **skeletons**)
1 the framework of bones of the body. **2** the shell or other hard part of a crab etc. **3** a framework, e.g. of a building.
skeletal *adjective*
[from Greek *skeletos* = dried-up]

sketch *noun* (*plural* **sketches**)
1 a rough drawing or painting. **2** a short account of something. **3** a short amusing play.
sketch *verb* (**sketches, sketching, sketched**)
make a sketch.

sketchy *adjective*
rough and not detailed or careful.

skewer *noun* (*plural* **skewers**)
a long pin pushed through meat to hold it together while it is being cooked.
skewer *verb*

ski (*say* skee) *noun* (*plural* **skis**)
each of a pair of long narrow strips of wood, metal, or plastic fixed under the feet for moving quickly over snow.
ski *verb* (**skies, skiing, skied**)
travel on skis.
skier *noun*
[from Norwegian]

skid *verb* (**skids, skidding, skidded**)
slide accidentally.

skid *noun* (*plural* **skids**)
1 a skidding movement. **2** a runner on a helicopter, for use in landing.
[probably from Old Norse *skith* = ski]

ski jump *noun* (*plural* **ski jumps**)
a steep slope with a sharp drop where it levels out at the bottom, for skiers to jump off as a sport.

skilful *adjective*
having or showing great skill.
skilfully *adverb*

skill *noun* (*plural* **skills**)
the ability to do something well.
skilled *adjective*
[from Old Norse]

skim *verb* (**skims, skimming, skimmed**)
1 remove something from the surface of a liquid; take the cream off milk. **2** move quickly over a surface or through the air. **3** read something quickly.
[from early French *escume* = scum]

skimp *verb* (**skimps, skimping, skimped**)
supply or use less than is needed ♦ *Don't skimp on the food.*

skimpy *adjective* (**skimpier, skimpiest**)
scanty or too small.

skin *noun* (*plural* **skins**)
1 the flexible outer covering of a person's or animal's body. **2** an outer layer or covering, e.g. of a fruit. **3** a skin-like film formed on the surface of a liquid.
skin *verb* (**skins, skinning, skinned**)
take the skin off something.

skinny *adjective* (**skinnier, skinniest**)
very thin.

skip[1] *verb* (**skips, skipping, skipped**)
1 move along lightly, especially by hopping on each foot in turn. **2** jump with a skipping rope. **3** go quickly from one subject to another. **4** miss something out ♦ *You can skip chapter six.*
skip *noun* (*plural* **skips**)
a skipping movement.
[probably from Scandinavian]

skip[2] *noun* (*plural* **skips**)
a large metal container for taking away builders' rubbish etc.
[from Old Norse *skeppa* = basket]

skipping rope *noun* (*plural* **skipping ropes**)
a rope, usually with a handle at each end, that is swung over your head and under your feet as you jump.

skirt *noun* (*plural* **skirts**)
1 a piece of clothing for a woman or girl that hangs down from the waist. **2** the part of a dress below the waist.
skirt *verb* (**skirts, skirting, skirted**)
go round the edge of something.

skittish *adjective*
frisky; lively and excitable.

skulk *verb* (**skulks, skulking, skulked**)
loiter stealthily.

skull *noun* (*plural* **skulls**)
the framework of bones of the head.

skunk *noun* (*plural* **skunks**)
a North American animal with black and white
fur that can spray a bad-smelling fluid.
[from a Native American word]

sky *noun* (*plural* **skies**)
the space above the earth, appearing blue in
daylight on fine days.
[from Old Norse]

skylight *noun* (*plural* **skylights**)
a window in a roof.

skyline *noun* (*plural* **skylines**)
the outline of buildings etc. against the sky.

skyscraper *noun* (*plural* **skyscrapers**)
a very tall building.

slab *noun* (*plural* **slabs**)
a thick flat piece.

slack *adjective*
1 not pulled tight. 2 not busy; not working hard.
slackly *adverb* **slackness** *noun*

slack *verb* (**slacks, slacking, slacked**)
avoid work; be lazy.
slacker *noun*

slacken *verb* (**slackens, slackening, slackened**)
make or become slack.

slacks *plural noun*
trousers for informal occasions.

slag *noun*
waste material separated from metal in smelting.

slag heap *noun* (*plural* **slag heaps**)
a mound of waste matter from a mine etc.

slain *past participle* of **slay**.

slake *verb* (**slakes, slaking, slaked**)
quench ♦ *slake your thirst*.

slam *verb* (**slams, slamming, slammed**)
1 shut loudly. 2 hit violently.
slam *noun*

slander *noun* (*plural* **slanders**)
a spoken statement that damages a person's
reputation and is untrue. (Compare **libel**.)
slanderous *adjective*

slander *verb* (**slanders, slandering, slandered**)
make a slander against someone.
slanderer *noun*

slang *noun*
words that are used very informally to add
vividness or humour to what is said, especially
those used only by a particular group of people
♦ *teenage slang*.
slangy *adjective*

slant *verb* (**slants, slanting, slanted**)
1 slope. 2 present news or information etc. from
a particular point of view.

slap *verb* (**slaps, slapping, slapped**)
1 hit with the palm of the hand or with
something flat. 2 put forcefully or carelessly
♦ *We slapped paint on the walls*.
slap *noun*

slapdash *adjective*
hasty and careless.

slapstick *noun*
comedy with people hitting each other, falling
over, etc.

slash *verb* (**slashes, slashing, slashed**)
1 make large cuts in something. 2 cut or strike
with a long sweeping movement. 3 reduce
greatly ♦ *Prices were slashed*.

slash *noun* (*plural* **slashes**)
1 a slashing cut. 2 a slanting line (/) used in
writing and printing.

slate *noun* (*plural* **slates**)
1 a kind of grey rock that is easily split into flat
plates. 2 a piece of this rock used in covering a
roof or (formerly) for writing on.
slaty *adjective*

slate *verb* (**slates, slating, slated**)
1 cover a roof with slates. 2 (*informal*) criticize
severely.

slaughter *verb* (**slaughters, slaughtering,
slaughtered**)
1 kill an animal for food. 2 kill people or animals
ruthlessly or in great numbers.
slaughter *noun*

slaughterhouse *noun* (*plural*
slaughterhouses)
a place where animals are killed for food.

slave *noun* (*plural* **slaves**)
a person who is owned by another and obliged to
work for him or her without being paid.
slavery *noun*

slave *verb* (**slaves, slaving, slaved**)
work very hard.
[from Latin *sclavus* = captive]

slavish *adjective*
1 like a slave. 2 showing no independence or
originality.

slay *verb* (**slays, slaying, slew, slain**) (*poetical*)
kill.

sledge *noun* (*plural* **sledges**)
a vehicle for travelling over snow, with strips of
metal or wood instead of wheels.
sledging *noun*

sledgehammer *noun* (*plural*
sledgehammers)
a very large heavy hammer.

sleek *adjective*
smooth and shiny.

sleep *noun*
the condition or time of rest in which the eyes are closed, the body relaxed, and the mind unconscious.
go to sleep (said about part of the body) become numb. **put to sleep** kill an animal painlessly, e.g. with an injection of a drug.
sleep *verb* (**sleeps, sleeping, slept**)
have a sleep.
sleep with have sexual intercourse with.
[from Old English]

sleeper *noun* (*plural* **sleepers**)
1 someone who is asleep. **2** each of the wooden or concrete beams on which the rails of a railway rest. **3** a railway carriage with beds or berths for passengers to sleep in; a place in this.

sleepwalker *noun* (*plural* **sleepwalkers**)
a person who walks about while asleep.
sleepwalking *noun*

sleepy *adjective*
feeling a need or wish to sleep.
sleepily *adverb* **sleepiness** *noun*

sleet *noun*
a mixture of rain and snow or hail.

sleeve *noun* (*plural* **sleeves**)
1 the part of a piece of clothing that covers the arm. **2** the cover of a record.
up your sleeve hidden but ready for you to use.

sleight (rhymes with *slight*) *noun*
sleight of hand skill in using the hands to do conjuring tricks etc.

slender *adjective*
1 slim and graceful. **2** slight or small ♦ *a slender chance.*
slenderness *noun*

sleuth (*say* slooth) *noun* (*plural* **sleuths**)
a detective.
[from Old Norse *sloth* = a track or trail]

slew *past tense* of **slay**.

slice *noun* (*plural* **slices**)
1 a thin piece cut off something. **2** a portion.
slice *verb* (**slices, slicing, sliced**)
1 cut into slices. **2** cut from a larger piece ♦ *Slice the top off the egg.* **3** cut cleanly ♦ *The knife sliced through the apple.*

slick *adjective*
1 done or doing things quickly and cleverly. **2** slippery.
slick *noun* (*plural* **slicks**)
1 a large patch of oil floating on water. **2** a slippery place.

slide *verb* (**slides, sliding, slid**)
1 move or cause to move smoothly on a surface. **2** move quietly or secretly ♦ *The thief slid behind a bush.*

slide *noun* (*plural* **slides**)
1 a sliding movement. **2** a smooth surface or structure on which people or things can slide. **3** a photograph that can be projected on a screen. **4** a small glass plate on which things are placed to be examined under a microscope. **5** a fastener to keep hair tidy.

slight *adjective*
very small; not serious or important.
slightly *adverb* **slightness** *noun*

slim *adjective* (**slimmer, slimmest**)
1 thin and graceful. **2** small; hardly enough ♦ *a slim chance.*
slimness *noun*
slim *verb* (**slims, slimming, slimmed**)
make yourself thinner, especially by dieting.
slimmer *noun*

slime *noun*
unpleasant wet slippery stuff.
slimy *adjective* **sliminess** *noun*

sling *noun* (*plural* **slings**)
1 a loop or band placed round something to support or lift it ♦ *He had his arm in a sling.* **2** a looped strap used to throw a stone etc.
sling *verb* (**slings, slinging, slung**)
1 hang or support something so that it hangs loosely. **2** (*informal*) throw carelessly.

slink *verb* (**slinks, slinking, slunk**)
move in a stealthy or guilty way.
slinky *adjective*

slip *verb* (**slips, slipping, slipped**)
1 slide accidentally; lose your balance by sliding. **2** move or put quickly and quietly ♦ *Slip it in your pocket.* ♦ *We slipped away from the party.* **3** escape from ♦ *The dog slipped its leash.* ♦ *It slipped my memory.*
slip up make a mistake.
slip *noun* (*plural* **slips**)
1 an accidental slide or fall. **2** a mistake. **3** a small piece of paper. **4** a petticoat. **5** a pillowcase.
give someone the slip escape or avoid someone skilfully.

slipper *noun* (*plural* **slippers**)
a soft comfortable shoe to wear indoors.

slippery *adjective*
smooth or wet so that it is difficult to stand on or hold.
slipperiness *noun*

slipshod *adjective*
careless; not systematic.

slipstream *noun* (*plural* **slipstreams**)
a current of air driven backward as an aircraft or vehicle is propelled forward.

slit *noun* (*plural* **slits**)
a narrow straight cut or opening.
slit *verb* (**slits, slitting, slit**)
make a slit or slits in something.

slither *verb* (slithers, slithering, slithered)
slip or slide unsteadily.

sliver (*say* sliv-er) *noun* (*plural* slivers)
a thin strip of wood or glass etc.

slog *verb* (slogs, slogging, slogged)
1 hit hard. 2 work or walk hard and steadily.
slog *noun* **slogger** *noun*

slogan *noun* (*plural* slogans)
a phrase used to advertise something or to sum
up the aims of a campaign etc. ♦ *Their slogan
was 'Ban the bomb!'*
[from Scottish Gaelic *sluagh-ghairm*
= battle-cry]

slope *verb* (slopes, sloping, sloped)
lie or turn at an angle; slant.
slope off (*informal*) go away.
slope *noun* (*plural* slopes)
1 a sloping surface. 2 the amount by which
something slopes.

sloppy *adjective* (sloppier, sloppiest)
1 liquid and splashing easily. 2 careless or
slipshod ♦ *sloppy work.* 3 weakly sentimental
♦ *a sloppy story.*
sloppily *adverb* **sloppiness** *noun*

slot *noun* (*plural* slots)
a narrow opening to put things in.
slotted *adjective*
slot *verb* (slots, slotting, slotted)
put something into a place where it fits.

sloth (rhymes with *both*) *noun* (*plural* sloths)
1 laziness. 2 a South American animal that lives
in trees and moves very slowly.
slothful *adjective*

slot machine *noun* (*plural* slot machines)
a machine worked by putting a coin in the slot.

slouch *verb* (slouches, slouching, slouched)
stand, sit, or move in a lazy awkward way, not
with an upright posture.
slouch *noun*

slovenly (*say* sluv-en-lee) *adjective*
careless or untidy.
slovenliness *noun*

slow *adjective*
1 not quick; taking more time than is usual.
2 showing a time earlier than the correct time
♦ *Your watch is slow.* 3 not clever; not able to
understand quickly or easily.
slowly *adverb* **slowness** *noun*
slow *adverb*
slowly ♦ *Go slow.*
slow *verb* (slows, slowing, slowed)
go more slowly; cause to go more slowly
♦ *The storm slowed us down.*

slow-worm *noun* (*plural* slow-worms)
a small European legless lizard that looks like a
snake, and gives birth to live young.

sludge *noun*
thick mud.

slug *noun* (*plural* slugs)
1 a small slimy animal like a snail without a
shell. 2 a pellet for firing from a gun.

sluggish *adjective*
slow-moving; not alert or lively.

sluice gate *noun* (*plural* sluice gates)
a sliding barrier for controlling a flow of water.

slum *noun* (*plural* slums)
an area of dirty overcrowded houses.

slumber *verb* (slumbers, slumbering,
slumbered)
sleep.
slumber *noun* **slumberer** *noun* **slumberous** or
slumbrous *adjective*

slump *verb* (slumps, slumping, slumped)
fall heavily or suddenly.
slump *noun* (*plural* slumps)
a sudden great fall in prices or trade.

slur *verb* (slurs, slurring, slurred)
1 pronounce words indistinctly by running the
sounds together. 2 mark with a slur in music.
slur *noun* (*plural* slurs)
1 a slurred sound. 2 something that harms a
person's reputation. 3 (in music) a curved line
placed over notes to show that they are to be
sung or played smoothly without a break.

slurp *verb* (slurps, slurping, slurped)
eat or drink with a loud sucking sound.
slurp *noun*

slush *noun*
partly melted snow on the ground.
slushy *adjective*

sly *adjective* (slyer, slyest)
1 unpleasantly cunning or secret. 2 mischievous
and knowing ♦ *a sly smile.*
slyly *adverb* **slyness** *noun*

smack¹ *noun* (*plural* smacks)
1 a slap. 2 a loud sharp sound ♦ *It hit the wall
with a smack.* 3 (*informal*) a loud kiss.
smack *verb* (smacks, smacking, smacked)
1 slap. 2 smash into.
smack your lips close and then part them noisily
in enjoyment.
smack *adverb* (*informal*)
forcefully or directly ♦ *The ball went smack
through the window.*
smack² *noun* (*plural* smacks)
a slight flavour of something; a trace.
smack *verb* (smacks, smacking, smacked)
have a slight flavour or trace ♦ *His manner
smacks of conceit.*

small *adjective*
1 not large; less than the usual size.
2 not important or significant.
smallness *noun*
the small of the back the lower part of a
person's back, where the spine curves in.

smallholding noun (plural **smallholdings**)
a small area of land used for farming.
smallholder noun

small hours plural noun
the early hours of the morning, after midnight.

small-minded adjective
selfish; petty.

smallpox noun
a serious contagious disease that causes a fever
and produces spots that leave scars on the skin.

smarmy adjective (informal)
trying to win someone's favour by being friendly
in an insincere or exaggerated way.

smart adjective
1 neat and elegant; dressed well. 2 clever.
3 forceful; brisk ♦ She ran at a smart pace.
smartly adverb **smartness** noun

smart card noun (plural **smart cards**)
a card like a credit card, which stores
information or enables you to use a cash
machine etc.

smarten verb (**smartens, smartening,
smartened**)
make or become smarter.

smash verb (**smashes, smashing, smashed**)
1 break noisily into pieces. 2 hit or move with
great force. 3 destroy or defeat completely.

smash noun (plural **smashes**)
1 the action or sound of smashing. 2 a collision
between vehicles.

smash hit noun (plural **smash hits**) (informal)
a very successful song, show, etc.

smashing adjective (informal)
excellent or beautiful.
smasher noun

smear verb (**smears, smearing, smeared**)
1 rub something greasy or sticky or dirty on a
surface. 2 try to damage someone's reputation.
smeary adjective

smear noun (plural **smears**)
1 smearing; something smeared. 2 material
smeared on a slide to be examined under a
microscope. 3 a false accusation. 4 a smear test.

smear test noun (plural **smear tests**)
the taking and examination of a sample of the
cervix lining, to check for faulty cells which may
cause cancer.

smell verb (**smells, smelling, smelt** or **smelled**)
1 be aware of something by means of the sense
organs of the nose ♦ I can smell smoke. 2 give
out a smell.

smell noun (plural **smells**)
1 something you can smell; a quality in
something that makes people able to smell it.
2 an unpleasant quality of this kind. 3 the ability
to smell things.
smelly adjective

smile noun (plural **smiles**)
an expression on the face that shows pleasure or
amusement, with the lips stretched and turning
upwards at the ends.

smile verb (**smiles, smiling, smiled**)
give a smile.

smirk noun (plural **smirks**)
a self-satisfied smile.

smirk verb (**smirks, smirking, smirked**)
give a smirk.

smite verb (**smites, smiting, smote, smitten**)
(old use) hit hard.

smith noun (plural **smiths**)
1 a person who makes things out of metal.
2 a blacksmith.

smithereens plural noun
small fragments.
[from Irish]

smock noun (plural **smocks**)
1 an overall shaped like a very long shirt.
2 a loose top with the upper part gathered into
stitched pleats.

smog noun
a mixture of smoke and fog.

smoke noun
1 the mixture of gas and solid particles given off
by a burning substance. 2 a period of smoking
tobacco ♦ He wanted a smoke.
smoky adjective

smoke verb (**smokes, smoking, smoked**)
1 give out smoke. 2 have a lighted cigarette,
cigar, or pipe between your lips and draw its
smoke into your mouth; do this as a habit.
3 preserve meat or fish by treating it with smoke
♦ smoked haddock.
smoker noun

smokescreen noun (plural **smokescreens**)
1 a mass of smoke used to hide the movement of
troops. 2 something that conceals what is
happening.

smooth adjective
1 having a surface without any lumps, wrinkles,
roughness, etc. 2 moving without bumps or jolts
etc. 3 not harsh ♦ a smooth flavour. 4 without
problems or difficulties.
smoothly adverb **smoothness** noun

smooth verb (**smooths, smoothing,
smoothed**)
make a thing smooth.

smote past tense of **smite**.

smother verb (**smothers, smothering,
smothered**)
1 suffocate. 2 put out a fire by covering it.
3 cover thickly ♦ The buns were smothered in
sugar. 4 restrain or conceal ♦ She smothered a
smile.

smoulder *verb* (smoulders, smouldering, smouldered)
1 burn slowly without a flame. **2** feel an emotion strongly without showing it ♦ *He was smouldering with jealousy.*

smudge *noun* (*plural* smudges)
a dirty mark made by rubbing something.
smudgy *adjective*

smudge *verb* (smudges, smudging, smudged)
make a smudge on something; become smudged.

smug *adjective*
self-satisfied; too pleased with your own good fortune or abilities.
smugly *adverb* **smugness** *noun*

smuggle *verb* (smuggles, smuggling, smuggled)
bring something into a country etc. secretly or illegally.
smuggler *noun*

snack *noun* (*plural* snacks)
1 a small meal. **2** food eaten between meals.

snag *noun* (*plural* snags)
1 an unexpected difficulty. **2** a sharp or jagged part sticking out from something. **3** a tear in material that has been caught on something sharp.

snail *noun* (*plural* snails)
a small animal with a soft body and a shell.

snake *noun* (*plural* snakes)
a reptile with a long narrow body and no legs.
snaky *adjective*

snap *verb* (snaps, snapping, snapped)
1 break suddenly or with a sharp sound. **2** bite suddenly or quickly. **3** say something quickly and angrily. **4** take something or move quickly. **5** take a snapshot of something.
snap your fingers make a sharp snapping sound with your thumb and a finger.

snap *noun* (*plural* snaps)
1 the action or sound of snapping. **2** a snapshot. **3** Snap a card game in which players shout 'Snap!' when they see two similar cards.

snappy *adjective*
1 snapping at people. **2** quick and lively.
snappily *adverb*

snapshot *noun* (*plural* snapshots)
an informal photograph.

snare *noun* (*plural* snares)
1 a trap for catching birds or animals. **2** something that attracts someone but is a trap or a danger.

snare *verb* (snares, snaring, snared)
catch in a snare.

snarl *verb* (snarls, snarling, snarled)
1 growl angrily. **2** speak in a bad-tempered way.
snarl *noun*
[imitating the sound]

snatch *verb* (snatches, snatching, snatched)
seize; take quickly, eagerly, or by force.

snatch *noun* (*plural* snatches)
1 snatching. **2** a short and incomplete part of a song, conversation, etc.

sneak *verb* (sneaks, sneaking, sneaked)
1 move quietly and secretly. **2** (*informal*) take secretly ♦ *He sneaked a biscuit from the tin.* **3** (*informal*) tell tales.

sneak *noun* (*plural* sneaks) (*informal*)
a telltale.

sneaky *adjective*
dishonest or deceitful.
sneakily *adverb* **sneakiness** *noun*

sneer *verb* (sneers, sneering, sneered)
speak or behave in a scornful way.
sneer *noun*

sneeze *verb* (sneezes, sneezing, sneezed)
send out air suddenly and uncontrollably through the nose and mouth in order to get rid of something irritating the nostrils.
sneeze *noun*
[from Old English *fneosan*, imitating the sound]

sniff *verb* (sniffs, sniffing, sniffed)
1 make a sound by drawing in air through the nose. **2** smell something.
sniff *noun* **sniffer** *noun*

sniffle *verb* (sniffles, sniffling, sniffled)
1 sniff slightly. **2** keep on sniffing.
sniffle *noun*

snigger *verb* (sniggers, sniggering, sniggered)
giggle slyly.
snigger *noun*

snip *verb* (snips, snipping, snipped)
cut with scissors or shears in small quick cuts.
snip *noun*

snipe *verb* (snipes, sniping, sniped)
1 shoot at people from a hiding place. **2** attack someone with critical remarks.
sniper *noun*

snippet *noun* (*plural* snippets)
a small piece of news, information, etc.

snivel *verb* (snivels, snivelling, snivelled)
cry or complain in a whining way.

snob *noun* (*plural* snobs)
a person who despises those who have not got wealth, power, or particular tastes or interests.
snobbery *noun* **snobbish** *adjective*

snooker *noun*
a game played with cues and 21 balls on a special cloth-covered table.

snoop *verb* (snoops, snooping, snooped)
pry; ask or look around secretly.
snooper *noun*

snooze *noun* (*plural* **snoozes**) (*informal*)
a short sleep.
snooze *verb*

snore *verb* (**snores, snoring, snored**)
breathe very noisily while sleeping.
snore *noun*

snort *verb* (**snorts, snorting, snorted**)
make a rough sound by breathing forcefully
through the nose.
snort *noun*

snout *noun* (*plural* **snouts**)
an animal's projecting nose and jaws.

snow *noun*
frozen drops of water that fall from the sky in
small white flakes.

snow *verb* (**snows, snowing, snowed**)
come down as snow.
be snowed under be overwhelmed with a mass
of letters or work etc.

snowball *noun* (*plural* **snowballs**)
a ball of snow pressed together for throwing.

snowball *verb* (**snowballs, snowballing,
snowballed**)
grow quickly in size or intensity.

snowdrop *noun* (*plural* **snowdrops**)
a small white flower that blooms in early spring.

snowdrift *noun* (*plural* **snowdrifts**)
a large heap or bank of snow piled up by the
wind.

snowflake *noun* (*plural* **snowflakes**)
a flake of snow.

snowshoe *noun* (*plural* **snowshoes**)
a frame rather like a tennis racket for walking on
soft snow.

snowstorm *noun* (*plural* **snowstorms**)
a storm in which snow falls.

snub *verb* (**snubs, snubbing, snubbed**)
treat in a scornful or unfriendly way.
snub *noun* (*plural* **snubs**)
scornful or unfriendly treatment.

snub-nosed *adjective*
having a short turned-up nose.

snuff¹ *noun*
powdered tobacco for taking into the nose by
sniffing.

snuff² *verb* (**snuffs, snuffing, snuffed**)
put out a candle by covering or pinching the
flame.
snuffer *noun*

snuffle *verb* (**snuffles, snuffling, snuffled**)
sniff in a noisy way.
snuffle *noun*

snug *adjective* (**snugger, snuggest**)
1 cosy. **2** fitting closely.
snugly *adverb* **snugness** *noun*

snuggle *verb* (**snuggles, snuggling, snuggled**)
curl up in a warm comfortable place.

so *adverb*
1 in this way; to such an extent ♦ *Why are
you so cross?* **2** very ♦ *Cricket is so boring.*
3 also ♦ *I was wrong but so were you.*
and so on and other similar things. **or so** or
about that number. **so far** up to now. **so long!**
(*informal*) goodbye. **so what?** (*informal*) that is
not important.

so *conjunction*
for that reason ♦ *They threw me out, so I came
here.*

soak *verb* (**soaks, soaking, soaked**)
make a person or thing very wet.
soak *noun*
soak up take in a liquid in the way that a sponge
does.

soap *noun* (*plural* **soaps**)
1 a substance used with water for washing and
cleaning things. **2** a soap opera.
soapy *adjective*

soap opera *noun* (*plural* **soap operas**)
a television serial about the everyday lives of a
group of people.
[originally American, where the serials were
sponsored by soap manufacturers]

soar *verb* (**soars, soaring, soared**)
1 rise high in the air. **2** increase by a lot
♦ *Prices are soaring.*

sob *verb* (**sobs, sobbing, sobbed**)
make a gasping sound when crying.
sob *noun*
[probably from early Dutch]

sober *adjective*
1 not drunk. **2** serious and calm. **3** (said about
colour) not bright or showy.
soberly *adverb* **sobriety** (*say* so-**bry**-it-ee) *noun*
sober *verb* (**sobers, sobering, sobered**)
make or become sober.

so-called *adjective*
named in what may be the wrong way
♦ *This so-called gentleman slammed the door.*

soccer *noun*
Association football.
[short for *Association*]

sociable *adjective*
liking to be with other people; friendly.
sociably *adverb* **sociability** *noun*

social *adjective*
1 living in a community, not alone ♦ *Bees are
social insects.* **2** to do with life in a community
♦ *social science.* **3** concerned with people's
welfare ♦ *a social worker.* **4** helping people to
meet each other ♦ *a social club.* **5** sociable.
socially *adverb*
[from Latin *sociare* = unite, associate]

socialism *noun*
a political system where wealth is shared equally between people, and the main industries and trade etc. are controlled by the government. (Compare **capitalism**.)

socialist *noun* (*plural* **socialists**)
a person who believes in socialism.

social security *noun*
money and other assistance provided by the government for those in need through being unemployed, ill, or disabled.

social services *plural noun*
welfare services provided by the government, including schools, hospitals, and pensions.

society *noun* (*plural* **societies**)
1 a community; people living together in a group or nation ♦ *We live in a multiracial society.* **2** a group of people organized for a particular purpose ♦ *the school dramatic society.* **3** company or companionship ♦ *We enjoy the society of our friends.*

sock *noun* (*plural* **socks**)
a piece of clothing that covers your foot and the lower part of your leg.
[from Old English]

socket *noun* (*plural* **sockets**)
1 a hollow into which something fits ♦ *a tooth socket.* **2** a device into which an electric plug or bulb is put to make a connection.

soda water *noun*
water made fizzy with carbon dioxide, used in drinks.

sodden *adjective*
made very wet.

sodium *noun*
a soft white metal.

sodium bicarbonate *noun*
a soluble white powder used in fire extinguishers and fizzy drinks, and to make cakes rise.

sofa *noun* (*plural* **sofas**)
a long soft seat with a back and arms.
[from Arabic *suffa* = long stone bench]

soft *adjective*
1 not hard or firm; easily pressed. **2** smooth, not rough or stiff. **3** gentle; not loud. **4** (said about drugs) not likely to be addictive.
softly *adverb* **softness** *noun*

soft drink *noun* (*plural* **soft drinks**)
a cold drink that is not alcoholic.

soften *verb* (**softens, softening, softened**)
make or become soft or softer.
softener *noun*

software *noun*
(in computing) programs and data, which are not part of the machinery of a computer. (Compare **hardware**.)

soggy *adjective* (**soggier, soggiest**)
very wet and heavy ♦ *soggy ground.*
[from a dialect word *sog* = swamp]

soil *noun* (*plural* **soils**)
1 the loose earth in which plants grow. **2** territory ♦ *on British soil.*
[from early French]

solar panel *noun* (*plural* **solar panels**)
a panel designed to catch the sun's rays and use their energy for heating or to make electricity.

solar power *noun*
electricity or other forms of power derived from the sun's rays.

solar system *noun*
the sun and the planets that revolve round it.

soldier *noun* (*plural* **soldiers**)
a member of an army.

sole¹ *noun* (*plural* **soles**)
1 the bottom surface of a foot or shoe. **2** a flat edible sea fish.
sole *verb* (**soles, soling, soled**)
put a sole on a shoe.

sole² *adjective*
single; only ♦ *She was the sole survivor.*
solely *adverb*

solemn *adjective*
1 not smiling or cheerful. **2** dignified or formal.
solemnly *adverb* **solemnity** *noun*

solicit *verb* (**solicits, soliciting, solicited**)
ask for or try to obtain ♦ *I've been soliciting opinions from rail users.*

solicitor *noun* (*plural* **solicitors**)
a lawyer who advises clients, prepares legal documents, etc.

solid *adjective*
1 not hollow; with no space inside. **2** keeping its shape; not liquid or gas. **3** continuous ♦ *for two solid hours.* **4** firm or strongly made; not flimsy ♦ *a solid foundation.* **5** showing solidarity; unanimous.
solidly *adverb* **solidity** *noun*
solid *noun* (*plural* **solids**)
1 a solid thing. **2** a shape that has three dimensions (length, width, and height or depth).

solids *plural noun*
solid food; food that is not liquid ♦ *Is your baby eating solids yet?*

soliloquy (*say* sol-il-ok-wee) *noun* (*plural* **soliloquies**)
a speech in which a person speaks his or her thoughts aloud when alone or without addressing anyone.
soliloquize *verb*
[from Latin *solus* = alone + *loqui* = speak]

solitary *adjective*
1 alone, without companions. **2** single ♦ *a solitary example.*

solitary confinement noun
a form of punishment in which a prisoner is kept alone in a cell and not allowed to talk to others.

solo noun (plural **solos**)
something sung, played, danced, or done by one person.
solo adjective & adverb **soloist** noun

soluble adjective
1 able to be dissolved. 2 able to be solved.
solubility noun

solution noun (plural **solutions**)
1 a liquid in which something is dissolved.
2 the answer to a problem or puzzle.

solve verb (**solves, solving, solved**)
find the answer to a problem or puzzle.
[from Latin solvere = unfasten]

solvent adjective
1 having enough money to pay all your debts.
2 able to dissolve another substance.
solvency noun

solvent noun (plural **solvents**)
a liquid used for dissolving something.

sombre adjective
dark and gloomy.

some adjective
1 a few; a little ♦ some apples; ♦ some money.
2 an unknown person or thing ♦ Some fool left the door open. 3 about ♦ We waited some 20 minutes.
some time 1 quite a long time ♦ I've been wondering about it for some time. 2 at some point in time ♦ You must come round for a meal some time.

some pronoun
a certain number or amount that is less than the whole ♦ Some of them were late.

somebody pronoun
1 some person. 2 an important or impressive person.

somehow adverb
in some way.

someone pronoun
somebody.

somersault noun (plural **somersaults**)
a movement in which you turn head over heels before landing on your feet.
somersault verb
[from Latin supra = above + saltus = a leap]

something noun
some thing; a thing which you cannot or do not want to name.
something like 1 rather like ♦ It's something like a rabbit. 2 approximately ♦ It cost something like £10.

sometimes adverb
at some times but not always ♦ We sometimes walk to school.

somewhat adverb
to some extent ♦ He was somewhat annoyed.

somewhere adverb
in or to some place.

son noun (plural **sons**)
a boy or man who is someone's child.

sonata noun (plural **sonatas**)
a piece of music for one instrument or two, in several movements.

song noun (plural **songs**)
1 a tune for singing. 2 singing ♦ He burst into song.
a song and dance (informal) a great fuss.
for a song bought or sold very cheaply.

sonic boom noun (plural **sonic booms**)
a loud noise caused by the shock wave of an aircraft travelling faster than the speed of sound.

son-in-law noun (plural **sons-in-law**)
a daughter's husband.

sonnet noun (plural **sonnets**)
a kind of poem with 14 lines.
[from Italian sonetto = a little sound]

soon adverb
1 in a short time from now. 2 not long after something.
as soon as willingly ♦ I'd just as soon stay here.
as soon as at the moment that. **sooner or later** at some time in the future.

soot noun
the black powder left by smoke in a chimney or on a building etc.
sooty adjective

soothe verb (**soothes, soothing, soothed**)
1 calm or comfort. 2 ease pain or distress.
soothingly adverb

sop verb (**sops, sopping, sopped**)
sop up soak up liquid like a sponge.

sophisticated adjective
1 having refined tastes or experienced about the world. 2 complicated ♦ a sophisticated machine.
sophistication noun

sopping adjective
very wet; drenched.

soppy adjective
1 very wet. 2 (informal) sentimental in a silly way.

soprano noun (plural **sopranos**)
a woman, girl, or boy with a high singing voice.

sorcerer noun (plural **sorcerers**)
a person who can perform magic.
sorceress noun **sorcery** noun

sordid adjective
1 dirty and nasty. 2 dishonourable; selfish and mercenary ♦ sordid motives.
sordidly adverb **sordidness** noun

sore *adjective*
1 painful or smarting. **2** (*informal*) annoyed or offended. **3** serious or distressing ♦ *in sore need*.
soreness *noun*

sore *noun* (*plural* **sores**)
a sore place.

sorrow *noun* (*plural* **sorrows**)
1 unhappiness or regret caused by loss or disappointment. **2** something that causes this.
sorrowful *adjective* **sorrowfully** *adverb*

sorry *adjective* (**sorrier, sorriest**)
1 feeling regret ♦ *I'm sorry I forgot your birthday*. **2** feeling pity or sympathy.
3 wretched ♦ *His clothes were in a sorry state*.

sort *noun* (*plural* **sorts**)
a group of things or people that are similar; a kind or variety.
out of sorts slightly unwell or depressed.
sort of (*informal*) rather; to some extent
♦ *I sort of expected it*.

---

❶ USAGE Correct use is *this sort of thing* or *these sorts of things* (not 'these sort of things').

---

sort *verb* (**sorts, sorting, sorted**)
arrange things in groups according to their size, kind, etc.
sorter *noun*
sort out **1** deal with and solve a problem or difficulty. **2** (*informal*) deal with and punish someone.

sortie *noun* (*plural* **sorties**)
1 an attack by troops coming out of a besieged place. **2** an attacking expedition by a military aircraft.
[from French *sortir* = go out]

SOS *noun* (*plural* **SOSs**)
an urgent appeal for help.
[the international Morse code signal of extreme distress, chosen because it is easy to recognize, but often said to stand for 'Save Our Souls']

sought *past tense* of **seek**.

soul *noun* (*plural* **souls**)
1 the invisible part of a person that is believed to go on living after the body has died. **2** a person's mind and emotions etc. **3** a person ♦ *There isn't a soul about*. **4** a kind of popular music that originated in gospel music.

sound¹ *noun* (*plural* **sounds**)
1 vibrations that travel through the air and can be detected by the ear; the sensation they produce. **2** sound reproduced in a film etc.
3 a mental impression ♦ *We don't like the sound of his plans*.

sound *verb* (**sounds, sounding, sounded**)
1 produce or cause to produce a sound. **2** give an impression when heard ♦ *He sounds angry*.
3 test by noting the sounds heard ♦ *A doctor sounds a patient's lungs with a stethoscope*.
[from Latin *sonus*]

sound² *verb* (**sounds, sounding, sounded**)
test the depth of water beneath a ship.
sound out try to find out what a person thinks or feels about something.
[from Latin *sub* = under + *unda* = a wave]

sound³ *adjective*
1 in good condition; not damaged. **2** healthy; not diseased. **3** reasonable or correct ♦ *His ideas are sound*. **4** reliable or secure ♦ *a sound investment*.
5 thorough or deep ♦ *a sound sleep*.
soundly *adverb* **soundness** *noun*
[from Old English *gesund* = healthy]

sound barrier *noun*
the resistance of the air to objects moving at speeds near the speed of sound.

sound bite *noun* (*plural* **sound bites**)
a short piece taken from a speech or statement because it has a special interest.

sound effects *plural noun*
sounds produced artificially to make a play, film, etc. seem more realistic.

soundtrack *noun* (*plural* **soundtracks**)
the sound that goes with a cinema film.

soup *noun* (*plural* **soups**)
liquid food made from stewed bones, meat, fish, vegetables, etc.
in the soup (*informal*) in trouble.
[from early French *soupe* = broth poured on bread, from Latin *suppa*]

sour *adjective*
1 tasting sharp like unripe fruit. **2** stale and unpleasant, not fresh ♦ *sour milk*.
3 bad-tempered.
sourly *adverb* **sourness** *noun*

source *noun* (*plural* **sources**)
1 the place from which something comes.
2 the starting point of a river.

sour grapes *plural noun*
pretending that something you want is no good because you know you cannot have it.

south *noun*
1 the direction to the right of a person who faces east. **2** the southern part of a country, city, etc.
south *adjective* & *adverb*
towards or in the south.
southerly (*say* suth-er-lee) *adjective* **southern** *adjective* **southerner** *noun* **southernmost** *adjective*

south-east *noun*, *adjective*, & *adverb*
midway between south and east.
south-easterly *adjective* **south-eastern** *adjective*

southward *adjective* & *adverb*
towards the south.
southwards *adverb*

south-west *noun*, *adjective*, & *adverb*
midway between south and west.
south-westerly *adjective* **south-western** *adjective*

souvenir (*say* soo-ven-**eer**) *noun* (*plural* **souvenirs**)
something that you keep to remind you of a person, place, or event.

sovereign *noun* (*plural* **sovereigns**)
1 a king or queen who is the ruler of a country; a monarch. **2** an old British gold coin, originally worth £1.

sow[1] (rhymes with *go*) *verb* (**sows, sowing, sowed, sown** or **sowed**)
1 put seeds into the ground so that they will grow into plants. **2** cause feelings or ideas to develop ♦ *Her words sowed doubt in my mind.*
sower *noun*
[from Old English *sawan*]

ⓘ USAGE Do not confuse with *sew*.

---

sow[2] (rhymes with *cow*) *noun* (*plural* **sows**)
a female pig.
[from Old English *sugu*]

soy sauce or **soya sauce** *noun*
a Chinese or Japanese sauce made from fermented **soya beans**.
[from Chinese words meaning 'salted beans' and 'oil']

space *noun* (*plural* **spaces**)
1 the whole area outside the earth, where the stars and planets are. **2** an area or volume ♦ *This table takes too much space.* **3** an empty area; a gap. **4** an interval of time ♦ *within the space of an hour.*

space *verb* (**spaces, spacing, spaced**)
arrange things with spaces between
♦ *Space them out.*

spacecraft *noun* (*plural* **spacecraft**)
a vehicle for travelling in outer space.

spaceship *noun* (*plural* **spaceships**)
a spacecraft, especially one carrying people.

space shuttle *noun* (*plural* **space shuttles**)
a spacecraft for repeated use to and from outer space.

space station *noun* (*plural* **space stations**)
a satellite which orbits the earth and is used as a base by scientists and astronauts.

spacious *adjective*
providing a lot of space; roomy.
spaciousness *noun*

spade[1] *noun* (*plural* **spades**)
a tool with a long handle and a wide blade for digging.

spade[2] *noun* (*plural* **spades**)
a playing card with black shapes like upside-down hearts on it, each with a short stem.

spaghetti *noun*
pasta made in long thin sticks.
[from Italian, = little strings]

span *noun* (*plural* **spans**)
1 the length from end to end or across something. **2** the part between two uprights of an arch or bridge. **3** the length of a period of time. **4** the distance from the tip of the thumb to the tip of the little finger when the hand is spread out.

span *verb* (**spans, spanning, spanned**)
reach from one side or end to the other ♦ *A bridge spans the river.*

spaniel *noun* (*plural* **spaniels**)
a kind of dog with long ears and silky fur.
[from early French *espaigneul* = Spanish (because the dog originally came from Spain)]

spank *verb* (**spanks, spanking, spanked**)
smack a person several times on the bottom as a punishment.

spanner *noun* (*plural* **spanners**)
a tool for gripping and turning the nut on a bolt etc.
[from German *spannen* = tighten]

spar[1] *noun* (*plural* **spars**)
a strong pole used for a mast or boom etc. on a ship.
[from Old Norse]

spar[2] *verb* (**spars, sparring, sparred**)
1 practise boxing. **2** quarrel or argue.
[from Old English]

spare *verb* (**spares, sparing, spared**)
1 afford to give something or do without it
♦ *Can you spare a moment?* **2** be merciful towards someone; not hurt or harm a person or thing. **3** avoid making a person suffer something ♦ *Spare me the details.* **4** use or treat economically ♦ *No expense will be spared.*
to spare left over without being needed
♦ *We arrived with five minutes to spare.*

spare *adjective*
1 not used but kept ready in case it is needed; extra ♦ *a spare wheel.* **2** thin; lean.
sparely *adverb* **spareness** *noun*
go spare (*slang*) become very annoyed.

spare time *noun*
time not needed for work.

sparing (*say* **spair**-ing) *adjective*
careful or economical; not wasteful.
sparingly *adverb*

spark *noun* (*plural* **sparks**)
1 a tiny glowing particle. **2** a flash produced electrically. **3** a trace ♦ *a spark of hope.*

spark *verb* (**sparks, sparking, sparked**)
give off a spark or sparks.

sparkle *verb* (**sparkles, sparkling, sparkled**)
1 shine with tiny flashes of light. **2** show brilliant wit or liveliness.
sparkle *noun*

sparkler *noun* (*plural* **sparklers**)
a hand-held firework that gives off sparks.

spark plug noun (plural **spark plugs**)
a device that makes a spark to ignite the fuel in
an engine.

sparrow noun (plural **sparrows**)
a small brown bird.

sparse adjective
thinly scattered; not numerous ♦ a sparse
population.
sparsely adverb **sparseness** noun

spasm noun (plural **spasms**)
1 a sudden involuntary movement of a muscle.
2 a sudden brief spell of activity etc.
[from Greek spasmos, from span = to pull]

spasmodic adjective
happening or done at irregular intervals.
spasmodically adverb

spastic noun (plural **spastics**) (offensive)
a person suffering from spasms of the muscles
and jerky movements, especially caused by
cerebral palsy.

spat past tense of **spit¹**.

spate noun (plural **spates**)
a sudden flood or rush.

spatter verb (spatters, spattering, spattered)
1 scatter in small drops. 2 splash ♦ spattered
with mud.
spatter noun

spawn noun
1 the eggs of fish, frogs, toads, or shellfish.
2 the thread-like matter from which fungi grow.

spawn verb (spawns, spawning, spawned)
1 produce spawn. 2 be produced from spawn.
3 produce something in great quantities.

speak verb (speaks, speaking, spoke, spoken)
1 say something; talk. 2 talk or be able to talk in
a foreign language ♦ Do you speak French?
speak up 1 speak more loudly. 2 give your
opinion.

speaker noun (plural **speakers**)
1 a person who is speaking. 2 someone who
makes a speech. 3 a loudspeaker.
the Speaker the person who controls the debates
in the House of Commons or a similar assembly.

spear noun (plural **spears**)
a weapon for throwing or stabbing, with a long
shaft and a pointed tip.

special adjective
1 not ordinary or usual; exceptional ♦ a special
occasion; ♦ Take special care of it. 2 meant for a
particular person or purpose ♦ You need a
special tool for this job.

special effects plural noun
illusions created for films or television by using
props, trick photography, or computer images.

specialist noun (plural **specialists**)
an expert in one subject ♦ a skin specialist.

speciality noun (plural **specialities**)
1 something in which a person specializes.
2 a special product, especially a food.

specialize verb (specializes, specializing,
specialized)
give particular attention or study to one subject
or thing ♦ She specialized in biology.
specialization noun

special needs plural noun
educational needs resulting from special reasons
such as learning difficulties or physical
disability.

species (say spee-shiz) noun (plural **species**)
a group of animals or plants that are very similar.

specific adjective
definite or precise; of or for a particular thing
♦ The money was given for a specific purpose.
specifically adverb

specific gravity noun
the weight of something as compared with the
same volume of water or air.

specimen noun (plural **specimens**)
1 a sample. 2 an example ♦ a fine specimen of an
oak tree.

speck noun (plural **specks**)
a small spot or particle.

speckle noun (plural **speckles**)
a small spot or mark.
speckled adjective

spectacle noun (plural **spectacles**)
1 an impressive sight or display. 2 a ridiculous
sight.

spectacles plural noun
a pair of glasses.
spectacled adjective

spectacular adjective
impressive or striking.

spectator noun (plural **spectators**)
a person who watches a game, show, incident,
etc.
[from Latin spectare = to look at]

spectre noun (plural **spectres**)
a ghost.
spectral adjective

spectrum noun (plural **spectra**)
1 the bands of colours seen in a rainbow.
2 a wide range of things, ideas, etc.

speculate verb (speculates, speculating,
speculated)
1 form opinions without having any definite
evidence. 2 invest in stocks, property, etc. in the
hope of making a profit but with the risk of loss.
speculation noun **speculator** noun **speculative**
adjective

sped past tense of **speed**.

speech *noun* (*plural* **speeches**)
1 the action or power of speaking. **2** a talk to an audience. **3** a group of lines spoken by a character in a play.

speechless *adjective*
unable to speak because of great emotion.

speed *noun* (*plural* **speeds**)
1 a measure of the time in which something moves or happens. **2** quickness or swiftness.
at speed quickly.

speed *verb* (**speeds, speeding, sped** (in sense 3 **speeded**))
1 go quickly ♦ *The train sped by.* **2** make or become quicker ♦ *This will speed things up.*
3 drive faster than the legal limit.

speed camera *noun* (*plural* **speed cameras**)
a camera by the side of a road which automatically photographs any vehicle which is going too fast.

speed limit *noun* (*plural* **speed limits**)
the maximum speed at which vehicles may legally travel on a particular road.

speedometer *noun* (*plural* **speedometers**)
a device in a vehicle, showing its speed.

speedy *adjective* (**speedier, speediest**)
quick or swift.
speedily *adverb*

spell¹ *noun* (*plural* **spells**)
a saying or action etc. supposed to have magical power.
[from Old English *spel* = speech, story]

spell² *noun* (*plural* **spells**)
1 a period of time. **2** a period spent doing a certain task or activity etc.
[from Old English *spelian* = take someone's place, take over a task]

spell³ *verb* (**spells, spelling, spelled** or **spelt**)
1 put letters in the right order to make a word or words. **2** (said about letters) form a word ♦ *C-A-T spells 'cat'.* **3** have as a result
♦ *Wet weather spells ruin for crops.*
speller *noun*
[from early French]

spellbound *adjective*
entranced as if by a magic spell.

spend *verb* (**spends, spending, spent**)
1 use money to pay for things. **2** use up
♦ *Don't spend too much time on it.* **3** pass time
♦ *We spent a holiday in Spain.*

sperm *noun* (*plural* **sperms** or **sperm**)
the male cell that fuses with an ovum to fertilize it.
[from Greek *sperma* = seed]

sphere *noun* (*plural* **spheres**)
1 a perfectly round solid shape; the shape of a ball. **2** a field of action or interest etc. ♦ *That country is in Russia's sphere of influence.*
spherical *adjective*

sphinx *noun* (*plural* **sphinxes**)
a stone statue with the body of a lion and a human head, especially the huge one (almost 5,000 years old) in Egypt.
[named after the Sphinx in Greek mythology, a winged creature with a woman's head and a lion's body]

spice *noun* (*plural* **spices**)
1 a strong-tasting substance used to flavour food, often made from dried parts of plants.
2 something that adds interest or excitement
♦ *Variety is the spice of life.*
spicy *adjective*

spick and span *adjective*
neat and clean.
[*span* is from Old Norse; *spick* is probably from early Dutch]

spider *noun* (*plural* **spiders**)
a small animal with eight legs that spins webs to catch insects on which it feeds.
[from Old English *spithra* = spinner]

spike *noun* (*plural* **spikes**)
a pointed piece of metal; a sharp point.
spiky *adjective*

spill *verb* (**spills, spilling, spilt** or **spilled**)
1 let something fall out of a container ♦ *Try not to spill your drink.* **2** become spilt ♦ *The coins came spilling out.*
spillage *noun*

spin *verb* (**spins, spinning, spun**)
1 turn round and round quickly. **2** make raw wool or cotton into threads by pulling and twisting its fibres. **3** (said about a spider or silkworm) make a web or cocoon out of threads from its body.
spin a yarn tell a story. **spin out** make something last as long as possible.

spinach *noun*
a vegetable with dark green leaves.
[via early French from Persian]

spinal cord *noun* (*plural* **spinal cords**)
the thick cord of nerves enclosed in the spine, that carries impulses to and from the brain.

spindly *adjective*
thin and long or tall.

spin doctor *noun* (*plural* **spin doctors**)
a person who works for a political party and publishes information in a way that shows it in the best possible light.

spine *noun* (*plural* **spines**)
1 the line of bones down the middle of the back. **2** a thorn or prickle. **3** the back part of a book where the pages are joined together.

spineless *adjective*
1 without a backbone. **2** lacking in determination or strength of character.

spinney *noun* (*plural* **spinneys**)
a small wood or thicket.

spin-off *noun* (*plural* **spin-offs**)
something extra produced while making
something else.

spinster *noun* (*plural* **spinsters**)
a woman who has not married.
[the original meaning was 'someone who spins'.
Many unmarried women used to earn their
living by spinning, which could be done at
home]

spiny *adjective*
covered with spines; prickly.

spiral *adjective*
going round and round a central point and
becoming gradually closer to it or further from it;
twisting continually round a central line or
cylinder etc.
spirally *adverb*

spiral *noun* (*plural* **spirals**)
a spiral line or course.

spiral *verb* (**spirals, spiralling, spiralled**)
1 move in a spiral. 2 increase or decrease
continuously and quickly ♦ *Prices are spiralling.*
[from Greek *speira* = winding]

spire *noun* (*plural* **spires**)
a tall pointed part on top of a church tower.

spirit *noun* (*plural* **spirits**)
1 the soul. 2 a person's mood or mind and
feelings ♦ *He was in good spirits.* 3 a ghost or
a supernatural being. 4 courage or liveliness
♦ *She answered with spirit.* 5 a kind of quality in
something ♦ *the romantic spirit of the book.*
6 a strong distilled alcoholic drink.

spirit *verb* (**spirits, spiriting, spirited**)
carry off quickly and secretly ♦ *They spirited her
away.*

spirit level *noun* (*plural* **spirit levels**)
a device consisting of a tube of liquid with an air
bubble in it, used to find out whether something
is level.

spiritual *adjective*
1 to do with the human soul; not physical.
2 to do with religion.
spiritually *adverb* **spirituality** *noun*

spiritual *noun* (*plural* **spirituals**)
a religious folk song, originally sung by black
Christians in America.

spiritualism *noun*
the belief that the spirits of dead people
communicate with living people.
spiritualist *noun*

spit¹ *verb* (**spits, spitting, spat** or **spit**)
1 send out drops of liquid etc. forcibly from
the mouth ♦ *He spat at me.* 2 fall lightly
♦ *It's spitting with rain.*

spit *noun*
saliva.

spit² *noun* (*plural* **spits**)
1 a long thin metal spike put through meat or
vegetables to hold them together while they are
being roasted. 2 a narrow strip of land sticking
out into the sea.

spite *noun*
a desire to hurt or annoy somebody.
spiteful *adjective* **spitefully** *adverb* **spitefulness**
noun
in spite of not being prevented by ♦ *We went
out in spite of the rain.*

spitting image *noun*
an exact likeness.

splash *verb* (**splashes, splashing, splashed**)
1 make liquid fly about in drops. 2 (said about
liquid) fly about in drops. 3 make wet by
splashing ♦ *The bus splashed us.*

splash *noun* (*plural* **splashes**)
1 the action or sound or mark of splashing.
2 a bright patch of colour or light.
make a splash attract a lot of attention.

splay *verb* (**splays, splaying, splayed**)
spread or slope apart.

splendid *adjective*
1 magnificent; full of splendour. 2 excellent.
splendidly *adverb*

splendour *noun*
a brilliant display or appearance.

splint *noun* (*plural* **splints**)
a straight piece of wood or metal etc. tied to a
broken arm or leg to hold it firm.

splinter *noun* (*plural* **splinters**)
a thin sharp piece of wood, glass, stone, etc.
broken off a larger piece.

splinter *verb* (**splinters, splintering,
splintered**)
break into splinters.

split *verb* (**splits, splitting, split**)
1 break apart, especially along the length of
something. 2 divide something into parts.
split up 1 end a marriage or other relationship.
2 go in different directions.

split *noun* (*plural* **splits**)
1 the splitting or dividing of something.
2 a place where something has split.
the splits an acrobatic position in which the legs
are stretched widely in opposite directions.

split second *noun*
a very brief moment of time; an instant.

splutter *verb* (**splutters, spluttering,
spluttered**)
1 make a quick series of spitting sounds.
2 speak quickly but not clearly.
splutter *noun*
[imitating the sound]

spoil *verb* (**spoils, spoiling, spoilt** or **spoiled**)
1 damage something and make it useless or
unsatisfactory. 2 make someone selfish by
always letting them have what they want.

spoke¹ *noun* (*plural* **spokes**)
each of the bars or rods that go from the centre of a wheel to its rim.

spoke² *past tense* of **speak**.

spokesperson *noun* (*plural* **spokespersons**)
a person who speaks on behalf of a group of people.
spokesman *noun* **spokeswoman** *noun*

sponge *noun* (*plural* **sponges**)
1 a sea creature with a soft porous body.
2 the skeleton of this creature, or a piece of a similar substance, used for washing or padding things. **3** a soft lightweight cake or pudding.
spongy *adjective*

sponge *verb* (**sponges, sponging, sponged**)
1 wipe or wash something with a sponge.
2 (*informal*) get money or food off other people without giving anything in return, ♦ *He's always sponging off his friends.*
sponger *noun*

sponsor *noun* (*plural* **sponsors**)
1 a person or organization that provides money for an arts or sports event or for a broadcast in return for advertising. **2** someone who gives money to a charity in return for something achieved by another person.
sponsorship *noun*

sponsor *verb* (**sponsors, sponsoring, sponsored**)
be a sponsor for a person or thing.
[from Latin *sponsum* = promised]

spontaneous (*say* spon-**tay**-nee-us) *adjective*
happening or done naturally; not forced or suggested by someone else.
spontaneously *adverb* **spontaneity** *noun*

spool *noun* (*plural* **spools**)
a rod or cylinder on which something is wound.

spoon *noun* (*plural* **spoons**)
a small device with a rounded bowl on a handle, used for lifting things to the mouth or for stirring or measuring things.
spoonful *noun* (*plural* **spoonfuls**)

spoonerism *noun* (*plural* **spoonerisms**)
an accidental exchange of the initial letters of two words, e.g. by saying *a boiled sprat* instead of *a spoiled brat.*
[named after Canon Spooner (1844–1930), who made mistakes of this kind]

spore *noun* (*plural* **spores**)
a tiny reproductive cell of a plant such as a fungus or fern.

sport *noun* (*plural* **sports**)
1 an athletic activity; a game or pastime, especially outdoors. **2** games of this kind ♦ *Are you keen on sport?* **3** (*informal*) a person who behaves fairly and generously ♦ *Thanks for being such a good sport.*

sporting chance *noun*
a reasonable chance of success.

sports car *noun* (*plural* **sports cars**)
an open low-built fast car.

sportsman *noun* (*plural* **sportsmen**)
1 a man who takes part in sport. **2** a person who shows sportsmanship.

sportsmanship *noun*
behaving fairly and generously to rivals.

sportswoman *noun* (*plural* **sportswomen**)
1 a woman who takes part in sport. **2** a woman who shows sportsmanship.

spot *noun* (*plural* **spots**)
1 a small round mark. **2** a pimple. **3** a small amount ♦ *We had a spot of trouble.* **4** a place. **5** a drop ♦ *a few spots of rain.*
on the spot without delay or change of place; under pressure to take action ♦ *This really puts him on the spot!* **spot on** (*informal*) exactly right or accurate.

spot *verb* (**spots, spotting, spotted**)
1 mark with spots. **2** (*informal*) notice or recognize ♦ *We spotted her in the crowd.*
3 watch for and take note of ♦ *train-spotting.*
spotter *noun*

spotlight *noun* (*plural* **spotlights**)
1 a strong light that can shine on one small area. **2** public attention ♦ *The Royal Family are used to being in the spotlight.*

spotty *adjective*
marked with spots.

spouse *noun* (*plural* **spouses**)
a person's husband or wife.

spout *noun* (*plural* **spouts**)
1 a pipe or similar opening from which liquid can pour. **2** a jet of liquid.

spout *verb* (**spouts, spouting, spouted**)
1 come or send out as a jet of liquid. **2** (*informal*) speak for a long time.

sprain *verb* (**sprains, spraining, sprained**)
injure a joint by twisting it.
sprain *noun*

sprawl *verb* (**sprawls, sprawling, sprawled**)
1 sit or lie with the arms and legs spread out loosely. **2** spread out loosely or untidily.
sprawl *noun*

spray¹ *verb* (**sprays, spraying, sprayed**)
scatter tiny drops of liquid over something.

spray *noun* (*plural* **sprays**)
1 tiny drops of liquid sent through the air. **2** a device for spraying liquid. **3** a liquid for spraying ♦ *fly spray.*

spray² *noun* (*plural* **sprays**)
1 a single shoot with its leaves and flowers. **2** a small bunch of flowers.

spread *verb* (spreads, spreading, spread)
1 open or stretch something out to its full size
♦ *The bird spread its wings.* **2** make something
cover a surface ♦ *We spread jam on the bread.*
3 become longer or wider ♦ *The stain was
spreading.* **4** make or become more widely
known or felt or distributed etc. ♦ *We spread the
news.* ♦ *The story quickly spread round the
village.*
spread *noun* (*plural* **spreads**)
1 the action or result of spreading. **2** a thing's
breadth or extent. **3** a paste for spreading on
bread. **4** (*informal*) a large or grand meal.

spreadeagled *adjective*
with arms and legs stretched out ♦ *He lay
spreadeagled on the bed.*
[a *spread eagle* was originally a picture of an
eagle with legs and wings stretched out, used as
an emblem in heraldry]

spreadsheet *noun* (*plural* **spreadsheets**)
(in computing) a program for handling
information, especially figures, displayed in a
table.

spree *noun* (*plural* **sprees**)
something you do with a lot of freedom and
enjoyment ♦ *a shopping spree.*

sprig *noun* (*plural* **sprigs**)
a small branch; a shoot.
[from early German]

sprightly *adjective* (sprightlier, sprightliest)
lively and full of energy.

spring *verb* (springs, springing, sprang,
sprung)
1 jump; move quickly or suddenly ♦ *He sprang
to his feet.* **2** originate or develop ♦ *The trouble
has sprung from carelessness.* ♦ *Weeds have
started to spring up.* **3** present or produce
suddenly ♦ *They sprang a surprise on us.*
spring *noun* (*plural* **springs**)
1 a springy coil or bent piece of metal.
2 a springing movement. **3** a place where
water comes up naturally from the ground.
4 the season when most plants begin to grow.
[from Old English]

springboard *noun* (*plural* **springboards**)
a springy board from which people jump in
diving and gymnastics.

spring-clean *verb* (spring-cleans,
spring-cleaning, spring-cleaned)
clean a house thoroughly in springtime.

springy *adjective* (springier, springiest)
able to spring back easily after being bent or
squeezed.
springiness *noun*

sprinkle *verb* (sprinkles, sprinkling, sprinkled)
make tiny drops or pieces fall on something.
sprinkler *noun*

sprint *verb* (sprints, sprinting, sprinted)
run very fast for a short distance.
sprint *noun* **sprinter** *noun*
[from Old Norse]

sprout *verb* (sprouts, sprouting, sprouted)
start to grow; put out shoots.
sprout *noun* (*plural* **sprouts**)
1 a shoot of a plant. **2** a Brussels sprout.

spruce[1] *noun* (*plural* **spruces**)
a kind of fir tree.

spruce[2] *adjective*
neat and trim; smart.
spruce *verb* (spruces, sprucing, spruced)
smarten ♦ *Spruce yourself up.*

spry *adjective* (spryer, spryest)
active, nimble, and lively.

spur *noun* (*plural* **spurs**)
1 a sharp device worn on the heel of a rider's
boot to urge a horse to go faster. **2** a stimulus or
incentive. **3** a ridge that sticks out from a
mountain.
on the spur of the moment on an impulse;
without planning.
spur *verb* (spurs, spurring, spurred)
urge on; encourage.

spurious *adjective*
not genuine.

spurn *verb* (spurns, spurning, spurned)
reject scornfully.

spurt *verb* (spurts, spurting, spurted)
1 gush out. **2** increase your speed suddenly.
spurt *noun* (*plural* **spurts**)
1 a sudden gush. **2** a sudden increase in speed or
effort.

spy *noun* (*plural* **spies**)
someone who works secretly for one country,
person, etc. to find out things about another.
spy *verb* (spies, spying, spied)
1 be a spy. **2** keep watch secretly ♦ *Have you
been spying on me?* **3** see or notice ♦ *She spied a
house in the distance.*
[from early French *espier* = catch sight of]

squabble *verb* (squabbles, squabbling,
squabbled)
quarrel or bicker.
squabble *noun*

squad *noun* (*plural* **squads**)
a small group of people working or being trained
together.

squadron *noun* (*plural* **squadrons**)
part of an army, navy, or air force.

squalid *adjective*
dirty and unpleasant.
squalidly *adverb* **squalor** *noun*

squall *noun* (*plural* **squalls**)
1 a sudden storm or gust of wind. **2** a baby's loud
cry.

squall *verb* (squalls, squalling, squalled)
(said about a baby) cry loudly.

squander *verb* (squanders, squandering, squandered)
spend money or time etc. wastefully.

square *noun* (*plural* **squares**)
1 a flat shape with four equal sides and four right angles. **2** an area surrounded by buildings ♦ *Leicester Square*. **3** the result of multiplying a number by itself ♦ *9 is the square of 3 (9 = 3 × 3)*.

square *adjective*
1 having the shape of a square. **2** forming a right angle ♦ *The desk has square corners*. **3** equal or even ♦ *The teams are all square with six points each*.
squarely *adverb* **squareness** *noun*
square foot, square metre etc. the area of a surface with sides that are one foot or one metre etc. long.

square *verb* (squares, squaring, squared)
1 make a thing square. **2** multiply a number by itself ♦ *5 squared is 25*. **3** match; make or be consistent ♦ *His story doesn't square with yours*. **4** settle or pay.

square deal *noun*
a deal that is honest and fair.

square meal *noun* (*plural* **square meals**)
a good satisfying meal.

square root *noun* (*plural* **square roots**)
the number that gives a particular number if it is multiplied by itself ♦ *3 is the square root of 9 (3 × 3 = 9)*.

squash *verb* (squashes, squashing, squashed)
1 press something so that it becomes flat or out of shape. **2** force into a small space; pack tightly. **3** suppress or quash.

squash *noun* (*plural* **squashes**)
1 a crowded condition. **2** a fruit-flavoured soft drink. **3** a game played with rackets and a soft ball in a special indoor court.

squat *verb* (squats, squatting, squatted)
1 sit on your heels; crouch. **2** live in an unoccupied building without permission.
squat *noun* **squatter** *noun*

squat *adjective*
short and fat.

squawk *verb* (squawks, squawking, squawked)
make a loud harsh cry.
squawk *noun*

squeak *verb* (squeaks, squeaking, squeaked)
make a short high-pitched cry or sound.
squeak *noun* **squeaky** *adjective* **squeakily** *adverb*

squeal *verb* (squeals, squealing, squealed)
make a long shrill cry or sound.
squeal *noun*

squeamish *adjective*
easily disgusted or shocked.
squeamishness *noun*

squeeze *verb* (squeezes, squeezing, squeezed)
1 press something from opposite sides, especially to get liquid out of it. **2** force into or through a place ♦ *We squeezed through a gap in the hedge*.
squeezer *noun*

squeeze *noun* (*plural* **squeezes**)
1 the action of squeezing. **2** a drop of liquid squeezed out ♦ *Add a squeeze of lemon*. **3** a time when money is difficult to get or borrow.

squelch *verb* (squelches, squelching, squelched)
make a sound like someone treading in thick mud.
squelch *noun*

squid *noun* (*plural* **squids**)
a sea animal with eight short tentacles and two long ones.

squint *verb* (squints, squinting, squinted)
1 be cross-eyed. **2** peer; look with half-shut eyes at something.
squint *noun*

squire *noun* (*plural* **squires**)
1 the man who owns most of the land in a country parish or district. **2** a young nobleman in the Middle Ages who served a knight.

squirm *verb* (squirms, squirming, squirmed)
wriggle about, especially when you feel embarrassed.

squirrel *noun* (*plural* **squirrels**)
a small animal with a bushy tail and red or grey fur, living in trees.
[via early French from Greek *skia* = shade + *oura* = tail]

squirt *verb* (squirts, squirting, squirted)
send or come out in a jet of liquid.
squirt *noun*

St. or **St** *abbreviation*
1 Saint. **2** Street.

stab *verb* (stabs, stabbing, stabbed)
pierce or wound with something sharp.

stab *noun* (*plural* **stabs**)
1 the action of stabbing. **2** a sudden sharp pain ♦ *She felt a stab of fear*. **3** (*informal*) an attempt ♦ *I'll have a stab at it*.

stability *noun*
being stable.

stable¹ *adjective*
1 steady and firmly fixed. **2** not likely to change or end suddenly ♦ *a stable relationship*. **3** sensible and dependable.
stably *adverb*

stable² *noun* (*plural* **stables**)
a building where horses are kept.

stable *verb* (**stables, stabling, stabled**)
put or keep in a stable.

stack *noun* (*plural* **stacks**)
1 a neat pile. **2** a haystack. **3** (*informal*) a large
amount ♦ *I have a stack of work to do.* **4** a single
tall chimney; a group of small chimneys.

stack *verb* (**stacks, stacking, stacked**)
pile things up.
[from Old Norse]

stadium *noun* (*plural* **stadiums**)
a sports ground surrounded by seats for
spectators.
[via Latin from Greek *stadion*]

staff *noun* (*plural* **staffs** or, in sense 4, **staves**)
1 the people who work in an office, shop, etc.
2 the teachers in a school or college. **3** a stick or
pole used as a weapon or support or as a symbol
of authority. **4** a set of five horizontal lines on
which music is written.

staff *verb* (**staffs, staffing, staffed**)
provide with a staff of people ♦ *The centre is
staffed by volunteers.*

stag *noun* (*plural* **stags**)
a male deer.

stage *noun* (*plural* **stages**)
1 a platform for performances in a theatre or
hall. **2** a point or part of a process, journey, etc.
♦ *Now for the final stage.*
the stage the profession of acting or working in
the theatre.

stage *verb* (**stages, staging, staged**)
1 present a performance on a stage. **2** organize
♦ *We decided to stage a protest.*

stagecoach *noun* (*plural* **stagecoaches**)
a horse-drawn coach that formerly ran regularly
from one point to another along the same route.

stage manager *noun* (*plural* **stage
managers**)
the person in charge of the scenery, lighting,
sound, etc. in a theatre during a performance.

stagger *verb* (**staggers, staggering,
staggered**)
1 walk unsteadily. **2** amaze or shock deeply
♦ *We were staggered at the price.* **3** arrange
things so that they do not all happen together
♦ *Please stagger your holidays so that there is
always someone here.*
stagger *noun*

stagnant *adjective*
1 not flowing. **2** not active or developing
♦ *business is stagnant.*

stain *noun* (*plural* **stains**)
1 a dirty mark on something. **2** a blemish on
someone's character or past record. **3** a liquid
used for staining things.

stain *verb* (**stains, staining, stained**)
1 make a stain on something. **2** colour with a
liquid that sinks into the surface.
[from an old word *distain* = dye]

stained glass *noun*
pieces of coloured glass held together in a lead
framework to make a picture or pattern.

stainless steel *noun*
steel that does not rust easily.

stair *noun* (*plural* **stairs**)
each of the fixed steps in a series that lead from
one level or floor to another in a building.

staircase *noun* (*plural* **staircases**)
a set of stairs.

stake *noun* (*plural* **stakes**)
1 a thick pointed stick to be driven into the
ground. **2** the post to which people used to
be tied for execution by being burnt alive.
3 an amount of money bet on something.
4 an investment that gives a person a share
or interest in a business etc.
at stake being risked.

stake *verb* (**stakes, staking, staked**)
1 fasten, support, or mark out with stakes.
2 bet or risk money etc. on an event.
stake a claim claim or obtain a right to
something.

stalactite *noun* (*plural* **stalactites**)
a stony spike hanging like an icicle from a cave
roof.
[from Greek *stalaktos* = dripping]

---

❶ USAGE See note at *stalagmite*.

---

stalagmite *noun* (*plural* **stalagmites**)
a stony spike standing like a pillar on the floor of
a cave.
[from Greek *stalagma* = a drop]

---

❶ USAGE Remember that a *stalagmite* stands up
from the **g**round, while a *stalactite* hangs down
from the **c**eiling.

---

stale *adjective*
1 not fresh. **2** bored and not having any good
ideas.
staleness *noun*

stalemate *noun*
1 a drawn position in chess when a player
cannot make a move without putting his or her
king in check. **2** a deadlock; a situation in which
neither side in an argument will give way.

stalk¹ *noun* (*plural* **stalks**)
a stem of a plant etc.

stalk² *verb* (**stalks, stalking, stalked**)
1 track or hunt stealthily. **2** walk in a stiff or
dignified way.

stall *noun* (*plural* **stalls**)
1 a table or counter from which things are sold.
2 a place for one animal in a stable or shed.

stall *verb* (**stalls, stalling, stalled**)
1 delay things or avoid giving an answer to give
yourself more time. **2** stop suddenly from lack of
power ♦ *The car engine stalled.* **3** put an animal
into a stall.

stallion noun (plural **stallions**)
a male horse.

stalls plural noun
the seats in the lowest level of a theatre.

stalwart adjective
strong and faithful ♦ my stalwart supporters.

stamen noun (plural **stamens**)
the part of a flower bearing pollen.
[from Latin, = thread]

stamina noun
strength and ability to endure hard effort over a
long time.
[from Latin, plural of stamen (referring to the
threads of life spun by the Fates, three
mythological godesses who were believed to
determine each person's birth and death)]

stammer verb (**stammers, stammering,
stammered**)
keep repeating the same syllables when you
speak.
stammer noun

stamp noun (plural **stamps**)
1 a small piece of gummed paper with a special
design on it; a postage stamp. 2 a small device for
pressing words or marks on something; the
words or marks made by this. 3 a distinctive
characteristic ♦ His story bears the stamp of
truth.
stamp verb (**stamps, stamping, stamped**)
1 bang your foot heavily on the ground.
2 walk with loud heavy steps. 3 stick a postage
stamp on a letter or packet. 4 press a mark or
design etc. on something.
stamp out 1 put out a fire by stamping.
 2 stop something ♦ We have stamped out
bullying.

stampede noun (plural **stampedes**)
a sudden rush by animals or people.
stampede verb
[from Spanish estampida = crash, uproar]

stand verb (**stands, standing, stood**)
1 be on your feet without moving ♦ We were
standing at the back of the hall. 2 rise to your feet
♦ Please all stand now. 3 set or be upright; place
♦ We stood the vase on the table. 4 stay the same
♦ My offer still stands. 5 be a candidate for
election ♦ She stood for Parliament. 6 tolerate or
endure ♦ I can't stand that noise. 7 provide and
pay for ♦ I'll stand you a drink.
it stands to reason it is reasonable or obvious.
stand by be ready for action. **stand for**
1 represent ♦ 'US' stands for 'United States'.
2 tolerate. **stand in for** take someone's place.
stand out be clear or obvious. **stand up for**
support or defend. **stand up to** 1 resist bravely.
2 stay in good condition in spite of prolonged
use.

stand noun (plural **stands**)
1 something made for putting things on
♦ a music stand. 2 a stall where things are sold
or displayed. 3 a grandstand. 4 a stationary
condition or position ♦ He took his stand near
the door. 5 resistance to attack ♦ The time has
come to make a stand.

standard noun (plural **standards**)
1 how good something is ♦ a high standard of
work. 2 a thing used to measure or judge
something else. 3 a special flag ♦ the royal
standard. 4 an upright support.
standard adjective
1 of the usual or average quality or kind.
2 regarded as the best and widely used
♦ the standard book on spiders.

standby noun
on standby ready to be used if needed.

stand-in noun (plural **stand-ins**)
a deputy or substitute.

standing order noun (plural **standing
orders**)
an instruction to a bank to make regular
payments, or to a trader to supply something
regularly.

stand-offish adjective
cold and formal; not friendly.

standpoint noun (plural **standpoints**)
a point of view.

standstill noun
a stop; an end to movement or activity.

staple¹ noun (plural **staples**)
1 a small piece of metal pushed through
papers and clenched to fasten them together.
2 a U-shaped nail.
staple verb **stapler** noun

staple² adjective
main or usual ♦ Rice is their staple food.
staple noun

star noun (plural **stars**)
1 a large mass of burning gas that is seen as a
speck of light in the sky at night. 2 a shape with
points or rays sticking out from it; an asterisk.
3 an object or mark of this shape showing rank
or quality ♦ a five-star hotel. 4 a famous
performer; one of the chief performers in a play,
film, or show.
star verb (**stars, starring, starred**)
1 be one of the main performers in a film or
show. 2 have someone as a main performer.
3 mark with an asterisk or star symbol.

starboard noun
the right-hand side of a ship or aircraft when you
are facing forward. (Compare port¹.)
[from Old English steor = paddle for steering
(usually mounted on the right-hand side),
+ board]

starch *noun* (*plural* **starches**)
1 a white carbohydrate in bread, potatoes, etc.
2 this or a similar substance used to stiffen clothes.
starchy *adjective*

starch *verb* (**starches, starching, starched**)
stiffen with starch.

stare *verb* (**stares, staring, stared**)
look at something intensely.
stare *noun*

starfish *noun* (*plural* **starfish** or **starfishes**)
a sea animal shaped like a star with five points.

stark *adjective*
1 complete or unmistakable ♦ *stark nonsense.*
2 desolate and bare ♦ *the stark lunar landscape.*
starkly *adverb* **starkness** *noun*

stark *adverb*
completely ♦ *stark naked.*

starling *noun* (*plural* **starlings**)
a noisy black bird with speckled feathers.

starry *adjective*
full of stars.

starry-eyed *adjective*
made happy by foolish dreams or unrealistic hopes.

start *verb* (**starts, starting, started**)
1 begin or cause to begin. 2 make an engine or machine begin running, ♦ *I'll start the car.*
3 begin a journey. 4 make a sudden movement because of pain or surprise.
starter *noun*

start *noun* (*plural* **starts**)
1 the beginning; the place where a race starts. 2 an advantage that someone starts with
♦ *We gave the young ones ten minutes' start.*
3 a sudden movement.

startle *verb* (**startles, startling, startled**)
surprise or alarm someone.

starve *verb* (**starves, starving, starved**)
1 suffer or die from lack of food; cause to do this.
2 deprive someone of something they need,
♦ *She was starved of love.*
starvation *noun*

starving *adjective*
(*informal*) very hungry.

state *noun* (*plural* **states**)
1 the quality of a person's or thing's characteristics or circumstances; condition.
2 an organized community under one government (*the state of Israel*) or forming part of a republic (*the 50 states of the USA*).
3 a country's government ♦ *Help for the earthquake victims was provided by the state.*
4 a grand style ♦ *She arrived in state.*
5 (*informal*) an excited or upset condition
♦ *Don't get into a state about the robbery.*

state *verb* (**states, stating, stated**)
express something in spoken or written words.

stately *adjective* (**statelier, stateliest**)
dignified, imposing, or grand.
stateliness *noun*

statement *noun* (*plural* **statements**)
1 words stating something. 2 a formal account of facts ♦ *The witness made a statement to the police.* 3 a written report of a financial account
♦ *a bank statement.*

state school *noun* (*plural* **state schools**)
a school which is funded by the government and which does not charge fees to pupils.

statesman *noun* (*plural* **statesmen**)
a person, especially a man, who is important or skilled in governing a country.
statesmanship *noun* **stateswoman** *noun*

static *adjective*
not moving or changing.

static electricity *noun*
electricity that is present in something, not flowing as current.

station *noun* (*plural* **stations**)
1 a stopping place for trains, buses, etc. with platforms and buildings for passengers and goods. 2 a building equipped for people who serve the public or for certain activities ♦ *the police station.* 3 a broadcasting company with its own frequency. 4 a place where a person or thing stands or is stationed; a position.
[from Latin *statio* = a stand, standing]

stationary *adjective*
not moving ♦ *The car was stationary when the van hit it.*

❶ USAGE Do not confuse with *stationery.*

stationery *noun*
paper, envelopes, and other articles used in writing or typing.

❶ USAGE Do not confuse with *stationary.*

statistician (*say* stat-is-**tish**-an) *noun* (*plural* **statisticians**)
an expert in statistics.

statistics *noun*
1 the study of information based on the numbers of things. 2 facts obtained from studying statistics.

statue *noun* (*plural* **statues**)
a model made of stone or metal etc. to look like a person or animal.

statuette *noun* (*plural* **statuettes**)
a small statue.

stature *noun*
1 the natural height of the body. 2 greatness gained by ability or achievement.

status (*say* **stay**-tus) *noun* (*plural* **statuses**)
1 a person's or thing's position or rank in relation to others. 2 high rank or prestige.

statute *noun* (*plural* **statutes**)
a law passed by a parliament.
statutory *adjective*

staunch *adjective*
firm and loyal ♦ *our staunch supporters.*
staunchly *adverb*

stave *verb* (**staves, staving, staved** or **stove**)
dent or break a hole in something ♦ *The collision stove in the front of the ship.*
stave off keep something away ♦ *We staved off the disaster.*

stave *noun* (*plural* **staves**)
a set of five horizontal lines on which music is written.

stay *verb* (**stays, staying, stayed**)
1 continue to be in the same place or condition; remain. **2** spend time in a place as a visitor. **3** satisfy temporarily ♦ *We stayed our hunger with a sandwich.* **4** pause. **5** show endurance in a race or task.
stay put (*informal*) remain in place.

stay *noun* (*plural* **stays**)
1 a time spent somewhere ♦ *We made a short stay in Rome.* **2** a postponement ♦ *a stay of execution.*

stead *noun*
in a person's or **thing's stead** instead of this person or thing. **stand a person in good stead** be very useful to him or her.

steadfast *adjective*
firm and not changing ♦ *a steadfast refusal.*

steady *adjective* (**steadier, steadiest**)
1 not shaking or moving; firm. **2** regular; continuing the same ♦ *a steady pace.*
steadily *adverb* **steadiness** *noun*

steak *noun* (*plural* **steaks**)
a thick slice of meat (especially beef) or fish.
[from Old Norse]

steal *verb* (**steals, stealing, stole, stolen**)
1 take and keep something that does not belong to you; take secretly or dishonestly. **2** move secretly or without being noticed ♦ *He stole out of the room.*

stealthy (*say* stelth-ee) *adjective* (**stealthier, stealthiest**)
quiet and secret, so as not to be noticed.
stealth *noun* **stealthily** *adverb* **stealthiness** *noun*

steam *noun*
1 the gas or vapour that comes from boiling water; this used to drive machinery. **2** energy ♦ *He ran out of steam.*
steamy *adjective*

steam *verb* (**steams, steaming, steamed**)
1 give off steam. **2** move by the power of steam ♦ *The ship steamed down the river.* **3** cook or treat by steam ♦ *a steamed pudding.*
steam up be covered with mist or condensation.

steam engine *noun* (*plural* **steam engines**)
an engine driven by steam.

steamroller *noun* (*plural* **steamrollers**)
a heavy vehicle with a large roller used to flatten surfaces when making roads.
[so called because the first ones were powered by steam]

steed *noun* (*plural* **steeds**) (*old or poetical use*)
a horse.
[from Old English]

steel *noun* (*plural* **steels**)
1 a strong metal made from iron and carbon.
2 a steel rod for sharpening knives.

steel *verb* (**steels, steeling, steeled**)
steel yourself find courage to face something difficult.

steely *adjective*
1 like or to do with steel. **2** cold, hard, and severe ♦ *a steely glare.*

steep[1] *adjective*
1 sloping very sharply, not gradually.
2 (*informal*) unreasonably high ♦ *a steep price.*
steeply *adverb* **steepness** *noun*
[from Old English]

steep[2] *verb* (**steeps, steeping, steeped**)
soak thoroughly; saturate.
be steeped in be completely filled or familiar with something, ♦ *The story is steeped in mystery.*
[probably from a Scandinavian language]

steepen *verb* (**steepens, steepening, steepened**)
make or become steeper.

steeple *noun* (*plural* **steeples**)
a church tower with a spire on top.

steer *verb* (**steers, steering, steered**)
make a car, ship, or bicycle etc. go in the direction you want; guide.
steersman *noun*
steer clear of take care to avoid.

steering wheel *noun* (*plural* **steering wheels**)
a wheel for steering a car, boat, etc.

stem[1] *noun* (*plural* **stems**)
1 the main central part of a tree, shrub, or plant. **2** a thin part on which a leaf, flower, or fruit is supported. **3** a thin upright part, e.g. the thin part of a wineglass between the bowl and the foot. **4** the main part of a verb or other word, to which endings are attached. **5** the front part of a ship ♦ *from stem to stern.*

stem *verb* (**stems, stemming, stemmed**)
stem from arise from; have as its source.
[from Old English]

stem[2] *verb* (**stems, stemming, stemmed**)
stop the flow of something.
[from Old Norse]

stench *noun* (*plural* **stenches**)
a very unpleasant smell.

stencil *noun* (*plural* **stencils**)
a piece of card, metal, or plastic with pieces cut
out of it, used to produce a picture or design etc.

step *noun* (*plural* **steps**)
1 a movement made by lifting the foot and
setting it down. 2 the sound of a person putting
down their foot when walking or running.
3 a level surface for placing the foot on in
climbing up or down. 4 each of a series of things
done in some process or action ♦ *The first step is
to find somewhere to practise.*
in step 1 stepping in time with others in
marching or dancing. 2 in agreement. **watch
your step** be careful.

step *verb* (**steps, stepping, stepped**)
tread or walk.
step in intervene. **step on it** (*informal*) hurry.
step up increase something.

stepfather *noun* (*plural* **stepfathers**)
a man who is married to your mother but is not
your natural father.

stepladder *noun* (*plural* **stepladders**)
a folding ladder with flat treads.

stepmother *noun* (*plural* **stepmothers**)
a woman who is married to your father but is not
your natural mother.

stepping stone *noun* (*plural* **stepping
stones**)
1 each of a line of stones put into a shallow
stream so that people can walk across. 2 a way of
achieving something, or a stage in achieving it
♦ *good exam results can be a stepping stone to a
career.*

stereo *noun* (*plural* **stereos**)
1 stereophonic sound or recording.
2 a stereophonic CD player, record player, etc.

stereophonic *adjective*
using sound that comes from two different
directions to give a natural effect.

stereotype *noun* (*plural* **stereotypes**)
a fixed idea or image of a person or thing
♦ *The stereotype of a hero is one who is tall,
strong, brave, and good-looking.*
stereotypical *adjective*

sterile *adjective*
1 not fertile; barren. 2 free from germs.
sterility *noun*

sterilize *verb* (**sterilizes, sterilizing, sterilized**)
1 make a thing free from germs, e.g. by heating
it. 2 make a person or animal unable to
reproduce.
sterilization *noun* **sterilizer** *noun*

sterling *noun*
British money.

sterling *adjective*
1 genuine ♦ *sterling silver.* 2 excellent; of great
worth ♦ *her sterling qualities.*

stern¹ *adjective*
strict and severe, not lenient or kindly.
sternly *adverb* **sternness** *noun*

stern² *noun* (*plural* **sterns**)
the back part of a ship.

stew *verb* (**stews, stewing, stewed**)
cook slowly in liquid.

stew *noun* (*plural* **stews**)
a dish of stewed food, especially meat and
vegetables.
in a stew (*informal*) very worried or agitated.

steward *noun* (*plural* **stewards**)
1 a man whose job is to look after the passengers
on a ship or aircraft. 2 an official who keeps
order or looks after the arrangements at a large
public event.

stewardess *noun* (*plural* **stewardesses**)
a woman whose job is to look after the
passengers on a ship or aircraft.

stick¹ *noun* (*plural* **sticks**)
1 a long thin piece of wood. 2 a walking stick.
3 the implement used to hit the ball in hockey,
polo, etc. 4 a long thin piece of something
♦ *a stick of rock.*

stick² *verb* (**sticks, sticking, stuck**)
1 push a thing into something ♦ *Stick a pin
in it.* 2 fix or be fixed by glue or as if by this
♦ *Stick stamps on the parcel.* 3 become fixed and
unable to move ♦ *The drawer keeps sticking.*
4 (*informal*) endure or tolerate ♦ *I can't stick
that noise!*
stick out 1 come or push out from a surface;
stand out from the surrounding area. 2 be very
noticeable. **stick to** 1 remain faithful to a friend
or promise etc. 2 keep to and not alter ♦ *He stuck
to his story.* **stick together** 1 stay together.
2 support each other. **stick up for** (*informal*)
stand up for. **be stuck with** (*informal*) be
unable to avoid something unwelcome.

stickler *noun* (*plural* **sticklers**)
a person who insists on something ♦ *a stickler
for punctuality.*

sticky *adjective* (**stickier, stickiest**)
1 able or likely to stick to things. 2 (said about
weather) hot and humid, causing perspiration.
3 (*informal*) difficult or awkward ♦ *a sticky
situation.*
stickily *adverb* **stickiness** *noun*
come to a sticky end (*informal*) die or end in a
painful or unpleasant way.

stiff *adjective*
1 not bending or moving or changing its shape
easily. 2 not fluid; hard to stir ♦ *a stiff dough.*
3 difficult ♦ *a stiff examination.* 4 formal in
manner; not friendly. 5 severe or strong
♦ *a stiff breeze.*
stiffly *adverb* **stiffness** *noun*

stiffen verb (stiffens, stiffening, stiffened)
make or become stiff.
stiffener noun

stifle verb (stifles, stifling, stifled)
1 suffocate. 2 suppress ♦ She stifled a yawn.

stigma noun (plural stigmas)
1 a mark of disgrace. 2 part of a flower's pistil
that receives the pollen.
[from Greek]

stile noun (plural stiles)
an arrangement of steps or bars for people to
climb over a fence.

stiletto heel noun (plural stiletto heels)
a high pointed shoe heel.

still adjective
1 not moving ♦ still water. 2 silent. 3 not fizzy.
stillness noun

still adverb
1 without moving ♦ Stand still. 2 up to this or
that time ♦ He was still there. 3 in a greater
amount or degree ♦ You can do still better.
4 nevertheless ♦ They've lost. Still, they tried,
and that was good.

stillborn adjective
born dead.

still life noun (plural still lifes)
a painting of lifeless things such as ornaments
and fruit.

stilted adjective
stiffly formal.

stilts plural noun
a pair of poles with supports for the feet so that
the user can walk high above the ground.

stimulate verb (stimulates, stimulating,
stimulated)
1 make someone excited or enthusiastic. 2 cause
or arouse ♦ The programme has stimulated a lot
of interest in her work.
stimulant noun **stimulation** noun

sting noun (plural stings)
1 a sharp-pointed part of an animal or plant,
often containing a poison, that can cause a
wound. 2 a painful wound caused by this part.

sting verb (stings, stinging, stung)
1 wound or hurt with a sting. 2 feel a sharp pain.
3 make someone feel upset or hurt ♦ I was stung
by this criticism. 4 (slang) cheat a person by
overcharging; extort money from someone.

stingy (say stin-jee) adjective (stingier,
stingiest)
mean, not generous; giving or given in small
amounts.
stingily adverb **stinginess** noun

stink noun (plural stinks)
1 an unpleasant smell. 2 (informal) an
unpleasant fuss or protest.

stink verb (stinks, stinking, stank or stunk)
have an unpleasant smell.

stint noun (plural stints)
1 a fixed amount of work to be done. 2 limitation
of a supply or effort ♦ They gave help without
stint.

stint verb (stints, stinting, stinted)
be sparing; restrict to a small amount
♦ Don't stint on the cream.

stir verb (stirs, stirring, stirred)
1 mix a liquid or soft mixture by moving a spoon
etc. round and round in it. 2 move slightly; start
to move. 3 excite or stimulate ♦ They stirred up
trouble.

stir noun
1 the action of stirring. 2 a disturbance;
excitement ♦ The news caused a stir.

stir-fry verb (stir-fries, stir-frying, stir-fried)
cook by frying quickly over a high heat while
stirring and tossing.
stir-fry noun

stirrup noun (plural stirrups)
a metal part that hangs from each side of a
horse's saddle, for a rider to put his or her foot in.

stitch noun (plural stitches)
1 a loop of thread made in sewing or knitting.
2 a method of arranging the threads ♦ cross
stitch. 3 a sudden sharp pain in the side of the
body, caused by running.

stitch verb (stitches, stitching, stitched)
sew or fasten with stitches.

stoat noun (plural stoats)
a kind of weasel.

stock noun (plural stocks)
1 a number of things kept ready to be sold or
used. 2 livestock. 3 a line of ancestors ♦ a man
of Irish stock. 4 a number of shares in a
company's capital. 5 liquid made by stewing
meat, fish, or vegetables, used for making soup
etc. 6 the main stem of a tree or plant. 7 the base,
holder, or handle of an implement, weapon, etc.
8 a garden flower with a sweet smell. 9 a kind of
cravat.

stock verb (stocks, stocking, stocked)
1 keep goods in stock. 2 provide a place with a
stock of something.
stock up buy a supply of goods etc.

stockade noun (plural stockades)
a fence made of stakes.

stockbroker noun (plural stockbrokers)
a broker who deals in stocks and shares.

stock exchange noun (plural stock
exchanges)
a country's central place for buying and selling
stocks and shares.

stocking noun (plural stockings)
a piece of clothing covering the foot and part or
all of the leg.

stock market noun (plural stock markets)
1 a stock exchange. 2 the buying and selling of
stocks and shares.

stockpile *noun* (*plural* **stockpiles**)
a large stock of things kept in reserve.
stockpile *verb*

stocks *plural noun*
a wooden structure in which people used to be
locked as a public punishment.

stock-still *adjective*
quite still.

stocktaking *noun*
the counting, listing, and checking of the amount
of stock held by a shop or business.

stocky *adjective* (**stockier, stockiest**)
short and solidly built ♦ *a stocky man*.

stodgy *adjective* (**stodgier, stodgiest**)
1 (said about food) heavy and filling. 2 dull and
boring ♦ *a stodgy book*.
stodginess *noun*

stoical (*say* stoh-ik-al) *adjective*
bearing pain or difficulties etc. calmly without
complaining.
stoically *adverb* **stoicism** *noun*

stoke *verb* (**stokes, stoking, stoked**)
put fuel in a furnace or on a fire.
stoker *noun*

stole *past tense* of **steal**.

stolid *adjective*
not showing much emotion or excitement.
stolidly *adverb* **stolidity** *noun*

stomach *noun* (*plural* **stomachs**)
1 the part of the body where food starts to be
digested. 2 the abdomen.

stomach *verb* (**stomachs, stomaching,
stomached**)
endure or tolerate.

stone *noun* (*plural* **stones**)
1 a piece of rock. 2 stones or rock as material,
e.g. for building. 3 a jewel. 4 the hard case round
the kernel of plums, cherries, etc. 5 a unit of
weight equal to 14 pounds (6.35 kg) ♦ *She
weighs 8 stone*.

stone *verb* (**stones, stoning, stoned**)
1 throw stones at somebody. 2 remove the
stones from fruit.
[from Old English]

Stone Age *noun*
the earliest period of human history, when tools
and weapons were made of stone.

stone-cold *adjective*
extremely cold.

stone-deaf *adjective*
completely deaf.

stony *adjective*
1 full of stones. 2 like stone; hard. 3 unfriendly
and not answering ♦ *a stony silence*.

stool *noun* (*plural* **stools**)
1 a movable seat without arms or a back.
2 a footstool. 3 a lump of faeces.

stoop *verb* (**stoops, stooping, stooped**)
1 bend your body forwards and down. 2 lower
yourself ♦ *He would not stoop to cheating*.
stoop *noun*

stop *verb* (**stops, stopping, stopped**)
1 bring or come to an end; no longer do
something. 2 be no longer moving or working
♦ *A car stopped in front of us*. 3 prevent or
obstruct something. 4 stay for a short time.
5 fill a hole.

stop *noun* (*plural* **stops**)
1 stopping; a pause or end. 2 a place where a bus
or train etc. regularly stops. 3 a punctuation
mark, especially a full stop. 4 a lever or knob
that controls pitch in a wind instrument or
allows organ pipes to sound.

stopcock *noun* (*plural* **stopcocks**)
a valve controlling the flow of liquid or gas in a
pipe.

stopgap *noun* (*plural* **stopgaps**)
a temporary substitute.

stoppage *noun* (*plural* **stoppages**)
1 an interruption in the work of a factory etc.
2 a blockage. 3 an amount taken off someone's
wages.

stopper *noun* (*plural* **stoppers**)
a plug for closing a bottle etc.

stopwatch *noun* (*plural* **stopwatches**)
a watch that can be started and stopped when
you wish, used for timing races etc.

store *noun* (*plural* **stores**)
1 a supply of things kept for future use. 2 a place
where things are kept until they are needed.
3 a shop, especially a large one.
in store 1 being stored. 2 going to happen
♦ *There's a surprise in store for you*. **set store by
something** value it greatly.

store *verb* (**stores, storing, stored**)
keep things until they are needed.
storage *noun*

storehouse *noun* (*plural* **storehouses**)
a building for storing goods.

storey *noun* (*plural* **storeys**)
one whole floor of a building.

---

❶ USAGE Do not confuse with *story*.

---

stork *noun* (*plural* **storks**)
a large bird with long legs and a long beak.

storm *noun* (*plural* **storms**)
1 a very strong wind usually with rain, snow,
etc. 2 a violent attack or outburst ♦ *a storm of
protest*.
stormy *adjective*
a storm in a teacup a great fuss over something
unimportant.

storm verb (storms, storming, stormed)
1 move or behave violently or angrily
♦ *He stormed out of the room.* 2 suddenly
attack and capture a place ♦ *They stormed the
castle.*

story noun (*plural* **stories**)
1 an account of a real or imaginary event.
2 the plot of a play or novel etc. 3 (*informal*) a lie
♦ *Don't tell stories!*
[from Latin *historia* = history]

❶ USAGE Do not confuse with *storey*.

stout adjective
1 rather fat. 2 thick and strong. 3 brave and
determined ♦ *a stout defender of human rights.*
stoutly adverb **stoutness** noun

stove¹ noun (*plural* **stoves**)
1 a device containing an oven or ovens.
2 a device for heating a room.

stove² past tense of **stave.**

stow verb (stows, stowing, stowed)
pack or store something away.
stowage noun
stow away hide on a ship or aircraft so as to
travel without paying. **stowaway** noun

straddle verb (straddles, straddling,
straddled)
have a position across or astride something.

straggle verb (straggles, straggling,
straggled)
1 grow or spread in an untidy way. 2 lag behind;
wander on your own.
straggler noun **straggly** adjective

straight adjective
1 going continuously in one direction;
not curving or bending. 2 level or upright
♦ *Is the picture straight?* 3 tidy; in proper order.
4 honest and frank ♦ *a straight answer.*
straightness noun

straight adverb
1 in a straight line or manner. 2 directly; without
delay ♦ *Go straight home.*
straight away immediately.

❶ USAGE Do not confuse with *strait.*

straighten verb (straightens, straightening,
straightened)
make or become straight.

straightforward adjective
1 easy, not complicated. 2 honest and frank.

strain¹ verb (strains, straining, strained)
1 injure or weaken something by stretching or
working it too hard. 2 stretch tightly. 3 make a
great effort. 4 put something through a sieve or
filter to separate liquid from solid matter.

strain¹ noun (*plural* **strains**)
1 straining; the force of straining. 2 an injury
caused by straining. 3 something that uses up
strength, patience, resources, etc. 4 exhaustion.
5 a part of a tune.

strain² noun (*plural* **strains**)
1 a breed or variety of animals, plants, etc.; a line
of descent. 2 an inherited characteristic
♦ *There's an artistic strain in the family.*

strait noun (*plural* **straits**)
a narrow stretch of water connecting two seas.

❶ USAGE Do not confuse with *straight.*

straits plural noun
1 a strait ♦ *the Straits of Dover.* 2 a difficult
condition ♦ *We were in dire straits when we lost
our money.*

strand¹ noun (*plural* **strands**)
1 each of the threads or wires etc. twisted
together to form a rope, yarn, or cable. 2 a single
thread or hair. 3 one idea or theme of several in
a story.

strand² verb (strands, stranding, stranded)
be stranded 1 (said about a boat) run onto sand
or rocks in shallow water. 2 be left in a difficult
or helpless position ♦ *We were stranded when
our car broke down.*

strange adjective
1 unusual or surprising. 2 not known or seen or
experienced before.
strangely adverb **strangeness** noun

stranger noun (*plural* **strangers**)
a person you do not know, or who is in a place
they do not know.

strangle verb (strangles, strangling,
strangled)
1 kill by squeezing the throat to prevent
breathing. 2 restrict something so that it does not
develop.
strangler noun

strap noun (*plural* **straps**)
a flat strip of leather or cloth etc. for fastening
things or holding them in place.

strap verb (straps, strapping, strapped)
fasten with a strap or straps; bind.

strapping adjective
tall and healthy-looking ♦ *a strapping lad.*

strata (*say* strah-ta *or* stray-ta) *plural noun*
layers or levels, especially of rock.

strategy noun (*plural* **strategies**)
1 a plan or policy to achieve something
♦ *our economic strategy.* 2 the planning of
a war or campaign. (Compare **tactics**.)
[from Greek *strategos* = a general]

stratosphere noun
a layer of the atmosphere between about 10 and
60 kilometres above the earth's surface.

straw *noun* (*plural* **straws**)
1 dry cut stalks of corn. 2 a narrow tube for drinking through.
[from Old English]

strawberry *noun* (*plural* **strawberries**)
a small red juicy fruit, with its seeds on the outside.

stray *verb* (**strays, straying, strayed**)
leave a group or proper place and wander; get lost.

stray *adjective*
that has become lost or separated ♦ *a stray cat*;
♦ *a stray sock*.

stray *noun*

streak *noun* (*plural* **streaks**)
1 a long thin line or mark. 2 a trace ♦ *a streak of cruelty*. 3 a spell of success, luck, etc. ♦ *on a winning streak*.

streaky *adjective*

streak *verb* (**streaks, streaking, streaked**)
1 mark with streaks. 2 move very quickly.
3 run naked in a public place for fun or to get attention.

streaker *noun*

stream *noun* (*plural* **streams**)
1 water flowing in a channel; a brook or small river. 2 a flow of liquid or of things or people.
3 a group in which children of similar ability are placed in a school.

stream *verb* (**streams, streaming, streamed**)
1 move in or like a stream. 2 produce a stream of liquid. 3 arrange schoolchildren in streams according to their ability.

streamline *verb* (**streamlines, streamlining, streamlined**)
1 give something a smooth shape that helps it to move easily through air or water. 2 organize something so that it works more efficiently.

streamlined *adjective*

street *noun* (*plural* **streets**)
a road with houses beside it in a city or village.
[via Old English from Latin *strata via* = paved way]

strength *noun* (*plural* **strengths**)
1 how strong a person or thing is; being strong.
2 an ability or good quality ♦ *Patience is your great strength*.

strengthen *verb* (**strengthens, strengthening, strengthened**)
make or become stronger.

stress *noun* (*plural* **stresses**)
1 a force that acts on something, e.g. by pressing, pulling, or twisting it; strain. 2 emphasis, especially the extra force with which you pronounce part of a word or phrase. 3 distress caused by having too many problems or too much to do.

stress *verb* (**stresses, stressing, stressed**)
1 emphasize a point or idea ♦ *I must stress the importance of arriving on time*. 2 pronounce part of a word or phrase with extra emphasis.
3 cause stress to someone.

stretch *verb* (**stretches, stretching, stretched**)
1 pull something or be pulled so that it becomes longer or wider or larger. 2 extend or be continuous ♦ *The wall stretches right round the estate*. 3 push out your arms and legs as far as you can. 4 make use of all your ability or intelligence ♦ *This course should really stretch you*.

stretch out lie down with your arms and legs at full length.

stretch *noun* (*plural* **stretches**)
1 the action of stretching. 2 a continuous period of time or area of land or water.

stretcher *noun* (*plural* **stretchers**)
a framework for carrying a sick or injured person.

strict *adjective*
1 demanding obedience and good behaviour
♦ *a strict teacher*. 2 complete or exact ♦ *in strict confidence*; ♦ *the strict truth*.

strictly *adverb* **strictness** *noun*

stride *verb* (**strides, striding, strode, stridden**)
walk with long steps.

stride *noun* (*plural* **strides**)
1 a long step when walking or running.
2 progress.

get into your stride settle into a fast and steady pace of working. **take something in your stride** manage or deal with something without difficulty.

strife *noun*
conflict; fighting or quarrelling.

strike *verb* (**strikes, striking, struck**)
1 hit. 2 attack suddenly ♦ *Plague struck the village*. 3 make an impression on someone's mind ♦ *She strikes me as truthful*. 4 light a match by rubbing it against a rough surface.
5 refuse to work as a protest against pay or conditions. 6 produce by pressing or stamping something ♦ *They are striking some special coins*.
7 sound ♦ *The clock struck ten*. 8 find gold or oil etc. by digging or drilling. 9 go in a certain direction ♦ *We struck north through the forest*.

strike off or **out** cross out. **strike up** 1 begin playing or singing. 2 start a friendship or conversation.

strike *noun* (*plural* **strikes**)
1 a hit. 2 an attack ♦ *an air strike*. 3 refusing to work as a way of making a protest. 4 a sudden discovery of gold or oil etc.

on strike (said about workers) striking.

striking *adjective*
attractive or impressive.

strikingly *adverb*

string *noun* (*plural* **strings**)
1 thin cord made of twisted threads, used to fasten or tie things; a piece of this or similar material. 2 a piece of wire or cord etc. stretched and vibrated to produce sounds in a musical instrument. 3 a line or series of things ♦ *a string of cars*.

string *verb* (**strings, stringing, strung**)
1 fit or fasten with string. 2 thread on a string. 3 remove the tough fibre from beans.
string along mislead someone over a period of time. **string out** 1 spread out in a line. 2 cause something to last a long time.

strings *plural noun*
musical instruments with strings.

stringy *adjective*
1 like string. 2 containing tough fibres.

strip¹ *verb* (**strips, stripping, stripped**)
1 take a covering or layer off something. 2 undress. 3 deprive a person of something.

strip *noun*
the distinctive clothes worn by a sports team while playing.

strip² *noun* (*plural* **strips**)
a long narrow piece or area.

strip cartoon *noun* (*plural* **strip cartoons**)
a series of drawings telling a story.

stripe *noun* (*plural* **stripes**)
1 a long narrow band of colour. 2 a strip of cloth worn on the sleeve of a uniform to show the wearer's rank.
striped *adjective* **stripy** *adjective*

striptease *noun* (*plural* **stripteases**)
an entertainment in which a person slowly undresses.

strive *verb* (**strives, striving, strove, striven**)
1 try hard to do something. 2 carry on a conflict.

stroke¹ *noun* (*plural* **strokes**)
1 a hit. 2 a movement; a style of swimming. 3 an action or effort ♦ *a stroke of genius*. 4 the sound made by a clock striking. 5 a sudden illness that often causes paralysis.

stroke² *verb* (**strokes, stroking, stroked**)
move your hand gently along something.
stroke *noun*

stroll *verb* (**strolls, strolling, strolled**)
walk in a leisurely way.
stroll *noun* **stroller** *noun*

strong *adjective*
1 having great power, energy, or effect. 2 not easy to break, damage, or defeat. 3 great in intensity ♦ *strong feelings*. 4 having a lot of flavour or smell. 5 having a certain number of members ♦ *an army 5,000 strong*.
strongly *adverb*
be going strong be making good progress.

stronghold *noun* (*plural* **strongholds**)
1 a fortified place. 2 an area where many people live or think in a particular way ♦ *a Tory stronghold*.

strove *past tense* of **strive**.

structure *noun* (*plural* **structures**)
1 something that has been constructed or built. 2 the way something is constructed or organized.
structural *adjective* **structurally** *adverb*

struggle *verb* (**struggles, struggling, struggled**)
1 move your arms, legs, etc. in trying to get free. 2 make strong efforts to do something. 3 try to overcome an opponent or a problem etc.

struggle *noun* (*plural* **struggles**)
the action of struggling; a hard fight or great effort.

strum *verb* (**strums, strumming, strummed**)
sound a guitar by running your fingers across its strings.

strut *verb* (**struts, strutting, strutted**)
walk proudly or stiffly.

strut *noun* (*plural* **struts**)
1 a bar of wood or metal strengthening a framework. 2 a strutting walk.

stub *noun* (*plural* **stubs**)
1 a short stump left when the rest has been used or worn down. 2 a counterfoil of a cheque, ticket, etc.

stub *verb* (**stubs, stubbing, stubbed**)
bump your toe painfully.
stub out put out a cigarette by pressing it against something hard.

stubble *noun*
1 the short stalks of corn left in the ground after the harvest is cut. 2 short hairs growing after shaving.

stubborn *adjective*
1 determined not to change your ideas or ways; obstinate. 2 difficult to remove or deal with ♦ *stubborn stains*.
stubbornly *adverb* **stubbornness** *noun*

stubby *adjective*
short and thick.

stuck-up *adjective* (*informal*)
conceited or snobbish.

stud *noun* (*plural* **studs**)
1 a small curved lump or knob. 2 a device like a button on a stalk, used to fasten a detachable collar to a shirt.

student *noun* (*plural* **students**)
a person who studies a subject, especially at a college or university.

studio *noun* (*plural* **studios**)
1 the room where a painter or photographer etc. works. 2 a place where cinema films are made. 3 a room from which radio or television broadcasts are made or recorded.

studious *adjective*
keen on studying; studying hard.
studiously *adverb* **studiousness** *noun*

study *verb* (**studies, studying, studied**)
1 spend time learning about something. 2 look at something carefully.

study *noun* (*plural* **studies**)
1 the process of studying. 2 a subject studied; a piece of research. 3 a room used for studying or writing. 4 a piece of music for playing as an exercise. 5 a drawing done for practice or in preparation for another work.

stuff *noun*
1 a substance or material. 2 things ♦ *Leave your stuff outside.*

stuff *verb* (**stuffs, stuffing, stuffed**)
1 fill tightly. 2 fill with stuffing. 3 push a thing into something ♦ *He stuffed the notebook into his pocket.* 4 (*informal*) eat greedily.

stuffing *noun*
1 material used to fill the inside of something; padding. 2 a savoury mixture put into meat or poultry etc. before cooking.

stuffy *adjective* (**stuffier, stuffiest**)
1 badly ventilated; without fresh air. 2 with blocked breathing passages ♦ *a stuffy nose.* 3 formal and boring.
stuffily *adverb* **stuffiness** *noun*

stumble *verb* (**stumbles, stumbling, stumbled**)
1 trip and lose your balance. 2 speak or do something hesitantly or uncertainly.
stumble *noun*
stumble across or **on** find accidentally.

stumbling block *noun* (*plural* **stumbling blocks**)
an obstacle; something that causes difficulty.

stump *noun* (*plural* **stumps**)
1 the bottom of a tree trunk left in the ground when the rest has fallen or been cut down. 2 something left when the main part is cut off or worn down. 3 each of the three upright sticks of a wicket in cricket.

stump *verb* (**stumps, stumping, stumped**)
1 put a batsman out by knocking the bails off the stumps while they are out of the crease. 2 be too difficult or puzzling for somebody♦ *The last question stumped everyone.*
stump up (*informal*) produce the money to pay for something.

stumpy *adjective*
short and thick.
stumpiness *noun*

stun *verb* (**stuns, stunning, stunned**)
1 knock a person unconscious. 2 daze or shock ♦ *She was stunned by the news.*

stunt[1] *verb*
prevent a thing from growing or developing normally ♦ *a stunted tree.*
[from a dialect word meaning 'foolish' or 'stubborn']

stunt[2] *noun* (*plural* **stunts**)
something unusual or difficult done as a performance or part of a film, or to attract attention.
[originally American: origin unknown]

stupendous *adjective*
amazing or tremendous.
stupendously *adverb*

stupid *adjective*
1 not clever or thoughtful. 2 without reason or common sense.
stupidly *adverb* **stupidity** *noun*

sturdy *adjective* (**sturdier, sturdiest**)
strong and vigorous or solid.
sturdily *adverb* **sturdiness** *noun*

stutter *verb* (**stutters, stuttering, stuttered**)
stammer.
stutter *noun*

style *noun* (*plural* **styles**)
1 the way something is done, made, said, or written. 2 fashion or elegance.
stylistic *adjective*

stylish *adjective*
in a fashionable style.

subconscious *adjective*
to do with mental processes of which we are not fully aware but which influence our actions.
subconscious *noun*

subdivide *verb* (**subdivides, subdividing, subdivided**)
divide again or into smaller parts.
subdivision *noun*

subdue *verb* (**subdues, subduing, subdued**)
1 overcome or bring under control. 2 make quieter or gentler.
subdued *adjective*

subject *noun* (*plural* **subjects**)
1 the person or thing being talked or written about or dealt with. 2 something that is studied. 3 (in grammar) the word or words naming who or what does the action of a verb, e.g. 'the book' in ♦ *The book fell off the table.* 4 someone who is ruled by a monarch or government.

subject *adjective*
ruled by a monarch or government; not independent.
subject to 1 having to obey. 2 liable to ♦ *Trains are subject to delays during fog.* 3 depending upon ♦ *Our decision is subject to your approval.*

subject (*say* sub-jekt) *verb* (**subjects, subjecting, subjected**)
1 make a person or thing undergo something ♦ *They subjected him to torture.* **2** bring a country under your control.
subjection *noun*
[from Latin *subicere* = bring under, include under a heading]

subjective *adjective*
1 existing in a person's mind and not produced by things outside it. **2** depending on a person's own taste or opinions etc. (Compare **objective**.)

subjunctive *noun* (*plural* **subjunctives**)
the form of a verb used to indicate what is imagined or wished or possible. There are only a few cases where it is commonly used in English, e.g. '*were*' in '*if I were you*' and '*save*' in '*God save the Queen*'.

sublime *adjective*
1 noble or impressive. **2** extreme; not caring about the consequences ♦ *with sublime carelessness.*

submarine *adjective*
under the sea ♦ *We laid a submarine cable.*

submarine *noun* (*plural* **submarines**)
a ship that can travel under water.

submerge *verb* (**submerges, submerging, submerged**)
go under or put under water.
submergence *noun* **submersion** *noun*

submit *verb* (**submits, submitting, submitted**)
1 let someone have authority over you; surrender. **2** put forward for consideration, testing, etc. ♦ *Submit your plans to the committee.*
submission *noun*

subnormal *adjective*
below normal.

subordinate *adjective*
1 less important. **2** lower in rank.

subordinate *noun* (*plural* **subordinates**)
a person working under someone's authority or control.

subordinate *verb* (**subordinates, subordinating, subordinated**)
treat as being less important than another person or thing.
subordination *noun*

subordinate clause *noun* (*plural* **subordinate clauses**)
a clause which adds details to the main clause of the sentence, but cannot be used as a sentence by itself.

sub-plot *noun* (*plural* **sub-plots**)
a secondary plot in a play etc.

subscribe *verb* (**subscribes, subscribing, subscribed**)
1 pay regularly in order to be a member of a society, receive a periodical, have the use of a telephone, etc. **2** contribute money to a project or charity etc. **3** apply to take part in something ♦ *The course is already fully subscribed.* **4** say that you agree ♦ *We cannot subscribe to this theory.*
subscriber *noun* **subscription** *noun*

subsequent *adjective*
coming after in time or order; later.
subsequently *adverb*

subside *verb* (**subsides, subsiding, subsided**)
1 sink into the ground. **2** become quieter or less intense ♦ *Her fear subsided.*
subsidence *noun*

subsidiary *adjective*
1 less important; secondary. **2** (said about a business) controlled by another ♦ *a subsidiary company.*
subsidiary *noun*

subsidize *verb* (**subsidizes, subsidizing, subsidized**)
pay a subsidy to a person or firm etc.

subsidy *noun* (*plural* **subsidies**)
money paid to an industry etc. that needs help, or to keep down the price at which its goods etc. are sold to the public.

subsoil *noun*
soil lying just below the surface layer.

substance *noun* (*plural* **substances**)
1 matter of a particular kind. **2** the main or essential part of something ♦ *We agree with the substance of your report but not with its details.*

substantial *adjective*
1 of great size, value, or importance ♦ *a substantial sum of money.* **2** solidly built ♦ *substantial houses.*
substantially *adverb*

substitute *noun* (*plural* **substitutes**)
a person or thing that acts or is used instead of another.

substitute *verb* (**substitutes, substituting, substituted**)
put or use a person or thing as a substitute.
substitution *noun*

subterranean *adjective*
underground.

subtitle *noun* (*plural* **subtitles**)
1 a secondary or additional title. **2** words shown on the screen during a film, e.g. to translate a foreign language.

subtle (*say* sut-el) *adjective*
1 faint or delicate ♦ *a subtle perfume.* **2** slight and difficult to detect or describe ♦ *a subtle distinction.* **3** ingenious; not immediately obvious ♦ *a subtle joke.*
subtly *adverb* **subtlety** *noun*

subtract verb (subtracts, subtracting, subtracted)
deduct; take away a part, quantity, or number from a greater one.
subtraction noun

suburb noun (plural suburbs)
a district with houses that is outside the central part of a city.
suburban adjective

subway noun (plural subways)
an underground passage for pedestrians.

succeed verb (succeeds, succeeding, succeeded)
1 do or get what you wanted or intended. 2 come after another person or thing; become the next king or queen ♦ She succeeded to the throne.
♦ Edward VII succeeded Queen Victoria.

success noun (plural successes)
1 doing or getting what you wanted or intended. 2 a person or thing that does well ♦ The show was a great success.

successful adjective
having success; being a success.
successfully adverb

succession noun (plural successions)
1 a series of people or things. 2 the process of following in order. 3 succeeding to the throne; the right of doing this.
in succession one after another.

successive adjective
following one after another ♦ on five successive days.
successively adverb

succumb (say suk-um) verb (succumbs, succumbing, succumbed)
give way to something overpowering.

such adjective
1 of the same kind; similar ♦ Cakes, biscuits, and all such foods are fattening. 2 of the kind described ♦ There's no such person. 3 so great or intense ♦ It gave me such a fright!
such as for example.

such-and-such adjective
particular but not now named ♦ He promises to come at such-and-such a time but is always late.

suck verb (sucks, sucking, sucked)
1 take in liquid or air through the mouth with the lips almost closed. 2 squeeze something in your mouth by using your tongue ♦ sucking a toffee. 3 draw in ♦ The canoe was sucked into the whirlpool.
suck noun

suck up to (informal) flatter someone in the hope of winning their favour.

sucker noun (plural suckers)
1 an organ or device that can stick to a surface by suction. 2 a shoot coming up from a root or underground stem. 3 (informal) a person who is easily deceived.

suckle verb (suckles, suckling, suckled)
feed on milk at the mother's breast or udder.

suction noun
1 sucking. 2 producing a vacuum so that things are sucked into the empty space ♦ Vacuum cleaners work by suction.

sudden adjective
happening or done quickly or without warning.
suddenly adverb **suddenness** noun

suds plural noun
froth on soapy water.

sue verb (sues, suing, sued)
start a lawsuit to claim money from somebody.

suet noun
hard fat from cattle and sheep, used in cooking.

suffer verb (suffers, suffering, suffered)
1 feel pain or sadness. 2 experience something bad ♦ The house suffered some damage. ♦ She suffers from hay fever. 3 be badly affected ♦ She's not sleeping and her work is suffering. 4 (old use) allow or tolerate.
sufferer noun **suffering** noun

suffice verb (suffices, sufficing, sufficed)
be enough for someone's needs.

sufficient adjective
enough.
sufficiently adverb **sufficiency** noun

suffix noun (plural suffixes)
a letter or set of letters joined to the end of a word to make another word (e.g. in forgetful, lioness, rusty) or a form of a verb (e.g. singing, waited).

suffocate verb (suffocates, suffocating, suffocated)
1 make it difficult or impossible for someone to breathe. 2 suffer or die because breathing is prevented.
suffocation noun

sugar noun
a sweet food obtained from the juices of various plants, such as sugar cane or sugar beet.
sugar verb **sugary** adjective
[via early French from Arabic]

suggest verb (suggests, suggesting, suggested)
1 put forward an idea or plan for someone to consider. 2 cause an idea or possibility to come into the mind.
suggestion noun **suggestive** adjective

suicide noun (plural suicides)
1 killing yourself deliberately ♦ He committed suicide. 2 a person who deliberately kills himself or herself.
suicidal adjective

suit *noun* (*plural* **suits**)
1 a matching jacket and trousers, or a jacket and skirt, that are meant to be worn together. **2** a set of clothing for a particular activity ♦ *a diving suit*. **3** any of the four sets of cards (clubs, hearts, diamonds, and spades) in a pack of playing cards. **4** a lawsuit.

❶ USAGE Do not confuse with *suite*.

suit *verb* (**suits, suiting, suited**)
1 be suitable or convenient for a person or thing. **2** make a person look attractive.

suitable *adjective*
satisfactory or right for a particular person, purpose, or occasion etc.
suitably *adverb* **suitability** *noun*

suitcase *noun* (*plural* **suitcases**)
a rectangular container for carrying clothes, usually with a hinged lid and a handle.

suite (rhymes with *sweet*) *noun* (*plural* **suites**)
1 a set of furniture. **2** a set of rooms. **3** a set of short pieces of music.

❶ USAGE Do not confuse with *suit*.

sulk *verb* (**sulks, sulking, sulked**)
be silent and bad-tempered because you are not pleased.
sulks *plural noun* **sulky** *adjective* **sulkily** *adverb* **sulkiness** *noun*

sullen *adjective*
sulking and gloomy.
sullenly *adverb* **sullenness** *noun*

sulphur *noun*
a yellow chemical used in industry and in medicine.
sulphurous *adjective*

sultry *adjective*
1 hot and humid ♦ *sultry weather*. **2** suggesting passion or sexual desire ♦ *her sultry smile*.
sultriness *noun*

sum *noun* (*plural* **sums**)
1 a total. **2** a problem in arithmetic. **3** an amount of money.

sum *verb* (**sums, summing, summed**)
sum up give a summary at the end of a talk etc.

summarize *verb* (**summarizes, summarizing, summarized**)
make or give a summary of something.

summary *noun* (*plural* **summaries**)
a statement of the main points of something said or written.

summary *adjective*
1 brief. **2** done or given hastily, without delay ♦ *summary punishment*.
summarily *adverb*

summer *noun* (*plural* **summers**)
the warm season between spring and autumn.
summery *adjective*

summer house *noun* (*plural* **summer houses**)
a small building providing shade in a garden or park.

summit *noun* (*plural* **summits**)
1 the top of a mountain or hill. **2** a meeting between the leaders of powerful countries ♦ *a summit conference*.

summon *verb* (**summons, summoning, summoned**)
1 order someone to come or appear. **2** call people together ♦ *A meeting of the governors was quickly summoned*.
summon up gather together your strength in order to do something ♦ *She summoned up all her courage and knocked on the door*.

sumptuous *adjective*
splendid and expensive-looking.
sumptuously *adverb*

sun *noun* (*plural* **suns**)
1 the star round which the earth travels. **2** light and warmth from the sun ♦ *Go and sit in the sun*. **3** any star in the universe round which planets travel.

sun *verb* (**suns, sunning, sunned**)
sun yourself sit or lie in the sunshine.

sunbathe *verb* (**sunbathes, sunbathing, sunbathed**)
expose your body to the sun, especially to get a tan.

sunbeam *noun* (*plural* **sunbeams**)
a ray of sun.

sunburn *noun*
redness of the skin caused by too much exposure to the sun.
sunburnt *adjective*

sundae (*say* sun-day) *noun* (*plural* **sundaes**)
a mixture of ice cream and fruit, nuts, cream, etc.

Sunday *noun*
the first day of the week, observed by Christians as a day of rest and worship.
[from Old English *sunnandaeg* = day of the sun]

sundial *noun* (*plural* **sundials**)
a device that shows the time by a shadow on a dial.

sundry *adjective*
various or several.
all and sundry everyone.

sunglasses *plural noun*
dark glasses to protect your eyes from strong sunlight.

sunken *adjective*
sunk deeply into a surface ♦ *Their cheeks were pale and sunken*.

sunlamp *noun* (*plural* **sunlamps**)
a lamp which uses ultraviolet light to give people an artificial tan.

sunlight *noun*
light from the sun.
sunlit *adjective*

sunny *adjective* (**sunnier, sunniest**)
1 full of sunshine. **2** cheerful ♦ *She was in a sunny mood.*
sunnily *adverb*

sunrise *noun* (*plural* **sunrises**)
the rising of the sun; dawn.

sunset *noun* (*plural* **sunsets**)
the setting of the sun.

sunshade *noun* (*plural* **sunshades**)
a parasol or other device to protect people from the sun.

sunshine *noun*
sunlight with no cloud between the sun and the earth.

sunstroke *noun*
illness caused by being in the sun too long.

suntan *noun* (*plural* **suntans**)
a brown colour of the skin caused by the sun.
suntanned *adjective*

super *adjective* (*informal*)
excellent or superb.

superb *adjective*
magnificent or excellent.
superbly *adverb*

superficial *adjective*
1 on the surface ♦ *a superficial cut.* **2** not deep or thorough ♦ *a superficial knowledge of French.*
superficially *adverb* **superficiality** *noun*

superfluous *adjective*
more than is needed.
superfluity *noun*

superhuman *adjective*
1 beyond ordinary human ability ♦ *their superhuman strength.* **2** higher than human; divine.

superimpose *verb* (**superimposes, superimposing, superimposed**)
place a thing on top of something else.
superimposition *noun*

superintend *verb* (**superintends, superintending, superintended**)
supervise.

superintendent *noun* (*plural* **superintendents**)
1 a supervisor. **2** a police officer above the rank of inspector.

superior *adjective*
1 higher in position or rank ♦ *She is your superior officer.* **2** better than another person or thing. **3** showing conceit.
superiority *noun*

superior *noun* (*plural* **superiors**)
a person who is higher in position or rank than someone else.

superlative *adjective*
of the highest degree or quality ♦ *superlative skill.*
superlatively *adverb*

superlative *noun* (*plural* **superlatives**)
the form of an adjective or adverb that expresses 'most' ♦ *The superlative of 'great' is 'greatest'.* (Compare **positive** and **comparative**.)

supermarket *noun* (*plural* **supermarkets**)
a large self-service shop that sells food and other goods.

supermodel *noun* (*plural* **supermodels**)
a very successful and famous fashion model.

supernatural *adjective*
not belonging to the natural world or having a natural explanation ♦ *supernatural beings such as ghosts.*

superpower *noun* (*plural* **superpowers**)
one of the most powerful nations of the world, such as the USA.

supersede *verb* (**supersedes, superseding, superseded**)
take the place of something.

supersonic *adjective*
faster than the speed of sound.

superstition *noun* (*plural* **superstitions**)
a belief or action that is not based on reason or evidence, e.g. the belief that it is unlucky to walk under a ladder.
superstitious *adjective*

supervise *verb* (**supervises, supervising, supervised**)
be in charge of a person or thing and inspect what is done.
supervision *noun* **supervisor** *noun* **supervisory** *adjective*

supper *noun* (*plural* **suppers**)
a meal eaten in the evening.

supple *adjective*
bending easily; flexible.
supplely *adverb* **suppleness** *noun*

supplement *noun* (*plural* **supplements**)
1 something added as an extra. **2** an extra section added to a book or newspaper ♦ *the colour supplement.*
supplementary *adjective*

supplement *verb* (**supplements, supplementing, supplemented**)
add to something ♦ *She supplements her pocket money by working on Saturdays.*

supply *verb* (**supplies, supplying, supplied**)
give or sell or provide what is needed or wanted.
supplier *noun*

supply *noun* (*plural* **supplies**)
1 an amount of something that is available for use when needed. **2** the action of supplying something.

support *verb* (**supports, supporting, supported**)
1 keep a person or thing from falling or sinking; hold something up. **2** give strength, help, or encouragement to someone ♦ *Support your local team.* **3** provide with the necessities of life ♦ *She has two children to support.*
supporter *noun* **supportive** *adjective*

support *noun* (*plural* **supports**)
1 the action of supporting. **2** a person or thing that supports.

suppose *verb* (**supposes, supposing, supposed**)
1 think that something is likely to happen or be true. **2** assume; consider as a suggestion ♦ *Suppose the world were flat.*
supposedly *adverb* **supposition** *noun*
be supposed to be expected to do something; have as a duty.

suppress *verb* (**suppresses, suppressing, suppressed**)
1 put an end to something forcibly or by authority ♦ *Troops suppressed the rebellion.*
2 keep something from being known or seen ♦ *They suppressed the truth.*
suppression *noun* **suppressor** *noun*

supreme *adjective*
1 most important or highest in rank. **2** greatest ♦ *supreme courage.*
supremely *adverb* **supremacy** *noun*

sure *adjective*
1 completely confident that you are right; feeling no doubt. **2** certain to happen or do something ♦ *Our team is sure to win.* **3** reliable; undoubtedly true.
sureness *noun*
for sure definitely. **make sure** **1** find out exactly. **2** make something happen or be true ♦ *Make sure the door is locked.*

surely *adverb*
1 in a sure or certain way. **2** I feel sure ♦ *Surely we met last year.*

surf *noun*
the white foam of waves breaking on a rock or shore.

surf *verb* (**surfs, surfing, surfed**)
1 go surfing. **2** browse through the Internet.

surface *noun* (*plural* **surfaces**)
1 the outside of something. **2** any of the sides of an object, especially the top part. **3** an outward appearance ♦ *On the surface he was a kindly man.*

surfboard *noun* (*plural* **surfboards**)
a board used in surfing.

surfeit (*say* **ser**-fit) *noun*
too much of something.
surfeited *adjective*

surfing *noun*
balancing yourself on a board that is carried to the shore on the waves.
surfer *noun*

surf-riding *noun*
surfing.
surf-rider *noun*

surge *verb* (**surges, surging, surged**)
1 move forwards or upwards like waves.
2 increase suddenly and powerfully.
surge *noun*

surgeon *noun* (*plural* **surgeons**)
a doctor who treats disease or injury by removing or repairing the affected parts of the body.

surgery *noun* (*plural* **surgeries**)
1 the work of a surgeon. **2** the place where a doctor or dentist etc. regularly gives advice and treatment to patients. **3** the time when patients can visit the doctor etc.
surgical *adjective* **surgically** *adverb*

surly *adjective* (**surlier, surliest**)
bad-tempered and unfriendly.
surliness *noun*

surname *noun* (*plural* **surnames**)
the name held by all members of a family.

surpass *verb* (**surpasses, surpassing, surpassed**)
do or be better than all others; excel.

surplus *noun* (*plural* **surpluses**)
an amount left over after spending or using all that was needed.
surplus *adjective*

surprise *noun* (*plural* **surprises**)
1 something unexpected. **2** the feeling caused by something that was not expected.
take someone by surprise happen to someone unexpectedly.

surprise *verb* (**surprises, surprising, surprised**)
1 be a surprise; make someone feel surprise.
2 come upon or attack somebody unexpectedly.
surprisingly *adverb*

surrender *verb* (**surrenders, surrendering, surrendered**)
1 stop fighting and give yourself up to an enemy.
2 hand something over to another person, especially when compelled to do so.
surrender *noun*

surreptitious (*say* su-rep-**tish**-us) *adjective*
stealthy.
surreptitiously *adverb*

surrogate mother *noun* (*plural* **surrogate mothers**)
a woman who agrees to conceive and give birth to a baby for a woman who cannot do so herself, using a fertilized egg of the other woman or sperm from the other woman's partner.

surround *verb* (**surrounds, surrounding, surrounded**)
come or be all round a person or thing ♦ *Police surrounded the building.*

surroundings *plural noun*
the conditions or area around a person or thing.

survey (*say* ser-vay) *noun* (*plural* **surveys**)
1 a general look at something. 2 an inspection of an area, building, etc.

survey (*say* ser-vay) *verb* (**surveys, surveying, surveyed**)
make a survey of something; inspect.
surveyor *noun*

survival *noun* (*plural* **survivals**)
1 surviving; the likelihood of surviving.
2 something that has survived from an earlier time.

survive *verb* (**survives, surviving, survived**)
1 stay alive; continue to exist. 2 remain alive after an accident or disaster ♦ *Only two people survived the crash.* 3 continue living after someone has died.
survivor *noun*

susceptible (*say* sus-**ept**-ib-ul) *adjective*
likely to be affected by something ♦ *She is susceptible to colds.*
susceptibility *noun*

suspect (*say* sus-**pekt**) *verb* (**suspects, suspecting, suspected**)
1 think that a person is not to be trusted or has committed a crime; distrust. 2 have a feeling that something is likely or possible.

suspect (*say* sus-pekt) *noun* (*plural* **suspects**)
a person who is suspected of a crime etc.
suspect *adjective*

suspend *verb* (**suspends, suspending, suspended**)
1 hang something up. 2 postpone; stop something temporarily. 3 remove a person from a job or position for a time. 4 keep something from falling or sinking in air or liquid,
♦ *Particles are suspended in the fluid.*

suspender *noun* (*plural* **suspenders**)
a fastener to hold up a sock or stocking by its top.

suspense *noun*
an anxious or uncertain feeling while waiting for something to happen or become known.

suspension *noun*
1 suspending. 2 the springs etc. in a vehicle that lessen the effect of rough road surfaces.
3 a liquid containing small pieces of solid material which do not dissolve.

suspicion *noun* (*plural* **suspicions**)
1 suspecting or being suspected; distrust.
2 a slight belief.

suspicious *adjective*
feeling or causing suspicion.
suspiciously *adverb*

sustain *verb* (**sustains, sustaining, sustained**)
1 keep someone alive. 2 keep something happening. 3 undergo or suffer ♦ *We sustained another defeat.* 4 support or uphold.
sustainable *adjective*

SW *abbreviation*
1 south-west. 2 south-western.

swab (*say* swob) *noun* (*plural* **swabs**)
1 a mop or pad for cleaning or wiping something; a small pad for cleaning a wound.
2 a specimen of fluid from the body taken on a swab for testing.

swab *verb* (**swabs, swabbing, swabbed**)
clean or wipe with a swab.

swagger *verb* (**swaggers, swaggering, swaggered**)
walk or behave in a conceited way; strut.
swagger *noun*

swallow¹ *verb* (**swallows, swallowing, swallowed**)
1 make something go down your throat.
2 believe something that ought not to be believed.
swallow *noun*
swallow up take in and cover; engulf ♦ *She was swallowed up in the crowd.*
[from Old English *swelgan*]

swallow² *noun* (*plural* **swallows**)
a small bird with a forked tail and pointed wings.
[from Old English *swealwe*]

swamp *noun* (*plural* **swamps**)
a marsh.
swampy *adjective*

swamp *verb* (**swamps, swamping, swamped**)
1 flood. 2 overwhelm with a great mass or number of things.

swan *noun* (*plural* **swans**)
a large white water bird with a long neck.

swank *verb* (**swanks, swanking, swanked**)
(*informal*)
boast or swagger; show off.
swank *noun* (*informal*)
showing yourself or your possessions off in a conceited way.

swansong *noun* (*plural* **swansongs**)
a person's last performance or work.

swap *verb* (**swaps, swapping, swapped**)
(*informal*)
exchange one thing for another.
swap *noun*
[formerly = seal a bargain by slapping each other's hands; imitating the sound]

swarm *noun* (*plural* **swarms**)
a large number of insects or birds etc. flying or moving about together.

swarm *verb* (**swarms, swarming, swarmed**)
1 gather or move in a swarm. 2 be crowded with people etc. ♦ *The town is swarming with tourists in the summer.*

swarthy *adjective*
having a dark complexion.
swarthiness *noun*

swastika *noun* (*plural* **swastikas**)
an ancient symbol formed by a cross with its
ends bent at right angles, adopted by the Nazis as
their sign.
[from Sanskrit *svasti* = well-being, luck]

swat *verb* (**swats, swatting, swatted**)
hit or crush a fly etc.
swatter *noun*

swathe (*say* swayth) *verb* (**swathes, swathing,
swathed**)
wrap in layers of bandages, paper, or clothes etc.

swathe *noun* (*plural* **swathes**)
a broad strip or area ♦ *vast swathes of
countryside.*

sway *verb* (**sways, swaying, swayed**)
1 move or swing gently from side to side.
2 influence ♦ *His speech swayed the crowd.*
sway *noun*

swear *verb* (**swears, swearing, swore, sworn**)
1 make a solemn promise ♦ *She swore to tell the
truth.* **2** make a person take an oath ♦ *We swore
him to secrecy.* **3** use curses or coarse words in
anger or surprise etc.
swear by have great confidence in something.

sweat (*say* swet) *noun*
moisture given off by the body through the pores
of the skin; perspiration.
sweaty *adjective*

sweat *verb* (**sweats, sweating, sweated**)
give off sweat; perspire.

sweater *noun* (*plural* **sweaters**)
a jersey or pullover.

sweatshirt *noun* (*plural* **sweatshirts**)
a thick cotton jersey worn for sports or casual
wear.

sweep *verb* (**sweeps, sweeping, swept**)
1 clean or clear with a broom or brush etc.
2 move or remove quickly ♦ *The floods swept
away the bridge.* **3** go smoothly and quickly
♦ *She swept out of the room.* **4** spread quickly
over an area ♦ *A new craze is sweeping the
country.*
sweeper *noun*

sweep *noun* (*plural* **sweeps**)
1 the process of sweeping ♦ *Give this room
a good sweep.* **2** a sweeping movement.
3 a chimney sweep. **4** a sweepstake.

sweeping *adjective*
general or wide-ranging ♦ *He made sweeping
changes.*

sweet *adjective*
1 tasting as if it contains sugar; not bitter.
2 very pleasant ♦ *a sweet smell.* **3** charming
or delightful.
sweetly *adverb* **sweetness** *noun*
a sweet tooth a liking for sweet things.

sweet *noun* (*plural* **sweets**)
1 a small shaped piece of sweet food made with
sugar, chocolate, etc. **2** a pudding; the sweet
course in a meal. **3** a beloved person.

sweeten *verb* (**sweetens, sweetening,
sweetened**)
make or become sweet.
sweetener *noun*

sweetheart *noun* (*plural* **sweethearts**)
a person you love very much.

swell *verb* (**swells, swelling, swelled, swollen**
or **swelled**)
1 make or become larger ♦ *My ankle was
starting to swell.* **2** increase in amount, volume,
or force.

swell *noun* (*plural* **swells**)
1 the process of swelling. **2** the rise and fall of the
sea's surface.

swelling *noun* (*plural* **swellings**)
a swollen place.

swerve *verb* (**swerves, swerving, swerved**)
turn to one side suddenly.
swerve *noun*

swift *adjective*
quick or rapid.
swiftly *adverb* **swiftness** *noun*

swift *noun* (*plural* **swifts**)
a small bird rather like a swallow.

swill *verb* (**swills, swilling, swilled**)
pour water over or through something; wash or
rinse.

swim *verb* (**swims, swimming, swam, swum**)
1 move the body through the water; be in
the water for pleasure. **2** cross by swimming
♦ *She swam the Channel.* **3** float. **4** be covered
with or full of liquid ♦ *Our eyes were swimming
in tears.* **5** feel dizzy ♦ *His head swam.*
swimmer *noun*

swim *noun* (*plural* **swims**)
the action of swimming ♦ *We went for a swim.*
swimsuit *noun*

swimming bath *noun* (*plural* **swimming
baths**)
a public swimming pool.

swimming pool *noun* (*plural* **swimming
pools**)
an artificial pool for swimming in.

swindle *verb* (**swindles, swindling, swindled**)
cheat a person in business etc.
swindle *noun* **swindler** *noun*
[from German *Schwindler* = a fool, a cheat]

swine *noun* (*plural* **swine**)
1 a pig. **2** (*informal*) a very unpleasant person.

swing *verb* (**swings, swinging, swung**)
1 move back and forth while hanging. **2** move or
turn in a curve ♦ *The door swung open.* **3** change
from one opinion or mood etc. to another.

swing *noun* (*plural* **swings**)
1 a swinging movement. 2 a seat hung on chains or ropes etc. so that it can be moved backwards and forwards. 3 the amount by which votes or opinions etc. change from one side to another. 4 a kind of jazz music.
in full swing at the height of activity.

swipe *verb* (**swipes, swiping, swiped**)
1 hit with a swinging blow. 2 (*informal*) steal something. 3 pass a credit card through an electronic reading device when making a payment.
swipe *noun*

swirl *verb* (**swirls, swirling, swirled**)
move round quickly in circles.
swirl *noun*
[probably from early German or Dutch]

swish *verb* (**swishes, swishing, swished**)
move with a hissing sound.
swish *noun*

Swiss roll *noun* (*plural* **Swiss rolls**)
a thin sponge cake spread with jam or cream and rolled up.

switch *noun* (*plural* **switches**)
1 a device that is pressed or turned to start or stop something working, especially by electricity. 2 a change of opinion, policy, or methods. 3 a mechanism for moving the points on a railway track. 4 a flexible rod or whip.
switch *verb* (**switches, switching, switched**)
1 turn something on or off by means of a switch. 2 change or replace something.

switchback *noun* (*plural* **switchbacks**)
a railway at a fair, with steep slopes up and down alternately.

switchboard *noun* (*plural* **switchboards**)
a panel with switches etc. for making telephone connections or operating electric circuits.

swivel *verb* (**swivels, swivelling, swivelled**)
turn round.
swivel *noun* (*plural* **swivels**)
a device joining two things so that one can revolve without turning the other.

swollen *past participle* of **swell**.

swoon *verb* (**swoons, swooning, swooned**)
(*old use* or *poetical*)
faint.
swoon *noun*

swoop *verb* (**swoops, swooping, swooped**)
1 come down with a rushing movement. 2 make a sudden attack or raid.
swoop *noun*

sword (*say* sord) *noun* (*plural* **swords**)
a weapon with a long pointed blade fixed in a handle or hilt.
swordsman *noun*

swordfish *noun* (*plural* **swordfish**)
a large sea fish with a long sword-like upper jaw.

sworn *adjective*
1 given under oath, ♦ *sworn testimony*.
2 determined to remain so ♦ *They are sworn enemies*.

swot *verb* (**swots, swotting, swotted**) (*slang*)
study hard.
swot *noun*
[originally a dialect word for *sweat*]

sycamore *noun* (*plural* **sycamores**)
a tall tree with winged seeds, often grown for its timber.

syllable *noun* (*plural* **syllables**)
a word or part of a word that has one vowel sound when you say it ♦ *'Cat' has one syllable, 'el-e-phant' has three syllables*.
syllabic *adjective*

syllabus *noun* (*plural* **syllabuses**)
a summary of the things to be studied by a class or for an examination etc.
[via Latin from Greek *sittuba* = label. The *tt* was misread in Latin as *ll*]

symbol *noun* (*plural* **symbols**)
1 a thing used as a sign ♦ *The crescent is a symbol of Islam*. 2 a mark or sign with a special meaning (e.g. +, −, and ÷ in mathematics).

---

❶ USAGE Do not confuse with *cymbal*.

---

symbolic *adjective*
acting as a symbol of something; representing something.
symbolical *adjective* **symbolically** *adverb*

symbolize *verb* (**symbolizes, symbolizing, symbolized**)
make or be a symbol of something.

symmetrical *adjective*
able to be divided into two halves which are exactly the same but the opposite way round.
symmetrically *adverb* **symmetry** *noun*

sympathize *verb* (**sympathizes, sympathizing, sympathized**)
show or feel sympathy.
sympathizer *noun*

sympathy *noun* (*plural* **sympathies**)
1 the sharing or understanding of other people's feelings, opinions, etc. 2 a feeling of pity or tenderness towards someone who is hurt, sad, or in trouble.
sympathetic *adjective* **sympathetically** *adverb*

symphony *noun* (*plural* **symphonies**)
a long piece of music for an orchestra.
symphonic *adjective*

symptom *noun* (*plural* **symptoms**)
a sign that a disease or condition exists ♦ *Red spots are a symptom of measles*.
symptomatic *adjective*

synagogue (*say* sin-a-gog) *noun* (*plural* **synagogues**)
a place where Jews meet for worship.

syndicate noun (plural **syndicates**)
1 a group of people or firms who work together in business. **2** a group of people who buy something together, or who gamble together, sharing the cost and any gains.

syndrome noun (plural **syndromes**)
a set of signs that are characteristic of a condition, especially of a disease.

synonym (say sin-o-nim) noun (plural **synonyms**)
a word that means the same or almost the same as another word ♦ 'Large' and 'great' are synonyms of 'big'.
synonymous (say sin-on-im-us) adjective

syntax (say sin-taks) noun
the way words are arranged to make phrases or sentences.
syntactic adjective **syntactically** adverb

synthesizer noun (plural **synthesizers**)
an electronic musical instrument that can make a large variety of sounds.

synthetic adjective
artificially made; not natural.
synthetically adverb

syringe noun (plural **syringes**)
a device for sucking in a liquid and squirting it out.
[from Greek syrinx = pipe, tube]

syrup noun
a thick sweet liquid.
syrupy adjective
[from Arabic sharab = a drink]

system noun (plural **systems**)
1 a set of parts, things, or ideas that are organized to work together. **2** a way of doing something ♦ a new system of training motorcyclists.

systematic adjective
methodical; carefully planned.
systematically adverb

Tt

tab noun (plural **tabs**)
a small flap or strip that sticks out.

tabby noun (plural **tabbies**)
a grey or brown cat with dark stripes.

table noun (plural **tables**)
1 a piece of furniture with a flat top supported on legs. **2** a list of facts or figures arranged in order. **3** a list of the results of multiplying a number by other numbers ♦ multiplication tables.

tablecloth noun (plural **tablecloths**)
a cloth for covering a table, especially at meals.

tablespoon noun (plural **tablespoons**)
a large spoon for serving food.
tablespoonful noun

tablet noun (plural **tablets**)
1 a pill. **2** a solid piece of soap. **3** a flat piece of stone or wood etc. with words carved or written on it.

table tennis noun
a game played on a table divided by a net, over which you hit a small ball with bats.

taboo adjective
not to be done or used or talked about.
taboo noun
[from Tongan (South Pacific) tabu = sacred]

tack¹ noun (plural **tacks**)
1 a short nail with a flat top. **2** a tacking stitch. **3** (in sailing) the direction taken when tacking. **4** a course of action or policy ♦ I think we need to change tack.
tack verb (tacks, tacking, tacked)
1 nail something down with tacks. **2** fasten material together with long stitches. **3** sail a zigzag course to take advantage of what wind there is.
tack on (informal) add an extra thing.

tack² noun
harness, saddles, etc.

tackle verb (tackles, tackling, tackled)
1 try to do something that needs doing. **2** try to get the ball from someone else in a game of football or hockey. **3** talk to someone about a difficult or awkward matter.
tackle noun (plural **tackles**)
1 equipment, especially for fishing. **2** a set of ropes and pulleys. **3** tackling someone in football or hockey.

tacky adjective
sticky, not quite dry ♦ The paint is still tacky.
tackiness noun

tact noun
skill in not offending people.
tactful adjective **tactfully** adverb **tactless** adjective **tactlessly** adverb

tactics noun
1 the method of arranging troops etc. skilfully for a battle. **2** the methods you use to achieve something or gain an advantage.
tactical adjective **tactically** adverb **tactician** noun
[from Greek taktika = things arranged]

ⓘ USAGE Strategy is a general plan for a whole campaign; tactics is for one part of this.

---

tadpole noun (plural **tadpoles**)
a young frog or toad that has developed from the egg and lives entirely in water.

tag¹ *noun* (*plural* **tags**)
1 a label tied on or stuck into something.
2 a metal or plastic point at the end of a shoelace.
tag *verb* (**tags, tagging, tagged**)
1 label something with a tag. 2 add as an extra thing ♦ *A postscript was tagged on to her letter.*
3 (*informal*) go with other people ♦ *Her sister tagged along.*
tag² *noun*
a game in which one person chases the others.

tail *noun* (*plural* **tails**)
1 the part that sticks out from the rear end of the body of a bird, fish, or animal. 2 the part at the end or rear of something. 3 the side of a coin opposite the head ♦ *Heads or tails?*
tail *verb* (**tails, tailing, tailed**)
1 remove stalks etc. from fruit ♦ *top and tail gooseberries.* 2 (*informal*) follow someone closely.
tail off become fewer, smaller, or slighter etc.; cease gradually.

tailor *noun* (*plural* **tailors**)
a person who makes men's clothes.

taint *noun* (*plural* **taints**)
a small amount of decay, pollution, or a bad quality that spoils something.
taint *verb* (**taints, tainting, tainted**)
give something a taint.

take *verb* (**takes, taking, took, taken**)
1 get something into your hands or possession or control etc. ♦ *Take this cup.* ♦ *We took many prisoners.* 2 carry or convey ♦ *Take this parcel to the post.* 3 make use of ♦ *Shall we take a taxi?* 4 indulge in or undertake ♦ *You need to take a holiday.* 5 perform or deal with ♦ *When do you take your music exam?* 6 study or teach a subject ♦ *Who takes you for maths?* 7 make an effort ♦ *Thanks for taking the trouble to see me.* 8 experience a feeling ♦ *Don't take offence.* 9 accept or endure ♦ *I'll take a risk.* 10 require ♦ *It takes a strong man to lift this.* 11 write down ♦ *take notes.* 12 make a photograph. 13 subtract ♦ *take 4 from 10.* 14 assume ♦ *I take it that you agree.*
taker *noun*
take after be like a parent etc. **take in** deceive somebody. **take leave of** say goodbye to. **take off** (said about an aircraft) leave the ground and become airborne. **take-off** *noun* **take on** 1 begin to employ someone. 2 play or fight against someone. 3 (*informal*) show that you are upset. **take over** take control. **takeover** *noun* **take place** happen or occur. **take up** 1 start something. 2 occupy space or time etc. 3 accept an offer.
[from Old Norse]

takeaway *noun* (*plural* **takeaways**)
1 a place that sells cooked meals for customers to take away. 2 a meal from this.

tale *noun* (*plural* **tales**)
a story.
[from Old English]

talent *noun* (*plural* **talents**)
a special or very great ability.
talented *adjective*
[from Greek *talanton* = sum of money. The meaning in English is based on the use of the word in a parable in the New Testament (Matthew 25:14–30), in which a man gives his servants 'talents' of money to put to good use]

talk *verb* (**talks, talking, talked**)
speak; have a conversation.
talker *noun*
talk *noun* (*plural* **talks**)
1 a conversation or discussion. 2 an informal lecture.

talkative *adjective*
talking a lot.

tall *adjective*
1 higher than the average ♦ *a tall tree.*
2 measured from the bottom to the top
♦ *It is 10 metres tall.*
tallness *noun*

tall story *noun* (*plural* **tall stories**) (*informal*)
a story that is hard to believe.

tally *verb* (**tallies, tallying, tallied**)
correspond or agree with something else
♦ *Does your list tally with mine?*

talon *noun* (*plural* **talons**)
a strong claw.

tambourine *noun* (*plural* **tambourines**)
a circular musical instrument with metal discs round it, tapped or shaken to make it jingle.

tame *adjective*
1 (said about animals) gentle and not afraid of people; not wild or dangerous. 2 not exciting; dull.
tamely *adverb* **tameness** *noun*
tame *verb* (**tames, taming, tamed**)
make an animal become tame.
tamer *noun*

tamper *verb* (**tampers, tampering, tampered**)
meddle or interfere with something.

tampon *noun* (*plural* **tampons**)
a plug of soft material that a woman puts into her vagina to absorb the blood during her period.

tan *noun* (*plural* **tans**)
1 a light brown colour. 2 a brown colour in skin that has been exposed to sun.
tan *verb* (**tans, tanning, tanned**)
1 make or become brown by exposing skin to the sun. 2 make an animal's skin into leather by treating it with chemicals.

tandem *noun* (*plural* **tandems**)
a bicycle for two riders, one behind the other.
in tandem one behind another; together.
[Latin, = at length]

tang *noun* (*plural* **tangs**)
a strong flavour or smell.

tangent *noun* (*plural* **tangents**)
a straight line that touches the outside of a curve or circle.
go off at a tangent move away suddenly from a subject or line of thought being considered.

tangerine *noun* (*plural* **tangerines**)
a kind of small orange.

tangle *verb* (**tangles, tangling, tangled**)
make or become twisted into a confused mass.
tangle *noun*

tango *noun* (*plural* **tangos**)
a ballroom dance with gliding steps.

tank *noun* (*plural* **tanks**)
1 a large container for a liquid or gas. **2** a heavy armoured vehicle used in war.

tankard *noun* (*plural* **tankards**)
a large mug for drinking beer from, usually made of silver or pewter.

tanker *noun* (*plural* **tankers**)
1 a large ship for carrying oil. **2** a large lorry for carrying a liquid.

tantalize *verb* (**tantalizes, tantalizing, tantalized**)
tease or torment a person by showing him or her something good but keeping it out of reach.

tantrum *noun* (*plural* **tantrums**)
an outburst of bad temper.

tap¹ *noun* (*plural* **taps**)
a device for letting out liquid or gas in a controlled flow.
tap *verb* (**taps, tapping, tapped**)
1 take liquid out of something, especially through a tap. **2** obtain supplies or information etc. from a source. **3** fix a device to a telephone line so that you can overhear conversations on it.

tap² *noun* (*plural* **taps**)
a quick light hit; the sound of this.
tap *verb* (**taps, tapping, tapped**)
hit a person or thing quickly and lightly.

tape *noun* (*plural* **tapes**)
1 a narrow strip of cloth, paper, plastic, etc.
2 a narrow plastic strip coated with a magnetic substance and used for making recordings.
3 a tape recording. **4** a tape measure.
tape *verb* (**tapes, taping, taped**)
1 fix, cover, or surround something with tape.
2 record something on magnetic tape.
get or **have something taped** (*slang*) know or understand it; be able to deal with it.

tape measure *noun* (*plural* **tape measures**)
a long strip marked in centimetres or inches for measuring things.

taper *verb* (**tapers, tapering, tapered**)
1 make or become thinner towards one end.
2 make or become gradually less.

tape recorder *noun* (*plural* **tape recorders**)
a machine for recording music or sound on magnetic tape and playing it back.
tape recording *noun*

tapestry *noun* (*plural* **tapestries**)
a piece of strong cloth with pictures or patterns woven or embroidered on it.

tapeworm *noun* (*plural* **tapeworms**)
a long flat worm that can live as a parasite in the intestines of people and animals.

tar *noun*
a thick black liquid made from coal or wood etc. and used in making roads.

target *noun* (*plural* **targets**)
something aimed at; a thing that someone tries to hit or reach.

tariff *noun* (*plural* **tariffs**)
a list of prices or charges.

tarmac *noun*
an area surfaced with a mixture of tar and broken stone (called **tarmacadam**), especially on an airfield.

tarnish *verb* (**tarnishes, tarnishing, tarnished**)
1 make or become less shiny ♦ *The silver had tarnished*. **2** spoil or blemish ♦ *The scandal tarnished his reputation*.
tarnish *noun*

tarpaulin *noun* (*plural* **tarpaulins**)
a large sheet of waterproof canvas.

tarry¹ (*say* **tar**-ee) *adjective*
covered with or like tar.

tarry² (*say* **ta**-ree) *verb* (**tarries, tarrying, tarried**) (*old use*)
stay for a while longer; linger.

tart¹ *noun* (*plural* **tarts**)
an open pastry case with a sweet filling.

tart² *adjective*
1 sour. **2** sharp in manner ♦ *a tart reply*.
tartly *adverb* **tartness** *noun*

tartan *noun*
a pattern with coloured stripes crossing each other, especially one that is used by a Scottish clan.

tartar¹ *noun* (*plural* **tartars**)
a person who is fierce or difficult to deal with.

tartar² *noun* (*plural* **tartars**)
a hard chalky deposit that forms on teeth.

task *noun* (*plural* **tasks**)
a piece of work to be done.
take a person to task rebuke him or her.

tassel *noun* (*plural* **tassels**)
a bundle of threads tied together at the top and used to decorate something.
tasselled *adjective*

taste *verb* (**tastes, tasting, tasted**)
1 take a small amount of food or drink to try its flavour. **2** be able to perceive flavours. **3** have a certain flavour.

taste noun (plural **tastes**)
1 the feeling caused in the tongue by something placed on it. **2** the ability to taste things. **3** the ability to enjoy beautiful things or to choose what is suitable ♦ She shows good taste in her choice of clothes. **4** a liking ♦ I've developed quite a taste for skiing. **5** a very small amount of food or drink.

tasteful adjective
showing good taste.
tastefully adverb **tastefulness** noun

tasteless adjective
1 having no flavour. **2** showing poor taste.
tastelessly adverb **tastelessness** noun

tasty adjective (**tastier, tastiest**)
having a strong pleasant taste.

tattered adjective
badly torn; ragged.

tatters plural noun
rags; badly torn pieces.
in tatters torn to pieces ♦ My coat was in tatters.

tattoo¹ verb (**tattoos, tattooing, tattooed**)
mark a person's skin permanently with a picture or pattern by using a needle and dye.

tattoo noun (plural **tattoos**)
a tattooed picture or pattern.
[from a Polynesian (South Pacific) language]

tattoo² noun (plural **tattoos**)
1 a drumming or tapping sound. **2** an entertainment consisting of military music, marching, etc.
[from Dutch taptoe = close the tap of a cask]

taunt verb (**taunts, taunting, taunted**)
jeer at or insult someone.
taunt noun

taut adjective
stretched tightly.
tautly adverb **tautness** noun

tautology noun (plural **tautologies**)
saying the same thing again in different words, e.g. ♦ You can get the book free for nothing (where free and for nothing mean the same).

tavern noun (plural **taverns**) (old use)
an inn or public house.

tawny adjective
brownish-yellow.

tax noun (plural **taxes**)
1 money that people or business firms have to pay to the government, to be used for public purposes. **2** a strain or burden ♦ The long walk was a tax on his strength.

tax verb (**taxes, taxing, taxed**)
1 put a tax on something. **2** charge someone a tax. **3** pay the tax on something ♦ I have taxed the car up to June. **4** put a strain or burden on a person or thing ♦ This will tax your strength. **5** accuse ♦ I taxed him with leaving the door open.
taxable adjective **taxation** noun

taxi noun (plural **taxis**)
a car that carries passengers for payment, usually with a meter to record the fare to be paid.
taxicab noun

taxi verb (**taxies, taxiing, taxied**)
(said about an aircraft) move along the ground or water, especially before or after flying.

tea noun (plural **teas**)
1 a drink made by pouring hot water on the dried leaves of an evergreen shrub. **2** these dried leaves. **3** a drink made with the leaves of other plants ♦ camomile tea. **4** a meal in the afternoon or early evening.
teacup noun **tea leaf** noun **teatime** noun
[via Dutch from Chinese]

tea bag noun (plural **tea bags**)
a small bag holding about a teaspoonful of tea.

teach verb (**teaches, teaching, taught**)
1 give a person knowledge or skill; train.
2 give lessons, especially in a particular subject. **3** show someone what to do or avoid ♦ That will teach you not to meddle!

teacher noun (plural **teachers**)
a person who teaches others, especially in a school.

team noun (plural **teams**)
1 a set of players forming one side in certain games and sports. **2** a set of people working together. **3** two or more animals harnessed to pull a vehicle or a plough etc.

teapot noun (plural **teapots**)
a pot with a lid and a handle, for making and pouring tea.

tear¹ (say teer) noun (plural **tears**)
a drop of the water that comes from the eyes when a person cries.
teardrop noun
in tears crying.

tear² (say tair) verb (**tears, tearing, tore, torn**)
1 pull something apart, away, or into pieces.
2 become torn ♦ Newspaper tears easily.
3 (informal) run or travel hurriedly.
tear noun (plural **tears**)
a split made by tearing.

tear gas noun
a gas that makes people's eyes water painfully.

tease verb (**teases, teasing, teased**)
1 amuse yourself by deliberately annoying or making fun of someone. **2** pick threads apart into separate strands.
tease noun (plural **teases**)
a person who often teases others.

teaspoon noun (plural **teaspoons**)
a small spoon for stirring tea etc.
teaspoonful noun

tea towel noun (plural **tea towels**)
a cloth for drying washed dishes, cutlery, etc.

technical *adjective*
1 to do with technology. 2 to do with a particular subject and its methods ♦ *the technical terms of chemistry.* 3 using language that only experts can understand.
technically *adverb*

technical college *noun* (*plural* **technical colleges**)
a college where technical subjects are taught.

technicality *noun* (*plural* **technicalities**)
1 being technical. 2 a technical word, phrase, or detail.

technician *noun* (*plural* **technicians**)
a person whose job is to look after scientific equipment and do practical work in a laboratory.

technique *noun* (*plural* **techniques**)
the method of doing something skilfully.

technology *noun* (*plural* **technologies**)
the study of machinery, engineering, and how things work.
technological *adjective* **technologist** *noun*

teddy bear *noun* (*plural* **teddy bears**)
a soft furry toy bear.

tedious *adjective*
annoyingly slow or long; boring.
tediously *adverb* **tediousness** *noun* **tedium** *noun*

tee *noun* (*plural* **tees**)
1 the flat area from which golfers strike the ball at the start of play for each hole. 2 a small piece of wood or plastic on which a golf ball is placed for being struck.

teem *verb* (**teems, teeming, teemed**)
be full of something ♦ *The river was teeming with fish.*

teenage *adjective*
to do with teenagers.

teenager *noun* (*plural* **teenagers**)
a person in his or her teens.

teens *plural noun*
the time of life between 13 and 19 years of age.

teething *noun*
(said about a baby) having its first teeth beginning to grow through the gums.

teetotal *adjective*
never drinking alcohol.
teetotaller *noun*

telecommunications *plural noun*
communications over a long distance, e.g. by telephone, telegraph, radio, or television.

telegram *noun* (*plural* **telegrams**)
a message sent by telegraph.

telegraph *noun*
a way of sending messages by using electric current along wires or by radio.
telegraphic *adjective* **telegraphy** *noun*

telepathy (*say* til-ep-ath-ee) *noun*
communication of thoughts from one person's mind to another without speaking, writing, or gestures.
telepathic *adjective*

telephone *noun* (*plural* **telephones**)
a device or system using electric wires or radio etc. to enable one person to speak to another who is some distance away.

telephone *verb* (**telephones, telephoning, telephoned**)
speak to a person on the telephone.

telescope *noun* (*plural* **telescopes**)
an instrument using lenses to magnify distant objects.
telescopic *adjective*

telescope *verb* (**telescopes, telescoping, telescoped**)
1 make or become shorter by sliding overlapping sections into each other. 2 compress or condense something so that it takes less space or time.
[from Greek *tele-* = far + *skopein* = look at]

televise *verb* (**televises, televising, televised**)
to show a programme on television.

television *noun* (*plural* **televisions**)
1 a system using radio waves to reproduce a view of scenes, events, or plays etc. on a screen.
2 an apparatus for receiving these pictures.
3 televised programmes.
[from Greek *tele-* = far + *vision*]

tell *verb* (**tells, telling, told**)
1 make a thing known to someone, especially by words. 2 speak ♦ *Tell the truth.* 3 order ♦ *Tell them to wait.* 4 reveal a secret ♦ *Promise you won't tell.* 5 decide or distinguish ♦ *Can you tell the difference between butter and margarine?*
6 produce an effect ♦ *The strain began to tell on him.*
all told in all, all together ♦ *There are ten of them, all told.* **tell off** (*informal*) reprimand.
tell tales report something wrong or bad that someone has done.

telling *adjective*
having a strong effect or meaning ♦ *It was a telling reply.*

tell-tale *adjective*
revealing or indicating something ♦ *There was a tell-tale spot of jam on his chin.*

temper *noun* (*plural* **tempers**)
1 a person's mood ♦ *He is in a good temper.*
2 an angry mood ♦ *She was in a temper.*
lose your temper become angry.

temper *verb* (**tempers, tempering, tempered**)
1 harden or strengthen metal etc. by heating and cooling it. 2 moderate or soften the effects of something ♦ *Justice needs to be tempered with mercy.*

temperament *noun* (*plural* **temperaments**)
a person's nature as shown in the way he or she usually behaves ♦ *a nervous temperament.*

temperamental *adjective*
1 likely to become excitable or moody suddenly.
2 to do with a person's temperament.
temperamentally *adverb*

temperate *adjective*
neither extremely hot nor extremely cold
♦ *Britain has a temperate climate.*

temperature *noun* (*plural* **temperatures**)
1 how hot or cold a person or thing is.
2 an abnormally high temperature of the body.

tempest *noun* (*plural* **tempests**)
a violent storm.

template *noun* (*plural* **templates**)
a thin sheet of shaped metal, plastic, etc. used as a guide for cutting or shaping things.

temple¹ *noun* (*plural* **temples**)
a building where a god is worshipped.
[from Latin *templum* = consecrated place]

temple² *noun* (*plural* **temples**)
the part of the head between the forehead and the ear.
[from Latin *tempora* = sides of the head]

tempo *noun* (*plural* **tempos** or **tempi**)
the speed or rhythm of something, especially of a piece of music.
[Italian, from Latin *tempus* = time]

temporary *adjective*
lasting for a limited time only; not permanent.
temporarily *adverb*

tempt *verb* (**tempts, tempting, tempted**)
try to persuade or attract someone, especially into doing something wrong or unwise.
temptation *noun* **tempter** *noun* **temptress** *noun*

ten *noun* & *adjective*(*plural* **tens**)
the number 10.

tenacious (*say* ten-**ay**-shus) *adjective*
1 holding or clinging firmly to something.
2 obstinate and persistent.
tenaciously *adverb* **tenacity** *noun*

tenant *noun* (*plural* **tenants**)
a person who rents a house, building, or land etc. from a landlord.
tenancy *noun*

tend¹ *verb* (**tends, tending, tended**)
be inclined or likely to do something
♦ *Prices tend to rise.*

tend² *verb* (**tends, tending, tended**)
look after ♦ *Shepherds were tending their sheep.*

tendency *noun* (*plural* **tendencies**)
the way a person or thing is likely to behave
♦ *She has a tendency to be lazy.*

tender¹ *adjective*
1 easy to chew; not tough or hard. 2 easily hurt or damaged; sensitive or delicate ♦ *tender plants.*
3 (said about a part of the body) painful when touched. 4 gentle and loving ♦ *a tender smile.*
tenderly *adverb* **tenderness** *noun*

tender² *verb* (**tenders, tendering, tendered**)
offer something formally ♦ *He tendered his resignation.*

tender *noun* (*plural* **tenders**)
a formal offer to supply goods or carry out work at a stated price ♦ *The council asked for tenders to build a school.*
legal tender kinds of money that are legal for making payments ♦ *Pound notes are no longer legal tender.*

tendril *noun* (*plural* **tendrils**)
1 a thread-like part by which a climbing plant clings to a support. 2 a thin curl of hair etc.

tennis *noun*
a game played with rackets and a ball on a court with a net across the middle.

tenor *noun* (*plural* **tenors**)
1 a male singer with a high voice. 2 the general meaning or drift of something♦ *What was the tenor of her speech?*

tenpin bowling *noun*
a game in which players try to knock over ten skittles set up at the end of a track by rolling hard balls down it.

tense¹ *noun* (*plural* **tenses**)
the form of a verb that shows when something happens, e.g. he *came* (**past tense**), he *comes* or *is coming* (**present tense**), he *will come* (**future tense**).

tense² *adjective*
1 tightly stretched. 2 nervous or worried and unable to relax. 3 making people tense
♦ *a tense moment.*
tensely *adverb* **tenseness** *noun*

tense *verb* (**tenses, tensing, tensed**)
make or become tense.

tension *noun* (*plural* **tensions**)
1 how tightly stretched a rope or wire is.
2 a feeling of anxiety or nervousness about something that is just about to happen.
3 voltage ♦ *high-tension cables.*

tent *noun* (*plural* **tents**)
a shelter made of canvas or other material.

tentacle *noun* (*plural* **tentacles**)
a long flexible part of the body of certain animals (e.g. snails or octopuses), used for feeling or grasping things or for moving.

tentative *adjective*
cautious; trying something out ♦ *a tentative suggestion.*
tentatively *adverb*

tenth *adjective & noun*
next after the ninth.

tenuous *adjective*
very slight or thin ♦ *tenuous threads*;
♦ *a tenuous connection*.

tepid *adjective*
only slightly warm; lukewarm ♦ *tepid water*.

term *noun* (*plural* **terms**)
1 the period of weeks when a school or college is
open. **2** a definite period ♦ *a term of
imprisonment*. **3** a word or expression
♦ *technical terms*.

term *verb* (**terms, terming, termed**)
name; call something by a certain term
♦ *This music is termed jazz*.

terminal *noun* (*plural* **terminals**)
1 the place where something ends; a terminus.
2 a building where air passengers arrive or
depart. **3** a place where a wire is connected in an
electric circuit or battery etc. **4** a monitor and
keyboard used for putting data into a computer,
or for receiving it.

terminal *adjective*
1 to do with or at the end or boundary of
something. **2** (said of a disease) leading to death.
terminally *adverb*

terminate *verb* (**terminates, terminating,
terminated**)
end; stop finally.
termination *noun*

terminology *noun* (*plural* **terminologies**)
the technical terms of a subject.
terminological *adjective*

terminus *noun* (*plural* **termini** or **terminuses**)
the last station on a railway or bus route.

termite *noun* (*plural* **termites**)
a small insect that is very destructive to timber.

terms *plural noun*
1 a relationship between people ♦ *They
remained on friendly terms*. **2** conditions offered
or accepted ♦ *peace terms*.
come to terms with become reconciled to a
difficulty or unwelcome situation.

terrace *noun* (*plural* **terraces**)
1 a level area on a slope or hillside. **2** a paved
area beside a house. **3** a row of houses joined
together. **4** a series of steps for spectators at a
sports ground
terraced *adjective*

terrestrial *adjective*
to do with the earth or land.

terrible *adjective*
very bad; awful.
terribly *adverb*

terrier *noun* (*plural* **terriers**)
a kind of small lively dog.

terrific *adjective* (*informal*)
1 very great ♦ *a terrific storm*. **2** excellent.
terrifically *adverb*

terrify *verb* (**terrifies, terrifying, terrified**)
fill someone with terror.

territory *noun* (*plural* **territories**)
an area of land, especially one that belongs to a
country or person.
territorial *adjective*

terror *noun* (*plural* **terrors**)
1 very great fear. **2** a terrifying person or thing.

terrorist *noun* (*plural* **terrorists**)
a person who uses violence for political
purposes.
terrorism *noun*

terrorize *verb* (**terrorizes, terrorizing,
terrorized**)
fill someone with terror; frighten someone by
threatening them.
terrorization *noun*

test *noun* (*plural* **tests**)
1 a short examination. **2** a way of discovering the
qualities, abilities, or presence of a person or
thing ♦ *a test for radioactivity*. **3** a test match.

test *verb* (**tests, testing, tested**)
carry out a test on a person or thing.
tester *noun*

testament *noun* (*plural* **testaments**)
1 a written statement. **2** either of the two main
parts of the Bible, the Old Testament or the New
Testament.

testicle *noun* (*plural* **testicles**)
either of the two glands where semen is
produced.

testify *verb* (**testifies, testifying, testified**)
1 give evidence; swear that something is true.
2 be evidence or proof of something.
[from Latin *testis* = witness]

testimonial *noun* (*plural* **testimonials**)
1 a letter describing someone's abilities,
character, etc. **2** a gift presented to someone as a
mark of respect.

test match *noun* (*plural* **test matches**)
a cricket or rugby match between teams from
different countries.

testosterone (*say* test-ost-er-ohn) *noun*
a male sex hormone.

test tube *noun* (*plural* **test tubes**)
a tube of thin glass with one end closed, used for
experiments in chemistry etc.

tether *verb* (**tethers, tethering, tethered**)
tie an animal so that it cannot move far.

tether *noun* (*plural* **tethers**)
a rope for tethering an animal.
at the end of your tether unable to endure
something any more.

tetrahedron noun (plural **tetrahedrons**)
a solid with four triangular sides (i.e. a pyramid with a triangular base).

text noun (plural **texts**)
1 the words of something written or printed.
2 a sentence from the Bible used as the subject of a sermon etc.

textbook noun (plural **textbooks**)
a book that teaches you about a subject.

text message noun (plural **text messages**)
a written message sent on a mobile phone.

texture noun (plural **textures**)
the way that the surface of something feels.

than conjunction
compared with another person or thing ♦ His brother is taller than he is or taller than him.

thank verb (**thanks, thanking, thanked**)
tell someone that you are grateful to him or her.
thank you an expression of thanks.

thankful adjective
grateful.

thankfully adverb
1 in a grateful way. **2** fortunately ♦ Thankfully, John remembered to bring some money

thankless adjective
not likely to win thanks from people
♦ a thankless task.

thanks plural noun
1 statements of gratitude. **2** (informal) thank you.
thanks to as a result of; because of ♦ Thanks to your help, we succeeded.

that adjective & pronoun (plural **those**)
the one there ♦ That book is mine. ♦ Whose is that?

that adverb
to such an extent ♦ I'll come that far but no further.

that relative pronoun
which, who, or whom ♦ This is the record that I wanted. ♦ We liked the people that we met on holiday.

that conjunction
used to introduce a wish, reason, result, etc.
♦ I hope that you are well. ♦ The puzzle was so hard that no one could solve it.

thatch noun
straw or reeds used to make a roof.

thatch verb (**thatches, thatching, thatched**)
make a roof with thatch.
thatcher noun

thaw verb (**thaws, thawing, thawed**)
melt; stop being frozen.

thaw noun (plural **thaws**)
a period of warm weather that thaws ice and snow.
[from Old English]

the adjective (called the definite article)
a particular one; that or those.

theatre noun (plural **theatres**)
1 a building where plays etc. are performed to an audience. **2** the writing, acting, and producing of plays. **3** a special room where surgical operations are done ♦ the operating theatre.
[from Greek theatron = place for seeing things]

theatrical adjective
1 to do with plays or acting. **2** (said about a person's behaviour) exaggerated and done for showy effect.
theatrically adverb

thee pronoun (old use)
you (referring to one person and used as the object of a verb or after a preposition).

theft noun (plural **thefts**)
stealing.

their adjective
1 belonging to them ♦ Their coats are over there.
2 belonging to a person ♦ Somebody has left their coat on the bus.
[from Old Norse]

ⓘ USAGE Do not confuse with there or they're.

---

theirs possessive pronoun
belonging to them ♦ These coats are theirs.

ⓘ USAGE It is incorrect to write their's.

---

them pronoun
the form of they used as the object of a verb or after a preposition ♦ We saw them.

theme noun (plural **themes**)
1 the subject about which a person speaks, writes, or thinks. **2** a melody.

themselves pronoun
they or them and nobody else.

then adverb
1 at that time ♦ We were younger then.
2 after that; next ♦ Make the tea, then pour it out.
3 in that case ♦ If this is yours, then this must be mine.

theology noun
the study of religion.
theological adjective **theologian** noun
[from Greek theos = a god]

theorem noun (plural **theorems**)
a mathematical statement that can be proved by reasoning.

theoretical adjective
based on theory not on practice or experience.
theoretically adverb

theory noun (plural **theories**)
1 an idea or set of ideas put forward to explain something ♦ Darwin's theory of evolution. **2** the principles of a subject rather than its practice.
in theory according to what should happen rather than what may in fact happen.

therapy *noun* (*plural* **therapies**)
a way of treating a physical or mental illness,
especially without using surgery or medicines.
therapeutic *adjective*

there *adverb*
1 in or to that place etc. **2** used to call attention
to something (*There's a good boy!*) or to
introduce a sentence where the verb comes
before its subject (*There was plenty to eat*).

❶ USAGE Do not confuse with *their* or *they're*.

thereabouts *adverb*
near there.

therefore *adverb*
for that reason.

thermodynamics *noun*
the science dealing with the relation between
heat and other forms of energy.

thermometer *noun* (*plural* **thermometers**)
a device for measuring temperature.

thermostat *noun* (*plural* **thermostats**)
a piece of equipment that automatically keeps
the temperature of a room or piece of equipment
steady.
thermostatic *adjective* **thermostatically** *adverb*

thesaurus (*say* thi-sor-us) *noun* (*plural*
thesauruses or **thesauri**)
a kind of dictionary containing sets of words
grouped according to their meaning.
[from Greek *thesauros* = storehouse, treasury]

these *plural* of **this**.

they *pronoun*
1 the people or things being talked about.
2 people in general ♦ *They say the show is a
great success.* **3** he or she; a person ♦ *I am never
angry with anyone unless they deserve it.*

they're (*mainly spoken*)
they are.

❶ USAGE Do not confuse with *their* or *there*.

thick *adjective*
1 measuring a lot between opposite surfaces.
2 measuring from one side to the other ♦ *The
wall is ten centimetres thick.* **3** (said about a line)
broad, not fine. **4** crowded with things; dense
♦ *a thick forest*; ♦ *thick fog.* **5** fairly stiff, not
flowing easily ♦ *thick cream.* **6** (*informal*)
stupid.
thickly *adverb* **thickness** *noun*

thicken *verb* (**thickens, thickening, thickened**)
make or become thicker.

thicket *noun* (*plural* **thickets**)
a number of shrubs and small trees etc. growing
close together.

thief *noun* (*plural* **thieves**)
a person who steals things.
thievish *adjective* **thievery** *noun* **thieving** *noun*

thigh *noun* (*plural* **thighs**)
the part of the leg between the hip and the knee.

thimble *noun* (*plural* **thimbles**)
a small metal or plastic cap worn on the end of
the finger to push the needle in sewing.

thin *adjective* (**thinner, thinnest**)
1 not thick; not fat. **2** feeble ♦ *a thin excuse.*
thinly *adverb* **thinness** *noun*

thin *verb* (**thins, thinning, thinned**)
make or become less thick.
thinner *noun*
thin out make or become less dense or crowded.

thine *adjective* & *possessive pronoun* (*old use*)
yours (referring to one person).

thing *noun* (*plural* **things**)
an object; something which can be seen,
touched, thought about, etc.

think *verb* (**thinks, thinking, thought**)
1 use your mind; form connected ideas. **2** have
as an idea or opinion ♦ *Do you think we have
enough time?*
think *noun* **thinker** *noun*

third *adjective*
next after the second.
thirdly *adverb*

third *noun* (*plural* **thirds**)
1 the third person or thing. **2** one of three equal
parts of something.

Third World *noun*
the poorer countries of Asia, Africa, and South
America, also called 'developing countries'.

thirst *noun*
1 a feeling of dryness in the mouth and throat,
causing a desire to drink. **2** a strong desire
♦ *a thirst for adventure.*
thirsty *adjective* **thirstily** *adverb*

thirteen *noun* & *adjective*
the number 13.
thirteenth *noun* & *adjective*

thirty *noun* & *adjective*(*plural* **thirties**)
the number 30.
thirtieth *adjective* & *noun*

this *adjective* & *pronoun*(*plural* **these**)
the one here ♦ *This house is ours.* ♦ *Whose is
this?*

this *adverb*
to such an extent ♦ *I'm surprised he got this far.*

thistle *noun* (*plural* **thistles**)
a prickly wild plant with purple, white, or yellow
flowers.

thong *noun* (*plural* **thongs**)
a narrow strip of leather etc. used for fastening
things.

thorn *noun* (*plural* **thorns**)
1 a small pointed growth on the stem of a plant.
2 a thorny tree or shrub.

thorny *adjective* (**thornier, thorniest**)
1 having many thorns; prickly. 2 difficult
♦ *a thorny problem.*

thorough *adjective*
1 done or doing things carefully and in detail.
2 complete in every way ♦ *a thorough mess.*
thoroughly *adverb* **thoroughness** *noun*

thoroughbred *adjective*
bred of pure or pedigree stock.
thoroughbred *noun*

thoroughfare *noun* (*plural* **thoroughfares**)
a public road or path that is open at both ends.

those *plural* of that.

thou *pronoun* (*old use*)
you (referring to one person).

though *conjunction*
in spite of the fact that; even if ♦ *We can try
phoning her, though she's probably left by now.*
though *adverb*
however ♦ *She's right, though.*

thought¹ *noun* (*plural* **thoughts**)
1 something that you think; an idea or opinion.
2 the process of thinking ♦ *She was deep in
thought.*

thought² *past tense* of think.

thoughtful *adjective*
1 thinking a lot. 2 showing thought for other
people's needs; considerate.
thoughtfully *adverb* **thoughtfulness** *noun*

thoughtless *adjective*
1 careless; not thinking of what may happen.
2 inconsiderate.
thoughtlessly *adverb* **thoughtlessness** *noun*

thousand *noun* & *adjective*(*plural* **thousands**)
the number 1,000.
thousandth *adjective* & *noun*

thrash *verb* (**thrashes, thrashing, thrashed**)
1 beat someone with a stick or whip; keep
hitting very hard. 2 defeat someone thoroughly.
3 move violently ♦ *The crocodile thrashed its
tail.*
thrash something out discuss a matter
thoroughly.

thread *noun* (*plural* **threads**)
1 a thin length of any substance. 2 a length of
spun cotton, wool, or nylon etc. used for making
cloth or in sewing or knitting. 3 the spiral ridge
round a screw. 4 a theme or idea running
through a story, argument, etc. ♦ *I'm afraid I've
lost the thread.*
thread *verb* (**threads, threading, threaded**)
1 put a thread through the eye of a needle.
2 pass a strip of film etc. through or round
something. 3 put beads on a thread.

threadbare *adjective*
(said about cloth) with the surface worn away so
that the threads show.

threat *noun* (*plural* **threats**)
1 a warning that you will punish, hurt, or
harm a person or thing. 2 a sign of something
undesirable. 3 a person or thing causing danger.

threaten *verb* (**threatens, threatening,
threatened**)
1 make threats against someone. 2 be a threat or
danger to a person or thing.

three *noun* & *adjective*(*plural* **threes**)
the number 3.

three-dimensional *adjective*
having three dimensions (length, width, and
height or depth).

threshold *noun* (*plural* **thresholds**)
1 a slab of stone or board etc. forming the
bottom of a doorway; the entrance. 2 the point
at which something begins to happen or change
♦ *We are on the threshold of a great discovery.*

thrift *noun*
1 careful spending or management of money or
resources. 2 a plant with pink flowers.
thrifty *adjective* **thriftily** *adverb*

thrill *noun* (*plural* **thrills**)
a feeling of excitement.
thrill *verb* (**thrills, thrilling, thrilled**)
have or give a feeling of excitement.
thrilling *adjective*

thriller *noun* (*plural* **thrillers**)
an exciting story, play, or film, usually about
crime.

thrive *verb* (**thrives, thriving, throve, thrived**
or **thriven**)
grow strongly; prosper or be successful.
[from Old Norse, = grasp, get hold of]

throat *noun* (*plural* **throats**)
1 the tube in the neck that takes food and drink
down into the body. 2 the front of the neck.
[from Old English]

throb *verb* (**throbs, throbbing, throbbed**)
beat or vibrate with a strong rhythm ♦ *My head
throbbed with pain.*
throb *noun*

thrombosis *noun*
the formation of a clot of blood in the body.

throne *noun* (*plural* **thrones**)
1 a special chair for a king, queen, or bishop at
ceremonies. 2 the position of being king or
queen ♦ *the heir to the throne.*

throng *noun* (*plural* **throngs**)
a crowd of people.
throng *verb* (**throngs, thronging, thronged**)
crowd ♦ *People thronged the streets.*

throttle *noun* (*plural* **throttles**)
a device that controls the flow of fuel to an
engine; an accelerator.

throttle *verb* (**throttles, throttling, throttled**)
strangle.
throttle back or **down** reduce the speed of an engine by partially closing the throttle.

through *preposition*
1 from one end or side to the other end or side of ♦ *Climb through the window.* 2 by means of; because of ♦ *We lost it through carelessness.* 3 at the end of; having finished successfully ♦ *He is through his exam.*

through *adverb*
1 through something ♦ *We squeezed through.* 2 with a telephone connection made ♦ *I'll put you through to the president.* 3 finished ♦ *Wait till I'm through with these papers.*

through *adjective*
1 going through something ♦ *No through road.* 2 going all the way to a destination ♦ *a through train.*

throughout *preposition & adverb*
all the way through; from beginning to end.

throve *past tense* of **thrive.**

throw *verb* (**throws, throwing, threw, thrown**)
1 send a person or thing through the air. 2 put something in a place carelessly or hastily. 3 move part of your body quickly ♦ *He threw his head back and laughed.* 4 put someone in a certain condition etc. ♦ *It threw us into confusion.* 5 confuse or upset ♦ *Your question threw me.* 6 move a switch or lever in order to operate it. 7 shape a pot on a potter's wheel. 8 hold a party.
throw *noun* **thrower** *noun*
throw away 1 get rid of something because it is useless or unwanted. 2 waste ♦ *You threw away an opportunity.* **throw up** (*informal*) vomit.

thrush *noun* (*plural* **thrushes**)
a songbird with a speckled breast.

thrust *verb* (**thrusts, thrusting, thrust**)
push hard.
thrust *noun*

thud *verb* (**thuds, thudding, thudded**)
make the dull sound of a heavy knock or fall.
thud *noun*

thug *noun* (*plural* **thugs**)
a rough and violent person.
thuggery *noun*

thumb *noun* (*plural* **thumbs**)
the short thick finger set apart from the other four.
be under a person's thumb be completely under his or her influence.

thump *verb* (**thumps, thumping, thumped**)
1 hit or knock something heavily. 2 punch.
thump *noun*

thunder *noun*
1 the loud noise that is heard with lightning. 2 a similar noise ♦ *a thunder of applause.*
thunderous *adjective* **thunderstorm** *noun*
thundery *adjective*

thunder *verb* (**thunders, thundering, thundered**)
1 sound with thunder. 2 make a noise like thunder; speak loudly.

thunderbolt *noun* (*plural* **thunderbolts**)
a lightning flash thought of as a destructive missile.

Thursday *noun*
the day of the week following Wednesday.
[from Old English *thuresdaeg* = day of thunder, named after Thor, the Norse god of thunder]

thus *adverb*
1 in this way ♦ *Hold the wheel thus.* 2 therefore.

thwart *verb* (**thwarts, thwarting, thwarted**)
frustrate; prevent someone from achieving something.

thy *adjective* (*old use*)
your (referring to one person).

tiara (*say* tee-ar-a) *noun* (*plural* **tiaras**)
a woman's jewelled crescent-shaped ornament worn like a crown.

tic *noun* (*plural* **tics**)
an unintentional twitch of a muscle, especially of the face.

tick¹ *noun* (*plural* **ticks**)
1 a mark (usually ✓) put by something to show that it is correct or has been checked. 2 a regular clicking sound, especially that made by a clock or watch. 3 (*informal*) a moment ♦ *I won't be a tick.*

tick *verb* (**ticks, ticking, ticked**)
1 put a tick by something. 2 make the sound of a tick.
tick off (*informal*) reprimand someone.

tick² *noun* (*plural* **ticks**)
a bloodsucking insect.

ticket *noun* (*plural* **tickets**)
1 a printed piece of paper or card that allows a person to travel on a bus or train, see a show, etc. 2 a label showing a thing's price.

tickle *verb* (**tickles, tickling, tickled**)
1 touch a person's skin lightly in order to produce a slight tingling feeling and laughter. 2 (said about a part of the body) have a slight tingling or itching feeling. 3 amuse or please somebody.

ticklish *adjective*
1 likely to laugh or wriggle when tickled. 2 awkward or difficult ♦ *a ticklish situation.*

tidal wave *noun* (*plural* **tidal waves**)
a huge sea wave.

tide *noun* (*plural* **tides**)
1 the regular rise and fall in the level of the sea which usually happens twice a day. **2** (*old use*) a time or season ◆ *Christmas-tide.*

tide *verb* (**tides, tiding, tided**)
tide a person over provide him or her with what is needed, for a short time.

tidy *adjective* (**tidier, tidiest**)
1 with everything in its right place; neat and orderly. **2** (*informal*) fairly large ◆ *It costs a tidy sum.*
tidily *adverb* **tidiness** *noun*

tidy *verb* (**tidies, tidying, tidied**)
make a place tidy.

tie *verb* (**ties, tying, tied**)
1 fasten something with string, ribbon, etc.
2 arrange something into a knot or bow.
3 make the same score as another competitor.
be tied up be busy.

tie *noun* (*plural* **ties**)
1 a strip of material worn passing under the collar of a shirt and knotted in front. **2** a result when two or more competitors have equal scores. **3** one of the matches in a competition.
4 a close connection or bond ◆ *the ties of friendship.*

tier (*say* teer) *noun* (*plural* **tiers**)
each of a series of rows or levels etc. placed one above the other.
tiered *adjective*

tiff *noun* (*plural* **tiffs**)
a slight quarrel.

tiger *noun* (*plural* **tigers**)
a large wild animal of the cat family, with yellow and black stripes.
[from Greek *tigris*]

tight *adjective*
1 fitting very closely. **2** firmly fastened. **3** fully stretched; tense. **4** in short supply ◆ *Money is tight at the moment.* **5** stingy ◆ *He is very tight with his money.* **6** severe or strict ◆ *tight security.*
7 (*slang*) drunk.
tightly *adverb* **tightness** *noun*

tighten *verb* (**tightens, tightening, tightened**)
make or become tighter.

tightrope *noun* (*plural* **tightropes**)
a tightly stretched rope high above the ground, on which acrobats perform.

tights *plural noun*
a piece of clothing that fits tightly over the feet, legs, and lower part of the body.

tile *noun* (*plural* **tiles**)
a thin square piece of baked clay or other hard material, used in rows for covering roofs, walls, or floors.
tiled *adjective*

till¹ *preposition* & *conjunction*
until.
[from Old English *til* = to]

> ❶ USAGE It is better to use *until* rather than *till* when the word stands first in a sentence (e.g. ◆ *Until last year we had never been abroad*) or when you are speaking or writing formally.

till² *noun* (*plural* **tills**)
a drawer or box for money in a shop; a cash register.
[origin unknown]

tilt *verb* (**tilts, tilting, tilted**)
move into a sloping position.
tilt *noun*
a sloping position.
at full tilt at full speed or force.

timber *noun* (*plural* **timbers**)
1 wood for building or making things.
2 a wooden beam.

time *noun* (*plural* **times**)
1 all the years of the past, present, and future; the continuous existence of the universe.
2 a particular point or portion of time.
3 an occasion ◆ *the first time I saw him.*
4 a period suitable or available for something ◆ *Is there time for a cup of tea?* **5** a system of measuring time ◆ *Greenwich Mean Time.* **6** (in music) rhythm depending on the number and stress of beats in the bar.
7 (**times**) multiplied by ◆ *Five times three is 15 (5 × 3 = 15).*
at times or **from time to time** sometimes; occasionally. **in time 1** not late. **2** eventually.
on time punctual.

time *verb* (**times, timing, timed**)
1 measure how long something takes. **2** arrange when something is to happen.
timer *noun*
[from Old English]

timeless *adjective*
not affected by the passage of time; eternal.

timely *adjective*
happening at a suitable or useful time ◆ *a timely warning.*

timetable *noun* (*plural* **timetables**)
a list showing the times when things will happen, e.g. when buses or trains will arrive and depart, or when school lessons will take place.

timid *adjective*
easily frightened.
timidly *adverb* **timidity** *noun*

timing *noun*
1 the choice of time to do something. **2** the time when something happens.

timpani *plural noun*
kettledrums.

tin *noun* (*plural* **tins**)
1 a silvery-white metal. **2** a metal container for food.

tinge *verb* (**tinges, tingeing, tinged**)
1 colour something slightly. **2** add a slight amount of another feeling ♦ *Our relief was tinged with sadness.*
tinge *noun*

tingle *verb* (**tingles, tingling, tingled**)
have a slight pricking or stinging feeling.
tingle *noun*

tinker *verb* (**tinkers, tinkering, tinkered**)
work at something casually, trying to improve or mend it.

tinkle *verb* (**tinkles, tinkling, tinkled**)
make a gentle ringing sound.
tinkle *noun*

tinny *adjective*
1 like tin. **2** (said about a sound) unpleasantly thin and high-pitched.

tinsel *noun*
strips of glittering material used for decoration.

tint *noun* (*plural* **tints**)
a shade of colour, especially a pale one.
tint *verb* (**tints, tinting, tinted**)
colour something slightly.

tiny *adjective* (**tinier, tiniest**)
very small.

tip¹ *noun* (*plural* **tips**)
the part right at the top or end of something.
tip *verb* (**tips, tipping, tipped**)
put a tip on something.

tip² *noun* (*plural* **tips**)
1 a small present of money given to someone who has helped you. **2** a small but useful piece of advice; a hint.
tip *verb* (**tips, tipping, tipped**)
1 give a person a tip. **2** name someone as a likely winner ♦ *Which team would you tip to win the championship?*
tipper *noun*
tip off give a warning or special information about something. **tip-off** *noun*

tip³ *verb* (**tips, tipping, tipped**)
1 tilt or topple. **2** empty rubbish somewhere.
tip *noun* (*plural* **tips**)
1 the action of tipping something. **2** a place where rubbish etc. is tipped.

tipsy *adjective*
slightly drunk.

tiptoe *verb* (**tiptoes, tiptoeing, tiptoed**)
walk on your toes very quietly or carefully.
on tiptoe walking or standing on your toes.

tire *verb* (**tires, tiring, tired**)
make or become tired.
tiring *adjective*

tired *adjective*
feeling that you need to sleep or rest.
be tired of have had enough of something and feel impatient or bored with it.

tireless *adjective*
having a lot of energy; not tiring easily.

tiresome *adjective*
annoying.

tissue *noun* (*plural* **tissues**)
1 tissue paper. **2** a paper handkerchief. **3** the substance forming any part of the body of an animal or plant ♦ *bone tissue.*

tissue paper *noun*
very thin soft paper used for wrapping and packing things.

tit¹ *noun* (*plural* **tits**)
a kind of small bird.

tit² *noun*
tit for tat something equal given in return; retaliation.

titbit *noun* (*plural* **titbits**)
a nice little piece of something, e.g. of food, gossip, or information.

titillate *verb* (**titillates, titillating, titillated**)
stimulate or excite you pleasantly.
titillation *noun*

title *noun* (*plural* **titles**)
1 the name of a book, film, song, etc. **2** a word used to show a person's rank or position, e.g. *Dr, Lord, Mrs.* **3** a championship in sport ♦ *the world heavyweight title.* **4** a legal right to something.

titter *verb* (**titters, tittering, tittered**)
giggle.
titter *noun*

to *preposition*
This word is used to show **1** direction or arrival at a position (*We walked to school. He rose to power*), **2** limit (*from noon to two o'clock*), **3** comparison (*We won by six goals to three*), **4** receiving or being affected by something (*Give it to me. Be kind to animals*). Also used before a verb to form an infinitive (*I want to see him*) or to show purpose etc. (*He does that to annoy us*), or alone when the verb is understood (*We meant to go but forgot to*).

to *adverb*
1 to or in the proper or closed position or condition ♦ *Push the door to.* **2** into a state of activity ♦ *We set to and cleaned the kitchen.*
to and fro backwards and forwards.

toad *noun* (*plural* **toads**)
a frog-like animal that lives mainly on land.

toadstool *noun* (*plural* **toadstools**)
a fungus (usually poisonous) with a round top on a stalk.

toast *verb* (**toasts, toasting, toasted**)
1 heat bread etc. to make it brown and crisp.
2 warm something in front of a fire etc. **3** drink
in honour of someone.

toast *noun* (*plural* **toasts**)
1 toasted bread. **2** the call to drink in honour of
someone; the person honoured in this way.

tobacco *noun*
the dried leaves of certain plants prepared for
smoking in cigarettes, cigars, or pipes or for
making snuff.
[via Spanish from a Central American language]

toboggan *noun* (*plural* **toboggans**)
a small sledge used for sliding downhill.
tobogganing *noun*
[via Canadian French from a Native American
language]

today *noun*
this present day ♦ *Today is Monday.*
today *adverb*
on this day ♦ *Have you seen him today?*

toddler *noun* (*plural* **toddlers**)
a young child who has only recently learnt to
walk.
toddle *verb*

to-do *noun* (*plural* **to-dos**)
a fuss or commotion.

toe *noun* (*plural* **toes**)
1 any of the separate parts (five in humans) at
the end of each foot. **2** the part of a shoe or sock
etc. that covers the toes.
on your toes alert.

toffee *noun* (*plural* **toffees**)
a sticky sweet made from heated butter and
sugar.

together *adverb*
with another person or thing; with each other
♦ *They went to the party together.*

toil *verb* (**toils, toiling, toiled**)
1 work hard. **2** move slowly and with difficulty.
toiler *noun*
toil *noun*
hard work.

toilet *noun* (*plural* **toilets**)
1 a bowl-like object, connected by pipes to a
drain, which you use to get rid of urine and
faeces.
2 a room containing a toilet. **3** the
process of washing, dressing, and tidying
yourself.

token *noun* (*plural* **tokens**)
1 a piece of metal or plastic that can be used
instead of money. **2** a voucher or coupon that
can be exchanged for goods. **3** a sign or signal of
something ♦ *a token of our friendship.*

tolerable *adjective*
able to be tolerated.
tolerably *adverb*

tolerant *adjective*
willing to accept or tolerate other people's
behaviour and opinions even if you do not agree
with them.
tolerantly *adverb* **tolerance** *noun*

tolerate *verb* (**tolerates, tolerating, tolerated**)
1 allow something even if you do not approve of
it. **2** bear or put up with something unpleasant.
toleration *noun*

toll[1] (rhymes with *hole*) *noun* (*plural* **tolls**)
1 a charge made for using a road, bridge, etc.
2 loss or damage caused ♦ *The death toll in the
earthquake is rising.*

toll[2] (rhymes with *hole*) *verb* (**tolls, tolling,
tolled**)
ring a bell slowly.
toll *noun*

tom *noun* (*plural* **toms**)
a male cat.
tomcat *noun*

tomato *noun* (*plural* **tomatoes**)
a soft round red fruit eaten as a vegetable.
[via French, Spanish, or Portuguese from
Nahuatl (a Central American language)]

tomb (*say* toom) *noun* (*plural* **tombs**)
a place where someone is buried; a monument
built over this.

tomboy *noun* (*plural* **tomboys**)
a girl who enjoys rough noisy games etc.

tombstone *noun* (*plural* **tombstones**)
a memorial stone set up over a grave.

tomorrow *noun* & *adverb*
the day after today.

ton *noun* (*plural* **tons**)
1 a unit of weight equal to 2,240 pounds or about
1,016 kilograms. **2** a large amount ♦ *There's tons
of room.* **3** (*slang*) a speed of 100 miles per hour.

tone *noun* (*plural* **tones**)
1 a sound in music or of the voice. **2** each of the
five larger intervals between notes in a musical
scale (the smaller intervals are **semitones**).
3 a shade of a colour. **4** the quality or character
of something ♦ *a cheerful tone.*
tonal *adjective* **tonally** *adverb*
tone *verb* (**tones, toning, toned**)
1 give a particular tone or quality to something.
2 be harmonious in colour.
tone down make a thing quieter or less bright or
less harsh.
[from Greek *tonos* = tension]

tongs *plural noun*
a tool with two arms joined at one end, used to
pick up or hold things.

tongue *noun* (*plural* **tongues**)
1 the long soft muscular part that moves about inside the mouth. **2** a language. **3** the leather flap on a shoe or boot underneath the laces. **4** a pointed flame.
[from Old English]

tongue-tied *adjective*
too shy to speak.

tonic *noun* (*plural* **tonics**)
1 a medicine etc. that makes a person healthier or stronger. **2** anything that makes a person more energetic or cheerful. **3** a fizzy mineral water with a bitter taste, often mixed with gin. **4** a keynote in music.
tonic *adjective*

tonight *noun* & *adverb*
this evening or night.

tonne *noun* (*plural* **tonnes**)
a metric ton (1,000 kilograms).

too *adverb*
1 also ♦ *Take the others too.* **2** more than is wanted or allowed etc. ♦ *That's too much sugar for me.*

tool *noun* (*plural* **tools**)
1 a device that helps you to do a particular job ♦ *A saw is a tool for cutting wood or metal.* **2** a thing used for a particular purpose ♦ *An encyclopedia is a useful study tool.*

tooth *noun* (*plural* **teeth**)
1 one of the hard white bony parts that are rooted in the gums, used for biting and chewing things. **2** one of a row of sharp parts ♦ *the teeth of a saw.*
toothache *noun* **toothbrush** *noun* **toothed** *adjective*
fight tooth and nail fight very fiercely.

toothpaste *noun* (*plural* **toothpastes**)
a paste for cleaning your teeth.

top[1] *noun* (*plural* **tops**)
1 the highest part of something. **2** the upper surface. **3** the covering or stopper of a bottle, jar, etc. **4** a piece of clothing for the upper part of the body.
on top of in addition to something.
top *adjective*
highest ♦ *at top speed.*
top *verb* (**tops, topping, topped**)
1 put a top on something. **2** be at the top of something ♦ *She tops the list.* **3** remove the top of something.
top up fill up something that is half empty ♦ *top up your glass.*

top[2] *noun* (*plural* **tops**)
a toy that can be made to spin on its point.

top hat *noun* (*plural* **top hats**)
a man's tall stiff black or grey hat worn with formal clothes.

top-heavy *adjective*
too heavy at the top and likely to overbalance.

topic *noun* (*plural* **topics**)
a subject to write, learn, or talk about.

topical *adjective*
connected with things that are happening now ♦ *a topical film.*
topically *adverb* **topicality** *noun*

topmost *adjective*
highest.

topple *verb* (**topples, toppling, toppled**)
1 fall over; totter and fall. **2** make something fall; overthrow.

top secret *adjective*
extremely secret ♦ *top secret information.*

topsy-turvy *adverb* & *adjective*
upside down; muddled.

torch *noun* (*plural* **torches**)
1 a small electric lamp that you can carry in your hand. **2** a stick with burning material on the end, used as a light.

torment *verb* (**torments, tormenting, tormented**)
1 make someone suffer greatly. **2** tease; keep annoying someone.
tormentor *noun*

torment *noun* (*plural* **torments**)
great suffering.

tornado (*say* tor-**nay**-doh) *noun* (*plural* **tornadoes**)
a violent storm or whirlwind.

torpedo *noun* (*plural* **torpedoes**)
a long tube-shaped missile that can be fired under water to destroy ships.

torrent *noun* (*plural* **torrents**)
1 a rushing stream; a great flow. **2** a heavy downpour of rain.
torrential *adjective*

torso *noun* (*plural* **torsos**)
the trunk of the human body.

tortoise *noun* (*plural* **tortoises**)
a slow-moving animal with a shell over its body.

tortoiseshell (*say* tort-a-shell) *noun* (*plural* **tortoiseshells**)
1 the mottled brown and yellow shell of certain turtles, used for making combs etc. **2** a cat or butterfly with mottled brown colouring.

torture *verb* (**tortures, torturing, tortured**)
make a person feel great pain or worry.
torture *noun* **torturer** *noun*

Tory *noun* (*plural* **Tories**)
a Conservative.
Tory *adjective*

toss *verb* (**tosses, tossing, tossed**)
1 throw something, especially up into the air. **2** spin a coin to decide something according to which side of it is upwards after it falls. **3** move restlessly or unevenly from side to side.
toss *noun*

toss-up *noun* (*plural* **toss-ups**)
1 the tossing of a coin. **2** an even chance.

tot¹ *noun* (*plural* **tots**)
1 a small child. **2** (*informal*) a small amount of spirits ♦ *a tot of rum.*

tot² *verb* (**tots, totting, totted**)
tot up (*informal*) add up.

total *adjective*
1 including everything ♦ *the total amount.*
2 complete ♦ *total darkness.*
totally *adverb*

total *noun* (*plural* **totals**)
the amount you get by adding everything together.

total *verb* (**totals, totalling, totalled**)
1 add up the total. **2** amount to something ♦ *The cost of the damage totalled £500.*

totalitarian *adjective*
using a form of government where people are not allowed to form rival political parties.

totem pole *noun* (*plural* **totem poles**)
a pole carved or painted by Native Americans with the symbols (**totems**) of their tribes or families.

totter *verb* (**totters, tottering, tottered**)
walk unsteadily; wobble.
tottery *adjective*

touch *verb* (**touches, touching, touched**)
1 put your hand or fingers etc. on something lightly. **2** be or come together so that there is no space between. **3** come into contact with something or hit it gently. **4** move or meddle with something. **5** reach ♦ *The thermometer touched 30° Celsius.* **6** affect someone's feelings, e.g. by making them feel sympathy ♦ *The sad story touched our hearts.*
touch and go an uncertain situation. **touch down 1** (said about an aircraft) land.
2 (in rugby football) touch the ball on the ground behind the goal line. **touch on** discuss a subject briefly. **touch up** improve something by making small additions or changes.

touch *noun* (*plural* **touches**)
1 the action of touching. **2** the ability to feel things by touching them. **3** a small amount; a small thing done ♦ *the finishing touches.*
4 a special skill or style of workmanship ♦ *She hasn't lost her touch.* **5** communication with someone ♦ *We lost touch with him.*
6 the part of a football field outside the playing area.

touching *adjective*
causing you to have kindly feelings such as pity or sympathy.

touchline *noun* (*plural* **touchlines**)
one of the lines that mark the side of a sports pitch.

touchstone *noun* (*plural* **touchstones**)
a test by which the quality of something is judged.

touchy *adjective* (**touchier, touchiest**)
easily offended.
touchily *adverb* **touchiness** *noun*

tough *adjective*
1 strong; difficult to break or damage. **2** difficult to chew. **3** able to stand hardship; not easily hurt. **4** firm or severe. **5** difficult ♦ *a tough decision.*
toughly *adverb* **toughness** *noun*

toughen *verb* (**toughens, toughening, toughened**)
make or become tough.

tour *noun* (*plural* **tours**)
a journey visiting several places.

tour *verb* (**tours, touring, toured**)
make a tour.

tourism *noun*
the industry of organizing holidays and visits to places of interest.

tourist *noun* (*plural* **tourists**)
a person who makes a tour or visits a place for pleasure.

tournament *noun* (*plural* **tournaments**)
a series of games or contests.

tow (rhymes with *go*) *verb* (**tows, towing, towed**)
pull something along behind you.
tow *noun*
on tow being towed.

toward *preposition*
towards.

towards *preposition*
1 in the direction of ♦ *She walked towards the sea.* **2** in relation to; regarding ♦ *He behaved kindly towards his children.* **3** as a contribution to ♦ *Put the money towards a new bicycle.*
4 near ♦ *towards four o'clock.*

towel *noun* (*plural* **towels**)
a piece of absorbent cloth for drying things.
towelling *noun*

tower *noun* (*plural* **towers**)
a tall narrow building.

tower *verb* (**towers, towering, towered**)
be very high; be taller than others ♦ *Skyscrapers towered over the city.*

town *noun* (*plural* **towns**)
a place with many houses, shops, offices, and other buildings.

town hall *noun* (*plural* **town halls**)
a building with offices for the local council and usually a hall for public events.

towpath *noun* (*plural* **towpaths**)
a path beside a canal or river, originally for use when a horse was towing a barge etc.

toxic *adjective*
poisonous; caused by poison.
toxicity *noun*

toy *noun* (*plural* **toys**)
a thing to play with.

toy *adjective*
1 made as a toy. 2 (said about a dog) of a very small breed ♦ *a toy poodle.*

toy *verb* (**toys, toying, toyed**)
toy with handle a thing or consider an idea casually.

trace *noun* (*plural* **traces**)
1 a mark left by a person or thing; a sign ♦ *There was no trace of the thief.* 2 a very small amount.

trace *verb* (**traces, tracing, traced**)
1 copy a picture or map etc. by drawing over it on transparent paper. 2 follow the traces of a person or thing; find ♦ *The police have been trying to trace her.*
tracer *noun*

tracery *noun*
a decorative pattern of holes in stone, e.g. in a church window.

track *noun* (*plural* **tracks**)
1 a mark or marks left by a moving person or thing. 2 a rough path made by being used. 3 a road or area of ground specially prepared for racing. 4 a set of rails for trains or trams etc. 5 one of the songs or pieces of music on a CD, tape, etc. 6 a continuous band round the wheels of a tank or tractor etc.
keep or **lose track of** keep or fail to keep yourself informed about where something is or what someone is doing.

track *verb* (**tracks, tracking, tracked**)
1 follow the tracks left by a person or animal. 2 follow or observe something as it moves.
tracker *noun*
track down find a person or thing by searching.

tract[1] *noun* (*plural* **tracts**)
1 an area of land. 2 a series of connected parts along which something passes ♦ *the digestive tract.*
[from Latin *tractus* = drawing, draught]

tract[2] *noun* (*plural* **tracts**)
a pamphlet containing a short essay, especially about religion or politics.
[via Old English from Latin]

tractor *noun* (*plural* **tractors**)
a motor vehicle for pulling farm machinery or other heavy loads.

trade *noun* (*plural* **trades**)
1 buying, selling, or exchanging goods. 2 business of a particular kind; the people working in this. 3 an occupation, especially a skilled craft.

trade *verb* (**trades, trading, traded**)
buy, sell, or exchange things.
trader *noun*
trade in give a thing as part of the payment for something new ♦ *He traded in his motorcycle for a car.*

trade mark *noun* (*plural* **trade marks**)
a firm's registered symbol or name used to distinguish its goods etc. from those of other firms.

tradesman *noun* (*plural* **tradesmen**)
a person employed in trade, especially one who sells or delivers goods.

trade union *noun* (*plural* **trade unions**)
a group of workers organized to help and protect workers in their own trade or industry.

tradition *noun* (*plural* **traditions**)
1 the passing down of beliefs or customs etc. from one generation to another. 2 something passed on in this way.
traditional *adjective* **traditionally** *adverb*

traffic *noun*
1 vehicles, ships, or aircraft moving along a route. 2 trading, especially when it is illegal or wrong ♦ *drug traffic.*

traffic lights *plural noun*
coloured lights used as a signal to traffic at road junctions etc.

traffic warden *noun* (*plural* **traffic wardens**)
an official who assists police to control the movement and parking of vehicles.

tragedy *noun* (*plural* **tragedies**)
1 a play with unhappy events or a sad ending. 2 a very sad or distressing event.
[from Greek *tragos* = goat + *oide* = song. The connection with goats is not known]

tragic *adjective*
1 very sad or distressing. 2 to do with tragedies ♦ *a great tragic actor.*
tragically *adverb*

trail *noun* (*plural* **trails**)
1 a track, scent, or other sign left where something has passed. 2 a path or track made through the countryside or a forest.

trail *verb* (**trails, trailing, trailed**)
1 follow the trail of something; track. 2 drag or be dragged along behind; lag behind. 3 follow someone more slowly or wearily. 4 hang down or float loosely. 5 become fainter ♦ *Her voice trailed away.*

trailer *noun* (*plural* **trailers**)
1 a truck or other container pulled along by a vehicle. 2 a short piece from a film or television programme, shown in advance to advertise it.

train *noun* (*plural* **trains**)
1 a railway engine pulling a line of carriages or trucks that are linked together. 2 a number of people or animals moving in a line ♦ *a camel train.* 3 a series of things ♦ *a train of events.* 4 part of a long dress or robe that trails on the ground at the back.

train *verb* (trains, training, trained)
1 give a person instruction or practice so that they become skilled. **2** practise, especially for a sporting event ♦ *She was training for the race.* **3** make something grow in a particular direction ♦ *We'd like to train roses up the walls.* **4** aim a gun or camera etc.

trainer *noun* (*plural* trainers)
1 a person who trains people or animals. **2** a soft rubber-soled shoe of the kind worn for running or by athletes etc. while exercising.

traitor *noun* (*plural* traitors)
a person who betrays his or her country or friends.
traitorous *adjective*

tram *noun* (*plural* trams)
a public passenger vehicle running on rails in the road.

tramp *noun* (*plural* tramps)
1 a person without a home or job who walks from place to place. **2** a long walk. **3** the sound of heavy footsteps.

tramp *verb* (tramps, tramping, tramped)
1 walk with heavy footsteps. **2** walk for a long distance.

trample *verb* (tramples, trampling, trampled)
tread heavily on something; crush something by treading on it.

trampoline *noun* (*plural* trampolines)
a large piece of canvas joined to a frame by springs, used by gymnasts for jumping on.

trance *noun* (*plural* trances)
a dreamy or unconscious state rather like sleep.

tranquil *adjective*
calm and quiet.
tranquilly *adverb* **tranquillity** *noun*

tranquillizer *noun* (*plural* tranquillizers)
a medicine used to make a person feel calm.

transatlantic *adjective*
across or on the other side of the Atlantic Ocean.

transcript *noun* (*plural* transcripts)
a written copy.

transfer *verb* (transfers, transferring, transferred)
1 move a person or thing to another place. **2** hand over.
transferable *adjective* **transference** *noun*
transfer *noun* (*plural* transfers)
1 the transferring of a person or thing. **2** a picture or design that can be transferred onto another surface.

transfigure *verb* (transfigures, transfiguring, transfigured)
change the appearance of something greatly.
transfiguration *noun*

transfix *verb* (transfixes, transfixing, transfixed)
1 make a person or animal unable to move because of fear or surprise etc. **2** pierce and fix with something pointed.

transform *verb* (transforms, transforming, transformed)
change the form or appearance or character of a person or thing.
transformation *noun*

transformer *noun* (*plural* transformers)
a device used to change the voltage of an electric current.

transfusion *noun* (*plural* transfusions)
putting blood taken from one person into another person's body.
transfuse *verb*

transistor *noun* (*plural* transistors)
1 a tiny semiconductor device that controls a flow of electricity. **2** (also **transistor radio**) a portable radio that uses transistors.
transistorized *adjective*

transit *noun*
the process of travelling from one place to another ♦ *The goods were damaged in transit.*

transition *noun* (*plural* transitions)
the process of changing from one condition or form etc. to another.
transitional *adjective*

transitive *adjective*
(said about a verb) used with a direct object after it, e.g. *change* in *change your shoes* (but not in *change into dry shoes*). (Compare **intransitive**.)
transitively *adverb*

translate *verb* (translates, translating, translated)
put something into another language.
translatable *adjective* **translation** *noun*
translator *noun*

transliterate *verb* (transliterates, transliterating, transliterated)
write a word in the letters of a different alphabet or language.
transliteration *noun*

translucent (*say* tranz-**loo**-sent) *adjective*
allowing some light to shine through but not transparent.

transmission *noun* (*plural* transmissions)
1 transmitting something. **2** a broadcast. **3** the gears by which power is transmitted from the engine to the wheels of a vehicle.

transmit *verb* (transmits, transmitting, transmitted)
1 send or pass on from one person or place to another. **2** send out a signal or broadcast etc.
transmitter *noun*

transmute verb (transmutes, transmuting, transmuted)
change something from one form or substance into another.
transmutation noun

transparent adjective
able to be seen through.

transplant verb (transplants, transplanting, transplanted)
1 remove a plant and put it to grow somewhere else. 2 transfer a part of the body to another person or animal.
transplantation noun

transplant noun (plural transplants)
1 the process of transplanting. 2 something transplanted.

transport verb (transports, transporting, transported)
take a person, animal, or thing from one place to another.
transportation noun **transporter** noun

transport noun
the process or means of transporting people, animals, or things ♦ The city has a good system of public transport.

transpose verb (transposes, transposing, transposed)
1 change the position or order of something. 2 put a piece of music into a different key.
transposition noun

trap noun (plural traps)
1 a device for catching and holding animals. 2 a plan or trick for capturing, detecting, or cheating someone. 3 a two-wheeled carriage pulled by a horse. 4 a bend in a pipe, filled with water to prevent gases from rising up from a drain.

trap verb (traps, trapping, trapped)
1 catch or hold a person or animal in a trap. 2 prevent someone from escaping ♦ The driver was trapped in the wreckage.
trapper noun

trapdoor noun (plural trapdoors)
a door in a floor, ceiling, or roof.

trapeze noun (plural trapezes)
a bar hanging from two ropes as a swing for acrobats.

trapezium noun (plural trapeziums or trapezia)
a quadrilateral in which two opposite sides are parallel and the other two are not.

trash noun
rubbish or nonsense.
trashy adjective

trauma (say traw-ma) noun (plural traumas)
a shock that produces a lasting effect on a person's mind.
traumatic adjective **traumatize** verb

travel verb (travels, travelling, travelled)
move from place to place.
travel noun

traveller noun (plural travellers)
1 a person who is travelling or who often travels. 2 a gypsy, or a person who does not settle in one place.

traveller's cheque noun (plural traveller's cheques)
a cheque for a fixed amount of money that is sold by banks and that can be exchanged for money in foreign countries.

trawl verb (trawls, trawling, trawled)
fish by dragging a large net along the seabed.

trawler noun (plural trawlers)
a boat used in trawling.

tray noun (plural trays)
1 a flat piece of wood, metal, or plastic, usually with raised edges, for carrying cups, plates, food, etc. 2 an open container for holding letters etc. in an office.

treacherous adjective
1 betraying someone; disloyal. 2 dangerous or unreliable ♦ It's snowing and the roads are treacherous.
treacherously adverb **treachery** noun

treacle noun
a thick sticky liquid produced when sugar is purified.

treacly adjective
[originally = ointment for an animal bite; from Greek therion = wild or poisonous animal]

tread verb (treads, treading, trod, trodden)
walk or put your foot on something.

tread noun (plural treads)
1 a sound or way of walking. 2 the top surface of a stair; the part you put your foot on. 3 the part of a tyre that touches the ground.

treadmill noun (plural treadmills)
1 a wide mill wheel turned by the weight of people or animals treading on steps fixed round its edge. 2 monotonous routine work.

treason noun
betraying your country.
treasonable adjective **treasonous** adjective

treasure noun (plural treasures)
1 a store of precious metals or jewels. 2 a precious thing or person.

treasure verb (treasures, treasuring, treasured)
value greatly something that you have.

treasurer noun (plural treasurers)
a person in charge of the money of a club, society, etc.

treasury noun (plural treasuries)
a place where money and valuables are kept.
the Treasury the government department in charge of a country's income.

treat *verb* (**treats, treating, treated**)
1 behave in a certain way towards a person or thing. **2** deal with a subject etc. **3** give medical care in order to cure a person or animal. **4** put something through a chemical or other process ♦ *The fabric has been treated to make it waterproof.* **5** pay for someone else's food, drink, or entertainment ♦ *I'll treat you to an ice cream.*

treat *noun* (*plural* **treats**)
1 something special that gives pleasure. **2** the process of treating someone to food, drink, or entertainment.
[from Latin *tractare* = to handle or manage]

treatment *noun* (*plural* **treatments**)
1 the process or manner of dealing with a person, animal, or thing. **2** medical care.

treaty *noun* (*plural* **treaties**)
a formal agreement between two or more countries.

treble *adjective*
three times as much or as many.

treble *noun* (*plural* **trebles**)
1 a treble amount. **2** a person with a high-pitched or soprano voice.

treble *verb* (**trebles, trebling, trebled**)
make or become three times as much or as many.
[from early French; related to *triple*]

tree *noun* (*plural* **trees**)
a tall plant with a single very thick hard stem or trunk that is usually without branches for some distance above the ground.
[from Old English]

trek *noun* (*plural* **treks**)
a long walk or journey.

trek *verb* (**treks, trekking, trekked**)
go on a long walk or journey.
[from South African Dutch *trekken* = to pull, to travel]

trellis *noun* (*plural* **trellises**)
a framework with crossing bars of wood or metal etc. to support climbing plants.

tremble *verb* (**trembles, trembling, trembled**)
shake gently, especially with fear.
tremble *noun*

tremendous *adjective*
1 very large; huge. **2** excellent.
tremendously *adverb*

tremor *noun* (*plural* **tremors**)
1 a shaking or trembling movement. **2** a slight earthquake.

trench *noun* (*plural* **trenches**)
1 a long narrow hole cut in the ground. **2** a ditch dig by troops to protect them from enemy fire.
trench *verb*
dig a trench or trenches.

trend *noun* (*plural* **trends**)
the general direction in which something is going.

trendy *adjective* (*informal*)
fashionable; following the latest trends.
trendily *adverb* **trendiness** *noun*

trespass *verb* (**trespasses, trespassing, trespassed**)
1 go on someone's land or property unlawfully. **2** (*old use*) do wrong; sin.
trespasser *noun*

trespass *noun* (*plural* **trespasses**) (*old use*)
wrongdoing; sin.

tress *noun* (*plural* **tresses**)
a lock of hair.

trestle *noun* (*plural* **trestles**)
each of a set of supports on which a board is rested to form a table.
trestle table *noun*

trial *noun* (*plural* **trials**)
1 the process of examining the evidence in a lawcourt to decide whether a person is guilty of a crime. **2** testing a thing to see how good it is. **3** a test of qualities or ability. **4** an annoying person or thing; a hardship.
on trial 1 being tried in a lawcourt. **2** being tested. **trial and error** trying out different methods of doing something until you find one that works.

triangle *noun* (*plural* **triangles**)
1 a flat shape with three sides and three angles. **2** a percussion instrument made from a metal rod bent into a triangle.
triangular *adjective*

tribe *noun* (*plural* **tribes**)
1 a group of families living in one area as a community, ruled by a chief. **2** a set of people.
tribal *adjective* **tribally** *adverb* **tribesman** *noun* **tribeswoman** *noun*

tribunal (*say* try-**bew**-nal) *noun* (*plural* **tribunals**)
a committee appointed to hear evidence and give judgements when there is a dispute.

tributary *noun* (*plural* **tributaries**)
a river or stream that flows into a larger one or into a lake.

tribute *noun* (*plural* **tributes**)
1 something said, done, or given to show respect or admiration. **2** payment that one country or ruler was formerly obliged to pay to a more powerful one.

trice *noun* (*old use*)
in a trice in a moment.
[from early Dutch *trisen* = to pull quickly, to tug]

trick *noun* (*plural* **tricks**)
1 a crafty or deceitful action; a practical joke ♦ *Let's play a trick on Jo.* **2** a skilful action, especially one done for entertainment ♦ *magic tricks.* **3** the cards picked up by the winner after one round of a card game such as whist.

trick *verb* (tricks, tricking, tricked)
1 deceive or cheat someone by a trick. **2** decorate
♦ *The building was tricked out with little flags.*

trickery *noun*
the use of tricks; deception.

trickle *verb* (trickles, trickling, trickled)
flow or move slowly.
trickle *noun*

tricky *adjective* (trickier, trickiest)
1 difficult; needing skill ♦ *a tricky job.* **2** cunning
or deceitful.
trickiness *noun*

tricycle *noun* (*plural* tricycles)
a vehicle like a bicycle but with three wheels.

trifle *noun* (*plural* trifles)
1 a pudding made of sponge cake covered in
custard, fruit, cream, etc. **2** a very small amount.
3 something that has very little importance or
value.

trifle *verb* (trifles, trifling, trifled)
treat a person or thing without seriousness or
respect ♦ *She is not a woman to be trifled with.*

trifling *adjective*
small in value or importance.

trigger *noun* (*plural* triggers)
a lever that is pulled to fire a gun.

trigger *verb* (triggers, triggering, triggered)
trigger off start something happening.

trigonometry (*say* trig-on-om-it-ree) *noun*
the calculation of distances and angles by using
triangles.

trill *verb* (trills, trilling, trilled)
make a quivering musical sound.
trill *noun*

trillion *noun* (*plural* trillions)
1 a million million. **2** (*old use*) a million million
million.

trim *adjective*
neat and orderly.
trimly *adverb* **trimness** *noun*

trim *verb* (trims, trimming, trimmed)
1 cut the edges or unwanted parts off something.
2 decorate a hat or piece of clothing by adding
lace, ribbons, etc. **3** arrange sails to suit the
wind.

trim *noun* (*plural* trims)
1 cutting or trimming ♦ *Your beard needs a trim.*
2 lace, ribbons, etc. used to decorate something.
in good trim in good condition; fit.

Trinity *noun*
God regarded as three persons (Father, Son, and
Holy Spirit).

trinket *noun* (*plural* trinkets)
a small ornament or piece of jewellery.

trio *noun* (*plural* trios)
1 a group of three people or things. **2** a group of
three musicians or singers. **3** a piece of music for
three musicians.

trip *verb* (trips, tripping, tripped)
1 catch your foot on something and fall; make
someone do this. **2** move with quick light steps.
3 operate a switch.
trip up 1 stumble. **2** make a mistake. **3** cause a
person to stumble or make a mistake.

trip *noun* (*plural* trips)
1 a journey or outing. **2** the action of tripping;
a stumble. **3** (*informal*) hallucinations caused by
taking a drug.

tripe *noun*
1 part of an ox's stomach used as food.
2 (*slang*) nonsense.

triple *adjective*
1 consisting of three parts. **2** involving three
people or groups ♦ *a triple alliance.* **3** three times
as much or as many.
triply *adverb*

triple *verb* (triples, tripling, tripled)
make or become three times as much or as many.

triplet *noun* (*plural* triplets)
each of three children or animals born to the
same mother at one time.

triplicate *noun*
in triplicate as three identical copies.

tripod (*say* try-pod) *noun* (*plural* tripods)
a stand with three legs, e.g. to support a camera.

trite (rhymes with *kite*) *adjective*
worn out by constant repetition; unoriginal
♦ *a few trite remarks.*

triumph *noun* (*plural* triumphs)
1 a great success or victory; a feeling of joy at
this. **2** a celebration of a victory.
triumphal *adjective* **triumphant** *adjective*
triumphantly *adverb*

triumph *verb* (triumphs, triumphing,
triumphed)
1 be successful or victorious. **2** rejoice in success
or victory.

trivia *plural noun*
unimportant details or pieces of information.

trivial *adjective*
small in value or importance.
trivially *adverb* **triviality** *noun*

troll (rhymes with *hole*) *noun* (*plural* trolls)
(in Scandinavian mythology) a supernatural
being, either a giant or a friendly but
mischievous dwarf.
[originally = witch: from Old Norse]

trolley *noun* (*plural* trolleys)
1 a small table on wheels or castors. **2** a small
cart or truck. **3** a basket on wheels, used in
supermarkets.

trombone noun (plural **trombones**)
a large brass musical instrument with a sliding tube.

troop noun (plural **troops**)
1 an organized group of soldiers, Scouts, etc.
2 a number of people moving along together.

ℹ️ USAGE Do not confuse with *troupe*.

troop verb (**troops, trooping, trooped**)
move along as a group or in large numbers
♦ *They all trooped in.*
[from Latin *troppus* = herd]

trooper noun (plural **troopers**)
a soldier in the cavalry or in an armoured unit.

troops plural noun
armed forces.

trophy noun (plural **trophies**)
1 a cup etc. given as a prize for winning a competition. 2 something taken in war or hunting as a souvenir of success.

tropic noun (plural tropics)
a line of latitude about $23\frac{1}{2}°$ north of the equator (**tropic of Cancer**) or $23\frac{1}{2}°$ south of the equator (**tropic of Capricorn**).
the tropics the hot regions between these two latitudes.

tropical adjective
to do with the tropics ♦ *tropical fish.*

trot verb (**trots, trotting, trotted**)
1 (said about a horse) run, going faster than when walking but more slowly than when cantering. 2 run gently with short steps.
trot out (*informal*) produce or repeat
♦ *He trotted out the usual excuses.*

trot noun
a trotting run.
on the trot (*informal*) one after the other without a break ♦ *She worked for ten days on the trot.*

trouble noun (plural **troubles**)
1 difficulty, inconvenience, or distress. 2 a cause of any of these.
take trouble take great care in doing something.

trouble verb (**troubles, troubling, troubled**)
1 cause trouble to someone. 2 give yourself trouble or inconvenience etc. ♦ *Nobody troubled to ask if he needed help.*

troublesome adjective
causing trouble or annoyance.

trough (*say* trof) noun (plural **troughs**)
1 a long narrow open container, especially one holding water or food for animals. 2 a channel for liquid. 3 the low part between two waves or ridges. 4 a long region of low air pressure.

troupe (rhymes with *troop*) noun (plural **troupes**)
a company of actors or other performers.

ℹ️ USAGE Do not confuse with *troop*.

trousers plural noun
a piece of clothing worn over the lower half of the body, with a separate part for each leg.
[from Irish or Scottish Gaelic]

trout noun (plural **trout**)
a freshwater fish that is caught as a sport and for food.

trowel noun (plural **trowels**)
1 a small garden tool with a curved blade for lifting plants or scooping things. 2 a small tool with a flat blade for spreading mortar etc.
[from Latin *trulla* = scoop]

truant noun (plural **truants**)
a child who stays away from school without permission.
truancy noun
play truant be a truant.
[from early French, = criminal]

truce noun (plural **truces**)
an agreement to stop fighting for a while.

truck[1] noun (plural **trucks**)
1 a lorry. 2 an open container on wheels for transporting loads; an open railway wagon.
3 an axle with wheels attached, fitted under a skateboard.

truck[2] noun
have no truck with refuse to have dealings with
♦ *I'll have no truck with fortune tellers!*

trudge verb (**trudges, trudging, trudged**)
walk slowly and heavily.

true adjective (**truer, truest**)
1 representing what has really happened or exists ♦ *a true story.* 2 genuine or proper; not false ♦ *He was the true heir.* 3 accurate.
4 loyal or faithful ♦ *Be true to your friends.*
trueness noun
come true actually happen as hoped or predicted.

truffle noun (plural **truffles**)
1 a soft sweet made with chocolate. 2 a fungus that grows underground and is valued as food because of its rich flavour.

truly adverb
1 truthfully. 2 sincerely or genuinely ♦ *We are truly grateful.* 3 accurately. 4 loyally or faithfully.
Yours truly see yours.

trump noun (plural **trumps**)
a playing card of a suit that ranks above the others for one game.

trump verb (**trumps, trumping, trumped**)
beat a card by playing a trump.
trump up invent an excuse or an accusation etc.

trumpet noun (plural **trumpets**)
1 a metal wind instrument with a narrow tube that widens near the end. 2 something shaped like this.

trumpet *verb* (**trumpets, trumpeting, trumpeted**)
1 blow a trumpet. 2 (said about an elephant) make a loud sound with its trunk. 3 shout or announce something loudly.
trumpeter *noun*

truncheon *noun* (*plural* **truncheons**)
a short thick stick carried as a weapon, especially by police.

trundle *verb* (**trundles, trundling, trundled**)
roll along heavily ♦ *He was trundling a wheelbarrow.* ♦ *A bus trundled up.*

trunk *noun* (*plural* **trunks**)
1 the main stem of a tree. 2 an elephant's long flexible nose. 3 a large box with a hinged lid for transporting or storing clothes etc. 4 the human body except for the head, arms, and legs.

trunk road *noun* (*plural* **trunk roads**)
an important main road.

trunks *plural noun*
shorts worn by men and boys for swimming, boxing, etc.

truss *noun* (*plural* **trusses**)
1 a framework of beams or bars supporting a roof or bridge etc. 2 a bundle of hay etc.

truss *verb* (**trusses, trussing, trussed**)
1 tie up a person or thing securely. 2 support a roof or bridge etc. with trusses.

trust *verb* (**trusts, trusting, trusted**)
1 believe that a person or thing is good, truthful, or strong. 2 let a person have or use something in the belief that they will behave responsibly ♦ *Don't trust him with your CD player!* 3 hope ♦ *I trust that you are well.*
trust to rely on ♦ *We're trusting to luck.*

trust *noun* (*plural* **trusts**)
1 the belief that a person or thing can be trusted. 2 responsibility; being trusted ♦ *Being a prefect is a position of trust.* 3 a legal arrangement in which money is entrusted to a person with instructions about how to use it.
trustful *adjective* **trustfully** *adverb*

trustworthy *adjective*
able to be trusted; reliable.

trusty *adjective* (*old use*)
trustworthy or reliable ♦ *my trusty sword.*

truth *noun* (*plural* **truths**)
1 something that is true. 2 the quality of being true.

truthful *adjective*
1 telling the truth ♦ *a truthful boy.* 2 true ♦ *a truthful account of what happened.*
truthfully *adverb* **truthfulness** *noun*

try *verb* (**tries, trying, tried**)
1 make an effort to do something; attempt. 2 test something by using or doing it ♦ *Try sleeping on your back.* 3 examine the evidence in a lawcourt to decide whether a person is guilty of a crime. 4 be a strain on ♦ *You are trying my patience.*
try on put on clothes etc. to see if they fit.
try out use something to see if it works.

try *noun* (*plural* **tries**)
1 an attempt. 2 (in rugby football) putting the ball down behind the opponents' goal line in order to score points.

trying *adjective*
putting a strain on someone's patience; annoying.

T-shirt or **tee shirt** *noun* (*plural* **T-shirts** or **tee-shirts**)
a short-sleeved casual shirt.

tub *noun* (*plural* **tubs**)
a round open container holding liquid, ice cream, soil for plants, etc.

tubby *adjective* (**tubbier, tubbiest**)
short and fat.
tubbiness *noun*

tube *noun* (*plural* **tubes**)
1 a long hollow piece of metal, plastic, rubber, glass, etc., especially for liquids or air etc. to pass along. 2 a container made of flexible material with a screw cap ♦ *a tube of toothpaste.* 3 the underground railway in London.

tuber *noun* (*plural* **tubers**)
a short thick rounded root (e.g. of a dahlia) or underground stem (e.g. of a potato) that produces buds from which new plants will grow.

tuberculosis *noun*
a disease of people and animals, producing small swellings in the parts affected by it, especially in the lungs.
tubercular *adjective*

tuck *verb* (**tucks, tucking, tucked**)
1 push a loose edge into something so that it is hidden or held in place. 2 put something away in a small space ♦ *Tuck this in your pocket.*
tuck in (*informal*) eat heartily. **tuck someone in** or **up** make someone comfortable in bed by folding the edges of the bedclothes tightly.

tuck *noun* (*plural* **tucks**)
1 a flat fold stitched in a piece of clothing. 2 (*informal, dated*) food, especially sweets and cakes etc. that children enjoy.
tuck shop *noun*

Tuesday *noun*
the day of the week following Monday.
[from Old English *Tiwesdaeg* = day of Tiw, a Norse god]

tuft *noun* (*plural* **tufts**)
a bunch of threads, grass, hair, or feathers etc. growing close together.
tufted *adjective*

tug *verb* (**tugs, tugging, tugged**)
1 pull something hard or suddenly. 2 tow a ship.
tug *noun* (*plural* **tugs**)
1 a hard or sudden pull. 2 a small powerful boat used for towing others.

tug of war *noun*
a contest between two teams pulling a rope from opposite ends.

tuition *noun*
teaching, especially when given to one person or a small group.

tulip *noun* (*plural* **tulips**)
a large cup-shaped flower on a tall stem growing from a bulb.
[from Persian *dulband* = turban (because the flowers are this shape)]

tumble *verb* (**tumbles, tumbling, tumbled**)
1 fall or roll over suddenly or clumsily.
2 move or push quickly and carelessly.
tumble *noun*
tumble to (*informal*) realize what something means.

tumbler *noun* (*plural* **tumblers**)
1 a drinking glass with no stem or handle.
2 a part of a lock that is lifted when a key is turned to open it. 3 an acrobat.

tummy *noun* (*plural* **tummies**) (*informal*)
the stomach.

tumour (*say* **tew**-mer) *noun* (*plural* **tumours**)
an abnormal lump growing on or in the body.

tumult (*say* **tew**-mult) *noun*
an uproar; a state of noisy confusion and agitation.
tumultuous *adjective*

tune *noun* (*plural* **tunes**)
a short piece of music; a pleasant series of musical notes.
tuneful *adjective* **tunefully** *adverb*
in tune at the correct musical pitch.
tune *verb* (**tunes, tuning, tuned**)
1 put a musical instrument in tune. 2 adjust a radio or television set to receive a certain channel. 3 adjust an engine so that it runs smoothly.
tuner *noun*
tune up (said about an orchestra) bring the instruments to the correct pitch.

tunic *noun* (*plural* **tunics**)
1 a jacket worn as part of a uniform. 2 a piece of clothing reaching from the shoulders to the hips or knees.

tunnel *noun* (*plural* **tunnels**)
an underground passage.
tunnel *verb* (**tunnels, tunnelling, tunnelled**)
make a tunnel.
[from early French *tonel* = barrel]

turban *noun* (*plural* **turbans**)
a covering for the head made by wrapping a strip of cloth round a cap.

turbine *noun* (*plural* **turbines**)
a machine or motor driven by a flow of water, steam, or gas.

turbulence *noun*
violent and uneven movement of air or water
♦ *We experienced turbulence during the flight.*

turbulent *adjective*
1 moving violently and unevenly ♦ *turbulent seas.* 2 involving much change and disagreement or violence ♦ *a turbulent period of history.*
turbulently *adverb*

turf *noun* (*plural* **turfs** or **turves**)
1 short grass and the earth round its roots.
2 a piece of this cut from the ground.
the turf horse racing.

turkey *noun* (*plural* **turkeys**)
a large bird kept for its meat.

turmoil *noun*
wild confusion or agitation ♦ *Her mind was in turmoil.*

turn *verb* (**turns, turning, turned**)
1 move round; move to a new direction.
2 change in appearance etc.; become
♦ *He turned pale.* 3 make something change
♦ *You can turn milk into butter.* 4 move a switch or tap etc. to control something ♦ *Turn that radio off.* 5 pass a certain time ♦ *It has turned midnight.* 6 shape something on a lathe.
turn down 1 fold down. 2 reduce the flow or sound of something. 3 reject ♦ *We offered her a job but she turned it down.* **turn out** 1 send out.
2 empty something, especially to search or clean it. 3 happen. 4 prove to be ♦ *The visitor turned out to be my uncle.* **turn up** 1 appear or arrive.
2 increase the flow or sound of something.

turn *noun* (*plural* **turns**)
1 the action of turning; a turning movement.
2 a change; the point where something turns.
3 an opportunity or duty etc. that comes to each person in succession ♦ *It's your turn to wash up.*
4 a short performance in an entertainment.
5 (*informal*) an attack of illness; a nervous shock
♦ *It gave me a nasty turn.*
a good turn a helpful action. **in turn** in succession; one after another.

turning *noun* (*plural* **turnings**)
a place where one road meets another, forming a corner.

turnip *noun* (*plural* **turnips**)
a plant with a large round white root used as a vegetable.

turnout *noun* (*plural* **turnouts**)
the number of people who attend a meeting, vote at an election, etc. ♦ *Despite the rain, there was a pretty good turnout.*

turnover noun (plural **turnovers**)
1 the amount of money received by a firm selling things. **2** the rate at which goods are sold or workers leave and are replaced. **3** a small pie made by folding pastry over fruit, jam, etc.

turnstile noun (plural **turnstiles**)
a revolving gate that lets one person in at a time.

turntable noun (plural **turntables**)
a circular revolving platform or support, e.g. for the record in a record player.

turquoise noun (plural **turquoises**)
1 a sky-blue or greenish-blue colour. **2** a blue jewel.

turret noun (plural **turrets**)
1 a small tower on a castle or other building. **2** a revolving structure containing a gun.
turreted adjective

turtle noun (plural **turtles**)
a sea animal that looks like a tortoise.
turn turtle capsize.

turtle dove noun (plural **turtle doves**)
a wild dove.

tusk noun (plural **tusks**)
a long pointed tooth that sticks out from the mouth of an elephant, walrus, etc.

tussle noun (plural **tussles**)
a struggle or conflict over something.

tussock noun (plural **tussocks**)
a tuft or clump of grass.

tutor noun (plural **tutors**)
1 a private teacher, especially of one pupil or a small group. **2** a teacher of students in a college or university.

TV abbreviation
television.

twain noun & adjective (old use)
two.

twang verb (**twangs, twanging, twanged**)
make a sharp sound like that of a wire when plucked.
twang noun

tweak verb (**tweaks, tweaking, tweaked**)
pinch and twist or pull something sharply.
tweak noun

tweed noun
thick woollen twill, often woven of mixed colours.

tweet noun (plural **tweets**)
the chirping sound made by a small bird.
tweet verb

tweezers plural noun
small pincers for picking up or pulling very small things.

twelve noun & adjective (plural **twelves**)
the number 12.
twelfth adjective & noun

twenty noun & adjective (plural **twenties**)
the number 20.
twentieth adjective & noun

twice adverb
1 two times; on two occasions. **2** double the amount.

twiddle verb (**twiddles, twiddling, twiddled**)
turn something round or over and over in an idle way ♦ He tried twiddling the knob on the radio.
twiddle noun **twiddly** adjective
twiddle your thumbs have nothing to do.

twig noun (plural **twigs**)
a small shoot on a branch or stem of a tree or shrub.

twilight noun
dim light from the sky just after sunset or just before sunrise.

twin noun (plural **twins**)
1 either of two children or animals born to the same mother at one time. **2** either of two things that are exactly alike.

twin verb (**twins, twinning, twinned**)
1 put things together as a pair. **2** if a town is twinned with a town in a different country, the two towns exchange visits and organize cultural events together.

twine verb (**twines, twining, twined**)
twist or wind together or round something.

twinge noun (plural **twinges**)
a sudden pain or unpleasant feeling.

twinkle verb (**twinkles, twinkling, twinkled**)
shine with tiny flashes of light; sparkle.
twinkle noun

twirl verb (**twirls, twirling, twirled**)
twist quickly.
twirl noun

twist verb (**twists, twisting, twisted**)
1 turn the ends of something in opposite directions. **2** turn round or from side to side ♦ The road twisted through the hills. **3** bend something out of its proper shape. **4** pass threads or strands round something or round each other. **5** distort the meaning of something ♦ You're twisting my words.
twister noun

twist noun (plural **twists**)
a twisting movement or action.
twisty adjective

twitch verb (**twitches, twitching, twitched**)
move or pull with a slight jerk.
twitch noun

twitter verb (**twitters, twittering, twittered**)
make quick chirping sounds.
twitter noun

two noun & adjective (plural **twos**)
the number 2.
be in two minds be undecided about something.

two-faced adjective
insincere or deceitful.

tycoon *noun* (*plural* **tycoons**)
a rich and influential business person.
[from Japanese *taikun* = great prince]

tying *present participle* of **tie**.

type *noun* (*plural* **types**)
1 a kind or sort. **2** letters or figures etc. designed
for use in printing.

type *verb* (**types, typing, typed**)
write something by using a typewriter.
typist *noun*

typewriter *noun* (*plural* **typewriters**)
a machine with keys that are pressed to print
letters or figures etc. on a piece of paper.
typewritten *adjective*

typhoon *noun* (*plural* **typhoons**)
a violent hurricane in the western Pacific or East
Asian seas.
[from Chinese *tai fung* = great wind]

typical *adjective*
1 having the usual characteristics or qualities of
a particular type of person or thing ♦ *a typical
school playground*. **2** usual in a particular person
or thing ♦ *He worked with typical carefulness*.
typically *adverb*

tyranny (*say* tirran-ee) *noun* (*plural* **tyrannies**)
1 government by a tyrant. **2** the way a tyrant
behaves towards people.
tyrannical *adjective* **tyrannous** *adjective*

tyrant (*say* ty-rant) *noun* (*plural* **tyrants**)
a person who rules cruelly and unjustly;
someone who insists on being obeyed.
[from Greek *tyrannos* = ruler with full power]

tyre *noun* (*plural* **tyres**)
a covering of rubber fitted round a wheel to
make it grip the road and run more smoothly.

Uu

ubiquitous (*say* yoo-**bik**-wit-us) *adjective*
found everywhere ♦ *Mobile phones are
ubiquitous these days*.
ubiquity *noun*

udder *noun* (*plural* **udders**)
the bag-like part of a cow, ewe, female goat, etc.
from which milk is taken.

ugly *adjective* (**uglier, ugliest**)
1 unpleasant to look at; not beautiful. **2** hostile
and threatening ♦ *The crowd was in an ugly
mood*.
ugliness *noun*
[from Old Norse *uggligr* = frightening]

UK *abbreviation*
United Kingdom.

ulcer *noun* (*plural* **ulcers**)
a sore on the inside or outside of the body.
ulcerated *adjective* **ulceration** *noun*

ulterior *adjective*
beyond what is obvious or stated ♦ *an ulterior
motive*.

ultimate *adjective*
furthest in a series of things; final ♦ *Our ultimate
destination is London*.
ultimately *adverb*
[from Latin *ultimus* = last]

ultimatum (*say* ul-tim-ay-tum) *noun* (*plural*
ultimatums)
a final demand or statement that unless
something is done by a certain time action will
be taken or war will be declared.

ultramarine *noun*
a deep bright blue.
[from Latin *ultra mare* = beyond the sea
(because it was originally imported 'across the
sea' from the East)]

ultrasound *noun*
sound of a frequency beyond the range of human
hearing, used in medical examinations.

ultraviolet *adjective*
(said about light rays) beyond the violet end of
the spectrum and so not visible to the human
eye.

umbilical cord *noun* (*plural* **umbilical cords**)
the tube through which a baby receives
nourishment before it is born, connecting its
body with the mother's womb.

umbrella *noun* (*plural* **umbrellas**)
1 a circular piece of material stretched over a
folding frame with a central stick used as a
handle, or a central pole, which you open to
protect yourself from rain or sun. **2** a general
protection.
[from Italian *ombrella* = a little shade]

umpire *noun* (*plural* **umpires**)
a referee in cricket, tennis, and some other
games.

umpire *verb* (**umpires, umpiring, umpired**)
act as an umpire.

UN *abbreviation*
United Nations.

un- *prefix*
1 not (as in *uncertain*). **2** (before a verb)
reversing the action (as in *unlock* = release from
being locked). Many words beginning with this
prefix are not listed here if their meaning is
obvious.

unable *adjective*
not able to do something.

unaccountable *adjective*
1 unable to be explained ♦ *For some unaccountable reason I completely forgot your birthday.* 2 not accountable for what you do.
unaccountably *adverb*

unanimous (*say* yoo-nan-im-us) *adjective*
with everyone agreeing ♦ *a unanimous decision.*
unanimously *adverb* **unanimity** (*say* yoo-nan-im-it-ee) *noun*
[from Latin *unus* = one + *animus* = mind]

unassuming *adjective*
modest; not arrogant or pretentious.

unavoidable *adjective*
not able to be avoided.

unawares *adverb*
unexpectedly; without warning ♦ *His question caught me unawares.*

unbearable *adjective*
not able to be endured.
unbearably *adverb*

unbeaten *adjective*
not defeated or surpassed.

unbecoming *adjective*
1 not making a person look attractive.
2 not suitable or fitting.

unbelievable *adjective*
not able to be believed; incredible.
unbelievably *adverb*

unbend *verb* (unbends, unbending, unbent)
1 change from a bent position; straighten up.
2 relax and become friendly.

unblock *verb* (unblocks, unblocking, unblocked)
remove an obstruction from something.

unborn *adjective*
not yet born.

unbroken *adjective*
not broken or interrupted.

uncalled for *adjective*
not justified or necessary ♦ *Such rudeness was quite uncalled for.*

uncanny *adjective* (uncannier, uncanniest)
strange or mysterious ♦ *an uncanny coincidence.*
uncannily *adverb* **uncanniness** *noun*

uncertain *adjective*
1 not known certainly. 2 not sure about something. 3 not reliable ♦ *His aim is rather uncertain.*
uncertainly *adverb* **uncertainty** *noun*
in no uncertain terms clearly and forcefully.

uncharitable *adjective*
making unkind judgements of people or actions.
uncharitably *adverb*

uncivilized *adjective*
not civilized; not having much culture.

uncle *noun* (*plural* uncles)
the brother of your father or mother; your aunt's husband.

uncomfortable *adjective*
not comfortable.
uncomfortably *adverb*

uncommon *adjective*
not common; unusual.

uncompromising (*say* un-komp-rom-I-zing) *adjective*
not allowing a compromise; inflexible.

unconcerned *adjective*
not caring about something; not worried.

unconditional *adjective*
without any conditions; absolute ♦ *unconditional surrender.*
unconditionally *adverb*

unconscious *adjective*
1 not conscious. 2 not aware of things.
unconsciously *adverb* **unconsciousness** *noun*

uncouth (*say* un-kooth) *adjective*
rude and rough in manner.

uncover *verb* (uncovers, uncovering, uncovered)
1 remove the covering from something.
2 reveal or expose ♦ *They uncovered a plot to kill the king.*

undecided *adjective*
1 not yet settled; not certain. 2 not having made up your mind yet.

undeniable *adjective*
impossible to deny; undoubtedly true.
undeniably *adverb*

under *preposition*
1 below or beneath ♦ *Hide it under the desk.*
2 less than ♦ *under 5 years old.* 3 governed or controlled by ♦ *The country prospered under his rule.* 4 in the process of; undergoing ♦ *The road is under repair.* 5 using ♦ *He writes under the name of 'Lewis Carroll'.* 6 according to the rules of ♦ *This is permitted under our agreement.*
under way in motion or in progress.

under *adverb*
in or to a lower place or level or condition ♦ *Slowly the diver went under.*

under *adjective*
lower ♦ *the under layers.*

undercarriage *noun* (*plural* undercarriages)
an aircraft's landing wheels and their supports.

undercover *adjective*
done or doing things secretly ♦ *an undercover agent.*

undercurrent *noun* (*plural* undercurrents)
1 a current that is below the surface or below another current. 2 an underlying feeling or influence ♦ *an undercurrent of fear.*

undercut *verb* (**undercuts, undercutting, undercut**)
sell something for a lower price than someone else sells it.

underdone *adjective*
not thoroughly done; undercooked.

underestimate *verb* (**underestimates, underestimating, underestimated**)
make too low an estimate of a person or thing.

undergo *verb* (**undergoes, undergoing, underwent, undergone**)
experience or endure something; be subjected to ♦ *The new aircraft underwent intensive tests.*

undergraduate *noun* (*plural* **undergraduates**)
a student at a university who has not yet taken a degree.

underground *adjective & adverb*
1 under the ground. 2 done or working in secret.

underground *noun*
a railway that runs through tunnels under the ground.

undergrowth *noun*
bushes and other plants growing close together, especially under trees.

underhand *adjective*
done or doing things in a sly or secret way.

underline *verb* (**underlines, underlining, underlined**)
1 draw a line under a word etc. 2 emphasize something.

underlying *adjective*
1 forming the basis or explanation of something ♦ *the underlying causes of the trouble.* 2 lying under something ♦ *the underlying rocks.*

undermine *verb* (**undermines, undermining, undermined**)
weaken something gradually.

underneath *preposition & adverb*
below or beneath.

underpants *plural noun*
a piece of men's underwear covering the lower part of the body, worn under trousers.

underprivileged *adjective*
having less than the normal standard of living or rights in a community.

understand *verb* (**understands, understanding, understood**)
1 know what something means or how it works or why it exists. 2 know and tolerate a person's ways. 3 have been told ♦ *I understand that you would like to speak to me.* 4 take something for granted ♦ *Your expenses will be paid, that's understood.*

understandable *adjective* **understandably** *adverb*

understanding *noun*
1 the power to understand or think; intelligence. 2 sympathy or tolerance. 3 agreement in opinion or feeling ♦ *a better understanding between nations.*

understatement *noun* (*plural* **understatements**)
an incomplete or very restrained statement of facts or truth ♦ *To say they disagreed is an understatement: they had a violent quarrel.*

understudy *noun* (*plural* **understudies**)
an actor who learns a part in order to be able to play it if the usual performer is ill or absent.

undertake *verb* (**undertakes, undertaking, undertook, undertaken**)
1 agree or promise to do something. 2 take on a task or responsibility.

undertaker *noun* (*plural* **undertakers**)
a person whose job is to arrange funerals and burials or cremations.

undertone *noun* (*plural* **undertones**)
1 a low or quiet tone ♦ *They spoke in undertones.* 2 an underlying quality or feeling etc. ♦ *His letter has a threatening undertone.*

underwear *noun*
clothes worn next to the skin, under indoor clothing.

underweight *adjective*
not heavy enough.

underwent *past tense* of **undergo**.

underworld *noun*
1 the people who are regularly involved in crime. 2 (in myths and legends) the place for the spirits of the dead, under the earth.

undeveloped *adjective*
not yet developed.

undo *verb* (**undoes, undoing, undid, undone**)
1 unfasten or unwrap. 2 cancel the effect of something ♦ *He has undone all our careful work.*

undoing *noun*
be someone's undoing be the cause of their ruin or failure.

undress *verb* (**undresses, undressing, undressed**)
take your clothes off.

undue *adjective*
excessive; too great.
unduly *adverb*

undulate *verb* (**undulates, undulating, undulated**)
move like a wave or waves; have a wavy appearance.
undulation *noun*

undying *adjective*
everlasting.

unearth *verb* (**unearths, unearthing, unearthed**)
1 dig something up; uncover something by digging. **2** find something by searching.

unearthly *adjective*
1 unnatural; strange and frightening.
2 (*informal*) very early or inconvenient
♦ *We had to get up at an unearthly hour.*

uneasy *adjective*
1 worried or anxious. **2** uncomfortable.
uneasily *adverb* **uneasiness** *noun*

unemployed *adjective*
without a job.
unemployment *noun*

unequal *adjective*
1 not equal in amount, size, or value.
2 not giving the same opportunities to everyone
♦ *an unequal society.*
unequalled *adjective* **unequally** *adverb*

unerring (*say* un-er-ing) *adjective*
making no mistake ♦ *unerring accuracy.*

uneven *adjective*
1 not level or regular. **2** not equally balanced
♦ *an uneven contest.*
unevenly *adverb* **unevenness** *noun*

unfair *adjective*
not fair; unjust.
unfairly *adverb* **unfairness** *noun*

unfaithful *adjective*
not faithful; disloyal.

unfamiliar *adjective*
not familiar.
unfamiliarity *noun*

unfasten *verb* (**unfastens, unfastening, unfastened**)
open the fastenings of something.

unfavourable *adjective*
not favourable.
unfavourably *adverb*

unfeeling *adjective*
not caring about other people's feelings; unsympathetic.

unfit *adjective*
1 unsuitable. **2** not in perfect health from lack of exercise.

unfold *verb* (**unfolds, unfolding, unfolded**)
1 open; spread out. **2** make or become known slowly ♦ *as the story unfolds.*

unfortunate *adjective*
1 unlucky. **2** unsuitable or regrettable
♦ *an unfortunate remark.*
unfortunately *adverb*

unfounded *adjective*
not based on facts.

unfriendly *adjective*
not friendly.
unfriendliness *noun*

unfurl *verb* (**unfurls, unfurling, unfurled**)
unroll; spread out ♦ *They unfurled a large flag.*

ungainly *adjective*
awkward-looking or clumsy.
ungainliness *noun*

ungodly *adjective*
1 not giving reverence to God; not religious.
2 (*informal*) outrageous; very inconvenient
♦ *She woke me at an ungodly hour.*
ungodliness *noun*

unguarded *adjective*
1 not guarded. **2** without thought or caution; indiscreet ♦ *He said this in an unguarded moment.*

unhappy *adjective*
1 not happy; sad. **2** unfortunate or unsuitable
♦ *an unhappy coincidence.*
unhappily *adverb* **unhappiness** *noun*

unhealthy *adjective*
not healthy.
unhealthiness *noun*

unheard of *adjective*
never known or done before; extraordinary.

unhinge *verb* (**unhinges, unhinging, unhinged**)
cause a person's mind to become unbalanced.

unicorn *noun* (*plural* **unicorns**)
(in legends) an animal that is like a horse with one long straight horn growing from its forehead.

uniform *noun* (*plural* **uniforms**)
special clothes showing that the wearer is a member of a certain organization, school, etc.

uniform *adjective*
always the same; not varying ♦ *The desks are of uniform size.*
uniformly *adverb* **uniformity** *noun*

unilateral *adjective*
done by one person or group or country etc.
♦ *a unilateral decision.*

uninhabitable *adjective*
unfit to live in.

union *noun* (*plural* **unions**)
1 the joining of things together; uniting.
2 a trade union.

Union Jack *noun* (*plural* **Union Jacks**)
the flag of the United Kingdom.

unique (*say* yoo-**neek**) *adjective*
being the only one of its kind ♦ *This jewel is unique.*
uniquely *adverb*
[from French, from Latin *unicus* = one and only]

unison *noun*
in unison 1 with all sounding or singing the same tune etc. together, or speaking in chorus. 2 in agreement.

unit *noun* (*plural* **units**)
1 an amount used as a standard in measuring or counting things ♦ *Centimetres are units of length.* 2 a group, device, piece of furniture, etc. regarded as a single thing but forming part of a larger group or whole ♦ *an army unit;* ♦ *a sink unit.* 3 (in mathematics) any whole number less than 10.

unite *verb* (**unites, uniting, united**)
join together; make or become one thing.

unity *noun*
1 being united; being in agreement. 2 something whole that is made up of parts. 3 (in mathematics) the number one.

universal *adjective*
to do with or including or done by everyone or everything.
universally *adverb*

universe *noun*
everything that exists, including the earth and living things and all the stars and planets.

university *noun* (*plural* **universities**)
a place where people go to study at an advanced level after leaving school.
[from Latin *universitas*, literally = the universe, and later = a community of teachers and students]

unjust *adjective*
not fair or just.

unkempt *adjective*
looking untidy or neglected.
[from *un-* = not + an old word *kempt* = combed]

unkind *adjective*
not kind.
unkindly *adverb* **unkindness** *noun*

unleaded *adjective*
(said about petrol) without added lead.

unleash *verb* (**unleashes, unleashing, unleashed**)
1 set a dog free from a leash. 2 let a strong feeling or force be released.

unless *conjunction*
except when; if ... not ♦ *We cannot go unless we are invited.*

unlike *preposition*
not like ♦ *Unlike me, she enjoys cricket.*
unlike *adjective*
not alike; different ♦ *The two children are very unlike.*

unlikely *adjective* (**unlikelier, unlikeliest**)
not likely to happen or be true.

unlimited *adjective*
not limited; very great or very many.

unload *verb* (**unloads, unloading, unloaded**)
remove the load of things carried by a ship, aircraft, vehicle, etc.

unlock *verb* (**unlocks, unlocking, unlocked**)
open something by undoing a lock.

unlucky *adjective*
not lucky; having or bringing bad luck.
unluckily *adverb*

unmask *verb* (**unmasks, unmasking, unmasked**)
1 remove a person's mask. 2 reveal what a person or thing really is.

unmentionable *adjective*
too bad or embarrassing to be spoken of.

unmistakable *adjective*
not able to be mistaken for another person or thing.
unmistakably *adverb*

unmitigated *adjective*
absolute ♦ *an unmitigated disaster.*

unnatural *adjective*
not natural or normal.
unnaturally *adverb*

unnecessary *adjective*
not necessary; more than is necessary.

unorthodox *adjective*
not generally accepted ♦ *an unorthodox method.*

unpack *verb* (**unpacks, unpacking, unpacked**)
take things out of a suitcase, bag, box, etc.

unpaid *adjective*
1 not yet paid ♦ *an unpaid bill.* 2 not receiving payment for work you do.

unpick *verb* (**unpicks, unpicking, unpicked**)
undo the stitching of something.

unpleasant *adjective*
not pleasant.
unpleasantly *adverb* **unpleasantness** *noun*

unpopular *adjective*
not popular.

unprecedented (*say* un-**press**-id-en-tid) *adjective*
that has never happened before.

unprepared *adjective*
not prepared beforehand; not ready or equipped.

unprintable *adjective*
too rude or indecent to be printed.

unprofessional *adjective*
not professional; not worthy of a member of a profession.

unqualified *adjective*
1 not officially qualified to do something. 2 not limited ♦ *We gave it our unqualified approval.*

unravel *verb* (**unravels, unravelling, unravelled**)
1 disentangle. 2 undo something that is knitted. 3 investigate and solve a mystery etc.

unready *adjective*
not ready; hesitating.

ℹ️ USAGE In the title of the English king *Ethelred the Unready* the word means 'lacking good advice or wisdom'.

---

unreal *adjective*
not real; existing in the imagination only.
unreality *noun*

unreasonable *adjective*
1 not reasonable. 2 excessive or unjust.
unreasonably *adverb*

unrelieved *adjective*
without anything to vary it ♦ *unrelieved gloom.*

unreserved *adjective*
1 not reserved. 2 without restriction; complete
♦ *unreserved loyalty.*
unreservedly *adverb*

unrest *noun*
trouble or rioting caused because people are dissatisfied.

unroll *verb* (**unrolls, unrolling, unrolled**)
open something that has been rolled up.

unruly *adjective*
difficult to control; disorderly.
unruliness *noun*

unsavoury *adjective*
unpleasant or disgusting.

unscrew *verb* (**unscrews, unscrewing, unscrewed**)
unfasten something by twisting it or loosening screws.

unscrupulous *adjective*
having no scruples about wrongdoing.

unseemly *adjective*
not proper or suitable; indecent.

unseen *adjective*
not seen; invisible.

unseen *noun* (*plural* **unseens**)
a passage for translation without previous preparation.

unsettled *adjective*
1 not settled or calm. 2 (said about weather) likely to change.

unshakeable *adjective*
not able to be shaken; firm.

unshaven *adjective*
(said about a man) not recently shaved.

unsightly *adjective*
not pleasant to look at; ugly.
unsightliness *noun*

unskilled *adjective*
not having or not needing special skill or training.

unsolicited *adjective*
not asked for ♦ *unsolicited advice.*

unsound *adjective*
1 nor reliable or firm. 2 not healthy.

unspeakable *adjective*
too bad to be described; very objectionable.

unstable *adjective*
not stable; likely to change or become unbalanced.

unstuck *adjective*
come unstuck 1 cease to stick. 2 (*informal*) fail or go wrong.

unsure *adjective*
not sure or confident.

unthinkable *adjective*
too bad or too unlikely to be worth considering.

unthinking *adjective*
thoughtless.

untidy *adjective* (**untidier, untidiest**)
not tidy.
untidily *adverb* **untidiness** *noun*

untie *verb* (**unties, untying, untied**)
undo something that has been tied.

until *preposition & conjunction*
up to a particular time or event.
[from an Old Norse word *und* = as far as, added to *till*]

ℹ️ USAGE See the note on *till*[1].

---

untold *adjective*
1 not told. 2 too much or too many to be counted
♦ *untold wealth.*

untruth *noun* (*plural* **untruths**)
an untrue statement; a lie.
untruthful *adjective* **untruthfully** *adverb*

unused *adjective*
1 (*say* un-**yoozd**) not yet used ♦ *an unused stamp.* 2 (*say* un-**yoost**) not accustomed
♦ *He is unused to eating meat.*

unusual *adjective*
not usual; strange or exceptional.
unusually *adverb*

unveil *verb* (**unveils, unveiling, unveiled**)
1 remove a veil or covering from something.
2 reveal.

unwarranted *adjective*
not justified; uncalled for.

unwell *adjective*
not in good health.

unwholesome *adjective*
not wholesome.

unwieldy *adjective*
awkward to move or control because of its size, shape, or weight.
unwieldiness *noun*

unwind *verb* (**unwinds, unwinding, unwound**)
1 unroll. 2 (*informal*) relax after a time of work or strain.

unwise *adjective*
not wise; foolish.
unwisely *adverb*

unworthy *adjective*
not worthy or deserving.

unwrap *verb* (**unwraps, unwrapping, unwrapped**)
open something that is wrapped.

up *adverb*
1 to or in a higher place or position or level
♦ *Prices have gone up.* **2** so as to be upright
♦ *Stand up.* **3** out of bed ♦ *It's time to get up.*
4 completely ♦ *Eat up your carrots.* **5** finished
♦ *Your time is up.* **6** (*informal*) happening
♦ *Something is up.*
up against 1 close to. **2** (*informal*) faced with
difficulties, dangers, etc. **ups and downs**
alternate good and bad luck. **up to 1** until.
2 busy with or doing something ♦ *What are
you up to?* **3** capable of ♦ *I don't think I'm up
to it.* **4** needed from ♦ *It's up to us to help her.*
up to date 1 modern or fashionable. **2** giving
recent information etc.

ⓘ USAGE Use hyphens when this is used as an
adjective before a noun, e.g. ♦ *up-to-date
information* (but ♦ *The information is up to
date*).

---

up *preposition*
upwards through or along or into ♦ *Water came
up the pipes.*
[from Old English]

upbringing *noun*
the way someone is trained during childhood.

update *verb* (**updates, updating, updated**)
bring a thing up to date.
update *noun*

upgrade *verb* (**upgrades, upgrading,
upgraded**)
improve a machine by installing new or better
parts in it.
upgrade *noun*

upheaval *noun* (*plural* **upheavals**)
a sudden violent change or disturbance.

uphill *adverb*
up a slope.
uphill *adjective*
1 going up a slope. **2** difficult ♦ *It was an uphill
struggle.*

uphold *verb* (**upholds, upholding, upheld**)
support or maintain a decision or belief etc.

upholster *verb* (**upholsters, upholstering,
upholstered**)
put a soft padded covering on furniture.
upholstery *noun*

upkeep *noun*
keeping something in good condition; the cost of
this.

uplifting *adjective*
making you feel more cheerful.

upon *preposition*
on.

upper *adjective*
higher in place or rank etc.

upper class *noun* (*plural* **upper classes**)
the highest class in society, especially the
aristocracy.
upper-class *adjective*

uppermost *adjective*
highest.
uppermost *adverb*
on or to the top or the highest place ♦ *Keep the
painted side uppermost.*

upright *adjective*
1 vertical or erect. **2** strictly honest or
honourable.
upright *noun* (*plural* **uprights**)
a post or rod etc. placed upright, especially as a
support.

uprising *noun* (*plural* **uprisings**)
a rebellion or revolt.

uproar *noun*
an outburst of noise or excitement or anger.

uproot *verb* (**uproots, uprooting, uprooted**)
1 remove a plant and its roots from the ground.
2 make someone leave the place where he or she
has lived for a long time.

upset *verb* (**upsets, upsetting, upset**)
1 overturn; knock something over. **2** make
a person unhappy or distressed. **3** disturb
the normal working of something; disrupt
♦ *This has really upset my plans.*
upset *adjective*
1 unhappy or distressed. **2** slightly ill ♦ *an upset
stomach.*
upset *noun* (*plural* **upsets**)
1 a slight illness ♦ *a stomach upset.*
2 an unexpected result or setback ♦ *There has
been a major upset in the quarter-finals.*

upshot *noun* (*plural* **upshots**)
the eventual outcome.

upside down *adverb* & *adjective*
1 with the upper part underneath instead
of on top. **2** in great disorder; very untidy
♦ *Everything had been turned upside down.*

upstairs *adverb* & *adjective*
to or on a higher floor.

upstart *noun* (*plural* **upstarts**)
a person who has risen suddenly to a high
position, especially one who then behaves
arrogantly.

uptake *noun*
quick on the uptake quick to understand.
slow on the uptake slow to understand.

uptight *adjective* (*informal*)
tense and nervous or annoyed.

upward *adjective* & *adverb*
going towards what is higher.
upwards *adverb*

uranium *noun*
a heavy radioactive grey metal used as a source
of nuclear energy.
[named after the planet Uranus]

urban *adjective*
to do with a town or city.
[from Latin *urbis* = of a city]

urchin *noun* (*plural* **urchins**)
1 a poorly dressed or mischievous boy.
2 a sea urchin.
[via early French from Latin *hericius* =
hedgehog]

urge *verb* (**urges, urging, urged**)
1 try to persuade a person to do something.
2 drive people or animals onward. 3 recommend
or advise.

urge *noun* (*plural* **urges**)
a strong desire or wish.

urgent *adjective*
needing to be done or dealt with immediately.
urgently *adverb* **urgency** *noun*

urinate (*say* yoor-in-ayt) *verb* (**urinates,
urinating, urinated**)
pass urine out of your body.
urination *noun*

urine (*say* **yoor**-in) *noun*
waste liquid that collects in the bladder and is
passed out of the body.
urinary *adjective*

urn *noun* (*plural* **urns**)
1 a large metal container with a tap, in which
water is heated. 2 a container shaped like a vase,
usually with a foot, especially a container for
holding the ashes of a cremated person.

US *abbreviation*
United States (said about America).

us *pronoun*
the form of *we* used when it is the object of a verb
or after a preposition.

USA *abbreviation*
United States of America.

use (*say* yooz) *verb* (**uses, using, used**)
perform an action or job with something
♦ *Use soap for washing.*
user *noun*
used to 1 was or were in the habit of doing
♦ *We used to go by train.* 2 accustomed to or
familiar with ♦ *I'm used to his strange behaviour.*
use up use all of something.

use (*say* yooss) *noun* (*plural* **uses**)
1 the action of using something; being used
♦ *the use of computers in schools.* 2 the purpose
for which something is used ♦ *Can you find a
use for this crate?* 3 the quality of being useful
♦ *These scissors are no use at all.*
[via early French from Latin *uti*]

used *adjective*
not new; second-hand ♦ *used cars.*

useful *adjective*
able to be used a lot or to do something that
needs doing.
usefully *adverb* **usefulness** *noun*

useless *adjective*
not useful; producing no effect ♦ *Their efforts
were useless.*
uselessly *adverb* **uselessness** *noun*

user-friendly *adjective*
designed to be easy to use.

usher *noun* (*plural* **ushers**)
a person who shows people to their seats in a
cinema, theatre, or church.

usher *verb* (**ushers, ushering, ushered**)
lead someone in or out; escort someone as an
usher.
[via early French from Latin *ostiarius* =
doorkeeper]

usherette *noun* (*plural* **usherettes**)
a woman who shows people to their seats in a
cinema or theatre.

usual *adjective*
such as happens or is done or used etc. always or
most of the time.
usually *adverb*

utensil (*say* yoo-ten-sil) *noun* (*plural* **utensils**)
a tool, device, or container, especially one for use
in the house ♦ *cooking utensils.*

utilitarian *adjective*
designed to be useful rather than decorative or
luxurious; practical.

utility *noun* (*plural* **utilities**)
1 usefulness. 2 an organization that supplies
water, gas, electricity, etc. to the community.

utilize *verb* (**utilizes, utilizing, utilized**)
use; find a use for something.
utilization *noun*

utmost *adjective*
extreme or greatest ♦ *Look after it with the
utmost care.*
utmost *noun*
do your utmost do the most that you are
able to.

Utopia (*say* yoo-toh-pee-a) *noun* (*plural*
Utopias)
an imaginary place or state of things where
everything is perfect.
Utopian *adjective*

utter[1] *verb* (**utters, uttering, uttered**)
say or speak; make a sound with your mouth.
utterance *noun*
[from early Dutch]

utter[2] *adjective*
complete or absolute ♦ *utter misery.*
utterly *adverb*
[from Old English *uttra* = outer]

uttermost *adjective* & *noun*
utmost.

U-turn *noun* (*plural* **U-turns**)
1 a U-shaped turn made in a vehicle so that
it then travels in the opposite direction.
2 a complete change of policy.

vacant *adjective*
1 empty; not filled or occupied ♦ *a vacant seat*;
♦ *a vacant post.* **2** without expression; blank
♦ *a vacant stare.*
vacantly *adverb* **vacancy** *noun*
[from Latin *vacans* = being empty]

vacation (*say* vak-**ay**-shun) *noun* (*plural*
vacations)
1 a holiday, especially between the terms at a
university. **2** vacating a place etc.

vaccinate (*say* **vak**-sin-ayt) *verb* (**vaccinates,
vaccinating, vaccinated**)
inoculate someone with a vaccine.
vaccination *noun*

vaccine (*say* **vak**-seen) *noun* (*plural* **vaccines**)
a substance used to give someone immunity
against a disease.
[from Latin *vacca* = cow (because serum from
cows was used to protect people from the disease
smallpox)]

vacuum *noun* (*plural* **vacuums**)
1 a completely empty space; a space without any
air in it. **2** (*informal*) a vacuum cleaner.

vacuum *verb* (**vacuums, vacuuming,
vacuumed**)
to clean a floor with a vacuum cleaner.

vacuum cleaner *noun* (*plural* **vacuum
cleaners**)
an electrical device that sucks up dust and dirt
etc.

vagabond *noun* (*plural* **vagabonds**)
a person with no settled home or regular work;
a vagrant.

vagina (*say* va-**jy**-na) *noun* (*plural* **vaginas**)
the passage that leads from the vulva to the
womb.

vagrant (*say* **vay**-grant) *noun* (*plural*
vagrants)
a person with no settled home or regular work;
a tramp.
vagrancy *noun*

vague *adjective*
1 not definite or clear. **2** not thinking clearly or
precisely.
vaguely *adverb* **vagueness** *noun*

vain *adjective*
1 conceited, especially about your appearance.
2 useless ♦ *They made vain attempts to save her.*
vainly *adverb*
in vain with no result; uselessly.

❶ USAGE Do not confuse with *vane* or *vein*.

valency *noun* (*plural* **valencies**)
(in science) the power of an atom to combine
with other atoms, measured by the number of
hydrogen atoms it is capable of combining with.

valentine *noun* (*plural* **valentines**)
1 a card sent on St Valentine's day (14 February)
to someone you are fond of. **2** the person you
send this card to.

valiant *adjective*
brave or courageous.
valiantly *adverb*

valid *adjective*
1 legally able to be used or accepted ♦ *a valid
passport.* **2** (said about reasoning) sound and
logical.
validity *noun*

valley *noun* (*plural* **valleys**)
1 a long low area between hills. **2** an area
through which a river flows ♦ *the Nile valley.*

valuable *adjective*
worth a lot of money; of great value.
valuably *adverb*

valuables *plural noun*
valuable things.

value *noun* (*plural* **values**)
1 the amount of money etc. that is considered to
be the equivalent of something, or for which it
can be exchanged. ♦ *They learned the value of regular
exercise.* **3** (in mathematics) the number or
quantity represented by a figure etc. ♦ *What is
the value of x?*

value *verb* (**values, valuing, valued**)
1 think that something is valuable. **2** estimate
the value of a thing.
valuation *noun* **valuer** *noun*

valve *noun* (*plural* **valves**)
1 a device for controlling the flow of gas or liquid through a pipe or tube. **2** a structure in the heart or in a blood vessel allowing blood to flow in one direction only. **3** a device that controls the flow of electricity in old televisions, radios, etc. **4** each piece of the shell of oysters etc.
valvular *adjective*

vampire *noun* (*plural* **vampires**)
a dead creature that is supposed to leave its grave at night and suck blood from living people.
[from Hungarian *vampir*, perhaps from a Turkish word *uber* = witch]

van *noun* (*plural* **vans**)
1 a covered vehicle for carrying goods. **2** a railway carriage for luggage or goods, or for the use of the guard.
[short for *caravan*]

vandal *noun* (*plural* **vandals**)
a person who deliberately breaks or damages things, especially public property.
vandalism *noun*
[named after the Vandals, a Germanic people who invaded the Roman Empire in the 5th century, destroying many books and works of art]

vandalize *verb* (**vandalizes, vandalizing, vandalized**)
damage things as a vandal.

vane *noun* (*plural* **vanes**)
1 a weathervane. **2** the blade of a propeller, sail of a windmill, or other device that acts on or is moved by wind or water.
[from Old English]

ℹ USAGE Do not confuse with *vain* or *vein*.

---

vanilla *noun*
a flavouring obtained from the pods of a tropical plant.
[from Spanish *vainilla* = little pod]

vanish *verb* (**vanishes, vanishing, vanished**)
disappear completely.

vanity *noun*
conceit; being vain.

vanquish *verb* (**vanquishes, vanquishing, vanquished**)
defeat thoroughly.

vantage point *noun* (*plural* **vantage points**)
a place from which you have a good view of scenery or something interesting.
[from Middle English *vantage* = advantage]

vaporize *verb* (**vaporizes, vaporizing, vaporized**)
change or be changed into vapour.
vaporization *noun* **vaporizer** *noun*

vapour *noun* (*plural* **vapours**)
a visible gas to which some substances can be converted by heat; steam or mist.

variable *adjective*
likely to vary; changeable.
variably *adverb* **variability** *noun*

variable *noun* (*plural* **variables**)
something that varies or can vary; a variable quantity.

variant *adjective*
differing from something ♦ *'Gipsy' is a variant spelling of 'gypsy'.*
variant *noun*

variation *noun* (*plural* **variations**)
1 varying; the amount by which something varies. **2** a different form of something.

varied *adjective*
of different sorts; full of variety.

variegated (*say* vair-ig-ay-tid) *adjective*
with patches of different colours.
variegation *noun*

variety *noun* (*plural* **varieties**)
1 a quantity of different kinds of things. **2** the quality of not always being the same; variation. **3** a particular kind of something. ♦ *There are several varieties of spaniel.* **4** an entertainment that includes short performances of various kinds.

various *adjective*
1 of several kinds; unlike one another ♦ *for various reasons.* **2** several ♦ *We met various people.*
variously *adverb*

varnish *noun* (*plural* **varnishes**)
a liquid that dries to form a hard, shiny, clear coating.

varnish *verb* (**varnishes, varnishing, varnished**)
coat something with varnish.

vary *verb* (**varies, varying, varied**)
1 make or become different; change. **2** be different.

vase *noun* (*plural* **vases**)
an open, usually tall, container used for holding cut flowers or as an ornament.

vast *adjective*
very great, especially in area ♦ *a vast expanse of water.*
vastly *adverb* **vastness** *noun*

VAT *abbreviation*
value added tax; a tax on goods and services.

vat *noun* (*plural* **vats**)
a very large container for holding liquid.

vault *verb* (**vaults, vaulting, vaulted**)
jump over something, especially while supporting yourself on your hands or with the help of a pole.

vault *noun* (*plural* **vaults**)
1 a vaulting jump. **2** an arched roof.
3 an underground room used to store things.
4 a room for storing money or valuables.
5 a burial chamber.

vaulted *adjective*
having an arched roof.

vaunt *verb* (**vaunts, vaunting, vaunted**) (*old use* or *poetical*)
boast.
vaunt *noun*

VCR *abbreviation*
video cassette recorder.

VDU *abbreviation*
visual display unit.

veal *noun*
calf's flesh used as food.

vector *noun* (*plural* **vectors**)
(in mathematics) a quantity that has size and direction, such as velocity (which is speed in a certain direction).
vectorial *adjective*
[from Latin, = carrier, traveller]

veer *verb* (**veers, veering, veered**)
change direction; swerve.

vegetable *noun* (*plural* **vegetables**)
a plant that can be used as food.
[from Latin *vegetare* = enliven, animate]

vegetarian *noun* (*plural* **vegetarians**)
a person who does not eat meat.
vegetarianism *noun*

vegetation *noun*
1 plants that are growing. **2** vegetating.

vehement (*say* vee-im-ent) *adjective*
showing strong feeling ♦ *a vehement refusal*.
vehemently *adverb* **vehemence** *noun*

vehicle *noun* (*plural* **vehicles**)
a means of transporting people or goods, especially on land.

veil *noun* (*plural* **veils**)
a piece of thin material worn to cover the face or head.
take the veil become a nun.
veil *verb* (**veils, veiling, veiled**)
1 cover something with a veil. **2** partially conceal something ♦ *veiled threats*.

vein *noun* (*plural* **veins**)
1 any of the tubes that carry blood from all parts of the body to the heart. (Compare **artery**.)
2 a line or streak on a leaf, rock, insect's wing, etc. **3** a long deposit of mineral or ore in the middle of a rock. **4** a mood or manner
♦ *She spoke in a serious vein*.

ℹ️ USAGE Do not confuse with *vain* or *vane*.

velocity *noun* (*plural* **velocities**)
speed in a given direction.

velvet *noun*
a woven material with very short soft furry fibres on one side.
velvety *adjective*

vendetta *noun* (*plural* **vendettas**)
a long-lasting bitter quarrel; a feud.
[from Italian, from Latin *vindicta* = vengeance]

vending machine *noun* (*plural* **vending machines**)
a slot machine from which you can obtain drinks, chocolate, cigarettes, etc.

veneer *noun* (*plural* **veneers**)
1 a thin layer of good wood covering the surface of a cheaper wood in furniture etc. **2** an outward show of some good quality ♦ *a veneer of politeness*.

venerable *adjective*
worthy of respect or honour, especially because of great age.

venerate *verb* (**venerates, venerating, venerated**)
honour with great respect or reverence.
veneration *noun*

venereal disease *noun* (*plural* **venereal diseases**)
a disease passed on by sexual intercourse.

vengeance *noun*
revenge.
with a vengeance with great intensity.

venison *noun*
deer's flesh as food.

Venn diagram *noun* (*plural* **Venn diagrams**)
(in mathematics) a diagram in which circles are used to show the relationships between different sets of things.

venom *noun*
1 the poisonous fluid produced by snakes, scorpions, etc. **2** strong bitterness or spitefulness.
venomous *adjective*

vent *noun* (*plural* **vents**)
an opening in something, especially to let out smoke or gas etc.
give vent to express your feelings openly.
vent *verb* (**vents, venting, vented**)
1 make a vent in something. **2** give vent to feelings.

ventilate *verb* (**ventilates, ventilating, ventilated**)
let air move freely in and out of a room etc.
ventilation *noun* **ventilator** *noun*

ventriloquist *noun* (*plural* **ventriloquists**)
an entertainer who makes his or her voice sound as if it comes from another source.
ventriloquism *noun*
[from Latin *venter* = abdomen + *loqui* = speak]

venture *noun* (*plural* **ventures**)
something you decide to do that is risky.

venture *verb* (**ventures, venturing, ventured**)
dare or be bold enough to do or say something or
to go somewhere ♦ *We ventured out into the
snow.*

venturesome *adjective*
ready to take risks; daring.

veracity (*say* ver-**as**-it-ee) *noun*
truth.
veracious (*say* ver-**ay**-shus) *adjective*

veranda *noun* (*plural* **verandas**)
a terrace with a roof along the side of a house.
[via Hindi from Portuguese *varanda* = railing,
balcony]

verb *noun* (*plural* **verbs**)
a word that shows what a person or thing is
doing, e.g. *bring, came, sing, were.*
[from Latin *verbum* = word]

verbal *adjective*
1 to do with or in words; spoken, not written
♦ *a verbal statement.* **2** to do with verbs.
verbally *adverb*

verdict *noun* (*plural* **verdicts**)
a judgement or decision made after considering
something, especially that made by a jury.

verge *noun* (*plural* **verges**)
a strip of grass along the edge of a road or path.
on the verge of very nearly doing something
♦ *I was on the verge of tears*

verge *verb* (**verges, verging, verged**)
verge on border on something; be close to
something ♦ *This puzzle verges on the
impossible.*

veritable *adjective*
real; rightly named ♦ *a veritable villain.*
veritably *adverb*

vermin *plural noun*
animals or insects that damage crops or food or
carry disease, such as rats and fleas.
verminous *adjective*

vernacular (*say* ver-**nak**-yoo-ler) *noun* (*plural*
vernaculars)
the language of a country or district, as distinct
from an official or formal language.

versatile *adjective*
able to do or be used for many different things.
versatility *noun*

verse *noun* (*plural* **verses**)
1 writing arranged in short lines, usually with a
particular rhythm and often with rhymes;
poetry. **2** a group of lines forming a unit in a
poem or song. **3** each of the short numbered
sections of a chapter in the Bible.
[via Old English from Latin *versus* = a line of
writing]

version *noun* (*plural* **versions**)
1 a particular person's account of something that
happened. **2** a translation ♦ *modern versions of
the Bible.* **3** a special or different form of
something ♦ *the latest version of this car.*

versus *preposition*
against; competing with ♦ *The final was
Germany versus Brazil.*

vertebra *noun* (*plural* **vertebrae**)
each of the bones that form the backbone.

vertebrate *noun* (*plural* **vertebrates**)
an animal that has a backbone. (The opposite is
invertebrate.)

vertical *adjective*
at right angles to something horizontal; upright.
vertically *adverb*

vertigo *noun*
a feeling of dizziness and loss of balance,
especially when you are very high up.

verve *noun*
enthusiasm and liveliness.

very *adverb*
1 to a great amount or intensity; extremely
♦ *It was very cold.* **2** (used to emphasize
something) ♦ *on the very next day*;
♦ *the very last drop.*

very *adjective*
1 exact or actual ♦ *It's the very thing we need.*
2 extreme ♦ *at the very end.*

vessel *noun* (*plural* **vessels**)
1 a ship or boat. **2** a container, especially for
liquid. **3** a tube carrying blood or other liquid in
the body of an animal or plant.

vest *noun* (*plural* **vests**)
a piece of underwear covering the trunk of the
body.

vest *verb* (**vests, vesting, vested**)
1 give something as a right ♦ *The power to make
laws is vested in Parliament.* **2** (*old use*) clothe.

vested interest *noun* (*plural* **vested
interests**)
a strong reason for wanting something to
happen, usually because you will benefit from it.

vet *noun* (*plural* **vets**)
a person trained to give medical and surgical
treatment to animals.

vet *verb* (**vets, vetting, vetted**)
make a careful check of a person or thing,
especially of someone's background before
employing them.

veteran *noun* (*plural* **veterans**)
a person who has long experience, especially in
the armed forces.

veterinary (*say* vet-rin-ree) *adjective*
to do with the medical and surgical treatment of
animals ♦ *a veterinary surgeon.*

veto (*say* vee-toh) *noun* (*plural* **vetoes**)
1 a refusal to let something happen. **2** the right to
prohibit something.

veto *verb* (**vetoes, vetoing, vetoed**)
refuse or prohibit something.
[from Latin, = I forbid]

vex *verb* (**vexes, vexing, vexed**)
annoy; cause somebody worry.
vexation *noun* **vexatious** *adjective*

VHF *abbreviation*
very high frequency.

via (*say* **vy**-a) *preposition*
through; by way of ♦ *The train goes from London to Exeter via Bristol.*
[from Latin, = by way of]

viable *adjective*
able to work or exist successfully ♦ *a viable plan.*
viability *noun*

viaduct *noun* (*plural* **viaducts**)
a long bridge, usually with many arches, carrying a road or railway over a valley or low ground.
[from Latin *via* = road + *ducere* = to lead]

vibrant *adjective*
full of energy; lively.

vibrate *verb* (**vibrates, vibrating, vibrated**)
1 shake very quickly to and fro. 2 make a throbbing sound.
vibration *noun*

vicar *noun* (*plural* **vicars**)
a member of the Church of England clergy who is in charge of a parish.

vice[1] *noun* (*plural* **vices**)
1 evil or wickedness. 2 an evil or bad habit; a bad fault.

vice[2] *noun* (*plural* **vices**)
a device for gripping something and holding it firmly while you work on it.

vice versa *adverb*
the other way round ♦ *Which do you prefer— blue spots on a yellow background or vice versa?*
[from Latin, = the position being turned round]

vicinity *noun*
the area near or round a place ♦ *Is there a newsagent in the vicinity?*
[from Latin *vicinus* = neighbouring, a neighbour]

vicious *adjective*
1 cruel and aggressive. 2 severe or violent.
viciously *adverb* **viciousness** *noun*

vicious circle *noun* (*plural* **vicious circles**)
a situation in which a problem produces an effect which in turn makes the problem worse.

victim *noun* (*plural* **victims**)
someone who is injured, killed, robbed, etc.

victimize *verb* (**victimizes, victimizing, victimized**)
single someone out for cruel or unfair treatment.
victimization *noun*

victor *noun* (*plural* **victors**)
the winner.

Victorian *adjective*
belonging to the time of Queen Victoria (1837–1901).
Victorian *noun*

victory *noun* (*plural* **victories**)
success won against an opponent in a battle, contest, or game.
victorious *adjective*

video *noun* (*plural* **videos**)
1 the recording on tape of pictures and sound. 2 a video recorder or cassette. 3 a television programme or a film recorded on a video cassette.

video *verb* (**videos, videoing, videoed**)
record something on videotape.
[from Latin, = I see]

video cassette recorder *noun* (*plural* **video cassette recorders**)
a device for recording television programmes on videotape and for playing video cassettes.

videotape *noun* (*plural* **videotapes**)
magnetic tape suitable for recording television programmes.

vie *verb* (**vies, vying, vied**)
compete; carry on a rivalry ♦ *vying with each other.*

view *noun* (*plural* **views**)
1 what can be seen from one place, e.g. beautiful scenery. 2 sight; range of vision ♦ *The ship sailed into view.* 3 an opinion ♦ *She has strong views about politics.*
in view of because of. **on view** displayed for inspection. **with a view to** with the hope or intention of.

view *verb* (**views, viewing, viewed**)
1 look at something. 2 consider or regard ♦ *He viewed us with suspicion.*
viewer *noun*

viewpoint *noun* (*plural* **viewpoints**)
an opinion or point of view.

vigorous *adjective*
full of strength and energy.
vigorously *adverb*

Viking *noun* (*plural* **Vikings**)
a Scandinavian trader and pirate in the 8th–10th centuries.
[from Old Norse]

vile *adjective*
1 extremely disgusting. 2 very bad or wicked.
vilely *adverb* **vileness** *noun*

villa *noun* (*plural* **villas**)
a house, especially a holiday home abroad.
[from Latin, = country house]

village *noun* (*plural* **villages**)
a group of houses and other buildings in a country district, smaller than a town and usually having a church.
villager *noun*
[from early French; related to *villa*]

villain *noun* (*plural* **villains**)
a wicked person or a criminal.
villainous *adjective* **villainy** *noun*

vindicate *verb* (**vindicates, vindicating, vindicated**)
1 clear a person of blame or suspicion. 2 prove something to be true or worthwhile.
vindication *noun*

vine *noun* (*plural* **vines**)
a climbing or trailing plant whose fruit is the grape.

vinegar *noun*
a sour liquid used to flavour food or in pickling.

vintage *noun* (*plural* **vintages**)
1 the harvest of a season's grapes; the wine made from this. 2 the period from which something comes.

vintage car *noun* (*plural* **vintage cars**)
a car made between 1917 and 1930.

viola (*say* vee-**oh**-la) *noun* (*plural* **violas**)
a musical instrument like a violin but slightly larger and with a lower pitch.

violate *verb* (**violates, violating, violated**)
1 break a promise, law, or treaty etc. 2 treat a person or place with disrespect and violence.
violation *noun* **violator** *noun*

violence *noun*
1 physical force that does harm or damage. 2 strength or intensity ♦ *the violence of the storm.*
violent *adjective* **violently** *adverb*

violet *noun* (*plural* **violets**)
1 a small plant with purple or blue flowers. 2 purple.

violin *noun* (*plural* **violins**)
a musical instrument with four strings, played with a bow.
violinist *noun*
[from Italian *violino* = small viola]

viper *noun* (*plural* **vipers**)
a small poisonous snake.

virgin *noun* (*plural* **virgins**)
a person, especially a girl or woman, who has never had sexual intercourse.
virginal *adjective* **virginity** *noun*

virgin *adjective*
not yet touched or used ♦ *virgin snow.*

virtual *adjective*
being something in effect though not strictly in fact ♦ *His silence was a virtual admission of guilt.*

virtually *adverb*
nearly or almost.

virtual reality *noun*
a computer image or environment that is so realistic it appears to be real.

virtue *noun* (*plural* **virtues**)
1 moral goodness, or a particular form of this ♦ *Honesty is a virtue.* 2 a good quality or advantage ♦ *Jamie's plan has the virtue of simplicity.*
virtuous *adjective* **virtuously** *adverb*
by virtue of because of.

virtuoso (*say* ver-tew-**oh**-soh) *noun* (*plural* **virtuosos** or **virtuosi**)
a person with outstanding skill, especially in singing or playing music.
virtuosity *noun*
[from Italian, = skilful]

virus *noun* (*plural* **viruses**)
1 a very tiny living thing, smaller than a bacterium, that can cause disease. 2 a disease caused by a virus. 3 a hidden set of instructions in a computer program that is designed to destroy data.

visa (*say* **vee**-za) *noun* (*plural* **visas**)
an official mark put on someone's passport by officials of a foreign country to show that the holder has permission to enter that country.

viscount (*say* **vy**-kownt) *noun* (*plural* **viscounts**)
a nobleman ranking below an earl and above a baron.
viscountess *noun*

visibility *noun*
the distance you can see clearly ♦ *Visibility is down to 20 metres.*

visible *adjective*
able to be seen or noticed ♦ *The ship was visible on the horizon.*
visibly *adverb*

---

❶ USAGE Do not confuse with *visual*.

---

vision *noun* (*plural* **visions**)
1 the ability to see; sight. 2 something seen in a person's imagination or in a dream. 3 foresight and wisdom in planning things. 4 a person or thing that is beautiful to see.

visionary *adjective*
extremely imaginative or fanciful.

visionary *noun* (*plural* **visionaries**)
a person with extremely imaginative ideas and plans.

visit *verb* (**visits, visiting, visited**)
1 go to see a person or place. 2 stay somewhere for a while.
visitor *noun*

visit *noun* (*plural* **visits**)
1 going to see a person or place. 2 a short stay somewhere.

vista *noun* (*plural* **vistas**)
a pleasing view.
[from Italian, = view]

visual *adjective*
to do with or used in seeing; to do with sight.
visually *adverb*

---

❶ USAGE Do not confuse with *visible*.

---

visual aid *noun* (*plural* **visual aids**)
a picture, slide, film, etc. used as an aid in teaching.

visual display unit *noun* (*plural* **visual display units**)
a device that looks like a television screen and displays data being received from a computer or fed into it.

visualize *verb* (**visualizes, visualizing, visualized**)
form a mental picture of something.
visualization *noun*

vital *adjective*
1 connected with life; necessary for life to continue ♦ *vital functions such as breathing*.
2 essential; very important.
vitally *adverb*

vitality *noun*
liveliness or energy.

vitamin (*say* **vit**-a-min or **vy**-ta-min) *noun* (*plural* **vitamins**)
any of a number of substances that are present in various foods and are essential to keep people and animals healthy.

vivacious (*say* viv-**ay**-shus) *adjective*
happy and lively.
vivaciously *adverb* **vivacity** *noun*

vivid *adjective*
1 bright and strong or clear ♦ *vivid colours*; ♦ *a vivid description*. **2** active and lively ♦ *her vivid imagination*.
vividly *adverb* **vividness** *noun*

vivisection *noun*
doing surgical experiments on live animals.

vixen *noun* (*plural* **vixens**)
a female fox.
[from Old English]

vocabulary *noun* (*plural* **vocabularies**)
1 all the words used in a particular subject or language, or that an individual person uses.
2 a list of words with their meanings.

vocal cords *plural noun*
two strap-like membranes in the throat that can be made to vibrate and produce sounds.

vocalist *noun* (*plural* **vocalists**)
a singer, especially in a pop group.

vocation *noun* (*plural* **vocations**)
1 a person's job or occupation. **2** a strong desire to do a particular kind of work, or a feeling of being called by God to do something.

vocational *adjective*
teaching you the skills you need for a particular job or profession ♦ *vocational training*.

vodka *noun* (*plural* **vodkas**)
a strong alcoholic drink very popular in Russia.

vogue *noun* (*plural* **vogues**)
the current fashion ♦ *Very short hair for women seems to be the vogue*.
in vogue in fashion ♦ *Stripy dresses are definitely in vogue*.

voice *noun* (*plural* **voices**)
1 sounds formed by the vocal cords and uttered by the mouth, especially in speaking, singing, etc. **2** the ability to speak or sing ♦ *She has lost her voice*. **3** someone expressing a particular opinion about something ♦ *Emma's the only dissenting voice*. **4** the right to express an opinion or desire ♦ *I have no voice in this matter*.
[via early French *vois* from Latin *vox*]

void *adjective*
1 empty. **2** having no legal validity.

void *noun* (*plural* **voids**)
an empty space or hole.

volatile (*say* **vol**-a-tyl) *adjective*
1 evaporating quickly ♦ *a volatile liquid*.
2 changing quickly from one mood or interest to another.
volatility *noun*

volcano *noun* (*plural* **volcanoes**)
a mountain or hill with an opening at the top from which lava, ashes, and hot gases from below the earth's crust are or have been thrown out.
volcanic *adjective*

vole *noun* (*plural* **voles**)
a small animal like a mouse.
[from Norwegian *vollmus* = field mouse]

volley *noun* (*plural* **volleys**)
1 a number of bullets or shells etc. fired at the same time. **2** hitting back the ball in tennis etc. before it touches the ground.

volley *verb* (**volleys, volleying, volleyed**)
send or hit something in a volley or volleys.

volt *noun* (*plural* **volts**)
a unit for measuring electric force.

voltage *noun* (*plural* **voltages**)
electric force measured in volts.

volume *noun* (*plural* **volumes**)
1 the amount of space filled by something.
2 an amount or quantity ♦ *The volume of work
has increased.* 3 the strength or power of sound.
4 a book, especially one of a set.
[from Latin *volumen* = a roll (because ancient
books were made in the form of rolled
parchment)]

voluntary *adjective*
1 done or doing something willingly, not
because you are forced to do it. 2 unpaid
♦ *voluntary work.*
voluntarily *adverb*

voluntary *noun* (*plural* **voluntaries**)
an organ solo, often improvised, played before or
after a church service.

volunteer *verb* (**volunteers, volunteering,
volunteered**)
give or offer something of your own accord,
without being asked or forced to.

volunteer *noun* (*plural* **volunteers**)
a person who volunteers to do something, e.g. to
serve in the armed forces.

vomit *verb* (**vomits, vomiting, vomited**)
bring up food etc. from the stomach and out
through the mouth; be sick.
vomit *noun*

voodoo *noun*
a form of witchcraft and magical rites, especially
in the West Indies.
[from a West African language]

vote *verb* (**votes, voting, voted**)
show which person or thing you prefer by
putting up your hand, making a mark on a
paper, etc.
voter *noun*

vote *noun* (*plural* **votes**)
1 the action of voting. 2 the right to vote.

vouch *verb* (**vouches, vouching, vouched**)
vouch for guarantee that something is true or
certain ♦ *I will vouch for his honesty.*

voucher *noun* (*plural* **vouchers**)
a piece of paper that can be exchanged for certain
goods or services; a receipt.

vow *noun* (*plural* **vows**)
a solemn promise, especially to God or a saint.
vow *verb* (**vows, vowing, vowed**)
make a vow.

vowel *noun* (*plural* **vowels**)
any of the letters a, e, i, o, u, and sometimes y,
which represent sounds in which breath comes
out freely. (Compare **consonant**.)

voyage *noun* (*plural* **voyages**)
a long journey on water or in space.
voyage *verb* (**voyages, voyaging, voyaged**)
make a voyage.
voyager *noun*

VSO *abbreviation*
Voluntary Service Overseas.

vulgar *adjective*
rude; without good manners.
vulgarly *adverb* **vulgarity** *noun*
[from Latin *vulgus* = the common or ordinary
people]

vulnerable *adjective*
able to be hurt or harmed or attacked.
vulnerability *noun*
[from Latin *vulnus* = wound]

vulture *noun* (*plural* **vultures**)
a large bird that feeds on dead animals.

vulva *noun* (*plural* **vulvas**)
the outer parts of the female genitals.

vying *present participle* of **vie**.

Ww

W. *abbreviation*
1 west. 2 western.

wad (*say* wod) *noun* (*plural* **wads**)
a pad or bundle of soft material or banknotes,
papers, etc.
[from Dutch]

waddle *verb* (**waddles, waddling, waddled**)
walk with short steps, swaying from side to side,
as a duck does.
waddle *noun*

wade *verb* (**wades, wading, waded**)
walk through water or mud etc.
wader *noun*
[from Old English]

wafer *noun* (*plural* **wafers**)
a kind of thin biscuit.
[from early French]

waffle[1] (*say* wof-el) *noun* (*plural* **waffles**)
a small cake made of batter and eaten hot.
[from Dutch]

waffle[2] (*say* wof-el) *noun* (*informal*)
vague wordy talk or writing.
waffle *verb*
[from a dialect word *waff* = to bark or yelp]

waft (*say* woft) *verb* (**wafts, wafting, wafted**)
carry or float gently through the air or over
water.
[originally = escort a ship: from early German or
Dutch]

wag[1] *verb* (**wags, wagging, wagged**)
move quickly to and fro ♦ *a dog wagging its tail.*
wag *noun*
[from Old English]

wag² *noun* (*plural* **wags**)
a person who makes jokes.
[from an old word *waghalter* = someone likely
to be hanged]

wage *noun* or **wages** *plural noun*
a regular payment to someone in return for his or
her work.

wage *verb* (**wages, waging, waged**)
carry on a war or campaign.

wager (*say* way-jer) *noun* (*plural* **wagers**)
a bet.
wager *verb*

waggle *verb* (**waggles, waggling, waggled**)
move quickly to and fro.
waggle *noun*

wagon *noun* (*plural* **wagons**)
1 a cart with four wheels, pulled by a horse or an
ox. **2** an open railway truck, e.g. for coal.

waif *noun* (*plural* **waifs**)
a homeless and helpless person, especially a
child.

wail *verb* (**wails, wailing, wailed**)
make a long sad cry.
wail *noun*

wainscot or **wainscoting** *noun*
wooden panelling on the wall of a room near the
floor.

waist *noun* (*plural* **waists**)
the narrow part in the middle of your body.

---

❶ USAGE Do not confuse with *waste*.

---

waistcoat *noun* (*plural* **waistcoats**)
a short close-fitting jacket without sleeves, worn
over a shirt and under a jacket.

waistline *noun* (*plural* **waistlines**)
the amount you measure around your waist,
which indicates how fat or thin you are.

wait *verb* (**waits, waiting, waited**)
1 stay somewhere or postpone an action until
something happens; pause. **2** be left to be dealt
with later ◆ *This question must wait until next
week.* **3** wait on people.
wait on 1 hand food and drink to people at a
meal. **2** be an attendant to someone.
wait *noun*
an act or time of waiting ◆ *We had a long wait
for the train.*

waiter *noun* (*plural* **waiters**)
a man who serves people with food and drink in
a restaurant.

waiting list *noun* (*plural* **waiting lists**)
a list of people waiting for something to become
available.

waiting room *noun* (*plural* **waiting rooms**)
a room provided for people who are waiting for
something.

waitress *noun* (*plural* **waitresses**)
a woman who serves people with food and drink
in a restaurant.

wake¹ *verb* (**wakes, waking, woke, woken**)
1 stop sleeping ◆ *I woke when I heard the bell.*
2 make someone stop sleeping ◆ *You have
woken the baby.*

wake *noun* (*plural* **wakes**)
(in Ireland) a party held after a funeral.
[from Old English]

wake² *noun* (*plural* **wakes**)
1 the track left on the water by a moving ship.
2 currents of air left behind a moving aircraft.
in the wake of following or coming after.
[probably from an Old Norse word = opening in
the ice (made by a ship)]

wakeful *adjective*
unable to sleep.

waken *verb* (**wakens, wakening, wakened**)
wake.

walk *verb* (**walks, walking, walked**)
move along on your feet at an ordinary speed.
walker *noun*

walk *noun* (*plural* **walks**)
1 a journey on foot. **2** the manner of walking.
3 a path or route for walking.

walking stick *noun* (*plural* **walking sticks**)
a stick used as a support while walking.

walk of life *noun* (*plural* **walks of life**)
a person's occupation or social position.

walkover *noun* (*plural* **walkovers**)
an easy victory.

wall *noun* (*plural* **walls**)
1 a continuous upright structure, usually made
of brick or stone, forming one of the sides of a
building or room or supporting something or
enclosing an area. **2** the outside part of
something ◆ *the stomach wall.*

wall *verb* (**walls, walling, walled**)
enclose or block something with a wall
◆ *a walled garden.*

wallet *noun* (*plural* **wallets**)
a small flat folding case for holding banknotes,
credit cards, documents, etc.

wallflower *noun* (*plural* **wallflowers**)
a garden plant with fragrant flowers, blooming
in spring.

wallop *verb* (**wallops, walloping, walloped**)
(*informal*)
hit or beat someone.
wallop *noun*

wallow *verb* (**wallows, wallowing, wallowed**)
1 roll about in water, mud, etc. **2** get great
pleasure by being surrounded by something
◆ *a week wallowing in luxury.*
wallow *noun*
[from Old English]

wallpaper *noun* (*plural* **wallpapers**)
paper used to cover the inside walls of rooms.

walnut *noun* (*plural* **walnuts**)
1 an edible nut with a wrinkled surface.
2 the wood from the tree that bears this nut,
used for making furniture.

walrus *noun* (*plural* **walruses**)
a large Arctic sea animal with two long tusks.
[probably from an Old Norse word = horse-
whale]

waltz *noun* (*plural* **waltzes**)
a dance with three beats to a bar.

waltz *verb* (**waltzes, waltzing, waltzed**)
dance a waltz.

wand *noun* (*plural* **wands**)
a thin rod, especially one used by a magician.

wander *verb* (**wanders, wandering,
wandered**)
1 go about without trying to reach a particular
place. 2 leave the right path or direction; stray.
3 be distracted or digress ♦ *He let his attention
wander.*
wanderer *noun*

wane *verb* (**wanes, waning, waned**)
1 (said about the moon) show a bright area that
becomes gradually smaller after being full. (The
opposite is **wax**.) 2 become less, smaller, or
weaker ♦ *His popularity waned.*

wangle *verb* (**wangles, wangling, wangled**)
(*informal*)
get or arrange something by trickery or clever
planning ♦ *He's managed to wangle himself a
trip to Paris.*
wangle *noun*

want *verb* (**wants, wanting, wanted**)
1 wish to have something. 2 need ♦ *Your hair
wants cutting.* 3 be without something; lack.

want *noun* (*plural* **wants**)
1 a wish to have something. 2 lack or need of
something.
[from Old Norse]

wanted *adjective*
(said about a suspected criminal) that the police
wish to find or arrest.

WAP *abbreviation*
Wireless Application Protocol, a means of
enabling a mobile phone to be connected to the
Internet.

war *noun* (*plural* **wars**)
1 fighting between nations or groups, especially
using armed forces. 2 a serious struggle or effort
against crime, disease, poverty, etc.
at war taking part in a war. **war crime** a crime
committed during a war that breaks the
international rules of war.

warble *verb* (**warbles, warbling, warbled**)
sing with a trilling sound, as some birds do.
warble *noun*

ward *noun* (*plural* **wards**)
1 a room with beds for patients in a hospital.
2 a child looked after by a guardian. 3 an area
electing a councillor to represent it.

ward *verb* (**wards, warding, warded**)
ward off keep something away.

warden *noun* (*plural* **wardens**)
an official who is in charge of a hostel, college,
etc., or who supervises something.

warder *noun* (*plural* **warders**)
an official in charge of prisoners in a prison.

wardrobe *noun* (*plural* **wardrobes**)
1 a cupboard to hang clothes in. 2 a stock of
clothes or costumes.

warhead *noun* (*plural* **warheads**)
the head of a missile or torpedo etc., containing
explosives.

warlike *adjective*
1 fond of making war. 2 threatening war.

warm *adjective*
1 fairly hot; not cold or cool. 2 keeping the body
warm ♦ *a warm coat.* 3 friendly or enthusiastic
♦ *a warm welcome.* 4 close to the right answer,
or to something hidden ♦ *You're getting warm
now.*
warmly *adverb* **warmness** *noun* **warmth** *noun*

warm *verb* (**warms, warming, warmed**)
make or become warm.

warm-blooded *adjective*
having blood that remains warm permanently.

warn *verb* (**warns, warning, warned**)
tell someone about a danger or difficulty that
may affect them, or about what they should do
♦ *I warned you to take your boots.*
warning *noun*
warn off tell someone to keep away or to avoid
a thing.

warp (*say* worp) *verb* (**warps, warping,
warped**)
1 bend or twist out of shape, e.g. by dampness.
2 distort a person's ideas, judgement, etc.
♦ *Jealousy warped his mind.*

warrant *noun* (*plural* **warrants**)
a document that authorizes a person to do
something (e.g. to search a place) or to receive
something.

warrant *verb* (**warrants, warranting,
warranted**)
1 justify ♦ *Nothing can warrant such rudeness.*
2 guarantee.

warren *noun* (*plural* **warrens**)
1 a piece of ground where there are many
burrows in which rabbits live and breed.
2 a building or place with many winding
passages.

warrior *noun* (*plural* **warriors**)
a person who fights in battle; a soldier.

warship *noun* (*plural* **warships**)
a ship used in war.

wart *noun* (*plural* **warts**)
a small hard lump on the skin, caused by a virus.

wary (*say* **wair**-ee) *adjective*
cautious; looking carefully for possible danger or difficulty.
warily *adverb* **wariness** *noun*

wash *verb* (**washes, washing, washed**)
1 clean something with water or other liquid.
2 suitable for washing ♦ *Cotton washes easily.*
3 flow against or over something ♦ *Waves washed over the deck.* **4** carry along by a moving liquid ♦ *A wave washed him overboard.*
5 (*informal*) be accepted or believed
♦ *That excuse won't wash.*
be washed out (*informal*) (said about an event) be abandoned because of rain. **wash up** wash dishes and cutlery etc. after use.
washing-up *noun*

wash *noun* (*plural* **washes**)
1 the action of washing. **2** clothes etc. being washed. **3** the disturbed water behind a moving ship. **4** a thin coating of colour.

washable *adjective*
able to be washed without becoming damaged.

washbasin *noun* (*plural* **washbasins**)
a small sink for washing your hands etc.

washer *noun* (*plural* **washers**)
1 a small ring of rubber or metal etc. placed between two surfaces (e.g. under a bolt or screw) to fit them tightly together. **2** a washing machine.

washing *noun*
clothes etc. that need washing or have just been washed.

washing machine *noun* (*plural* **washing machines**)
a machine for washing clothes etc.

wasn't (*mainly spoken*)
was not.

wasp *noun* (*plural* **wasps**)
a stinging insect with black and yellow stripes round its body.

wastage *noun*
loss of something by waste.

waste *verb* (**wastes, wasting, wasted**)
1 use something in an extravagant way or without getting enough results. **2** fail to use something ♦ *You are wasting a good opportunity.* **3** become gradually weaker or thinner from lack of nourishment.

waste *adjective*
1 left over or thrown away because it is not wanted. **2** not used; not usable ♦ *waste land.*
lay waste destroy the crops and buildings etc. of an area.

waste *noun* (*plural* **wastes**)
1 wasting a thing, not using it well ♦ *a waste of time.* **2** things that are not wanted or not used.
3 an area of waste land ♦ *the wastes of the Sahara Desert.*
wasteful *adjective* **wastefully** *adverb*
wastefulness *noun*

❶ USAGE Do not confuse with *waist.*

watch *verb* (**watches, watching, watched**)
1 look at a person or thing for some time.
2 be on guard or ready for something to happen
♦ *Watch for the traffic lights to change.*
3 pay careful attention to something ♦ *Watch where you put your feet.* **4** take care of something
♦ *His job is to watch the sheep.*
watcher *noun*

watch *noun* (*plural* **watches**)
1 a device like a small clock, usually worn on the wrist. **2** the action of watching. **3** a turn of being on duty in a ship.

watchful *adjective*
watching closely; alert.
watchfully *adverb* **watchfulness** *noun*

watchman *noun* (*plural* **watchmen**)
a person employed to look after an empty building etc., especially at night.

watchtower *noun* (*plural* **watchtowers**)
a tall tower used as an observation post.

water *noun* (*plural* **waters**)
1 a colourless liquid that is a compound of hydrogen and oxygen. **2** a lake or sea. **3** the tide
♦ *at high water.*
pass water urinate.

water *verb* (**waters, watering, watered**)
1 sprinkle or supply something with water.
2 produce tears or saliva ♦ *It makes my mouth water.*
water down dilute.

watercolour *noun* (*plural* **watercolours**)
1 paint made with pigment and water (not oil).
2 a painting done with this kind of paint.

waterfall *noun* (*plural* **waterfalls**)
a place where a river or stream flows over the edge of a cliff or large rock.

waterlogged *adjective*
completely soaked or swamped in water.

waterproof *adjective*
that keeps out water ♦ *a waterproof jacket.*
waterproof *verb*

waterskiing *noun*
the sport of skimming over the surface of water on a pair of flat boards (**waterskis**) while being towed by a motor boat.

watertight *adjective*
1 made or fastened so that water cannot get in or out. **2** so carefully put together that it cannot be changed or set aside or proved to be untrue
♦ *a watertight excuse.*

waterworks *plural noun*
a place with pumping machinery etc. for supplying water to a district.

watery *adjective*
1 like water. **2** full of water. **3** containing too much water.

watt *noun* (*plural* **watts**)
a unit of electric power.

wave *noun* (*plural* **waves**)
1 a ridge moving along the surface of the sea etc. or breaking on the shore. **2** a curling piece of hair. **3** (in science) the wave-like movement by which heat, light, sound, or electricity etc. travels. **4** the action of waving.

wave *verb* (**waves, waving, waved**)
1 move your hand to and fro as a greeting or signal etc. **2** move loosely to and fro or up and down. **3** make a thing wavy. **4** be wavy.

wavelength *noun* (*plural* **wavelengths**)
the size of a sound wave or electromagnetic wave.

waver *verb* (**wavers, wavering, wavered**)
1 be unsteady; move unsteadily. **2** hesitate; be uncertain.

wavy *adjective*
full of waves or curves.
wavily *adverb* **waviness** *noun*

wax¹ *noun* (*plural* **waxes**)
1 a soft substance that melts easily, used to make candles, crayons, and polish. **2** beeswax.
waxy *adjective*

wax *verb* (**waxes, waxing, waxed**)
coat or polish something with wax.

wax² *verb* (**waxes, waxing, waxed**)
1 (said about the moon) show a bright area that becomes gradually larger. (The opposite is **wane**.) **2** become stronger or more important.

waxwork *noun* (*plural* **waxworks**)
a model of a person etc. made in wax.

way *noun* (*plural* **ways**)
1 how something is done; a method or style. **2** a manner ♦ *She spoke in a kindly way.* **3** a line of communication between places, e.g. a path or road. **4** a route or direction. **5** a distance to be travelled ♦ *Is it a long way away?* **6** a respect ♦ *It's a good idea in some ways.* **7** a condition or state ♦ *Things were in a bad way.*
get or **have your own way** make people let you do what you want. **give way** **1** collapse. **2** let somebody else move first. **3** yield.
in the way forming an obstacle or hindrance. **no way** (*informal*) that is impossible!
under way see **under**.

waylay *verb* (**waylays, waylaying, waylaid**)
lie in wait for a person or people, especially in order to talk to them or rob them.

wayside *noun*
fall by the wayside fail to continue doing something.

wayward *adjective*
disobedient; wilfully doing what you want.

we *pronoun*
a word used by a person to refer to himself or herself and another or others.

weak *adjective*
1 having little power, energy, or effect. **2** easy to break, damage, or defeat. **3** not great in intensity.
weakness *noun*

weaken *verb* (**weakens, weakening, weakened**)
make or become weaker.

weakling *noun* (*plural* **weaklings**)
a weak person or animal.

wealth *noun*
1 a lot of money or property; riches. **2** a large quantity ♦ *The book has a wealth of illustrations.*

wealthy *adjective* (**wealthier, wealthiest**)
having wealth; rich.
wealthiness *noun*

wean *verb* (**weans, weaning, weaned**)
make a baby take food other than its mother's milk.
wean off make someone give up a habit etc. gradually.

weapon *noun* (*plural* **weapons**)
something used to harm or kill people in a battle or fight.
weaponry *noun*

wear *verb* (**wears, wearing, wore, worn**)
1 have clothes, jewellery, etc. on your body. **2** have a certain look on your face ♦ *She wore a frown.* **3** damage something by rubbing or using it often; become damaged in this way ♦ *The carpet has worn thin.* **4** last while in use ♦ *It has worn well.*
wearable *adjective* **wearer** *noun*
wear off **1** be removed by wear or use. **2** become less intense. **wear on** pass gradually ♦ *The night wore on.* **wear out** **1** use or be used until it becomes weak or useless. **2** exhaust.

wear *noun*
1 what you wear; clothes ♦ *evening wear.* **2** (also **wear and tear**) gradual damage done by rubbing or using something.

weary *adjective* (**wearier, weariest**)
1 tired. **2** tiring ♦ *It's weary work.*
wearily *adverb* **weariness** *noun*

weary *verb* (**wearies, wearying, wearied**)
make or become weary.

weasel *noun* (*plural* **weasels**)
a small fierce animal with a slender body and reddish-brown fur.

weather *noun*
the rain, snow, wind, sunshine etc. at a particular time or place.
under the weather feeling ill or depressed.

weather verb (weathers, weathering, weathered)
1 expose something to the effects of the weather.
2 come through something successfully
♦ *The ship weathered the storm.*

weathercock or **weathervane** noun (plural weathercocks or weathervanes)
a pointer, often shaped like a cockerel, that turns in the wind and shows from which direction it is blowing.

weave verb (weaves, weaving, wove, woven)
1 make material or baskets etc. by crossing threads or strips under and over each other.
2 put a story together ♦ *She wove a thrilling tale.*
3 (past tense & past participle weaved) twist and turn ♦ *He weaved through the traffic.*
weaver noun

weave noun (plural weaves)
a style of weaving ♦ *a loose weave.*

web noun (plural webs)
1 a cobweb. 2 a network.
the Web the World Wide Web.
[from Old English *webb* = a piece of woven cloth]

webbed or **web-footed** adjective
having toes joined by pieces of skin, as ducks and frogs do.

website noun (plural websites)
a place on the Internet where you can get information about a subject, company, etc.

wed verb (weds, wedding, wedded)
1 marry. 2 unite two different things.

wedding noun (plural weddings)
the ceremony when a man and woman get married.

wedge noun (plural wedges)
1 a piece of wood or metal etc. that is thick at one end and thin at the other. It is pushed between things to force them apart or prevent something from moving. 2 a wedge-shaped thing.

wedge verb (wedges, wedging, wedged)
1 keep something in place with a wedge.
2 pack tightly together ♦ *Ten of us were wedged in the lift.*

Wednesday noun
the day of the week following Tuesday.
[from Old English *Wodnesdaeg* = day of Woden or Odin, the chief Norse god]

weed noun (plural weeds)
a wild plant that grows where it is not wanted.

weed verb (weeds, weeding, weeded)
remove weeds from the ground.

weedy adjective (weedier, weediest)
1 full of weeds. 2 thin and weak.

week noun (plural weeks)
a period of seven days, especially from Sunday to the following Saturday.

weekday noun (plural weekdays)
a day other than Saturday or Sunday.

weekend noun (plural weekends)
Saturday and Sunday.

weekly adjective & adverb
happening or done once a week.

weep verb (weeps, weeping, wept)
1 shed tears; cry. 2 ooze moisture in drops.
weep noun **weepy** adjective

weeping adjective
(said about a tree) having drooping branches
♦ *a weeping willow.*

weigh verb (weighs, weighing, weighed)
1 measure the weight of something. 2 have a certain weight ♦ *What do you weigh?*
3 be important or have influence ♦ *Her evidence weighed with the jury.*
weigh anchor raise the anchor and start a voyage. **weigh down** 1 keep something down by its weight. 2 depress or trouble somebody.
weigh up estimate or assess something.

weight noun (plural weights)
1 how heavy something is; the amount that something weighs. 2 a piece of metal of known weight, especially one used on scales to weigh things. 3 a heavy object. 4 importance or influence.
weighty adjective **weightless** adjective
weight verb (weights, weighting, weighted)
put a weight on something.

weir (say weer) noun (plural weirs)
a small dam across a river or canal to control the flow of water.

weird adjective
very strange; uncanny.
weirdly adverb **weirdness** noun

ⓘ USAGE When spelling this word, note that the 'e' comes before the 'i', not the other way round.

welcome noun (plural welcomes)
a greeting or reception, especially a kindly one.
welcome adjective
1 that you are glad to receive or see ♦ *a welcome gift.* 2 allowed or invited to do or take something
♦ *You are welcome to come.*
welcome verb (welcomes, welcoming, welcomed)
1 show that you are pleased when a person or thing arrives. 2 be glad to receive or hear of something ♦ *We welcome this decision.*

weld verb (welds, welding, welded)
1 join pieces of metal or plastic by heating and pressing or hammering them together. 2 unite people or things into a whole.

welfare noun
people's health, happiness, and comfort.

welfare state *noun*
a system in which a country's government provides money to pay for health care, social services, benefits, etc.

well¹ *noun* (*plural* **wells**)
1 a deep hole dug to bring up water or oil from underground. **2** a deep space, e.g. containing a staircase.

well *verb* (**wells, welling, welled**)
rise or flow up ♦ *Tears welled up in our eyes.*

well² *adverb* (**better, best**)
1 in a good or suitable way ♦ *She swims well.*
2 thoroughly ♦ *Polish it well.* **3** probably or reasonably ♦ *This may well be our last chance.*
well off 1 fairly rich. **2** in a good situation.

well *adjective*
1 in good health ♦ *He is not well.* **2** satisfactory ♦ *All is well.*

well-being *noun*
good health, happiness, and comfort.

wellingtons *plural noun*
rubber or plastic waterproof boots.
wellies *plural noun* (*informal*)
[named after the first Duke of Wellington (1769–1852), who wore long leather boots]

well-known *adjective*
known to many people.

well-mannered *adjective*
having good manners.

well-meaning *adjective*
having good intentions.

well-read *adjective*
having read a lot of good books.

well-to-do *adjective*
fairly rich.

weren't (*mainly spoken*)
were not.

werewolf *noun* (*plural* **werewolves**)
(in legends and stories) a person who sometimes changes into a wolf.
[from Old English *wer* = man + *wolf*]

west *noun*
1 the direction where the sun sets, opposite east.
2 the western part of a country, city, etc.

west *adjective*
1 situated in the west ♦ *the west coast.*
2 coming from the west ♦ *a west wind.*

west *adverb*
towards the west ♦ *We sailed west.*

westerly *adjective*
to or from the west.

western *adjective*
of or in the west.

western *noun* (*plural* **westerns**)
a film or story about cowboys or American Indians in western North America during the 19th and early 20th centuries.

westward *adjective* & *adverb*
towards the west.
westwards *adverb*

wet *adjective* (**wetter, wettest**)
1 soaked or covered in water or other liquid.
2 not yet dry ♦ *wet paint.* **3** rainy ♦ *wet weather.*
wetly *adverb* **wetness** *noun*

wet *verb* (**wets, wetting, wet** or **wetted**)
make a thing wet.

whale *noun* (*plural* **whales**)
a very large sea animal.
a whale of a (*informal*) very good or great
♦ *We had a whale of a time.*

whaling *noun*
hunting whales.

what *adjective*
used to ask the amount or kind of something (*What kind of bike have you got?*) or to say how strange or great a person or thing is (*What a fool you are!*).

what *pronoun*
1 what thing or things ♦ *What did you say?*
2 the thing that ♦ *This is what you must do.*
what's what (*informal*) which things are important or useful.

whatever *pronoun*
1 anything or everything ♦ *Do whatever you like.*
2 no matter what ♦ *Keep calm, whatever happens.*

whatever *adjective*
of any kind or amount ♦ *Take whatever books you need.* ♦ *There is no doubt whatever.*

wheat *noun*
a cereal plant from which flour is made.
wheaten *adjective*

wheedle *verb* (**wheedles, wheedling, wheedled**)
persuade by coaxing or flattering.

wheel *noun* (*plural* **wheels**)
1 a round device that turns on a shaft that passes through its centre. **2** a horizontal revolving disc on which clay is made into a pot.

wheel *verb* (**wheels, wheeling, wheeled**)
1 push a bicycle or trolley etc. along on its wheels. **2** move in a curve or circle; change direction and face another way ♦ *He wheeled round in astonishment.*

wheelbarrow *noun* (*plural* **wheelbarrows**)
a small cart with one wheel at the front and legs at the back, pushed by handles.

wheelchair *noun* (*plural* **wheelchairs**)
a chair on wheels for a person who cannot walk.

wheeze *verb* (**wheezes, wheezing, wheezed**)
make a hoarse whistling sound as you breathe.
wheeze *noun* **wheezy** *adjective*

when *adverb*
at what time; at which time ♦ *When can you come to tea?*

when *conjunction*
1 at the time that ♦ *The bird flew away when I moved.* 2 although; considering that ♦ *Why do you smoke when you know it's dangerous?*

whence *adverb*
from where; from which.

whenever *conjunction*
at whatever time; every time ♦ *Whenever I see it, I smile.*

where *adverb*
in or to what place or that place ♦ *Where did you put it? Leave it where it is.*

whereabouts *adverb*
in or near what place ♦ *Whereabouts are you going?*

whereabouts *plural noun*
the place where something is ♦ *Do you know the whereabouts of my radio?*

whereas *conjunction*
but in contrast ♦ *Some people enjoy sport, whereas others hate it.*

whereupon *conjunction*
after which; and then.

wherever *adverb*
in or to whatever place.

whet *verb* (**whets, whetting, whetted**)
whet your appetite stimulate it.

---

❶ USAGE Do not confuse with *wet*.

---

whether *conjunction*
as one possibility; if ♦ *I don't know whether to believe her or not.*

which *adjective*
what particular ♦ *Which way did he go?*

which *pronoun*
1 what person or thing ♦ *Which is your desk?*
2 the person or thing referred to ♦ *The film, which is a western, will be shown on Saturday.*

whichever *pronoun & adjective*
no matter which; any which ♦ *Take whichever you like.*

whiff *noun* (*plural* **whiffs**)
a puff or slight smell of smoke, gas, etc.

while *conjunction*
1 during the time that; as long as ♦ *Whistle while you work.* 2 although; but ♦ *She is dark, while her sister is fair.*

while *noun*
a period of time ♦ *a long while.*

while *verb* (**whiles, whiling, whiled**)
while away pass time ♦ *We whiled away the afternoon on the river.*

whim *noun* (*plural* **whims**)
a sudden wish to do or have something.

whimper *verb* (**whimpers, whimpering, whimpered**)
cry or whine softly.
whimper *noun*

whimsical *adjective*
quaint and playful.
whimsically *adverb* **whimsicality** *noun*

whine *verb* (**whines, whining, whined**)
1 make a long high miserable cry or a shrill sound. 2 complain in a petty or feeble way.
whine *noun*

whip *noun* (*plural* **whips**)
1 a cord or strip of leather fixed to a handle and used for hitting people or animals. 2 an official of a political party in Parliament. 3 a pudding made of whipped cream and fruit or flavouring.

whip *verb* (**whips, whipping, whipped**)
1 hit a person or animal with a whip. 2 beat cream until it becomes thick. 3 move or take something suddenly ♦ *He whipped out a gun.*
4 (*informal*) steal something.
whip up stir up people's feelings etc.
♦ *She whipped up support for her plans.*

whirl *verb* (**whirls, whirling, whirled**)
turn or spin very quickly.
whirl *noun*

whirlpool *noun* (*plural* **whirlpools**)
a whirling current of water.

whirlwind *noun* (*plural* **whirlwinds**)
a strong wind that whirls round a central point.

whirr *verb* (**whirrs, whirring, whirred**)
make a continuous buzzing sound.
whirr *noun*

whisk *verb* (**whisks, whisking, whisked**)
1 move or brush something away quickly and lightly ♦ *A waiter whisked away our plates.*
2 beat eggs etc. until they are frothy.

whisk *noun* (*plural* **whisks**)
1 a kitchen tool used for whisking things.
2 a whisking movement.
[from Old Norse]

whisker *noun* (*plural* **whiskers**)
1 a hair of those growing on a man's face, forming a beard or moustache if not shaved off.
2 a long bristle growing near the mouth of a cat etc.
whiskery *adjective*

whisky *noun* (*plural* **whiskies**)
a strong alcoholic drink.
[from Scottish Gaelic *uisge beatha* = water of life]

whisper *verb* (**whispers, whispering, whispered**)
1 speak very softly. 2 talk secretly.
whisper *noun*

whist *noun*
a card game usually for four people.

whistle *verb* (**whistles, whistling, whistled**)
make a shrill or musical sound, especially by blowing through your lips.
whistler *noun*

whistle *noun* (*plural* **whistles**)
1 a whistling sound. **2** a device that makes a shrill sound when air or steam is blown through it.

white *noun* (*plural* **whites**)
1 the very lightest colour, like snow or salt.
2 the transparent substance (**albumen**) round the yolk of an egg, which turns white when it is cooked. **3** a person with a light-coloured skin.

white *adjective*
1 of the colour white. **2** (said of a person) having light-coloured skin. **3** very pale from the effects of illness or fear etc. **4** (said about coffee) with milk.
whiteness *noun*

white elephant *noun* (*plural* **white elephants**)
a useless possession, especially one that is expensive to keep.

white-hot *adjective*
extremely hot; so hot that heated metal looks white.

white lie *noun* (*plural* **white lies**)
a harmless or trivial lie that you tell in order to avoid hurting someone's feelings.

whiten *verb* (**whitens, whitening, whitened**)
make or become whiter.

whitewash *noun*
1 a white liquid containing lime or powdered chalk, used for painting walls and ceilings etc.
2 concealing mistakes or other unpleasant facts so that someone will not be punished.
whitewash *verb*

whither *adverb* (*old use*)
to what place.

ℹ USAGE Do not confuse with *wither*.

---

whittle *verb* (**whittles, whittling, whittled**)
1 shape wood by trimming thin slices off the surface. **2** reduce something by removing various things from it ♦ *We need to whittle down the cost.*

whizz or **whiz** *verb* (**whizzes, whizzing, whizzed**)
1 move very quickly. **2** sound like something rushing through the air.

who *pronoun*
which person or people; the particular person or people ♦ *This is the boy who stole the apples.*

whoever *pronoun*
1 any or every person who. **2** no matter who.

whole *adjective*
1 complete. **2** not injured or broken.

whole *noun*
1 the full amount. **2** a complete thing.
on the whole considering everything; mainly.

wholefood *noun*
food that is free of additives and has been processed as little as possible.

wholehearted *adjective*
without doubts or reservations ♦ *You have my wholehearted support.*

wholemeal *adjective*
made from the whole grain of wheat.

whole number *noun* (*plural* **whole numbers**)
a number without fractions.

wholesale *noun*
selling goods in large quantities to be resold by others. (Compare **retail**.)
wholesaler *noun*

wholesale *adjective* & *adverb*
1 on a large scale; including everybody or everything ♦ *wholesale destruction.* **2** in the wholesale trade.

wholesome *adjective*
good for health; healthy ♦ *wholesome food.*
wholesomeness *noun*

wholly *adverb*
completely or entirely.

whom *pronoun*
the form of **who** used when it is the object of a verb or comes after a preposition, as in ♦ *the boy whom I saw* or *to whom we spoke.*

whoop (*say* woop) *noun* (*plural* **whoops**)
a loud cry of excitement.
whoop *verb*

whooping cough (*say* hoop-ing) *noun*
an infectious disease that causes spasms of coughing and gasping for breath.

whopper *noun* (*plural* **whoppers**) (*slang*)
something very large.

whopping *adjective* (*slang*)
very large or remarkable ♦ *a whopping lie.*

who's (*mainly spoken*)
who is; who has.

ℹ USAGE Do not confuse with *whose*.

---

whose *pronoun*
belonging to what person or people; of whom; of which ♦ *Whose house is that?*

ℹ USAGE Do not confuse with *who's*.

---

why *adverb*
for what reason or purpose; the particular reason on account of which ♦ *This is why I came.*

wick *noun* (*plural* **wicks**)
1 the string that goes through the middle of a candle and is lit. **2** the strip of material that you light in a lamp or heater etc. that uses oil.

wicked *adjective*
1 morally bad or cruel. **2** mischievous
♦ *a wicked smile.* **3** (*informal*) very good.
wickedly *adverb* **wickedness** *noun*

wicket *noun* (*plural* **wickets**)
1 a set of three stumps and two bails used in cricket. 2 the strip of ground between the wickets.

wicketkeeper *noun* (*plural* **wicketkeepers**)
the fielder in cricket who stands behind the batsman's wicket.

wide *adjective*
1 measuring a lot from side to side; not narrow. 2 measuring from side to side ♦ *The cloth is one metre wide.* 3 covering a great range ♦ *a wide knowledge of birds.* 4 fully open ♦ *eyes wide with excitement.* 5 missing the target ♦ *The shot was wide of the mark.*
widely *adverb* **wideness** *noun*

wide *adverb*
1 to the full extent; far apart ♦ *Open wide.* 2 missing the the target ♦ *The shot went wide.* 3 over a large area ♦ *She travelled far and wide.*

widen *verb* (**widens, widening, widened**)
make or become wider.

widespread *adjective*
existing in many places or over a wide area ♦ *a widespread belief.*

widow *noun* (*plural* **widows**)
a woman whose husband has died.

widowed *adjective*
made a widow or widower.

widower *noun* (*plural* **widowers**)
a man whose wife has died.

width *noun* (*plural* **widths**)
how wide something is; wideness.

wield *verb* (**wields, wielding, wielded**)
1 hold and use a weapon or tool ♦ *wielding a sword.* 2 have and use power or influence.

wife *noun* (*plural* **wives**)
the woman to whom a man is married.
[from Old English *wif* = woman]

wig *noun* (*plural* **wigs**)
a covering for the head, made of real or artificial hair.

wiggle *verb* (**wiggles, wiggling, wiggled**)
move from side to side.

wigwam *noun* (*plural* **wigwams**)
a tent formerly used by Native Americans, made by fastening skins or mats over poles.

wild *adjective*
1 living or growing in its natural state, not looked after by people. 2 not cultivated ♦ *a wild landscape.* 3 not civilized ♦ *the Wild West.* 4 not controlled; very violent or excited. 5 very foolish or unreasonable ♦ *You do have wild ideas.*
wildly *adverb* **wildness** *noun*

wilderness *noun* (*plural* **wildernesses**)
a wild uncultivated area; a desert.

wildfire *noun*
spread like wildfire (said about rumours etc.) spread very fast.

wildlife *noun*
wild animals in their natural setting.

wilful *adjective*
1 obstinately determined to do what you want ♦ *a wilful child.* 2 deliberate ♦ *wilful murder.*
wilfully *adverb* **wilfulness** *noun*

will¹ *auxiliary verb*
used to express the future tense, questions, or promises ♦ *They will arrive soon.* ♦ *Will you shut the door?* ♦ *I will get my revenge.*
[from Old English]

---

❶ USAGE See the entry for *shall.*

---

will² *noun* (*plural* **wills**)
1 the mental power to decide and control what you do. 2 a desire; a chosen decision ♦ *I wrote the letter against my will.* 3 determination to do something ♦ *They set to work with a will.* 4 a written statement of how a person's possessions are to be disposed of after his or her death.
at will whenever you like ♦ *You can come and go at will.*

will *verb* (**wills, willing, willed**)
use your will power; influence something by doing this ♦ *I was willing you to win!*
[from Old English *willa*]

willing *adjective*
ready and happy to do what is wanted.
willingly *adverb* **willingness** *noun*

willow *noun* (*plural* **willows**)
a tree or shrub with flexible branches, usually growing near water.

will power *noun*
strength of mind to control what you do.

willy-nilly *adverb*
whether you want to or not.

wilt *verb* (**wilts, wilting, wilted**)
lose freshness or strength.

wily (*say* wy-lee) *adjective*
cunning or crafty.
wiliness *noun*

win *verb* (**wins, winning, won**)
1 defeat your opponents in a battle, game, or contest. 2 get or achieve something by a victory or by using effort or skill etc. ♦ *She won the prize.*
win over gain someone's favour or support ♦ *By the end he had won over the audience.*

win *noun* (*plural* **wins**)
a victory.

wince *verb* (**winces, wincing, winced**)
make a slight movement because of pain or embarrassment etc.

wind¹ (rhymes with *tinned*) *noun* (*plural* **winds**)
1 a current of air. **2** gas in the stomach or intestines that makes you feel uncomfortable. **3** breath used for a purpose, e.g. for running or speaking. **4** the wind instruments of an orchestra.
get or **have the wind up** (*informal*) feel frightened. **get wind of** hear a rumour of something.

wind *verb* (**winds, winding, winded**)
put a person out of breath ♦ *The climb had winded us.*

wind² (rhymes with *find*) *verb* (**winds, winding, wound**)
1 go or turn something in twists, curves, or circles. **2** make a clock or watch work by tightening its spring.
winder *noun*
wind up 1 make a clock or watch work by tightening its spring. **2** close a business. **3** (*informal*) end up in a place or condition ♦ *He wound up in jail.*

windfall *noun* (*plural* **windfalls**)
1 a piece of unexpected good luck, especially a sum of money. **2** a fruit blown off a tree by the wind.

wind instrument *noun* (*plural* **wind instruments**)
a musical instrument played by blowing, e.g. a trumpet.

windmill *noun* (*plural* **windmills**)
a mill worked by the wind turning its sails.

window *noun* (*plural* **windows**)
1 an opening in a wall or roof etc. to let in light and often air, usually filled with glass. **2** the glass in this opening. **3** (in computing) an area on a VDU screen used for a particular purpose. [from Old Norse *vind* = wind, air + *auga* = eye]

windpipe *noun* (*plural* **windpipes**)
the tube by which air passes from the throat to the lungs.

windscreen *noun* (*plural* **windscreens**)
the window at the front of a motor vehicle.

windsurfing *noun*
surfing on a board that has a sail fixed to it.
windsurfer *noun*

windy *adjective*
with much wind ♦ *It's windy outside.*

wine *noun* (*plural* **wines**)
1 an alcoholic drink made from grapes or other plants. **2** a dark red colour.

wing *noun* (*plural* **wings**)
1 one of the pair of parts used by a bird, bat, or insect for flying. **2** one of the pair of long flat parts that stick out from the side of an aircraft and support it while it flies. **3** a part of a large building that extends from the main part. **4** the part of a motor vehicle's body above a

wheel. **5** a player whose place is at one of the far ends of the forward line in football or hockey etc. **6** a section of a political party, with more extreme opinions than the others.
on the wing flying. **take wing** fly away.
under your wing under your protection.
the wings the sides of a theatre stage out of sight of the audience.

wing *verb* (**wings, winging, winged**)
1 fly; travel by means of wings ♦ *The bird winged its way home.* **2** wound a bird in the wing or a person in the arm.

winged *adjective*
having wings.

wink *verb* (**winks, winking, winked**)
1 close and open your eye quickly, especially as a signal to someone. **2** (said about a light) flicker or twinkle.

wink *noun* (*plural* **winks**)
1 the action of winking. **2** a very short period of sleep ♦ *I didn't sleep a wink.*

winkle *verb* (**winkles, winkling, winkled**)
winkle out extract or obtain something with difficulty ♦ *I managed to winkle out some information.*

winner *noun* (*plural* **winners**)
1 a person or animal etc. that wins. **2** something very successful ♦ *Her latest book is a winner.*

winnings *plural noun*
money won.

winter *noun* (*plural* **winters**)
the coldest season of the year, between autumn and spring.
wintry *adjective*

wipe *verb* (**wipes, wiping, wiped**)
dry or clean something by rubbing it.
wipe *noun*
wipe out 1 cancel ♦ *wipe out the debt.* **2** destroy something completely.

wiper *noun* (*plural* **wipers**)
a device for wiping something, especially on a vehicle's windscreen.

wire *noun* (*plural* **wires**)
1 a strand or thin flexible rod of metal. **2** a piece of wire used to carry electric current. **3** a fence etc. made from wire. **4** a telegram.

wire *verb* (**wires, wiring, wired**)
1 fasten or strengthen something with wire. **2** fit or connect something with wires to carry electric current.

wireless *noun* (*plural* **wirelesses**) (*old use*)
a radio.

wiring *noun*
the system of wires carrying electricity in a building or in a device.

wiry *adjective*
1 like wire. **2** lean and strong.

wisdom *noun*
1 being wise. 2 wise sayings or writings.

wisdom tooth *noun* (*plural* **wisdom teeth**)
a molar tooth that may grow at the back of the jaw of a person aged about 20 or more.

wise *adjective*
knowing or understanding many things, and making good judgements.
wisely *adverb*

wish *verb* (**wishes, wishing, wished**)
1 feel or say that you would like to have or do something or would like something to happen.
2 say that you hope someone will get something ♦ *Wish me luck!*

wish *noun* (*plural* **wishes**)
1 something you wish for; a desire. 2 the action of wishing ♦ *Make a wish when you blow out the candles.*

wishbone *noun* (*plural* **wishbones**)
a forked bone between the neck and breast of a chicken or other bird.

wishful thinking *noun*
believing something because you want it to be true rather than because it is likely.

wisp *noun* (*plural* **wisps**)
1 a few strands of hair or bits of straw etc.
2 a small streak of smoke or cloud etc.
wispy *adjective*

wistful *adjective*
sadly longing for something.
wistfully *adverb* **wistfulness** *noun*

wit *noun* (*plural* **wits**)
1 intelligence or cleverness ♦ *Use your wits.*
2 a clever kind of humour. 3 a witty person.
at your wits' end not knowing what to do.
keep your wits about you stay alert.

witch *noun* (*plural* **witches**)
a person, especially a woman, who uses magic to do things.

witchcraft *noun*
the use of magic, especially for evil purposes.

witch-hunt *noun* (*plural* **witch-hunts**)
a campaign to find and punish people who hold views that are considered to be unacceptable or dangerous.

with *preposition*
used to indicate 1 being in the company or care etc. of (*Come with me*), 2 having (*a man with a beard*), 3 using (*Hit it with a hammer*),
4 because of (*shaking with laughter*), 5 feeling or showing (*We heard it with pleasure*), 6 towards or concerning (*I was angry with him*), 7 in opposition to; against (*Don't argue with your father*), 8 being separated from (*We had to part with it*).

withdraw *verb* (**withdraws, withdrawing, withdrew, withdrawn**)
1 take back or away; remove ♦ *She withdrew money from the bank.* 2 go away from a place or people ♦ *The troops withdrew from the frontier.*

withdrawal *noun* (*plural* **withdrawals**)
1 taking something out, especially money from a bank. 2 the process of stopping taking addictive drugs ♦ *withdrawal symptoms.*

withdrawn *adjective*
very shy or reserved.

wither *verb* (**withers, withering, withered**)
1 shrivel or wilt. 2 make something shrivel or wilt.

---

❶ USAGE Do not confuse with *whither*.

---

withering *adjective*
scornful or sarcastic ♦ *a withering remark.*

withhold *verb* (**withholds, withholding, withheld**)
refuse to give or allow information or permission.

within *preposition* & *adverb*
inside; not beyond something.

without *preposition*
1 not having ♦ *without food.* 2 free from
♦ *without fear.* 3 (*old use*) outside ♦ *without the city wall.*

without *adverb* (*old use*)
outside ♦ *We looked at the house from within and without.*

withstand *verb* (**withstands, withstanding, withstood**)
endure something successfully; resist.

witness *noun* (*plural* **witnesses**)
1 a person who sees or hears something happen
♦ *There were no witnesses to the accident.*
2 a person who gives evidence in a lawcourt.

witness *verb* (**witnesses, witnessing, witnessed**)
1 be a witness of something ♦ *Did anyone witness the accident?* 2 sign a document to confirm that it is genuine.

witticism *noun* (*plural* **witticisms**)
a witty remark.

witty *adjective* (**wittier, wittiest**)
clever and amusing; full of wit.
wittily *adverb* **wittiness** *noun*

wizard *noun* (*plural* **wizards**)
1 a male witch; a magician. 2 a person with amazing abilities.
wizardry *noun*

wobble *verb* (**wobbles, wobbling, wobbled**)
move unsteadily from side to side; shake slightly.
wobble *noun* **wobbly** *adjective*

woe *noun* (*plural* **woes**)
1 sorrow. **2** misfortune.
woeful *adjective* **woefully** *adverb*

woebegone *adjective*
looking unhappy.

wok *noun* (*plural* **woks**)
a Chinese cooking pan shaped like a large bowl.
[from Chinese]

wolf *noun* (*plural* **wolves**)
a fierce wild animal of the dog family, often
hunting in packs.
wolf *verb* (**wolfs, wolfing, wolfed**)
eat something greedily.

woman *noun* (*plural* **women**)
a grown-up female human being.
womanhood *noun*
[from Old English]

womanly *adjective*
having qualities that are thought to be typical of
women.

womb (*say* woom) *noun* (*plural* **wombs**)
the hollow organ in a female's body where
babies develop before they are born.

women's lib or **women's liberation** *noun*
the freedom of women to have the same rights,
opportunities, and status as men.

wonder *noun* (*plural* **wonders**)
1 a feeling of surprise and admiration or
curiosity. **2** something that causes this feeling;
a marvel.
no wonder it is not surprising.
wonder *verb* (**wonders, wondering,
wondered**)
1 feel that you want to know; try to decide
♦ *We are still wondering what to do next.*
2 feel wonder.

wonderful *adjective*
marvellous or excellent.
wonderfully *adverb*

won't (*mainly spoken*)
will not.

woo *verb* (**woos, wooing, wooed**) (*old use*)
1 court a woman. **2** seek someone's favour or
support.
wooer *noun*

wood *noun* (*plural* **woods**)
1 the substance of which trees are made.
2 many trees growing close together.

wooded *adjective*
covered with growing trees.

wooden *adjective*
1 made of wood. **2** stiff and showing no
expression or liveliness.
woodenly *adverb*

woodlouse *noun* (*plural* **woodlice**)
a small crawling creature with seven pairs of
legs, living in rotten wood or damp soil etc.

woodpecker *noun* (*plural* **woodpeckers**)
a bird that taps tree trunks with its beak to find
insects.

woodwind *noun*
wind instruments that are usually made of wood,
e.g. the clarinet and oboe.

woodwork *noun*
1 making things out of wood. **2** things made out
of wood.

woodworm *noun* (*plural* **woodworms**)
the larva of a kind of beetle that bores into wood;
the damage done by this.

woody *adjective*
1 like wood; consisting of wood. **2** full of trees.

wool *noun* (*plural* **wools**)
1 the thick soft hair of sheep and goats etc.
2 thread or cloth made from this.

woollen *adjective*
made of wool.

woolly *adjective*
1 covered with wool or wool-like hair.
2 like wool; woollen. **3** not thinking clearly;
vague or confused ♦ *woolly ideas.*
woolliness *noun*

word *noun* (*plural* **words**)
1 a set of sounds or letters that has a meaning,
and when written or printed has no spaces
between the letters. **2** a brief conversation
♦ *Can I have a word with you?* **3** a promise
♦ *He kept his word.* **4** a command or spoken
signal ♦ *Run when I give the word.* **5** a message;
information ♦ *We sent word of our safe arrival.*
have words quarrel. **word for word** in exactly
the same words.
word *verb* (**words, wording, worded**)
express something in words ♦ *Word the question
carefully.*

word class *noun* (*plural* **word classes**)
any of the groups (also called **parts of speech**)
into which words are divided in grammar (noun,
pronoun, adjective, verb, adverb, preposition,
conjunction, and interjection).

wording *noun*
the way something is worded.

word of honour *noun*
a solemn promise.

word-perfect *adjective*
having memorized every word perfectly
♦ *He was word-perfect at the rehearsal.*

word processor *noun* (*plural* **word
processors**)
a type of computer or program used for editing
and printing letters and documents.

wordy *adjective*
using too many words; not concise.

wore *past tense* of **wear**.

work *noun* (*plural* **works**)
1 something you have to do that needs effort or
energy ♦ *Digging is hard work.* 2 a job;
employment. 3 something produced by work
♦ *The teacher marked our work.* 4 (in science)
the result of applying a force to move an object.
5 a piece of writing, painting, music, etc.
♦ *the works of William Shakespeare.*
at work working. **out of work** having no work;
unable to find paid employment.
work *verb* (**works, working, worked**)
1 do work. 2 have a job; be employed ♦ *She
works in a bank.* 3 act or operate correctly or
successfully ♦ *Is the lift working?* 4 make
something act; operate ♦ *Can you work the lift?*
5 shape or press etc. ♦ *Work the mixture into a
paste.* 6 gradually move into a particular position
or state ♦ *The screw had worked loose.*
work out 1 find an answer by thinking or
calculating. 2 have a particular result.
work up make people become excited; arouse.

workable *adjective*
that can be used or will work.

worker *noun* (*plural* **workers**)
1 a person who works. 2 a member of the
working class. 3 a bee or ant etc. that does the
work in a hive or colony but does not produce
eggs.

workforce *noun* (*plural* **workforces**)
the number of people who work in a particular
factory, industry, country, etc.

working class *noun* (*plural* **working classes**)
people who work for wages, especially in
manual or industrial work.

workman *noun* (*plural* **workmen**)
a man employed to do manual labour.

workmanship *noun*
a person's skill in working; the result of this.

work of art *noun* (*plural* **works of art**)
a fine picture, building, etc.

workout *noun* (*plural* **workouts**)
a session of physical exercise or training.

works *plural noun*
1 the moving parts of a machine. 2 a factory or
industrial site.

workshop *noun* (*plural* **workshops**)
a place where things are made or mended.

world *noun* (*plural* **worlds**)
1 the earth with all its countries and peoples.
2 all the people on the earth; everyone ♦ *He felt
that the world was against him.* 3 a planet
♦ *creatures from another world.* 4 everything to
do with a certain subject or activity ♦ *the world
of sport.* 5 a very great amount ♦ *It will do him a
world of good.*

worldwide *adjective & adverb*
over the whole world.

World Wide Web *noun*
an international information system that
connects related sites and documents which can
be accessed using the Internet.

worm *noun* (*plural* **worms**)
1 a small animal with a long thin soft body.
2 (*informal*) an unpleasant person.
wormy *adjective*

worm *verb* (**worms, worming, wormed**)
move along by wriggling or crawling.
worm out gradually get someone to tell you
something by constantly and cleverly
questioning them ♦ *We eventually managed to
worm the truth out of them.*

worn *past participle* of **wear**.

worn-out *adjective*
1 exhausted. 2 damaged by too much use.

worried *adjective*
feeling or showing worry.

worry *verb* (**worries, worrying, worried**)
1 be troublesome to someone; make a person feel
slightly afraid. 2 feel anxious. 3 hold something
in the teeth and shake it ♦ *The dog was worrying
a rat.*
worrier *noun*

worry *noun* (*plural* **worries**)
1 the condition of worrying; being uneasy.
2 something that makes a person worry.

worse *adjective & adverb*
more bad or more badly; less good or less well.
worse off less fortunate or well off.

worship *verb* (**worships, worshipping,
worshipped**)
1 give praise or respect to God or a god.
2 love or respect a person or thing greatly.
worshipper *noun*

worship *noun* (*plural* **worships**)
1 worshipping; religious ceremonies.
2 a title of respect for a mayor or certain
magistrates ♦ *his worship the mayor.*

worst *adjective & adverb*
most bad or most badly; least good or least well.

worth *adjective*
1 having a certain value ♦ *This stamp is worth
£100.* 2 deserving something; good or important
enough for something ♦ *That book is worth
reading.*

worth *noun*
1 value or usefulness. 2 the amount that a
certain sum will buy ♦ *a pound's worth of
stamps.*

worthwhile *adjective*
important or good enough to deserve the time or
effort needed ♦ *a worthwhile job.*

worthy *adjective*
having great merit; deserving respect or support
♦ *a worthy cause.*
worthiness *noun*
worthy of deserving ♦ *This charity is worthy of
your support.*

would *auxiliary verb*
1 used as the past tense of *will*[1] (*We said we would do it*), in questions (*Would you like to come?*), and in polite requests (*Would you come in, please?*). **2** used instead of *should* with *I* and *we* and the verbs *like, prefer be glad*, etc. (e.g. *I would like to do it. We would be glad to help*). **3** used of something to be expected (*That's just what he would do!*).

ℹ️ USAGE For sense 2, see the note on *should* 4.

would-be *adjective*
wanting or pretending to be ♦ *a would-be comedian*.

wouldn't (*mainly spoken*)
would not.

wound[1] (*say* woond) *noun* (*plural* **wounds**)
1 an injury done by a cut, stab, or hit.
2 an injury to a person's feelings.

wound *verb* (**wounds, wounding, wounded**)
1 cause a wound to a person or animal.
2 hurt a person's feelings ♦ *She was wounded by these remarks.*

wound[2] (*say* wownd) *past tense* of **wind**[2].

wrap *verb* (**wraps, wrapping, wrapped**)
put paper or cloth etc. round something as a covering.
wrap up put on warm clothes.

wrapper *noun* (*plural* **wrappers**)
a piece of paper etc. wrapped round something.

wrapping *noun* (*plural* **wrapping**)
paper or other material for wrapping things in.

wreath (*say* reeth) *noun* (*plural* **wreaths**)
1 flowers or leaves etc. fastened into a circle ♦ *wreaths of holly.* **2** a curving line of mist or smoke.

wreathe (*say* reeth) *verb* (**wreathes, wreathing, wreathed**)
1 surround or decorate something with a wreath.
2 cover ♦ *Their faces were wreathed in smiles.*
3 move in a curve ♦ *Smoke wreathed upwards.*

wreck *verb* (**wrecks, wrecking, wrecked**)
damage or ruin something so badly that it cannot be used again.

wreck *noun* (*plural* **wrecks**)
1 a wrecked ship or building or car etc.
2 a person who is in a very bad state ♦ *a nervous wreck.* **3** the wrecking of something.

wreckage *noun*
the pieces of a wreck.

wren *noun* (*plural* **wrens**)
a very small brown bird.

wrench *verb* (**wrenches, wrenching, wrenched**)
twist or pull something violently.

wrench *noun* (*plural* **wrenches**)
1 a wrenching movement. **2** pain caused by parting ♦ *Leaving home was a great wrench.*
3 an adjustable tool rather like a spanner, used for gripping and turning bolts, nuts, etc.

wrestle *verb* (**wrestles, wrestling, wrestled**)
1 take part in a fight in which opponents grapple with each other and try to throw each other to the ground. **2** struggle with a problem etc.
wrestle *noun* **wrestler** *noun*

wretch *noun* (*plural* **wretches**)
1 a person who is very unhappy or who you pity.
2 a person who is disliked.

wretched *adjective*
1 miserable or unhappy. **2** of bad quality.
3 not satisfactory; causing a nuisance
♦ *This wretched car won't start.*
wretchedly *adverb* **wretchedness** *noun*

wriggle *verb* (**wriggles, wriggling, wriggled**)
move with short twisting movements.
wriggle *noun* **wriggly** *adjective*
wriggle out of avoid work or blame etc. cunningly.

wring *verb* (**wrings, wringing, wrung**)
1 twist and squeeze a wet thing to get water etc. out of it. **2** squeeze something firmly or forcibly.
3 get something by a great effort ♦ *We wrung a promise out of him.*
wring *noun*
wringing wet so wet that water can be squeezed out of it.

wrinkle *noun* (*plural* **wrinkles**)
1 a small furrow or ridge in the skin.
2 a small crease in something.

wrinkle *verb* (**wrinkles, wrinkling, wrinkled**)
make wrinkles in something; form wrinkles.

wrist *noun* (*plural* **wrists**)
the joint that connects the hand and arm.

wristwatch *noun* (*plural* **wristwatches**)
a watch for wearing on the wrist.

write *verb* (**writes, writing, wrote, written**)
1 put letters or words etc. on paper or another surface. **2** be the author or composer of something. **3** send a letter to somebody.
4 (in computing) enter data into a computer memory.
writer *noun*
write off think something is lost or useless.
write up write an account of something.

writhe *verb* (**writhes, writhing, writhed**)
1 twist your body because of pain. **2** wriggle.
3 suffer because of great shame.

writing *noun* (*plural* **writings**)
something you write; the way you write.

wrong *adjective*
1 incorrect; not true ♦ *the wrong answer.*
2 not fair or morally right ♦ *It is wrong to cheat.*
3 not working properly ♦ *There's something wrong with the engine.*
wrongly *adverb* **wrongness** *noun*

wrong *adverb*
wrongly ♦ *You guessed wrong.*

wrong *noun* (*plural* **wrongs**)
something morally wrong; an injustice.
in the wrong having done or said something
wrong.

wrong *verb* (**wrongs, wronging, wronged**)
do wrong to someone; treat a person unfairly.

wrought *adjective*
(said about metal) worked by being beaten out
or shaped by hammering or rolling etc.
♦ *wrought iron.*
[an old past participle of *work*]

wry *adjective* (**wryer, wryest**)
1 slightly mocking or sarcastic ♦ *a wry smile.*
2 twisted or bent out of shape. (Compare **awry**.)
wryly *adverb* **wryness** *noun*

#

Xmas *noun* (*informal*)
Christmas.

X-ray *noun* (*plural* **X-rays**)
a photograph or examination of the inside of
something, especially a part of the body, made
by a kind of radiation (called **X-rays**) that can
penetrate solid things.

X-ray *verb* (**X-rays, X-raying, X-rayed**)
make an X-ray of something.

xylophone (*say* zy-lo-fohn) *noun* (*plural*
xylophones)
a musical instrument made of wooden bars that
you hit with small hammers.
[from Greek *xylon* = wood + *phone* = sound]

#

yacht (*say* yot) *noun* (*plural* **yachts**)
1 a sailing boat used for racing or cruising.
2 a private ship.
yachting *noun* **yachtsman** *noun* **yachtswoman**
noun
[from Dutch *jaghtschip* = fast pirate ship]

yak *noun* (*plural* **yaks**)
an ox with long hair, found in central Asia.
[from Tibetan]

yank *verb* (**yanks, yanking, yanked**) (*informal*)
pull something strongly and suddenly.
yank *noun*

Yankee *noun* (*plural* **Yankees**) (*informal*)
an American, especially of the northern USA.

yap *verb* (**yaps, yapping, yapped**)
bark shrilly.
yap *noun*

yard¹ *noun* (*plural* **yards**)
1 a measure of length, 36 inches or about 91
centimetres. **2** a long pole stretched out from a
mast to support a sail.
[from Old English *gerd*]

yard² *noun* (*plural* **yards**)
an enclosed area beside a building or used for a
certain kind of work ♦ *a timber yard.*
[from Old English *geard*]

yarn *noun* (*plural* **yarns**)
1 thread spun by twisting fibres together, used in
knitting etc. **2** (*informal*) a tale or story.

yawn *verb* (**yawns, yawning, yawned**)
1 open the mouth wide and breathe in deeply
when feeling sleepy or bored. **2** form a wide
opening ♦ *A pit yawned in front of us.*
yawn *noun*

ye *pronoun* (*old use*)
you (referring to two or more people).

year *noun* (*plural* **years**)
1 the time the earth takes to go right round the
sun, about 365¼ days. **2** the time from 1 January
to 31 December; any period of twelve months.
3 a group of students of roughly the same age.
yearly *adjective* & *adverb*

yearn *verb* (**yearns, yearning, yearned**)
long for something.

yeast *noun*
a substance that causes alcohol and carbon
dioxide to form as it develops, used in making
beer and wine and in baking bread etc.

yell *verb* (**yells, yelling, yelled**)
give a loud cry; shout.
yell *noun*

yellow *noun* (*plural* **yellows**)
the colour of buttercups and ripe lemons.

yellow *adjective*
1 of yellow colour. **2** (*informal*) cowardly.
yellowness *noun*

yellow pages *plural noun*
a special telephone directory giving addresses
and telephone numbers of businesses, arranged
according to what services they provide.

yelp *verb* (**yelps, yelping, yelped**)
give a shrill bark or cry.
yelp *noun*

yen¹ *noun* (*plural* **yen**)
a unit of money in Japan.
[from Japanese *en* = round]

yen² *noun* (*plural* **yens**)
a longing for something.
[from Chinese]

yes *adverb*
used to agree to or accept something or as an
answer meaning 'I am here'.

yesterday *noun & adverb*
the day before today.

yet *adverb*
1 up to this time; by this time ♦ *The post hasn't
come yet.* **2** eventually ♦ *I'll get even with him
yet!* **3** in addition; even ♦ *She became yet more
excited.*

yet *conjunction*
nevertheless ♦ *It is strange, yet it is true.*

yew *noun* (*plural* **yews**)
an evergreen tree with dark green needle-like
leaves and red berries.

yield *verb* (**yields, yielding, yielded**)
1 give in or surrender. **2** agree to do what is
asked or ordered; give way ♦ *He yielded to
persuasion.* **3** produce as a crop or as profit etc.

yoga (*say* yoh-ga) *noun*
a Hindu system of meditation and self-control;
a system of physical exercises based on this.

yoghurt (*say* yog-ert) *noun*
milk thickened by the action of certain bacteria,
giving it a sharp taste.
[from Turkish]

yoke *noun* (*plural* **yokes**)
1 a curved piece of wood put across the
necks of animals pulling a cart or plough etc.
2 a shaped piece of wood fitted across a person's
shoulders, with a pail or load hung at each end.
3 a close-fitting upper part of a piece of clothing,
from which the rest hangs.

yoke *verb* (**yokes, yoking, yoked**)
harness or join things by means of a yoke.
[from Old English]

❶ USAGE Do not confuse with *yolk*.

yolk (rhymes with *coke*) *noun* (*plural* **yolks**)
the round yellow part inside an egg.

❶ USAGE Do not confuse with *yoke*.

yonder *adjective & adverb*
over there.

you *pronoun*
1 the person or people being spoken to
♦ *Who are you?* **2** anyone or everyone;
one ♦ *You can't tell what will happen next.*

young *adjective*
having lived or existed for only a short time;
not old.

youngster *noun* (*plural* **youngsters**)
a young person; a child.

your *adjective*
belonging to you.

❶ USAGE Do not confuse with *you're*.

you're (*mainly spoken*)
you are.

❶ USAGE Do not confuse with *your*.

yours *possessive pronoun*
belonging to you.
Yours faithfully, Yours sincerely ways of
ending a letter before you sign it. (*Yours
faithfully* is more formal than *Yours sincerely*.)

❶ It is incorrect to write ♦ *your's*.

yourself *pronoun* (*plural* **yourselves**)
you and nobody else.

youth *noun* (*plural* **youths**)
1 being young; the time when you are young.
2 a young man. **3** young people.
youthful *adjective* **youthfulness** *noun*

youth hostel *noun* (*plural* **youth hostels**)
a place where young people can stay cheaply
when they are hiking or on holiday.

yo-yo *noun* (*plural* **yo-yos**)
a round wooden or plastic toy that moves up and
down on a string that you hold.
[probably from a language spoken in the
Philippines]

Yule *noun* (*old use*)
the Christmas festival, also called **Yuletide**.
[originally the name of a pagan festival: from Old
English or Old Norse]

Zz

zap *verb* (**zaps, zapping, zapped**) (*slang*)
1 attack or destroy something forcefully,
especially in electronic games. **2** use a remote
control to change television channels quickly.

zeal *noun*
enthusiasm or keenness.
zealous (*say* zel-us) *adjective* **zealously** *adverb*

zebra (*say* zeb-ra) *noun* (*plural* **zebras**)
an African animal of the horse family, with black
and white stripes all over its body.
[from Italian, Spanish, or Portuguese]

zebra crossing *noun* (*plural* **zebra crossings**)
a place for pedestrians to cross a road safely,
marked with broad white stripes.

zero *noun* (*plural* **zeros**)
1 nought; the figure 0. **2** the point marked 0 on a
thermometer etc.
[from Arabic *sifr* = cipher]

zero hour *noun*
the time when something is planned to start.

zest *noun*
1 great enjoyment or interest. 2 the coloured part of orange or lemon peel.
zestful *adjective* **zestfully** *adverb*

zigzag *noun* (*plural* **zigzags**)
a line or route that turns sharply from side to side.

zigzag *verb* (**zigzags, zigzagging, zigzagged**)
move in a zigzag.

zinc *noun*
a white metal.
[from German *Zink*]

zip *noun* (*plural* **zips**)
1 a zip fastener. 2 a sharp sound like a bullet going through the air. 3 liveliness or vigour.
zippy *adjective*

zip *verb* (**zips, zipping, zipped**)
1 fasten something with a zip fastener.
2 move quickly with a sharp sound.

zip fastener or **zipper** *noun* (*plural* **zip fasteners** or **zippers**)
a fastener consisting of two strips of material, each with rows of small teeth that interlock when a sliding tab brings them together.

zodiac (*say* zoh-dee-ak) *noun*
a strip of sky where the sun, moon, and main planets are found, divided into twelve equal parts (called **signs of the zodiac**), each named after a constellation.
[from Greek *zoidion* = image of an animal]

zone *noun* (*plural* **zones**)
an area of a special kind or for a particular purpose ♦ *a war zone;* ♦ *a no-parking zone.*
[from Greek, = girdle]

zoo *noun* (*plural* **zoos**)
a place where wild animals are kept so that people can look at them or study them.

zoology (*say* zoh-ol-o-jee) *noun*
the scientific study of animals.
zoological *adjective* **zoologist** *noun*
[from Greek *zoion* = animal]

zoom *verb* (**zooms, zooming, zoomed**)
1 move very quickly, especially with a deep buzzing sound. 2 rise quickly ♦ *Prices had zoomed.* 3 (in photography) use a zoom lens to change from a distant view to a close-up.
zoom *noun*
[imitating the sound]

zoom lens *noun* (*plural* **zoom lenses**)
a camera lens that can be adjusted continuously to make things appear close up or far away.

Appendices

Appendix 1

Prefixes and suffixes

Prefixes

A prefix is placed at the beginning of a word to change its meaning or to form a new word.

Prefix	Meaning	Example
a-	not, without	asymmetrical
ab-	away, from	abduct
ad-	to, towards	admit
aero-	to do with air or aircraft	aeronautics
ante-	before	antenatal
anti-	against, opposed to	antifreeze
arch-	chief, principal	arch-enemy
auto-	of or by yourself or itself	autograph
be-	used to make verbs from nouns	befriend
bene-	well, good	benefactor
bi-	two, twice	bicycle, biennial
bio-	life	biology
cata-	down	catapult
centi-	centi-	centimetre
co-	with, together	coalition
com-	with, together	combine
con-	with, together	concise
contra-	against, opposed to	contraception
counter-	against, opposing	counterbalance
cross-	across, crossing	crossbar
de-	removing, away from	decapitate, decompose
deca-	ten	decathlon
deci-	one tenth	decimal
demi-	half	demigod
di-	two, double	dilemma
dia-	through, across	diagonal
dis-	not, the opposite of	dishonest, disarm
dys-	bad, difficult	dyslexia
electro-	to do with or using electricity	electromagnet
en-	on, into	encamp
epi-	above, over	epidemic
equi-	equal, equally	equilateral
eu-	well	euphemism
ex-	out, away; former	extract; ex-president
extra-	outside, beyond	extraterrestrial
for-	going without, preventing	forbid

Prefix	Meaning	Example
fore-	before, in advance	forecast
geo-	to do with the earth	geography
hecto-	one hundred	hectogram = 100 grams
hepta-	seven	heptagon = a shape with seven sides
hetero-	other, different	heterosexual
hexa-	six	hexagon
homo-	the same	homosexual
hydro-	to do with water	hydroelectric
hyper-	above, beyond	hyperactive
hypo-	below, less than	hypothermia
in-	towards, against; not	invade; invalid
infra-	below	infra-red
inter-	between, among	interactive
intra-	within	intravenous
iso-	equal	isotope
kilo-	one thousand	kilometre
mal-	bad, badly	malfunction
mega-	large	megaphone
micro-	small	microscope
milli-	one thousandth	milligram = 0.001 gram
mini-	small	minidress = a very short dress
mis-	badly, wrong	misbehave
mono-	one, single	monopoly
multi-	many	multicultural
neo-	new	neolithic
non-	not	non-existent
ob-	against, blocking	obstruct
octo-	eight	octopus
omni-	all, everything	omnivorous
ortho-	right, correct	orthodox
out-	out of, away from; more than	outcast; outdo
over-	too much	overact

Prefix	Meaning	Example
pan-	to do with all of something	pan-African = to do with all Africa
penta-	five	pentagon
per-	through, thoroughly	perception
peri-	around	perimeter
philo-	fond of	philosophy
photo-	to do with light	photography
poly-	many	polygamy
post-	after	post-war
pre-	before	prehistoric
pro-	in favour of; forward	pro-British; proceed
proto-	first	prototype
pseudo-	false, pretended	pseudonym
psycho-	to do with the mind	psychoanalysis
quadri-	four	quadrilateral
quasi-	seeming to be but not really or not fully	quasi-scientific
radio-	to do with radiation or radio	radioactive
re-	again	refill

Prefix	Meaning	Example
retro-	back, backward	retrograde
self-	done by yourself or itself	self-catering
semi-	half, partly	semi-detached
step-	related by the remarriage of one parent	stepmother
sub-	under; subordinate	submarine; submit
super-	above, over	superfluous
sym-	with, together	sympathy
syn-	with, together	synthesize
tele-	far, at a distance	telephone
tetra-	four	tetrahedron
thermo-	to do with heat	thermodynamics
trans-	across, through	transatlantic, transfer
tri-	three	triangle
ultra-	beyond	ultraviolet
un-	not; the reverse of	unhappy; undo
under-	not enough	underdone
uni-	one, single	universe
vice-	deputy, substitute	vice-president

Suffixes

A suffix is placed at the end of a word to form another word or to form a plural, past tense, comparative, superlative, etc.

Suffix	Meaning	Example
-ability	forming nouns from adjectives in -able	readability
-able	forming adjectives meaning 'able to be done'	readable
-archy	forming nouns meaning 'a type of rule'	monarchy
-arian	forming nouns and adjectives meaning 'members of a group'	vegetarian
-ary	forming nouns and adjectives	primary, dictionary
-ate	forming nouns and adjectives	passionate, magistrate
-ate	used in scientific and technical terms	nitrate
-ation	forming nouns from verbs	organization
-cide	forming nouns meaning 'killing' or 'killer'	homicide
-cle	forming nouns meaning 'something small'	particle
-cracy	forming nouns meaning 'a type of government'	democracy
-crat	forming nouns meaning 'believer in a type of government'	democrat
-cule	forming nouns meaning 'something small'	molecule
-cy	forming nouns	piracy
-dom	forming nouns	freedom
-ed	forming past tenses and past participles of verbs	greeted, pasted
-ee	forming nouns meaning 'a person affected by something'	employee, refugee
-er	forming nouns meaning 'someone who does something'	painter
-er	forming adjectives and adverbs meaning 'more –'	bigger, slower

Suffix	Meaning	Example
-ess	forming female nouns	lioness
-est	forming adjectives and adverbs meaning 'most –'	biggest, slowest
-ette	forming nouns meaning 'something small'	cigarette
-faction	forming nouns from verbs that end in **-fy**	satisfaction
-fication	forming nouns from verbs that end in **-fy**	purification
-fold	forming adjectives and adverbs meaning 'multiplied by'	twofold
-ful	forming adjectives meaning 'having this quality' and nouns meaning 'containing this amount'	beautiful; cupful
-fy	forming verbs	purify
-gen	used in scientific language to form nouns meaning 'producing' or 'produced'	oxygen
-gon	forming nouns meaning 'having a certain number of angles and sides'	hexagon
-gram	forming nouns meaning 'something written or drawn'	diagram
-graph	forming nouns meaning 'something written or drawn or recorded'	photograph
-graphy	forming nouns for a scientific study	geography
-hood	forming nouns	parenthood
-ibility	forming nouns from adjectives that end in **-ible**	accessibility
-ible	forming adjectives meaning 'able to be done'	accessible
-ic	forming adjectives and nouns	comic, public
-ical	forming adjectives	comical
-ician	forming nouns meaning 'a person who is skilled in something'	musician
-icity	forming nouns from words that end in **-ic**	publicity
-ics	forming nouns for a subject	mathematics
-ie	forming nouns for pet names	auntie
-ing	forming parts of verbs, which can also be adjectives	asking, missing
-ion	forming nouns	attraction, dominion
-ise	forming verbs	advise
-ish	forming adjectives meaning 'rather, somewhat'	greenish
-ism	forming nouns	criticism, heroism
-ist	forming nouns meaning 'someone who does something or believes in or supports something'	communist
-ite	used in scientific and technical terms	dynamite
-itis	forming nouns for diseases involving inflammation	appendicitis
-ive	forming adjectives, mostly from verbs	active
-ize	forming verbs	privatize
-less	forming adjectives meaning 'without' or 'lacking'	helpless
-ling	forming nouns meaning 'something small'	fledgeling
-logical	forming adjectives from nouns that end in **-logy**	archaeological
-logist	forming nouns meaning 'an expert in'	archaeologist
-logy	forming nouns for a subject of study	archaeology
-ly	forming adverbs from adjectives and forming some adjectives	quickly; friendly
-most	forming adjectives meaning 'most'	innermost
-ness	forming nouns from adjectives	blindness, happiness
-or	forming nouns meaning 'someone who does something'	sailor
-ous	forming adjectives	dangerous
-pathy	forming nouns meaning 'feeling or suffering something'	sympathy
-phobia	forming nouns meaning 'fear or great dislike of something'	claustrophobia
-ship	forming nouns	friendship

Suffix	Meaning	Example
-some	forming adjectives	quarrelsome
-teen	forming numbers from 13 to 19	sixteen
-tude	forming nouns	solitude
-uble	forming adjectives meaning 'able to be done'	soluble
-vore	forming nouns meaning 'feeding on'	carnivore
-vorous	forming adjectives from nouns that end in -**vore**	carnivorous
-ward	forming adjectives and adverbs showing direction	backward
-wards	forming adverbs showing direction	backwards
-ways	forming adverbs showing direction or manner	sideways
-wise	forming adverbs	clockwise, otherwise
-y	forming adjectives	messy, sticky

Appendix 2

Some foreign words and phrases used in English

ad hoc
done or arranged only when necessary and not planned in advance. [Latin, = for this]

ad infinitum (*say* in-fin-I-tum)
without limit; for ever. [Latin, = to infinity]

ad nauseam (*say* naw-see-am)
until people are sick of it. [Latin, = to sickness]

aide-de-camp (*say* ayd-der-**kahm**)
a military officer who is the assistant to a senior officer. [French, = camp-helper]

à la carte
ordered and paid for as separate items from a menu. (Compare *table d'hôte*.) [French, = from the menu]

alfresco
in the open air ♦ *an alfresco meal*. [from Italian *al fresco* = in the fresh air]

alter ego
another, very different, side of someone's personality. [Latin, = other self]

au fait (*say* oh fay)
knowing a subject or procedure etc. well. [French, = to the point]

au gratin (*say* oh grat-an)
cooked with a crisp topping of breadcrumbs or grated cheese. [French]

au revoir (*say* oh rev-**wahr**)
goodbye for the moment. [French, = to be seeing again]

avant-garde (*say* av-ahn-**gard**)
people who use a very modern style in art or literature etc. [French, = vanguard]

bête noire (*say* bayt **nwahr**)
a person or thing you greatly dislike. [French, = black beast]

bona fide (*say* boh-na **fy**-dee)
genuine; without fraud ♦ *Are they bona fide tourists or spies?* [Latin, = in good faith]

bona fides (*say* boh-na **fy**-deez)
honest intention; sincerity ♦ *We do not doubt his bona fides.* [Latin, = good faith]

bon voyage (*say* bawn vwah-**yah**zh)
pleasant journey! [French]

carte blanche (*say* kart **blahnsh**)
freedom to act as you think best. [French, = blank paper]

c'est la vie (*say* sel la **vee**)
life is like that. [French, = that is life]

chef-d'oeuvre (*say* shay **dervr**)
a masterpiece. [French, = chief work]

compos mentis
in your right mind; sane. (The opposite is *non compos mentis*.) [Latin, = having control of the mind]

cordon bleu (*say* kor-dawn **bler**)
(of cooks and cookery) first-class. [French, = blue ribbon]

corps de ballet (*say* kor der **bal**-ay)
the whole group of dancers (not the soloists) in a ballet. [French]

corps diplomatique (*say* kor dip-lom-at-**eek**)
the diplomatic service. [French]

coup de grâce (*say* koo der **grahs**)
a stroke or blow that puts an end to something. [French, = mercy-blow]

coup d'état (*say* koo day-**tah**)
the sudden overthrow of a government. [French, = blow of State]

crème de la crème (*say* krem der la krem)
the very best of something. [French, = cream of the cream]

curriculum vitae (*say* **veet**-I)
a brief account of a person's education, career, etc. [Latin, = course of life]

déjà vu (*say* day-*zh*a **vew**)
a feeling that you have already experienced what is happening now. [French, = already seen]

de rigueur (*say* der rig-**er**)
proper; required by custom or etiquette. [French, = of strictness]

de trop (*say* der **troh**)
not wanted; unwelcome. [French, = too much]

doppelgänger (*say* **dop**-el-geng-er)
the ghost of a living person. [German, = double-goer]

dramatis personae (*say* dram-a-tis per-**sohn**-I)
the characters in a play. [Latin, = persons of the drama]

en bloc (*say* ahn blok)
all at the same time; in a block. [French]

en masse (*say* ahn mass)
all together. [French, = in a mass]

en passant (*say* ahn pas-ahn)
by the way. [French, = in passing]

en route (*say* ahn root)
on the way. [French]

entente (*say* ahn-**tahnt** or on-**tont**)
a friendly understanding between nations. [French]

esprit de corps (*say* es-pree der **kor**)
loyalty to your group. [French, = spirit of the body]

eureka (*say* yoor-**eek**-a)
I have found it! [Greek]

exeunt (*say* eks-ee-unt)
they leave the stage. [Latin, = they go out]

ex gratia (*say* eks **gray**-sha)
given without being legally obliged to be given ♦ *an ex gratia payment.* [Latin, = from favour]

faux pas (*say* foh **pah**)
an embarrassing blunder. [French, = false step]

hara-kiri
a form of suicide formerly used by Japanese officers when in disgrace. [from Japanese *hara* = belly, *kiri* = cutting]

hoi polloi
the ordinary people; the masses. [Greek, = the many]

Homo sapiens
human beings regarded as a species of animal. [Latin, = wise man]

hors-d'oeuvre (*say* or-**dervr**)
food served as an appetizer at the start of a meal. [French, = outside the work]

in camera
in a judge's private room, not in public. [Latin, = in the room]

in extremis (*say* eks-**treem**-iss)
at the point of death; in very great difficulties. [Latin, = in the greatest danger]

in memoriam
in memory (of). [Latin]

in situ (*say* **sit**-yoo)
in its original place. [Latin]

joie de vivre (*say* *zh*wah der **veevr**)
a feeling of great enjoyment of life. [French, = joy of life]

laissez-faire (*say* lay-say-**fair**)
a government's policy of not interfering. [French, = let (them) act]

maître d'hôtel (*say* metr doh-**tel**)
a head waiter. [French, = master of house]

milieu (*say* **meel**-yer)
environment; surroundings. [French, from *mi* = mid + *lieu* = place]

modus operandi (*say* moh-dus op-er-**and**-ee)
1 a person's way of working. **2** the way a thing works. [Latin, = way of working]

nem. con.
unanimously. [short for Latin *nemine contradicente* = with nobody disagreeing]

nom de plume
a writer's pseudonym. [French, = pen-name (this phrase is not used in France)]

non sequitur (*say* non **sek**-wit-er)
a conclusion that does not follow from the evidence given. [Latin, = it does not follow]

nota bene (*say* noh-ta **ben**-ee)
(usually shortened to NB) note carefully. [Latin, = note well]

nouveau riche (*say* noo-voh **reesh**)
a person who has only recently become rich. [French, = new rich]

objet d'art (*say* ob-*zh*ay **dar**)
a small artistic object. [French, = object of art]

par excellence (*say* par eks-el-**ahns**)
more than all the others; to the greatest degree. [French, = because of special excellence]

pas de deux (*say* pah der **der**)
a dance (e.g. in a ballet) for two persons. [French, = step of two]

pâté de foie gras (*say* pat-ay der fwah **grah**)
a paste or pie of goose-liver. [French, = paste of fat liver]

per annum
for each year; yearly. [Latin]

per capita (*say* **kap**-it-a)
for each person. [Latin, = for heads]

persona grata (*say* per-soh-na **grah**-ta)
a person who is acceptable to someone, especially a diplomat acceptable to a foreign government. (The opposite is *persona non grata*.) [Latin, = pleasing person]

pièce de résistance (*say* pee-ess der ray-zees-**tahns**)
the most important item. [French]

placebo (*say* plas-**ee**-boh) (*plural* **placebos**)
a harmless substance given as if it were medicine, usually to reassure a patient. [Latin, = I shall be pleasing]

poste restante (*say* rest-**ahnt**)
a part of a post office where letters etc. are kept until called for. [French, = letters remaining]

prima facie (*say* pry-ma **fay**-shee)
at first sight; judging by the first impression. [Latin, = on first appearance]

quid pro quo (*say* kwoh)
something given or done in return for something. [Latin, = something for something]

raison d'être (*say* ray-zawn **detr**)
the purpose of a thing's existence. [French, = reason for being]

rigor mortis (*say* ry-ger **mor**-tis)
stiffening of the body after death. [Latin, = stiffness of death]

RIP
may he or she (or they) rest in peace. [short for Latin *requiescat* (or *requiescant*) *in pace*]

sang-froid (*say* sahn-**frwah**)
calmness in danger or difficulty. [French, = cold blood]

savoir faire (*say* sav-wahr **fair**)
knowledge of how to behave socially. [French,
= knowing how to do]

sotto voce (*say* sot-oh **voh**-chee)
in a very quiet voice. [Italian, = under the voice]

status quo (*say* stay-tus **kwoh**)
the state of affairs as it was before a change.
[Latin, = the state in which]

sub judice (*say* **joo**-dis-ee)
being decided by a judge or lawcourt. [Latin,
= under a judge]

table d'hôte (*say* tahbl **doht**)
a restaurant meal served at a fixed inclusive
price. (Compare *à la carte.*) [French, = host's
table]

terra firma
dry land; the ground. [Latin, = firm land]

tête-à-tête (*say* tayt-ah-**tayt**)
a private conversation, especially between two
people. [French, = head to head]

vis-à-vis (*say* veez-ah-**vee**)
1 in a position facing one another; opposite to.
2 as compared with. [French, = face to face]

viva voce (*say* vy-va **voh**-chee)
in a spoken test or examination. [Latin, = with
the living voice]

volte-face (*say* volt-**fahs**)
a complete change in your attitude towards
something. [French]

Appendix 3

Signs of the zodiac

The strip of sky called the zodiac is divided into twelve equal sections, each named after a group of stars (its sign) that was formerly situated in it. When seen from the Earth, the sun appears to move through each section in turn during one year. The dates given below are the approximate times when it enters and leaves each sign.

In ancient times, people believed that stars and planets influenced the entire world and all that happened in it, including medicine, and people's lives. The key to a person's whole life was thought to lie in the way the planets were arranged (called a horoscope) at his or her birth. Many newspapers and magazines print forecasts of what is about to happen to those born under each sign, but only a few people treat them seriously.

The names of the signs are derived from the Latin word with the same meaning.

Aries	the Ram	12 March–20 April
Taurus	the Bull	12 April–20 May
Gemini	the Twins	21 May–20June
Cancer	the Crab	21 June–21 July
Leo	the Lion	22 July–22 August
Virgo	the Virgin	23 August–21 Spetember
Libra	the Scales	22 September–22 October
Scorpio	the Scorpion	23 October–21November
Sagittarius	the Archer	22 November–21 December
Capricorn	the Goat	22 December–20 January
Aquarius	the Water-carrier	21 January–19 February
Pisces	the Fishes	20 February–20 March

Appendix 4

Countries of the world

Country	People
Afghanistan	Afghans
Albania	Albanians
Algeria	Algerians
Andorra	Andorrans
Angola	Angolans
Antigua and Barbuda	Antiguans, Barbudans
Argentina	Argentinians
Armenia	Armenians
Australia	Australians
Austria	Austrians
Azerbaijan	Azerbaijanis or Azeris
Bahamas	Bahamians
Bahrain	Bahrainis
Bangladesh	Bangladeshis
Barbados	Barbadians
Belarus	Belorussians
Belgium	Belgians
Belize	Belizians
Benin	Beninese
Bermuda	Bermudans
Bhutan	Bhutanese
Bolivia	Bolivians
Bosnia-Herzegovina	Bosnians
Botswana	Batswana or Citizens of Botswana
Brazil	Brazilians
Brunei Darussalam	People of Brunei
Bulgaria	Bulgarians
Burkina Faso	Burkinans
Burundi	People of Burundi
Cambodia	Cambodians
Cameroon	Cameroonians
Canada	Canadians
Cape Verde	Cape Verdeans
Central African Republic	People of the Central African Republic
Chad	Chadians
Chile	Chileans
China, People's Republic of	Chinese
Colombia	Colombians
Comoros	Comorans
Congo, Democratic Republic of the	Congolese
Congo, Republic of the	Congolese
Costa Rica	Costa Ricans
Côte d'Ivoire	People of the Côte d'Ivoire
Croatia	Croats

Country	People
Cuba	Cubans
Cyprus	Cypriots
Czech Republic	Czechs
Denmark	Danes
Djibouti	Djiboutians
Dominica	Dominicans
Dominican Republic	Dominicans
East Timor	East Timorese
Ecuador	Ecuadoreans
Egypt	Egyptians
El Salvador	Salvadoreans
Equatorial Guinea	Equatorial Guineans
Eritrea	Eritreans
Estonia	Estonians
Ethiopia	Ethiopians
Fiji	Fijians
Finland	Finns
France	French
Gabon	Gabonese
Gambia, The	Gambians
Georgia	Georgians
Germany	Germans
Ghana	Ghanaians
Greece	Greeks
Grenada	Grenadians
Guatemala	Guatemalans
Guinea	Guineans
Guinea-Bissau	People of Guinea-Bissau
Guyana	Guyanese
Haiti	Haitians
Honduras	Hondurans
Hungary	Hungarians
Iceland	Icelanders
India	Indians
Indonesia	Indonesians
Iran	Iranians
Iraq	Iraqis
Ireland, Republic of	Irish
Israel	Israelis
Italy	Italians
Jamaica	Jamaicans
Japan	Japanese
Jordan	Jordanians

Country	People
Kazakhstan	Kazakhs
Kenya	Kenyans
Kiribati	Kiribatians
Kuwait	Kuwaitis
Kyrgyzstan	Kyrgyz
Laos	Laotians
Latvia	Latvians
Lebanon	Lebanese
Lesotho	Basotho
Liberia	Liberians
Libya	Libyans
Liechtenstein	Liechtensteiners
Lithuania	Lithuanians
Luxembourg	Luxembourgers
Macedonia (Former Yugoslav Republic of Macedonia)	Macedonians
Madagascar	Malagasies
Malawi	Malawians
Malaysia	Malaysians
Maldives	Maldivians
Mali	Malians
Malta	Maltese
Marshall Islands	Marshall Islanders
Mauritania	Mauritanians
Mauritius	Mauritians
Mexico	Mexicans
Micronesia	Micronesians
Moldova	Moldovans
Monaco	Monégasques
Mongolia	Mongolians
Morocco	Moroccans
Mozambique	Mozambicans
Myanmar (Burma)	Burmese
Namibia	Namibians
Nauru	Nauruans
Nepal	Nepalese
Netherlands	Dutch
New Zealand	New Zealanders
Nicaragua	Nicaraguans
Niger	Nigeriens
Nigeria	Nigerians
North Korea (People's Democratic Republic of Korea)	North Koreans
Norway	Norwegians
Oman	Omanis
Pakistan	Pakistanis
Palau	Palauans
Panama	Panamanians
Papua New Guinea	Papua New Guineans
Paraguay	Paraguayans
Peru	Peruvians
Philippines	Filipinos
Poland	Poles

Country	People
Portugal	Portuguese
Qatar	Qataris
Romania	Romanians
Russia (Russian Federation)	Russians
Rwanda	Rwandans
St Kitts and Nevis	People of St Kitts and Nevis
St Lucia	St Lucians
St Vincent and the Grenadines	St Vincentians
Samoa	Samoans
San Marino	People of San Marino
São Tomé and Principe	People of São Tomé and Principe
Saudi Arabia	Saudi Arabians
Senegal	Senegalese
Seychelles	Seychellois
Sierra Leone	Sierra Leoneans
Singapore	Singaporeans
Slovakia	Slovaks
Slovenia	Slovenes
Solomon Islands	Solomon Islanders
Somalia	Somalis
South Africa	South Africans
South Korea (Republic of Korea)	South Koreans
Spain	Spaniards
Sri Lanka	Sri Lankans
Sudan	Sudanese
Suriname	Surinamers
Swaziland	Swazis
Sweden	Swedes
Switzerland	Swiss
Syria	Syrians
Taiwan	Taiwanese
Tajikistan	Tajiks
Tanzania	Tanzanians
Thailand	Thais
Togo	Togolese
Tonga	Tongans
Trinidad and Tobago	Trinidadians and Tobagans or Tobagonians
Tunisia	Tunisians
Turkey	Turks
Turkmenistan	Turkmens
Tuvalu	Tuvaluans
Uganda	Ugandans
Ukraine	Ukrainians
United Arab Emirates	People of the United Arab Emirates
United Kingdom	British
United States of America	Americans

Country	People	Country	People
Uruguay	Uruguayans	**Yemen**	Yemenis
Uzbekistan	Uzbeks	**Yugoslavia (Montenegro and Serbia)**	Yugoslavians (Montenegrins and Serbians)
Vanuatu	People of Vanuatu		
Vatican City	Vatican citizens		
Venezuela	Venezuelans	**Zambia**	Zambians
Vietnam	Vietnamese	**Zimbabwe**	Zimbabweans

Appendix 5

Weights and measures

1 Metric, with British equivalents

Note The conversion factors are not exact unless so marked. They are given only to the accuracy likely to be needed in everyday calculations.

Linear Measure

1 millimetre	= 0.039 inch
1 centimetre = 10 mm	= 0.394 inch
1 decimetre = 10 cm	= 3.94 inches
1 metre = 10 dm	= 1.094 yards
1 decametre = 10 m	= 10.94 yards
1 hectometre = 100 m	= 109.4 yards
1 kilometre = 1,000 m	= 0.6214 mile

Square Measure

1 square centimetre	= 0.155 sq. inch
1 square metre	= 1.196 sq.yards
= 10,000 sq. cm	
1 are = 100 sq. metres	= 119.6 sq.yards
1 hectare = 100 ares	= 2.471 acres
1 square kilometre	= 0.386 sq. mile
= 100 hectares	

Cubic Measure

1 cubic centimetre	= 0.061 cu. inch
1 cubic metre	= 1.308 cu.yards
= 1,000,000 cu. cm	

Capacity Measure

1 millilitre	= 0.002 pint (British)
1 centilitre = 10 ml	= 0.018 pint
1 decilitre = 10 cl	= 0.176 pint
1 litre = 10 dl	= 1.76 pints
1 decalitre = 10 l	= 2.20 gallons
1 hectolitre = 100 l	= 2.75 bushels
1 kilolitre = 1,000 l	= 3.44 quarters

Weight

1 milligram	= 0.015 grain
1 centigram = 10 mg	= 0.154 grain
1 decigram = 10 cg	= 1.543 grains
1 gram = 10 dg	= 15.43 grains
1 decagram = 10 g	= 5.63 drams
1 hectogram = 100 g	= 3.527 ounces
1 kilogram = 1,000 g	= 2.205 pounds
1 tonne (metric ton)	= 0.984 (long) ton
= 1,000 kg	

2 British and American, with metric equivalents

Linear Measure

1 inch	= 25.4 mm (exactly)
1 foot = 12 inches	= 0.3048 metre
1 yard = 3 feet	= 0.9144 metre (exactly)
1 (statute) mile	= 1.609 km
= 1,760 yards	

Square Measure

1 square inch	= 6.45 sq. cm
1 square foot	= 9.29 sq. dm
= 144 sq. in.	
1 square yard	= 0.836 sq. metre
= 9 sq. ft.	

1 acre = 4,840 sq. yd.	= 0.405 hectare
1 square mile	= 259 hectares
= 640 acres	

Cubic Measure

1 cubic inch	= 16.4 cu. cm
1 cubic foot	= 0.0283 cu. metre
= 1,728 cu. in.	
1 cubic yard	= 0.765 cu. metre
= 27 cu. ft.	

Capacity Measure
British

1 pint = 34.68 cu. in.	= 20 fluid oz
	= 0.568 litre

1 quart = 2 pints	= 1.136 litres		1 quart = 2 pints	= 1.101 litres
1 gallon = 4 quarts	= 4.546 litres		1 peck = 8 quarts	= 8.81 litres
1 peck = 2 gallons	= 9.092 litres		1 bushel = 4 pecks	= 35.3 litres
1 bushel = 4 pecks	= 36.4 litre			
1 quarter = 8 bushels	= 2.91 hectolitres			

American liquid

1 pint = 16 fluid oz. = 28.88 cu. in.	= 0.550 litre

American dry

1 pint = 33.60 cu. in.	= 0.550 litre

1 quart = 2 pints	= 0.946 litre
1 gallon = 4 quarts	= 3.785 litres

Avoirdupois Weight

1 grain	= 0.065 gram		1 hundredweight = 4 quarters	= 50.80 kilograms
1 dram	= 1.772 grams			
1 ounce = 16 drams	= 28.35 grams		1 (long) ton = 20 hundredweight	= 1.016 tonnes
1 pound = 16 ounces = 7,000 grains	= 0.4536 kilogram (0.45359237 exactly)			
1 stone = 14 pounds	= 6.35 kilograms		1 short ton = 2,000 pounds	= 0.907 tonne
1 quarter = 2 stones	= 12.70 kilograms			

3 Power Notation

This expresses concisely any power of ten (any number that is composed of factors 10), and is sometimes used in the dictionary. 10^2 or ten squared $= 10 \times 10 = 100$; 10^3 or ten cubed $= 10 \times 10 \times 10 = 1,000$. Similarly, $10^4 = 10,000$ and $10^{10} = 1$ followed by ten noughts $= 10,000,000,000$. Proceeding in the opposite direction, dividing by ten and subtracting one from the index, we have $10^2 = 100$, $10^1 = 10$, $10^0 = 1$, $10^{-1} = \frac{1}{10}$, $10^{-2} = \frac{1}{100}$, and so on; $10^{-10} = 1/1010 = 1/10,000,000,000$.

4 Temperature

Fahrenheit: water boils (under standard conditions) at 212° and freezes at 32°.
Celsius or Centigrade: water boils at 100° and freezes at 0°.
Kelvin: water boils at 373.15 K and freezes at 273.15 K.

Celsius	Fahrenheit		Celsius	Fahrenheit
−17.8°	0°		50°	122°
−10°	14°		60°	140°
0°	32°		70°	158°
10°	50°		80°	176°
20°	68°		90°	194°
30°	86°		100°	212°
40°	104°			

To convert Celsius into Fahrenheit: multiply by 9, divide by 5, and add 32.
To convert Fahrenheit into Celsius: subtract 32, multiply by 5, and divide by 9.